slow cooking
& one pot recipes

CONTENTS

INTRODUCTION

Long, slow cooking techniques have been used for centuries. From the earliest times, cooks discovered that meat roasted in the dying embers of the fire, or in a pot of gently bubbling stock suspended well above the flames, produced the tenderest results with rich, well-balanced flavours.

Cooking methods have developed and improved over the years, but no drastic changes were seen until the reduction of staff employed in richer households meant that very few people still had a cook who would spend the entire day preparing food.

Along with the gradual introduction of controllable range cookers and, eventually, the introduction of modern gas and electric ovens came an increased demand for dishes requiring less cooking time. In the latter half of the 20th century, more women went out to work, and time-saving became all-important.

Food manufacturers thrived on the sale of prepared ingredients that could reduce the number of hours spent in

Below: The gentle heat of the slow cooker means that delicate fish cooks beautifully.

the kitchen. Canned and dried soups, dehydrated prepared vegetables, main meals and "instant" desserts became very popular at the end of the 1960s and continued to be so throughout the 1970s.

The story of slow cooking

In the mid-1970s, the slow cooker was invented. It was originally designed for making baked beans and was marketed to the public as an appliance that would cook a wholesome meal unattended, ready to be served after a hard day's work. As such it caught the attention of those with busy working lives. It lived up to its promise, and busy working mothers, families and students soon discovered its delights. The slow cooker's popularity continued for a decade.

However, with the booming economy years in the late 1980s and 1990s, the demand for economical cuts of meat fell. They were replaced by lean prime cuts, such as chicken breast portions and beef steak, which were more suited to fast cooking methods, such as grilling, broiling and stir-frying. Time-saving appliances appeared on the scene,

Above: Impressive terrines can be made using the slow cooker as a bain-marie.

including the microwave – and with their arrival, many slow cookers were left to gather dust.

Changing attitudes

Towards the end of the 20th century and in the new millennium, there has been a change in attitudes towards food and a reverse in eating trends. Many people now demand natural food, with fewer artificial chemicals and more nutrients and flavour, rather than instant, quick-fix food. Genetically modified produce has not been welcomed and sales of organic food have rocketed, along with requests for less tender, tastier cuts of meat. Slow-simmered casseroles, home-made soups and traditional desserts are back in fashion, and so are slow cookers.

From tasty, wholesome family food to sophisticated entertaining, a slow cooker is a superb way to create wonderfully tender and flavour-packed meals. Its reputation for making delicious soups and succulent stews is well known, and the slow cooker is far more versatile than many people realize.

Because the slow cooker cooks gently, without the vigorous bubbling or fierce heat of some other cooking methods, delicate food, such as fish, fruit and vegetables, won't break up even after

long cooking. Used as a bain-marie the slow cooker can produce divine creamy "baked" custards, the lightest sponge desserts, and tasty terrines and pâtés. The constant temperature makes it perfect for keeping party punches steaming hot and simmering preserves so that the flavours mingle, making ready-to-eat preserves that don't need to be left to mature.

There are many advantages to using a slow cooker. Not only does it produce delicious dishes with well-developed flavours, but once the food is in the slow cooker you can usually turn it on and forget about it. Because the slow cooker uses less electricity than a light bulb, it can be left unattended, which means you can be away from the kitchen all day and return when ready to serve.

Some slow cookers have timers that automatically switch to the warm setting when the food is cooked, and this is ideal for households who eat at different times. The remaining portions will still be deliciously moist for latecomers, and won't be overcooked or dry. As an added bonus, little steam or smell escapes from slow cookers.

You will be pleasantly surprised at the range of uses of the slow cooker. Although traditionally associated with cold weather foods, such as warming

Below: Pastry toppings for traditional pies are oven-cooked to retain their crispness.

casseroles, soups and stews, you can also make delicious hot weather dishes, such as chilled pâtés and terrines, light fish dishes and summery Mediterranean-style pasta meals. The slow cooker really is invaluable when it is warm outside and you don't want to be confined to a steamy kitchen, with the oven pumping out heat. Simply switch on the slow cooker and leave it to it while you get on with more important things.

Below: Individual servings can be cooked in single-portion ramekins in the slow cooker.

Above: The slow cooker makes excellent steamed chocolate and fruit puddings.

One-pot and clay-pot cooking

You can still take advantage of the benefits that a slow cooker brings by making meals cooked in just one pot, whether it be a large casserole dish, a clay baking dish or a wok. Nourishing soups, delectable stews, spicy stir fries, robust roasts, creamy risottos and citrus custards all can be cooked in one-pot dishes. They are easy to prepare, a pleasure to serve and the perfect choice for family and friends.

As with the slow cooker, cooking in a single pot is wonderfully liberating. All that is needed is a bit of leisurely preparation, and then the cook can relax, secure in the knowledge that there will be no last-minute sauces to make, and no tricky toppings to produce. Serving a selection of side dishes would defeat the object of one-pot cooking (and is largely unnecessary when vegetables are included anyway), so you have the perfect excuse for offering only the simplest accompaniments, sparing yourself the anxiety that comes with trying to get everything ready at precisely the same time.

One-pot dishes will seldom spoil if not eaten the moment they are ready. Some, like curries and casseroles, actually improve if made the day before, so that all the flavours can bed down together and blend. Stir-fries, pasta and rice dishes need last-minute cooking, but if the preparation is done in advance, the effort is minimal.

This style of cooking is perfect for everyone from single students to those cooking for a large family. The meal can be cooked in the oven, on top of the stove or even in a free-standing appliance like a microwave oven or electric frying pan. There's very little washing up, and if there are any leftovers, you may well be able to transform them into tasty pie fillings, simply by sandwiching them inside ready-rolled puff pastry or filo.

The benefits of one-pot and clay-pot cooking

One-pot cooking can also be extremely healthy, especially if you use a clay pot, which ensures that vitamins and minerals are retained. This ancient form of cooking seals in all the food's natural juices by enclosing it in a porous clay container that has been soaked in water. As the container heats up, the water turns to steam, keeping the contents beautifully moist and tender. The only other liquid is that which comes from the food itself, so the full flavour of the food can be appreciated.

There's nothing new about cooking in clay. Thousands of years ago, hunters discovered that coating small birds and animals in clay before baking them in an open fire kept the meat juicy and

Above: Paella, a classic one-pot seafood and rice dish from Spain, is traditionally cooked in a shallow, two-handled pan.

Left: A whole chicken cooked with forty cloves of garlic makes the perfect pot-roast, and it, like other one-pot dishes, needs little attention once it is in the oven.

Below: Clay pots come in a whole host of sizes and shapes. These tiny shallow cazuelas can be used to bake individual portions of both savoury and sweet tarts, roasted vegetables and custards.

Left: *The tall, conical tagine from north Africa is one of the many ancient clay pot designs that are still widely used today.*

results every time. For each type of dish there is a chapter devoted to slow cooker recipes followed by a chapter for one-pot and clay-pot recipes so that you can easily find recipes to suit your chosen method of cooking.

Most recipes are based on a family of four people, but if you have a small or large slow cooker or pan the quantities can easily be halved to serve two, or doubled for eight. All recipes have been thoroughly tested, but it is important to get to know your slow cooker, as times can vary from one model to another. After trying a few recipes, you will know whether your slow cooker is faster or slower, and you will be able to adjust the recipe cooking times accordingly.

Below: *A glazed clay pot ensures that the flavours don't soak into the pot, which means that it can be used for both sweet and savoury dishes.*

prevented it from burning. Chipping off the clay and throwing it away was wasteful and time-consuming, however. Clay pots were a huge improvement, and this material was used by many of the ancient civilizations. Today, clay pots based on ancient designs are still widely used all over the world. In North Africa, it is the conical tagine; in China, the sand pot; in Spain, the cazuela; and in France, the daubière and tian.

Chicken bricks, bean pots and clay pots come in all shapes and sizes. They need to be treated kindly, but are surprisingly durable. If you've never used one – or have forgotten just how good they make food taste – there is plenty of inspiration, along with ideas for other delicious one-pot dishes of every kind, contained within these pages.

Using this book
Ideal for the first-time slow-cooker user, as well as the more experienced slow-cooker fan, this book also offers practical advice and plenty more recipes that can be cooked just on the hob in any large pan or slowly in the oven in a clay pot. It contains a wonderfully detailed reference section with everything you need to know about ingredients, equipment and techniques, so that you can feel completely confident.

Once you have mastered the basics, turn to the recipe chapters for a selection of all-time classics as well as unusual recipes that are sure to become household favourites. Step-by-step photographs show the key preparation stages of each recipe to give successful

SLOW COOKER BASICS

The basic principle behind the slow cooker is that it cooks food very slowly at a low temperature. The heat gradually builds up and is then maintained at an even temperature throughout cooking, to give perfect, tender results. Slow cookers are very simple and economical to use. They have a low wattage that consumes about the same amount of electricity as a light bulb, which makes them environmentally friendly as well.

Choosing a slow cooker

There is a very wide selection of slow cookers available. They come in a range of sizes, shapes, colours and prices, and it is these factors that you will need to think about before you decide which type of slow cooker is right for you.

When slow cookers were first manufactured, the earthenware or ceramic pots were permanently fixed into the heat-resistant plastic or aluminium outer casing. While it is still possible to buy models made this way, most modern versions have a removable cooking pot that fits snugly into an inner metal casing. The heating elements are safely situated between the inner and outer casings. This newer style not only simplifies washing up, but allows the cooking pot to be lifted out and taken to the table as a serving dish. In addition, food can be browned in the oven or under the grill (broiler) without causing damage to the outer casing.

The heat-resistant lid may be made of toughened glass or ceramic. The former has the advantage of allowing you to monitor the food's cooking progress without lifting off the lid and losing heat and moisture, although this may be hindered to some extent by steam and condensation gathering on the inside of the lid.

The range of designs and colours of slow cookers has increased in recent years. The original round-shaped rustic

cream and brown design with ceramic lid is still available, but alongside it you will now find much more contemporary-looking white, stainless steel and brightly coloured models that will fit well in a bright, modern kitchen.

Slow cookers may be round or oval in shape. Round ones are superb for cooking casseroles, steaming desserts and cooking cakes in round tins (pans), while the oval version is better for pot-roasted meats and for use with loaf tins (pans) and terrines.

The size of different slow cookers can vary enormously – from a small 600ml/ 1 pint/2½ cup cooking pot to a huge 6.5 litre/11¼ pint/26¼ cup one. Of all the sizes, the most popular size is probably 3.5 litres/6 pints/14¼ cups, which will enable you to cook a wide range of dishes and easily cater for four people. However, the smaller versions, intended for cooking just one or two portions at a time, are a great asset for single people and couples and take up less space in the kitchen. They are also perfect for making hot dips and fondues.

Below: Oval-shaped slow cookers are perfect for cooking certain types of food, such as pot-roasted joints of meat, long, loaf-shaped terrines, and small whole fish.

Temperature settings

The cooking temperatures and settings on slow cookers vary slightly from model to model. The most basic (but perfectly adequate) models have three settings: off, low and high. When the slow cooker is switched to low, the food will barely simmer, and at the highest setting it will cook at a simmer or even boil.

Other models have an additional medium setting and some also have an auto setting. The auto setting is thermostatically controlled, so that the cooking temperature builds up to high, maintains it for a short time, then automatically switches to low to maintain the heat. It normally takes about an hour for the slow cooker to reach the "high" temperature, but this depends on the quantity of food being cooked and its initial temperature.

Most slow cooker models also have a power indicator light that remains on constantly during cooking – although in a few models it may switch off to indicate that the optimum temperature has been reached, so check the instructions.

Using a new slow cooker

Every model of slow cooker varies slightly, so it is important to read the manufacturer's instructions carefully before using. Even when using the same settings, some cookers will cook slower or faster than others.

To cover all models of slow cooker, the recipes in this book offer a range of cooking times. Depending on whether your own model cooks more slowly or quickly, you will either need to use the longer or shorter timing, or somewhere in between. Once you have used your new cooker a few times, it will be easy to know at a glance which cooking time you need to use.

Preheating

Some slow cookers need to be preheated on high for 15–20 minutes before cooking. However, always check the instructions first because some models heat up quickly, making this step unnecessary, and the manufacturer may advise against heating the slow cooker when empty.

To preheat the slow cooker, place the empty cooking pot and lid in the slow cooker base and switch the temperature on to the high setting. While the slow cooker heats up, prepare the ingredients for the recipe.

Slow cooker care

Always remove any labels and tags from a new slow cooker, then wash the ceramic cooking pot well in hot soapy water, rinse and dry thoroughly.

After use, the slow cooker should be switched off before removing the ceramic cooking pot. If you don't want to wash the pot immediately after serving the food, it can be filled with warm water and left to soak for as long as necessary. However, do not immerse the entire pot in water for long periods of time because the base is usually porous and soaking may damage the pot. Very few cooking pots are dishwasher-proof, but it is worth checking the manufacturer's instructions; these should also inform you whether the cooking pot can be used on the stovetop or in the oven, microwave or freezer.

Never plunge the hot cooking pot into cold water immediately after use, or pour boiling water into an empty cold cooking pot. Subjecting it to a sudden change in temperature could cause it to crack. As with all electrical appliances, never immerse the outer casing in water or fill it with water. Nor should you use the metal inner casing without the ceramic cooking pot.

Scouring pads and abrasive cleaners will damage the outside of the cooker, so use a damp soapy cloth to clean it.

Above: Smaller slow cookers intended for cooking just one or two portions at a time are an asset for single people and couples.

During cooking, the cooking pot and lid will become very hot, so always use oven gloves when handling. The outer casing may also become hot after long cooking, so care should be taken when touching this, too.

The first few times you use a slow cooker, you may notice a slight odour. This is caused by the burning off of manufacturing residues, which is normal, and will lessen and disappear after time. After several months, the glaze on the cooking pot may become crackled; this is common with glazed stoneware and will not affect the slow cooker's efficiency.

Adapting your own recipes

Conventional recipes can be adapted for cooking in a slow cooker. The easiest way to adapt a recipe is to find a similar one in this book and use it as a guide to adapt the original recipe. As a general rule, the liquid content of a dish cooked conventionally can be reduced by as much as half in a slow cooker. Check towards the end of cooking time and add more hot liquid if necessary.

Tips for success

During cooking, steam will condense on the lid of the slow cooker, then slowly trickle back into the pot. This helps to form a seal around the lid, retaining heat, flavour and cooking smells.

If possible, avoid lifting the lid during cooking because this will cause heat loss and lengthen the cooking time. Unless a recipe states otherwise, the slow cooker should be left undisturbed. There is no need to stir food frequently because the even cooking and low temperature help to prevent food from sticking or bubbling over. Should you need to lift the lid though, add an extra 15–20 minutes to the cooking time to make up for the heat lost.

If at the end of the cooking time the food is not quite ready, replace the lid and switch the slow cooker to high to speed up the cooking process. Once ready, many dishes can be kept hot for an hour or so without risk of spoiling, by switching the slow cooker to low.

Guide to cooking times

You can often introduce some flexibility to the total cooking time by adjusting the temperature setting. Certain foods, however, are only successful if cooked at the specified setting. Cakes, for example, should always be cooked on high for the entire cooking time, and pot-roasted meats and egg-based recipes should usually be started on high (or auto) for the first hour of cooking, then reduced. For dishes such as soups and casseroles, the cooking time may be shortened or extended to suit your needs by cooking on a higher or lower setting. As a rough guide, the cooking time on high is just over half that on low.

Low	Medium	High
6–8 hours	4–6 hours	3–4 hours
8–10 hours	6–8 hours	5–6 hours
10–12 hours	8–10 hours	7–8 hours

SLOW COOKER EQUIPMENT

To make most slow cooker recipes, you will only need a slow cooker. Stocks, soups, stews, casseroles, compotes and pot roasts can all simply be cooked in the ceramic cooking pot. However, to make other dishes, such as cakes and pâtés that are cooked in a bain-marie, you will need suitable cookware that is watertight and which will fit inside the ceramic cooking pot.

Cake tins/pans

When cooking cakes in the slow cooker, always use cake tins that have a fixed, non-removable base, rather than loose-based or springform tins. Before use, check that the tin is completely watertight by filling it with water and leaving it to stand for an hour; if it leaks it is not suitable. You should also check that the tin will fit inside the ceramic cooking pot before you prepare and fill it with mixture.

While it is important that the tin has a strong rigid shape, heat will penetrate more quickly if lighter, thinner tins are used. When using heavy-gauge metal tins, you will need to allow an extra 15–20 minutes cooking time.

Generally, round slow cookers can accommodate larger round and square cake tins than oval cookers. A 20cm/8in round tin or a 17.5cm/6½in square tin should fit comfortably in a 5 litre/8¾ pint/20 cup round cooker, providing the sides of the tins are straight and

there is no protruding lip or side handle. Oval cookers can also be used for round and square tins, if necessary, but the size will obviously be more limited.

The recipes in this book state which size and shape of tin to use. Try to stick to these as closely as possible – if the tin is too large you will end up with a shallow cake; if it is too small the mixture may overflow. Bear in mind, too, that the length of cooking time and the texture of the cake may be affected if the wrong tin is used.

Loaf tins/pans

Perfect for making terrines, pâtés and loaf-shaped cakes, these sturdy long, narrow metal tins are better suited to cooking in an oval-shaped slow cooker, which will accommodate their shape conveniently. A 3.5 litre/6 pint/14 cup oval slow cooker will hold a straight-sided 900g/2lb loaf tin or Balmoral – a barrel-shaped ridged tin.

Ring tins/pans

Kugelhopf tins and deep, ring-shaped tins that are not too wide, are excellent for using in a slow cooker. The hollow tube in the centre conducts heat into the middle of the cake, helping it to cook quickly and evenly. Ideally choose

Above: Rectangular, round and heart-shaped tins can be used in the slow cooker as long as they fit comfortably inside the pot.

a tin with a central tube that is just a little higher than the outer rim of the tin. However, you should also check that the tin fits inside the slow cooker, and that the cooker lid can still fit tightly on top of the ceramic cooking pot when the tin is inside.

Other shaped tins/pans

There are many other shapes of tin that may also be used in the slow cooker. These include small heart-, petal-, oval-, and hexagon-shaped tins. Before buying a tin to use in a slow cooker, it may be worth taking the internal measurement of the ceramic cooking pot first, to be sure the tin will fit inside.

Dariole moulds

These little sandcastle-shaped tins are usually made of matt aluminium and come in various sizes, although moulds with a 65mm/2½in diameter are the most popular. Dariole moulds are useful for making single-portion sized cakes, desserts and timbales, and are particularly good for making individual baked custards.

Below: Classic rectangular loaf tins are very useful for making terrines and chunky, country-style cooked pâtés.

Soufflé and ramekin dishes

These pretty round dishes can be used as an alternative to metal cake tins, as well as for cooking pâtés and mousses. They are always straight-sided and may be made of glass, heatproof porcelain or stoneware. Glass or porcelain are preferable because they conduct heat more quickly to the food inside. When using these dishes for cake making, it is better to choose one with a perfectly flat base; occasionally they are slightly domed. Individual soufflé and ramekin dishes are miniature versions and can be used to make small, individual cakes, pâtés and desserts such as baked custards.

Terrines

Usually rectangular in shape, these dishes may be made of porcelain, cast iron or earthenware. When used to make pâté, they may double up as a serving dish. Some earthenware terrines aren't glazed, so are unsuitable for use in a bain-marie in a slow cooker. A loaf tin makes a good substitute.

Left: Thermometers are used to check that meat is cooked through.

Pudding bowls

Traditionally made of white earthenware, but also made of toughened glass, aluminium or polypropylene, pudding bowls have sloping sides, which make the top much wider than the base. They are ideal for making sweet and savoury steamed puddings and can also be used to melt chocolate, butter and similar ingredients in a bain-marie in the slow cooker. Bowls made from aluminium may have a clip-on lid with a handle attached. They are very good for making steamed meat and plain sponge puddings, because heat is conducted quickly. They are unsuitable for making acidic fruit desserts or similarly acidic recipes because the acid will react with the metal.

Below: Soufflé dishes and ramekins can be used inside the slow cooker to make steamed desserts, custards and pâtés.

Above: Metal pudding bowls with a clip-on lid and handle for easy lifting are great for making steamed meat puddings.

Meat thermometers

These useful instruments are the most reliable way of checking that meat is thoroughly cooked – this is particularly important for poultry, which can pass on the salmonella bacteria when raw or partially cooked. Most thermometers have a stainless steel body and a glass dial. By piercing the meat near the centre towards the end of the cooking time, you can check the temperature inside the meat. The meat is ready to eat when the pointer on the dial reaches the appropriate wording; there are indications for types of meat including chicken, beef, lamb and pork, as well as readings within some of those categories for rare, medium and well-cooked meat. Choose a thermometer with a thin probe, so that it doesn't make large holes in the meat, causing juices to be lost. Do not leave the thermometer inside the meat during cooking because exposure to steam in the slow cooker could damage the dial. Immediately after use, rinse the probe in hot soapy water and wipe it clean; don't immerse the thermometer in water.

ONE-POT EQUIPMENT

If you are going to do a lot of cooking in just one pot, make it a good one. There's no point in planning a pot-roast for the whole family, only to find you haven't got a big enough pan, or that the one you have has a wobbly base. It is equally irritating to discover that your only decent casserole has a crack in it, or can only be used in the oven and not on top of the stove. Choose your cookware with care; it is worth investing in good quality equipment that will last.

Right:
Stainless-
steel pans
with a heavy
base are a good
choice for one-pot cooking.

Above: Frying pans with metal handles can be used under the grill (broiler) and in the oven.

For one-pot cooking, you need a large pan with a heavy base, which will conduct the heat evenly and help to prevent the food from scorching should you inadvertently allow the amount of liquid to get too low. A good quality stainless-steel pan would be an excellent choice, but it is important to choose one with an aluminium or copper base, since stainless steel does not conduct heat well. For long, slow cooking, cast-iron pans coated in vitreous enamel, are ideal, as they can also be used in the oven. When buying a frying pan, choose one with a heavy base. When cooking a frittata or a dessert such as tarte Tatin, it is essential to use a frying pan with a handle that can withstand the heat of the grill (broiler) or oven; a point worth considering when you are buying a new frying pan.

Woks

One of the most useful items in the kitchen, the wok need not be reserved solely for stir-frying. It is the ideal pan for quick-cooked creamy dishes such as beef Stroganoff. The wok can also be used for making a risotto. Woks that

Pots and Pans

When you are buying cooking equipment, it is very tempting to opt for a set of shiny pans, rather than individual items that might suit your purposes – and your personal circumstances – better.

Below left: A large pot with metal handles can be used on top of the stove and in the oven.

Left:
Woks have
either one or
two handles.

Right: When buying casseroles, it is a good idea to choose different shapes and sizes.

FREE-STANDING ELECTRIC COOKING POTS
It isn't vital to have a stove in order to cook a one-pot meal. Electric frying pans; slow-cookers (and combinations of the two); multi-purpose appliances, in which you can shallow fry, deep fry or even cook a casserole, all have the advantage that they have easy temperature control, use very little electricity and are easy to clean.

Casseroles

For one-pot cooking, choose a casserole that is big enough to serve six, even if you usually cook for four. This will give you plenty of room for stirring the contents without risking splashes and scalds. The ideal pot will be one that can be used on top of the stove as well as inside it, so that if you do need to do any pre-cooking, or if cooking juices need to be reduced by boiling, you will not need a second container. If you buy several casseroles, vary the shapes as well as the sizes. For cooking a whole chicken, for instance, an oval is more useful than a round dish. Look at the handles, too. It is important that they are easy to grasp, and that they do not become so hot that they are liable to burn you, even when you are using an oven glove. Appearance will obviously be a consideration, since you will be serving straight from the casserole, but consider practical aspects too.

have a flat base can be used on all types of cooker. They can have either one or two handles. Those with two handles are good for deep-frying and general cooking, while the wok with one handle is designed especially for stir-frying. The single handle makes the wok easy to pick up so that the ingredients can be stirred and tossed in the wok at the same time.

Baking Dishes

There are plenty of one-pot recipes that benefit from being cooked in large, shallow dishes, from oven-roasted vegetables to layered potato bakes. Buy several different shapes, bearing in mind the size of your oven. Having two rectangular dishes that will fit side by side can be a real boon if you want to cook one meal for serving immediately and another for the freezer.

Ramekins

You will also find it useful to have six or eight ovenproof ramekin dishes, for baking single portions, such as individual soufflés and oven-baked desserts.

Below: Choose two ovenproof baking dishes that will fit next to each other in your oven.

FLAMEPROOF CASSEROLES

The most versatile casseroles are also flameproof and so can be used on top of the stove and under the grill (broiler) as well as in the oven.

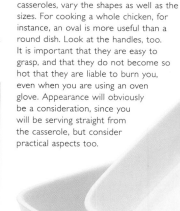

CLAY-POT EQUIPMENT

Visit any market in any town the world over, and you will find clay cooking pots for sale. Some will be rough, rustic items, only suitable for display, but others – like the Spanish cazuela or the North African tagine – will be intended not for the tourist trade, but for everyday cooking. Before buying, always seek local advice as to the durability and safety of the items, especially as regards any glazes that might be used. Buying a boxed item from a reputable store may not be as romantic, but it is probably more sensible. Clay cooking pots need special treatment, and it makes sense to follow the instructions that come with your particular utensil.

Left: The classic, high, domed Romertopf dish (top) and a large oval clay pot that is especially designed for cooking whole fish.

Romertopfs

Perhaps the most familiar unglazed clay pots are those produced by Romertopf. Their extensive range includes items suitable for cooking meat, fish, vegetables, fruit, even bread and cakes. The classic Romertopf is a rectangular pot with a deep, wide base and a domed lid. These come in several sizes. Other shapes include a long oval, suitable for accommodating a whole fish. This has a glazed base, to prevent liquid from penetrating the porous clay and leaving behind a lingering fishy smell.

Lids are designed to fit snugly, so that they cannot accidentally slip off, but there is a narrow gap between the lid and the base that allows any excess steam to escape from the clay pot.

Right: This deep, pan-shaped clay pot is designed for cooking bean dishes, but would also be good for baking potatoes, and for cooking soups and stews that have lots of liquid.

Bean Pot/Potato Brick

There are several shapes of these deep, round pots. Some have a handle for easy lifting. Made entirely from clay, the pots have a domed lid. Although these pots are especially suitable for slowly cooking beans and pulses, they can also be used for soups and stews, and the shape is ideal for cooking both large and small potatoes. The potatoes are bathed in a layer of steam, which keeps them moist during cooking.

Whatever you are cooking, the pot and lid should first be soaked in water, then placed in a cold oven after the ingredients have been added.

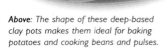

Above: The shape of these deep-based clay pots makes them ideal for baking potatoes and cooking beans and pulses.

COOKING BEANS

If you are cooking beans, check the recipe or the manufacturer's handbook. Before being added to the pot, such varieties as kidney, cannellini and soya beans need to be brought to the boil in a pan of water, then boiled vigorously for about 10 minutes to eliminate toxins from the beans. Drain the beans and leave them to cool before adding them to the bean pot. Any liquid added to the pot should be cold. This will prevent the pot from cracking or breaking.

Garlic Baker

This small terracotta dish with a domed lid is used for baking garlic. Like all clay pots, it must be placed in a cold oven and heated gradually. There is no need

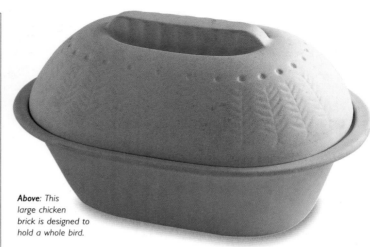

Above: This large chicken brick is designed to hold a whole bird.

to soak the pot in water first. The inside of the dish is glazed, so the garlic juices will not permeate it. The baker will accommodate four to six garlic bulbs. A small cross must be cut in the top of each garlic bulb, or the tops can be sliced off, to prevent them from bursting during cooking. The steam they release will be trapped under the domed lid of the garlic baker, and will keep the garlic cloves beautifully moist and tender. The garlic baker can also be used in a microwave oven.

Onion Baker

This clay pot looks like a larger version of the garlic baker. It consists of a shallow terracotta dish with a high, domed lid; it will accommodate four medium-sized onions, and can also be used for cooking onion wedges, shallots or baby onions. The lid can be soaked in water first, so that it releases steam during cooking. The steam helps to tenderize the onions. Towards the end of cooking, the lid should be removed so that the onions turn brown and become caramelized.

Chicken Brick

This is a large, unglazed fire clay cooking dish with a high lid. The largest ones are designed to hold a whole chicken, guinea fowl or duck, but can also be used to cook any large piece of meat or poultry. Smaller chicken bricks are ideal for small birds and portions. There is no need to add fat or liquid to the pot unless the recipe specifically requires this.

ADDING FLAVOURINGS

Roasting onions in a clay pot gives them a wonderful, sweet taste, but the flavour can be enhanced even further by adding sprigs of fresh herbs. Pungent fresh herbs such as rosemary, thyme and oregano work well; tuck small sprigs in among the vegetables for the best result.

Above: The onion baker (left) and the garlic baker both have high, domed lids that are designed to trap steam during cooking.

Chinese Sand Pot

This covered earthenware pot, which is sometimes called a Chinese casserole, is usually glazed on the inside only and reinforced on the outside with wire. It comes from China, where it was originally used to cook stews over a slow charcoal fire. Several shapes and sizes are available. They are not expensive and can be bought in Asian and Chinese food and cooking equipment stores. The sand pot is ideal for slow-cooked dishes such as soups and stews that are baked in the oven. Do not use sand pots on top of the stove unless the manufacturer recommends this. Sand pots are fairly fragile, and are prone to crack easily. They do not need to be soaked before baking but like other clay pots are best placed in a cold oven.

Left: The Chinese sand pot was designed for cooking over a slow charcoal fire, but it is equally at home in a modern oven.

Tagine

This North African cooking pot consists of a large, shallow base and a tall, conical lid. The dish that is cooked in it is also known as a tagine.

Above: The traditional tagine (above left) has a shallow base and a tall, conical lid, while the contemporary version (right) has a deeper, larger base.

The food is placed in the base. As it cooks, steam rises and is trapped in the lid, keeping the food moist. Tagines are traditionally made from glazed brown earthenware, sometimes with a slightly rounded base. They come in a range of sizes, from small individual tagines to family-size ones that measure at least 20cm/8in across. There is also a modern version, with a heavy, cast-iron base and a glazed earthenware lid. Unlike the traditional tagine, which can only be used in the oven, or on a barbecue whose coals have been dowsed with sand, this design can also be used on top of the stove. This is very convenient, since it means that onions, vegetables and other ingredients such as meat and poultry can be browned in the base before the lid is fitted and the tagine is placed in the oven. Some glazed earthenware tagines can be used on top of the stove on a low heat, but it is best to use a heat diffuser; always check the manufacturer's instructions.

WHAT'S IN A NAME?

Clay, earthenware, terracotta, stoneware – we use the terms interchangeably, but are they all the same thing? Clay is essentially the raw material; it is a fine-grained mix of mineral origin that occurs in sedimentary rocks and soils. It is malleable when moist, but hardens when it is heated. When pots that are made from clay are baked, they become earthenware.

Terracotta is an Italian word that means "baked earth". It has come to refer to a type of hard, brownish-red earthenware that is traditionally left unglazed.

Stoneware is stronger than earthenware, having been fired at a higher temperature. It is usually perfectly safe to put stoneware in a hot oven, but always check the manufacturer's instructions.

Cazuelas

These shallow, lidless earthenware dishes originated in Spain. They are made in a variety of sizes. The smallest, suitable for Catalan-style sweet custards, measure 10–12.5cm/4–5in across, while the largest – used for cooking savoury dishes in the oven – measure 38cm/15in or even more. They vary in depth from about 2.5cm/1in to 7.5cm/3in. Cazuelas are either partially glazed on the outside, and fully glazed inside, or glazed inside and out. Neither type are soaked in water before use. After a while, the glaze on the cazuela may develop a slightly "crazed" appearance, but this is completely natural and will not affect the performance of the dish.

Individual cazuelas can be used for cooking single portions of all sorts of one-pot dishes, but they are ideal for making individual upside-down tarts. The lightly fried vegetables are spread out on the cazuelas, topped with rounds of puff pastry, then baked in the oven. The tarts are then inverted on serving plates.

Left: Spanish cazuelas come in a range of sizes and depths. The smallest are perfect for individual oven-baked custards, while the largest are good for slow-cooked stews and vegetable bakes, but will also accommodate whole fish and poultry as well as large joints of meat.

Tian

This traditional French baking dish originated in Provence. It is a shallow, usually oval, earthenware dish, and is used for baking vegetables, sometimes with rice and eggs. The dish that is cooked in it is also called a tian.

Right: Oval-shaped tians originated in Provence and are traditionally used for baking vegetables, but the shape is ideal for other oven-baked, one-pot dishes.

Glazed Earthenware Bakeware

A wide selection of glazed ovenproof earthenware is available. These dishes can often be put straight into a hot oven, or used under a hot grill (broiler) for browning. They are also suitable for use in the freezer. Unlike clay pots and porous earthenware, they do not need to be soaked in water before use and will not absorb food flavours and become tainted.

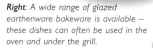

Right: A wide range of glazed earthenware bakeware is available – these dishes can often be used in the oven and under the grill.

INGREDIENTS: BEEF

Enjoyed all over the world, there are dozens of classic beef dishes, from the British Sunday roast, to French boeuf bourguignonne, German sauerbraten and Russian stroganoff. Beef's popularity is partly due to its versatility. There are many different cuts of beef, and many of these are suitable for a range of cooking methods. Tender fillet, for example, is perfect for cutting into steaks for grilling (broiling), strips for stir-frying, or baked whole, wrapped in pastry. Other cuts, such as the less expensive shin of beef, are unsuitable for roasting or grilling but are wonderful in stews and braised dishes – and are perfect for slow cooker cooking.

Buying and storing

As with all meat, the flavour and texture of beef is determined by the breed of the animal, its feed, the environment in which it is reared and, ultimately, by the process of slaughtering and the treatment of meat before it is cooked. While pork and lamb tend to come from very young animals, beef usually comes from those aged between 18 months and 2 years.

Beef should be hung to allow the flavour to develop and the texture to improve, preferably for at least two weeks. Well-matured beef has a deep, rich burgundy colour, not a bright red hue, and the fat is a creamy colour, or yellow, if the animal was grass-fed. Maturing is an expensive process because some water content will be lost through evaporation, so expect to pay a little more for well-hung meat. The leanest looking joint isn't always the best: for pot-roasting, casseroling

Above: Topside, also known as top round or top rump, is a fairly lean cut of beef that is best slowly braised or pot-roasted.

and braising, a marbling of fat running through the meat will provide flavour and basting to keep the meat moist.

Beef should be kept on a low shelf in the refrigerator, below any cooked foods and ingredients that will be eaten raw. When buying pre-packed meat, check and observe the eat-by date. Whether pre-packed or loose, minced (ground) and cubed beef should be used within 1–2 days of buying; chops and small joints should be used within 3 days, and larger joints within 4–5 days.

Cuts of beef

Butchering techniques differ according to regional and cultural traditions, and also from country to country. Good butchers and larger supermarkets offer a range of cuts and it is worth asking for their advice when buying.

Generally, cuts from the top of the animal, along the middle of the back, are tender because the muscles in this area do relatively little work. These are prime cuts that are good for quick cooking techniques, such as grilling (broiling) and pan-frying, and tend to be the most expensive. Cuts from the neck, shoulders and lower legs are full of flavour, but the texture is coarser and tougher because these are the parts of the animal that work the hardest. They require longer cooking by moist methods to ensure tender results – it is these cuts that are perfectly suited to cooking in the slow cooker. Slow, gentle stewing results in meltingly tender meat and a further developed flavour.

Left (from top): Thick flank makes good braising steak; thin flank produces rich-flavoured steaks and is best suited to slow, moist methods of cooking. Skirt and onglet, which is taken from the skirt area, are lean cuts with a coarse texture that become moist and tender when slowly braised.

Below: Neck is one of the less tender beef cuts but is delicious braised or stewed.

Blade or chuck These cuts come from the top forequarter and are relatively lean, marbled with just a little fat that keeps the meat moist. They are usually boned and sold together as braising steak. The long, gentle cooking of a slow cooker helps to tenderize the meat and intensifies its flavour. These cuts suit pot-roasting, casseroling and braising.

Brisket This may be bought on the bone or boned and rolled and comes from the lower part of the shoulder. It can be a fatty and somewhat tough cut of meat, but is excellent pot-roasted, braised or stewed in the slow cooker. It may also be salted or spiced before cooking, and served cold in thin slices.

Clod and neck Sometimes referred to as "sticking", these cuts come from the neck area and are fairly lean. They are often sold cut up as "stewing" steak. Slightly leaner than blade or chuck, they may also be sold minced (ground).

Fillet/tenderloin, rump/round, sirloin steak These lean, tender cuts from the back are usually cut into steaks for grilling (broiling) or frying, or into strips for stir-frying, and occasionally they are used for roasting. They may be included in braised slow cooker recipes, particularly those cooked on a high setting, but there is little point in using such cuts in casseroles and similar long-cooked dishes, where less expensive cuts produce more flavourful results.

Flank Lean thick flank, or top rump, comes from the hindquarter. In a whole

piece, it is ideal for pot-roasting in the slow cooker. It is also sold thickly sliced as braising steak. Thin flank can be fatty and gristly. It can be stewed but is often sold minced (ground).

Leg and shin/foreshank The leg cut comes from the hind legs of the animal and the shin from the forelegs. The shin is a tough cut that responds well to slow cooking. It is usually sold in slices with the bone in the centre and sinews and connective tissue running though; these and the marrow from the bones give the cooked meat a rich, gelatinous quality.

Minced/ground beef This is made from meat from any part of the animal, which has been passed through a mincer. It can be used to make meat sauces and meatballs in the slow cooker. As a general rule, the paler the meat the higher the fat content, so look for dark meat with less fat.

Rib Fore rib and wing, or prime rib, are expensive joints, best served roasted. For the slow cooker, choose middle rib. It is a fairly lean joint, and best boned before braising or pot-roasting.

Silverside/round pot roast This is lean, but tough, and is excellent for pot-roasts and braised dishes. It is often salted and gently cooked, then pressed and served cold.

Skirt/flank steak This thin braising cut can also be pot-roasted. It has a lean but somewhat coarse texture, and can be fast-fried or cooked very slowly, making it an ideal cut for the slow cooker.

VEAL

This meat comes from young calves so is very tender and lean. Most cuts are not well suited to cooking in the slow cooker. Exceptions are shoulder of veal, also known as the oyster, which is sometimes cut into chunks for casseroles; and the knuckle, the bonier end of the hind leg, which can be cut into slices and used to make the Italian stew osso bucco.

Above: Chuck steak (top) and brisket (bottom) are tough cuts, but both have an excellent flavour. They are perfectly suited to long, slow stewing, which gives deliciously moist results.

Below: Knuckle (top) and shoulder (bottom) are two of the few cuts of veal suitable for slow cooker cooking.

BRING OUT THE TASTE

Beef is a well-flavoured meat that is delicious cooked with robust ingredients and served with spicy accompaniments. Peppery mustards and spicy horseradish are classic accompaniments, while wasabi, a sharp-tasting Japanese horseradish gives a more unusual twist.

Other Asian flavourings, such as soy sauce and ginger, also work well. Perfect vegetable partners include potatoes, leeks, onions, parsnips, celery and celeriac.

LAMB

Though lamb cuts do not usually need tenderizing, the fragrant flavour of the meat is intensified by slow cooking. It is enjoyed around the world in a wealth of pot-roasts, casseroles, stews, tagines, curries and braised dishes.

Buying and storing

Lamb comes from animals that are less than a year old; spring lamb comes from animals that are between five and seven months old. Meat from older sheep is known as mutton and has a darker colour and stronger flavour; it is rarely available. Look for firm, slightly pink lamb with a fine-grained texture. The younger the animal, the paler the meat. The fat should be creamy white, firm and waxy. Avoid any meat that looks dark, dry or grainy.

Lamb should be kept covered on a low shelf in the refrigerator. Pre-packed meat can be left in its packaging and used by the date given on the packet. When buying loose meat, steaks and chops will keep for 2–3 days, while larger joints will keep for up to 5 days.

Above: Tender chump chops are good pan-fried, grilled or braised.

Below: A small leg of lamb can be pot-roasted in the slow cooker; steaks cut from the leg are good for braises and casseroles.

Cuts of lamb

The lean, tender prime cuts are taken from the top of the lamb along the middle of the back and are often grilled (broiled), fried or roasted. However, they may also be cooked using slow, moist methods. Tougher cuts from the neck and lower legs respond well to slow cooker methods.

Breast This inexpensive cut is fairly fatty and is often served boned and rolled, sometimes with stuffing. It can be braised in the slow cooker, but trim off the visible fat.

Chops and cutlets Chump or loin chops and leg chops are thick tender chops. Best-end chops or cutlets and middle neck cutlets are thinner and should be trimmed of fat before slow cooking.

Leg This is the prime roasting joint and is often divided into two pieces: the knuckle or shank end, and the leg fillet. The shank is a flavourful cut and is good pot-roasted or gently braised. A small leg of lamb may be pot-roasted on the bone in a large or oval slow cooker, or it can be boned and stuffed. It may also be cut into leg steaks or cubed.

Middle neck and scrag end Relatively cheap and made tender by long, slow cooking, these are used in dishes such as Lancashire hot-pot and Irish stew.

Saddle of lamb Also called a double loin of lamb, this tender roasting joint is too big to cook in a slow cooker.

Shoulder This roasting joint from the forequarter is fattier than the leg, so should be trimmed before pot-roasting on or off the bone. Boneless shoulder can be cubed for casseroles.

Above: Tender noisettes cut from the rolled, boned loin (top) are better suited to quick cooking techniques, while lamb cutlets (bottom) are great for braised dishes.

> ### PERFECT PARTNERS
> Fragrant herbs and fruity flavours go well with lamb. Dried fruit is a common addition to lamb dishes all over the world; rosemary, thyme and mint are popular herbs; and garlic and salty additions, such as anchovies and olives, are widely used in Mediterranean dishes. Vegetables that go well with lamb include new potatoes, peas, carrots and beans such as haricot (navy) and flageolet.
>
> *Below*: Dried prunes make a tasty addition to a Moroccan lamb tagine.

PORK

This light meat is rich-tasting and very versatile. It is also particularly good for slow cooking: whole joints can be pot-roasted, bacon and gammon can be poached, chops can be braised, and cubes of meat stewed. Pork products, such as sausages and minced (ground) pork, are also fabulous cooked in the slow cooker, in dishes such as hearty stews and chunky pâtés and terrines.

Buying and storing

Traditionally, fresh pork was a food for late autumn. Pigs were fattened through the summertime to provide fresh and cured meats during the colder months. However, with modern storage techniques, pork is no longer a seasonal meat and is available all the year round.

Pork should be a pale brownish-pink in colour with a smooth, moist, fine-grained texture. The fat should look white and firm. In older animals, the meat darkens to a deeper colour and the flesh is coarser and less tender.

Hygiene is very important when handling pork, and great care should be taken not to contaminate other foods with the meat juices. Store pork on a low shelf in the refrigerator, below any food that will be eaten raw. Keep pre-packed meat in its packaging and observe the use-by dates. Minced (ground) pork can be kept for up to 2 days, while pork chops and joints can be kept for 3 days.

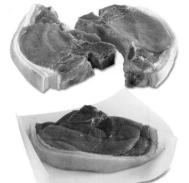

Above: Loin chops (top) and chump chops (bottom) are very good for braising.

Cuts of pork

Belly/side This cut can be rolled and tied to make a neat joint and pot-roasted, or used for mincing and making sausages or terrines. Once a very fatty cut, today's belly pork tends to be leaner.
Chops Large and bony chump chops come from the hind loin, and leaner loin chops from the foreloin. Both are good for braising. (A loin joint is better suited to oven-roasting than slow cooking.)
Leg/ham Often weighing more than 4.5kg/10lb, this cut is too big to be cooked in the slow cooker. However, it can be cut into two joints: the knuckle (shank) and the fillet. The knuckle can be pot-roasted, but is better oven-roasted. Leg fillet is cut across the top of the leg and is very tender. Leg steaks, cut from the top of the leg, are good for braising.
Neck end Cuts from this area include the spare rib, which is often cut into spare rib chops (different from Chinese-style spare ribs, which are cut from the belly). They are good for braising.
Shoulder/blade Taken from the fore end and sold on or off the bone, this can be pot-roasted, but is usually trimmed, cubed and casseroled.
Fillet/tenderloin This lean, boneless, fine-textured piece of meat can be sliced into medallions or split lengthways, stuffed and tied. It may be cooked on a high setting in the slow cooker.

Bacon, ham and gammon

These are cured cuts of pork. Bacon is usually cured meat taken from the back and sides of the pig. Ham is the hind leg of a pig cut from the whole side, then cured separately. Gammon is the name of the whole hind leg cut from a side of bacon after curing. Cooked gammon is now often referred to as ham. These joints respond well to poaching in the slow cooker, as long cooking makes them very tender. Bacon chops and gammon steaks are also good braised. Strips of bacon are often fried in a pan before adding to slow cooker stews.

Above: Rolled belly of pork is perfect for pot-roasting in the slow cooker.

POULTRY and GAME

The term poultry covers domesticated birds, including chicken, turkey, duck, goose and guinea fowl, while game refers to wild birds and animals hunted for food, including pheasant, quail, wild rabbit and venison. However, many game birds and animals are now farmed.

SMALL POULTRY

Chicken is probably the most popular of all small poultry, but there are many other types that are just as good.

Buying and storing

When buying fresh or chilled poultry, choose birds with soft blemish-free skin. Because poultry is highly susceptible to bacterial growth, keep poultry well chilled. Place loose poultry in a deep dish and cover loosely, check pre-packed poultry to make sure that the packs are sealed and place on a plate, then store in the coldest part of the refrigerator. Check inside whole birds and remove any giblets. Always wash hands, utensils and surfaces after handling poultry.

When using frozen poultry, the safest way to thaw it is in the refrigerator. Place in a suitable container and leave to defrost: for a 900g–1.3kg/2–3lb bird, allow about 30 hours in the refrigerator, or 8 hours at room temperature; for a 2.25kg/5lb chicken, allow about 48 hours in the refrigerator, or 10 hours at room temperature. Once thawed or partially thawed, it should not be refrozen.

Below (from left to right):
Corn-fed, free-range and
organic chickens are
widely available.

Types of small poultry

Poussin This is the French name for a young chicken that is only four to six weeks old and weighs 350–675g/ 12oz–1½lb. These are very tender, with little fat, and will serve one or two people. They are ideal for pot-roasting, which gives moist, tender results.

Spring chicken These are sometimes called double poussins and will easily serve two. They are slightly larger birds, between six and ten weeks old, and weigh about 900g/2lb.

Roasting chicken Sometimes known as a roaster, these prime birds are about 12 weeks old. They usually weigh about 1.3kg/3lb but they may be as big as 3kg/ 6–7lb. The larger the bird, the better its value. The proportion of meat to bone will be higher. They can be pot-roasted whole or in portions, poached, braised or stewed.

Stewing or boiling chicken Rarely available from supermarkets, these birds are over one year old and tend to be large. Too tough for roasting, they are full of flavour and perfect for the slow cooker as they need slow simmering. Either poach or use for soups and stews.

Guinea fowl These domestic fowl originated from the coast of Guinea in West Africa, hence their name. These birds are about the same size as a spring chicken. The flesh is delicate with a slightly gamey flavour. They can be cooked in the same way as chicken, but because they are quite dry, they respond best to moist cooking such as pot-roasting, braising and stewing.

Cuts of chicken

A wide range of chicken portions are available fresh and frozen and are sold either individually, or in large, more economical packs. They may be sold on or off the bone.

Chicken quarters may be either leg joints or wing joints that have a portion of breast meat attached. The leg joint may be divided into thighs, small well-flavoured dark meat joints, and drumsticks. Both need relatively long cooking in the slow cooker because the meat is compact.

Tender breast portions are entirely white meat; they are sold on or off the bone and may be skinned or unskinned. Portions on the bone have the most flavour when stewed or braised. Boneless chicken breast portions are sometimes referred to as fillets. The very small strips of chicken that can be found under the chicken breast are often sold separately. Supremes are chicken breast portions that include the wingbone, while part-boned breasts still have the short piece of bone leading into the wing and the fine strip of breastbone.

Jointing small poultry

This method of jointing can also be used for game birds, such as pheasant.

1 With the breast uppermost, use a sharp knife to remove the leg between the thigh and carcass. Cut, angling the knife inwards, through the ball and socket joint. Repeat with the other leg.

2 Using poultry shears, cut along the breastbone, between the breast sections. Turn the bird over and cut out the backbone. Using poultry shears, cut off the wing tips at the first joint.

3 Cut each breast section in half, leaving a portion of the breast attached to the wing. Next, cut each leg through the knee joint to separate the thigh and drumstick, making eight portions in all.

TURKEY

These substantial birds have dense meat that is lean and succulent. Fully grown, a turkey can weigh over 9kg/20lb and feed over twenty people. Whole birds won't fit in a slow cooker, but prepared joints and cuts are perfect for slow cooking.

Skinless, boneless breast fillets can be used in many different dishes. Turkey drumsticks can be large enough to provide a meal for three to four people. They can be pot-roasted, but are better braised or stewed until tender. Diced turkey is usually darker meat from the thigh or leg, and is ideal for casseroles and pâtés. Minced (ground) turkey can be used as an alternative to minced beef.

DUCK

Flavourful, juicy and rich, duck is much fattier than chicken or turkey, with a higher proportion of bone to meat. Birds under 2 months old are called ducklings and are slightly leaner and more tender, but with less flavour. Wild duck has a stronger, more gamey taste than farmed duck, but can be cooked in the same way. The slow cooker is unsuitable for cooking whole birds because of their awkward shape and fat content. However, duck breast portions can be used, providing the thick layer of fat is removed. Breast portions weigh about 225g/8oz, making a generous serving for one. Skinned duck portions are ideal for braising, especially in citrus or fruit sauces, which tenderize and flavour.

Jointing a duck

Because ducks have a high proportion of bone to meat, it is better to cut the bird into four portions, dividing an equal amount of meat between them.

1 Place the duck, breast side up, on a board. Using poultry shears, trim off the wing tips at the first joint. Pull back the skin at the neck end and cut out the wishbone. Cut the breast in half from the tail end to the neck.

Above: Turkey is a versatile as well as economical meat.

2 Separate the bird into two halves by cutting along each side of the backbone. Remove the backbone and discard.

3 Cut each portion in half, sharing the meat as evenly as possible between the four portions.

GOOSE

These large, fatty birds are difficult to rear intensively, so fresh birds are usually only available from the late autumn until Christmas. Goose is much better suited to oven-roasting than cooking gently in the slow cooker.

GAME
Once hard to come by, game is now readily available from the supermarket. Fresh wild game remains seasonal and is only available during the months when hunting is allowed. Many types of game are now farmed and available year-round, while wild game is available frozen. Game can be divided into two types: game birds and furred game, which includes rabbit, hare, wild boar and venison.

Buying and storing
Larger supermarkets and specialist butchers offer a good choice of game when in season and should be able to offer you advice on preparation and cooking. Game birds will not look as perfect as poultry, but check that they are not too damaged. Pheasant should be even in shape with a pleasant gamey aroma. Partridge will have a slightly stronger game smell and soft pale flesh. When buying grouse and quail, look for a moist fresh skin and choose birds with a high proportion of meat to bone.

Right: A brace of pheasant.

Below: Tiny quail are often farmed.

Below: Mallard is the most commonly available wild duck.

Birds that are sold in sealed packaging should be left in their packing and used by the date indicated. If you buy a bird "loose" from the butcher, remove the packaging when you get home, rinse the bird under cold running water and pat dry with kitchen paper. Put the bird in a deep dish to catch any drips and cover it tightly with clear film (plastic wrap). Store game birds in the coldest part of the refrigerator and use within two days of purchase or freeze straight away. Before cooking wild game birds, rub your fingertips over the surface to try to locate any tiny balls of lead shot that may be left in them, then carefully cut them out with kitchen scissors or a filleting knife and discard.

Types of game bird
Very young and tender birds are often roasted or spatchcocked and grilled (broiled), but most older game birds benefit from moist cooking techniques, such as pot-roasting, stewing or braising. When pot-roasting dry game birds, such as cock pheasant, wrap rashers (slices) of streaky (fatty) bacon around the bird, then tie in place with string. This will help to baste and flavour the meat.

Pheasant One of the most plentiful of game birds, these are usually raised on managed estates in a similar manner to free-range farming. Traditionally they were sold in pairs, known as a brace (one male and one female). The tender hen pheasant would be roasted and the cock pheasant hung and stewed. In practice, supermarket pheasants are always young and tender. For the best results, pot-roast or stew pheasants. One bird should serve three or four people.

Grouse Native to Scotland, these birds feed on highland heather, which gives them a rich gamey flavour. They are quite small and

Below: Pigeon.

MARINATING GAME BIRDS
Leaving game birds to marinate for several hours or overnight in the refrigerator adds moisture and flavour as well as tenderizing the meat. Place the whole bird or pieces in a deep non-metallic dish, then pour over the marinade. Cover and marinate, turning at least once. Try one of the following combinations:
- Fruity red wine and crushed juniper berries
- Dry white wine and orange rind
- Dry cider and fresh root ginger
- Fresh orange juice and fragrant herbs such as thyme or rosemary

will serve one or two people. Ptarmigan and capercaillie are members of the grouse family, but are considered to have an inferior flavour compared to grouse. Young birds may be pot-roasted, but need to be kept moist with a layer of fat or streaky bacon over the breast. They are good stewed.

Partridge There are two main types: French or red-legged partridge, and the smaller English or grey-legged partridge, which has a better flavour. At their prime (around three months old), they weigh about 450g/1lb and it is usual to serve one per person. Older birds should always be casseroled or braised.

Wild duck These are less fatty than farmed ducks, so smaller ones may be cooked whole in a large slow cooker. Choose inland ducks because those from saltwater areas may have a fishy flavour.

Pigeon Wild and wood pigeon has a strong flavour and can be cooked slowly to tenderize the meat. Another traditional way of cooking an older bird is in a steamed pudding, often with beef steak inside a suet crust. Young pigeon is known as squab. They are reared commercially, although they are usually only available in the spring.

Quail This is now a protected species, so quail on sale will have been farmed. They are tiny, so you will need two per person for a main course. They may be pot-roasted whole.

FURRED GAME

Most game needs to be hung before cooking to tenderize the flesh and develop the flavour. However, this is usually done by the butcher, so the meat is ready for cooking when you buy it.

Game is cooked in the same way as other meats and recipes for similar types of meat are usually interchangeable. For example, wild boar can often be used instead of pork, farmed rabbit instead of chicken, and venison in place of beef in many recipes. Mature game should always be cooked using gentle, moist heat, such as braising and stewing, making it ideal for the slow cooker.

Deer

The word venison was once used to describe the meat of any animal killed for food by hunting. Today, in Britain and Australia, the term venison only refers to the meat from deer, although in North America it also includes meat from the reindeer, moose, caribou, elk and antelope. Venison from deer is a lean, dark, close-textured meat. Much of it is now farmed and is more tender, with a slightly milder flavour, than venison from wild deer. Prime cuts, such as loin and fillet, are best roasted and served rare. Other cuts, such as shin, neck and shoulder, benefit from marinating (red wine and juniper is traditional); they then need long and gentle cooking to tenderize and bring out the flavour of the meat.

Wild boar

Although hunted to extinction in Britain in the 17th century, wild boar is still found in Europe, central Asia and North Africa. The meat is dark-coloured with a strong flavour and little fat, so it benefits from marinades with a little added oil. It can be cooked in exactly the same way as pork, but care must be taken because the meat is dry and can easily become tough. Moist cooking methods work best.

Rabbit and hare

Although these animals belong to the same family, the meat is very different. Rabbit, especially if it has been farmed, is a paler, milder meat, similar to chicken. Hare, or jack rabbit as it is known in the United States, has a very strong, dark gamey flesh. The saddle of both can be roasted, but other cuts are best slowly stewed. Boneless rabbit and hare meat can be used in steamed puddings, terrines and pâtés. Older hares are traditionally jugged (cooked in a casserole set over a pan of simmering water to temper the heat) to give deliciously tender results. Cooking gently in the slow cooker gives similar results.

Jointing a rabbit

A whole rabbit can be jointed into five pieces or more, depending on its size.

1 To joint a skinned and cleaned rabbit, use a large filleting knife to cut between the ball and socket joint at the top of each thigh to remove the hind legs.

2 Cut the body into three pieces. This will give you five pieces – two forelegs, two hind legs and the saddle.

Above and right: Rabbit saddle is best roasted. Other rabbit cuts should be stewed.

Above and left: Cultivated hare has lean, dark meat and is available whole or in pieces.

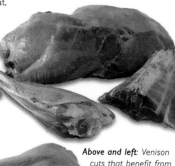

Above and left: Venison cuts that benefit from long, slow cooking include shin, shoulder and neck (above left to right) and haunch (left).

FISH and SHELLFISH

The slow cooker is great for cooking fish, allowing the subtle flavour to develop slowly and also helping to retain the fish's shape as it cooks. Fish dishes that can be made in the slow cooker include terrines, soups, risottos and pasta dishes, as well as simple steamed and poached fish. The slow cooker is also good for cooking many dishes containing raw and cooked shellfish. However, it is not suitable for cooking live shellfish, such as mussels and lobsters, because these require brief, fast boiling.

Most shellfish benefit from short cooking and should be added towards the end of cooking time, particularly when using pre-cooked shellfish. One exception is squid, which requires either very brief or very long, slow cooking; anything in between gives tough results.

Buying and cooking

Always buy the freshest fish and shellfish available, from a supplier with a high turnover, and prepare and cook it within 24 hours. Fish and shellfish should smell fresh; if it has an unpleasant fishy or ammoniac odour, it is past its best. Most fish and shellfish from the supermarket has already been frozen, so shouldn't be refrozen; check this when you buy.

PREPARING FISH

Fish can be divided into two types: white and oily. These, in turn, can be divided into round and flat fish, which require slightly different preparation and cooking.

Round fish

This group includes white-fleshed fish such as cod, coley and haddock, and oily fish such as salmon and mackerel. They have rounded bodies and eyes on either side of the head. The flesh is usually firm with largish flakes when cooked. Many are too big to be cooked whole in the slow cooker, so need to be sliced into steaks or filleted. A good fishmonger will often do this for you.

I To remove the scales, place the fish on a large sheet of newspaper. Scrape a fish scaler or knife against the skin, working from the tail to the head.

2 Using a filleting knife or thin, sharp knife, slit the fish open along the belly from the gills to the tail vent. Carefully scrape out the innards with a spoon, then rinse well under running water, inside and out. Cut off the head using a sharp knife.

3 To fillet the fish, lay it on its side, tail away from you. Make an incision along the backbone from head to tail, cutting through behind the gills. Starting at the head end, slide the knife between the fillet and bones to release the fillet.

4 To skin the fillet, lay it skin side down. Make a cut at the tail end, cutting through the flesh, but not the skin, so that the fillet can be lifted away slightly. Hold the tail firmly and "saw" the knife between the skin and flesh.

Flat fish

This group includes sole and plaice. Both eyes lie on their upper side and, because they lead an inactive life on the seabed, the flesh tends to be very delicate.

I Place the fish, light side down, on a board. Make a cut down the centre using a sharp filleting knife, following the backbone, then make a second cut round the head.

2 Slide the knife under one fish fillet, inserting the blade between the flesh and bones. Holding the loosened corner, cut the flesh from the bones. Remove the second fillet in the same way, then turn the fish over and repeat.

3 The skins may be removed in the same manner as for round fish.

PREPARING SHELLFISH

You can often ask the fishmonger to prepare shellfish for you, but it is also easy to prepare at home.

Prawns/shrimp

Raw prawns may be cooked in their shells or peeled first. The dark intestinal vein is usually removed.

1 To peel, grip the head between your forefinger and thumb. Holding the body with your other hand, gently pull until the head comes off. Remove the legs and peel the shell from the body. The tail may be pulled away or left on.

2 To remove the dark intestinal vein, make a shallow cut down the centre of the back and pull out the vein using a knife blade or a cocktail stick (toothpick).

Preparing squid

Unlike other shellfish, which have their protective shell on the outside, the shell of the squid is found inside its body.

1 Hold the body of the squid in one hand and the tentacles in the other and gently pull apart. Cut the tentacles away from the head just below the eyes and discard the head.

2 Remove the "quill" and soft innards from the body and discard. Peel off the thin membrane, then rinse the body and tentacles under cold running water.

3 Using a sharp knife, slice the body into rings, or cut it into large pieces and lightly score in a criss-cross pattern.

COOKING FISH

Fish is well suited to simple cooking methods that retain its natural juices. Unlike meat, fish should be removed from the slow cooker as soon as it is done, otherwise it will become dry. It is ready when the flesh is still slightly translucent when eased away from the bone, and flakes easily.

Poaching

This is a good method for cooking large, fairly firm pieces of fish, such as steaks or chunky fillets. It can also be used for small whole fish. Fish stock, wine, water and milk can all be used for poaching.

1 Lightly grease the base of the ceramic cooking pot. Place four 175–225g/6–8oz salmon fillets or similar in the base, leaving space between each one.

2 Pour over 150ml/¼ pint/⅔ cup dry white wine and 300ml/½ pint/1¼ cups of boiling fish stock or water. Add a pinch of salt, 2 black peppercorns, a few slices of onion, 1 bay leaf and a sprig of fresh parsley.

3 Cover the pot with the lid and switch the slow cooker to high. Cook for 45 minutes–1½ hours, or until cooked. Serve with melted butter or a sauce, or leave to cool and serve with salad.

Braising

This method cooks the fish in a small amount of liquid, so that it is partly poached and partly steamed. It is a good technique for delicate flat fish fillets. Rolling the fish fillets helps to protect them during cooking and allows you to add a filling for extra flavour.

1 Pour slightly less than 5mm/¼in white wine, cider or fish stock into the ceramic cooking pot and switch the slow cooker to high. Cover with the lid.

2 Blend 25g/1oz butter with lemon or orange rind, salt and pepper. Place four large, skinned lemon sole fillets on a board and spread each with the butter.

3 Roll up the fillet to enclose the filling and carefully place in the base of the ceramic cooking pot, with the loose end tucked underneath.

4 Sprinkle the fish with 15ml/1 tbsp lemon juice. Cover with the lid and cook for 45 minutes–1½ hours, or until the fish is opaque and cooked. Transfer to serving plates. Stir a little sour cream and chopped fresh parsley, dill or coriander (cilantro) into the cooking juices and spoon over the fish.

FRUITS

The gentle simmering of the slow cooker makes it ideal for cooking all kinds of fruit to perfection. It is particularly good for poaching delicate fruits that have a tendency to break up during cooking, including soft fruits, such as currants and rhubarb. It can also be used to make desserts, such as cobblers and crumbles.

PREPARING FRUIT
Many fruits need only simple preparation, such as washing, while others need to be peeled, cored, seeded or stoned (pitted) before they are cooked.

Peeling
Fruits such as apples, pears and peaches should be peeled before cooking.

To peel fruits such as apples and pears, use a vegetable peeler or a small paring knife to pare off the skin in thin strips. Apples can also be peeled in one single, spiral strip.

To peel fruits such as peaches and apricots, loosen the skins first. Make a tiny nick in the skin, then place in a bowl. Pour over boiling water to cover and leave for 20–30 seconds. Lift out using a slotted spoon, rinse under cold water, and the skin should peel off easily.

Coring
Tough cores, pips and stems should be removed from fruit before cooking so that they do not spoil the dish.

When cooking chunks of fruit, first cut the fruit lengthways into quarters. Remove the central core and pips using a small knife, then peel and chop into smaller pieces as required.

When cooking whole fruits (for example, baked apples) you will need a special corer. Place the sharp "blade" of the corer over the stem end of the fruit, press down firmly and twist. The core will come out with the corer.

Removing stones/pits
Hard stones should always be removed from fruit before cooking, since they will become loose as the fruit cooks.

To stone larger fruits such as plums and apricots, cut around the crease in the fruit. Twist the halves apart, then carefully lever out the stone using the point of a small knife.

To stone cherries, it is easiest to use a special cherry stoner. Put the fruit in the stoner, with the end where the stalk was facing upwards. Push the bar into the fruit to eject the stone.

COOKING FRUIT
Fruit can be cooked in all kinds of ways in a slow cooker, which is good for stewing and poaching, and can be used for "baking" as well.

Poaching and stewing
These techniques are slightly different. Poaching cooks fruit in a hot syrup, and is good for pears, stone fruits, and figs. Stewing is used for fruit such as apples, berries and rhubarb.

1 To stew rhubarb, cut 900g/2lb rhubarb into 2.5cm/1in pieces. Put into the ceramic cooking pot with 150–200g/5–7oz/¾–1 cup caster (superfine) sugar, sprinkling it between the layers. Pour over the juice of 1 large orange and 120ml/4fl oz/½ cup water.

2 Switch the slow cooker to high and cook for 1½ hours, or until the rhubarb is tender but still holds its shape. Stir gently halfway through cooking.

Baking
Fruits such as whole apples, halved peaches and figs can be "baked" in the slow cooker, with just a tiny amount of liquid to start the cooking process.

1 To make baked apples, you can use either cooking or eating apples. Keeping the fruits whole, remove the cores, then score the skin around the circumference.

2 Blend together 115g/4oz/½ cup soft light brown sugar and 50g/2oz/¼ cup finely chopped dried fruit and use to fill the apples. Top each with a piece of butter and place in the ceramic pot on a square of foil shaped to form a saucer.

3 Pour 150ml/¼ pint/⅔ cup very hot water around the foil squares. Cover and cook on high for 2–3 hours. If using cooking apples, check frequently and remove as soon as they are tender; if overcooked, they may collapse.

To bake nectarines, figs and oranges, place the halved or sliced fruits in the buttered ceramic cooking pot. Sprinkle a little lemon juice and sugar over each one and dot with butter. Pour 75ml/5 tbsp water around the fruit, cover and cook on high for 1½–2 hours, or until tender.

Making compotes

Compotes can be made with a single fruit, or several different types, cooked in a flavoured syrup. They may be served hot or cold, as a dessert or for breakfast. The fruits should be ripe but still firm.

When using a slow cooker, all the fruits can be added at the same time, rather than in order of their cooking time. When using dried fruit, less extra sugar is needed because the fruit is already very sweet.

1 Put 200g/7oz/1 cup sugar in the ceramic cooking pot with 300ml/½ pint/1¼ cups cold water. Add flavouring ingredients such as lemon rind.

2 Switch the slow cooker to high and heat for about 30 minutes, then stir until the sugar dissolves completely. Cover the cooking pot with the lid and heat for a further 30–45 minutes.

3 Add the fruit to the syrup. This could be 450g/1lb each prepared peaches, apricots and cherries, or 450g/1lb each halved pears, plums and apple slices. Cover and cook for 1–3 hours, or until the fruit is tender. Serve hot or allow to cool and transfer to a bowl before chilling. The compote will keep for several days in the refrigerator.

Making cobblers

Stewed and canned fruit are perfect for making these traditional baked desserts. Adding a little of the juice or syrup with the fruit produces steam and helps the cobbler to rise.

1 Lightly grease the ceramic cooking pot with unsalted (sweet) butter. Add the fruit, cover the cooking pot with the lid and switch the slow cooker to high. Canned fruit, such as peaches and berries, should be cooked for about 1 hour until hot and steaming; uncooked fruit, such as apple slices, should be cooked for 2–3 hours until tender.

2 When the fruit is nearly ready, make the cobbler topping. Sift 50g/2oz/½ cup plain (all-purpose) flour, 5ml/1 tsp baking powder and a pinch of salt into a bowl. Rub in 40g/1½oz/3 tbsp butter, then add the finely grated rind of ½ lemon. Stir in 75ml/2½fl oz/⅓ cup milk to make a thick batter and spoon over the fruit. Cover and cook on high for 45 minutes–1 hour, or until a skewer inserted into the topping comes out clean.

Making crumbles

Crumbles made in a slow cooker do not brown in the same way as conventional crumbles, but using brown flour, oats, butter and crunchy sugar and a fairly dry fruit mixture gives similar results.

1 Combine prepared fruit such as apple and peach slices with a little sugar and 5ml/1 tsp cornflour (cornstarch). Add 30ml/2 tbsp fruit juice or water and switch the slow cooker to high.

2 Place 75g/3oz/¾ cup wholemeal (whole-wheat) flour and 50g/2oz/½ cup jumbo oats in a mixing bowl. Rub in 75g/3oz/6 tbsp butter. Stir in 50g/2oz/¼ cup demerara (raw) sugar, then sprinkle over the fruit. Cover and cook for 3–4 hours, or until the fruit and topping are cooked.

HERBS, SPICES and FLAVOURINGS

The judicious use of flavourings is the key to successful cooking. Some dishes require just a subtle hint, while others need more robust flavourings.

HERBS

While fresh herbs are usually considered superior, for slow cooker dishes dried herbs are often better. Delicate fresh leaves lose their pungency and colour with long cooking, whereas dried herbs release their flavour slowly. As a general rule, fresh herbs should be added about 30 minutes before the end of cooking, or just before serving.

Some herbs dry more successfully than others. Thyme, marjoram, oregano and sage dry very well, while parsley and chives lose their potency and colour; it is better to use these herbs fresh at the end of cooking. Dried herb mixtures are often well flavoured and worth using.

Buy dried herbs from a reliable source with a quick turnover and look for small packets. "Freeze dried" herbs have a good fresh flavour. Store dried herbs in a cool, dark place for 6–9 months. Try to buy fresh herbs on the day you need them. They will keep for several days stored in the refrigerator.

Below: Robustly flavoured rosemary and sage should be used sparingly.

Tender herbs

These herbs have soft, fragile leaves and need careful handling. They should be added in the last few minutes of cooking time, or to the finished dish. Popular tender herbs include pungent basil, which goes well with tomatoes and Mediterranean-style dishes; anise-scented chervil, dill and tarragon, which go well with fish, eggs and cream sauces; strong, refreshing mint; aromatic coriander (cilantro); lovage with its mild taste of celery; and the great all-rounder, parsley.

Robust herbs

These usually have tough, woody stems and pungent leaves and can withstand long cooking. They should be added at the start of slow cooking to extract and mellow their flavour, then removed just before serving. Popular robust herbs include richly flavoured bay leaves, which are used in stocks, casseroles, marinades and some sweet dishes; fragrant, aromatic oregano, marjoram and thyme, which are very good in Mediterranean-style dishes; robust rosemary, which goes well with lamb; pungent sage, which complements pork; and aromatic kaffir lime leaves, which are used in Thai and Malaysian dishes.

SPICES

Warm, fragrant spices are usually added at the beginning of cooking time. However, some may become bitter if cooked for many hours, and should be added partway through cooking. Most spices are better used whole, rather than ground, in slow cooker dishes. Store spices in a cool, dark place and check the sell-by date before using; they lose their taste and aroma with age. Whole spices will keep for up to 1 year; ground spices start to lose their pungency after about 6 months.

Left: Delicate dill has a mild aniseed flavour that goes well with fish.

Hot spices

Many spices add heat to dishes – some give just a hint of warmth, others a fierce heat. The main hot spices are chilli, ginger, pepper and mustard.

There are more than 200 types of chilli, with varying shape, size, colour and potency. They can be bought fresh, dried, flaked or ground. Chilli powder may be hot or mild – from red hot cayenne pepper to mild, sweet paprika. There are also chilli sauces, such as Tabasco or Thai chilli sauce. All chillies and chilli products can become bitter with long cooking and should be added partway through cooking.

Sweet, peppery ginger is used in both sweet and savoury dishes and is available fresh, dried, ground and preserved in syrup. Its close relative, galangal, is used in many South-east Asian dishes. Warm, spicy fresh turmeric looks similar to fresh root ginger and is used in curries.

Black, white and green peppercorns add a peppery bite to dishes. Black are the most aromatic. Black, brown and white mustard seeds have a much more pungent aroma and kick, with the black seeds being the hottest. The heat diminishes with cooking, so add towards the end of cooking time.

Fragrant spices

Some plants are grown for their fragrant, aromatic seeds. These are sold whole and ground. Long, slow cooking softens the whole seeds and releases their taste. Popular seed spices include warm, aromatic cumin and coriander, which are used in Indian, North African and Middle Eastern dishes; pungent caraway seeds, which feature in many European dishes, especially pork- and cabbage-based ones, as well as baked recipes such as rye bread and sweet seed cake; and poppy seeds, which are often used in desserts in eastern Europe, and are also a popular topping for crusty bread. Other fragrant spices include warming allspice, cinnamon, cassia and nutmeg; aromatic cardamom pods; pungent cloves; scented star anise; vanilla, which is mainly used in sweet dishes; gin-scented juniper berries, which go well with pork, game and cabbage; delicate, bitter-sweet saffron, which is often used in rice and fish dishes; and sour tamarind, which is widely used in Indian and South-east Asian cooking.

Spice mixtures

As well as individual spices, there are a number of ground spice mixes that are widely used in both sweet and savoury dishes. Popular mixes include mixed spice (apple pie spice), which is used in cakes and desserts; Chinese five-spice powder, which is used in many savoury Chinese and Asian dishes; garam masala, a popular Indian spice mix that is added towards the end of cooking; and a wide variety of curry powders that vary in strength from mild to very hot. Jars of curry paste are also available.

OTHER FLAVOURINGS

As well as herbs and spices, there are many other flavourings that can be used to enliven dishes – ranging from pungent sauces to delicate flower waters.

Savoury sauces

There are many savoury sauces that can be used to boost the flavour of dishes. They are strongly flavoured and often salty, so usually only a splash or two is required. Mushroom ketchup and Worcestershire sauce can add a rich, rounded flavour to stews and casseroles. Dark and light soy sauce and other soy-based sauces, such as hoisin, are good in Asian-style braised dishes and soups. Fermented fish sauces are common in many cuisines and include anchovy sauce, oyster sauce and nam pla (Thai fish sauce). They should be added at the beginning of cooking.

Sweet extracts

These have a rich, fragrant aroma and are usually used to flavour sweet dishes. You only need a little, sometimes just a few drops, to flavour a whole dish. Look for the real thing, and avoid artificial flavourings. Almond and vanilla extract are used to flavour cakes and desserts. Orange flower water and rose water have a delicate fragrance and should be added towards the end of cooking for the best flavour.

Above: There are many different varieties of chilli.

Alcohol

Because of the gentle heat, alcohol evaporates more slowly in a slow cooker, resulting in a stronger flavour. When adapting conventional recipes, the amount of alcohol should be reduced slightly. Beer, cider and wine can be used in marinades and casseroles. Fortified wines, such as sherry, port, Marsala and Madeira, can be used to enrich both sweet and savoury dishes; a few spoonfuls should be added towards the end of cooking. Colourless fruit spirits, such as kirsch, and sweet liqueurs, such as amaretto, can be used to flavour desserts and sweet dishes.

GRINDING SPICES

Where ground spices are called for in a recipe, it is better to use whole spices and grind them yourself.

1 Dry-fry whole spices in a heavy frying pan, shaking the pan over a medium-high heat for 1–2 minutes until the aroma is released.

2 Place the spices in a mortar and grind to a powder. To grind a larger quantity of spices, it is easier to use an electric spice grinder or a coffee grinder used solely for the purpose.

MAKING STOCK

A good stock forms the foundation of many dishes, from simple soups and classic sauces to warming casseroles and pot-roasts. Although ready-made stocks are available from supermarkets, making your own is easy and inexpensive. Most butchers and fishmongers will supply meat and fish bones and trimmings.

Making stock in a large pan on the stovetop is a simple process, but using a slow cooker is even easier because it can be left to bubble unattended for hours. A good stock must be simmered gently (rapid boiling will make it go cloudy) so the slow cooker comes into its own, keeping the stock at a bare simmer.

There are two types of stock: brown stock, where the bones and vegetables are roasted in the oven first, and white stock, where ingredients are only boiled. Clean vegetable peelings, celery leaves and the stalks from fresh herbs are useful additions, providing extra flavour.

Always start making a stock with cold water; ideally this and any vegetables should be at room temperature. Use whole peppercorns because long cooking makes ground pepper taste bitter. If you make stock without salt, it can be used in dishes that include salty ingredients, such as smoked meats and fish, and as a base for reduced sauces.

Below: The ingredients used for stock can be varied according to what is available.

A good stock should be beautifully clear. Fat and other impurities will make it cloudy, so it is important to skim these off as the stock comes to simmering point, and at least once during cooking. Strain the stock through a sieve placed over a bowl and leave to drip slowly, rather than squeezing the vegetables, which will spoil the clarity.

For the following recipes, you will need a slow cooker with a capacity of at least 3.5 litres/6 pints/10¼ cups. If your slow cooker is too small, the recipes can be halved, but the cooking times remain the same.

Basic meat stock

Used for meat dishes, such as casseroles, and as a base for light soups, basic meat stock is traditionally made from veal bones. Beef bones will also make a good stock but with a stronger flavour. Lamb bones may also be used, but this stock can only be used for lamb dishes. Some recipes include lean stewing meat, such as shin of beef, which gives a much meatier flavour. For this option, you will need 450g/1lb each bones and meat.

MAKES ABOUT 1.2 LITRES/2 PINTS/5 CUPS

675g/1½lb beef or veal bones
1 onion, unpeeled and quartered
1 carrot, sliced
1 stick celery, sliced
6 black peppercorns
1 fresh bouquet garni
about 1.2 litres/2 pints/5 cups cold water

1 Using a meat cleaver, chop any large bones, so that they will fit into the slow cooker. (Cutting the bones into pieces will increase the flavour of the stock.)

2 Place the vegetables in the ceramic cooking pot. Add the peppercorns and bouquet garni, then place the bones on top, packing them tightly so that they fit in a single layer. Pour over the water, adding a little more, if necessary, to cover the bones, but leaving a space of at least 4cm/1½in between the water and the top of the pot. Cover and cook on high or auto for 2 hours.

3 Using a slotted spoon, skim off any scum and turn the temperature to low or leave on auto and cook for 5 hours.

4 Strain the stock through a fine strainer and leave to cool. This should be done quickly, ideally over a bowl of iced water.

5 Chill the stock for at least 4 hours, then remove the fat from the surface.

Brown meat stock

This stock is used as the base for classic beef consommé and other clear soups such as French onion soup. It also adds depth to the colour and flavour of casseroles and braised meat dishes. The secret to the stock's rich colour and flavour lies in the way the onion and bones are caramelized before simmering. However, take care not to let them burn, or the final stock will taste bitter.

MAKES ABOUT 1.2 LITRES/2 PINTS/5 CUPS

675g/1½lb beef or veal bones
1 onion, unpeeled and quartered
1 carrot, sliced
1 stick celery, sliced
6 black peppercorns
1 fresh bouquet garni
about 1.2 litres/2 pints/5 cups cold water

1 Preheat the oven to 220°C/425°F/ Gas 7. Using a meat cleaver, chop up the large bones, then place in a large, heavy roasting pan. Roast for 15 minutes, turning several times during cooking.

2 Add the vegetables to the pan and cook for 15 minutes more, until the bones are well browned and the vegetables lightly tinged with colour.

3 Transfer the bones and vegetables to the slow cooker, adding the peppercorns and bouquet garni. Pour in enough water to just cover, allowing a space of at least 4cm/1½in between the water and the top of the cooking pot. Cover with the lid and cook on high or auto for 2 hours.

4 Using a slotted spoon, skim off any scum, then reduce the temperature to low or leave on auto. Cook for 4 hours.

5 Strain the stock through a fine strainer into a bowl and cool quickly. Cover and chill or freeze. Remove the fat from the surface of the stock before using.

STORING STOCK

Fresh stock should be covered and stored in the refrigerator as soon as it is cool, then used within 3 days. If it will not be needed in this time, freeze it in small quantities – 300ml/ ½ pint/1¼ cups is ideal. Line square-sided containers with freezer bags, leaving plenty overhanging the sides. Pour the measured stock into the bags, then freeze until solid. Remove the bags of stock, seal, label and stack the blocks in the freezer.

White poultry stock

Raw poultry bones, chicken wings or a cooked poultry carcass can be used to make this stock. It makes an excellent base for soups, white sauces and for braising or stewing white meats. Including the onion skins does not add a great deal of extra flavour, but gives the stock a lovely, rich golden colour.

MAKES ABOUT 1 LITRE/1¾ PINTS/4 CUPS

1 fresh or cooked poultry carcass
1 onion, unpeeled and roughly chopped
1 leek, roughly chopped
1 celery stick, sliced
1 carrot, sliced
6 white peppercorns
2 sprigs fresh thyme
2 bay leaves
about 1 litre/1¾ pints/4 cups cold water

1 Using poultry shears, cut the carcass into pieces, so that they will fit into the slow cooker. (This will also help to extract the flavour from the bones.)

2 Place the chopped onion, leek, celery and carrot in the base of the ceramic cooking pot. Sprinkle over the peppercorns, then add the herbs and top with the chopped poultry carcass.

3 Pour over the water, adding a little more to cover the chicken carcass, if necessary, but leaving a space of at least 4cm/1½in between the water and the top of the ceramic cooking pot. Cover the pot with the lid, then cook on high or auto for 2 hours.

4 Using a slotted spoon, skim off any scum that has risen to the surface of the stock. Reduce the temperature to low or leave on auto, re-cover and cook for a further 3–4 hours.

5 Strain the stock through a fine strainer into a bowl and cool quickly, ideally over a bowl of iced water.

6 Cover the stock and store in the refrigerator, or freeze. Before using, remove the fat that has risen to the surface of the stock.

TURKEY GIBLET STOCK

This stock can be made in exactly the same way as white poultry stock. Use the giblets (including the liver) and neck of the turkey in place of the poultry carcass and pour over 900ml/1½ pints/3¾ cups water.

Fish Stock

This light broth can be used as the base for delicate fish soups and hearty stews, as well as for poaching. It is the quickest and most easily made of all stocks.

Unlike other stocks, fish stock should not be simmered for very long, otherwise it will become bitter. Once the stock has come to simmering point (which will take about 1 hour), it should be kept at a bare simmer for no more than 1 hour.

Use only the bones of white fish such as sole and plaice. (The bones of oily fish such as mackerel are unsuitable.) Heads may be added, but the eyes and gills should be removed because these will spoil the final flavour. You can also use prawn (shrimp) shells. The vegetables should be sliced finely to extract as much flavour as possible during cooking. To make a stock with a richer flavour, you can replace about 150ml/¼ pint/⅔ cup of the water with dry white wine.

MAKES ABOUT 900ML/1½ PINTS/3¾ CUPS

900g/2lb fish bones and trimmings
2 carrots, finely sliced
1 onion, peeled and sliced
6 white peppercorns
1 bouquet garni
900ml/1½ pints/3¾ cups water

1 Rinse the fish bones and trimmings well under cold water and cut any larger bones or pieces into several chunks so that they will easily fit inside the ceramic cooking pot.

2 Arrange the vegetables in the base of the cooking pot. Sprinkle over the peppercorns, add the bouquet garni and place the fish bones on top.

3 Pour the cold water into the pot, adding a little more to cover the bones, if necessary, but leaving a space of at least 4cm/1½in between the water and the top of the cooking pot. Cover with the lid, then cook on high or auto for 1 hour until simmering.

4 Using a slotted spoon, skim off any scum that has risen to the surface. Reduce the temperature to low or leave on auto, re-cover and cook for 1 hour. (Do not cook for longer than this.)

5 Using a fine sieve – or a course sieve lined with muslin (cheesecloth) that has been briefly held under running water – pour the stock into a bowl, then cool quickly, ideally in a bowl of iced water. Cover with clear film (plastic wrap) and store in the refrigerator, or freeze.

Vegetable stock

You can vary the vegetables used in this recipe, but be sure to wash them well and chop fairly small. Strong-tasting vegetables, such as turnips and parsnips, should be used in small quantities; their flavour will dominate otherwise. Starchy vegetables, such as potatoes, should be avoided; they will make the stock cloudy.

MAKES ABOUT 1.5 LITRES/2½ PINTS/
6¼ CUPS

1 large onion, left unpeeled
   and chopped
1 leek, roughly chopped
2 carrots, thinly sliced
1 celery stick, thinly sliced
2 bay leaves
1 sprig fresh thyme
a few fresh parsley stalks
6 white peppercorns
about 1.5 litres/2½ pints/6¼ cups water

1 Put the vegetables, herbs and peppercorns in the ceramic cooking pot and pour over the water. Cover and cook on high or auto for 2 hours.

2 Using a slotted spoon, skim off any scum. Reduce the temperature to low, or leave on auto, and cook for 2 hours.

3 Strain the stock through a fine sieve into a bowl and leave to cool. Cover and store in the refrigerator, or freeze.

Removing fat

Before using stock, the fat should be removed. The easiest way to do this is by cooling, then chilling the stock.

Pour the stock into a bowl, cover and leave undisturbed in the refrigerator for at least 4 hours, or overnight. The fat will rise to the surface, setting in visible globules or a single layer if there is a lot of fat in the stock. Simply lift the fat from the top, or scoop off with a spoon.

1 If you don't have time to let the stock cool, let it settle for a few minutes, then skim off as much fat as possible, using a slotted spoon.

2 Next, draw a sheet of absorbent kitchen paper across the top to soak up any remaining surface fat. You may need to use two or three pieces of paper to remove the fat completely.

Another way to remove the fat is to leave the stock to cool, then lower several ice cubes into it. Gently move the ice cubes around for a few seconds, then remove. The fat will solidify and cling to the ice cubes, making it easy to remove. (This method will only work if the stock is cool.)

Reducing stocks

After straining and removing the fat from stock, it can be concentrated by returning it to the slow cooker and cooking uncovered on high for several hours to allow some of the water to evaporate. However, if you need a very concentrated stock, for a reduced sauce for example, the slow cooker is not suitable. To make very concentrated stocks, pour the stock into a pan and boil rapidly on the stovetop.

READY-MADE STOCKS

If you do not have time to make your own stock, cartons of fresh stock can be found in the chiller cabinets of many supermarkets. These make a good substitute. Good-quality bouillon powders and liquid stocks may also be used, but take care with stock cubes because they are often strongly flavoured and high in salt. Make them only in the recommended strength and use in robustly flavoured dishes.

MAKING SOUPS

Although many slow cooker soup recipes have lengthy cooking times, the actual preparation time for most is minimal, and they can then be left simmering on a low setting all day or overnight. Most soups benefit from long, gentle cooking, so there is no need to worry if they are left for a little longer than intended.

A good home-made stock forms the base of many soups so it is well worth making large batches of stock and freezing it in convenient quantities. Alternatively, use good-quality ready-made stock from the supermarket.

There are two basic techniques for making slow cooker soups. The easiest is to place the prepared ingredients in the ceramic cooking pot with either cold or near-boiling stock. This produces a fresh-flavoured soup with a low fat content and is a good method for vegetable soups. However, it is less suitable for recipes containing onions, which take a long time to soften. The second, more usual, method is to sauté or fry onions, other vegetables and/or meat in a frying pan before placing in the cooking pot. In some recipes, vegetables are simply softened, but in others they may be lightly browned, giving a richer flavour and deeper colour.

Mixed vegetable soup

Almost any vegetable can be made into soup, but for the best results, use the freshest, seasonal ingredients.

SERVES 4–6

675g/1½lb mixed vegetables, such as
   carrots, celery, parsnips, potatoes
25g/1oz/2 tbsp butter
1 onion, finely chopped
5ml/1 tsp dried mixed herbs
900ml/1½ pints/3¾ cups near-boiling
   vegetable stock
150ml/¼ pint/⅔ cup milk or single
   (light) cream (optional)
salt and ground black pepper

1 Prepare the mixed vegetables, then cut them into 5mm/¼in slices, sticks or dice to ensure that they cook evenly and within the recommended time.

2 Melt the butter in a frying pan, add the onion and fry gently, stirring frequently, for 10 minutes, until softened, but not coloured.

3 Add the chopped vegetables to the pan and fry for 2–3 minutes. Transfer the vegetables to the ceramic cooking pot and switch the slow cooker to low.

4 Sprinkle over the dried mixed herbs, then pour in the stock. If you are using vegetables with a high water content, such as courgettes (zucchini) or squash, reduce the quantity of liquid. Others, such as potatoes and dried vegetables, soak up cooking juices, so add a little more liquid to compensate. (Bear in mind that it is easier to dilute the soup at the end of cooking, than to try to thicken a watery soup.)

5 Make sure that there is a gap of at least 2cm/¾in between the liquid and the top of the slow cooker, then cover with the lid and cook for 7–12 hours, or until the vegetables are tender.

6 If using milk or cream, stir this in and cook for a further 30 minutes to bring the soup back to boiling point. (Do not heat for longer than this because long heating may cause the soup to separate.) Season to taste, then serve.

ADAPTING SOUP RECIPES
Use this simple mixed vegetable soup recipe as a guide for making other soups. If you want to add meat or poultry to the soup, add it to the ceramic cooking pot at the start of cooking on high for at least 1 hour before reducing the heat to low. If you want to use fresh rather than dried herbs, stir in twice the quantity at the end of cooking time. Rather than using plain stock, use a mixture of stock and tomato juice, or a moderate amount of white wine or cider. Instead of stirring in cream, try adding crème fraîche instead.

Above: *Using a hand blender is one of the easiest ways to make smooth soups, but be sure to keep the blade submerged in the soup to avoid spattering.*

Puréeing soups

A few ladlefuls of soup can be puréed, then stirred back into the remaining soup to thicken it, or the entire soup can be puréed to make a wonderfully smooth, velvety soup. When making chilled puréed soup, it is best to adjust the consistency after chilling because the soup will thicken considerably as it cools.

The simplest way to make puréed soup is using a hand-held blender. It can be puréed while still in the slow cooker, and will not need reheating. You can also use a food processor or blender, but do not over-fill it because it may flood over the top. Most soups will need to be processed in two or more batches and, unless being served cold, will need to be reheated in the slow cooker or in a pan on the stovetop.

Soft vegetable soups can be puréed by hand. Press the mixture through a fine stainless steel or plastic sieve, using a wooden "mushroom" or a large spoon. Alternatively, press the vegetables through a mouli-légumes, then stir in the cooking liquid. The soup will need to be reheated if serving hot.

Thickening soups

There are several ways to thicken soups. Cornflour (cornstarch) or arrowroot are probably the simplest. They can be blended with a little cold water to make a smooth paste, then stirred or whisked into the hot soup. Cornflour will thicken boiling liquid instantly, but takes about 10 minutes to lose its raw flavour. Arrowroot thickens as soon as it reaches boiling point, but will become slightly thinner with prolonged cooking, so add in the last few minutes of cooking.

Plain (all-purpose) flour can be sprinkled over fried onions before stirring in the stock, or blended with an equal quantity of softened butter or double (heavy) cream and whisked into the finished soup a little at a time, cooking for a few minutes to thicken. Allow the soup to cook for at least 5 minutes to avoid a raw flour flavour.

Beaten eggs, egg yolks or a mixture of eggs and cream can be used to thicken and enrich smooth soups. Always turn off the heat and allow the soup to cool slightly before whisking in the egg mixture, otherwise it may curdle.

Breadcrumbs are sometimes used to thicken rustic and chilled soups. The breadcrumbs are stirred into the finished soup to soak up and thicken the liquid.

Garnishing soups

Adding a pretty garnish gives the final flourish as you serve soup, and can be as simple or complex as you like. A swirl of cream, crème fraîche or yogurt, followed by a sprinkling of paprika or ground black pepper, can look great with smooth soups. Fresh chopped herbs make another simple but stylish garnish, adding colour, flavour and texture. Use strong herbs, such as sage and rosemary, in moderation.

For a richly flavoured garnish, try adding a spoonful or swirl of pesto. It works especially well with Italian and Mediterranean soups. Grated, shaved or crumbled cheeses also work well and are particularly good with vegetable and bean soups. Strongly flavoured cheeses, such as Parmesan, Cheddar or a crumbly cheese, such as Stilton, are ideal.

To add more substance, flavour and texture to soups, try sprinkling over croûtons or fried breadcrumbs. These are a classic soup garnish and they add a crunchy texture that works with both smooth and chunky soups. To make croûtons, cut thick slices of day-old bread (any type will do) into cubes. Shallow-fry in hot olive oil, turning them continuously, so that the cubes brown evenly, then drain on kitchen paper. Fried breadcrumbs can be made in the same way, but need less cooking time. To oven-bake croûtons, toss them in a little oil, then bake in a shallow roasting pan at 200°C/400°F/Gas 6 for 12–15 minutes.

Grilled cheesy croûtes are the classic topping for French onion soup and can make a dramatic impact floating on top of a bowl of steaming hot soup. Simply rub thin slices of day-old baguette with peeled garlic cloves, then lightly toast both sides under a hot grill (broiler). Sprinkle one side with grated Cheddar or Parmesan cheese, or sliced goat's cheese, and put under a hot grill until melted. Float one or two croûtes on top of the soup just before serving.

Below: *Crispy croûtes coated in melted, bubbling cheese make an impressive garnish for a simple blended soup.*

MAKING MARINADES

Marinating tenderizes and flavours meat, poultry, game, fish and even vegetables and cheese. Although tenderizing may not be necessary when using a slow cooker, it is worth doing for the flavour. There are three basic types of marinade: moist, dry and paste. Always use a non-metallic dish for marinating.

Basic moist marinade

Moist marinades are usually made with oil and vinegar, or other acidic ingredients, such as wine, fruit juice or yogurt. They add moisture as well as flavour.

Red meat, poultry and game can be marinated for up to 2 hours at room temperature, or up to 24 hours in the refrigerator; small pieces of meat, such as steaks, chops and cutlets, should be marinated for no more than 2 hours at room temperature, or 12 hours in the refrigerator; whole fish, fish fillets and steaks should be marinated for up to 30 minutes at room temperature, or 2 hours in the refrigerator; vegetables need 30 minutes at room temperature, or 2 hours in the refrigerator; cheeses and tofu can be marinated for 1 hour at room temperature, or about 8 hours in the refrigerator.

SUFFICIENT FOR 900G/2LB MEAT OR FISH OR 675G/1½LB VEGETABLES

90ml/6 tbsp olive oil
15–30ml/1–2 tbsp cider vinegar
1 garlic clove, crushed
5ml/1 tsp dried thyme
2.5ml/½ tsp crushed peppercorns

1 Combine all the ingredients, using 15ml/1 tbsp vinegar for fish and 30ml/2 tbsp vinegar for meat or vegetables.

2 If you are marinating meat or fish with skin, make several shallow slashes in each piece, then place in a shallow dish.

3 Drizzle or brush the marinade over the food, making sure the pieces are completely covered, then leave to marinate, turning the pieces regularly.

Other moist marinades

You can make several other marinades, using the same techniques and timings as for the basic moist marinade.

Spicy yogurt marinade: Combine 175ml/6fl oz/1 cup plain yogurt, 2 crushed garlic cloves, 2.5ml/½ tsp each ground cumin and cinnamon and crushed black peppercorns, a pinch each of ground ginger, ground cloves, cayenne pepper and salt. Use for chicken, lamb and fish.

Hoisin marinade: Combine 175ml/6fl oz/1 cup hoisin sauce, 30ml/2 tbsp each sesame oil, dry sherry and rice vinegar, 4 finely chopped garlic cloves, 2.5ml/½ tsp soft light brown sugar, 1.5ml/¼ tsp five-spice powder. Use this Chinese marinade for chops and chicken pieces.

Coconut and pineapple: Blend ¼ peeled, chopped pineapple, juice of ½ lime and 150ml/¼ pint/⅔ cup coconut milk in a food processor. Use for chicken and pork.

Thai: Soak 30ml/2 tbsp tamarind pulp in 45ml/3 tbsp boiling water until softened, then press through a fine sieve into a pan. Finely chop 1 lemon grass stalk, 2.5cm/1in piece fresh galangal or ginger, 2 shallots, 2 garlic cloves, 2 seeded green chillies and 2 kaffir lime leaves and place in a blender with 30ml/2 tbsp each groundnut (peanut) oil and dark soy sauce. Blend to a paste and add to the pan. Bring to the boil, then leave to cool. Use for beef, pork or chicken.

Wine: Combine 75ml/5 tbsp wine, 30ml/2 tbsp olive oil, 2 finely chopped shallots, a pinch of dried herbs or 10ml/2 tsp chopped fresh herbs, such as rosemary. Use red wine for red meat and duck, and white wine for chicken and fish.

Basic dry marinade

Also known as dry rubs, these herb and spice mixtures are rubbed into food shortly before cooking. They are used purely for flavouring and so are best used on fattier pieces of meat, oily fish, or for braised dishes. You can vary the flavour by using different spices, such as cardamom, dry-roasted cumin seeds or a little chilli powder, or try a dried herb mixture with some grated citrus rind.

SUFFICIENT FOR 900G/2LB MEAT OR FISH

15ml/1 tbsp dried thyme
15ml/1 tbsp dried oregano
15ml/1 tbsp garlic granules
15ml/1 tbsp ground cumin
15ml/1 tbsp ground paprika
2.5ml/½ tsp cayenne pepper
2.5ml/½ tsp ground black pepper

1 Combine the ingredients in a bowl, then transfer the mixture to a shallow dish and spread out in an even layer.

2 Press each piece of meat or fish into the mixture to coat evenly, then gently shake off any excess. Arrange on a dish, cover with clear film (plastic wrap) and leave to marinate at room temperature for 30 minutes, or use immediately.

Paste marinades

Because these coat the food, it should be cooked above the level of the liquid – such as on a bed of vegetables.

Herb paste: Heat 50g/2oz/¼ cup butter in a frying pan and gently fry 115g/4oz finely chopped shallots and 1.5ml/¼ tsp fennel seeds until the shallots are soft. Remove from the heat and stir in 2.5cm/1in piece grated fresh ginger, 30ml/2 tbsp each chopped fresh dill and parsley and 15ml/1 tbsp finely chopped capers. Stir in 15–30ml/1–2 tbsp sunflower oil to make a paste. Spread over chicken pieces or tuck under the skin, or use to fill the cavity of whole fish. Marinate for up to 1 hour at room temperature, or cook straight away. Use for food with a short cooking time.

Mexican chilli paste: Combine the finely grated rind of 1 lime, 4 crushed garlic cloves, 30ml/2 tbsp mild chilli powder, 15ml/1 tbsp ground paprika, 5ml/1 tsp ground cumin, 2.5ml/½ tsp dried oregano and a pinch each of ground cinnamon and salt. Stir in 15ml/1 tbsp olive oil and enough lime juice to make into a paste. Use for chicken and pork. Marinate for up to 1 hour at room temperature, or cook straight away.

Tandoori paste: Mix together 30ml/2 tbsp each ground coriander, cumin and garlic powder, 15ml/1 tbsp each paprika and ground ginger and 10ml/2 tsp each ground turmeric and chilli powder with enough groundnut (peanut) oil to make a paste. Use for lamb, beef, chicken and oily fish. Marinate for up to 2 hours at room temperature, or cover and leave overnight in the refrigerator. Scrape off the excess paste before cooking.

Fruit marinades

Certain fruits contain enzymes that soften the fibres of meat and tougher seafood, such as squid. Papaya, pineapple and kiwi fruit all contain papain, which breaks down protein and is used in commercial tenderizers. Add a little of the juice to a marinade, or slice the fruit and place on top of the meat or fish and leave for no longer than 15 minutes.

MARINATING TIPS

• The thicker a piece of food is, the longer it will need to marinate.
• When marinating meats such as game and white fish that can become dry during cooking, choose marinades containing less vinegar, wine or fruit juice. These are suitable for fattier meats, such as lamb, and oily fish.
• During humid weather or in a warm kitchen, it is safer to marinate meat and fish in the refrigerator. In cooler weather, or for short marinating times, it is safe to leave the food at room temperature.
• As a general rule, dry herbs are better than fresh for marinades. When using fresh woody herbs, such as rosemary and thyme, crush the leaves to release their aroma.
• If you are frying or grilling (broiling) marinated food before adding it to the slow cooker, pat it dry on kitchen paper first.
• Avoid adding salt to marinades; this will draw moisture from the food. If you want to season with salt, do so after marinating.

MAKING STEWS and CASSEROLES

The slow cooker's gentle, constant heat makes it perfect for making stews and casseroles. The lengthy cooking allows all cuts of meat to become tender and succulent, and even the toughest pieces can be turned into a flavoursome meal.

Stews, casseroles, carbonnades, hot-pots and navarins are all names for what is, essentially, the same type of dish – meat and/or vegetables cooked in liquid in a cooking pot. Originally, the word stew described such dishes cooked on the stovetop, while casserole described dishes cooked in the oven, but now the names are largely interchangeable.

Choosing the right cut

Ideal meats for slow cooking are the cheaper cuts, such as brisket, chuck steak, blade-bone, shank and knuckle. These cuts come from the part of the animal (usually the front) that has worked hardest, so have a looser texture and a good marbling of fat. During cooking, the connective tissues and fat dissolve to create a rich gravy and the fibres open up and allow moisture to penetrate, making them juicy. These cuts also have far greater flavour than very lean ones.

More expensive cuts of meat, such as fine-grained and densely-textured sirloin steak and pork fillet, are delicious when cooked to rare or medium by quick-frying or grilling (broiling). However, they are less suitable for slow cooking because the tightness of the fibres prevents them absorbing the liquid around them. This means that although they become tender when cooked in a slow cooker, the final stew will lack succulence and flavour.

Cutting meat into cubes

Tougher cuts of meat, such as stewing steak, cook more evenly and quickly if they are cut into small, even-size cubes; 2.5cm/1in is ideal. They should be slightly larger than the vegetables being cooked in the stew because these will take a little longer to cook than the meat. Although excess fat should be removed, some marbling is useful for keeping the meat moist. Any excess fat can be skimmed off after cooking.

1 Trim the meat, cutting off the excess fat and any gristle, sinew or membranes while it is in one piece.

2 Using a large sharp knife, cut the meat across the grain into 2.5cm/1in thick slices. These slices can be used for stews and casseroles. Cutting across the grain makes the fibres shorter so that the meat is more tender.

3 To cut the meat into cubes, first cut the slices lengthways into thick strips. Remove any fat or gristle as you go.

4 Cut each strip crossways into 2.5cm/1in cubes. (When preparing meats such as shoulder of lamb, it may not be possible to cut into perfect cubes. Simply cut into evenly-sized pieces, removing any fat or gristle as you go.)

Preparing chops

These are usually sold ready-prepared and fairly lean, but it is usually worth trimming a little before cooking. This will help them cook, look and taste better.

1 Using sharp kitchen scissors or a sharp knife, remove the excess fat, cutting around the contours of the chop and leaving a little less than 5mm/¼in fat on the edge of each chop.

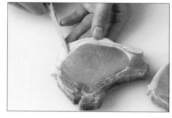

2 If you are going to pre-fry chops, such as bacon or gammon, before adding to the slow cooker, make shallow cuts with the knife all around the edge. The edge of the meat will then fan out during frying, preventing the meat curling up, so that it stays in constant contact with the frying pan.

Preparing poultry

A variety of chicken and game portions can be used in stews and casseroles – from whole or diced breast portions, to drumsticks and thighs. Leaving the bones in the meat during cooking will enhance the flavour, or you may remove them (saving to use for stock) if you prefer. Generally, it is better to remove poultry skin before casseroling because it won't crispen during the moist cooking.

To skin breast fillets, carefully pull the skin and thin membrane away from the meat. If you like, use a small, sharp knife to cut the meat off the rib bone and any remaining breastbone. Turn the breast portion over and remove the thin, white central tendons from the meat.

To prepare escalopes (scallops), cut the breast in half horizontally, holding your hand on top of the chicken breast as you cut. A chicken breast portion will yield two escalopes, a duck breast portion three, and turkey four or more.

To skin and bone chicken thighs, use a sharp knife to loosen the skin, then pull it away from the meat. Carefully cut the flesh lengthways along the main thigh bone, then cut the bone out, trimming the meat close to it.

Preparing vegetables

One of the unusual characteristics of slow cooking is that many types of vegetables take longer to cook than meat. To ensure that they cook within the recommended time, they should be cut into even-size pieces slightly smaller than the meat.

When preparing onions, slice them thinly or chop finely. If you want to have chunkier pieces, fry them until they are soft before adding to the slow cooker, because onion takes a long time to cook in a slow cooker.

Hard root vegetables such as carrots, potatoes and turnips take the longest time to cook in the slow cooker. Cut them into 5mm/¼in dice, slices or sticks. (Potatoes discolour when exposed to air, so make sure they are covered with liquid during cooking.)

COOK'S TIP

Some vegetables, such as (bell) peppers, become bitter if cooked too long and some types, especially green peppers, may discolour. They cook fairly quickly, so add these to the slow cooker 45 minutes–1 hour before the end of cooking time.

LIQUIDS FOR CASSEROLES AND STEWS

The finished sauce is provided by a mixture of the juices from the meat and vegetables and the liquid that is added at the start of cooking. The long cooking time ensures plenty of flavour if you use water, although other liquids will give the dish a richer finish. You may need to adjust the quantity of liquid used, according to the main ingredients in the dish; vegetables such as mushrooms, for example, will give out a lot of moisture that will thin the sauce.

Stock Home-made stock is preferable, but you can use ready-made fresh stock, or good-quality stock cubes or bouillon powder. Make these to the correct strength (you may only need a small portion of stock cube) because too much can produce an over-salty, artificial flavour. Try to use the flavour of stock that matches the dish. If you haven't got the appropriate meat stock, use vegetable stock instead.

Wine Red or white wine will add extra flavour and its acidity will help to tenderize the meat. Choose a wine that you enjoy drinking because a really cheap, acidic wine will spoil the finished dish. Generally, it is preferable to use a mixture of wine and stock, rather than wine alone.

Cider This flavours and tenderizes meat in the same way as wine, and is excellent in chicken and pork dishes, especially ones containing fruit. Unless you require a very sweet finish, use dry (hard) or medium cider.

Beer Pale or brown ale or stout makes a rich dark sauce and cooks without a hint of its original bitterness. Too much can be overpowering, though, so use a mixture of beer and stock.

Tomatoes These add flavour to the dish. You can use chopped fresh or canned tomatoes, passata (bottled strained tomatoes), concentrated purée (paste), or tomato juice.

BASIC TECHNIQUES

There are two basic ways of making slow cooker stews and casseroles: a simple one-step method, where cold raw ingredients are placed in the ceramic cooking pot, and a second method in which the meat and some or all of the vegetables are fried beforehand.

Making a one-step stew

Irish stew is a classic one-step stew, and the recipe given here is a perfect guide to cooking any stew using this technique. All the ingredients are placed in the ceramic cooking pot without pre-frying. This reduces preparation time and is also suitable for those on a reduced-fat diet.

The stock or cooking liquid is usually cold, but may be hot to speed up the cooking process. For the tenderest results, casseroles should be cooked on a low setting. However, when the ingredients are cold to begin with, and especially if cooking larger pieces of meat, it is better to start the cooking on the high or auto setting for 1–2 hours.

SERVES 4

900g/2lb boned shoulder of lamb
    or 8 neck of lamb chops
450g/1lb onions
900g/2lb potatoes
1 carrot, sliced (optional)
sprig of thyme or bay leaf (optional)
about 600ml/1 pint/2½ cups lamb
    or vegetable stock
salt and ground black pepper

1 Using a sharp knife, trim all excess fat from the lamb, then cut the meat into 3cm/1¼in pieces. (If using lamb chops, these may be left whole.)

2 Using a sharp knife, slice the onions and potatoes as thinly as possible.

3 Place the onions at the bottom of the ceramic cooking pot, then arrange the potatoes, carrot and herbs, if using, on top and finally the meat. Lightly season each layer with salt and pepper.

4 Pour the stock over the meat. If necessary, add a little more stock to cover the meat. Cover the slow cooker with the lid and cook on auto or high for 2 hours.

5 Using a large spoon, skim off any scum that has risen to the surface. Re-cover the pot and leave on auto or switch to low and cook for a further 4–6 hours, or until the meat and vegetables are very tender and juicy.

Making a pre-fried stew

This method is used for the majority of stews and casseroles, because it adds colour and an intense rich flavour. The natural sugars in the ingredients are broken down by pre-frying and the sweet, complex flavours are released. While pre-cooking meat improves the taste and appearance of the cooked casserole, it is also useful to give vegetables the same treatment, especially onions because they take much longer to tenderize than meat in a slow cooker.

SERVES 4–6

900g/2lb lean stewing steak
45ml/3 tbsp plain (all-purpose) flour
50g/2oz/¼ cup butter
30ml/2 tbsp oil
12 baby (pearl) onions, peeled
115g/4oz button (white) mushrooms
1 garlic clove, crushed
300ml/½ pint/1¼ cups red wine
150ml/¼ pint/⅔ cup near-boiling
    beef stock
1 bay leaf
30ml/2 tbsp chopped fresh parsley
salt and ground black pepper

1 Trim the meat and cut into 2.5cm/1in cubes. Season the flour with salt and black pepper and either spread out on a plate or place in a plastic bag. Roll the meat in the flour, or add a few cubes at a time to the bag, shaking until coated, then remove and coat the next batch. Shake off any excess and reserve.

2 Melt half the butter with half of the oil in a large frying pan. (If you prefer, you can reduce the fat slightly by using a non-stick frying pan.)

3 When the butter sizzles, fry the meat in two or three batches. (Do not try to cook too much meat at once because it will start to stew, rather than brown.) Turn the meat frequently, so that it browns on all sides. Lift the meat out of the pan with a slotted spoon and transfer to the ceramic cooking pot.

4 Heat the remaining butter and oil in the frying pan, then add the onions and cook until glazed and golden brown. Transfer to the ceramic cooking pot using a slotted spoon. Add the mushrooms and garlic to the pan and cook for 2–3 minutes until browned, then transfer to the cooking pot.

5 Sprinkle any remaining flour into the pan juices and stir to mix. Gradually mix in the red wine, followed by the stock.

6 Stir the sauce to loosen any sediment from the base of the pan and heat to simmering point. Pour over the meat and vegetables, and add the bay leaf, pressing it down into the liquid.

7 Cover the slow cooker with the lid and switch to high or auto. Cook for 1 hour, then leave on auto or switch to low and cook for a further 6–8 hours, or until the meat and vegetables are tender. Alternatively, cook on high throughout for 4–5 hours. Sprinkle over the parsley just before serving.

Thickening stews

There are many different ways to thicken the sauces of stews and casseroles.
Flour Meat is often fried before being put in the ceramic cooking pot, and can be first dusted in flour, which will act as a thickener for the juices as the meat cooks. Do not over-brown the flour as this gives it a bitter flavour; only fry until light brown.

Alternatively, you can add flour towards the end of cooking time by whisking in a paste made from equal quantities of flour and butter. Allow extra cooking time to allow the flour to cook and lose its "raw" flavour.

Cornflour/cornstarch or arrowroot These very fine flours can both be used as thickeners. They should be blended with a little water or other cold liquid before being stirred into the stew.

Pasta and rice If it becomes obvious part-way through cooking that the stew or casserole will be too thin, you can stir in a little pasta or easy-cook (converted) rice, which will absorb some of the liquid. These should be added about 45 minutes before the end of cooking time. (Lentils and grains, such as pearl barley, will also act as thickeners, but these must be added early in the cooking time to cook thoroughly.)
Reduction If the sauce is too thin when cooking is complete, lift out the meat and vegetables with a slotted spoon and set aside. Pour the liquid into a wide pan or frying pan and boil fast to reduce the liquid. Add the meat and vegetables to the reduced sauce and gently reheat. This is a useful technique with delicate fish and chicken, which may break up if overcooked.

Skimming off fat

If the dish has produced a lot of fat during cooking, you may wish to remove it before serving. Most will rise to the surface so that you can simply skim it off the top, using a large kitchen spoon. Further fat can be removed using absorbent kitchen paper. Simply rest the kitchen paper on the surface of the stew and remove as soon as it has soaked up the fat. If you have made the dish in advance, chill it in the refrigerator so that the fat solidifies on the top of the stew or casserole. It can then be lifted or scooped off.

BRAISING

This technique involves slow cooking in very little liquid in a dish with a tight-fitting lid; the trapped steam keeps the food moist during cooking. Instead of cutting meat into small chunks, it is sliced into larger, even-size pieces, or in some cases, such as chops or lamb shanks, left whole. Braising also works well for large pieces of firm, meaty fish which can be placed on a bed of vegetables, with just enough liquid to cover these.

The slow cooker is perfect for braising because the heat is so gentle, and the lid forms a tight seal, so that any steam condenses on the inside of the lid and trickles back into the pot.

Preparing meat for braising

Always trim excess fat from meat before braising, then skim any fat from the surface before serving. To ensure even cooking, all the pieces of meat should be of a similar thickness.

I Cut the meat into slices about 2cm/¾in thick. At the narrower end cut slightly thicker slices.

2 Place the thicker slices on a chopping board, cover with a sheet of greaseproof (waxed) paper and gently beat with a rolling pin or meat mallet to flatten.

If you want to pound all the meat, to help tenderize it, you can start by cutting it all into thick slices, about 3cm/1in thick, then pounding it to flatten.

Braising lamb shanks

On the whole lamb joints are tender and quite fatty and do not benefit from being braised. Lamb shanks, however, are lean and tough so benefit from long, slow, moist cooking. Thickly sliced meat, such as braising steak, and small joints, such as topside, can be cooked in the same way.

SERVES 4

4 lamb shanks
I red onion, very finely chopped
I garlic clove, crushed
sprig of fresh thyme
5ml/I tsp chopped fresh rosemary
5ml/I tsp ground paprika
15ml/I tbsp balsamic vinegar
60ml/4 tbsp olive oil
175ml/6fl oz/¾ cup red wine
150ml/¼ pint/⅔ cup lamb
   or vegetable stock
chopped fresh parsley
salt and ground black pepper

I Using the point of a sharp knife, gently prick the shanks at intervals all over.

2 Combine the onion, garlic, thyme, rosemary, paprika, vinegar and 30ml/2 tbsp of the oil. Brush over the shanks, place in a shallow, non-metallic dish, cover and leave to marinate for 2 hours at room temperature, or up to 24 hours in the refrigerator. (Marinating starts the tenderizing process, but is not essential.)

3 Brush the marinade off the lamb and set aside. Heat the remaining 30ml/2 tbsp oil in a frying pan and lightly brown the shanks all over. Transfer to the ceramic cooking pot and season with salt and pepper.

4 Add the reserved marinade to the frying pan and pour in the wine and stock. Bring almost to the boil, stirring, then pour over the shanks.

5 Cover with the lid and switch to high or auto. Cook for I hour, then leave on auto or reduce to low and cook for a further 6–8 hours, or until very tender, turning the meat halfway through.

6 Using a slotted spoon, transfer the lamb shanks to a warmed serving plate. Skim off any fat from the cooking juices, then check the seasoning. Stir in the parsley and spoon over the shanks.

Braising red cabbage

Many types of vegetable respond well to braising, becoming meltingly tender with an intense flavour. Red cabbage is used here, but fennel and celery are also very good braised. Fennel should be cut into thin, even slices from the top through the root end; sticks of celery can be left whole or cut into shorter pieces.

SERVES 4–6

1 red cabbage, about 900g/2lb
450g/1lb cooking apples, peeled, cored
    and chopped
30ml/2 tbsp soft light or dark brown sugar
30ml/2 tbsp red wine vinegar
175g/6fl oz/3/4 cup near-boiling water
salt and ground black pepper

1 Discard the tough outer leaves of the cabbage, cut it into quarters and remove the hard stalk. Shred the cabbage finely.

2 Put the cabbage, apples, sugar, vinegar, salt and pepper into the ceramic cooking pot and toss together. Pack down firmly, then pour over the water.

3 Cover with the lid and switch to high for 3–4 hours, or to low for 6–8 hours, stirring halfway through.

Reheating braised dishes, casseroles and stews

Braised dishes, casseroles and stews are often served the day after they are made because their flavour improves with keeping and reheating. The improvement in taste is less obvious in dishes made in the slow cooker because the long gentle cooking has already allowed the flavours to develop and mingle. However, if you do plan to reheat a dish, it is important to cool it as quickly as possible – but you should never plunge the hot ceramic cooking pot into cold water because this may cause it to crack.

1 When cooking is complete, remove the ceramic cooking pot from the slow cooker, and place on a pot stand for at least 10 minutes, taking off the lid to allow steam to escape. (Do not remove the lid for braised vegetables; you want to retain the moisture with these.)

2 Place the ceramic cooking pot in a washing-up bowl of cool but not very cold water. Leave for about 15 minutes, or until the surrounding water starts to feel warm. (Don't overfill the bowl or the water may overflow into the prepared dish; the water should come just over halfway up the cooking pot.)

3 Remove the ceramic cooking pot and pour away the warmed water. Refill the bowl with very cold water, replace the ceramic cooking pot and add a few ice cubes or frozen ice packs to speed up the cooling process. Leave until the food is completely cool.

4 Cover the ceramic cooking pot with the lid and place in the refrigerator until needed, or transfer the contents to another container, if you prefer.

5 The slow cooker is not suitable for reheating the dish. It will take too long for the contents to reheat to ensure food safety. Check whether the ceramic cooking pot is suitable for use on the stovetop or in the oven. Remove the dish from the refrigerator at least 30 minutes before reheating.

6 If necessary, transfer the food to a suitable pan or casserole dish, then reheat gently over a low heat on the stovetop, or in the oven at 170°C/325°F/ Gas 3, until simmering. For safety, meat dishes must come to a gentle simmer and be maintained at that temperature for at least 30 minutes. Any fresh herbs should be added at this stage, a few minutes before serving.

POT-ROASTING

This method of cooking small or large joints of meat and whole poultry in a small amount of liquid, usually with herbs and vegetables, is ideal for less tender cuts of meat, poultry and game that are low in natural fat. It makes them wonderfully succulent and tender and minimizes shrinkage. The meat is nearly always browned before being placed in the slow cooker with a little liquid and other ingredients. Sometimes the meat is marinated before cooking, especially beef and game, which can be dry.

When choosing joints of meat for pot-roasting, small pieces weighing no more than 1.2kg/2½lb are ideal. If the meat is irregularly shaped it will cook less uniformly and may be awkward to carve, so boned joints such as sirloin, silverside and topside should be tied; shoulder of lamb should be both boned and tied before pot-roasting.

Tying a boneless joint

You will need fine string for tying joints of meat. Store it in a plastic bag or box, rather than leaving loose in a drawer, so that it does not get dirty.

I Roll or arrange the meat joint into a neat shape. Tie it lengthways with a piece of string. This should be pulled tightly and double-knotted because the meat will shrink a little during cooking. (You may need to ask someone to help you do this.)

2 Tie the joint widthways at regular intervals about 2.5cm/1in apart, knotting and trimming the ends of string as you go. Apply even pressure when tying each length of string to keep the shape of the joint as neat as possible.

Boning a shoulder of lamb

Lamb shoulder is made up of three bones: the flat blade bone, the thin arm bone and the knuckle.

I Place the shoulder on a board and trim off any excess fat. Insert a sharp knife into the larger end of the lamb joint, then slice it along the flat blade bone, working towards the centre. Turn the meat over and repeat on the other side. Twist out the blade bone.

2 Put the lamb, skin side down, on the board. Cut along the line of the arm and knuckle bones, scraping the meat off the bones, then remove them.

3 Cut through the flesh where the blade bone was and open out the meat. It can now be stuffed, then rolled and tied.

Tying a shoulder *en ballon*

As an alternative to rolling and tying a shoulder of lamb, it can be tied *en ballon*; this is a round cushion shape that is served sliced into wedges.

I Lay the meat out flat, skin side down. If you like, spoon stuffing into the middle. Pull one corner of the joint into the centre and secure it with a skewer.

2 Do the same with the other four corners, tucking in the remains of the shank and securing them by tying a loop of string around the "ballon".

3 Turn the joint over and continue tying loops of string at even spaces around the ballon, to make six or eight sections. Tie a knot at the crossover point on each side as you go.

Pot-roasting brisket of beef

Other cuts of beef, such as silverside and topside of beef, can be cooked in this way. Stuffed breast or shoulder of lamb also work very well.

SERVES 4–6

1.2kg/2½lb rolled brisket
25g/1oz/2 tbsp beef dripping
    or white vegetable fat
2 onions, cut into 8 wedges
2 carrots, quartered
2 sticks celery, cut into 5cm/2in lengths
2 bay leaves
2 sprigs of fresh thyme
300ml/½ pint/1¼ cups near-boiling
    beef stock
salt and ground black pepper

1 Season the meat well with salt and pepper. Heat the dripping or vegetable fat in a large, heavy pan until hot. Add the meat and turn frequently using two spoons until browned. If the fat gets too hot before the meat is browned, add a little cold butter to cool it. Lift out the meat and transfer to a plate.

2 Pour away some of the fat, leaving about 15ml/1 tbsp in the pan. Add the onions, carrots and celery and cook for a few minutes or until lightly browned and beginning to soften. Browning the vegetables will add flavour and colour to the pot-roast, but take care not to darken them too much or the stock will become bitter. Arrange a single layer of vegetables in the base of the cooking pot, then place the meat on top, adding any juices from the plate. Put the remaining vegetables around the sides of the meat and tuck in the fresh herbs.

3 Pour the stock into the pan and bring to the boil, stirring in any sediment.

4 Pour the stock over the meat and vegetables; it should barely cover them, leaving most of the meat exposed.

5 Cover the slow cooker with the lid and switch to high. Cook for 4 hours, then reduce the temperature to low and cook for a further 2–3 hours, or until the meat is cooked through and very tender. Once or twice during cooking, turn the meat and baste. Avoid using any sharp utensils when doing so because they may puncture the outer layer and allow juices to escape.

6 Lift out the meat and place on a warmed serving dish. Cover with a piece of foil and leave it to rest; 15 minutes will be sufficient to allow the fibres to relax and let the juices settle, making the meat easier to carve.

7 Meanwhile, skim any fat from the juices and stock in the cooking pot. Serve as a gravy with the meat. (If you like, thicken the juices with cornflour or arrowroot first.) Normally the vegetables are discarded, but these may be served with the meat as well.

Pot-roasting chicken

A whole chicken can be pot-roasted in exactly the same way as a joint of beef or lamb, but this technique is unsuitable for large chickens weighing more than 1.6kg/3½lb. Avoid stuffing the cavity, although you may add a quartered onion or lemon for flavouring.

SERVES 4

150ml/¼ pint/⅔ cup dry white wine
    or dry (hard) cider
2 bay leaves
1.2–1.3kg/2½–3lb chicken
1 lemon, quartered
15ml/1 tbsp sunflower oil
25g/1oz/2 tbsp unsalted (sweet) butter
150ml/¼ pint/⅔ cup boiling chicken stock
15ml/1 tbsp cornflour (cornstarch) blended
    with 30ml/2 tbsp water or wine
salt and ground black pepper

1 Pour the wine into the ceramic cooking pot. Add the bay leaves and switch the slow cooker to high. Meanwhile, rinse or wipe the chicken and pat dry using kitchen paper. Season the cavity, then add the lemon quarters.

2 Heat the oil and butter in a heavy frying pan. Brown the chicken on all sides, then transfer it to the ceramic cooking pot. If the chicken has been trussed, untie it before placing in the cooking pot. This will allow the heat to penetrate more easily.

3 Pour the stock over the chicken, then cover with the lid and cook on high for 3½–4½ hours, or until the juices run clear when pierced with a thin knife or skewer, or a meat thermometer inserted into the thickest part of the thigh reads 77°C/170°F. (Chicken and other poultry must be cooked on high throughout.)

4 Lift the chicken out of the cooking pot, place on a warmed serving dish, cover with foil and leave to rest for 10–15 minutes before serving. Meanwhile, skim the juices, stir in the cornflour mixture and cook on high for 10 minutes, then serve as a sauce.

POACHING

This gentle method of cooking keeps food wonderfully moist. It differs from boiling because the heat is so low that only the occasional bubble breaks the surface of the liquid. It is ideal for delicate meats, such as poultry and fish, which can overcook and disintegrate if fiercely boiled. Poaching also allows you to skim off the scum and fat that faster boiling would bubble back into the liquid, making it cloudy and spoiling the flavour. The slow cooker is perfect for poaching because it keeps the heat constant and steady and needs little attention.

Poaching chicken

Unlike pot-roasting, the slow cooker can be used for poaching large chickens and other poultry, although it is important to check that it will fit comfortably in the ceramic cooking pot. There should be enough space for it to be completely immersed in liquid and room for liquid to circulate around the sides. Because the cavity of the bird will be filled with poaching liquid, the bird will be cooked from the inside and the outside.

SERVES 4

1.3kg/3lb oven-ready chicken
1 onion
2 carrots
2 leeks
2 celery sticks
a few fresh parsley stalks
2 bay leaves
6 black peppercorns
2.5ml/½ tsp salt

1 Remove any trussing string from the chicken. Remove any loose pieces of fat from inside the chicken, then rinse the cavity under cold water and place the chicken in the ceramic cooking pot.

2 Trim the onion at the stem and root end, but do not peel (the skin will add a rich golden colour to the stock). Cut the onion into six or eight wedges. Wash and trim the carrots, leeks and celery, then roughly chop or slice them and add to the cooking pot, packing them in around the chicken.

3 Tie the herbs together and add to the pot with the peppercorns and salt.

4 Pour in enough near-boiling water to just cover the chicken, pouring it over the vegetables and the chicken. Cover with the lid, switch the slow cooker to high and cook for 1 hour.

5 Skim off any scum and fat using a slotted spoon. Re-cover the pot and cook for 2–2½ hours, or until the chicken is cooked and tender. To check the chicken is cooked, insert a meat thermometer into the thickest part, where the thigh joins the body; it should read 77°C/170°F. (Alternatively, insert a skewer into the thickest part; the juices should show no traces of pink. If they are clear, lift the chicken out of the pot and double-check on the other side.)

6 Remove the chicken from the pot, using a large fork inserted into the cavity to lift it up. Leave the chicken to rest for 10 minutes before carving. Alternatively, if you plan to eat the chicken cold, leave it to cool completely on a wire rack placed over a large plate to catch any drips. (The wire rack will allow air to circulate around the chicken, helping it to cool more quickly.)

7 Leave the cooking liquid to cool for a few minutes, then ladle into a colander set over a large bowl. Leave to drip; do not press the vegetables or the stock will become cloudy. Cool the stock quickly by placing the bowl in cold water.

8 If you plan to eat the chicken cold, as soon as it is cool, cover with clear film (plastic wrap) and store in the refrigerator. (Leave the skin on because this will help to keep the meat moist.) Use within 2 days of cooking.

9 When the stock is cool, cover with clear film and place in the refrigerator. Any fat in the stock will rise to the surface and can be removed easily and discarded. The stock can be kept for up to 3 days, or it can be frozen in airtight containers for up to 6 months.

Poaching gammon

Gammon is the cured hind leg of the bacon pig. Once cooked, it is known as ham. When serving the meat in slices, poaching is the best cooking method, producing tender, juicy results. However, if you wish to serve it whole, it can be glazed after poaching and briefly baked.

SERVES 6–8

1.8kg/4lb boned middle gammon joint
1 onion
6 whole cloves
2 carrots, halved
1 bouquet garni
10 black peppercorns
dry (hard) cider (optional)

1 Place the meat in the ceramic cooking pot, cover with cold water and leave to soak for 2–24 hours to remove the salt. (Mild cured gammon shouldn't need long soaking, but it is preferable to soak smoked gammon for the longer time.)

2 Drain the gammon, then return it to the cooking pot. Peel the onion, stud with the cloves and add to the pot with the carrots, herbs and peppercorns. If you find it difficult to squeeze the onion down the side of the gammon, halve it.

3 Pour in enough cold water, or cider or a mixture of the two, to just cover the gammon. Switch the slow cooker to high, cover with the lid and cook for 1 hour. Skim off any scum using a slotted spoon, then re-cover and cook for a further 4–5 hours. Check and skim the surface once or twice during cooking.

4 Lift the ham out of the pot and place on a board. Slice and serve hot, or allow to cool, then wrap in foil and store in the refrigerator for up to 5 days.

5 Strain the cooking liquid into a bowl and leave to cool. (Taste the stock when hot; if it is very salty, use sparingly in dishes and do not add additional salt.) Chill the stock and remove any fat from the surface. Store in the refrigerator and use within 2 days. Alternatively, freeze for up to 6 months.

GLAZING HAMS

After poaching, lift the ham into a foil-lined baking dish and leave to cool for 15 minutes. Snip the string off the ham, then slice off the rind, leaving a thin, even layer of fat. Score the fat in diagonal lines, then score in the opposite direction to make a diamond pattern. Brush the warm joint with about 45ml/3 tbsp lime marmalade and sprinkle with 45ml/3 tbsp demerara (raw) sugar. Push whole cloves into the corners of the diamond shapes after glazing, if you like. Bake at 220°C/425°F/Gas 7 for about 20 minutes, until the fat is brown and crisp. Serve hot or cold.

Poaching fish

The delicate texture of fish benefits from simple cooking. Poaching brings out its flavour and keeps it moist. Both whole fish and fillets can be poached in the slow cooker, but first check that there is enough room for the fish, as well as space to manoeuvre a fish slice (spatula).

Fish can be poached in cold liquid, but it will retain its shape and texture if added to hot liquid. Larger pieces of fish, such as steaks or cutlets, will take no more than 45 minutes on high, or 1½–2 hours on low, but take care not to overcook and check frequently. Fish is ready when the flesh is only slightly translucent when eased away from the bone, or flakes easily when tested with the point of a sharp knife or skewer.

Poaching fruit

Apples, pears, stone fruits, such as plums, and soft fruit, such as figs, can be poached whole, halved or sliced. Even fragile fruit, such as rhubarb, will retain its shape when cooked in a slow cooker. Cooking times will depend on the size and ripeness of the fruit, but as a rough guide, tender fruit, such as figs and rhubarb, will take about 1½ hours on high; ripe or near-ripe fruit, such as plums or apples, will take about 2 hours on high; and harder, less ripe fruit, such as pears, will take 3–5 hours on high, or 6–8 hours on low.

The classic poaching liquid is syrup and usually consists of 1 part sugar to 2 parts water. Flavouring ingredients such as a pared strip of lemon rind or spices can be added to the liquid, as can red or white wine, cider or fruit juice sweetened with sugar.

1 Put the sugar, poaching liquid and any flavourings into the ceramic cooking pot and switch the slow cooker to high. Cook for 1 hour, stirring occasionally to dissolve the sugar.

2 Add the fruit, cover and cook until the fruit is barely tender. Leave the fruit to cool in the syrup, or remove and place in a serving dish. Strain the syrup over the fruit, or simmer gently to thicken.

USING the SLOW COOKER as a BAIN-MARIE

While many dishes are cooked directly in the ceramic cooking pot, others may be cooked in a bain-marie – in a tin (pan) or dish placed inside the cooking pot and surrounded by barely simmering water. This technique is good for making pâtés, terrines, cakes, steamed puddings and custard-based desserts. To allow the water to move freely around the cooking container, an upturned saucer or metal pastry ring is often placed on the base of the cooking pot. This is important if the cooking pot has a slightly concave base.

MAKING PÂTÉS AND TERRINES

When raw meat and eggs are used, make sure that the depth of the mixture is no greater than 6cm/2¼in, otherwise the pâté may not cook thoroughly. This is especially important with pork and chicken. A 450g/1lb terrine or loaf tin measuring about 20 × 10 × 5.5cm/ 8 × 4 × 2¼in and holding a volume of 900ml/1½ pints/3¾ cups is an ideal size.

Making classic pork pâté
You can use this recipe as a guide for making other pâtés. You can vary the proportions of the main ingredients, and can use lean minced (ground) beef or pork in place of the veal.

SERVES 6

225g/8oz rindless smoked streaky
    (fatty) bacon rashers (strips)
225g/8oz boneless belly of pork
175g/6oz veal
115g/4oz chicken livers
45ml/3 tbsp dry white wine
15ml/1 tbsp brandy
2.5ml/½ tsp dried thyme
2.5ml/½ tsp dried rosemary
1 garlic clove, crushed
2.5ml/½ tsp salt
1.5ml/¼ tsp ground mace
ground black pepper

1 Place an upturned saucer or metal pastry cutter in the base of the ceramic cooking pot. Pour in about 2.5cm/1in of very hot water, then turn the slow cooker to high.

2 Taking 150g/5oz of the bacon, stretch one rasher at a time on a board using the back of a large knife. Use to line a 450g/1lb loaf tin, or a 900ml/1½ pint/ 3¾ cup round dish, leaving the bacon overhanging the sides.

3 Finely chop the remaining bacon and place in a large bowl. Trim the belly of pork, veal and chicken livers, then mince (grind) using the medium blade of a mincer, or place in a food processor and chop roughly. Add to the bowl.

4 Spoon the white wine and brandy over the meat. Add the herbs, garlic and seasonings, then mix well. Transfer the mixture to the tin or dish, pressing down lightly. Fold the overhanging bacon over the top of the filling, then cover with a piece of foil.

5 Place the pâté in the slow cooker, then pour enough very hot water around it to come nearly to the top. Cook on high for 4–6 hours. To test whether the pâté is cooked, push a thin skewer into the centre and press lightly around the edges of the hole; the liquid should be clear, not cloudy or pink.

6 Carefully remove the pâté from the slow cooker and leave to cool on a wire rack. Cover and chill for several hours, then unmould and keep covered until ready to serve. (If you like, the pâté can be pressed before chilling.)

PRESSING PÂTÉS

After cooling the cooked pâté, you may "press" it to give it a slightly firmer texture and to make it easier to slice. Cover the pâté with greaseproof (waxed) paper or clear film (plastic wrap). Top with a board that fits exactly inside the tin (pan) and place several weights or cans on the board. (Alternatively, use bags of rice or lentils, which can be moulded to fit into the top of the tin.) Leave until completely cool, then chill overnight (still weighted if you want a really firm texture).

Making mousseline pâté

A mousseline pâté has a light, smooth, creamy texture. Allow plenty of time to prepare it because you will need to chill the mixture between each stage. Mousseline pâtés are extremely rich, so serve thinly sliced with bread or salad.

SERVES 8

15g/½oz/1 tbsp butter
1 shallot, finely chopped
15ml/1 tbsp brandy or sherry
225g/8oz skinless chicken breast portion
50g/2oz chicken livers, trimmed
15ml/1 tbsp fresh white breadcrumbs
1 egg, separated
300ml/½ pint/1¼ cups double
 (heavy) cream
salt and ground white pepper

1 Lightly oil and line a 450g/1lb loaf or terrine tin (pan), or a 900ml/1½ pint/ 3¾ cup baking dish, with baking parchment. Melt the butter in a small pan, add the shallot and cook for about 5 minutes until soft. Turn off the heat, then stir in the brandy or sherry. Place the mixture in a bowl and leave to cool.

2 Meanwhile, roughly chop the chicken breast portion and livers, then place in a food processor and purée for about 30 seconds. Add the shallot mixture and breadcrumbs to the chicken and process until very smooth. Return the mixture to the bowl and chill for 30 minutes.

3 Meanwhile, place an upturned saucer or metal pastry cutter in the bottom of the ceramic cooking pot. Pour in about 2.5cm/1in of very hot water, then turn the slow cooker to high.

4 Set the bowl of chicken purée over a larger bowl filled with crushed ice and water. Lightly whisk the egg white with a fork until frothy and beat into the purée, a little at a time. Beat in the egg yolk.

5 Gradually add the cream, mixing well between each addition. Season with salt and white pepper, then spoon the mixture into the prepared tin and level the top. Cover with clear film (plastic wrap) or foil.

6 Place the tin or terrine in the slow cooker, then pour enough hot water around to come nearly to the top. Cook on high for 3–4 hours, or until firm.

7 Carefully remove the pâté from the slow cooker and leave to cool on a wire rack. Chill well before slicing and serving.

Making a studded terrine

Attractive terrines can be made using the mousseline mixture and studding it with vegetables or layering it with other meats, such as strips of chicken or ham.

SERVES 8

75g/3oz fine asparagus stalks
75g/3oz green beans, topped and tailed
115g/4oz carrots, peeled and cut into
 matchstick strips
½ quantity mousseline pâté mixture

1 Lightly oil and line a 450g/1lb loaf tin or terrine, or a 900ml/1½ pint/3¾ cup baking dish, with baking parchment. Cook the vegetables, one type at a time, in boiling water for 1 minute. Drain, plunge into cold water, then drain again.

2 Spread a layer of the mixture in the bottom of the tin. Arrange the asparagus lengthways, with gaps between each, then cover with a thin layer of the pâté.

3 Repeat the layers using the beans and carrots and finishing with the remaining pâté mixture. Smooth the top. Cover with clear film (plastic wrap) or foil and cook in the same way as the chicken mousseline for 2½–3½ hours.

MAKING STEAMED PUDDINGS and DESSERTS

The slow cooker is perfect for cooking sticky steamed sponges and custards. It keeps the water at a very gentle simmer, reducing the risk of the water bubbling up and spoiling the dish.

Making a steamed sponge

Sponge puddings cooked in steam have a surprisingly light, moist texture. They were traditionally made using shredded beef or vegetarian suet, but this modern version uses a creamed cake mixture. Make sure that all the ingredients are at room temperature before you start.

SERVES 4–6

115g/4oz/½ cup butter, at room
   temperature
115g/4oz/generous ½ cup caster
   (superfine) sugar
2.5ml/½ tsp vanilla essence
   (extract)
2 eggs, lightly beaten
175g/6oz/1½ cups self-raising
   (self-rising) flour
about 45ml/3 tbsp milk

1 Place an upturned saucer or metal pastry cutter in the bottom of the ceramic cooking pot. Pour in 2.5cm/1in very hot water, then preheat the slow cooker on high. Grease a 900ml/ 1½ pint/3¾ cup pudding bowl and line the base with a piece of greaseproof (waxed) paper or baking parchment.

2 Cream the butter, sugar and vanilla essence together in a large mixing bowl until pale and fluffy. Add the eggs, a little at a time, beating thoroughly. If the mixture begins to curdle, beat in a spoonful of the flour.

3 Sift half the flour over the creamed mixture and fold in using a large metal spoon. Sift over the rest and fold in with 30ml/2 tbsp of the milk. If necessary, add the remaining milk to make a soft dropping consistency, then spoon into the pudding bowl.

4 Cover the pudding with greaseproof paper and foil and tie with string. Lower into the slow cooker, then pour enough water around the bowl to come halfway up the sides. Cover with the lid and cook on high for 4–5 hours, or until well risen and springy to the touch. Lift out of the slow cooker and remove the foil. Turn out on to a serving plate, peel off the paper and serve.

**HOW TO COVER A
STEAMED PUDDING**

1 Brush a sheet of greaseproof (waxed) paper with softened butter, then place the unbuttered side on a sheet of foil. Make a pleat about 2cm/¾in wide in the middle to allow the pudding to rise. (If fresh fruit is included in the pudding, you must use greaseproof paper; otherwise, a double piece of foil may be used.)

2 Cover the bowl with the pleated greaseproof paper and foil, allowing it to overlap the rim by 2.5cm/1in. Tie the foil securely with fine string.

3 Make a loop with the string at the top of the bowl to make a secure handle. This will enable the bowl to be lifted in and out of the ceramic cooking pot easily.

Making baked egg custard

A lightly set, creamy-textured custard is ideal for serving hot or cold. It can be enjoyed on its own or with all manner of desserts, such as fruit pies, steamed sponges and crumbles.

SERVES 4–6

butter or flavourless oil, for greasing
475ml/16fl oz/2 cups milk
3 eggs
45ml/3 tbsp caster (superfine) sugar
pinch of freshly grated nutmeg

1 Place an upturned saucer or metal pastry cutter in the bottom of the ceramic cooking pot. Pour in about 2.5cm/1in of very hot water, then turn the slow cooker to high.

2 Lightly grease the base and sides of a 900ml/1½ pint/3¾ cup heatproof dish. Heat the milk in a pan until it is steaming hot, without letting it boil.

3 Whisk the eggs and sugar lightly in a bowl, then slowly pour over the hot milk, whisking all the time. Strain the mixture through a fine sieve (strainer) into the prepared dish and sprinkle the top with a little grated nutmeg.

4 Cover the dish with clear film (plastic wrap) and place in the slow cooker. Pour in enough near-boiling water to come just over halfway up the sides of the dish. Put the lid on the slow cooker, then switch to the low setting and cook for 4 hours, or until the custard is lightly set. Serve hot or cold.

Making crème brûlée

You can use the basic baked egg custard mixture to make other custard-based desserts, such as crème brûlée, which is a rich, creamy baked custard topped with a crisp layer of caramelized sugar.

1 Make the custard, whisking 5ml/1 tsp vanilla essence (extract) into the egg and sugar mixture, then use 150ml/¼ pint/ ⅔ cup double (heavy) cream and 300ml/ ½ pint/1¼ cups single (light) cream in place of the milk.

2 Strain the custard into a jug (pitcher), then pour into four or six individual ramekins (custard cups), first making sure that the ramekins will fit inside the cooking pot in a single layer.

3 Cover each dish with clear film (plastic wrap), then place in the ceramic cooking pot. Pour enough near-boiling water around the dishes to come three-quarters of the way up the sides. Cover with the lid and cook on low for about 3 hours, or until set.

4 Remove the custards from the slow cooker and leave to cool. Sprinkle the tops with 115g/4oz/½ cup caster (superfine) sugar. Place under a hot grill (broiler) and cook until the sugar melts and caramelizes. Cool, then chill.

Making bread and butter pudding

This favourite dessert can be made using the classic baked custard mixture.

1 Make the custard using 300ml/½ pint/ 1¼ cups milk and 75ml/2½fl oz/⅓ cup double (heavy) cream.

2 Butter 8 medium slices of bread, then cut each in half diagonally. Arrange the slices in a 1 litre/1¾ pint/4 cup, buttered baking dish, first making sure that it will fit in the cooking pot.

3 Pour the custard over the bread and sprinkle 30ml/2 tbsp demerara (raw) sugar and a little grated nutmeg over the top. Cover with clear film (plastic wrap) and put the dish in the cooking pot. Pour enough near-boiling water around the dish to come two-thirds up the sides. Cover with a lid and cook on high for 3–4 hours, or until the custard has set. Serve the pudding warm.

Making cheese and vegetable strata

This savoury bread and butter pudding can be made using the baked custard mixture. Simply leave out the sugar and season well with salt and black pepper.

1 Cook 1 thinly sliced leek and 1 large finely chopped onion in 25g/1oz/2 tbsp butter until soft. Stir in 30ml/2 tbsp chopped fresh chives or parsley.

2 Remove the crusts from 8 slices of bread, then cut into fingers. Arrange one-third of the bread fingers in a buttered 1.75 litre/3 pint/7½ cup soufflé dish. Top with half the vegetable mixture. Repeat the layers, ending with bread.

3 Pour the custard mixture over the strata, then sprinkle 75g/3oz/¾ cup finely grated Cheddar cheese over the top. Cover with buttered foil, then put in the ceramic cooking pot and pour enough near-boiling water around the dish to come halfway up the sides. Cover and cook on high for 3–4 hours until lightly set. Cut into wedges and serve warm.

Making rice pudding

Cooked in the slow cooker, rice pudding is wonderfully rich and creamy. Unlike baked versions it doesn't form a thick skin on the top. Add flavourings such as grated nutmeg at the beginning, or part-way through cooking.

SERVES 4–6

25g/1oz/2 tbsp softened butter
75g/3oz/generous ⅓ cup pudding rice, rinsed and drained
50g/2oz/4 tbsp caster (superfine) sugar
750ml/1¼ pints/3 cups milk
175ml/6fl oz/¾ cup evaporated (unsweetened condensed) milk

1 Thickly butter the ceramic cooking pot, taking it about half-way up the sides. Add the rice, sugar, milk, evaporated milk and any flavourings and stir to mix.

2 Cover with the lid and cook on high for 3–4 hours, or on low for 5–6 hours, until the rice is cooked and most of the milk has been absorbed.

3 Stir the pudding at least twice during the last 2 hours of cooking. If the mixture gets too thick towards the end, stir in a little more milk.

MAKING CAKES

Many cakes can be made successfully in a slow cooker – in particular, moist cake mixtures, such as carrot cake and gingerbread, that normally require long cooking at low temperatures. These types of cake usually benefit from being left to mature before eating, but this is not necessary when they are cooked in the slow cooker. The slow cooker is also good for making lightly textured, rich-flavoured sponge cakes. However, it is not suitable for whisked sponges and cakes because these need fast cooking at a high temperature.

Cakes can be cooked either in a tin (pan) with a fixed base or in a straight-sided soufflé dish. Before you line a tin and fill it with cake mixture, make sure it will fit in the ceramic cooking pot. It is a good idea to test that the tin is watertight: fill it with water and leave for a few minutes to check for leakages.

The baking tin should be lined with greaseproof (waxed) paper that has been greased with a little flavourless oil, or baking parchment. This makes it easier to remove the cake from the tin.

Base-lining

Some recipes only require the base of the tin (pan) to be lined. This technique can be used to line any shape of tin, whether round, square or rectangular.

Place the tin on a sheet of greaseproof (waxed) paper or baking parchment and, using a pencil, draw round the tin. Cut just inside the line so that the paper will fit neatly inside the tin. Using a sheet of kitchen paper drizzled with a flavourless oil, grease the inside of the tin and place the lining paper in the base, pressing it right into the corners.

Lining round cookware

The sides, as well as the base, of a tin or soufflé dish will often need to be lined.

1 Place the tin (pan) or soufflé dish on a sheet of greaseproof (waxed) paper and draw round it. Cut inside the line. Cut strips of paper, about 1cm/½in wider than the depth of the tin or dish. Fold up the bottom edge by 1cm/½in, then make cuts about 1cm/½in apart from the edge of the paper to the fold.

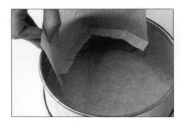

2 Brush the inside of the tin or dish with oil, then position the paper strips around the side of the tin so that the snipped edge sits on the base. Place the paper circle in the base.

Lining a square tin

You can line a square tin (pan) with a single piece of greaseproof paper.

Put the tin on a square of greaseproof paper, which allows the depth of the tin on all four sides. Draw around the base of the tin. Cut in from the edge to each corner of the square. Fold in each side along its pencil line, making a firm crease. Lightly brush the inside of the tin with oil, then fit the paper inside, making sure it fits well into the corners.

Lining a loaf tin

Unlike a square tin (pan), it is easier to line a loaf tin with two strips of paper.

1 Cut a strip of greaseproof paper the length of the tin base and wide enough to cover the base and long sides. Cut another strip of paper, the same width as the tin base and long enough to cover the base and ends of the tin.

2 Lightly brush the inside of the tin with oil, then press the two pieces of paper into position, creasing it where it meets the edges of the base of the tin.

Making dark chocolate cake

Steaming in the slow cooker gives this rich cake a deliciously moist texture.

SERVES 8–10

175g/6oz/¾ cup butter, at room temperature
115g/4oz/½ cup soft light brown sugar
50g/2oz/¼ cup clear honey
3 eggs, lightly beaten
150g/5oz/1¼ cups self-raising (self-rising) flour
25g/1oz/¼ cup unsweetened cocoa powder
10ml/2 tsp milk
5ml/1 tsp vanilla essence (extract)
whipped cream, for the filling (optional)

1 Place an upturned saucer or metal pastry cutter in the ceramic cooking pot. Pour in 2.5cm/1in of very hot water, then switch the slow cooker to high.

2 Grease and line a 16cm/7in fixed-base round cake tin (pan) or soufflé dish, at least 7.5cm/3in deep.

3 Put the butter, sugar and honey in a bowl and cream together until pale and fluffy. Beat the eggs into the creamed mixture a little at a time, beating well after each addition. If the mixture curdles, mix in a little of the measured flour.

4 Sift the flour and cocoa over the cake mixture. Using a large metal spoon, gently fold in with the milk and vanilla essence. Spoon the mixture into the prepared tin and level the surface.

5 Loosely cover the cake tin with lightly oiled foil. Put the tin in the ceramic cooking pot and then pour enough near-boiling water around the tin to come just over halfway up the sides.

6 Cover with the lid and cook on high for 3 hours. To test if the cake is cooked, insert a skewer into the centre of the cake. Leave for a few seconds, then remove; it should come away clean. If any mixture sticks to the skewer, re-cover and cook for 30 minutes more.

7 Remove the cake from the ceramic cooking pot and place on a wire rack for 10 minutes before turning out of the tin. Leave to cool, then cut in half and fill with whipped cream, if you like.

DECORATING CAKES

Cakes cooked in a slow cooker darken in colour but they do not brown in the same way as an oven-baked cake. As a result, many will benefit from decorating.

Decorating uncooked cakes
Many cakes can be decorated before they are cooked in the slow cooker. Note that light sponges and wet cake mixtures cannot hold heavy decorations.

Glistening sugar is an easy and effective way of decorating cakes. Different types of sugar can be sprinkled over the top of an uncooked cake. Good choices include caster (superfine) sugar, larger crystals of granulated or demerara (raw) sugar, and brown sugar crystals.

Chopped and flaked (sliced) nuts can be sprinkled over cakes in the same way as sugar. Toast them first.

Halved nuts and glacé (candied) fruits can be arranged in decorative patterns on fruit cakes and stiff cake batters. After cooking, brush over a little warmed honey or sugar syrup to glaze.

Decorating cooked cakes
After cooking, cakes can be decorated in a number of different ways.

Icing or frosting can transform a simple cake into something special. To make fudge frosting, break 50g/2oz plain (semisweet) chocolate into the cooking pot and add 225g/8oz/2 cups sifted icing (confectioners') sugar, 50g/2oz/¼ cup butter, 45ml/3 tbsp milk and 5ml/1 tsp vanilla essence (extract). Switch the slow cooker to high for 15–25 minutes, or until the chocolate has melted. Remove the cooking pot, stir to mix, then beat until thick and spread over the cake.

American frosting can be made by placing a bowl in the ceramic cooking pot, then pouring enough near-boiling water around the bowl to come just over halfway up the sides. Switch the slow cooker to high. Place 350g/12oz caster (superfine) sugar in the bowl with 2.5ml/½ tsp cream of tartar and 2 egg whites. Whisk continuously until the mixture holds its shape. Spread over the cake in peaks.

MAKING SAVOURY SAUCES

Sauces add flavour, colour, texture and moisture to food. Many can be made in the slow cooker, from classic simmered sauces to emulsions that are made by using the slow cooker as a bain-marie. Here are just a selection of classic sauces that can be used for cooking or for serving with other dishes.

Making fresh tomato sauce

This sauce can be used as the base for pasta dishes, or can be combined with meat or poultry to make a rich cooking sauce. You can use 2 × 400g/14oz cans chopped plum tomatoes instead of fresh, if you prefer. This recipe will make about 475ml/16fl oz/2 cups.

I Pour 15ml/1 tbsp olive oil into the ceramic cooking pot. Add 2 crushed garlic cloves and the finely grated zest of ½ lemon. Stir, then cover with the lid and switch the slow cooker to high. Cook for 15 minutes.

2 Peel and roughly chop 900g/2lb ripe tomatoes and add to the cooking pot with 60ml/4 tbsp vegetable stock or red wine, 5ml/1 tsp dried oregano and a pinch of caster (superfine) sugar. Stir to combine, then cover with the lid and cook on low for 3 hours.

3 Stir in 30–45ml/2–3 tbsp chopped fresh basil and season to taste with salt and ground black pepper.

Making white sauce

To make white sauce in a slow cooker, heat the milk, then whisk in a mixture of butter and flour. This recipe will make about 475ml/16fl oz/2 cups.

I Pour 400ml/14fl oz/1⅔ cups milk into the ceramic cooking pot. Add flavouring ingredients (such as a bay leaf, a blade of mace, a few parsley stalks, half a peeled onion and 4 black peppercorns). Switch the slow cooker to high and heat for 1 hour, or until simmering.

2 Blend 20g/¾oz/1½ tbsp softened butter with 20g/¾oz/scant ¼ cup plain (all-purpose) flour to make a paste.

3 Remove the flavouring ingredients from the milk using a slotted spoon. Add the paste in small spoonfuls and whisk into the hot milk until thickened.

4 Cover with the lid and cook for about 30 minutes, stirring occasionally. Season with salt and extra pepper if needed.

HOT EMULSION SAUCES

These rich, creamy sauces can be made very successfully using the slow cooker as a bain-marie.

Making hollandaise sauce

The rich flavour of hollandaise sauce goes well with fish, shellfish and many vegetables. Take your time making it because it may curdle if the butter is added too quickly. This recipe will make about 300ml/½ pint/1¼ cups.

I About 30 minutes before making the sauce, remove 150g/5oz/¾ cup unsalted (sweet) butter from the refrigerator. Cut into tiny cubes and leave to come to room temperature.

2 Pour about 5cm/2in near-boiling water into the ceramic cooking pot. Cover the slow cooker with the lid to retain the heat and switch to high.

3 Put 60ml/4 tbsp white wine vinegar in a pan with 4 black peppercorns, 1 bay leaf and 1 blade of mace (optional). Bring to the boil and simmer until reduced to 15ml/1 tbsp. Remove from the heat and dip the base of the pan into cold water to prevent further evaporation.

4 Beat 3 egg yolks with 15g/½oz/1 tbsp of the butter and a pinch of salt in a heatproof bowl that will fit in the slow cooker. Strain in the reduced vinegar. Place the bowl in the ceramic cooking pot and pour enough boiling water around the bowl to come just over halfway up the sides. Whisk for about 3 minutes until beginning to thicken.

5 Beat in the remaining butter a little at a time, making sure that each addition of butter is completely incorporated before adding the next. The mixture will slowly thicken and emulsify. Season with salt and ground black pepper. Switch the slow cooker to low and keep the hollandaise warm for up to 1 hour. (If the sauce starts to curdle, add an ice cube and whisk vigorously; the sauce should combine. If this doesn't work, whisk 1 egg yolk with 15ml/1 tbsp lukewarm water and slowly whisk into the separated sauce.)

Making beurre blanc

This simple butter sauce is served with poached or grilled (broiled) fish and poultry. It can be varied by adding chopped fresh herbs, such as chives or chervil, to the finished sauce. It is extremely rich, and only a small amount is needed per serving. This recipe will make about 250ml/8fl oz/1 cup.

1 Pour about 5cm/2in of near-boiling water into the ceramic cooking pot. Cover with the lid and switch the slow cooker to high.

2 Pour 45ml/3 tbsp each of white wine and white wine vinegar into a pan. Add 2 finely chopped shallots and bring to the boil. Simmer until reduced to about 15ml/1 tbsp liquid.

3 Strain the mixture into a heatproof bowl that will fit in the slow cooker, then pour enough boiling water around the bowl to come halfway up the sides.

4 Whisk in 225g/8oz/1 cup chilled diced butter, adding it piece by piece and making sure that each addition is completely incorporated before adding the next. Season with salt and ground black pepper before serving.

Making a sabayon sauce

Light and airy sabayon sauce is thickened with egg. It goes well with vegetable and pastry dishes. This recipe will make about 300ml/½ pint/1¼ cups.

1 Half-fill the ceramic cooking pot with near-boiling water, cover with the lid and switch to high.

2 Place a heatproof bowl over the water in the slow cooker; the base should just touch the water but the rest of the bowl should be above the water. Place 4 egg yolks with 15ml/1 tbsp white wine vinegar in the bowl and whisk until pale. Add 90ml/6 tbsp red or white wine or stock and whisk again.

3 When the sauce is thick and frothy, season to taste and serve immediately.

MAKING SWEET SAUCES

A sweet sauce adds the finishing touch to a dessert, and the slow cooker is excellent for making fruit purées, creamy custards and rich chocolate sauces.

Making fresh fruit coulis
Cooking soft fruits, such as raspberries, blackberries, blueberries, blackcurrants, plums, cherries and apricots, brings out their natural flavour. This recipe will make about 350ml/12fl oz/1½ cups.

I Put 350g/12oz/3 cups prepared fruit in the ceramic cooking pot with 45ml/ 3 tbsp water. Stir in a little sugar and add a dash of lemon juice. Cover with the lid and cook on high for 1–1½ hours or until very soft.

2 Remove the cooking pot from the slow cooker and leave to cool slightly. Pour the fruit into a food processor or blender and process until smooth. Press the purée through a sieve (strainer) to remove any seeds or skins.

3 Taste the sauce and stir in a little more sugar or lemon juice, if needed. Cover and chill until required. If you like, stir in 45ml/3 tbsp liqueur, such as Kirsch, before serving. The coulis can be stored in the refrigerator for up to 5 days.

Making dried fruit sauce
Dried fruits, such as apricots, can also be made into sauces. This recipe will make about 600ml/1 pint/scant 2½ cups.

I Place 175g/6oz dried apricots in the ceramic cooking pot, pour over 475ml/ 16fl oz/2 cups orange juice, cover and leave to soak overnight.

2 Place the ceramic pot in the slow cooker and cook on high for 1 hour, or until the apricots are tender. Purée in a food processor or blender and serve warm or cold. If necessary, dilute the sauce with a little extra fruit juice.

Making custard
Custard is the classic dessert sauce and can also be used as the basis for many desserts. The slow cooker maintains a gentle, constant heat, so the custard can be made directly in the ceramic cooking pot, rather than in a bain-marie. It can be served hot or cold, and can also be flavoured: try stirring 75g/3oz chopped plain (semisweet) chocolate or 45ml/ 3 tbsp rum or brandy into hot custard. For extra richness, replace some of the milk with single (light) or double (heavy) cream. This recipe will make about 600ml/1 pint/2½ cups.

I Pour 475ml/16fl oz/2 cups of milk into the ceramic cooking pot. Split a vanilla pod (bean) lengthways and add it to the milk. Heat on high for 1 hour, or until the milk reaches boiling point.

2 Meanwhile, whisk together 5 egg yolks and 90g/3½ oz/scant ½ cup caster (superfine) sugar in a bowl until the mixture is pale and thick.

3 Whisk 5ml/1 tsp cornflour (cornstarch) into the egg mixture. (This will help the custard to thicken and prevent curdling.)

4 Remove the vanilla pod and pour the hot milk over the egg mixture, whisking all the time. Pour the mixture back into the ceramic cooking pot and stir until slightly thickened. Bring the custard to simmering point; do not let it boil or it may curdle. Cook until it is thick enough to coat the back of a wooden spoon.

Making sabayon sauce
This frothy sauce goes well with elegant desserts and dainty pastries. This recipe makes about 450ml/¾ pint/scant 2 cups.

I Pour about 5cm/2in near-boiling water into the ceramic cooking pot. Cover with the lid and switch to high.

2 Put 4 eggs and 50g/2oz/¼ cup caster (superfine) sugar in a heatproof bowl, first checking that it will fit comfortably in the slow cooker. Beat well until the mixture becomes a paler colour, then whisk in 100ml/3½fl oz/generous ½ cup sweet white wine.

3 Place the bowl in the ceramic cooking pot and pour enough boiling water around it to come just over halfway up the sides. Continue whisking the sauce for 10 minutes until it is very thick and frothy. Serve hot or cold.

Making creamy chocolate sauce

This dark, velvety smooth sauce should be served with desserts that can stand up to its deep, rich flavour.

1 Pour 200ml/7fl oz/scant 1 cup double (heavy) cream, 60ml/4 tbsp milk and 2.5ml/½ tsp vanilla essence (extract) into the ceramic cooking pot. Switch the slow cooker to high and heat for about 45 minutes.

2 Turn off the slow cooker. Add 150g/5oz chopped dark (bittersweet) chocolate and stir continuously until it has melted. Serve warm.

Making glossy chocolate sauce

This sweet pouring sauce is ideal for serving with profiteroles and ice cream.

Put 225g/8oz chopped plain (semisweet) chocolate, 60ml/4 tbsp golden (light corn) syrup, 60ml/4 tbsp water and 25g/1oz/ 2 tbsp unsalted (sweet) butter into the ceramic cooking pot. Switch the slow cooker to high and heat, stirring, for 30 minutes until melted. Serve warm.

Making white chocolate sauce

This sweet creamy sauce is good served warm with fresh summer fruits.

1 Pour about 5cm/2in very hot water into the cooking pot. Cover with the lid and switch the slow cooker to high.

2 Put 200g/7oz white chocolate and 30ml/2 tbsp double (heavy) cream into a heatproof bowl. Place in the cooking pot and pour enough near-boiling water around the bowl to touch the base.

3 Stir until melted, then stir in 60ml/ 4 tbsp double (heavy) cream and 60ml/4 tbsp milk. Heat for 5 minutes, then remove from the heat and whisk.

Making caramel sauce

This rich, creamy sauce is delicious poured over sweet pastries and pastry desserts.

1 Put 25g/1oz/2 tbsp unsalted (sweet) butter and 75g/3oz/6 tbsp soft dark brown sugar in the ceramic cooking pot. Switch the slow cooker to high and heat for about 20 minutes, stirring occasionally, until the butter has melted and the sugar has dissolved.

2 Stir 150ml/¼ pint/⅔ cup double (heavy) cream into the sauce and cook for 20 minutes, stirring occasionally, until smooth. Serve warm or cold.

Making butterscotch sauce

This buttery sauce is very sweet and rich and should be served in small quantities.

1 Put 50g/2oz/¼ cup unsalted (sweet) butter, 75g/3oz/6 tbsp soft light brown sugar, 50g/2oz/¼ cup caster (superfine) sugar and 150g/5oz/scant ½ cup golden (light corn) syrup into the ceramic cooking pot. Heat on high for 20 minutes, stirring, until the sugar has dissolved.

2 Gradually stir in 150ml/¼ pint/⅔ cup double (heavy) cream and 5ml/1 tsp vanilla essence (extract). Serve warm.

SLOW COOKER SAFETY

The slow cooker is an extremely efficient and safe way to cook food. It is however an electrical appliance, and some basic common-sense safety precautions should be followed. Because slow cooker models vary, always take the time to read the instruction manual supplied by the manufacturer before use.

Cooker care

Looking after your cooker is simple but very important. When you first unwrap and remove your slow cooker from its box, check that it isn't damaged in any way, that the plug (which has hopefully been provided) is attached properly and, if you bought your slow cooker in another country, that the voltage on the rating plate of the appliance corresponds with your house electricity supply. If you are in any doubt, consult a qualified electrician before using the slow cooker.

Before you use the slow cooker for the first time, wash the ceramic cooking pot in warm soapy water and dry it thoroughly. Stand the slow cooker on a heat-resistant surface when in use, making sure that the mains lead is tucked away safely; the slow cooker should not touch anything hot or hang over the edge of the table or work-top in case it falls off accidentally.

Take extra care if you have young children (or curious pets) and position the slow cooker out of reach. After an hour or so of cooking, the slow cooker can become very hot; not just the

Below: Do not submerge the slow cooker in water. If it needs cleaning, make sure it is unplugged and use a damp, soapy sponge.

Above: Protect your hands from the hot cooker and escaping steam with a pair of padded oven gloves.

ceramic cooking pot, but the outer casing and the lid as well. Always use oven gloves when lifting the lid (do this away from you to prevent scalding from steam or drips), and when removing the cooking pot from inside the slow cooker.

Do not switch on the slow cooker if the ceramic cooking pot is empty (the only exception to this would be if the manufacturer recommends preheating). As soon as you have finished cooking, remove the plug from the socket to prevent the slow cooker being switched on accidentally.

Never immerse the outer casing of the slow cooker in water – this would be extremely dangerous, risking electric shock and fatal injury, because the outer casing contains the electrical elements that heat the ceramic cooking pot.

You should never use the outer casing for cooking without the ceramic cooking pot in place. If you need to clean the casing, do so with warm soapy water and a damp cloth, and be absolutely sure that the appliance is unplugged before you put it in contact with water.

Ensuring food safety

Slow cookers cook food slowly using a gentle heat – the precise temperature will vary from model to model but the average is from about 90°C/200°F on the low setting to about 150°C/300°F on the high setting. Bacteria in food is destroyed at a temperature of 74°C/165°F, so as long as the food is cooked

for the appropriate length of time, as stated in the recipe, this temperature will be reached quickly enough to ensure that the food is safe to eat. However, additional factors may affect the slow cooker's ability to reach the desired temperature and you should be aware of the following to ensure food safety:
• Avoid placing the slow cooker near an open window or in a draught.
• Do not lift the lid during cooking time unless instructed to do so in the recipe.
• Do not add ingredients that are frozen or part-frozen to the ceramic cooking pot because they will increase the length of time needed to reach the required cooking temperature, and the timings given in the recipe will not be sufficient.
• Increase the cooking time in extreme cold temperatures, where the kitchen temperature is considerably lower than normal, and check food is cooked before serving, particularly poultry and pork.

Checking meat is cooked

When it comes to food safety, one of the main things to look out for is that meat is properly cooked – in particular, poultry and pork. A meat thermometer is a worthwhile investment if you are planning to cook whole joints of meat and poultry in your slow cooker. It is the most reliable way to ensure that the inside of the meat has reached a high enough temperature to kill any potentially harmful bacteria, without losing its juices and becoming dry and overcooked.

Below: A meat thermometer is easy to use and gives an accurate temperature reading to let you know when meat is safe to eat.

Above: A skewer or the tip of a sharp knife can be inserted into a thick part of a meat joint to check that it is thoroughly cooked.

When using a meat thermometer, the tip of the stainless steel probe should be inserted as near the centre of the meat as possible, but not touching any bone. Meat thermometers have different markings for various meats, indicating rare and pinkish lamb and beef, through to medium and well cooked. Pork and poultry must always be cooked thoroughly to avoid the risk of food poisoning as they can pass on harmful bacteria when raw or partially cooked; always err on the side of caution and go for well cooked, rather than risk the meat being underdone and therefore unsafe.

To check that meat is cooked without a thermometer, insert the tip of a thin sharp knife or skewer into the thickest part of the meat joint and hold it there for 20 seconds. For medium to well-cooked lamb or beef, the juices will be almost clear and the knife will feel hot on the back of the hand. When cooking pork or poultry, it is essential that the meat juices should be completely clear. If there is any trace of pink, the meat is not ready to eat and should be cooked for a further 30 minutes; check again with the skewer or knife before serving.

With poultry, you can double check by giving the leg a tug – it should have some give in it and not be resistant. If you are still unsure, make a deep cut where the thigh joins the body; there should be no visible trace of pink meat. If there is, cook the meat for a further 30 minutes, then check again.

FOOD SAFETY TIPS

Basic food safety recommendations should be followed when preparing or using food in the slow cooker.

• Food should always be at room temperature when it is added to the slow cooker, otherwise it will take longer to reach the safe cooking temperature. However, ingredients such as meat and fish should not be left out of the refrigerator for longer than is necessary, so remove from the refrigerator just to take off the chill and keep covered with cling film or plastic wrap.

• Marinating food in the ceramic cooking pot before cooking saves on washing up, but the cooking pot will become cold in the refrigerator, so remove it at least 1 hour before you plan to start cooking.

• Large joints of meat and whole poultry should be cooked at a high temperature for the first 1–2 hours to accelerate the cooking process. Switch the slow cooker to low for the remaining cooking time.

• Avoid lifting the lid of the ceramic cooking during the cooking time, especially in the early stages. It takes 15–20 minutes to recover the lost heat each time the lid is removed, so it will take much longer to reach a safe temperature.

• Don't be tempted to partially cook meat or poultry, then refrigerate for subsequent cooking. Also avoid reheating pre-cooked dishes in the slow cooker.

• Frozen foods should always be thoroughly thawed before being placed in the slow cooker. If added when frozen, they will increase the time the food takes to reach a safe temperature. If adding frozen vegetables towards the end of cooking time, thaw them first under cold running water.

• Soak dried beans, in particular red kidney beans, overnight and then fast-boil them on the stovetop for 10 minutes in a pan of fresh cooking water to destroy toxins before adding to the slow cooker.

ONE-POT COOKING TECHNIQUES

Cooking a dish in a single pot doesn't demand any particular expertise, but mastering a few simple techniques will make for greater efficiency, especially when preparing the ingredients. Many one-pot dishes need very little attention while they are actually cooking, but it is important to follow the instructions in individual recipes as regards stirring.

Stewing, Braising and Casseroling Meat

These are long, slow and moist methods of cooking either in the oven or on top of the stove. The meat is browned first to seal in the natural juices and improve the flavour and colour of the finished dish, then it is simmered slowly at a low temperature in liquid – wine, water, beer or stock.

I Trim off any excess fat from the meat. For stewing and casseroling, cut the meat into 2.5cm/1in cubes. For braising use thickly cut steaks or cut the meat into thick slices.

2 Toss the meat a few pieces at a time in seasoned flour, then shake off any excess. The flour coating browns to give the casserole a good flavour and also thickens the liquid.

3 Heat 30ml/2 tbsp sunflower oil in a flameproof casserole. Add the meat in batches and cook over a high heat. When the meat is well browned on all sides, use a draining spoon to remove the meat before adding the next batch.

4 Add the sliced or chopped onions and other vegetables to the remaining fat and juices in the casserole and cook, stirring occasionally, for about 5 minutes.

5 Return the meat to the casserole, add herbs and pour in the cooking liquid. Stir to loosen the cooking residue from the base of the pan and then heat until simmering. Simmer gently on the hob or in the oven until the meat is tender. The casserole may be covered for the entire cooking time or uncovered towards the end to allow excess liquid to evaporate.

CUTS FOR STEWS, BRAISES AND CASSEROLES
These slow-cooked dishes are ideal for tough, inexpensive cuts of meat, such as cubes of stewing steak or slices of braising steak, less tender cuts of lamb such as shoulder, and diced or thickly sliced pork. Lamb leg steaks, although fairly tender, are also a good choice for braising.

Pot-roasting Meat

This long, slow method of cooking is ideal for slightly tough joints of meat such as topside of beef, lamb shoulder and shanks, and knuckle of pork.

I Heat a little sunflower oil in a large flameproof casserole until very hot. Add the meat and cook over a high heat, turning frequently, until browned on all sides. Remove the meat from the pan.

2 Add the onions, leeks and any root vegetables to the pan, then cook, stirring, for a few minutes. Replace the meat on top of the vegetables and pour in a little liquid, such as stock, wine or beer. Cover and cook gently in the oven until the meat is tender.

Casseroling Chicken

Moist cooking methods not only bring out the flavour of poultry but also offer the opportunity for allowing herbs and spices and aromatics to infuse the light meat thoroughly. Whole birds and joints can be casseroled.

Pan-frying Meat

This is the traditional cooking method for steaks such as sirloin and fillet, and it is also good for veal escalopes (US scallops) and veal chops, lamb chops, cutlets and noisettes, and pork chops, steaks and escalopes.

Pan-frying Poultry

This quick cooking method is ideal for chicken breast fillets and portions. Once the meat is cooked, the cooking juices can be made into a tasty sauce, simply stir in a little cream, add some chopped herbs and season to taste.

I Brown the poultry pieces or bird all over first. Remove from the pan before softening chopped onion, carrot, celery and other flavouring ingredients in the fat remaining in the pan.

I Cook steaks and chops in the minimum of fat, then add flavoured butter when serving, if you like. Dab a little sunflower oil on kitchen paper and use to grease the pan lightly. Heat the pan until it is very hot (almost smoking). Add the steak or chops and cook for 2–4 minutes on each side.

When frying poultry, remember that it must be cooked through. Escalopes and boneless breasts cook quickly, so are ideal for pan-frying over a high heat, but uneven thicker portions require careful cooking. With larger pieces, reduce the heat to low once the chicken is browned and cook it slowly for up to 30 minutes to ensure that the centre is cooked.

Stir-frying

This is a fast method of cooking tender meat. The meat should be cut into thin slices across the grain, and then cut into fine, long strips. Use a wok or a heavy frying pan.

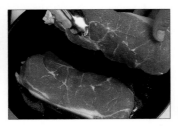

2 Replace the poultry before adding the chosen liquid – stock, wine or canned tomatoes. Season the casserole well, then bring it just to simmering point. Cover it closely and allow it to simmer very gently on top of the stove, or cook in the oven at 180°C/350°F/Gas 4.

2 Pan-fry other lean cuts of meat in a mixture of butter and oil. Butter burns easily, so heat the oil in the pan first and add the butter just before the meat to avoid this. Make sure that the butter and oil are sizzling before adding the meat. Cook on both sides until browned. Beef and thin cuts of meat such as escalopes will be ready to serve. For some thicker cuts and meat such as pork that needs to be well-cooked, reduce the heat to low once the meat is browned and cook for 10–15 minutes, or until cooked through. Test by piercing the centre of the meat with the point of a sharp knife.

Heat a little oil in a wok or frying pan until it is smoking hot. Add the meat in batches and stir-fry over a high heat. Remove the cooked meat before adding a fresh batch. When all the meat is cooked, add the other ingredients and stir-fry over a slightly lower heat.

COOKING TIMES FOR CASSEROLING CHICKEN

• For a whole bird allow 20 minutes per 450g/1lb, plus 20 minutes.
• Large portions 45–60 minutes.
• Boneless breasts about 30 minutes.
• Chunks or diced poultry 20–40 minutes, depending on their size.

CLAY-POT COOKING TECHNIQUES

Used with care, clay cooking pots last for years, but it is very important to follow the manufacturer's instructions closely. The advice that follows should be read in conjunction with your handbook.

Preparing a Clay Pot
All unglazed clay cooking pots must be soaked in cold water before every use. This is essential because it is the water retained in the clay that provides the moisture required during cooking. Ideally, the soaking time should be about 20 minutes. If it is the first time you have used the pot, leave it to soak for at least 30 minutes.

Place both the pot and its lid in a sink of cold water, inverting the lid on top of the base if necessary. The entire pot and the lid must be submerged. This thorough soaking is recommended before every use. If you are really short of time, you can just hold the pot under cold running water for about 1 minute, but this is not as satisfactory as soaking.

You can use your clay pot for lots of different recipes, but should avoid cooking fish or any highly flavoured dish in it the first time you use it. If you have more than one clay pot, consider keeping separate pots for savoury and sweet dishes.

Partially Glazed Clay Pots
Also available are clay pots that are glazed on the inside, but which have unglazed lids. With this type of pot, only the lid needs to be soaked, and this is done by holding it under running cold water for a few minutes. The ingredients are put into the pot, seasoned, and moistened with stock. The lid is fitted

and the pot is placed in a cold oven, which is then heated to 220°C/425°F/Gas 7. Steam released from the soaked lid helps to keep the food moist as it bakes. The lid can be removed towards the end of cooking to allow the food to brown, if necessary.

Cooking with a Clay Pot
Most clay pots should only be used in the oven. Unglazed pots are sensitive to sudden changes of temperature, which can cause the pot to crack or break if it is placed directly over the heat.

Some clay pots can be used on top of the stove on a very low heat, but it is recommended that a heat diffuser or flame-tamer is used. These are available from specialist cookware stores.

1 Some recipes suggest sautéing vegetables or meat in a frying pan to brown them before adding them to the clay pot. If you do this, let the browned foods cool slightly before putting them into the cold clay pot.

2 Once the browned foods have been added, it is okay to pour in warm or hand-hot cooking liquids. If what is in the pot is cold, any liquid added should be at room temperature.

USING A HEAT DIFFUSER

If your handbook states that your pot can safely be used on top of the stove you can obviously do so, but always use a heat diffuser between the heat source and the pot.

Some cazuelas can be used on top of the stove with a heat diffuser.

Cooking in an Oven
An unglazed clay pot must always be heated gradually.

Place the clay pot in a cold oven and then heat to the required temperature. It might crack if subjected to a sudden change of temperature.

You will notice that the recipes in this book advise you to place the clay pot, which will be cold, in a cold oven, then set the oven temperature to allow the oven and clay pot to heat slowly.

An electric oven heats up gradually, giving the clay pot time to acclimatize. If, however, you are using a traditional gas oven, the flames may be too fierce for the cold clay pot. You should start by setting the oven temperature to 190°C/375°F/Gas 5. After 5 minutes, increase the temperature to 200°C/400°F/Gas 6. Continue to increase the temperature of the oven gradually, each time raising it to the next setting on your cooker, until the required temperature is reached.

The exact cooking times for recipes containing liquids may vary from oven to oven, as the time taken for the liquid to come to the boil will differ.

Cooking with a Cast-iron Tagine on a Stovetop

In addition to the classic all-earthenware tagines, which can't be used on a stovetop, there is a modern version that has an earthenware lid and cast-iron base. The base can be used on the top of any type of stove, be it gas, electric or wood-burning, to brown ingredients such as onions, vegetables or meat before the other ingredients and liquid are added. The pot is then covered and the tagine or stew is simmered gently on top of the stove or in the oven.

Place the cast-iron tagine base on the stovetop, add a little oil and heat. Add the vegetables or other ingredients and cook over a medium-high heat, stirring occasionally, until browned.

Browning in a Clay Pot

A certain amount of browning will occur during cooking, depending on the cooking temperature, cooking time and type of food. Some recipes suggest removing the lid for a short period of time towards the end of the cooking time to enhance the colour of baked items and roasts, and also to develop a crisper finish. The oven temperature for clay-pot cooking is fairly high, so the browning process will only take a few minutes; keep a close check on the food.

To remove the lid, lift the clay pot out of the oven using oven gloves and place it on a pot stand, wooden board or folded dishtowel. Take care when lifting the lid to avoid any escaping steam.

Adding Liquids to a Clay Pot

Never add boiling liquids – or even very hot liquids – to a cold clay pot or the sudden change in temperature may cause the clay pot to crack.

If you need to add liquid to the clay pot during the cooking period, this liquid should be hot. This not only avoids a sudden temperature change, but also ensures that the food isn't cooled too much, which would slow the cooking.

Adding Flavourings

To get the best results, place herb sprigs and spices in among vegetables that are to be roasted or underneath joints of meat. This will ensure that the flavour penetrates as deeply as possible.

Adding Ingredients during Cooking

In some recipes, ingredients that don't need to be cooked for long, such as prawns or cooked ham, are added towards the end of the cooking time.

Remove the pot from the oven using oven gloves and remove the lid. Add the cold food and stir well to ensure that it is distributed evenly, then re-cover the pot and return it to the oven.

Cooking on a Barbecue

Moroccan tagines are sometimes placed on a barbecue, but they should not be too near the heat source. It is best to wait until the coals have all turned grey. Cover the coals with some sand, to make the heat less concentrated, and then allow the tagine to heat up slowly by initially placing it at the edge of the barbecue and gradually moving it to the hottest part.

Using a Clay Pot for Baking

Clay pots can be used for baking cakes, breads and sponge-based desserts. It is, however, best to keep a separate clay pot for sweet foods or, alternatively, use earthenware that is glazed inside.

If you use a clay pot for baking, it is a good idea to line the base of the clay pot with a piece of baking parchment, so that the food doesn't stick to the base and is easy to remove after baking.

SAFETY FIRST

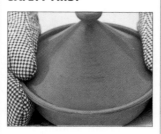

When you remove any type of clay pot from the oven, either to add extra ingredients or to serve the food, protect your hands with oven gloves. Place the pot on a folded towel, wooden board, heatproof mat or pot stand, as sudden contact with a cold surface could cause the pot to crack. Do the same with the lid, when you lift it off.

Clay pots should not be used under the grill (broiler) or in the freezer as the sudden change in temperature could cause the clay pot to crack or break.

Microwave Cooking

Clay pots can be used to cook foods in the microwave oven, as well as in a conventional oven. One of the advantages with using a clay pot for microwave cooking is that, because it is moist from soaking, it will absorb some of the microwave energy. This slows down the cooking process, which is perfect for protecting delicate foods, cooking foods more evenly and pot-roasting less tender cuts of meat, whole chickens or game birds.

Select a clay pot that will fit inside your microwave oven. The smaller, rectangular or round pots are ideal.

Prepare the pot as for oven cooking, by soaking it in water for 20 minutes. When setting the cooking time, refer to your microwave handbook for detailed instructions on using a clay pot, as each appliance is different. If you are adapting an existing microwave recipe, expect the food to take slightly longer to cook in a clay pot. The food is usually cooked on full (100%) power, but it may also be cooked on medium-high (70%) or medium (50%) settings so that the food simmers, rather than boils.

A safety note worth remembering is that because a clay pot is moist and absorbs microwave energy it will become hot; hotter, in fact, than many other types of microwave cookware. Make sure you use oven gloves to lift the clay pot out of the microwave, and always place the pot on a pot stand, wooden board or mat, or folded dishtowel when removing it from the oven, both for your own safety, and to avoid subjecting the pot to severe temperature changes.

ADAPTING RECIPES FOR CLAY-POT COOKING

A wide range of foods can be cooked in a clay pot, and you may wish to try using it for some of your favourite dishes. Find a clay-pot recipe in this book that is similar to the one you want to make, and use it as a blueprint. The main differences in cooking techniques that need to be observed are these:

• When an unglazed or partially glazed clay pot is used, the oven must not be preheated.

• When the pot is put into the cold oven, it is heated gradually until it reaches the required cooking temperature. If the dish contains liquid, it must be heated until it boils. This is likely to be at a higher temperature than when cooking in another type of container, because the pot forms an insulating layer between the heat of the oven and the food. When the liquid boils, the oven temperature may then be reduced, so that the contents of the pot simmer.

• If you are using a gas stove, it is essential that you increase the temperature gradually or the transition from cold to blasting heat may cause the pot to crack.

• You will probably have to extend the cooking time to take into account the fact that the ingredients, including any liquids, are cold when put into the oven, which also starts off cold. When foods are roasted with little or no liquid, however, the cooking time stays about the same because the higher cooking temperature compensates for the insulation of the clay pot.

• Because of the moist environment, food cooked in a clay pot doesn't overcook quickly when the lid is on, however, it is important to check the food frequently if the lid is removed towards the end of cooking to promote browning as the top of the food can easily scorch.

Cleaning and Storing Clay Pots

Before using a clay pot for the first time, brush it thoroughly inside and out to remove any loose clay particles left from the manufacturing process. Rinse the pot after brushing, then drain it. If you intend to cook in it straight away, then soak it thoroughly in cold water first.

After using the pot a few times, you may notice a colour change. This is completely natural and is part of the character of a clay pot. As with a well-seasoned frying pan or wok, this effect is due to a protective layer that builds up with use and enhances the cooking qualities of the pot.

Washing the Pot

I Wash a clay pot promptly after every use, using a brush and hot water. A soft-bristled brush is fine if the pot is not too dirty, otherwise use a firm-bristled washing-up brush, Add washing-up (dishwashing) liquid to the water if this is recommended in your handbook, as this helps to get rid of stubborn stains. Avoid using abrasive cleaning materials, as these may affect the porous nature of the clay and may impair its cooking qualities.

2 Having washed the pot, rinse it under hot water, then stand it upside down on kitchen paper to drain thoroughly.

Using a Dishwasher

Most glazed earthenware dishes can be put in the dishwasher, but some manufacturers do not recommend washing clay pots that way. Check your manufacturer's handbook.

Removing Food Residue

Sometimes food may bake on to the surface of a clay pot, especially if it has been used for cooking without the cover. Soaking the pot in hot water to which a little washing-up liquid has been added is usually sufficient to release the residue. Leave the pot to soak overnight if the residue is particularly stubborn. Some earthenware dishes can be filled with hot water to remove baked-on food, but do not leave them immersed in hot soapy water.

I If an unglazed clay pot becomes tainted with residual flavours, soak it overnight in cold water containing bicarbonate of soda (baking soda). If the problem is severe, or if smells still linger, fill the pot with water, add bicarbonate of soda and place it in a cold oven.

2 Set the oven to 180°C/350°F/Gas 4 and leave the clay pot to heat in the oven for about 20 minutes. Increase the temperature of the oven to 200°C/400°F/Gas 6 and heat for another 20 minutes, then increase the oven temperature again to 230°C/450°F/Gas 8 and leave the pot at this temperature for 30 minutes to I hour.

3 Carefully lift the pot out of the oven using oven gloves and then discard the contents. Scrub the interior of the pot gently before rinsing it thoroughly with very hot water. Turn the pot and lid upside-down on a rack and leave to dry at room temperature. It is worth following this cleaning procedure after about a hundred uses, to clean the pores of your clay pot. This will allow it to take up water with the same efficiency as when it was brand new.

Storing the Pot

Before you put a clay pot away, make sure that it is not only completely clean but also thoroughly dried.

Invert the lid into the base. This is not only for safety and so that it takes up less room in your storecupboard, but also because placing the lid on the pot as for cooking could encourage moulds and mildew to grow on the inside surface of the pot and lid.

It is for this reason that the pot must also be stored somewhere dry and airy. Do not leave it in a damp place. It is the nature of a clay pot to absorb moisture, so it is important to keep it completely dry during storage. Do not wrap the clay pot or seal it in a plastic bag during storage.

SLOW COOKER SOUPS

The slow cooker truly excels when it comes to soup-making – the long, gentle cooking allows the flavours to develop fully over time, giving rich, flavoursome results. This chapter draws on recipes from around the world – from North African Spiced Soup, Asian-Style Duck Consommé and Galician Broth, to French Onion Soup with Cheese Croûtes, Chicken Soup with Knaidlach and Genoese Minestrone. There are also soups for every occasion – from Spicy Pumpkin Soup for a hearty lunch and Chilled Tomato and Sweet Pepper Soup for a summer lunch party to delicate Greek Avgolemono for an elegant start to a meal.

FRENCH ONION SOUP with CHEESE CROÛTES

Probably the most famous of all onion soups, this hearty, warming dish was traditionally
served as a sustaining early morning meal to the porters and workers of Les Halles
market in Paris. Use large yellow Spanish onions for the best result.

3 Add the sugar and stir well. Cover again with the lid and folded dish towel and continue cooking on high for 4 hours, stirring two or three times, to ensure the onions are colouring evenly. At the end of this time, they should be a dark golden colour.

4 Sprinkle the flour over the onions and stir to mix. Next, stir in the vinegar followed by the brandy, then slowly blend in the wine. Stir in the stock and thyme and season with salt and pepper. Cook on high for a further 2 hours, or until the onions are very tender.

SERVES 4

40g/1½oz/3 tbsp butter
10ml/2 tsp olive oil
1.2kg/2½lb onions, peeled and sliced
5ml/1 tsp caster (superfine) sugar
15ml/1 tbsp plain (all-purpose) flour
15ml/1 tbsp sherry vinegar
30ml/2 tbsp brandy
120ml/4fl oz/½ cup dry white wine
1 litre/1¾ pints/4 cups boiling beef,
    chicken or duck stock
5ml/1 tsp chopped fresh thyme
salt and ground black pepper

For the croûtes

4 slices day-old French stick or baguette,
    about 2.5cm/1in thick
1 garlic clove, halved
5ml/1 tsp French mustard
50g/2oz/½ cup grated Gruyère cheese

1 Put the butter and olive oil in the ceramic cooking pot and heat on high for about 15 minutes until melted.

2 Add the onions to the pot and stir to coat well in the melted butter and oil. Cover with the lid, then place a folded dish towel over the top to retain all the heat and cook for 2 hours, stirring halfway through cooking time.

5 For the croûtes, place the bread slices under a low grill (broiler) and cook until dry and lightly browned. Rub the bread with the cut surface of the garlic and spread with mustard, then sprinkle the grated Gruyère cheese over the slices.

6 Turn the grill to high and cook the croûtes for 2–3 minutes, until the cheese melts, bubbles and browns. Ladle the soup into warmed bowls and float a Gruyère croûte on top of each. Serve straight away.

Energy 418Kcal/1747kJ; Protein 11.5g; Carbohydrate 51.8g, of which sugars 19.4g; Fat 15.9g, of which saturates 8.2g; Cholesterol 33mg; Calcium 209mg; Fibre 5.3g; Sodium 1195mg.

CARROT and CORIANDER SOUP

Root vegetables, such as carrots, are great for slow cooker soups. Their earthy flavour becomes rich and sweet when cooked slowly over a gentle heat and goes perfectly with robust herbs and spices, and their texture becomes beautifully smooth when puréed.

SERVES 4

450g/1lb carrots, preferably young
   and tender
15ml/1 tbsp sunflower oil
40g/1½oz/3 tbsp butter
1 onion, chopped
1 stick celery, plus 2–3 pale leafy tops
2 small potatoes, peeled
900ml/1½ pints/3¾ cups boiling
   vegetable stock
10ml/2 tsp ground coriander
15ml/1 tbsp chopped fresh coriander
   (cilantro)
150ml/¼ pint/⅔ cup milk
salt and ground black pepper

3 Pour the boiling vegetable stock over the vegetables, then season with salt and ground black pepper. Cover the pot with the lid and cook on low for 4–5 hours until the vegetables are tender.

4 Reserve 6–8 tiny celery leaves from the leafy tops for the garnish, then finely chop the remaining celery tops. Melt the remaining butter in a large pan and add the ground coriander. Fry for about 1 minute, stirring constantly, until the aromas are released.

5 Reduce the heat under the pan and add the chopped celery tops and fresh coriander. Fry for about 30 seconds, then remove the pan from the heat.

6 Ladle the soup into a food processor or blender and process until smooth, then pour into the pan with the celery tops and coriander. Stir in the milk and heat gently until piping hot. Check the seasoning, then serve garnished with the reserved celery leaves.

1 Trim and peel the carrots and cut into chunks. Heat the oil and 25g/1oz/2 tbsp of the butter in a pan and fry the onion over a gentle heat for 3–4 minutes until slightly softened. Do not let it brown.

2 Slice the celery and chop the potatoes, and add them to the onion in the pan. Cook for 2 minutes, then add the carrots and cook for a further 1 minute. Transfer the fried vegetables to the ceramic cooking pot.

Energy 168Kcal/697kJ; Protein 3g; Carbohydrate 11.9g, of which sugars 9.2g; Fat 12.4g, of which saturates 6g; Cholesterol 24mg; Calcium 94mg; Fibre 3.1g; Sodium 758mg.

TOMATO and FRESH BASIL SOUP

Peppery, aromatic basil is the perfect partner for sweet, ripe tomatoes – and it is easy
to grow at home in a pot on a sunny kitchen windowsill. Make this soup in late summer
when fresh tomatoes are at their best and most flavoursome.

SERVES 4

15ml/1 tbsp olive oil
25g/1oz/2 tbsp butter
1 onion, finely chopped
900g/2lb ripe tomatoes, roughly chopped
1 garlic clove, roughly chopped
about 600ml/1 pint/2½ cups
    vegetable stock
120ml/4fl oz/½ cup dry white wine
30ml/2 tbsp sun-dried tomato paste
30ml/2 tbsp shredded fresh basil
150ml/¼ pint/⅔ cup double
    (heavy) cream
salt and ground black pepper
whole basil leaves, to garnish

1 Heat the oil and butter in a large saucepan until foaming. Add the onion and cook gently for about 5 minutes, stirring, until the onion is softened but not brown, then add the chopped tomatoes and garlic.

2 Add the stock, white wine and sun-dried tomato paste to the pan and stir to combine. Heat until just below boiling point, then carefully pour the mixture into the ceramic cooking pot.

3 Switch the slow cooker to the high or auto setting, cover with the lid and cook for 1 hour. Leave the slow cooker on auto or switch to low and cook for a further 4–6 hours, until tender.

4 Leave the soup to cool for a few minutes, then ladle into a food processor or blender and process until smooth. Press the puréed soup through a sieve (strainer) into a clean pan.

5 Add the shredded basil and the cream to the soup and heat through, stirring. Do not allow the soup to reach boiling point. Check the consistency and add a little more stock if necessary. Season, then pour into warmed bowls and garnish with basil. Serve immediately.

Energy 335Kcal/1387kJ; Protein 3.1g; Carbohydrate 11.7g, of which sugars 10.8g; Fat 28.9g, of which saturates 16.4g; Cholesterol 65mg; Calcium 50mg; Fibre 3g; Sodium 168mg.

CHILLED TOMATO and SWEET PEPPER SOUP

Inspired by the classic Spanish soup, gazpacho, *which is made with raw salad vegetables, this soup is cooked first and then chilled. Grilling the peppers gives a slightly smoky flavour, but you can leave out this step to save on preparation time, if you like.*

SERVES 4

2 red (bell) peppers
30ml/2 tbsp olive oil
1 onion, finely chopped
2 garlic cloves, crushed
675g/1½lb ripe, well-flavoured
    tomatoes
120ml/4fl oz/½ cup red wine
450ml/¾ pint/scant 2 cups vegetable
    or chicken stock
2.5ml/½ tsp caster (superfine) sugar
salt and ground black pepper
chopped fresh chives, to garnish

For the croûtons
2 slices white bread, crusts removed
45ml/3 tbsp olive oil

1 Cut each pepper into quarters and remove the core and seeds. Place each quarter, skin side up, on a grill (broiler) rack. Grill (broil) until the skins are blistered and charred, then transfer to a bowl and cover with a plate.

2 Heat the oil in a frying pan. Add the onion and garlic and cook gently for about 10 minutes until soft, stirring occasionally. Meanwhile, remove the skin from the peppers and roughly chop the flesh. Cut the tomatoes into chunks.

3 Transfer the onions to the ceramic cooking pot and add the peppers, tomatoes, wine, stock and sugar. Cover and cook on high for 3–4 hours, or until the vegetables are very tender. Leave the soup to stand for about 10 minutes to cool slightly.

4 Ladle the soup into a food processor or blender and process until smooth. Press through a fine sieve (strainer) into a bowl. Leave to cool before chilling in the refrigerator for at least 3 hours.

5 Meanwhile, make the croûtons. Cut the bread into cubes. Heat the oil in a frying pan, add the bread and fry until golden. Drain well on kitchen paper.

6 Season the soup to taste with salt and pepper, then ladle into chilled bowls. Serve topped with a few croûtons and a sprinkling of chopped chives.

Energy 262Kcal/1090kJ; Protein 3.5g; Carbohydrate 17.6g, of which sugars 11.5g; Fat 18g, of which saturates 2.6g; Cholesterol 0mg; Calcium 47mg; Fibre 3.4g; Sodium 499mg.

SPICY PUMPKIN SOUP

*This stunning golden-orange soup has a smooth velvety texture, and a delicate taste,
which is subtly spiced with cumin and garlic. Long, slow cooking really gives the flavours
time to develop and come together to make a wonderful autumnal dish.*

SERVES 4

900g/2lb pumpkin, peeled
   and seeds removed
30ml/2 tbsp olive oil
2 leeks, trimmed and sliced
1 garlic clove, crushed
5ml/1 tsp ground ginger
5ml/1 tsp ground cumin
750ml/1¼ pints/3 cups near-boiling
   chicken stock
salt and ground black pepper
60ml/4 tbsp natural (plain) yogurt, to serve
coriander (cilantro) leaves, to garnish

COOK'S TIP
To save time, reheat the soup on the
stovetop rather than in the slow cooker.

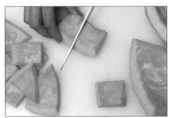

1 Using a sharp knife, cut the pumpkin
into large chunks. Place the chunks in
the ceramic cooking pot.

2 Heat the oil in a large pan and add
the leeks and garlic. Cook gently until
softened but not coloured.

3 Add the ginger and cumin to the pan
and cook, stirring, for a further minute.
Tip the mixture into the ceramic cooking
pot, pour over the chicken stock and
season with salt and black pepper.

4 Cover the slow cooker with the lid,
switch to low and cook for 6–8 hours,
or until the pumpkin is very tender.

5 Ladle the soup, in batches if necessary,
into a food processor or blender and
process until smooth. Return the soup
to the rinsed out cooking pot, cover and
cook on high for 1 hour, or until piping
hot. Serve in warmed individual bowls,
with a swirl of natural yogurt and a few
coriander leaves.

Energy 89Kcal/372kJ; Protein 2.3g; Carbohydrate 6.2g, of which sugars 4.7g; Fat 6.3g, of which saturates 1.1g; Cholesterol 0mg; Calcium 75mg; Fibre 3.1g; Sodium 127mg.

WILD MUSHROOM SOUP

This robust, creamy soup is ideal for a simple lunch or supper, served with chunks of nutty wholegrain bread spread with fresh butter. The rich flavour and colour of the soup are further enhanced by the addition of dried wild mushrooms and a dash of Madeira.

SERVES 4

15g/½oz/¼ cup dried wild mushrooms, such as morels, ceps or porcini
600ml/1 pint/2½ cups hot chicken or vegetable stock
25g/1oz/2 tbsp butter
1 onion, finely chopped
1 garlic clove, crushed
450g/1lb button (white) or other cultivated mushrooms, trimmed and sliced
15ml/1 tbsp plain (all-purpose) flour
fresh nutmeg
1.5ml/¼ tsp dried thyme
60ml/4 tbsp Madeira or dry sherry
60ml/4 tbsp crème fraîche or sour cream
salt and ground black pepper
chopped fresh chives, to garnish

1 Put the dried mushrooms in a sieve (strainer) and rinse under cold running water to remove any grit, then place in the ceramic cooking pot. Pour over half of the hot chicken or vegetable stock and cover with the lid. Switch the slow cooker to the auto or high setting.

2 Place the butter in a large pan and melt over a medium heat. Add the chopped onion and cook for 5–7 minutes until softened and just golden.

3 Add the garlic and fresh mushrooms to the pan and cook for 5 minutes. Sprinkle over the flour, then grate some nutmeg into the mixture and add the thyme. Cook for 3 minutes more, stirring all the time, until blended.

4 Stir in the Madeira or sherry and the remaining stock, and season with salt and pepper. Bring to the boil, then transfer to the ceramic cooking pot. Cook for 1 hour, then switch to low or leave on auto and cook for a further 3–4 hours, or until the mushrooms are very tender.

5 Ladle the soup into a food processor or blender and process until smooth. Strain it back into the pan, pressing it with the back of a spoon to force the purée through the sieve.

6 Reheat the soup until piping hot, then stir in half the crème fraîche or sour cream. Ladle into warmed bowls, swirl a little of the remaining crème fraîche or sour cream on top of each and sprinkle with chives.

COOK'S TIP

Dried mushrooms have a rich, intense flavour and are perfect for boosting the flavour of cultivated mushrooms, which can often be rather bland.

Energy 143Kcal/592kJ; Protein 3.7g; Carbohydrate 8.2g, of which sugars 3.2g; Fat 9g, of which saturates 5.3g; Cholesterol 22mg; Calcium 41mg; Fibre 2g; Sodium 174mg.

GALICIAN BROTH

This classic Galician soup from the north coast of Spain needs long, slow cooking to give the flavours time to develop fully. Traditionally it would be made with young, green leafy turnip tops, but in this version tasty spring greens are used instead.

SERVES 6

450g/1lb gammon, in one piece, soaked
   overnight in cold water
2 bay leaves
2 onions, sliced
10ml/2 tsp paprika
675g/1½lb baking potatoes, cut into
   2.5cm/1in chunks
225g/8oz spring greens (collards)
425g/15oz can haricot (navy) or cannellini
   beans, drained
ground black pepper

COOK'S TIP
Bacon knuckles can be used instead of
the gammon. The bones will give the
stock a delicious flavour. If there is any
broth left over, you can freeze it and use
it as stock for another soup.

1 Drain the gammon and put it in the
ceramic cooking pot with the bay leaves
and onions. Pour over just enough fresh
cold water to cover the gammon. Switch
to high, cover and cook for 1 hour.

2 Skim off any scum, then re-cover and
cook for 3 hours. Check and skim the
broth once or twice if necessary.

3 Using a slotted spoon and a large
fork, carefully lift the gammon out of the
slow cooker and on to a board. Add the
paprika and potatoes to the broth and
cook for 1 hour.

4 Meanwhile, discard the skin and fat
from the gammon and cut the meat into
small chunks. Add it to the slow cooker
and cook for a further 2 hours, or until
the meat and potatoes are tender.

5 Remove the cores from the greens,
then roll up the leaves and cut into thin
shreds. Add to the slow cooker with the
beans and cook for 30 minutes.

6 Remove the bay leaves from the
broth, season with black pepper to taste
and serve piping hot.

Energy 273Kcal/1147kJ; Protein 21.4g; Carbohydrate 33.7g, of which sugars 5.3g; Fat 6.7g, of which saturates 2g; Cholesterol 17mg; Calcium 113mg; Fibre 6.7g; Sodium 974mg.

GENOESE MINESTRONE

In the Italian city of Genoa, pesto is stirred into minestrone to add extra flavour and colour. This tasty version is packed with vegetables and makes an excellent vegetarian supper dish when served with bread. To save time, you can use ready-made bottled pesto.

SERVES 4

30ml/2 tbsp olive oil
1 onion, finely chopped
2 celery sticks, finely chopped
1 large carrot, finely chopped
1 potato, weighing about 115g/4oz,
    cut into 1cm/½in cubes
1 litre/1¾ pints/4 cups vegetable stock
75g/3oz green beans, cut into 5cm/
    2in pieces
1 courgette (zucchini), thinly sliced
2 Italian plum tomatoes, peeled
    and chopped
200g/7oz can cannellini beans, drained
    and rinsed
¼ Savoy cabbage, shredded
40g/1½oz dried "quick-cook" spaghetti
    or vermicelli, broken into short lengths
salt and ground black pepper

For the pesto
about 20 fresh basil leaves
1 garlic clove
10ml/2 tsp pine nuts
15ml/1 tbsp freshly grated
    Parmesan cheese
15ml/1 tbsp freshly grated Pecorino cheese
30ml/2 tbsp olive oil

1 Heat the olive oil in a pan, then add the chopped onion, celery and carrot and cook, stirring, for about 7 minutes, until the vegetables begin to soften.

2 Transfer the fried vegetables to the ceramic cooking pot. Add the potato cubes and vegetable stock, cover the cooking pot with the lid and cook on high for 1½ hours.

3 Add the green beans, courgette, tomatoes and cannellini beans to the pot. Cover and cook for 1 hour, then stir in the cabbage and pasta and cook for a further 20 minutes.

4 Meanwhile, place all the pesto ingredients in a food processor. Blend to make a smooth sauce, adding 15–45ml/ 1–3 tbsp water through the feeder tube to loosen the mixture if necessary.

5 Stir 30ml/2 tbsp of the pesto sauce into the soup. Check the seasoning, adding more if necessary. Serve hot, in warmed bowls, with the remaining pesto spooned on top of each serving.

Energy 263Kcal/1098kJ; Protein 8.5g; Carbohydrate 25.1g, of which sugars 7g; Fat 14.9g, of which saturates 2.8g; Cholesterol 5mg; Calcium 103mg; Fibre 5.4g; Sodium 1034mg.

NORTH AFRICAN SPICED SOUP

The great advantage of cooking soup in the slow cooker is that all the flavours have a chance to develop and mingle. This technique is particularly well suited to richer soups with complex spicing, such as this version of the Moroccan national soup harira.

3 Mix together the cinnamon, turmeric, ginger, cayenne pepper and 30ml/2 tbsp of stock to form a paste, then add to the pot with the carrots, celery and remaining stock. Stir well and season. Cover and cook for 1 hour.

4 Add the chopped tomatoes, potatoes, chickpeas and saffron to the pot. Cook for 4–5 hours until the vegetables are tender. Stir in the coriander and lemon juice, then check the seasoning and adjust if necessary. Ladle into warmed bowls and serve piping hot, with fried wedges of lemon, if you like.

SERVES 6

1 large onion, very finely chopped
1 litre/1¾ pints/4 cups near-boiling
   vegetable stock
5ml/1 tsp ground cinnamon
5ml/1 tsp ground turmeric
15ml/1 tbsp grated fresh root ginger
pinch cayenne pepper
2 carrots, finely diced
2 celery sticks, finely diced
400g/14oz can chopped tomatoes
450g/1lb potatoes, finely diced
400g/14oz can chickpeas, drained
5 strands saffron
30ml/2 tbsp chopped fresh coriander
   (cilantro)
15ml/1 tbsp lemon juice
salt and ground black pepper
fried wedges of lemon, to serve (optional)

1 Place the chopped onion in the ceramic cooking pot and add 600ml/1 pint/2½ cups of the nearly-boiling vegetable stock.

2 Switch the slow cooker to high or auto, cover with the lid and cook for about 1 hour, until the onion is soft and translucent.

Energy 166Kcal/705kJ; Protein 7.5g; Carbohydrate 30.3g, of which sugars 7.4g; Fat 2.5g, of which saturates 0.3g; Cholesterol 0mg; Calcium 62mg; Fibre 5.3g; Sodium 335mg.

AVGOLEMONO

This light, delicate soup is a great favourite in Greece and is a fine example of a few carefully chosen ingredients combining to make a delicious dish. It is essential to use a stock that is well flavoured, so use home-made if you can.

SERVES 4

900ml/1½ pints/3¾ cups near-boiling
  chicken stock
50g/2oz/⅓ cup easy-cook (converted)
  white rice
3 egg yolks
30–60ml/2–4 tbsp lemon juice
30ml/2 tbsp finely chopped fresh parsley
salt and ground black pepper
lemon slices and parsley sprigs, to garnish

1 Pour the stock into the ceramic cooking pot. Cover with a lid and cook on high for 30 minutes, or until it reaches boiling point.

2 Stir in the rice, cover and cook for 45 minutes, or until the rice is tender. Season to taste with salt and pepper. Switch off the slow cooker, remove the lid and leave to stand for 5 minutes.

3 Meanwhile, whisk the egg yolks in a bowl, then add about 30ml/2 tbsp of the lemon juice, whisking constantly until the mixture is smooth and bubbly. Add a ladleful of the hot soup to the egg mixture, whisking continuously.

4 Slowly add the egg mixture to the soup in the ceramic cooking pot, whisking all the time. The soup will thicken slightly and turn a pretty yellow.

5 Taste and add more lemon juice and seasoning if necessary. Stir in the parsley and serve immediately, garnished with lemon slices and parsley sprigs.

COOK'S TIP
When adding the egg mixture, you need to be careful not to let the soup curdle. You should avoid whisking the mixture into boiling liquid, so allow the soup to cool very slightly before whisking in the egg mixture in a slow, steady stream. Do not reheat the soup.

Energy 98Kcal/410kJ; Protein 3.3g; Carbohydrate 11.1g, of which sugars 0.3g; Fat 4.8g, of which saturates 1.3g; Cholesterol 151mg; Calcium 26mg; Fibre 0.1g; Sodium 211mg.

CABBAGE, BEETROOT and TOMATO BORSCHT

There are numerous versions of this classic soup, which originates in eastern Europe. Beetroot and soured cream are the traditional ingredients in every borscht, but other ingredients tend to be many and varied. This version has a deliciously sweet and sour taste and can be served piping hot or refreshingly chilled.

SERVES 6

1 onion, chopped
1 carrot, chopped
6 raw or vacuum-packed (cooked, not
    pickled) beetroot (beets), 4 diced
    and 2 coarsely grated
400g/14oz can chopped tomatoes
6 new potatoes, cut into bitesize pieces
1 small white cabbage, thinly sliced
600ml/1 pint/2½ cups vegetable stock
45ml/3 tbsp sugar
30–45ml/2–3 tbsp white wine vinegar
    or cider vinegar
45ml/3 tbsp chopped fresh dill
salt and ground black pepper
sour cream and dill, to garnish
buttered rye bread, to serve

1 Put the onion, carrot, diced beetroot, tomatoes, potatoes and cabbage into the ceramic cooking pot and pour over the vegetable stock. Cover the cooking pot with the lid and cook on high for about 4 hours, or until the vegetables are just tender.

2 Add the grated beetroot, sugar and vinegar to the pot and stir to combine. Cook for a further hour until the beetroot is cooked.

3 Taste the soup, checking for a good sweet/sour balance, and add more sugar and/or vinegar if necessary. Season to taste with plenty of salt and freshly ground black pepper.

4 Just before serving, stir the chopped dill into the soup and ladle into warmed soup bowls. Garnish each serving with a generous spoonful of sour cream and plenty more fresh dill, then serve with thick slices of buttered rye bread.

VARIATIONS
• Borscht is often served cold in summer. To serve chilled, leave it to cool at room temperature, then chill in the refrigerator for at least 4 hours. Ladle into bowls, each containing an ice cube, and top with a large spoonful of soured cream.
• For a different garnish, try scattering finely chopped hard-boiled egg or spring onions (scallions) over the top.

Energy 125Kcal/531kJ; Protein 3.5g; Carbohydrate 27.8g, of which sugars 7g; Fat 0.7g, of which saturates 0.1g; Cholesterol 0mg; Calcium 58mg; Fibre 3.2g; Sodium 357mg.

POTAGE of LENTILS

In this soup, red lentils and vegetables are cooked slowly until very soft, then puréed to give a rich and velvety consistency. On a hot day, serve chilled with extra lemon juice.

SERVES 4

45ml/3 tbsp olive oil
1 onion, chopped
2 celery sticks, chopped
1 carrot, sliced
2 garlic cloves, peeled and chopped
1 potato, peeled and diced
250g/9oz/generous 1 cup red lentils
750ml/1¼ pints/3 cups near-boiling
　　vegetable stock
2 bay leaves
1 small lemon
2.5ml/½ tsp ground cumin
cayenne pepper or Tabasco sauce, to taste
salt and ground black pepper
lemon slices and chopped fresh flat leaf
　　parsley, to serve

1 Heat the oil in a frying pan. Add the onion and cook, stirring frequently, for 5 minutes, or until beginning to soften. Stir in the celery, carrot, garlic and potato. Cook for a further 3–4 minutes.

2 Tip the fried vegetables into the ceramic cooking pot and switch to high. Add the lentils, vegetable stock, bay leaves and a pared strip of lemon rind and stir briefly to combine.

3 Cover the slow cooker with a lid and cook on auto or high for 1 hour.

4 Leave the cooker on auto or switch to low and cook for a further 5 hours, or until the vegetables and lentils are soft and tender.

5 Remove and discard the bay leaves and lemon rind. Process the soup in a food processor or blender until smooth. Tip the soup back into the cleaned cooking pot, stir in the cumin and cayenne pepper or Tabasco, and season.

6 Cook the soup on high for a further 45 minutes, or until piping hot. Squeeze in lemon juice to taste and check the seasoning. Ladle into warmed bowls and top each portion with lemon slices and a sprinkling of chopped fresh parsley.

Energy 300Kcal/1265kJ; Protein 15.8g; Carbohydrate 40.1g, of which sugars 3.6g; Fat 9.6g, of which saturates 1.3g; Cholesterol 0mg; Calcium 47mg; Fibre 3.9g; Sodium 456mg.

CHICKEN SOUP with KNAIDLACH

This famous Jewish soup is often made using a whole chicken cut into portions and slowly simmered in a huge stockpot. If you have a very large slow cooker you can double the quantities given here, using a small whole chicken; the cooking times will remain the same. The knaidlach are cooked separately, so that the clarity of the soup is retained.

SERVES 4

2 chicken portions, about 275g/10oz each
1 onion
1.2 litres/2 pints/5 cups boiling
   chicken stock
2 carrots, thickly sliced
2 celery sticks, thickly sliced
1 small parsnip, cut into large chunks
small pinch of ground turmeric
30ml/2 tbsp roughly chopped fresh parsley,
   plus extra to garnish
15ml/1 tbsp chopped fresh dill
salt and ground black pepper

For the knaidlach
175g/6oz/¾ cup medium matzo meal
2 eggs, lightly beaten
45ml/3 tbsp vegetable oil
30ml/2 tbsp chopped fresh parsley
½ onion, finely grated
pinch of chicken stock cube (optional)
about 90ml/6 tbsp water
salt and ground black pepper

1 Rinse the chicken pieces and put them in the ceramic cooking pot. Peel the onion, keeping it whole. Cut a small cross to the stem end and add to the pot with the stock, carrots, celery, parsnip, turmeric, salt and pepper.

2 Cover with the lid and cook on high for 1 hour. Skim off the scum that comes to the surface. (Scum will continue to form but it is only the first scum that rises that will detract from the appearance and flavour of the soup.)

3 Cook for a further 3 hours, or until the chicken is tender. Remove the chicken, discard the skin and bones and chop the flesh. Skim the fat off the soup, then return the pieces of chicken. Stir in the parsley and dill and continue cooking while you make the knaidlach.

4 Put the matzo meal, eggs, oil, parsley, onion, chicken stock, if using, and water in a large bowl. Mix together well; it should be the consistency of a thick, soft paste. Cover and chill for 30 minutes, until the mixture has become firm.

5 Bring a pan of water to the boil and have a bowl of cold water next to the stove. Dip two tablespoons into the cold water, then take a spoonful of the matzo batter. With wet hands, roll it into a ball, then slip it into the boiling water and reduce the heat so that the water simmers. Continue with the remaining matzo batter, then cover the pan and cook for 15–20 minutes.

6 Remove the knaidlach from the pan with a slotted spoon and divide between individual serving bowls. Leave them to firm up for a few minutes. Ladle the hot soup over the knaidlach and serve sprinkled with extra chopped parsley.

VARIATIONS
• Instead of knaidlach, the soup can be served over cooked rice or noodles.
• To make knaidlach with a lighter texture, separate the eggs and add the yolks to the matzo mixture. Whisk the whites until stiff, then fold into the batter.

Energy 586Kcal/2451kJ; Protein 38.2g; Carbohydrate 42.6g, of which sugars 6.3g; Fat 30.3g, of which saturates 7.7g; Cholesterol 272mg; Calcium 131mg; Fibre 3.7g; Sodium 802mg.

SPINACH and ROOT VEGETABLE SOUP

This is a typical Russian soup, traditionally prepared when the first vegetables of spring appear. You will need to use a large slow cooker to accommodate the spinach.

SERVES 4

1 small turnip, cut into chunks
2 carrots, diced
1 small parsnip, cut into large dice
1 potato, peeled and diced
1 onion, chopped
1 garlic clove, finely chopped
¼ celeriac bulb, diced
750ml/1¼ pints/3 cups boiling vegetable
   or chicken stock
175g/6oz fresh spinach, roughly chopped
1 small bunch fresh dill, chopped
salt and ground black pepper

For the garnish
2 hard-boiled eggs, sliced lengthways
1 lemon, sliced
30ml/2 tbsp fresh parsley and dill

COOK'S TIP
For best results, use a really good-quality vegetable or chicken stock.

1 Put the turnip, carrots, parsnip, potato, onion, garlic, celeriac and stock into the ceramic cooking pot. Cook on high or auto for 1 hour, then either leave on auto or switch to low and cook for a further 5–6 hours, until the vegetables are soft and tender.

2 Stir the spinach into the cooking pot and cook on high for 45 minutes, or until the spinach is tender but still green and leafy. Season with salt and pepper.

3 Stir in the dill, then ladle the soup into warmed bowls and serve garnished with egg, lemon and a sprinkling of fresh parsley and dill.

Energy 67Kcal/280kJ; Protein 3g; Carbohydrate 11.5g, of which sugars 7g; Fat 1.3g, of which saturates 0.1g; Cholesterol 0mg; Calcium 121mg; Fibre 3.9g; Sodium 499mg.

ASIAN-STYLE DUCK CONSOMMÉ

*The Vietnamese community in France has had a profound influence on French cooking.
As a result, you will find many classic French dishes brought together with Asian flavours.*

SERVES 4

1 small carrot
1 small leek, halved lengthwise
4 shiitake mushrooms, thinly sliced
soy sauce
2 spring onions (scallions), thinly sliced
finely shredded watercress
    or Chinese cabbage
ground black pepper

For the consommé

1 duck carcass (raw or cooked), plus
    2 legs or any giblets, trimmed of fat
1 large onion, unpeeled, with root
    end trimmed
2 carrots, cut into 2.5cm/1in pieces
1 parsnip, cut into 2.5cm/1in pieces
1 leek, cut into 2.5cm/1in pieces
2 garlic cloves, crushed
15ml/1 tbsp black peppercorns
2.5cm/1in piece fresh root ginger,
    peeled and sliced
4 thyme sprigs or 5ml/1 tsp dried thyme
1 small bunch fresh coriander (cilantro)

1 To make the consommé, put the duck
carcass, legs or giblets, onion, carrots,
parsnip, leek and garlic in the ceramic
cooking pot. Add the peppercorns, ginger,
thyme and coriander stalks (reserve the
leaves) and enough cold water to cover
the bones, leaving at least 4cm/1½in
space at the top of the pot.

2 Cover the pot with the lid and cook
on high or auto for 2 hours. Skim off
any surface scum, then reduce the
temperature to low or leave on auto.
Cover and cook for a further 4 hours,
removing the lid for the last hour.

3 Line a sieve (strainer) with muslin
(cheesecloth) and strain the consommé
into a bowl, discarding the bones and
vegetables. Leave to cool, then chill for
several hours or overnight. Skim off any
congealed fat and blot the surface with
kitchen paper to remove all traces of fat.

4 Cut the carrot and leek into 5cm/2in
pieces. Cut each piece lengthways into
thin slices, then stack and slice into thin
julienne strips. Place the julienne strips
in the clean ceramic cooking pot with
the sliced shiitake mushrooms.

5 Pour over the consommé and add
a few dashes of soy sauce and some
ground black pepper. Cover and cook on
high for about 45 minutes, or until piping
hot, skimming off any foam that rises to
the surface with a slotted spoon.

6 Adjust the seasoning and stir in the
spring onions and watercress or Chinese
cabbage. Ladle into warmed bowls and
sprinkle with the fresh coriander leaves.

Energy 96Kcal/406kJ; Protein 7.1g; Carbohydrate 12.1g, of which sugars 7.9g; Fat 2.5g, of which saturates 0.6g; Cholesterol 28mg; Calcium 51mg; Fibre 4g; Sodium 47mg.

HOT and SOUR PRAWN SOUP

This salty, sour, spicy hot Thai soup, known as Tom Yam Kung, *is a real classic. Cooking the stock in the slow cooker maximizes the flavour before the final ingredients are added.*

SERVES 4

450g/1lb raw king prawns (jumbo shrimp),
   thawed if frozen
900ml/1½ pints/3¾ cups near-boiling light
   chicken stock or water
3 lemon grass stalks
6 kaffir lime leaves, torn in half
225g/8oz straw mushrooms, drained
45ml/3 tbsp Thai fish sauce
60ml/4 tbsp fresh lime juice
30ml/2 tbsp chopped spring onion
   (scallion)
15ml/1 tbsp fresh coriander
   (cilantro) leaves
4 fresh red chillies, seeded and
   thickly sliced
salt and ground black pepper

1 Peel the prawns, reserving the shells. Using a sharp knife, make a shallow cut along the back of each prawn and use the point of the knife to remove the thin black vein. Place the prawns in a bowl, cover and place in the refrigerator until ready to use.

2 Rinse the reserved prawn shells under cold running water, then put them in the ceramic cooking pot and add the chicken stock or water. Cover with the lid and switch the slow cooker to high.

3 Using a pestle, bruise the bulbous end of the lemon grass stalks. Lift the lid of the ceramic pot and quickly add the lemon grass stalks and half the torn kaffir lime leaves to the stock. Stir well, then re-cover with the lid and cook for about 2 hours until the stock is fragrant and aromatic.

4 Strain the stock into a large bowl and rinse out the ceramic cooking pot. Pour the stock back into the cleaned pot. Add the drained mushrooms and cook on high for 30 minutes.

5 Add the prawns to the soup and cook for a further 10 minutes until the prawns turn pink and are cooked.

6 Stir the fish sauce, lime juice, spring onion, coriander, chillies and remaining lime leaves into the soup. Taste and adjust the seasoning if necessary. The soup should be sour, salty, spicy and hot.

Energy 127Kcal/536kJ; Protein 27g; Carbohydrate 1.4g, of which sugars 1.2g; Fat 1.4g, of which saturates 0.3g; Cholesterol 315mg; Calcium 133mg; Fibre 0.7g; Sodium 2715mg.

ONE-POT AND CLAY-POT SOUPS

There's something supremely comforting about hot soup,
and when you prepare it yourself, the aroma ensures
that the pleasure starts long before you lift the ladle.
Nourishing, easy to digest, quick to cook and convenient,
soup provides the perfect meal-in-a-bowl at lunchtime or
a warming after-school snack, and when served as a
first course, it gives guests a real sense of welcome.
Mediterranean Sausage and Pesto Soup, Italian Farmhouse
Soup, Chicken and Leek Soup with Prunes, Seafood
Chowder, and Bean and Pistou Soup are just some
of the treats in store.

CATALAN POTATO and BROAD BEAN SOUP

While they are in season fresh broad beans are perfect, but canned or frozen are just as good in this creamy, richly flavoured soup.

SERVES 6

30ml/2 tbsp olive oil
2 onions, chopped
3 large floury potatoes, diced
450g/1lb fresh shelled broad
   (fava) beans
1.75 litres/3 pints/7½ cups vegetable or
   chicken stock
1 bunch coriander (cilantro),
   finely chopped
150ml/¼ pint/⅔ cup single (light) cream
salt and ground black pepper
coriander (cilantro) leaves, to garnish

COOK'S TIP
Broad beans sometimes have a tough outer skin, particularly if they are large. To remove this, first cook the beans briefly in boiling water, then peel off the skin, and add the tender, bright green centre part to the soup.

1 Heat the olive oil in a large pan, add the chopped onions and fry, stirring occasionally with a wooden spoon, for about 5 minutes until they are just softened but not brown.

2 Add the diced potatoes, shelled broad beans (reserving a few for garnishing) and vegetable or chicken stock to the pan. Bring to the boil, then simmer for 5 minutes.

3 Stir in the finely chopped coriander and simmer for a further 10 minutes.

4 Process the soup in batches in a food processor or blender, then return the soup to the rinsed-out pan.

5 Stir in the cream (reserving a little for garnishing), season, and bring to a simmer. Serve garnished with more coriander leaves, beans and cream.

SPANISH POTATO and GARLIC SOUP

Traditionally served in shallow earthenware dishes, this delicious, classic Spanish soup is a great choice for vegetarians.

SERVES 6

30ml/2 tbsp olive oil
1 large onion, finely sliced
4 garlic cloves, crushed
1 large potato, halved and cut
   into thin slices
5ml/1 tsp paprika
400g/14oz can chopped tomatoes, drained
5ml/1 tsp thyme leaves, plus extra chopped
   thyme leaves, to garnish
900ml/1½ pints/3¾ cups vegetable stock
5ml/1 tsp cornflour (cornstarch)
salt and ground black pepper

COOK'S TIP
Paprika is a popular spice in many Spanish dishes. It is made from red peppers that are dried and powdered into a coarse-grained spice. It has a slightly sweet, mild flavour and a rich red colour.

1 Heat the oil in a large, heavy pan, add the onion, garlic, potato and paprika and cook, stirring occasionally, for about 5 minutes, or until the onions have softened, but not browned.

2 Add the chopped tomatoes, thyme leaves and vegetable stock to the pan and simmer for 15–20 minutes until the potatoes have cooked through.

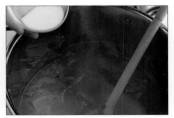

3 In a small bowl, mix the cornflour with a little water to form a smooth paste, then stir into the soup. Bring to the boil, stirring, then simmer for about 5 minutes until the soup has thickened.

4 Using a wooden spoon, break up the potatoes slightly, then season to taste. Serve the soup garnished with the extra chopped thyme leaves.

Catalan Potato and Broad Bean Soup: Energy 236Kcal/990kJ; Protein 9.3g; Carbohydrate 30.3g, of which sugars 4.6g; Fat 9.4g, of which saturates 3.8g; Cholesterol 14mg; Calcium 94mg; Fibre 6.8g; Sodium 30mg.
Spanish Potato and Garlic Soup: Energy 86Kcal/359kJ; Protein 1.5g; Carbohydrate 11.5g, of which sugars 4.4g; Fat 4.1g, of which saturates 0.6g; Cholesterol 0mg; Calcium 15mg; Fibre 1.5g; Sodium 12mg.

LENTIL and PASTA SOUP

This rustic vegetarian soup makes a warming winter meal and goes especially well with Granary or crusty Italian bread.

SERVES 4–6

175g/6oz/¾ cup brown lentils
3 garlic cloves, unpeeled
1 litre/1¾ pints/4 cups water
45ml/3 tbsp olive oil
25g/1oz/2 tbsp butter
1 onion, finely chopped
2 celery sticks, finely chopped
30ml/2 tbsp sun-dried tomato
    purée (paste)
1.75 litres/3 pints/7½ cups vegetable stock
a few fresh marjoram leaves
a few fresh basil leaves
leaves from 1 fresh thyme sprig
50g/2oz/½ cup dried small pasta shapes,
    such as macaroni or tubetti
salt and ground black pepper
tiny fresh herb leaves, to garnish

1 Put the lentils in a large pan. Smash one of the garlic cloves using the blade of a large knife (there's no need to peel it first), then add it to the lentils. Pour in the water and bring to the boil. Simmer for about 20 minutes, or until the lentils are tender. Tip the lentils into a sieve, remove the garlic and set it aside. Rinse the lentils under the cold tap and leave to drain.

2 Heat 30ml/2 tbsp of the oil with half the butter in the pan. Add the onion and celery and cook gently for 5 minutes.

3 Crush the remaining garlic, then peel and mash the reserved garlic. Add to the pan with the remaining oil, the tomato purée and the lentils. Stir, then add the stock, herbs and salt and pepper. Bring to the boil, stirring. Simmer for 30 minutes, stirring occasionally.

4 Add the pasta and bring the soup back to the boil, stirring. Reduce the heat and simmer until the pasta is just tender. Add the remaining butter to the pan and stir until melted. Taste the soup for seasoning, then serve hot in warmed bowls, sprinkled with herb leaves.

Energy 206Kcal/865kJ; Protein 8.1g; Carbohydrate 23.5g, of which sugars 1.7g; Fat 9.5g, of which saturates 3g; Cholesterol 9mg; Calcium 24mg; Fibre 1.9g; Sodium 42mg.

ITALIAN FARMHOUSE SOUP

Root vegetables form the base of this chunky, minestrone-style main meal soup. You can vary the vegetables according to what you have to hand.

SERVES 4

30ml/2 tbsp olive oil
1 onion, roughly chopped
3 carrots, cut into large chunks
175–200g/6–7oz turnips, cut into
    large chunks
about 175g/6oz swede (rutabaga), cut into
    large chunks
400g/14oz can chopped Italian tomatoes
15ml/1 tbsp tomato purée (paste)
5ml/1 tsp dried mixed herbs
5ml/1 tsp dried oregano
50g/2oz dried (bell) peppers, washed and
    thinly sliced (optional)
1.5 litres/2½ pints/6¼ cups vegetable stock
    or water
50g/2oz/½ cup dried small macaroni
    or conchiglie
400g/14oz can red kidney beans, rinsed
    and drained
30ml/2 tbsp chopped fresh flat leaf parsley
salt and ground black pepper
freshly grated Parmesan cheese, to serve

1 Heat the olive oil in a large pan, add the onion and cook over a low heat for about 5 minutes until softened. Add the carrot, turnip and swede chunks, canned chopped tomatoes, tomato purée, dried mixed herbs, dried oregano and dried peppers, if using. Stir in salt and pepper to taste.

2 Pour in the vegetable stock or water and bring to the boil. Stir well, cover the pan, then lower the heat and simmer for 30 minutes, stirring occasionally.

3 Add the pasta to the pan and bring quickly to the boil, stirring. Lower the heat and simmer, uncovered, for about 5 minutes until the pasta is only just tender, or according to the instructions on the packet. Stir frequently.

4 Stir in the kidney beans. Heat through for 2–3 minutes, then remove the pan from the heat and stir in the parsley. Taste the soup for seasoning. Serve hot in warmed soup bowls, with grated Parmesan cheese handed separately.

Energy 248Kcal/1047kJ; Protein 10.2g; Carbohydrate 38.6g, of which sugars 14.9g; Fat 7g, of which saturates 1.1g; Cholesterol 0mg; Calcium 139mg; Fibre 10.6g; Sodium 422mg.

BROCCOLI, ANCHOVY and PASTA SOUP

This wonderfully chunky and flavourful soup is from Puglia in the south of Italy, where anchovies and broccoli are often used together.

SERVES 4

30ml/2 tbsp olive oil
1 small onion, finely chopped
1 garlic clove, finely chopped
¼–⅓ fresh red chilli, seeded and
   finely chopped
2 drained canned anchovies
200ml/7fl oz/scant 1 cup passata (bottled
   strained tomatoes)
45ml/3 tbsp dry white wine
1.2 litres/2 pints/5 cups vegetable or light
   chicken stock
300g/11oz broccoli florets
200g/7oz/1¾ cups dried orecchiette pasta
   or other medium-size pasta shapes
salt and ground black pepper
freshly grated Pecorino cheese, to serve

1 Heat the oil in a large pan. Add the onion, garlic, chilli and anchovies and cook over a low heat, stirring constantly, for 5–6 minutes.

2 Add the passata and wine, with salt and pepper to taste. Bring to the boil, cover, then cook over a low heat, stirring occasionally, for 12–15 minutes.

3 Pour in the stock. Bring to the boil, then add the broccoli and simmer for about 5 minutes. Add the pasta and bring back to the boil, stirring. Simmer, stirring frequently for 7–8 minutes until the pasta is just tender, or according to the packet instructions. Taste for seasoning. Serve hot, in warmed bowls. Hand around grated Pecorino separately.

PASTA SQUARES and PEAS in BROTH

This thick, filling Italian soup, flavoured with pancetta or bacon and prosciutto, is traditionally made with home-made pasta and fresh peas. In this modern, more convenient version, ready-made fresh lasagne sheets are used with frozen peas, to save time.

SERVES 4–6

25g/1oz/2 tbsp butter
50g/2oz pancetta or rindless smoked
   streaky (fatty) bacon, roughly chopped
1 small onion, finely chopped
1 celery stick, finely chopped
400g/14oz/3½ cups frozen peas
5ml/1 tsp tomato purée (paste)
5–10ml/1–2 tsp finely chopped fresh flat
   leaf parsley
1 litre/1¾ pints/4 cups chicken stock
300g/11oz fresh lasagne sheets
about 50g/2oz prosciutto, cut into cubes
salt and ground black pepper
freshly grated Parmesan cheese, to serve

1 Melt the butter in a large pan and add the pancetta or rindless smoked streaky bacon, with the chopped onion and chopped celery. Cook together over a low heat, stirring constantly, for 5 minutes.

2 Add the frozen peas to the pan and cook, stirring, for 3–4 minutes. Stir in the tomato purée and finely chopped parsley, then add the chicken stock, with salt and pepper to taste. Bring to the boil. Cover, lower the heat and simmer the soup for 10 minutes.

3 Meanwhile, using a large, sharp knife and a ruler, cut the lasagne sheets into 2cm/¾in squares.

4 Taste the soup for seasoning. Drop the pasta into the pan, then stir and bring to the boil. Simmer for 2 minutes, or until the pasta is just tender, then stir in the prosciutto. Serve hot with grated Parmesan handed around separately.

COOK'S TIP
Take care when seasoning the soup with salt, because of the saltiness of the pancetta and the prosciutto.

Broccoli, Anchovy and Pasta Soup: Energy 268Kcal/1131kJ; Protein 10.3g; Carbohydrate 41.2g, of which sugars 5.2g; Fat 7.3g, of which saturates 1.1g; Cholesterol 1mg; Calcium 69mg; Fibre 3.9g; Sodium 182mg.
Pasta Squares and Peas in Broth: Energy 175Kcal/730kJ; Protein 9.5g; Carbohydrate 19.7g, of which sugars 2.6g; Fat 7.1g, of which saturates 3.2g; Cholesterol 19mg; Calcium 24mg; Fibre 4g; Sodium 236mg.

CORN and POTATO CHOWDER

This creamy yet chunky soup is rich with the sweet taste of corn. It's excellent served with thick, crusty bread and topped with some grated Cheddar cheese.

2 Heat until the oil and butter are sizzling, then reduce the heat to low. Cover the pan and cook gently for about 10 minutes until the vegetables are just softened, shaking the pan occasionally.

3 Pour in the stock, season with salt and pepper to taste and bring to the boil. Reduce the heat, cover the pan again and simmer gently, stirring occasionally, for about 15 minutes, or until the vegetables are tender.

SERVES 4

1 onion, chopped
1 garlic clove, crushed
1 medium baking potato, chopped
2 celery sticks, sliced
1 green (bell) pepper, seeded and sliced
30ml/2 tbsp sunflower oil
25g/1oz/2 tbsp butter
600ml/1 pint/2½ cups vegetable stock
300ml/½ pint/1¼ cups milk
200g/7oz can flageolet, cannellini or
   haricot (navy) beans
300g/11oz can sweetcorn
good pinch of dried sage
salt and ground black pepper
freshly grated Cheddar cheese, to serve

1 Put the onion, garlic, potato, celery and green pepper into a large, heavy pan with the sunflower oil and butter.

4 Add the milk, canned beans and sweetcorn – including their liquids. Stir in the dried sage and simmer, uncovered, for 5 minutes, then check the seasoning and adjust to taste. Serve hot in bowls, sprinkled with the grated Cheddar cheese.

Energy 275Kcal/1161kJ; Protein 9.6g; Carbohydrate 43.3g, of which sugars 16.5g; Fat 8.3g, of which saturates 1.8g; Cholesterol 4mg; Calcium 141mg; Fibre 5.5g; Sodium 441mg.

BEAN and PISTOU SOUP

This hearty vegetarian soup is a typical Provençal-style soup, richly flavoured with a home-made garlic and fresh basil pistou sauce.

SERVES 4–6

150g/5oz/scant 1 cup dried haricot (navy) beans, soaked overnight in cold water
150g/5oz/scant 1 cup dried flageolet or cannellini beans, soaked overnight in cold water
1 onion, chopped
1.2 litres/2 pints/5 cups hot vegetable stock
2 carrots, roughly chopped
225g/8oz Savoy cabbage, shredded
1 large potato, about 225g/8oz, roughly chopped
225g/8oz French (green) beans, chopped
salt and ground black pepper
basil leaves, to garnish

For the pistou
4 garlic cloves
8 large sprigs basil leaves
90ml/6 tbsp olive oil
60ml/4 tbsp freshly grated Parmesan cheese

1 Soak a bean pot in cold water for 20 minutes then drain. Drain the soaked haricot and flageolet or cannellini beans and place in the bean pot. Add the chopped onion and pour over sufficient cold water to come 5cm/2in above the beans. Cover and place the pot in an unheated oven. Set the oven to 200°C/400°F/Gas 6 and cook for about 1½ hours, or until the beans are tender.

2 Drain the beans and onions. Place half the beans and onions in a food processor or blender and process to a paste. Return the drained beans and the bean paste to the bean pot. Add the hot vegetable stock.

3 Add the chopped carrots, shredded cabbage, chopped potato and French beans to the bean pot. Season with salt and pepper, cover and return the pot to the oven. Reduce the oven temperature to 180°C/350°F/Gas 4 and cook for 1 hour, or until all the vegetables are cooked right through.

4 Meanwhile place the garlic and basil in a mortar and pound with a pestle, then gradually beat in the oil. Stir in the grated Parmesan. Stir half the pistou into the soup and then ladle into warmed soup bowls. Top each bowl of soup with a spoonful of the remaining pistou and serve garnished with basil.

Energy 305Kcal/1281kJ; Protein 17.2g; Carbohydrate 34.6g, of which sugars 7.5g; Fat 11.8g, of which saturates 3.3g; Cholesterol 10mg; Calcium 215mg; Fibre 10.8g; Sodium 133mg.

MEDITERRANEAN SAUSAGE and PESTO SOUP

This hearty soup makes a satisfying one-pot meal that brings the summery flavour of basil to midwinter meals. Thick slices of warm crusty bread make the perfect accompaniment.

SERVES 4

oil, for deep-frying
450g/1lb smoked pork sausages
a handful of fresh basil leaves
15ml/1 tbsp olive oil
1 red onion, chopped
225g/8oz/1 cup red lentils
400g/14oz can chopped tomatoes
   with herbs
1 litre/1¾ pints/4 cups chicken stock
   or water
salt and ground black pepper
60ml/4 tbsp pesto, to serve

COOK'S TIP

The flavour of smoked sausages is very good in this soup, but you could use ordinary fresh sausages if you like. Choose course-textured sausages, such as Toulouse.

1 Heat the oil for deep-frying to 190°C/375°F or until a cube of day-old bread browns in about 60 seconds. Slice one of the sausages diagonally and deep-fry for 2–3 minutes, or until brown and crisp. Add the basil leaves and fry for a few seconds until crisp. Lift out the sausage slices and basil leaves using a slotted spoon and drain them on kitchen paper. Strain the oil into a bowl.

2 Heat the olive oil in the pan, add the chopped red onion and cook until softened. Coarsely chop the remaining sausages and add them to the pan. Cook for about 5 minutes, stirring, or until the sausages are cooked.

3 Stir in the lentils, tomatoes and stock or water and bring to the boil. Reduce the heat, cover and simmer for about 20 minutes. Cool the soup slightly before puréeing it in a blender. Return the soup to the rinsed-out pan.

4 Reheat the soup, add seasoning to taste, then ladle into warmed individual soup bowls. Sprinkle the soup with the deep-fried sausage slices and basil and swirl a little pesto through each portion just before serving. Serve with plenty of warm crusty bread.

Energy 738Kcal/3075kJ; Protein 26.2g; Carbohydrate 46.7g, of which sugars 6.9g; Fat 50.9g, of which saturates 15.8g; Cholesterol 53mg; Calcium 86mg; Fibre 4.5g; Sodium 885mg.

MOROCCAN SPICED LAMB SOUP

Classic north African spices – ginger, turmeric and cinnamon – are combined with chickpeas and lamb to make this hearty, warming soup.

SERVES 6

75g/3oz/½ cup chickpeas, soaked overnight
15g/½oz/1 tbsp butter
225g/8oz lamb, cut into cubes
1 onion, chopped
450g/1lb tomatoes, peeled and chopped
a few celery leaves, chopped
30ml/2 tbsp chopped fresh parsley
15ml/1 tbsp chopped fresh
    coriander (cilantro)
2.5ml/½ tsp ground ginger
2.5ml/½ tsp ground turmeric
5ml/1 tsp ground cinnamon
1.75 litres/3 pints/7½ cups water
75g/3oz/scant ½ cup green lentils
75g/3oz vermicelli or soup pasta
2 egg yolks
juice of ½–1 lemon
salt and ground black pepper
fresh coriander (cilantro), to garnish
lemon wedges, to serve

1 Drain the chickpeas, rinse under cold water and set aside. Melt the butter in a large flameproof casserole or pan and fry the lamb and onion for 2–3 minutes, stirring, until the lamb is just browned.

2 Add the chopped tomatoes, celery leaves, herbs and spices and season well with ground black pepper. Cook for about 1 minute, then stir in the water and add the green lentils and the soaked, drained and rinsed chickpeas.

3 Slowly bring to the boil and skim the surface to remove the froth. Boil rapidly for 10 minutes, then reduce the heat and simmer very gently for 2 hours, or until the chickpeas are very tender.

4 Season with salt and pepper, then add the vermicelli or soup pasta to the pan and cook for 5–6 minutes until it is just tender. If the soup is very thick at this stage, add a little more water.

5 Beat the egg yolks with the lemon juice and stir into the simmering soup. Immediately remove the soup from the heat and stir until thickened. Pour into warmed serving bowls and garnish with plenty of fresh coriander. Serve the soup with lemon wedges.

COOK'S TIP
If you have forgotten to soak the chickpeas overnight, place them in a pan with about four times their volume of cold water. Bring very slowly to the boil, then cover the pan, remove it from the heat and leave to stand for 45 minutes before using as described in the recipe.

Energy 248Kcal/1042kJ; Protein 16.3g; Carbohydrate 25.8g, of which sugars 4.1g; Fat 9.5g, of which saturates 4g; Cholesterol 101mg; Calcium 64mg; Fibre 3.6g; Sodium 70mg.

CHINESE CHICKEN and CHILLI SOUP

Ginger and lemon grass add an aromatic note to this tasty, refreshing soup, which can be served as a light lunch or appetizer.

2 Place the Chinese sand pot in an unheated oven. Set the temperature to 200°C/400°F/Gas 6 and cook the soup for 30–40 minutes, or until the stock is simmering and the chicken and vegetables are tender.

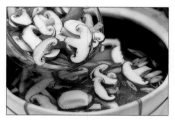

3 Add the spring onions and mushrooms, cover and return the pot to the oven for 10 minutes. Meanwhile place the noodles in a large bowl and cover with boiling water – soak for the required time, following the packet instructions.

4 Drain the noodles and divide among four warmed serving bowls. Stir the soy sauce into the soup and season with salt and pepper. Divide the soup between the bowls and serve immediately.

COOK'S TIP
Rice noodles are available in a variety of thicknesses and can be bought in straight lengths or in coils or loops. They are a creamy white colour and very brittle in texture. Rice noodles are pre-cooked so they only require a very short soaking time – check the packet for exact timings. Vermicelli rice noodles are very fine and will only need to be soaked for a few minutes.

SERVES 4

150g/5oz boneless chicken breast portion, cut into thin strips
2.5cm/1in piece fresh root ginger, finely chopped
5cm/2in piece lemon grass stalk, finely chopped
1 red chilli, seeded and thinly sliced
8 baby corn cobs, halved lengthwise
1 large carrot, cut into thin sticks
1 litre/1¾ pints/4 cups hot chicken stock
4 spring onions (scallions), thinly sliced
12 small shiitake mushrooms, sliced
115g/4oz/1 cup vermicelli rice noodles
30ml/2 tbsp soy sauce
salt and ground black pepper

1 Place the chicken strips, chopped ginger, chopped lemon grass and sliced chilli in a Chinese sand pot. Add the halved baby corn and the carrot sticks. Pour over the hot chicken stock and cover the pot.

Energy 168Kcal/707kJ; Protein 13.7g; Carbohydrate 26.1g, of which sugars 3.1g; Fat 1g, of which saturates 0.2g; Cholesterol 26mg; Calcium 25mg; Fibre 1.7g; Sodium 853mg.

CHICKEN and LEEK SOUP with PRUNES

This recipe is based on the traditional Scottish soup, Cock-a-leekie. The unusual combination of leeks and prunes is surprisingly delicious.

SERVES 6

115g/4oz/²⁄₃ cup pearl barley
1 chicken, weighing about 2kg/4¼lb
900g/2lb leeks
1 fresh bay leaf
a few fresh parsley stalks and
    thyme sprigs
1 large carrot, thickly sliced
2.4 litres/4 pints/10 cups chicken or
    beef stock
400g/14oz ready-to-eat prunes
salt and ground black pepper
chopped fresh parsley, to garnish

1 Rinse the pearl barley thoroughly in a sieve under cold running water, then cook it in a large pan of boiling water for about 10 minutes. Drain the barley, rinse well again and drain thoroughly. Set aside in a cool place.

2 Cut the breast portions off the chicken and set aside, then place the remaining chicken carcass in the pan. Cut half the leeks into 5cm/2in lengths and add them to the pan. Tie the herbs together into a bouquet garni and add to the pan with the carrot and stock.

3 Bring the stock to the boil, then reduce the heat and cover the pan. Simmer gently for 1 hour. Skim off any scum when the water first starts to boil and occasionally during simmering.

4 Add the chicken breast portions to the pan and continue to cook for another 30 minutes until they are just cooked. Leave until cool enough to handle, then strain the stock.

5 Reserve the chicken breast portions and take all the meat from the carcass. Discard all the skin, bones, cooked vegetables and herbs. Skim as much fat as you can from the stock, then return it to the pan.

6 Add the pearl barley to the stock. Bring to the boil over a medium heat, then lower the heat and cook very gently for 15–20 minutes, until the barley is just cooked and tender. Season the soup with 5ml/1 tsp each salt and ground black pepper.

7 Add the ready-to-eat prunes to the pan, then thinly slice the remaining leeks and add them to the pan. Bring to the boil, then cover the pan and simmer gently for about 10 minutes, or until the leeks are just cooked.

8 Slice the chicken breast portions and then add them to the soup with the remaining chicken meat from the carcass, sliced or cut into neat pieces. Reheat the soup, if necessary, then ladle it into warm, deep soup plates and sprinkle with plenty of chopped parsley to serve.

Energy 273Kcal/1158kJ; Protein 21.7g; Carbohydrate 44.4g, of which sugars 27.2g; Fat 2.1g, of which saturates 0.4g; Cholesterol 47mg; Calcium 70mg; Fibre 7.5g; Sodium 55mg.

BOUILLABAISSE

Perhaps the most famous of all Mediterranean fish soups, this recipe, originating from Marseilles in the south of France, is a rich and colourful mixture of fish and shellfish, flavoured with tomatoes, saffron and orange.

SERVES 4–6

1.3–1.6kg/3–3½lb mixed fish and shellfish,
   such as red mullet, John Dory, monkfish,
   large prawns (shrimp) and clams
1.2 litres/2 pints/5 cups water
225g/8oz tomatoes
pinch of saffron threads
90ml/6 tbsp olive oil
1 onion, sliced
1 leek, sliced
1 celery stick, sliced
2 garlic cloves, crushed
bouquet garni
1 strip pared orange rind
2.5ml/½ tsp fennel seeds
15ml/1 tbsp tomato purée (paste)
10ml/2 tsp Pernod
4–6 thick slices French bread
45ml/3 tbsp chopped fresh parsley
salt and ground black pepper

1 Remove the heads, tails and fins from the fish and put in a large pan, with the water. Bring to the boil, and simmer for 15 minutes. Strain, and reserve the liquid.

2 Cut the fish into large chunks. Leave the shellfish in their shells.

3 Scald the tomatoes, then drain and refresh in cold water. Peel and chop them. Soak the saffron in 15–30ml/1–2 tbsp hot water. Heat the oil in the cleaned pan, add the onion, leek and celery and cook until softened. Add the garlic, bouquet garni, orange rind, fennel seeds and tomatoes, then stir in the saffron and liquid and the fish stock. Season with salt and pepper, then bring to the boil and simmer for 30–40 minutes.

4 Add the shellfish and boil for about 6 minutes. Discard any clams that remain closed. Add the fish and cook for a further 6–8 minutes until it flakes easily. Using a slotted spoon, transfer the fish to a warmed serving platter. Keep the liquid boiling and add the tomato purée and Pernod, then check the seasoning. Place a slice of bread in each soup bowl, pour the broth over and serve the fish separately, sprinkled with the parsley.

Energy 338Kcal/1418kJ; Protein 42.2g; Carbohydrate 12.8g, of which sugars 3.8g; Fat 13.2g, of which saturates 1.9g; Cholesterol 100mg; Calcium 55mg; Fibre 1.6g; Sodium 239mg.

COCONUT and SEAFOOD SOUP with GARLIC CHIVES

The long list of ingredients in this Thai-inspired recipe could mislead you into thinking that this soup is complicated. In fact, it is very easy to put together.

SERVES 4

600ml/1 pint/2½ cups fish stock
5 thin slices fresh root ginger
2 lemon grass stalks, chopped
3 kaffir lime leaves, shredded
25g/1oz garlic chives (1 bunch), chopped
15g/½oz fresh coriander (cilantro)
15ml/1 tbsp vegetable oil
4 shallots, chopped
400ml/14fl oz can coconut milk
30–45ml/2–3 tbsp Thai fish sauce
45–60ml/3–4 tbsp Thai green curry paste
450g/1lb uncooked large prawns (jumbo shrimp), peeled and deveined
450g/1lb prepared squid
a little lime juice (optional)
salt and ground black pepper
60ml/4 tbsp fried shallot slices, to serve

4 Stir in the curry paste and the peeled prawns and cook for 3 minutes. Add the squid, cook for a further 2 minutes. Add the lime juice, if using, and season.

1 Pour the stock into a pan and add the slices of fresh ginger, the chopped lemon grass and half the lime leaves.

2 Add half the chopped chives to the pan with the coriander stalks. Bring to the boil, then reduce the heat. Cover the pan, then simmer gently for 20 minutes. Strain the stock.

3 Rinse the pan, then add the oil and shallots. Cook over a medium heat for 5–10 minutes, stirring occasionally, until the shallots are just beginning to brown. Stir in the stock, coconut milk, the remaining lime leaves and half the fish sauce. Heat gently until the soup is just simmering and cook over a low heat for 5–10 minutes.

5 Stir in the remaining fish sauce, chopped chives and the chopped coriander leaves. Serve in warmed, shallow bowls sprinkled with fried shallots.

VARIATIONS
• Instead of squid, you could add 400g/14oz firm white fish, such as monkfish, cut into small pieces.
• You could also replace the squid with fresh mussels. Steam 675g/1½lb closed mussels in a tightly covered pan for about 3 minutes, or until the shells have opened. Discard any that remain shut, then remove the mussels from their shells.

Energy 282Kcal/1185kJ; Protein 37.9g; Carbohydrate 7.7g, of which sugars 6g; Fat 11.3g, of which saturates 1.9g; Cholesterol 473mg; Calcium 156mg; Fibre 0.7g; Sodium 451mg.

SEAFOOD CHOWDER

Chowder takes its name from the French word for cauldron – chaudière – the type of pot once traditionally used for soups and stews. Like most chowders, this is a substantial dish, which is good served with crusty bread for a lunch or supper.

SERVES 4–6

200g/7oz/generous 1 cup drained, canned sweetcorn
600ml/1 pint/2½ cups milk
15g/½oz/1 tbsp butter
1 small leek, sliced
1 small garlic clove, crushed
2 rindless smoked streaky (fatty) bacon rashers (strips), finely chopped
1 small green or red (bell) pepper, seeded and diced
1 celery stick, chopped
115g/4oz/generous ½ cup white long grain rice
5ml/1 tsp plain (all-purpose) flour
about 450ml/¾ pint/scant 2 cups hot chicken or vegetable stock
4 large scallops
115g/4oz white fish fillet, such as monkfish, plaice or flounder
15ml/1 tbsp finely chopped fresh flat leaf parsley
good pinch of cayenne pepper
30–45ml/2–3 tbsp single (light) cream (optional)
salt and ground black pepper
crusty bread, to serve

1 Place half the drained sweetcorn in a food processor or blender. Add a little of the milk and then process until the mixture is thick and creamy. Set aside.

COOK'S TIP
If you don't have a food processor, then simply chop the sweetcorn finely and transfer to a bowl. Beat in the milk a little at time until the mixture is thick and creamy.

2 Melt the butter in a large, heavy pan. add the leek, garlic and bacon and gently fry for 4–5 minutes until the leek has softened but not browned.

3 Add the diced green or red pepper and the chopped celery and cook over a very gentle heat for 3–4 minutes more, stirring frequently, until the pepper and celery have softened slightly.

4 Stir in the rice and cook for a few minutes, stirring occasionally, until the grains begin to swell, then sprinkle the flour evenly over the top of the rice and vegetables. Cook for about 1 minute, stirring all the time, then gradually stir in the remaining milk and the hot stock.

VARIATIONS
You can use other shellfish in place of the scallops if you prefer – try fresh or frozen prawns (shrimp), or mussels or clams, which are equally good in or out of their shells. Allow frozen shellfish to thaw at room temperature before adding to the chowder. Undyed, naturally smoked haddock or cod would make a delicious alternative fish.

5 Bring the mixture to the boil over a medium heat, then lower the heat and stir in the creamed sweetcorn mixture, with the whole sweetcorn. Season well.

6 Cover the pan and simmer very gently for about 20 minutes, or until the rice is tender, stirring occasionally. Add a little more chicken or vegetable stock or water to the pan if the mixture thickens too quickly or if the rice begins to stick to the base of the pan.

7 Cut the corals away from the scallops and set them aside, slice the white flesh into 5mm/¼in pieces. Cut the white fish fillet into bitesize chunks.

8 Add the scallops and chunks of fish to the chowder. Stir gently, then cook for 4 minutes.

9 Stir in the scallop corals, chopped parsley and cayenne pepper. Cook for a few minutes more until the scallops are just cooked and heated through, then stir in the cream, if using. Adjust the seasoning and serve the chowder with thick slices of crusty bread.

Energy 263Kcal/1106kJ; Protein 19.2g; Carbohydrate 32.8g, of which sugars 10.4g; Fat 6.5g, of which saturates 3.2g; Cholesterol 40mg; Calcium 149mg; Fibre 1.6g; Sodium 353mg.

SLOW COOKER FIRST COURSES AND LIGHT MEALS

Whether you are planning a light lunch with friends, or a delicate first course for a special dinner party, the slow cooker is perfect for cooking a beautiful dish while giving you the time to concentrate on something else. Among the tasty appetizers here are a pretty Haddock and Smoked Salmon Terrine, Cardamom Chicken Mousselines and Red Lentil and Goat's Cheese Pâté. For a delicious trouble-free lunch there are mouthwatering Baked Eggs with Creamy Leeks, Mushroom and Courgette Lasagne, and a Savoury Nut Loaf which is sensational when served with a spicy fresh tomato sauce.

RED LENTIL and GOAT'S CHEESE PÂTÉ

The slightly smoky, earthy flavour of red lentils provides a perfect partner to tangy goat's cheese, making a pâté that will be a hit with vegetarians and non-vegetarians alike.

SERVES 8

225g/8oz/1 cup red lentils
1 shallot, very finely chopped
1 bay leaf
475ml/16fl oz/2 cups near-boiling
    vegetable stock
115g/4oz/½ cup soft goat's cheese
5ml/1 tsp ground cumin
3 eggs, lightly beaten
salt and ground black pepper
melba toast and rocket (arugula) leaves,
    to serve

1 Place the lentils in a sieve (strainer) and rinse well under cold running water. Drain, then tip the lentils into the ceramic cooking pot and add the shallot, bay leaf and hot vegetable stock.

2 Switch the slow cooker to high, cover and cook for 2 hours, or until all the liquid has been absorbed and the lentils are soft and pulpy. Stir once or twice towards the end of cooking time to prevent the lentils sticking to the pot.

3 Turn off the slow cooker. Tip the lentil mixture into a bowl, remove the bay leaf and leave to cool uncovered, so that the steam can evaporate. Meanwhile, wash and dry the ceramic cooking pot.

4 Lightly grease the base of a 900ml/ 1½ pint/3¾ cup loaf tin (pan) with oil and line the base with greaseproof (waxed) paper. Put an upturned saucer or metal pastry ring in the bottom of the ceramic cooking pot and pour in about 2.5cm/1in of hot water. Turn the slow cooker to high.

5 Put the goat's cheese in a bowl with the cumin and beat together until soft and creamy. Gradually mix in the eggs until blended. Stir in the lentil mixture and season well with salt and pepper.

6 Tip the mixture into the prepared tin. Cover with clear film (plastic wrap) or foil. Put the tin in the slow cooker and pour in enough boiling water to come just over halfway up the sides. Cover the slow cooker with the lid and cook for 3–3½ hours, until the pâté is lightly set.

7 Carefully remove the tin from the slow cooker and place on a wire rack to cool completely. Chill in the refrigerator for several hours, or overnight.

8 To serve, turn the pâté out of the tin, peel off the lining paper and cut into slices. Serve with melba toast and rocket.

Energy 136Kcal/573kJ; Protein 9.8g; Carbohydrate 16g, of which sugars 0.9g; Fat 4.1g, of which saturates 2.6g; Cholesterol 13mg; Calcium 34mg; Fibre 1.4g; Sodium 97mg.

CHEESE-STUFFED PEARS

These pears, with their scrumptious creamy topping, make a sublime dish when served with a simple salad. If you don't have a very large slow cooker, choose short squat pears rather than long, tapering ones, so that they will fit in a single layer.

SERVES 4

50g/2oz/¼ cup ricotta cheese
50g/2oz/¼ cup dolcelatte cheese
15ml/1 tbsp honey
½ celery stick, finely sliced
8 green olives, pitted and
  roughly chopped
4 dates, stoned and cut into
  thin strips
pinch of paprika
2 medium barely ripe pears
150ml/¼ pint/⅔ cup apple juice
salad leaves, to serve (optional)

4 Pour the apple juice around the pears, then cover with the lid. Cook on high for 1½–2 hours, or until the fruit is tender. (The cooking time will depend on the ripeness of the pears.)

5 Remove the pears from the slow cooker. If you like, brown them under a hot grill (broiler) for a few minutes. Serve with salad leaves, if you like.

COOK'S TIP
These pears go particularly well with slightly bitter and peppery leaves, such as chicory and rocket. Try them tossed in a walnut oil dressing.

1 Place the ricotta cheese in a bowl and crumble in the dolcelatte. Add the honey, celery, olives, dates and paprika and mix together well until creamy and thoroughly blended.

2 Halve the pears lengthways. Use a melon baller or teaspoon to remove the cores and make a hollow for the filling.

3 Divide the ricotta filling equally between the pears, packing it into the hollow, then arrange the fruit in a single layer in the ceramic cooking pot.

Energy 236Kcal/992kJ; Protein 6.9g; Carbohydrate 35.6g, of which sugars 35.6g; Fat 8.2g, of which saturates 5.0g; Cholesterol 24mg; Calcium 141mg; Fibre 4.1g; Sodium 261mg.

BAKED EGGS with CREAMY LEEKS

Enjoy these deliciously creamy eggs for a light lunch or supper with toast and a salad.
You can use other vegetables in place of the leeks, such as puréed spinach or ratatouille.

3 Melt the butter in a small frying pan and cook the leeks over a medium heat, stirring frequently, until softened.

4 Add 45ml/3 tbsp of the cream and cook gently for about 5 minutes, or until the leeks are very soft and the cream has thickened a little. Season with salt, black pepper and nutmeg.

5 Spoon the leeks into the ramekins or soufflé dishes, dividing the mixture equally. Using the back of the spoon, make a hollow in the centre of each pile of leeks, then break an egg into the hollow. Spoon 5–10ml/1–2 tsp of the remaining cream over each egg and season lightly with salt and pepper.

6 Cover each dish with clear film (plastic wrap) and place in the slow cooker. If necessary, pour in a little more boiling water to come halfway up the sides of the dishes. Cover and cook for 30 minutes, or until the egg whites are set and the yolks are still soft, or a little longer if you prefer the eggs firmer.

SERVES 4

15g/½oz/1 tbsp butter, plus extra
    for greasing
225g/8oz small leeks, thinly sliced
60–90ml/4–6 tbsp whipping or double
    (heavy) cream
freshly grated nutmeg
4 eggs
salt and ground black pepper

VARIATION
To make herb and cheese eggs, put 15ml/
1 tbsp double (heavy) cream in each dish
with some chopped herbs. Break in the
eggs, add 15ml/1 tbsp double cream and
a little grated cheese, then cook as
before. This is the perfect recipe for
a lazy weekend brunch.

1 Pour about 2.5cm/1in hot water into the ceramic cooking pot and switch the slow cooker to high.

2 Using a pastry brush, lightly butter the base and insides of four 175ml/ 6fl oz/¾ cup ramekins or individual soufflé dishes.

Energy 239Kcal/990kJ; Protein 8.5g; Carbohydrate 2g, of which sugars 1.6g; Fat 21.9g, of which saturates 11.4g; Cholesterol 266mg; Calcium 58mg; Fibre 1.2g; Sodium 110mg.

SAVOURY NUT LOAF

Ideal as an alternative to the traditional meat roast, this wholesome dish is perfect for special occasions. It is also particularly good served with a spicy fresh tomato sauce.

SERVES 4

30ml/2 tbsp olive oil, plus extra
    for greasing
I onion, finely chopped
I leek, finely chopped
2 celery sticks, finely chopped
225g/8oz/3 cups mushrooms, chopped
2 garlic cloves, crushed
425g/15oz can lentils, rinsed and drained
115g/4oz/1 cup mixed nuts, such as
    hazelnuts, cashew nuts and almonds,
    finely chopped
50g/2oz/1/2 cup plain (all-purpose) flour
50g/2oz/1/2 cup grated mature (sharp)
    Cheddar cheese
I egg, beaten
45–60ml/3–4 tbsp chopped fresh
    mixed herbs
salt and ground black pepper
chives and sprigs of fresh flat leaf parsley,
    to garnish

I Place an upturned saucer or metal pastry ring in the base of the ceramic cooking pot. Pour in about 2.5cm/1in hot water and switch the slow cooker to high.

2 Lightly grease the base and sides of a 900g/2lb loaf tin (pan) or terrine – first making sure it will fit in the slow cooker – and line the base and sides of the tin with baking parchment.

3 Heat the oil in a large pan, add the onion, leek, celery, mushrooms and garlic, then cook for 10 minutes, until the vegetables have softened. Do not let them brown.

4 Remove the pan from the heat, then stir in the lentils, mixed nuts and flour, grated cheese, beaten egg and herbs. Season well with salt and black pepper and mix thoroughly.

5 Spoon the nut mixture into the prepared loaf tin or terrine, pressing right into the corners. Level the surface with a fork, then cover the tin with a piece of foil. Place the loaf tin in the ceramic cooking pot and pour in enough near-boiling water to come just over halfway up the side of the dish.

6 Cover the slow cooker with the lid and cook for 3–4 hours, or until the loaf is firm to the touch.

7 Leave the loaf to cool in the tin for about 15 minutes, then turn out on to a serving plate. Serve the loaf hot or cold, cut into thick slices and garnished with fresh chives and sprigs of flat leaf parsley.

Energy 484Kcal/2019kJ; Protein 23.7g; Carbohydrate 34.1g, of which sugars 5.1g; Fat 29g, of which saturates 5.4g; Cholesterol 69mg; Calcium 238mg; Fibre 8.7g; Sodium 128mg.

PASTA with MUSHROOMS

Slow-cooking a mixture of mushrooms, garlic and sun-dried tomatoes together with white wine and stock makes a rich and well-flavoured pasta sauce. Served with warm ciabatta, this makes a truly excellent vegetarian lunch dish.

SERVES 4

15g/½oz dried porcini mushrooms
120ml/4fl oz/½ cup hot water
2 cloves garlic, finely chopped
2 large pieces drained sun-dried tomato
  in olive oil, sliced into thin strips
120ml/4fl oz/½ cup dry white wine
120ml/4fl oz/½ cup vegetable stock
225g/8oz/2 cups chestnut mushrooms,
  thinly sliced
1 handful fresh flat leaf parsley, roughly
  chopped
450g/1lb/4 cups dried short pasta shapes,
  such as ruote, penne, fusilli or eliche
salt and ground black pepper
rocket and/or fresh flat leaf parsley,
  to garnish

1 Put the dried porcini mushrooms in a large bowl. Pour over the hot water and leave to soak for 15 minutes.

2 While the mushrooms are soaking, put the garlic, tomatoes, wine, stock and chestnut mushrooms into the ceramic cooking pot and switch the slow cooker to high.

3 Tip the porcini mushrooms into a sieve (strainer) set over a bowl, then squeeze them with your hands to release as much liquid as possible. Reserve the soaking liquid. Chop the porcini finely. Add the liquid and the chopped porcini to the ceramic cooking pot, and cover the slow cooker with the lid. Cook on high for 1 hour, stirring halfway through cooking time to make sure that the mushrooms cook evenly.

4 Switch the slow cooker to the low setting and cook for a further 1–2 hours, until the mushrooms are tender.

5 Cook the pasta in boiling salted water for 10 minutes, or according to the instructions on the packet. Drain the pasta and tip it into a warmed large bowl. Stir the chopped parsley into the sauce and season to taste with salt and black pepper. Add the sauce to the pasta and toss well. Serve immediately, garnished with rocket and/or parsley.

VARIATIONS
Fresh wild mushrooms can be used instead of chestnut mushrooms, although they are seasonal and often expensive. A cheaper alternative is to use a box of mixed wild mushrooms, available from good supermarkets and delicatessens.

Energy 420Kcal/1787kJ; Protein 15.1g; Carbohydrate 84.9g, of which sugars 5.1g; Fat 2.6g, of which saturates 0.3g; Cholesterol 0 mg; Calcium 61mg; Fibre 4.8g; Sodium 14mg.

MUSHROOM AND COURGETTE LASAGNE

This is the perfect lasagne for vegetarians. Adding dried porcini to fresh chestnut mushrooms intensifies the flavour. The dish can be made and assembled in the slow cooker early in the day, then left to cook. Serve with crusty Italian bread.

SERVES 6

For the tomato sauce
15g/½oz dried porcini mushrooms
120ml/4fl oz/½ cup hot water
1 onion
1 carrot
1 celery stick
30ml/2 tbsp olive oil
2 x 400g/14oz cans chopped tomatoes
15ml/1 tbsp sun-dried tomato paste
5ml/1 tsp granulated sugar
5ml/1 tsp dried basil or mixed herbs

For the lasagne
30ml/2 tbsp olive oil
50g/2oz/¼ cup butter
450g/1lb courgettes (zucchini), thinly sliced
1 onion, finely chopped
450g/1lb/6 cups chestnut mushrooms,
   thinly sliced
2 garlic cloves, crushed
6–8 non-pre-cook lasagne sheets
50g/2oz/½ cup freshly grated Parmesan
   cheese
salt and ground black pepper
fresh oregano leaves, to garnish
Italian-style bread, to serve (optional)

For the white sauce
40g/1½oz/3 tbsp butter
40g/1½oz/⅓ cup plain (all-purpose) flour
900ml/1½ pints/3¾ cups milk
freshly grated nutmeg

1 Put the dried porcini mushrooms in a bowl. Pour over the hot water and leave to soak for 15 minutes. Tip the porcini and liquid into a sieve (strainer) set over a bowl and squeeze the mushrooms with your hands to release as much liquid as possible. Chop the mushrooms finely and set aside. Strain the soaking liquid through a fine sieve and reserve.

2 Chop the onion, carrot and celery finely. Heat the olive oil in a pan and fry the vegetables until softened. Place in a food processor with the tomatoes, tomato paste, sugar, herbs, porcini and soaking liquid, and blend to a purée.

3 For the lasagne, heat the olive oil and half the butter in a large pan. Add half the courgette slices and season to taste. Cook over a medium heat, turning the courgettes frequently, for 5–8 minutes, until lightly coloured on both sides. Remove from the pan with a slotted spoon and transfer to a bowl. Repeat with the remaining courgettes.

4 Melt the remaining butter in the pan, and cook the onion for 3 minutes, stirring. Add the chestnut mushrooms, chopped porcini and garlic and cook for 5 minutes. Add to the courgettes.

5 For the white sauce, melt the butter in a large pan, then add the flour and cook, stirring, for 1 minute. Turn off the heat and gradually whisk in the milk. Bring to the boil and cook, stirring, until the sauce is smooth and thick. Season with salt, black pepper and nutmeg.

6 Ladle half of the tomato sauce into the ceramic cooking pot and spread out to cover the base. Add half the vegetable mixture, spreading it evenly. Top with about one-third of the white sauce, then about half the lasagne sheets, breaking them to fit the cooking pot. Repeat these layers, then top with the remaining white sauce and sprinkle with grated Parmesan cheese.

7 Cover the ceramic cooking pot with the lid and cook on low for 2–2½ hours or until the lasagne is tender. If you like, brown the top under a medium grill (broiler). Garnish with a sprinkling of fresh oregano leaves, and serve with fresh Italian-style bread.

Energy 421Kcal/1757kJ; Protein 15.5g; Carbohydrate 32.9g, of which sugars 15g; Fat 26.2g, of which saturates 12.4g; Cholesterol 49mg; Calcium 346mg; Fibre 3.8g; Sodium 310mg.

CHICKEN and PISTACHIO PÂTÉ

This easy version of a classic French charcuterie can be made with white chicken breast portions or a mixture of light and dark meat for a more robust flavour. Serve it as an elegant appetizer for a special dinner, or with salad for a light lunch.

SERVES 8

oil, for greasing
800g/1¾lb boneless chicken meat
40g/1½oz/¾ cup fresh white breadcrumbs
120ml/4fl oz/½ cup double (heavy) cream
1 egg white
4 spring onions (scallions) finely chopped
1 garlic clove, finely chopped
75g/3oz cooked ham, cut into small cubes
75g/3oz/½ cup shelled pistachio nuts
30ml/2 tbsp green peppercorns
    in brine, drained
45ml/3 tbsp chopped fresh tarragon
pinch of grated nutmeg
salt and ground black pepper
French bread and salad, to serve

3 Cut the chicken meat into cubes, then put in a food processor and blend until fairly smooth. (You may need to do this in batches depending on the capacity of your food processor.) Alternatively, pass the meat through the medium blade of a food mill. Remove any white stringy pieces from the minced (ground) meat.

4 Place the breadcrumbs in a large mixing bowl, pour over the cream and leave to soak.

5 Meanwhile, lightly whisk the egg white with a fork, then add it to the soaked breadcrumbs. Add the minced chicken, spring onions, garlic, ham, pistachio nuts, green peppercorns, tarragon, nutmeg, salt and pepper. Using a wooden spoon or your fingers, mix thoroughly.

7 To check whether the pâté is cooked, pierce with a skewer or fine knife – the juices should run clear. Carefully lift out of the slow cooker and leave the pâté to cool in the dish. Chill in the refrigerator, preferably overnight.

8 To serve, turn out the pâté on to a serving dish and cut into slices. Serve with crusty French bread and salad.

VARIATIONS
• You can use turkey breast fillet in place of some or all of the chicken, and serve with a tangy cranberry sauce.
• Pale green pistachio nuts look very pretty in this pâté but you can use hazelnuts instead; they are equally good.
• This pâté also makes a perfect dish for a special picnic or a cold buffet. Serve with a delicately flavoured herb mayonnaise.

1 Line the base of a 1.2 litre/2 pint/5 cup round or oval heatproof dish (such as a soufflé dish) with greaseproof (waxed) paper, then lightly brush the base and sides with oil.

2 Put an upturned saucer or metal pastry ring in the base of the ceramic cooking pot and pour in about 2.5cm/1in of hot water. Switch the slow cooker to high.

6 Spoon the mixture into the prepared dish and cover with foil. Place the dish in the ceramic cooking pot and pour a little more boiling water around the dish to come just over halfway up the sides. Cover the slow cooker with the lid and cook for about 4 hours until the pâté is cooked through.

Energy 321Kcal/1344kJ; Protein 36.6g; Carbohydrate 3.7g, of which sugars 1.2g; Fat 17.9g, of which saturates 7.7g; Cholesterol 125mg; Calcium 37mg; Fibre 0.7g; Sodium 379mg.

CARDAMOM CHICKEN MOUSSELINES

These light chicken mousselines, served with a tangy tomato vinaigrette, make an elegant appetizer. They should be served warm rather than hot, so as soon as they are cooked, turn off the slow cooker and leave to cool for half an hour before eating.

SERVES 6

350g/12oz skinless, boneless
   chicken breast portions
1 shallot, finely chopped
115g/4oz/1 cup full-fat soft cheese
1 egg, lightly beaten
2 egg whites
crushed seeds of 2 cardamom pods
60ml/4 tbsp white wine
150ml/¼ pint/⅔ cup double (heavy) cream
oregano sprigs, to serve

For the tomato vinaigrette
350g/12oz ripe tomatoes
10ml/2 tsp balsamic vinegar
30ml/2 tbsp olive oil
sea salt and ground black pepper

1 Roughly chop the chicken and put in a food processor with the finely chopped shallot. Process until the mixture becomes fairly smooth.

2 Add the soft cheese, beaten egg, egg whites, crushed cardamom seeds and white wine to the chicken mixture and season with salt and ground black pepper. Process again until the ingredients are thoroughly blended.

3 Gradually add the cream, using the pulsing action, until the mixture has a smooth and creamy texture. Transfer the mixture to a bowl, cover with clear film (plastic wrap) and chill in the refrigerator for about 30 minutes.

4 Meanwhile, prepare six 150ml/¼ pint/⅔ cup ramekins or dariole moulds, checking first that they will all fit in the slow cooker. Lightly grease the base of each one, then line. Pour about 2cm/¾in hot water into the ceramic cooking pot and switch the cooker to high.

5 Divide the chicken mixture among the prepared dishes and level the tops. Cover each with foil and place in the ceramic cooking pot. Pour in a little more near-boiling water to come half-way up the dishes. Cover and cook for 2½–3 hours, or until the mousselines are firm; a skewer or thin knife inserted into the middle should come out clean.

6 Meanwhile, peel, quarter, seed and finely dice the tomatoes. Place them in a bowl, sprinkle with balsamic vinegar and season with a little salt. Stir well.

7 To serve, unmould the mousselines on to warmed plates. Place small spoonfuls of the tomato vinaigrette around each plate, then drizzle over a little olive oil and grind over a little black pepper. Garnish with sprigs of fresh oregano.

Energy 191Kcal/795kJ; Protein 18.1g; Carbohydrate 2g, of which sugars 2g; Fat 11.6g, of which saturates 5g; Cholesterol 96mg; Calcium 30mg; Fibre 0.7g; Sodium 130mg.

FISH TERRINE

This colourful layered terrine makes a spectacular appetizer or main course on a special occasion. It is particularly good for entertaining because it can be made in advance, chilled until ready to serve, then arranged on plates at the last minute.

SERVES 6

450g/1lb skinless white fish fillets
225g/8oz thinly sliced smoked salmon
2 egg whites, chilled
1.5ml/¼ tsp each salt and ground
    white pepper
pinch of freshly grated nutmeg
250ml/8fl oz/1 cup double (heavy) cream
50g/2oz small tender fresh spinach leaves
lemon mayonnaise, to serve

1 Cut the white fish fillets into 2.5cm/1in pieces, removing any bones. Spread out the fish pieces on a plate, cover with clear film (plastic wrap) and chill in the freezer for 15 minutes until very cold.

2 Lightly oil a 1.2 litre/2 pint/5 cup terrine or loaf tin (pan). Line the base and sides of the tin with the smoked salmon slices, making sure they overlap each other all the way around and letting them hang over the edges of the tin.

3 Remove the white fish from the freezer, then place in a food processor and blend to make a very smooth purée. (You may need to stop the machine and scrape down the sides two or three times as you do this.)

4 Add the egg whites, one at a time, processing after each addition, then add the salt, pepper and nutmeg. With the machine running, pour in the cream and stop as soon as it is blended. (If over-processed the cream will thicken.)

5 Transfer the fish mixture to a large glass bowl. Put the spinach leaves into the food processor and process to make a smooth purée. Add one-third of the fish mixture to the spinach and process briefly until just combined, scraping down the sides once or twice.

6 Pour about 2.5cm/1in of very hot water into the ceramic cooking pot. Place an upturned saucer or metal pastry ring in the base, then turn the slow cooker on to high.

7 Spread half the plain fish mixture in the base of the tin. Spoon the green fish mixture over the top and smooth it level, then cover with the remaining plain mixture. Fold the overhanging pieces of smoked salmon over the top to enclose the mixture. Tap the tin to settle the mixture and remove any air pockets, then cover the tin with a double layer of lightly oiled foil.

8 Put the tin in the slow cooker and pour in enough boiling water to come just over halfway up the sides. Cook for 3–3½ hours, or until a skewer inserted into the terrine comes out clean. Leave the terrine to cool in the tin, then chill in the refrigerator until firm.

9 To serve the terrine, turn out on to a board, remove the lining paper and slice. Arrange the slices on individual plates and serve with lemon mayonnaise.

Energy 340Kcal/1409kJ; Protein 23.2g; Carbohydrate 0.8g, of which sugars 0.8g; Fat 27.1g, of which saturates 14.7g; Cholesterol 110mg; Calcium 50mg; Fibre 0.2g; Sodium 201mg.

HADDOCK and SMOKED SALMON TERRINE

This substantial terrine makes a superb dish for a summer buffet. It is very good served with dill mayonnaise or a tangy mango salsa instead of the crème fraîche or sour cream.

SERVES 6

15ml/1 tbsp sunflower oil, for greasing
350g/12oz smoked salmon
900g/2lb haddock fillets, skinned
2 eggs, lightly beaten
105ml/7 tbsp low-fat crème fraîche
   or sour cream
30ml/2 tbsp drained bottled capers
30ml/2 tbsp drained soft green or pink
   peppercorns
salt and ground white pepper
low-fat crème fraîche or sour cream,
   peppercorns, fresh dill and rocket
   (arugula), to serve

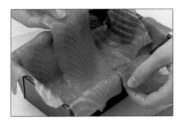

1 Pour about 2.5cm/1in of warm water into the ceramic cooking pot. Place an upturned saucer or metal pastry ring in the base, then turn the slow cooker on to high. Lightly grease a 1 litre/1¾ pint/4 cup loaf tin (pan) or terrine. Use some of the smoked salmon slices to line the tin or terrine, letting them hang over the edge. Reserve the remaining salmon.

2 Cut two long slices of the haddock the length of the tin or terrine, and cut the remaining haddock into small pieces. Season with salt and pepper.

3 Combine the eggs, crème fraîche or sour cream, capers and soft peppercorns in a bowl. Season with salt and pepper, then stir in the small pieces of haddock. Spoon half the mixture into the mould and smooth the surface with a spatula.

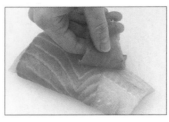

4 Wrap the long haddock fillets in the reserved smoked salmon. (Don't worry if there isn't enough salmon to cover them completely.) Lay the wrapped haddock fillets on top of the fish mixture in the tin or terrine.

5 Spoon the rest of the fish mixture into the tin or terrine and smooth the surface. Fold the overhanging pieces of smoked salmon over the top and cover tightly with a double thickness of foil.

6 Tap the terrine to settle the contents, then place in the slow cooker and pour in enough boiling water to come just over halfway up the sides. Cook for 3–4 hours, or until a skewer inserted into the terrine comes out clean.

7 Remove the terrine from the slow cooker, but do not remove the foil cover. Place two or three large heavy cans on the foil to weight it, and leave until cold. Chill in the refrigerator for 24 hours.

8 About 1 hour before serving, remove the terrine from the refrigerator, lift off the weights and carefully remove the foil. Gently invert the terrine on to a serving plate and lift off the mould.

9 Cut the terrine into thick slices using a sharp knife. Serve with crème fraîche or sour cream, peppercorns, dill sprigs and rocket leaves.

Energy 316Kcal/1326kJ; Protein 46.1g; Carbohydrate 0.4g, of which sugars 0.4g; Fat 14.5g, of which saturates 6.2g; Cholesterol 170mg; Calcium 653mg; Fibre 0g; Sodium 1228mg.

ONE-POT AND CLAY-POT FIRST COURSES AND LIGHT MEALS

When you are cooking a first course, appetizer or snack for family or friends, the most successful dishes are often the simplest, so anything that can be cooked in one pot is a sure winner. Whether you opt for a simple pasta dish such as Spaghetti with Cheese and Black Pepper, a hot and spicy clay-pot treat such as Potato Wedges with Tomato and Chilli Salsa, or Fillet of Beef Stroganoff, or use your wok to make a stunning Sweet-and-sour Pork Stir-fry or Stir-fried Crispy Duck, everyone will be glad you chose the easy option.

BRAISED BABY LEEKS in RED WINE with AROMATICS

Coriander seeds and oregano lend a Greek flavour to this dish of braised leeks. Serve it as part of a mixed hors d'oeuvre or as a partner for baked white fish.

SERVES 6

12 baby leeks or 6 thick leeks
15ml/1 tbsp coriander seeds,
    lightly crushed
5cm/2in piece of cinnamon stick
120ml/4fl oz/½ cup olive oil
3 fresh bay leaves
2 strips pared orange rind
5–6 fresh or dried oregano sprigs
5ml/1 tsp sugar
150ml/¼ pint/⅔ cup fruity red wine
10ml/2 tsp balsamic or
    sherry vinegar
30ml/2 tbsp coarsely chopped fresh
    oregano or marjoram
salt and ground black pepper

1 If using baby leeks, simply trim the ends, but leave them whole. Cut thick leeks into 5–7.5cm/2–3in lengths.

2 Place the coriander seeds and cinnamon in a pan wide enough to take all the leeks in a single layer. Cook over a medium heat for 2–3 minutes, until the spices give off a fragrant aroma, then stir in the olive oil, bay leaves, orange rind, fresh or dried oregano, sugar, wine and balsamic or sherry vinegar. Bring to the boil and simmer for 5 minutes.

3 Add the leeks to the pan. Bring back to the boil, reduce the heat and cover the pan. Cook the leeks gently for 5 minutes. Uncover and simmer gently for another 5–8 minutes, until the leeks are just tender when tested with the tip of a sharp knife.

4 Use a slotted spoon to transfer the leeks to a serving dish. Boil the pan juices rapidly until reduced to about 75–90ml/5–6 tbsp. Add salt and pepper to taste and pour the liquid over the leeks. Leave to cool.

5 The leeks can be left to stand for several hours. If you chill them, bring them back to room temperature again before serving. Sprinkle the chopped herbs over the leeks just before serving.

COOK'S TIP
Genuine balsamic vinegar from Modena in northern Italy has been produced for over 1,000 years. It has a high sugar content and wonderfully strong bouquet. It is a very dark brown colour and has a deep, rich flavour with hints of herbs and port. Nowadays you can find quite good balsamic vinegar in supermarkets. It is expensive, but the flavour is so rich that you only need to use a little.

Energy 185Kcal/768kJ; Protein 2.9g; Carbohydrate 5.7g, of which sugars 4.5g; Fat 15.1g, of which saturates 2.2g; Cholesterol 0mg; Calcium 52mg; Fibre 3.9g; Sodium 7mg.

POTATO WEDGES with TOMATO and CHILLI SALSA

This is a healthier version of traditionally baked potato skins; the clay pot keeps the potato flesh wonderfully moist and fluffy.

SERVES 4

6 potatoes, about 115g/4oz each
45ml/3 tbsp olive oil
salt and ground black pepper

For the tomato and chilli salsa
4 juicy ripe tomatoes
1 sun-dried tomato in olive
   oil, drained
3 spring onions (scallions)
1–2 red or green chillies, halved
   and seeded
15ml/1 tbsp extra virgin
   olive oil
10ml/2 tsp lemon juice

COOK'S TIP
Varieties of floury potatoes that produce a fluffy texture when baked are best for these wedges. Good types to use include Maris Piper, Désirée, King Edward and Pentland Squire.

1 Soak the clay pot or a potato pot in cold water for 20 minutes, then drain. Scrub the potatoes and dry with kitchen paper. Cut each potato lengthwise into four wedges. Brush with a little of the oil and sprinkle with salt and pepper.

2 Place the potatoes in the clay pot and cover with the lid. Place in an unheated oven, set the temperature to 200°C/400°F/Gas 6 and cook for 55–60 minutes, or until the potatoes are tender.

3 Meanwhile, finely chop the tomatoes, sun-dried tomato, spring onions and chilli and mix together with the olive oil and lemon juice. Cover and leave to stand to allow the flavours to mingle.

4 Uncover the potatoes, brush with the remaining olive oil and bake, uncovered, for a further 15 minutes until slightly golden. Divide the potato wedges and salsa among four serving bowls and plates, and serve immediately.

Energy 238Kcal/1001kJ; Protein 4g; Carbohydrate 30.8g, of which sugars 4.9g; Fat 11.9g, of which saturates 1.8g; Cholesterol 0mg; Calcium 23mg; Fibre 2.6g; Sodium 28mg.

BRAISED VINE LEAVES

This popular eastern Mediterranean dish keeps moist when cooked slowly in a clay pot.

SERVES 4

12 fresh vine leaves
30ml/2 tbsp olive oil
1 small onion, chopped
30ml/2 tbsp pine nuts
1 garlic clove, crushed
115g/4oz cooked long grain rice
2 tomatoes, skinned, seeded and
    finely chopped
15ml/1 tbsp chopped fresh mint
1 lemon, sliced
150ml/¼ pint/⅔ cup dry white wine
200ml/7fl oz/scant 1 cup vegetable stock
salt and ground black pepper
lemon wedges, to serve

3 Stir into the cooked rice, with the tomatoes, mint and seasoning, to taste.

4 Place a spoonful of the rice mixture at the stalk end of each vine leaf. Fold the sides over the filling and roll up tightly.

1 Soak the clay pot in cold water for 20 minutes, then drain. Blanch the vine leaves in a pan of boiling water for about 2 minutes or until they darken and soften. Rinse the leaves under cold running water and leave to drain.

2 Heat the oil in a frying pan, add the onion and fry for 5–6 minutes, stirring frequently, until softened. Add the pine nuts and crushed garlic and cook, stirring continuously until the onions and pine nuts are a golden brown colour.

5 Place the stuffed vine leaves close together, seam side down in the clay pot. Place the lemon slices on top. Pour over the wine and sufficient stock to just cover the lemon slices.

6 Cover with the lid and place in an unheated oven. Set the oven to 200°C/400°F/Gas 6 and cook for 30 minutes. Reduce to 160°C/325°F/Gas 3 and cook for a further 30 minutes. Serve hot or cold, with lemon wedges.

Energy 258Kcal/1072kJ; Protein 4.6g; Carbohydrate 28.8g, of which sugars 5.5g; Fat 11.1g, of which saturates 1.2g; Cholesterol 0mg; Calcium 49mg; Fibre 2.1g; Sodium 11mg.

LINGUINE with ROCKET

*This is a first course that you will find in many a fashionable restaurant in Italy. It is very
quick and easy to make at home and is worth trying for yourself.*

SERVES 4

350g/12oz fresh or dried linguine
120ml/4fl oz/½ cup extra virgin olive oil
1 large bunch rocket (arugula), about
    150g/5oz, stalks removed, shredded
    or torn
75g/3oz/1 cup freshly grated
    Parmesan cheese
salt and ground black pepper

VARIATION
Oil-based pasta sauces such as this one
are best served with fine, long pastas
such as linguine. Spaghetti, capelli
d'angelo, bucatini or fettucine would
work just as well in this recipe.

1 Cook the pasta in a large pan of
salted boiling water for 8–10 minutes
until it is just tender, or according to the
instructions on the packet. As soon as
the pasta is cooked, drain thoroughly.

2 Heat about 60ml/4 tbsp of the olive
oil in the pasta pan, then add the drained
pasta, followed by the rocket. Toss over
a medium to high heat for 1–2 minutes
or until the rocket is just wilted, then
remove the pan from the heat.

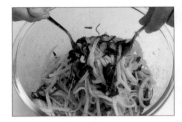

3 Tip the pasta and rocket into a
warmed, large serving bowl. Add half the
freshly grated Parmesan cheese and the
remaining olive oil. Add a little salt and
black pepper to taste.

4 Toss the mixture quickly to mix and
serve immediately. Hand round the
remaining Parmesan cheese.

COOK'S TIP
Buy rocket by the bunch from the
greengrocer. The type sold in small
cellophane packets in supermarkets is
usually very expensive. Always check
when buying rocket that all the leaves
are bright green. In hot weather, rocket
leaves quickly turn yellow.

Energy 585Kcal/2451kJ; Protein 19g; Carbohydrate 65.4g, of which sugars 3.5g; Fat 29.2g, of which saturates 7.1g; Cholesterol 19mg; Calcium 311mg; Fibre 3.3g; Sodium 260mg.

SPAGHETTI with GARLIC and OIL

This simple Roman pasta dish can be made in less than 15 minutes. Use fresh chillies if you prefer and, since the oil is so important, the very best extra virgin olive oil.

SERVES 4

400g/14oz fresh or dried spaghetti
90ml/6 tbsp extra virgin olive oil
2–4 garlic cloves, crushed
1 dried red chilli
1 small handful fresh flat leaf parsley,
   roughly chopped
salt

COOK'S TIP
Don't use salt when you are preparing the hot oil, garlic and chilli mixture, because the salt will not dissolve sufficiently. This is why plenty of salt is recommended for cooking the pasta.

1 Cook the pasta in a large pan of salted boiling water, according to the packet instructions, until it is just tender, adding plenty of salt to the water (see Cook's Tip).

2 When the pasta is just tender, drain it by tipping it into a large colander, then transfer it to a warmed, large serving bowl. Rinse out the pasta pan and dry.

3 Heat the olive oil in the pan. Add the crushed garlic and the whole dried chilli and stir over a low heat for a minute or two until the garlic is just beginning to brown. Remove the chilli and discard.

4 Pour the hot olive oil and cooked garlic mixture over the pasta, add the roughly chopped fresh flat leaf parsley and toss vigorously until the pasta glistens, then serve immediately.

Energy 495Kcal/2084kJ; Protein 12.4g; Carbohydrate 74.5g, of which sugars 3.6g; Fat 18.5g, of which saturates 2.6g; Cholesterol 0mg; Calcium 50mg; Fibre 3.5g; Sodium 7mg.

SPAGHETTI with BUTTER and HERBS

This is a versatile recipe. You can use just one favourite herb or several — basil, flat leaf parsley, rosemary, thyme, marjoram or sage would all work well.

SERVES 4

400g/14oz fresh or dried spaghetti
    alla chitarra
2 good handfuls mixed fresh herbs,
    plus extra herb leaves and flowers
    to garnish
115g/4oz/½ cup butter, diced
salt and ground black pepper
freshly grated Parmesan cheese, to serve

1 Cook the pasta in a large pan of salted boiling water for 10–12 minutes until just tender or according to the instructions on the packet.

2 Using a large sharp knife, chop the fresh herbs roughly or finely, whichever you prefer.

COOK'S TIP
Square-shaped chitarra spaghetti is the traditional type for this sauce, but you can use any type of long thin pasta, such as ordinary spaghetti or spaghettini, or even linguine.

VARIATION
If you like the flavour of garlic, add one or two crushed cloves to the pan when melting the butter.

3 Drain the pasta in a colander and then return the pasta to the pan. Add the butter and heat until it melts and sizzles, then add the chopped herbs and salt and pepper to taste.

4 Toss the pasta over a medium heat until it is thoroughly coated in the butter and herbs.

5 Serve the pasta immediately in warmed shallow bowls, sprinkled with some extra herb leaves and flowers. Hand around a bowl of freshly grated Parmesan separately.

SPAGHETTI with CHEESE and BLACK PEPPER

This dish is very quick and easy to cook, perfect for a midweek supper. The flavours are very simple, so choose a strong-tasting cheese and a good extra virgin olive oil. Pecorino is traditional in this dish, but Parmesan could also be used.

SERVES 4

400g/14oz fresh or
    dried spaghetti
115g/4oz/1 cup freshly grated
    Pecorino cheese
about 5ml/1 tsp coarsely ground
    black pepper
extra virgin olive oil, to taste
salt

1 Cook the fresh or dried pasta in a large pan of salted boiling water until it is just tender, or according to the instructions on the packet.

2 As soon as the spaghetti is cooked, drain it, leaving it a little moister than usual, then tip the spaghetti straight into a large warmed serving bowl.

3 Add the freshly grated cheese, lots of black pepper, and salt to taste. Toss the pasta well to mix, then moisten with as much olive oil as you like. Serve the pasta immediately.

Spaghetti with Butter and Herbs: Energy 565Kcal/2371kJ; Protein 12.9g; Carbohydrate 75g, of which sugars 4.1g; Fat 25.8g, of which saturates 15.2g; Cholesterol 61mg; Calcium 80mg; Fibre 4.2g; Sodium 186mg.
Spaghetti with Cheese and Black Pepper: Energy 472Kcal/1997kJ; Protein 23.3g; Carbohydrate 74.1g, of which sugars 3.3g; Fat 11.2g, of which saturates 6.1g; Cholesterol 29mg; Calcium 370mg; Fibre 2.9g; Sodium 317mg.

LAMB'S LIVER and BACON CASSEROLE

The trick when cooking liver is to seal it quickly, then simmer it gently and briefly.
Prolonged and/or fierce cooking makes liver hard and grainy. Boiled new potatoes
tossed in lots of butter go well with this simple casserole.

SERVES 4

30ml/2 tbsp extra virgin olive oil or
   sunflower oil
225g/8oz rindless unsmoked lean bacon
   rashers (strips), cut into pieces
2 onions, halved and sliced
175g/6oz/2 cups chestnut
   mushrooms, halved
450g/1lb lamb's liver, trimmed
   and sliced
25g/1oz/2 tbsp butter
15ml/1 tbsp soy sauce
30ml/2 tbsp plain (all-purpose) flour
150ml/¼ pint/⅔ cup hot, well-flavoured
   chicken stock
salt and ground black pepper

1 Heat the oil in a frying pan, add the bacon and fry until crisp. Add the sliced onions to the pan and cook for about 10 minutes, stirring frequently, or until softened. Add the mushrooms to the pan and fry for a further 1 minute.

2 Use a slotted spoon to remove the bacon and vegetables from the pan and keep warm. Add the liver to the fat remaining in the pan and cook over a high heat for 3–4 minutes, turning once to seal the slices on both sides. Remove the liver from the pan and keep warm.

3 Melt the butter in the pan, add the soy sauce and flour and blend together. Stir in the stock and bring to the boil, stirring until thickened. Return the liver, bacon and vegetables to the pan and heat through for 1 minute. Season with salt and pepper to taste, and serve immediately with new potatoes and lightly cooked green beans.

Energy 418Kcal/1739kJ; Protein 34.2g; Carbohydrate 9.3g, of which sugars 2.6g; Fat 27.3g, of which saturates 9.5g; Cholesterol 527mg; Calcium 34mg; Fibre 1.3g; Sodium 1257mg.

FILLET of BEEF STROGANOFF

Legend has it that this Russian recipe was devised by Count Paul Stroganov's cook to use beef frozen by the Siberian climate. The only way that it could be prepared was cut into very thin strips. The strips of lean beef were served in a brandy-flavoured cream sauce.

3 Cook the onion and garlic over a low heat, stirring occasionally until the onion has softened. Add the mushrooms and stir-fry over a high heat for 1–2 minutes. Transfer the vegetables and their juices to a dish and set aside.

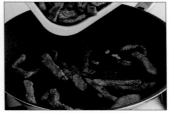

4 Wipe the pan, then add and heat the remaining oil. Coat a batch of meat with flour, then fry over a high heat until well browned. Remove from the pan, then coat and fry another batch. When the last batch is cooked, replace all the meat and vegetables. Add the brandy and simmer until it has almost evaporated.

5 Stir in the beef stock or consommé and seasoning and cook for 10–15 minutes, stirring frequently with a wooden spoon, or until the meat is tender and the sauce is thick and glossy. Add the sour cream, stir well and sprinkle with the chopped fresh flat leaf parsley. Serve immediately with plain boiled rice and a simple salad.

SERVES 8

1.2kg/2½lb beef fillet (tenderloin)
30ml/2 tbsp plain (all-purpose) flour
large pinch each of cayenne pepper
    and paprika
75ml/5 tbsp sunflower oil
1 large onion, chopped
3 garlic cloves, finely chopped
450g/1lb/6½ cups chestnut
    mushrooms, sliced
75ml/5 tbsp brandy
300ml/½ pint/1¼ cups beef stock
    or consommé
300ml/½ pint/1¼ cups sour cream
45ml/3 tbsp chopped fresh flat leaf parsley
salt and ground black pepper

1 Thinly slice the beef fillet across the grain, then cut it into fine strips. Season the flour with the cayenne and paprika.

2 Heat half the oil in a large frying pan and add the chopped onion and garlic.

COOK'S TIP

If you do not have a very large frying pan, it may be easier to cook this dish in a large, flameproof casserole.

Energy 399Kcal/1659kJ; Protein 34.6g; Carbohydrate 6.5g, of which sugars 3g; Fat 23.9g, of which saturates 9.8g; Cholesterol 114mg; Calcium 56mg; Fibre 1.1g; Sodium 85mg.

SWEET-and-SOUR PORK STIR-FRY

This is a great idea for a quick family lunch. Remember to cut the carrots into thin matchstick strips so that they cook in time.

SERVES 4

450g/1lb pork fillet (tenderloin)
30ml/2 tbsp plain (all-purpose) flour
45ml/3 tbsp oil
1 onion, roughly chopped
1 garlic clove, crushed
1 green (bell) pepper, seeded and sliced
350g/12oz carrots, cut into thin strips
225g/8oz can bamboo shoots, drained
15ml/1 tbsp white wine vinegar
15ml/1 tbsp soft brown sugar
10ml/2 tsp tomato purée (paste)
30ml/2 tbsp light soy sauce
salt and ground black pepper

1 Thinly slice the pork. Season the flour and toss the pork in it to coat.

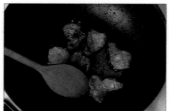

2 Heat the oil in a wok or large frying pan and cook the pork over a medium heat for about 5 minutes, until golden and cooked through. Remove the pork with a slotted spoon and drain on kitchen paper. You may need to do this in several batches.

3 Add the onion and garlic to the pan and cook for 3 minutes. Stir in the pepper and carrots and stir-fry over a high heat for 6–8 minutes, or until beginning to soften slightly.

4 Return the meat to the pan with the bamboo shoots. Add the remaining ingredients with 120ml/4fl oz/½ cup water and bring to the boil. Simmer gently for 2–3 minutes, or until piping hot. Adjust the seasoning, if necessary, and serve immediately.

VARIATION
Finely sliced strips of skinless chicken breast fillet can be used in this recipe instead of the pork.

Energy 324Kcal/1357kJ; Protein 27.9g; Carbohydrate 23.9g, of which sugars 16.2g; Fat 13.6g, of which saturates 3g; Cholesterol 71mg; Calcium 63mg; Fibre 4.2g; Sodium 646mg.

PORK CHOW MEIN

This is a very speedy dish to cook, but make sure that you prepare all the ingredients before you start to cook. If you don't have a wok, use a very large frying pan instead.

SERVES 4

175g/6oz medium egg noodles
350g/12oz pork fillet (tenderloin)
30ml/2 tbsp sunflower oil
15ml/1 tbsp sesame oil
2 garlic cloves, crushed
8 spring onions (scallions), sliced
1 red (bell) pepper, seeded and
   roughly chopped
1 green (bell) pepper, seeded and
   roughly chopped
30ml/2 tbsp dark soy sauce
45ml/3 tbsp dry sherry
175g/6oz/¾ cup beansprouts
45ml/3 tbsp chopped fresh flat leaf parsley
15ml/1 tbsp toasted sesame seeds

1 Soak the noodles according to the packet instructions, then drain well.

2 Thinly slice the pork fillet. Heat the sunflower oil in a wok or large frying pan and cook the pork over a high heat until golden brown and cooked through.

3 Add the sesame oil to the pan, with the garlic, spring onions and peppers. Cook over a high heat for 3–4 minutes, or until beginning to soften.

4 Reduce the heat slightly, then stir in the soaked noodles, with the dark soy sauce and dry sherry. Stir-fry for about 2 minutes. Add the beansprouts and cook for a further 1–2 minutes. If the noodles begin to stick to the pan, add a splash of water. Stir in the chopped parsley and serve the chow mein sprinkled with the toasted sesame seeds.

Energy 404Kcal/1696kJ; Protein 26.9g; Carbohydrate 40.2g, of which sugars 8.5g; Fat 14.8g, of which saturates 3.3g; Cholesterol 68mg; Calcium 45mg; Fibre 3.7g; Sodium 683mg.

MINTED LAMB STIR-FRY

Lamb and mint have a long-established partnership that works particularly well in this full-flavoured stir-fry. Serve simply, with noodles or rice.

SERVES 2

275g/10oz lamb neck fillet or boneless
   leg steaks
30ml/2 tbsp sunflower oil
10ml/2 tsp sesame oil
1 onion, roughly chopped
2 garlic cloves, crushed
1 red chilli, seeded and
   finely chopped
75g/3oz fine green beans, halved
225g/8oz fresh spinach, shredded
30ml/2 tbsp oyster sauce
30ml/2 tbsp Thai fish sauce (*nam pla*)
15ml/1 tbsp lemon juice
5ml/1 tsp sugar
45ml/3 tbsp chopped fresh mint
salt and ground black pepper
mint sprigs, to garnish
noodles or rice, to serve

1 Trim the lamb of any excess fat and cut into thin slices. Heat the sunflower and sesame oils in a wok or large frying pan and cook the lamb over a high heat until browned. Remove with a slotted spoon and drain on kitchen paper.

2 Add the onion, garlic and chilli to the wok, cook for 2–3 minutes, then add the beans and stir-fry for 3 minutes.

3 Stir in the shredded spinach with the browned meat, oyster sauce, Thai fish sauce, lemon juice and sugar. Stir-fry for a further 3–4 minutes, or until the lamb is cooked through.

4 Sprinkle in the chopped mint and toss lightly, then adjust the seasoning. Serve piping hot, garnished with mint sprigs and accompanied by noodles or rice.

Energy 438Kcal/1819kJ; Protein 31.9g; Carbohydrate 9.3g, of which sugars 8g; Fat 30.6g, of which saturates 9.1g; Cholesterol 105mg; Calcium 229mg; Fibre 3.6g; Sodium 1879mg.

STIR-FRIED CRISPY DUCK

This stir-fry would be delicious wrapped in flour tortillas or steamed Chinese pancakes, with a little extra warm plum sauce.

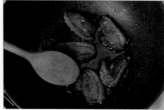

2 Heat the oil in a wok or large frying pan and cook the duck over a high heat until golden and crisp. Keep stirring to prevent the duck from sticking. Remove the duck with a slotted spoon and drain on kitchen paper. You may need to cook the duck in several batches.

3 Add the spring onions to the pan and cook for 2 minutes. Stir in the cabbage and cook for 5 minutes, or until it is softened and golden.

SERVES 2

275–350g/10–12oz boneless duck breast
30ml/2 tbsp plain (all-purpose) flour
60ml/4 tbsp oil
1 bunch spring onions (scallions), halved
    lengthwise and cut into 5cm/2in strips,
    plus extra to garnish
275g/10oz/2½ cups finely shredded
    green cabbage
225g/8oz can water chestnuts, drained
    and sliced
50g/2oz/½ cup unsalted cashew nuts
115g/4oz cucumber, cut into strips
45ml/3 tbsp plum sauce
15ml/1 tbsp light soy sauce
salt and ground black pepper

1 Remove any skin from the duck breast, then trim off a little of the fat. Thinly slice the meat into even-size pieces. Season the flour with plenty of salt and pepper and use it to completely coat each piece of duck.

4 Return the duck to the pan with the water chestnuts, cashews and cucumber. Stir-fry for 2 minutes. Add the plum sauce and soy sauce and season to taste, then heat for 2 minutes. Serve garnished with the sliced spring onions.

Energy 682Kcal/2846kJ; Protein 36.9g; Carbohydrate 41.3g, of which sugars 26.3g; Fat 44.4g, of which saturates 7.5g; Cholesterol 151mg; Calcium 174mg; Fibre 5.8g; Sodium 844mg.

MUSSELS and CLAMS with LEMON GRASS and COCONUT CREAM

Lemon grass has an incomparable flavour and aroma and is widely used in Thai cooking, especially with seafood. If you have difficulty obtaining fresh baby clams for this recipe, then use a few extra mussels instead.

SERVES 6

1.8–2kg/4–4½lb mussels
450g/1lb baby clams
120ml/4fl oz/½ cup dry white wine
1 bunch spring onions (scallions), chopped
2 lemon grass stalks, chopped
6 kaffir lime leaves, chopped
10ml/2 tsp Thai green curry paste
200ml/7fl oz/scant 1 cup coconut cream
30ml/2 tbsp chopped fresh
    coriander (cilantro)
salt and ground black pepper
garlic chives, to garnish

1 Clean the mussels by pulling off the beards, scrubbing the shells well and removing any barnacles. Discard any broken mussels or any that do not close when tapped sharply. Wash the clams.

COOK'S TIP
The kaffir lime tree is native to South-east Asia and both the leaves and fruit rind are used in cooking. Dried kaffir lime leaves, available from supermarkets, can be used in place of fresh – add them at the beginning of the cooking time and remove and discard just before serving.

2 Put the white wine in a large, heavy pan with the spring onions, chopped lemon grass stalks, kaffir lime leaves and Thai green curry paste. Simmer all the ingredients together until the wine has almost evaporated.

3 Add the mussels and clams to the pan, cover tightly and steam the shellfish over a high heat for 5–6 minutes, or until they open.

4 Using a slotted spoon, transfer the cooked mussels and clams to a heated serving bowl and keep hot. At this stage discard any shellfish that remain closed. Strain the cooking liquid into the clean pan and gently simmer until it is reduced to about 250ml/8fl oz/1 cup.

5 Stir in the coconut cream and fresh coriander, with plenty of salt and pepper to taste. Increase the heat and simmer gently until the sauce is piping hot. Pour the sauce over the mussels and clams and serve immediately, garnished with garlic chives.

Energy 132Kcal/563kJ; Protein 19.6g; Carbohydrate 3.1g, of which sugars 3g; Fat 3.4g, of which saturates 0.6g; Cholesterol 44mg; Calcium 239mg; Fibre 0.3g; Sodium 288mg.

SAFFRON MUSSELS with WHITE WINE and GARLIC

Mussels are easy to cook in a clay pot and they stay deliciously moist. The saffron adds a lovely pungent flavour as well as its characteristic yellow colour to the creamy sauce.

SERVES 4

few threads of saffron
1kg/2¼lb mussels in their shells
25g/1oz/2 tbsp butter
2 shallots, finely chopped
2 garlic cloves, finely chopped
200ml/7fl oz/scant 1 cup dry white wine
60ml/4 tbsp double (heavy) cream or
    crème fraîche
30ml/2 tbsp chopped fresh parsley
salt and ground black pepper
French bread, to serve

1 Soak a large clay pot in cold water for about 20 minutes, then drain. Put the saffron in a small bowl, add 15ml/1 tbsp boiling water and leave to soak.

2 Scrub the mussels, pull off the beards and discard any open mussels that don't close when tapped. Place all the closed mussels in the soaked clay pot.

3 Melt the butter in a frying pan, add the shallots and garlic and cook gently for 5 minutes, to soften. Stir in the wine and saffron water and bring to the boil. Pour the liquid over the mussels.

4 Cover the clay pot and place in an unheated oven. Set the oven to 220°C/425°F/Gas 7. Cook the mussels for 15 minutes, then remove the pot from the oven and, firmly holding the lid on, shake the pot. Return the pot to the oven and cook for another 10 minutes, or until the mussels have opened.

COOK'S TIP
Saffron is the stigma of a type of crocus. It is an expensive spice and is sold as thin, wiry threads. It has a mild aroma and adds a slightly pungent flavour to both sweet and savoury dishes, and also to buns, cakes and breads. However, the main characteristic of saffron is the distinctive yellow colour it imparts once diluted in a liquid.

5 Using a slotted spoon, transfer the mussels to four warmed serving bowls (discard any that have not opened). Mix the cream or crème fraîche and parsley into the cooking liquid and season to taste. Pour the cooking liquid over the mussels and serve immediately with French bread to soak up the sauce.

Energy 224Kcal/935kJ; Protein 13.5g; Carbohydrate 1.8g, of which sugars 1.4g; Fat 14.7g, of which saturates 8.5g; Cholesterol 64mg; Calcium 164mg; Fibre 0.2g; Sodium 201mg.

PENNE with CREAM and SMOKED SALMON

This modern way of serving pasta is popular all over Italy. The three essential ingredients combine together beautifully, and the dish is very quick and easy to make. Accompany with a green salad, ciabatta bread and some sparkling wine for an easy but impressive meal.

SERVES 4

350g/12oz/3 cups dried penne
115g/4oz thinly sliced
    smoked salmon
2–3 fresh thyme sprigs
25g/1oz/2 tbsp unsalted (sweet)
    butter, diced
150ml/¼ pint/⅔ cup single (light) cream
salt and ground black pepper

VARIATION

Although penne is the traditional pasta to serve with this sauce, it also goes very well with fresh ravioli stuffed with spinach and ricotta.

COOK'S TIP

This dish can be served as an appetizer or a main course.

1 Cook the dried pasta in a large pan of lightly salted boiling water for 10 minutes until it is just tender or according to the instructions on the packet.

2 Meanwhile, using sharp kitchen scissors, cut the smoked salmon slices into thin strips, about 5mm/¼in wide. Strip the leaves from the thyme sprigs and rinse in cold water.

3 Drain the pasta and return it to the pan. Add the butter and heat gently until melted, then stir in the cream with about one-quarter of the smoked salmon and thyme leaves, then season with pepper. Heat gently for 3–4 minutes, stirring all the time. Check the seasoning. Divide among four warmed bowls, top with the remaining salmon and thyme leaves and serve immediately.

Energy 459Kcal/1936kJ; Protein 19.1g; Carbohydrate 65.7g, of which sugars 3.8g; Fat 15.2g, of which saturates 8.2g; Cholesterol 44mg; Calcium 62mg; Fibre 2.6g; Sodium 592mg.

PRAWNS with BAKED GARLIC and ROASTED TOMATOES

Packed full of wonderful Mediterranean flavours, this simple, gutsy dish makes a marvellous first course for a dinner party.

SERVES 4

4 small garlic bulbs
60–75ml/4–5 tbsp olive oil
500g/1¼lb baby plum tomatoes on
    the vine
16 raw large prawns (jumbo shrimp), in
    their shells
a few sprigs of fresh thyme
salt and ground black pepper
lemon wedges and warm crusty bread,
    to serve

COOK'S TIPS
• If you can't find small garlic bulbs use one large one and bake it in the oven for about 50 minutes, or until the cloves are soft and creamy.
• Spread a little of the baked garlic on the bread and drizzle with olive oil.

1 Cut a small cross in the top of each bulb of garlic. Place the bulbs in a garlic baker, brush with half the olive oil and sprinkle with a little salt and ground black pepper.

2 Place the garlic baker in an unheated oven, set the temperature to 200°C/400°F/Gas 6 and bake the garlic for about 40 minutes. The garlic cloves should be soft and creamy – if not, bake for a further 10 minutes.

3 Place the tomatoes and prawns in a shallow earthenware baking dish. Drizzle over the remaining olive oil, sprinkle with thyme sprigs and season. Place the dish in the oven after the garlic has been cooking for 30 minutes; turn the prawns after 7 minutes.

4 Arrange the garlic, tomatoes and prawns on a warmed serving plate and serve with lemon wedges and plenty of crusty bread.

Energy 183Kcal/761kJ; Protein 11.7g; Carbohydrate 8g, of which sugars 4.3g; Fat 11.8g, of which saturates 1.8g; Cholesterol 98mg; Calcium 53mg; Fibre 2.3g; Sodium 107mg.

TUNA FRITTATA

This is the ultimate meal in a pan – easy to prepare and easy to serve. For a stronger
cheese flavour, try a creamy goat's cheese in place of the soft white cheese.

SERVES 2–3

25g/1oz/2 tbsp butter
15ml/1 tbsp olive oil
1 onion, finely chopped
175g/6oz courgettes (zucchini), halved
  lengthwise and sliced
75g/3oz/1¼ cups brown cap (cremini)
  mushrooms, sliced
50g/2oz asparagus tips
4 eggs, beaten
75g/3oz/⅜ cup soft white (farmer's) cheese
  or ricotta cheese
30ml/2 tbsp chopped fresh thyme
200g/7oz can tuna, in olive oil, drained and
  roughly flaked
115g/4oz cooked, peeled
  prawns (shrimp)
salt and ground black pepper

1 Heat the butter and oil in a non-stick
frying pan. Add the chopped onion and
cook for 3 minutes, then add the sliced
courgettes, mushrooms and asparagus
tips and cook for a further 10 minutes,
or until beginning to soften and brown.

2 Beat together the eggs, soft or ricotta
cheese, chopped thyme and plenty of
seasoning until they are well combined.

3 Stir the tuna into the pan, add the
prawns and season well. Heat through
gently. Pour over the egg mixture and
cook over a gentle heat for 5 minutes.

4 Push the egg away from the sides to
allow the uncooked egg to run on to the
pan. Preheat the grill (broiler) to medium
and grill (broil) the omelette to set and
brown the surface. Serve cut in wedges.

Energy 465Kcal/1935kJ; Protein 39.6g; Carbohydrate 3.9g, of which sugars 2.5g; Fat 32.6g, of which saturates 13g; Cholesterol 435mg; Calcium 174mg; Fibre 1.4g; Sodium 1033mg.

FISH STEW with LEMON GRASS

Lemon grass and ginger give this delicate stew of fish, prawns, new potatoes and broccoli an appetizing aromatic flavour.

SERVES 4

25g/1oz/2 tbsp butter
175g/6oz onions, chopped
20ml/4 tsp plain (all-purpose) flour
400ml/14fl oz/1⅔ cups light fish stock
150ml/¼ pint/⅔ cup white wine
2.5cm/1in piece fresh root ginger, peeled
   and finely chopped
2 lemon grass stalks, trimmed and
   finely chopped
450g/1lb new potatoes, scrubbed and
   halved if necessary
450g/1lb white fish fillets
175g/6oz large, cooked, peeled
   prawns (shrimp)
275g/10oz small broccoli florets
150ml/¼ pint/⅔ cup double (heavy) cream
60ml/4 tbsp chopped fresh garlic chives
salt and ground black pepper
crusty bread, to serve

3 Remove the skin from the fish fillets and cut the fillets into large chunks. Add the chunks of fish to the pan with the prawns, broccoli and cream. Stir gently.

4 Simmer gently for 5 minutes, taking care not to break up the fish. Adjust the seasoning and sprinkle in the chives. Serve with plenty of crusty bread.

1 Melt the butter in a large pan. Add the onions and cook for 3–4 minutes. Stir in the flour and cook for 1 minute.

2 Stir in the stock, wine, ginger, lemon grass and potatoes. Season and bring to the boil. Cover and cook for 15 minutes, or until the potatoes are almost tender.

Energy 515Kcal/2148kJ; Protein 34.9g; Carbohydrate 27.6g, of which sugars 5.9g; Fat 27.4g, of which saturates 16.2g; Cholesterol 202mg; Calcium 131mg; Fibre 3.7g; Sodium 218mg.

SLOW COOKER FISH AND SHELLFISH

Delicious, healthy and perfectly suited to cooking in a slow cooker, fish and shellfish can be used in a fabulous range of dishes. The gentle heat of this method cooks the delicate flesh to perfection every time. Although large whole fish, such as salmon, are too big for the slow cooker, smaller fish, such as herring and red mullet, fillets, fish steaks and shellfish are perfect. Unlike meat, fish cooks relatively quickly in the slow cooker, so is ideal for combining with rice or pasta. It is incredibly versatile and can be cooked in all manner of ways, to make both light and hearty dishes. Try Salmon Risotto with Cucumber for a light and sophisticated summer dish, or comforting Fish Pie as a winter warmer.

CREAMY ANCHOVY and POTATO BAKE

This classic Scandinavian dish of potatoes, onions and anchovies cooked with cream makes a hearty winter lunch or simple supper, served with a refreshing salad. In Norway and Sweden, it is often served as a hot appetizer.

2 Use half of the butter to grease the base and sides of the ceramic cooking pot, and layer half the potatoes and onions in the base of the dish.

3 Drain the anchovies, reserving 15ml/ 1 tbsp of the oil. Cut the anchovies into thin strips and lay these over the potatoes and onions, then layer the remaining potatoes and onions on top.

4 Combine the single cream and anchovy oil in a small jug (pitcher) and season with a little ground black pepper. Pour the mixture evenly over the potatoes and dot the surface with butter.

5 Cover and cook on high for 3½ hours, or until the potatoes and onions are tender. Brown under a hot grill (broiler), if you like, then drizzle over the double cream and sprinkle with parsley and pepper. Serve with fresh crusty bread.

SERVES 4

1kg/2¼lb maincrop potatoes
2 onions
25g/1oz/2 tbsp butter
2 x 50g/2oz cans anchovy fillets
150ml/¼ pint/⅔ cup single (light) cream
150ml/¼ pint/⅔ cup double (heavy) cream
15ml/1 tbsp chopped fresh parsley
ground black pepper
fresh crusty bread, to serve

COOK'S TIP
This recipe can also be served as an appetizer for six, or as a side dish to accompany a main meal.

1 Peel the potatoes and cut into slices slightly thicker than 1cm/½in. Cut the slices into strips slightly more than 1cm/½in wide. Peel the onions and cut into very thin rings.

Energy 378Kcal/1580kJ; Protein 11.3g; Carbohydrate 37.9g, of which sugars 6.4g; Fat 21.2g, of which saturates 11.4g; Cholesterol 54mg; Calcium 1460mg; Fibre 11.5g; Sodium 133mg.

SALMON RISOTTO with CUCUMBER

A classic risotto is time-consuming to make because the stock needs to be added very gradually and requires constant attention from the cook. Here, the wine and stock are added in one go, making it far easier, yet still giving a delicious, creamy texture.

SERVES 4

25g/1oz/2 tbsp butter
small bunch of spring onions (scallions),
   finely sliced
½ cucumber, peeled, seeded
   and chopped
225g/8oz/generous 1 cup easy-cook
   (converted) Italian rice
750ml/1¼ pints/3 cups boiling vegetable
   or fish stock
120ml/4fl oz/½ cup white wine
450g/1lb salmon fillet, skinned
   and diced
45ml/3 tbsp chopped fresh tarragon
salt and ground black pepper

1 Put the butter in the ceramic cooking pot and switch the slow cooker to high. Leave to melt for 15 minutes, then stir in the spring onions and cucumber. Cover and cook for 30 minutes.

2 Add the rice to the pot and stir, then pour in the stock and wine. Cover with the lid and cook for 45 minutes, stirring once halfway through cooking.

3 Stir the diced salmon into the risotto and season with salt and pepper. Cook for a further 15 minutes, or until the rice is tender and the salmon just cooked. Switch off the slow cooker and leave the risotto to stand for 5 minutes.

4 Remove the lid, add the chopped tarragon and mix lightly. Spoon the risotto into individual warmed serving bowls or plates and serve immediately.

COOK'S TIP
Frozen peas can be used instead of cucumber, if you like. These should be defrosted and stirred into the risotto at the same time as the salmon.

Energy 506Kcal/2122kJ; Protein 28.4g; Carbohydrate 51.3g, of which sugars 2.8g; Fat 20g, of which saturates 5.9g; Cholesterol 70mg; Calcium 91mg; Fibre 1.4g; Sodium 266mg.

SPECIAL FISH PIE

Fish pie topped with melting, cheesy breadcrumbs is the ultimate comfort food and is always a firm family favourite. Serve with plenty of lightly steamed green vegetables such as asparagus spears, green beans or sugar snap peas.

SERVES 4

350g/12oz haddock fillet, skinned
30ml/2 tbsp cornflour (cornstarch)
175g/6oz/1 cup drained, canned corn
115g/4oz/1 cup frozen peas, defrosted
115g/4oz peeled cooked prawns (shrimp)
115g/4oz/½ cup cream cheese
150ml/¼ pint/⅔ cup milk
15g/½oz/¼ cup wholemeal (whole-wheat)
   breadcrumbs
50g/2oz/½ cup grated Cheddar cheese
salt and freshly ground black pepper

1 Cut the haddock into bitesize pieces and place in a mixing bowl. Sprinkle with the cornflour and toss thoroughly to coat the pieces evenly.

2 Add the corn, peas and prawns to the coated haddock pieces and mix together well. In a separate mixing bowl, blend together the cream cheese and milk, season with salt and ground black pepper and pour over the fish mixture. Stir well to combine.

3 Spoon the fish mixture into the ceramic cooking pot. Switch the slow cooker to high, cover with the lid and cook for 2 hours.

4 Meanwhile, combine the breadcrumbs and grated cheese. Spoon the mixture evenly over the top of the dish. Remove the ceramic cooking pot from the slow cooker and brown the top under a moderate grill (broiler) for 5 minutes until golden and crisp. Serve hot.

COOK'S TIP
To make a more economical dish, you can leave out the prawns and replace them with the same weight of haddock. Alternatively, to make a more extravagant dish, use more shellfish, replacing some of the haddock with the same weight of scallops and shelled mussels.

Energy 306Kcal/1283kJ; Protein 31.3g; Carbohydrate 12.2g, of which sugars 2.1g; Fat 15.1g, of which saturates 9.2g; Cholesterol 153mg; Calcium 224mg; Fibre 0.6g; Sodium 736mg.

SMOKED TROUT CANNELLONI

This delicious dish makes a great change to the classic meat or spinach and cheese cannelloni that are usually served. You can also buy smoked trout ready-filleted, which can save on preparation time. If you buy fillets you will need only about 225g/8oz.

SERVES 4

25g/1oz/2 tbsp butter, plus extra
    for greasing
1 large onion, finely chopped
400g/14oz can chopped tomatoes
2.5ml/½ tsp dried mixed herbs
1 smoked trout, weighing
    about 400g/14oz
75g/3oz/¾ cup frozen peas, thawed
75g/3oz/1½ cups fresh white breadcrumbs
16 cannelloni tubes
15g/½oz/1½ tbsp freshly grated
    Parmesan cheese
salt and ground black pepper
mixed salad, to serve (optional)

For the sauce
40g/1½oz/3 tbsp butter
40g/1½oz/⅓ cup plain (all-purpose)
    flour
550ml/18fl oz/2½ cups milk
1 bay leaf
freshly grated nutmeg

VARIATION
To make a more economical dish, use a drained 200g/7oz can of tuna in oil in place of the trout.

1 Melt the butter in a frying pan, add the onion and cook gently for about 10 minutes until soft, stirring frequently. Stir in the chopped tomatoes and dried herbs and simmer uncovered for a further 10 minutes, or until the sauce is very thick.

2 Meanwhile, skin the smoked trout using a sharp knife. Carefully flake the flesh and discard all the bones. Add the fish to the tomato sauce, then stir in the peas and breadcrumbs and season with plenty of salt and black pepper.

3 Lightly grease the base and halfway up the sides of the ceramic cooking pot. Carefully spoon the trout filling into the cannelloni tubes and arrange the filled tubes in the base of the slow cooker, placing them side by side.

4 To make the sauce, melt the butter in the pan and add the flour. Cook for 1 minute, stirring, then gradually whisk in the milk and add the bay leaf. Cook over a medium heat, whisking constantly until the sauce thickens, then simmer for 2–3 minutes, continuing to stir. Remove the bay leaf and season to taste with salt, pepper and nutmeg.

5 Pour the sauce over the cannelloni and sprinkle with grated Parmesan. Cover and cook on high or auto for 1 hour.

6 Switch the slow cooker to low or leave on auto and cook for 1–1½ hours, or until the cannelloni is tender. If you like, brown the top under a moderate grill (broiler) before serving. Serve with a mixed salad, if using.

Energy 669Kcal/2811kJ; Protein 41.5g; Carbohydrate 74.5g, of which sugars 15.1g; Fat 24.9g, of which saturates 11.9g; Cholesterol 116mg; Calcium 353mg; Fibre 3.1g; Sodium 390mg.

CANNELLONI SORRENTINA-STYLE

There is more than one way of making cannelloni. For this fresh-tasting dish, sheets of cooked lasagne are rolled around a tomato, ricotta and anchovy filling. You can, of course, use traditional cannelloni tubes, if you prefer.

SERVES 4–6

15ml/1 tbsp olive oil, plus extra for greasing
1 small onion, finely chopped
900g/2lb ripe Italian tomatoes, peeled and finely chopped
2 garlic cloves, crushed
5ml/1 tsp dried mixed herbs
150ml/¼ pint/⅔ cup vegetable stock
150ml/¼ pint/⅔ cup dry white wine
30ml/2 tbsp sun-dried tomato paste
2.5ml/½ tsp sugar
16 dried lasagne sheets
250g/9oz/generous 1 cup ricotta cheese
130g/4½oz packet mozzarella cheese, drained and diced
30ml/2 tbsp shredded fresh basil, plus extra basil leaves to garnish
8 bottled anchovy fillets in olive oil, drained and halved lengthways
50g/2oz/⅔ cup freshly grated Parmesan cheese
salt and ground black pepper

1 Heat the oil in a pan, add the onion and cook gently, stirring, for 5 minutes until softened. Transfer to the ceramic cooking pot and switch on to high. Stir in the tomatoes, garlic and herbs. Season with salt and black pepper to taste, then cover the slow cooker with the lid and cook for 1 hour.

2 Ladle about half of the tomato mixture out of the cooking pot, place in a bowl and set aside to cool.

3 Stir the vegetable stock, white wine, tomato paste and sugar into the tomato mixture remaining in the slow cooker. Cover with the lid and cook for a further hour. Turn off the slow cooker.

4 Meanwhile, cook the lasagne sheets in batches in a pan of salted boiling water for 3 minutes or according to the instructions on the packet. Drain the sheets of lasagne. Separate them, and lay them out on a clean dishtowel until needed.

5 Add the ricotta and mozzarella to the tomato mixture in the bowl. Stir in the shredded fresh basil and season to taste with salt and black pepper. Spread a little of the mixture over each lasagne sheet. Place one halved anchovy fillet across the width of each sheet, close to one of the short ends. Starting from the end with the anchovy, roll up each lasagne sheet to form a tube.

6 Transfer the tomato sauce in the slow cooker to a food processor or blender, and purée until smooth. Wash and dry the ceramic cooking pot, then lightly grease the base and halfway up the sides with a little oil.

7 Spoon about a third of the puréed sauce into the ceramic cooking pot, covering the base evenly. Arrange the filled cannelloni seam-side down on top of the sauce. Spoon the remaining sauce over the top.

8 Sprinkle with the Parmesan. Cover the slow cooker with the lid and cook on high or auto for 1 hour, then switch to low or leave on auto and cook for a further hour until the cannelloni is tender. Brown under the grill (broiler), if you like, then serve garnished with basil.

Energy 546Kcal/2293kJ; Protein 25.5g; Carbohydrate 54.3g, of which sugars 9.7g; Fat 24.1g, of which saturates 13.4g; Cholesterol 58mg; Calcium 301mg; Fibre 3.5g; Sodium 282mg.

TUNA LASAGNE

This delicious, comforting dish is perfect for a family supper or casual entertaining, and is incredibly simple to make. Use pre-cooked sheets of lasagne, breaking them into smaller pieces as necessary to fit the shape of your slow cooker.

SERVES 6

65g/2½oz/5 tbsp butter, plus extra
    for greasing
1 small onion, finely chopped
1 garlic clove, finely chopped
115g/4oz mushrooms, thinly sliced
40g/1½oz/⅓ cup plain (all-purpose)
    flour
50ml/2fl oz/¼ cup dry white wine
150ml/¼ pint/⅔ cup double (heavy) cream
600ml/1 pint/2½ cups milk
45ml/3 tbsp chopped fresh parsley
2 × 200g/7oz cans tuna in oil
2 canned pimientos, cut into strips
115g/4oz/1 cup mozzarella cheese, grated
8–12 sheets pre-cooked lasagne
25g/1oz/3 tbsp freshly grated
    Parmesan cheese
salt and ground black pepper
Italian-style bread, such as ciabatta,
    and green salad, to serve

1 Lightly grease the base and halfway up the sides of the ceramic cooking pot.

2 Melt 25g/1oz/2 tbsp of the butter in a large pan, add the onion and fry gently for 5 minutes until almost soft but not coloured. Add the garlic and mushrooms and cook for a further 3 minutes, stirring occasionally. Tip the vegetables into a bowl and set aside.

3 Melt the remaining 40g/1½oz/3 tbsp of butter in the pan. Sprinkle over the flour and stir in. Turn off the heat, then gradually blend in the wine, followed by the cream and milk. Gently heat, stirring constantly, until the mixture bubbles and thickens. Stir in the parsley and season well with salt and ground black pepper.

4 Reserve 300ml/½ pint/1¼ cups of the sauce, then stir the mushroom mixture into the remaining sauce.

5 Drain the tuna well and tip into a bowl. Flake the fish with a fork, then gently mix in the pimiento strips, grated mozzarella and a little salt and pepper.

6 Spoon a thin layer of the mushroom sauce over the base of the ceramic cooking pot and cover with 2–3 lasagne sheets, breaking them to fit. Sprinkle half of the tuna mixture over the pasta. Spoon half of the remaining sauce evenly over the top and cover with another layer of lasagne sheets. Repeat, ending with a layer of lasagne. Pour over the reserved plain sauce, then sprinkle with the Parmesan cheese.

7 Cover the slow cooker with the lid and cook on low for 2 hours, or until the lasagne is tender.

8 If you like, brown the top of the lasagne under a medium grill (broiler) and serve with bread and a green salad.

Energy 554Kcal/2315kJ; Protein 32.2g; Carbohydrate 28.9g, of which sugars 7.4g; Fat 34.7g, of which saturates 18.5g; Cholesterol 110mg; Calcium 371mg; Fibre 0.6g; Sodium 616mg.

COCONUT SALMON

Salmon is quite a robust fish, and responds well to being cooked with this fragrant blend
of spices, garlic and chilli. Coconut milk adds a mellow touch and a creamy taste.

SERVES 4

15ml/1 tbsp oil
1 onion, finely chopped
2 fresh green chillies, seeded and chopped
2 garlic cloves, crushed
2.5cm/1in piece fresh root ginger, grated
175ml/6fl oz/¾ cup coconut milk
10ml/2 tsp ground cumin
5ml/1 tsp ground coriander
4 salmon steaks, each about 175g/6oz
10ml/2 tsp chilli powder
2.5ml/½ tsp ground turmeric
15ml/1 tbsp white wine vinegar
1.5ml/¼ tsp salt
fresh coriander (cilantro) sprigs, to garnish
rice tossed with spring onions (scallions),
    to serve

VARIATION

Trout fillets go well with spices and can
be used instead of salmon in this dish.

1 Heat the oil in a pan, add the onion,
chillies, garlic and ginger and fry for 5-6
minutes, until fairly soft. Place in a food
processor with 120ml/4fl oz/½ cup of
the coconut milk and blend until smooth.

2 Tip the paste into the ceramic cooking
pot. Stir in 5ml/1 tsp of the cumin, the
ground coriander and the rest of the
coconut milk. Cover and cook on high
for 1½ hours.

3 About 20 minutes before the end of
cooking time, arrange the salmon steaks
in a single layer in a shallow glass dish.
Combine the remaining 5ml/1 tsp cumin,
the chilli powder, turmeric, vinegar and
salt in a bowl to make a paste. Rub the
mixture over the salmon steaks and
leave to marinate at room temperature
while the sauce finishes cooking.

4 Add the salmon steaks to the sauce,
arranging them in a single layer and
spoon some of the coconut sauce over
the top to keep the fish moist while it
cooks. Cover with the lid, reduce the
temperature to low and cook for
45 minutes–1 hour, or until the salmon
is opaque and tender.

5 Transfer the fish to a serving dish,
spoon over the sauce and garnish with
fresh coriander. Serve with the rice.

Energy 363Kcal/1512kJ; Protein 35.9g; Carbohydrate 5.1g, of which sugars 4.2g; Fat 22.2g, of which saturates 3.8g; Cholesterol 88mg; Calcium 59mg; Fibre 0.5g; Sodium 275mg.

POACHED FISH in SPICY TOMATO SAUCE

This traditional Jewish dish is known as Samak. *It is usually served with flatbreads, such as pitta or matzos, but you can serve it with plain boiled rice or noodles, if you prefer.*

SERVES 4

15ml/1 tbsp vegetable or olive oil
1 onion, finely chopped
150ml/¼ pint/⅔ cup passata (bottled
    strained tomatoes)
75ml/2½fl oz/⅓ cup boiling fish
    or vegetable stock
2 garlic cloves, crushed
1 small red chilli, seeded and
    finely chopped
pinch of ground ginger
pinch of curry powder
pinch of ground cumin
pinch of ground turmeric
seeds from 1 cardamom pod
juice of 1 lemon, plus extra if needed
900g/2lb mixed firm white fish fillets
30ml/2 tbsp chopped fresh
    coriander (cilantro)
30ml/2 tbsp chopped fresh parsley
salt and ground black pepper

1 Heat the oil in a frying pan, add the onion and cook gently, stirring, for 10 minutes until soft but not coloured.

2 Transfer the onions to the ceramic cooking pot, then stir in the passata, stock, garlic, chilli, ginger, curry powder, cumin, turmeric, cardamom, lemon juice, salt and pepper. Cover and cook on high or auto for 1½ hours, until the mixture is just simmering.

3 Add the fish to the pot, cover and continue cooking on auto or low for 45 minutes–1 hour, or until the fish is tender. (The flesh should flake easily.)

4 Lift the fish on to warmed serving plates. Stir the fresh herbs into the sauce, then taste and adjust the seasoning, adding more lemon juice, if necessary. Spoon the sauce over the fish and serve immediately.

Energy 224Kcal/942kJ; Protein 42g; Carbohydrate 4.1g, of which sugars 3.1g; Fat 4.4g, of which saturates 0.6g; Cholesterol 104mg; Calcium 34mg; Fibre 0.8g; Sodium 151mg.

HOKI BALLS in TOMATO SAUCE

This simple fish dish is ideal for serving to young children because there is no risk of bones. For adults, it can be spiced up with a dash of chilli sauce. It is low in fat and therefore ideal for anyone on a low-fat or low-cholesterol diet.

2 Meanwhile, cut the fish into large chunks and place in a food processor. Add the breadcrumbs and the chives or spring onions and season with salt and pepper. Process until the fish is finely chopped, but still has some texture.

3 Divide the mixture into 16 even-size pieces, then roll them into balls with damp hands. Put the fish balls on a plate and chill in the refrigerator until needed.

4 About 30 minutes before the end of the sauce's cooking time, take the fish balls out of the refrigerator and leave them to stand at room temperature.

5 Add the fishballs to the sauce in a single layer. Cook for 1 hour on high, then reduce the temperature to low and cook for a further hour, or until the fish balls are thoroughly cooked. Serve hot, garnished with chives and accompanied by steamed green vegetables.

SERVES 4

400g/14oz can chopped tomatoes
50g/2oz button mushrooms, sliced
450g/1lb hoki or other firm white fish
    fillets, skinned
15g/½oz/¼ cup wholemeal
    (whole-wheat) breadcrumbs
30ml/2 tbsp chopped fresh chives or
    spring onions (scallions)
salt and ground black pepper
chopped fresh chives, to garnish
steamed green vegetables, to serve

COOK'S TIP
If hoki is not available, you can use the same weight of cod, haddock or whiting.

1 Pour the chopped tomatoes into the ceramic cooking pot, then add the sliced mushrooms and a little salt and ground black pepper. Cover with the lid, switch the slow cooker to high and cook for about 2 hours.

Energy 116Kcal/490kJ; Protein 22.2g; Carbohydrate 4.6g, of which sugars 2.9g; Fat 1.0g, of which saturates 0.1g; Cholesterol 52mg; Calcium 27mg; Fibre 1.0g; Sodium 125mg.

MIXED FISH JAMBALAYA

As with the Spanish paella, the ingredients used to make this classic Creole dish can be varied according to what is available. The name Jambalaya is thought to have come from the French word for ham – jambon – and the Creole word for rice – à la ya.

SERVES 4

30ml/2 tbsp oil
6 rashers (strips) rinded smoked streaky
    (fatty) bacon, chopped
I onion, chopped
2 sticks celery, sliced
2 garlic cloves, crushed
5ml/I tsp cayenne pepper
2 bay leaves
5ml/I tsp dried oregano
2.5ml/½ tsp dried thyme
4 tomatoes, skinned, seeded and chopped
750ml/1¼ pints/3 cups boiling vegetable
    or fish stock
I5ml/I tbsp tomato purée (paste)
300g/10oz/1½ cups easy-cook
    (converted) rice
225g/8oz firm white fish, such as haddock,
    skinned, boned and cubed
115g/4oz cooked prawns (shrimp)
salt and ground black pepper
4 spring onions (scallions) and 4 cooked
    prawns (shrimp) in their shells,
    to garnish

I Heat the oil in a frying pan and cook the bacon over a medium-high heat for 2 minutes. Reduce the heat, add the onion and celery and cook for a further 5–10 minutes, or until soft and beginning to turn brown.

2 Transfer the mixture to the ceramic cooking pot and switch the slow cooker to high. Add the garlic, cayenne pepper, bay leaves, oregano, thyme, tomatoes, boiling stock and tomato purée. Stir well to mix, then cover with the lid and cook for about I hour.

3 Sprinkle the rice over the tomato mixture, followed by the cubes of fish. Season with salt and pepper and stir. Re-cover and cook for 45 minutes.

4 Add the prawns and stir, then cook for 15 minutes, or until the fish and rice are tender and most of the liquid has been absorbed. Serve garnished with spring onions and prawns in their shells.

COOK'S TIP
If you like a really hot, spicy bite to your jambalaya, serve with a little hot chilli sauce for sprinkling over at the table.

Energy 243Kcal/1015kJ; Protein 23.2g; Carbohydrate 6.5g, of which sugars 5.4g; Fat 14g, of which saturates 3.4g; Cholesterol 126mg; Calcium 64mg; Fibre 1.6g; Sodium 1303mg.

RED MULLET BRAISED on a BED of FENNEL

These pretty pink fish have a wonderful firm flesh and sweet flavour. They are usually cooked whole, but you can remove the heads if there is not enough room in your slow cooker to fit them all in a single layer. Other small whole fish, such as sardines, or fish fillets, such as salmon, cod and hake, can also be cooked in this way.

SERVES 4

10ml/2 tsp fennel seeds
5ml/1 tsp chopped fresh thyme
30ml/2 tbsp chopped fresh parsley
1 clove garlic, crushed
10ml/2 tsp olive oil
4 red mullet, weighing about
    225g/8oz each
lemon wedges, to serve

For the fennel
8 ripe tomatoes
2 fennel bulbs
30ml/2 tbsp olive oil
120ml/4fl oz/½ cup boiling fish
    or vegetable stock
10ml/2 tsp balsamic vinegar
salt and ground black pepper

1 Crush the fennel seeds using a mortar and pestle, then work in the chopped thyme and parsley, garlic and olive oil.

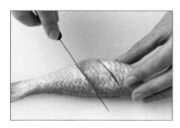

2 Clean and scale the fish and trim off the fins. Use a sharp knife to make deep slashes on each side of the fish.

3 Push the herb paste into the cuts in the fish and spread any excess inside the body cavities. Place the fish on a plate, loosely cover with clear film (plastic wrap) and leave to marinate. On a warm day, it is best to place the marinating fish in the refrigerator and then bring to room temperature about 20 minutes before cooking.

4 Meanwhile, prepare the bed of fennel. Put the tomatoes in a heatproof bowl, add boiling water to cover and leave to stand for 1 minute. Drain and cool under cold running water and peel off the skins. Quarter the tomatoes, seed and cut into small dice.

5 Trim the feathery fronds from the fennel (these can be kept for garnishing), then cut the bulbs into 1cm/½ in slices from the top to the root end.

6 Heat the olive oil in a frying pan and cook the fennel slices over a medium heat for about 10 minutes, or until just starting to colour.

7 Transfer the fennel to the ceramic cooking pot. Add the diced tomatoes, hot stock, balsamic vinegar, salt and pepper, cover with the lid and cook on high for 2 hours.

8 Give the fennel sauce a stir, then place the red mullet on top in a single layer. Cover and cook for 1 hour, or until the fish is cooked through and tender. Serve immediately, with lemon wedges for squeezing over.

COOK'S TIP
Red mullet is highly perishable, so be sure to buy very fresh fish. Look for specimens with bright eyes and skin, and that feel firm. The liver is considered a delicacy, so if your fishmonger will clean them for you, ask for the liver along with the fish.

Energy 194Kcal/816kJ; Protein 26.5g; Carbohydrate 4.2g, of which sugars 4.1g; Fat 8.1g, of which saturates 1.2g; Cholesterol 63mg; Calcium 95mg; Fibre 3.0g; Sodium 239mg.

SKATE with TOMATO and OLIVE SAUCE

The classic way of serving skate is with a browned butter sauce, but here it is given a Mediterranean twist with tomatoes, olives, orange and a dash of Pernod. If time allows, soak the skate in salted water for a few hours before cooking, to firm up the flesh.

SERVES 4

15ml/1 tbsp olive oil
1 small onion, finely chopped
2 fresh thyme sprigs
grated rind of ½ orange
15ml/1 tbsp Pernod
400g/14oz can chopped tomatoes
50g/2oz/1 cup stuffed green olives
1.5ml/¼ tsp caster (superfine) sugar
4 small skate wings
plain (all-purpose) flour, for coating
salt and ground black pepper
15ml/1 tbsp basil leaves, to garnish
lime wedges, to serve

COOK'S TIP
Pernod gives this dish a deliciously distinctive taste of aniseed, but for those who don't like the flavour, use 15ml/1 tbsp vermouth instead.

1 Heat the oil in a pan, add the onion and fry gently for 10 minutes. Stir in the thyme and orange rind and cook for 1 minute. Add the Pernod, tomatoes, olives, sugar and a little salt and pepper, and heat until just below boiling point.

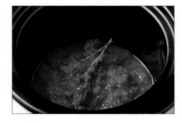

2 Tip the mixture into the ceramic pot and switch on to high. Cover with the lid and cook for 1½ hours.

3 Meanwhile, rinse the skate wings under cold water and pat dry on kitchen paper. Sprinkle the flour on a large, flat dish and season well with salt and ground black pepper. Coat each skate wing in the flour, shaking off any excess, then place on top of the tomato sauce.

4 Re-cover the ceramic cooking pot and reduce the temperature to low. Cook for 1½–2 hours, or until the skate is cooked and flakes easily.

5 Place the fish on to warmed serving plates and spoon over the sauce. Sprinkle over the basil leaves and serve with a wedge of lime for squeezing over.

Energy 144Kcal/606kJ; Protein 15.5g; Carbohydrate 8.1g, of which sugars 3.7g; Fat 4.8g, of which saturates 0.7g; Cholesterol 35mg; Calcium 37mg; Fibre 1.4g; Sodium 366mg.

HADDOCK with SPICY PUY LENTILS

Dark brown Puy lentils have a delicate taste and texture and hold their shape during cooking, which makes them particularly good for slow cooker dishes. Red chilli pepper and ground cumin add a hint of heat and spice without overpowering the flavour of the fish.

SERVES 4

175g/6oz/¾ cup Puy lentils
600ml/1 pint/2½ cups near-boiling
    vegetable stock
30ml/2 tbsp olive oil
1 onion, finely chopped
2 celery sticks, finely chopped
1 red chilli, halved, seeded
    and finely chopped
2.5ml/½ tsp ground cumin
four thick 150g/5oz pieces of haddock
    fillet or steak
10ml/2 tsp lemon juice
25g/1oz/2 tbsp butter, softened
5ml/1 tsp finely grated lemon rind
salt and ground black pepper
lemon wedges, to garnish

1 Put the lentils in a sieve (strainer) and rinse under cold running water. Drain well, then tip into the ceramic cooking pot. Pour over the hot vegetable stock, cover with the lid and switch the slow cooker on to high.

2 Heat the oil in a frying pan, add the onion and cook gently for 8 minutes. Stir in the celery, chilli and cumin, and cook for a further 2 minutes, or until soft but not coloured. Add the mixture to the lentils, stir, re-cover and cook for about 2½ hours.

3 Meanwhile, rinse the haddock pieces and pat dry on kitchen paper. Sprinkle them with the lemon juice. In a clean bowl, beat together the butter, lemon rind, salt and a generous amount of ground black pepper.

4 Put the haddock on top of the lentils, then dot the lemon butter over the top. Cover and cook for 45 minutes–1 hour, or until the fish flakes easily, the lentils are tender and most of the stock has been absorbed. Serve immediately, garnished with the lemon wedges.

COOK'S TIP
Any firm white fish can be cooked in this way. Both cod and swordfish give particularly good results.

Energy 366Kcal/1538kJ; Protein 38.9g; Carbohydrate 25.2g, of which sugars 3.2g; Fat 12.8g, of which saturates 4.3g; Cholesterol 82mg; Calcium 64mg; Fibre 4.7g; Sodium 353mg.

LEMON SOLE and PROSCIUTTO ROULADES

In this elegant dish, prosciutto and delicately textured lemon sole are rolled around a subtle herb and lemon stuffing. Serve this dish for a special dinner party with new potatoes tossed in butter, and lightly steamed asparagus.

2 Remove most of the fat from the prosciutto. Lay two overlapping slices on a board and place a sole fillet on top, skinned side up.

3 Mix the walnuts, breadcrumbs, parsley, eggs, lemon rind and pepper together and spread a quarter of the mixture over the fish fillet, then press down gently. Starting at the thicker end of the fillet, carefully roll up the fish and ham to enclose the filling.

4 Repeat with the remaining prosciutto, fish and filling, then secure each roll with a cocktail stick (toothpick).

5 Place the fish seam-side down in the ceramic cooking pot. Cover with the lid, then turn the temperature down to low. Cook for 1½–2 hours, or until the fish flakes easily. Remove the cocktail sticks and serve straight away with freshly cooked vegetables.

SERVES 4

10ml/2 tsp unsalted (sweet) butter,
    at room temperature
120ml/4fl oz/½ cup dry white wine
4 large lemon sole fillets, about
    150g/5oz each
8 thin slices of prosciutto, about
    130g/4½oz in total
50g/2oz/½ cup chopped toasted walnuts
75g/3oz/1½ cups fresh white breadcrumbs
30ml/2 tbsp finely chopped fresh parsley
2 eggs, lightly beaten
5ml/1 tsp finely grated lemon rind
ground black pepper
new potatoes and steamed green
    vegetables, to serve

1 Smear the inside of the ceramic cooking pot with the butter. Pour in the wine and switch the slow cooker to high. Skin the fish fillets and check that all the bones have been removed, then pat dry with kitchen paper.

Energy 363Kcal/1521kJ; Protein 38g; Carbohydrate 9.6g, of which sugars 1.5g; Fat 17.3g, of which saturates 3.6g; Cholesterol 201mg; Calcium 134mg; Fibre 0.8g; Sodium 714mg.

BASQUE-STYLE TUNA

In Spain, this traditional fisherman's stew is known as marmitako. *It used to be cooked at sea on the fishing boats, and takes its name from the cooking pot, known in France as a* marmite. *The rich flavourings go perfectly with the robust taste of chunky tuna.*

SERVES 4

30ml/2 tbsp olive oil
1 onion, finely chopped
1 clove garlic, finely chopped
75ml/2½fl oz/⅓ cup white wine,
    preferably Spanish
150ml/¼ pint/⅔ cup boiling fish
    or vegetable stock
200g/7oz can chopped tomatoes
5ml/1 tsp paprika
2.5ml/½ tsp dried crushed chillies
450g/1lb waxy new potatoes, cut into
    1cm/½in chunks
1 red and 1 yellow (bell) pepper, seeded
    and chopped
1 small sprig of fresh rosemary
1 bay leaf
450g/1lb fresh tuna, cut into 2.5cm/
    1in chunks
salt and ground black pepper
crusty bread, to serve

3 Stir the chunks of tuna into the sauce. Cover and cook for 15–20 minutes, or until the fish is firm and opaque.

4 Remove the rosemary and bay leaf, then ladle the stew into warmed dishes, grind over a little more black pepper and serve with crusty bread.

1 Heat the oil in a large frying pan, add the onion and fry gently for 10 minutes until soft and translucent. Stir in the garlic, followed by the wine, stock, tomatoes, paprika and chillies. Bring to just below boiling point, then carefully pour the mixture into the ceramic cooking pot.

2 Add the chunks of potato, red and yellow pepper, rosemary and bay leaf to the pot and stir to combine. Cover the slow cooker with the lid and cook on high for 2–2½ hours, or until the potatoes are just tender, then season the sauce to taste with salt and a little ground black pepper.

Energy 297Kcal/1256kJ; Protein 30.1g; Carbohydrate 27.5g, of which sugars 9.6g; Fat 6.g, of which saturates 1.2g; Cholesterol 57mg; Calcium 39mg; Fibre 3.2g; Sodium 397mg.

COD with CARAMELIZED ONIONS

After very long slow cooking, sliced onions become caramelized and turn a deep golden colour with a fabulously rich, sweet flavour, which is further enhanced here by the addition of balsamic vinegar. Tangy caper and coriander butter adds a fresh, sharp contrast.

SERVES 4

40g/1½oz/3 tbsp butter
10ml/2 tsp olive oil
1.2kg/2½lb yellow onions, peeled
    and finely sliced
5ml/1 tsp caster (superfine) sugar
30ml/2 tbsp balsamic vinegar
30ml/2 tbsp vegetable stock, white wine
    or water
4 x 150g/5oz thick cod fillets

For the butter
115g/4oz/½ cup butter, softened
30ml/2 tbsp capers, drained and chopped
30ml/2 tbsp chopped fresh
    coriander (cilantro)
salt and ground black pepper

1 Put the butter and oil in the ceramic cooking pot and heat on high for about 15 minutes, until melted.

2 Add the sliced onions and stir to coat well in the butter and oil. Cover the pot with the lid, then place a folded dish towel over the top to retain all the heat. Cook for 2 hours, stirring halfway through cooking time.

3 Sprinkle the sugar over the onions and stir well to mix. Replace the lid and folded dish towel and cook on high for 4 hours, stirring two or three times, to ensure the onions colour evenly. At the end of the cooking time, they should be a dark golden colour.

4 Add the vinegar to the onions and stir in the stock, wine or water. Cover again and cook for 1 hour; the onions should now be fairly tender. Season with a little salt and pepper and stir well. Arrange the cod fillets on top of the onions and cook for a final 45 minutes–1 hour, or until the fish flakes easily.

5 Meanwhile, make the caper and coriander butter. Cream the butter in a small bowl until soft, then beat in the capers, coriander, salt and pepper. Roll up the butter in foil, clear film (plastic wrap) or greaseproof (waxed) paper to form a short log shape, twisting the ends to secure them. Chill in the refrigerator or freezer until firm.

6 To serve, spoon the onions and fish on to warmed serving plates. Slice off discs of the butter and top each piece of fish with one or two slices. Serve immediately, with the butter melting over the hot fish.

Energy 534Kcal/2213kJ; Protein 31.3g; Carbohydrate 25g, of which sugars 18.1g; Fat 35g, of which saturates 20.6g; Cholesterol 152mg; Calcium 96mg; Fibre 4.2g; Sodium 334mg.

SWORDFISH in BARBECUE SAUCE

This is an ideal way to cook any firm fish steaks. The warmly spiced smoky sauce goes particularly well with meaty fish, such as swordfish, shark and tuna. Choose smaller, thicker fish steaks rather than large, thinner ones, so that they will fit in the slow cooker.

SERVES 4

15ml/1 tbsp sunflower oil
1 small onion, very finely chopped
1 garlic clove, crushed
2.5ml/½ tsp chilli powder
15ml/1 tbsp Worcestershire sauce
15ml/1 tbsp soft light brown sugar
15ml/1 tbsp balsamic vinegar
15ml/1 tbsp American mustard
150ml/¼ pint/⅔ cup tomato juice
4 swordfish steaks, about 115g/4oz each
salt and ground black pepper
fresh flat leaf parsley, to garnish
boiled or steamed rice, to serve

1 Heat the oil in a frying pan, add the onion and cook gently for 10 minutes, until soft. Stir in the garlic and chilli powder and cook for a few seconds, then add the Worcestershire sauce, sugar, vinegar, mustard and tomato juice. Heat gently, stirring, until nearly boiling.

2 Pour half the sauce into the ceramic cooking pot. Rinse the swordfish steaks, pat dry on kitchen paper and arrange in a single layer on top of the sauce. Top with the remaining sauce.

3 Cover the slow cooker with a lid and switch on to high. Cook for 2–3 hours, or until the fish is tender and cooked.

4 Carefully transfer the fish to warmed serving plates and spoon the barbecue sauce over the top. Garnish with sprigs of flat-leaf parsley and serve immediately with boiled or steamed rice.

COOK'S TIP
For a really smoky barbecue flavour use a crushed dried chipotle chilli instead of the chilli powder.

Energy 158Kcal/670kJ; Protein 27.3g; Carbohydrate 4.9g, of which sugars 4.5g; Fat 3.5g, of which saturates 0.6g; Cholesterol 59mg; Calcium 21mg; Fibre 0.2g; Sodium 414mg.

SPINACH and NUT STUFFED HERRINGS

It is difficult to cook large whole fish in a slow cooker, but smaller fish, such as sardines and herrings, are ideal. Their slightly oily flesh is perfectly suited to slow cooking, too, because it helps to keep the fish wonderfully moist.

SERVES 4

40g/1½oz/3 tbsp unsalted (sweet) butter
5ml/1 tsp sunflower oil
25g/1oz/¼ cup pine nuts
1 small onion, finely chopped
175g/6oz frozen spinach, thawed
50g/2oz/1 cup white breadcrumbs
25g/1oz/⅓ cup grated Parmesan cheese
pinch of freshly grated nutmeg
75ml/5 tbsp fish or vegetable stock
    or white wine
4 small herrings, heads removed,
    and boned
salt and ground black pepper
lemon wedges, to serve

1 Heat 25g/1oz/2 tbsp of the butter and sunflower oil in a frying pan until melted. Add the pine nuts and gently fry for 3–4 minutes until golden. Lift them from the pan with a slotted spoon, leaving the fat behind, and place in a mixing bowl.

2 Add the finely chopped onion to the pan and cook gently for 10 minutes, stirring frequently, until soft.

3 Meanwhile, place the thawed spinach in a fine sieve (strainer) and press out as much liquid as possible. (Use your hands to squeeze out the liquid, or press firmly with the back of a spoon.)

VARIATIONS
• Other kinds of nuts can be used in place of pine nuts in the stuffing. Try chopped hazelnuts or walnuts instead.
• As an alternative to nuts, add 15ml/1 tbsp chopped dried apricots to the stuffing.

4 Put the onion and spinach in the mixing bowl with the pine nuts and add the breadcrumbs, cheese, nutmeg, salt and pepper. Mix the ingredients with a fork until thoroughly combined.

5 Smear the remaining 15g/½oz/1 tbsp of butter over the base of the ceramic cooking pot and pour in the stock or wine. Cover with the lid and switch the slow cooker on to high.

6 Using a sharp knife, make three shallow cuts down each side of the fish, then spoon the stuffing into the cavities, packing it in quite firmly. Bring the edges of the fish together and secure with wooden cocktail sticks (toothpicks).

7 Arrange the fish on the base of the ceramic cooking pot in a single layer. Cover the pot with the lid and cook for 1½–2½ hours, or until the fish is cooked. (Test the flesh with a fork; it should flake easily when ready.)

8 Carefully lift the stuffed fish out of the slow cooker on to warmed serving plates, and serve with lemon wedges.

COOK'S TIP
This dish is perfect for a simple, tasty supper, but it is great for entertaining, too. Serve with a tasty couscous salad tossed with plenty of herbs and raisins. The sweetness of the dried fruit goes particularly well with the spinach and pine nut stuffing, and complements the rich flavour of the fish.

Energy 351Kcal/1462kJ; Protein 24g; Carbohydrate 7.6g, of which sugars 1.9g; Fat 23.9g, of which saturates 6.9g; Cholesterol 78mg; Calcium 619mg; Fibre 1.5g; Sodium 624mg.

NORTHERN THAI FISH CURRY

Thin, soupy, strongly flavoured curries are typical of the northern region of Thailand. Fragrant lemon grass, zesty galangal and salty Thai fish sauce come together to give this dish its characteristic Thai flavour. Serve with lots of sticky rice to soak up the juices.

5 Add the shallots, garlic, galangal or ginger, lemon grass, chilli flakes, fish sauce and sugar to the pot and stir to combine. Cover with the lid and cook for 2 hours.

6 Add the cubes of salmon to the stock and cook for 15 minutes. Turn off the slow cooker and leave to stand for a further 10–15 minutes, or until the fish is cooked through. Serve immediately.

SERVES 4

450g/1lb salmon fillet
475ml/16fl oz/2 cups near-boiling
   vegetable stock
4 shallots, very finely chopped
1 garlic clove, crushed
2.5cm/1in piece fresh galangal or ginger,
   finely chopped
1 lemon grass stalk, finely chopped
2.5ml/½ tsp dried chilli flakes
15ml/1 tbsp Thai fish sauce
5ml/1 tsp palm sugar or light muscovado
   (brown) sugar

COOK'S TIP
Allow the fish to return to room temperature before adding to the stock, so that the temperature of the liquid doesn't fall below simmering point.

1 Wrap the salmon fillet in clear film (plastic wrap) and place in the freezer for 30–40 minutes to firm up slightly.

2 Unwrap the fish, and carefully remove and discard the skin. Using a sharp knife, cut the fish into 2.5cm/1in cubes and remove any stray bones with your fingers or a pair of tweezers.

3 Place the cubed fish in a bowl, cover with clear film (plastic wrap) and leave to stand at room temperature.

4 Meanwhile, pour the hot vegetable stock into the ceramic cooking pot and switch the slow cooker to high.

Energy 216Kcal/902kJ; Protein 23.2g; Carbohydrate 2.7g, of which sugars 2.2g; Fat 12.6g, of which saturates 2.1g; Cholesterol 56mg; Calcium 30mg; Fibre 0.2g; Sodium 522mg.

GREEN FISH CURRY

Fresh-tasting, spicy curries made with coconut milk are a classic of Thai cuisine. This slow-cooker version of green curry uses desiccated coconut and cream to give a really rich taste and texture, which is offset by the generous use of spices, chilli and fragrant herbs.

SERVES 4

I onion, chopped
I large fresh green chilli, halved, seeded
  and chopped, plus extra slices to
  garnish
I garlic clove, crushed
50g/2oz/½ cup cashew nuts
2.5ml/½ tsp fennel seeds
30ml/2 tbsp desiccated (dry unsweetened
  shredded) coconut
150ml/¼ pint/⅔ cup water
30ml/2 tbsp vegetable oil
1.5ml/¼ tsp cumin seeds
1.5ml/¼ tsp ground coriander
1.5ml/¼ tsp ground cumin
150ml/¼ pint/⅔ cup double (heavy) cream
4 white fish fillets, such as cod or
  haddock, skinned
1.5ml/¼ tsp ground turmeric
30ml/2 tbsp lime juice
salt
45ml/3 tbsp chopped fresh coriander
  (cilantro), plus extra to garnish
boiled rice, to serve

I Place the onion, chilli, garlic, cashew nuts, fennel seeds and desiccated coconut in a food processor with 45ml/ 3 tbsp of the water and blend to make a smooth paste. Alternatively, work the dry ingredients to a paste in a mortar with a pestle, then stir in the water.

2 Heat the oil in a frying pan and fry the cumin seeds for I minute, until they give off their aroma. Add the coconut paste and fry for 5 minutes, then stir in the ground coriander, cumin and remaining water. Bring to the boil, then let the mixture bubble for I minute.

3 Transfer the mixture to the ceramic cooking pot. Stir in the cream, cover with the lid and switch the slow cooker to high. Cook for 1½ hours.

COOK'S TIP
Do not leave the fish to marinate for longer than 15 minutes because the texture will be spoilt.

4 Towards the end of cooking time, prepare and marinate the fish. Cut the fillets into 5cm/2in chunks and put them in a glass bowl. Combine the turmeric, lime juice and a pinch of salt in a separate bowl and pour it over the fish. Use your hands to rub it into the fish. Cover with clear film (plastic wrap) and leave to marinate for 15 minutes.

5 Stir the fish into the sauce, re-cover and cook for 30 minutes–I hour, or until the fish flakes easily. Stir in the coriander. Spoon the curry into a warmed bowls. Garnish with chopped coriander and sliced green chilli, and serve with rice.

Energy 511Kcal/2118kJ; Protein 36.1g; Carbohydrate 6.4g, of which sugars 3.9g; Fat 37.9g, of which saturates 18.8g; Cholesterol 132mg; Calcium 50mg; Fibre 2g; Sodium 153mg.

ONE-POT AND CLAY-POT FISH AND SHELLFISH

For a healthy, speedy meal with superb flavour, fish and shellfish are the perfect choice. Cooking on top of the stove means you can check the dish frequently, and serve it the moment it is ready. Italian Fish Stew or Seafood Pie with Rösti Topping would make a fine dish for a family meal, Seafood Risotto is a good choice for an impromptu supper with friends, while a more formal dinner would provide the perfect opportunity for trying Octopus and Red Wine Stew, Fillets of Brill in Red Wine Sauce or a colourful Seafood Paella.

OCTOPUS and RED WINE STEW

*Fresh octopus can be quite tricky to prepare so unless you're happy to clean and prepare
it for this traditional Greek dish, buy one that's ready for cooking.*

SERVES 4

900g/2lb prepared octopus
450g/1lb onions, sliced
2 bay leaves
450g/1lb ripe tomatoes
60ml/4 tbsp olive oil
4 garlic cloves, crushed
5ml/1 tsp sugar
15ml/1 tbsp chopped fresh oregano
    or rosemary
30ml/2 tbsp chopped fresh parsley
150ml/¼ pint/⅔ cup red wine
30ml/2 tbsp red wine vinegar
chopped fresh herbs, to garnish
warm bread and pine nuts, to serve

COOK'S TIP

The octopus, along with cuttlefish and
squid, is a member of the mollusc family –
their main shared characteristic is that
they have no shell. Octopus can be very
tough, so it needs long, slow cooking to
tenderize it.

1 Put the octopus in a large pan of
gently simmering water with one-quarter
of the onions and the bay leaves. Cover
the pan and cook gently for 1 hour.

2 While the octopus is cooking, plunge
the tomatoes into boiling water for
30 seconds, then refresh in cold water.
Peel away the skins and chop roughly.

3 Drain the octopus and, using a small
sharp knife, cut it into bitesize pieces.
Discard the head.

4 Heat the oil in the pan and fry the
octopus, the remaining onions and the
garlic for 3 minutes. Add the tomatoes,
sugar, herbs, wine and vinegar and cook,
stirring, for 5 minutes.

5 Cover the pan and cook over the
lowest possible heat for about 1½ hours
until the red wine and tomato sauce is
thickened and the octopus is tender.
To serve, garnish with fresh herbs and
serve with plenty of warm bread, and
pine nuts to scatter on top.

Energy 371Kcal/1556kJ; Protein 42.5g; Carbohydrate 12.5g, of which sugars 9.9g; Fat 14.5g, of which saturates 2.4g; Cholesterol 108mg; Calcium 113mg; Fibre 2.7g; Sodium 16mg.

ITALIAN FISH STEW

Italians are renowned for enjoying good food and this stew is a veritable feast of fish and shellfish in a delicious tomato broth — ideal for a family lunch.

SERVES 4

30ml/2 tbsp olive oil
1 onion, thinly sliced
a few saffron threads
5ml/1 tsp dried thyme
large pinch of cayenne pepper
2 garlic cloves, finely chopped
2 x 400g/14oz cans tomatoes, drained
    and chopped
175ml/6fl oz/¾ cup dry white wine
2 litres/3½ pints/8 cups hot fish stock
350g/12oz white, skinless fish fillets, such
    as haddock or cod, cut into pieces
450g/1lb monkfish, cut into pieces
450g/1lb mussels, scrubbed
225g/8oz small squid, cleaned and cut
    into rings
30ml/2 tbsp chopped fresh basil
    or parsley
salt and ground black pepper
thickly sliced bread, to serve

1 Heat the olive oil in a large, heavy pan. Add the onion, saffron threads, thyme, cayenne pepper and salt, to taste. Stir well and cook over a low heat for 10 minutes, until the onion is soft. Add the garlic and cook for 1 minute more.

2 Stir in the chopped tomatoes, dry white wine and hot fish stock. Bring to the boil and boil for 1 minute, then reduce the heat and simmer gently for 15 minutes.

COOK'S TIP

Cayenne pepper has quite a hot, spicy flavour and was originally made from a type of chilli from the Cayenne region of French Guiana. It should be used sparingly.

3 Add the fish pieces to the tomato mixture in the pan and stir gently. Simmer the stew over a low heat for a further 3 minutes.

4 Add the mussels and squid rings and simmer for about 2 minutes, until the mussels open. Discard any that remain closed. Stir in the basil or parsley and season to taste. Ladle into warmed soup bowls and serve with bread.

Energy 337Kcal/1423kJ; Protein 49.8g; Carbohydrate 8.3g, of which sugars 7.3g; Fat 8.8g, of which saturates 1.5g; Cholesterol 196mg; Calcium 112mg; Fibre 2.2g; Sodium 226mg.

GOAN FISH CASSEROLE

The cooking of Goa is a mixture of Portuguese and Indian; the addition of tamarind gives a slightly sour note to the spicy coconut sauce.

SERVES 4

7.5ml/1½ tsp ground turmeric
5ml/1 tsp salt
450g/1lb monkfish fillet, cut into
    eight pieces
15ml/1 tbsp lemon juice
5ml/1 tsp cumin seeds
5ml/1 tsp coriander seeds
5ml/1 tsp black peppercorns
1 garlic clove, chopped
5cm/2in piece fresh root ginger,
    finely chopped
25g/1oz tamarind paste
150ml/¼ pint/⅔ cup hot water
30ml/2 tbsp vegetable oil
2 onions, halved and sliced lengthways
400ml/14fl oz/1⅔ cups coconut milk
4 mild green chillies, seeded and cut into
    thin strips
16 large raw prawns (shrimp), peeled
30ml/2 tbsp chopped fresh coriander
    (cilantro) leaves, to garnish

2 Put the cumin seeds, coriander seeds and black peppercorns in a blender or small food processor and blend to a powder. Add the garlic and ginger and process for a few seconds more.

5 Add the fish fillets to the oil remaining in the frying pan, and fry briefly over a high heat, turning them to seal on all sides. Remove the fish from the pan and place on top of the onions.

6 Add the ground spice mixture to the frying pan and cook over a medium heat, stirring constantly, for 1–2 minutes. Stir in the tamarind liquid, coconut milk and chilli strips and bring to the boil. Pour the sauce into the earthenware dish to coat the fish completely.

3 Preheat the oven to 200°C/400°F/ Gas 6. Mix the tamarind paste with the hot water and set aside.

1 Mix together the ground turmeric and salt in a small bowl. Place the monkfish in a shallow dish and sprinkle over the lemon juice, then rub the turmeric and salt mixture over the fish fillets to coat them completely. Cover and chill until ready to cook.

4 Heat the oil in a frying pan, add the onions and cook for 5–6 minutes, until softened and golden. Transfer the onions to a shallow earthenware dish.

7 Cover the earthenware dish and cook the fish casserole in the oven for about 10 minutes. Add the prawns, pushing them into the liquid, then cover the dish again and return it to the oven for 5 minutes, or until the prawns turn pink. Do not overcook them or they will toughen. Check the seasoning, sprinkle with coriander leaves and serve.

COOK'S TIP

Tamarind, which is also known as Indian date, is a popular spice throughout India, South-east Asia and the Caribbean. It has little smell, but the distinctive sour, yet fruity taste makes up for this. It is often used in curries and spicy dishes and is available from Indian and South-east Asian stores and some large supermarkets.

VARIATION
You may use any firm white fish fillets such as cod, halibut or hake instead of the monkfish in this casserole.

Energy 220Kcal/926kJ; Protein 28g; Carbohydrate 12.8g, of which sugars 10.5g; Fat 6.8g, of which saturates 1g; Cholesterol 113mg; Calcium 103mg; Fibre 1.4g; Sodium 720mg.

FISH PLAKI

Greece has so much coastline, it's no wonder that fish is so popular there. Generally, it is treated simply, but in this recipe the fish is cooked with onions and tomatoes.

SERVES 6

300ml/½ pint/1¼ cups olive oil
2 onions, thinly sliced
3 large, well-flavoured tomatoes,
    roughly chopped
3 garlic cloves, thinly sliced
5ml/1 tsp sugar
5ml/1 tsp chopped fresh dill
5ml/1 tsp chopped fresh mint
5ml/1 tsp chopped fresh celery leaves
15ml/1 tbsp chopped fresh flat
    leaf parsley
300ml/½ pint/1¼ cups water
6 hake or cod steaks
juice of 1 lemon
salt and ground black pepper
extra fresh dill, mint or parsley sprigs,
    to garnish

1 Heat the oil in large heavy sauté pan or flameproof casserole. Add the onions and cook, stirring, until pale golden, then add the tomatoes, garlic, sugar, dill, mint, celery leaves and parsley with the water. Season with salt and pepper, then simmer, uncovered, for 25 minutes, until the liquid has reduced by one-third.

2 Add the fish steaks and cook gently for 10–12 minutes until the fish is just cooked. Remove the pan or casserole from the heat and add the lemon juice. Cover and leave to stand for 20 minutes before serving. Arrange the cod in a dish and pour the sauce over. Garnish with herbs and serve warm or cold.

Energy 455Kcal/1885kJ; Protein 29g; Carbohydrate 6.5g, of which sugars 5.3g; Fat 34.9g, of which saturates 5g; Cholesterol 69mg; Calcium 64mg; Fibre 2.2g; Sodium 103mg.

MOROCCAN FISH TAGINE

This spicy, aromatic dish proves just how exciting an ingredient fish can be. Serve it with couscous, which you can steam in the traditional way in a colander on top of the tagine.

SERVES 8

1.3kg/3lb firm fish fillets, skinned and cut into 5cm/2in chunks
60ml/4 tbsp olive oil
1 large aubergine (eggplant), cut into 1cm/½in cubes
2 courgettes (zucchini), cut into 1cm/½in cubes
4 onions, chopped
400g/14oz can chopped tomatoes
400ml/14fl oz/1⅔ cups passata (bottled strained tomatoes)
200ml/7fl oz/scant 1 cup fish stock
1 preserved lemon, chopped
90g/3½oz/scant 1 cup olives
60ml/4 tbsp chopped fresh coriander (cilantro), plus extra coriander leaves to garnish
salt and ground black pepper

For the harissa
3 large fresh red chillies, seeded and chopped
3 garlic cloves, peeled
15ml/1 tbsp ground coriander
30ml/2 tbsp ground cumin
5ml/1 tsp ground cinnamon
grated rind of 1 lemon
30ml/2 tbsp sunflower oil

3 Heat half the olive oil in a shallow heavy pan. Add the aubergine cubes and fry for about 10 minutes, or until they are golden brown. Add the courgettes and fry for a further 2 minutes. Remove the vegetables from the pan using a slotted spoon and set aside.

4 Add the remaining olive oil to the pan, add the onions and cook over a low heat for about 10 minutes until golden brown. Stir in the remaining harissa and cook for 5 minutes, stirring occasionally.

5 Add the vegetables and combine with the onions, then stir in the chopped tomatoes, the passata and fish stock. Bring to the boil, then lower the heat and simmer for about 20 minutes.

6 Stir the fish chunks and preserved lemon into the pan. Add the olives and stir gently. Cover and simmer over a low heat for about 15–20 minutes. Season to taste. Stir in the chopped coriander. Serve with couscous, if you like, and garnish with coriander leaves.

1 Make the harissa. Whizz everything in a food processor to a smooth paste.

2 Put the fish in a wide bowl and add 30ml/2 tbsp of the harissa. Toss to coat, cover and chill for at least 1 hour.

COOK'S TIP
To make the fish go further, add 225g/8oz/1¼ cups cooked chickpeas to the tagine.

Energy 263Kcal/1099kJ; Protein 32.3g; Carbohydrate 8.3g, of which sugars 7g; Fat 11.3g, of which saturates 1.7g; Cholesterol 75mg; Calcium 57mg; Fibre 3.2g; Sodium 360mg.

SEAFOOD PIE with RÖSTI TOPPING

In this variation of a classic fish pie, a mixture of white fish and shellfish are combined with a creamy herb-flavoured sauce and finished with a grated potato topping.

SERVES 4

750g/1lb 10oz potatoes, unpeeled
   and scrubbed
50g/2oz/¼ cup butter, melted
350g/12oz cod or haddock fillets, skinned
   and cut into bitesize pieces
115g/4oz cooked, peeled prawns (shrimp)
115g/4oz cooked, shelled mussels
8–12 shelled queen scallops
50g/2oz/¼ cup butter
1 onion, finely chopped
50g/2oz/½ cup plain (all-purpose) flour
200ml/7fl oz/scant 1 cup dry white wine
300ml/½ pint/1¼ cups fish or
   vegetable stock
105ml/7 tbsp double (heavy) cream
30ml/2 tbsp chopped fresh dill, plus extra
   sprigs to garnish
15ml/1 tbsp chopped fresh parsley
60ml/4 tbsp freshly grated
   Parmesan cheese
salt and ground black pepper

1 Place the potatoes in a large pan. Cover with cold water and bring to the boil. Cook for 10–15 minutes, or until they are only just tender.

VARIATIONS

• For a speedy version of these individual pies, buy ready-prepared potato rösti and sprinkle it evenly over the fish and sauce as in step 6.
• To make an alternative topping, cook the potatoes until soft, drain and mash with a little milk and butter. Spoon the mashed potato over the fish and sauce and top with cheese as in step 6.
• Add 30ml/2 tbsp chopped capers to the sauce at the end of step 5.

2 Drain the potatoes well, and set aside until they are cool enough to handle. Peel and coarsely grate the par-boiled potatoes into a large mixing bowl. Stir in the melted butter and season well with salt and pepper.

3 Preheat the oven to 220°C/425°F/ Gas 7. Divide the pieces of cod or haddock and the prawns, mussels and scallops among four individual 19cm/ 7½in rectangular earthenware dishes.

4 Melt the butter in a large pan, add the onion and cook for 6–8 minutes, stirring occasionally with a wooden spoon, or until softened and light golden. Sprinkle in the flour and stir thoroughly with a wooden spoon until well blended.

5 Remove the pan from the heat and gradually pour in the wine and stock, stirring constantly until smooth. Bring to the boil, stirring constantly, then stir in the cream, dill and parsley and season to taste. Pour the sauce over the fish.

6 Sprinkle the grated potato evenly over the fish and sauce in the dishes and top with the grated Parmesan cheese. Bake for 25 minutes, or until the topping is crisp and golden and the fish is cooked. Serve hot, garnished with dill.

COOK'S TIP

Choose waxy potatoes for this dish and cook until barely tender. Floury potatoes are too soft and will break up, so if you only have floury potatoes, opt for the mashed potato option (see Variations).

Energy 770Kcal/3215kJ; Protein 47.3g; Carbohydrate 44.5g, of which sugars 4.5g; Fat 42.4g, of which saturates 25.5g; Cholesterol 236mg; Calcium 298mg; Fibre 2.7g; Sodium 626mg.

SHELLFISH TAGINE

The distinctive mixture of spices and chillies used in this tagine is known as charmoula –
a classic Moroccan marinade for fish, meat and vegetable dishes.

SERVES 4

60ml/4 tbsp olive oil
4 garlic cloves, sliced
1–2 green chillies, seeded and chopped
a large handful of flat leaf parsley,
    roughly chopped
5ml/1 tsp coriander seeds
2.5ml/½ tsp ground allspice
6 cardamom pods, split open
2.5ml/½ tsp ground turmeric
15ml/1 tbsp lemon juice
350g/12oz scorpion fish, red mullet or red
    snapper fillets, cut into large chunks
225g/8oz squid, cleaned and cut into rings
1 onion, chopped
4 tomatoes, seeded and chopped
300ml/½ pint/1¼ cups warm fish or
    vegetable stock
225g/8oz large, raw prawns (shrimp)
15ml/1 tbsp chopped fresh
    coriander (cilantro)
salt and ground black pepper
lemon wedges, to garnish
couscous or rice and crusty bread,
    to serve

1 Place the olive oil, garlic, chillies, parsley, coriander seeds, allspice and cardamom pods in a mortar and pound to a smooth paste using a pestle. Stir in the ground turmeric, salt, pepper and lemon juice.

VARIATIONS
Scorpion fish is the traditional choice for this dish and red mullet or snapper makes a good, authentic alternative, but there's no reason why you shouldn't substitute other fish – try red bream, porgy or even halved cod or hake steaks.

2 Place the chunks of fish in a large glass or china bowl with the squid rings, add the spice paste and toss together. Cover and leave the fish to marinate in the refrigerator for about 2 hours, or longer, if time allows.

3 Place the chopped onion, seeded and chopped tomatoes and fish or vegetable stock in a tagine (see Cook's Tip) and cover. Place the tagine in an unheated oven and set the oven to 200°C/400°F/ Gas 6. Cook the vegetables for 20 minutes.

4 Remove the fish from the marinade, then drain well. Set aside the squid and any excess marinade, then place the fish in the tagine with the vegetables. Cover and cook in the oven for 5 minutes.

5 Add the prawns, squid rings and the remaining marinade to the tagine and stir to combine. Cover the tagine and return it to the oven for 5–10 minutes, or until all the fish, prawns and squid are cooked right through.

6 Taste the sauce and season to taste with salt and pepper if necessary, then stir in the chopped coriander. Serve immediately, garnished with lemon wedges. Serve the tagine with couscous or rice and crusty bread to soak up the juices.

COOK'S TIPS
• A tagine is a traditional Moroccan stew and it is also the name given to the shallow earthenware cooking dish with a tall, conical, earthenware lid in which the stew is traditionally cooked. A shallow, earthenware baking dish or a soaked, shallow clay pot can be used in place of a tagine.
• To ensure that the fish fillets have no tiny bones left in the flesh after filleting, lay the fillets on a board, skin-side down, and run your hand gently over the surface of the flesh. Pull out any bones that you find using a pair of tweezers.

Energy 301Kcal/1261kJ; Protein 37.2g; Carbohydrate 7.1g, of which sugars 5.5g; Fat 14g, of which saturates 2.2g; Cholesterol 269mg; Calcium 128mg; Fibre 2.2g; Sodium 251mg.

FISH with SPINACH and LIME

Fresh herbs and hot spices are combined to make the charmoula marinade that is used to flavour this delicious Moroccan-style dish. Crusty bread makes a good accompaniment.

SERVES 4

675g/1½lb white fish, such as haddock,
    cod, sea bass or monkfish
sunflower oil, for frying
500g/1¼lb potatoes, sliced
1 onion, chopped
1–2 garlic cloves, crushed
5 tomatoes, peeled and chopped
375g/13oz fresh spinach, chopped
lime wedges, to garnish

For the charmoula
6 spring onions (scallions), chopped
10ml/2 tsp fresh thyme
60ml/4 tbsp chopped flat leaf parsley
30ml/2 tbsp chopped fresh
    coriander (cilantro)
10ml/2 tsp paprika
generous pinch of cayenne pepper
60ml/4 tbsp olive oil
grated rind of 1 lime and 60ml/4 tbsp
    lime juice
salt

1 Cut the white fish into large even-size pieces, discarding any skin and bones. Place the fish in a large shallow dish.

2 Blend together the ingredients for the charmoula. Season with salt. Pour over the fish, stir to mix and leave in a cool place, covered with clear film (plastic wrap), to marinate for 2–4 hours.

3 Heat about 5mm/¼in oil in a large heavy pan, add the potato slices and cook, turning them occasionally, until they are cooked right through and golden brown. Drain the fried potatoes on kitchen paper.

4 Pour off all but 15ml/1 tbsp of the oil from the pan and add the onion, garlic and tomatoes. Cook over a gentle heat for 5–6 minutes, stirring occasionally, until the onion is soft. Place the potatoes on top and then add the spinach.

5 Place the marinated fish pieces on top of the chopped spinach in the pan and pour over all of the marinade. Cover the pan tightly and cook for 15–18 minutes. After about 8 minutes of the cooking time, carefully stir the contents of the pan with a wooden spoon, so that the pieces of fish at the top are distributed throughout the dish.

6 Cover the pan again and continue cooking, but check occasionally – the dish is cooked once the fish is just tender and opaque and the spinach has wilted. Serve the dish hot, with wedges of lime and plenty of warm crusty bread, if you like.

Energy 433Kcal/1810kJ; Protein 37.3g; Carbohydrate 28.9g, of which sugars 9.4g; Fat 19.3g, of which saturates 2.8g; Cholesterol 78mg; Calcium 206mg; Fibre 5.2g; Sodium 260mg.

FISH with FREGOLA

This Sardinian speciality is a cross between a soup and a stew. Serve it with crusty Italian country bread to mop up the juices.

SERVES 4–6

75ml/5 tbsp olive oil
4 garlic cloves, finely chopped
½ small fresh red chilli, seeded and
  finely chopped
1 large handful fresh flat leaf parsley,
  roughly chopped
1 red snapper, about 450g/1lb, cleaned,
  with head and tail removed
1 grey mullet or porgy, about 500g/1¼lb,
  cleaned, with head and tail removed
350–450g/12oz–1lb thick cod fillet
400g/14oz can chopped plum tomatoes
175g/6oz/1½ cups dried fregola
250ml/8fl oz/1 cup water
salt and ground black pepper

1 Heat 30ml/2 tbsp of the olive oil in a large flameproof casserole. Add the chopped garlic and chilli, with about half the chopped fresh parsley. Fry over a medium heat, stirring occasionally, for about 5 minutes.

2 Cut all of the fish into large chunks – including the skin and the bones in the case of the snapper and mullet – and add the pieces to the casserole. Sprinkle with a further 30ml/2 tbsp of the olive oil and fry for a few minutes more.

3 Add the tomatoes, then fill the empty can with water and add to the pan. Bring to the boil. Season to taste, lower the heat and cook for 10 minutes.

4 Add the fregola and simmer for about 5 minutes, then add the water and the remaining oil. Simmer for 15 minutes until the fregola is just tender.

5 If the sauce becomes too thick, add more water, then taste for seasoning. Serve hot, in warmed bowls, sprinkled with the remaining parsley.

VARIATION

Any white fish fillet can be used instead of cod in this dish. Monkfish, haddock, hake or plaice could all be used.

COOK'S TIPS
• Fregola is a tiny pasta shape from Sardinia. If you can't get it, use a tiny soup pasta (*pastina*), such as *corallini* or *semi de melone*.
• You can make the basic fish sauce several hours in advance or even the day before, bringing it to the boil and adding the fregola just before serving.

Energy 300Kcal/1256kJ; Protein 29.6g; Carbohydrate 17.3g, of which sugars 2.3g; Fat 12.9g, of which saturates 1.7g; Cholesterol 44mg; Calcium 79mg; Fibre 1.1g; Sodium 126mg.

SEAFOOD PAELLA

There are as many versions of paella as there are regions of Spain. Those from near the coast contain a lot of seafood, while inland versions add chicken or pork. Here the only meat is the chorizo – essential for an authentic flavour.

SERVES 4

45ml/3 tbsp olive oil
1 large onion, chopped
2 fat garlic cloves, chopped
150g/5oz chorizo, sliced
300g/11oz small squid, cleaned
1 red (bell) pepper, seeded and sliced
4 tomatoes, peeled, seeded and diced,
    or 200g/7oz can tomatoes
about 500ml/17fl oz/generous 2 cups
    chicken stock
105ml/7 tbsp dry white wine
200g/7oz/1 cup short grain Spanish rice
    or risotto rice
a large pinch of saffron threads
150g/5oz/1¼ cups fresh or frozen peas
12 large cooked prawns (shrimp), in the
    shell, or 8 langoustines
450g/1lb mussels, scrubbed
450g/1lb clams, scrubbed
salt and ground black pepper

1 Heat the olive oil in a large sauté pan or a paella pan, add the onion and garlic and fry until the onion is translucent. Add the chorizo and fry until golden.

2 If the squid are very small, you can leave them whole; otherwise cut the bodies into rings and the tentacles into pieces. Add the squid to the pan and sauté over a high heat for 2 minutes, stirring occasionally.

3 Stir in the pepper slices and the seeded and diced tomatoes and simmer gently for 5 minutes, until the pepper slices are tender. Pour in the stock and wine, stir well and bring to the boil.

4 Stir in the rice and saffron and season to taste with salt and pepper. Spread the contents of the pan in an even layer over the base. Bring the liquid back to the boil, then lower the heat and simmer gently for 10 minutes.

5 Add the peas, prawns or langoustines, mussels and clams, stirring them gently into the rice. Cook gently for another 15–20 minutes, until the rice is tender and all the mussels and clams have opened. If any remain closed, discard them. If the paella seems dry, add a little more stock. Gently stir everything together and serve piping hot.

Energy 613Kcal/2566kJ; Protein 43.1g; Carbohydrate 57.7g, of which sugars 10g; Fat 21.8g, of which saturates 5.4g; Cholesterol 313mg; Calcium 246mg; Fibre 4.4g; Sodium 639mg.

SEAFOOD RISOTTO

Creamy, saffron-flavoured rice makes the perfect foil for shellfish. Ready-prepared, frozen seafood mixtures, which include prawns, squid and mussels, are ideal for making this quick and easy dish – remember to thaw them before cooking.

SERVES 4

1 litre/1¾ pints/4 cups hot fish or
   shellfish stock
50g/2oz/¼ cup unsalted (sweet) butter
2 shallots, chopped
2 garlic cloves, chopped
350g/12oz/1¾ cups risotto rice
150ml/¼ pint/⅔ cup dry white wine
2.5ml/½ tsp powdered saffron, or a
   pinch of saffron threads
400g/14oz mixed prepared seafood,
   thawed if frozen
30ml/2 tbsp freshly grated
   Parmesan cheese
30ml/2 tbsp chopped fresh flat leaf parsley,
   to garnish
salt and ground black pepper

1 Pour the fish or shellfish stock into a large, heavy pan. Bring it to the boil, then pour it into a large, heatproof jug (pitcher) or bowl and keep warm.

2 Melt the butter in the rinsed-out pan pan, add the shallots and garlic and cook over a low heat for 3–5 minutes, stirring occasionally, until the shallots are soft but not coloured. Add the rice, stir well to coat the grains completely with butter, then pour in the dry white wine. Cook over a medium heat, stirring occasionally, until the wine has been absorbed by the rice.

COOK'S TIP
It is essential to use proper risotto rice, such as arborio or carnaroli for this dish, it has a wonderfully creamy texture when cooked but still retains a "bite".

3 Add a ladleful of hot stock and the saffron, and cook, stirring continuously, until the liquid has been absorbed. Add the seafood and stir well. Continue to add hot stock a ladleful at a time, waiting until each quantity has been absorbed before adding more. Stir the mixture for about 20 minutes in all until the rice is swollen and creamy, but still with a little bite in the middle.

VARIATION
Use peeled prawns (shrimp), or cubes of fish such as cod or salmon in place of the mixed prepared seafood.

4 Vigorously mix in the freshly grated Parmesan cheese and season to taste, then sprinkle over the chopped parsley and serve immediately.

Energy 547Kcal/2284kJ; Protein 27.3g; Carbohydrate 71.3g, of which sugars 1.2g; Fat 13.8g, of which saturates 8.2g; Cholesterol 229mg; Calcium 195mg; Fibre 0.2g; Sodium 350mg.

BAKED SEA BREAM with TOMATOES

John Dory, halibut or sea bass can all be cooked this way. If you prefer to use filleted fish, choose a chunky fillet, such as cod, and roast it skin-side up. Roasting the tomatoes brings out their sweetness, which contrasts beautifully with the flavour of the fish.

SERVES 4–6

8 ripe tomatoes
10ml/2 tsp sugar
200ml/7fl oz/scant 1 cup olive oil
450g/1lb new potatoes
1 lemon, sliced
1 bay leaf
1 fresh thyme sprig
8 fresh basil leaves
1 sea bream, about 900g–1kg/2–2¼lb,
    cleaned and scaled
150ml/¼ pint/⅔ cup dry white wine
30ml/2 tbsp fresh white breadcrumbs
2 garlic cloves, crushed
15ml/1 tbsp finely chopped fresh parsley
salt and ground black pepper
fresh flat leaf parsley or basil leaves,
    chopped, to garnish

1 Preheat the oven to 240°C/475°F/ Gas 9. Cut the tomatoes in half lengthwise and arrange them in a single layer in a baking dish, cut-side up. Sprinkle with sugar, salt and pepper and drizzle over a little of the olive oil. Roast for 30–40 minutes, until lightly browned. Remove the tomatoes from the dish and set aside.

2 Meanwhile, cut the potatoes into 1cm/½in slices. Place in a large pan of salted water and par-boil for 5 minutes. Drain and set aside.

3 Grease the baking dish with a little more of the oil. Arrange the potatoes in a single layer with the lemon slices over; sprinkle on the herbs. Season and drizzle with half the remaining oil. Lay the fish on top and season. Pour over the wine and the rest of the oil. Arrange the tomatoes around the fish.

4 Mix together the breadcrumbs, garlic and parsley; sprinkle over the fish. Bake for 30 minutes. Garnish with chopped parsley or basil.

Energy 440Kcal/1840kJ; Protein 26g; Carbohydrate 21.5g, of which sugars 6.6g; Fat 26.7g, of which saturates 3.4g; Cholesterol 51mg; Calcium 76mg; Fibre 2g; Sodium 205mg.

FILLETS of BRILL in RED WINE SAUCE

Forget the old maxim that red wine and fish do not go well together. The robust sauce adds colour and richness to this excellent dish, which is more than elegant enough for a dinner party. Halibut and John Dory are also good cooked this way.

SERVES 4

4 fillets of brill, about 175–200g/6–7oz
    each, skinned
150g/5oz/10 tbsp chilled butter, diced, plus
    extra for greasing
115g/4oz shallots, thinly sliced
200ml/7fl oz/scant 1 cup robust red wine
200ml/7fl oz/scant 1 cup fish stock
salt and ground black and white pepper
fresh flat leaf parsley leaves or chervil,
    to garnish

1 Preheat the oven to 180°C/350°F/ Gas 4. Season the fish fillets on both sides with salt and ground black pepper. Generously butter a shallow flameproof dish, which is large enough to take all the brill fillets in a single layer. Spread the shallots in an even layer in the dish and lay the fish fillets on top. Season well with salt and ground black pepper.

2 Pour in the red wine and fish stock, cover the dish with a lid or foil and then bring the liquid to just below boiling point. Transfer the dish to the oven and bake for 6–8 minutes, or until the brill is just cooked.

3 Using a fish slice (metal spatula), lift the fish and shallots on to a serving dish, cover with foil and keep hot.

4 Transfer the dish to the stove and bring the cooking liquid to the boil over a high heat. Cook it until it has reduced by half. Lower the heat and whisk in the chilled butter, one piece at a time, to make a smooth, shiny sauce. Season with salt and ground white pepper, set the sauce aside and keep hot.

5 Divide the shallots among four warmed plates and lay the brill fillets on top. Pour the sauce over and around the fish and garnish with the fresh flat leaf parsley or chervil.

Energy 515Kcal/2142kJ; Protein 35.6g; Carbohydrate 2.6g, of which sugars 1.9g; Fat 36.7g, of which saturates 19.5g; Cholesterol 156mg; Calcium 98mg; Fibre 0.4g; Sodium 452mg.

MONKFISH with ROCKET PESTO, PEPPERS and ONIONS

Colourful Mediterranean vegetables complement richly flavoured monkfish layered with pesto sauce in this impressive-looking clay pot dish.

SERVES 4

900g/2lb monkfish tail
50g/2oz rocket (arugula)
30ml/2 tbsp pine nuts
1 garlic clove, chopped
25g/1oz/⅓ cup freshly grated
   Parmesan cheese
90ml/6 tbsp olive oil
45ml/3 tbsp lemon juice
2 red (bell) peppers, halved
2 yellow (bell) peppers, halved
1 red onion, cut into wedges
2 courgettes (zucchini), cut into
   2.5cm/1in slices
4 fresh rosemary sprigs
salt and ground black pepper

3 Place the rocket, pine nuts, garlic, freshly Parmesan, 45ml/3 tbsp of the olive oil and 15ml/1 tbsp of the lemon juice in a food processor or blender and process to form a smooth paste.

1 Remove any skin or membrane from the monkfish. Using a large, sharp knife cut along one side of the central bone, as close to the bone as possible and then remove the fish fillet. Repeat on the other side. Set aside.

2 Soak a fish clay pot in cold water for 20 minutes, then drain and set aside.

VARIATIONS

• Salmon tail fillets, or thick fillets of cod or haddock could be used in place of the monkfish. Remove the skin from the fish and run your hand along the other side to check for any hidden bones and, if necessary, remove these with tweezers.
• Rocket makes an interestingly peppery pesto, but other leafy herbs can be used to make this sauce. Basil is the classic choice, but flat leaf parsley is also good.

4 Lay one fish fillet out flat, cut-side up and spread with the pesto. Place the remaining fillet on top, cut-side down, on top of the layer of pesto. Tie the fish with string at regular intervals to seal together. Sprinkle with plenty of salt and pepper to season and set aside.

5 Cut each pepper half into three lengthwise. Remove and discard the core, the white membranes and the seeds.

6 Place the pieces of pepper in the clay pot with the onion wedges and slices of courgette. In a small bowl, mix together 15ml/1 tbsp of the olive oil and the remaining lemon juice and sprinkle over the vegetables. Mix well and season with salt and plenty of black pepper.

7 Tuck the fresh rosemary sprigs in among the vegetables. Cover the clay pot and place in an unheated oven. Set the temperature to 220°C/425°F/Gas 7 and cook the vegetables for 20 minutes.

8 Remove the clay pot from the oven, place the monkfish parcel in the centre of the vegetables and brush it with 15ml/1 tbsp of the olive oil. Sprinkle the remaining oil over the vegetables. Cover the pot again, then return the pot to the oven and cook for 20–25 minutes more, or until the monkfish is cooked through and turns opaque.

9 To serve, cut the fish into thick slices, removing the string, if you prefer, and serve with the cooked vegetables.

COOK'S TIP

• Although monkfish is usually skinned before being sold, check that the tough, transparent membrane has been completely removed from the monkfish tail. If any membrane does remain, strip it off the fish, because the membrane shrinks during cooking and becomes tough and unappetizing.

Energy 477Kcal/1991kj; Protein 47g; Carbohydrate 14.7g, of which sugars 13.7g; Fat 25.8g, of which saturates 4.5g; Cholesterol 42mg; Calcium 160mg; Fibre 4.3g; Sodium 139mg.

BAKED MONKFISH with POTATOES and GARLIC

This simple supper dish can be made with other fish. Sauce tartare or a thick vinaigrette flavoured with chopped gherkins and hard-boiled egg are delicious accompaniments.

3 Pour the main batch of stock over the potatoes and bake, uncovered, stirring once or twice, for about 50 minutes, or until the potatoes are just tender.

4 Nestle the monkfish tail into the potatoes and season well with salt and ground black pepper. Mix the 45ml/ 3 tbsp stock with the wine and use to baste the monkfish two or three times during cooking. Bake the monkfish and potatoes for 10–15 minutes.

5 Finely chop the remaining garlic. Melt the remaining butter and toss it with the fresh breadcrumbs, chopped garlic, most of the chopped parsley and seasoning. Spread the crumb mixture over the monkfish, pressing it down gently with the back of a spoon.

6 Drizzle the olive oil over the crumb-covered fish, then return the dish to the oven and bake for a final 10–15 minutes, or until the breadcrumbs are crisp and golden brown and all the liquid has been absorbed. Sprinkle the remaining chopped parsley on to the potatoes and fish and serve immediately.

SERVES 4

50g/2oz/¼ cup butter
2 onions, thickly sliced
1kg/2¼lb waxy potatoes, peeled and cut
   into small chunks
4 garlic cloves
a few fresh thyme sprigs
2–3 fresh bay leaves
450ml/¾ pint/scant 2 cups vegetable
   or fish stock, plus 45ml/3 tbsp
900g/2lb monkfish tail in one piece,
   membrane removed
30–45ml/2–3 tbsp white wine
50g/2oz/1 cup fresh white breadcrumbs
15g/½oz fresh flat leaf parsley,
   finely chopped
15ml/1 tbsp olive oil
salt and ground black pepper

1 Preheat the oven to 190°C/375°F/ Gas 5. Melt half the butter in a shallow flameproof dish and cook the onions for 5 minutes until soft. Stir in the potatoes.

2 Slice two of the garlic cloves and add them to the dish with the thyme and bay leaves, and season with salt and pepper.

Energy 529Kcal/2230kJ; Protein 45.8g; Carbohydrate 54g, of which sugars 6.5g; Fat 15g, of which saturates 7.4g; Cholesterol 63mg; Calcium 67mg; Fibre 3.5g; Sodium 245mg.

JANSSON'S TEMPTATION

A traditional Swedish favourite, this rich gratin is utterly moreish. As food writer Jane Grigson pointed out, the name probably does not refer to a specific Jansson but means "everyone's temptation" as Jansson is a common Swedish surname.

SERVES 4–6

50g/2oz/¼ cup butter
900g/2lb potatoes
2 large, sweet onions, sliced
2 × 50g/2oz cans anchovies in olive
    oil, drained
450ml/¾ pint/scant 2 cups whipping cream
    or half and half double (heavy) and
    single (light) cream
a little milk (optional)
salt and ground black pepper

1 Preheat the oven to 200°C/400°F/Gas 6. Use 15g/½oz/1 tbsp of the butter to grease a shallow 1.5 litre/2½ pint/6¼ cup earthenware baking dish.

4 Lay half of the onions on top of the potatoes, season with black pepper and dot with butter. Lay the anchovies on top of the onions, then add the rest of the sliced onions and top with the remaining potatoes.

5 Mix the cream with 30ml/2 tbsp cold water and pour this mixture over the potatoes and onions in the dish. Add a little milk, if necessary, to bring the liquid to just below the top of the final layer of potato matchstick strips.

6 Dot the potatoes with the remaining butter, then cover the dish with foil and bake for 1 hour.

7 Reduce the oven temperature to 180°C/350°F/Gas 4 and remove the foil from the top of the dish. Bake for a further 40–50 minutes, or until the potatoes are tender when tested with a knife and brown in colour.

2 Using a small sharp knife, carefully cut the potatoes into thin slices, then cut the slices into fine matchstick strips.

3 Toss the potato strips with salt and ground black pepper and sprinkle half of them in the base of the prepared ovenproof dish.

COOK'S TIPS

• It is important to cover the gratin with foil for the first half of the cooking time so that the potatoes don't brown or dry out too much.
• If using whole, salted anchovies or Swedish salted sprats (US small whitebait or smelts) they will need to be boned. If they are very salty, soak in a little milk for about 30 minutes before using.
• Serve with small glasses of chilled schnapps and cold beer for an authentic Swedish flavour.

Energy 509Kcal/2111kJ; Protein 9.1g; Carbohydrate 31.5g, of which sugars 7.8g; Fat 39.3g, of which saturates 23.7g; Cholesterol 107mg; Calcium 121mg; Fibre 2.4g; Sodium 743mg.

SALMON BAKED with POTATOES and THYME

This is a mouthwatering combination of potatoes and onions braised in thyme-flavoured stock and topped with perfectly tender pepper-crusted salmon fillets.

SERVES 4

675g/1½lb waxy potatoes, thinly sliced
1 onion, thinly sliced
10ml/2 tsp fresh thyme leaves
450ml/¾ pint/scant 2 cups vegetable or
    fish stock
40g/1½oz/3 tbsp butter,
    finely diced
4 skinless salmon fillets, about
    150g/5oz each
30ml/2 tbsp olive oil
15ml/1 tbsp black peppercorns,
    roughly crushed
salt and ground black pepper
fresh thyme, to garnish
mangetouts (snow peas) or sugar snap
    peas, to serve

1 Soak a fish clay pot in cold water for 20 minutes, then drain.

2 Layer the potato and onion slices in the clay pot, seasoning each layer and sprinkling with thyme. Pour over the stock, dot with butter, cover and place in an unheated oven.

3 Set the oven to 190°C/375°F/Gas 5. Bake the potatoes for 40 minutes then remove the lid and bake for a further 20 minutes, or until they are almost cooked.

4 Meanwhile brush the salmon fillets with olive oil and coat with crushed black peppercorns, pressing them in, if necessary, with the back of a spoon. Place the salmon on top of the potatoes, cover and cook for 15 minutes, or until the salmon is opaque, removing the lid for the last 5 minutes. Serve garnished with fresh thyme sprigs and with mangetouts or sugar snap peas to accompany.

Energy 517Kcal/2160kJ; Protein 33.4g; Carbohydrate 28.4g, of which sugars 3.1g; Fat 30.8g, of which saturates 9g; Cholesterol 96mg; Calcium 47mg; Fibre 1.9g; Sodium 147mg.

SWORDFISH STEAKS with MANGO SALSA

*Meaty swordfish steaks, marinated in a tangy mix of lime juice, coriander and chilli,
served with a vibrant fruity salsa.*

SERVES 4

4 swordfish steaks, about 150g/5oz each
lime wedges and shredded spring onions
    (scallions), to garnish

For the marinade
rind and juice of 2 limes
2 garlic cloves, crushed
I red chilli, seeded and finely chopped
30ml/2 tbsp olive oil
30ml/2 tbsp chopped fresh
    coriander (cilantro)
salt and ground black pepper

For the salsa
I mango
4 spring onions (scallions), thinly sliced
I red chilli, seeded and finely chopped
30ml/2 tbsp chopped fresh dill or
    coriander (cilantro)
30ml/2 tbsp lime juice
30ml/2 tbsp olive oil
I ripe avocado

3 Place the swordfish steaks in the clay
pot and pour over the marinade. Cover
and place in an unheated oven. Set the
oven to 220°C/425°F/Gas 7 and bake
for 15–20 minutes, or until the fish is
cooked. The time will vary depending
on the thickness of the steaks.

4 To complete the salsa, using a sharp
knife, cut the avocado in half, remove the
stone (pit), then roughly dice the flesh.
Stir it into the prepared salsa ingredients
and mix well. Serve the swordfish steaks
with a mound of salsa, garnished with
lime wedges and shredded spring onions.

1 Place the swordfish steaks in a shallow
non-metallic dish. Mix together the
marinade ingredients and pour over the
swordfish. Cover and leave to marinate
in the refrigerator for 2 hours, or longer
if time allows.

2 Soak a fish clay pot in cold water for
20 minutes, then drain. To prepare the
salsa, peel the mango and slice the flesh
off the stone (pit). Cut the flesh into
rough dice. Add the spring onions, chilli,
dill or coriander, lime juice and olive oil.
Toss the ingredients together, cover and
set aside to allow the flavours to blend.

Energy 311Kcal/1297kJ; Protein 29g; Carbohydrate 5.5g, of which sugars 5.3g; Fat 19.4g, of which saturates 3.3g; Cholesterol 69mg; Calcium 30mg; Fibre 1.3g; Sodium 212mg.

SLOW COOKER POULTRY AND GAME

The slow cooker is perfect for making all manner of stews, casseroles and curries, and this chapter is packed with fantastic, healthy recipe ideas using poultry and game as the basis. Chicken is always a firm favourite, and the versatility of the slow cooker means that there is something here for everyone. In addition, there are plenty of other poultry and game dishes to whet the appetite, using turkey, guinea fowl and rabbit. All of these recipes draw their inspiration from favourite cuisines around the world, giving a wonderful choice of dishes for every occasion. Try Chicken Fricassée, Chicken Korma, Chicken with Chipotle Sauce or Duck Stew with Olives.

TURKEY and TOMATO HOT-POT

Often reserved for festive meals, turkey makes a great choice for any occasion. Here the
meat is shaped into balls and simmered with rice in a richly flavoured tomato sauce.

SERVES 4

white bread loaf, unsliced
30ml/2 tbsp milk
1 garlic clove, crushed
2.5ml/½ tsp caraway seeds
225g/8oz minced (ground) turkey
1 egg white
350ml/12fl oz/1½ cups near-boiling
   chicken stock
400g/14oz can chopped tomatoes
15ml/1 tbsp tomato purée (paste)
90g/3½oz/½ cup easy-cook
   (converted) rice
salt and ground black pepper
15ml/1 tbsp chopped fresh basil, to garnish
courgette (zucchini) ribbons, to serve

1 Using a serrated knife, remove the
crusts and cut the bread into cubes.

2 Place the bread in a mixing bowl and
sprinkle with the milk, then leave to soak
for about 5 minutes.

3 Add the garlic clove, caraway seeds,
turkey, and salt and pepper to the bread
and mix together well.

4 Whisk the egg white until stiff, then
fold, half at a time, into the turkey
mixture. Chill in the refrigerator.

5 Pour the stock into the ceramic
cooking pot. Add the tomatoes and
tomato purée, then switch to high,
cover with the lid and cook for 1 hour.

6 Meanwhile, shape the turkey mixture
into 16 small balls. Stir the rice into the
tomato mixture, then add the turkey
balls. Cook on high for a further hour,
or until the turkey balls and rice are
cooked. Serve with the courgettes.

Energy 187Kcal/797kJ; Protein 18.2g; Carbohydrate 26.6g, of which sugars 3.9g; Fat 1.7g, of which saturates 0.5g; Cholesterol 32mg; Calcium 44mg; Fibre 1g; Sodium 212mg.

LAYERED CHICKEN and MUSHROOM BAKE

*This rich, creamy dish makes a hearty winter supper. The thick sauce combines with
juices from the mushrooms and chicken during cooking to make a well-flavoured gravy.*

2 Add 25g/1oz/2 tbsp of the butter to
the pan and heat gently until melted.
Stir in the leek and fry gently for about
10 minutes. Sprinkle the flour over the
leeks, then turn off the heat and
gradually blend in the milk until smooth.
Slowly bring the mixture to the boil,
stirring all the time, until thickened.

3 Remove the pan from the heat and
stir in the Worcestershire sauce, if using,
mustard, diced carrot, mushrooms and
chicken. Season generously.

4 Arrange enough potato slices to cover
the base of the ceramic cooking pot.
Spoon one-third of the chicken mixture
over the top, then cover with another
layer of potatoes. Repeat layering,
finishing with a layer of potatoes. Dot
the remaining butter on top.

5 Cover and cook on high for 4 hours,
or until the potatoes are cooked and
tender when pierced with a skewer.
If you like, place the dish under a
moderate grill (broiler) for 5 minutes
to brown, then serve.

SERVES 4

15ml/1 tbsp olive oil
4 large chicken breast portions,
   cut into chunks
40g/1½oz/3 tbsp butter
1 leek, finely sliced into rings
25g/1oz/¼ cup plain (all-purpose) flour
550ml/18fl oz/2½ cups milk
5ml/1 tsp Worcestershire sauce (optional)
5ml/1 tsp wholegrain mustard
1 carrot, finely diced
225g/8oz/3 cups button (white)
   mushrooms, thinly sliced
900g/2lb potatoes, thinly sliced
salt and ground black pepper

1 Heat the olive oil in a large pan. Add
the chicken and fry gently until beginning
to brown. Remove the chicken from the
pan using a slotted spoon, leaving any
juices behind. Set aside.

Energy 461Kcal/1943kJ; Protein 42.4g; Carbohydrate 43.8g, of which sugars 5.2g; Fat 14.1g, of which saturates 6.4g; Cholesterol 126.3mg; Calcium 49mg; Fibre 4.3g; Sodium 351mg.

APRICOT and ALMOND STUFFED CHICKEN

Couscous makes a delicious and simple base for this sweet-and-sour stuffing flavoured with dried apricots and crunchy toasted almonds. A couple of spoonfuls of orange jelly marmalade adds tanginess to the sauce, as well as thickening it slightly.

3 Put the couscous in a bowl and spoon over 50ml/2fl oz/¼ cup of the stock. Leave to stand for 2–3 minutes, or until all the stock has been absorbed.

4 Drain the apricots, reserving the juice, then stir them into the couscous along with the chopped almonds and tarragon. Season with salt and black pepper, then stir in just enough egg yolk to bind the mixture together.

5 Divide the stuffing equally between the chicken portions, packing it firmly into the pockets, then securing with wooden cocktail sticks (toothpicks). Place the stuffed chicken portions in the base of the ceramic cooking pot.

6 Stir the orange marmalade into the remaining hot stock until dissolved, then stir in the orange juice. Season with salt and pepper and pour over the chicken. Cover the pot and cook on high for 3–5 hours, or until the chicken is cooked through and tender.

7 Remove the chicken from the sauce and keep warm. Tip the sauce into a wide pan and boil rapidly until reduced by half. Carve the chicken into slices on the diagonal and arrange on serving plates. Spoon over the sauce and serve immediately with basmati and wild rice.

COOK'S TIP
Sautéed spinach or steamed green vegetables make a great accompaniment to this dish. They go particularly well with the sweet, fruity stuffing.

SERVES 4

50g/2oz/¼ cup dried apricots
150ml/¼ pint/⅔ cup orange juice
4 skinned boneless chicken breast portions
50g/2oz/⅓ cup instant couscous
150ml/¼ pint/⅔ cup boiling chicken stock
25g/1oz/¼ cup chopped toasted almonds
1.5ml/¼ tsp dried tarragon
1 egg yolk
30ml/2 tbsp orange jelly marmalade
salt and ground black pepper
boiled or steamed basmati and wild rice,
    to serve

1 Put the dried apricots in a small bowl and pour over the orange juice. Leave to soak at room temperature while you prepare the remaining ingredients.

2 Using a sharp knife, cut a deep pocket horizontally in each chicken breast portion, taking care not to cut all the way through. Put the chicken portions between two sheets of oiled baking parchment or clear film (plastic wrap), then gently beat with a rolling pin or mallet until slightly thinner.

Energy 379Kcal/1604kJ; Protein 40.2g; Carbohydrate 38g, of which sugars 27g; Fat 8.5g, of which saturates 1.3g; Cholesterol 155mg; Calcium 61mg; Fibre 1.6g; Sodium 117mg.

CHICKEN with CHIPOTLE SAUCE

Spicy-hot and deliciously rich and smoky, this dish of chicken cooked in a rich chilli sauce is great served with rice for a tasty, healthy supper. The purée can be prepared ahead of time, making this recipe ideal for casual entertaining.

SERVES 6

6 chipotle chillies
200ml/7fl oz/scant 1 cup boiling water
about 200ml/7fl oz/scant 1 cup chicken
  stock
45ml/3 tbsp vegetable oil
3 onions
6 boneless chicken breast portions
salt and ground black pepper
fresh oregano, to garnish

COOK'S TIP

Spicy-hot, wrinkled, dark red chipotle chillies are smoke-dried jalepeños and have a really rich taste. To really bring out their flavour, they need long, slow cooking – making them perfect for slow cooker casseroles.

1 Put the dried chillies in a bowl and cover with the boiling water. Leave to stand for about 30 minutes until very soft. Drain, reserving the soaking water in a measuring jug (pitcher). Cut off the stalk from each chilli, then slit the chilli lengthways and scrape out the seeds with a small, sharp knife.

2 Chop the chillies roughly and put in a food processor or blender. Add enough chicken stock to the soaking water to make it up to 400ml/14fl oz/1⅔ cups, then pour into the food processor or blender. Process until smooth.

3 Heat the oil in a frying pan. Halve and slice the onions and add them to the pan. Cook, stirring, over a medium heat for 5 minutes, or until soft but not coloured.

4 Transfer the onions to the ceramic cooking pot and switch to high. Sprinkle the onion slices with a little salt and ground black pepper.

5 Remove the skin from the chicken breast portions and trim off any pieces of fat. Arrange in a single layer on top of the onion slices. Sprinkle with a little salt and several grindings of black pepper.

6 Pour the chilli purée over the chicken, making sure that each piece is evenly coated. Cover with the lid and cook for 3–4 hours, or until the chicken is cooked through but still moist and tender. Garnish with fresh oregano and serve.

Energy 235Kcal/989kJ; Protein 36.9g; Carbohydrate 5.9g, of which sugars 4.2g; Fat 7.3g, of which saturates 1.1g; Cholesterol 105mg; Calcium 26mg; Fibre 1.1g; Sodium 92mg.

CHICKEN FRICASSÉE

Traditionally made with chicken, rabbit or veal, this fricassée dish has a wonderfully rich and flavoursome sauce that is further enhanced with cream and fresh herbs. The meat is first seared in fat, then braised in stock with vegetables until tender. It is a perfect dish for entertaining because you can prepare it in advance and then simply leave it to simmer while you enjoy the company of your guests.

SERVES 4

20 small even-size button (pearl) onions or
    shallots
1.2–1.3kg/2½–3lb chicken, cut into pieces
25g/1oz/2 tbsp butter
30ml/2 tbsp sunflower oil
45ml/3 tbsp plain (all-purpose) flour
250ml/8fl oz/1 cup dry white wine
600ml/1 pint/2½ cups boiling chicken stock
1 bouquet garni
5ml/1 tsp lemon juice
225g/8oz/3 cups button (white) mushrooms
75ml/2½fl oz/⅓ cup double (heavy) cream
45ml/3 tbsp chopped fresh parsley
salt and ground black pepper
mashed potatoes and steamed seasonal
    vegetables, to serve

1 Put the onions or shallots in a bowl, add just enough boiling water to cover them, and leave to soak.

2 Meanwhile, rinse the chicken pieces well in cold water, and pat dry with kitchen paper.

3 Melt half the butter with the oil in a large frying pan. Add the chicken pieces and cook, turning occasionally, until lightly browned all over. Using a slotted spoon or tongs, transfer the chicken pieces to the ceramic cooking pot, leaving the juices behind.

4 Stir the flour into the pan juices, then blend in the wine. Stir in the stock and add the bouquet garni and the lemon juice. Bring the mixture to the boil, stirring all the time, until the sauce has thickened. Season well and pour over the chicken. Cover the pot with the lid and switch the slow cooker to high.

5 Drain and peel the onions or shallots. (Soaking them in boiling water loosens the skins, making them easy to peel.) Trim the stalks from the mushrooms.

6 Clean the frying pan, then add the remaining butter and heat gently until melted. Add the mushrooms and onions or shallots and cook for 5 minutes, turning frequently until they are lightly browned. Tip into the ceramic cooking pot with the chicken.

7 Re-cover the slow cooker with the lid and cook on high for 3–4 hours, or until the chicken is cooked and tender. (To test that the chicken is cooked through, pierce the thickest part of one of the portions with a skewer or thin knife; the juices should run clear.)

8 Using a slotted spoon, remove the chicken and vegetables to a warmed serving dish. Add the cream and 30ml/2 tbsp of the parsley to the sauce and whisk to combine. Check the seasoning and adjust if necessary, then pour the sauce over the chicken and vegetables.

9 Sprinkle the fricassée with the remaining parsley and serve with mashed potatoes and seasonal vegetables.

COOK'S TIP
A classic bouquet garni is made up of parsley stalks, a sprig of thyme and a bay leaf. You can tie these together with a piece of string, or tie the herbs in a small square of muslin (cheesecloth). Some people like to add rosemary as well.

Energy 613Kcal/2563kJ; Protein 53.1g; Carbohydrate 36.4g, of which sugars 17.9g; Fat 25g, of which saturates 11.1g; Cholesterol 196mg; Calcium 128mg; Fibre 5.3g; Sodium 396mg.

SPRING CHICKEN SLOW-BRAISED in SMOKY BACON SAUCE

Sweet, succulent and tangy with the flavour of apples and aromatic thyme, this delicious stew makes a great alternative to the classic roast. Baby spring chickens are also known as poussin and can weigh 350–500g/12oz–1¼lb. Be sure to buy large ones because the smaller birds are only big enough for a single serving.

SERVES 4

2 large spring chickens
25g/1oz/2 tbsp unsalted
   (sweet) butter
10ml/2 tsp sunflower oil
115g/4oz chopped bacon pieces
   or smoked streaky (fatty) bacon
2 leeks, washed and sliced
175g/6oz/2¼ cup small button (white)
   mushrooms, trimmed
120ml/4fl oz/½ cup apple juice,
   plus a further 15ml/1 tbsp
120ml/4fl oz/½ cup chicken stock
30ml/2 tbsp clear honey
10ml/2 tsp chopped fresh thyme
   or 2.5ml/½ tsp dried
225g/8oz crisp red apples
10ml/2 tsp cornflour (cornstarch)
salt and ground black pepper
creamy mashed potatoes and
   pan-fried or steamed baby leeks,
   to serve

1 Using a sharp, heavy knife or a meat cleaver, carefully split the spring chickens in half to make four portions. Rinse the portions well under cold running water, then pat dry using kitchen paper.

2 Heat the butter and sunflower oil in a large pan and add the spring chicken portions. Fry, turning the pieces over, until lightly browned on all sides. Transfer the chicken portions to the ceramic cooking pot, leaving the cooking fat in the pan.

3 Add the chopped bacon to the pan and cook for about 5 minutes, stirring occasionally, until beginning to brown.

4 Using a slotted spoon transfer the bacon to the ceramic cooking pot, leaving all the fat and juices behind.

5 Add the leeks and mushrooms to the pan and cook for a few minutes until they begin to soften and the mushrooms begin to release their juices.

6 Pour 120ml/4fl oz/½ cup apple juice and the chicken stock into the pan, then stir in the honey and thyme. Season well with salt and ground black pepper.

7 Bring the mixture almost to boiling point, then pour over the chicken and bacon. Cover the ceramic cooking pot with the lid, switch the slow cooker to high and cook for 2 hours.

8 Quarter, core and thickly slice the apples. Add them to the cooking pot, submerging them in the liquid to stop them turning brown. Cook for a further 2 hours, or until the chicken and vegetables are cooked and tender.

9 Remove the chicken from the cooking pot, place on a plate and keep warm.

10 Blend the cornflour with the 15ml/1 tbsp apple juice and stir into the cooking liquid until thickened. Taste and adjust the seasoning, if necessary.

11 Serve the chicken on warmed plates with sauce poured over the top. Accompany with mashed potatoes and pan-fried or steamed baby leeks.

COOK'S TIP
Always check that chicken is thoroughly cooked before serving to avoid any risk of salmonella. To test, pierce the thickest part of the meat with a skewer or thin knife; the juices should run clear.

Energy 465Kcal/1945kJ; Protein 32.8g; Carbohydrate 25.9g, of which sugars 20.7g; Fat 26.3g, of which saturates 9.5g; Cholesterol 172mg; Calcium 40mg; Fibre 3.3g; Sodium 632mg.

TARRAGON CHICKEN in CIDER

Aromatic tarragon has a distinctive flavour that goes wonderfully with both cream and chicken. This recipe is truly effortless, yet provides an elegant dish for entertaining or a special family meal. Serve with sautéed potatoes and a green vegetable.

SERVES 4

350g/12oz small button (pearl) onions
15ml/1 tbsp sunflower oil
4 garlic cloves, peeled
4 boneless chicken breast portions,
    skin on
350ml/12fl oz/1½ cups dry (hard) cider
1 bay leaf
200g/7oz/scant 1 cup crème fraîche
    or sour cream
30ml/2 tbsp chopped fresh tarragon
15ml/1 tbsp chopped fresh parsley
salt and ground black pepper

1 Put the button onions in a heatproof bowl and pour over enough boiling water to cover. Leave to stand for at least 10 minutes, then drain and peel off the skins. (They should come off very easily after soaking.)

2 Heat the oil in a frying pan, add the onions and cook gently for 10 minutes, or until lightly browned, turning them frequently. Add the garlic and cook for a further 2–3 minutes. Using a slotted spoon, transfer the onions and garlic to the ceramic cooking pot.

3 Place the chicken breast portions in the frying pan and cook for 3–4 minutes, turning once or twice until lightly browned on both sides. Transfer the chicken to the ceramic cooking pot.

4 Pour the cider into the pan, add the bay leaf and a little salt and pepper, and bring to the boil.

5 Pour the hot cider and bay leaf over the chicken. Cover the ceramic cooking pot with the lid and cook on low for 4–5 hours, or until the chicken and onions are cooked and very tender. Lift out the chicken breasts. Set aside while you finish preparing the cider sauce.

COOK'S TIP

When preparing and cooking poultry, always be sure to wash utensils, surfaces and hands afterwards to avoid risk of contamination or food poisoning. Use a plastic or glass chopping board when cutting all poultry, meat or fish because they are easier to wash and much more hygienic. Wooden boards are absorbent and should therefore be avoided.

6 Stir the crème fraîche or sour cream and the herbs into the sauce. Return the chicken breasts to the pot and cook for a further 30 minutes on high, or until piping hot. Serve the chicken immediately, with lightly sautéed potatoes and a green vegetable, such as cabbage.

VARIATIONS

• Guinea fowl and pheasant portions can also be cooked in this way. Try using white wine in place of the cider and serve with creamy mashed potatoes and steamed baby carrots drizzled with a little melted butter.
• Try using 1 or 2 sprigs of fresh thyme in place of the tarragon. It gives a very different flavour but is equally good. Serve with rice and roasted tomatoes.

Energy 520Kcal/2167kJ; Protein 36.9g; Carbohydrate 12.1g, of which sugars 9.2g; Fat 33.9g, of which saturates 12.9g; Cholesterol 184mg; Calcium 90mg; Fibre 1.5g; Sodium 138mg.

CARIBBEAN PEANUT CHICKEN

Peanut butter adds a delicious richness and depth of flavour to this spicy rice dish.
It is a classic ingredient used in many slow-cooked Caribbean curries and stews.

3 Meanwhile, heat the remaining oil in a frying pan, add the onion and fry for 10 minutes until soft. Transfer to the ceramic cooking pot and switch the slow cooker to high. Add the chopped tomatoes and chilli and stir to combine.

4 Put the peanut butter into a bowl, then blend in the stock, adding a little at a time. Pour the mixture into the ceramic cooking pot, season and stir. Cover with the lid and cook for 1 hour.

5 About 30 minutes before the end of cooking time, remove the chicken from the refrigerator and leave it to come to room temperature.

6 Add the chicken and the marinade to the ceramic cooking pot and stir to mix. Re-cover and cook for 1 hour.

7 Sprinkle the rice over the casserole, then stir to mix. Cover and cook for a final 45 minutes–1 hour, or until the chicken and rice are cooked and tender. Serve straight away, garnished with lemon or lime wedges for squeezing over, and sprigs of fresh parsley.

SERVES 4

4 skinless, boneless chicken
   breast portions
45ml/3 tbsp groundnut (peanut) or
   sunflower oil
1 garlic clove, crushed
5ml/1 tsp chopped fresh thyme
15ml/1 tbsp curry powder
juice of half a lemon
1 onion, finely chopped
2 tomatoes, peeled, seeded and chopped
1 fresh green chilli, seeded and sliced
60ml/4 tbsp smooth peanut butter
750ml/1¼ pints/3 cups boiling
   chicken stock
300g/10oz/1½ cups easy-cook (converted)
   white rice
salt and ground black pepper
lemon or lime wedges and sprigs of fresh
   flat leaf parsley, to garnish

1 Cut the chicken breast portions into thin strips. In a bowl, mix together 15ml/1 tbsp of the oil with the garlic, thyme, curry powder and lemon juice.

2 Add the chicken strips to the ingredients in the bowl and stir well to combine. Cover with clear film (plastic wrap) and leave to marinate in the refrigerator for 1½–2 hours.

Energy 635Kcal/2677kJ; Protein 45.8g; Carbohydrate 70.7g, of which sugars 4.4g; Fat 20.8g, of which saturates 4.1g; Cholesterol 105mg; Calcium 65mg; Fibre 2.1g; Sodium 354mg.

JAMAICAN JERK CHICKEN

The word "jerk" refers to the herb and spice seasoning traditionally used to marinate meat in Jamaica. It was originally used only for pork, but jerked chicken is just as good.

SERVES 4

8 chicken pieces, such as thighs and legs
15ml/1 tbsp sunflower oil
15g/½ oz/1 tbsp unsalted (sweet) butter

For the sauce
1 bunch of spring onions (scallions),
    trimmed and finely chopped
2 garlic cloves, crushed
1 hot red chilli pepper, halved, seeded
    and finely chopped
5ml/1 tsp ground allspice
2.5ml/½ tsp ground cinnamon
5ml/1 tsp dried thyme
1.5ml/¼ tsp freshly grated nutmeg
10ml/2 tsp demerara (raw) sugar
15ml/1 tbsp plain (all-purpose) flour
300ml/½ pint/1¼ cups chicken stock
15ml/1 tbsp red or white wine vinegar
15ml/1 tbsp lime juice
10ml/2 tsp tomato purée (paste)
salt and ground black pepper
salad leaves or rice, to serve

VARIATION
For jerked pork, sauté 4 pork loin steaks
(each about 90g/3½oz) in oil for 30 seconds
on each side. Make the jerk sauce as above,
using vegetable instead of chicken stock.
Cook in the same way as the chicken recipe
above, and serve with plain boiled rice and
chargrilled pineapple wedges.

1 Wipe the chicken pieces, then pat dry on kitchen paper. Heat the oil and butter in a frying pan until melted, then add the chicken, in batches if necessary, and cook until browned on all sides. Remove with a slotted spoon, leaving the fat in the pan, and transfer to the ceramic cooking pot. Switch the slow cooker to high.

2 Add the spring onions, garlic and chilli to the frying pan and cook gently for 4–5 minutes, or until softened, stirring frequently. Stir in the allspice, cinnamon, thyme, nutmeg and sugar. Sprinkle in the flour and stir to mix, then gradually add the chicken stock, stirring until the mixture bubbles and thickens. Remove the pan from the heat.

3 Stir the vinegar, lime juice, tomato purée and some salt and ground black pepper into the sauce. Pour over the chicken pieces, cover with a lid and cook on high for 3–4 hours, or until the chicken is cooked and very tender.

4 Remove the chicken from the sauce and place on a serving dish. Taste the sauce and adjust the seasoning, then serve separately, with salad leaves or rice as an accompaniment.

COOK'S TIP
There are many recipes for jerk seasoning, but all include chillies, allspice and thyme. The spicy sauce not only flavours the meat, it also tenderizes it.

Energy 189Kcal/794kJ; Protein 21g; Carbohydrate 7g, of which sugars 3.1g; Fat 8.8g, of which saturates 3.1g; Cholesterol 107mg; Calcium 24mg; Fibre 0.5g; Sodium 238mg.

FRAGRANT CHICKEN CURRY

Lentils are used to thicken the sauce in this mild, fragrant curry, and fresh coriander gives the dish a really distinctive, fresh taste. The generous quantities of spinach mean that you won't need an additional vegetable dish to balance the meal.

2 Add the chicken to the lentil mixture, pressing it down in a single layer. Cover and cook on high for 3 hours, or until the chicken is just tender.

3 Add the spinach to the pot, pressing it down into the hot liquid. Cover and cook for a further 30 minutes until wilted. Stir in the chopped coriander.

4 Season the curry with salt and pepper to taste, then serve garnished with fresh coriander sprigs and accompanied with basmati rice and poppadums.

COOK'S TIP
You will need a large slow cooker to accommodate all the spinach in this recipe. It will shrink down during cooking, but the initial volume is large. If you have a small slow cooker, use thawed, well-drained frozen spinach instead.

SERVES 4

75g/3oz/scant ½ cup red lentils
30ml/2 tbsp mild curry powder
10ml/2 tsp ground coriander
5ml/1 tsp cumin seeds
350ml/12fl oz/1½ cups boiling vegetable
    or chicken stock
8 chicken thighs, skinned
225g/8oz fresh shredded spinach
15ml/1 tbsp chopped fresh
    coriander (cilantro)
salt and ground black pepper
sprigs of fresh coriander (cilantro),
    to garnish
white or brown basmati rice
    and poppadums, to serve

1 Place the lentils in a sieve (strainer) and rinse under cold running water. Drain well, then put in the ceramic cooking pot with the curry powder, ground coriander, cumin seeds and stock. Cover and cook on high for 2 hours.

Energy 591Kcal/2490kJ; Protein 75.5g; Carbohydrate 38.2g, of which sugars 3.9g; Fat 16.1g, of which saturates 3.9g; Cholesterol 171mg; Calcium 426mg; Fibre 9.4g; Sodium 880mg.

CHICKEN in a CASHEW NUT SAUCE

The Moguls had a profound impact on the Indian cuisine, and the resulting style of cooking is known as Mughlai food. One of their legacies is the use of nut paste, which is used here to give the curry a rich yet delicately flavoured sauce.

SERVES 4

1 large onion, roughly chopped
1 clove garlic, crushed
15ml/1 tbsp tomato purée (paste)
50g/2oz/½ cup cashew nuts
7.5ml/1½ tsp garam masala
5ml/1 tsp chilli powder
1.5ml/¼ tsp ground turmeric
5ml/1 tsp salt
15ml/1 tbsp lemon juice
15ml/1 tbsp natural (plain) yogurt
30ml/2 tbsp vegetable oil
450g/1lb chicken breast fillets, skinned
    and cubed
175g/6oz/2¼ cups button (white)
    mushrooms
15ml/1 tbsp sultanas (golden raisins)
300ml/½ pint/1¼ cups chicken
    or vegetable stock
30ml/2 tbsp chopped fresh coriander
    (cilantro), plus extra to garnish
rice and fruit chutney, to serve

1 Put the onion, garlic, tomato purée, cashew nuts, garam masala, chilli powder, turmeric, salt, lemon juice and yogurt in a food processor and process to a paste.

2 Heat the oil in a large frying pan or wok and fry the cubes of chicken for a few minutes, or until just beginning to brown. Using a slotted spoon, transfer the chicken to the ceramic cooking pot, leaving the oil in the pan.

3 Add the spice paste and mushrooms to the pan, lower the heat and fry gently, stirring frequently, for 3–4 minutes. Tip the mixture into the ceramic pot.

4 Add the sultanas to the pot and stir in the chicken or vegetable stock. Cover with the lid and switch the slow cooker to high. Cook for 3–4 hours, stirring halfway through the cooking time. The chicken should be cooked through and very tender, and the sauce fairly thick.

5 Stir the chopped coriander into the sauce, then taste and add a little more salt and pepper, if necessary. Serve the curry from the ceramic cooking pot, or transfer to a warmed serving dish, and garnish with a sprinkling of chopped fresh coriander. Serve with rice and a fruit chutney, such as mango.

Energy 239Kcal/1006kJ; Protein 31.6g; Carbohydrate 10.7g, of which sugars 7.6g; Fat 8.1g, of which saturates 1.7g; Cholesterol 78.9mg; Calcium 39mg; Fibre 1.9g; Sodium 696mg.

CHICKEN and SPLIT PEA KORESH

A traditional Persian Koresh – a thick saucy stew served with rice – is usually made with lamb, but here chicken is used to create a lighter, lower-fat dish.

SERVES 4

50g/2oz/¼ cup green split peas
45ml/3 tbsp olive oil
1 large onion, finely chopped
450g/1lb boneless chicken thighs
350ml/12fl oz/1½ cups boiling
    chicken stock
5ml/1 tsp ground turmeric
2.5ml/½ tsp ground cinnamon
1.5ml/¼ tsp grated nutmeg
30ml/2 tbsp dried mint
2 aubergines (eggplant), diced
8 ripe tomatoes, diced
2 garlic cloves, crushed
salt and ground black pepper
fresh mint, to garnish
plain boiled rice, to serve

1 Put the split peas in a large bowl. Pour in cold water to cover and leave to soak for at least 6 hours or overnight.

2 Tip the split peas into a sieve (strainer) and drain well. Place in a large pan, cover with fresh cold water and bring to the boil. Boil rapidly for 10 minutes, then rinse, drain and set aside.

3 Heat 15ml/1 tbsp of the oil in a pan, add the onion and cook for about 5 minutes. Add the chicken and cook until golden on all sides, then transfer to the ceramic cooking pot. Add the split peas, hot chicken stock, turmeric, cinnamon, nutmeg and mint and season well with salt and black pepper.

4 Cover the pot with the lid and cook on high or auto for 1 hour. Switch the slow cooker to low or leave on auto and cook for a further 3 hours, or until the chicken is just cooked and the split peas are nearly tender.

5 Heat the remaining 30ml/2 tbsp of oil in a frying pan, add the diced aubergines and cook for about 5 minutes until lightly browned. Add the tomatoes and garlic and cook for a further 2 minutes.

6 Transfer the aubergines to the ceramic cooking pot, stir to combine, then cook for about 1 hour. Sprinkle with fresh mint leaves to garnish and serve with plain boiled rice.

Energy 298Kcal/1251kJ; Protein 29.1g; Carbohydrate 18.5g, of which sugars 10.2g; Fat 12.5g, of which saturates 2.3g; Cholesterol 118mg; Calcium 48mg; Fibre 4.5g; Sodium 206mg.

CHICKEN KORMA

*The use of ground almonds to thicken the sauce gives this mild, fragrant curry a
beautifully creamy texture. Its mild taste makes it particularly popular with children.*

SERVES 4

75g/3oz/¾ cup flaked (sliced) almonds
15ml/1 tbsp ghee or butter
675g/1½lb skinless, boneless chicken
   breast portions, cut into bitesize
   pieces
about 15ml/1 tbsp sunflower oil
1 onion, chopped
4 green cardamom pods
2 garlic cloves, crushed
10ml/2 tsp ground cumin
5ml/1 tsp ground coriander
pinch of ground turmeric
1 cinnamon stick
good pinch of chilli powder
250ml/8fl oz/1 cup coconut milk
120ml/4fl oz/½ cup boiling chicken stock
5ml/1 tsp tomato purée (paste) (optional)
75ml/5 tbsp single (light) cream
15–30ml/1–2 tbsp fresh lime
   or lemon juice
10ml/2 tsp grated lime or lemon rind
5ml/1 tsp garam masala
salt and ground black pepper
saffron rice and poppadums, to serve

1 Dry-fry the flaked almonds in a frying
pan until pale golden. Transfer about
two-thirds of the almonds to a plate and
continue to dry-fry the remainder until
they are slightly deeper in colour. Put the
darker almonds on a separate plate and
set them aside to use for the garnish.
Leave the paler almonds to cool, then
grind them until fine in a spice grinder
or coffee mill used for the purpose.

2 Heat the ghee or butter in the frying
pan and gently fry the chicken pieces
until evenly brown. Transfer to a plate.

3 Add a little sunflower oil to the fat in
the pan, if necessary, then fry the onion
for 8 minutes. Stir in the cardamom
pods and garlic and fry for a further
2 minutes, until the onion is soft and
just starting to colour.

4 Add the ground almonds, cumin,
coriander, turmeric, cinnamon stick and
chilli powder to the frying pan and cook
for about 1 minute. Transfer the mixture
to the ceramic cooking pot and switch
the slow cooker to high.

5 Add the coconut milk, stock and
tomato purée, if using, to the pot and
stir in. Add the chicken and season with
salt and pepper. Cover and cook on high
for 3 hours, until the chicken is tender.

6 Stir the single cream, citrus juice and
rind and the garam masala into the curry
and cook on high for 30 minutes. Season
with salt and pepper to taste, garnish
with the reserved almonds, then
serve immediately with saffron rice
and poppadums.

Energy 410Kcal/1714kJ; Protein 45.7g; Carbohydrate 7.8g, of which sugars 6.4g; Fat 22g, of which saturates 6g; Cholesterol 136mg; Calcium 98mg; Fibre 1.9g; Sodium 202mg.

BRAISED GUINEA FOWL with RED CABBAGE

The slightly gamey flavour of guinea fowl is complemented perfectly by the sweet, fruity flavour of red cabbage, braised in apple juice and scented with juniper berries.

SERVES 4

15ml/1 tbsp unsalted (sweet) butter
½ red cabbage, weighing
    about 450g/1lb
1.3kg/3lb oven-ready guinea
    fowl, jointed
15ml/1 tbsp sunflower oil
3 shallots, very finely chopped
15ml/1 tbsp plain (all-purpose) flour
120ml/4fl oz/½ cup chicken stock
150ml/¼ pint/⅔ cup apple juice
15ml/1 tbsp soft light brown sugar
15ml/1 tbsp red wine vinegar
4 juniper berries, lightly crushed
salt and ground black pepper

VARIATIONS

• Other mild-tasting poultry or game such as chicken or pheasant can be used in place of the guinea fowl, if preferred.
• Add to the fruity flavour of the cabbage by adding 15ml/1tbsp sultanas (golden raisins) to the pot before cooking.

1 Use half the butter to grease the ceramic cooking pot. Cut the cabbage into wedges, removing any tough outer leaves and the central core. Shred the cabbage finely, then place in the ceramic cooking pot, packing it down tightly.

2 Rinse the guinea fowl portions and pat dry with kitchen paper. Heat the remaining butter and the oil in a pan and brown the guinea fowl on all sides. Lift from the pan, leaving the fat behind, and place on top of the red cabbage.

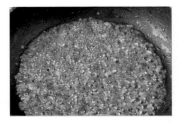

3 Add the shallots to the frying pan and cook gently for 5 minutes. Sprinkle with the flour, cook for a few seconds, then gradually stir in the stock followed by the apple juice. Bring to the boil, stirring continuously, until thickened. Remove from the heat, stir in the sugar, vinegar and juniper berries, and season.

4 Pour the sauce over the guinea fowl, cover and cook on high for 4 hours, or until the meat and cabbage are tender. Check the seasoning and serve.

Energy 456Kcal/1907kJ; Protein 44.5g; Carbohydrate 20g, of which sugars 15g; Fat 22.5g, of which saturates 6.7g; Cholesterol 225mg; Calcium 96mg; Fibre 3.1g; Sodium 15mg

GUINEA FOWL and SPRING VEGETABLE STEW

Resembling a well-flavoured chicken stew, this tasty dish of guinea fowl cooked with spring vegetables and flavoured with mustard and herbs is a sure winner.

SERVES 4

1.6kg/3½lb guinea fowl
45ml/3 tbsp plain (all-purpose) flour
45ml/3 tbsp olive oil
115g/4oz pancetta, cut into tiny cubes
1 onion, chopped
3 cloves garlic, chopped
200ml/7fl oz/scant 1 cup white wine
225g/8oz baby carrots
225g/8oz baby turnips
6 baby leeks, cut into 7.5cm/3in lengths
sprig of fresh thyme
1 bay leaf
10ml/2 tsp Dijon mustard
150ml/¼ pint/⅔ cup boiling chicken
   or vegetable stock
225g/8oz shelled peas
30ml/2 tbsp chopped fresh parsley
15ml/1 tbsp chopped fresh mint
salt and ground black pepper

1 Joint the guinea fowl into eight pieces. Wipe or lightly rinse them, then pat dry on kitchen paper. Season the flour with salt and pepper and toss the guinea fowl portions in it. Set aside any leftover flour.

2 Heat 30ml/2 tbsp of the oil in a large frying pan, add the pancetta and fry over a medium heat until lightly browned, stirring occasionally. Using a slotted spoon, transfer the pancetta to the ceramic cooking pot, leaving any fat and juices in the frying pan.

3 Add the guinea fowl portions to the pan and fry, turning, until browned on all sides. Arrange the guinea fowl portions in a single layer in the cooking pot on top of the pancetta.

4 Add the remaining 15ml/1 tbsp oil to the frying pan, add the onion and cook for 3–4 minutes, until just beginning to soften. Add the garlic and cook for about 1 minute, then stir in the reserved flour. Gradually stir in the wine and bring to the boil. Pour over the guinea fowl.

5 Add the carrots, turnips and leeks to the cooking pot with the thyme and bay leaf. Blend the mustard with the stock, season with salt and pepper and pour over. Cover with the lid and cook on high for 3–4 hours, or until the guinea fowl and vegetables are tender.

6 Add the peas to the stew and cook for a further 45 minutes. Taste and adjust the seasoning, then stir in most of the fresh herbs. Divide the stew among four warmed serving plates, sprinkle the remaining fresh herbs over the top and serve immediately.

COOK'S TIPS
• To save time on preparation, ask your butcher to joint the guinea fowl for you.
• Rabbit has a delicate flavour that goes well with the tender spring vegetables and herbs used in this stew. Try using eight rabbit joints in place of the guinea fowl.

Energy 581Kcal/2425kJ; Protein 50.5g; Carbohydrate 29.1g, of which sugars 11.2g; Fat 26.5g, of which saturates 7.4g; Cholesterol 224mg; Calcium 109mg; Fibre 6.9g; Sodium 668mg.

DUCK STEW with OLIVES

Cooking duck with olives, onions and wine has its roots in Provence in France. The sweetness brought out by slow-cooking the onions balances the saltiness of the olives.

SERVES 4

4 duck quarters or breast portions
225g/8oz baby (pearl) onions, peeled
2.5ml/½ tsp caster (superfine) sugar
30ml/2 tbsp plain (all-purpose) flour
250ml/8fl oz/1 cup dry red wine
250ml/8fl oz/1 cup duck or chicken stock
1 bouquet garni
115g/4oz/1 cup pitted green or black olives, or a combination
salt and ground black pepper

1 Put the duck skin side down in a large frying pan and cook for 10–12 minutes, turning to colour evenly, until browned on both sides. Lift out with a slotted spoon and place skin side up in the ceramic cooking pot. Switch the slow cooker to high.

2 Pour off most of the fat from the pan, leaving about 15ml/1 tbsp behind. Add the onions and cook over a medium-low heat until beginning to colour. Sprinkle over the sugar and cook for 5 minutes until golden, stirring frequently. Sprinkle the onions with the flour and cook, uncovered, for 2 minutes, stirring frequently so it does not stick.

3 Gradually stir the red wine into the onions, followed by the stock. Bring to the boil, then pour over the duck. Add the bouquet garni to the pot, cover with the lid and cook on high for 1 hour.

4 Turn the slow cooker to low and cook for a further 4–5 hours, or until the duck and onions are very tender.

5 Put the olives in a heatproof bowl and pour over very hot water to cover. Leave to stand for about 1 minute, then drain thoroughly. Add the olives to the casserole, re-cover with the lid and cook for a further 30 minutes.

6 Transfer the duck, onions and olives to a warm serving dish or individual plates. Skim all the fat from the cooking liquid and discard the bouquet garni. Season the sauce to taste with black pepper and a little salt, if needed, then spoon over the duck and serve immediately.

COOK'S TIPS
• Taste the stew before adding more salt; if the olives were salty, the stew will not need any more.
• The skin may be removed from the duck before cooking, if you prefer, and the duck pieces cooked in 15ml/1 tbsp oil for a few minutes to brown them.

Energy 414Kcal/1736kJ; Protein 47.3g; Carbohydrate 8.2g, of which sugars 2.3g; Fat 18.5g, of which saturates 5.2g; Cholesterol 257mg; Calcium 67mg; Fibre 1.6g; Sodium 917mg.

PAPPARDELLE with RABBIT

This rich-tasting dish comes from northern Italy, where rabbit sauces are very popular.
It is ideal for entertaining as the sauce can be kept warm in the slow cooker until needed.

SERVES 4

15g/½oz dried porcini mushrooms
150ml/¼ pint/⅔ cup warm water
1 small onion
½ carrot
½ celery stick
2 bay leaves
25g/1oz/2 tbsp butter or 15ml/1 tbsp
   olive oil
40g/1½oz pancetta or rindless streaky
   (fatty) bacon, chopped
15ml/1 tbsp roughly chopped fresh flat leaf
   parsley, plus extra to garnish
250g/9oz boneless rabbit meat
60ml/4 tbsp dry white wine
200g/7oz can chopped Italian plum
   tomatoes or 200ml/7fl oz/scant 1 cup
   passata (bottled strained tomatoes)
300g/11oz fresh or dried pappardelle
salt and ground black pepper

1 Put the dried mushrooms in a bowl, pour over the warm water and leave to soak for 15 minutes. Finely chop the vegetables, either in a food processor or by hand. Make a tear in each bay leaf, so that they will release their flavour when added to the sauce.

2 Heat the butter or oil in a large frying pan until just sizzling. Add the chopped vegetables, pancetta or bacon and the parsley and cook for about 5 minutes.

3 Add the rabbit pieces and fry on both sides for 3–4 minutes. Transfer the mixture to the ceramic cooking pot and switch to the high or auto setting. Add the wine and tomatoes or passata.

4 While the mixture is starting to heat through, drain the mushrooms and strain the soaking liquid into the slow cooker through a fine sieve (strainer). Chop the mushrooms and add to the mixture, with the bay leaves. Season to taste with salt and black pepper. Stir well, cover with the lid and cook for 1 hour. Reduce the setting to low or leave on auto, and cook for a further 2 hours, or until the meat is tender.

5 Lift out the rabbit pieces, cut them into bite-size chunks and stir them back into the sauce. Remove and discard the bay leaves. Taste the sauce and season, as necessary. The sauce is now ready to serve, but can be kept hot in the slow cooker for 1–2 hours.

6 About 10 minutes before serving, cook the pasta according to the instructions on the packet. Drain the pasta, add to the sauce and toss well to mix. Serve immediately, sprinkled with fresh parsley.

VARIATION
If you prefer, or if rabbit is not available, this dish can be made with chicken instead.

Energy 393Kcal/1653kJ; Protein 23g; Carbohydrate 46g, of which sugars 4.9g; Fat 13.3g, of which saturates 5g; Cholesterol 46mg; Calcium 80mg; Fibre 1.1g; Sodium 128mg.

HARE POT PIES

The full, gamey flavour of hare is perfect for this dish, but boneless rabbit, venison, pheasant or any other game meat can be used instead. The meat filling is cooked in the slow cooker until tender and succulent – this can be done the day before if you like – before being topped with pastry and finished in the oven.

SERVES 4

45ml/3 tbsp olive oil
1 leek, sliced
225g/8oz parsnips, sliced
225g/8oz carrots, sliced
1 fennel bulb, sliced
675g/1½lb boneless hare, diced
30ml/2 tbsp plain (all-purpose) flour
60ml/4 tbsp Madeira
300ml/½ pint/1¼ cups game
    or chicken stock
45ml/3 tbsp chopped fresh parsley
450g/1lb puff pastry, thawed
    if frozen
beaten egg yolk, to glaze

VARIATION
You can make one large single pie, instead of four individual ones, if you like.

1 Heat 30ml/2 tbsp of the oil in a large pan. Add the leek, parsnips, carrots and fennel and cook for about 10 minutes, stirring frequently, until softened.

2 Using a slotted spoon, transfer the vegetables to the ceramic cooking pot. Cover with the lid and switch the slow cooker to the high or auto setting.

3 Heat the remaining oil in the pan and fry the hare in batches until well browned. When all the meat has been cooked, return it to the pan. Sprinkle over the flour and cook, stirring, for a few seconds, then gradually stir in the Madeira and stock and bring to the boil.

4 Transfer the hare mixture to the ceramic cooking pot and cook for 1 hour. Switch the slow cooker to low or leave on auto and cook for a further 5–6 hours, until the meat and vegetables are tender. Stir in the chopped parsley, then set aside to cool.

5 To make the pies, preheat the oven to 220°C/425°F/Gas 7. Spoon the hare mixture into four individual pie dishes. Cut the pastry into quarters and roll out on a lightly floured work surface to make the pie covers. Make the pieces larger than the dishes. Trim off any excess pastry and use the trimmings to line the rim of each dish.

6 Dampen the pastry rims with cold water and cover with the pastry lids. Pinch the edges together to seal in the filling. Brush each pie with beaten egg yolk and make a small hole in the top of each one to allow steam to escape.

7 Stand the pies on a baking tray and bake for 25 minutes, or until the pastry is well risen and dark golden. If the pastry is browning too quickly, cover with foil after 15 minutes to prevent it from overbrowning.

Energy 906Kcal/3784kJ; Protein 45g; Carbohydrate 60.4g, of which sugars 10g; Fat 53.7g, of which saturates 15.9g; Cholesterol 107mg; Calcium 180mg; Fibre 7.6g; Sodium 553mg.

RABBIT CASSEROLE with JUNIPER

Because rabbit is such a lean meat, casseroling is an ideal way to cook it, helping to keep it really moist and juicy. Using a well-flavoured marinade improves both the taste and texture of the meat. Chicken leg portions make an excellent alternative to rabbit if you prefer. Serve with steamed new potatoes and whole baby carrots.

SERVES 4

900g/2lb prepared rabbit pieces
1 onion, roughly chopped
2 garlic cloves, crushed
1 bay leaf
350ml/12fl oz/1½ cups fruity red wine
2 sprigs of fresh thyme
1 sprig of fresh rosemary
15ml/1 tbsp juniper berries
30ml/2 tbsp olive oil
15g/½oz dried porcini mushrooms
30ml/2 tbsp chopped fresh parsley
25g/1oz/2 tbsp chilled butter
salt and ground black pepper

1 Put the rabbit pieces in a glass or ceramic dish with the onion, garlic, bay leaf and wine. Bruise the thyme and rosemary to release their flavour and lightly crush the juniper berries and add them to the dish. Toss to combine. Cover and marinate in the refrigerator for at least 4 hours or overnight, turning the pieces once or twice, if possible.

2 Remove the rabbit from the marinade, reserving the marinade, and pat dry with kitchen paper. Heat the oil in a frying pan, add the rabbit pieces and fry for 3–5 minutes, turning to brown all over. Transfer the meat to the ceramic cooking pot.

3 Pour the marinade into the frying pan and bring to boiling point. Pour over the rabbit, cover the ceramic cooking pot with the lid and switch the slow cooker to high. Cook for about 1 hour.

4 Meanwhile, put the mushrooms in a heatproof bowl and pour over 150ml/¼ pint/⅔ cup boiling water. Leave to soak for 1 hour, then drain, reserving the soaking liquid, and finely chop the mushrooms. Put the mushrooms in a small bowl and cover with clear film (plastic wrap) to keep them moist.

5 Pour the soaking liquid from the mushrooms into the ceramic cooking pot. Cook for a further 2 hours. Lift out the rabbit pieces with a slotted spoon and strain the cooking liquid, discarding the vegetables, herbs and juniper berries. Wipe the ceramic cooking pot clean, then return the rabbit and cooking liquid. Add the mushrooms and season.

6 Cover and cook for a further hour, or until the meat and mushrooms are cooked and tender. Stir in the chopped parsley, then lift out the rabbit pieces and arrange on a warmed serving dish. Cut the chilled butter into small cubes and whisk it into the sauce, one or two pieces at a time, to thicken. Spoon the sauce over the rabbit and serve.

Energy 356Kcal/1483kJ; Protein 32g; Carbohydrate 3.2g, of which sugars 2.3g; Fat 17.5g, of which saturates 6.3g; Cholesterol 163mg; Calcium 30mg; Fibre 0.6g; Sodium 66mg.

ONE-POT AND CLAY-POT POULTRY AND GAME

This chapter lifts the lid on delicious main courses using chicken, duck, pheasant, grouse, guinea fowl, pigeon, venison and rabbit. All are made effortlessly on top of the stove or in a free-standing electric cooker. You'll be reminded of old favourites like Coq au Vin, Chicken Casserole with Winter Vegetables and Hunter's Chicken, and invited to try some exciting new flavours, such as Guinea Fowl with Beans and Curly Kale, Mediterranean Duck with Harissa and Saffron, or Grouse with Orchard Fruit Stuffing. For a great experience you'll be sure to repeat, try Spicy Venison Casserole.

HUNTER'S CHICKEN

This traditional dish sometimes has strips of green pepper in the sauce instead of the
mushrooms. Creamed potato or polenta makes a good accompaniment.

2 Heat the oil and butter in a large, flameproof casserole until foaming. Add the chicken portions and sauté over a medium heat for 5 minutes, or until golden brown. Remove the pieces and drain on kitchen paper.

3 Add the sliced onion and chopped porcini mushrooms to the pan. Cook gently, stirring frequently, for about 3 minutes until the onion has softened but not browned. Stir in the chopped tomatoes, red wine and reserved mushroom soaking liquid, then add the crushed garlic and chopped rosemary, with salt and pepper to taste. Bring to the boil, stirring constantly.

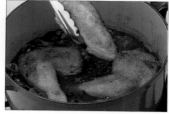

4 Return the chicken to the casserole and turn to coat with the sauce. Cover with a tightly fitting lid and simmer gently for 30 minutes.

SERVES 4

15g/½oz/¼ cup dried porcini mushrooms
30ml/2 tbsp olive oil
15g/½oz/1 tbsp butter
4 chicken portions, on the bone, skinned
1 large onion, thinly sliced
400g/14oz can chopped tomatoes
150ml/¼ pint/⅔ cup red wine
1 garlic clove, crushed
leaves of 1 fresh rosemary sprig,
    finely chopped
115g/4oz/1¾ cups fresh field (portabello)
    mushrooms, thinly sliced
salt and ground black pepper
fresh rosemary sprigs, to garnish

1 Put the porcini in a bowl, add 250ml/ 8fl oz/1 cup warm water and soak for 20 minutes. Squeeze the porcini over the bowl, strain the liquid and reserve. Finely chop the porcini.

5 Add the fresh mushrooms to the casserole and stir well to mix into the sauce. Continue simmering gently for 10 minutes, or until the chicken is tender. Taste for seasoning. Serve hot, with creamed potato or polenta, if you like. Garnish with the rosemary sprigs.

Energy 310Kcal/1299kJ; Protein 38.2g; Carbohydrate 9.2g, of which sugars 7.5g; Fat 10.8g, of which saturates 3.3g; Cholesterol 113mg; Calcium 38mg; Fibre 2.4g; Sodium 128mg.

SEVILLE CHICKEN

Oranges and almonds are a favourite ingredient in southern Spain, especially around
Seville, where the orange and almond trees are a familiar and wonderful sight.

SERVES 4

1 orange
8 chicken thighs
plain (all-purpose) flour, seasoned with
    salt and pepper
45ml/3 tbsp olive oil
1 large Spanish (Bermuda) onion,
    roughly chopped
2 garlic cloves, crushed
1 red (bell) pepper, seeded and sliced
1 yellow (bell) pepper, seeded and sliced
115g/4oz chorizo, sliced
50g/2oz/½ cup flaked (sliced) almonds
225g/8oz/generous 1 cup brown
    basmati rice
about 600ml/1 pint/2½ cups chicken
    or vegetable stock
400g/14oz can chopped tomatoes
175ml/6fl oz/¾ cup white wine
generous pinch of dried thyme
salt and ground black pepper
fresh thyme sprigs, to garnish

3 Add the chorizo, stir-fry for a few
minutes, then sprinkle over the almonds
and rice. Cook, stirring, for 1–2 minutes.

4 Pour in the chicken or vegetable stock,
chopped tomatoes and white wine, then
add the reserved orange peel and the
dried thyme. Season well. Bring the
sauce to simmering point, stirring, then
return the chicken to the pan.

5 Cover tightly and cook over a very
low heat for 1–1¼ hours until the rice
and chicken are tender. Just before
serving, add the orange segments and
juice, and allow to cook briefly to heat
through. Season to taste, garnish with
sprigs of fresh thyme and serve.

1 Pare a thin strip of peel from the
orange using a vegetable peeler and set
it aside. Peel the orange, then cut it into
even segments, working over a bowl to
catch any excess juice. Dust the chicken
thighs with plenty of seasoned flour.

2 Heat the olive oil in a large frying pan
and fry the chicken pieces on both sides
until nicely brown. Transfer the browned
chicken to a plate. Add the chopped
onion and crushed garlic to the pan and
fry for 4–5 minutes until the onion
begins to brown. Add the sliced red
and yellow peppers to the pan and fry,
stirring occasionally with a wooden
spoon, until they are slightly softened.

Energy 861Kcal/3598kJ; Protein 65.3g; Carbohydrate 67.1g, of which sugars 17.1g; Fat 34g, of which saturates 5.6g; Cholesterol 155mg; Calcium 172mg; Fibre 6.3g; Sodium 453mg.

MUSTARD BAKED CHICKEN

In this recipe, a mild, aromatic wholegrain mustard makes a tasty way of cooking chicken.
Speciality mustards are freely available in delicatessens and wholefood shops. Serve with
new potatoes and peas or mangetouts.

SERVES 4–6

8–12 chicken joints, or 1 medium chicken,
   about 1kg/2¼lb, jointed
juice of ½ lemon
15–30ml/2–3 tbsp whiskey mustard
10ml/2 tsp chopped fresh tarragon
sea salt and ground black pepper

VARIATION
A whole chicken can also be baked this
way. Allow about 1½ hours in an oven
preset to 180°C/350°F/Gas 4. When
cooked, the juices will run clear without
any trace of blood.

1 Preheat the oven to 190°C/375°F/
Gas 5. Put the chicken joints into a large
shallow baking dish in a single layer and
sprinkle the lemon juice over the chicken
to flavour the skin. Season well with sea
salt and black pepper.

2 Spread the mustard over the joints
and sprinkle with the chopped tarragon.
Bake in the preheated oven for 20–30
minutes or until thoroughly cooked,
depending on the size of the chicken
pieces. Serve immediately.

Per portion Energy 426Kcal/1768kJ; Protein 40.3g; Carbohydrate 0g, of which sugars 0g; Fat 29.3g, of which saturates 8.1g; Cholesterol 215mg; Calcium 13mg; Fibre 0g; Sodium 146mg.

ROAST FARMYARD DUCK with APPLES and CIDER

Sharp fruit flavours offset the richness of duck: orange is the classic, but cooking apples are used here with dry cider. Serve with a selection of vegetables.

SERVES 4

2kg/4½lb oven-ready duck or duckling
300ml/½ pint/1¼ cups dry (hard) cider
60ml/4 tbsp double (heavy) cream
sea salt and ground black pepper

For the stuffing
75g/3oz/6 tbsp butter
115g/4oz/2 cups fresh white
    breadcrumbs
450g/1lb cooking apples, peeled, cored
    and diced
15ml/1 tbsp sugar, or to taste
freshly grated nutmeg

1 Preheat the oven to 200°C/400°F/ Gas 6. To make the stuffing, melt the butter in a pan and gently fry the breadcrumbs until golden brown. Add the apples to the breadcrumbs with salt, pepper, the sugar and a pinch of nutmeg. Mix together well.

2 Wipe the duck out with a clean, damp cloth, and remove any obvious excess fat (including the flaps just inside the vent). Rub the skin with salt. Stuff the duck with the prepared mixture, then secure the vent with a small skewer.

COOK'S TIP
The giblets aren't required for this recipe, but you can remove the liver and set it aside to use in a warm salad. The remaining giblets can be used later, with the duck carcass, to make a delicious stock for soup.

3 Weigh the stuffed duck and calculate the cooking time, allowing 20 minutes per 450g/1lb. Prick the skin in several places with a fork or skewer, to allow the fat to run out during the cooking time, then place the duck on top of a wire rack in a roasting pan, then sprinkle the skin with freshly ground black pepper and put it into the preheated oven to roast.

4 About 20 minutes before the end of the estimated cooking time, remove the duck from the oven and pour off all the fat that has accumulated under the rack (reserve it for frying). Slide the duck off the rack into the roasting pan and pour the cider over it. Return to the oven and finish cooking, basting occasionally.

5 When the duck is cooked through, remove it from the pan and keep in a warm place while you make the sauce. Set the roasting pan over a medium heat and bring the cider to to the boil. Heat until it is reduced by half. Stir in the cream, heat through and season. Meanwhile, remove the stuffing from the duck. Carve the duck into slices or quarter it using poultry shears. Serve with a portion of stuffing and the cider sauce.

Energy 572Kcal/2397kJ; Protein 31.5g; Carbohydrate 34.6g, of which sugars 13.1g; Fat 33.1g, of which saturates 17.8g; Cholesterol 211mg; Calcium 74mg; Fibre 2.4g; Sodium 498mg.

CHICKEN GUMBO with OKRA, HAM, TOMATOES and PRAWNS

This classic Creole dish is really a very hearty soup, but is usually served over rice as a delicious and filling main course, like a stew.

SERVES 4

30ml/2 tbsp olive oil
1 onion, chopped
225g/8oz skinless, boneless chicken
   breast portions, cut into
   small chunks
25g/1oz/¼ cup plain (all-purpose) flour
5ml/1 tsp paprika
30ml/2 tbsp tomato purée (paste)
600ml/1 pint/2½ cups well-flavoured
   chicken stock
400g/14oz can chopped tomatoes
   with herbs
a few drops of Tabasco
175g/6oz okra
1 red, orange or yellow (bell) pepper,
   seeded and chopped
2 celery sticks, sliced
225g/8oz/1⅓ cups diced lean
   cooked ham
225g/8oz large prawns (shrimp), peeled,
   deveined and heads removed, but with
   tails intact
salt and ground black pepper
boiled rice, to serve

1 Soak a large clay pot or chicken brick in cold water for 20 minutes, then drain. Heat the oil in a large frying pan, add the chopped onion and cook over a medium heat for about 5 minutes, stirring occasionally, until softened and lightly golden.

2 Add the chicken chunks to the pan and sauté for 1–2 minutes, to seal. Stir in the flour, paprika and tomato purée and cook, stirring constantly, for 1–2 minutes.

3 Gradually add the stock, stirring constantly, then bring the sauce to the boil, stirring. Add the chopped tomatoes, then remove the pan from the heat. Add a few drops of Tabasco and season with salt and pepper.

4 Cut the okra pods in half if they are large, then add them to the clay pot or chicken brick with the chopped red, orange or yellow pepper and the sliced celery. Add the chicken and tomato mixture and stir well to mix.

5 Cover the clay pot or chicken brick and place it in an unheated oven. Set the oven to 200°C/400°F/Gas 6 and cook for 30 minutes.

6 Remove the clay pot or chicken brick from the oven, then add the diced ham and the prawns and stir well to combine. Cover the pot or brick and return it to the oven for about 10 minutes, or until the ham is heated through and the prawns are just cooked. To serve, spoon some freshly boiled rice into four warmed, individual serving plates or bowls and ladle over the gumbo.

VARIATIONS
Replace the cooked ham with crab meat or cooked and shelled mussels or, for a special occasion, replace the peeled prawns with crayfish and replace the ham with cooked and shelled oysters.

COOK'S TIPS
• Okra is a favourite ingredient in the southern states of the USA and in African and Caribbean cooking. When buying, look for firm, bright green pods that are less than 10cm/4in long. Larger pods may be slightly tough and fibrous. When cooked, okra produces a rather viscous substance that thickens the liquid in which it is cooked – an essential part of many traditional okra recipes.
• If you don't have a bottle of Tabasco sauce to hand, add about 2.5ml/½ tsp chilli powder, or a finely chopped fresh or dried chilli. Remove the seeds from the chilli if you would prefer the gumbo to be only medium-hot.

Energy 290Kcal/1221kJ; Protein 37.3g; Carbohydrate 15g, of which sugars 9.6g; Fat 9.4g, of which saturates 1.9g; Cholesterol 182mg; Calcium 153mg; Fibre 4.2g; Sodium 858mg.

CHICKEN with FORTY CLOVES of GARLIC

This dish does not have to be mathematically exact, so do not worry if you have 35 or even 50 cloves of garlic – the important thing is that there should be lots. The smell that emanates from the oven as the chicken and garlic cook is indescribably delicious.

SERVES 4–5

5–6 whole heads of garlic
15g/½oz/1 tbsp butter
45ml/3 tbsp olive oil
1.8–2kg/4–4½lb chicken
150g/5oz/1¼ cups plain (all-purpose) flour,
    plus 5ml/1 tsp
75ml/5 tbsp white port, Pineau
    de Charentes or other white,
    fortified wine
2–3 fresh tarragon or rosemary sprigs
30ml/2 tbsp crème fraîche (optional)
a few drops of lemon juice (optional)
salt and ground black pepper

1 Separate three of the heads of garlic into cloves and peel them. Remove the first layer of papery skin from the remaining heads of garlic and cut off the tops to expose the cloves, if you like, or leave them whole. Preheat the oven to 180°C/350°F/Gas 4.

2 Heat the butter and 15ml/1 tbsp of the olive oil in a flameproof casserole that is just large enough to take the chicken and garlic. Add the chicken and cook over a medium heat, turning it frequently, for 10–15 minutes, until it is browned all over.

3 Sprinkle in 5ml/1 tsp flour and cook for 1 minute. Add the port or wine. Tuck in the whole heads of garlic and the peeled cloves with the sprigs of tarragon or rosemary. Pour over the remaining oil and season to taste with salt and pepper.

4 Mix the main batch of flour with sufficient water to make a firm dough. Roll it out into a long sausage and press it around the rim of the casserole, then press on the lid, folding the dough up and over it to create a tight seal. Cook in the oven for 1½ hours.

5 To serve, lift off the lid to break the seal and remove the chicken and whole garlic to a serving platter and keep warm. Remove and discard the herb sprigs, then place the casserole on the stove top and whisk the remaining ingredients to combine the garlic cloves with the juices. Add the crème fraîche, if using, and a little lemon juice to taste, if using. Process the sauce in a food processor or blender until smooth. Reheat the garlic sauce in a clean pan if necessary and serve it with the chicken.

Energy 616Kcal/2565kJ; Protein 37.7g; Carbohydrate 31.6g, of which sugars 2.9g; Fat 36.5g, of which saturates 10.4g; Cholesterol 173mg; Calcium 64mg; Fibre 2.6g; Sodium 151mg.

POUSSINS and NEW POTATO POT-ROAST

Pot roasts are traditionally associated with the colder months, but this delicious version is a simple summer dish that makes the most of new season potatoes. Lemons and red onion with rosemary liven up the chicken and potatoes.

SERVES 4

2 poussins, about 500g/1¼lb each
25g/1oz/2 tbsp butter
15ml/1 tbsp clear honey
500g/1¼lb small new potatoes
1 red onion, halved lengthwise and cut
   into thin wedges
4–5 small rosemary sprigs
2 bay leaves
1 lemon, cut into wedges
450ml/¾ pint/scant 2 cups hot
   chicken stock
salt and ground black pepper

1 Soak a clay chicken brick in cold water for at least 20 minutes, then drain. Cut the poussins in half, along the breast bone.

2 Melt the butter, then add it to a small bowl with the honey. Mix together then brush over the poussins. Season with salt and pepper.

3 Place the potatoes and onions in the chicken brick. Tuck the rosemary sprigs, bay leaves and lemon wedges among the vegetables. Pour over the chicken stock.

4 Place the halved poussins on top of the vegetables. Cover the chicken brick and place it in an unheated oven. Set the oven to 200°C/400°F/Gas 6 and cook for 55–60 minutes, or until the poussin juices run clear and the vegetables are tender. Uncover the chicken for the last 10 minutes of cooking to add more colour to the poussins, if necessary.

COOK'S TIPS
• Make sure the stock is hot, but not boiling when it is added to the chicken brick otherwise the chicken brick may crack.
• A poussin is a baby chicken – usually around 4–6 weeks old. Poussins can be cooked by grilling (broiling), roasting or pot-roasting, but are especially tender and moist cooked in a chicken brick.

Energy 443Kcal/1852kJ; Protein 30.1g; Carbohydrate 24.2g, of which sugars 5.4g; Fat 25.8g, of which saturates 8.9g; Cholesterol 158mg; Calcium 23mg; Fibre 1.5g; Sodium 153mg.

STOVED CHICKEN

"Stovies" were originally potatoes slowly cooked on the stove with onions and dripping or butter until falling to pieces. This version includes a delicious layer of bacon and chicken.

2 Heat the butter and oil in a large, heavy frying pan, add the chopped bacon and chicken pieces and cook, turning occasionally, until brown on all sides. Using a slotted spoon, transfer the chicken and bacon to the earthenware dish. Reserve the fat in the pan.

3 Sprinkle the remaining chopped thyme over the chicken, season with salt and pepper, then cover with the remaining onion slices, followed by a neat, overlapping layer of the remaining potato slices. Season the top layer of potatoes with more salt and ground black pepper.

SERVES 4

1kg/2¼lb baking potatoes, cut into
  5mm/¼in slices
butter, for greasing
2 large onions, thinly sliced
15ml/1 tbsp chopped fresh thyme
25g/1oz/2 tbsp butter
15ml/1 tbsp vegetable oil
2 large bacon rashers (strips), chopped
4 large chicken portions, halved
600ml/1 pint/2½ cups chicken stock
1 bay leaf
salt and ground black pepper

COOK'S TIP

Instead of chicken portions, choose eight chicken thighs or chicken drumsticks.

1 Preheat the oven to 150°C/300°F/ Gas 2. Arrange a thick layer of half the potato slices in a large lightly greased, earthenware baking dish, then cover with half the onions. Sprinkle with half of the thyme, and season with salt and pepper to taste.

4 Pour the chicken stock into the casserole, add the bay leaf and brush the potatoes with the reserved fat from the frying pan. Cover tightly with foil and bake for about 2 hours, or until the chicken is cooked and tender.

5 Preheat the grill (broiler) to medium-hot, then remove the foil from the earthenware dish and place the dish under the grill. Cook until the slices of potato are beginning to turn golden brown and crisp. Remove the bay leaf and serve immediately.

Energy 500Kcal/2107kJ; Protein 50g; Carbohydrate 48.2g, of which sugars 8.9g; Fat 13.2g, of which saturates 5.4g; Cholesterol 144mg; Calcium 51mg; Fibre 3.9g; Sodium 405mg.

POT-ROAST CHICKEN with LEMON and GARLIC

This is a rustic dish that is easy to prepare. Lardons are thick strips of bacon fat; if you can't get them, use fatty bacon instead. Serve with thick bread to mop up the juices.

SERVES 4

30ml/2 tbsp olive oil
25g/1oz/2 tbsp butter
175g/6oz/1 cup smoked lardons, or
    roughly chopped streaky (fatty) bacon
8 garlic cloves, peeled
4 onions, quartered
10ml/2 tsp plain (all-purpose) flour
600ml/1 pint/2½ cups chicken stock
2 lemons, thickly sliced
45ml/3 tbsp chopped fresh thyme
1 chicken, about 1.3–1.6kg/3–3½lb
2 × 400g/14oz cans flageolet, cannellini
    or haricot (navy) beans, drained
    and rinsed
salt and ground black pepper

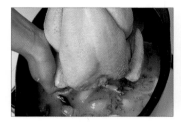

3 Bring the sauce to the boil, stirring constantly until thickened, then place the chicken on top. Season well. Transfer the casserole to the oven. Cook for 1 hour, basting the chicken once or twice during cooking to ensure it stays moist.

4 Baste the chicken again. Stir the beans into the casserole and return it to the oven for a further 30 minutes, or until the chicken is cooked through and tender. Carve the chicken into thick slices and serve with the beans.

1 Preheat the oven to 190°C/375°F/ Gas 5. Heat the oil and butter in a flameproof casserole that is large enough to hold the chicken with a little room around the sides. Add the lardons and cook until golden. Remove with a slotted spoon and drain on kitchen paper.

2 Add the garlic and onions and brown over a high heat. Stir in the flour, then the stock. Return the lardons to the pan with the lemon, thyme and seasoning.

Energy 887Kcal/3696kJ; Protein 62.5g; Carbohydrate 45.5g, of which sugars 12.9g; Fat 51.7g, of which saturates 16g; Cholesterol 256mg; Calcium 187mg; Fibre 13.9g; Sodium 1519mg.

CHICKEN and PRAWN JAMBALAYA

*This colourful mixture of rice, peppers and tomatoes with chicken, gammon and prawns is
flavoured with garlic and fresh herbs and a few dashes of fiery Tabasco sauce.*

SERVES 10

2 chickens, each about 1.3–1.6kg/3–3½lb
450g/1lb piece raw smoked gammon
   (smoked or cured ham)
50g/2oz/⅓ cup lard or
   bacon fat
50g/2oz/½ cup plain (all-purpose) flour
3 onions, finely sliced
2 green (bell) peppers, seeded and sliced
675g/1½lb tomatoes, peeled and chopped
2–3 garlic cloves, crushed
10ml/2 tsp chopped fresh thyme or
   5ml/1 tsp dried thyme
24 raw Mediterranean prawns (jumbo
   shrimp), peeled with tails intact
500g/1¼lb/2½ cups white long grain rice
1.2 litres/2 pints/5 cups water
2–3 dashes Tabasco sauce
45ml/3 tbsp chopped fresh flat leaf parsley,
   plus tiny fresh parsley sprigs to garnish
salt and ground black pepper

4 Add the diced gammon, onions, green
peppers, tomatoes, garlic and thyme and
stir well to mix. Cook, stirring regularly,
for about 10 minutes, then add the
prawns and mix lightly.

5 Stir the rice into the frying pan and
pour in the water. Season well with salt,
black pepper and Tabasco sauce. Bring
to the boil, then cook gently, stirring
occasionally, until the rice is tender and
all the liquid has been fully absorbed.
Add a little extra boiling water if the rice
looks like drying out before it is cooked.
Check the seasoning and add salt,
pepper and more Tabasco if necessary.

6 Mix the chopped fresh flat leaf parsley
into the finished dish, garnish with tiny
sprigs of flat leaf parsley and serve the
jambalaya immediately with plenty of
crusty bread.

1 Cut each chicken into ten pieces and
season the pieces well with salt and
pepper. Dice the gammon, discarding
the rind and fat.

2 Melt the lard or bacon fat in a large,
heavy frying pan. Add the chicken pieces
in several batches, cook them until they
are golden brown all over, then lift
them out with a slotted spoon and
set them aside.

3 Reduce the heat. Sprinkle the flour
into the fat in the pan and stir with a
wooden spoon until the roux turns a
golden brown colour. Return the chicken
pieces to the pan.

Energy 740Kcal/3079kJ; Protein 50.6g; Carbohydrate 52.9g, of which sugars 7.7g; Fat 36.1g, of which saturates 11.1g; Cholesterol 240mg; Calcium 79mg; Fibre 2.2g; Sodium 593mg.

RISOTTO with CHICKEN

This is a classic risotto combination of creamy rice and tender cubes of chicken, flavoured with aromatic saffron, prosciutto, white wine and Parmesan cheese.

SERVES 6

30ml/2 tbsp olive oil
225g/8oz skinless, boneless chicken breast
   portions, cut into 2.5cm/1in cubes
1 onion, finely chopped
1 garlic clove, finely chopped
450g/1lb/2¼ cups risotto rice
120ml/4fl oz/½ cup dry white wine
1.5ml/¼ tsp saffron threads
1.75 litres/3 pints/7½ cups simmering
   chicken stock
50g/2oz prosciutto, cut into
   thin strips
25g/1oz/2 tbsp butter, diced
25g/1oz/⅓ cup freshly grated Parmesan
   cheese, plus extra to serve
salt and ground black pepper
sprigs of flat leaf parsley, to garnish

1 Heat the olive oil in a large frying pan over a medium-high heat. Add the cubes of chicken and cook, stirring occasionally with a wooden spoon, until they start to turn white.

2 Reduce the heat to low and add the chopped onion and garlic. Cook, stirring occasionally, until the onion is soft. Stir in the risotto rice, then sauté for 2 minutes, stirring constantly, until all the rice grains are coated in oil.

3 Add the dry white wine to the rice mixture and cook, stirring constantly, until the wine has been absorbed. Add the saffron threads to the simmering stock and stir well, then add ladlefuls of hot stock to the rice mixture, allowing each ladleful to be fully absorbed before adding the next.

4 When the rice is about three-quarters cooked, add the strips of prosciutto and stir well. Continue cooking, stirring occasionally, until the rice is just tender and the risotto is creamy.

5 Add the butter and the Parmesan and stir in well. Season with salt and pepper to taste. Serve the risotto hot, sprinkled with a little more Parmesan, and garnish with flat leaf parsley.

Energy 418Kcal/1744kJ; Protein 17.9g; Carbohydrate 60.9g, of which sugars 0.8g; Fat 9.5g, of which saturates 3.8g; Cholesterol 44mg; Calcium 72mg; Fibre 0.1g; Sodium 194mg.

CHICKEN PIRI-PIRI

This is a classic Portuguese dish, based on a hot sauce made from Angolan chillies.

SERVES 4

4 chicken breast portions
30–45ml/2–3 tbsp olive oil
I large onion, finely sliced
2 carrots, cut into thin strips
I large parsnip or 2 small parsnips,
    cut into thin strips
I red (bell) pepper, seeded and sliced
I yellow (bell) pepper, seeded
    and sliced
I litre/1¾ pints/4 cups chicken or
    vegetable stock
3 tomatoes, peeled, seeded and chopped
generous dash of piri-piri sauce
15ml/1 tbsp tomato purée (paste)
½ cinnamon stick
I fresh thyme sprig, plus extra fresh
    thyme to garnish
I bay leaf
275g/10oz/1½ cups white long grain rice
15ml/1 tbsp lime or lemon juice
salt and ground black pepper

I Preheat the oven to 180°C/350°F/
Gas 4. Rub the chicken skin with a little
salt and ground black pepper. Heat
30ml/2 tbsp of the olive oil in a large
frying pan, add the chicken portions and
cook, turning occasionally until browned
on all sides. Transfer to a plate using a
metal spatula.

2 Add some more oil to the pan if
necessary, add the sliced onion and fry
for 2–3 minutes until slightly softened.
Add the carrot and parsnip strips and
the pepper slices and stir-fry for a few
minutes more. Cover the pan and cook
for 4–5 minutes until all the vegetables
are quite soft.

3 Pour in the chicken or vegetable stock,
then add the chopped tomatoes, piri-piri
sauce, tomato purée and cinnamon stick.
Stir in the thyme and bay leaf. Season to
taste with salt and ground black pepper
and bring to the boil. Using a ladle,
spoon off 300ml/½ pint/1¼ cups of the
liquid and set aside in a small pan.

4 Put the rice in the base of a large
earthenware dish. Using a slotted spoon,
scoop the vegetables out of the frying pan
and spread them over the rice. Arrange
the chicken pieces over the top of the
rice. Pour over the spicy chicken stock
from the frying pan, cover tightly and
cook in the oven for about 45 minutes,
until both the rice and chicken are
completely tender.

5 Meanwhile, heat the reserved chicken
stock, adding a few more drops of piri-
piri sauce and the lime or lemon juice.

6 To serve, spoon the piri-piri chicken
and rice on to warmed serving plates.
Serve the remaining sauce separately or
poured over the chicken.

Energy 557Kcal/2337kJ; Protein 44.3g; Carbohydrate 75.4g, of which sugars 15.5g; Fat 8.8g, of which saturates 1.5g; Cholesterol 105mg; Calcium 73mg; Fibre 5.8g; Sodium 122mg.

CHICKEN BIRYANI

Easy to make and very tasty, this is the ideal one-pot dish for a family supper.

SERVES 4

10 green cardamom pods
275g/10oz/1½ cups basmati rice, soaked
    and drained
2.5ml/½ tsp salt
2–3 cloves
5cm/2in cinnamon stick
45ml/3 tbsp vegetable oil
3 onions, sliced
4 chicken breast portions, each about
    175g/6oz, cubed
1.5ml/¼ tsp ground cloves
5ml/1 tsp ground cumin
5ml/1 tsp ground coriander
2.5ml/½ tsp ground black pepper
3 garlic cloves, chopped
5ml/1 tsp finely chopped fresh root ginger
juice of 1 lemon
4 tomatoes, sliced
30ml/2 tbsp chopped fresh
    coriander (cilantro)
150ml/¼ pint/⅔ cup natural (plain) yogurt
4–5 saffron threads, soaked in 10ml/2 tsp
    hot milk
150ml/¼ pint/⅔ cup water
toasted flaked (sliced) almonds and fresh
    coriander (cilantro) sprigs, to garnish
natural (plain) yogurt, to serve

1 Preheat the oven to 190°C/375°F/
Gas 5. Remove the seeds from half the
cardamom pods and grind them finely, using
a mortar and pestle. Set the seeds aside.

2 Bring a flameproof casserole of water
to the boil and add the soaked and
drained basmati rice, then stir in the salt,
the remaining whole cardamom pods,
whole cloves and cinnamon stick. Boil
the rice for 2 minutes, then drain,
leaving the whole spices in the rice.

3 Heat the oil in the flameproof
casserole and fry the onions for about
8 minutes, until softened and browned.
Add the cubed chicken and the ground
spices, including the ground cardamom
seeds. Mix well, then add the chopped
garlic, ginger and lemon juice. Stir-fry the
mixture together for 5 minutes.

4 Arrange the sliced tomatoes on top.
Sprinkle on the coriander, spoon the
yogurt on top and cover with the rice.

5 Drizzle the saffron milk over the rice
and add the water. Cover and bake for
1 hour. Garnish with almonds and
coriander and serve with extra yogurt.

Energy 563Kcal/2359kJ; Protein 45.4g; Carbohydrate 70g, of which sugars 12.5g; Fat 11.3g, of which saturates 1.7g; Cholesterol 105mg; Calcium 152mg; Fibre 3.2g; Sodium 138mg.

CHICKEN CASSEROLE with WINTER VEGETABLES

A casserole of wonderfully tender chicken, root vegetables and lentils, finished with a tangy mixture of crème fraîche, mustard and tarragon.

SERVES 4

350g/12oz onions
350g/12oz leeks
225g/8oz carrots
450g/1lb swede (rutabaga)
30ml/2 tbsp oil
4 chicken portions, about 900g/2lb total weight
115g/4oz/½ cup green lentils
475ml/16fl oz/2 cups chicken stock
300ml/½ pint/1¼ cups apple juice
10ml/2 tsp cornflour (cornstarch)
45ml/3 tbsp crème fraîche
10ml/2 tsp wholegrain mustard
30ml/2 tbsp chopped fresh tarragon
salt and ground black pepper
fresh tarragon sprigs, to garnish

1 Preheat the oven to 190°C/375°F/Gas 5. Prepare the onions, leeks, carrots and swede and roughly chop them.

COOK'S TIP
Chop the vegetables into similarly sized pieces so that they cook evenly.

2 Heat the oil in a large flameproof casserole. Season the chicken portions with plenty of salt and pepper and brown them in the hot oil until golden. Drain on kitchen paper.

3 Add the onions to the casserole and cook for 5 minutes, stirring, until they begin to soften and colour. Add the leeks, carrots, swede and lentils to the casserole and stir over a medium heat for 2 minutes.

4 Return the chicken to the pan, then add the stock, apple juice and seasoning. Bring to the boil and cover tightly. Cook in the oven for 50–60 minutes, or until the chicken and lentils are tender.

5 Place the casserole on the stove-top over a medium heat. In a small bowl, blend the cornflour with about 30ml/2 tbsp water to make a smooth paste and add to the casserole with the crème fraîche, wholegrain mustard and chopped tarragon. Adjust the seasoning, then simmer gently for about 2 minutes, stirring, until thickened slightly, before serving, garnished with tarragon sprigs.

Energy 477Kcal/2010kJ; Protein 46.8g; Carbohydrate 45.7g, of which sugars 24.9g; Fat 13.2g, of which saturates 4.5g; Cholesterol 118mg; Calcium 151mg; Fibre 8.1g; Sodium 141mg.

COQ au VIN

This French country casserole was traditionally made with an old boiling bird, marinated overnight in red wine, then simmered gently until tender. Modern recipes use tender roasting birds to save time and because boiling fowl are not readily available.

SERVES 6

45ml/3 tbsp light olive oil
12 shallots
225g/8oz rindless streaky (fatty) bacon
   rashers (strips), chopped
3 garlic cloves, finely chopped
225g/8oz small mushrooms, halved
6 boneless chicken thighs
3 boneless chicken breast
   portions, halved
1 bottle red wine
salt and ground black pepper
45ml/3 tbsp chopped fresh parsley,
   to garnish

For the bouquet garni
3 sprigs each parsley, thyme and sage
1 bay leaf
4 peppercorns

For the beurre manié
25g/1oz/2 tbsp butter, softened
25g/1oz/¼ cup plain (all-purpose) flour

1 Heat the oil in a large, flameproof casserole and cook the shallots for about 5 minutes, or until golden. Increase the heat, then add the chopped bacon, garlic and mushrooms and cook for a further 10 minutes, stirring frequently.

2 Use a slotted spoon to transfer the cooked ingredients to a plate, then brown the chicken portions in the oil remaining in the pan, turning them until they are golden brown all over. Return the cooked shallots, garlic, mushrooms and bacon to the casserole and pour in the red wine.

3 Tie the ingredients for the bouquet garni in a bundle in a small piece of muslin (cheesecloth) and add to the casserole. Bring to the boil, reduce the heat and cover the casserole with a tightly fitting lid, then simmer for 30–40 minutes.

4 To make the beurre manié, cream the butter and flour together in a small bowl using your fingers or a spoon to make a smooth paste.

5 Add small lumps of the beurre manié paste to the bubbling casserole, stirring well until each piece has melted into the liquid before adding the next. When all the paste has been added, bring the casserole back to the boil and simmer for 5 minutes.

6 Season the casserole to taste with salt and pepper and serve garnished with chopped fresh parsley and accompanied by boiled potatoes.

Energy 538Kcal/2240kJ; Protein 43.5g; Carbohydrate 7g, of which sugars 2.8g; Fat 28.2g, of which saturates 8.9g; Cholesterol 170mg; Calcium 50mg; Fibre 1.1g; Sodium 610mg.

BRAISED SAUSAGES with ONIONS, CELERIAC and APPLE

This richly flavoured casserole is comfort food at its best – serve with mashed potatoes and a glass or two of full-bodied red wine on a cold winter night.

SERVES 4

45ml/3 tbsp sunflower oil
450g/1lb duck or venison sausages
2 onions, sliced
15ml/1 tbsp plain (all-purpose) flour
400ml/14fl oz/1⅔ cups dry (hard) cider
350g/12oz celeriac, cut into
    large chunks
15ml/1 tbsp Worcestershire sauce
15ml/1 tbsp chopped fresh sage
2 small tart cooking apples, cored
    and sliced
salt and ground black pepper

1 Preheat the oven to 180°C/350°F/ Gas 4. Heat the oil in a frying pan, add the sausages and fry until evenly browned, about 5 minutes. Transfer to an earthenware casserole dish.

2 Drain off any excess oil from the pan to leave 15ml/1 tbsp. Add the onions and sauté for a few minutes until golden.

3 Stir in the flour, then gradually add the cider and bring to the boil, stirring. Add the celeriac and cook for 2 minutes. Stir in the Worcestershire sauce and sage. Season well with salt and black pepper.

4 Pour the cider and celeriac mixture over the sausages, then cover and cook in the oven for 30 minutes. Add the apples and cook for 10–15 minutes, or until the apples are just tender.

VARIATION
You can use good-quality pork and herb sausages instead, if you like.

Energy 538Kcal/2240kJ; Protein 43.5g; Carbohydrate 7g, of which sugars 2.8g; Fat 28.2g, of which saturates 8.9g; Cholesterol 170mg; Calcium 50mg; Fibre 1.1g; Sodium 610mg.

MEDITERRANEAN DUCK with HARISSA and SAFFRON

Harissa is a fiery chilli sauce from north Africa. Mixed with cinnamon, saffron and preserved lemon, it gives this colourful casserole an unforgettable flavour.

SERVES 4

15ml/1 tbsp olive oil
1.8–2kg/4–4½lb duck, quartered
1 large onion, thinly sliced
1 garlic clove, crushed
2.5ml/½ tsp ground cumin
400ml/14fl oz/1⅔ cups duck or
    chicken stock
juice of ½ lemon
5–10ml/1–2 tsp harissa
1 cinnamon stick
5ml/1 tsp saffron threads
50g/2oz/⅓ cup black olives
50g/2oz/⅓ cup green olives
peel of 1 preserved lemon, rinsed, drained
    and cut into fine strips
2–3 lemon slices
30ml/2 tbsp chopped fresh coriander
    (cilantro), plus extra leaves
        to garnish
salt and ground black pepper

1 Heat the oil in a flameproof casserole. Add the duck quarters and cook until browned all over. Remove the duck with a slotted spoon and set aside. Add the onion and garlic to the oil remaining in the casserole and cook for 5 minutes until soft. Add the ground cumin and cook, stirring, for 2 minutes.

COOK'S TIP
The term "duck" refers to birds over two months old. The rich flavour of duck is best appreciated when a duck reaches its full-grown size. Look for a duck with a supple, waxy skin with a dry appearance. It should have a long body with tender, meaty breasts.

2 Pour in the stock and lemon juice, then add the harissa, cinnamon and saffron. Bring to the boil. Return the duck to the casserole and add the olives, preserved lemon peel and lemon slices. Season with salt and pepper.

3 Lower the heat, partially cover the casserole and simmer gently for about 45 minutes, or until the duck is cooked through. Discard the cinnamon stick. Stir in the chopped coriander and garnish with the coriander leaves.

Energy 262Kcal/1095kJ; Protein 26.6g; Carbohydrate 8.3g, of which sugars 5.9g; Fat 34g, of which saturates 13.5g; Cholesterol 135mg; Calcium 79mg; Fibre 2.8g; Sodium 709mg.

CASSOULET

Based on the traditional French dish, this recipe is full of delicious flavours and makes a welcoming and warming meal.

SERVES 6

3–4 boneless duck breast portions, about
   450g/1lb total weight
225g/8oz thick-cut streaky (fatty) pork
   or unsmoked streaky (fatty) bacon
   rashers (strips)
450g/1lb Toulouse or garlic sausages
45ml/3 tbsp vegetable oil
450g/1lb onions, chopped
2 garlic cloves, crushed
2 × 425g/15oz cans cannellini beans, rinsed
   and drained
225g/8oz carrots, roughly chopped
400g/14oz can chopped tomatoes
15ml/1 tbsp tomato purée (paste)
bouquet garni
30ml/2 tbsp chopped fresh thyme or
   15ml/1 tbsp dried
475ml/16fl oz/2 cups well-flavoured
   chicken stock
115g/4oz/2 cups fresh white or wholemeal
   (whole-wheat) breadcrumbs
salt and ground black pepper
fresh thyme sprigs, to garnish
warm crusty bread, to serve

1 Preheat the oven to 160°C/325°F/
Gas 3. Cut the duck portions and pork
or bacon rashers into large pieces. Twist
the sausages to shorten them and then
cut them into short lengths.

COOK'S TIP
Cannellini beans are large white beans
with a nutty flavour. They are especially
popular in Italy, particularly in Tuscany,
where they are included in a variety of
pasta and soup dishes. Cannellini beans
are sometimes referred to as white
kidney beans or fazola beans.

2 Heat the oil in a large flameproof
casserole. Cook the meat in batches,
until well browned. Remove from the
pan with a slotted spoon and drain on
kitchen paper.

3 Add the onions and garlic to the pan
and cook for 3–4 minutes, or until
beginning to soften, stirring frequently.

4 Stir in the beans, carrots, tomatoes,
tomato purée, bouquet garni, thyme and
seasoning. Return the meat to the
casserole and mix until well combined.

VARIATION
Canned butter (lima) beans or borlotti
beans can be used in this recipe instead
of the cannellini beans.

5 Add enough of the stock just to cover
the meat and beans. (The cassoulet
shouldn't be swimming in juices; if the
mixture becomes too dry during the
cooking time, add a little more stock or
water.) Bring to the boil. Cover the
casserole tightly and cook in the oven
for 1 hour.

6 Remove the cassoulet from the oven
and add a little more stock or water, if
necessary. Remove the bouquet garni.

7 Sprinkle the breadcrumbs in an even
layer over the top of the cassoulet and
return to the oven, uncovered, for a
further 40 minutes, or until the meat is
tender and the top crisp and lightly
brown. Garnish with fresh thyme sprigs
and serve hot with plenty of warm
crusty bread to mop up the juices.

Energy 739Kcal/3085kJ; Protein 40.2g; Carbohydrate 49.6g, of which sugars 11.6g; Fat 44.8g, of which saturates 14.2g; Cholesterol 142mg; Calcium 118mg; Fibre 9.4g; Sodium 1848mg.

PIGEONS in STOUT

Pigeons are usually sold in breast portions, as the edible meat is mainly on the breast.
The flesh is dark and, like most small birds, dry, so casseroling them in stout is an ideal
cooking method. When buying the pigeon breasts, ask your poulterer for the carcasses for
stock, if possible. Serve with spiced rice and a watercress or rocket salad.

SERVES 6

175g/6oz thick streaky (fatty) bacon
2 medium onions, finely chopped
2 or 3 garlic cloves, crushed
seasoned flour, for coating
50g/2oz/¼ cup butter
15ml/1 tbsp olive oil
6 pigeon breasts
30ml/2 tbsp Irish whiskey (optional)
600ml/1 pint/2½ cups chicken stock
300ml/½ pint/1¼ cups stout
175g/6oz button (white) mushrooms
beurre manié, if needed (see Cook's tip)
15–30ml/1–2 tbsp rowan jelly
sea salt and ground black pepper

1 Preheat the oven to 150°C/300°F/
Gas 2. Trim the streaky bacon and cut it
into strips. Cook gently in a large,
flameproof casserole until the fat runs
out, then add the two chopped onions
and crushed garlic and continue cooking
until they are soft. Remove from the
casserole and set aside.

2 Coat the breast portions thickly with
seasoned flour. Add the butter and oil to
the pan, heat until the butter is foaming,
then add the meat and brown well on all
sides. Pour in the Irish whiskey, if using.
Carefully set it alight and shake the pan
until the flames go out – this improves
the flavour.

3 Stir in the stock, stout and the
mushrooms, and bring slowly to the boil.
Cover closely and cook in the preheated
oven for 1½–2 hours, or until the
pigeons are tender.

4 Remove from the oven and lift the
pigeons on to a serving dish. Thicken the
gravy, if necessary, by adding small pieces
of beurre manié, stirring until the sauce
thickens. Stir in rowan jelly to taste and
adjust the seasoning. Serve the pigeons
with the gravy while hot.

COOK'S TIP
To make beurre manié mix together
15g/½oz/1 tbsp of butter with 15ml/
1 tbsp flour. Add small pieces of the
mixture to the boiling gravy or sauce and
stir until thickened.

Energy 436Kcal/1817kJ; Protein 38.7g; Carbohydrate 6.7g, of which sugars 5.3g; Fat 27.2g, of which saturates 6.2g; Cholesterol 33mg; Calcium 48mg; Fibre 1.7g; Sodium 639mg.

MARINATED PIGEON in RED WINE

The time taken to marinate and cook this casserole is well rewarded by the fabulous rich flavour of the finished dish. Stir-fried green cabbage and celeriac purée are delicious accompaniments to this casserole.

SERVES 4

4 pigeons (US squabs), about 225g/
   8oz each
30ml/2 tbsp olive oil
I onion, coarsely chopped
225g/8oz/3¼ cups chestnut
   mushrooms, sliced
15ml/1 tbsp plain (all-purpose) flour
300ml/½ pint/1¼ cups game stock
30ml/2 tbsp chopped fresh parsley
salt and ground black pepper
flat leaf parsley, to garnish

For the marinade
15ml/1 tbsp light olive oil
I onion, chopped
I carrot, peeled and chopped
I celery stick, chopped
3 garlic cloves, sliced
6 allspice berries, bruised
2 bay leaves
8 black peppercorns, bruised
150ml/¼ pint/⅔ cup red wine vinegar
150ml/¼ pint/⅔ cup red wine
45ml/3 tbsp redcurrant jelly

I Mix together all the ingredients for the marinade in a large bowl. Add the pigeons and turn them in the marinade, then cover the bowl and chill for about 12 hours, turning the pigeons frequently.

VARIATIONS
If you are unable to buy pigeon, this recipe works equally well with chicken or rabbit. Buy portions and make deep slashes in the flesh so that the marinade soaks into, and flavours right to the centre of the pieces of meat.

2 Preheat the oven to 150°C/300°F/ Gas 2. Heat the oil in a large, flameproof casserole and cook the onion and mushrooms for about 5 minutes, or until the onion has softened.

3 Meanwhile, drain the pigeons and strain the marinade into a jug (pitcher), then set both aside separately.

4 Sprinkle the flour over the pigeons and add them to the casserole, breast-sides down. Pour in the marinade and stock, and add the chopped parsley and seasoning. Cover and cook for 2½ hours.

5 Check the seasoning, then serve the pigeons on warmed plates and ladle the sauce over them. Garnish with parsley.

Energy 428Kcal/1785kJ; Protein 32.8g; Carbohydrate 16.7g, of which sugars 12.4g; Fat 23.3g, of which saturates 1.3g; Cholesterol 0mg; Calcium 51mg; Fibre 2g; Sodium 135mg.

GUINEA FOWL with BEANS and CURLY KALE

Cooking lean poultry such as guinea fowl, chicken or turkey in a clay pot or chicken brick
gives a delicious, moist result. Here the guinea fowl is cooked atop a colourful bed of
herb-flavoured beans and vegetables.

2 Remove the shallots, garlic and celery with a slotted spoon and place in the chicken brick. Stir in the tomatoes and beans. Tuck in the thyme and bay leaves.

3 Put the guinea fowl in the frying pan and brown on all sides, then pour in the wine and stock and bring to the boil. Lift the bird out of the pan, place it on top of the vegetables in the chicken brick and then pour the liquid over the top. Cover and place in an unheated oven and set to 200°C/400°F/Gas 6. Cook for 1 hour.

4 Add the curly kale to the chicken brick, nestling it among the beans. Cover and cook for 10–15 minutes, or until the guinea fowl is tender. Season the bean mixture and serve.

COOK'S TIP

Guinea fowl and quail were both originally classified as game birds but nowadays farmed varieties are sold, making them available in the stores all year round.

VARIATION

Use chard, spring greens (collards) or Savoy cabbage in place of curly kale.

SERVES 4

1.3kg/3lb guinea fowl
45ml/3 tbsp olive oil
4 shallots, chopped
1 garlic clove, crushed
3 celery sticks, sliced
400g/14oz can chopped tomatoes
2 × 400g/14oz cans mixed
    beans, drained
5 fresh thyme sprigs
2 bay leaves
150ml/¼ pint/⅔ cup dry white wine
300ml/½ pint/1¼ cups well-flavoured
    chicken stock
175g/6oz curly kale
salt and ground black pepper

1 Soak a clay chicken brick in cold water for 20 minutes, then drain. Rub the guinea fowl with 15ml/1 tbsp of the olive oil and season. Place the remaining oil in a frying pan, add the shallots, garlic and celery and sauté for 4–5 minutes.

Energy 617Kcal/2585kJ; Protein 53.1g; Carbohydrate 32.9g, of which sugars 8.7g; Fat 28.6g, of which saturates 1.5g; Cholesterol 0mg; Calcium 98mg; Fibre 11.6g; Sodium 1017mg.

BRAISED PHEASANT with WILD MUSHROOMS, CHESTNUTS and BACON

Pheasant at the end of their season are not suitable for roasting, so consider this tasty casserole enriched with wild mushrooms and chestnuts. Allow two birds for four people.

SERVES 4

2 mature pheasants
50g/2oz/¼ cup butter
75ml/5 tbsp brandy
12 baby (pearl) onions, peeled
1 celery stick, chopped
50g/2oz unsmoked rindless bacon,
    cut into strips
45ml/3 tbsp plain (all-purpose) flour
550ml/18fl oz/2¼ cups chicken
    stock, boiling
175g/6oz peeled, cooked chestnuts
350g/12oz/4 cups fresh ceps, trimmed and
    sliced, or 15g/½oz/¼ cup dried porcini
    mushrooms, soaked in warm water for
    20 minutes
15ml/1 tbsp lemon juice
salt and ground black pepper
watercress sprigs, to garnish

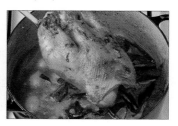

2 Wipe out the casserole and melt the remaining butter. Add the onions, celery and bacon and brown lightly. Stir in the flour. Remove from the heat.

3 Stir in the stock gradually so that it is completely absorbed by the flour. Add the chestnuts, mushrooms, the pheasants and their juices. Bring back to a gentle simmer, then cover and cook in the oven for 1½ hours.

4 Transfer the cooked pheasants and vegetables to a warmed serving plate. Bring the sauce back to the boil, add the lemon juice and season to taste. Pour the sauce into a jug (pitcher) or gravy boat and garnish the birds with watercress.

COOK'S TIP
Cooking and peeling fresh chestnuts can be hard work, so look out for ready-peeled canned or vacuum-packed varieties.

1 Preheat the oven to 160°C/325°F/ Gas 3. Season the pheasants with salt and pepper. Melt half of the butter in a large flameproof casserole and brown the pheasants over a medium heat. Transfer the pheasants to a shallow dish and pour off the cooking fat. Return the casserole to the heat and brown the sediment. Add the brandy, stir well to loosen the sediment using a flat wooden spoon, then pour all the cooking juices over the pheasant.

COOK'S TIP
When buying pheasant choose birds that look fresh. They should be plump and firm, with supple skin. Game birds have a strong odour but they should never smell unpleasant or "off".

Energy 883Kcal/3699kJ; Protein 86.8g; Carbohydrate 32.3g, of which sugars 6.9g; Fat 41.6g, of which saturates 15.8g; Cholesterol 35mg; Calcium 205mg; Fibre 2.9g; Sodium 920mg.

GROUSE with ORCHARD FRUIT STUFFING

Tart apples, plums and pears make a fabulous orchard fruit stuffing that complements the rich gamey flavour of grouse perfectly.

SERVES 2

juice of ½ lemon
2 young grouse
50g/2oz/¼ cup butter
4 Swiss chard leaves
50ml/2fl oz/¼ cup Marsala
salt and ground black pepper

For the stuffing
2 shallots, finely chopped
1 tart cooking apple, peeled, cored
  and chopped
1 pear, peeled, cored and chopped
2 plums, halved, stoned (pitted)
  and chopped
large pinch of mixed (apple pie) spice

1 Sprinkle the lemon juice over the grouse and season well. Melt half the butter in a flameproof casserole, add the grouse and cook for 10 minutes, or until browned. Use tongs to remove the grouse from the casserole and set aside.

2 Add the shallots to the fat remaining in the casserole and cook until softened but not coloured. Add the apple, pear, plums and mixed spice, and cook for about 5 minutes, or until the fruits are just beginning to soften. Remove the casserole from the heat and spoon the hot fruit mixture into the body cavities of the birds.

3 Truss the birds neatly with string. Smear the remaining butter over the birds and wrap them in the chard leaves, then replace them in the casserole.

4 Pour in the Marsala and heat until simmering. Cover tightly and simmer for 20 minutes, or until the birds are tender, taking care not to overcook them. Leave to rest in a warm place for about 10 minutes before serving.

COOK'S TIP
There isn't a lot of liquid in the casserole for cooking the birds – they are steamed rather than boiled, so it is very important that the casserole has a heavy base and a tight-fitting lid, otherwise the liquid may evaporate and the chard will burn on the base of the pan.

Energy 508Kcal/2121kJ; Protein 46.9g; Carbohydrate 19.5g, of which sugars 18.7g; Fat 24.3g, of which saturates 13.8g; Cholesterol 53mg; Calcium 185mg; Fibre 4.2g; Sodium 406mg.

SPICY VENISON CASSEROLE

Being low in fat but high in flavour, venison is an excellent choice for healthy, yet rich,
casseroles. Cranberries and orange bring a festive fruitiness to this spicy recipe. Serve
with small baked potatoes and green vegetables.

SERVES 4

15ml/1 tbsp olive oil
1 onion, chopped
2 celery sticks, sliced
10ml/2 tsp ground allspice
15ml/1 tbsp plain (all-purpose) flour
675g/1½lb stewing venison, cubed
225g/8oz fresh or frozen cranberries
grated rind and juice of 1 orange
900ml/1½ pints/3¾ cups beef or
    venison stock
salt and ground black pepper

1 Heat the oil in a flameproof casserole.
Add the onion and celery and fry for
about 5 minutes, or until softened.

2 Meanwhile, mix the ground allspice
with the flour and either spread the
mixture out on a large plate or place
in a large plastic bag. Toss a few pieces
of venison at a time (to prevent them
becoming soggy) in the flour mixture
until they are all lightly coated. Spread
the floured venison out on a large plate
until ready to cook.

3 When the onion and celery are
just softened, remove them from the
casserole using a slotted spoon and set
aside. Add the venison pieces to the
casserole in batches and cook until well
browned and sealed on all sides.

COOK'S TIP

Freshly made stock is always best, but if
you are short of time, look for cartons
or tubs of fresh stock in the chilled food
cabinets of large supermarkets.

4 Add the cranberries and the orange
rind and juice to the casserole along
with the stock, and stir well. Return the
vegetables and the browned venison to
the casserole and heat until simmering.
Cover tightly and reduce the heat.

5 Simmer for about 45 minutes, or
until the venison is tender, stirring
occasionally. Season the venison
casserole to taste with salt and pepper
before serving.

VARIATIONS

Farmed venison is increasingly easy to
find and is available from good butchers
and many large supermarkets. It makes a
rich and flavourful stew, but lean pork or
braising steak could be used in place of
the venison, if you prefer. You could
also replace the cranberries with pitted
and halved ready-to-eat prunes and, for
extra flavour, use either ale or stout
instead of about half the stock.

Energy 242Kcal/1025kJ; Protein 38.3g; Carbohydrate 10.4g, of which sugars 7.1g; Fat 6.6g, of which saturates 1.8g; Cholesterol 84mg; Calcium 27mg; Fibre 1.4g; Sodium 105mg.

VENISON SAUSAGES with RED WINE GRAVY

Strongly flavoured, meaty sausages are delicious with a robust red wine gravy flavoured with assertive shiitake mushrooms. Serve with soft polenta, mashed potatoes or plenty of thickly sliced crusty bread to mop up the delicious gravy.

SERVES 4

15ml/1 tbsp sunflower oil (optional)
12 venison or wild boar sausages
2 leeks, sliced
2 plump garlic cloves, sliced
225g/8oz/3 cups shiitake
   mushrooms, quartered
15ml/1 tbsp plain (all-purpose) flour
600ml/1 pint/2½ cups red wine
30ml/2 tbsp chopped mixed fresh herbs,
   such as flat leaf parsley and marjoram
salt and ground black pepper

1 Pour the sunflower oil, if using, into a large frying pan, add the venison or wild boar sausages and cook over a medium heat for 15–20 minutes, turning frequently.

2 Add the leeks, garlic and mushrooms and mix well. Cook the vegetables for 10–15 minutes, or until the leeks are soft and beginning to brown.

3 Sprinkle in the flour and gradually pour in the red wine, stirring with a wooden spoon and pushing the sausages around to mix the flour and the liquid smoothly with the leeks.

4 Bring slowly to the boil, reduce the heat and simmer for 10–15 minutes, stirring occasionally, or until the gravy is smooth and glossy. Season the gravy with salt and pepper to taste and then sprinkle the mixed herbs over the sausages. Serve immediately with polenta or mashed potatoes.

COOK'S TIP
Shiitake mushrooms have a slightly floury-looking medium to dark grey-brown cap. They have a firm and meaty texture that becomes silky when cooked. The stalks can be tough so discard if necessary.

Energy 246Kcal/1026kJ; Protein 7.8g; Carbohydrate 11.7g, of which sugars 2.9g; Fat 7.8g, of which saturates 3g; Cholesterol 15mg; Calcium 71mg; Fibre 3g; Sodium 447mg.

CASSEROLED VENISON with STOUT

Venison, both wild and (more usually) farmed, is now widely available. It is popular on restaurant menus and, increasingly, available for home cooks from butchers and the better supermarkets. Serve with boiled or baked potatoes and red cabbage.

SERVES 6

900g/2lb stewing venison, such as shoulder
45ml/3 tbsp seasoned flour
30ml/2 tbsp olive oil
2 or 3 large onions, sliced
5 or 6 juniper berries, crushed
3 allspice berries
rind of ½ lemon or orange
25g/1oz/2 tbsp butter
about 300ml/½ pint/1¼ cups chicken or
    beef stock
150ml/¼ pint/⅔ cup red wine vinegar or
    cider vinegar
300ml/½ pint/1¼ cups stout or red wine
salt and ground black pepper

1 Preheat the oven to 180°C/350°F/ Gas 4. Cut the meat into 5cm/2in cubes. Toss the meat in the seasoned flour. Shake off and reserve the excess flour.

2 Heat the olive oil in a heavy frying pan and fry the meat in it until well browned all over. Lift out the pieces with a slotted spoon and put them into a casserole.

3 Add the onions to the casserole with the juniper berries and allspice, a little salt and black pepper and the lemon or orange rind.

4 Melt the butter in the pan in which the meat was browned, add the reserved flour, and stir and cook for 1 minute. Mix the stock, vinegar and stout or red wine together and gradually add to the pan, stirring until it boils and thickens.

5 Pour the sauce over the meat in the casserole, cover closely and cook in the oven for 1 hour. Reduce the temperature to 150°C/300°F/Gas 2 and cook for a further 2 hours, or until the venison is tender. Check the casserole occasionally and add a little extra stock or water if required. Serve piping hot.

COOK'S TIP
Venison is not difficult to cook but, like other game, it is lean, so marinating, basting and braising all help to offset any tendency to dryness.

Energy 294Kcal/1233kJ; Protein 34.7g; Carbohydrate 9.3g, of which sugars 4.9g; Fat 10.6g, of which saturates 3.9g; Cholesterol 84mg; Calcium 37mg; Fibre 1.3g; Sodium 114mg.

BRAISED RABBIT

Rabbit now features frequently on restaurant menus. It is delicious served with potatoes boiled in their skins and a lightly cooked green vegetable.

SERVES 4–6

1 rabbit, prepared and jointed by
   the butcher
30ml/2 tbsp seasoned flour
30ml/2 tbsp olive oil or vegetable oil
25g/1oz/2 tbsp butter
115g/4oz streaky (fatty) bacon
1 onion, roughly chopped
2 or 3 carrots, sliced
1 or 2 celery sticks, trimmed and sliced
300ml/½ pint/1¼ cups chicken stock
300ml/½ pint/1¼ cups dry (hard) cider
   or stout
a small bunch of parsley leaves, chopped
salt and ground black pepper

1 Soak the joints in cold salted water for at least two hours, then pat them dry with kitchen paper and toss them in seasoned flour. Preheat the oven to 200°C/400°F/Gas 6.

2 Heat the oil and butter together in a heavy flameproof casserole. Shake off (and reserve) any excess flour from the rabbit joints and brown them on all sides. Lift out and set aside.

3 Add the bacon to the casserole and cook for a few minutes, then remove and set aside with the rabbit. Add the vegetables to the casserole and cook gently until just colouring, then sprinkle over any remaining seasoned flour to absorb the fats in the casserole. Stir over a low heat for 1 minute, to cook the flour. Add the stock and cider or stout, stirring, to make a smooth sauce.

4 Return the rabbit and bacon to the casserole, and add half of the chopped parsley and a light seasoning of salt and pepper. Mix gently together, then cover with a lid and put into the preheated oven. Cook for 15–20 minutes, then reduce the temperature to 150°C/300°F/Gas 2 for about 1½ hours, or until the rabbit is tender. Add the remaining parsley and serve.

COOK'S TIP
Buy rabbit whole or jointed, from butchers and good supermarkets.
To make Rabbit Pie, prepare as above then allow to cool. Remove the meat from the bones, and then return the meat to the casserole, taste for seasoning and turn into a suitable pie dish, ensuring that the meat is covered by the sauce. (Add a sliced hard-boiled egg and a few quartered button (white) mushrooms, if you like.) Cover with shortcrust or rough-puff pastry and cook in the oven heated to 200°C/400°F/Gas 6 for about 30 minutes, or until the filling is hot and the pastry is golden brown and cooked through.

Energy 368Kcal/1535kJ; Protein 32.9g; Carbohydrate 10.5g, of which sugars 5.8g; Fat 19.7g, of which saturates 8g; Cholesterol 133mg; Calcium 88mg; Fibre 1.4g; Sodium 567mg.

RABBIT with RED WINE and PRUNES

This is a favourite French dish and is often found on the menus of small country restaurants. It has a wonderfully rich flavour and the prunes add a delicious sweetness to the sauce. Serve with crisp, golden sautéed potatoes.

SERVES 4

8 rabbit portions
30ml/2 tbsp vegetable oil
2 onions, finely chopped
2 garlic cloves, finely chopped
60ml/4 tbsp Armagnac or brandy
300ml/½ pint/1¼ cups dry red wine
5ml/1 tsp soft light brown sugar
16 ready-to-eat prunes
150ml/¼ pint/⅔ cup double (heavy) cream
salt and ground black pepper

VARIATIONS
• Chicken can also be cooked in this way. Use 4 chicken drumsticks and 4 thighs in place of the rabbit portions.
• The prunes can be replaced with ready-to-eat dried apricots if you prefer – these go well with the rabbit and particularly well with chicken.

1 Season the rabbit portions liberally with salt and pepper. Heat the vegetable oil in a large, flameproof casserole and fry the rabbit portions in batches until they are golden brown on all sides.

2 Remove the browned rabbit portions from the casserole, add the chopped onion and garlic, and cook, stirring occasionally, until the onion is softened.

3 Return the rabbit to the casserole, add the Armagnac or brandy and ignite it. When the flames have died down, pour in the wine. Stir in the sugar and prunes, cover and simmer for 30 minutes.

4 Remove the rabbit from the casserole and keep warm. Add the cream to the sauce and simmer for 3–5 minutes, then season to taste and serve immediately.

Energy 543Kcal/2259kJ; Protein 29.3g; Carbohydrate 19.4g, of which sugars 18.2g; Fat 29.9g, of which saturates 15.3g; Cholesterol 156mg; Calcium 99mg; Fibre 3g; Sodium 81mg.

SLOW COOKER MEAT

Slow cooking is suitable for all kinds of meat, but it works its magic best on less tender cuts, helping to improve and enhance their flavour and texture. Although beef and pork are great for robust dishes, such as Beef and Mushroom Pudding, they can also be used to make lighter modern meals, like Spicy Pork Casserole with Dried Fruit. Most lamb cuts are naturally tender and succulent and the slow cooker ensures they stay that way – try Moroccan Lamb with Honey and Prunes for a delicious meal. Whatever meat you choose and whether you are looking for a simple supper or an impressive dinner, you will find plenty of recipes here for delicious pot roasts, braised dishes, casseroles and stews.

STEAK and KIDNEY PIE with MUSTARD GRAVY

Peppery mustard gravy flavoured with bay leaves and parsley complements the tasty chunks of succulent beef and kidney in this classic pie. Cooking the puff pastry topping separately from the filling ensures it remains perfectly crisp – and is a perfect technique to use when making the pie using a slow cooker.

SERVES 4

675g/1½lb stewing steak
225g/8oz ox or lamb's kidney
45ml/3 tbsp oil
15g/½oz/1 tbsp unsalted (sweet) butter
2 onions, chopped
30ml/2 tbsp plain (all-purpose) flour
300ml/½ pint/1¼ cups beef stock
15ml/1 tbsp tomato purée (paste)
10ml/2 tsp English mustard
2 bay leaves
375g/13oz puff pastry
beaten egg, to glaze
15ml/1 tbsp chopped fresh parsley
salt and ground black pepper
creamed potatoes and green vegetables,
    to serve

1 Using a sharp knife, cut the stewing steak into 2.5cm/1in cubes. Remove all fat and skin from the kidney and cut into cubes or thick slices.

2 Heat 30ml/2 tbsp of the oil in a frying pan and brown the beef on all sides. Remove from the pan with a slotted spoon and place in the ceramic cooking pot. Switch the slow cooker on to high.

3 Add the kidney to the frying pan and brown for 1–2 minutes before adding to the beef. Add the remaining oil and the butter to the pan, add the onions and cook for 5 minutes, until just beginning to colour. Sprinkle with the flour and stir in, then remove the pan from the heat.

4 Gradually stir the stock into the pan, followed by the tomato purée and mustard. Return to the heat and bring to the boil, stirring constantly, until thickened. Pour the gravy over the meat, then add the bay leaves and season. Stir well and cover with the lid. Reduce the cooker to low and cook for 5–7 hours, or until the meat is very tender.

VARIATION
To make a richer version, use half the quantity of stock and add 150ml/¼ pint/⅔ cup stout or red wine.

5 While the beef is cooking, roll out the pastry and, using a dinner plate as a guide, cut out a 25cm/10in round. Transfer the pastry round to a baking sheet lined with baking parchment.

6 Using a sharp knife, mark the pastry into quarters, cutting almost but not quite through it. Decorate with pastry trimmings, then flute the edge. Cover with clear film (plastic wrap) and place in the refrigerator until ready to cook.

7 Towards the end of the beef's cooking time, preheat the oven to 200°C/400°F/ Gas 6. Brush the pastry all over with beaten egg to glaze, then bake for about 25 minutes, or until well risen, golden-brown and crisp.

8 To serve, stir the chopped parsley into the steak and kidney stew and spoon on to warmed serving plates. Cut the baked pie crust into four, using the markings as a guide, and top each portion of stew with a wedge of pastry. Serve immediately with rich, creamed potatoes and green vegetables.

Energy 637Kcal/2652kJ; Protein 18.7g; Carbohydrate 46.2g, of which sugars 5.2g; Fat 43.4g, of which saturates 13.1g; Cholesterol 259mg; Calcium 99mg; Fibre 2.7g; Sodium 578mg.

PROVENÇAL BEEF STEW

Known in France as daube de boeuf à la Provençal, *after the earthernware pot it was originally cooked in, this deliciously rich, fruity stew makes a perfect winter supper dish. Serve with mashed or boiled new potatoes and green vegetables.*

SERVES 4

45ml/3 tbsp olive oil
115g/4oz lean salt pork or
    thick-cut bacon, diced
900g/2lb stewing steak cut into
    4cm/1½in pieces
1 large onion, chopped
2 carrots, sliced
2 ripe tomatoes, peeled, seeded
    and chopped
10ml/2 tsp tomato purée (paste)
2 garlic cloves, very finely chopped
250ml/8fl oz/1 cup fruity red wine
150ml/¼ pint/⅔ cup beef stock
1 bouquet garni
1 small onion, studded with 2 cloves
grated zest and juice of ½ unwaxed orange
15ml/1 tbsp chopped fresh parsley
salt and ground black pepper

1 Heat 15ml/1 tbsp of the oil in a large heavy frying pan, then add the salt pork or bacon and cook over a medium heat for 4–5 minutes, stirring frequently, until browned and the fat is rendered.

2 Using a slotted spoon, transfer the pork or bacon to the ceramic cooking pot and switch the slow cooker to high.

3 Working in batches, add the beef to the pan in a single layer (do not overcrowd the pan, or the meat will stew in its own juices and not brown). Cook for 6–8 minutes until browned, turning to colour all sides.

4 Transfer the beef to the ceramic cooking pot and continue browning the rest of the meat in the same way, adding more oil when needed.

5 Pour the wine and stock over the beef in the ceramic cooking pot, then add the bouquet garni and the onion. Add the remaining oil and the onion to the frying pan and cook gently for 5 minutes. Stir in the carrots and cook for a further 5 minutes, until softened. Stir in the tomatoes, tomato purée and garlic, then transfer to the ceramic cooking pot.

6 Cover with the lid and switch the slow cooker to low. Cook for 5–7 hours, or until the beef and vegetables are very tender. Uncover and skim off any fat. Season, discard the bouquet garni and clove-studded onion, and stir in the orange zest and juice and the parsley.

Energy 547Kcal/2286kJ; Protein 55.8g; Carbohydrate 8.7g, of which sugars 7.2g; Fat 27.8g, of which saturates 8.9g; Cholesterol 170mg; Calcium 43mg; Fibre 2g; Sodium 682mg.

BRAISED BEEF in a RICH PEANUT SAUCE

Like many dishes brought to the Philippines by the Spanish, this slow-cooking Estofado, *renamed by the Philippinos as* Kari Kari, *retains much of its original charm. Peanuts are used to thicken the juices, yielding a rich, sweet, glossy sauce.*

SERVES 4

900g/2lb stewing (braising) chuck,
   shin or blade steak
45ml/3 tbsp vegetable oil
2 onions, chopped
2 cloves garlic, crushed
5ml/1 tsp paprika
pinch of ground turmeric
225g/8oz celeriac or swede (rutabaga),
   peeled and cut into 2cm/¾in dice
425ml/15fl oz/1¾ cups boiling beef stock
15ml/1 tbsp fish or anchovy sauce
30ml/2 tbsp tamarind sauce (optional)
10ml/2 tsp soft light brown sugar
1 bay leaf
1 sprig thyme
30ml/2 tbsp smooth peanut butter
45ml/3 tbsp easy-cook (converted)
   white rice
5ml/1 tsp white wine vinegar
salt and ground black pepper

1 Using a sharp knife, cut the beef into 2.5cm/1in cubes. Heat 30ml/2 tbsp of the oil in a pan and fry the beef, turning until well browned all over.

2 Transfer the meat and any juices to the ceramic cooking pot and switch the slow cooker to high.

3 Add the remaining 15ml/1 tbsp oil to the frying pan, add the onions and fry gently for 10 minutes until softened.

4 Add the garlic, paprika and turmeric to the pan and cook for 1 minute. Transfer the mixture to the ceramic pot and add the celeriac or swede.

5 Pour in the stock, fish or anchovy sauce and taramind sauce, if using, and add the sugar, bay leaf and thyme. Cover with the lid, then reduce the heat to low and cook for 4 hours, or until the beef and vegetables are just tender.

6 Turn the slow cooker up to high, then remove about 60ml/4 tbsp of the cooking juices to a bowl and blend with the peanut butter. Stir the mixture into the casserole, sprinkle with the rice, and stir again to combine.

7 Cover the pot and cook for about 45 minutes, or until the rice is cooked and the sauce has thickened slightly. Stir in the wine vinegar and season to taste.

COOK'S TIP
This stew makes a meal in itself so needs no accompaniments. However, a simple green salad served on the side makes a refreshing palate cleanser.

Energy 577Kcal/2408kJ; Protein 48.9g; Carbohydrate 14.1g, of which sugars 8.9g; Fat 36.8g, of which saturates 12.2g; Cholesterol 141mg; Calcium 70mg; Fibre 2.4g; Sodium 561mg.

BEEF and MUSHROOM PUDDING

Based on a great British classic, this steamed savoury pudding has a light herb pastry crust made with a mixture of suet and butter for both taste and colour. A mouthwatering mixture of dried porcini and chestnut mushrooms gives the filling an intense flavour.

SERVES 4

25g/1oz/½ cup dried porcini mushrooms
475ml/16fl oz/2 cups near-boiling
  beef stock
675g/1½lb stewing (braising) steak
60ml/4 tbsp plain (all-purpose) flour
45ml/3 tbsp sunflower oil
1 large onion, finely chopped
225g/8oz chestnut or flat mushrooms,
  thickly sliced
1 bay leaf
15ml/1 tbsp Worcestershire sauce
75ml/2½fl oz/⅓ cup port or red wine
salt and ground black pepper

For the pastry
275g/10oz/2½ cups self-raising
  (self-rising) flour
2.5ml/½ tsp baking powder
2.5ml/½ tsp salt
15ml/1 tbsp each chopped parsley
  and fresh thyme
75g/3oz/1½ cups beef or vegetable suet
  (chilled, grated shortening)
50g/2oz/¼ cup butter, frozen and grated
1 egg, lightly beaten
about 150ml/¼ pint/⅔ cup cold water

1 Put the dried mushrooms in a bowl and pour over the stock. Leave to soak for about 20 minutes.

2 Meanwhile, trim the meat and cut into 2cm/¾in pieces. Place the flour in a bowl, season, then add the meat and toss to coat. Heat the oil in a frying pan and fry the meat in batches until browned on all sides. Transfer to the ceramic cooking pot.

3 Add the onion to the pan and cook gently for 10 minutes, or until softened. Transfer to the ceramic cooking pot, then add the chestnut mushrooms and the bay leaf.

4 In a bowl or jug (pitcher), combine the Worcestershire sauce with the port or wine, then pour into the ceramic cooking pot. Drain the soaked porcini mushrooms, pouring the stock into the pot, then chop them and add to the pot.

5 Stir the ingredients together, then cover with the lid and cook on high or auto for 1 hour. Reduce the heat to low and cook for a further 5–6 hours, or until the meat and onions are tender. Remove the bay leaf, then leave the mixture to cool completely.

6 To make the pastry, butter a deep 1.7 litre/3 pint/7½ cup heatproof pudding basin. Sift the flour, baking powder and salt into a mixing bowl and stir in the herbs followed by the suet and butter. Make a well in the centre, add the egg and enough cold water to mix, and gather into a soft dough.

7 Lightly knead the dough for a few seconds on a floured surface until smooth. Cut off a quarter of the dough and wrap in clear film (plastic wrap). Shape the rest into a ball and roll out into a round large enough to line the basin or bowl. Lift up the pastry and carefully place in the basin, pressing it against the sides and allowing the excess to fall over the sides. Roll out the reserved pastry to make a round large enough to use as a lid for the pudding.

8 Spoon in the cooled filling and enough of the gravy to come to within 1cm/½in of the rim. (Reserve the remaining gravy to serve with the pudding.) Brush the top edge of the pastry with water and place the lid on top. Press the edges together to seal and trim off any excess.

9 Cover the pudding basin with a pleated, double thickness layer of baking parchment and secure under the rim using string. Cover with pleated foil to allow the pudding to rise.

10 Put an inverted saucer or metal pastry ring in the base of the cleaned ceramic cooking pot and place the pudding basin on top. Pour in enough near-boiling water to come just over halfway up the sides of the basin. Cover with the lid and cook on high for 3 hours.

11 Carefully remove the pudding from the slow cooker, then take off the foil, string and greaseproof paper. Loosen the edges of the pudding and invert on to a warmed serving plate.

Energy 1061Kcal/4444kJ; Protein 70g; Carbohydrate 75.1g, of which sugars 4.8g; Fat 54.3g, of which saturates 24.5g; Cholesterol 265mg; Calcium 319mg; Fibre 4.4g; Sodium 941mg.

BRAISED BEEF with HORSERADISH

This dark rich beef with a spicy kick makes an ideal alternative to a meat roast. The meat slowly tenderizes in the slow cooker and all the flavours blend together beautifully. It is also a great dish for entertaining because it can be prepared in advance and then simply left to simmer on its own until you are ready to serve.

SERVES 4

30ml/2 tbsp plain (all-purpose) flour
4 × 175g/6oz braising steaks
30ml/2 tbsp sunflower oil
12 small shallots, peeled and halved
1 garlic clove, crushed
1.5ml/¼ tsp ground ginger
5ml/1 tsp curry powder
10ml/2 tsp dark muscovado (molasses) sugar
475ml/16fl oz/2 cups near-boiling beef stock
15ml/1 tbsp Worcestershire sauce
30ml/2 tbsp creamed horseradish
225g/8oz baby carrots, trimmed
1 bay leaf
salt and ground black pepper
30ml/2 tbsp chopped fresh chives, to garnish
roast vegetables, to serve

1 Place the flour in a large, flat dish and season with salt and black pepper. Toss the steaks in the flour to coat.

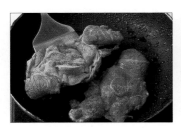

2 Heat the oil in a pan and quickly brown the steaks on both sides. Transfer them to the ceramic cooking pot.

3 Add the halved shallots to the pan and cook gently for 10 minutes, or until golden and beginning to soften. Stir in the garlic, ginger and curry powder and cook for 1 minute more, then remove the pan from the heat.

4 Tip the shallot mixture into the ceramic cooking pot, spreading it over the meat, and sprinkle with the sugar.

5 Pour the beef stock over the shallots and meat, then add the Worcestershire sauce, horseradish, baby carrots and bay leaf. Stir to combine, then season with salt and black pepper. Cover with the lid and cook on high or auto for 1 hour.

6 Reduce the slow cooker to low, or leave on auto, and continue to cook the stew for a further 5–6 hours, or until the beef and vegetables are very tender.

7 Remove the bay leaf from the stew and sprinkle with the chopped chives before serving with roast vegetables.

COOK'S TIPS
• Choose a medium curry powder for flavouring the stew. There is already plenty of bite from the horseradish, so you don't want to overpower the meat flavours entirely with a very strong, spicy curry powder.
• To give the stew a really robust flavour, replace 175ml/6fl oz/¾ cup of the stock with red wine.
• The sweet flavour of roasted parsnips and butternut squash goes particularly well with the spicy bite of horseradish. Cook plenty of roast potatoes too – they are the perfect accompaniment to braised beef, and are great for mopping up the delicious gravy.

Energy 478Kcal/2010kJ; Protein 62.5g; Carbohydrate 17.7g, of which sugars 9.6g; Fat 18.1g, of which saturates 7.4g; Cholesterol 176mg; Calcium 65mg; Fibre 2.5g; Sodium 423mg.

HUNGARIAN CHOLENT

A traditional Sabbath dish of the Ashkenazi Jews, cholent *is a long-simmered dish of beans, grains, meat and vegetables. The addition of whole boiled eggs is a classic feature. Don't forget to start soaking the beans the day before; they need at least 8 hours.*

3 Meanwhile, heat the oil in a pan, add the onion and cook gently for about 10 minutes, or until soft. Transfer the onions to the ceramic cooking pot.

4 Add the garlic, beans, barley, paprika, cayenne pepper, celery, tomatoes, carrots, turnip, potatoes, beef and stock to the onions and stir to combine.

5 Cover the pot with the lid and cook on low for 5–6 hours, or until the meat and vegetables are tender. Add the rice, stir, and season with salt and pepper.

6 Rinse the eggs in tepid water, then lower them, one at a time, into the hot stock. Cover and cook for a further 45 minutes, or until the rice is cooked. Serve hot, making sure each portion contains a whole egg.

SERVES 4

250g/9oz/1⅓ cups dried haricot (navy) beans
30ml/2 tbsp olive oil
1 onion, chopped
4 garlic cloves, finely chopped
50g/2oz pearl barley
15ml/1 tbsp ground paprika
pinch of cayenne pepper
1 celery stick, chopped
400g/14oz can chopped tomatoes
3 carrots, sliced
1 small turnip, diced
2 baking potatoes, peeled and cut into chunks
675g/1½lb mixture of beef brisket, stewing beef and smoked beef, cut into cubes
1 litre/1¾ pints/4 cups boiling beef stock
30ml/2 tbsp easy-cook (converted) white rice
4 eggs, at room temperature
salt and ground black pepper

1 Place the beans in a large bowl. Pour over plenty of cold water to cover and leave to soak for at least 8 hours, or overnight if you like.

2 Drain the beans well, then place them in a large pan, cover with fresh cold water and bring to the boil. Boil them steadily for about 10 minutes, skimming off any froth that rises to the surface, then drain well and set aside.

Energy 860Kcal/3607kJ; Protein 58.9g; Carbohydrate 74.2g, of which sugars 13.7g; Fat 38.8g, of which saturates 12.7g; Cholesterol 341mg; Calcium 164mg; Fibre 10.9g; Sodium 639mg.

SPICED BEEF

This is a classic Irish dish, although it is a modern version of the traditional recipe, as it omits the initial pickling stage and takes only three or four days to cure in comparison with ten days for the older method. Serve on thinly sliced brown bread, with chutney.

SERVES 6

15ml/1 tbsp coarsely ground
   black pepper
10ml/2 tsp ground ginger
15ml/1 tbsp juniper berries, crushed
15ml/1 tbsp coriander seeds, crushed
5ml/1 tsp ground cloves
15ml/1 tbsp ground allspice
45ml/3 tbsp soft dark brown sugar
2 bay leaves, crushed
1 small onion, finely chopped
1.8kg/4lb corned beef, silverside or tail end
300ml/½ pint/1¼ cups Guinness
fruit chutney and brown bread, to serve

COOK'S TIP

• As a first course, serve the beef thinly sliced with home-made brown bread and a fruit chutney, such as apple and sultana.
• Spiced beef is excellent as finger food for parties, sliced thinly and served with sour cream lightly flavoured with horseradish and black pepper.

3 When the joint is cooked, leave it to cool in the cooking liquid. Wrap in foil and keep in the refrigerator until required, then slice thinly to serve. It will keep for about 1 week.

1 First, spice the beef: blend the pepper, spices and sugar thoroughly, then mix in the bay leaves and onion. Rub the mixture into the meat, then put it into a suitable lidded container and refrigerate for 3–4 days, turning and rubbing with the mixture daily.

2 Put the meat into the ceramic cooking pot and barely cover with cold water. Cover with the lid and switch on to auto or high. Cook for 3 hours, then leave on auto or reduce to low and cook for a further 3–4 hours, until the meat is very tender. For the last hour add the Guinness.

Energy 309Kcal/1301kJ; Protein 53.6g; Carbohydrate 2g, of which sugars 2g; Fat 9.7g, of which saturates 3.6g; Cholesterol 137mg; Calcium 15mg; Fibre 0g; Sodium 140mg.

HOT and SOUR PORK

This has all the flavour of a stir-fry without the hassle of last-minute cooking. Using lean pork fillet and reducing the temperature to low after an hour means that the meat remains wonderfully moist and tender, while the vegetables retain their crunchy texture.

SERVES 4

15ml/1 tbsp dried Chinese mushrooms
150ml/¼ pint/⅔ cup boiling
    vegetable stock
350g/12oz pork fillet
115g/4oz baby corn kernels
1 green (bell) pepper
225g/8oz pineapple chunks
    in natural juice
20ml/4 tsp cornflour (cornstarch)
15ml/1 tbsp sunflower oil
115g/4oz water chestnuts
2.5cm/1 in piece root ginger, grated
1 red chilli, seeded and finely chopped
5ml/1 tsp Chinese five-spice powder
15ml/1 tbsp sherry vinegar
15ml/1 tbsp dark soy sauce
15ml/1 tbsp hoisin sauce
plain boiled or fried rice, to serve

1 Put the mushrooms in a heatproof bowl, then pour over the hot stock and leave to soak for 15–20 minutes.

2 Trim away any visible fat from the pork and cut into 1cm/½ in slices. Slice the baby corn kernels lengthways. Halve, seed and slice the green pepper. Drain the pineapple chunks, reserving the juice. Drain the mushrooms, reserving the stock, and slice any large ones.

3 In a bowl, blend the cornflour with a little of the reserved pineapple juice, then slowly stir in the remainder.

4 Heat the oil in a non-stick frying pan. Add the pork and sear for 30 seconds on each side, or until lightly browned. Transfer to the ceramic cooking pot and add the vegetables, pineapple chunks and water chestnuts.

5 In a bowl, combine the ginger, chilli and five-spice powder with the vinegar, soy sauce, hoisin sauce and reserved stock. Pour in the pineapple juice mixture, then tip into the frying pan and bring to the boil, stirring constantly. As soon as the mixture thickens, pour over the pork and vegetables.

6 Cover with the lid and switch the slow cooker to high. Cook for 1 hour, then reduce the temperature to low and cook for 1–2 hours, or until the pork is cooked and the vegetables retain some crispness. Serve with rice.

Energy 358Kcal/1509kJ; Protein 19.9g; Carbohydrate 49.4g, of which sugars 36.3g; Fat 10.3g, of which saturates 2.8g; Cholesterol 60.4mg; Calcium 43mg; Fibre 2.7g; Sodium 405mg.

BOSTON BAKED BEANS

The slow cooker was actually invented for making baked beans. Molasses gives the beans
a very rich flavour and dark colour, but you can replace it with maple syrup if you prefer.

SERVES 8

450g/1lb/2½ cups dried haricot
   (navy) beans
4 whole cloves
2 onions, peeled
1 bay leaf
90ml/6 tbsp tomato ketchup
30ml/2 tbsp molasses
30ml/2 tbsp dark brown sugar
15ml/1tbsp Dijon-style mustard
475ml/16fl oz/2 cups unsalted
   vegetable stock
225g/8oz piece of salt pork
salt and ground black pepper

1 Rinse the beans, then place in a large
bowl. Cover with cold water and leave
to soak for at least 8 hours or overnight.

2 Drain and rinse the beans. Place them
in a large pan, cover with plenty of cold
water and bring to the boil. Boil gently
for about 10 minutes, then drain and tip
into the ceramic cooking pot.

3 Stick 2 cloves in each of the onions.
Add them to the pot with the bay leaf,
burying them in the beans.

4 In a bowl, blend together the ketchup,
molasses, sugar, mustard and stock, and
pour over the beans. Add more stock,
or water, if necessary, so that the beans
are almost covered with liquid. Cover
with the lid and switch the slow cooker
to low. Cook for 3 hours.

5 Towards the end of the cooking time,
place the salt pork in a pan of boiling
water and cook for 3 minutes.

6 Using a sharp knife, score the pork
rind in deep 1.5cm/½in cuts. Add the
salt pork to the ceramic cooking pot,
pushing it down just below the surface
of the beans, skin side up. Cover the
pot with the lid and cook for a further
5–6 hours, until the beans are tender.

7 Remove the pork from the beans and
set aside until cool enough to handle,
Using a sharp knife, slice off the rind and
fat and finely slice the meat.

8 Using a spoon, skim off any fat from
the top of the beans, then stir in the
pieces of meat. Season to taste with salt
and black pepper, and serve hot.

COOK'S TIPS
• Be sure to taste the beans before adding
any more salt. The salt pork will have
already added plenty, so you may only
need to season with black pepper.
• To make a vegetarian version of these
beans, simply leave out the salt pork.
They are just as good cooked without.

Energy 228Kcal/968kJ; Protein 13.4g; Carbohydrate 43.9g, of which sugars 19.4g; Fat 1g, of which saturates 0.1g; Cholesterol 0mg; Calcium 140mg; Fibre 9.5g; Sodium 334mg.

ITALIAN PORK SAUSAGE STEW

This hearty casserole, made with spicy sausages and haricot beans, is flavoured with
fragrant fresh herbs and dry Italian wine. Serve with Italian bread for mopping up the
delicious juices. Remember to leave time for the beans to soak before cooking.

SERVES 4

225g/8oz/1¼ cups dried haricot
   (navy) beans
2 sprigs fresh thyme
30ml/2 tsp olive oil
450g/1lb fresh Italian pork sausages
1 onion, finely chopped
2 sticks celery, finely diced
300ml/½ pint/1¼ cups dry red or white
   wine, preferably Italian
1 sprig of fresh rosemary
1 bay leaf
300ml/½ pint/1¼ cups boiling
   vegetable stock
200g/7oz can chopped tomatoes
¼ head dark green cabbage such as cavolo
   nero or Savoy, finely shredded
salt and ground black pepper
chopped fresh thyme, to garnish
crusty Italian bread, to serve

1 Put the haricot beans in a large bowl and cover with cold water. Leave to soak for at least 8 hours, or overnight.

2 Drain the beans and place in a pan with the thyme sprigs and at least twice their volume of cold water. Bring to the boil and boil steadily for 10 minutes, then drain and place in the ceramic cooking pot, discarding the thyme.

3 Meanwhile, heat the oil in a pan and cook the sausages until browned all over. Transfer to the ceramic cooking pot and tip away all but 15ml/1 tbsp of the fat in the frying pan.

4 Add the onion and celery to the pan and cook gently for 5 minutes until softened but not coloured. Add the wine, rosemary and bay leaf and bring to the boil. Pour over the sausages, add the stock and season with salt and pepper. Cover with the lid, switch the slow cooker to high and cook for 5–6 hours, until the beans are tender.

5 Stir the chopped tomatoes and the shredded cabbage into the stew. Cover and cook for 30–45 minutes, or until the cabbage is tender but not overcooked. Divide between warmed plates, garnish with a little chopped fresh thyme and serve with crusty Italian bread.

COOK'S TIP
The tomatoes are added towards the end of cooking because their acidity would prevent the beans from becoming tender if added earlier.

Energy 620Kcal/2593kJ; Protein 28.4g; Carbohydrate 47.4g, of which sugars 9.9g; Fat 30.9g, of which saturates 10.8g; Cholesterol 67.5mg; Calcium 205mg; Fibre 7.6g; Sodium 1139mg.

PORK and POTATO HOT-POT

Long, slow cooking makes the pork chops meltingly tender and allows the potato slices to soak up all the delicious juices from the meat. Perfect for a family meal or casual supper with friends, simply serve with lightly cooked green vegetables.

SERVES 4

25g/1oz/2 tbsp butter
15ml/1 tbsp oil
1 large onion, very thinly sliced
1 garlic clove, crushed
225g/8oz/generous 3 cups button (white)
    mushrooms, sliced
1.5ml/¼ tsp dried mixed herbs
900g/2lb potatoes, thinly sliced
4 thick pork chops
750ml/1¼ pints/3 cups vegetable
    or chicken stock
salt and ground black pepper

1 Use 15g/½oz/1 tbsp of the butter to grease the base and halfway up the sides of the ceramic cooking pot.

2 Heat the oil in a frying pan, add the sliced onion and cook gently for about 5 minutes, until softened and translucent.

3 Add the garlic and mushrooms to the pan and cook for a further 5 minutes until softened. Remove the pan from the heat and stir in the mixed herbs.

4 Spoon half the mushroom mixture into the base of the ceramic cooking pot, then arrange half the potato slices on top and season with salt and ground black pepper.

5 Using a sharp knife, trim as much fat as possible from the pork chops, then place them on top of the potatoes in a single layer. Pour about half the stock over the top to cover the potatoes and prevent them discolouring.

6 Repeat the layers of the mushroom mixture and potatoes, finishing with a layer of neatly overlapping potatoes. Pour over the remaining stock; it should just cover the potatoes, so use a little more or less if necessary. Dot the remaining butter on top of the potatoes and cover with the lid.

7 Cook the stew on high for 4–5 hours, or until the potatoes and meat are tender when pierced with a thin skewer. If you like, place the hot-pot under a medium grill (broiler) for 5–10 minutes to brown before serving.

Energy 511Kcal/2132kJ; Protein 17.9g; Carbohydrate 41.5g, of which sugars 6.5g; Fat 31.5g, of which saturates 12.1g; Cholesterol 67mg; Calcium 40mg; Fibre 3.7g; Sodium 529mg.

POTATO and SAUSAGE CASSEROLE

There are many variations of this traditional Irish supper dish, known as Irish coddle, but the basic ingredients are the same wherever you go – potatoes, sausages and bacon.

SERVES 4

15ml/1 tbsp vegetable oil
8 large pork sausages
4 bacon rashers (slices), cut into 2.5cm/
    1in pieces
1 large onion, chopped
2 garlic cloves, crushed
4 large baking potatoes, peeled
    and thinly sliced
1.5ml/¼ tsp fresh sage
300ml/½ pint/1¼ cups vegetable stock
salt and ground black pepper

COOK'S TIPS

• For an authentic Irish feel, serve this delicious, hearty casserole with braised green cabbage.
• Choose good-quality sausages because it will make all the difference to the final result. Many Irish artisan butchers export quality Irish sausages, so it is well worth keeping an eye out for them.

1 Heat the oil in a frying pan. Gently fry the sausages for about 5 minutes, turning frequently until they are golden but not cooked through. Remove from the frying pan and set aside. Tip away all but about 10ml/2 tsp of fat from the pan.

2 Add the bacon to the pan and fry for 2 minutes. Add the onion and fry for about 8 minutes, stirring frequently until golden. Add the garlic and fry for a further 1 minute, then turn off the heat.

3 Arrange half the potato slices in the base of the ceramic cooking pot. Spoon the bacon and onion mixture on top. Season well with salt and ground black pepper, and sprinkle with the fresh sage. Cover with the remaining potato slices.

4 Pour the stock over the potatoes and top with the sausages. Cover with the lid and cook on high for 3–4 hours, or until the potatoes are tender and the sausages cooked through. Serve hot.

Energy 717Kcal/2984kJ; Protein 20.5g; Carbohydrate 49.9g, of which sugars 6.1g; Fat 49.8g, of which saturates 18.1g; Cholesterol 78.1mg; Calcium 73mg; Fibre 4g; Sodium 1322mg.

PORK FILLETS with PRUNE STUFFING

The sweet flavour and rich texture of dried fruit, such as prunes, goes particularly well
with pork. If you want to ring the changes, dried apricots or figs can be used instead.

SERVES 4

15g/½oz/1 tbsp butter
1 shallot, very finely chopped
1 stick celery, very finely chopped
finely grated rind of ½ orange
115g/4oz/½ cup (about 12) stoned
  (pitted), ready-to-eat prunes, chopped
25g/1oz/½ cup fresh white breadcrumbs
30ml/2 tbsp chopped fresh parsley
pinch of grated nutmeg
two 225g/8oz pork fillets (tenderloin), trimmed
6 slices Parma ham or prosciutto
15ml/1 tbsp olive oil
150ml/¼ pint/⅔ cup dry white wine
salt and ground black pepper
mashed root vegetables and wilted pak
  choi (bok choy), to serve

1 Melt the butter in a frying pan, add the shallot and celery, and fry gently until soft. Tip into a bowl and stir in the orange rind, prunes, breadcrumbs, parsley and nutmeg. Season and leave to cool.

2 Slice down the length of each fillet, cutting three-quarters of the way through.

3 Open out each pork fillet and lay it out on a board. Cover the meat with a piece of oiled clear film (plastic wrap), then gently bash with a rolling pin until the meat is about 5mm/¼in thick.

4 Arrange 3 slices of the ham on a board and place one pork fillet on top. Repeat with the remaining ham and fillet.

5 Divide the prune and breadcrumb stuffing between the pork fillets, then fold over to enclose the filling.

6 Wrap the ham around one stuffed pork fillet, and secure with one or two wooden cocktail sticks (toothpicks). Repeat with the remaining ham and fillet.

7 Heat the oil in the clean frying pan and quickly brown the wrapped pork fillets all over, taking care not to dislodge the cocktail sticks, before transferring them to the ceramic cooking pot.

8 Pour the white wine into the frying pan and bring almost to the boil, then pour over the pork.

9 Cover the ceramic cooking pot with the slow cooker lid and cook on high for 1 hour, then reduce the temperature to low and cook for a further 2–3 hours, or until the pork is cooked completely through and tender.

10 Remove the cocktail sticks from the meat and cut the pork into slices. Arrange on warmed plates and spoon over some of the cooking juices. Serve with mashed root vegetables and wilted pak choi leaves.

Energy 245Kcal/1027kJ; Protein 17.3g; Carbohydrate 14.6g, of which sugars 11.3g; Fat 10.8g, of which saturates 4g; Cholesterol 59mg; Calcium 34mg; Fibre 2g; Sodium 378mg.

SPICY PORK CASSEROLE with DRIED FRUIT

Inspired by the South American mole *– a paste of chilli, shallots and nuts – this casserole is thickened and flavoured with a similar mixture, which really brings out the taste of the onions, meat and sweet dried fruit. Part of the* mole *is added at the end of cooking to retain its fresh flavour. Serve the casserole with rice and a green salad.*

SERVES 6

25ml/1½ tbsp plain (all-purpose) flour
1kg/2¼lb shoulder or leg of pork,
    cut into 4cm/1½in cubes
30ml/2 tbsp olive oil
450ml/¾ pint/scant 2 cups fruity
    white wine
150ml/¼ pint/⅔ cup vegetable stock
    or water
115g/4oz/1½ cups ready-to-eat prunes
115g/4oz/1½ cups ready-to-eat dried
    apricots
grated rind and juice of 1 small orange
pinch of muscovado (molasses) sugar
30ml/2 tbsp chopped fresh parsley
1 fresh green or red chilli, seeded
    and finely chopped
salt and ground black pepper
plain boiled rice, to serve

For the *mole*
3 ancho chillies and 2 pasilla chillies
    (or other varieties of large,
    medium-hot dried red chillies)
30ml/2 tbsp olive oil
2 large onions, finely chopped
3 garlic cloves, chopped
1 fresh green chilli, seeded and
    chopped
10ml/2 tsp ground coriander
5ml/1 tsp mild Spanish paprika
    or pimenton
50g/2oz/½ cup blanched almonds,
    toasted
15ml/1 tbsp chopped fresh oregano
    or 2.5ml/½ tsp dried oregano

1 Make the *mole* paste first. Toast the dried chillies in a dry frying pan over a low heat for 1–2 minutes, stirring, until they are aromatic. Remove the chillies from the heat, place in a small bowl and pour over warm water to cover. Leave to soak for about 30 minutes.

2 Drain the chillies, reserving the soaking water, then remove and discard the woody stalks and seeds.

3 Heat the oil in a frying pan and fry the onions over a low heat for about 10 minutes until soft. Remove two-thirds of the onions from the pan and set aside. Add the garlic, fresh green chilli and ground coriander to the pan and cook for a further 5 minutes.

4 Transfer the onion mixture to a food processor and add the drained chillies, paprika or pimenton, almonds and oregano. Process the mixture, adding 45–60ml/3–4 tbsp of the chilli soaking liquid to make a workable paste.

5 Place the flour in a shallow dish and season with salt and black pepper. Add the pork and toss well to coat.

6 Wipe the frying pan clean with kitchen paper and heat the olive oil. Fry the pork in two batches over a high heat for 5–6 minutes, stirring frequently, until it is sealed on all sides. Transfer the pork to the ceramic cooking pot with a slotted spoon and switch the slow cooker to high.

7 Add the reserved fried onions to the pan. Pour in the wine and stock or water and simmer for 1 minute. Stir in half the *mole* paste, bring back to the boil and bubble for a few seconds before pouring over the pork. Stir to mix, then cover with the lid and cook for 2 hours.

8 Stir the fruit, orange juice and sugar into the stew. Switch the slow cooker to low and cook for a further 2–3 hours, or until the pork is very tender.

9 Stir in the remaining *mole* paste and cook for 30 minutes. Serve sprinkled with orange rind, parsley and fresh chilli.

Energy 477Kcal/1999kJ; Protein 40.7g; Carbohydrate 25.6g, of which sugars 21g; Fat 19.1g, of which saturates 3.8g; Cholesterol 105mg; Calcium 86mg; Fibre 4.1g; Sodium 149mg.

CIDER-GLAZED GAMMON

This is a classic buffet centrepiece, which is ideal for Christmas or Thanksgiving. A fresh cranberry sauce provides the perfect foil to the richness of the meat and can be made in the slow cooker the day before if you want to serve the gammon hot, rather than cold. Soaking smoked gammon overnight helps to remove the excess salts.

SERVES 8

2kg/4½lb middle gammon joint, soaked
    overnight, if smoked
2 small onions
about 30 whole cloves
3 bay leaves
10 black peppercorns
150ml/¼ pint/⅔ cup medium-dry
    (hard) cider
45ml/3 tbsp soft light brown sugar

For the cranberry sauce
350g/12oz/3 cups cranberries
175g/6oz/scant 1 cup caster (superfine)
    sugar
grated rind and juice of 2 clementines
30ml/2 tbsp port

1 Drain the gammon joint, if soaked overnight, then place it in the ceramic cooking pot. Stud the onions with 6 of the cloves and add to the cooking pot with the bay leaves and peppercorns.

2 Pour over enough cold water to just cover the gammon. Switch the slow cooker to high, cover with the lid and cook for 1 hour. Skim off any scum from the surface, re-cover and cook for a further 4–5 hours. Check once during cooking and skim the surface, if necessary.

COOK'S TIP
The gammon should remain barely covered with water during cooking. There should be little evaporation from the slow cooker, but if necessary, top up with a small amount of boiling water.

3 Carefully lift the gammon joint out of the slow cooker using large forks or slotted spoons, and place it in a roasting tin (pan) or ovenproof dish. Leave to stand for about 15 minutes until cool enough to handle.

4 Meanwhile, make the glaze. Pour the cider into a small pan, add the soft brown sugar and heat gently, stirring, until dissolved. Simmer for 5 minutes to make a sticky glaze, then remove from the heat and leave to cool for a few minutes so that it thickens slightly.

5 Preheat the oven to 220°C/425°F/ Gas 7. Using a pair of scissors, snip the string off the gammon then carefully slice off the rind, leaving a thin, even layer of fat over the meat.

6 Using a sharp knife, score the fat into a neat diamond pattern. Press a clove into the centre of each diamond, then spoon over the glaze. Bake for about 25 minutes, or until the fat is brown, glistening and crisp. Remove from the oven and set aside until ready to serve.

7 Meanwhile, make the cranberry sauce. Wash the ceramic cooking pot, then add all the ingredients for the cranberry sauce to it. Switch the slow cooker to high and cook uncovered for 20 minutes, stirring continuously, until the sugar has dissolved completely.

8 Cover the pot with the lid and cook on high for 1½–2 hours, or until the cranberries are tender. Transfer the sauce to a jug (pitcher) or bowl, or keep warm in the slow cooker until ready to serve with the gammon. (The sauce can be served hot or cold.)

COOK'S TIPS
• If serving hot, cover the gammon with foil and leave to rest for 15 minutes before carving.
• If you prefer, serve the ham with redcurrant sauce or jelly. You can also use honey in place of the soft brown sugar for the glaze, if you like.

Energy 404Kcal/1689kJ; Protein 44.1g; Carbohydrate 15.2g, of which sugars 14.8g; Fat 18.8g, of which saturates 6.3g; Cholesterol 57mg; Calcium 25mg; Fibre 1g; Sodium 220mg.

VEAL STEW with TOMATOES

This classic French dish is traditionally made with lean and mildly flavoured veal.
Pork fillet makes an excellent, and economical, alternative.

SERVES 4

30ml/2 tbsp plain (all-purpose) flour
675g/1½lb boneless veal shoulder,
  trimmed and cut into cubes
30ml/2 tbsp sunflower oil
4 shallots, very finely chopped
300ml/½ pint/1¼ cups boiling vegetable
  or chicken stock
150ml/¼ pint/⅔ cup dry white wine
15ml/1 tbsp tomato purée (paste)
225g/8oz tomatoes, peeled, seeded
  and chopped
115g/4oz mushrooms, quartered
grated zest and juice of 1 small
  unwaxed orange
bouquet garni
salt and ground black pepper
30ml/2 tbsp chopped fresh parsley,
  to garnish

1 Put the flour in a small plastic bag and season with salt and pepper. Drop the pieces of meat into the bag a few at a time and shake to coat with the flour.

2 Heat 15ml/1 tbsp of the oil in a pan, add the shallots and cook gently for 5 minutes. Transfer to the ceramic cooking pot and switch to high or auto.

3 Add the remaining 15ml/1 tbsp oil to the pan and fry the meat in batches until well browned on all sides, then transfer to the ceramic cooking pot.

4 Pour the stock and white wine into the pan. Add the tomato purée and bring to the boil, stirring. Pour the sauce over the meat. Add the tomatoes, mushrooms, orange zest and juice, and bouquet garni to the pot and stir briefly to mix the ingredients. Cover with the lid and cook for about 1 hour.

5 Reduce the temperature to low or leave on auto and cook for 3–4 hours, or until the meat and mushrooms are very tender. Remove the bouquet garni, check the seasoning and add more salt and ground black pepper if necessary. Garnish with fresh parsley and serve.

Energy 323Kcal/1358kJ; Protein 38.2g; Carbohydrate 13.8g, of which sugars 5.4g; Fat 10.6g, of which saturates 2.3g; Cholesterol 141mg; Calcium 47mg; Fibre 1.7g; Sodium 314mg.

GREEK MEATBALLS in RICH TOMATO SAUCE

There are many versions of these sausage-shaped meatballs, known as yiouvarlakia
or soudzoukakia. These are made with lamb, but beef makes an excellent alternative.

SERVES 4

50g/2oz/1 cup fresh white breadcrumbs
1 egg, lightly beaten
finely grated rind of ½ small orange
2.5ml/½ tsp dried oregano
450g/1lb minced (ground) lamb
1 small onion, peeled and grated
2 cloves garlic, crushed
15ml/1 tbsp plain (all-purpose) flour
30ml/2 tbsp olive oil
salt and ground black pepper
flat leaf parsley, to garnish

For the sauce
1 onion, very finely chopped
400g/14oz can chopped tomatoes
150ml/¼ pint/⅔ cup hot lamb or beef
    stock
1 bay leaf

1 Put the breadcrumbs, beaten egg,
orange rind and oregano in a bowl and
stir together. Add the lamb, onion and
garlic and season with salt and pepper.
Mix together until thoroughly combined.

2 Using dampened hands, so that the
mixture doesn't stick, press the meat
mixture into small sausage-shapes, about
5cm/2in long, and roll them in flour.
Place in the refrigerator for 30 minutes
to firm up slightly.

COOK'S TIP
Serve these meatballs with a refreshing
salad and plenty of fresh, country-style
crusty bread for mopping up the juices.
Alternatively, serve with pitta bread so
that guests can stuff the breads with
meatballs and fresh green salad.

3 Heat the oil in a large frying pan and
add the meatballs, working in batches if
necessary. Cook for 5–8 minutes, turning
the meatballs, until evenly browned all
over. Transfer to a plate and set aside,
leaving the fat and juices in the pan.

4 To make the sauce, add the onion to
the pan and cook for 3–4 minutes, until
beginning to soften. Pour in the chopped
tomatoes, bring to the boil and cook
gently for 1 minute.

5 Transfer the sauce to the ceramic
cooking pot and stir in the stock. Add
the bay leaf and season with salt and
ground black pepper.

6 Arrange the meatballs in a single layer
in the sauce. Cover with the lid and
cook on high or auto for 1 hour. Reduce
the temperature to low or leave on auto
and cook for a further 4–5 hours. Serve
garnished with sprigs of fresh parsley.

Energy 363Kcal/1515kJ; Protein 26.1g; Carbohydrate 15g, of which sugars 5.3g; Fat 22.5g, of which saturates 8.3g; Cholesterol 141mg; Calcium 68mg; Fibre 1.5g; Sodium 239mg.

LANCASHIRE HOT-POT

This dish is traditionally made without browning the lamb or vegetables, and relies on long, slow cooking to develop the flavour. You can brown the top under the grill, if you like.

SERVES 4

8 middle neck or loin lamb chops,
    about 900g/2lb in total weight
900g/2lb potatoes, thinly sliced
2 onions, peeled and sliced
2 carrots, peeled and sliced
1 stick celery, trimmed and sliced
1 leek, peeled and sliced
225g/8oz/generous 3 cups button (white)
    mushrooms, sliced
5ml/1 tsp dried mixed herbs
small sprig of rosemary
475ml/16fl oz/2 cups lamb or beef stock
15g/½oz/1 tbsp butter, melted
salt and ground black pepper

3 Pour the meat stock into the ceramic cooking pot, then cover with the lid and switch the slow cooker to high or auto. Cook for 1 hour, then reduce the temperature to low or leave on auto and cook for 6–8 hours or until tender.

4 Brush the top layer of potatoes with melted butter. Place under a preheated grill (broiler) and cook for 5 minutes, or until the potatoes are lightly browned. Serve immediately.

1 Trim the lamb chops of excess fat. Place a layer of sliced potatoes in the base of the ceramic cooking pot, and top with some sliced vegetables and a sprinkling of dried herbs, salt and black pepper. Place four of the chops on top.

2 Repeat the layers of sliced potato, vegetables, dried herbs and meat, tucking the rosemary sprig down the side of the pot. Continue layering up the remaining vegetables, finishing with a neat layer of potatoes on the top.

Energy 850Kcal/3544kJ; Protein 44.7g; Carbohydrate 45.3g, of which sugars 10.1g; Fat 55.8g, of which saturates 26.5g; Cholesterol 186mg; Calcium 72mg; Fibre 4.3g; Sodium 274mg.

LAMB PIE with MUSTARD THATCH

Here, a traditional shepherd's pie is given a contemporary twist with a tangy topping of mashed potato flavoured with peppery mustard. Serve with vegetables.

SERVES 4

450g/1lb lean minced (ground) lamb
1 onion, very finely chopped
2 celery sticks, thinly sliced
2 carrots, finely diced
15ml/1 tbsp cornflour (cornstarch)
    blended into 150ml/¼ pint/⅔ cup
    lamb stock
15ml/1 tbsp Worcestershire sauce
30ml/2 tbsp chopped fresh rosemary,
    or 10ml/2 tsp dried
800g/1¾lb floury potatoes, diced
60ml/4 tbsp milk
15ml/1 tbsp wholegrain mustard
25g/1oz/2 tbsp butter
salt and ground black pepper

1 Heat a non-stick frying pan, then add the lamb, breaking it up with a wooden spoon, and cook until lightly browned all over. Add the onion, celery and carrots to the pan and cook for 2–3 minutes, stirring frequently.

2 Stir the stock and cornflour mixture into the pan. Bring to the boil, stirring constantly, then remove from the heat. Stir in the Worcestershire sauce and rosemary, and season well with salt and ground black pepper.

3 Transfer the mixture to the ceramic cooking pot and switch the slow cooker to high. Cover and cook for 3 hours.

4 Towards the end of the cooking time, cook the potatoes in a large pan of boiling salted water until tender. Drain well, mash, and stir in the milk, mustard and butter. Season to taste.

5 Spoon the mashed potatoes on top of the lamb, spreading the mixture out evenly. Cook for a further 45 minutes. Brown the topping under a pre-heated grill (broiler) for a few minutes, if you like, then serve immediately.

Energy 458Kcal/1920kJ; Protein 26.5g; Carbohydrate 42.2g, of which sugars 8.1g; Fat 21.5g, of which saturates 10.6g; Cholesterol 101mg; Calcium 84mg; Fibre 3.5g; Sodium 264mg.

MOUSSAKA

This classic Greek dish topped with a light egg and cheese sauce is delicious in summer or winter, served with a crisp leafy salad. Try to find small, sweet aubergines with firm, shiny skins because they have much the best flavour. For an authentic touch, look out for Kefolotiri cheese in delicatessens and specialist food stores – although if you can't find it, Cheddar cheese will give equally good results.

SERVES 6

900g/2lb small or medium aubergines
   (eggplant), thinly sliced
60ml/4 tbsp olive oil
1 onion, finely chopped
2 garlic cloves, crushed
450g/1lb lean minced (ground) lamb
400g/14oz can chopped tomatoes
5ml/1 tsp dried oregano
pinch of ground cinnamon
salt and ground black pepper

For the topping
50g/2oz/¼ cup butter
50g/2oz/½ cup plain (all-purpose) flour
600ml/1 pint/2½ cups milk
pinch of freshly grated nutmeg
75g/3oz/¾ cup grated Kefolotiri or
   mature Cheddar cheese
1 egg yolk
30ml/2 tbsp fresh white breadcrumbs

2 Lightly brush the aubergine slices with about half the oil, then arrange the slices in a single layer on a baking sheet. Place the baking sheet under a medium grill (broiler) and cook, turning once, until the aubergine slices are softened and golden brown on both sides.

3 Arrange half the aubergine slices in the bottom of the ceramic cooking pot and switch the slow cooker to high. Set aside the remaining slices.

6 Spoon the lamb mixture into the slow cooker, covering the aubergine slices. Arrange the remaining aubergine slices on top, cover and cook for 2 hours.

7 Meanwhile, make the cheese topping. Melt the butter in a pan, stir in the flour and cook for one minute. Gradually stir in the milk, bring to the boil over a low heat, stirring constantly, and cook until thick and creamy. Lower the heat and simmer for 1 minute. Remove from the heat, season, then stir in the nutmeg and two-thirds of the cheese.

1 Layer the aubergine slices in a sieve (strainer) or colander, sprinkling each layer with salt. Place the sieve over a bowl and leave to drain for 20 minutes. Rinse the aubergine slices thoroughly under cold running water and pat dry with kitchen paper.

VARIATION
You can use courgettes (zucchini) in place of the aubergines, if you prefer. Simply slice the courgettes, brush with olive oil and grill as before. There is no need to salt the courgette slices.

4 Heat the remaining olive oil in a heavy pan, add the onion and fry gently for about 10 minutes, or until softened. Add the garlic and lamb and cook, stirring and breaking up the meat with a wooden spoon, until the meat is evenly browned.

5 Stir the tomatoes, oregano and cinnamon into the meat mixture, season generously with salt and ground black pepper and slowly bring to the boil over a gentle heat.

8 Leave the sauce to cool for 5 minutes, then beat in the egg yolk. Pour the sauce over the aubergine slices. Cover and cook for a further 2 hours, or until the topping is lightly set.

9 Sprinkle the remaining cheese and the breadcrumbs over the top and cook under a grill (broiler) for 3–4 minutes, or until golden brown. Leave to stand for 5–10 minutes before serving.

Energy 444Kcal/1850kJ; Protein 24.1g; Carbohydrate 1.5g, of which sugars 11.2g; Fat 31g, of which saturates 14g; Cholesterol 93.5mg; Calcium 268mg; Fibre 4.1g; Sodium 266mg.

MOROCCAN LAMB with HONEY and PRUNES

*This classic dish of the Moroccan Jews is eaten at Rosh Hashanah – the Jewish
New Year – when sweet foods are served in anticipation of a sweet new year to come.*

SERVES 6

130g/4½oz/generous ½ cup stoned
   (pitted) prunes
350ml/12fl oz/1½ cups hot tea
1kg/2¼lb stewing or braising lamb,
   such as shoulder
30ml/2 tbsp olive oil
1 onion, chopped
2.5ml/½ tsp ground ginger
2.5ml/½ tsp curry powder
pinch of freshly grated nutmeg
10ml/2 tsp ground cinnamon
1.5ml/¼ tsp saffron threads
30ml/2 tbsp hot water
75ml/5 tbsp clear honey
200ml/7fl oz/scant 1 cup near-boiling lamb
   or beef stock
salt and ground black pepper
115g/4oz/1 cup blanched almonds, toasted
30ml/2 tbsp chopped fresh coriander
   (cilantro) and 3 hard-boiled eggs,
   cut into wedges, to garnish

1 Put the prunes in a heatproof bowl,
then pour over the tea and leave to
soak. Meanwhile, trim the lamb and cut
into chunky pieces, no larger than 2.5cm/
1in. Heat the oil in a frying pan and
sauté the lamb in batches for 5 minutes,
stirring frequently, until well-browned.
Remove with a slotted spoon and
transfer to the ceramic cooking pot.

2 Add the onion to the frying pan and
cook for 5 minutes, until starting to
soften. Stir in the ginger, curry powder,
nutmeg, cinnamon, salt and a large pinch
of black pepper, and cook for 1 minute.
Add to the ceramic cooking pot with the
meat and their juices.

3 Drain the prunes, adding the soaking
liquid to the lamb. Cover the prunes.

4 Soak the saffron in the hot water for
1 minute, then add to the cooking pot
with the honey and stock. Cover with
the lid and cook on high or auto for
1 hour. Reduce the temperature to low
and cook for a further 5–7 hours, or
until the lamb is very tender.

5 Add the prunes to the cooking pot
and stir to mix. Cook for 30 minutes, or
until warmed through. Serve sprinkled
with the toasted almonds and chopped
coriander, and topped with the wedges
of hard-boiled egg.

Energy 490Kcal/2051kJ; Protein 43.6g; Carbohydrate 23.8g, of which sugars 23.4g; Fat 25.2g, of which saturates 10.3g; Cholesterol 279mg; Calcium 41mg; Fibre 1.4g; Sodium 197mg.

LAMB in DILL SAUCE

In this recipe, the lamb is cooked with vegetables to make a clear well-flavoured broth,
which is then thickened with an egg and cream mixture to make a smooth delicate sauce.

SERVES 6

1.3kg/3lb lean boneless lamb
1 small onion, trimmed and quartered
1 carrot, peeled and thickly sliced
1 bay leaf
4 sprigs of fresh dill, plus 45ml/3 tbsp
    chopped
1 thinly pared strip of lemon rind
750ml/1¼ pints/3 cups near-boiling lamb
    or vegetable stock
225g/8oz small shallots
15ml/1 tbsp olive oil
15g/½oz/1 tbsp unsalted (sweet) butter
15ml/1 tbsp plain (all-purpose) flour
115g/4oz frozen petits pois, defrosted
1 egg yolk
75ml/2½fl oz/⅓ cup single (light) cream, at
    room temperature
salt and ground black pepper
new potatoes and carrots, to serve

1 Trim the lamb and cut into 2.5cm/1in
pieces. Place in the ceramic cooking pot
with the onion, carrot, bay leaf, sprigs of
dill and lemon rind. Pour over the stock,
cover and cook on high for 1 hour. Skim
off any scum, then re-cover and cook for
a further 2 hours on high or 4 hours on
low, until the lamb is fairly tender.

2 Meanwhile, put the shallots in a
heatproof bowl and pour over enough
boiling water to cover. Leave to cool,
then drain and peel off the skins.

3 Remove the meat from the pot. Strain
the stock, discarding the vegetables and
herbs. Clean the pot. Return the meat
and half the stock (reserving the rest),
cover and switch to high.

4 Heat the oil and butter in a pan, add
the shallots and cook gently, stirring, for
10–15 minutes, or until browned and
tender. Turn off the heat, then transfer
the shallots to the cooking pot, using a
slotted spoon.

5 Sprinkle the flour over the fat
remaining in the pan, then stir in the
reserved stock, a little at a time. Bring
to the boil, stirring all the time until
thickened, then stir into the lamb and
shallot mixture. Stir in the peas and
season with salt and pepper. Cook on
high for 30 minutes until piping hot.

6 Blend the egg yolk and the cream
together, then stir in a few spoonfuls
of the hot stock. Add to the casserole
in a thin stream, stirring until slightly
thickened. Stir in the chopped dill and
serve immediately, with steamed new
potatoes and carrots.

Energy 631Kcal/2629kJ; Protein 60.9g; Carbohydrate 7g, of which sugars 3.5g; Fat 40g, of which saturates 17.5g; Cholesterol 249mg; Calcium 123mg; Fibre 1.9g; Sodium 566mg.

TUSCAN POT-ROASTED SHOULDER of LAMB

This delicious boned and rolled shoulder of lamb, studded with rosemary sprigs and garlic, then cooked on a bed of vegetables, makes a perfect alternative to a traditional meat roast. Check that the lamb will fit comfortably in the slow cooker before you start.

SERVES 6

15ml/1 tbsp olive oil
1.3kg/3lb lamb shoulder, trimmed, boned and tied
3 large garlic cloves
12 small fresh rosemary sprigs
115g/4oz lean rinded smoked bacon, chopped
1 onion, chopped
3 carrots, finely chopped
3 celery sticks, finely chopped
1 leek, finely chopped
150ml/¼ pint/⅔ cup red wine
300ml/½ pint/1¼ cups lamb or vegetable stock
400g/14oz can chopped tomatoes
3 sprigs of fresh thyme
2 bay leaves
400g/14oz can flageolet (small cannellini) beans, drained and rinsed
salt and ground black pepper
potatoes or warm crusty bread, to serve

1 Heat the oil in a large frying pan and brown the lamb on all sides. Remove from the pan and leave to stand until it is cool enough to handle.

2 Meanwhile, cut the garlic cloves into quarters. When the lamb is cool enough, make twelve deep incisions all over the meat. Push a piece of garlic and a small sprig of rosemary into each incision.

COOK'S TIP
Lamb can be quite a fatty meat, so ask your butcher to trim off as much excess fat as possible from the joint, before boning, rolling and tying it.

3 Add the bacon, onion, carrot, celery and leek to the pan and cook for about 10 minutes until soft, then transfer to the ceramic cooking pot. Stir the red wine into the cooking pot.

4 Add the stock and chopped tomatoes to the pot and season with salt and pepper. Add the thyme and bay leaves, submerging them in the liquid. Place the lamb on top, cover with the lid and cook on high for 4 hours.

5 Lift the lamb out of the pot and stir the beans into the vegetable mixture. Return the lamb, re-cover and cook for a further 1–2 hours, or until the lamb is cooked and tender.

6 Remove the lamb from the ceramic cooking pot using slotted spoons, cover with foil to keep warm, and leave to rest for 10 minutes.

7 Remove the string from the lamb and carve the meat into thick slices. Remove the thyme and bay leaves from the vegetable and bean mixture and carefully skim off any fat from the surface. Spoon the vegetables on to warmed serving plates and arrange the sliced lamb on top. Serve with potatoes or warm bread.

VARIATIONS
• Flageolet beans have a delicate yet distinctive flavour that goes particularly well in this dish. However, you can use other mildly flavoured beans instead, such as butter beans or cannellini beans.
• Try using 15ml/1 tsp fresh oregano in place of the thyme, if you prefer. This classic Italian herb tastes just as good.

Energy 710Kcal/2958kJ; Protein 60.2g; Carbohydrate 13.7g, of which sugars 4.8g; Fat 44.6g, of which saturates 19.4g; Cholesterol 229mg; Calcium 58mg; Fibre 4.7g; Sodium 864mg.

LAMB and CARROT CASSEROLE with BARLEY

Barley and carrots make natural partners for lamb and mutton. In this convenient casserole the barley extends the meat and adds to the flavour and texture as well as thickening the sauce. This warming dish is comfort food at its very best.

SERVES 6

675g/1½lb stewing (braising) lamb
15ml/1 tbsp vegetable oil
2 onions
675g/1½lb carrots, thickly sliced
4–6 celery sticks, sliced
45ml/3 tbsp pearl barley, rinsed
600ml/1 pint/2½ cups near-boiling lamb or
  vegetable stock
5ml/1 tsp fresh thyme leaves or pinch of
  dried mixed herbs
salt and ground black pepper
spring cabbage and jacket potatoes,
  to serve

1 Trim all excess fat from the lamb, then cut the meat into 3cm/1¼in pieces. Heat the oil in a frying pan, add the lamb and fry until browned. Remove from with a slotted spoon and set aside.

2 Slice the onions and add to the pan. Fry gently for 5 minutes until golden. Add the carrots and celery and cook for a further 3–4 minutes or until beginning to soften. Transfer the vegetables to the ceramic cooking pot and switch the slow cooker to high.

3 Sprinkle the pearl barley over the vegetables in the cooking pot, then arrange the lamb pieces on top.

4 Lightly season with salt and ground black pepper, then scatter with the herbs. Pour the stock over the meat, so that all of the meat is covered.

5 Cover the slow cooker with the lid and cook on auto or high for 2 hours. Lift the lid and, using a large spoon, skim off any scum that has risen to the surface of the casserole.

6 Re-cover the pot and leave on auto or switch to low and cook for a further 4–6 hours or until the meat, vegetables and barley are tender. Serve with spring cabbage and jacket potatoes.

Energy 304Kcal/1263kJ; Protein 23.2g; Carbohydrate 13g, of which sugars 11.3g; Fat 18g, of which saturates 7.5g; Cholesterol 84mg; Calcium 53mg; Fibre 3.6g; Sodium 110mg.

LAMB STEWED with TOMATOES and GARLIC

This simple rustic stew comes from the plateau of Puglia in Italy, where sheep graze
beside the vineyards. Serve simply, with fresh crusty bread and a green leaf salad.

SERVES 4

1.2kg/2½lb stewing (braising) lamb
30ml/2 tbsp plain (all-purpose) flour,
    seasoned with ground black pepper
60ml/4 tbsp olive oil
2 large cloves garlic, finely chopped
1 sprig fresh rosemary
150ml/¼ pint/⅔ cup dry white wine
150ml/¼ pint/⅔ cup lamb or beef stock
2.5ml/½ tsp salt
450g/1lb fresh tomatoes, peeled and
    chopped, or 400g/14oz can chopped
    tomatoes
salt and ground black pepper

4 Season with salt and pepper and stir
in the tomatoes. Cover the cooking pot
with the lid and switch the slow cooker
to high or auto. Cook for 1 hour.

5 Reduce the heat to low or leave on
auto and cook for a further 6–8 hours,
or until the lamb is tender. Taste and
adjust the seasoning before serving.

VARIATION
For Lamb with Butternut Squash, sauté
675g/1½lb cubed lamb fillet in 15ml/1 tbsp
oil, then transfer to the ceramic cooking
pot. Fry 1 chopped onion and 2 crushed
garlic cloves until soft, and add to the lamb
with 1 cubed butternut squash, 400g/14oz
can chopped tomatoes, 150ml/¼ pint/⅔ cup
lamb stock and 5ml/1 tsp dried marjoram.
Cover and cook on low for 5–6 hours.

1 Trim all fat and gristle from the lamb
and cut into 2.5cm/1in cubes. Toss in the
flour to coat. Set aside the excess flour.

2 Heat the oil in a pan and fry the lamb,
in two batches for 5 minutes, stirring,
until browned. Lift out the lamb and
transfer to the ceramic cooking pot.

3 Add the garlic and cook for a few
seconds before adding the rosemary,
wine and stock. Bring almost to the boil,
stirring, to remove any meat sediment
from the pan. Pour over the lamb.

Energy 636Kcal/2656kJ; Protein 62.4g; Carbohydrate 11.5g, of which sugars 3.9g; Fat 35.5g, of which saturates 12.2g; Cholesterol 222mg; Calcium 62mg; Fibre 1.4g; Sodium 508mg.

ONE-POT AND CLAY-POT MEAT

Nothing quite matches the flavour of meat that has simmered in the oven for hours with tasty root vegetables and aromatic herbs, especially when a little beer or wine has been poured into the pot, as in Pot-roast Beef with Guinness, Pork Cooked in Cider with Parsley Dumplings, or Osso Bucco with Risotto Milanese. Equally delicious are sustaining stews, such as Boeuf Bourguignon and Braised Lamb with Apricots and Herb Dumplings. For sophisticated entertaining, why not try Calf's Liver with Slow-cooked Onions, Marsala and Sage, or Noisettes of Pork with Creamy Calvados and Apple Sauce?

CITRUS BEEF CURRY

This superbly aromatic Thai-style curry is not too hot but full of flavour. For a special meal, it goes perfectly with fried noodles.

SERVES 4

450g/1lb rump (round) steak
30ml/2 tbsp sunflower oil
30ml/2 tbsp medium curry paste
2 bay leaves
400ml/14fl oz/1⅔ cups coconut milk
300ml/½ pint/1¼ cups beef stock
30ml/2 tbsp lemon juice
45ml/3 tbsp Thai fish sauce
    (*nam pla*)
15ml/1 tbsp sugar
115g/4oz baby (pearl) onions, peeled but
    left whole
225g/8oz new potatoes, halved
115g/4oz/1 cup unsalted roasted peanuts,
    roughly chopped
115g/4oz fine green beans, halved
1 red (bell) pepper, seeded and
    thinly sliced
unsalted roasted peanuts, to
    garnish (optional)

1 Trim any fat off the beef and cut the beef into 5cm/2in strips.

2 Heat the sunflower oil in a large, heavy pan, add the curry paste and cook over a medium heat for 30 seconds, stirring constantly.

3 Add the beef and cook, stirring, for 2 minutes until it is beginning to brown and is thoroughly coated with the spices.

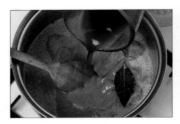

4 Stir in the bay leaves, coconut milk, stock, lemon juice, fish sauce and sugar, and bring to the boil, stirring.

5 Add the onions and potatoes, then bring back to the boil, reduce the heat and simmer, uncovered, for 5 minutes.

6 Stir in the peanuts, beans and pepper and simmer for a further 10 minutes, or until the beef and potatoes are tender. Serve in shallow bowls, with a spoon and fork, to enjoy all the rich and creamy juices. Sprinkle with extra unsalted roasted peanuts, if you like.

Energy 476Kcal/1990kJ; Protein 33.8g; Carbohydrate 27.5g, of which sugars 16.3g; Fat 26.4g, of which saturates 6.6g; Cholesterol 69mg; Calcium 77mg; Fibre 4.1g; Sodium 169mg.

IRISH STEW

Simple and delicious, this is the quintessential Irish main course. Traditionally, mutton chops are used, but as they are harder to find these days you can use lamb instead.

SERVES 4

1.3kg/3lb boneless lamb chops, cut into
　large chunks
15ml/1 tbsp vegetable oil
3 onions
4 large carrots
900ml/1½ pints/3¾ cups water
4 large potatoes, cut into
　large chunks
1 large fresh thyme sprig
15g/½oz/1 tbsp unsalted
　(sweet) butter
15ml/1 tbsp chopped fresh parsley
salt and ground black pepper

1 Trim any fat from the lamb. Heat the oil in a large, flameproof casserole and brown the meat on all sides. Remove from the casserole.

2 Cut the onions into quarters and thickly slice the carrots. Add them to the casserole and cook for 5 minutes, stirring, or until the onions are browned. Return the meat to the pan with the water. Bring to the boil, reduce the heat, cover and simmer for 1 hour.

3 Add the potatoes to the pan with the thyme and cook for a further 1 hour.

4 Leave the stew to settle for a few minutes. Remove the fat from the liquid with a spoon, then stir in the butter and the parsley. Season well before serving.

Energy 898Kcal/3763kJ; Protein 70.4g; Carbohydrate 60g, of which sugars 19.1g; Fat 43.6g, of which saturates 19.5g; Cholesterol 255mg; Calcium 104mg; Fibre 7g; Sodium 359mg.

POT-ROAST BEEF with GUINNESS

This heart-warming, rich pot-roast is ideal for a winter supper. Brisket of beef has the best flavour but this dish works equally well with rolled silverside or topside.

SERVES 6

30ml/2 tbsp vegetable oil
900g/2lb rolled brisket of beef
275g/10oz onions, roughly chopped
2 celery sticks, thickly sliced
450g/1lb carrots, cut into large chunks
675g/1½lb potatoes, peeled and cut into
   large chunks
30ml/2 tbsp plain (all-purpose) flour
475ml/16fl oz/2 cups beef stock
300ml/½ pint/1¼ cups Guinness
1 bay leaf
45ml/3 tbsp chopped fresh thyme
5ml/1 tsp soft light brown sugar
30ml/2 tbsp wholegrain mustard
15ml/1 tbsp tomato purée (paste)
salt and ground black pepper

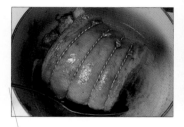

1 Preheat the oven to 180°C/350°F/ Gas 4. Heat the oil in a large flameproof casserole and brown the meat all over until golden.

3 Add the celery, carrot and potato to the casserole and cook over a medium heat for 2–3 minutes, or until they are just beginning to colour.

5 Add the bay leaf, thyme, sugar, mustard, tomato purée and plenty of seasoning. Place the meat on top, cover tightly and transfer to the oven.

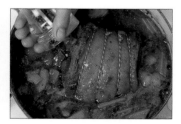

2 Remove the meat from the pan and drain it on a double layer of kitchen paper. Add the chopped onions to the pan and cook for about 4 minutes, or until they are just beginning to soften and turn brown, stirring all the time.

4 Stir in the flour and cook for a further 1 minute stirring continuously. Pour in the beef stock and the Guinness and stir until well combined. Bring the sauce to the boil, stirring continuously with a wooden spoon.

6 Cook for about 2½ hours, or until the vegetables and meat are tender. Adjust the seasoning and add another pinch of sugar, if necessary. To serve, remove the meat and carve into thick slices. Serve with the vegetables and plenty of gravy.

Energy 402Kcal/1691kJ; Protein 35.5g; Carbohydrate 33.8g, of which sugars 11.9g; Fat 13.6g, of which saturates 4.4g; Cholesterol 81mg; Calcium 58mg; Fibre 4g; Sodium 142mg.

CLAY-POT BEEF with RED PEPPERS

Using a clay pot to cook lean meat keeps it moist and juicy. Here it is cooked with sweet peppers and onion in a rich red wine sauce.

SERVES 6

1.2kg/2½lb top rump (round) steak
   or silverside (pot roast) of beef,
   neatly tied
2 garlic cloves
30ml/2 tbsp sunflower oil
1 large onion, chopped
300ml/½ pint/1¼ cups beef stock
15ml/1 tbsp tomato purée (paste)
150ml/¼ pint/⅔ cup red wine
bouquet garni
4 sweet romano red (bell) peppers, halved
   lengthwise and seeded
15ml/1 tbsp butter, softened
15ml/1 tbsp plain (all-purpose) flour
salt and ground black pepper

1 Soak the clay pot in cold water for 20 minutes, then drain. Using a sharp knife, make about 20 small incisions in the beef. Cut the garlic cloves into thin slivers and insert into the cuts.

2 Season the beef with salt and pepper. Heat the sunflower oil in a large frying pan, add the beef and cook, stirring frequently with a wooden spoon until browned on all sides. Remove the beef from the pan and set aside.

3 Add the onion to the frying pan and fry gently for 5–8 minutes, stirring occasionally, until light golden. Transfer the onion to the clay pot.

4 Place the beef on top of the onion in the clay pot, then mix together the beef stock, tomato purée and wine and pour over the beef.

5 Add the bouquet garni to the pot, then cover the pot and place it in an unheated oven. Set the oven to 200°C/400°F/Gas 6 and cook for 1 hour. Uncover, baste the meat and add the pepper halves, arranging them around the meat. Cook uncovered for a further 45 minutes until the beef is tender, basting occasionally.

6 To serve, transfer the beef to a large warmed serving dish with the peppers and onion. Drain the juices from the clay pot into a pan and heat gently.

7 Blend together the butter and flour to make a smooth paste, then gradually add small pieces of the paste to the sauce, whisking until well blended. Bring the sauce to the boil and simmer gently for about 1 minute, whisking all the time, until the sauce is thickened slightly. Pour into a sauce boat and serve with the beef and vegetables.

VARIATIONS

Romano peppers are an elongated variety that are available in large supermarkets. If you can't find them, use ordinary bell-shaped peppers instead – the dish will be just as good. If you prefer, use green, orange or yellow peppers in place of red.

COOK'S TIPS

• The butter and flour paste used in step 7 to thicken the sauce is known as a beurre manié. The paste is always made from equal quantities of plain flour and softened butter. It is used for thickening casseroles, sauces and occasionally soups.

• A bouquet garni is a selection of aromatic herbs used to flavour soups, stocks or casseroles. The most widely used herbs include thyme, parsley, rosemary and bay leaves. Fresh herbs can be tied together with string or dried herbs can be wrapped in a small muslin (cheesecloth) square and secured with string. Ready-made bouquet garnis of dried herbs are sold in many supermarkets.

Energy 420Kcal/1760kJ; Protein 44.7g; Carbohydrate 15.5g, of which sugars 11.7g; Fat 18.6g, of which saturates 6.9g; Cholesterol 113mg; Calcium 42mg; Fibre 3g; Sodium 154mg.

BEEF CARBONADE

*This rich, dark stew of beef cooked slowly with lots of onions, garlic and beer is a classic
casserole from the north of France and neighbouring Belgium.*

SERVES 6

45ml/3 tbsp vegetable oil or beef dripping
3 onions, sliced
45ml/3 tbsp plain (all-purpose) flour
2.5ml/½ tsp mustard powder
1kg/2¼lb stewing beef (shin, shank or
    chuck), cut into large cubes
2–3 garlic cloves, finely chopped
300ml/½ pint/1¼ cups dark beer or ale
150ml/¼ pint/⅔ cup water
5ml/1 tsp dark brown sugar
1 fresh thyme sprig
1 fresh bay leaf
1 celery stick
salt and ground black pepper

For the topping
50g/2oz/¼ cup butter
1 garlic clove, crushed
15ml/1 tbsp Dijon mustard
45ml/3 tbsp chopped fresh parsley
6–12 slices of French baguette

1 Preheat the oven to 160°C/325°F/
Gas 3. Heat 30ml/2 tbsp of the oil or
dripping in a pan and cook the onions
over a low heat until softened. Remove
from the pan and set aside.

2 Meanwhile, mix together the flour and
mustard and season. Toss the beef in the
flour. Add the remaining oil or dripping
to the pan and heat over a high heat.
Brown the beef all over, then transfer it
to a deep, earthenware baking dish.

3 Reduce the heat and return the
onions to the pan. Add the garlic, cook
briefly, then add the beer or ale, water
and sugar. Tie the thyme and bay leaf
together and add to the pan with the
celery. Bring to the boil, stirring, then
season with salt and pepper.

4 Pour the sauce over the beef and mix
well. Cover tightly, then place in the
oven and cook for 2½ hours. Check the
beef once or twice to make sure that it
is not too dry, adding a little extra water,
if necessary. Test for tenderness, allowing
an extra 30–40 minutes' cooking time
if necessary.

5 To make the topping, beat together
the butter, crushed garlic, Dijon mustard
and 30ml/2 tbsp of the chopped fresh
parsley. Spread the flavoured butter
thickly over the bread. Increase the oven
temperature to 190°C/375°F/Gas 5.
Taste and season the stew, then arrange
the prepared bread slices, buttered side
uppermost, on top. Bake for 20 minutes,
or until the bread is browned and crisp.
Sprinkle the remaining chopped fresh
parsley over the top to garnish and
serve immediately.

Energy 532Kcal/2234kJ; Protein 41.1g; Carbohydrate 40g, of which sugars 10.7g; Fat 21.8g, of which saturates 9.1g; Cholesterol 108mg; Calcium 102mg; Fibre 2.7g; Sodium 409mg.

BOEUF BOURGUIGNON

The classic French dish of beef cooked in Burgundy style, with red wine, small pieces of bacon, shallots and mushrooms, is baked for several hours at a low temperature.

SERVES 6

175g/6oz rindless streaky (fatty) bacon
   rashers (strips), chopped
900g/2lb lean braising steak, such as top
   rump (round) steak
30ml/2 tbsp plain (all-purpose) flour
45ml/3 tbsp sunflower oil
25g/1oz/2 tbsp butter
12 shallots
2 garlic cloves, crushed
175g/6oz/2⅓ cups mushrooms, sliced
450ml/¾ pint/scant 2 cups robust
   red wine
150ml/¼ pint/⅔ cup beef stock
   or consommé
1 bay leaf
2 sprigs each of fresh thyme, parsley
   and marjoram
salt and ground black pepper

1 Preheat the oven to 160°C/325°F/ Gas 3. Heat a large flameproof casserole, then add the bacon and cook, stirring occasionally, until the pieces are crisp and golden brown.

2 Meanwhile, cut the beef into 2.5cm/ 1in cubes. Season the flour and use to coat the meat. Use a slotted spoon to remove the bacon from the casserole and set aside. Add and heat the oil, then brown the beef in batches and set aside with the bacon.

COOK'S TIP
Beef consommé, which can be used as an alternative to beef stock in this recipe, is a clear, light soup. It is sold in cans, or in cartons as a fresh soup. Fresh beef stock is also available in cartons.

3 Add the butter to the fat remaining in the casserole. Cook the shallots and garlic until they are just beginning to colour, then add the mushrooms and cook for a further 5 minutes. Return the bacon and beef to the casserole, and stir in the wine and stock or consommé. Tie the herbs together into a bouquet garni and add to the casserole.

4 Cover and cook in the oven for 1½ hours, or until the meat is tender, stirring once or twice during the cooking time. Season to taste and serve the casserole with creamy mashed root vegetables, such as celeriac and potatoes.

COOK'S TIP
Boeuf Bourguignon freezes very well. Transfer the mixture to a dish so that it cools quickly, then pour it into a rigid plastic container. Push all the cubes of meat down into the sauce or they will dry out. Freeze for up to 2 months. Thaw overnight in the refrigerator, then transfer to a flameproof casserole and add 150ml/ ¼ pint/⅔ cup water. Stir well, then bring to the boil, stirring occasionally, and simmer steadily for at least 10 minutes, or until the meat is piping hot.

Energy 459Kcal/1913kJ; Protein 39g; Carbohydrate 8.1g, of which sugars 3.1g; Fat 24.7g, of which saturates 8.9g; Cholesterol 122mg; Calcium 37mg; Fibre 1.2g; Sodium 497mg.

BEEF HOTPOT with HERB DUMPLINGS

Tender chunks of beef braised in beer, flavoured with shallots and mushrooms and finished with parsley- and thyme-flavoured dumplings.

SERVES 4

20g/¾oz/⅓ cup dried porcini mushrooms
60ml/4 tbsp warm water
40g/1½oz/3 tbsp butter
30ml/2 tbsp sunflower oil
115g/4oz/⅔ cup lardons or cubed pancetta
900g/2lb lean braising steak, cut
    into chunks
45ml/3 tbsp plain (all-purpose) flour
450ml/¾ pint/scant 2 cups beer
450ml/¾ pint/scant 2 cups beef stock
bouquet garni
8 shallots
175g/6oz/2 cups button (white) mushrooms
salt and ground black pepper
sprigs of thyme, to garnish

For the herb dumplings
115g/4oz/1 cup self-raising
    (self-rising) flour
50g/2oz/scant ½ cup shredded suet
2.5ml/½ tsp salt
2.5ml/½ tsp mustard powder
15ml/1 tbsp chopped fresh parsley
15ml/1 tbsp chopped fresh thyme

1 Soak a clay pot in cold water for 20 minutes, then drain. Place the porcini mushrooms in a bowl, add the warm water and leave to soak. In a frying pan, melt half the butter with half the oil, add the lardons or pancetta and quickly brown. Remove with a slotted spoon and transfer to the clay pot.

2 Add the beef to the frying pan and brown in batches, then, using a slotted spoon, transfer to the clay pot. Sprinkle the flour into the fat remaining in the frying pan and stir well.

3 Stir the beer and stock into the flour and bring to the boil, stirring constantly. Strain the mushroom soaking liquid and add to the frying pan along with the porcini. Season well. Pour the sauce over the meat in the clay pot, then add the bouquet garni. Cover the pot and place in an unheated oven. Set the oven to 200°C/400°F/Gas 6. Cook for 30 minutes, then reduce the oven temperature to 160°C/325°F/Gas 3 and cook for a further 1 hour.

4 Heat the remaining butter and oil in a frying pan and cook the shallots until golden. Remove and set aside. Add the button mushrooms and sauté for 2–3 minutes. Stir the shallots and mushrooms into the pot and cook for 30 minutes.

5 In a bowl, mix together the dumpling ingredients with sufficient cold water to bind to a soft, sticky dough. Divide into 12 small balls and place on top of the hotpot. Cover and cook for 25 minutes.

Energy 527Kcal/2194kJ; Protein 10.3g; Carbohydrate 39.1g, of which sugars 6.4g; Fat 35.5g, of which saturates 14.9g; Cholesterol 50mg; Calcium 169mg; Fibre 3.1g; Sodium 789mg.

SLOW-BAKED BEEF with a POTATO CRUST

This recipe makes the most of braising beef by marinating it in red wine and topping it with a cheesy grated potato crust that bakes to a golden, crunchy consistency.

SERVES 4

675g/1½lb stewing beef, diced
300ml/½ pint/1¼ cups red wine
3 juniper berries, crushed
pared strip of orange peel
30ml/2 tbsp olive oil
2 onions, cut into chunks
2 carrots, cut into chunks
1 garlic clove, crushed
225g/8oz/3 cups button
   (white) mushrooms
150ml/¼ pint/⅔ cup beef stock
30ml/2 tbsp cornflour (cornstarch)
salt and ground black pepper

For the crust
450g/1lb potatoes, grated
15ml/1 tbsp olive oil
30ml/2 tbsp creamed horseradish
50g/2oz/½ cup grated mature (sharp)
   Cheddar cheese
salt and ground black pepper

1 Place the diced beef in a non-metallic bowl. Add the wine, juniper berries and orange peel and season with pepper. Mix the ingredients together, then cover and leave to marinate for at least 4 hours or overnight if possible.

COOK'S TIP
Use a large-holed, coarse grater on the food processor for the potatoes. They will hold their shape better while being blanched than if you use a finer blade.

2 Preheat the oven to 160°C/325°F/ Gas 3. Drain the diced stewing beef, reserving the marinade.

3 Heat the oil in a large flameproof casserole and fry the meat in batches for 5 minutes to brown and seal. Add the onions, carrots and garlic and cook for 5 minutes. Stir in the mushrooms, red wine marinade and beef stock.

4 Mix the cornflour with water to make a smooth paste and stir into the beef mixture. Season, cover and cook in the oven for 1½ hours.

5 Prepare the crust about 45 minutes before the end of the cooking time for the beef. Start by blanching the grated potatoes in boiling water for 5 minutes. Drain well and then squeeze out all the extra liquid.

6 Stir in the olive oil, horseradish, grated cheese and seasoning, then sprinkle the mixture evenly over the surface of the beef. Increase the oven temperature to 200°C/400°F/Gas 6 and cook for a further 30 minutes until the potato crust is crisp and lightly browned.

Energy 641Kcal/2678kJ; Protein 45.9g; Carbohydrate 36.6g, of which sugars 10.8g; Fat 29.6g, of which saturates 10.6g; Cholesterol 111mg; Calcium 152mg; Fibre 4.2g; Sodium 306mg.

CALFS' LIVER with SLOW-COOKED ONIONS, MARSALA and SAGE

Liver and onions are an international favourite, from British liver with onion gravy to the famous Venetian dish of Fegato alla Veneziana. Inspired by Italian cooking, this dish is good served with polenta, either soft or set and grilled.

3 Add the remaining oil to the pan and fry the remaining sage leaves for about 30 seconds, then leave them to drain on kitchen paper.

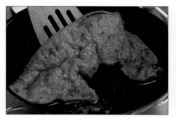

4 Add the remaining butter and extra oil to the pan and increase the heat to high. Season the flour, then dip the liver in it and fry quickly for about 2 minutes on each side until browned, but still pink in the middle. Use a slotted spoon or metal spatula to transfer the liver to warm plates and keep warm.

5 Immediately add the Marsala to the pan and let it bubble fiercely until reduced to a few tablespoons of sticky glaze. Distribute the onions over the liver and spoon over the Marsala juices. Sprinkle with the fried sage leaves and extra parsley and serve immediately.

VARIATION

Chicken liver and onion bruschetta
Cook the onions as above, replacing the sage with 5ml/1 tsp chopped fresh thyme. Fry 400g/14oz chicken livers in 25g/1oz/2 tbsp butter and 15ml/1 tbsp olive oil until browned but still pink in the centre. Flame the chicken livers with 45ml/3 tbsp cognac, and add 150g/5oz seeded, skinned grapes (optional). Heat the grapes through, then toss them into the cooked onions. Heap the mixture on to thick slices of toasted country bread rubbed with oil and garlic or on to thick slices of grilled (broiled) polenta. Serve sprinkled with chopped fresh parsley.

SERVES 4

45ml/3 tbsp olive oil, plus extra for shallow frying
25g/1oz/2 tbsp butter
500g/1¼lb mild onions, thinly sliced
small bunch of fresh sage leaves
30ml/2 tbsp chopped fresh parsley, plus a little extra to garnish
2.5ml/½ tsp sugar
15ml/1 tbsp balsamic vinegar
30ml/2 tbsp plain (all-purpose) flour
675g/1½lb calfs' liver, thinly sliced
150ml/¼ pint/⅔ cup Marsala
salt and ground black pepper

1 Heat half the oil with half the butter in a large, wide, heavy pan and cook the onions, covered, over a very gentle heat for 30 minutes. Stir once or twice.

2 Chop five of the sage leaves and add them to the pan with the chopped parsley, a pinch of salt, the sugar and balsamic vinegar. Cook, uncovered and stirring frequently with a wooden spoon, until the onions are very tender and a golden brown colour. Taste for seasoning and add salt and pepper as necessary. Tip the onions into a heatproof dish and keep warm.

Energy 427Kcal/1777kJ; Protein 32.5g; Carbohydrate 14.9g, of which sugars 12.1g; Fat 22.1g, of which saturates 6.5g; Cholesterol 638mg; Calcium 44mg; Fibre 1.8g; Sodium 163mg.

BLACK BEAN CHILLI CON CARNE

Fresh green and dried red chillies add plenty of fire to this classic Tex-Mex dish of tender beef cooked in a spicy tomato sauce.

SERVES 6

225g/8oz/1¼ cups dried black beans
500g/1¼lb braising steak
30ml/2 tbsp vegetable oil
2 onions, chopped
I garlic clove, crushed
I fresh green chilli, seeded and
    finely chopped
15ml/1 tbsp paprika
10ml/2 tsp ground cumin
10ml/2 tsp ground coriander
400g/14oz can chopped tomatoes
300ml/½ pint/1¼ cups beef stock
I dried red chilli, crumbled
5ml/1 tsp hot pepper sauce
I fresh red (bell) pepper, seeded and chopped
salt
fresh coriander (cilantro), to garnish
boiled rice, to serve

I Put the beans in a large pan. Add enough cold water to cover them, bring to the boil and boil vigorously for about 10 minutes. Drain, tip into a clean bowl, cover with cold water and leave to soak for about 8 hours or overnight.

2 Preheat the oven to 150°C/300°F/ Gas 2. Cut the braising steak into small dice. Heat the vegetable oil in a large, flameproof casserole. Add the chopped onion, crushed garlic and chopped green chilli and cook them gently for 5 minutes until soft, using a slotted spoon to transfer the mixture to a plate.

3 Increase the heat to high, add the meat to the casserole and brown on all sides, then stir in the paprika, ground cumin and ground coriander.

4 Add the tomatoes, beef stock, dried chilli and hot pepper sauce. Drain the beans and add them to the casserole, with enough water to cover. Bring to simmering point, cover and cook in the oven for 2 hours. Stir occasionally and add extra water, if necessary.

5 Season the casserole with salt and add the chopped red pepper. Replace the lid, return the casserole to the oven and cook for 30 minutes more, or until the meat and beans are tender. Sprinkle over the fresh coriander and serve with rice.

COOK'S TIP
Red kidney beans are traditionally used in chilli con carne, but in this recipe black beans are used instead. They are the same shape and size as red kidney beans but have a shiny black skin. They are also known as Mexican or Spanish black beans.

VARIATION
Use minced (ground) beef in place of the braising steak.

Energy 289Kcal/1216kJ; Protein 27.3g; Carbohydrate 24.7g, of which sugars 7.8g; Fat 9.7g, of which saturates 2.8g; Cholesterol 45mg; Calcium 61mg; Fibre 7.8g; Sodium 65mg.

NOISETTES of PORK with CREAMY CALVADOS and APPLE SAUCE

This dish gives the impression of being far more difficult to prepare than it really is, so it is ideal as part of a formal menu to impress guests. Buttered gnocchi or griddled polenta and red cabbage are suitable accompaniments.

SERVES 4

30ml/2 tbsp plain (all-purpose) flour
4 noisettes of pork, about 175g/6oz each,
    firmly tied
25g/1oz/2 tbsp butter
4 baby leeks, finely sliced
5ml/1 tsp mustard seeds,
    coarsely crushed
30ml/2 tbsp Calvados
150ml/¼ pint/⅔ cup dry white wine
2 eating apples, peeled, cored
    and sliced
150ml/¼ pint/⅔ cup double (heavy) cream
30ml/2 tbsp chopped fresh flat
    leaf parsley
salt and ground black pepper

1 Place the flour in a bowl and add plenty of seasoning. Turn the noisettes in the flour mixture to coat them lightly.

2 Melt the butter in a heavy frying pan and cook the noisettes until golden on both sides. Remove from the pan and set aside.

3 Add the leeks to the fat remaining in the pan and cook for 5 minutes. Stir in the mustard seeds and pour in the Calvados, then carefully ignite it to burn off the alcohol. When the flames have died down pour in the wine and replace the pork. Cook gently for 10 minutes, turning the pork frequently.

4 Add the sliced apples to the pan and pour in the cream. Simmer for about 5 minutes, or until the apples are tender and the sauce is thick and creamy. Taste for seasoning, then stir in the chopped fresh parsley and serve immediately.

Energy 553Kcal/2304kJ; Protein 40.6g; Carbohydrate 14.3g, of which sugars 6.1g; Fat 32.9g, of which saturates 18.3g; Cholesterol 175mg; Calcium 72mg; Fibre 2.8g; Sodium 173mg.

PANCETTA and BROAD BEAN RISOTTO

This delicious risotto makes a healthy and filling meal, when served with a mixed green salad. Use smoked bacon instead of pancetta, if you like.

SERVES 4

225g/8oz frozen baby broad (fava) beans
15ml/1 tbsp olive oil
1 onion, chopped
2 garlic cloves, finely chopped
175g/6oz smoked pancetta, diced
350g/12oz/1¾ cups risotto rice
1.2 litres/2 pints/5 cups chicken stock
30ml/2 tbsp chopped fresh mixed herbs,
    such as parsley, thyme and oregano
salt and ground black pepper
coarsely chopped fresh parsley, to garnish
shavings of Parmesan cheese, to serve
    (see Cook's Tip)

1 First, cook the broad beans in a large flameproof casserole of lightly salted boiling water for about 3 minutes until tender. Drain and set aside.

2 Heat the olive oil in the casserole. Add the chopped onion, chopped garlic and diced pancetta and cook gently for about 5 minutes, stirring occasionally.

3 Add the rice to the pan and cook for 1 minute, stirring. Add 300ml/½ pint/1¼ cups of the stock and simmer, stirring frequently until it has been absorbed.

4 Continue adding the stock, a ladleful at a time, stirring frequently until the rice is just tender and creamy, and almost all of the liquid has been absorbed. This will take 30–35 minutes. It may not be necessary to add all the stock.

5 Stir the beans, mixed herbs and seasoning into the risotto. Heat gently, then serve garnished with the chopped fresh parsley and sprinkled with shavings of Parmesan cheese.

COOK'S TIP
To make thin Parmesan cheese shavings, take a rectangular block or long wedge of Parmesan and firmly scrape a vegetable peeler down the side of the cheese to make shavings. The swivel-bladed type of peeler is best for this job.

Energy 511Kcal/2132kJ; Protein 18g; Carbohydrate 77.6g, of which sugars 1.6g; Fat 13.9g, of which saturates 4g; Cholesterol 28mg; Calcium 55mg; Fibre 3.9g; Sodium 556mg.

POT-ROAST LOIN of PORK with APPLE

Roasted pork loin with crisp crackling and a lightly spiced apple and raisin stuffing makes a wonderful Sunday-lunch main course.

SERVES 6–8

1.8kg/4lb boned loin of pork
300ml/½ pint/1¼ cups dry (hard) cider
150ml/¼ pint/⅔ cup sour cream
7.5ml/1½ tsp salt

For the stuffing
25g/1oz/2 tbsp butter
1 small onion, chopped
50g/2oz/1 cup fresh white breadcrumbs
2 apples, cored, peeled and chopped
50g/2oz/scant ½ cup raisins
finely grated rind of 1 orange
pinch of ground cloves
salt and ground black pepper

1 Preheat the oven to 220°C/425°F/ Gas 7. To make the stuffing, melt the butter in a frying pan and gently fry the onion for 10 minutes until soft. Stir in the remaining stuffing ingredients.

2 Put the pork, rind side down, on a board. Make a horizontal cut between the meat and outer layer of fat, cutting to within 2.5cm/1in of the edges to make a pocket.

3 Push the prepared stuffing into the pocket. Roll up the pork lengthwise and tie firmly with string. Score the rind at 2cm/¾in intervals with a sharp knife.

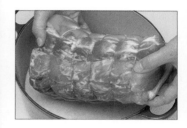

4 Pour the cider and sour cream into a large casserole. Stir to combine, then add the pork, rind-side down. Transfer to the oven and cook, uncovered, for 30 minutes.

5 Turn the joint over, so that the rind is on top. Baste with the juices, then sprinkle the rind with salt. Cook for a further 1 hour, basting after 30 minutes. Reduce the oven temperature to 180°C/ 350°F/Gas 4. Cook for 1½ hours, then remove the casserole from the oven and leave the joint to stand for 20 minutes before carving.

COOK'S TIP
Do not baste during the final 1½ hours of roasting, so the crackling becomes crisp.

Energy 398Kcal/1667kJ; Protein 49.7g; Carbohydrate 13g, of which sugars 8.2g; Fat 15.5g, of which saturates 7.1g; Cholesterol 160mg; Calcium 50mg; Fibre 0.7g; Sodium 239mg.

BRAZILIAN PORK and RICE CASSEROLE

We tend to associate Brazil with beef recipes, but there are also some excellent pork recipes, including this hearty dish of marinated pork, vegetables and rice.

SERVES 4–6

500g/1¼lb lean pork, such as fillet
    (tenderloin), cut into strips
60ml/4 tbsp vegetable oil
1 onion, chopped
1 garlic clove, crushed
1 green (bell) pepper, cut into pieces
about 300ml/½ pint/1¼ cups chicken or
    vegetable stock
225g/8oz/generous 1 cup white long
    grain rice
150ml/¼ pint/⅔ cup single (light) cream
150g/5oz/1½ cups freshly grated
    Parmesan cheese
salt and ground black pepper

For the marinade
120ml/4fl oz/½ cup dry white wine
30ml/2 tbsp lemon juice
1 onion, chopped
4 juniper berries, lightly crushed
3 cloves
1 fresh red chilli, seeded and finely sliced

1 Mix the marinade ingredients in a shallow dish, add the pork strips and leave to marinate for 3–4 hours, stirring occasionally. Transfer the pork to a plate using a slotted spoon and pat dry. Strain the marinade and set aside.

2 Heat the oil in a heavy pan, add the pork strips and fry for a few minutes until evenly brown. Transfer to a plate using a slotted spoon.

3 Add the chopped onion and the garlic to the pan and fry for 3–4 minutes. Stir in the pieces of pepper and cook for 3–4 minutes more, then return the pork strips to the pan. Pour in the reserved marinade and the stock. Bring to the boil and season with salt and pepper, then lower the heat, cover the pan and simmer gently for 10 minutes, or until the meat is nearly tender.

VARIATION
Strips of chicken breast meat can be used in this recipe instead of the lean pork fillet.

4 Preheat the oven to 160°C/325°F/ Gas 3. Cook the rice in plenty of lightly salted boiling water for 8 minutes or until three-quarters cooked. Drain well. Spread half the rice over the base of a buttered, earthenware dish. Using a slotted spoon, make a neat layer of meat and vegetables on top, then spread over the remaining rice.

5 Stir the cream and 30ml/2 tbsp of the grated Parmesan into the liquid in which the pork was cooked. Tip into a jug (pitcher) and then carefully pour the cream mixture over the rice and sprinkle with the remaining Parmesan. Cover with foil and bake for 20 minutes, then remove the foil and cook for 5 minutes more, until the top is lightly brown.

Energy 490Kcal/2040kJ; Protein 31.7g; Carbohydrate 33.3g, of which sugars 3g; Fat 23.9g, of which saturates 10.2g; Cholesterol 91mg; Calcium 342mg; Fibre 0.6g; Sodium 340mg.

PORK COOKED in CIDER with PARSLEY DUMPLINGS

Pork and fruit are a perfect combination. If you don't want to make dumplings, serve creamy mashed potatoes with the stew.

SERVES 6

115g/4oz/½ cup pitted prunes, roughly chopped
115g/4oz/½ cup ready-to-eat dried apricots, roughly chopped
300ml/½ pint/1¼ cups dry (hard) cider
30ml/2 tbsp plain (all-purpose) flour
675g/1½lb lean boneless pork, cut into cubes
30ml/2 tbsp vegetable oil
350g/12oz onions, roughly chopped
2 garlic cloves, crushed
6 celery sticks, roughly chopped
475ml/16fl oz/2 cups stock
12 juniper berries, lightly crushed
30ml/2 tbsp chopped fresh thyme
425g/15oz can black-eyed beans (peas), drained
salt and ground black pepper

For the dumplings
115g/4oz/1 cup self-raising (self-rising) flour
50g/2oz/scant ½ cup vegetable suet
45ml/3 tbsp chopped fresh parsley
90ml/6 tbsp water

1 Preheat the oven to 180°C/350°F/ Gas 4. Place the roughly chopped prunes and apricots in a small bowl. Pour over the cider and leave to soak for at least 20 minutes.

VARIATION
This recipe can also be made with lean lamb – leg steaks or diced shoulder would be ideal cuts to choose. Omit the juniper berries, try cannellini beans in place of the black-eyed beans and use red onions rather than brown ones.

2 Season the flour, then toss the pork in the flour to coat. Reserve any leftover flour. Heat the oil in a large flameproof casserole. Brown the meat in batches, adding a little more oil if necessary. Remove the meat with a slotted spoon and drain on kitchen paper.

3 Add the onions, garlic and celery to the casserole and cook for 5 minutes. Add any reserved flour and cook for a further 1 minute.

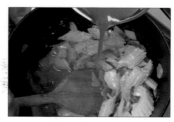

4 Blend in the stock until smooth. Add the cider and fruit, juniper berries, thyme and plenty of seasoning. Bring to the boil, add the pork, cover tightly and then cook in the oven for 50 minutes.

5 Just before the end of the cooking time prepare the dumplings. Sift the flour into a large bowl, add a pinch of salt, then stir in the suet and chopped fresh parsley. Add the water gradually and mix all the ingredients together to form a smooth, slightly sticky dough.

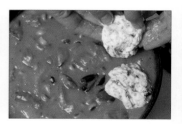

6 Remove the casserole from the oven, then stir in the black-eyed beans and adjust the seasoning. Divide the dumpling mixture into six, form into rough rounds and place on top of the stew. Return the casserole to the oven, then cover and cook for a further 20–25 minutes, or until the dumplings are cooked and the pork is tender.

COOK'S TIP
Black-eyed beans or peas, as they are called in America, are also sometimes referred to as cowpeas. They are a medium-size cream-coloured bean with a distinctive black spot or "eye" on the inner curve. They have a smooth, creamy texture and a subtle flavour. Black-eyed beans are a popular addition to soups and casseroles and are widely used in southern American cuisines.

Energy 468Kcal/1968kJ; Protein 32.6g; Carbohydrate 46.9g, of which sugars 21g; Fat 16.5g, of which saturates 5.9g; Cholesterol 71mg; Calcium 174mg; Fibre 8.2g; Sodium 437mg.

PORK TENDERLOIN with SPINACH and PUY LENTILS

Lean pork tenderloin, wrapped in spinach and cooked in a clay pot on a bed of tiny French green lentils, flavoured with coconut.

SERVES 4

500–675g/1¼–1½lb pork tenderloin
15ml/1 tbsp sunflower oil
15g/½oz/1 tbsp butter
8–12 large spinach leaves
1 onion, chopped
1 garlic clove, finely chopped
2.5cm/1in piece fresh root ginger,
    finely grated
1 red chilli, finely chopped (optional)
250g/9oz/generous 1 cup Puy lentils
750ml/1¼ pints/3 cups chicken or
    vegetable stock
200ml/7fl oz/scant 1 cup coconut cream
salt and ground black pepper

1 Soak a small clay pot in cold water for about 15 minutes, then drain. Cut the pork tenderloin widthwise into two equal pieces. Season the pork well with salt and ground black pepper.

2 Heat the sunflower oil and butter in a heavy frying pan, add the pork tenderloin and cook over a high heat until browned on all sides. Remove the meat from the pan using a metal spatula and set aside.

3 Meanwhile, add the spinach leaves to a large pan of boiling water and cook for 1 minute. Drain in a colander and refresh under cold water. Drain well.

4 Lay the spinach leaves on the work surface, overlapping them slightly to form a rectangle. Place the pork on top and wrap the leaves around the pork to enclose it completely.

5 Add the onion to the oil in the frying pan and cook for about 5 minutes, stirring occasionally, until softened. Add the chopped garlic, grated ginger and finely chopped chilli, if using, and fry for a further 1 minute.

6 Add the lentils to the onion mixture in the frying pan and then stir in the chicken or vegetable stock. Bring to the boil, then boil rapidly for 10 minutes. Remove the pan from the heat and stir in the coconut cream until well blended. Transfer the onion and lentil mixture to the clay pot and arrange the pork tenderloins on top.

7 Cover the clay pot and place it in an unheated oven. Set the oven to 190°C/375°F/Gas 5 and cook for 45 minutes, or until the lentils and pork are cooked.

8 To serve, remove the spinach-wrapped pork tenderloins from the clay pot using a slotted spoon or tongs and cut the pork into thick slices. Stir the lentils and spoon them, with some of the cooking juices, on to warmed, individual plates and top each portion with a few of the pork slices.

VARIATIONS
• Wrap the pork in slices of prosciutto, instead of the spinach leaves, and tie in place with string or secure with wooden cocktail sticks (toothpicks).
• Use 4 large chicken or duck breast portions in place of the pork tenderloin. Check the chicken or duck after about 30 minutes cooking time. Cut the breast portions into thick, diagonal slices to serve. The chicken would also be good wrapped with prosciutto.

Energy 399Kcal/1683kJ; Protein 42.3g; Carbohydrate 39.1g, of which sugars 5g; Fat 9.2g, of which saturates 4g; Cholesterol 87mg; Calcium 81mg; Fibre 3.5g; Sodium 206mg.

SAUSAGE, BACON and POTATO CASSEROLE

This simple supper dish will become a firm favourite with all the family. Warming and nourishing, it is perfect for those long winter evenings by the fire.

2 Heat the oil in a frying pan, then add the bacon and fry for 2 minutes, stirring. Add the onions and fry for 5–6 minutes until golden. Add the garlic and fry for 1 minute, then remove the mixture from the pan and set aside.

3 Fry the sausages in the same pan for 5–6 minutes until golden brown.

4 Arrange the potatoes in the base of the prepared dish. Spoon the bacon and onion mixture on top. Season with the salt and pepper and sprinkle with the fresh sage. Pour on the stock and top with the sausages. Cover and bake for about 1 hour, or until the potatoes and sausages are tender. Serve hot with crusty bread.

SERVES 4

15ml/1 tbsp vegetable oil
4 bacon rashers (strips), cut into
    2.5cm/1in pieces
2 large onions, chopped
2 garlic cloves, crushed
8 large pork sausages
4 large baking potatoes, peeled and
    thinly sliced
1.5ml/¼ tsp fresh sage
300ml/½ pint/1¼ cups vegetable stock
salt and ground black pepper
crusty bread, to serve

1 Preheat the oven to 180°C/350°F/Gas 4. Lightly grease a large, shallow earthenware baking dish and set aside.

Energy 526Kcal/2201kJ; Protein 19.6g; Carbohydrate 53.4g, of which sugars 7.5g; Fat 27.4g, of which saturates 9.7g; Cholesterol 56mg; Calcium 71mg; Fibre 3.8g; Sodium 1214mg.

TOAD-in-the-HOLE

This is one of those dishes that is classic comfort food – perfect for lifting the spirits on cold days. Use only the best sausages for this grown-up version, which includes chives.

SERVES 4–6

175g/6oz/1½ cups plain (all-purpose) flour
30ml/2 tbsp chopped fresh chives (optional)
2 eggs
300ml/½ pint/1¼ cups milk
50g/2oz/⅓ cup white vegetable fat
   or lard
450g/1lb Cumberland sausages or good-
   quality pork sausages
salt and ground black pepper

VARIATION

For a young children's supper, make small individual toad-in-the-holes: omit the chopped fresh chives from the batter and cook small cocktail sausages in patty tins (muffin pans) until golden. Add the batter and cook for 10–15 minutes, or until puffed and golden brown.

1 Preheat the oven to 220°C/425°F/ Gas 7. Sift the flour into a bowl with a pinch of salt and pepper. Make a well in the centre of the flour. Whisk the chives, if using, with the eggs and milk, then pour this into the well in the flour. Gradually whisk the flour into the liquid to make a smooth batter. Cover and leave to stand for at least 30 minutes.

2 Put the vegetable fat or lard into a small roasting pan and place in the oven for 3–5 minutes until very hot. Add the sausages and cook for 15 minutes. Turn the sausages twice during cooking.

3 Pour the batter over the sausages and cook for about 20 minutes, or until the batter is risen and golden. Serve immediately.

Energy 448Kcal/1871kJ; Protein 15.6g; Carbohydrate 33.1g, of which sugars 4.9g; Fat 29.2g, of which saturates 11.7g; Cholesterol 111mg; Calcium 188mg; Fibre 1.7g; Sodium 692mg.

ROAST LAMB with BEANS and GREEN PEPPERCORNS

Roasting the lamb slowly on a bed of beans results in a dish that combines meltingly tender meat with vegetables all in one pot.

SERVES 6

8–10 garlic cloves, peeled
1.8–2kg/4–4½lb leg of lamb
30ml/2 tbsp olive oil
400g/14oz spinach leaves
400g/14oz can flageolet, cannellini or
    haricot (navy) beans, drained
400g/14oz can butter (lima) beans, drained
2 large, fresh rosemary sprigs, plus extra
    to garnish
15–30ml/1–2 tbsp drained, bottled
    green peppercorns

1 Preheat the oven to 150°C/300°F/ Gas 2. Set four garlic cloves aside and slice the rest lengthwise into three or four pieces. Make shallow slits in the skin of the lamb and insert a piece of garlic in each.

2 Heat the olive oil in a heavy, shallow flameproof casserole or a roasting pan that is large enough to hold the leg of lamb. Add the reserved garlic cloves and the fresh spinach leaves to the casserole or pan and cook over a medium heat, stirring occasionally, for 4–5 minutes, or until the spinach is wilted.

3 Add the beans and tuck the rosemary sprigs and peppercorns among them. Place the lamb on top, then cover the casserole or roasting pan with foil or a lid. Roast the lamb for 3–4 hours until it is cooked to your taste. Serve the lamb and beans hot, garnished with the remaining fresh rosemary sprigs.

Energy 705Kcal/2945kJ; Protein 74.3g; Carbohydrate 22.2g, of which sugars 4.2g; Fat 35.9g, of which saturates 15.4g; Cholesterol 246mg; Calcium 186mg; Fibre 8.7g; Sodium 775mg.

MIDDLE-EASTERN ROAST LAMB and POTATOES

When the Eastern aroma of the garlic and saffron come wafting out of the oven, this deliciously garlicky lamb won't last very long.

SERVES 6–8

2.75kg/6lb leg of lamb
4 garlic cloves, halved
60ml/4 tbsp olive oil
juice of 1 lemon
2–3 saffron threads, soaked in
    15ml/1 tbsp boiling water
5ml/1 tsp mixed dried herbs, oregano
    or marjoram
450g/1lb small baking potatoes,
    thickly sliced
2 large or 4 small onions,
    thickly sliced
salt and ground black pepper
fresh thyme, to garnish

1 Make eight evenly-spaced incisions in the leg of lamb, press the halved garlic cloves into the slits and place the lamb in a large non-metallic dish.

2 Mix together the olive oil, lemon juice, saffron mixture and herbs. Rub over the lamb and marinate for 2 hours.

3 Preheat the oven to 180°C/350°F/ Gas 4. Layer the potato and onion slices in a large roasting pan. Lift the lamb out of the marinade and place it on top of the sliced potato and onions, fat side up and season well with plenty of salt and ground black pepper.

4 Pour the marinade over the lamb, then roast for 2 hours, basting occasionally. Remove from the oven and cover with foil, then rest for 10 minutes before carving. Garnish with thyme.

Energy 719Kcal/2997kJ; Protein 74.4g; Carbohydrate 13g, of which sugars 3.5g; Fat 41.2g, of which saturates 17.7g; Cholesterol 282mg; Calcium 33mg; Fibre 1.3g; Sodium 169mg.

LAMB SHANKS with BEANS and HERBS

A hearty winter meal, the lamb shanks are slowly cooked in a clay pot until tender on a bed of tasty beans and vegetables.

SERVES 4

175g/6oz/1 cup dried cannellini beans,
    soaked overnight in cold water
150ml/¼ pint/⅔ cup water
45ml/3 tbsp olive oil
4 large lamb shanks, about 225g/8oz each
1 large onion, chopped
450g/1lb carrots, cut into thick chunks
2 celery sticks, cut into thick chunks
450g/1lb tomatoes, quartered
250ml/8fl oz/1 cup vegetable stock
4 fresh rosemary sprigs
2 bay leaves
salt and ground black pepper

1 Soak a large clay pot in cold water for 20 minutes, then drain. Drain and rinse the cannellini beans and place in a large pan of unsalted boiling water and boil rapidly for 10 minutes, then drain.

2 Place the 150ml/¼ pint/⅔ cup water in the soaked clay pot and then add the drained cannellini beans.

3 Heat 30ml/2 tbsp of the olive oil in a large frying pan, add the lamb shanks and cook over a high heat, turning the lamb shanks occasionally until brown on all sides. Remove the lamb shanks with a slotted spoon and set aside.

4 Add the remaining oil to the pan, then add the onion and sauté for 5 minutes, until soft and translucent.

5 Add the carrots and celery to the pan and cook for 2–3 minutes. Stir in the quartered tomatoes and vegetable stock and mix well. Transfer the vegetable mixture to the clay pot and season well with salt and pepper, then add the fresh rosemary and bay leaves and stir again to combine.

6 Place the lamb shanks on top of the beans and vegetables. Cover the clay pot and place it in an unheated oven. Set the oven to 220°C/425°F/Gas 7 and cook for about 30 minutes, or until the liquid is bubbling.

7 Reduce the oven temperature to 160°C/325°F/Gas 3 and cook for about 1½ hours, or until the meat is tender. Check the seasoning and serve on warmed plates, placing each lamb shank on a bed of beans and vegetables.

COOK'S TIP

Lamb shanks are small joints cut from the lower end of the leg. One shank is an ideal-sized portion for one. Until recently you would have had to order them from the butcher, but they are now becoming increasingly available from larger supermarkets. To obtain a tender result, shanks should be cooked for a long time at a low heat.

VARIATIONS

• Dried butter (lima) beans or the smaller haricot (navy) beans can be used in place of the cannellini beans.
• If you prefer, two 400g/14oz cans cannellini beans can be used in this dish – simply place the drained beans in the soaked clay pot with the water and continue from step 3.
• A variety of other root vegetables would work well in this recipe – try chopped swede (rutabaga), sweet potatoes, butternut squash, parsnips or celeriac instead of the carrots. In spring, a mixture of baby turnips and baby carrots would also be good.

Energy 743Kcal/3121kJ; Protein 79.2g; Carbohydrate 39.7g, of which sugars 18.7g; Fat 30.9g, of which saturates 10.1g; Cholesterol 225mg; Calcium 127mg; Fibre 12.3g; Sodium 200mg.

SPICED LAMB with TOMATOES and PEPPERS

Select lean tender lamb from the leg for this lightly spiced curry with juicy peppers and
wedges of onion. Serve warm naan bread to mop up the tomato-rich juices.

3 Cut two of the onions into wedges (six from each onion) and add to the oil remaining in the pan. Fry the onions over a medium heat for 10 minutes, or until they are beginning to colour. Add the peppers and cook for 5 minutes. Use a slotted spoon to remove the vegetables from the pan and set aside.

4 Meanwhile, chop the remaining onion. Add it to the oil remaining in the pan with the chopped garlic, chilli and ginger, and cook for 4–5 minutes, stirring frequently, until the onion has softened.

5 Stir in the curry paste and canned tomatoes with the reserved yogurt. Return the lamb to the pan, season and stir well. Bring to the boil, then reduce the heat and simmer for 30 minutes.

SERVES 6

1.5kg/3¼lb lean boneless lamb, cubed
250ml/8fl oz/1 cup natural (plain) yogurt
30ml/2 tbsp sunflower oil
3 onions
2 red (bell) peppers, seeded and cut
  into chunks
3 garlic cloves, finely chopped
1 red chilli, seeded and chopped
2.5cm/1in piece fresh root ginger, peeled
  and chopped
30ml/2 tbsp mild curry paste
2 × 400g/14oz cans chopped tomatoes
large pinch of saffron threads
800g/1¾lb plum tomatoes, halved, seeded
  and cut into chunks
salt and ground black pepper
chopped fresh coriander (cilantro),
  to garnish

1 Mix the lamb with the yogurt in a bowl. Cover and chill for about 1 hour.

2 Heat the oil in a large pan. Drain the lamb and reserve the yogurt, then cook the lamb in batches until it is golden on all sides – this will take about 15 minutes in total. Remove the lamb from the pan using a slotted spoon and set aside.

6 Pound the saffron to a powder in a mortar, then stir in a little boiling water to dissolve the saffron. Add this liquid to the curry and stir well. Return the onion and pepper mixture to the pan, then stir in the fresh tomatoes. Bring the curry back to simmering point and cook for 15 minutes. Garnish with chopped fresh coriander to serve.

Energy 559Kcal/2343kJ; Protein 54.4g; Carbohydrate 20.5g, of which sugars 18.8g; Fat 29.6g, of which saturates 13.5g; Cholesterol 191mg; Calcium 139mg; Fibre 4.6g; Sodium 278mg.

BRAISED SHOULDER of LAMB with PEARL BARLEY and BABY VEGETABLES

In this wonderful, slow-cooked stew, the pearl barley absorbs all the rich meat juices and stock to become full-flavoured and nutty in texture when cooked.

SERVES 4

60ml/4 tbsp olive oil
1 large onion, chopped
2 garlic cloves, chopped
2 celery sticks, sliced
a little plain (all-purpose) flour
675g/1½lb boned shoulder of lamb, cut into cubes
900ml–1 litre/1½–1¾ pints/3¾–4 cups lamb stock
115g/4oz/⅔ cup pearl barley
225g/8oz baby carrots
225g/8oz baby turnips
salt and ground black pepper
30ml/2 tbsp chopped fresh marjoram, to garnish

1 Heat 45ml/3 tbsp of the oil in a flameproof casserole. Cook the onion and garlic until softened, add the celery, then cook until the vegetables brown.

2 Season the flour and toss the lamb in it. Use a slotted spoon to remove the vegetables from the casserole.

3 Add and heat the remaining oil with the juices in the casserole. Brown the lamb in batches until golden. When all the meat is browned, return it to the casserole with the onion mixture. Stir in 900ml/1½ pints/3¾ cups of the stock. Add the pearl barley. Cover, then bring to the boil, reduce the heat and simmer for 1 hour, or until the pearl barley and lamb are tender.

4 Add the baby carrots and turnips to the casserole for the final 15 minutes of cooking. Stir the meat occasionally during cooking and add the remaining stock, if necessary. Stir in seasoning to taste, and serve piping hot, garnished with marjoram. Warm, crusty bread would make a good accompaniment.

Energy 565Kcal/2364kJ; Protein 37.2g; Carbohydrate 37.2g, of which sugars 11g; Fat 30.9g, of which saturates 10.4g; Cholesterol 128mg; Calcium 85mg; Fibre 3.9g; Sodium 180mg.

BRAISED LAMB with APRICOTS and HERB DUMPLINGS

A rich and fruity lamb casserole, topped with light, herby dumplings, which is delicious served with baked potatoes and broccoli.

SERVES 6

30ml/2 tbsp sunflower oil
675g/1½lb lean lamb fillet, cut into
    2.5cm/1in cubes
350g/12oz baby (pearl) onions, peeled
1 garlic clove, crushed
225g/8oz/3 cups button
    (white) mushrooms
175g/6oz/¾ cup small ready-to-eat
    dried apricots
about 250ml/8fl oz/1 cup well-flavoured
    lamb or beef stock
250ml/8fl oz/1 cup red wine
15ml/1 tbsp tomato purée (paste)
salt and ground black pepper
fresh herb sprigs, to garnish

For the dumplings
115g/4oz/1 cup self-raising
    (self-rising) flour
50g/2oz/scant ½ cup shredded
    vegetable suet
15–30ml/1–2 tbsp chopped fresh
    mixed herbs

1 Preheat the oven to 160°C/325°F/Gas 3. Heat the oil in a large, flameproof casserole, add the lamb and cook over a high heat until browned all over, stirring occasionally. Remove the meat from the casserole using a slotted spoon, then set aside and keep warm.

2 Reduce the heat slightly, then add the baby onions, crushed garlic and whole mushrooms to the oil remaining in the casserole and cook them gently for about 5 minutes, stirring occasionally with a wooden spoon.

3 Return the meat to the casserole, then add the dried apricots, stock, wine and tomato purée. Season to taste with salt and pepper and stir to mix.

4 Bring to the boil, stirring, then remove the casserole from the heat and cover. Transfer the casserole to the oven and cook for 1½–2 hours until the lamb is cooked and tender, stirring once or twice during the cooking time and adding a little extra stock, if necessary.

5 Meanwhile, make the dumplings. Place the flour, suet, herbs and seasoning in a bowl and stir to mix. Add enough cold water to make a soft, elastic dough. Divide the dough into small, marble-size pieces and, using lightly floured hands, roll each piece into a small ball.

6 Remove the lid from the casserole and place the dumplings on top of the braised lamb and vegetables.

7 Increase the oven temperature to 190°C/375°F/Gas 5. Return the casserole to the oven and cook for a further 20–25 minutes until the herb dumplings are cooked. Serve, garnished with the fresh herb sprigs.

VARIATIONS
Use lean beef or pork in place of the lamb and substitute shallots for the baby onions, if you prefer.

Energy 499Kcal/2091kJ; Protein 28.5g; Carbohydrate 36.7g, of which sugars 20.2g; Fat 24.4g, of which saturates 10.1g; Cholesterol 86mg; Calcium 132mg; Fibre 4.8g; Sodium 277mg.

ITALIAN LAMB MEATBALLS with CHILLI TOMATO SAUCE

Serve these piquant Italian-style meatballs with pasta and a leafy salad. Sprinkle with a little grated Parmesan cheese for that extra Italian touch.

SERVES 4

450g/1lb lean minced (ground) lamb
1 large onion, grated
1 garlic clove, crushed
50g/2oz/1 cup fresh white breadcrumbs
15ml/1 tbsp chopped fresh parsley
1 small egg, lightly beaten
30ml/2 tbsp olive oil
salt and ground black pepper
60ml/4 tbsp finely grated Parmesan cheese
    and rocket (arugula) leaves, to serve

For the sauce
1 onion, finely chopped
400g/14oz can chopped tomatoes
200ml/7fl oz/scant 1 cup passata (bottled
    strained tomatoes)
5ml/1 tsp granulated sugar
2 green chillies, seeded and finely chopped
30ml/2 tbsp chopped fresh oregano
salt and ground black pepper

1 Soak a small clay pot in cold water for 15 minutes, then drain. Place the minced lamb, onion, garlic, breadcrumbs, parsley and seasoning in a bowl and mix well. Add the beaten egg and mix to bind the meatball mixture together.

2 Shape the mixture into 20 small even-size balls. Heat the olive oil in a frying pan, add the meatballs and cook over a high heat, stirring occasionally, until they are browned all over.

VARIATIONS
Minced (ground) beef or sausage meat (bulk sausage) can be used in place of the minced lamb in this dish.

3 Meanwhile, to make the sauce, mix together the chopped onion, tomatoes, passata, sugar, seeded and chopped chillies and oregano. Season well and pour the sauce into the clay pot.

4 Place the meatballs in the sauce, then cover and place in an unheated oven. Set the oven to 200°C/400°F/Gas 6 and cook for 1 hour, stirring after 30 minutes. Serve with Parmesan cheese and rocket.

Energy 443Kcal/1853kJ; Protein 33.1g; Carbohydrate 22.5g, of which sugars 11.1g; Fat 25.3g, of which saturates 10.3g; Cholesterol 148mg; Calcium 246mg; Fibre 3g; Sodium 389mg.

FRAGRANT LAMB CURRY
with CARDAMOM-SPICED RICE

Wonderfully aromatic, this Indian-style lamb biriani, with the meat and rice cooked
together, is a delicious meal in itself.

SERVES 4

I large onion, quartered
2 garlic cloves
I small green chilli, halved and seeded
5cm/2in piece fresh root ginger
15ml/I tbsp ghee
15ml/I tbsp vegetable oil
675 g/1½lb boned shoulder or leg of lamb,
    cut into chunks
15ml/I tbsp ground coriander
10ml/2 tsp ground cumin
I cinnamon stick, broken into 3 pieces
150ml/¼ pint/⅔ cup thick natural
    (plain) yogurt
150ml/¼ pint/⅔ cup water
75g/3oz/⅓ cup ready-to-eat dried apricots,
    cut into chunks
salt and ground black pepper

For the rice
250g/9oz/1¼ cups basmati rice
6 cardamom pods, split open
25g/1oz/2 tbsp butter, cut into small pieces
45ml/3 tbsp toasted cashew nuts or flaked
    (sliced) almonds

For the garnish
I onion, sliced and fried until golden
a few sprigs of fresh coriander (cilantro)

I Soak a large clay pot or chicken brick
in cold water for 20 minutes, then drain.
Place the onion, garlic, chilli and ginger in
a food processor or blender and process
with 15ml/I tbsp water, to a smooth paste.

COOK'S TIP
Serve a cooling yogurt raita and a fresh
fruit chutney or relish as an accompaniment.

2 Heat the ghee and vegetable oil in a
heavy frying pan. Fry the lamb chunks
in batches over a high heat until golden
brown. Remove from the pan using a
slotted spoon and set aside.

3 Add the onion paste to the remaining
oil left in the frying pan, stir in the ground
coriander and cumin, add the cinnamon
stick pieces and fry for 1–2 minutes,
stirring constantly with a wooden spoon.

4 Return the meat to the frying pan,
then gradually add the yogurt, a spoonful
at a time, stirring well between each
addition with a wooden spoon. Season
the meat well with plenty of salt and
pepper and stir in the water.

5 Transfer the contents of the frying pan
to the prepared clay pot, cover with the
lid and place in an unheated oven. Set
the oven to 180°C/350°F/Gas 4 and
cook for 45 minutes.

6 Meanwhile prepare the basmati rice.
Place it in a bowl, cover with cold water
and leave to soak for 20 minutes. Drain
the rice and place it in a large pan of
boiling salted water, bring back to the boil
and cook for 10 minutes. Drain and stir
in the split cardamom pods.

7 Remove the clay pot from the oven
and stir in the chopped ready-to-eat
apricots. Pile the cooked rice on top of
the lamb and dot with the butter. Drizzle
over 60ml/4 tbsp water, then sprinkle
the cashew nuts or flaked almonds on
top. Cover the pot, reduce the oven
temperature to 150°C/300°F/Gas 2 and
cook the meat and rice for 30 minutes.

8 Remove the lid from the pot and fluff
up the rice with a fork. Spoon into
warmed individual bowls, then sprinkle
over the fried onion slices and garnish
with the sprigs of fresh coriander.

Energy 769Kcal/3208kJ; Protein 43.6g; Carbohydrate 67.6g, of which sugars 14.5g; Fat 36.2g, of which saturates 15g; Cholesterol 142mg; Calcium 134mg; Fibre 2.6g; Sodium 252mg.

OSSO BUCCO with RISOTTO MILANESE

Two one-pot dishes in one recipe, both so utterly delicious that it seemed churlish to omit them from this collection. Osso Bucco is a traditional Milanese veal stew and is classically accompanied by this saffron-scented risotto.

SERVES 4

50g/2oz/¼ cup butter
15ml/1 tbsp olive oil
1 large onion, chopped
1 leek, finely chopped
45ml/3 tbsp plain (all-purpose) flour
4 large portions of veal shin, hind cut
600ml/1 pint/2½ cups dry white wine
salt and ground black pepper

For the risotto
25g/1oz/2 tbsp butter
1 onion, finely chopped
350g/12oz/1¾ cups risotto rice
1 litre/1¾ pints/4 cups chicken stock
2.5ml/½ tsp saffron threads
60ml/4 tbsp white wine
50g/2oz/⅔ cup freshly grated
    Parmesan cheese

For the gremolata
grated rind of 1 lemon
30ml/2 tbsp chopped fresh parsley
1 garlic clove, finely chopped

1 Heat the butter and oil until sizzling in a large heavy frying pan. Add the onion and leek, and cook gently for about 5 minutes. Season the flour and toss the veal in it, then add to the pan and cook over a high heat until it browns.

2 Gradually stir in the wine and heat until simmering. Cover the pan and simmer for 1½ hours, stirring occasionally. Use a slotted spoon to transfer the veal to a warmed serving dish, then boil the sauce over a high heat until it is reduced and thickened to the required consistency.

3 Make the risotto about 30 minutes before the end of the cooking time for the stew. Melt the butter in a large pan and cook the onion until softened.

4 Stir in the rice to coat all the grains in butter. Add a ladleful of boiling chicken stock and mix well. Continue adding the boiling stock a ladleful at a time, allowing each portion to be completely absorbed before adding the next.

5 Pound the saffron threads in a mortar, then stir in the wine. Add the saffron-scented wine to the risotto and cook for a final 5 minutes. Remove the pan from the heat and stir in the Parmesan.

6 Mix the lemon rind, chopped parsley and garlic together for the gremolata. Spoon some risotto on to each plate, then add some veal. Sprinkle each with a little gremolata and serve immediately.

Energy 899Kcal/3754kJ; Protein 46.3g; Carbohydrate 90.6g, of which sugars 7.1g; Fat 27.4g, of which saturates 14.2g; Cholesterol 178mg; Calcium 249mg; Fibre 2.4g; Sodium 427mg.

OSTRICH STEW with SWEET POTATOES and CHICKPEAS

Lean and firm, ostrich meat marries well with the soft-textured sweet potatoes and chickpeas in this quick and easy, rich-flavoured stew.

SERVES 4

45ml/3 tbsp olive oil
1 large onion, chopped
2 garlic cloves, finely chopped
675g/1½lb ostrich fillet, cut into
    short strips
450g/1lb sweet potatoes, peeled
    and diced
2 × 400g/14oz cans chopped tomatoes
400g/14oz can chickpeas, drained
salt and ground black pepper
fresh oregano, to garnish

COOK'S TIP
Steamed couscous is a quick and easy accompaniment to this healthy stew, but it would also be good served with rice, or simply some warm, crusty bread.

1 Heat half the oil in a flameproof casserole. Add the chopped onion and garlic, and cook for about 5 minutes, or until softened but not coloured, stirring occasionally. Remove from the casserole using a slotted spoon and set aside. Add the remaining oil to the casserole and heat.

2 Fry the meat in batches over a high heat until browned. When the last batch is cooked, replace the meat and onions and stir in the potatoes, tomatoes and chickpeas. Bring to the boil, reduce the heat and simmer for 25 minutes, or until the meat is tender. Season and serve, garnished with the fresh oregano.

Energy 639Kcal/2682kJ; Protein 49g; Carbohydrate 51.2g, of which sugars 16.5g; Fat 27.9g, of which saturates 8.2g; Cholesterol 98mg; Calcium 108mg; Fibre 9.7g; Sodium 393mg.

SLOW COOKER VEGETARIAN AND SIDE DISHES

Just because you follow a vegetarian diet doesn't mean you need to miss out on fabulous-tasting food. This chapter makes use of all kinds of wonderful vegetables, beans and grains to make fabulous slow-cooked main meals that will appeal just as much to meat eaters as they do to vegetarians. Try rich and creamy Rosemary Risotto with Borlotti Beans, or Sweet Pumpkin and Peanut Curry for a hearty main meal. Or if you are looking for a special side dish, why not try Potato, Onion and Garlic Gratin, or Spicy Tamarind Chickpeas. Whatever you are in the mood for, you are sure to find the perfect meat-free recipe in this chapter.

MUSHROOM and FENNEL HOT-POT

Hearty and richly flavoured, this tasty stew makes a marvellous vegetarian main dish, but it can also be served as an accompaniment to meat dishes. Dried mushrooms swell up a great deal after soaking, so a little goes a long way in terms of both flavour and quantity.

SERVES 4

25g/1oz/½ cup dried shiitake mushrooms
1 small head of fennel
30ml/2 tbsp olive oil
12 shallots, peeled
225g/8oz/3 cups button (white)
   mushrooms, trimmed and halved
250ml/8fl oz/1 cup dry (hard) cider
25g/1oz/½ cup sun-dried tomatoes
30ml/2 tbsp/½ cup sun-dried
   tomato paste
1 bay leaf
salt and ground black pepper
chopped fresh parsley,
   to garnish

1 Place the dried shiitake mushrooms in a heatproof bowl. Pour over just enough hot water to cover them and leave to soak for about 15 minutes. Meanwhile, trim and slice the fennel.

2 Heat the oil in a heavy pan. Add the shallots and fennel, then sauté for about 10 minutes over a medium heat, until the vegetables are softened and just beginning to brown. Add the button mushrooms to the pan and cook for a further 2–3 minutes, stirring occasionally.

3 Transfer the vegetable mixture to the ceramic cooking pot. Drain the shiitake mushrooms, adding 30ml/2 tbsp of the soaking liquid to the cooking pot. Chop them and add them to the pot.

4 Pour the cider into the pot and stir in the sun-dried tomatoes and tomato paste. Add the bay leaf. Cover with the lid and cook on high for 3–4 hours, or until the vegetables are tender.

5 Remove the bay leaf and season to taste with salt and black pepper. Serve sprinkled with plenty of chopped parsley.

Energy 94Kcal/394kJ; Protein 2.1g; Carbohydrate 4.2g, of which sugars 4g; Fat 6g, of which saturates 0.9g; Cholesterol 0mg; Calcium 28mg; Fibre 2.4g; Sodium 17mg.

SWEET and SOUR MIXED-BEAN HOT-POT

This impressive-looking dish, topped with sliced potatoes, is incredibly easy, making the most of dried and canned ingredients from the kitchen cupboard and combining them with a deliciously rich and tangy tomato sauce.

SERVES 6

40g/1½oz/3 tbsp butter
4 shallots, peeled and finely chopped
40g/1½oz/⅓ cup plain (all-purpose)
   or wholemeal (whole-wheat) flour
300ml/½ pint/1¼ cups passata (bottled
   strained tomatoes)
120ml/4fl oz/½ cup unsweetened
   apple juice
60ml/4 tbsp soft light brown sugar
60ml/4 tbsp tomato ketchup
60ml/4 tbsp dry sherry
60ml/4 tbsp cider vinegar
60ml/4 tbsp light soy sauce
400g/14oz can butter beans
400g/14oz can flageolet (small cannellini)
   beans
400g/14oz can chickpeas
175g/6oz green beans, cut into 2.5cm/
   1in lengths
225g/8oz/3 cups mushrooms, sliced
450g/1lb unpeeled potatoes
15ml/1 tbsp olive oil
15ml/1 tbsp chopped fresh thyme
15ml/1 tbsp fresh marjoram
salt and ground black pepper
fresh herbs, to garnish

1 Melt the butter in a pan, add the shallots and fry gently for 5–6 minutes, until softened. Add the flour and cook for 1 minute, stirring all the time, then gradually stir in the passata.

2 Add the apple juice, sugar, tomato ketchup, sherry, vinegar and light soy sauce to the pan and stir in. Bring the mixture to the boil, stirring constantly until it thickens.

VARIATIONS
• You can vary the proportions and types of beans used, depending on what you have in the store cupboard (pantry). Kidney beans and borlotti beans would work well and can be either interchanged with any of the beans used here, or combined with them.
• Try using mangetout or sugar snap peas in place of the green beans, if you prefer.

3 Rinse the beans and chickpeas and drain well. Place them in the ceramic cooking pot with the green beans and mushrooms and pour over the sauce. Stir well, then cover with the lid and cook on high for 3 hours.

4 Meanwhile, thinly slice the potatoes and par-boil them for 4 minutes. Drain well, then toss them in the oil so that they are lightly coated all over.

5 Stir the fresh herbs into the bean mixture and season with salt and pepper. Arrange the potato slices on top of the beans, overlapping them slightly so that they completely cover them. Cover the pot and cook for a further 2 hours, or until the potatoes are tender.

6 Place the ceramic cooking pot under a medium grill (broiler) and cook for 4–5 minutes to brown the potato topping. Serve garnished with herbs.

Energy 483Kcal/2042kJ; Protein 18.5g; Carbohydrate 73.3g, of which sugars 24.8g; Fat 13.8g, of which saturates 4.5g; Cholesterol 14mg; Calcium 134mg; Fibre 10.9g; Sodium 826mg.

ROOT VEGETABLE CASSEROLE
with CARAWAY DUMPLINGS

Stirring soft cheese into the cooking juices gives this incredibly easy casserole a wonderfully creamy richness, while thickening and flavouring it at the same time. Light courgette dumplings spiced with caraway complete the meal.

SERVES 3

300ml/½ pint/1¼ cups dry (hard) cider
175ml/6fl oz/¾ cup boiling vegetable stock
2 leeks
2 carrots
2 small parsnips
225g/8oz potatoes
1 sweet potato, weighing about 175g/6oz
1 bay leaf
7.5ml/1½ tsp cornflour (cornstarch)
115g/4oz full-fat soft cheese with garlic
    and herbs
salt and ground black pepper

For the dumplings
115g/4oz/1 cup self-raising
    (self-rising) flour
5ml/1 tsp caraway seeds
50g/2oz/½ cup shredded vegetable suet
    (chilled, grated shortening)
1 courgette (zucchini), grated
about 75ml/5 tbsp cold water

1 Reserve 15ml/1 tbsp of the cider and pour the rest into the ceramic cooking pot with the stock. Cover with the lid and switch the slow cooker to high.

2 Meanwhile, prepare the vegetables. Trim the leeks and cut into 2cm/¾in slices. Peel the carrots, parsnips, potatoes and sweet potato and cut into 2cm/¾in chunks.

3 Add the vegetables to the ceramic cooking pot with the bay leaf. Cover with the lid and cook for 3 hours.

4 In a small bowl, blend the cornflour with the reserved cider. Add the cheese and mix together until combined, then gradually blend in a few spoonfuls of the cooking liquid. Pour over the vegetables and stir until thoroughly mixed. Season with salt and black pepper. Cover and cook for a further 1–2 hours, or until the vegetables are almost tender.

5 Towards the end of the cooking time, make the dumplings. Sift the flour into a bowl and stir in the caraway seeds, suet, courgettes, salt and black pepper. Stir in the water, adding a little more if necessary, to make a soft dough. With floured hands, shape the mixture into 12 dumplings, about the size of walnuts.

6 Carefully place the dumplings on top of the casserole, cover with the lid and cook for a further hour, or until the vegetables and dumplings are cooked. Adjust the seasoning and serve in warmed deep soup plates.

VARIATION
To make a non-vegetarian version of this dish, add some fried chopped bacon or pancetta to the pot with the vegetables.

Energy 616Kcal/2584kJ; Protein 11.9g; Carbohydrate 74.9g, of which sugars 17.1g; Fat 28.9g, of which saturates 15.9g; Cholesterol 35mg; Calcium 256mg; Fibre 9.5g; Sodium 369mg.

SPICY-HOT MIXED-BEAN CHILLI
with CORNBREAD TOPPING

Inspired by traditional Texan cooking, this chilli combines Tex-mex with classic Texan cornbread. The delicious topping offers the starch component of the dish, making this dish a filling one-pot meal with no need for accompaniments.

SERVES 4

115g/4oz/generous ½ cup dried red
   kidney beans
115g/4oz/generous ½ cup dried
   black-eyed beans
1 bay leaf
15ml/1 tbsp vegetable oil
1 large onion, finely chopped
1 garlic clove, crushed
5ml/1 tsp ground cumin
5ml/1 tsp chilli powder
5ml/1 tsp mild paprika
2.5ml/½ tsp dried marjoram
450g/1lb mixed vegetables such
   as potatoes, carrots, aubergines
   (eggplant), parsnips and celery
1 vegetable stock cube
400g/14oz can chopped tomatoes
15ml/1 tbsp tomato purée (paste)
salt and ground black pepper

For the cornbread topping
250g/9oz/2¼ cups fine cornmeal
30ml/2 tbsp wholemeal
   (whole-wheat) flour
7.5ml/1½ tsp baking powder
1 egg, plus 1 egg yolk lightly beaten
300ml/½ pint/1¼ cups milk

1 Put the dried beans in a large bowl and pour over at least twice their volume of cold water. Leave to soak for at least 6 hours, or overnight.

2 Drain the beans and rinse well, then place in a pan with 600ml/1 pint/ 2½ cups of cold water and the bay leaf. Bring to the boil and boil rapidly for 10 minutes. Turn off the heat, leave to cool for a few minutes, then tip into the ceramic cooking pot and switch the slow cooker to high.

3 Heat the oil in a pan, add the onion and cook for 7–8 minutes. Add the garlic, cumin, chilli powder, paprika and marjoram and cook for 1 minute. Tip into the ceramic cooking pot and stir.

4 Prepare the vegetables, peeling or trimming them as necessary, then cut into 2cm/¾ in chunks.

5 Add the vegetables to the mixture, making sure that those that may discolour, such as potatoes and parsnips, are submerged. It doesn't matter if the other vegetables are not completely covered. Cover with the lid and cook for 3 hours, or until the beans are tender.

6 Add the stock cube and chopped tomatoes to the cooking pot, then stir in the tomato purée and season with salt and ground black pepper. Replace the lid and cook for a further 30 minutes until the mixture is at boiling point.

7 To make the topping, combine the cornmeal, flour, baking powder and a pinch of salt in a bowl. Make a well in the centre and add the egg, egg yolk and milk. Mix, then spoon over the bean mixture. Cover and cook for 1 hour, or until the topping is firm and cooked.

Energy 613Kcal/2595kJ; Protein 29.6g; Carbohydrate 97.4g, of which sugars 15.8g; Fat 14.5g, of which saturates 3.4g; Cholesterol 112mg; Calcium 257mg; Fibre 13.4g; Sodium 413mg.

SWEET PUMPKIN and PEANUT CURRY

Rich, sweet, spicy and fragrant, the flavours of this delicious Thai-style curry really come together with long, slow cooking. Serve with rice or noodles for a substantial supper dish.

3 Add the lime leaves, galangal, pumpkin and sweet potatoes to the cooking pot. Pour the stock and 150ml/¼ pint/⅔ cup of the coconut milk over the vegetables, and stir to combine. Cover with the lid and cook on high for 1½ hours.

4 Stir the mushrooms, soy sauce and Thai fish sauce into the curry, then add the chopped peanuts and pour in the remaining coconut milk. Cover and cook on high for a further 3 hours, or until the vegetables are very tender.

5 Spoon the curry into warmed serving bowls, garnish with the pumpkin seeds and chillies, and serve immediately.

SERVES 4

30ml/2 tbsp vegetable oil
4 garlic cloves, crushed
4 shallots, finely chopped
30ml/2 tbsp yellow curry paste
400ml/14fl oz/1⅔ cups near-boiling
    vegetable stock
300ml/½ pint/1¼ cups coconut milk
2 kaffir lime leaves, torn
15ml/1 tbsp chopped fresh galangal
450g/1lb pumpkin, peeled, seeded
    and diced
225g/8oz sweet potatoes, diced
90g/3½oz/1½ cups chestnut
    mushrooms, sliced
15ml/1 tbsp soy sauce
30ml/2 tbsp Thai fish sauce
90g/3½ oz/scant 1 cup peanuts, roasted
    and chopped
50g/2oz/⅓ cup pumpkin seeds, toasted,
    and fresh green chilli flowers, to garnish

1 Heat the oil in a frying pan. Add the garlic and shallots and cook over a medium heat, stirring occasionally, for 10 minutes, until softened and beginning to turn golden.

2 Add the yellow curry paste to the pan and stir-fry over a medium heat for 30 seconds, until fragrant. Tip the mixture into the ceramic cooking pot.

COOK'S TIP
Fresh chilli flowers make an impressive garnish for a special occasion dinner, and will make the curry look authentically Thai. To make chilli flowers, hold each chilli by the stem and slit the chilli in half lengthways, keeping the stem end intact. Continue slitting the chilli in the same way to make thin strips. Put the chillies in a bowl of iced water and leave for several hours to curl up like flower petals.

Energy 337Kcal/1404kJ; Protein 10.3g; Carbohydrate 21.7g, of which sugars 10.8g; Fat 23.8g, of which saturates 4g; Cholesterol 0mg; Calcium 168mg; Fibre 5.1g; Sodium 554mg.

POTATO, ONION and GARLIC GRATIN

This tasty side dish makes the perfect accompaniment to roasts, stews and grilled meat or fish. Cooking the potatoes in stock with onions and garlic gives them a really rich flavour.

3 Pour just enough of the stock into the pot to cover the potatoes. Cover with the lid and cook on low for 8–10 hours, or on high for 4–5 hours, until the potatoes are tender.

4 If you like, brown the potatoes under a hot grill (broiler) for 3–4 minutes. Serve sprinkled with a little salt and ground black pepper.

VARIATIONS
• To make this dish more substantial, sprinkle 115g/4oz/1 cup of grated Gruyère cheese over the top of the cooked potatoes and brown under a preheated grill (broiler) for 3–4 minutes until golden-brown and bubbling.
• Alternatively, crumble 165g/5½oz/scant 1 cup soft goat's cheese on the gratin 30 minutes before the end of cooking.
• To vary the flavour, try using chopped rosemary or sage in place of the thyme, or use crushed juniper berries instead.

SERVES 4

40g/1½oz/3 tbsp butter
1 large onion, finely sliced into rings
2–4 garlic cloves, finely chopped
2.5ml/½ tsp dried thyme
900g/2lb waxy potatoes, very finely sliced
450ml/¾ pint/scant 2 cups boiling
    vegetable stock
sea salt and ground black pepper

1 Grease the inside of the ceramic cooking pot with 15g/½oz/1 tbsp of the butter. Spoon a thin layer of onions on to the base of the cooking pot, then sprinkle over a little of the chopped garlic, thyme, salt and pepper.

2 Carefully arrange an overlapping layer of potato slices on top of the onion mixture in the ceramic cooking pot. Continue to layer the ingredients in the pot until all the onions, garlic, herbs and potatoes are used up, finishing with a layer of sliced potatoes.

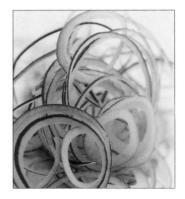

Energy 260Kcal/1092kJ; Protein 5.1g; Carbohydrate 41.9g, of which sugars 6.4g; Fat 9.1g, of which saturates 5.4g; Cholesterol 21mg; Calcium 31mg; Fibre 3.3g; Sodium 171mg.

ROSEMARY RISOTTO with BORLOTTI BEANS

Using easy-cook Italian rice means that all the wine and stock can be added at the same time, rather than ladleful by ladleful, as with a traditional risotto. The gentle, constant heat of the slow cooker produces a delicious risotto that is still thick and creamy.

SERVES 3

400g/14oz can borlotti beans
15g/½oz/1 tbsp butter
15ml/1 tbsp olive oil
1 onion, finely chopped
2 garlic cloves, crushed
120ml/4fl oz/½ cup dry white wine
225g/8oz/generous 1 cup easy-cook
    (converted) Italian rice
750ml/1¼ pints/3 cups boiling
    vegetable stock
60ml/4 tbsp mascarpone cheese
5ml/1 tsp chopped fresh rosemary
65g/2½oz/¾ cup freshly grated
    Parmesan cheese, plus extra
    to serve (optional)
salt and ground black pepper

1 Drain the borlotti beans in a sieve, rinse well under cold running water and drain again. Place about two-thirds of the beans in a food processor or blender and process to a coarse purée. Tip the remaining beans into a bowl and set aside for later.

2 Heat the butter and oil in a pan, add the onion and garlic and fry gently for 7–8 minutes until soft. Transfer the mixture to the ceramic cooking pot and stir in the wine and bean purée. Cover with the lid and cook on high for 1 hour.

3 Add the rice to the pot, then stir in the stock. Re-cover with the lid and cook for about 45 minutes, stirring once halfway through cooking. The rice should be almost tender and most of the stock should have been absorbed.

4 Stir the reserved beans, mascarpone and rosemary into the risotto. Cover again with the lid and cook for a further 15 minutes, until the rice is tender but still has a little bite.

5 Stir the Parmesan cheese into the risotto and season to taste with salt and ground black pepper. Turn off the slow cooker, cover and leave to stand for about 5 minutes, so that the risotto absorbs the flavours fully and the rice completes cooking.

6 Spoon the rice into warmed serving bowls and serve immediately, sprinkled with extra Parmesan, if you like.

VARIATIONS
• Try using different herbs to vary the flavour. Fresh thyme or marjoram would make a good alternative to rosemary.
• To make a lower-fat version of this dish, use Quark cheese in place of the mascarpone. It offers the same creamy texture with much less fat.

Energy 651Kcal/2740kJ; Protein 25g; Carbohydrate 87g, of which sugars 4.6g; Fat 22.2g, of which saturates 10.5g; Cholesterol 41.9mg; Calcium 357mg; Fibre 7.1g; Sodium 1462mg.

COUSCOUS-STUFFED SWEET PEPPERS

The peppers are softened in boiling water before filling to ensure really tender results.
Choose red, yellow or orange peppers for this dish, but avoid green ones because they
tend to discolour after a couple of hours of cooking and do not have such a sweet taste.

SERVES 4

4 (bell) peppers
75g/3oz/½ cup instant couscous
75ml/2½ fl oz/⅓ cup boiling
    vegetable stock
15ml/1 tbsp olive oil
10ml/2 tsp white wine vinegar
50g/2oz dried apricots, finely chopped
75g/3oz feta cheese, cut into tiny cubes
3 ripe tomatoes, skinned, seeded
    and chopped
45ml/3 tbsp toasted pine nuts
30ml/2 tbsp chopped fresh parsley
salt and ground black pepper
flat leaf parsley, to garnish

1 Halve the peppers lengthways, then remove the core and seeds. Place the peppers in a large heatproof bowl and pour over boiling water to cover. Leave to stand for about 3 minutes, then drain thoroughly and set aside.

2 Meanwhile, put the couscous in a small bowl and pour over the stock. Leave to stand for about 5 minutes until all the water has been absorbed.

3 Using a fork, fluff up the couscous, then stir in the oil, vinegar, apricots, feta cheese, tomatoes, pine nuts and parsley, and season to taste with salt and ground black pepper.

COOK'S TIP
Be sure to taste the stuffing before adding any more salt. Feta cheese can be very salty already, so you may not need to add any extra.

4 Fill the peppers with the couscous mixture, gently packing it down using the back of a spoon.

5 Place the peppers, filling side up, in the ceramic cooking pot, then pour 150ml/¼ pint/⅔ cup near-boiling water around them.

6 Cover with the lid, switch the slow cooker to high and cook for 2–3 hours, or until the peppers are tender. Brown under a hot grill (broiler) for 2 minutes and serve garnished with fresh parsley.

Energy 303Kcal/1266kJ; Protein 33.7g; Carbohydrate 33.6g, of which sugars 17g; Fat 15.8g, of which saturates 3.9g; Cholesterol 13mg; Calcium 105mg; Fibre 4.3g; Sodium 285mg.

PARSNIPS and CHICKPEAS in GARLIC, ONION, CHILLI and GINGER PASTE

The sweet flavour of parsnips goes very well with the spices in this Indian-style vegetable stew. It makes an ideal meal for vegetarians, because chickpeas are high in protein. Complete the meal with warm Indian breads, such as chapati or naan.

SERVES 4

5 garlic cloves, finely chopped
1 small onion, chopped
5cm/2in piece fresh root ginger, chopped
2 green chillies, seeded and finely chopped
75ml/5 tbsp cold water
60ml/4 tbsp groundnut (peanut) oil
5ml/1 tsp cumin seeds
10ml/2 tsp coriander seeds
5ml/1 tsp ground turmeric
2.5ml/½ tsp chilli powder or mild paprika
50g/2oz/½ cup cashew nuts, toasted and ground
225g/8oz tomatoes, peeled and chopped
400g/14oz can chickpeas, drained and rinsed
900g/2lb parsnips, cut into 2cm/¾in chunks
350ml/12 fl oz/1½ cups boiling vegetable stock
juice of 1 lime, to taste
salt and ground black pepper
chopped fresh coriander (cilantro) leaves, toasted cashew nuts and natural (plain) yogurt, to serve

1 Reserve 10ml/2 tsp of the garlic, then place the remainder in a food processor or blender with the onion, ginger and half the chilli. Add the water and process to make a smooth paste.

2 Heat the oil in a large frying pan, add the cumin seeds and cook for about 30 seconds. Stir in the coriander seeds, turmeric, chilli powder or paprika and the ground cashew nuts. Add the ginger and chilli paste and cook, stirring frequently, until the paste bubbles and the water begins to evaporate.

COOK'S TIPS
• Buy spices in small quantities and store them in a cool, dark place. Try to use them within a few months because they quickly lose their flavour.
• Frying spices before adding to the cooking pot intensifies their taste.

3 Add the tomatoes to the pan and cook for 1 minute. Transfer the mixture to the ceramic cooking pot and switch the slow cooker to high.

4 Add the chickpeas and parsnips to the pot and stir to coat in the spicy tomato mixture, then stir in the stock and season with salt and pepper. Cover with the lid and cook on high for 4 hours, or until the parsnips are tender.

5 Stir half the lime juice, the reserved garlic and green chilli into the stew. Re-cover and cook for 30 minutes more, then taste and add more lime juice if needed. Spoon on to plates and sprinkle with fresh coriander leaves and toasted cashew nuts. Serve immediately with a generous spoonful of natural yogurt.

Energy 453Kcal/1899kJ; Protein 14.8g; Carbohydrate 50.1g, of which sugars 16.6g; Fat 23g, of which saturates 4.3g; Cholesterol 0mg; Calcium 148mg; Fibre 15.8g; Sodium 394mg.

ONIONS STUFFED with GOAT'S CHEESE and SUN-DRIED TOMATOES

Long, slow cooking is the best way to get maximum flavour from onions, so the slow cooker is the natural choice for these delicious stuffed onions. Serve with a rice or cracked wheat pilaff to make a great vegetarian main course.

SERVES 4

2 large onions
30ml/2 tbsp olive oil (or use oil from
    the sun-dried tomatoes)
150g/5oz/²⁄₃ cup firm goat's cheese,
    crumbled or cubed
50g/2oz/1 cup fresh white breadcrumbs
8 sun-dried tomatoes in olive oil, drained
    and chopped
1 garlic clove, finely chopped
2.5ml/½ tsp fresh thyme
30ml/2 tbsp chopped fresh parsley
1 small egg, beaten
45ml/3 tbsp pine nuts
150ml/¼ pint/²⁄₃ cup near-boiling
    vegetable stock
salt and ground black pepper
chopped fresh parsley, to garnish

1 Bring a large pan of water to the boil. Add the whole onions in their skins and boil for 10 minutes.

2 Drain the onions and leave until cool enough to handle, then cut each onion in half horizontally and peel. Using a teaspoon, remove the centre of each onion, leaving a thick shell.

3 Very finely chop the flesh from one of the scooped-out onion halves and place in a bowl. Stir in 5ml/1 tsp of the olive oil or oil from the sun-dried tomatoes, then add the goat's cheese, breadcrumbs, sun-dried tomatoes, garlic, thyme, parsley, egg and pine nuts. Season with salt and pepper and mix well.

4 Divide the stuffing among the onions and cover each one with a piece of oiled foil. Brush the base of the ceramic cooking pot with 15ml/1 tbsp of the oil, then pour in the stock. Arrange the onions in the base of the cooking pot, cover with the lid and cook on high for 4 hours, or until the onions are very tender but still hold their shape.

5 Carefully remove the onions from the slow cooker and transfer them to a grill (broiler) pan. Remove the foil and drizzle the tops with the remaining 10ml/1 tsp oil. Brown under a medium grill for 3–4 minutes, taking care not to burn the nuts. Serve immediately, garnished with fresh chopped parsley.

VARIATIONS
• Try using feta cheese in place of the goat's cheese and add chopped fresh mint, currants and pitted black olives in place of the other flavourings.
• Alternatively, use 175g/6oz Roquefort or Gorgonzola in place of the goat's cheese and add about 75g/3oz/¾ cup chopped walnuts and 115g/4oz/1 cup very finely chopped celery in place of the sun-dried tomatoes and pine nuts.

Energy 330Kcal/1370kJ; Protein 13.8g; Carbohydrate 14.3g, of which sugars 11.3g; Fat 24.7g, of which saturates 8.4g; Cholesterol 83.7mg; Calcium 98mg; Fibre 1.9g; Sodium 349mg.

BROWN RICE with LIME and LEMON GRASS

It is unusual to find brown rice given the Thai treatment, but the nutty flavour of the grains is enhanced by the fragrance of limes and lemon grass in this delicious dish.

3 Heat the oil in a large pan. Add the onion and cook over a low heat for 5 minutes. Stir in the ginger, coriander and cumin seeds, lemon grass and lime rind and cook for 2–3 minutes. Tip the mixture into the ceramic cooking pot.

4 Pour the stock into the pot, briefly stir to combine, then cover with the lid and switch the slow cooker to high. Cook for 1 hour.

5 Rinse the rice in cold water until the water runs clear, then drain and add to the ceramic cooking pot. Cook for 45 minutes–1½ hours, or until the rice is tender and has absorbed the stock.

6 Stir the fresh coriander into the rice and season with salt and pepper. Fluff up the grains with a fork and serve garnished with strips of spring onions and toasted coconut, and lime wedges.

SERVES 4

2 limes
1 lemon grass stalk
15ml/1 tbsp sunflower oil
1 onion, chopped
2.5cm/1in piece fresh root ginger, peeled and very finely chopped
7.5ml/1½ tsp coriander seeds
7.5ml/1½ tsp cumin seeds
750ml/1¼ pints/3 cups boiling vegetable stock
275g/10oz/1½ cups easy-cook (converted) brown rice
60ml/4 tbsp chopped fresh coriander (cilantro)
salt and ground black pepper
spring onions (scallion), toasted coconut strips and lime wedges, to garnish

1 Using a cannelle knife (zester) or fine grater, pare the rind from the limes, taking care not to remove any of the bitter white pith. Set the rind aside.

2 Cut off the lower portion of the lemon grass stalk, discarding the papery top end of the stalk. Finely chop the lemon grass and set aside.

Energy 308Kcal/1304kJ; Protein 5.6g; Carbohydrate 64g, of which sugars 5.1g; Fat 5.1g, of which saturates 0.9g; Cholesterol 0mg; Calcium 17mg; Fibre 2g; Sodium 129mg.

SPICY TAMARIND CHICKPEAS

Chickpeas make a good base for many vegetarian dishes. Here, they are tossed with sharp tamarind and spices to make a deliciously light vegetarian lunch or side dish.

SERVES 4

225g/8oz/1¼ cups dried chickpeas
50g/2oz tamarind pulp
45ml/3 tbsp vegetable oil
2.5ml/½ tsp cumin seeds
1 onion, very finely chopped
2 garlic cloves, crushed
2.5cm/1in piece of fresh root ginger,
   peeled and grated
1 fresh green chilli, finely chopped
5ml/1 tsp ground cumin
5ml/1 tsp ground coriander
1.5ml/¼ tsp ground turmeric
2.5ml/½ tsp salt
225g/8oz tomatoes, skinned
   and finely chopped
2.5ml/½ tsp garam masala
chopped fresh chillies and chopped
   onion, to garnish

1 Put the chickpeas in a large bowl and pour over cold water to cover. Leave to soak for at least 8 hours, or overnight.

2 Drain the chickpeas and put in a pan with at least double the volume of cold water. (Do not add salt to the water because this will toughen the chickpeas and spoil the final dish.)

3 Bring the water to the boil and boil vigorously for at least 10 minutes. Skim off any scum, then drain the chickpeas and tip into the ceramic cooking pot.

4 Pour 750ml/1¼ pints/3 cups of near-boiling water over the chickpeas and switch the slow cooker to high. Cover with the lid and cook for 4–5 hours, or until the chickpeas are just tender.

5 Towards the end of the cooking time, put the tamarind in a bowl and break up with a fork. Pour over 120ml/4fl oz/ ½ cup of boiling water and leave to soak for about 15 minutes.

6 Tip the tamarind into a sieve (strainer) and discard the water. Rub the pulp through, discarding any stones and fibre.

7 Heat the oil in a large pan, add the cumin seeds and fry for 2 minutes, until they splutter. Add the onion, garlic and ginger and fry for 5 minutes. Add the cumin, coriander, turmeric, chilli and salt and fry for 3–4 minutes. Add the tomatoes, garam masala and tamarind pulp and bring to the boil.

8 Stir the tamarind mixture into the chickpeas, cover and cook for a further 1 hour. Either serve straight from the ceramic cooking pot, or spoon into a warmed serving dish and garnish with chopped chilli and onion.

COOK'S TIP

To save time, make double the quantity of tamarind pulp and freeze in ice-cube trays. It will keep for up to 2 months.

Energy 277Kcal/1164kJ; Protein 12.8g; Carbohydrate 32.6g, of which sugars 5.3g; Fat 11.5g, of which saturates 1.3g; Cholesterol 0mg; Calcium 103mg; Fibre 7.1g; Sodium 274mg.

SLOW COOKER DESSERTS AND CAKES

From baked custards and poached fruit to steamed puddings and luscious cakes, this tempting chapter is perfect for anyone with a sweet tooth. Try old-fashioned favourites such as Poached Pears in Red Wine, Baked Stuffed Apples, and Tapioca Pudding, or indulge yourself with a really wicked treat such as Chocolate Chip and Banana Pudding. When you are looking for a little something to enjoy mid-afternoon with a cup of tea or coffee, try any one of the fabulous cakes – Frosted Carrot and Parsnip Cake, Chocolate Cheesecake Brownies or Moist Golden Ginger Cake. One mouthful of any of these delights and you will be in heaven.

COCONUT CUSTARD

This classic Thai dessert, made with rich, creamy coconut milk, is often served with a selection of fresh fruit. Mangoes and tamarillos go particularly well.

2 Strain the mixture into a jug (pitcher), then pour into four individual heatproof glasses, ramekins or one single ovenproof dish. Cover the containers with clear film (plastic wrap).

3 Place the dishes in the slow cooker and, if necessary, pour a little more boiling water around them to reach just over halfway up their sides.

4 Cover the ceramic cooking pot with the lid, then cook for 3 hours, or until the custards are lightly set. Test with a fine skewer or cocktail stick (toothpick); it should come out clean.

5 Carefully lift the dishes out of the slow cooker and leave to cool. Once cool, chill in the refrigerator until ready to serve. Decorate the custards with a light dusting of icing sugar, and serve with sliced fruit.

SERVES 4

4 eggs
75g/3oz/generous ⅓ cup soft light brown
    sugar
250ml/8fl oz/1 cup coconut milk
5ml/1 tsp vanilla, rose or jasmine extract
icing (confectioners') sugar, to decorate
sliced fresh fruit, to serve

COOK'S TIP
Line the bases of individual ramekins with rounds of baking parchment, then lightly oil the sides. After cooking and chilling, run a knife around the insides of the custards and turn out on to individual dessert plates.

1 Pour about 2.5cm/1in of hot water into the base of the ceramic cooking pot and switch the slow cooker on to low. Whisk the eggs and sugar in a bowl until smooth. Gradually add the coconut milk and flavoured extract, and whisk well.

Energy 175Kcal/738kJ; Protein 7.5g; Carbohydrate 22.7g, of which sugars 22.7g; Fat 6.7g, of which saturates 2g; Cholesterol 227mg; Calcium 57mg; Fibre 0g; Sodium 151mg.

TAPIOCA PUDDING

*Another Thai-style dessert, this version of the classic tapioca pudding is made from large
pearl tapioca and coconut milk and is served warm. It is very good served with lychees.*

SERVES 4

115g/4oz/²⁄₃ cup large pearl tapioca
475ml/16fl oz/2 cups very hot water
115g/4oz/generous ½ cup caster
    (superfine) sugar
pinch of salt
250ml/8fl oz/1 cup coconut milk
250g/9oz prepared tropical fruits
shredded lime rind and shaved fresh
    coconut, to decorate (optional)

COOK'S TIP
This dish includes a lot of sugar – as it
would in Thailand – but you may prefer
to reduce the sugar according to taste.

1 Put the tapioca in a bowl and pour
over enough warm water to cover
generously. Leave the tapioca to soak for
1 hour until the grains swell, then drain
well and set aside.

2 Pour the measured water into the
ceramic cooking pot and switch the slow
cooker to high. Add the sugar and salt
and stir until dissolved. Cover with the
lid and heat for about 30 minutes, until
the water reaches boiling point.

3 Add the tapioca and coconut milk and
stir well. Cover and cook for a further
1–1½ hours, or until the tapioca grains
become transparent.

4 Spoon into one large dish or four
individual bowls and serve warm with
tropical fruits, decorated with the lime
rind and coconut shavings, if using.

Energy 273Kcal/1164kJ; Protein 2.7g; Carbohydrate 66.7g, of which sugars 41.9g; Fat 1.3g, of which saturates 0.4g; Cholesterol 0mg; Calcium 43mg; Fibre 1.7g; Sodium 73mg.

POACHED PEARS in RED WINE

The pears take on a red blush from the wine and make a very pretty dessert. It works best in a small slow cooker, which ensures that the pears stay submerged during cooking.

SERVES 4

1 bottle fruity red wine
150g/5oz/¾ cup caster (superfine) sugar
45ml/3 tbsp clear honey
1 cinnamon stick
1 vanilla pod (bean), split lengthwise
large strip of lemon or orange rind
2 whole cloves
2 black peppercorns
4 firm ripe pears
juice of ½ lemon
mint leaves, to garnish
whipped cream or sour cream, to serve

1 Pour the red wine into the ceramic cooking pot. Add the sugar, honey, cinnamon stick, vanilla pod, lemon or orange rind, cloves and peppercorns. Cover with the lid and cook on high for 30 minutes, stirring occasionally.

2 Meanwhile, peel the pears using a vegetable peeler, leaving the stem intact. Take a very thin slice off the base of each pear so it will stand square and upright. As each pear is peeled, toss it in the lemon juice to prevent the flesh browning when exposed to the air.

3 Place the pears in the spiced wine mixture. Cover with the lid and cook for 2–4 hours, turning the pears occasionally, until they are just tender; be careful not to overcook them.

COOK'S TIP
The cooking time will depend on the size and ripeness of the pears. Small, ripe pears will cook quickly; large, hard pears will take longer.

4 Transfer the pears to a bowl using a slotted spoon. Continue to cook the wine mixture uncovered for a further hour, until reduced and thickened a little, then turn off the slow cooker and leave to cool. Alternatively, to save time, pour the cooking liquor into a pan and boil briskly for 10–15 minutes.

5 Strain the cooled liquid over the pears and chill for at least 3 hours. Place the pears in four individual serving dishes and spoon a little of the wine syrup over each one. Garnish with fresh mint and serve with whipped or sour cream.

Energy 87Kcal/367kJ; Protein 0.5g; Carbohydrate 16.6g, of which sugars 16.6g; Fat 0.2g, of which saturates 0g; Cholesterol 0mg; Calcium 19mg; Fibre 3.3g; Sodium 7mg.

WINTER FRUIT POACHED in MULLED WINE

Poaching fresh apples and pears with dried apricots and figs in a spicy wine syrup makes a delicious winter dessert. Serve on its own or with a generous spoonful of thick cream.

SERVES 4

300ml/½ pint/1¼ cups fruity red wine
300ml/½ pint/1¼ cups fresh apple
    or orange juice
thinly pared strip of orange or
    lemon peel
45ml/3 tbsp clear honey
1 small cinnamon stick
4 whole cloves
4 cardamom pods, split
2 pears, such as Comice or William
8 ready-to-eat figs
12 ready-to-eat dried unsulphured apricots
2 eating apples, peeled, cored and thickly
    sliced

1 Pour the wine and apple or orange juice into the ceramic cooking pot. Add the citrus peel, honey, cinnamon stick, cloves and cardamom pods. Cover with the lid and cook on high for 1 hour.

2 Peel, core and halve the pears, keeping the stalk intact if possible. Place in the slow cooker with the figs and apricots. Cook for 1 hour. Gently turn the pears, then add the sliced apples and cook for a further 1½–2 hours, or until all the fruit is tender.

3 Using a slotted spoon, carefully remove the fruit from the cooking pot and place in a serving dish. Set aside while you finish making the syrup.

4 Strain the syrup into a pan, discarding the spices, then bring to the boil. Boil vigorously for about 10 minutes, until reduced by about one-third. Pour over the fruit and serve hot or cold.

COOK'S TIP
Choose tart, well-tasting apples such as Cox's Orange Pippin, Braeburn or Granny Smith. They stand up particularly well against the sweet dried fruits and spicy, robust red wine syrup.

Energy 347Kcal/1476kJ; Protein 5g; Carbohydrate 78.1g, of which sugars 78.1g; Fat 1.9g, of which saturates 0g; Cholesterol 0mg; Calcium 284mg; Fibre 11.4g; Sodium 72mg.

BAKED STUFFED APPLES

Using Italian amaretti to stuff the apples gives a lovely almondy flavour, while dried cranberries and glacé fruit add sweetness and colour. Make sure that you choose a variety of apple that will remain firm during the long cooking time.

3 Add the nuts and dried cranberries or sour cherries and glacé fruit to the bowl and mix well, then set aside the filling while you prepare the apples.

4 Wash and dry the apples. Remove the cores using an apple corer, then carefully enlarge each core cavity to twice its size, using the corer to shave out more flesh. Using a sharp knife, score each apple around its equator.

5 Divide the filling among the apples, packing it into the hole, then piling it on top. Stand the apples in the cooking pot and cover with the lid. Reduce the temperature to low and cook for 4 hours, or until tender. Transfer the apples to warmed serving plates and spoon the sauce over the top. Serve with cream, crème fraîche or vanilla ice cream.

SERVES 4

75g/3oz/6 tbsp butter, softened
45ml/3 tbsp orange or apple juice
75g/3oz/scant ½ cup light muscovado (brown) sugar
grated rind and juice of ½ orange
1.5ml/¼ tsp ground cinnamon
30ml/2 tbsp crushed amaretti
25g/1oz/¼ cup pecan nuts, chopped
25g/1oz/¼ cup dried cranberries or sour cherries
25g/1oz/¼ cup luxury mixed glacé (candied) fruit, chopped
4 large cooking apples, such as Bramleys
cream, crème fraîche or vanilla ice cream, to serve

1 Grease the ceramic cooking pot with 15g/½oz/1 tbsp of the butter, then pour in the fruit juice and switch to high.

2 Put the remaining butter, the sugar, orange rind and juice, cinnamon and amaretti crumbs in a bowl and mix well.

COOK'S TIP
The cooking time will depend on the type and size of apples used.

Energy 347Kcal/1457kJ; Protein 1.6g; Carbohydrate 42.4g, of which sugars 41.3g; Fat 20.3g, of which saturates 10.3g; Cholesterol 40mg; Calcium 27mg; Fibre 3g; Sodium 131mg.

PAPAYA COOKED with GINGER

Spicy ginger enhances the delicate flavour of papaya perfectly. This recipe is excellent for busy people because it takes no more than 10 minutes to prepare and can then just be left to cook gently. Be careful not to overcook papaya or the flesh will become watery.

SERVES 4

150ml/¼ pint/⅔ cup hot water
45ml/3 tbsp raisins
shredded finely pared rind and juice
    of 1 lime
2 ripe papayas
2 pieces stem ginger in syrup, drained,
    plus 15ml/1 tbsp syrup from the jar
8 amaretti or other dessert biscuits
    (cookies), coarsely crushed
25g/1oz/¼ cup pistachio nuts, chopped
15ml/1 tbsp light muscovado
    (brown) sugar
60ml/4 tbsp crème fraîche, plus extra
    to serve

VARIATION
Try using chopped almonds and Greek (US strained plain) yogurt in place of the pistachio nuts and crème fraîche.

1 Pour the water into the base of the ceramic cooking pot and switch the slow cooker to high. Put the raisins in a small bowl and pour over the lime juice. Stir to combine, then leave to soak for at least 5 minutes, while preparing the remaining ingredients.

2 Cut the papayas in half and scoop out and discard their seeds using a teaspoon.

3 Finely chop the stem ginger and combine with the biscuits, raisins and lime juice, lime rind, two-thirds of the nuts, the sugar and crème fraîche.

4 Fill the papayas with the mixture and place in the cooking pot. Cover and cook for 1–1½ hours. Drizzle with the ginger syrup, sprinkle with the remaining nuts and serve with crème fraîche.

Energy 302Kcal/1272kJ; Protein 4.1g; Carbohydrate 45.6g, of which sugars 36.6g; Fat 12.8g, of which saturates 5.7g; Cholesterol 17mg; Calcium 70mg; Fibre 5.7g; Sodium 136mg.

VERMONT BAKED MAPLE CUSTARD

Maple syrup has a really distinctive flavour and gives these little baked custards a wonderfully rich taste. Try to find pure maple syrup – it will make all the difference.

SERVES 6

3 eggs
120ml/4fl oz/½ cup maple syrup
250ml/8fl oz/1 cup warm milk
150ml/¼ pint/⅔ cup warm single
    (light) cream
5ml/1 tsp vanilla extract
whole nutmeg, to grate

COOK'S TIP
Warming the milk and cream until tepid will help the custard cook and set more quickly. You can do this in a pan on the stovetop, or more simply, pour the milk and cream into a heatproof bowl or jug (pitcher) and place in the slow cooker filled with near-boiling water to a depth of about 5cm/2in. Switch the slow cooker to high and leave for 30 minutes. Remove the milk, then turn the slow cooker to low and use the hot water in the ceramic cooking pot to cook the custards.

1 Beat the eggs in a large bowl, then whisk in the maple syrup, followed by the warm milk, cream and the vanilla extract. Grate in a little nutmeg.

2 Strain the custard mixture into six individual ramekins – first checking that the dishes will all fit inside the ceramic cooking pot in a single layer. Carefully cover each ramekin with a piece of kitchen foil, then place them in the ceramic cooking pot.

3 Pour very hot water around the dishes to come three-quarters of the way up their sides. Cover with the lid and cook on low for 2½–3 hours, or until set. To test, insert a skewer in the middle; it should come out clean.

4 Transfer the custards to a wire rack. Leave for 5 minutes and serve warm, or leave to cool completely, then chill. Remove from the refrigerator about 30 minutes before serving.

Energy 174Kcal/735kJ; Protein 8.6g; Carbohydrate 24.5g, of which sugars 18.7g; Fat 5.3g, of which saturates 1.6g; Cholesterol 116mg; Calcium 97mg; Fibre 9.1g; Sodium 120mg.

PETITS POTS de CRÈME au MOCHA

The name of these classic French baked custards comes from the baking cups, called pots de crème. The addition of coffee gives the dessert an even richer, more indulgent flavour.

SERVES 4

5ml/1 tsp instant coffee powder
15ml/1 tbsp soft light brown sugar
300ml/½ pint/1¼ cups milk
150ml/¼ pint/⅔ cup double (heavy) cream
115g/4oz plain (semisweet) chocolate
15ml/1 tbsp coffee liqueur (optional)
4 egg yolks
whipped cream and candied cake
    decorations, to decorate (optional)

1 Put the instant coffee and sugar in a pan and stir in the milk and cream. Bring to the boil over a medium heat, stirring constantly, until the coffee and sugar have dissolved completely.

2 Remove the pan from the heat and add the chocolate. Stir until the chocolate has melted, then stir in the coffee liqueur, if using.

3 In a bowl, whisk the egg yolks, then slowly whisk in the chocolate mixture until well blended. Strain the custard mixture into a large jug (pitcher) and divide equally among *pots de crème* or ramekins – first checking that they will all fit inside the ceramic cooking pot.

4 Cover each *pot de crème* or ramekin with a piece of foil, then transfer to the ceramic cooking pot. Pour enough hot water around the dishes to come just over halfway up their sides. Cover the slow cooker with the lid and cook on high for 2½–3 hours, or until they are just set and a knife inserted into the middle comes out clean.

5 Carefully remove the pots from the cooker and leave to cool. Cover and chill until ready to serve, then decorate with whipped cream and candied cake decorations, if you like.

Energy 443Kcal/1840kJ; Protein 8.3g; Carbohydrate 23.7g, of which sugars 23.7g; Fat 35.7g, of which saturates 20.2g; Cholesterol 264mg; Calcium 196mg; Fibre 0.2g; Sodium 74mg.

HOT BANANAS with RUM and RAISINS

These sticky, sweet baked bananas are utterly moreish and make a great dessert all year round. The rich sauce becomes almost toffee-like during cooking, and is irresistible.

3 Add the bananas to the melted butter and sugar mixture, cover with the lid and cook for about 30 minutes, or until the fruit is almost tender, turning over the bananas halfway through cooking time.

4 Sprinkle the nutmeg and cinnamon over the bananas, then pour in the rum and raisins. Stir very gently to mix, then re-cover and cook for 10 minutes.

5 Carefully lift the bananas out of the ceramic cooking pot and arrange on a serving dish or individual plates. Spoon over the sauce, then sprinkle with almonds, if using. Serve hot with whipped cream or vanilla ice cream.

COOK'S TIP
Choose almost-ripe bananas with even-coloured skins. Over-ripe bananas will not hold their shape during cooking, and will give mushy results.

SERVES 4

30ml/2 tbsp seedless raisins
45ml/3 tbsp dark rum
40g/1½oz/3 tbsp unsalted (sweet) butter
50g/2oz/¼ cup soft light brown sugar
4 slightly under-ripe bananas, peeled and halved lengthways
1.5ml/¼ tsp grated nutmeg
1.5ml/¼ tsp ground cinnamon
25g/1oz/¼ cup flaked (sliced) almonds, toasted (optional)
whipped cream or vanilla ice cream, to serve

VARIATION
If you don't like the taste of rum, try using an orange liqueur, such as Cointreau, instead. It makes a very good alternative and is a little less overpowering.

1 Put the raisins in a bowl and spoon over 30ml/2 tbsp of the rum. Set aside and leave to soak.

2 Cut the butter into small cubes and place in the ceramic cooking pot with the sugar and remaining 15ml/1 tbsp rum. Switch the slow cooker to high and leave uncovered for 15 minutes, until the butter and sugar have melted.

CHOCOLATE CHIP and BANANA PUDDING

Rich, dense and sticky, this steamed pudding served with a glossy chocolate sauce is a great winter dessert. For an extra treat, serve with a scoop of vanilla ice cream.

SERVES 4

200g/7oz/1¾ cups self-raising
  (self-rising) flour
75g/3oz/6 tbsp unsalted (sweet) butter
2 ripe bananas
75g/3oz/6 tbsp caster (superfine) sugar
50ml/2fl oz/1¼ cups milk
1 egg, lightly beaten
75g/3oz/⅔ cup chocolate chips or
  chopped unsweetened chocolate

For the chocolate sauce
90g/3½oz/½ cup caster (superfine) sugar
50ml/2fl oz/¼ cup water
175g/6oz/1¼ cups plain (semisweet)
  chocolate chips or chopped
  unsweetened chocolate
25g/1oz/2 tbsp unsalted (sweet) butter
30ml/2 tbsp brandy or orange juice

1 Grease and line the base of a 1 litre/
1¾ pint/4 cup pudding basin with baking
parchment. Put an inverted saucer in the
bottom of the ceramic cooking pot and
pour in about 2.5cm/1in of hot water.
Turn the slow cooker to high.

2 Sift the flour into a large mixing bowl
and rub in the butter until the mixture
resembles coarse breadcrumbs. In a
separate bowl, mash the bananas, then
stir into the flour and butter mixture.
Add the sugar and mix well.

3 In a clean bowl, whisk together the
milk and egg, then beat into the banana
mixture. Stir in the chocolate chips or
chopped chocolate and spoon into the
prepared pudding basin. Cover with
a double thickness of buttered foil and
place in the ceramic cooking pot. Pour
enough boiling water around the basin
to come just over halfway up the sides.

4 Cover the slow cooker and cook on
high for 3–4 hours, or until the pudding
is well risen and a skewer inserted in the
middle comes out clean. Turn off the
slow cooker and leave the pudding in
the water while you make the sauce.

5 Put the sugar and water in a heavy
pan and heat gently, stirring occasionally
with a wooden spoon, until all the sugar
has dissolved. Remove from the heat,
add the chocolate and stir until melted,
then add the butter in the same way.
Stir in the brandy or orange juice.

6 Remove the pudding from the slow
cooker and run a knife around the inside
of the basin to loosen it. Turn it out on
to a warmed serving dish and serve hot,
with the sauce poured over.

Energy 926Kcal/3890kJ; Protein 11.1g; Carbohydrate 131.9g, of which sugars 93.2g; Fat 41.1g, of which saturates 24.6g; Cholesterol 118mg; Calcium 266mg; Fibre 3.3g; Sodium 378mg.

STICKY COFFEE and PEAR PUDDING

This dark and moist fruity pudding is complemented with a tangy citrus-flavoured cream. It is delicious served hot, but is equally good cold; serve at room temperature rather than chilled to enjoy its rich flavour and wonderful texture at their best.

SERVES 6

115g/4oz/½ cup butter, softened, plus
    extra for greasing
30ml/2 tbsp ground coffee
15ml/1 tbsp near-boiling water
50g/2oz/½ cup toasted skinned hazelnuts
4 small ripe pears
juice of ½ orange
115g/4oz/generous ½ cup golden caster
    (superfine) sugar, plus 15ml/1 tbsp for
    baking
2 eggs, beaten
50g/2oz/½ cup self-raising (self-rising) flour
45ml/3 tbsp maple syrup
fine strips of orange rind, to decorate

For the orange cream
300ml/½ pint/1¼ cups whipping cream
15ml/1 tbsp icing (confectioners') sugar,
    sifted
finely grated rind of ½ orange

1 Pour about 2.5cm/1in of hot water into the ceramic cooking pot. Place an upturned saucer or metal pastry ring in the base, then turn on to high. Grease and line the base of a deep 18cm/7in fixed-base cake tin (pan) or soufflé dish.

COOK'S TIPS
• If you can't find ready-toasted skinned hazelnuts, prepare your own. Toast the nuts under a hot grill (broiler) for about 3 minutes, turning frequently until well browned. Leave to cool and rub off the skins before grinding.
• Many supermarkets and specialist food stores sell flavoured coffees. Try using a hazelnut-flavoured coffee for this dessert.

2 Put the ground coffee in a small bowl and pour the water over. Leave to infuse for 4 minutes, then strain through a fine sieve. Place the hazelnuts in a coffee grinder and grind until fine.

3 Peel, halve and core the pears. Thinly slice across the pear halves part of the way through, then brush them all over with the orange juice.

4 Beat the butter and the larger quantity of caster sugar together in a bowl until very light and fluffy. Gradually beat in the eggs. Sift the flour, then fold into the mixture in the bowl. Add the hazelnuts and coffee. Spoon the mixture into the tin or soufflé dish, and level the surface.

5 Pat the pears dry on kitchen paper and arrange in a circle in the sponge mixture, flat side down. Brush them with some of the maple syrup, then sprinkle with the 15ml/1 tbsp caster sugar.

6 Cover the top of the tin or soufflé dish with kitchen foil and place in the ceramic cooking pot. Pour enough boiling water around the tin or dish to come slightly more than halfway up the sides. Cover with a lid and cook for 3–3½ hours, until firm and well risen.

7 Meanwhile, make the orange cream. Whip the cream, icing sugar and orange rind until soft peaks form. Spoon into a serving dish and chill until needed.

8 Leave the sponge to cool in the tin for about 10 minutes, then turn over on to a serving plate. Lightly brush with the remaining maple syrup, then decorate with orange rind and serve with the orange cream.

Energy 852Kcal/3571kJ; Protein 12.5g; Carbohydrate 107g, of which sugars 45g; Fat 44.5g, of which saturates 23.8g; Cholesterol 169mg; Calcium 362mg; Fibre 5.3g; Sodium 493mg.

STEAMED CHOCOLATE and FRUIT PUDDINGS

Drenched in a rich chocolate syrup, this wickedly indulgent steamed pudding makes a great alternative to a traditional Christmas pudding – although it is a fabulous treat at any time of year, the addition of cranberries gives it an unmistakably festive flavour.

SERVES 4

vegetable oil, for greasing
1 apple
25g/1oz/¼ cup cranberries, thawed
    if frozen
175g/6oz/¾ cup soft dark brown sugar
115g/4oz/½ cup soft margarine
2 eggs, lightly beaten
50g/2oz/½ cup self-raising (self-rising)
    flour, sifted
45ml/3 tbsp (unsweetened) cocoa powder

For the syrup
115g/4oz plain (semisweet) chocolate,
    chopped
30ml/2 tbsp clear honey
15g/½oz/1 tbsp unsalted (sweet) butter
2.5ml/½ tsp vanilla extract

1 Pour 2.5cm/1in of hot water into the cooking pot and switch the slow cooker to high. Grease four pudding basins with oil, then line with baking parchment.

2 Peel and core the apple, then dice the flesh. Place in a mixing bowl, then add the cranberries and 15ml/1 tbsp of the sugar. Mix well, then divide the fruit mixture among the prepared basins, gently patting it down into the base of each one.

3 Place the remaining sugar in a clean mixing bowl and add the margarine, eggs, flour and cocoa. Beat together with a wooden spoon until combined and smooth and creamy.

4 Spoon the mixture into the pudding basins and cover each with a double thickness of greased foil. Place the puddings in the ceramic cooking pot and pour in enough very hot water to come about two-thirds up the sides.

5 Cover with a lid and cook on high for 1½–2 hours, or until the puddings are well-risen and firm to the touch. Carefully remove from the slow cooker and leave to stand for 10 minutes.

6 Meanwhile, make the chocolate syrup. Put the chocolate, honey, butter and vanilla extract in a heatproof bowl and place in the hot water in the slow cooker. Leave for 10 minutes, until the butter has melted, then stir until smooth.

7 Run a knife around the edge of the puddings to loosen, then turn over on to warmed individual plates. Serve immediately with the chocolate syrup.

Energy 739Kcal/3094kJ; Protein 9.1g; Carbohydrate 88.3g, of which sugars 77.2g; Fat 41.3g, of which saturates 14.4g; Cholesterol 124mg; Calcium 103mg; Fibre 3.1g; Sodium 438mg.

HOT DATE PUDDINGS with TOFFEE SAUCE

Fresh dates make this pudding less rich than the classic dried date version, but it still makes an utterly indulgent dessert. Ideally, peel the dates because their skins can be tough. Squeeze them between your thumb and forefinger, and the skins will slip off.

3 Put the dates in a heatproof bowl, pour over the boiling water and mash well with a potato masher to make a fairly smooth paste.

4 Sift the flour and bicarbonate of soda over the creamed butter and sugar mixture, and fold in. Add the date paste and gently fold in.

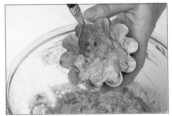

SERVES 6

50g/2oz/¼ cup butter, softened
75g/3oz/½ cup light muscovado (brown) sugar
2 eggs, beaten
175g/6oz/generous 1 cup fresh dates, peeled, stoned (pitted) and chopped
75ml/5 tbsp boiling water
115g/4oz/1 cup self-raising (self-rising) flour
2.5ml/½ tsp bicarbonate of soda (baking soda)

For the sauce
50g/2oz/¼ cup butter, at room temperature
75g/3oz/½ cup light muscovado (brown) sugar
60ml/4 tbsp double (heavy) cream
30ml/2 tbsp brandy

1 Grease six individual pudding moulds or tins (pans) – first making sure that they will all fit in the slow cooker. Pour enough very hot water into the ceramic cooking pot to reach a depth of 2cm/¾in. Switch the slow cooker to high.

2 Put the butter and sugar in a mixing bowl and beat until pale and fluffy. Gradually beat in the eggs.

5 Spoon the mixture into the greased moulds or tins. Cover each with a piece of foil. Place in the ceramic cooking pot and pour enough boiling water around the puddings to come just over halfway up the sides. Cover with the lid and cook on high for 1½–2 hours, or until well risen and firm. Remove the puddings from the slow cooker.

6 Meanwhile, make the sauce. Put the butter, sugar, cream and brandy in a pan and heat very gently, stirring occasionally, until the mixture is smooth. Increase the heat and boil for 1 minute.

7 Turn the warm puddings out on to individual dessert plates. Spoon sauce over each one and serve immediately.

Energy 462Kcal/1932kJ; Protein 5.1g; Carbohydrate 50.3g, of which sugars 35.9g; Fat 26.9g, of which saturates 16g; Cholesterol 138mg; Calcium 109mg; Fibre 1.1g; Sodium 244mg.

FRESH FRUIT BREAD and BUTTER PUDDING

Fresh currants add a tart touch to this scrumptious hot pudding. For the best results, use a wide, shallow dish rather than a narrow, deep one, but make sure it fits comfortably in the slow cooker. Serve drenched with a generous splash of fresh cream.

SERVES 4

40g/1½oz/3 tbsp butter, softened,
   plus extra for greasing
6 medium-thick slices of day-old bread,
   crusts removed
115g/4oz/1 cup prepared redcurrants
   and raspberries
3 eggs, beaten
50g/2oz/¼ cup golden caster
   (superfine) sugar
300ml/½ pint/1¼ cups creamy milk
5ml/1 tsp vanilla extract
freshly grated nutmeg
30ml/2 tbsp demerara (raw) sugar
single (light) cream, to serve

1 Generously butter a 1 litre/1¾ pints/4 cup round or oval baking dish – first checking that it fits in your slow cooker.

2 Pour about 2.5cm/1in of very hot water into the ceramic cooking pot. Place an upturned saucer or metal pastry ring in the base and switch the cooker to high.

3 Spread the slices of bread generously with the butter, then use a long serrated knife to cut them in half diagonally.

VARIATIONS

• Try using slices of Italian panettone in place of the white bread. It gives a particularly rich, indulgent result.
• Use fresh blueberries or blackcurrants in place of the fruit used here.
• When fresh berries and currants are unavailable, use chopped ready-to-eat dried apricots instead.

4 Arrange the buttered bread triangles in the dish in neat layers, overlapping the slices, with the buttered side facing up.

5 Scatter the fresh currants and berries over the bread and between the slices, ensuring that there is an even quantity of fruit throughout the pudding.

6 Place the eggs and caster sugar in a large mixing bowl and briefly beat together. Gradually whisk in the milk, vanilla extract and a large pinch of freshly grated nutmeg until well mixed.

COOK'S TIP

Always buy whole nutmegs. Once grated, the spice loses its flavour quickly.

7 Place the baking dish in the ceramic cooking pot, then slowly pour the egg and milk mixture over the bread, pushing the bread slices down to submerge them and making sure they are thoroughly soaked. Sprinkle the demerara sugar and a little nutmeg over the top, then cover the dish with foil.

8 Pour near-boiling water around the dish, so that the water level comes just over halfway up the sides of the dish. Cover with the lid and cook on high for 3–4 hours, or until a skewer inserted into the centre comes out clean.

9 Carefully remove the dish from the slow cooker and, if you like, briefly brown the top of the pudding under a hot grill (broiler). Cool slightly, then serve with the single cream.

Energy 405Kcal/1700kJ; Protein 12.6g; Carbohydrate 53.7g, of which sugars 30.7g; Fat 16.9g, of which saturates 8.6g; Cholesterol 202mg; Calcium 234mg; Fibre 2.1g; Sodium 405mg.

RICH CHOCOLATE CAKE

This rich, dense steamed chocolate cake filled with a decadently creamy buttercream makes a perfect teatime treat. Serve with a big cup of strong coffee.

SERVES 8

115g/4oz plain (semisweet) chocolate,
    chopped into small pieces
45ml/3 tbsp milk
150g/5oz/10 tbsp butter, at room
    temperature
200g/7oz/scant 1 cup soft light
    brown sugar
3 eggs, lightly beaten
200g/7oz/1¾ cups self-raising
    (self-rising) flour
15ml/1 tbsp (unsweetened) cocoa powder
icing (confectioners') sugar and
    (unsweetened) cocoa powder,
    for dusting

For the chocolate buttercream
75g/3oz/6 tbsp butter, at room
    temperature
115g/4oz/1 cup icing (confectioners') sugar
15ml/1 tbsp (unsweetened) cocoa powder
2.5ml/½ tsp vanilla extract

1 Grease and line a deep 18cm/7in fixed-base cake tin (pan) or soufflé dish with baking parchment. Pour about 5cm/2in very hot water into the ceramic cooking pot, then turn the slow cooker to high.

2 Put the chocolate and milk into a heatproof bowl and place in the cooking pot. Leave for about 10 minutes, until the chocolate softens, then stir until smooth. Remove and leave to cool for a few minutes.

3 Meanwhile, place the butter and sugar in a mixing bowl and beat together until light and fluffy. Beat in the eggs, a little at a time, then stir in the chocolate mixture until well mixed.

4 Sift the flour and cocoa over the chocolate mixture and fold in until evenly mixed. Spoon into the prepared tin or dish and cover the top with a piece of foil. Put a saucer in the bottom of the ceramic cooking pot, then rest the tin on top. If necessary, pour in more boiling water to come just over halfway up the sides of the tin.

5 Cover the slow cooker with the lid and cook for 3–3½ hours, or until firm to the touch and a fine skewer inserted into the middle comes out clean. Carefully lift the tin out of the cooking pot and leave to stand on a wire rack for 10 minutes. Turn out and leave to cool. Remove the lining paper.

6 To make the buttercream, put the butter in a large bowl and beat until very soft. Sift over the icing sugar and cocoa powder, then stir together. Add the vanilla extract and beat until the buttercream is light and fluffy.

7 Very carefully, cut the cake in half horizontally and spread a thick, even layer of the buttercream on one of the cut halves. Sandwich the cakes back together, then dust with a mixture of icing sugar and cocoa and serve.

Energy 564Kcal/2363kJ; Protein 6.6g; Carbohydrate 70g, of which sugars 51g; Fat 30.5g, of which saturates 18.2g; Cholesterol 146mg; Calcium 129mg; Fibre 1.5g; Sodium 321mg.

CHOCOLATE CHIP WALNUT CAKE

The tangy flavour of orange works well in this chocolate and nut loaf. It can be finished simply with a generous dusting of icing sugar, or as here with a zesty orange topping.

SERVES 8

115g/4oz/1 cup plain (all-purpose) flour
25g/1oz/¼ cup cornflour (cornstarch)
5ml/1 tsp baking powder
115g/4oz/½ cup butter, at room
  temperature
115g/4oz/½ cup golden caster (superfine)
  sugar
2 eggs, lightly beaten
75g/3oz/½ cup plain (semisweet), milk or
  white chocolate chips
50g/2oz/½ cup chopped walnuts
finely grated rind of ½ orange

For the topping
115g/4oz/1 cup icing (confectioners') sugar,
  sifted, plus 5ml/1 tsp for dusting
20–30ml/4 tsp–2 tbsp freshly squeezed
  orange juice
walnut halves, to decorate

1 Grease and line a 450g/1lb loaf tin (pan), with a capacity of 900ml/1½ pints/3¾ cups, with baking parchment. Place a metal pastry ring or upturned saucer in the base of the ceramic cooking pot and pour in about 2.5cm/1in very hot water. Switch the slow cooker to high.

2 Sift the flour, cornflour and baking powder together twice, so that the dry ingredients are well mixed and aerated, then set aside.

3 Place the butter in a large mixing bowl and beat until creamy. Add the golden caster sugar and continue beating until light and fluffy. Add the eggs a little at a time, beating well after each addition.

4 Gently fold about half of the sifted flour mixture into the creamed butter and sugar mixture, then add the rest with the chocolate chips, walnuts and orange rind. Fold in until just blended, taking care not to overmix.

5 Spoon the mixture into the prepared loaf tin and loosely cover with a piece of foil, allowing some space at the top for the cake to rise as it cooks.

6 Put the loaf tin on the pastry ring or saucer inside the ceramic cooking pot. Pour enough boiling water around the loaf tin to come two-thirds of the way up the sides.

7 Cover the slow cooker with a lid and cook for 2½–3 hours, or until a fine skewer pushed into the centre of the cake comes out clean. Carefully remove the cake from the slow cooker and stand it on a wire rack for 10 minutes, then turn out and leave to cool on the rack.

8 To decorate the cake, place the 115g/4oz/1 cup icing sugar in a mixing bowl. Stir in 20ml/4 tsp of the orange juice, adding a little more if needed to make the consistency of thick cream. Drizzle the mixture over the cake, then decorate with walnut halves dusted with the 5ml/1 tsp icing sugar. Leave the topping to set before serving.

Energy 395Kcal/1655kJ; Protein 4.7g; Carbohydrate 51g, of which sugars 36.9g; Fat 20.5g, of which saturates 9.9g; Cholesterol 87mg; Calcium 49mg; Fibre 0.9g; Sodium 171mg.

FROSTED CARROT and PARSNIP CAKE

A delicious twist on the classic plain carrot cake, this version is wonderfully light and crumbly. The grated vegetables help to keep it moist, and account for its excellent keeping qualities. Cooked meringue spread over the top makes a change from the usual cream cheese topping, and makes a stunning contrast to the wholesome, crumbly cake.

SERVES 8

oil, for greasing
1 orange or lemon
10ml/2 tsp caster (superfine) sugar
175g/6oz/¾ cup butter or margarine
175g/6oz/¾ cup soft light brown sugar
3 eggs, lightly beaten
175g/6oz carrots and parsnips, grated
50g/2oz/⅓ cup sultanas
   (golden raisins)
115g/4oz/1 cup self-raising
   (self-rising) flour
50g/2oz/½ cup self-raising (self-rising)
   wholemeal (whole-wheat) flour
5ml/1 tsp baking powder

For the topping
50g/2oz/¼ cup caster (superfine) sugar
1 egg white
pinch of salt

1 Put an upturned saucer or metal pastry cutter in the base of the ceramic cooking pot and pour in about 2.5cm/1in hot water. Turn the slow cooker to high. Lightly grease a deep 18cm/7in round fixed-based cake tin (pan) or soufflé dish with oil and line the base with baking parchment.

2 Finely grate the orange or lemon rind, taking care not to take off any of the white pith. Selecting the longest shreds, put about half the rind in a bowl and mix with the caster sugar. Arrange the sugar-coated rind on a sheet of greaseproof (waxed) paper and leave in a warm place to dry.

3 Put the butter or margarine and brown sugar in a large mixing bowl and beat together until pale and fluffy. Add the eggs a little at a time, beating well after each addition. Stir in the unsugared orange or lemon rind, grated carrots and parsnips and sultanas.

4 Sift the flours and baking powder together, adding any bran left in the sieve (strainer), then gradually fold into the carrot and parsnip mixture.

5 Transfer the mixture to the prepared tin and level the surface. Cover loosely with greased foil, then place in the ceramic cooking pot, on top of the saucer or pastry cutter. Pour sufficient boiling water around the tin to come just over halfway up the sides.

6 Cover the slow cooker with the lid and cook for 3–5 hours, or until a skewer inserted in the centre of the cake comes out clean. Carefully lift the tin out of the slow cooker and leave to stand for 5 minutes. Turn the cake out on to a wire rack and leave until cool.

7 To make the topping, place the caster sugar in a bowl over the near-simmering water in the slow cooker. Squeeze the juice from the orange or lemon and add 30ml/2 tbsp of the juice to the sugar. Stir over the heat until the sugar dissolves. Remove from the heat, add the egg white and salt, and whisk for 1 minute with an electric beater.

8 Return the bowl to the heat and whisk for about 6 minutes until the mixture becomes stiff and glossy, holding a good shape. Remove from the heat and allow to cool for about 5 minutes, whisking frequently.

9 Swirl the meringue topping over the cake and leave for 1 hour to firm up. To serve, sprinkle with the sugared orange or lemon rind.

VARIATION
If you do not like parsnips, you can make this cake with just carrots, or replace the parsnips with the same weight of grated courgettes (zucchini). Add a pinch of cinnamon and nutmeg to the mixture.

Energy 410Kcal/1718kJ; Protein 5.9g; Carbohydrate 53g, of which sugars 38.2g; Fat 20.8g, of which saturates 12.2g; Cholesterol 132mg; Calcium 98mg; Fibre 1.9g; Sodium 290mg.

CHOCOLATE CHEESECAKE BROWNIES

A very dense chocolate brownie mixture is swirled with creamy cheese to give a marbled effect. Cut into small squares for little mouthfuls of absolute heaven.

MAKES 9

50g/2oz dark (bittersweet) chocolate
   (minimum 70 per cent cocoa solids),
   chopped
50g/2oz/¼ cup unsalted (sweet) butter
65g/2½oz/5 tbsp light muscovado
   (brown) sugar
1 egg, beaten
25g/1oz/¼ cup plain (all-purpose) flour

For the cheesecake mixture
115g/4oz/½ cup full-fat cream cheese
25g/1oz/2 tbsp caster (superfine) sugar
5ml/1 tsp vanilla extract
½ beaten egg

1 Line the base and sides of a 15cm/6in square fixed-base cake tin (pan) with baking parchment. Pour about 5cm/2in of very hot water into the ceramic cooking pot and switch to high.

2 Put the chocolate and butter in a heatproof bowl and place in the slow cooker. Leave to stand for 10 minutes.

3 Meanwhile, make the cheesecake mixture. Put the cream cheese, sugar and vanilla extract in a clean mixing bowl and beat together. Gradually beat in the egg until the mixture is very smooth and creamy. Set aside.

4 Stir the chocolate and butter mixture until completely melted and smooth, then remove the bowl from the slow cooker. Add the muscovado sugar and stir to combine. Place an upturned saucer or metal pastry ring in the base of the ceramic cooking pot.

5 Add the beaten egg to the melted chocolate mixture a little at a time, and beat well until thoroughly mixed, then sift over the flour and gently fold in.

6 Spoon the chocolate mixture into the base of the tin. Drop small spoonfuls of the cheesecake mixture on top. Using a skewer, swirl the mixtures together.

7 Cover the tin with foil and place in the slow cooker. Pour in more boiling water around the tin to come just over halfway up the sides. Cook for 2 hours, or until just set in the centre. Remove the tin from the slow cooker and place on a wire rack to cool. Cut into squares.

Energy 174Kcal/727kJ; Protein 2.9g; Carbohydrate 16.2g, of which sugars 14g; Fat 11.3g, of which saturates 6.8g; Cholesterol 65mg; Calcium 25mg; Fibre 0.2g; Sodium 86mg.

LIGHT FRUIT CAKE

This incredibly easy all-in-one fruit cake has a crumbly texture. The combination of wholemeal flour and long slow cooking ensures that it stays beautifully moist.

SERVES 12

2 eggs
130g/4½oz/generous ½ cup butter,
    at room temperature
225g/8oz/1 cup light muscovado
    (brown) sugar
150g/5oz/1¼ cups self-raising
    (self-rising) flour
150g/5oz/1¼ cups wholemeal
    (whole-wheat) self-raising
    (self-rising) flour
pinch of salt
5ml/1 tsp mixed (apple pie) spice
450g/1lb/2½ cups luxury mixed
    dried fruit

1 Line the base and sides of a deep 18cm/7in round or 15cm/6in square fixed-base cake tin (pan) with baking parchment. Place an upturned saucer or metal pastry ring in the base of the ceramic cooking pot, then pour in about 2.5cm/1in of very hot water. Switch the slow cooker to high.

2 Crack the eggs into a large mixing bowl. Add the butter and sugar, then sift over the flours, salt and spice, adding any bran left in the sieve (strainer). Stir together with a wooden spoon until mixed, then add the dried fruit and beat for 2 minutes until the mixture is smooth and glossy.

COOK'S TIP
Choose a good-quality brand of luxury dried fruits. It should contain a good mix of currants, sultanas (golden raisins), mixed peel and glacé (candied) cherries, as well as other dried fruits.

3 Spoon the mixture into the prepared cake tin and level the surface. Cover the tin with a piece of buttered foil.

4 Put the tin in the slow cooker and pour in enough boiling water to come just over halfway up the sides of the tin. Cover with the lid and cook for 4–5 hours, or until a skewer inserted into the middle of the cake comes out clean.

5 Remove the cake from the slow cooker and place on a wire rack. Leave the cake to cool in the tin for about 15 minutes, then turn out and leave to cool completely. To store, wrap the cake in greaseproof (waxed) paper and then foil, and keep in a cool place.

Energy 351Kcal/1482kJ; Protein 4.9g; Carbohydrate 63g, of which sugars 46g; Fat 10.6g, of which saturates 6g; Cholesterol 60.8mg; Calcium 78.6mg; Fibre 2.3g; Sodium 148mg.

MARBLED SPICE CAKE

This cake can be baked in a fluted ring-shaped cake mould called a kugelhupf *or* gugelhupf, *which originates from Germany and Austria, or in a plain ring-shaped cake tin. The marbled effect looks particularly good when the cake is baked in a ring like this.*

SERVES 8

75g/3oz/6 tbsp butter, at room
  temperature, plus extra for greasing
130g/4½oz/generous 1 cup plain
  (all-purpose) flour, plus extra for
  dusting
115g/4oz/½ cup soft light brown sugar
2 eggs
few drops of vanilla extract
7.5ml/1½ tsp baking powder
45ml/3 tbsp milk
30ml/2 tbsp malt extract or black treacle
5ml/1 tsp mixed (apple pie) spice
2.5ml/½ tsp ground ginger
75g/3oz/¾ cup icing (confectioners') sugar,
  sifted, to decorate

1 Grease and flour a 1.2 litre/2 pint/
5 cup *kugelhupf* mould or ring-shaped
cake tin (pan). Put an inverted saucer
or large metal pastry cutter in the base
of the slow cooker and pour in about
5cm/2in hot water. Switch the slow
cooker to high.

2 Put the butter and sugar in a bowl
and beat together until light and fluffy.

3 In a separate bowl, beat together the
eggs and vanilla extract, then gradually
beat into the butter and sugar mixture,
adding a little at a time and beating well
after each addition.

COOK'S TIP
To make a marbled chocolate and vanilla
cake, stir 15ml/1 tbsp chocolate essence
into the cake mixture, in place of the
malt extract or treacle and spices.

4 Sift together the flour and baking
powder to combine, then fold the flour
into the butter and sugar mixture, adding
a little of the milk between each addition
until evenly combined.

5 Spoon about one-third of the mixture
into a small bowl and stir in the malt
extract or treacle, mixed spice and
ginger until just combined.

6 Drop a large spoonful of the light
mixture into the cake tin, followed by a
spoonful of the dark mixture. Continue
alternating spoonfuls of the light and
dark mixtures until all the mixture has
been used. Run a knife or skewer through
the mixtures to give a marbled effect.

7 Cover the tin with foil and place in
the ceramic cooking pot. Pour a little
more boiling water around the tin to
come just over halfway up the sides.
Cover the slow cooker with the lid and
cook for 3–4 hours. To test if it is done,
insert a skewer into the middle of the
cake; it should come out clean.

8 Carefully lift the cake out of the slow
cooker and leave in the tin for about
10 minutes before turning out on to
a wire rack to cool.

9 To decorate, place the icing sugar in
a bowl and add just enough warm water
to make a smooth icing (frosting) with
the consistency of single (light) cream.
Quickly drizzle the mixture over the
cake, then leave to set before serving
the cake in thick slices.

Energy 215Kcal/902kJ; Protein 2.8g; Carbohydrate 33g, of which sugars 20.3g; Fat 8.8g, of which saturates 5.2g; Cholesterol 49mg; Calcium 84mg; Fibre 0.5g; Sodium 172mg.

BLUEBERRY MUFFIN PUDDING

You can't cook traditional muffins in a slow cooker but this delicious alternative will satisfy your cravings. It's especially good served barely warm with custard or crème fraîche. Take the eggs and buttermilk out of the refrigerator at least an hour before you start mixing.

SERVES 4

75g/3oz/6 tbsp butter, plus extra
   for greasing
75g/3oz/6 tbsp soft light brown sugar
105ml/7 tbsp buttermilk, at room
   temperature
2 eggs, lightly beaten, at room temperature
225g/8oz/2 cups self raising
   (self-rising) flour
pinch of salt
5ml/1 tsp ground cinnamon
150g/5oz/1¼ cup fresh blueberries
10ml/2 tsp demerara (raw) sugar,
   for sprinkling
custard or crème fraîche, to serve

1 Place an upturned saucer or metal pastry ring in the base of the slow cooker. Pour in about 5cm/2in of very hot water, then switch the slow cooker to high. Lightly grease a 1.5 litre/2½ pint/6¼ cup heatproof dish with butter – first making sure that it will fit the inside of your slow cooker.

2 Put the butter and sugar in a heatproof jug (pitcher) and place in the ceramic cooking pot. Leave uncovered for 20 minutes, stirring, until melted.

3 Remove the jug from the slow cooker and leave to cool until tepid, then stir in the buttermilk followed by the beaten egg, until well mixed.

COOK'S TIP
Because less liquid evaporates from the pudding in a slow cooker, the mixture is thicker than a conventional muffin batter.

4 Sift the flour, salt and cinnamon into a mixing bowl. Stir in the blueberries, then make a hollow in the middle. Pour in the buttermilk mixture and quickly stir until just combined. Do not overmix.

5 Spoon the mixture into the prepared dish, then sprinkle the top with the demerara sugar. Cover with a piece of buttered foil and place in the ceramic cooking pot. Pour in a little more boiling water around the dish, if necessary, to come halfway up the sides.

6 Cover the slow cooker with the lid and cook for 3–4 hours, until a skewer inserted in the middle comes out clean. Remove from the slow cooker and let the pudding cool slightly before serving with custard or crème fraîche.

Energy 499Kcal/2101kJ; Protein 10.1g; Carbohydrate 76.2g, of which sugars 34.4g; Fat 19.2g, of which saturates 10.7g; Cholesterol 153mg; Calcium 262mg; Fibre 2.2g; Sodium 367mg.

PUMPKIN and BANANA CAKE

Rather like a cross between a carrot cake and banana bread, this luscious cake is an excellent way of using some of the scooped-out pumpkin flesh after making Hallowe'en lanterns. A cream cheese topping provides a delicious contrast with the dense moist cake.

SERVES 12

225g/8oz/2 cups self-raising
   (self-rising) flour
7.5ml/1½ tsp baking powder
2.5ml/½ tsp ground cinnamon
2.5ml/½ tsp ground ginger
pinch of salt
125g/5oz/10 tbsp soft light brown sugar
75g/3oz/¾ cup pecans or walnuts,
   chopped
115g/4oz pumpkin flesh, coarsely grated
2 small bananas, peeled and mashed
2 eggs, lightly beaten
150ml/¼ pint/⅔ cup sunflower oil

For the topping
50g/2oz/¼ cup butter, at room
   temperature
150g/5oz/⅔ cup soft cheese
1.5ml/¼ tsp vanilla extract
115g/4oz/1 cup icing (confectioners') sugar
pecan halves, to decorate

1 Line the base and sides of a deep 20cm/8in round fixed-base cake tin (pan) or soufflé dish with baking parchment. Place an upturned saucer or metal pastry ring in the base of the ceramic cooking pot, then pour in about 2.5cm/1in of very hot water. Switch the slow cooker to high.

2 Sift the flour, baking powder, cinnamon, ginger and salt into a large mixing bowl to combine. Stir in the sugar, chopped pecans or walnuts and grated pumpkin until thoroughly mixed. Make a slight hollow in the middle of the dry ingredients.

3 In a separate bowl, combine the bananas, eggs and sunflower oil, then stir into the dry ingredients. Turn into the prepared tin and level the surface.

4 Cover the tin with a piece of buttered foil and place in the slow cooker. Pour in sufficient boiling water to come just over halfway up the sides of the tin.

5 Cover the pot with the lid and cook on high for 4–4½ hours, or until the cake is firm and a skewer inserted into the middle comes out clean.

6 Carefully remove the cake from the slow cooker and stand the tin on a wire rack to cool for 15 minutes. Turn out and leave to cool completely, then peel off the lining paper.

7 To make the topping, put the butter, soft cheese and vanilla extract in a bowl and beat until blended and smooth. Sift in the icing sugar and beat again until smooth and creamy. Thickly spread the topping over the top of the cake and decorate with pecan halves. Chill in the refrigerator for at least 1 hour before serving, to allow the topping to harden.

Energy 374Kcal/1567kJ; Protein 5.1g; Carbohydrate 43.2g, of which sugars 28.7g; Fat 21.3g, of which saturates 6.5g; Cholesterol 58mg; Calcium 101.7mg; Fibre 1g; Sodium 203mg.

MOIST GOLDEN GINGER CAKE

This is the ultimate ginger cake: instead of the traditional black treacle, a mixture of golden syrup and malt extract gives a really sticky, moist texture. Because of the long slow cooking, the cake matures sufficiently to eat straight away. However, the flavour improves and the texture becomes stickier if it is wrapped and kept for a day or two.

SERVES 10

175g/6oz/generous ¾ cup light muscovado
  (brown) sugar
115g/4oz/½ cup butter
150g/5oz/⅔ cup golden (light corn)
  syrup
25g/1oz malt extract
175g/6oz/1½ cups self-raising
  (self-rising) flour
50g/2oz/½ cup plain (all-purpose) flour
10ml/2 tsp ground ginger
pinch of salt
1 egg, lightly beaten
120ml/4fl oz/½ cup milk, at room
  temperature
2.5ml/½ tsp bicarbonate of soda
  (baking soda)

1 Line the base of a deep 18cm/7in round fixed-base cake tin (pan) or soufflé dish with baking parchment. Pour 5cm/2in of very hot water into the ceramic cooking pot. Switch to high.

2 Place the sugar, butter, golden syrup and malt extract in a heatproof bowl that will fit inside the slow cooker. Place in the ceramic cooking pot and leave for 15 minutes, or until melted.

3 Remove the bowl from the slow cooker and stir until smooth. Place an upturned saucer or metal pastry ring in the base of the ceramic cooking pot.

4 Sift the flours, ginger and salt into a separate mixing bowl. Pour the melted butter and sugar mixture into the flour and beat until smooth. Stir in the beaten egg until well mixed.

VARIATION
To turn this moist cake into a tempting treat for kids, try decorating it with plain lemon icing (frosting) and scattering with multi-coloured sugar sprinkles. To make the icing, put 75g/3oz/¾ cup icing sugar in a bowl and stir in just enough lemon juice to make a smooth icing with the consistency of single (light) cream. Drizzle over the cake and scatter with sprinkles.

5 Pour the milk in a jug (pitcher) and stir in the bicarbonate of soda. Pour the mixture into the ginger cake mixture and stir until combined.

6 Pour the cake mixture into the prepared cake tin or soufflé dish, cover with foil and place in the cooking pot.

7 Pour a little more boiling water around the tin or dish to come just over halfway up the sides. Cover with the lid and cook for 5–6 hours, or until firm and a fine skewer inserted into the middle of the cake comes out clean.

8 Remove the cake from the slow cooker and place the tin or dish on a wire cooling rack. Leave to cool for 15 minutes, then turn out and leave to cool completely before serving in slices.

COOK'S TIP
Because this cake improves with keeping, it is the perfect choice when you are expecting guests because you can make it several days in advance.

Energy 289Kcal/1216kJ; Protein 3.4g; Carbohydrate 48g, of which sugars 31.1g; Fat 10.6g, of which saturates 6.4g; Cholesterol 48mg; Calcium 98mg; Fibre 0.7g; Sodium 211mg.

ONE-POT AND CLAY-POT DESSERTS AND CAKES

The clever cook who saves time and effort by mastering one-pot and clay-pot cooking deserves a sweet reward, and what better way to celebrate success than with Baked Maple and Pecan Croissant Pudding or Honey-baked Figs – cooked in a clay pot, of course – served with Hazelnut Ice Cream. Black Cherry Clafoutis is another treat and, for pots of pleasure, try sweet and tangy Citrus and Caramel Custards, which are baked in individual cazuelas, or elegant and impressive Plum Charlottes with Foamy Kirsch Sauce. There are also classic tarts and pies to bake, including Tarte Tatin, and Pear, Almond and Ground Rice Pie.

PLUM CHARLOTTES with FOAMY KIRSCH SAUCE

These individual puddings, cooked in mini earthenware dishes, conceal a fresh plum filling and are served on a pool of light, frothy Kirsch-flavoured sauce.

SERVES 4

115g/4oz/½ cup butter, melted
50g/2oz/4 tbsp demerara (raw) sugar
450g/1lb ripe plums, stoned (pitted) and
    thickly sliced
25g/1oz/2 tbsp caster (superfine) sugar
30ml/2 tbsp water
1.5ml/¼ tsp ground cinnamon
25g/1oz/¼ cup ground almonds
8–10 large slices of white bread

For the Kirsch sauce
3 egg yolks
40g/1½oz/3 tbsp caster
    (superfine) sugar
30ml/2 tbsp Kirsch

2 Place the stoned plum slices in a pan with the caster sugar, water and ground cinnamon and cook gently for 5 minutes, or until the plums have softened slightly. Cool, then stir in the ground almonds.

5 Divide the plum mixture among the dishes. Top with the bread rounds and brush with the remaining butter. Place on a baking sheet, bake for 25 minutes.

1 Preheat the oven to 190°C/375°F/ Gas 5. Line the base of four individual 10cm/4in-diameter deep, earthenware ramekin dishes with baking parchment. Brush evenly and thoroughly with a little of the melted butter, then sprinkle each dish with a little of the demerara sugar, rotating the dish in your hands to coat each dish evenly.

VARIATIONS
• Slices of peeled pear or eating apples can be used in this recipe instead of the stoned, sliced plums.
• If using apples or pears substitute the Kirsch in the foamy sauce with Calvados or another apple brandy.
• If you are short on time, drained canned fruit such as pineapple, apricots, pears or plums can be used – simply stir in the ground almonds as in step 2 and add to the prepared ramekins.

3 Cut the crusts off the bread and then use a plain pastry cutter to cut out four rounds to fit the bases of the ramekins. Dip the bread rounds into the melted butter and fit them into the dishes. Cut four more rounds to fit the tops of the dishes and set aside.

4 Cut the remaining bread into strips, dip into the melted butter and use to line the sides of the ramekins completely.

6 Just before the charlottes are ready place the egg yolks and caster sugar for the sauce in a bowl. Whisk together until pale. Place the bowl over a pan of simmering water and whisk in the Kirsch. Continue whisking until the mixture is very light and frothy.

7 Remove the charlottes from the oven and turn out on to warm serving plates. Pour a little sauce over and around the charlottes and serve immediately.

COOK'S TIP
For an extra indulgent dessert, serve the puddings with lightly whipped double (heavy) cream flavoured with extra Kirsch and sweetened to taste with a little sieved icing (confectioners') sugar.

Energy 600Kcal/2513kJ; Protein 9.1g; Carbohydrate 69.6g, of which sugars 44.2g; Fat 32.5g, of which saturates 16.5g; Cholesterol 218mg; Calcium 128mg; Fibre 3.1g; Sodium 467mg.

BAKED MAPLE and PECAN CROISSANT PUDDING

This variation of the classic English bread and butter pudding uses croissants, which give a light fluffy texture. Pecans, brandy-laced sultanas and maple syrup-flavoured custard complete this mouthwatering dessert.

SERVES 4

75g/3oz/generous ½ cup sultanas
  (golden raisins)
45ml/3 tbsp brandy
50g/2oz/¼ cup butter, plus extra for greasing
4 large croissants
40g/1½oz/⅓ cup pecan nuts,
  roughly chopped
3 eggs, lightly beaten
300ml/½ pint/1¼ cups milk
150ml/¼ pint/⅔ cup single (light) cream
120ml/4fl oz/½ cup maple syrup
25g/1oz/2 tbsp demerara (raw) sugar
maple syrup and pouring (half-and-half)
  cream, to serve (optional)

1 Place the sultanas and brandy in a small pan and heat gently, until warm. Leave to stand for 1 hour. Soak a small clay pot in cold water for 15 minutes, then drain, leave for 2–3 minutes and lightly grease the base and sides.

2 Cut the croissants (see Cook's Tip) into thick slices, then spread with butter on one side.

3 Arrange the croissant slices, butter-side uppermost and slightly overlapping in the soaked clay pot. Sprinkle the brandy-soaked sultanas and the roughly chopped pecan nuts over the buttered croissant slices.

4 In a large bowl, beat the eggs and milk together, then gradually beat in the single cream and maple syrup.

5 Pour the egg custard through a sieve, over the croissants, fruit and nuts in the dish. Leave the uncooked pudding to stand for 30 minutes, so that some of the egg custard liquid is absorbed by the croissants.

6 Sprinkle the demerara sugar evenly over the top, then cover the dish and place in an unheated oven. Set the oven to 180°C/350°F/Gas 4 and bake for 40 minutes. Remove the lid and continue to cook for about 20 minutes, or until the custard is set and the top is golden.

7 Leave the pudding to cool for about 15 minutes before serving warm with extra maple syrup and a little pouring cream, if you like.

COOK'S TIPS
• This dessert is perfect for using up leftover croissants. Slightly stale one-day-old croissants are easier to slice and butter; they also soak up the custard more easily. Thickly sliced one-day-old bread or large slices of brioche could be used instead.
• Pecan nuts are an elongated nut in a glossy red oval-shaped shell, but are usually sold shelled. They are native to the USA and have a sweet, mild flavour. Pecans are most commonly used in pecan pie but are also popular in ice creams and cakes. Walnuts can be substituted for pecans in most recipes, and they would be perfect in this one if you don't have any pecan nuts.

Energy 731Kcal/3056kJ; Protein 15g; Carbohydrate 72.3g, of which sugars 49.4g; Fat 45.6g, of which saturates 19.5g; Cholesterol 226mg; Calcium 217mg; Fibre 1.8g; Sodium 507mg.

COCONUT RICE PUDDING

A delicious adaptation of the classic creamy rice pudding, this dessert is flavoured with coconut milk and finished with a coconut crust.

SERVES 4

75g/3oz/scant ½ cup short grain
   pudding rice
40g/1½oz/3 tbsp caster
   (superfine) sugar
2.5ml/½ tsp vanilla extract
300ml/½ pint/1¼ cups milk
400ml/14fl oz/1⅔ cups coconut milk
105ml/7 tbsp single (light) cream
30ml/2 tbsp desiccated (dry unsweetened
   shredded) coconut or slivers of
   fresh coconut

VARIATION
If preferred, this pudding can be made
with extra milk instead of the single
cream. Use full cream (whole) milk, for
a rich, creamy flavour.

1 Soak a small clay pot in cold water
for 15 minutes, then drain. Add the rice,
sugar, vanilla extract, milk, coconut milk
and cream.

2 Cover the clay pot and place in a cold
oven. Set the oven to 180°C/350°F/
Gas 4 and cook for 1 hour.

3 Remove the lid from the clay pot, stir
the pudding gently, then re-cover and
cook for a further 30–45 minutes, or
until the rice is tender.

4 Remove the lid, stir the pudding, then
sprinkle with desiccated or fresh coconut
and bake uncovered for 10–15 minutes.

Energy 259Kcal/1087kJ; Protein 5.8g; Carbohydrate 34g, of which sugars 19.9g; Fat 11.6g, of which saturates 8.2g; Cholesterol 19mg; Calcium 153mg; Fibre 1g; Sodium 153mg.

CITRUS and CARAMEL CUSTARDS

These Spanish-style custards, made rich with cream and egg yolks, are delicately scented with tangy citrus flavours and aromatic cinnamon.

SERVES 4

450ml/¾ pint/scant 2 cups milk
150ml/¼ pint/⅔ cup single
   (light) cream
1 cinnamon stick, broken in half
thinly pared rind of ½ lemon
thinly pared rind of ½ orange
4 egg yolks
5ml/1 tsp cornflour (cornstarch)
40g/1½oz/3 tbsp caster (superfine) sugar
grated rind of ½ lemon
grated rind of ½ orange
a little icing (confectioner's) sugar,
   for sprinkling

1 Place the milk and cream in a pan. Add the cinnamon stick and the strips of pared citrus rind. Bring to the boil, then simmer for 10 minutes.

2 Preheat the oven to 160°C/325°F/ Gas 3. Whisk the egg yolks, cornflour and caster sugar together. Remove the rinds and cinnamon from the hot milk and cream and discard. Whisk the hot milk and cream into the egg yolk mixture.

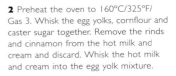

3 Stir the grated citrus rind into the custard mixture. Pour into four individual cazuelas, each about 13cm/5in in diameter. Place in a roasting pan and pour warm water into the pan to reach three-quarters of the way up the sides. Bake for 25–30 minutes, or until the custards are just set. Remove the dishes from the water; leave to cool, then chill.

4 Preheat the grill (broiler) to high. Sprinkle the custards liberally with icing sugar and place under the grill until the tops turn golden brown and caramelize.

COOK'S TIPS
• Prepare the grated rind first, then cut a few strips of rind from the ungrated side of the citrus fruits using a swivel-bladed vegetable peeler.
• You can use a special cook's gas-gun or salamander to caramelize the tops instead of grilling (broiling) them.

Energy 225Kcal/939kJ; Protein 8g; Carbohydrate 16.6g, of which sugars 16.6g; Fat 14.6g, of which saturates 7.3g; Cholesterol 229mg; Calcium 197mg; Fibre 0g; Sodium 69mg.

HONEY-BAKED FIGS with HAZELNUT ICE CREAM

This is a delectable dessert – fresh figs are baked in a lightly spiced lemon and honey syrup and served with a gorgeous, home-made roasted hazelnut ice cream.

SERVES 4

1 lemon grass stalk, finely chopped
1 cinnamon stick, roughly broken
60ml/4 tbsp clear honey
200ml/7fl oz/scant 1 cup water
8 large figs

For the hazelnut ice cream
450ml/¾ pint/scant 2 cups double
  (heavy) cream
50g/2oz/¼ cup caster (superfine) sugar
3 egg yolks
1.5ml/¼ tsp vanilla extract
75g/3oz/¾ cup hazelnuts

1 To make the ice cream, place the cream in a pan and heat slowly until almost boiling. Place the sugar and egg yolks in a bowl and beat until creamy.

2 Pour a little of the cream on to the egg yolk mixture and stir. Pour into the pan and mix with the rest of the cream. Cook over a low heat, stirring constantly, until the mixture thickens slightly and lightly coats the back of the spoon – do not allow it to boil. Pour into a bowl, then stir in the vanilla and leave to cool.

3 Preheat the oven to 180°C/350°F/ Gas 4. Place the hazelnuts on a baking sheet and roast for 10–12 minutes, or until golden. Leave the nuts to cool, then place them in a food processor or blender and process until they are coarsely ground.

4 Transfer the ice cream mixture to a metal or plastic freezer container and freeze for 2 hours, or until the mixture feels firm around the edge. Remove the container from the freezer and whisk the ice cream to break down the ice crystals. Stir in the ground hazelnuts and freeze the mixture again until half-frozen. Whisk again, then freeze until firm.

COOK'S TIPS
• If you prefer, rather than whisking the semi-frozen ice cream, tip it into a food processor and process until smooth.
• There are several different types of figs available and they can all be used in this recipe. Choose from green-skinned figs that have an amber-coloured flesh, dark purple-skinned fruit with a deep red flesh or green/yellow-skinned figs with a pinky-coloured flesh.

5 Place the lemon grass, cinnamon stick, honey and water in a small pan and heat slowly until boiling. Simmer the mixture for 5 minutes, then leave the syrup to stand for 15 minutes.

6 Meanwhile, soak a small clay pot in cold water for 15 minutes. Cut the figs into quarters, leaving them intact at the bases. Place the figs in the clay pot and pour over the honey-flavoured syrup.

7 Cover the clay pot and place in an unheated oven. Set the oven to 200°C/ 400°F/Gas 6 and bake the figs for about 15 minutes, or until tender.

8 Take the ice cream from the freezer about 10 minutes before serving, to soften slightly. Transfer the figs to serving plates. Strain a little of the cooking liquid over the figs and then serve them with a scoop or two of hazelnut ice cream.

VARIATION
This recipe also works well with halved, stoned (pitted) nectarines or peaches – simply cook as from step 6 and serve with the home-made ice cream.

Energy 909Kcal/3770kJ; Protein 8.2g; Carbohydrate 48.7g, of which sugars 48.4g; Fat 77.1g, of which saturates 39.6g; Cholesterol 305mg; Calcium 206mg; Fibre 4.2g; Sodium 60mg.

SPICED PEARS with NUT CRUMBLE

An all-time favourite, this crumble has a crunchy pecan nut and oat topping,
which complements the spicy pears hidden beneath.

SERVES 4–6

900g/2lb pears
30ml/2 tbsp lemon juice
40g/1½oz/3 tbsp caster (superfine) sugar
5ml/1 tsp mixed (apple pie) spice
2.5ml/½ tsp grated nutmeg
vanilla ice cream, to serve

For the crumble topping
75g/3oz/⅔ cup plain (all-purpose) flour
75g/3oz/6 tbsp butter
50g/2oz/¼ cup light muscovado
    (brown) sugar
50g/2oz/½ cup pecan nuts or
    walnuts, chopped
40g/1½oz/scant ½ cup rolled oats

COOK'S TIP
Look out for golden-skinned Forelle pears,
which are especially good for cooking, or
try Anjou, Williams or Conference pears.

1 Soak a small clay pot in cold water for
15 minutes, then drain. Peel the pears
if wished, then halve them and remove
the cores. Cut each pear into six wedges
and toss in the lemon juice.

2 Place the pears in the clay pot, add
the sugar, mixed spice and nutmeg and
mix together. Place in an unheated oven,
set the oven to 200°C/400°F/Gas 6 and
cook for 25 minutes.

3 Meanwhile, prepare the crumble
topping. Sift the flour into a bowl and
rub in the butter, then stir in the sugar,
nuts and rolled oats.

4 Uncover the clay pot and stir gently to
rearrange the fruit. Spoon the crumble
mixture over the pears, then return the
clay pot to the oven for 25–30 minutes,
or until the crumble is golden. Serve
warm, with vanilla ice cream.

Energy 365Kcal/1523kJ; Protein 3.5g; Carbohydrate 42.9g, of which sugars 33.2g; Fat 21g, of which saturates 7.4g; Cholesterol 27mg; Calcium 57mg; Fibre 4.3g; Sodium 82mg.

NECTARINES BAKED with ALMONDS and PISTACHIO NUTS

Fresh nectarines stuffed with a ground almond and chopped pistachio nut filling, baked in a clay pot until meltingly tender, then served with a passion fruit sauce.

SERVES 4

50g/2oz/½ cup ground almonds
15ml/1 tbsp caster (superfine) sugar
1 egg yolk
50g/2oz/⅓ cup shelled pistachio
    nuts, chopped
4 nectarines
200ml/7fl oz/scant 1 cup orange juice
2 ripe passion fruits
45ml/3 tbsp Cointreau or other
    orange liqueur

1 Soak a small clay pot, if using, in cold water for 15 minutes. Mix the ground almonds, sugar and egg yolk to a paste, then stir in the pistachio nuts.

2 Cut the nectarines in half and carefully remove the stones (pits). Pile the ground almond and pistachio filling into the nectarine halves and then place them in a single layer in the base of the clay pot or cazuela.

3 Pour the orange juice around the nectarines, then cover the pot or dish and place in an unheated oven. Set the oven to 200°C/400°F/Gas 6 and cook for 15 minutes.

4 Remove the lid from the pot or dish and bake for a further 5–10 minutes, or until the nectarines are soft. Transfer the nectarines to individual, warmed serving plates and keep warm.

5 Cut the passion fruits in half, scoop out the seeds and stir into the cooking juices in the clay pot or dish with the liqueur. Spoon the sauce around the nectarines and serve.

Energy 277Kcal/1159kJ; Protein 7.5g; Carbohydrate 27.8g, of which sugars 27.2g; Fat 14.1g, of which saturates 1.5g; Cholesterol 0mg; Calcium 63mg; Fibre 3.8g; Sodium 78mg.

BREAD and BUTTER PUDDING
with WHISKEY SAUCE

This is comfort food at its very best. The whiskey sauce is heavenly, but if you are not keen on the alcohol, the pudding can also be served with chilled cream or vanilla ice cream — the contrast between the hot and cold is delicious.

SERVES 6

8 slices of white bread, buttered
115–150g/4–5oz/⅔–¾ cup sultanas
    (golden raisins), or mixed dried fruit
2.5ml/½ tsp grated nutmeg
150g/5oz/¾ cup caster (superfine) sugar
2 large (US extra large) eggs
300ml/½ pint/1¼ cups single
    (light) cream
450ml/¾ pint/scant 2 cups milk
5ml/1 tsp of vanilla extract
light muscovado (brown) sugar, for
    sprinkling (optional)

For the whiskey sauce
150g/5oz/10 tbsp butter
115g/4oz/generous ½ cup caster
    (superfine) sugar
1 egg
45ml/3 tbsp Irish whiskey

1 Preheat the oven to 180°C/350°F/ Gas 4. Remove the crusts from the bread and put four slices, buttered side down, in the base of an ovenproof dish. Sprinkle with the fruit, some of the nutmeg and 15ml/1 tbsp sugar.

2 Place the remaining four slices of bread on top, buttered side down, and sprinkle again with nutmeg and 15ml/1 tbsp sugar.

3 Beat the eggs lightly, add the cream, milk, vanilla extract and the remaining sugar, and mix well to make a custard. Pour this mixture over the bread, and sprinkle light muscovado sugar over the top, if you like to have a crispy crust. Bake in the preheated oven for 1 hour, or until all the liquid has been absorbed and the pudding is risen and brown.

4 Meanwhile, make the whiskey sauce: melt the butter in a heavy pan, add the caster sugar and dissolve over gentle heat. Remove from the heat and add the egg, whisking vigorously, and then add the whiskey. Serve the pudding on hot serving plates, with the whiskey sauce poured over the top.

Energy 757Kcal/3168kJ; Protein 11.7g; Carbohydrate 82g, of which sugars 65.2g; Fat 40.8g, of which saturates 24.3g; Cholesterol 207mg; Calcium 232mg; Fibre 0.9g; Sodium 472mg.

FRESH CURRANT BREAD and BUTTER PUDDING

*Fresh mixed red- and blackcurrants add a tart touch to this scrumptious hot pudding in
which layers of custard-soaked bread are cooked to a crisp golden crust.*

SERVES 6

8 medium-thick slices day-old white bread,
    crusts removed
50g/2oz/¼ cup butter, softened
115g/4oz/1 cup redcurrants
115g/4oz/1 cup blackcurrants
4 eggs, beaten
75g/3oz/6 tbsp caster (superfine) sugar
475ml/16fl oz/2 cups creamy milk
5ml/1 tsp vanilla extract
freshly grated nutmeg
30ml/2 tbsp demerara (raw) sugar
single (light) cream, to serve

1 Preheat the oven to 160°C/325°F/
Gas 3. Butter a 1.2 litre/2 pint/5 cup
ovenproof earthenware dish.

VARIATION

A mixture of blueberries and raspberries
would work just as well as the currants.

2 Spread the slices of bread generously
with the butter, then cut them in half
diagonally. Layer the slices in the dish,
buttered side up, sprinkling the currants
between the layers.

3 Beat the eggs and caster sugar lightly
together in a large mixing bowl, then
gradually whisk in the creamy milk and
vanilla extract along with a large pinch
of freshly grated nutmeg.

4 Pour the milk mixture over the bread,
pushing the slices down into the liquid.
Sprinkle the demerara sugar and a little
more nutmeg over the top. Place the
dish in a roasting pan and fill with hot
water to come halfway up the sides of
the dish. Bake for 40 minutes, then
increase the oven temperature to
180°C/350°F/Gas 4 and bake for about
20 minutes more, or until the top is
golden. Serve warm, with single cream.

Energy 328Kcal/1377kJ; Protein 10.3g; Carbohydrate 42.2g, of which sugars 25.4g; Fat 14.3g, of which saturates 7.4g; Cholesterol 156mg; Calcium 186mg; Fibre 1.9g; Sodium 321mg.

APRICOT PANETTONE PUDDING

Panettone and pecan nuts make a rich addition to this "no-butter" version of a traditional bread and butter pudding.

SERVES 6

sunflower oil, for greasing
350g/12oz panettone, sliced
    into triangles
25g/1oz/¼ cup pecan nuts
75g/3oz/⅓ cup ready-to-eat dried
    apricots, chopped
500ml/17fl oz/generous 2 cups full-cream
    (whole) milk
5ml/1 tsp vanilla extract
1 large (US extra large) egg, beaten
30ml/2 tbsp maple syrup
nutmeg
demerara (raw) sugar,
    for sprinkling

1 Lightly grease a 1 litre/1¾ pint/4 cup ovenproof earthenware dish. Arrange half of the panettone triangles in the dish, sprinkle over half the pecan nuts and all of the chopped, dried apricots, then add another layer of panettone on top.

COOK'S TIP

Panettone is a light fruit cake originally from northern Italy but now popular all over the world. It is traditionally eaten at festivals such as Christmas or Easter. Panettone is baked in cylindrical moulds, giving it a distinctive shape. You can now find panettone in different flavours – the coffee-flavoured type is particularly good.

2 Heat the milk and vanilla extract in a small pan until the milk just simmers. Put the egg and maple syrup in a large bowl, grate in about 2.5ml/½ tsp nutmeg, then whisk in the hot milk.

3 Preheat the oven to 200°C/400°F/Gas 6. Pour the egg mixture over the panettone, lightly pressing down the bread so that it is submerged. Leave the pudding to stand for about 10 minutes, to allow the panettone slices to soak up a little of the liquid.

4 Sprinkle over the reserved pecan nuts and sprinkle a little demerara sugar and freshly grated nutmeg over the top. Bake for 40–45 minutes until the pudding is risen and golden brown. Serve hot.

Energy 294Kcal/1237kJ; Protein 9.4g; Carbohydrate 43.2g, of which sugars 21.8g; Fat 10.4g, of which saturates 3.7g; Cholesterol 44mg; Calcium 180mg; Fibre 2.3g; Sodium 248mg.

PEAR, ALMOND and GROUND RICE PIE

Ground rice gives a distinctive, slightly grainy texture to puddings that goes particularly well with autumn fruit. Pears and almonds are a divine combination.

2 Place the butter and caster sugar in a mixing bowl and beat together using a wooden spoon or electric mixer until light and fluffy, then beat in the eggs, one at a time, and the almond extract. Fold in the flour and the ground rice.

3 Carefully spoon the creamed mixture over the quartered pears in the flan or pie dish and then level the surface with a palette knife or metal spatula.

4 Sprinkle the flaked almonds evenly over the top of the creamed mixture, then bake the flan for about 30 minutes, or until the topping springs back when touched lightly and is a golden brown colour. Serve warm or cold with custard or crème fraîche.

SERVES 6

4 ripe pears
25g/1oz/2 tbsp soft light brown sugar
115g/4oz/½ cup unsalted (sweet) butter,
    at room temperature
115g/4oz/generous ½ cup caster
    (superfine) sugar
2 eggs
a few drops of almond extract
75g/3oz/⅔ cup self-raising
    (self-rising) flour
50g/2oz/⅓ cup ground rice
25g/1oz/¼ cup flaked (sliced) almonds
pouring custard or crème fraîche,
    to serve

1 Preheat the oven to 180°C/350°F/ Gas 4. Grease a shallow 25cm/10in flan or pie dish, then peel and quarter the pears and arrange them in the dish. Sprinkle with the brown sugar.

Energy 396Kcal/1656kJ; Protein 5.2g; Carbohydrate 50.9g, of which sugars 34.8g; Fat 20.2g, of which saturates 10.7g; Cholesterol 104mg; Calcium 92mg; Fibre 2.9g; Sodium 190mg.

SPICED BLACKBERRY and APPLE CRUMBLE

Any fruit can be used in this popular dessert, but you can't beat the favourites of blackberry and apple. Hazelnuts and cardamom seeds give the topping extra flavour.

SERVES 4–6

butter, for greasing
450g/1lb tart cooking apples
115g/4oz/1 cup blackberries
grated rind and juice of 1 orange
50g/2oz/¼ cup soft light brown sugar
custard, to serve

For the topping
175g/6oz/1½ cups plain (all-purpose) flour
75g/3oz/6 tbsp butter
75g/3oz/⅓ cup caster (superfine) sugar
25g/1oz/¼ cup chopped hazelnuts
2.5ml/½ tsp crushed cardamom seeds

VARIATIONS

This pudding can be made with all kinds of fruit. Try plums, apricots, peaches or pears, alone or in combination with apples. Rhubarb is especially good when partnered with bananas.

1 Preheat the oven to 200°C/400°F/ Gas 6. Generously butter a 1.2 litre/ 2 pint/5 cup baking dish. Peel and core the apples, then slice them into the prepared baking dish. Level the surface with the back of a spoon, then sprinkle the blackberries over. Sprinkle the orange rind and light brown sugar evenly over the top, then pour over the orange juice. Set the fruit mixture aside while you make the crumble topping.

2 Sift the flour into a large bowl and rub in the butter until the mixture resembles coarse breadcrumbs. Stir in the caster sugar, hazelnuts and cardamom seeds, then sprinkle the topping over the top of the fruit.

3 Press the topping around the edges of the dish to seal in the juices. Bake for 30–35 minutes, or until the crumble is golden. Serve hot, with custard.

Energy 336Kcal/1413kJ; Protein 4g; Carbohydrate 53.2g, of which sugars 30.8g; Fat 13.4g, of which saturates 6.8g; Cholesterol 27mg; Calcium 72mg; Fibre 3g; Sodium 81mg.

TARTE TATIN

This upside-down apple tart is remarkably easy to make – especially if you use ready-rolled pastry. The apples are cooked in butter and sugar to make a caramel topping.

SERVES 6–8

3 eating apples
juice of ½ lemon
50g/2oz/¼ cup butter, softened
75g/3oz/⅓ cup caster (superfine) sugar
250g/9oz ready-rolled puff pastry
cream, to serve

COOK'S TIPS
• Tarte Tatin is a popular traditional French dessert. It is basically an upside-down apple pie cooked in a pan. The tart is inverted before serving to reveal a rich caramel topping.
• To turn out the tarte Tatin, place the serving plate upside down on top of it, then, protecting your arms with oven gloves, hold both pan and plate firmly together and deftly turn them over. Lift off the pan.

I Preheat the oven to 220°C/425°F/Gas 7. Cut the apples in quarters and then remove the cores. Toss the apple quarters in the lemon juice.

2 Spread the butter over the base of a 20cm/8in heavy, ovenproof omelette pan. Sprinkle the caster sugar over the base of the pan and arrange the apple wedges on top, rounded side down.

3 Cook over a medium heat for about 15 minutes, or until the sugar and butter have melted and the apples are golden. Cut the pastry into a 25cm/10in round and place on top of the apples; tuck the edges in with a knife. Place the pan in the oven and bake for 15–20 minutes or until the pastry is golden. Carefully invert the tart on to a serving plate, then cool slightly before serving with cream.

Energy 208Kcal/872kJ; Protein 1.9g; Carbohydrate 23.5g, of which sugars 12.4g; Fat 12.8g, of which saturates 3.3g; Cholesterol 13mg; Calcium 25mg; Fibre 0.4g; Sodium 136mg.

BLACK CHERRY CLAFOUTIS

Clafoutis is a batter pudding that originated in the Limousin area of central France. It is often made with cream in place of milk and traditionally uses slightly tart black cherries.

SERVES 6

butter, for greasing
450g/1lb/2 cups fresh black
  cherries, pitted
25g/1oz/¼ cup plain (all-purpose) flour
50g/2oz/½ cup icing (confectioner's) sugar,
  plus extra for dusting
4 eggs, beaten
250ml/8fl oz/1 cup full-cream
  (whole) milk
30ml/2 tbsp cherry liqueur, such as Kirsch
  or maraschino
vanilla ice cream, to serve

1 Preheat the oven to 180°C/350°F/ Gas 4. Grease a 1.2 litre/2 pint/5 cup baking dish and add the cherries.

2 Sift the flour and icing sugar into a large mixing bowl, then gradually whisk in the beaten eggs until the mixture is smooth. Whisk in the milk until well blended, then stir in the liqueur.

3 Pour the batter into the baking dish and then stir gently to ensure that the cherries are evenly distributed. Transfer to the oven and bake for about 40 minutes, or until just set and light golden brown. Insert a small knife into the centre of the pudding to test if it is cooked in the middle; the blade should come out clean.

4 Allow the pudding to cool for at least 15 minutes, then dust liberally with icing sugar just before serving, either warm or at room temperature. Vanilla ice cream makes a good accompaniment.

VARIATIONS
Try other fruit or nut liqueurs in this dessert. Almond-flavoured liqueur is delicious teamed with cherries, while hazelnut, raspberry or orange liqueurs will also work well. Other fruits that can be used in this pudding include blackberries, blueberries, plums, peaches, nectarines and apricots.

Energy 167Kcal/704kJ; Protein 6.7g; Carbohydrate 23.8g, of which sugars 20.6g; Fat 4.5g, of which saturates 1.5g; Cholesterol 129mg; Calcium 89mg; Fibre 0.8g; Sodium 66mg.

LEMON SURPRISE PUDDING

This is a much-loved dessert that many of us remember from childhood. The surprise is the unexpected sauce concealed beneath the delectable sponge.

SERVES 4

50g/2oz/¼ cup butter, plus extra
   for greasing
grated rind and juice of 2 lemons
115g/4oz/½ cup caster (superfine) sugar
2 eggs, separated
50g/2oz/½ cup self-raising (self-rising) flour
300ml/½ pint/1¼ cups milk

1 Preheat the oven to 190°C/375°F/
Gas 5. Use a little butter to grease a
1.2 litre/2 pint/5 cup baking dish.

COOK'S TIP
Lemons are often waxed before packing.
If a recipe uses the rind of the lemons
either buy unwaxed lemons or scrub the
peel thoroughly to remove the wax.

2 Beat the lemon rind, remaining butter
and caster sugar in a bowl until pale and
fluffy. Add the egg yolks and flour and
beat together well. Gradually whisk in
the lemon juice and milk (don't be
alarmed – the mixture will curdle
horribly). In a grease-free bowl, whisk
the egg whites until they form stiff peaks.

3 Fold the egg whites lightly into the
lemon mixture using a metal spoon, then
pour into the prepared baking dish.

4 Place the dish in a roasting pan and
pour in hot water to come halfway up
the side of the dish. Bake for 45 minutes
until golden. Serve immediately.

Energy 319Kcal/1341kJ; Protein 7g; Carbohydrate 43.1g, of which sugars 33.8g; Fat 14.5g, of which saturates 8.1g; Cholesterol 126mg; Calcium 166mg; Fibre 0.4g; Sodium 190mg.

INDEX

Technical Communication
Canadian Edition

John M. Lannon
UNIVERSITY OF MASSACHUSETTS

Don Klepp
OKANAGAN UNIVERSITY COLLEGE

LONGMAN

Addison Wesley Longman
Toronto

Canadian Cataloguing in Publication Data

Lannon, John M.
   Technical communication

Canadian ed.
Includes index.
ISBN 0-201-61379-4

1. Technical writing.   2. Communication of technical information.
I. Klepp, Don, 1944–.   II. Title.

T11.L36 2000   808'.0666   C99-932716-X

ISBN 0-201-61379-4
Vice President, Editorial Director: Laura Pearson
Acquisitions Editor: David Stover
Marketing Manager: Sophia Fortier
Developmental Editor: Laura Paterson Forbes
Production Editor: Cathy Zerbst
Production Coordinator: Wendy Moran
Art Director: Mary Opper
Interior Design: Kyle Gell
Cover Design: Kevin Connolly
Cover Image: Sherman Hines/Masterfile
Page Layout: Quadratone

1 2 3 4 5   04 03 02 01 00

Printed and bound in Canada.

Visit the Prentice Hall Canada Web site! Send us your comments, browse our catalogues, and more at www.phcanada.com.

Brief Contents

Contents

Web Connect

Chapter 1

www.smartbiz.com/sbs/cats/comm.htm
http://www.inkspot.com/genres/tech.html
http://www.chss.iup.edu/wc/resources/
http://www.stcloudstate.edu/~scogdill/collaboration/biblio.html
http://owl.english.purdue.edu/files/101.html

Chapter 2

http://www.inkspot.com/genres/tech.html
http://www.chss.iup.edu/wc/resources/audience.html

Chapter 3

http://www.clarkson.edu/~wcenter/draft.html

Chapter 4

http://www.tc.cc.va.us/writcent/handouts/writing/argument.htm
http://www.wuacc.edu/services/zzcwwctr/you-attitude.txt

Chapter 5

http://www.yorku.ca/faculty/osgoode/ohlj/search_by_subject.html
http://www.siu.edu/departments/coba/mgmt/iswnet/isethics/biblio/part5.htm

Chapter 6

www.monash.com/spidap.html   A comprehensive guide to search engines
www.megresearch.com/focus.html
http://www.mtroyal.ab.ca/programs/academserv/lib/Timesavers/tswrit.htm

Chapter 7

http://discoveryschool.com/schrockguide/eval.html

Chapter 8

www.english.uiuc.edu/cws/wworkshop/bibliostyles.htm
www.westwords.com./guffey/students.html

http://www.columbia.edu/cu/cup/cgos/idx_basic.html

Chapter 9

http://www.english.uiuc.edu/cws/wworkshop/summaries.htm
http://www.esc.edu/htmlpages/writer/menub.htm
http://www.chss.iup.edu/wc/resources/summary.html

Chapter 10

http://www.inkspot.com/genres/tech.html

Chapter 11

http://owl.english.purdue.edu/Files/90.html
www.stetson.edu/~hansen/writguid.html
http://andromeda.rutgers.edu/~jlynch/Writing/
www.sti.larc.nasa.gov/html/Chapt3/Chapt3-TOC.html
www.gsu.edu/~esljmm/studyskills/writing.htm
www.spartanburg2.k12.sc.us/links/grammar.htm
http://www.io.com/~hcexres/tcm1603/acchtml/lists.html

Chapter 12

www.arcm.com/illustra.html
http://ltid.grc.nasa.gov/Publishing/graphics/samillus.htm
www.darkstar.engr.wisc.edu/zwickel/397/graphexc.html
www.arcm.com/techill.html
http://ltid.grc.nasa.gov/Publishing/graphics/

Chapter 13

http://trace.wisc.edu/world/web/

Chapter 14

http://www.rpgroup.org/define.shtml
http://www.pinellas.k12.fl.us/qa/stratplan/opdef.htm
http://www.kcmetro.cc.mo.us/longview/ctac/psychexer1.htm
http://www.lhup.edu/~dsimanek/glossary.htm
http://www.io.com/~hcexres/tcm1603/acchtml/def_ex.html

Chapter 15

http://www.cisco.com/warp/public/cc/cisco/mkt/servprod/voip/prodlit/ptelb_rg.htm
http://english.ttu.edu/grad/AHanson/2309/description.html
http://www.uwec.edu/Academic/Curric/jerzdg/English305/formats/mechanism.htm
http://www.dsu.edu/departments/liberal/english/techwrit/

Chapter 16

http://www.cisco.com/warp/public/cc/cisco/mkt/servprod/voip/prodlit/ptelb_rg.htm
http://www.cpmc.org/liver/process.htm

http://www.microsoft.com/opentype/otspec/ttch01.htm
http://www.fishingnorthwest.com/flypterns.htm
http://www.dsu.edu/departments/liberal/english/techwrit/

Chapter 17

http://www.westworld.com/~ayale/TechWrtg.html
http://www.animatedsoftware.com/hightech/donaldno.htm
http://pip.dknet.dk/~pip323/index.html

Chapter 18

http://www.uspto.gov/web/offices/ac/comp/proc/acquisitions/itpa/itpa-rfp.htm
http://contractscanada.gc.ca
http://www.io.com/~hcexres/tcm1603/acchtml/props.html
http://darkstar.engr.wisc.edu/zwickel/397/397refs.html

Chapter 19

http://search.netscape.com/cgi-bin/search?search=+technical+reports
http://www.lerc.nasa.gov/WWW/STI/editing/chp3.htm
http://jaring.nmhu.edu/Chaut98/rwojtecki/report.html
http://www.cics.uvic.ca/climate/change/cimpact.htm
http://www.newenergy.org/newenergy/publications.html
www.ec.gc.ca
http://www.pipeline.com/~bkyaffe/altfuel/

Chapter 20

None

Chapter 21

http://www.io.com/~hcexres/tcm1603/acchtml/progrepx2a_non.html
http://www.ecf.toronto.edu/~writing/shrtrept.htm#Attachments
www.rpi.edu/dept/llc/writecenter/web/text/labreport.html
www.iit.edu/~writer/mmae_out.htm engineering
http://www.io.com/~hcexres/tcm1603/acchtml/progrep.html
http://www.io.com/~hcexres/tcm1603/acchtml/feas.html

Chapter 22

Letters and Memos:
www.smartbiz.com/sbs/arts/bly48.htm
www.wuacc.edu:80/services/zzcwwctr/you-attitude.txt
www.rpi.edu/dept/llc/writecenter/web/text/memo.html

E-mail Usage:
www.wadham.ox.ac.uk/graphics/rules/etiquette.html
www.pimall.com/nais/n.pgp.faq.html
insight.mcmaster.ca/org/efc/efc.html

Chapter 23
Résumés:
http://www.contractengineering.com/data1/ResCivil.htm
www.golden.net/~archeus/reswri.htm
www.careermosaic.com/cm/crc/crc15.html
www.provenresumes.com
www.stantongp.com/resume.htm
www.hiwriting.com
Job Market Research:
www.kenevacorp.mb.ca/
www.monster.com/home.html
www.jobtrak.com/jobguide/what-now.html
www.cacee.com
www.irus.vri.uwo.ca/~jlaw/job_can.html
www.schoolnet.ca/ngr
www.careermosaic.com
www.careerpath.com
www.tripod.com/tripod/
www.webpost.net/th/TheJobMarket/employ.html
www.sfu.ca/jfremont/jobs.html

Chapter 24
Preparing Speeches:
speeches.com/index.shtml
www.columbia.edu/acis/br\artleby/bartlett
www.coffingo.com/doc/tjwrite.html
www.mwc.edu/~bchirico/psanxinf.html
speeches.com/writer.html
www.access.digex.net/~nuance/keystep1.html
www.eeicom.com/eye/shyness.html
Technical Presentations:
www.ieee.org/pcs/creimold.html
www.botany.uwc.ac.za/botany/talks.htm
www.access.digex.net/~nuance/keystep1.html
darkstar.engr.wisc.edu/zwickel/397/presgraf.html
www.eeicom/eye/shyness.html

Chapter 25
None

Preface

Technical Communication, First Canadian Edition, provides a comprehensive, flexible introduction to technical and professional communication. This book focuses primarily on writing, but it also discusses interpersonal and group collaborative processes, oral communications, intercultural communication, and information-gathering methods.

This edition is based on the 7th and 8th U.S. editions of John Lannon's *Technical Writing*. A Canadian edition was commissioned to meet the requirements of Canadian students and workplace writers. Thus, this new edition presents Canadian examples and Canadian perspective throughout.

Organization

The text has five main sections:

Part I: Primary Considerations (Chapters 1–5) considers the bases of successful technical and workplace communication: the nature of technical writing and other forms of workplace communication; rhetorical analysis (of the sender's purpose and the receiver's needs and priorities); and a process for writing effective documents quickly. Factors in persuasive communication and the ethics of persuading others round out Part I.

Part II: Information Gathering, Analysis, and Manipulation (Chapters 6–9) illustrates various stages of successful research. Students learn to formulate useful research questions; to explore primary and secondary sources (including electronic sources); to record, evaluate, interpret, and document their findings; and to summarize for economy, accuracy, and emphasis.

Part III: Structural, Style, and Format Elements (Chapters 10–13) demonstrates strategies for organizing and expressing messages that readers can follow and understand. Students learn to control their material and to develop a style that connects with readers. Also, students learn to enhance a document's readability and appeal by using page design, graphics, and visuals.

Part IV: Descriptive Writing (Chapters 14–17) applies principles of audience/purpose analysis, style, and format to descriptive writing: definitions, descriptions, instructions, and manuals. Students learn to clearly distinguish among varieties of descriptive writing in order to choose effective structures and phrasing.

Part V: Applications (Chapters 18–25) applies earlier concepts and strategies to the preparation of proposals, reports, and workplace correspondence, all of which are illustrated by examples taken from workplace and student communication. The concluding chapters on job-search communications and oral presentations demonstrate strategies for "real-world" success.

Finally, the Appendix offers a brief handbook of grammar, usage, and mechanics.

The Foundations of Technical Writing

- More than a value-neutral exercise in "information transfer," workplace communication—whether handwritten, electronically mediated, or face-to-face—is a complex social transaction. Each rhetorical situation places specific interpersonal, ethical, legal, and cultural demands on the message sender.

- Writers with no rhetorical awareness overlook the decisions that are crucial for effective writing. However, defining their rhetorical challenge and asking the important questions allow writers to meet that challenge.

- As well as being *communicators,* today's workplace professionals increasingly are *consumers* of information, who need to be skilled in the methods of enquiry, retrieval, evaluation, and interpretation that comprise the research process.

- Successful workplace writing requires an organized, sensible, efficient approach. Only rarely does the workplace writer use the discovery process frequently used by the academic essay writer. People at work can't afford the time to write, and re-write, and re-write again.

- A technical writing classroom typically contains an assortment of students with varied backgrounds. *Technical Communication* offers thorough explanations, broadly intelligible examples and models, and practical methods for dealing with workplace demands. Moreover, it is flexible enough to allow for various course plans.

New to This Edition

- Concepts, structures, and techniques are illustrated by current *Canadian* and international examples.

- Chapter 2 presents an expanded explanation of the factors to consider in analyzing the audiences for one's written and spoken messages.

- Chapter 3 is designed to help writers produce documents efficiently.

- Material retained from Lannon's 7th edition has been condensed and, in some cases reorganized, for greater clarity, conciseness, and emphasis.

- New information about Internet research techniques is accompanied by advice on how to evaluate Internet sources. There is also a comprehensive list of useful Web sites on pages xiii–xvi.

- Chapter 11 adds objective indexes designed to help writers evaluate and improve the readability of their writing.

- Chapter 13 presents new advice about headings format. This advice is designed to make the sample headings adaptable to a wide range of applications and to reflect current usage.

- Chapter 16 clearly distinguishes among process analyses, instructions, and procedures.

- A new chapter, 17, discusses the content and structure of a variety of manuals and describes a process for them.

- Chapter 18 presents a new approach to planning and producing proposals.

- Chapter 19 is a fully revised version of Lannon's 7th Edition chapter on formal analytical reports.

- Chapter 21, dealing with short reports, presents all new material, including expanded sections on progress reports and other commonly written reports. The chapter features an action structure that can be adapted to various reports.

- The chapter on workplace correspondence, Chapter 22, combines discussions of letters, memos, e-mail, and faxes. The chapter incorporates some material from the 7th edition, but the material has been substantially rewritten from a current Canadian perspective. New material on e-mail issues, fax usage, Canadian format standards, and an action structure for workplace messages highlight this chapter.

- Chapter 23 presents a step-by-step process for gaining a position, which will help the successful candidate find job satisfaction, not just a job with a salary. The chapter has new self-help material and current examples of job-search materials.

- Chapter 24 takes a positive approach to preparing for oral presentations. The chapter adds advice about impromptu speaking and a self-evaluation exercise.

- Chapter 25 provides detailed information on Web pages, including guidelines for creating a Web site.

Acknowledgments

Much of the new material in this edition has been requested by the following perceptive reviewers, who participated in a Canada-wide review of the 7th edition: Trish Campbell, Red Deer College; Ann Gasior, Okanagan

University College; Anne Mackenzie-Rivers, George Brown College; Lance Moen, Saskatchewan Institute of Applied Science and Technology; and Mary Silas, Concordia University. Jennie Bedford has added insights and updated information about workplace writing.

Student contributors Chris Hendsbee, Grant Perkins, Thanh Pham, Todd Trann, and Curtis Willis have generously allowed their work to be included in this book. Civil Engineering Technology students at Okanagan University College have tested new chapters of this edition. Their comments have been very helpful. In particular, Tim Audy and Richard Ferrier have suggested practical changes.

Ross Tyner and Garth Homer, Okanagan University College librarians, have been very helpful in identifying the new array of research tools available to student and workplace researchers.

A special thank-you goes to my wife, Betty Chan Klepp, whose patience and support has allowed me to complete this project.

Don Klepp

The *Inukshuk*, featured on the cover, is an example of a traditional method of communication still used today by the Native and Inuit people of northern Canada and the Arctic. Built with rocks, ice, or anything found in nature, the *Inukshuk* is created in human form, often in such a large size that it can be seen from a great distance away.

An *Inukshuk* is a signpost. It can be found on land or water and often indicates the direction of safe passage, a body of water, or a store of supplies. The limbs of an *Inukshuk* are constructed to communicate the vicinity of these important landmarks to the weary Arctic traveller.

Introduction to Technical Writing

A S A TECHNICAL writer, you communicate and interpret specialized information for your readers' use. Readers may need your information to perform a task, answer a question, solve a problem, or make a decision. Whether you write a memo, letter, report, or manual, the document must advance the goals of your readers and of the company or organization you represent.

Technical Writing Serves Practical Needs

Unlike poetry or fiction, which appeal mainly to our *imagination*, technical documents appeal to our *understanding*. Technical writing therefore rarely seeks to entertain, create suspense, or invite differing interpretations. Those of you who have written any type of lab or research report already know that technical writing has little room for ambiguity.

To serve practical needs in the workplace, technical documents must be reader oriented and efficient.

Technical Documents Meet Reader Needs

Instead of focusing on the writer's desire for self-expression, a technical document addresses the reader's desire for information. This doesn't mean your writing should sound like something produced by a robot, without any personality (or *voice*) at all. Your document may in fact reveal a lot about you (your competence, knowledge, integrity, and so on), but it rarely focuses on you personally. Readers are interested in *what you have done*, in *what you recommend*, or in *how you speak for your company*; they have only a professional interest in *who you are* (your feelings, hopes, dreams, visions). A personal essay, then, would not be technical writing. Consider this essay fragment:

Focuses on the feelings

> Computers are not a particularly forgiving breed. The wrong key struck or the wrong command entered is almost sure to avenge itself on the inattentive user by banishing the document to some electronic trash can.

This personal view communicates a good deal about the writer's resentment and anxiety but very little about computers themselves.

The following example can be called technical writing because it focuses (see italics) on the subject, on what the writer has done, and on what the reader should do:

Focuses on the subject, actions taken, and actions required

> On MK 950 terminals, *the BREAK key* is adjacent to keys used for text editing and special functions. Too often, users inadvertently strike the BREAK key, causing the program to quit prematurely. To prevent the problem, *we have modified all database management terminals:* to quit a program, *you must now strike BREAK twice successively.*

This next example also can be called technical writing because it focuses on what the writer recommends:

*Focuses on the
recommendation*

> I recommend that our Linux server be upgraded. This expansion will (1) increase the number of simultaneous users from 60 to 80, (2) increase the system's responsiveness, and (3) provide sorely needed disk storage for word processing and company databases.

As the above example illustrates, documents should not make the writer "disappear," but they should focus on that which is most important to the readers.

Technical Documents Strive for Efficiency

Educators read to *test* our knowledge; colleagues, customers, and supervisors read to *use* our knowledge. Workplace readers hate waste and demand efficiency; instead of reading a document from beginning to end, they are more likely to use it for reference, and want only as much as they need: "When it comes to memos, letters, proposals, and reports, there's no extra credit for extra words. And no praise for elegant prose. Bosses want employees to get to the point—quickly, clearly, and concisely" (Spruell 32). Efficient documents save time, energy, and money in the workplace.

In any system, efficiency is the rate of useful output to input. For the product that comes out, how much energy goes in?

When a system is efficient, the output nearly equals the input.

Similarly, a document's efficiency can be measured by how hard readers work to understand the message. Is the product worth the reader's effort?

No reader should have to spend ten minutes deciphering a message worth only five minutes. Consider, for example, this wordy message:

An inefficient message

> At this point in time, we are presently awaiting an on-site inspection by vendor representatives relative to electrical utilization adaptations necessary for the new computer installation. Meanwhile, all staff are asked to respect the off-limits designation of said location, as requested, due to liability insurance provisions requiring the on-line status of the computer.

Inefficient documents drain the readers' energy; they are too easily misinterpreted; they waste time and money. Notice how hard you had to work with the previous message to extract information that could be expressed this efficiently:

A more efficient message

> Hardware consultants soon will inspect our new computer room to recommend appropriate wiring. Because our insurance covers only an *operational* computer, this room must remain off limits until the computer is fully installed.

When readers sense they are working too hard, they tune out the message—or they stop reading altogether.

Inefficient documents have varied origins. Even when the information is accurate, errors like the following make readers work too hard:

Causes of inefficient documents

- more (or less) information than readers need
- irrelevant or uninterpreted information
- confusing organization
- jargon or vague technical expressions readers cannot understand
- more words than readers need
- uninviting appearance or confusing layout
- no visual aids when readers need or expect them

An efficient document sorts, organizes, and interprets its information to suit the audience's needs, abilities, and interests.

Instead of merely happening, an efficient document is carefully designed to include these elements:

Elements of efficient documents

- *content* that makes the document worth reading
- *organization* that guides readers and emphasizes important material
- *style* that is economical and easy to read
- *visuals* (graphs, diagrams, pictures) that clarify concepts and relationships, and that substitute for words whenever possible
- *format* (layout, typeface) that is accessible and appealing
- *supplements* (abstracts, appendices) that enable readers with different needs to read only those sections required for their work

Reader orientation and efficiency are more than abstract rules: Writers are accountable for their documents. In questions of liability, faulty writing is no different from any other faulty product. If your inaccurate, or unclear, or incomplete information leads to injury, or damage, or loss, *you* can be held legally responsible.

Writing Is Part of Most Careers

Although you might not anticipate a career as a "writer," your writing skills will be tested routinely in situations like these:

Ways in which your career may test your writing skills

- proposing various projects to management or to clients
- writing progress reports to supervisors, managers, and executives
- contributing articles to employee newsletters
- describing a product to employees or customers
- writing procedures and instructions for employees or customers
- justifying to management a request for funding or personnel
- editing and reviewing documents written by colleagues
- designing material that will be read on a computer screen or transformed into sound and pictures

You might write alone or as part of a collaborative team, and you will face strict deadlines.

Your value to any organization will depend on how clearly and persuasively you communicate. Many working professionals spend at least 40 percent of their time writing or dealing with someone else's writing. The higher their position, the more they write (Barnum and Fisher 9–11). Here is a corporate executive's description of some audiences you can expect:

> The technical graduate entering industry today will, in all probability, spend a portion of his or her career explaining technology to lawyers—some friendly and some not—to consumers, to legislators or judges, to bureaucrats, to environmentalists and to representatives of the press. (Florman 23)

These audiences, among countless others, expect to read efficient documents.

Here is what two top managers for an automaker say about the effect a document can have on the organization *and* on the writer:

Writing is an indicator of job performance

> A written report is often the only record which is made of results that have come out of years of thought and effort. It is used to judge the value of the *person's* work and serves as the foundation for all future action on the project. If it is written clearly and precisely, it is accepted as the result of sound reasoning and careful observation. If it is poorly written, the results presented in it are placed in a bad light and are often dismissed as the work of a careless or incompetent worker. (Richards and Richards 6)

Good writing gives you and your ideas *visibility* and *authority* within your organization. Bad writing, on the other hand, is not only useless to readers and politically damaging to the writer, but also expensive: Written communication[1] in North American business and industry costs billions of dollars yearly. More than 60 percent of the writing is inefficient: unclear, misleading, irrelevant, deceptive, or otherwise wasteful of time and money (Max 5–6).

Whatever your career plans, you can expect to be a part-time technical writer. Employers first judge your writing by your application letter and résumé.

---

1. "Written communication" includes the full range of activities involved in preparing, producing, processing, storing, and retrieving documents for re-use.

In a large organization, your future may be decided by executives you've never met. One concrete measure of your job performance will be your letters, memos, and reports. As you advance, communication skill becomes more important than technical background. The higher your goals, the better you need to communicate.

The Information Age Requires Excellent Writing Skills

Desktop publishing (DTP) systems have eliminated clerical support positions in countless organizations. Gone are the days in which writers could count on secretarial help in "fixing up" a document. In today's electronic office, each writer is responsible for a document's creation, proofreading, editing, page layout, and distribution.

More importantly, information has become our prized commodity:

Information is the ultimate product

> The new source of wealth is not material; it is information, knowledge applied to work to create value. The pursuit of wealth is now largely the pursuit of information, and the application of information to the means of production. (Wriston 8)

In education, industry, business, and government, people create, gather, analyze, and distribute information electronically around the world. But whether the information itself finally appears on a printed page or a computer screen, it usually needs to be *written*. A computer can transmit information, but it cannot give *meaning* to the information—only the writer and reader can do so.

Computer networks have increased the speed and volume of communication, but excessive information actually can *impede* or *prevent* communication. Despite our advances in communication technology, information still needs to be processed by the human brain, as depicted in Figure 1.1 on page 9. Unfortunately, it is easy for people to process information erroneously (to wrongly interpret the *meaning*).

Accidents that make headlines often result from human error in processing information—situations in which the complexity of information overwhelms the person receiving it (Wickens 2). The 1979 release of radiation and near-meltdown at Three-Mile Island; the 1984 chemical explosion in Bhopal, India; the 1989 runway collision at Los Angeles airport—these disasters occurred because vital information had been misunderstood. Similar but less publicized disasters occur routinely in the workplace. Today, more than ever, writers need to sort, organize, and interpret their material so readers can understand it.

Today's readers often lack technical expertise, but they do *use* the technology. Some non-technical workers who rely on technology include the manager using a teleconferencing network, the data-entry clerk using a computer terminal, or the bank teller using a cheque-verification system. Writers tell laypeople how to use software, or how to operate hardware, medical equipment, telephone systems, precision instruments, and all types of automated products, from computer games to microwave ovens. With so much information required, and so much available, no writer can afford to "let the facts speak for themselves."

Figure 1.1   The Brain Processes Information to Find Meaning

IN BRIEF

Writing Reaches a Global Audience

Electronically linked, our global community shares social, political, and financial interests that demand cooperation as well as competition. Multi-national corporations often use parts that are manufactured in one country and shipped to another for assembly into a product that will be marketed elsewhere. For example, cars may be assembled in North America for a German automaker, or farm equipment may be manufactured in East Asia for a Canadian company. Medical, environmental, and other research crosses national boundaries, and professionals in all fields transact with colleagues from other cultures.

What kinds of documents might address global audiences? Here is a sample (Weymouth 143):

- Scientific reports and articles on AIDS and other diseases.
- Studies of global pollution and industrial emissions.
- Specifications for hydroelectric dams and other engineering projects.
- Operating instructions for appliances and electronic equipment.
- Catalogues, promotional literature, and repair manuals.
- Contracts and business agreements.

To communicate effectively across cultural and national boundaries, any document must respect not only language differences, but also *cultural* differences. One writer offers this helpful definition of *culture:*

Our accumulated knowledge and experiences, beliefs and values, attitudes and roles—in other words, our cultures—shape us as individuals and differentiate us as a people. Our cultures, inbred through family life, religious training, and educational and work experiences. . . . manifest themselves . . . in our thoughts and feelings, our actions and reactions, and our views of the world.

Most important for communicators, our cultures manifest themselves in our information needs and our styles of communication. In other words, our cultures define our expectations as to how information should be organized, what should be included in its content, and how it should be expressed. (Hein 125)

Cultures differ over which behaviours seem appropriate or inappropriate for social interaction, business relationships, contract negotiation, and communication practices. A communication style considered perfectly acceptable in one culture may be offensive elsewhere.

Effective communicators recognize these differences but withhold judgment or evaluation, focusing instead on *similarities*. For example, needs assessment and needs satisfaction know no international boundaries; technical solutions are technical solutions without regard to nationality, creed, or language; courtesy and goodwill are universal values. In the diverse global context, the writer's challenge is to establish trust and enhance human relationships.

 ★ ★ ★

Technical Writers Face Interrelated Challenges

No matter how sophisticated our communication technology, computers cannot *think* for us. More specifically, computers cannot offer solutions to the challenges encountered by all people who write in the technical professions. These challenges include:

- *the information challenge:* different readers in different situations have different information needs
- *the persuasion challenge:* people often disagree about what the information means and about what should be done
- *the ethics challenge:* the interests of your company may conflict with the interests of your readers
- *the global context challenge:* diverse people work together on information for a diverse audience

An earlier section of this chapter explains that information has to have meaning for its audience. But people differ in their interpretations of facts, and so they may need persuading that one viewpoint is preferable to another. Persuasion, however, is a powerful and sometimes unethical strategy. Even the most useful and efficient document could deceive or harm. Therefore, solving the persuasion challenge doesn't mean manipulating readers by using "whatever works," but rather building a case from honest and reasonable interpretation of the facts. Figure 1.2 offers one way of visualizing how these challenges relate.

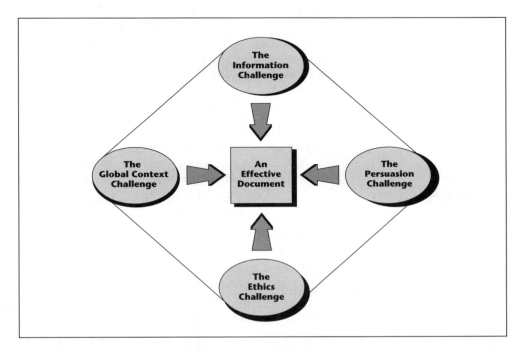

Figure 1.2   Writers Face Four Related Challenges

The scenarios that follow illustrate how a typical professional confronts the challenges of communicating in the workplace.

The Information Challenge

"Can I provide accurate and useful information?"

Sarah Habib was hired two months ago as a chemical engineer for Millisun, a leading maker of cameras, multipurpose film, and photographic equipment. Sarah's first major assignment is to evaluate the plant's incoming and outgoing water. (Waterborne contaminants can taint film during production, and the production process itself can pollute outgoing water.) Management wants an answer to this question: How often should we change water filters? The filters are very expensive and difficult to change, halting production for up to a day at a time. The company wants as much usage as possible from these filters, without incurring government fines or tainting its film production.

Sarah will study endless printouts of chemical analysis, review current research, do some testing of her own, and consult with her colleagues. When she finally decides on what all the data mean, Sarah will prepare a recommendation report for her manager.

Later, she will collaborate with the company training manager and the maintenance supervisor to prepare a manual, instructing employees how to check and change the filters. Trying to cut administrative assistant and printing costs, the company has asked Sarah to design this manual using its desktop publishing system. ∎

Sarah's report, above all, needs to be accurate; otherwise, the company gets fined or lowers production. Once she has processed all of the information, she has to solve the challenge of giving readers what they need. She has to answer questions such as: *How much explaining should I do? How will I organize the information? Do I need visuals?* And so on.

In other situations, Sarah will face a persuasion challenge as well: for example, when decisions must be made or actions taken on the basis of incomplete or inconclusive facts or conflicting interpretations (Hauser 72). In these instances, Sarah will seek reader acceptance for *her* view. Her writing will have to be persuasive as well as informative.

The Persuasion Challenge

"Can I influence readers to see things my way?"

Millisun and other electronics producers are located on the shores of a small harbour, the port for a major fishing fleet. For twenty years, these companies discharged directly into the harbour effluents containing metal compounds, PCBs, and other toxins. Sarah is on a multi-company team, assigned to work with the Canadian Environmental Assessment Agency to clean up the harbour. Much of the team's collaboration occurs via electronic mail.

Enraged local citizens and environmental groups are demanding immediate action, and the companies themselves are anxious to end this public-relations nightmare. But the team's analysis reveals that any type of clean-up would stir up harbour sediment, possibly dispersing the solution into surrounding waters and the atmosphere. (Many of the contaminants are airborne.) Premature action actually might *increase* danger, but team members disagree on the degree of risk and on how to proceed.

Sarah's communication here takes on a persuasive dimension: She and her team members first have to resolve their own conflicts and produce an environmental-impact report that reflects the team's consensus. If the report recommends further study, Sarah will have to justify the delays to her manager and the public relations office. She will have to make readers understand the dangers as well as she understands them. ■

In the above situation, the facts are neither complete nor conclusive, and views differ about what these facts mean. Sarah will have to balance the various political pressures and make a case for *her* interpretation. Moreover, as company *spokesperson*, Sarah will be expected to take a position that protects her company's interests. Some elements of Sarah's persuasion challenge are: *Are other interpretations possible? Is there a better way? Can I expect political fallout?*

Whenever she writes, Sarah will have to reckon with the ethical implications of her writing, with the question of "doing the right thing." Some situations will present hard choices. For instance, Sarah might feel pressured to overlook, sugarcoat, or suppress facts that would be costly or embarrassing to her company. Sometimes the best technical solution to a challenge might be a poor solution in human terms (as when a heavy industry decreases local pollution by building a smokestack to disperse the emissions over hundreds of miles).

The Ethics Challenge

"Can I be honest and still keep my job?"

To ensure compliance with OHS[2], WCB[3], and WHMIS[4] regulations for worker safety, Sarah is assigned to test the air purification system in Millisun's chemical division. After finding the filters hopelessly clogged, she decides to test the air quality and discovers dangerous levels of benzene (a potent carcinogen). She reports these findings in a memo to the production manager, with an urgent recommendation that all employees be tested for benzene poisoning. The manager phones and tells Sarah to "have the filters replaced, and forget about it." Now Sarah has to decide what to do next: bury the memo in some file cabinet or defy her manager and send copies to other readers who might take action. ■

Situations that jeopardize truth and fairness present the hardest choices of all: remain silent and look the other way or speak out and risk being dismissed. Some elements of Sarah's ethics challenge are: *Is this fair? Who might benefit or suffer? What other consequences could this have?*

---

2. Occupational Health and Safety
3. Workers' Compensation Board
4. Workplace Hazardous Materials Information System

In addition to meeting these various challenges, Sarah has to reckon with the implications of communication technology: Much of her writing, done at the computer, will be produced in collaboration with others (editors, managers, graphic artists), and her audience will extend beyond her own culture.

The Global Context Challenge

"Can I connect with all these different audiences?"

Recent mergers have transformed Millisun into a multi-national corporation with branches in eleven countries, all connected by computer network. Sarah can expect to collaborate with co-workers from diverse cultures on research and development; and with government agencies of the host countries on safety issues, patents and licensing rights, product liability laws, and environmental concerns.

In order to standardize the sensitive management of the toxic, volatile, and even explosive chemicals used in film production, Millisun is developing automated procedures for quality control, troubleshooting, and emergency response to chemical leakage. Sarah has been assigned to work with a group of colleagues to prepare Web-based instructional packages for all personnel involved in Millisun's chemical management worldwide. ◼

Sarah will have to develop working relationships with people she has never met, people she knows only via an electronic medium.

For Sarah Habib or any of us, writing is a process of *discovering* what we want to say, "a way to end up thinking something [we] couldn't have started out thinking" (Elbow 15). Throughout this process in the workplace, we rarely work alone, but instead rely on others for information, help in writing, and feedback (Grice 29–30). We must satisfy not only our audience, but also our employer, whose goals and values ultimately shape the document (Selzer 46–47). Almost any writing for readers outside our organization will be *reviewed* for accuracy, appropriateness, usefulness, and legality before it is finally approved (Kleimann 521).

Many Technical Writers Collaborate

Electronic communication allows more and more writing to be done collaboratively. Workplace documents (especially long reports, proposals, or manuals) are produced by teams who share information, expertise, ideas, and responsibilities. Production of a software manual, for instance, relies on writers, programmers, software engineers, graphic artists, editors, reviewers, marketing personnel, and lawyers (Debs, "Recent Research" 477).

Successful collaboration brings together the best that each team member has to offer. It enhances critical thinking by providing feedback, new perspectives, group support, and the chance to test one's ideas in group discussion.

Not all members of a collaborative team do the actual writing; some might research, edit, proofread, or test the document's *usability*. But even a document with a single author can be a collaborative product, as depicted in Figure 1.3. The more important the document, the more it will be reviewed.

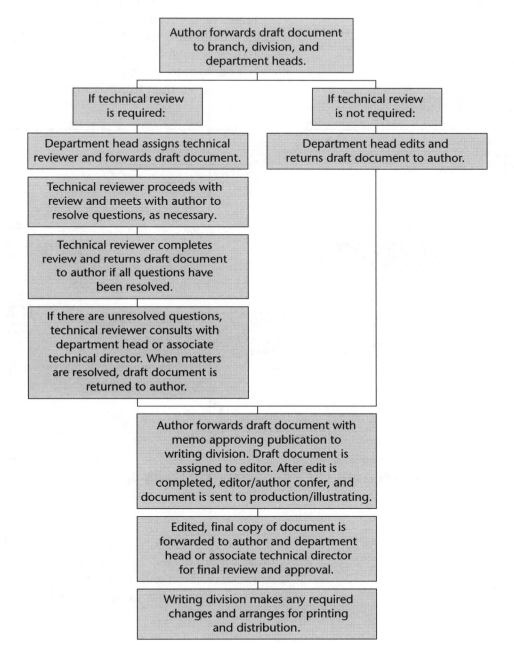

Figure 1.3   How One Organization Collaborates to Produce a Report
Adapted from *NUSC Technical Publication Guidelines.* Naval Underwater Systems Center, Technical Information Dept.

As in any group effort, collaborative writers can experience the types of conflict depicted in Figure 1.4. Members might fail to get along because of differences in personality, working style, commitment, standards, or ability to take criticism. Some might disagree about exactly what or how much the group should accomplish, who should do what, or who should have the final say. Some might feel intimidated or hesitant to speak out.[5] These interpersonal problems actually can worsen when the group communicates exclusively via e-mail.

Figure 1.4   How Pressures of a Group Effort Can Add Up

In any group, members have to find ways of expressing their views persuasively, of accepting constructive criticism, or getting along and reaching agreement with others who hold different views. These skills are essential for overcoming personal differences so that the group can achieve its goal.

---

5. Adapted from Bogert and Butt 51; Burnett 533–34; Hill Duin 45–46; Debs, "Collaborative Writing" 38; Nelson and Smith 61.

Guidelines for Writing Collaboratively

The following guidelines[6] focus on projects in which people meet face-to-face but can apply as well to electronically mediated collaboration.

1. *Appoint a project or group manager.* This person assigns tasks, enforces deadlines, conducts meetings, consults with supervisors, and generally runs the show.

2. *Define a clear and definite goal.* Compose a purpose statement that spells out the project's goal and the group's plan for achieving it. Be sure each member understands the goal.

3. *Decide how the group will be organized.* Some possibilities:

   a. The group researches and plans together, but each person writes a different part of the document.

   b. Some members plan and research; one person writes a complete draft; others review, edit, revise, and produce the final version.

   Whatever the arrangement, the final revision should display a consistent style throughout—as if written by one person only.

4. *Divide the task.* Who will be responsible for which parts of the document or which phases of the project? Should one person alone do the final revision? Which jobs are the most difficult? Who is best at doing what (writing, editing, layout, graphics, oral presentation)? Who will make final decisions?

5. *Establish a timetable.* Specific completion dates for each phase will keep everyone focused on what is due, and when.

6. *Decide on a meeting schedule and format.* How often will the group meet, and for how long? In or out of office? Who will take notes (or minutes)? Will the supervisor attend or participate?

7. *Establish a procedure for responding to the work of other members.* Will reviewing and editing be done in writing, face-to-face, as a group, one-on-one, or via computer? Will this process be supervised by the project manager?

8. *Establish procedures for dealing with group problems.* How will gripes and disagreements be aired (to the manager, the whole group, the offending individual)? How will disputes be resolved (by vote, the manager)? How will irrelevant discussion be avoided or curtailed? Expect some conflict, but try to use it positively, and try to identify a natural peacemaker in the group.

9. *Decide how to evaluate each member's contribution.* Will the manager assess each member's performance and, in turn, be evaluated by each member? Will members evaluate each other? What are the criteria?

---

6. Adapted from Debs, "Collaborative Writing" 38–41; Hill-Duin 45–46; Hulbert, "Developing" 53–54; McGuire 467–68; Morgan 540–41.

Figure 1.5 depicts one possible form for a manager's evaluation of members. Equivalent criteria for evaluating the manager include open mindedness, ability to organize the team, fairness in assigning tasks, ability to resolve conflicts, or ability to motivate. (Members might keep a journal of personal observations, for overall evaluation of the project.)

10. *Prepare a project management plan.* Figure 1.6 depicts a sample plan sheet. Distribute completed copies to members.

11. *Submit progress reports regularly.* Progress reports enable everyone to track activities, problems, and rate of progress.

Beyond these guidelines, respect for other people's views and willingness to listen are essential ingredients for successful collaboration.

Performance Appraisal for _____
(After each item place an X in the column that applies.)

	Superior	**Acceptable**	**Unacceptable**
Dependability			
Cooperation			
Effort			
Quality of work			
Ability to meet deadlines			

Project Manager's signature

Figure 1.5   Sample Form for Evaluating Team Members

Management Plan Sheet

Project title:

Audience:

Project manager:

Team members:

Purpose statement:

Specific Assignments	**Due Dates**
Research:	Research due:
Planning:	Plan and outline due:
Drafting:	First draft due:
Revising:	Reviews due:
Preparing final document:	Revisions due:
Presenting oral briefing:	Final document due:
	Progress report(s) due:

Work Schedule

Group meetings:	*Date*	*Place*	*Time*	*Note-taker*
#1				
#2				
#3				
etc.				
Mtgs. w/manager				
#1				
#2				
etc.				

Miscellaneous

How will disputes and grievances be resolved?

How will performances be evaluated?

Other matters (Internet searches, e-mail routing, computer conferences, etc.)?

Figure 1.6   Sample Plan Sheet for Managing a Collaborative Project

Effective Roles in Groups[7]

Groups function best when certain key roles are established and followed. Two main types of roles have been identified: *task roles* and *maintenance roles*. Often, such roles are established informally.

Task Roles. In order to accomplish its set task, a group has to have its members successfully complete a number of task roles. Some people play one or two of these roles almost exclusively, but most people slide easily in and out of most of the roles.

- *initiators* propose and define tasks; they also suggest solutions to problems or ways of solving problems
- *information seekers* notice where facts are needed; they push the group to find those facts. *Information givers* have the information at hand or they know how to find the needed information.
- *opinion seekers* actively canvas group members for their ideas and opinions concerning a problem. *Opinion givers* volunteer input, respond readily when asked, and help set the criteria for solving problems.
- *summarizers* draw together various ideas, facts, and opinions into a coherent whole; they review solutions, decisions, or problem-solving criteria. Often, the summarizing role is assumed by the group's elected chair or appointed manager.

Group Maintenance Roles. All successful groups need a supportive group climate in order for group members to give their best efforts. A positive group climate does not usually happen by accident; members have to consciously perform some of the following roles in order to develop and sustain a good working relationship.

- *encouragers* help other group members feel accepted and valued. In particular, they go out of their way to reward those group members who are shy or lazy about contributing to the group's tasks.
- *feeling expressers* try to get all group members to state their feelings about the group and those members' roles in the group.
- *harmonizers* help deal with unproductive conflict by removing the personal, emotional aspects of disputes and concentrating on the objective issues. They recognize the good points made by the respective disputants and they help the "warring members" recognize the merits of each other's positions.
- *gatekeepers* try to draw quiet group members into the discussion so that the louder, more aggressive group members do not dominate. When everyone contributes, two main advantages result: (1) the group has a better chance of getting the ideas and information it needs, and (2) group morale improves.

---

7. Source: Barker, Larry J. et al. *Groups in Process*. Third edition. Englewood Cliffs, New Jersey: Prentice-Hall, Inc., 1987.

IN BRIEF

Gender and Cultural Differences in Collaborative Groups

Any collaborative effort stands the best chance of succeeding when each group member feels included. A big mistake is to ignore personal differences, to assume everyone shares one viewpoint, one communication style, one approach to problem solving.

Collaboration often involves working with peers—those considered of equal status, rank, and expertise. In addition to the personality differences that lead to group conflict, gender and cultural differences in collaborative groups can create perceptions of inequality.

Gender Differences

Research on ways men and women communicate in meetings indicates a definite gender gap. Communication specialist Kathleen Kelley-Reardon offers this assessment of gender differences in workplace communication:

> "Women and men operate according to communication rules for their gender, what experts call 'gender codes.' They learn, for example, to show gratitude, ask for help, take control, and express emotion, defer-ence, and commitment in different ways." (88–89)

Professor Kelley-Reardon describes specific elements of a female gender code: Women are more likely than men to take as much time as needed to explore an issue, build consensus and relationship among members, use tact in expressing views, use care in choosing their words, consider the listener's feelings, speak softly, allow interruptions, make requests instead of giving commands ("Could I have the report by Friday?" versus "Have this ready by Friday."), preface assertions in ways that avoid offending ("I don't want to seem disagreeable here, but . . .").

One study of mixed-gender interaction among peers indicates that women tend to be more agreeable, solicit and admit the merits of other opinions, ask questions, and express uncertainty (e.g., with qualifiers such as *maybe, probably, it seems as if*) more often than men (Wojahn 747).

None of these traits, of course, is gender specific. Some people—regardless of gender—are more soft-spoken, contemplative, and reflective. But such traits most often are attributed to the "feminine" stereotype. Moreover, any woman who breaches the gender code, for instance, by being assertive, may be seen by peers as "too controlling" (Kelley-Reardon 6). In fact, studies suggest that women have less freedom than male peers to alter their communication strategies: less-assertive males often are still considered persuasive whereas more-assertive females often are not (Perloff 273).

Cultural Differences

International business expert David A. Victor describes cultural codes that influence inter-action in collaborative groups: Some cultures value silence more than speech, intuition and ambiguity more than hard evidence or data, politeness and personal relationships more than business relationships.

Cultures differ in their perceptions of time. Some want to get the job done immediately; others take as long as needed to weigh all the issues, engage in small talk and digressions, enquire about family, health, and other personal matters.

Cultures may differ in their willingness to express disagreement, question or be ques-tioned, leave things unstated, touch, shake hands, kiss, hug, or backslap.

IN BRIEF

Direct eye contact is not always a good indicator of listening. In some cultures it is offensive. Other eye movements such as squinting, closing the eyes, staring away, staring at legs or other body parts are acceptable in some cultures but insulting in others.

Influence of On-line Communication

Some observers argue that on-line communication eliminates many such problems encountered in face-to-face meetings, because every participant, in effect, has as much time as needed to contribute to the electronically mediated discussion. Also, "status cues" such as age, gender, appearance, or ethnicity virtually disappear on-line. Other observers disagree, arguing that the interpersonal chemistry of communication transcends specific media (Wojahn 747–48).

✔ EXERCISES

1. Locate a brief example of a technical document (or a section of one). Make a photocopy, bring it to class, and explain why your selection can be called technical writing.

2. Research the kinds of writing you will do in your future career. (Begin with the *Dictionary of Occupational Titles* in your library.) You might interview a member of your chosen profession. Why will you write on the job? For whom will you write? Explain in a memo to your instructor. (See Chapter 22 for memo elements and format.)

3. In a memo to your instructor, describe the skills you seek to develop in your technical writing course. How exactly will you apply these skills to your career?

4. Assume a friend in your major thinks that writing skills are obsolete, and that administrative assistants or word processors can fix any writing. Write your friend a letter, explaining why you think these assumptions are mistaken. Use examples to support your position. (See Chapter 22 for letter elements and format.)

✔ COLLABORATIVE PROJECT

Divide into small groups of mixed genders. Read "In Brief" (pages 21–22) and complete the following tasks to test the hypothesis that women and men communicate differently in the workplace.

Each group member prepares the following brief messages—without consulting with other members:

- A thank-you note to a co-worker who has done you a favour.
- A note asking a co-worker for help with a problem or project.
- A note asking a collaborative peer to be more cooperative or stop interrupting or complaining.
- A note expressing impatience, frustration, confusion, or satisfaction to members of your group.
- A recommendation for a friend who is applying for a position with your company.
- A note offering support to a good friend and co-worker.
- A note to a new colleague, welcoming this person to the company.
- A request for a raise, based on your hard work.
- The meeting is out of hand, so you decide to take control. Write what you would say.
- Some members of your group are dragging their feet on a project. Write what you would say.

As a group, compare messages, draw conclusions about the original hypothesis, and appoint one member to present the findings to the class.

Preparing to Write:
Audience/Purpose Analysis

As a TECHNICAL writer, you'll need to know your reader's needs, in order to meet those needs. At the same time, you'll need to consider your own role needs. Perhaps you want to persuade your reader to support a proposal; perhaps you are simply responding to your supervisor's request for information about your progress on a project. Whatever you write, you must first think very carefully about your audience and your purpose for writing.

Actually, you should analyze your audience and purpose for *any* kind of technical or business communication, written or spoken. For example, when you prepare for a job interview, you need to consider more than the points you hope to make about your qualifications and skills; you also need to consider what the interviewer hopes to accomplish by interviewing you. By analyzing the interviewer's role-dominated needs, you'll be able to anticipate some of the tough questions that the interviewer necessarily asks.

Can you know for certain how a listener will react to your statements in a job interview? Can you know how a reader will interpret your report's statements of fact and conclusions? The answer to both questions is that you can't know *for certain*. However, you *can* make some shrewd guesses. The following communications model can help you anticipate receiver reactions so that you can successfully adapt the content and presentation of your messages.

Use a Communications Model

Whether you have a quiet talk with a friend at a doughnut shop or whether you write a high-powered report for an important client, certain key factors affect the nature and outcome of that communication. We will now place those factors in a communications model, which will be developed in stages, so that you will be able to fully understand how the various factors interact and contribute to the success of the communications exchange.

Let's analyze a conversation between a consulting mechanical engineer, Daphne McCrae, and McCrae's client, Max Lauder, the maintenance supervisor for the Trendmark Ski Resort. Lauder has heard about a neighbouring ski hill's problem with the massive cast metal gripping mechanisms that clamp the chairs of a high-speed chairlift onto the cable of that lift. Lauder wants McCrae's advice about whether to replace the grips on Trendmark's high-speed quad lift. Thus, McCrae has tested several grips and is giving a preliminary oral report of her findings.

First, in order to develop a communications model, let's identify the conversation's primary *message* as Daphne McCrae's semi-technical answer to Lauder's question. McCrae is the *sender* of that message; Lauder is the *receiver*. Their conversation, which occurs in the ski resort's maintenance building, uses an oral verbal *channel* and several non-verbal *channels*.

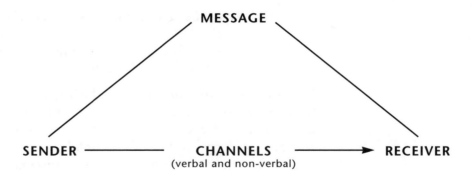

The conversation between McCrae and Lauder seems to depend on the verbal channel of speech. After all, McCrae uses words to convey her knowledge about the factors that might contribute to cast-alloy failure. However, several non-verbal channels such as facial expressions, vocal inflections, posture, and gestures send accompanying messages about the sender's confidence in her own knowledge, her degree of certainty, and her level of concern for her client's current problem. How Max Lauder receives these non-verbal messages affects how he judges the accuracy and value of McCrae's words.

Has Daphne McCrae chosen an appropriate channel to convey her initial reaction to her client's question? The answer is "yes," especially if she wants to alleviate her receiver's immediate concerns. However, if McCrae were to communicate a full technical analysis of the grips she has tested, she should use a formal written report to present her findings. McCrae's choice of communications channels illustrates a basic communications principle: Senders need to choose their primary communication channels carefully in order to reach their receivers.

Here are some other questions to help assess which channels should be used in a given situation:

1. *Has the sender chosen a channel used by the receiver?* For example, Daphne McCrae won't reach Max Lauder via e-mail on days when Lauder is working on the lifts, away from his office computer.
2. *Has the sender taken advantage of the chosen channel's particular strengths?* The main advantage of presenting McCrae's initial analysis *orally* is that it allows her to accompany her semi-technical comments with reassuring vocal tones and other non-verbal messages.
3. *Have both the sender and receiver blocked out external "noise"?* The maintenance building could be very noisy, as workers repair and maintain equipment, so perhaps the conversation should be held in Lauder's office. In this case, the two participants need to examine the equipment as they talk, so they meet in the maintenance shed, where they need to block out the noise in order to focus on each other's messages.

4. *Has the sender considered both the verbal and non-verbal aspects of the transmission?* McCrae's subsequent written analysis will need to use a formal report format, to correspond to the subject's serious nature and to signal the writer's credibility.

Choosing the right channel is only the beginning. The sender also has to *encode* the message so that the receiver has at least a hope of *decoding* it as the sender intended. Proper encoding means choosing the right words, sentence patterns, and message structures to suit the sender's purpose *and* the reader's interests and needs. This collection of choices requires careful thought; that's why this text emphasizes audience/purpose analysis for all writing and speaking assignments.

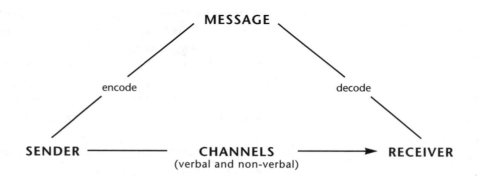

Does Max Lauder understand Daphne McCrae's explanations? Perhaps. If McCrae uses a great deal of technical jargon, Lauder may be perplexed. And if McCrae oversimplifies her message, Lauder won't get the full picture and thus will not understand McCrae's advice about the grips.

Indeed, decoding messages is often harder than encoding them. To start with, many receivers do not know how to listen or read effectively and so they miss much of the intended message. Even the alert, skilled receiver may have difficulty following the sender's train of thought if the encoded message has been poorly organized, or if the sender has chosen an inappropriate level of phrasing or detail, or if the sender's verbal and non-verbal messages contradict each other.

Even when the receiver is confident that she or he has understood the message, communication can break down. That's because senders and receivers often have different meanings for the same words. (Your English professor, for example, might intend the word "decode" to interpret written and spoken words, but you might think of deciphering Morse code and other coded messages if you have a military background or a passion for spy novels.)

Now let's introduce more psychology to our communications model:

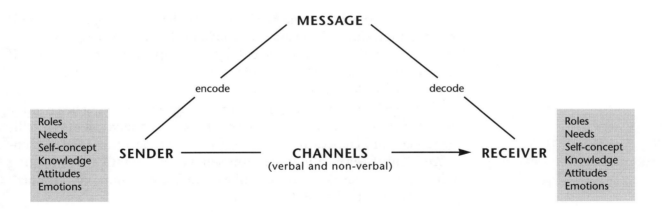

The terms beside *sender* and *receiver* in the model refer to factors that may affect each person at the time the communication occurs. These terms will now be discussed. The discussion will analyze the McCrae/Lauder conversation, but you might also like to stop at various points to think of a recent conversation you've had, or a letter you've sent, in order to see how each of the following factors may have affected the communication's outcome in each of those cases.

1. *Role.* Daphne McCrae's role is the expert analyst, which compels her to think and speak carefully and rationally. In that role, she must not jump to conclusions or make rash statements. Why? First, her job role requires her to make sense of the available technical data. Second, she has to maintain credibility, in order to convince her listener to consider her expert advice.

   Max Lauder's role requires him to understand and absorb McCrae's analysis and advice. Thus, Max listens very attentively.

   Now, think of how your role influences your behaviour at this moment. Probably, you're reading this page because your student role requires you to do so. So, your receiving behaviour is role-dominated. But what if you find yourself getting really interested in this subject? What if you are now starting to think of how *role* affects your communications with your friends and your colleagues at work or school? If so, your *personal needs* are starting to influence your receiving behaviour.

2. *Needs.* It's obvious that we all have strong reasons for communicating with others: *practical needs* associated with making a living, basic *physical needs,* and *social needs* for acceptance, affection, and control. Also, *identity needs* seem always to influence our behaviour, even when we're taking care of our basic physical needs or our practical business needs. Much of our communications has us trying to determine who we are and then trying to assert that identity to others. If we allow our identity needs to dominate, however, problems may result.

For example, if Daphne McCrae were to have a strong identity need to appear forceful and infallible, she might be driven to make definite conclusions even if there's insufficient data to support such conclusions. If her identity need overruns her role requirement, she might provide disastrous advice to her client.

3. *Self-concept.* Our self-beliefs affect our sending and receiving behaviours. If, for example, Daphne McCrae sees herself as analytical and intelligent, her word choices and speaking pace will reflect those self-perceptions. And if Max Lauder sees himself as very practical but lacking education, he may defer to some of McCrae's conclusions even if Max's instincts tell him that McCrae is wrong.

4. *Knowledge.* A sender like Daphne McCrae has to know her subject well before she can successfully explain, for example, resistance to stress in cast metal chairlift grips. Similarly, Max Lauder has to have a rudimentary knowledge in order to understand any of the complexities in McCrae's analysis. From a practical viewpoint, Max probably understands these stresses well: he has observed the chairlift in action. However, he probably does not understand how to measure shear forces or how metal breaks down.

5. *Attitude.* In the conversation we've been analyzing, both participants have a serious attitude toward the topic being discussed. They concentrate on the technical and practical aspects of a potential problem.

Another factor lies in their degree of respect for each other. As it turns out, each of them is in his/her late 30s with over 15 years' experience in their field. Each is aware of the other's expertise, so each chooses words carefully.

Actually, our attitudes are usually shown non-verbally. In the McCrae/Lauder conversation, the most likely channels revealing their attitudes toward the situation and each other would be posture, facial expressions, and tone of voice.

6. *Emotions.* You have experienced many situations where your emotions have affected how you spoke or how you listened. Indeed, one's emotions can totally block effective communications. In business, we should not allow that to happen, and it's not likely to happen in the conversation between Max and Daphne.

As this chapter has hinted, communication can break down for many reasons:

- poor choice of channels
- receiver inattentiveness
- poor sender decoding
- lack of knowledge by sender or receiver
- conflicting roles or contrasting personal needs

However, most misunderstandings can be prevented by timely and useful *feedback* that is so important for two-way channels such as face-to-face conversations, telephone calls, and e-mail. Let's introduce that feedback loop next.

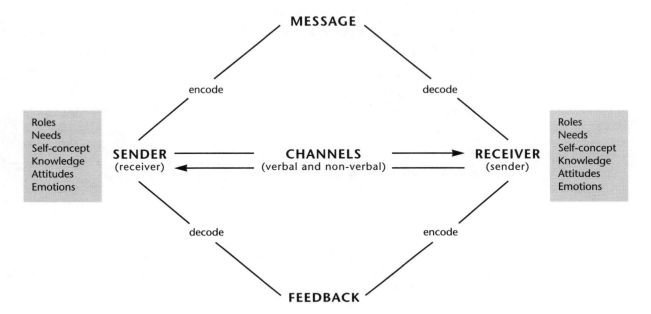

Feedback could be particularly useful in the McCrae/Lauder meeting—Max could immediately signal that he didn't understand some aspect of the message he heard and Daphne could use different terminology or a different order of explanation to convey her message.

While two-way channels provide timely, direct feedback, written channels (letters, memos, reports) do not. That's why you should consider the reader's role, needs, and knowledge levels when you choose the content, structure, and style of your written messages.

Let's look at assessing your readers' information needs now.

Assess Readers' Information Needs

Good writing connects with readers by recognizing their different backgrounds, needs, and preferences. A single message may appear in several versions for several audiences. For instance, an article describing a new cancer treatment might appear in a medical journal read by doctors and nurses. A less technical version might appear in a medical textbook read by medical and nursing students. An even simpler version might appear in *Reader's Digest*. All three versions treat the same topic, but each meets the needs of a different audience.

Technical writing is intended to be *used*. You become the teacher and the reader becomes the student. Because your readers may know less than you, they may have questions.

Typical Reader Questions About Workplace Documents

- What is the purpose of this document?
- Who should read the document?
- What is being described or explained?
- What does it look like?
- How do I do it?
- How did you do it?
- Why did it happen?
- When will it happen?
- Why should we do it?
- How much will it cost?
- What are the risks?

You always write to enable a specific audience to grasp the information and follow the discussion. In order to be useful, the writing must connect with the reader's level of understanding.

Identify Levels of Technicality

When you write for a close acquaintance (friend, computer crony, co-worker, professor, or supervisor), you know a good deal about your reader's background. You deliberately adapt your document to that reader's knowledge, interests, and needs. But sometimes you write for less defined audiences, particularly when the audience is large (when you are writing a journal article, a computer manual, a set of first-aid procedures, or a report of an accident). When you have only a general notion about your audience's background, you must decide whether your document should be *highly technical, semi-technical,* or *non-technical,* as depicted in Figure 2.1.

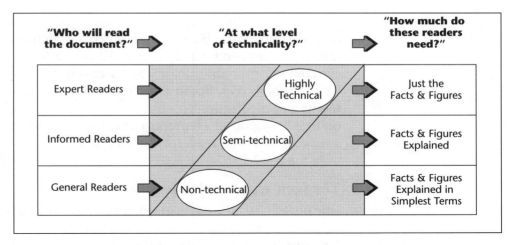

Figure 2.1   Deciding on a Document's Level of Technicality

The Highly Technical Document

Readers at the specialized level expect the technical facts and figures they need, without long explanations. The following report of treatment given to a heart attack victim is highly technical. The writer, an emergency room physician, is reporting to the patient's doctor. This reader needs an exact record of the patient's symptoms and treatment.

A Technical Version

Expert readers need merely the facts and figures, which they can interpret for themselves

The patient was brought to the emergency room by ambulance at 0100 hours, September 27, 2008. The patient complained of severe chest pains, dyspnea, and vertigo. Auscultation and EKG revealed a massive cardiac infarction and pulmonary edema marked by pronounced cyanosis. Vital signs: blood pressure, 80/40; pulse 140/min; respiration, 35/min. Lab: wbc, 20,000; elevated serum transaminase; urea nitrogen, 60 mg%. Urinalysis showed 4+ protein and 4+ granular casts/field, indicating acute renal failure secondary to the hypotension.

The patient received 10 mg of morphine stat, subcutaneously, followed by nasal oxygen and D_5W intravenously. At 0125 the cardiac monitor recorded an irregular sinus rhythm, indicating left ventricular fibrillation. The patient was defibrillated stat and given a 50 mg bolus of Xylocaine intravenously. A Xylocaine drip was started, and sodium bicarbonate administered until a normal heartbeat was established. By 0300, the oscilloscope was recording a normal sinus rhythm.

As the heartbeat stabilized and cyanosis diminished, the patient received 5 cc of heparin intravenously, to be repeated every six hours. By 0500 the BUN had fallen to 20 mg% and vital signs had stabilized: blood pressure, 110/60; pulse, 105/min; respiration, 22/min. The patient was now conscious and responsive. ■

This highly technical report is clear only to the medical expert. Because her reader has extensive background, this writer defines no technical terms (pulmonary edema, sinus rhythm). Nor does she interpret lab findings (4+ protein, elevated serum transaminase). She uses abbreviations her reader understands (wbc, BUN, D_5W). Because her reader knows the reasons for specific treatments and medications (defibrillation, Xylocaine drip), she includes no theoretical background. Her report answers concisely the main questions she can anticipate from her reader: What happened? What treatment was given? What were the results?

The Semi-technical Document

One broad class of readers may have some technical background, but less than the experts. For instance, first-year medical students have specialized knowledge, but not as much as second-, third-, and fourth-year students. Yet students in all four groups could be considered semi-technical readers. When you write for a semi-technical audience, identify the *lowest* level of understanding in the group, and write to that level. Too much explanation is better than too little.

Here is a partial version of the earlier medical report. Written at a semi-technical level, it might appear in a textbook for first-year medical or nursing students, in a report for a medical social worker, in a patient's history for the medical technology department, or in a monthly report for the hospital administration.

A Semi-technical Version

Informed but non-expert readers need enough explanations to understand what the facts mean

Examination by stethoscope and electrocardiogram revealed a massive failure of the heart muscle along with fluid build-up in the lungs, which produced a cyanotic **discolouration of the lips and fingertips from lack of oxygen.**

The patient's blood pressure at 80 mm Hg (systolic)/40 mm Hg (diastolic) was **dangerously below its normal measure of 130/70.** A pulse rate of 140/minute was **almost twice the normal rate of 60–80.** Respiration at 35/minute was more than **twice the normal rate of 12–16.**

Laboratory blood tests yielded a white blood cell count of 20,000/cu mm (normal value: 5,000–10,000), **indicating a severe inflammatory response by the heart muscle.** The elevated serum transaminase enzymes **(produced in quantity only when the heart muscle fails)** confirmed the earlier diagnosis. A blood urea nitrogen level of 60 mg% (normal value: 12–16 mg%) indicated **that the kidneys had ceased to filter out metabolic waste products.** The 4+ protein and casts reported from the urinalysis (normal value: 0) **revealed that the kidney tubules were degenerating as a result of the lowered blood pressure.**

The patient immediately received **morphine to ease the chest pain**, followed by **oxygen to relieve strain on the cardiopulmonary system,** and an intravenous solution of **dextrose and water to prevent shock.** ■

The version explains (in boldface) the raw data. Exact dosages are not mentioned because the readers are not treating the patient. Normal values of lab tests and vital signs, however, make interpretation easier. (Expert readers would know these values.) Knowing what medications the patient received would be especially important to the lab technician, because some medications affect test results. For a non-technical audience, however, the message needs further translation.

The Non-technical Document

Readers with no specialized training expect technical data to be translated into terms they understand. Non-technical readers are impatient with abstract theories but want enough background to help them make the right decision or take the right action. They are bored by long explanations but frustrated by bare facts not explained or interpreted. They expect a report that is clear on first reading, not one that requires review or study.

The following is a non-technical version of our medical report. The physician might write this version for the patient's spouse who is overseas on business, or as part of a script for a documentary film about emergency room treatment.

A Non-technical Version

General readers need everything translated into terms they understand

Heart sounds and electrical impulses both were abnormal, **indicating a massive heart attack caused by failure of a large part of the heart muscle.** The lungs were swollen with fluid and the lips and fingertips showed **a bluish discolouration from lack of oxygen.**

Blood pressure was **dangerously low, creating the risk of shock.** Pulse and respiration were **almost twice the normal rate, indicating that the heart and lungs were being overworked** in keeping oxygenated blood circulating freely.

Blood tests confirmed the heart attack diagnosis and **indicated that waste products usually filtered out by the kidneys were building up in the bloodstream. Urine tests showed that the kidneys were failing as a result of the lowered blood pressure.**

The patient was given **medication to ease the chest pain, oxygen to ease the strain on the heart and lungs, and intravenous solution to prevent the blood vessels from collapsing and causing irreversible shock.** ■

This non-technical version explains (in boldface) the situation using everyday language. It omits any mention of medications, lab tests, or normal values, because these have no meaning for the reader. The writer merely summarizes events and explains the causes of the crisis and the reasons for the particular treatment.

In some other situation, however (say, in a jury trial for malpractice), the non-technical audience might need information about specific medication and treatment. Such a report would, of course, be much longer—a short course in emergency coronary treatment.

Each version of the medical report is useful *only* to readers at a specific level. Doctors and nurses have no need for the explanations in the two latter versions, but they do need the specialized data in the first. Beginning medical students and paramedics might be confused by the first version and bored by the third. Non-technical readers would find both the first and second versions meaningless.

Primary and Secondary Readers

Whenever you prepare a single document for multiple readers, classify your readers as *primary* or *secondary.* Primary readers usually are those who requested the document and who will use it as a basis for decisions or actions. Secondary readers are those who will carry out the project, who will advise the primary readers about their decision, or who will somehow be affected by this decision. They will read your document (or perhaps only part of it) for information that will help them get the job done, for educated advice, or to keep up with new developments.

Often these two audiences differ in technical background. Primary readers may require highly technical messages, and secondary readers may need semi-technical or non-technical messages—or vice versa. When you must write for audiences at different levels, follow these guidelines:

How to tailor a single document for multiple readers

1. If the document is short (a letter, memo, or anything less than two pages), rewrite it at various levels for various readers.
2. If the document exceeds two pages, address the primary readers. Then provide appendices for secondary readers (technical appendices when secondary readers are technical, or vice versa). Letters of transmittal, informative abstracts, and glossaries are other supplements that help non-specialized audiences understand a highly technical report. (See Chapter 20 for how to use and prepare appendices and other supplements.)

The next scenario shows how some documents must be tailored for both primary and secondary readers.

Tailoring a Document for Different Readers

When Daphne McCrae writes the results of her tests on potentially damaged ski-lift grips, her primary reader will be the client, Trendmark Ski Resort. That audience will include Max Lauder, the maintenance supervisor who has some technical knowledge of metal and metal fatigue. The audience will also include Trendmark's management board and its lawyer, all of whom have little or no technical knowledge.

Daphne's report may eventually have legal implications, so it must be presented in meticulous detail. But her non-specialist readers will need explanations of her testing methods. These readers will also need photos of the test equipment to fully understand the processes involved. The report will have to define specialized terms such as "fractographs" (microscopic photographs of fractured surfaces) and "HSLA" (high-strength, low-alloy) steel such as ASTM grade A 242 (which has 0.4% copper alloyed to the steel to provide greater weathering resistance).

The report's secondary readers will include Daphne McCrae's supervisor and outside consulting engineers who may evaluate Daphne's test procedures and assess the validity of her findings. Consultants will focus on various parts of the report, to verify that Daphne's procedure has been exact and faultless. For these readers, she will have to include appendices spelling out the technical details of her analysis: *how* light-microscopic fractographs revealed the presence and direction of fractures, and *how* the pattern of these fractures indicates a casting flaw in the original grip, not torsional fatigue. Finally, Daphne will need to present the technical details of her finding that only one grip has the casting flaw and that the other grips are safe for operation. ■

In Daphne McCrae's situation, primary readers need to know *what her findings mean*, whereas secondary readers need to know *how she arrived at her conclusions*. Unless she serves the needs of each group independently, her information will be worthless.

Develop an Audience/Purpose Profile

When you write for a particular reader or a small group of readers, you can focus sharply on your audience by asking the questions listed below. To answer these questions consider the suggestions that follow, and use a version of the Audience/Purpose Profile Sheet (Figure 2.2 on page 36) for all of your writing.

Questions About a Document's Intended Audience and Purpose

- Who wants the document? Who else will read it?
- Why do they want the document? How will they use it? What is the purpose of my document? What do I want to achieve?
- What is the technical background of the primary audience? Of the secondary audience?
- How might cultural differences shape readers' expectations and interpretations?

- How much does the audience already know about the subject? What material will have informative value?
- What exactly does the audience need to know, and in what format? How much is enough?
- When is the document due?

Reader Characteristics

Identify the primary readers by name, job title, and specialty (Martha Jones, Director of Quality Control, B.S. and M.S. in mechanical engineering). Are they superiors, colleagues, or subordinates? Are they inside or outside your organization? What is their attitude toward this topic likely to be? Are they apt to accept or reject your conclusions and recommendations? Will your report be good or bad news? For readers from other cultures, how might cultural differences affect their expectations and interpretations?

AUDIENCE/PURPOSE PROFILE

Audience Identity and Needs

Primary reader(s): _____ *(name, title)*

Secondary reader(s): _____

Relationship: _____ *(client, employer, other)*

Intended use of document: _____ *(perform a task, solve a problem, other)*

Prior knowledge about this topic: _____ *(knows nothing, a few details, other)*

Additional information needed: _____ *(background, only bare facts, other)*

Probable questions: _____

_____

_____

_____

_____

_____

Audience's Probable Attitude and Personality

Attitude toward topic: _____ *(indifferent, skeptical, other)*

Probable objections: _____ *(cost, time, none, other)*

Probable attitude toward this writer: _____ *(intimidated, hostile, receptive, other)*

Persons most affected by this document: _____

Temperament: _____ *(cautious, impatient, other)*

Probable reaction to document: _____ *(resistance, approval, anger, guilt, other)*

Risk of alienating anyone: _____

Audience Expectations About the Document

Reason document originated: _____ *(audience request, my idea, other)*

Acceptable length: _____ *(comprehensive, concise, other)*

Material important to this audience: _____ *(interpretations, costs,*

_____ *conclusions, other)*

Most useful arrangement: _____ *(problem-causes-solutions, other)*

Tone: _____ *(businesslike, apologetic, enthusiastic, other)*

Intended effect on this audience: _____ *(win support, change behaviour, other)*

Due date: _____

Figure 2.2   Audience/Purpose Profile Sheet

Identify also those secondary readers who might be interested in or affected by your document, or who will affect the primary reader's perception or use of your document.

Purpose of the Document

Learn why readers want the document and how they will use it. Do they merely want a record of activities or progress? Do they expect only raw data, or conclusions and recommendations as well? Will readers act immediately on the information? Do they need step-by-step instructions? Will the document be read and discarded, filed, published, distributed electronically? In your audience's view, *what* is most important? What purpose should this document achieve?

Readers' Technical Background

Colleagues who speak your technical language will understand raw data. Supervisors responsible for several technical areas may want interpretations and recommendations. Managers who have limited technical knowledge expect definitions and explanations. Clients with no technical background expect versions that spell out what the facts mean to *them* (to their health, pocketbook, business prospects). However, none of these generalizations might apply to *your* situation. When in doubt, aim for low technicality.

Readers' Cultural Background

Some information needs can be culturally determined. For example, readers in certain cultures might value thoroughness and complexity above all: lists of data, with every relevant detail included and explained. Readers in other cultures might prefer an overview of the material, with multiple perspectives and liberal use of graphics (Hein 125–26).

North American business culture generally values plain talk that spells out the meaning directly, but some cultures prefer indirect and somewhat ambiguous messages, which leave explanations and interpretation for readers to decipher (Leki 151; Martin and Chaney 276–77). To avoid seeming impolite, some readers might hesitate to request clarification or additional information. Even disagreement or refusal might be expressed as "We will do our best" or "This is very difficult," instead of "No"—to avoid offending and to preserve harmony (Rowland 47).

Correspondence practices vary from culture to culture. In British business letters, for example, the salutation is followed by a comma (Dear Ms. Morrison,); in North America, it is followed by a colon (Dear Ms. Morrison:). Also, European data formats vary from North American practices, as Table 2.1 illustrates.

Table 2.1   Typical Data Formats

	North American	United Kingdom	France	Germany	Portugal
Dates	May 15, 2008	15th May, 2008	15 Mai 2008	15. Mai 2008	08.05.15
	5/15/08	15/5/08	15.05.08	15.5.08	
Time	10:32 p.m.	10:32 p.m.	22.32	22:32 Uhr	22H32m
			22 h 32	22.32	
Currency	$123.45	£123.45	123F45	DM 123,45	123$45
	C$123.45	GB£123.45	123,45 F	123,45 DM	ESC 123.45
	Can $123.45				
	123.45$ (Quebec)				
	US$123.45				
Large Number	1,234,567.89	1,234,567.89	1.234.567,89	1.234.567,89	1.234.567,89
Phone Numbers	(905) 555-1234	(081) 987 1234	(15) 61-87-34-02	(089) 2 61 39 12	056-244 33
		0255 876543	(15) 61.87.34.02		056 45 45 45

Source: Adapted from Guffey, M.E. et al. *Business Communication.* 2nd Canadian Edition. Toronto: Nelson, 1999, p. 59.

The following general advice may help with your intercultural communication:

1. Where feasible, hire a translator to convert your proposal or report to the *buyer's* language.

2. Where that's not feasible, or where your reader prefers to receive your document in English, keep your sentences and paragraphs short. Use direct, simple, precise words. Use relative pronouns such as "that," "which," and "who" to introduce clauses. Avoid technical jargon and North American idioms ("hit the ceiling," "at the drop of a hat," "been there, done that").

3. Pay special attention to the openings of letters and memos, and to the introductions of reports—North Americans like to get straight to the point; Asians and Latin Americans like to build relationships first.

4. When writing recommendations, consider whether your client's culture favours careful, deliberate team consultation or quick individual action.

5. Look at the physical format of reports produced in the reader's culture, and incorporate some aspects of that format in your report.

6. Learn whether it's best to deliver reports in person, by messenger, by courier, or by mail.

So far, we've assumed readers outside North America. But we also need to remember that our own culture is not homogeneous. Canadians and Americans have different attitudes and political systems. Within Canada, each region has distinctive characteristics that could affect how a reader interprets a given document.

Readers' Knowledge of the Subject

Do not waste time rehashing information readers already have. Readers expect something *new* and *significant*. Writing has informative value[1] when it (1) conveys knowledge that will be new *and* worthwhile to the intended audience; (2) reminds the audience about something they know but ignore; or (3) offers fresh insight about something familiar, a new perspective.

The informative value of any document is measured by its relevancy to the writer's purpose and the audience's needs. As this book's audience, for instance, you expect to learn about technical writing, and our purpose is to help you do so. In this situation, which of these statements would you find useful?

1. Technical writing is hard work.
2. Technical writing is a process of making deliberate decisions in response to a specific situation. In this process, you discover important meanings in your topic, and give your readers the information they need to understand your meanings.[2]

Statement 1 offers no news to anyone who has ever picked up a pencil, and so it has no informative value for you. But 2 offers a new perspective on something familiar. No matter how much you might have struggled through decisions about punctuation, organization, and grammar, chances are you haven't viewed writing as entailing the critical thinking discussed in this book. Because 2 provides new insight, you can say it has informative value.

The more non-essential information readers receive, the more they are likely to overlook or misinterpret the important material. Take the time to determine what your readers need, and try to give them just that.

Appropriate Details and Format

The amount of detail in your document *(How much is enough?)* will depend on what you have learned about your readers' needs. Were you asked to "keep it short" or to "be comprehensive"? Can you summarize, or does everything need spelling out? What length will they tolerate? Are the primary readers most interested in conclusions and recommendations, or do they want all of the details? Have they requested a letter, a memo, a short report, or a long, formal report with supplements (title page, table of contents, appendices, and so on)? What kinds of visuals (charts, graphs, drawings, photographs) make this material more accessible? What level of technicality will connect with primary readers?

---

1. Adapted from James L. Kinneavy's assertion that discourse ought to be unpredictable, in *A Theory of Discourse* (Englewood Cliffs: Prentice, 1971).
2. Our thanks to Robert M. Hogge, Weber State University, for this definition.

High Technicality	The diesel engine generates 10 BTUs per gallon of fuel, as opposed to the conventional gas engine's 8 BTUs.
Low Technicality	The diesel engine yields 25 percent better fuel mileage than its gas-burning counterpart.

Every professional in the Information Age has to keep abreast of technology in order to use it effectively. What one has to know changes quickly and often.

Due Date

Does your document have a deadline? Workplace documents almost always do. Allow plenty of time to collect data, to write, and to revise. Whenever possible, ask primary readers to review an early draft and to suggest improvements.

☑ EXERCISES

1. Locate a short article from your field (or part of a long article or a selection from your textbook for an advanced course). Choose a piece written at the highest level of technicality you understand and then translate the piece for a layperson, as in the example on page 33. Exchange translations with a colleague from a different major. Read your colleague's translation and write a paragraph evaluating its level of technicality. Submit to your instructor a copy of the original, your translated version, and your evaluation of your colleague's translation.

2. Assume that a new employee is taking over your job because you have been promoted. Identify a specific problem in the job that could cause difficulty for the new employee. Write for the employee instructions for avoiding or dealing with the problem. Before writing, create an audience/purpose profile by answering (on paper) the questions on page 35. Then brainstorm for details. Submit to your instructor your audience/purpose analysis, brainstorming list, and instructions.

☑ COLLABORATIVE PROJECT

Form teams according to major (electrical engineering, biology, etc.), and respond to the following situation.

Assume your team has received the following assignment from your major department's chairperson: An increasing number of first-year students are dropping out of the major because of low grades, stress, or inability to keep up with the work. Your task is to prepare a "Survival Guide," for distribution to incoming students. This one- or two-page memo should focus on the challenges and the pitfalls and should include a brief motivational section, along with whatever else team members think readers need.

ANALYZE YOUR AUDIENCE

Use Figure 2.2 as a guide for developing your audience/purpose profile.

Writing Efficiently

AT WORK, writers need to produce effective documents quickly. Most employers will not tolerate inefficient work habits, including writing habits. Here are three scenarios that illustrate that it's just as important to write *efficiently* as it is to create effective documents.

> *Bill,* a Halifax civil engineering technologist, returns to his office from a site inspection. As he sits down at his desk, his office manager tells him that Bill must write a proposal that afternoon for a soils-testing contract. Bill checks his watch; he has two hours to gather relevant data from company files and produce a two-page proposal before Bill has to catch a plane for a company meeting in Toronto.
>
> Bill spends 20 minutes gathering, choosing, and arranging the data and supporting arguments. Then, working from a standard proposal structure for soils-testing contracts, he composes a 550-word proposal on his personal computer in 35 minutes. He spends another 15 minutes polishing the document and sends it to two colleagues for proofreading. They find four mechanical errors and two minor errors in logic. Bill corrects the errors and prints three copies of the proposal; he takes two copies to the office manager. In total, Bill produces the proposal in 90 minutes.
>
> *George* works for a national research organization in Saskatoon. He has a master's degree in chemistry and a doctorate in biology. His company bills his services for $85 an hour, a rate that his company's clients are glad to pay because George's research methods, data, and analyses are thorough and accurate. His reports feature clear structures and phrasing.
>
> However, George is required to take a three-day technical writing course because typically it takes him a full work week (plus his own time in the evenings) to produce a project completion report that other researchers could produce in half the time.
>
> *Rita* has a background in electronics and computers; she has a 10-month contract to write software documentation manuals for an Ottawa-based software development company. The company is very pleased with the quality of Rita's work but its Director of Development, Martin Lefebvre, has told Rita that her contract will be renewed only if she can decrease the time it takes her to produce a manual. Martin suggests a minimum improvement of 25% in writing efficiency. ∎

Bill is an efficient writer. George and Rita are not, partly because both have perfectionist tendencies, but more because each has learned bad writing and time-wasting habits. Rita, for example, writes through a discovery method that requires several complete re-writes of each document. George's main problem is that he frequently reorganizes his reports as he composes drafts and thus wastes time re-writing whole sections in order to make the material read smoothly.

Why does Bill write more efficiently than Rita and George? Bill has learned to:

- identify several related but separate writing tasks
- focus on one task at a time and perform each task well
- identify the best sequence for completing the various writing tasks
- reduce writing time by starting quickly and by writing a first draft that requires relatively little revision

Efficient writers such as Bill have learned, primarily through trial and error, to use a writing process that is broken down into the following stages.

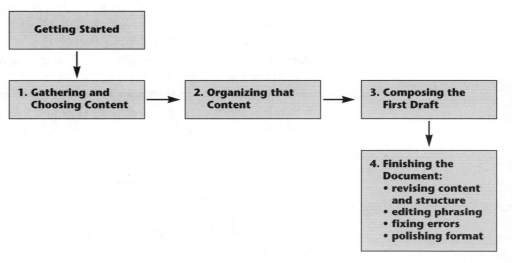

Figure 3.1   An Efficient Writing Process

Getting Started

Figure 3.1 shows the first section, "Getting Started," as preliminary to the other four stages. Technical and business writers benefit from immediately asking: *What does my reader need and expect?* and *What purpose am I trying to fulfill?* (The Audience/Purpose Profile described in Chapter 2 provides an excellent starting point for people who write business correspondence and technical documents.)

Technical writing differs from essay writing. Essayists often have to discover their subject as they progress. This process of writing until the writer discovers what she or he really wants to say is called *free-writing;* it may be necessary, but it results in many crumpled pages and in lengthy writing sessions.

Re-writing draft after draft is simply not necessary for most business and technical writing projects. Nor do you have to wait for that first "golden phrase" to start the river of words flowing. As a technical/business writer, you can be productive within 30 seconds of sitting down to write. Here's how:

- *Use an Audience/Purpose Profile* to determine the types of information and analysis to include. List the types of questions your reader would ask (or which your reader has already asked).

- *Choose an appropriate, proven structure* and then "fill in the blanks." Several of this book's chapters suggest structures for frequently written documents; progress reports, proposals, feasibility reports, and application letters are among those described. Then, use elements of an Audience/Purpose Profile to modify the suggested structure to meet your reader's needs and preferences.

The foregoing two methods will help you start writing almost any job-related document. However, occasionally you'll tackle a subject that is not clearly defined, or perhaps your reader's needs and priorities will be difficult to pin down. For those "open-ended" situations, here are two methods for getting your mind in gear:

1. *Brainstorm a list of ideas and topics.* A random listing of possible topics and ideas works precisely because it takes advantage of the natural chaos that exists in our minds. Often, we are most creative when we allow free thought association to generate a series of loosely related points and topics. It's important to simply record these points as they come, and not to edit them. Later, when the creative frenzy has abated, you can discard the points that don't seem relevant. Then, you can organize the material that remains.

   Now let's look at a list of topics and ideas that might be generated by the writer of an in-house product description of a new camera-style scanner. (The writer is part of a design team at GlobeTech that has recently developed the device in response to a request from GlobeTech's general manager to produce a new consumer product. GlobeTech is seeking to diversify.)

   The writer, Thanh Pham, has not previously written such a product description. Also, the product is radically different from the industrial controls manufactured by his company, so he doesn't have a model to emulate.) Here's Thanh's list:

   - limitation of previous digital cameras—why inadequate for scanning images
   - solution:
     – appearance and size
     – weight
     – features and controls
   - how it works (just an overview): (1) the optical process (2) storage of images—floppy disk; on-board storage
   - downloading images to a PC
   - performance specs: resolution; size of images that can be scanned; storage capacity

Notice that Thanh's thoughts contain some order and "connections," even though he was just letting the ideas "flow." The first items in the list reflect a problem-solution sequence, and the last three items a chronological pattern.

2. *Brainstorm ideas in a cluster diagram.* Cluster diagramming suits people who think visually. It also suits those who are used to following hypertext links through the Internet. Here's how Thanh could use clustering to generate ideas for his product description. He could:

- circle the main topic ("Camscan") which he writes in the centre of a clean page
- record any ideas that pop into his mind and circle those ideas
- avoid censoring ideas, but simply record them
- join related ideas with lines, but not make these organizational connections his main priority. Instead, he should keep on recording ideas until the flow stops.

The resulting diagram might look like this:

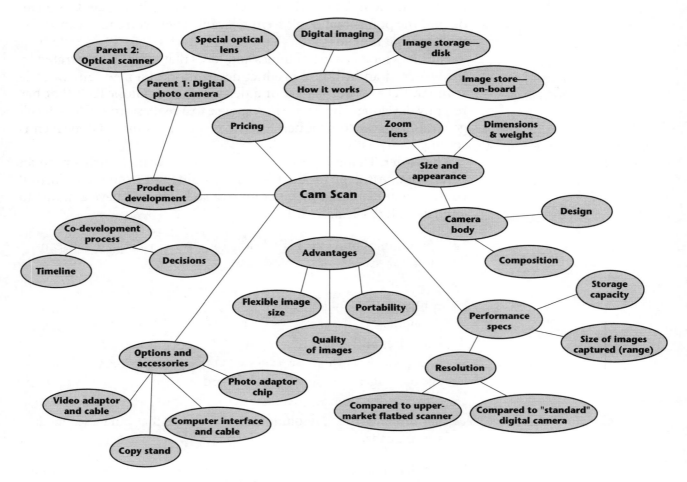

Figure 3.2   Sample Cluster Diagram

How To Save Writing Time

Whether you have generated ideas by brainstorming or by one of the more structured approaches described earlier, you are now well underway and you can complete four writing tasks in turn:

1. *Choose the content,* based on:

    - technical or research notes
    - personal observations
    - arguments and evidence
    - deductions and conclusions
    - available illustrations

    Then, check to see if anything has been omitted, or if any material should be deleted.

    Revising content now takes less time than revising material later in the process.

2. *Organize the blocks of material.* If you're writing a letter, decide what goes in each paragraph. If you're writing a longer document, start with larger blocks of material and work your way to the paragraph level. Next, organize the ideas and information *within* each block.

    Again, determine whether any material should be added, rearranged or omitted; **such changes take much more time** after **a draft's been phrased.**

3. *Write the first draft.* Since you know what to include, and where to place it, you will be able to concentrate on the best way to phrase each sentence, and you will understand where to inject transition statements. If you have done steps 1 and 2 properly, this draft will be close to a finished product. The very act of phrasing sentences can sometimes change your perception of your message, so you might have to modify your writing plan as you go.

    By working from an outline, you will save composition time. After all, you only have to think of *how* to phrase things; you've already chosen the content and arranged it. Your mind is free to concentrate on phrasing; you're not burdened by three writing tasks at once.

4. *Evaluate, revise, edit, proofread, and correct.* Wait as long as possible before polishing the writing. You may gain a new perspective on the best way to structure and express parts of the document. Also, you'll proofread more effectively if you distance yourself from the material.

    Use objective indexes such as the Fog Index (Chapter 11, page 277) to help evaluate your writing and to make it more readable. Finally, proofread the material at least three times to locate errors. Ideally, you should use at least two other proofreaders in addition to yourself.

Compared to a process of writing and re-writing (and more re-writing), this four-stage writing process will save you a great deal of revision and editing. **Investing a little time early in the process pays large dividends later in the process!**

Writing efficiently in the manner just described also will help you produce more *effective* writing; concentrating on one task at a time allows you to better perform each of those tasks.

Composing With a Word Processor

If you type as fast as you handwrite, and if you're accustomed to reading a computer screen, consider using a word processor to plan and compose the first draft of a document.

Composing with a computer has several advantages:

- *Brainstorming* lists of ideas suits word processing, especially if you type quickly
- *Choosing content* is easy to do—you can add, delete, or move points with little effort
- Today's sophisticated word processing software makes it easy to *arrange the chosen content into an outline.* Most software includes an outliner function that helps you divide topics into main headings and levels of sub-headings. The computer tracks levels in the outline so that you can easily add, subtract, or rearrange parts of the outline. The outliner functions are especially useful for long, complicated reports.
- *Key phrases* can be placed within the outline to represent paragraphs. Later, when you compose each paragraph, each key phrase gets expanded into a topic sentence for its corresponding paragraph. Essentially, then, the computer eliminates the drudgery of re-typing headings and key phrases. You simply fill in the paragraphs under each heading or key phrase. (Some writers type several key notes for each intended paragraph and then expand the notes into a series of closely linked sentences. They find that a pre-meditated list of points for each paragraph helps them write tight, clear paragraphs that require little subsequent revision.)
- Word processors help *identify and correct errors in spelling, punctuation, and grammar.* However, automated checkers have many limitations: a synonym offered by an electronic thesaurus may not accurately convey your intended meaning; the spell checker cannot differentiate between incorrectly used words such as "they're," "their," and "there," or "it's" and "its." And although spell and grammar checkers help, they cannot evaluate those subtle choices of phrasing that can be very important—no automated checker will tell you whether "you can reach me at …" or "call me at …" is more appropriate in a given situation.

Using word processors and printers has other potential drawbacks, so remember the following guidelines:

1. *Decide whether to create the draft by hand or computer.* Experiment to learn which works best for you.

2. *Beware of computer junk.* The ease of cranking out words on a computer can result in long, windy pieces that say nothing. Edit final drafts to eliminate anything that fails to advance your meaning.

3. *Never confuse style with substance.* With laser printers, desktop publishing, and graphics software, documents can be made highly attractive, but not even the most attractive design can redeem a document whose content is worthless or inaccessible.

4. *Save and print your work often.* One way to court disaster is to write without saving or printing often enough. One wrong keystroke might cause pages of writing to disappear forever—unless you have saved them beforehand. Try to save each paragraph and print each page as you complete it.

5. *Make a back-up disk.* A single electrical surge or malfunction can wipe out an entire file, floppy disk, or hard disk!

6. *Consider the benefits of revising from hard copy.* Many writers find they edit more productively by scribbling on the page. The printed page provides the whole text, in front of you.

7. *Print final copies on the right type of paper for your printer.* Ink jet printers, for example, require different paper from laser printers, to get the same high quality. Also, use colour only for special effects, in special circumstances.

8. *Decide how to design and transmit your document.* Should the document be primarily verbal (text), visual, or some combination? Should it travel by conventional mail, interoffice mail, fax, or e-mail? Would your reader(s) prefer the solid feel of paper or the lure of the computer screen? Research indicates that younger readers prefer flashy graphics, older readers prefer traditional text, and readers in general trust text more than visual images (Horton, "Mix Media" 781).

The Process in Action

The following situation illustrates how a busy person, who must balance the technical and management components of his job, uses his time efficiently to write a proposal to his supervisor.

Process to Write a Proposal

The company is MMT Consulting, an engineering firm with its headquarters in Calgary and with branch offices in Sudbury, Winnipeg, Edmonton, Kelowna, and Prince George. MMT specializes in feasibility studies, design projects, and construction management for the mining and petroleum sectors.

Art Basran manages MMT's Kelowna branch. He is responsible for MMT's contract to help the Jackson Mining Company choose a method of hauling coal from Jackson Mining's projected new mine site in the mountains north of Grand Forks, British Columbia. As Art and his staff start to investigate the project, they learn that they need to use specialized accounting methods to evaluate four alternatives for hauling the coal to the railhead.

Art's team, at Jackson Mining's request, examines the proposed route and calculates grade resistances and energy requirements along the route. The team then researches capital costs for constructing road beds and a railroad. Capital costs are also calculated for purchasing diesel trucks, a diesel train, an electric train, and a fleet of electric trains. Finally, annual operating costs are computed for the four options.

After gathering all of the data, Art realizes that he does not have a uniform method of applying the three main evaluation criteria (capital costs, annual operating costs, and potential for expanding the delivery system) to all four transportation options. He consults Brendan Winters, a chartered accountant who works with mining companies. Brendan recommends an accounting vehicle called Equivalent Uniform Annual Costs (EUAC), which combines all the variables and thus allows a uniform comparison of the four haul methods.

Now, Art faces the task of convincing his regional manager, Brenda Backstrom, to accept the EAUC method. Backstrom, a conservative thinker, tends to resist new ways of doing things. ■

Art **gets started** by:

- checking notes of his meeting with Brendan Winters
- jotting questions that Brenda Backstrom will have
- brainstorming a list of points to make in explaining EUAC

Time to **get started**: 10 minutes.

Art's next step is to choose **an approach.** He decides to write a direct proposal because he knows that his reader prefers direct communication, not a lengthy analysis that eventually leads to a recommendation. Art also knows that his reader prefers short messages, so Art chooses a memo that will not exceed two pages.

With the format decision made, Art turns to the **choice of content.** His word-processed list includes:

- situation more complex than usual—financial considerations
- solution: EUAC (Brendan's idea)
- process of preparing EUAC (see my notes)
- Note: we already do 5 of the 6 steps
- advantages of EUAC
  1) relatively easy—Brendan's software
  2) qualitative and quantitative

- our qualifications: Peter, John, Brendan
- why our "normal" method won't work: too complex, not reliable, too diffuse
- request authorization

Before thinking about the order of his material, Art **edits the contents** he's listed. He decides that discussing the inadequacies of the "normal" method could be too negative and that it would take the memo beyond two pages, so he deletes that part. He also thinks of a third EUAC advantage (using the EUAC method makes MMT look good), and adds that point, so his list now includes:

- situation more complex than usual—financial considerations
- <u>solution</u>: EUAC (Brendan's idea)
- process of preparing EUAC (see my notes)
- <u>Note</u>: we already do 5 of the 6 steps
- advantages of EUAC
  1) relatively easy—Brendan's software
  2) qualitative <u>and</u> quantitative
  3) using this innovative method gives us a competitive advantage
- our qualifications: Peter, John, Brendan
- request authorization

<u>Time to **choose and edit content**</u>: 8 minutes

At this point, Art's writing is interrupted by a phone call, which leads to other conversations between Art and two technologists in the office. After 40 minutes, Art returns to organize the content of his proposal. As he looks at his edited contents list, Art realizes that he has jotted down his points in the order he has successfully used for proposals in the past:

1. reader connection and statement of problem
2. proposed solution
3. description of proposal
4. supporting arguments
5. request for authorization

However, Art decides to place his team's qualifications *before* his supporting arguments, to establish that his Kelowna team can handle the proposed approach.

Using the cut-and paste function on his word processor, Art places his list of points as follows:

- situation more complex than usual—financial considerations
- <u>solution</u>: EUAC (Brendan's idea)
- process of preparing EUAC (see my notes)
- <u>Note</u>: we already do 5 of the 6 steps

- our qualifications: Peter, John, Brendan
- advantages of EUAC
  1) relatively easy—Brendan's software
  2) merges qualitative <u>and</u> quantitative methods
  3) using this innovative method gives us a competitive advantage
- request authorization

Before using this outline to compose his memo, Art **reviews its structure**. He realizes that he should start his supporting arguments with his strongest point, so he arranges the EUAC advantages as follows: (1) merges qualitative and quantitative methods; (2) gives us a competitive advantage; (3) Brendan's software—easy to use and inexpensive.

<u>Time to **organize content**</u>: 3 minutes

Feeling in control of the writing process, Art **composes the first draft**, working quickly from his outline and detailed notes. He composes the 757-word document in 33 minutes. At that point, Art has to leave for a meeting, which takes the rest of the afternoon. This is Art's draft:

Re: Recommending a Coal-haul Method to Jackson Mining

As you requested, I have begun to prepare a recommendation for Jackson Mining's consideration. Its situation, however, is considerably much more complex than other transportation issues we have analyzed in the past. In this case, we must consider the factor of fluctuating interest rates as well as varying amortization periods for carrying the capital debt. This problem is additionally compounded by not knowing how long Jackson Mining expects to operate the proposed Othello mine and haul coal from it.

Consulting with Brendan Winters, a Penticton C.A. who has a special interest in mining projects, we should use Equivalent Uniform Annual Costs (EUAC) as the main method of comparing Jackson Mining's four alternative transportation methods. EUAC provides a comprehensive, as well as a clear, way of comparing the four alternatives.

The Process

Preparing a comprehensive set of EUAC requires a six-step process. You will note from the following list of steps that we would normally preform the first five steps in this kind of analysis, the sixth step, the actual EUAC calculations, uses data generated during the first five steps of the process. These, then, are the steps:

1. Gather field data about the proposed road and railroad routes. This step will require doing our own surveys as well as gathering data from existing maps and surveys.

Figure 3.3   Draft document   **(Continued)**

2. Research specifications of the diesel trucks and train options that are suitable for the type of terrain found on the proposed routes. We will need physical and mechanical specifications as well as the capital costs of this equipment.

3. Determine the fuel consumption figures for each of the four options. This set of calculations will be quite extensive, particularly in this case, because of the length of the haul road and because of the grade variances on that road.

4. Combine the fuel costs with projected labour and maintenance costs to determine the annual operating costs for each alternative.

5. Determine the capital costs for the four alternatives.

6. Combine the annual operating costs and the capital costs with varying interest rates to produce an EUAC for each of the study periods of one to twenty years. Please see the attached sample table and sample figure which show the results for three of the twenty years that could be considered. These samples are based on roughly estimated data.

Qualifications

I believe our team is well equipped to handle this inovative method of assessing Jackson Mining's transportation needs. Peter Bondra, the engineer who will lead the research team, has degrees in both civil and mechanical engineering and useful experience in railbed construction. His main assistant will be John Housley who graduated two years ago from the Civil Engineering Technology program here in Kelowna. John has 15 years' experience in road construction and knows the area north of Grand Forks because of his frequent hunting trips in that area. In addition, John is well versed in a variety of surveying techniques. He'll be able to deal with the area's rough terrain.

After the data has been collected, Brendan Winters has indicated his willingness to be available to direct the cost analysis. He has particular expertise in calculating and presenting EUAC data.

Advantages of Using the EUAC Comparisons

The main advantage of using EUAC comparisons is that it provides qualitative comparisons as well as quantitative data. In effect, an EUAC creatively merges enginerring analysis with the maximal kind of accounting techniques to help our client see what the data really means.

Providing this kind of innovative analysis will position our firm as a creative, advanced engineering firm. Brendan Winters and I have recently surveyed a variety of resource-based companies, and not one of them had used the EUAC method. I believe its use will give us a competitive advantage in this bid and in others.

Furthermore, the complicated EUAC calclations will only take an extra day

Figure 3.3   Draft document   (*Continued*)

of work on this project because Brendan Winters has modified an accounting software program to help do the computations. His contribution will cost our firm an additional $1200.00, a relatively small part of our budget for this project.

Conclusion

I need to talk to you about using Equivalent Uniform Annual Costs in the Jackson Mining project before the end of this week. If I'm out of the office when you call, call me at my new cellular phone number, (250) 863-2999. If you would like a more comprehensive view of how EUAC can be used, I can prepare such a document in three hours and fax it to you immediately.

Art Basran

Figure 3.3   Draft document

Art returns to the memo the next morning. As he reads through his draft, he finds a dangling modifier ("Consulting with Brendan Winters, …, we") and two spelling errors ("preform", "inovative"), even though he is primarily checking the readability and tone of the document. As he **edits the draft** of his memo, Art asks himself:

- Does the content explain my ideas clearly?
- Have I established the need for my proposed action?
- Is everything accurate, complete, and correct?
- Will my supporting arguments appeal to my reader?
- Is the style readable? (concise? direct? natural?)
- Are the sentences and paragraphs about the right length?
- Have I used too much jargon? Have I used the right descriptive words?

His evaluation leaves him satisfied with the content of the proposal, but he sees wordy phrases and some phrases whose tone needs changing. Some of these are shown in the following table:

Paragraph	Phrasing	Concern/problem	Improvements
1	Its situation, however, is <u>considerably much</u> more complex than other transportation issues we have analyzed <u>in the past.</u> This problem is <u>additionally compounded by not knowing</u> ... operate the proposed Othello mine <u>and haul coal from it.</u>	wordy (see underlined words) wordy, pompous	Its situation, however, is more complex than other transport issues we have analyzed. Also, we don't know... operate the proposed Othello mine.
2	EUAC provides a comprehensive, <u>as well as</u> a clear, way of comparing the four alternatives.	wordy	EUAC provides a complete, clear comparison of the four options.
5	Brendan Winters has indicated his willingness to be available	wordy	Brendan Winters will be available
7	...surveyed a variety of resource-based companies	inexact and therefore not persuasive	surveyed 12 mining and forestry companies
9	I need to talk to you about using Equivalent Uniform Annual Costs ... before the end of this week.	the tone is too aggressive for addressing one's supervisor	May we discuss using EUAC... by this Friday?

Art's paring of unnecessary words reduces the word count from 757 to 663 and makes several sentences easier to read. Then, also confident that he has established the right tone in the memo, Art puts the document through his software's spell checker, which detects two errors ("calclations" and "enginerring"). But, not trusting either his own proofreading or the spell checker, Art gives the document to engineering technologist, Cathy Haldane, who finds a comma splice in paragraph 3 and a pronoun agreement error ("advantage of using EUAC comparisons is that <u>it</u> provides") in paragraph 6.

Art's <u>**revision, editing, and proofreading** time</u>: 18 minutes

Finally, Art takes 4 minutes to apply some final touch-ups and print the proposal.

Art's finished document is shown in Figure 3.4 on pages 54 and 55. His time to produce the memo, including time in discussion with Cathy Haldane, totals 84 minutes. Every minute of that time has been productive.

MMT Consulting   Inter-Office MEMORANDUM

To: Brenda Backstrom   **Date:** December 3, 2009
          Western Regional Manager

From: Art Basran
           Kelowna Branch Manager

Re: Method of Comparing Transportation Alternatives for Jackson Mining's
          Proposed Othello Mine

As you requested, I'm preparing a proposal for Jackson Mining's consideration. Its situation, however, is more complex than other transport issues we have analyzed. In this case, we must consider fluctuating interest rates and varying amortization periods for carrying the capital debt. Also, we don't know how long Jackson Mining expects to operate the proposed Othello mine.

After consulting with Brendan Winters, a Penticton C.A. who has a special interest in mining projects, I propose that we use Equivalent Uniform Annual Costs (EUAC) as the main method of comparing Jackson Mining's four alternative transportation methods. EUAC provides a complete, clear comparison of the four options.

The Process
Preparing a comprehensive set of EUAC requires a six-step process, the first five of which we would normally perform in this kind of analysis; the sixth step, the actual EUAC calculations, uses data generated during the first five steps of the process. Here are the steps:

1. *Gather field data about the proposed road and railroad routes.* This step will require doing our own surveys as well as gathering data from existing maps and surveys.

2. *Research specifications of the diesel trucks and train options* that are suitable for the type of terrain found on the proposed routes. We will need physical and mechanical specifications as well as the capital costs of this equipment.

3. *Determine the fuel consumption figures* for each of the four options. This set of calculations will be quite extensive for the Othello Mine road, which is about 80 kilometres and which has many grade variances.

4. *Combine the fuel costs* with projected labour and maintenance costs to *determine the annual operating costs for each alternative.*

5. *Determine the capital costs* for the four alternatives.

6. *Combine the annual operating costs and the capital costs with varying interest rates* to produce an EUAC for each of the study periods of one to twenty years. Please see the attached sample table and figure that show the results for three of the twenty years which could be considered. These samples are based on estimated data.

Qualifications
Our team is well equipped to handle this innovative method of assessing Jackson Mining's transportation needs. Peter Bondra, the engineer who will lead the research team, has degrees in both civil and mechanical engineering and useful experience in railbed construction. His main assistant will be John Housley who graduated two years ago from the Civil Engineering Technology program here in Kelowna.

...2

Figure 3.4   An Efficiently Produced Document   (*Continued*)

Brenda Backstrom
December 3, 2009
Page 2

John has 15 years' experience in road construction and knows the area north of Grand Forks because of his frequent hunting trips in that area. He'll be able to deal with the area's rough terrain. In addition, John is well versed in a variety of surveying techniques.

After the data has been collected, Brendan Winters will be available to direct the cost analysis. He's expert in calculating and presenting EUAC data.

Advantages of Using the EUAC Comparisons

The main advantage of using EUAC comparisons is that they provide qualitative comparisons as well as quantitative data. EUAC combines engineering and accounting ideas to help our client see what the data really means.

Providing this kind of innovative analysis will position MMT as a creative, advanced engineering firm. Brendan Winters and I have recently surveyed 12 mining and forestry companies, not one of which has used the EUAC method. I believe its use will give us a competitive advantage in this and future bids.

Furthermore, the complicated EUAC calculations will take only an extra day of work on this project because Brendan Winters has modified some accounting software to do the computations. His work will cost our firm an additional $1200, a small part of our project budget.

Conclusion

By this Friday, may we discuss using EUAC for Jackson Mining? If I'm out ofthe office when you call, you can reach me at my new cellular phone, (250) 863-2999. If you would like a fuller explanation of how EUAC can be used, I could fax one to you.

Art Basran

Attachments: Sample Calculations

Figure 3.4 An Efficiently Produced Document

☑ EXERCISES

1. Assume that you are a training manager for XYZ Corporation. After completing this first section of the text and the course, what advice would you have for a beginning writer who will frequently need to write reports on the job? In a one- or two-page, single-spaced memo to new employees, explain the writing process briefly, and give a list of guidelines these writers should follow.

2. Use the following form (Figure 3.5) to audit your writing habits as you produce your next few assignments. The time log should give you an idea of how efficiently you write, and where you could begin to save time in the writing process.

Stage of Writing Process	Time Spent	Methods and Results
1. Getting started		
2. Gathering/choosing content: information, ideas, and analysis		
3. Organizing		
4. Phrasing first draft		
5. Revising content and structure Editing style and paragraphs Finding and correcting errors		

Figure 3.5   Time Audit

☑ COLLABORATIVE PROJECT

Reviewing, Editing, and Revising a Document

After several weeks in a technical writing class, you have a good sense of *what* material is covered and of *how* the material is taught. Imagine that at a recent meeting your school's Advanced Writing Committee passed this motion:

> Because of the popularity of the technical writing course, and the 200 percent enrollment increase within two years, many new sections have been added. To ensure a unified program, we suggest that all sections follow a standard syllabus and similar teaching approaches.

For help in developing a standard model, the committee has decided to survey students about to complete the technical writing course. Each student has been asked to submit a memo evaluating the section, with suggestions for improvement. The responses will form a database for the committee's decisions about a course model that meets students' needs.

As a guide for evaluation, the committee has provided this question:

> How well do the content and teaching approach in your technical writing course fulfill your needs and expectations? How can this course best be taught, and what material should be covered? Be specific in your evaluation of strengths and weaknesses. Along with suggestions for improvement, explain how a specific change or improvement would benefit you.

Assume that Fran White, a student in some other section, has responded with this memo:

> To: The Advanced Writing Committee
> From: Fran White, Technical Writing Student
> Subject: Section 1499: Evaluation and
>   Recommendation
>
> This course is providing me with a great deal of useful information. Also, the teacher usually manages to hold the attention of the class very well. Learning about writing can be a pretty boring experience, but this class hardly ever is bored because the teacher does such a good job of making the material interesting. Also, the teacher is a very nice person. I'm happy to say that I've learned a number of approaches that have helped me improve my writing.
>
> Writing skills are important in just about anyone's career, so I'm glad we have the chance to take a technical writing course before graduation. Having the course as a requirement is a good idea, because many students (myself included) probably would avoid any course that requires this much writing. It isn't until we get there that we realize how worthwhile (and difficult!) this course is for everyone. I'd like to see every section taught the way this one is: by a teacher who knows how to get a tough job done.
>
> The only complaint I have against this teacher is the fact that he talks too much about computers. I know that computers are important, but I'd like to learn to use one for my writing instead of just being exposed to computers in general. And too many writing assignments have been saved for the latter part of the course. Everything is just stacking up, leaving me buried and confused.
>
> Also, the class is much too large, and the layout is awful. With so many students, the teacher has no way of providing individual attention, and so too many students get lost in the crowd. We need a classroom layout that would make group editing easier.
>
> I really enjoyed the audiovisual presentations in class and would like to see more of them. All in all, the concrete stuff was always the most useful.
>
> In general, the material has been covered well, except for the material on oral communication.
>
> With a few minor changes, this course would be excellent.

Before Fran can submit this memo, it will need heavy revision for content that is informative, persuasive, and ethical; organization that is easy to follow; and style that is readable. Working in teams, review, edit, and revise Fran's memo.

a. As a first step, complete an audience/purpose profile sheet based on the following data, as well as on the details given earlier.

Primary audience: The writing committee and the department chair. Several committee members also are on the tenure committee, and they are likely to use this information for an additional purpose: to evaluate Fran's instructor for tenure. These are the decision makers. Above all, Fran wants to convey a *positive* impression of her instructor.

Secondary audience: Fran's instructor (whom Fran likes, but who deserves an honest and detailed evaluation). Fran wants to be fair to her instructor but also wants to make some realistic suggestions for improving a course so important to everyone's career.

b. Assume you helped Fran prepare the brainstorming list she should have prepared *before* writing the previous draft. To visualize what it was that specifically pleased or displeased Fran, imagine that these items appeared on her list:

- instructor is always willing to help students individually
- instructor always takes time in class to answer all questions thoroughly
- emphasis on planning, drafting, and revising for a specific audience is helpful
- instructor spends a lot of time encouraging us
- instructor spends too much time talking about computers and automated offices—what I need is to develop strong writing skills by *using* the computer
- now and then we should have a guest lecturer from business and industry
- we should spend more time discussing the documents *we* have prepared
- instructor spends too much time emphasizing mistakes—not enough time on the positive
- instructor should spend more time on writing, and less than the present four weeks on oral communication
- when they are used (which is not often enough), the overhead, slide, and data projectors make things more vivid and interesting
- instructor gives a lot of feedback on our papers
- the class should have the same type of computers that are in our campus micro labs so that we have hands-on knowledge of how automation can affect the writing and revising process
- we should have a class with several round tables that seat 4–6 students for editing groups
- class size should be reduced from 30 to no more than 20 students
- tutoring should be available on a regularly scheduled basis for students with any type of writing problem
- we should spend at least one full week on job applications
- too few editing assignments early in the course; thus, too many at the end
- instructor should begin discussing the long report (term project) as early as the first or second week

From Fran's original draft and from the brainstorming list, select only that which is useful and appropriate for *this* audience and purpose. Compose a final draft of Fran's memo. Appoint one team member to present the document in class.

C HAPTER 1 explained how writers face the *information challenge: How can I make readers understand exactly what I mean?* But writers face a persuasion challenge as well, outlined in Figure 4.1. Persuasion means trying to influence people's thinking or win their cooperation. In the workplace, persuasive efforts often are aimed at building group consensus. The size of your persuasion challenge depends on who your readers are, how you want them to respond, and how firmly individuals are committed to their position.

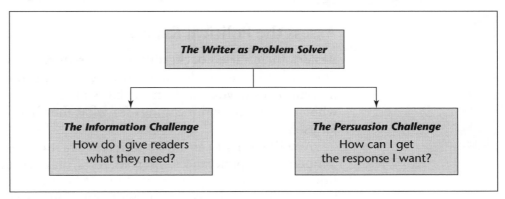

Figure 4.1   Two Challenges Confronted by Writers

You face a persuasion challenge whenever you express a viewpoint readers might dispute. Viewpoints ordinarily are expressed in a thesis or a *claim* (a statement of the point you are trying to prove). For instance, you might want readers to *recognize* facts they've ignored:

A claim about what the facts are

> The O-rings in the space shuttle's booster rockets have a serious defect that could have disastrous consequences.

Or you might want to influence how they *evaluate* the facts:

A claim about what the facts mean

> Taking time to redesign and test the O-rings is better than taking unacceptable risks to keep the shuttle program on schedule.

Or you might want readers to *take immediate action*:

A claim about what should be done

> We should call for a delay of tomorrow's shuttle launch because the risks simply are too great.

Whenever an audience disagrees about what things mean or what is better or worse or what should be done, you face a persuasion challenge.

Your own letters, memos, and reports will be asking readers to accept and act on claims like these:[1]

- We cannot meet this production deadline without sacrificing quality.
- We're doing all we can to correct your software problem.
- This hiring policy is discriminatory.

---

1. This list of claims was inspired by Gilsdorf, "Executives' and Academics' Perception."

- Our software is superior to the competing brand.
- We all need to work harder.
- I deserve a raise.

Your goal might be to convert readers to a different way of thinking, to reinforce one particular way of thinking, or to create a new way of thinking. In any event, you need to make the best case for seeing things *your* way.

Assess the Political Realities

Besides their varied backgrounds, different readers have different attitudes. On one level, your readers are consumers of information; on another they are human beings, who react on the basis of their personality and feelings, and who create their own meanings for what they have just read (Littlejohn and Jabusch 5).

Any document can evoke different reactions—depending on a reader's temperament, preferences, interests, fears, biases, preconceptions, misconceptions, ambitions, or general attitude. Whenever readers feel their views are being challenged, they respond with questions like these:

Typical Reader Questions About a Document That Attempts to Persuade	
■ Says who?	■ What are you up to?
■ So what?	■ What's in it for you?
■ Why should I?	■ What does this *really* mean?
■ Why rock the boat?	■ Will it mean more work for me?
■ What's in it for me?	■ Will it make me look bad?

Some readers might be impressed and pleased by your suggestions for increasing productivity; some might feel offended or threatened; others might think you are trying to make yourself look good or make them look bad. People can read much more between the lines than what actually is on the page. Such are the political realities of writing in any organization.

If you have worked with others, you already know something about office politics: how some people seek favour, influence, status, or power; how some resent, envy, or intimidate others; how some are easily threatened. Writing consultant Robert Hays sums up the writer's political situation this way:[2] "A writer must labour under political pressures from boss, peers, and subordinates. Any conclusion affecting other people can arouse resistance" (19). Some readers might resist your suggestion for shortening lunch breaks, cutting expenses, or automating the assembly line. Or your document might be seen as an attempt to undermine your supervisor.

---

2. Hays' "Political Realities" has excellent suggestions for analyzing and addressing political realities faced by writers.

No-one wants bad news; some people prefer to ignore it (as the O-ring flaw on the shuttle *Challenger's* booster rockets made all too clear). If you know something is wrong, that a project or product is unsafe, inefficient, or worthless, you have to decide whether "to try to change company plans; to keep silent; to 'blow the whistle'; or to quit" (Hays 19). Does your organization encourage or discourage outspokenness and constructive criticism? Find out—preferably before you accept the job. Ignoring political realities, you might write something that violates expectations and hurts your career.

Expect Reader Resistance

People who haven't made up their minds about what to do or think are more likely to be receptive to persuasive influence:

We rely on persuasion to help us make up our minds

> We are all consumers as well as providers of persuasion. Daily, we open OUR-SELVES to the persuasion of others. We need others' arguments and evidence. We're busy. We can't and don't want to discover and reason out everything for ourselves. We look for help, for short cuts, in making up our minds. (Gilsdorf, "Write Me" 12)

In a world overwhelmed by information, persuasion can help people "process" the information and decide on its meaning.

People who already have decided what to do or think, however, don't like to change their minds without good reason. Sometimes, even for the best reasons, people refuse to budge. The O-ring claims cited earlier were made—and convincingly supported—by engineers before the shuttle *Challenger* exploded on January 28, 1986. That such claims were ignored by decision makers illustrates how audiences can resist the most compelling arguments.

Whenever you question people's stand on an issue or try to change their behaviour, expect resistance. One researcher explains why persuasion is so difficult:

Once our minds are made up, we tend to hold stubbornly to our views

> By its nature, informing "works" more often than persuading does. While most people do not mind taking in some new facts, many people do resist efforts to change their opinions, attitudes, or behaviours. (Gilsdorf, "Executives' and Academics' Perception" 61)

The bigger the readers' stake in the issue, the more personal their involvement will be, and the more resistance you can expect. Research indicates that inducing permanent change in behaviour is especially difficult because people tend to revert to the familiar patterns and activities that are part of their lifestyle or work habits (Perloff 321).

*Some ways of yielding
to persuasion are better
than others*

When people do yield to persuasion, they yield either grudgingly, willingly, or enthusiastically (as in Figure 4.2). Researchers categorize these responses as *compliance, identification,* or *internalization* (Kelman 51–60):

- *Compliance:* "I'm yielding to your demand in order to get a reward or to avoid punishment. I really don't accept it, but I feel pressured and so I'll go along to get along."
- *Identification:* "I'm yielding to your appeal because I like and believe you, I want you to like me, and I feel we have something in common."
- *Internalization:* "I'm yielding because what you're saying makes good sense and it fits my goals and values."

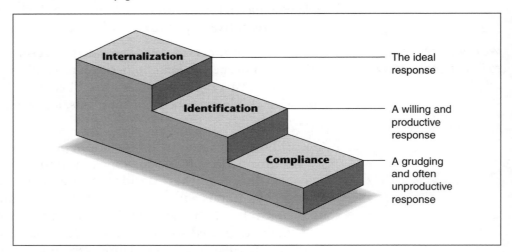

Figure 4.2   The Levels of Response to Persuasion

Although compliance is sometimes a necessary response (as in military orders or workplace safety regulations) nobody likes to be coerced. Effective persuasion relies on identification or internalization. If readers merely comply because they feel they have no choice, then you probably have lost their loyalty and goodwill—and as soon as the threat or reward disappears, you will lose their compliance as well.

Know How to Connect with Readers

Persuasive people know when to merely declare what they want, when to reach out and create a relationship, when to appeal to reason—or when to employ some combination of these strategies. These three strategies for connecting have been categorized as *hard, soft,* and *rational* (Kipnis and Schmidt 40–46). Let's call them the *power connection,* the *relationship connection,* and the *rational connection,* as shown in Figure 4.3.

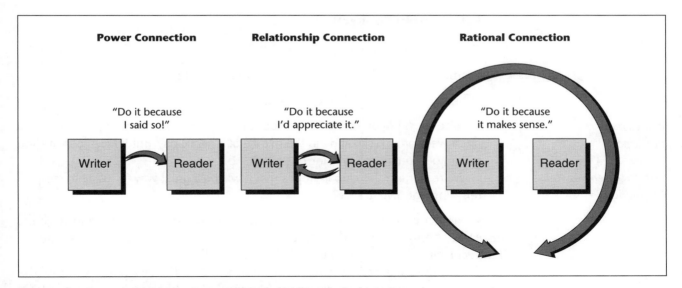

Figure 4.3   Three Strategies for Connecting with an Audience

For an illustration of these different connections, picture the following situation:

Your Company, XYZ Engineering, has just developed a fitness program, based on findings that healthy employees work better, take fewer sick days, and cost less to insure. This program offers clinics for smoking, stress reduction, and weight loss, along with group exercise. In your second month on the job you receive this notice through e-mail:

Power Connection

To: All Employees   1/20/07

From: G. Maximus, Human Resources Director

Subject: Physical Fitness

Orders readers to show up

On Monday, June 10, all employees will report to the company gymnasium at 8:00 a.m. for the purpose of choosing a walking or jogging group. Each group will meet 30 minutes three times weekly during lunch time.

How would you react to this memo—and to the person who wrote it? Here the writer seeks nothing more than compliance. Although the writer speaks of "choosing," you are given no real choice but simply ordered to show up. This kind of *power connection* is typically used by supervisors and others in power. Although it may or may not achieve its goal, the power connection almost surely will alienate its audience.

Now assume instead that you received the following version of our memo. How would you react to this message and its writer?

Relationship Connection

To:	All Employees	1/20/07
From:	G. Maximus, Human Resources Director	
Subject:	An Invitation to Physical Fitness	

Invites readers to participate

Leaves the choice to the reader

I realize most of you spend lunch hour playing cards, reading, or just enjoying a bit of well-earned relaxation in the middle of a hectic day. But I'd like to invite you to join our lunchtime walking/jogging club.

We're starting this club in hopes that it will be a great way for us all to feel better. Why not give it a try?

This version evokes a sense of identification, of shared feelings and goals. Instead of being commanded, readers are invited—they are given a real choice. This *relationship connection* establishes goodwill.

Often, the biggest factor in persuasion is an audience's perception of the writer. Audiences are more receptive to people they like, trust, and respect. Of course, you would be unethical in appealing to the relationship or in faking the relationship merely to hide the fact that you had no evidence to support your claim (Ross 28). Audiences need to find the claim believable ("Exercise will help me feel better") and relevant ("I personally need this kind of exercise"). The relationship connection, moreover, might strike some readers as too "chummy" to carry any real authority—and so the request might be ignored.

Here is a third version of our memo. As you read, think about the ways it makes a persuasive case.

Rational Connection

To:	All Employees	1/20/07
From:	G. Maximus, Human Resources Director	
Subject:	Invitation to Join One of Our Jogging or Walking Groups	

Presents authoritative evidence

I want to share a recent study from the *New England Journal of Medicine,* which reports that adults who walk two miles a day could increase their life expectancy by three years.

Other research shows that 30 minutes of moderate aerobic exercise, at least three times weekly, has a significant and long-term effect in reducing stress, lowering blood pressure, and improving job performance.

Offers alternatives

As a first step in our exercise program, XYZ Engineering is offering a variety of daily jogging groups: The One-Milers, Three-Milers, and Five-Milers. All groups will meet at designated times on our brand new, quarter-mile, rubberized clay track.

For beginners or skeptics, we're offering daily two-mile walking groups. For the truly resistant, we offer the option of a Monday-Wednesday-Friday two-mile walk.

Offers a compromise

Leaves the choice to the reader

Offers incentives

> Coffee and lunch breaks can be rearranged to accommodate whichever group you select.
>
> Why not take advantage of our hot new track? As small incentives, XYZ will reimburse anyone who signs up as much as $100 for running or walking shoes, and will even throw in an extra fifteen minutes for lunch breaks. And with a consistent turnout of 90 percent or better, our company insurer may be able to eliminate everyone's $200 yearly deductible in medical costs.

Here the writer shows willingness to compromise ("If you do this, I'll do that"). This *rational connection* communicates respect for the reader's intelligence *and* for the relationship by presenting good reasons, a variety of alternatives, and attractive incentives—all framed as an invitation. Whenever an audience is willing to listen to reason, the rational connection stands the best chance of succeeding.

Keep in mind that each kind of connection (or some combination) can work in particular situations. But no cookbook formula exists, and in many situations, your persuasive attempts may fail.

Ask for a Specific Decision

Unless you are giving an order, diplomacy is essential in persuasion. But don't be afraid to ask for the specific decision you want, preferably at the end of the message:

Let people know exactly what you want

> Studies show that the moment of decision is made easier for people when we show them what the desired action is, rather than leaving it up to them. . . . Without this directive, people may misunderstand or lose interest in the entire message. No one likes to make decisions: there is always a risk involved. But if the writer asks for the action, and makes it look easy and urgent, the decision itself looks less risky and the entire persuasive effort has a better chance of succeeding. (Cross 3)

Let readers know what you want them to do or think.

Never Ask for Too Much

No amount of persuasion will move people to accept something they consider unreasonable. And the definition of *reasonable* depends on the individual. Employees at XYZ, for example, will differ as to which walking/jogging option they might accept.

To the jock writing the memo, a daily five-mile jog might seem perfectly reasonable, but some employees would think it outrageous. XYZ's program therefore has to offer something most of its audience (except, say, couch potatoes and those in poor health) accept as reasonable. Any request that exceeds its audience's "latitude of acceptance" (Sherif 39–59) is doomed (see Figure 4.4).

Identify your audience's latitude of acceptance

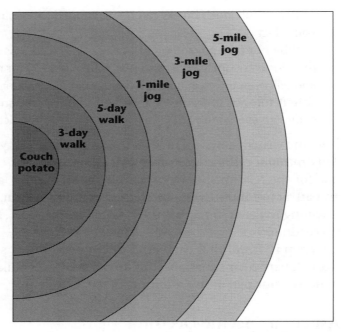

Options offered by XYZ

Figure 4.4   Options and Latitude of Acceptance

Recognize All Constraints

Persuasive communicators observe certain limits or restrictions imposed by their situation. These are the *constraints,* and they govern what should or should not be said, who should say it and to whom, when and how it should be said, and through which medium (printed document, on-line, telephone, face to face, and so on). In the workplace you need to account for constraints like those in Figure 4.5.

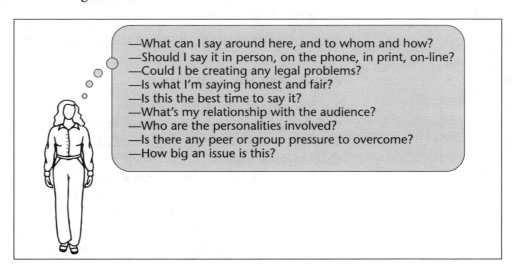

Figure 4.5   Every Writing Situation Poses Its Own Constraints

Organizational Constraints

Organizations often have their own official constraints; for instance, schedules, deadlines, budget limitations, writing style, the way a document is organized and formatted, and its chain and medium of distribution throughout the organization. But writers also face unofficial constraints:

Decide carefully when to say what to whom

> Most organizations have clear rules for interpreting and acting on (or responding to) statements made by colleagues. Even if the rules are unstated, we know who can initiate interaction, who can be approached, who can propose a delay, what topics can or cannot be discussed, who can interrupt or be interrupted, who can order or be ordered, who can terminate interaction, and how long interaction should last. (Littlejohn and Jabusch 143)

The exact rules vary among organizations, depending on whether communication channels are open and flexible or closed and rigid, on whether employee participation in decision making is encouraged or discouraged.

Although the rules of the game mostly are unspoken, anyone who ignores them (for example, going over a supervisor's head with a complaint or suggestion) invites disaster.

Airing even the most legitimate gripe in the wrong way through the wrong medium to the wrong person can be fatal to your work relationships and your career. The following memo, for instance, is likely to be interpreted by the executive officer as petty and whining behaviour, and by the maintenance director as a public attack.

Wrong way to the wrong person

> Dear Chief Executive Officer:
>
> Please ask the Maintenance Director to get his people to do their job for a change. I realize we're all short-staffed, but I've received fifty complaints this week about the filthy restrooms and overflowing wastebaskets in my department. If he wants us to empty our own wastebaskets, why doesn't he let us know?
>
> c: Maintenance Director

Instead, why not address the memo directly to the key person—or better yet, phone the person?

A better way to the right person

> Dear Maintenance Director:
>
> I wonder if we could meet to exchange some ideas about how our departments might be able to help one another during these staff shortages.

Can you identify the unspoken rules where you have worked? What happens when such rules are ignored?

Legal Constraints

Sometimes what you can say is limited by contract or by laws protecting confidentiality or customers' rights, or laws affecting product liability. For example, in a collection letter for non-payment, you can threaten legal action but cannot threaten any kind of violence or to publicize the refusal to pay, or pretend to be a lawyer (Varner and Varner 31–40). If someone requests information on one of your employees, you can "respond only to specific requests that have been approved by the employee. Further, your comments should relate only to job performance which is documented" (Harcourt 64). When writing sales literature or manuals, you and your company are liable for faulty information that leads to injury or damage.

Know how the law applies to any document you prepare. Suppose, for instance, an employee drops dead while participating in the new jogging program you've marketed so persuasively. Could you and your company be liable? Perhaps you should require physical exams and stress tests (at company expense) for participants.

Ethical Constraints

While legal constraints are defined by federal and provincial laws, ethical constraints are defined by good conscience, honesty, and fair play. For example, it may be perfectly legal to promote a new pesticide by emphasizing its effectiveness, while downplaying its carcinogenic effects; whether such action is *ethical*, however, is another issue entirely. To earn people's trust, you will find that "saying the right thing" involves more than legal considerations.

Persuasive skills carry tremendous potential for abuse. There is a difference between honestly presenting your best case and using deception to manipulate the reader. (Chapter 5 is devoted to various ethics problems in communication.)

Time Constraints

Persuasion often is a matter of good timing. Do you have a deadline? If not, should you delay your message, release it immediately, or what? Let's assume you're trying to "bring out the vote" among members of your professional society on some hotly debated issue; for example, whether to refuse work on any project related to biological warfare. You might want to wait until you have all of the information you need or until you've analyzed the situation and planned a strategy. But you don't want to delay so long that rumours, misinformation, or paranoia cause people to harden their position *and* their resistance to your appeals. If delay might place the situation beyond your control, you might have to speak out sooner than you would like.

Social and Psychological Constraints

Too often, what we say can be misunderstood or misinterpreted. Here are just a few of the human constraints routinely encountered by communicators.

- *Relationship between communicator and audience:* Are you writing to a superior, a subordinate, or an equal? (Try not to appear dictatorial to subordinates nor to shield superiors from bad news.) How well do you and your audience know each other? Can you joke around or should you be serious? Do you get along or have a history of conflict? Do you trust and like one another? What you say and how you say it—and how it is interpreted—will be influenced by the relationship.

- *Audience's personality:* Researchers claim that "some people are easier to persuade than others, regardless of the topic or situation" (Littlejohn 136). Any reader's ability to be persuaded might depend on such personality traits as confidence, optimism, self-esteem, willingness to be different, desire to conform, open- or closed-mindedness, or regard for power (Stonecipher 188–89). The less your audience is open to persuasion, the harder you have to work. If you sense that your audience is totally resistant, you may want to back off—or give up altogether.

- *Audience's sense of identity and affiliation as a group:* How close-knit is the group? Does it have a strong sense of identity (as, for example, union members, conservationists, or engineering majors)? Will group loyalty or pressure to conform prevent certain appeals from working? Address the group's collective concerns.

- *Perceived size and urgency of the problem or issue:* In the audience's view, how big is this issue or problem? Has it been understated or overstated? Big problems are more likely to cause people to exaggerate their fears, anxieties, loyalties, and resistance to change—or to desperately seek some quick and easy solution. Assess the problem realistically. You don't want to downplay it, but you don't want to cause panic, either.

Writers who can assess a situation's constraints avoid serious blunders and can develop their message for greatest effectiveness.

Support Your Claims Convincingly

The persuasive argument is the one that makes the best case in the audience's view. The strength of your case depends on the *reasons* you offer to support your claims.

Persuasive claims are backed up by reasons that have meaning for the reader

> When we seek a project extension, argue for a raise, interview for a job, justify our actions, advise a friend, speak out on issues of the day . . . we are involved in acts that require good reasons. Good reasons allow our audience and ourselves to find a shared basis for cooperating. . . . In speaking and writing, you can use marvellous language, tell great stories, provide exciting metaphors, speak in enthralling tones, and even use your reputation to advantage, but what it comes down to is that you must speak to your audience with reasons they understand. (Hauser 71)

To see how reasons support persuasive claims, imagine yourself in the following situation: As documentation manager for Bemis Software, a rapidly growing company, you supervise preparation and production of all user manuals. The present system for producing manuals is inefficient because three respective departments are involved in, (1) assembling the required material, (2) word processing and designing, and (3) publishing the manuals. As a result, much time and energy are wasted as a manual goes back and forth among software specialists, communication specialists, and the art and printing department. After studying the problem and calling in a consultant, you decide that greater efficiency could be achieved if desktop publishing software were installed on all computers. This way, all employees involved could contribute to all three phases of the process. To sell this plan to supervisors and co-workers you will need good reasons, in the form of *evidence* and *appeals to readers' needs and values* (Rottenberg 104–06).

Offer Convincing Evidence

Evidence is any factual support from an outside source. Evidence is a powerful element in persuasion—as long as it measures up to readers' standards. Discerning readers evaluate evidence by using these criteria (Perloff 157–58):

- *The evidence has quality.* Instead of sheer quantity, readers expect evidence that is strong, specific, new, or different.
- *The sources are credible.* Readers want to know where the evidence comes from, how it was collected, and who collected it.
- *The evidence is considered reasonable.* It falls within a reader's "latitude of acceptance" (Sherif 39–59).

Common types of evidence include factual statements, statistics, examples, and expert testimony.

Factual Statements. A *fact* is something whose existence can be demonstrated by observation, experience, research, or measurement.

Offer the facts

Many of our competitors already have desktop publishing networks in place.

When your space and your reader's tolerance are limited—as they usually are—be selective. Decide which facts best support your case.

Statistics. Numbers can be highly convincing. Before considering other details of your argument, many workplace readers are interested in the "bottom line": costs, savings, profits (Goodall and Waagen 57).

Give the numbers

After a cost/benefit analysis, our accounting office estimates that an integrated desktop publishing network will save Bemis 30 percent in production costs and 25 percent in production time—savings that will enable the system to pay for itself within one year.

Numbers also can be highly misleading. Any statistics you present have to be accurate, trustworthy, and easy for readers to understand and verify. (See pages 162–166 for ways to avoid faulty statistical reasoning.) Always cite your source.

Examples. By showing specific instances of your point, examples help audiences *visualize* the idea or the concept. For example, the best way to explain what you mean by "inefficiency" in your company is to show one or more instances of it:

Show what you mean

> The following figure illustrates the inefficiency of Bemis' present system for producing manuals:

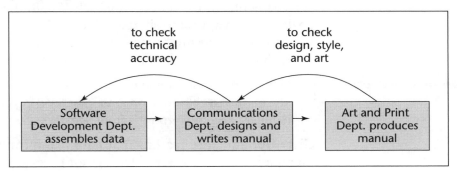

> A manual typically goes back and forth through this cycle three or four times, wasting time and effort in all three departments.

Good examples have persuasive force; they give readers something solid, a way of understanding even the most surprising or unlikely claim. Use examples that the audience can identify with and that fit the point they are designed to illustrate.

Expert Testimony. Expert testimony lends authority and credibility to any claim.

Cite the experts

> Ron Catabia, nationally recognized networking consultant, has studied our needs and strongly recommends we move ahead with the integrated network.

To be credible, however, an expert has to be unbiased and considered reliable by the audience.

Although solid evidence can be persuasive, evidence alone isn't always enough to influence the reader. At Bemis, for example, the bottom-line might be very persuasive for company executives but could mean little to some managers and employees who will be asking: *Does this threaten my authority? Will I have to work harder? Will I fall behind? Is my job in danger?* These readers will have to perceive some benefit beyond company profit.

Appeal to Common Goals and Values

Audiences expect a writer to share their goals and values. If you hope to create any kind of consensus, you have to identify at least one goal you and your audience have in common: "What do we all want most?"

Bemis employees, like most people, share these goals: job security, a sense of belonging, control over their jobs and destinies, a growing and fulfilling career. Any persuasive recommendation will have to take these goals into account. For example:

Appeal to shared goals

> I'd like to show how desktop publishing skills, instead of threatening anyone's job, would only increase career mobility for all of us.

Our goals are shaped by our values (qualities we believe in, ideals we stand for): friendship, loyalty, ambition, honesty, self-discipline, equality, fairness, achievement, among others (Rokeach 57–58). Beyond appealing to common goals, you can appeal to shared values.

At Bemis, you might appeal to the commitment to quality and achievement shared by the company and by individual employees:

Appeal to shared values

> None of us needs reminding of the fierce competition in the software industry. The improved collaboration among networking departments will result in better manuals, keeping us on the front line of quality and achievement.

Give your audience reasons that have real meaning for *them* personally. For example, in a recent study of teenage attitudes about the negative consequences of smoking, respondents listed these reasons for not smoking: bad breath, difficulty concentrating, loss of friends, and trouble with adults. None of them listed dying of cancer—presumably because this last reason carries little meaning for young people personally (Bauman et al. 510–30).

Consider the Cultural Context

Reaction to persuasive appeals can be influenced by a culture's customs and values.[3] Cultures might differ in their willingness to debate, criticize, or express disagreement or emotion. They might differ in their definitions of "convincing support," or they might observe special formalities in communicating. Expressions of feelings and concern for one's family might be valued more than logic, fact, statistics, research findings, or expert testimony. Some cultures consider the *source* of a message as important as its content. Establishing trust and building a relationship might weigh more heavily than proof and might be an essential prelude to getting down to business.

Cultures might differ in their attitudes toward the environment, big business, technology, or competition. They might value delayed gratification more than immediate reward, stability more than progress, time more than profit, politeness more than candour, age more than youth.

One essential element of reader expectations in all cultures is the primacy of *face saving*:

Face saving is every reader's bottom line

> *Face saving* [is] the act of preserving one's prestige or outward dignity. People of all cultures, to a greater or lesser degree, are concerned with face saving. Yet ... [its] importance ... varies significantly from culture to culture. ... Indirectness in high face-saving cultures is viewed as consideration for another's sense of dignity; in low face-saving cultures, indirectness is seen as dishonesty. (Victor 159–61)

---

3. Adapted from Beamer 293–95; Gestelend 24; Hulbert, "Overcoming" 42; Jameson 9–11; Kohl et al. 65; Martin and Chaney 271–77; Nydell 61; Thrush 276–77; Victor 159–66.

Readers lose face when they are offended by overly explicit argument, confused by a message that seems too vague, or embarrassed by the plain, unvarnished truth. They lose face when they think they are being contradicted, blatantly criticized, or addressed too informally. They lose face when their customs are ignored or their values trivialized.

Intentional or not, any perceived insult to a person's dignity ends all possibility for meaningful communication. Without violating ethical standards for honesty and fairness, effective communication in any cultural context enables recipients to save face.

CAUTION: Violating a reader's cultural frame of reference is offensive, but so is reducing individual complexity to a simplistic set of cultural stereotypes. Any generalization about any group presents a highly limited picture and in no way accurately characterizes all members of the group—or any members, for that matter. No laundry list of cultural features can replace our intuitive sensitivity toward those with whom we transact.

No particular formula for persuasion can guarantee positive results. Your approach depends on the people involved, the setting, the relationships, the issue, and the variables discussed earlier.

People rarely change their minds quickly or without good reason. A truly resistant audience will dismiss even our best arguments and may end up feeling threatened and resentful. Even when the audience is receptive, our initial attempts can fail. Often, the best we can do is avoid disaster and create an opportunity for people to appreciate the merits of our case.

IN BRIEF

Questions for Analyzing Cross-cultural Audiences[4]

About Accepted Behaviour?

- Formalities for making requests, expressing disagreement, criticism, or praise
- Preferred form for greetings or introductions (first or family names, titles)
- Willingness to criticize or request clarification
- Willingness to argue, debate, or express disagreement
- Willingness to be contradicted
- Willingness to express emotion (pleasure, gratitude, anger)
- Importance of trust and relationship building
- Importance of politeness and euphemism and leaving certain things unsaid
- Preference for casual or formal interaction
- Preference for directness and plain talk or for indirectness and ambiguity
- Preference for rapid decision making or for extensive analysis of a topic

About the Social and Legal System?

- Social/political system inflexible or open
- Class distinctions
- Democratic, egalitarian ideals or rank-conscious, authoritarian system
- Relative importance of the law versus interpersonal trust
- Formality of the contract process: a mere handshake or extensive legal documents
- Extent of lawyer involvement
- Extent to which the legal system enforces contractual agreements
- Role of gift giving (viewed as bribery or as a display of respect)

About Values and Attitudes?

- Attitude toward the environment, big business, technology, competition, risk taking, status, youth versus age, rugged individualism versus group loyalty
- Preference for immediate reward or delayed gratification, progress or stability
- Importance of gender equality, interaction, and differences in the workplace
- Importance of the personal relationship in a business transaction
- Importance of time ("Time is money!" or "Never rush!")
- Importance of feelings versus logic and facts, results versus relationships
- Importance of candour versus saving face and sparing other people's feelings
- Extent of belief in fate, luck, or destiny
- View of our culture (admiration, contempt, envy, fear)

---

4. Adapted from Beamer 293–95; Gestelend 24; Hulbert, "Overcoming" 42; Jameson 9–11; Kohl et al. 65; Martin and Chaney 271–77; Nydell 61; Thrush 276–77; Victor 159–66.

Observe Persuasion Guidelines

Later chapters offer specific guidelines for various persuasive documents. But beyond attending to specific requirements of a particular document, remember this principle:

No matter how brilliant, any argument rejected by its audience is a failed argument.

If readers find cause to dislike you or conclude that your argument has no meaning for them personally, they usually reject *anything* you say. Connecting with an audience means being able to see things from their perspective. The following guidelines can help you make that connection.

1. *Assess the political climate.* Can you be outspoken? Who will be affected by your document? How will they react? How will your motives be interpreted? Will the document enhance your reputation or damage it? The better you assess readers' political feelings, the less likely your document will backfire. Do what you can to earn confidence and good-will:

   - Be diplomatic; try not to make anyone look bad or lose face.
   - Be aware of your status in the organization; don't overstep.
   - Don't expect anyone to be perfect—including yourself.
   - Ask your intended readers to review early drafts.

   When reporting company negligence, dishonesty, stupidity, or incompetence, expect political fallout. Decide beforehand whether you want to keep your job or your dignity (more in Chapter 5).

2. *Learn the unspoken rules.* Know the constraints on what you can say, to whom you can say it, and how and when you can say it.

3. *Be clear about what you want.* Diplomacy is important, but people won't like having to guess about your purpose.

4. *Never make a claim or ask for something you know readers will reject outright.* Be sure readers can live with whatever you're requesting or proposing. Offer a genuine choice.

5. *Anticipate your audience's reaction.* Will they be defensive, surprised, annoyed, angry, or what? Try to address their biggest objections beforehand. Express your judgments ("We could do better") without making people defensive ("It's your fault").

6. *Decide on a connection (or combination of connections).* Does the situation call for you to merely declare your position, appeal to the relationship, or appeal to common sense and reason?

7. *Avoid an extreme persona.* Persona is the image or impression of the writer's personality suggested by a document's tone. Resist the urge to "sound off," no matter how strongly you feel, because audiences tune

out aggressive people, no matter how sensible the argument. Try to be likable and reasonable. Admit the imperfections in your case—a little humility never hurts. Don't hesitate to offer praise when it's deserved.

8. *Find points of agreement with your audience.* Focusing early on a shared value, goal, or concern can reduce conflict and help win agreement on later points.

9. *Never distort the opponent's position.* A sure way to alienate people is to cast the opponent as more of a villain or simpleton than the facts warrant.

10. *Try to concede something to the opponent.* Surely the opposing case is based on at least one good reason. Acknowledge the merits of that case before arguing for your own. Instead of seeming like a know-it-all, show some empathy and willingness to compromise.

11. *Use only your best material.* Not all your reasons or appeals will have equal strength or significance. Decide which material—from your *audience's* view—best advances your case.

12. *Make no claim or assertion unless you can support it with good reasons.* "Just because" does not constitute adequate support!

13. *Use your skills responsibly.* Persuasive skills are easily abused. People who feel they have been bullied, manipulated, or deceived most likely will become your enemies. Know when to back off.

14. *Seek a second opinion of your document before you release it.* Ask someone you trust and who has no stake in the issue at hand.

15. *Decide on the appropriate medium.* Given the specific issue and audience, should you communicate in person, in print, by phone, e-mail, fax, newsletter, bulletin board, or what? Should all recipients receive your message via the same medium?

Figure 4.6 illustrates how our guidelines are employed in an actual persuasive situation. This letter is from a company that distributes systems for generating electrical power from recycled steam (cogeneration). President Tom Ewing writes a persuasive answer to a potential customer's question: "Why should I invest in the cogeneration system you are proposing for my plant?" As you read the letter, notice the kinds of evidence and appeals that support the opening claim. Notice also how the writer focuses on reasons important to the reader.

July 20, 2009

Mr. Richard White, President
Southern Wood Products
4985 Johnston Road
Port Alberni, BC   V9Y 5L8

Dear Mr. White:

The writer states his claim

In our meeting last week, you asked me to explain why we have such confidence in the project we are proposing. Let me outline what I think are excellent reasons.

Offers first reason

Gives examples

First, you and Delia Smith have given us a clear idea of your needs, and our recent discussions confirm that we fully understand these needs. For instance, our proposal specifies an air-cooled condenser rather than a water-cooled condenser for your project because water in Port Alberni is expensive. And besides saving money, an air-cooled condenser will be easier to operate and maintain.

Offers second reason
Appeals to shared value (quality)

Gives example

Further examples

Second, we have confidence in our component suppliers and they have confidence in this project. We don't manufacture the equipment; instead, we integrate and package cogeneration systems by selecting for each application the best components from leading manufacturers. For example, Alias Engineering, the turbine manufacturer, is the world's leading producer of single-stage turbines, having built more than 40,000 turbines in 70 years. Likewise, each component manufacturer leads the field and has a proven track record. We have reviewed your project with each major component supplier, and each guarantees the equipment. This guarantee is of course transferable to you and is supplemented by our own performance guarantee.

Appeals to reader's goal (security)
Offers third reason
Cites experts

Third, we have confidence in the system design. We developed the CX Series specifically for applications like yours, in which there is a need for both a condensing and a backpressure turbine. In our last meeting, I pointed out the cost, maintenance, and performance benefits of the CX Series. And although the CX Series is an innovative design, all components are fully proven in many other applications, and our suppliers fully endorse this design.

Figure 4.6   Supporting a Claim with Good Reasons   (*Continued*)
Adapted from a communication by Thomas S. Ewing, President, Ewing Power Systems, So. Deerfield, MA 01373.

Mr. Richard White
July 20, 2009
Page 2

Closes with best reason

Finally, and perhaps most important, you should have confidence in this project because we will stand behind it. As you know, we are eager to establish ourselves in Vancouver Island industries. If we plan to succeed, this project must succeed. We have a tremendous amount at stake in keeping you happy.

Appeals to shared value (trust) and shared goals (success)

If I can answer any questions, please phone me. We look forward to working with you.

Sincerely,

EWING POWER SYSTEMS, INC.

Tom Ewing

Thomas S. Ewing
President

Figure 4.6   Supporting a Claim with Good Reasons

A Checklist for Cross-cultural Documents

Use this checklist[5] to verify that your documents respect audience diversity.

- ❑ Does the document enable everyone to save face?
- ❑ Is the document sensitive to the culture's customs and values?
- ❑ Does the document conform to the safety and regulatory standards of the province and/or country?
- ❑ Does the document provide the expected level of detail?
- ❑ Does the document avoid possible misinterpretation?
- ❑ Is the document organized in a way that readers will consider appropriate?

- ❑ Does the document observe interpersonal conventions important to the culture (accepted forms of greeting or introduction, politeness requirements, first names, family names, titles, and so on)?
- ❑ Does the document's tone reflect the appropriate level of formality or casualness one would expect?
- ❑ Is the document's style appropriately direct or indirect?
- ❑ Is the document's format consistent with the culture's expectations?
- ❑ Does the document embody universal standards for ethical communication?

✔ EXERCISES

1. Assume that you work for a technical marketing firm proud of its reputation for honesty and fair dealing. A handbook being prepared for new personnel includes a section titled "How to Avoid Abusing Your Persuasive Skills." All employees have been asked to contribute to this section by preparing a written response to the following:

   Share a personal experience in which you or a friend were the victim of persuasive abuse in a business transaction. In a one- or two-page memo, describe the situation and explain exactly how the intimidation, manipulation, or deception occurred.

   Write the memo and be prepared to discuss it in class.

2. Find an example of an effective persuasive letter. In a memo to your instructor, explain why and how the message succeeds. Base your evaluation on the persuasion guidelines listed on pages 79–80. Attach a copy of the letter to your evaluation memo. Be prepared to discuss your evaluation in class.

   Now, evaluate a poorly written document, explaining how and why it fails.

3. Think about some change you would like to see on your campus or at your part-time job. Perhaps you would like to make something happen, such as a campus-wide policy on plagiarism, changes in course offerings or requirements, more access to computers, a policy on sexist language, or a day-care centre. Or perhaps you would like to improve something, such as the grading system, campus lighting, the system for student

---

5. This list was largely adapted from Caswell-Coward 265; Weymouth 144; Beamer 293–95; Martin and Chaney 271–77; Victor 159–61.

evaluation of teachers, or the promotion system at work. Or perhaps you would like to stop something from happening, such as noise in the library or sexual harassment at work.

Decide whom you want to persuade, and write a memo to that audience. Anticipate carefully your audience's implied questions, such as:

- Do we really have a problem or need?
- If so, should we care enough about it to do anything?
- Can the problem be solved?
- What are some possible solutions?
- What benefits can we anticipate? What liabilities?

Can you envision additional audience questions? Complete an audience/purpose profile (see page 85).

Don't think of this memo as the final word but as a consciousness-raising introduction that gets the reader to acknowledge that the issue deserves attention. At this early stage, highly specific recommendations would be premature and inappropriate.

4. Challenge an attitude or viewpoint that is widely held by your audience. Maybe you want to persuade your colleagues that the time required to earn a bachelor's degree should be extended to five years or that grade inflation is watering down your school's education. Maybe you want to claim that the campus police should (or should not) wear guns. Or maybe you want to ask students to support a 10 percent tuition increase in order to make more computers and software available.

Complete an audience/purpose profile (see page 85). Write specific answers to the following questions: What are the political realities? What kind of resistance could you anticipate? How would you connect with readers? What about their latitude of acceptance? Are there any other constraints? What reasons could you offer to support your claim?

In a memo to your instructor, submit your plan for presenting your case. Be prepared to discuss your plan in class.

☑ COLLABORATIVE PROJECTS

Assume that you work for an environmental consulting firm that is under contract with various countries for a range of projects, including these:

- A plan for rain forest regeneration in Latin America and Sub-Saharan Africa.
- A plan to decrease industrial pollution in Eastern and Western Europe.
- A plan for "clean" industries in developing countries.
- A plan for organic agricultural development in Africa and India.
- A joint Canadian/American plan to decrease acid rain.
- A plan for developing alternative energy sources in Southeast Asia.

Each project will require environmental impact statements, feasibility studies, grant proposals, and a legion of other documents. These are often prepared in collaboration with members of the host country, and in some cases prepared by your company for audiences in the host country: from political, social, and industrial leaders to technical experts and so on. For such projects to succeed, people from different cultures have to communicate effectively and sensitively, creating goodwill and cooperation. Before your company begins work in earnest with a particular country, your co-workers will need to develop a degree of cultural awareness. Your assignment is to select a country and to research that culture's behaviours, attitudes, values, and social system in terms of how these variables influence the culture's communication preferences and expectations. What should your colleagues know about this culture in order to communicate effectively and diplomatically? Do the necessary research using the questions from In Brief on page 78 as a guide.

AUDIENCE/PURPOSE PROFILE

Audience Identity and Needs

Primary reader(s): _____ *(name, title)*

Secondary reader(s): _____

Relationship: _____ *(client, employer, other)*

Intended use of document: _____ *(perform a task, solve a problem, other)*

Prior knowledge about this topic: _____ *(knows nothing, a few details, other)*

Additional information needed: _____ *(background, only bare facts, other)*

Probable questions: _____

_____

_____

_____

_____

_____

Audience's Probable Attitude and Personality

Attitude toward topic: _____ *(indifferent, skeptical, other)*

Probable objections: _____ *(cost, time, none, other)*

Probable attitude toward this writer: _____ *(intimidated, hostile, receptive, other)*

Persons most affected by this document: _____

Temperament: _____ *(cautious, impatient, other)*

Probable reaction to document: _____ *(resistance, approval, anger, guilt, other)*

Risk of alienating anyone: _____

_____

Audience Expectations About the Document

Reason document originated: _____ *(audience request, my idea, other)*

Acceptable length: _____ *(comprehensive, concise, other)*

Material important to this audience: _____ *(interpretations, costs,*

conclusions, other)

Most useful arrangement: _____ *(problem-causes-solutions, other)*

Tone: _____ *(businesslike, apologetic, enthusiastic, other)*

Intended effect on this audience: _____ *(win support, change behaviour, other)*

Due date: _____

Figure 4.7 Audience/Purpose Profile Sheet

Writing Ethically

C HAPTERS 2 and 4 explained how audience analysis helps us tailor informative and persuasive communication (so we can complete the project, win the contract, or the like). But an *effective* message (one that achieves its purpose) isn't necessarily an *ethical* message. Think of examples from advertising: "Our artificial sweetener is composed of proteins that occur naturally in the human body (amino acids)" or "Our potato chips contain no cholesterol." Such claims are technically accurate but misleading: amino acids in certain sweeteners can alter body chemistry to cause headaches, seizures, and possibly brain tumours; potato chips contain saturated fat—which produces cholesterol. While the advertisers' facts may be accurate, they often are incomplete and imply misleading conclusions.

Whether the miscommunication occurs deliberately or through neglect, a message is unethical when it leaves readers at a disadvantage or prevents readers from making their best decision. Therefore, writers ultimately face the threefold problem outlined in Figure 5.1. Ethical communication is measured by standards of honesty, fairness, and concern for everyone involved (Johannesen 1).

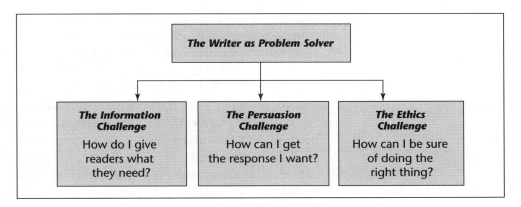

Figure 5.1   Three Challenges Confronted by Writers

Recognize Unethical Communication

Thousands of people are injured or killed yearly in avoidable accidents—the result of faulty communication that prevented intelligent decision making. Following are descriptions of tragedies caused ultimately by unethical communication.

Unethical communication has consequences

- On March 3, 1974, as a Turkish Airlines DC-10 leaving Paris reached 12,000 feet, a cargo door burst open, causing a crash that killed all 346 people. Immediate cause: a poorly designed locking mechanism gave way under high pressure. Ultimate cause: the faulty design had been recognized and documented since 1969, and cargo doors had burst open during a 1970 test and a 1972 flight (in which the pilot managed to land safely). On January 27, 1972, a head engineer wrote a memo to his superiors warning that "in the twenty years ahead of us, DC-10 cargo doors will come open, and I expect this to usually result in the loss of the airplane." This flaw easily could have been corrected. But, unwilling to admit design errors and under pressure from competitors to get the DC-10 flying as early as possible, manufacturers suppressed these data (Burghardt 4–5).

- In the early 1980s, thousands of workers (or their survivors) filed personal-injury suits against a leading manufacturer of asbestos products. The plaintiffs held the company responsible for respiratory afflictions ranging from lung cancer to emphysema. Immediate cause: exposure to asbestos fibres. Ultimate cause: for roughly fifty years the company hid from its workers the deadly facts about asbestos exposure—and even denied workers access to their own medical records. In 1963, the company's medical director offered this reason to justify the suppression of information: "As long as [the employee] is not disabled, it is felt that he should not be told of his condition so that he can live and work in peace, and the company can benefit from his many years of experience." When the cover-up finally was revealed, the company tried to evade lawsuits by filing for bankruptcy (Mokhiber 15).

- On May 9, 1992, 26 men were killed in an explosion at the Westray Coal mining operation in Plymouth, Nova Scotia. The mine, employing the latest mining technology, had been operating for about eight months when the explosion occurred. In a subsequent report of the Westray Mine Public Inquiry, Justice K. Peter Richard said that the Westray disaster was a "complex mosaic of actions, omissions, mistakes, incompetence, apathy, cynicism, stupidity, and neglect."[1] As the evidence emerged during the inquiry, it became clear that many people and entities had not communicated appropriately, had not acted on clear directives, and had not applied or enforced coal mine and occupational health and safety regulations. While criminal negligence and manslaughter charges were withdrawn late in 1998, in 1999 the families of the victims of the disaster commenced a negligence lawsuit against the federal and Nova Scotia governments, former mine officials, and equipment manufacturers.

These catastrophes make for dramatic headlines, but more routine examples of deliberate miscommunication rarely are publicized. Messages like the following succeed by saying whatever works.

- A person lands a great job by exaggerating his credentials, experience, or expertise.
- A marketing specialist for a chemical company negotiates a huge bulk sale of its powerful new pesticide by downplaying its carcinogenic hazards.
- To meet the production deadline on a new auto model, the test engineer suppresses, in her final report, data indicating that the fuel tank could explode upon impact.

---

1. The Westray Story: A Predictable Path to Disaster. Executive Summary (www.gov.ns.ca/legi/inquiry/westray/conclusn).

■ A manager writes a strong recommendation to get a friend promoted, while overlooking someone more deserving.

Can you recall some instances of deliberate miscommunication from your personal experience or that you learned about in the news? What were some of the effects of this miscommunication? How might the problems have been avoided?

To save face, escape blame, or get ahead, anyone might be tempted to say what people want to hear or to suppress bad news or make it seem "rosier." Some of these decisions are not simply black and white. Here is one engineer's description of the grey area in which issues of product safety and quality often are decided:

Ethical decisions are not always "black and white"

> The company must be able to produce its products at a cost low enough to be competitive. . . . To design a product that is of the highest quality and consequently has a high and uncompetitive price may mean that the company will not be able to remain profitable, and be forced out of business. (Burghardt 92)

Do you emphasize to a customer the need for extra careful maintenance of a highly sensitive computer—and risk losing the sale? Or do you downplay maintenance requirements, focusing instead on the computer's positive features? Do you tell a white lie so as not to hurt a colleague's feelings, or do you "tell it like it is" because you're convinced that lying is wrong in any circumstance? The decisions we make in these situations often are influenced by the pressures we feel.

Expect Social Pressure to Produce Unethical Communication

Pressure to get the job done can cause normally honest people to break the rules. At some point in your career you might have to choose between doing what your employer wants ("just follow orders" or "look the other way") and doing what you know is right. Maybe you will be pressured to ignore a safety hazard in order to meet a project deadline:

Pressure to "look the other way"

> Just as your automobile company is about to unveil its hot, new pickup truck, your safety engineering team discovers that the reserve gas tanks (installed beneath the truck but *outside* the frame) can explode on impact in a side collision. The company has spent a small fortune developing and producing this new model and doesn't want to hear about this problem.

Companies often face the contradictory goals of *production* (which means *making* money on the product) and *safety* (which means *spending* money to avoid accidents that may or may not happen). When productivity receives exclusive priority, safety concerns may suffer (Wickens 434–36). Thus it seems no surprise that well over 50 percent of managers studied nationwide feel "pressure to compromise personal ethics for company goals" (Golen et al. 75). These pressures come in varied forms (Lewis and Reinsch 31):

- the drive for profit
- the need to beat the competition (other organizations or co-workers)
- the need to succeed at any cost, as when superiors demand more productivity or savings without questioning the methods
- an appeal to loyalty—to the organization and to its way of doing things

Figure 5.2 depicts how such pressures can add up.

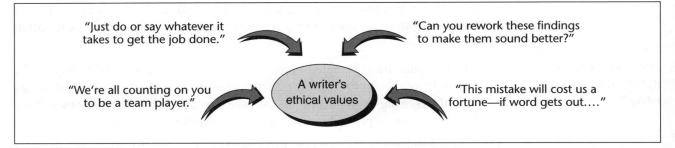

Figure 5.2   How Workplace Pressures Can Influence Ethical Values

Here is a vivid reminder of how organizational pressure can result in disastrous communication: On January 28, 1986, the space shuttle *Challenger* exploded 43 seconds after launch, killing all seven crew members. Immediate cause: two rubber O-ring seals in a booster rocket permitted hot exhaust gases to escape, igniting the adjacent fuel tank (see Figure 5.3 on page 92). Ultimate cause: the O-ring hazard had been recognized since 1977 and documented by engineers but largely ignored by management. (Managers had claimed that the O-ring system was safe because it was "redundant": each primary O-ring was backed up by a secondary O-ring.)

Moreover, in the final hours, engineers argued against launching because that day's low temperature would drastically increase the danger of both primary and secondary O-rings failing. But, under pressure to meet schedules and deadlines, managers chose to relay only a highly downplayed version of these warnings to the NASA decision makers who were to make *Challenger's* fatal launch decision.

The following analysis of key events and documents illustrates the role of miscommunication in the *Challenger* accident.[2]

1. More than six months before the explosion, officials at Morton Thiokol, Inc., manufacturer of the booster rockets, received a memo from engineer R. M. Boisjoly (Presidential Commission 49). Boisjoly described how exhaust gas leakage on an earlier flight had eroded O-rings in certain non-critical joints. The memo emphatically warned of possible "catastrophe" in some future shuttle flight if O-rings should fail to seal

---

2. Adapted from Winsor; Pace; Rowland; and Gouran et al.

a critical joint. Boisjoly called for renewed attention to the O-ring problem. Marked COMPANY PRIVATE, Boisjoly's urgent message never was passed on to top-level decision makers at NASA.

2. During the months preceding *Challenger's* fatal launch, Boisjoly and other Morton Thiokol engineers complained, in writing, about the lack of management attention or support on the O-ring issue. These complaints were largely ignored within the company—and they never reached the customer, NASA decision makers.

3. On the evening of January 27, managers and engineers at Morton Thiokol debated whether to recommend the January 28 launch. In addition to the yet-unsolved problem of O-ring erosion from exhaust gases, engineers were especially concerned that predicted low temperatures could harden the rubber O-rings, preventing them from sealing the joint at all. No prior flight had launched below 11.67°C (53°F). At this temperature—and even up to 23.89°C (75°F)—some blow-by (exhaust leakage) had occurred. O-ring temperature on January 28 would be barely above -1.1°C (30°F).

    Arguing against the launch, Roger Boisjoly presented a chart to his Thiokol colleagues (Presidential Commission 89). The chart showed that the O-rings would take longer to seal because lower temperatures would make the rubber hard and less pliable, and that the worst exhaust leakage had occurred on a January 1985 flight, when the O-ring temperature was 11.67°C (53°F). At -1.1°C (30°F), the O-rings might not seal at all, Boisjoly warned.

    Boisjoly and his supporters made their point, and Thiokol management decided to recommend no launch until the temperature reached at least 11.67°C (53°F).

4. In a teleconference with NASA's Marshall Space Center, Thiokol managers relayed their no-launch recommendation to the next level of decision makers. But the recommendation was rejected. One Thiokol manager's testimony:

    Mr. Mulloy [a NASA official] said he did not accept that recommendation, and Mr. Hardy said he was appalled that we would make such a recommendation (Presidential Commission 94).

    Refusing to accept the facts or the engineers' assessment of risk, NASA asked Thiokol to reconsider its recommendation.

5. The Thiokol staff met once again, the engineers and one manager continuing to oppose the launch. The managers then met without the engineers, and the reluctant manager was told to "take off your engineering hat and put on your management hat" (Presidential Commission 93). Despite the engineering evidence to the contrary, Thiokol managers finally concluded that the O-ring system had an acceptable margin of safety (Presidential Commission 108).

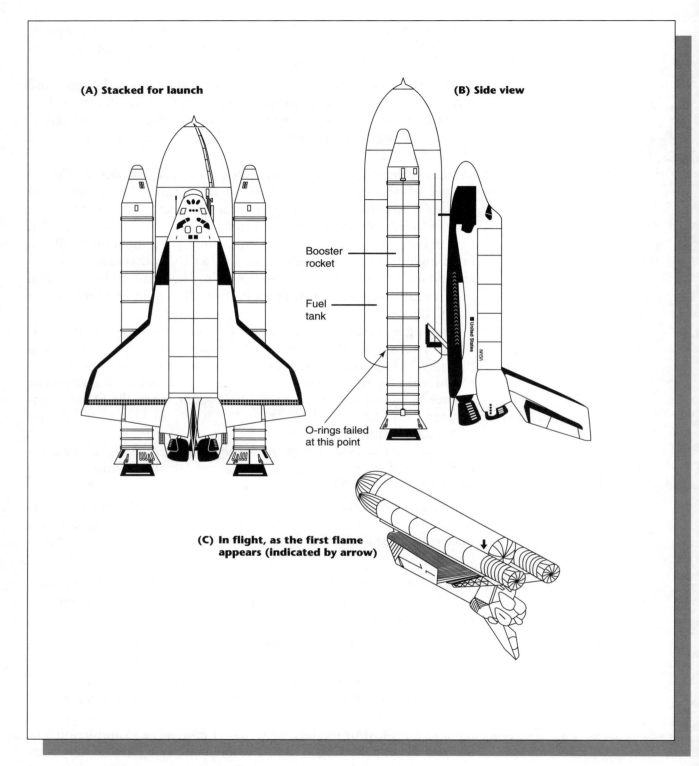

(A) Stacked for launch

(B) Side view

Booster rocket

Fuel tank

O-rings failed at this point

(C) In flight, as the first flame appears (indicated by arrow)

Figure 5.3   Views of the Challenger
Source: *Report to the Presidential Commission on the Space Shuttle Challenger Accident*. Washington, D.C.: U.S. Government Printing Office, 1986: 3, 26.

6. Despite continued engineering objections, Thiokol management reversed its recommendation (Presidential Commission 97) to Marshall and Kennedy Space Centers. Top NASA decision makers never were told about Thiokol engineers' objections to the low-temperature launch or about the level of concern about O-ring erosion in prior shuttle flights. The launch took place on schedule.

Here are some conclusions of the Presidential Commission investigating the fatal launch decision (104):

- The Commission was troubled by what appeared to be a propensity of management at Marshall to contain potentially serious problems and to attempt to resolve them internally rather than communicate them forward.
- The Commission concluded that the Thiokol management reversed its position and recommended the launch . . . at the urging of Marshall and contrary to the views of its engineers in order to accommodate a major customer.

Unethical communication played a key role in the *Challenger* disaster.

Never Confuse Teamwork with Groupthink

Any successful organization relies on teamwork, everyone cooperating to get the job done. But teamwork is not the same as *groupthink* (Janis 9).

Groupthink occurs when group pressure prevents individuals from questioning, criticizing, or "making waves." Group members feel a greater need for acceptance and a sense of belonging than for critically examining the issues. In a conformist climate, critical thinking is impossible. Anyone who has lived through adolescent peer pressure has already experienced a version of groupthink.

Yielding to pressure can be especially tempting in a large company or on a complex project, in which individual responsibility is easy to camouflage in the crowd:

How some corporations evade responsibility for their actions

Lack of accountability is deeply embedded in the concept of the corporation. Shareholders' liability is limited to the amount of money they invest. Managers' liability is limited to what they choose to know about the operation of the company. The corporation's liability is limited by governments, . . . by insurance, and by laws allowing corporations to duck liability by altering their . . . structure. (Mokhiber 16)

All kinds of people work at all levels on a major project (for instance, the production of a new passenger airplane). Countless decisions at any level have far-reaching effects on the whole project (as in the decision to ignore the DC-10's faulty locking mechanism). But with so many people collaborating, identifying those responsible for an error often is impossible—especially when the error is one of omission, that is, of *not* doing something that should have been done (Unger 137).

"I was only following orders!"

People commit unethical acts inside corporations that they never would commit as individuals representing only themselves. (Bryan 86)

After completing their assigned task, employees too often assume their job is done. Figure 5.4 depicts the kind of thinking that enables people to deny personal responsibility for the consequences of their communication[3].

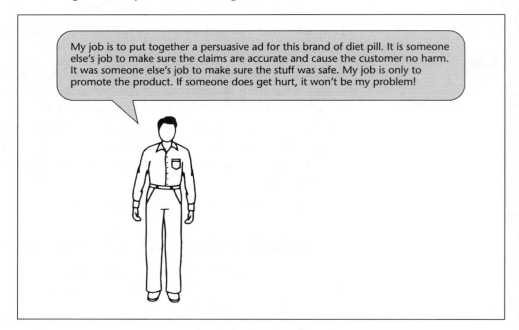

Figure 5.4   Groupthink Can Be a Handy Hiding Place

Groupthink was exemplified by the decision to relay to top NASA officials only downplayed warnings about *Challenger's* launch. In such cases, the group suffers an "illusion of invulnerability," which creates "excessive optimism and encourages taking extreme risks" (Janis 197).

Groupthink encourages subordinates to downplay or suppress bad news in their reports to superiors, instead "stressing what they think the superior wants to hear" (Littlejohn and Jabusch 159). Morton Thiokol's final launch recommendation to NASA serves as a memorable example.

Rely on Critical Thinking for Ethical Decisions

Because of their impact on people and on your career, ethical decisions challenge your critical thinking skills:

Ethical decisions require critical thinking

- *How can I know the "right thing" in this situation?*
- *What are my obligations, and to whom, in this situation?*

---

3. Our thanks to Judith Kaufman for this idea.

- *What values or ideals do I want to stand for in this situation?*
- *What is likely to happen if I do X, or Y?*

Can you rely on more than intuition or conscience in navigating the grey areas of ethical decisions? How will you make a convincing case against danger or folly to a roomful of people caught up in groupthink, people who ask "How do we know your way is right? Says who?" or who urge you to "take off your engineering hat and put on your management hat"?

Although ethical issues resist simple formulas, you can avoid two major fallacies that obstruct good judgment: the fallacy of "doing one's thing" and the fallacy of "one rule fits all."

The Fallacy of "Doing One's Thing"

One way to oversimplify a complex ethical issue is through a misguided notion known as *ethical relativism:* "Since we have no way to agree on right or wrong, it all depends on personal preference. *Right,* then, is what I think is right!" Such denial of any reasonable criteria of course legitimizes *any* action, including the atrocities of Hitler, Milosevic, or other fanatics who claim the "right" intentions.

The Fallacy of "One Rule Fits All"

The opposite extreme of ethical relativism is *absolutism,* the inflexible notion that one set of criteria governs all ethical decisions. If, for example, you abide absolutely by the rule "Thou shall not lie," you would violate this rule under no circumstance (even to save your family from harm).

Reasonable Criteria for Ethical Judgment

Somewhere between the extremes of relativism and absolutism are *reasonable criteria* (standards of measurement that most people would consider acceptable). These criteria for ethical judgment take the form of *obligations, ideals,* and *consequences* (Ruggiero 55–56; Christians et al. 17–18).

Obligations are the responsibilities we have to everyone involved:

- *Obligation to ourselves,* to act in our own self-interest and according to good conscience.
- *Obligation to clients and customers,* to stand by the people to whom we are bound by contract—and who pay the bills.
- *Obligation to our company,* to advance its goals, respect its policies, protect confidential information, and expose misconduct that would harm the organization.
- *Obligation to co-workers,* to promote their safety and well-being.
- *Obligation to the community,* to preserve the local economy, welfare, and quality of life.
- *Obligation to society,* to consider the national and global impact of our actions.

When the interests of these parties conflict—as they often do—we have to decide very carefully where our primary obligations lie. Can we honour all these obligations all of the time?

Ideals are "notions of excellence" (Ruggiero 55), the positive values that we believe in or stand for: loyalty, friendship, courage, compassion, dignity, fairness, and whatever qualities that make us who we are.

Consequences are the beneficial or harmful results of our actions. Consequences may be immediate or delayed, intentional or unintentional, obvious or subtle (Ruggiero 56). Some consequences are easy to predict; some aren't so easy; some are impossible.

Figure 5.5 depicts the relationship among these three criteria.

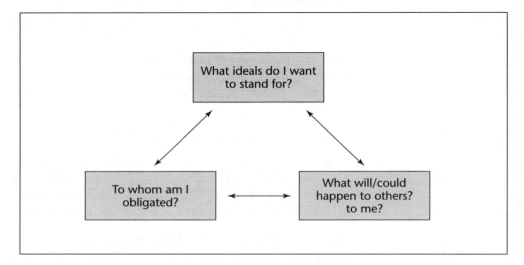

Figure 5.5   Reasonable Criteria for Ethical Judgment

The above criteria help us understand why even good intentions can produce bad judgments, as in the following situation:

What seems like the "right thing" might be the wrong thing

> Someone observes . . . that waste from the local mill is seeping into the water table and polluting the water supply. This is a serious situation and requires a remedy. But before one can be found, extremists condemn the mill for lack of conscience and for exploiting the community. People get upset and clamour for the mill to be shut down and its management tried on criminal charges. The next thing you know, the plant does close, 500 workers are without jobs, and no solution has been found for the pollution problem. (Hauser 96)

Because of their zealous dedication to the *ideal* of a pollution-free environment, the above group failed to anticipate the *consequences* of their protest or to respect their *obligation* to the community's economic welfare.

In the miscommunication surrounding the *Challenger* disaster, the group's sense of *obligation* to its client (i.e., NASA) caused it to ignore the *ideal* of honesty and the probable *consequences* of its recommendation to launch.

Ethical Dilemmas

Ethics decisions are especially frustrating when no single answer seems acceptable:

Ethical questions often resist easy answers

> [An ethical] dilemma exists whenever the conflicting obligations, ideals, and consequences are so very nearly equal in their importance that we feel we cannot choose among them, even though we must. (Ruggiero 91)

In private and public ways, such dilemmas are inescapable. For example, political candidates speak of drastic plans to eliminate the federal deficit in five years. One could argue that such a dedication to the *consequences* (or results) would violate our *obligations* (to the poor, the sick, etc.) and our *ideals* (of compassion, fairness, etc.). On the basis of our three criteria, how else might the deficit issue be considered?

Ethical dilemmas confront the medical community. For instance, in late 1992, a brain-dead, pregnant woman in Western Europe was kept alive for several weeks until her child could be delivered. Also in 1992, a California court debated the ethics of using medical findings of Nazi doctors who had experimented on prisoners in concentration camps. In terms of our three criteria, how might these dilemmas be considered?

As impossible as such dilemmas may seem, critical thinking directs our decision; without oversimplifying the issue or reaching a hasty judgment, we must consider all of the criteria involved.

Anticipate Some Hard Choices

Communicators' ethical choices basically are concerned with honesty in choosing to reveal or conceal information:

- *What exactly do I report, and to whom?*
- *How much do I reveal or conceal?*
- *How do I say what I have to say?*
- *Could misplaced obligation to one party be causing me to deceive others?*

For an illustration of a hard choice in a workplace communication, consider the following scenario:

A Hard Choice

You are an assistant structural engineer working on the construction of a nuclear power plant near a northern city. After years of construction delays and cost overruns, the plant finally has received its limited operating licence from the Atomic Energy Control Board (AECB).

During your final inspection of the nuclear core containment unit on February 15, you discover a 10-foot-long, hairline crack in a section of the reinforced concrete floor, within 20 feet of the area where the cooling pipes enter the containment unit. (The especially cold and snowless winter likely has caused a frost heave under a small part of the foundation.) The crack has either just appeared or was overlooked by AECB inspectors on February 10.

The crack could be perfectly harmless, caused by normal settling of the structure; and this is, after all, a "redundant" containment system (a shell within a shell). But then again, the crack could signal some kind of serious stress on the entire containment unit, which furthermore could damage the entry and exit cooling pipes or other vital structures.

You phone your supervisor, who is just about to leave on a ski vacation, and who tells you, "Forget it; no problem," and hangs up.

You may have to choose between the goals of your organization and what you know is right

You know that if the crack is reported, the whole start-up process scheduled for February 16 will be delayed indefinitely. More money will be lost; excavation, reinforcement, and further testing will be required—and many people with a stake in this project (from company executives to construction officials to shareholders) will be furious—especially if your report turns out to be a false alarm. All segments of plant management are geared up for the final big moment. Media coverage will be widespread. As the bearer of bad news—and bad publicity—you suspect that, even if you turn out to be right, your own career could be hurt by what some people will see as your overreaction that has made them look bad.

On the other hand, ignoring the crack could compromise the system's safety, with unforeseeable consequences. Of course, no-one would ever be able to implicate you. The AECB has already inspected and approved the containment unit, leaving you, your supervisor, and your company in the clear. You have very little time to decide. Start-up is scheduled for tomorrow, at which time the containment system will become intensely radioactive. ■

Working professionals commonly face similar choices, the product of conflicting goals and expectations, the pressure to meet deadlines and achieve results, to be a "loyal" employee, a "team player," to consider "the bottom line." Often, these choices have to be made alone or on the spur of the moment, without the luxury of meditation or consultation.

Never Depend Only on Legal Guidelines

Can the law tell you how to communicate ethically? Sometimes. If you stay within the law, are you being ethical? Not always. Legal standards "sometimes do no more than delineate minimally acceptable behaviour." In contrast, ethical standards "often attempt to describe ideal behaviour, to define the best possible practices for corporations" (Porter 183). Consider these legal actions:

Deception often is legal

- The investigative TV show "20/20" exposed the common and legal practice for trucks to haul garbage or toxic substances (such as formaldehyde) one way and then haul food products (such as juice concentrates) on the return trip—without ever informing the customer.
- It is perfectly legal to advertise a cereal made with oat bran (which allegedly lowers cholesterol) without mentioning that another ingredient in the cereal is coconut oil (which raises cholesterol).

Lying is rarely illegal, except in cases of lying under oath or breaking a contractual promise (Wicclair and Farkas 16). But putting aside these and other illegal lies, such as defamation of character or lying about a product so as to cause injury, we see plenty of room for the kinds of legal lies depicted in Figure 5.6. Later chapters cover other kinds of legal lying, such as page design that distorts the real emphasis or words that are deliberately unclear, misleading, or ambiguous.

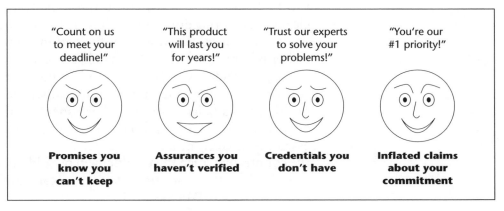

"Count on us to meet your deadline!"   "This product will last you for years!"   "Trust our experts to solve your problems!"   "You're our #1 priority!"

Promises you know you can't keep   **Assurances you haven't verified**   **Credentials you don't have**   **Inflated claims about your commitment**

Figure 5.6   Some Legal Lies in the Workplace

What then are a communicator's legal guidelines? Besides obscenity laws (not especially relevant here), workplace writing is regulated by the types of laws described below.

- *Laws against libel* prohibit any false written statement that maliciously attacks or ridicules anyone. A statement is considered libelous when it damages someone's reputation, character, career, or livelihood or when it causes humiliation or mental suffering. Material that is damaging but *truthful* would not be considered libelous unless it were used intentionally to cause harm. In the event of a libel suit, a writer's ignorance is no defence; even when the damaging material has been obtained from a source presumed reliable, the writer (and publisher) are legally accountable.[4]

- *Copyright laws* protect the ownership rights of authors—or of their employers, in cases where the writing was done as part of one's employment (Girill 48). You will find a copy of the Copyright Act posted at insight.mcmaster.ca/org/efc/pages/law/canada/canada. C-42. html#42.

- *Laws protecting software* provide penalties for illegally duplicating copyrighted software. (Guidelines for ethical, legal use of software are provided through CANCOPY's Web site: www.cancopy.com). Also, in Canada and internationally, the Software and Information Industry Association fights

---

4. Thanks to Peter Owens for the material on libel.

software piracy through education and enforcement measures.

- *Laws against deceptive or fraudulent advertising* make it illegal, for example, to falsely claim or imply that a product or treatment will cure cancer, or to represent and sell a used product as new. Fraud can be defined as "lying that causes another person monetary damage" (Harcourt 64).

- *Liability laws* define the responsibilities of authors, editors, and publishers for damages resulting from the use of incomplete, unclear, misleading, or otherwise defective information. The misinformation might be about a product (failure to warn about the toxic fumes from a spray-on oven cleaner) or a procedure (misleading instructions in an owner's manual for using a tyre jack). Even if misinformation is given out of ignorance, the writer is liable (Walter and Marsteller 164–65).

   Legal standards with which product literature must comply vary from country to country. A document must satisfy the legal standards for safety, health, accuracy, language, or other issues for any country in which it will be distributed. For example, instructions for any product requiring assembly or operation have to carry warnings as stipulated by the laws of the country in which the product will be sold. Inadequate documentation, as judged by that country's standards, can result in a lawsuit (Caswell-Coward 264–66; Weymouth 145).

Laws regulating communication practices are few because such laws traditionally have been seen as threats to our freedom of speech (Johannesen 86). Many companies, however, have legal departments you can turn to with questions about a document's legality.

Recognizing that ethical behaviour is a matter of commitment, and not of legislation, most professions have developed their own ethics guidelines. If your field has its own formal code, obtain a copy.

Understand the Potential for Communication Abuse

On the job, you write in the service of your employer. Your effectiveness is judged by how well your documents speak for the company and advance its interests and agendas (Ornatowski 100–01). You walk the proverbial line between telling the truth and doing what your employer expects (Dombrowski 97).

Workplace writing influences the thinking, actions, and welfare of different people: customers, investors, co-workers, the public, policy makers—to name a few. These people are victims of communication abuse whenever we give them information that is less than the truth as we know it. Following are some examples of such abuses.

Suppressing Knowledge the Public Deserves

Except for disasters that make big news (Bhopal, *Challenger,* Chernobyl, Westray Mines) people hear plenty about the *wonders* of technology: how fluoride eradicates tooth decay, how smart bombs and cruise missiles never miss their targets, how nuclear power will solve our energy problems—but they rarely hear about the failures or the dangers (Staudenmaier 67).

In fact, the pressure to downplay failure sometimes results in censorship. For instance, some prestigious science journals have refused to publish studies linking chlorine and fluoride in drinking water with cancer risk, and fluorescent lights with childhood leukemia. The papers allegedly were rejected as part of widespread suppression of news about dangers of technological products (Begley 63).

Exaggerating Claims About Technology

Organizations that have a stake in a particular technology are especially tempted to exaggerate its benefits, potential, or safety.

Unwarranted claims help technology sell

> An entrepreneur needs financiers. Scientists in a large corporation need advocates high enough in the hierarchy to allocate funds. And government-supported researchers at universities and national labs have an obvious incentive to overstate their progress and understate the problems that lie ahead: the better the chances for success, the more money an agency is willing to shell out. (Brody 40)

If your organization depends on outside funding (as in the defence or space industry), you might find yourself pressured to make unrealistic promises.

Stealing or Divulging Proprietary Information

Proprietary information is any document or idea that can be considered the exclusive property of the company in which it originated. Proprietary documents may include company records, test and experiment results, surveys paid for by clients, market research, minutes of meetings, plans, and specifications (Lavin 5). In theory, such information is legally protected,[5] but it remains vulnerable to sabotage or theft. Rapid developments in technology create fierce competition among rival companies for the very latest intelligence, giving rise to measures like these:

Examples of corporate espionage

> Companies have been known to use business school students to garner information on competitors under the guise of conducting "research." Even more commonplace is interviewing employees for slots that don't exist and wringing them dry about their current employer. (Gilbert 24)

Moreover, employees within a company can leak confidential information to the press or to anyone else who has no legal right to know.

Mismanaging Electronic Information

With so much information stored in databases (by schools, employers, government agencies, mail order retailers, credit bureaus, banks, credit card companies, insurance companies, pharmacies, etc.) questions of how we combine,

---

5. Although various Trade Secrets Acts around the world are designed to curb such abuses, these laws are subject to broad and varied interpretation by individual courts.

use, and disseminate the information become increasingly important (Finkelstein 471). Moreover, a database is easier to alter than its printed equivalent; one simple command can wipe out or transform the facts.

Withholding Information People Need to Do Their Jobs

Nowhere is the adage that "information is power" more true than among co-workers. One sure way to sabotage a colleague is to withhold vital information about the task at hand.

Beyond these deliberate communication abuses is this reality: *all* information is a matter of personal or social interpretation (Dombrowski 97); therefore, "objective reporting," practically speaking, is impossible. What we say on the job and how we say it are influenced by the expectations of our employer and by our own self-interest.

Exploiting Cultural Differences

Cross-cultural documents carry great potential for communication abuse. Based on its level of business experience, technological development, or financial need, a particular culture might be especially vulnerable to manipulation or deception. Some countries, for instance, are persuaded to purchase, from North American companies, pesticides and other chemicals whose use is banned in North America. Other countries witness depletion of their natural resources or exploitation of their labour force by more developed countries—all in the name of progress. All communication in all cultural contexts should embody universal standards of honesty and fairness.

Know Your Communication Guidelines

How do you balance self-interest with the interests of others—the organization, the public, your customers? How can you be practical and responsible at the same time? Here are two practical guidelines for ethical communication (Clark 194):

1. *Give the audience everything it needs to know.* To see things as clearly as you do, people need more than just a partial view. Don't bury readers in needless details, but do make sure they get all of the facts and get them straight.

2. *Give the audience a clear understanding of what the information means.* Even when all of the facts are known, they can be misinterpreted. Do all you can to ensure that your readers understand the facts as you do.

We have seen how the *Challenger* tragedy resulted from decision makers knowing too little or misunderstanding what they did know (Clark 194): "Low temperatures will harden the O-rings and will compromise their ability to seal the rocket joint." The *meaning* of this data depended on whether it was interpreted as a technical fact ("Exhaust leakage means an explosion") or a social fact ("Another launch delay means our company looks bad") (Ornatowski 98).

- To the engineers—the technical experts, but not the decision makers—the technical fact meant that the risk was serious enough to warrant a launch delay.
- To lower-level decision makers, the social fact meant that the risk was acceptable because of the social pressure to launch on schedule.
- To the ultimate decision makers at NASA, the data meant little, because lower-level decision makers provided information that was neither sufficient nor clear enough for the risk to be understood, or even recognized.

Because of social pressure to keep an employer happy, vital facts and truthful interpretations were suppressed.

The Ethics Checklist on page 105 incorporates additional guidelines from various chapters. Use the checklist for any document you prepare or for which you are responsible.

Decide Where and How to Draw the Line

Suppose your employer asks you to do something unethical—for example, alter data to cover up a violation of federal pollution standards. If you decide to resist, your choices seem limited: resign or go public (i.e., blow the whistle).

Walking away from a job isn't easy, however, and whistle-blowing can spell career disaster (Rubens 330). Many organizations refuse to hire anyone black-listed as a whistle-blower (Wicclair and Farkas 19). Even if you aren't fired, expect your job to become hellish. Here is one communicator's gloomy assessment, based on personal experience:

Know what to expect

> Most of the ethical infractions [you] witness will be so small that blowing the whistle will seem fruitless and self-destructive. And leaving one company for another may prove equally fruitless, given the pervasiveness of the problem. (Bryan 86)

Anglo-Canadian law tends to protect employees who blow the whistle and are then dismissed. An employee has the right to bring a wrongful dismissal law-suit and, in certain circumstances, to include human rights and/or labour relations claims. The outcome of these claims varies.

Employees covered by a contract or collective agreement, normally seek advice from their shop steward and/or union executive as well as a personal and/or union lawyer. Employees not covered by a contract or collective agreement, often seek initial advice from local Departments of Labour to establish employment standards law provisions. It is quite common for these people to also seek advice from their personal lawyer.

- Anyone who reports employer violations to a regulatory agency such as Occupational Health and Safety (OHS) and who is punished can request a Department of Labour investigation. Employees whose claims are ruled valid can win reinstatement and reimbursement for back pay and legal expenses.[6]

Even with such protections, an employee who takes on a company without the backing of a labour union or other powerful group can expect lengthy court battles, high legal fees (which may or may not be recouped) and disruption of life and career. Exactly where you draw the line (on having your integrity or health instead of your job) will be strictly your own decision.

If you do decide to take a stand, be reasonable and cautious, and follow these suggestions (Unger 127–30):

- *Get your facts straight, and get them on paper.* Don't blow matters out of proportion, but do keep a paper trail in case of legal proceedings.
- *Appeal your case in terms of the company's interests.* Instead of being pious and judgmental ("This is a racist and sexist policy, and you'd better get your act together"), focus on what the company stands to gain or lose ("Promoting too few women and minorities makes us vulnerable to legal action").
- *Aim your appeal toward the right person.* If you have to go to the top, find someone who knows enough to appreciate the problem and who has enough clout to make something happen.
- *Get professional advice.* Contact a lawyer and your professional society for advice about your legal rights.

Before accepting a job offer, do some discreet research about the company's ethical reputation. (Of course you can learn only so much about a company before actually working there.) Some companies have ombudspersons, who help employees lodge complaints. Others offer hotlines for advice on ethics problems or for reporting violations. Also, realizing that good ethics are good business, companies increasingly are developing codes for personal and organizational behaviour. Without such supports, don't expect to last long as an ethical employee in an unethical organization.

Remember that very few employers tolerate any public statement, no matter how truthful, that makes the company look bad.

A Final Note: Sometimes the right choice is obvious, but often not so obvious. No-one has any sure way of always knowing what to do. This chapter is only an introduction to the inevitable hard choices that, throughout your career, will be yours to make and to live with.

---

6. Although employees legally are entitled to speak confidentially with OHS and WCB inspectors about violations of health and safety in their company, a survey revealed that the inspectors themselves feel such laws offer employees little actual protection against company retribution (Kraft 5).

An Ethics Checklist for Communicators

Use this checklist[7] to help your documents reflect reasonable, ethical judgment.

❑ Do I avoid exaggeration, understatement, sugarcoating, or any distortion or omission that leaves readers at a disadvantage?

❑ Do I make a clear distinction between "certainty" and "probability"?

❑ Am I being honest and fair?

❑ Have I explored all sides of the issue and all possible alternatives?

❑ Are my information sources valid, reliable, and unbiased?

❑ Do I actually believe what I'm saying, instead of being a mouthpiece for groupthink or advancing some hidden agenda?

❑ Would I still advocate this position if I were held publicly accountable for it?

❑ Do I provide enough information and interpretation for readers to understand the facts as I know them?

❑ Am I reasonably sure this document will harm no innocent persons or damage their reputation?

❑ Am I respecting all legitimate rights to privacy and confidentiality?

❑ Do I inform readers of the consequences or risks (as I am able to predict) of what I'm advocating?

❑ Do I state the case clearly, instead of hiding behind jargon and generalities?

❑ Do I give candid feedback or criticism, if it is warranted?

❑ Am I distributing copies of this document to every person who has the right to know about it?

❑ Do I credit all contributors and sources of ideas and information?

---

7. Adapted from Brownell and Fitzgerald 18; Bryan 87; Johannesen 21–22; Larson 39; Unger 39–46; Yoos 50–55.

☑ EXERCISES

1. Prepare a memo (one or two pages) for distribution to first-year college students in which you introduce the ethical dilemmas they will face in college. For instance:

   - If you receive a final grade of A by mistake, would you inform your instructor or professor?
   - If the library loses the record of books you've signed out, would you return them anyway?
   - Would you plagiarize—and would that change in your professional life?
   - Would you support lowering standards for student athletes if the team's success was important for the school's funding and status?
   - Would you allow a friend to submit a paper you've written for some other course?

   What other ethical dilemmas can you envision? Tell your audience what to expect, and give them some *realistic* advice for coping. No sermons, please.

2. In your workplace communications, you may end up facing hard choices concerning what to say, how much to say, how to say it, and to whom. Whatever your choice, it will have definite consequences. Be prepared to discuss the following cases in terms of the obligations, ideals, and consequences involved. Can you think of similar choices you or someone you know has already faced? What happened?

   - While travelling on assignment that is being paid for by your employer, you visit an area in which you would really like to live and work, an area in which you have lots of contacts but never can find time to visit on your own. You have five days to complete your assignment, and then you must report on your activities. You complete the assignment in three days. Should you spend the remaining two days checking out other job possibilities, without reporting this activity?
   - As a marketing specialist, you are offered a lucrative account from a cigarette manufacturer; you are expected to promote the product. Should you accept the account? Suppose instead the account were for beer, junk food, suntanning parlours, or ice cream. Would your choice be different? Why, or why not?
   - You have been authorized to hire a technical assistant, and so you are about to prepare an advertisement. This is a time of threatened cutbacks for your company. People hired as "temporary," however, have never seemed to work out well. Should your ad include the warning that this position could be only temporary?
   - You are one of three employees being considered for a yearly production bonus, which will be awarded in six weeks. You've just accepted a better job, at which you can start anytime in the next two months. Should you wait until the bonus decision is made before announcing your plans to leave?
   - You are marketing director for a major importer of coffee beans. Your testing labs report that certain African beans contain roughly twice the caffeine of South American varieties. Many of these African varieties are big sellers, from countries whose coffee bean production helps prop otherwise desperate economies. Should your advertising of these varieties inform the public about the high caffeine content? If so, how much emphasis should this fact be given?
   - You are research director for a biotechnology company working on an AIDS vaccine. At a national conference, a researcher from a competing company secretly offers to sell your company crucial data that could speed discovery of an effective vaccine. Should you accept the offer?

3. Review the scenario entitled "A Hard Choice." What would you do? Come to the class prepared to justify your decision on the basis of the obligations, ideals, and consequences involved.

✓ COLLABORATIVE PROJECT

After dividing into groups, study the following scenario and complete the assignment: You belong to the Forestry Management Division in a province whose year-round economy depends almost totally on forest products (lumber, paper, etc.) but whose summer economy is greatly enriched by tourism, especially from fishing, kayaking, and other outdoor activities. The province's poorest area is also its most scenic, largely because of the virgin stands of hardwoods. Your division has been facing growing political pressure from this area to allow logging companies to harvest the trees. Logging here would have good and bad consequences: for the foreseeable future, the area's economy would benefit greatly from the jobs created; but traditional logging practices would erode the soil, pollute waterways, and decimate wildlife, including several endangered species—besides posing a serious threat to the area's tourist industry. Logging, in short, would give a desperately needed boost to the area's standard of living, but would put an end to many tourist-oriented businesses and would change the landscape forever.

Your group has been assigned to weigh the economic and environmental impacts of logging, and prepare recommendations (to log or not to log) for your managers, who will use your report in making their final decision. To whom do you owe the most loyalty here: the unemployed or underemployed residents, the tourist businesses (mostly owned by residents), the wildlife, the land, future generations? The choices are by no means simple. In cases like this, it isn't enough to say that we should "do the right thing," because we are sometimes unable to predict the consequences of a particular action—even when it seems the best thing to do. In a memo to your supervisor, outline what action you would recommend and explain why. Be prepared to defend your group's ethical choice in class on the basis of the obligations, ideals, and consequences involved.

Gathering Information

CHAPTER

6

MAJOR DECISIONS in the workplace typically are based on careful research, with the findings recorded in a written report. The report's readers expect current information that can help answer their specific questions.

Research is classified as *primary* or *secondary*. Primary research involves an original, first-hand study of your topic or problem: observations, interviews, questionnaires, enquiry letters, personal experiments, analysis of samples, fieldwork, or company records. Secondary research includes materials published by other researchers: journal articles, books, encyclopedias, reports, textbooks, handbooks, on-line articles, electronic databases, government documents, internet sites, and material held by public agencies and special interest groups.

Research strategies and resources differ widely among disciplines. This chapter focuses on research for preparing a formal report.

Thinking Critically About the Research Process

Research is a deliberate form of enquiry, a process of problem solving, in which certain procedures follow a recognizable sequence, as shown in Figure 6.1.

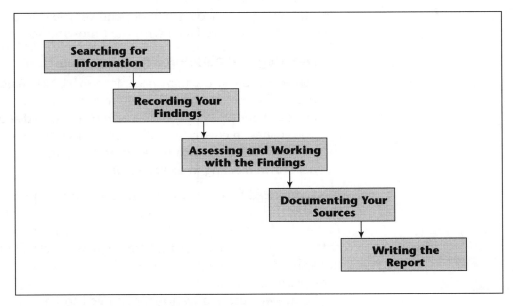

Figure 6.1   Procedural Stages of the Research Process

But research does not simply follow a numbered set of procedures ("First, do this; then, do that"). The procedural stages depend on the many decisions that accompany any legitimate enquiry (see Figure 6.2).

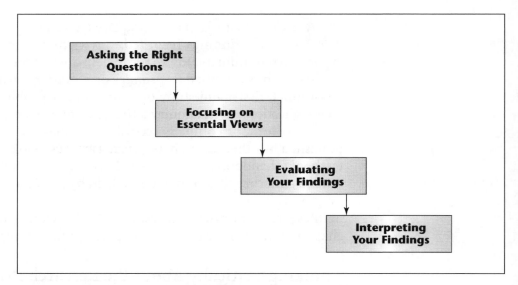

Figure 6.2   The Inquiry Stages of the Research Process

Asking the Right Questions

The answers you uncover will depend on the questions you ask. Assume, for instance, that you are faced with the following scenario:

Defining and Refining a Research Question

You are the public health manager for a small, New Brunswick town in which high-tension power lines run within 30 m of the elementary school. Parents are concerned about the danger from electromagnetic radiation (EMR) emitted by these power lines, in energy waves known as electromagnetic fields (EMFs). Town officials ask you to research the issue and prepare a report to be distributed at the next town meeting in six weeks. ■

First, you need to identify the exact question or questions you want answered. Initially, the major question might be: *Do the power lines pose any real danger to our children?* After some telephone calls around town and discussions at the coffee shop, you discover that townspeople actually have three major questions about electromagnetic fields: *What are they? Do they endanger our children? If so, what can be done?*

To answer these questions, you need to consider a range of subordinate questions, like those in the Figure 6.3 tree chart.

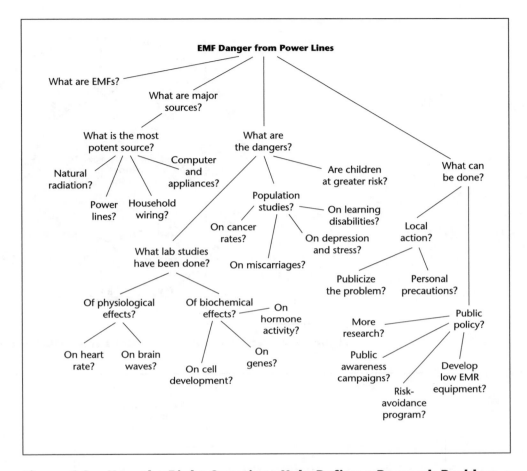

Figure 6.3   How the Right Questions Help Define a Research Problem

As research progresses, this chart will grow. For instance, after some preliminary reading, you learn that electromagnetic fields radiate not only from power lines but also from *all* electrical equipment, and even from the earth itself. So you face this additional question: *Do power lines present the greatest hazard as a source of EMFs?*

You now wonder whether the greater hazard comes from power lines or from other sources of EMF exposure. Critical thinking, in short, has enabled you to define and refine the essential questions.

Focusing on Essential Views

Assume you've settled on this research question: *Do electromagnetic fields from various sources endanger our children?* Now you can start considering information sources to consult (journals, interviews, reports, database searches). For a fair and accurate picture, you need all sides of the story from up-to-date and reputable sources, as depicted in Figure 6.4. Figure 6.5 illustrates some likely sources of information.

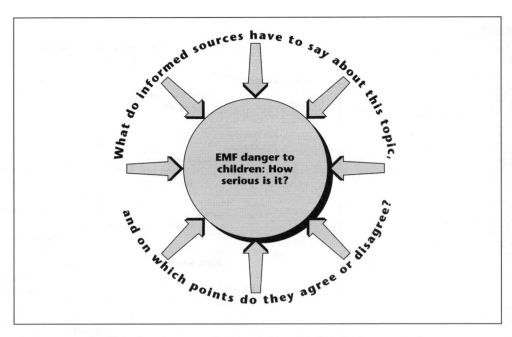

Figure 6.4   Effective Research Considers Multiple Perspectives

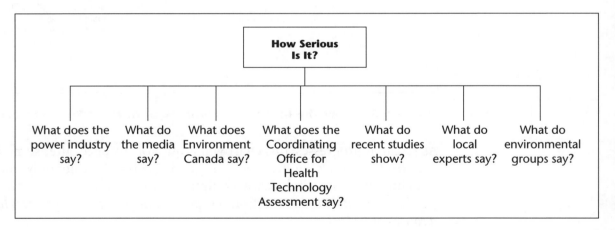

Figure 6.5   A Range of Essential Viewpoints

We do research to discover the right answer—or the answer that stands the best chance of being right. Rather than settling for the first or most comforting or most convenient answer, we have an ethical obligation to consider a variety of perspectives. Even expert testimony may not be the final word, because experts can disagree or they can be mistaken. To reach a balanced and informed conclusion, you need to survey the entire spectrum of significant viewpoints.

Achieving Adequate Depth in Your Search

Balanced research examines a broad *range* of evidence; thorough research, however, examines that evidence at an appropriate *depth*. As depicted in Figure 6.6, different types of secondary information about any topic occupy different levels of detail and dependability.

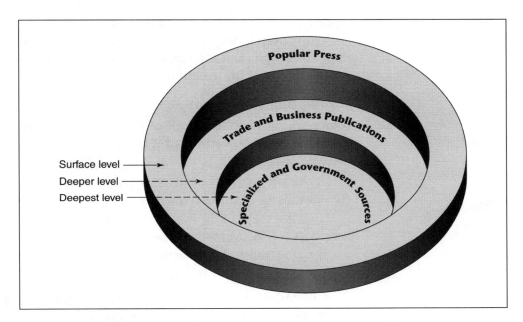

Figure 6.6 Effective Research Achieves Adequate Depth

1. At the surface level are items from the popular press (newspapers, radio, TV, general magazines). Designed for general consumption, this layer of information often contains more journalistic interpretation than factual detail.

2. At the next level are trade and business publications (*Frozen Food World, Publisher's Weekly,* etc.). Designed for readers who range from moderately informed to highly specialized, this level of information focuses more on practice than on theory, on items considered newsworthy to group members, on issues affecting the field, on public relations, on viewpoints that tend to reflect the particular biases of that field.

3. At a deeper level is the specialized literature (journals from professional associations: medical, legal, engineering, etc.). Designed for practising professionals, this level of information focuses on theory as well as practice, on descriptions of the latest studies—written by the researchers themselves and scrutinized by others for accuracy and objectivity, on debates among scholars and researchers, and on reviews and critiques and refutations of prior studies and publications.

Also at this deeper level are government sources and corporate documents available through the Freedom of Information Act. Designed for anyone willing to investigate its complex resources, this layer of information offers hard facts and highly detailed and (in many instances) *relatively* impartial views of virtually any issue or topic in any field.

Web pages, of course, offer links to increasingly specific levels of detail. But the actual "depth" and quality of a Web site's information depends on the sponsorship and reliability of that site.

How deep is deep enough? This depends on your purpose, your audience, and your topic. But the real story and the hard facts more likely reside at the deeper levels of information.

Evaluating Your Findings

Once you have collected all of the essential evidence about your topic, you need to decide how much of it is legitimate and then decide what it means.

QUESTIONS FOR EVALUATING A PARTICULAR FINDING
- Is this information accurate, reliable, and relatively unbiased?
- Can the claim be verified by the facts?
- How much of the information is useful?
- Is this the whole or the real story?
- Does something seem to be missing?
- Do I need more information?

Not all findings have equal value. Some information might be distorted, incomplete, or misleading. Information might be tainted by *source bias*. With an emotional issue involving children, a source might understate or overstate certain facts, depending on whose interests that source represents (power company, government agency, parent organization, etc.).

Ethical researchers rely on evidence that represents a fair balance of views. They don't merely emphasize findings that support their own biases or assumptions.

Interpreting Your Findings

Once you have decided which of your findings seem legitimate, you need to decide what they all mean.

QUESTIONS FOR INTERPRETING YOUR FINDINGS
- What do all these facts or observations mean?
- Do any findings conflict?
- Are other interpretations possible?
- Should I reconsider the evidence?
- What are my conclusions?
- What, if anything, should be done?

Perhaps you will reach a definite conclusion; for example, "The evidence about EMF dangers seems persuasive enough for us to be concerned and to take the following actions"—perhaps you will not.

Even the best research can produce contradictory or indefinite conclusions. For instance, some scientists show that studies linking electromagnetic radiation to health hazards are flawed. They point out that some studies indicate increased cancer risk while others indicate beneficial health effects. Other scientists claim that stronger EMFs are emitted by natural sources, such as earth's magnetic field, than by electrical sources (McDonald 5). An accurate conclusion would have to come from your analyzing all views and then deciding that one outweighs the others—or that only time will tell.

Never force a simplistic conclusion on a complex issue. Sometimes the best you can come up with is an indefinite conclusion: "Although controversy continues over the extent of EMF hazards, we all can take simple precautions to reduce our exposure." A wrong conclusion is far worse than no definite conclusion at all.

Figure 6.7 on page 118 shows the critical-thinking decisions crucial to worthwhile research: asking the right questions about your topic, your sources, your findings, and your conclusions. The quality of your entire research project will be determined by the quality of your thinking at each stage.

Exploring Secondary Sources

Although electronic searches for information are becoming the norm, a *thorough* search often requires careful examination of hard copy sources as well.

Hard Copy versus Electronic Sources

Advantages and drawbacks of each search medium (Table 6.1) often provide good reason for exploring both.

Table 6.1

Hard Copy v. Electronic Sources: Benefits and Drawbacks		
	Benefits	Drawbacks
Hard Copy Sources	• organized and searched by librarians • easier to preserve and keep secure	• time-consuming and inefficient to search • difficult to update
Electronic Sources	• more current, efficient, and accessible • searches can be narrowed or broadened • can offer material that has no hard copy equivalent	• access to recent material only • not always reliable • user might get lost

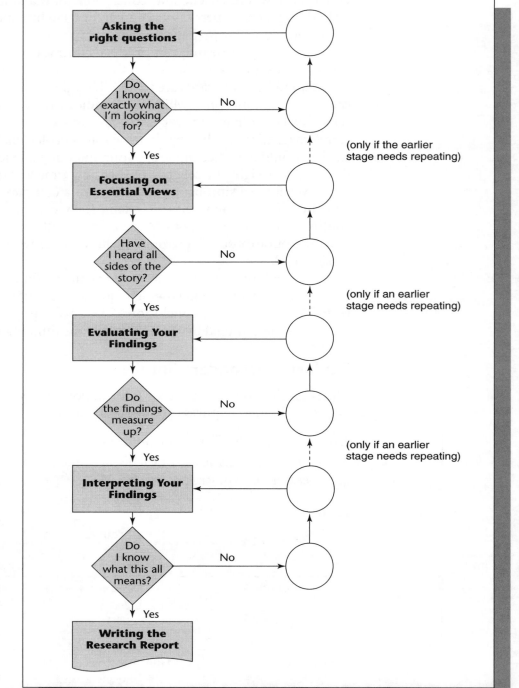

No single stage is complete until all stages are complete

Figure 6.7   Critical Thinking in the Research Process

Benefits of Hard Copy Sources. Hard copy libraries offer the judgment and expertise of librarians who organize and search for information. Compared with electronic files (on disks, tapes, and hard drives), hard copy is easier to protect from tampering and to preserve from aging. An electronic file's life-span can be as brief as ten years.

For many automated searches, a manual search of hard copy usually is needed as well. One recent study found greater than 50 percent inconsistency among database indexers. Thus, even an electronic search by a trained librarian can miss improperly indexed material (Lang and Secic 174-75). In contrast, a manual search provides the whole "database" (the bound index or abstracts). As you browse, you often randomly discover something useful.

Drawbacks of Hard Copy Sources. Manual searches (flipping pages by hand), however, are time-consuming and inefficient: books can get lost; relevant information has to be pinpointed and retrieved, or "pulled" by the user. Also, hard copy cannot be updated easily (Davenport 109-111).

Benefits of Electronic Sources. Compared with hard copy, electronic sources are more current, efficient, and accessible. Sources are updated rapidly. Ten or fifteen years of an index can be reviewed in minutes. Searches can be customized; for example, narrowed to specific dates or topics. They also can be broadened: A keyword search can uncover material that a hard copy search may have overlooked; Web pages can provide links to material of all sorts—much of which exists in no hard copy form.

Drawbacks of Electronic Sources. Drawbacks of electronic sources include the fact that databases rarely contain entries published before the mid-1960s and that material, especially on the Internet, can change or disappear overnight or be highly unreliable. Also, given the potential for getting lost in cyberspace, a thorough electronic search calls for a preliminary conference with a trained librarian.

Types of Hard Copy Sources

Where you begin your hard copy search depends on whether you are searching background and basic facts or the latest information. Library sources are shown in Figure 6.8.

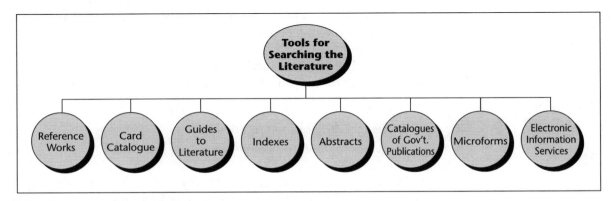

Figure 6.8   Library Sources

If you are an expert in the field, you might simply do a computerized database search or browse through specialized journals and listservs. If you have limited knowledge or you need to focus your topic, you probably will want to begin with general reference sources.

Reference Works

Reference sources, which provide background information, include encyclopedias, almanacs, handbooks, dictionaries, histories, and biographies. These provide background and bibliographies that can lead to more specific information. Make sure the work is current by checking the last copyright date.

Bibliographies. These comprehensive lists of publications about a subject are issued yearly, or even weekly. However, others can quickly become dated. Annotated bibliographies (which include an abstract for each entry) are most helpful. The following are sample listings (with annotations):

Bibliographies

> *Bibliographic Index.* A list (by subject) of bibliographies that contain at least 50 citations; to see which bibliographies are published in your field, begin here.
>
> *A Guide to Canadian Government Scientific and Technical Resources.* A list of everything published by the government in these broad fields.
>
> *Health Hazards of Video Display Terminals: An Annotated Bibliography.* One of many bibliographies focused on a specific subject.

Encyclopedias. Encyclopedias provide basic information (which might be outdated). The following are sample listings:

Encyclopedias

> *Encyclopedia of Building and Construction Terms*
>
> *Encyclopedia of Banking and Finance*
>
> *Encyclopedia of Food Technology*
>
> *The Encyclopedia of Associations.* A list of over 30,000 professional organizations worldwide (Canadian Medical Association, Institute of Electrical and Electronics Engineers, etc.). Many such organizations can be accessed via their Internet home pages.

Dictionaries. Dictionaries can be generalized or they can focus on specific disciplines or give biographical information. The following are sample listings:

Dictionaries

> *Dictionary of Engineering and Technology*
>
> *Dictionary of Telecommunications*
>
> *Dictionary of Scientific Biography*

Handbooks. These research aids amass key facts (formulas, tables, advice, examples) about a field in condensed form. The following are sample listings:

Handbooks

Business Writer's Handbook
Civil Engineering Handbook
The McGraw-Hill Computer Handbook

Almanacs. Almanacs contain factual and statistical data. The following are sample listings:

Almanacs

World Almanac and Book of Facts
Almanac for Computers
Almanac of Business and Industrial Financial Ratios

Directories. In directories you will find updated information about organizations, companies, people, products, services, or careers, often including addresses and phone numbers. The following are sample listings:

Directories

The Career Guide: Dun's Employment Opportunities Directory
The Internet Directory

Reference works increasingly are accessible by computer. Some, such as the *Free Online Dictionary of Computing*, are wholly electronic.

The Card Catalogue

All books, reference works, indexes, periodicals, and other materials held by a library are usually listed in its card catalogue under three headings: author, title, and subject.

Access points for an electronic card catalogue

Most libraries have automated their card catalogues. These electronic catalogues offer additional access points (beyond *author, title,* and *subject*) including:

- *Descriptor:* for retrieving works on the basis of a key word or phrase (for example, "electromagnetic" or "power lines and health") in the subject heading, in the work's title, or in the full text of its bibliographic record (its catalogue entry or abstract).
- *Document type:* for retrieving works in a specific format (videotape, audiotape, compact disk, motion picture).
- *Organizations and conferences:* for retrieving works produced under the name of an institution or professional association (for example, Brookings Institute or Canadian Heart and Stroke Foundation).
- *Publisher:* for retrieving works produced by a particular publisher (for example, Prentice Hall Canada Inc.).
- *Combination:* for retrieving works by combining any available access points (a book about a particular subject by a particular author or institution).

Figure 6.9 displays the first three computer screens you might encounter in an automated search using the descriptor ELECTROMAGNETIC. Through the Internet, a library's electronic catalogue can be searched from anywhere in the world.

You begin by pressing any key, and the computer responds with the screeen:

This first screen lists your options for getting help or for searching the catalogue from various access points

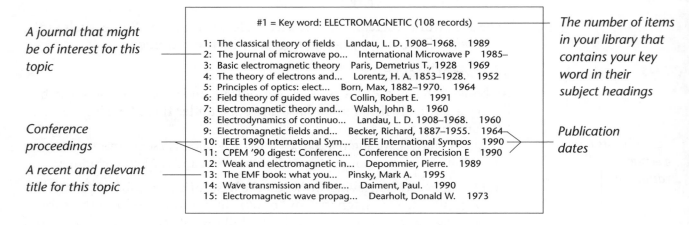

After selecting the DE search mode, you enter your key word (ELECTRO-MAGNETIC), and then press RETURN. This next screen appears (the first of several with all 108 entries):

A journal that might be of interest for this topic

Conference proceedings

A recent and relevant title for this topic

The number of items in your library that contains your key word in their subject headings

Publication dates

You select entry #13 and then press RETURN. The computer responds with detailed bibliographic information on your selected item.

This screen shows the electronic equivalent of the printed catalogue entry

Figure 6.9   Searching an Electronic Card Catalogue

Indexes

Indexes are lists of books, newspaper articles, journal articles, or other works, as shown in Figure 6.10. They are excellent sources for current information. Because different indexes list sources in different ways, always read the introductory pages for instructions, or ask a librarian for help.

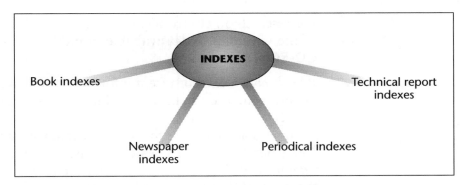

Figure 6.10   Useful Indexes for Technical Disciplines

Book Indexes. All books currently published (up to a set date) are listed in book indexes by author, title, or subject. The following are sample indexes (shown with annotations):

Book indexes

> *Books in Print.* An annual listing of all books published in Canada.
>
> *Cumulative Book Index.* A monthly worldwide listing of books in English.
>
> *Forthcoming Books.* A listing every two months of Canadian books to be published.
>
> *Scientific and Technical Books and Serials in Print.* An annual listing of literature in science and technology.
>
> *New Technical Books: A Selective List with Descriptive Annotations.* Issued ten times yearly.
>
> *Technical Book Review Index.* A monthly listing (with excerpts) of book reviews.
>
> *Medical Books and Serials in Print.* An annual listing of works from medicine and psychology.

In research on electromagnetic radiation, you might check the current issue of *New Technical Books in Print* or *Scientific and Technical Books and Serials in Print.* But no book is likely to offer the very latest information because of the time required to publish a book manuscript (from several months to over one year).

Newspaper Indexes. Most newspaper indexes list articles by subject. The *New York Times Index* is best known, but other major newspapers have their own indexes. The following are sample titles:

Newspaper indexes

> *The Globe and Mail Index* (www.theglobeandmail.com)
> *Christian Science Monitor Index*
> *Wall Street Journal Index*

For research on electromagnetic radiation, you might check recent editions of the *Canadian Index* available monthly in print or every six months on CD-ROM.

Periodical Indexes. For recent information in magazines and journals, consult periodical indexes. To find useful indexes, first decide whether you seek general or specialized information.

One general index is the *Magazine Index,* a subject index (on microfilm) of 400 general periodicals. A popular index is the *Readers' Guide to Periodical Literature,* listing articles from 150 general magazines and journals. Because the *Readers' Guide* is updated every few weeks, you can locate current material. In research on electromagnetic radiation, you would find numerous entries under the subject heading, "Electromagnetic waves."

For specialized information, consult indexes that list journal articles in specific disciplines, such as *Ulrich's International Periodicals Directory.* Another comprehensive source of specialized information, the *Applied Science and Technology Index* carries a monthly listing, by subject, of articles in more than 200 scientific and technical journals. In research on electromagnetic radiation, you would find multiple entries under the heading "Electromagnetic fields" in recent issues of the *AS&T Index.*

Other broad indexes that cover specialized fields in general include the *General Science Index.* The *Statistical Reference Index* lists statistical works not published by the government.

Along with these broad indexes, some disciplines have their own specific indexes. The following are sample listings:

Periodical indexes

> *Agricultural Index*
> *Canadian Business and Current Affairs Index*
> *Canadian Periodical Index*
> *Canadian Education Index*
> *Energy Index*
> *F&S Index of Corporations and Industries*
> *Environment Index*
> *Index to Legal Periodicals*
> *International Nursing Index*

Ask your librarian about the best indexes for your topic and about the many indexes that can be searched by computer.

Citation Indexes. Citation indexes enable researchers to trace, through the literature, the development and refinement of a published idea, concept, or theory. Using a citation index, you can track down the specific publications in which the original material has been cited, quoted, applied, critiqued, verified, or otherwise amplified (Garfield 200). In short, you can answer this question: Who else has said what about this idea?

Citation indexes

The *Science Citation Index,* a quarterly publication, provides a system for cross-referencing important articles on science and technology worldwide. Both the *Science Citation Index* and its counterpart, the *Social Science Citation Index,* can be searched by computer.

Technical Report Indexes. Countless government and private-sector reports written worldwide offer specialized and highly current information. (Proprietary or security restrictions, of course, restrict public access to certain corporate or government documents.) The following are sample indexes for these reports:

Technical report indexes

> *Canadian Research Index*
> *CISTI (The National Research Council of Canada's "Canada's Institute for Scientific and Technical Information")*
> *Monthly Catalog of United States Government Publications*

Abstracts

Beyond indexing various works, abstracts summarize each article. The abstract can save you from going all the way to the journal in order to decide whether to read the article.

Abstracts usually are titled by discipline. The following is a sample list:

Collection of abstracts

> *Biological Abstracts*
> *Computer Abstracts*
> *Environment Abstracts*
> *Excerpta Medica*
> *Forestry Abstracts*
> *International Aerospace Abstracts*
> *Metals Abstracts*

In researching electromagnetic radiation, you might consult *Energy Research Abstracts* under the subject heading "Electromagnetic Fields." Abstracts (such as *Energy Research Abstracts* and *Pollution Abstracts*) increasingly are searchable by computer. Check with your librarian.

For some current research, you might consult abstracts of doctoral dissertations in *Dissertation Abstracts International.*

Locating the Source. If your library does not hold the article you need, you can search an on-line database to identify a holding library, then request the article through interlibrary loan.

Access Tools for Government Publications

The Canadian and U.S. federal governments publish maps, periodicals, books, pamphlets, manuals, monographs, annual reports, research reports, and a bewildering array of other information. The *Canadian Research Index* lists a wide range of Canadian federal and provincial government publications.

Types of Canadian information available to the public include ministerial and government proclamations, government bills and reports, judiciary rulings, and publications from all other government agencies (Departments of Agriculture, Transportation, etc.). A few of the countless titles available are:

Government publications

> *Electromagnetic Fields in Your Environment*
> *Economic Report of the President*
> *Major Oil and Gas Fields of the Free World*
> *Decisions of the Federal Trade Commission*
> *Journal of Research of the National Bureau of Standards*
> *Siting Small Wind Turbines*

Much of this information can be searched on-line as well as in printed volumes. Your best bet for tapping this valuable but complex resource is to request assistance from the librarian in charge of government documents. If your library does not hold the publication you seek, it can be obtained through electronic access or interlibrary loan.

Here are the basic access tools for documents issued or published at government expense and access tools for privately sponsored documents. Though most of these access tools charge fees, you can use many of them free at your college library.

- *Micromedia's Canadian News and Periodical Reference Services* provides access to the CBCA, *Canadian Index, Canadian Serialism Microform, Canadian Education Index, Canadian NewsDisc,* and the *Canadian Research Index* and its microlog collection.
- *Canadian Research Index.* This comprehensive research guide includes all depository publications of research value issued by federal and provincial government agencies and departments. It also indexes scientific and technical reports issued by research institutes and government laboratories. It even lists policy, social, economic, and political reports and theses and dissertations from Canadian universities.
- The *Monthly Catalog of the United States Government,* the major access to government publications and reports, is indexed by author, subject, and title.
- *Government Reports Announcements & Index* is a listing published every two weeks by the National Technical Information Service (NTIS), a U.S. federal clearinghouse for scientific and technical information—all stored in a database. The collection has summaries of over one million federally sponsored research reports published and patents issued since 1964. About

70,000 new summaries are added annually in 22 subject categories, from aeronautics to medicine and biology. Full copies of reports are available from NTIS.

A growing body of government information is posted to the Internet. One starting point is the Government of Canada's federal organizations' home page: <http://canada.gc.ca/depts/major/depind_e.html>.

Examples of government agency postings include:

1. The Canadian Council for Tobacco Control (a Health Canada agency) and the British Columbia Ministry of Health combined in December 1968 to post the results of testing constituents of tobacco smoke.
2. The U.S. Food and Drug Administration's electronic bulletin board lists information on experimental drugs to fight AIDS, drug and device approvals, recalls and litigations involving drugs or devices, health fraud, and a host of related items.

Microforms

Microform technology enables vast quantities of printed information to be reproduced and stored on rolls of microfilm or packets of microfiche. (This material is read on machines that magnify the reduced image. Ask your librarian for assistance.) Among the growing array of microform products are government documents, technical reports, newspapers, business directories, and translated documents from around the world (Lavin 12).

Internet Sources

Today's Internet connects computer users by the tens of millions. Web sites and addresses (*uniform resource locators*, or *URLs*) numbering in the hundreds of millions continue to multiply across the globe.

Internet Service Providers (ISPs), including *Sympatico*, *Compuserve*, and *Microsoft Network* provide Internet access via "gateways," along with aids for navigating their many resources (see Figure 6.11).

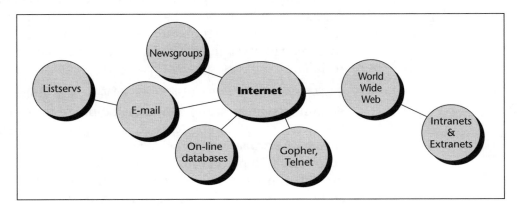

Figure 6.11   Various Parts of the Internet

Usenet. Usenet denotes a worldwide system for on-line discussions via *newsgroups,* a form of electronic bulletin board where users post and share information and discuss topics of common interest via e-mail. Newsgroups offer public access to countless topics ranging from rain forest protection, to intellectual property laws, to professional hockey.

Newsgroups are either *moderated* or *unmoderated.* In a moderated group, all contributions are reviewed by a moderator who must approve the material before it can be posted. In an unmoderated group, all contributions are posted. Most groups are unmoderated. Also available are *newsfeed* newsgroups, which gather and post items from wire services such as the Associated Press.

Newsgroups typically publish answers to "frequently asked questions" (FAQ lists) about their particular topic of interest (acupuncture, the North American Free Trade Agreement, abortion or anti-abortion, etc.). While these can be a good source of any group's distilled wisdom, FAQs reflect the biases of those who contribute to and edit them. A group's particular convictions might politicize information and produce all sorts of inaccuracies.

Listservs. Like newsgroups, *listservs* are special-interest groups for e-mail discussion and information sharing. In contrast to newsgroups, listserv discussions usually focus on specialized topics, with discussions usually among experts (say, cancer researchers), often before their findings or opinions appear in published form. Many listservs include FAQ listings.

Listserv access is available to subscribers who receive mailings automatically via e-mail. Instead of delivering messages to a newsgroup bulletin board, listservs deliver to each subscriber's electronic "mailbox." Like a newsgroup, a listserv may be moderated or unmoderated, but subscribers/contributors are expected to observe proper Internet etiquette, and stick to the discussed topic, without digressions or "flaming" (attacking someone) or "spamming" (posting irrelevant messages). Some lists allow anyone to subscribe, while others require that subscription requests be approved by the list owner. Only subscribers can post messages to the list.

E-mail Enquiries. The global e-mail network is excellent for contacting knowledgeable people in any field worldwide. E-mail addresses are increasingly accessible via locator programs that search various local directories listed on the Internet. However, unsolicited and indiscriminate enquiries might offend the recipient.

World Wide Web ("the Web"). The Web is a global network of databases, documents, images, and sounds. All types of information from anywhere in the Web network can be accessed and explored through navigation programs such as *Netscape Navigator, Lynx,* or *Microsoft Internet Explorer,* known as "browsers." Hypertext links among Web resources enable users to explore information along different paths by clicking on key words or icons that reveal additional paths for browsing and discovery.

Telnet and Gopher. Telnet and Gopher are older portions of the Internet which have been largely supplanted by the World Wide Web. These networks can still be explored by means of patched-together search engines such as *WAIS* (Wide Area Information Service), *Archie,* and *Veronica* (the Very Easy Rodent-oriented Net-wide Index to Computerized Archives).

Web Usage. Each Web site has its own *home page* that serves as introduction to the site and is linked to additional "pages" that individual users can explore according to their information needs.

Through your campus or office network, or using a modem, a phone line, and an Internet service provider, you can search Internet files, databases, and home pages. You can participate in various newsgroups, subscribe to discussion lists, send e-mail enquiries, and gain access to publications that exist only in electronic form. Using a browser, you can explore sites on the Web, locate experts in all types of specialties, read the latest articles in journals such as *Nature* or *Science,* or review the latest listings of jobs in your specialty. For on-line databases in your field, ask your librarian.

Assume that any material obtained from the Internet is protected by copyright. Before using such material any place other than in a college paper (properly documented), obtain written permission from its owner.

Intranets and Extranets. An *intranet* is an in-house computer network that employs Internet technology for information access within a company.

Invaluable for on-the-job research, training, and collaboration, a customized intranet provides authorized users access to the company's document library, price lists, on-line discussions, and progress reports—even the data files of colleagues. Fast-food chains and other franchises increasingly use intranets to respond to franchisee questions and to distribute advice, industry/company news, sales figures, and other timely messages (Wallace 12). An intranet puts the company's knowledge and expertise at everyone's fingertips. Some organizations have their company "yellow pages," listing the expertise and information possessed by each employee.

An *extranet* integrates a company's intranet with the global Internet. External users (customers, subcontractors, outside vendors) with an Internet connection and a password can browse non-restricted areas of a company's Web site and download selected information, including customized reports. Extranets eliminate the need for the traditional printing and mailing of information to clients or suppliers (Stedman 49). They also enable collaboration among organizations. At Caterpillar Tractors, Inc., for example, when a customer's equipment breaks down, the entire company can mobilize immediately, contact experts inside and outside the organization, access records of previous solutions to similar problems, and collaborate on a solution—for example, designing an improved mechanical part for the equipment (Haskin 57–60).

The extranet blend of in-house information and Internet access raises security issues for any organization, leaving its network vulnerable to hackers, spies, or saboteurs (Meyerson 35). Therefore, each extranet site has its own *firewall* (software that keeps out uninvited users and that controls the data they can access) that includes password protection and *encryption* (coding) of sensitive information (Haskin 59).

Keyword Searches Using Boolean Operators. Most search engines that retrieve by keyword allow the use of Boolean[1] operators (commands such as "AND", "OR," "NOT," etc.), to define relationships among various key words. Table 6-2 shows how these commands can expand a search of narrow it by generating fewer "hits."

Table 6-2

Using Boolean Operators to Expand or Limit a Search	
If you enter these terms ...	The computer searches for ...
■ electromagnetism AND health	■ only entries that contain both words
■ electromagnetism OR health	■ all entries that contain either word
■ electromagnetism NOT health	■ only entries that contain Word 1 and do not contain Word 2
■ electromag*	■ all entries that contain this root within other words

Boolean commands also can be combined, as in

(electromagnetic *or* radiation) *and* (fields *or* tumours)

The results (hits) produced from this query would contain any of these combinations:

electromagnetic fields, electromagnetic and tumours, radiation and fields, radiation and tumours

Using *truncation* (cropping a word to its root and adding an asterisk), as in *electromag**, would produce a broad array of hits, including these:

electromagnet, electromagnetic energy, electromagnetic pulse, electromagnetic wave. . . .

Different search engines use Boolean operators in slightly different ways; many include additional options (such as NEAR, to search for entries that contain search terms within ten or twenty words of each other). Click on the HELP option of your particular search engine to see which strategies it supports.

---

1. British mathematician and logician George Boole (1815–1864) developed the system of symbolic logic (Boolean logic) now widely used in electronic information retrieval.

Exploring Primary Sources

Work-related research is often based on primary research, an original, first-hand study of the topic, involving sources like those in Figure 6.12 on page 132.

IN BRIEF

Guidelines for Internet Research[2]

1. *Try to focus your search beforehand.* The more precisely you identify the information you seek, the lower your chance of wandering aimlessly through cyberspace.

2. *Select key words or search phrases that are varied and technical, rather than general.* Some search terms generate better hits than others. In addition to "electro-magnetic radiation," for example, try "electromagnetic fields," "power lines and health," or "electrical fields." Specialized terms (for example, *vertigo* versus *dizziness*) offer the best access to sites that are reliable, professional, and specific. Always check your spelling.

3. *Look for Web sites that are specific.* Compile a *hotlist* of sites that are most relevant to your needs and interests. (Specialized newsletters and trade publications are good sources for site listings.)

4. *Set a time limit for searching.* It's no secret that Internet searching ("surfing") can be addictive. Recent surveys indicate that employees spend sizable amounts of time surfing for personal instead of business-related information. As you begin a search set a 10-15 minute time limit, and avoid tangents that, no matter how engaging, are irrelevant to your search.

5. *Expect limited results from any search.* Each search engine (*Alta Vista, Excite, Hot Bot, Infoseek, WebCrawler, Yahoo,* etc.) has its own strengths and weaknesses. Some are faster and more thorough while others yield more targeted and updated hits. Some search titles only—instead of the full text—for keywords. In addition, studies show that "Web content is increasing so rapidly that no single search engine indexes more than about one-third of it" (Peterson 286). Broaden your coverage by using multiple engines.

6. *Use bookmarks and hotlists for quick access to favourite Web sites.* Mark a useful site with a bookmark which you then add to your hotlist.

7. *Expect material on the Internet to have a brief life span.* Site addresses can change overnight; material is rapidly updated or discarded. If you find something of special value, save or print it before it changes or disappears.

8. *Be selective about what you download.* Download only what you need. Unless they are crucial to your research, omit graphics, sound, and video files because these consume time and disk space. Focus on text files only.

9. *Never download copyrighted material without written authorization from the copyright holder.* According to the 1997 No Electronic Theft Act (NET), you commit a federal crime if you possess or distribute "unauthorized electronic copies of copyrighted material valued over $1,000, even when no profit is involved" (Grossman 37). Only material in the public domain (page 152) is exempted.

IN BRIEF

Such crimes are punishable by heavy fines and/or prison sentences.

Before downloading *anything* from the Internet, ask yourself: "Am I violating someone's privacy (as in forwarding an e-mail or a newsgroup entry)? or "Am I decreasing, in any way, the value of this material for the person who owns it?" Obtain permission beforehand and cite the source.

10. *Consider using information retrieval services.* An electronic service such as *Inquisit* or *Dialog* protects copyright holders by selling access to all materials in its database. For a monthly fee and or per-page fee, users can download full texts of articles from countless periodicals, ranging from general to highly specialized. Subscribers to these Internet-accessible databases include companies and educational institutions.

Although these services effectively filter out a lot of Internet junk, they do not catalogue material that exists only in electronic form (E-zines, newsgroup and listserv entries, etc.). Therefore, these databases exclude potentially valuable material (such as research studies not yet available in hard copy) accessible only through a general Web search.

Note: Rick Broadhead and Jim Carroll publish several titles dealing with the Internet in Canada:

Canadian Internet Directory
Canadian Internet Handbook
Canadian Internet New Users Handbook
Canadian Internet Access Kit
Canadian Internet Advantage

To learn more about these titles (and their updates), see your bookseller.

---

2. Guidelines adapted from Baker 57+; Branscrum 78; Busiel and Maeglin 39-40, 76; Fugate 40-41; Kawasaki 156; Matson 249-52.

The Informative Interview

An excellent primary source of information unavailable in any publication is the personal interview. Much of what an expert knows may never be published (Pugliano 6). Also, a respondent might refer you to other experts or sources of information.

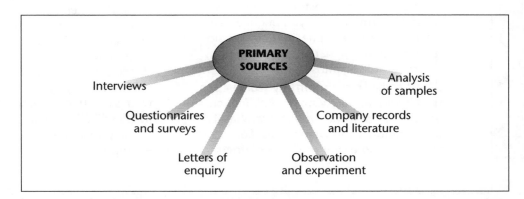

Figure 6.12   Sources for Primary Research

Of course, an expert opinion can be just as mistaken or biased as anyone else's. Like patients who seek second opinions about serious medical conditions, researchers seek a balanced range of expert opinions about a complex problem or controversial issue—not only from a company engineer and environmentalist, for example, but also from independent and presumably more objective third parties such as a professor or journalist who has studied the issue.

Selecting an Interview Medium.   Once you decide whom to interview about what, select your medium carefully:

- *In-person interviews* are most productive because they allow human contact (Hopkins-Tanne 24).
- *Phone interviews* can be convenient and productive, but they lack the human contact of in-person interviews—especially when the interviewer and respondent have not met.
- *E-mail interviews* are convenient and inexpensive, and they allow plenty of time for respondents to consider their answers.
- *Fax interviews* are highly impersonal, and using them is generally a bad idea.

Whatever your medium, obtain a respondent's approval *beforehand*—instead of waylaying this person with an unwanted surprise.

Guidelines for Informative Interviews[3]

Planning the Interview

1. *Focus on your purpose.* Determine exactly what you hope to learn from this interview. Write out your purpose.

Purpose statement

> I will interview Anne Hector, Chief Engineer at Northport Electric, to ask her about the company's approaches to EMF risk avoidance—within the company as well as in the community.

2. *Do your homework.* Learn all you can about the topic beforehand. The more you know, the better your chance of getting the facts straight. If the respondent has published anything relevant, read it before the interview. Be sure the information this person might provide is unavailable in print.

---

3. Several guidelines are adapted from Blum 88; Dowd, 13-14; Hopkins, Kotulak 147; McDonald 190; Rensberger 15; Hopkins-Tanne 23, 29; Young 114, 115, 177.

3. *Contact the intended respondent.* Do this by telephone, letter, or e-mail, and be sure to introduce yourself and your purpose.

4. *Request the interview at your respondent's convenience.* Give the respondent ample notice and time to prepare, and ask whether she/he objects to being quoted or taped. If you use a tape recorder, insert fresh batteries and a new tape, and set the recording volume loud enough.

Preparing the Questions

1. *Make each question clear and specific.* Vague, unspecific questions elicit vague, unspecific answers.

A vague question

> How is this utility company dealing with the problem of electromagnetic fields?

> Which problem—public relations, potential liability, danger to electrical workers, to the community, or what?

Clear and specific question

> What safety procedures have you developed for risk avoidance among electrical work crews?

2. *Avoid questions that can be answered with a mere "yes" or "no."*

An unproductive question

> In your opinion, can technology find ways to decrease EMF hazards?

> Instead, phrase your question to elicit a detailed response:

A productive question

> Of the various technological solutions being proposed or considered, which do you consider most promising?

> This is one instance in which your earlier homework pays off.

3. *Avoid loaded questions.* A loaded question invites or promotes a particular bias:

A loaded question

> Wouldn't you agree that EMF hazards have been overstated?

> An impartial question does not lead the interviewee to respond in a certain way.

An impartial question

> In your opinion, have EMF hazards been accurately stated, overstated, or understated?

4. *Save the most difficult, complex, or sensitive questions for last.* Leading off with your toughest question might annoy respondents, making them uncooperative.

5. *Write out each question on a separate page.* Use a three-ring binder with 21.5 cm x 28 cm (8½" x 11") pages to arrange your questions in logical order, to flip to a new page for each question, and to record responses easily.

Conducting the Interview

1. *Make a good start.* Dress appropriately and arrive on time. Thank your respondent: restate your purpose; explain why you believe he/she can be helpful; explain exactly how you will use the information.

2. *Be sensitive to cultural differences.* If the respondent belongs to a culture different from your own, then consider the level of formality, politeness, directness, relationship building, and other behaviours considered appropriate in that culture.

3. *Let the respondent do the most talking.* Keep opinions to yourself.

4. *Be a good listener.* Don't doodle or let your eyes wander. People reveal more when the listener seems genuinely interested.

5. *Stick to your interview plan.* If the respondent wanders, politely nudge the conversation back on track (unless the added information is useful).

6. *Ask for clarification or explanation whenever necessary.* If you don't understand an answer, say so. Request an example, an analogy, or a simplified version—and keep asking until you understand.

Clarifying questions

> Would you go over that again please?
> Is there a simpler explanation?

Science writer Ronald Kotulak argues that, "No question is dumb if the answer is necessary to help you understand something. . . . Don't pretend to know more than you do" (144).

7. *Keep checking on your understanding.* Repeat major points in your own words and ask if the technical details are accurate and if your interpretation is correct.

8. *Be ready with follow-up questions.* Some answers may lead to additional questions.

Follow-up questions

> Why is it like that?
> Could you say something more about that?
> What more needs to be done?
> What happened next?

9. *Keep note-taking to a minimum.* Record statistics, dates, names, and other precise data, but not every word. Jot key terms or phrases that later can refresh your memory.

Concluding the Interview

1. *Ask for closing comments.* Perhaps the respondent can lead you to additional information.

Concluding questions

> Have I missed anything?
> Would you care to add anything?
> Is there anything I've neglected to ask?

> Is there anyone else I should talk to?
> Is there anyone who has a different point of view?

2. *Invite the respondent to review your version.* If the interview will be published, ask the respondent to check your final draft (for misspelled names, inaccurate details, misquotations, and so on) and to approve it. Offer to provide copies of any document in which this information appears.

3. *Thank your respondent and leave promptly.*

4. *As soon as you leave the interview, write a complete summary* (or record one verbally). Do this while responses are fresh in your memory.

A Sample Interview

Figure 6.13 shows the partial text of an interview on persuasive challenges in the workplace. Notice how the interviewer probes, seeks clarification, and follows up on certain responses.

Q. *Would you please summarize your communication responsibilities?*
A. The corporate relations office oversees three departments: customer service (which handles claims, adjustments, and queries), public relations, and employee relations. My job is to supervise the production of all documents generated by this office.

Probing and following up

Q. *Isn't that a lot of responsibility?*
A. It is, considering we're trying to keep some people happy, getting others to cooperate, and trying to get everyone to change their thinking and see things in a positive light. Just about every document we write has to be persuasive.

Seeking clarification

Q. *What exactly do you mean by "persuasive"?*
A. The best way to explain is through examples of what we do. The customer service department responds to problems like these: some users are unhappy with our software because it won't work for a particular application, or they find a glitch in one of our programs, or they're confused by the documentation, or someone wants the software modified to meet a specific need. For each of these complaints or requests we have to persuade our audience that we've resolved the problem or that we're making a genuine effort to resolve it quickly. The public relations department works to keep up our reputation through links outside the company. For instance, we keep in touch with this community, with consumers, the general public, government and educational agencies. . . .

Seeking clarification

Q. *Can you be more specific? "Keeping in touch" doesn't sound much like persuasion.*
A. Okay, right now we're developing programs with colleges and universities, in which we offer heavily discounted software, backed up by an extensive support network (regional consultants, an 800 phone hotline, and workshops). We're hoping to persuade them that our software is superior to our well-entrenched competitor's. And locally we're offering the same kind of service and support to business clients.

Figure 6.13   Partial Text of an Informative Interview   **(Continued)**

Following up

> **Q. *What about employee relations?***
> **A.** Day to day we face the usual kinds of problems: trying to get 100 percent employee contributions to the United Way, or persuading employees to help out in the community, or getting them to abide by new company regulations restricting smoking or to limit personal phone calls. Right now, we're facing a real persuasive challenge. Because of market saturation, software sales have flattened across the board. This means temporary layoffs for roughly 28 percent of our employees. Our only alternative is to persuade *all* employees to accept a 10 percent salary and benefit cut until the market improves.
>
> **Q. *How, exactly, do you persuade employees to accept a cut in pay and benefits?***
> **A.** Basically, we have to make them see that by taking the cut, they're really investing in the company's future—and, of course, in their own.
>
> (The interview continues.)

Probing

Figure 6.13   Partial Text of an Informative Interview

Surveys and Questionnaires

Surveys help us develop profiles and estimates about the concerns, preferences, attitudes, beliefs, or perceptions of a large, identifiable group (a *target population*) by studying representatives of that group (a *sample group*).

Surveys help us make assessments like these:

- *Do consumers prefer brand A or brand B?*
- *What percentage of students feel safe on our campus?*
- *Is public confidence in technology increasing or decreasing?*

The questionnaire is the tool for conducting surveys. While interviews allow for greater clarity and depth, questionnaires offer an inexpensive way to survey a large group. Respondents can answer privately and anonymously—and often more candidly than in an interview.

Questionnaires carry certain limitations:

Limitations of survey research

- *A low rate of response (often less than 30 percent).* People refuse to respond to a questionnaire that seems too long, complicated, or in some way threatening. They might be embarrassed by the topic or afraid of how their answers could be used.
- *Responses that might be non-representative.* A survey will get responses from the people who want to respond, but you will know nothing about the people who didn't respond. Those who responded might have extreme views, a particular stake in the outcome, or some other motive that represents inaccurately the population being surveyed (Plumb and Spyridakis 625–26).
- *Lack of follow-up.* Survey questions do not allow for the kind of follow-up and clarification possible with interview questions.

Even surveys by professionals carry potential for error. As consumers of survey research, we need to understand how surveys are designed, administered, and interpreted, and what can go wrong in the process. The following is an introduction to creating surveys and to avoiding pitfalls along the way.

Defining the Survey's Purpose. Why is this survey being done? What, exactly, is it measuring? How much background research is needed? How will the survey findings be used?

Defining the Target Population. Who is the exact population being studied ("the chronically unemployed," "part-time students," "computer users")? For example, in its research on science and technology activity, the *1997 Statistical Abstract of the United States* differentiates "scientists and engineers" from "technicians":

Target populations clearly defined

> Scientists and engineers are defined as persons engaged in scientific and engineering work at a level requiring a knowledge of sciences equivalent at least to that acquired through completion of a 4-year college course. Technicians are defined as persons engaged in technical work at a level requiring knowledge acquired through a technical institute, junior college, or other type of training less extensive than 4-year college training. Craftspersons and skilled workers are excluded. (603)

Identifying the Sample Group. How will intended respondents be selected? How many respondents will there be? Generally, the larger the sample surveyed, the more dependable the results (assuming a well-chosen and representative sample). Will the sample be randomly chosen? In the statistical sense, "random" does not mean "chosen haphazardly": a random sample means that any member of the target population stands an equal chance of being included in the sample group.

Even a sample that is highly representative of the target population carries a measure of *sampling error*.

A type of survey error

> The particular sample used in a survey is only one of a large number of possible samples of the same size which could have been selected using the same sampling procedures. Estimates derived from the different samples would, in general, differ from each other. (Statistical Abstract 949)

The larger the sampling error (usually expressed as the *margin of error*, page 164) the less dependable the survey findings.

Defining the Survey Method. What type of data (opinions, ideas, facts, figures) will be collected? Is timing important? How will the survey be administered—in person, by mail, by telephone? How will the data be collected, recorded, analyzed, and reported (Lavin 277)?

Telephone, e-mail, and in-person surveys yield fast results, but respondents consider telephone surveys annoying and, without anonymity, people tend to be less candid. They generate high response rates, but mail surveys are less expensive and more confidential. Computerized surveys create the sense of a video game: the program analyzes each response and automatically designs the next question. Respondents who dislike being quizzed by a human researcher seem more comfortable with this automated format (Perelman 89–90).

Guidelines for Developing a Questionnaire

1. *Choose the types of questions.* (Adams and Schvaneveldt 202–12; Velotta 390). Questions can be *open-ended* or *closed-ended*. Open-ended questions allow respondents to express exactly what they're thinking or feeling in a word, phrase, sentence, or short essay:

Open-ended questions

How much do you know about electromagnetic radiation at our school?

What do you think should be done about electromagnetic fields (EMFs) at our school?

Since one never knows what people will say, open-ended questions are a good way to uncover attitudes and obtain unexpected information. But essay-type questions are difficult to answer and tabulate.

When you want to measure where people stand on an issue, choose close-ended questions:

Close-ended questions

Are you interested in joining a group of concerned parents?
YES_____ NO_____

Rate your degree of concern about EMFs at our school.
HIGH_____ MODERATE_____ LOW_____ NO CONCERN_____

Circle the number that indicates your view about the town's proposal to spend $20,000 to hire its own EMF consultant.

1........ 2.......... 3..........4........ 5........ 6........7
Strongly   No   Strongly
Approve   Opinion   Disapprove

Respondents may be asked to *rate* one item on a scale (from high to low, best to worse), to *rank* two or more items (by importance desirability), or to *select* items from a list. Other questions measure percentages or frequency.

How often do you . . . ?
ALWAYS _____ OFTEN _____ SOMETIMES _____ RARELY_____ NEVER _____

Although closed-ended questions are easy to answer, tabulate, measure, and analyze, they might elicit biased responses. Some people, for instance, automatically prefer items near the top of a list or the left side of a rating scale (Plumb and Spyridakis 633). Also, people are prone to agree rather than disagree with assertions in a questionnaire (Sherblom, Sullivan, and Sherblom 61).

2. *Design an engaging introduction and opening questions.* Persuade respondents that the survey relates to their concerns, that their answers matter, and that their anonymity is assured. Explain how respondents will benefit from your findings, or offer an incentive (say, a copy of your final report).

A survey introduction

Your answers will enable our school board to speak accurately for your views at our next town meeting. Results of this survey will appear in our campus newspaper. Thank you.

Researchers often include a cover letter with the questionnaire.

Begin with the easiest questions. Once respondents commit to these, they are likely to complete more difficult questions later.

3. *Make each question unambiguous.* All respondents should be able to interpret identical questions identically. An ambiguous question leaves room for misinterpretation.

An ambiguous question

Do you favour weapons for campus police?   YES_____   NO_____

"Weapons" might mean tear gas, clubs, handguns, all three, or two out of three. Consequently, responses to the above question would produce a misleading statistic, such as "Over 95 percent of students favour handguns for campus police" when the accurate conclusion might be "Over 95 percent of students favour some form of weapon." Moreover, the limited choice ("yes/no") reduces an array of possible opinions to an either/or choice.

A clear, incisive question

Do you favour (check all that apply):
_____ Having campus police carry mace and a club?
_____ Having campus police carry non-lethal "stun guns"?
_____ Having campus police store handguns in their cruisers?
_____ Having campus police carry small-caliber handguns?
_____ Having campus police carry large-caliber handguns?
_____ Having campus police carry no weapons?
_____ Don't know

To ensure a full range of possible responses, include options such as "Other_____," "Don't know," "Not Applicable," or an "Additional Comments" section.

4. *Make each question unbiased.* Avoid *loaded questions* that invite or advocate a particular viewpoint or bias:

A loaded question

Should our campus tolerate the needless endangerment of innocent students by lethal weapons?

YES_____   NO_____

Emotionally loaded and judgmental words ("endangerment," "innocent," "tolerate," "needless," "lethal") in a survey are unethical because their built-in judgments manipulate people's responses (Hayakawa 40).

5. *Make it brief, simple, and inviting.* Try to limit questions and response space to two sides of a single page. Include a stamped, return-addressed envelope, and give a specific return date. Address each respondent by name, sign your letter or your introduction, and give your title.

A Sample Questionnaire

The student-written questionnaire in Figure 6.14 sent to presidents of local companies, is designed to elicit responses that can be tabulated easily.

Written reports of survey findings usually include an appendix that contains a copy of the questionnaire as well as the tabulated responses.

Enquiries

Letters, phone calls, or e-mail enquiries to experts listed in Web pages are handy for obtaining specific information from government agencies, legislators, private companies, university research centres, trade associations, and research foundations.

Office Files

Organization records (reports, memos, computer printouts, etc. are good primary sources. Most organizations also publish pamphlets, brochures, annual reports, or prospectuses for consumers, employees, investors, or voters. But be alert for bias in company literature. If you were evaluating the safety measures at a local nuclear power plant, you would want the complete picture. Along with the company's literature, you would also want studies and reports from government agencies and publications from environmental groups.

Personal Observation and Experiment

If possible, amplify and verify your findings with a first-hand look. Observation should be your final step because you now know what to look for. Have a plan. Know how, where, and when to look, and jot down observations immediately. You might even take photos or make drawings.

Informed observations can pinpoint real problems. Here is an excerpt from a report investigating low morale at an electronics firm. This researcher's observations and interpretation are crucial in defining the problem:

Direct observation is often essential

Our on-site communications audit revealed that employees were unaware of any major barriers to communication. Over 75 percent of employees claimed they felt free to talk to their managers, but the managers, in turn, estimated that fewer than 50 percent of employees felt free to talk to them.

Communication Questionnaire

1. Describe your type of company (e.g., manufacturing, high tech) _____
   _____

2. Number of employees? (Please check one.)

   _____ 5–25   _____ 51–100   _____ 151–300

   _____ 26–50   _____ 101–150   _____ 301–450

3. What types of written communication occur in your company? (Label by frequency:
   never, rarely, sometimes, often.)

   _____ memos   _____ letters   _____ advertising

   _____ manuals   _____ reports   _____ newsletters

   _____ procedures _____ proposals   _____ other (Specify.)

   _____ e-mail   _____ catalogues   _____

4. Who does most of the writing? (Pls. give titles.) _____
   _____

5. Please characterize your employees' writing effectiveness.

   _____ good   _____ fair   _____ poor

6. Does your company have formal guidelines for writing?

   _____ no   _____ yes   (Pls. describe briefly.) _____
   _____

7. Do you offer in-house communication training?

   _____ no   _____ yes   (Pls. describe briefly.) _____
   _____

8. Please rank the usefulness of the following areas in communication training (from 1 through 10).

   _____ organization information   _____ audience awareness

   _____ summarizing information   _____ persuasive writing

   _____ editing for style   _____ grammar

   _____ document design   _____ researching

   _____ e-mail etiquette   _____ Web page design

   _____ other   (Pls. specify.) _____

9. Please rank these skills in order of importance (from 1-6).

   _____ reading   _____ listening   _____ speaking to groups

   _____ writing   _____ collaborating _____ speaking face-to-face

10. Do you provide tuition reimbursement for employees?

    _____ no   _____ yes

11. Would you consider having UMD communication interns work for you part-time?

    _____ no   _____ yes

12. Should UMD offer Saturday seminars in communication?

    _____ no   _____ yes

    Additional comments/suggestions: _____
    _____

Figure 6.14   A Sample Survey

> The problem involves misinterpretation. Because managers don't ask for complaints, employees are afraid to make them, and because employees never ask for an evaluation, they never get one. Each side has inaccurate perceptions of what the other side expects, and because of ineffective communications, each side fails to realize that its perceptions are wrong.

Even direct observation is not foolproof; for instance, you might be biased about what you see (focusing on the wrong events or ignoring something important), or, instead of behaving normally, people being observed might behave in ways they think they expect (Adams and Schvanveldt 244).

An experiment is a controlled form of observation designed to verify an assumption (e.g., the role of fish oil in preventing heart disease) or to test something untried (the relationship between background music and worker productivity). Each specialty has its own guidelines for experiment design.

Analysis of Samples

Workplace research can involve collecting and analyzing samples: water, soil, or air, for contamination and pollution; foods, for nutritional value; ore, for mineral value; or plants, for medicinal value. Investigators analyze material samples to find the cause of an airline accident. Engineers analyze samples of steel, concrete, or other building materials to determine their load-bearing capacity. Medical specialists analyze tissue samples for disease.

☑ EXERCISES

1. Begin researching for the analytical report (Chapter 19) due at semester's end. Complete these steps. (Your instructor might establish a timetable.)

   Phase One: Preliminary Steps

   a. Choose a topic of *immediate practical importance,* something that affects you or your community directly.

   b. Identify a specific audience and its intended use of your information. Complete an audience/purpose profile (page 36).

   c. Narrow your topic, and check with your instructor for approval.

   d. Make a working bibliography to ensure sufficient primary and secondary resources. Don't delay this step!

   e. List things you already know about your topic.

   f. Write a clear statement of purpose and submit it in a proposal memo (pages 49–57) to your instructor.

   g. Develop a tree chart of possible questions (as on page 113).

   h. Make a working outline.

   Phase Two: Collecting Data (Read Chapter 7 in preparation for this phase.)

   a. In your research, move from general to specific; begin with general reference works for an overview.

   b. Skim your material, looking for high points.

   c. Take selective notes. Don't write everything down! Use notecards.

   d. Plan and administer questionnaires, interviews, and letters of enquiry.

   e. Whenever possible, conclude your research with direct observation.

   f. Evaluate and interpret your findings.

   g. Use the checklist on page 168 to reassess your research methods and reasoning.

   Phase Three: Organizing Your Data and Writing Your Report

   a. Revise and adjust your working outline, as needed.

   b. Compose an audience/purpose analysis, like the sample on pages 355 and 357.

c. Fully document all sources of information.

d. Proofread carefully and add all needed supplements (title page, letter of transmittal, abstract, summary, appendix, glossary).

Due Dates: To Be Assigned by Your Instructor

List of possible topics due:

Final topic due:

Proposal memo due:

Working bibliography and working outline due:

Notecards due:

Copies of questionnaires, interview questions, and enquiry letters due:

Revised outline due:

First draft of report due:

Final draft with supplements and documentation due:

2. Using the printed or electronic card catalogue, locate and record the full bibliographic data for five books in your field or on your semester report topic, all published within the past year.

3. List the title of each of these specialized reference works in your field or on your topic: a bibliography, an encyclopedia, a dictionary, a handbook, an almanac (if available), and a directory.

4. Identify the major periodical index in your field or on your topic. Locate a recent article on a specific topic (e.g., use of artificial intelligence in medical diagnosis). Photocopy the article (get CANCOPY clearance) and write an informative abstract.

5. Consult the appropriate librarian and identify two databases you would search for information on the topic in Exercise 1.

6. Using technical report indexes, locate abstracts of three recent reports on one specific topic in your field. Provide complete bibliographic information.

7. Most Web browsers allow you to do keyword searches (page 131) by using a search engine such as *Yahoo, Lycos, Alta Vista,* or *Infoseek*. Each engine has its own guidelines and peculiarities; these usually are explained in a "help" file or user guide. Learn to use at least one search engine; for your colleagues, write instructions for designing and conducting a Web search using that engine.

URLs: *http://www.yahoo.com*
http://www.lycos.com
http://www.altavista.com
http://www.infoseek.com

8. Locate an Internet newsgroup or discussion list related to your report topic. Download and print out the group's FAQ list.

9. Using *Netscape Navigator, Internet Explorer,* or a similar browser, search Web sites to locate resources for your report topic.

10. If your library belongs to a consortium of electronically networked libraries, search the holdings of other libraries on the network for topic resources not available in your library. Prepare a list of promising possibilities.

11. Revise these questions to make them appropriate for inclusion in a questionnaire:

a. Would a female prime minister do the job as well as a male?

b. Don't you think that euthanasia is a crime?

c. Do you oppose increased government spending?

d. Do you think welfare recipients are too lazy to support themselves?

e. Are teachers responsible for the decline in literacy among students?

f. Aren't humanities studies a waste of time?

g. Do you prefer Rocket Cola to other leading brands?

h. In meetings, do you think men are more interruptive than women?

12. Arrange an interview with someone in your field. Decide on general areas for questioning: job opportunities, chances for promotion, salary range, requirements, outlook for the next decade, working conditions, job satisfaction, etc.

Compose specific interview questions; conduct the interview, and summarize your findings in a memo to your instructor.

✔ COLLABORATIVE PROJECT

Divide into small groups, and decide on a campus or community issue or some other topic worthy of research. Elect a group manager to assign and coordinate tasks. At project's end, the manager will provide a performance appraisal by summarizing, in writing, the contribution of each team member. Assigned tasks will include planning, information gathering from primary and secondary sources, document preparation (including visuals) and revision, and classroom presentation. (See pages 17–18 for collaboration guidelines.)

Do the research, write the report, and present your findings to the class. (In conjunction with this project, your instructor may assign Chapter 23.)

As you discover material during research, you confront questions like these: *How much is worth keeping? How should I record it? Can I trust this information? What, exactly, does it mean? How will I credit the source?* These latter stages of the research process require the same quality of critical thinking as the earlier stages in Chapter 6.

Recording the Findings

Findings should be recorded in ways that enable you to easily locate, organize, and control the material as you work with it. Record primary research findings by using a laptop computer, photographs, drawings, tape recorder, videotape, or whichever medium suits your purpose. Record secondary research findings in the form of notes.

Taking Notes

Notecards are convenient because they are easy to organize and reorganize. In place of notecards, many researchers take notes on a laptop computer, using information or database management software that allows notes to be filed, rearranged, and retrieved by author, title, topic, date, etc.

Follow these suggestions when using notecards:

1. Make a separate bibliography card for each work you plan to consult (Figure 7.1). Record the complete entry, using the identical citation format that will appear in your document (see pages 175–182 for sample entries). When searching an on-line catalogue, you often can print out the full bibliographic record for each work, thereby ensuring accurate citation.

Record each bibliographic citation exactly as it will appear in your final report

Pinsky, Mark A. *The EMF Book: What You Should Know About Electromagnetic Fields, Electromagnetic Radiation, and Your Health.* New York: Warner, 1995.

Figure 7.1   Bibliography Card

2. Skim the entire work to locate relevant material.

3. Go back and decide what to record. Use a separate card for each item.

4. Decide how to record the item: as a quotation or a paraphrase. When quoting others directly, be sure to record words and punctuation accurately. When restating or adapting material in your own words, be sure to preserve the original meaning and emphasis.

Quoting the Work of Others

When you borrow exact wording, whether the words were written or spoken (as in an interview or presentation) or whether they appeared in electronic form, you must place quotation marks around all borrowed material. Even a single borrowed sentence or phrase, or a single word used in a special way, needs quotation marks, with the exact source properly cited.

If your notes fail to identify quoted material accurately, you may forget to credit the source in your report. Even when this omission is unintentional, writers face the charge of *plagiarism* (misrepresenting as one's own the words or ideas of someone else). Possible consequences of plagiarism include expulsion from school, the loss of your job, or a lawsuit.

In recording a direct quotation, copy the selection word for word (Figure 7.2) and include the page numbers.

Place quotation marks around all directly quoted material

> Pinsky, Mark A. pp. 29–30.
>
> "Neither electromagnetic fields nor electromagnetic radiation cause cancer per se, most researchers agree. What they may do is promote cancer. Cancer is a multistage process that requires an "initiator" that makes a cell or group of cells abnormal. Everyone has cancerous cells in his or her body. Cancer—the disease as we think of it—occurs when these cancerous cells grow uncontrollably."

Figure 7.2   Notecard for a Quotation

If your quotation omits parts of a sentence, use an *ellipsis* (three periods: ...) to indicate each part that you have omitted from the original. If your quotation omits the end of a sentence, the beginning of the subsequent sentence, or whole sentences or paragraphs, show the ellipsis with four periods (....).

Ellipsis within and between sentences

> If your quotation omits parts . . . use an ellipsis. . . . If your quotation omits the end. . . .

Be sure that your elliptical expression is grammatically correct and that the omitted material in no way distorts the original meaning.

If you insert your own words within the quotation, place them inside brackets to distinguish them from those of your source:

Brackets setting off personal comments within quoted material

> "This profession [aircraft ground controller] requires exhaustive attention."

(For more on brackets, see the Appendix.)

Sentences and paragraphs that include quotations must be clear and understandable. Read your sentences aloud to be sure they make sense and they read smoothly and grammatically. Generally, integrated quotations are introduced by phrases such as "Wong argues that," "Dupuis suggests that," so that readers know who said what. More importantly, readers must see the relationship between the quoted idea and the sentence that precedes it. Use a transitional phrase that emphasizes this relationship by looking back as well as ahead:

An introduction that unifies a quotation with the discussion

> After you decide to develop a program, "the first step in the programming process . . . ."

Besides showing how each quotation helps advance the main idea you are developing, your integrated sentences should be grammatically correct:

Quoted material integrated grammatically with the writer's words

> "The agricultural crisis," Marx acknowledges, "resulted primarily from unchecked land speculation."

> "She has rejuvenated the industrial economy of our region," Smith writes of Berry's term as regional planner.

(For quoting long passages and for punctuating at the end of a quotation, see the Appendix.)

Use a direct quotation only when precision, clarity, or emphasis requires the exact words from the original. Avoid excessively long quoted passages. Research writing is more a process of independent thinking, in which you work with the ideas of others in order to reach your own conclusions; you should therefore paraphrase, instead of quoting, much of your borrowed material.

Paraphrasing the Work of Others

We paraphrase not only to preserve the original idea, but also to express it in a clear, simple, direct, or emphatic way—without distorting the idea. *Paraphrasing* means more than changing or shuffling a few words; it means restating the original idea in your own words and giving full credit to the source.

To borrow or adapt someone else's ideas or reasoning without properly documenting the source is plagiarism. To offer as a paraphrase an original passage only slightly altered—even when you document the source—also is plagiarism. It is equally unethical to offer a paraphrase, although documented, that distorts the original meaning.

An effective paraphrase generally displays all or most of the following elements (Weinstein 3):

Elements of an effective paraphrase

- reference to the author early in the paraphrase, to indicate the beginning of the borrowed passage
- key words retained from the original, to preserve the meaning
- original sentences restructured and combined, for emphasis and fluency
- needless words from the original deleted, for conciseness
- your own words and phrases that help explain the author's ideas, for clarity
- a citation (in parentheses) of the exact source, to mark the end of the borrowed passage and to give full credit
- preservation of the author's original intent

Figure 7.3 shows an entry paraphrased from the passage in Figure 7.2. Paraphrased material does not have quotation marks, but you must acknowledge your debt to the source. Failing to acknowledge ideas, findings, judgments, lines of reasoning, opinions, facts, or insights not considered *common knowledge* (page 172) is plagiarism—even when these are expressed in your own words.

Signal the beginning of the paraphrase by citing the author, and the end by citing the source

Pinsky, Mark A.

Pinsky explains that electromagnetic waves probably do not directly cause cancer. However, they might contribute to the uncontrollable growth of those cancer cells normally present—but controlled—in the human body (29–30).

Figure 7.3　Notecard for a Paraphrase

Evaluating and Interpreting Information

Not all information is equal. Not all interpretations are equal. Whether you work with your own findings or the findings of other researchers, you need to decide if the information is valid and reliable. Then you need to decide what your information means. Figure 7.4 outlines this challenge.

Evaluating the Sources

Not all data sources are equally dependable. A source might offer information that is out of date, inaccurate, incomplete, mistaken, or biased.

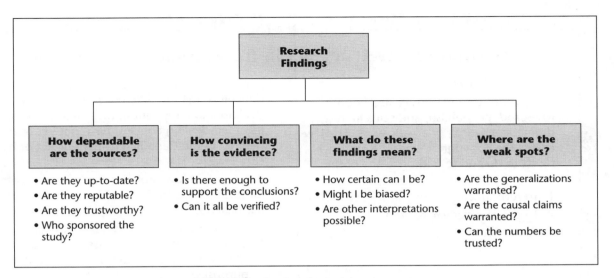

Figure 7.4   Decisions in Reviewing Research Findings

"How current is the information?"

Is the Source Up-to-Date? Newly published books contain information that can be more than one year old, and journal articles often undergo a lengthy process of peer review.

Certain types of information become outdated more quickly than others. For topics that focus on *technology* (superconductivity, multimedia law, Internet censorship, alternative cancer treatments), information more than a few months old may be outdated. Except for historical or background research, sources in those areas generally should offer the most recent information available. For topics that focus on *people* (business ethics, management practices, workplace gender equality, employee motivation), information several decades old might offer valuable perspective on present situations.

"What is the source's reputation?"

Is the Source Reputable? Some sources enjoy better reputations than others. For research on alternative cancer treatments, you could depend more on reports in the *New England Journal of Medicine* or *Scientific American* than on those in scandal sheets or movie magazines. Even researchers with expert credentials, however, can disagree or be mistaken.

One way to assess a publication's reputation is to check its copyright page for information. Is the work published by a university, professional society, museum, or respected news organization? Do members of the editorial and advisory board have distinguished titles and degrees? Is the publication *refereed* (all submissions reviewed by experts prior to acceptance)?

One way to assess an author's reputation is to check citation indexes (page 125) to see what others have said about this research. Many periodicals also provide brief biographies or descriptions of authors' earlier publications and other achievements.

IN BRIEF

Copyright Protection and Fair Use of Printed Information

Copyright Law

A copyright is the exclusive legal right to reproduce, publish, and sell a literary, dramatic, musical, or artistic work. The law grants the copyright owner the exclusive rights to do and to authorize any of the following:

1. To reproduce the copyrighted work.
2. To prepare derivative works.
3. To distribute copies of the copyrighted work to the public by sale, rental, lease, or lending.
4. In certain cases, such as for literary and musical works, to perform the copyrighted work publicly.
5. In certain cases, such as for graphics, images, or other audiovisuals, to display the copyrighted work publicly.

You must obtain written permission to use all copyrighted material. Works are copyrighted for the author's life plus 50 years. If the author is unknown, the copyright lasts for 50 years from the document's publication date.

Public Domain

Public domain refers to material on which copyright has expired or material that is not protected by copyright. Most government publications and commonplace information such as height and weight charts are in the public domain. These works occasionally contain copyrighted material used with permission and properly acknowledged. **However, a new translation or version of a work in the public domain can be protected by copyright;** if you are not sure whether something is in the public domain, obtain permission.

Fair Dealing

Fair dealing allows quotes from, or reproduction of, minor excerpts of a copyrighted work, if the quote or reproduction is for bona fide private study, research, criticism, or news-paper summary. But there's a problem: It's difficult to tell the difference between fair dealing and copyright infringement. The limits of fair dealing copying have not yet been defined in the Canadian Copyright Act or by case law.

Copyright law provides the following criteria to be considered in the determination of fair dealing:

1. The purpose and character of the use, including whether such use is of a commercial nature or is for non-profit educational purposes.
2. The nature of the copyrighted work.
3. The amount and substantiality of the portion used in relation to the whole.
4. The effect of the use upon the potential market for or value of the copyrighted work.

When the quoted material forms the core, distinguishable creative effort of the work being cited, then use of the material isn't considered fair.

Fair dealing ordinarily does not apply to use of: poetry, musical lyrics, dialogue of a play, entries in a diary, case studies, charts and graphs, author's notes, private letters, testing materials, or quotations for use as epigraphs.

Copying Under the CANCOPY Licence

Many Canadian college, university, high school, and public libraries have signed licence agreements with CANCOPY, a non-profit organization representing Canadian and foreign authors and publishers. Under such licences, library users can copy certain portions of certain kinds of documents without permission. HOWEVER, EACH LICENCE IMPOSES CLEAR LEGAL RESTRICTIONS, so ask your librarian for details.

Based on *HarperCollins Author's Guide*. Copyright ©1995, and on Canada's Copyright Act, as amended by Bill C-32.

Copyright Protection and Fair Dealing of Electronic Information

The Problem

Copyright and fair dealing law is quite specific for printed works or works in other tangible form (paintings, photographs, music). But how do we define "fair dealing" (page 152) of intellectual property in electronic form? How does copyright protection apply (Dyson 137)? How do fair-dealing restrictions apply to material used in multimedia presentations or to text or images that have been altered or reshaped to suit the user's specific needs (Steinberg, "Travels" 30)?

Information obtained via e-mail or discussion groups presents additional problems: Sources often do not wish to be quoted or named or to have early drafts made public. How do we protect source confidentiality? How do we avoid infringing on works in progress that have not yet been published? How do we quote and cite this material without violating ownership and privacy rights (Howard 40–41)?

Present Status of Electronic Copyright Law

Subscribers to commercial on-line databases pay fees, and copyholders in turn receive royalties (Communication Concepts, Inc. 13). But as of this writing, few specific legal protections exist for non-commercial types of electronic information. Since April 1989, however, most works are considered copyrighted as soon as they are produced—even if they carry no copyright notice. Fair dealing of electronic information generally is limited to brief excerpts that serve as a basis for response—for example, in a discussion group. Except for certain government documents, no Internet posting is in the public domain unless it is expressly designated as such by its author (Templeton).

Until specific laws are enacted, the following examples can be considered violations of copyright (Communication Concepts, Inc. 13; Templeton):

- Downloading a work from the Internet and forwarding copies to other readers.
- Editing, altering, or incorporating an original work as part of your own document or multimedia presentation.
- Putting someone else's printed work on-line without the author's written permission.
- Copying and forwarding an e-mail message without the sender's authorization. The e-mail *text* is copyrighted, but its *content* legally may be revealed—except for proprietary information (page 101).

Penalties for Copyright Infringement

Individuals, businesses, or organizations that hold copyright may sue those who infringe copyright. Canadian legislation stipulates minimum penalties for copyright infringements. Violations of copyright on printed or electronic works may exceed the boundaries of civil law and may be prosecuted as summary convictions under criminal law. When in doubt, assume the work is copyrighted and obtain written permission for its use.

★　★　★

"Can the source be trusted?"

Is the Source Trustworthy? The Internet offers information that may never appear in other sources, for example from listservs and newsgroups. But much of this information may reflect the bias of the special interest groups that provide it. Moreover, anyone can publish almost anything on the Internet—including a great deal of misinformation—without having it verified, edited, or reviewed for accuracy (Snyder 89–90).

Even in a commercial database, decisions about what to include and what to leave out depend on the biases, priorities, or interests of those who assemble that database. In general, try not to rely on any single information source.

"Who sponsored the study?"

Is the Information Biased? Much of today's research is paid for by private companies or special-interest groups that have their own social, political, or economic agendas (Crossen 14, 19). Medical research may be sponsored by drug or tobacco companies; nutritional research, by food manufacturers; and environmental research, by oil or chemical companies. Public policy research (on gun control, school prayer, seat-belt laws, endangered species) may be sponsored by opposing groups (environmentalists versus the logging industry) producing opposing results. Instead of a neutral and balanced enquiry, this kind of "strategic research" is designed to support one special interest group or another. Those who pay for strategic research are not likely to publicize findings that contradict their original claims, opinions, or beliefs (profits lower than expected, losses or risks greater than expected). As consumers of research, we should try to determine exactly what the sponsors of a particular study stand to gain or lose from the results.

IN BRIEF

Guidelines for Evaluating Web Sites[1]

1. *Consider the site's domain type and sponsor.* In this typical address, http://www.umass.edu the site or *domain* information follows the *www*. The *.edu* signifies the type of organization from which the site originates. Standard domain types in North America are:

   .com = business/commercial organization

   .edu = educational institution

   .gov = government organization

   .mil = military organization

   .net = any group or individual with simple software and Internet access

   .org = non-profit organization

   The domain type might signal a certain bias or agenda that could skew the data. For example, at a *.com* site, you might find accurate information, but also some type of sales pitch. At an *.org* site, you might find a political or ideological bias (say, The Heritage Foundation's conservative ideology versus the Brookings Institution's more liberal slant). Knowing about a site's sponsor can help you evaluate the credibility of its postings.

2. *Identify the purpose of the page or message.* Decide whether the message is intended to merely relay information, to sell something, or to promote a particular ideology or agenda.

IN BRIEF

3. *Look beyond the style of a site.* Fancy graphics, video, and sound do not always translate into dependable information. Sometimes the most reliable material resides in the less attractive, text-only sites. People can design flashy-looking pages without necessarily knowing what they are talking about. Even something written in clear, plain English instead of in difficult scientific terms (as in medical information) might be inaccurate.

4. *Assess the site's/material's currency.* An up-to-date site should clearly indicate when the material was created or published, and when it was posted and updated.

5. *Assess the author's credentials.* Learn all you can about the author's reputation, level of expertise on the topic, and institutional affiliation (a university, a Fortune 500 company, a reputable environmental group). Do this by following links to other sites that mention the author or by using search engines to track the author's name. Newsgroup postings often contain "a *signature file* that includes the author's name, location, institutional or organizational affiliation, and often a quote that suggests something of the writer's personality, political leanings, or sense of humour" (Goubil-Gambrell).

6. *Compare the site with other sources.* Check related sites, publications, and other sources to compare the quality of information and to discover what others might have said about this site or author. Comparing many similar sites helps you create a *benchmark*, a standard for evaluating any particular site (based on the criteria in these guidelines). Ask a librarian for help.

7. *Decide whether the assertions/claims make sense.* Based on what you know about the issue, decide where, on the spectrum of informed opinion and accepted theory, this author's position resides. How well is each assertion supported? Never accept any claim that seems extreme without verifying it through other sources, such as a professor, a librarian, or a specialist in the field.

8. Look for other indicators of quality.

   * *Worthwhile content*: The material displays a clear and sharply focused main point, technical accuracy, opinions based on fact or good sense, and assertions supported by evidence that is documented (citing all sources of data presented as "factual").

   * *Sensible organization*: The material is organized for the reader's understanding, with a clear line of reasoning.

   * *Readable style*: The material is well written (clear, concise, and easy to understand), and free of typos, misspellings, and other errors.

   * *Objective coverage*: Debatable topics are addressed in a balanced and impartial way, with fair, accurate representation of opposing views. The tone is reasonable, with no "sounding off."

   * *Expertise*: The author refers to related theory and other work in the field and uses specialized terminology accurately and appropriately.

   * *Peer review*: The material has been evaluated and verified by related experts.

   * *Links to reputable sites*: The site offers a gateway to related sites that meet quality criteria.

   * *Follow-up option*: The material includes a signature block or a link for contacting the author or organization for clarification or verification.

1. Guidelines adapted from Barnes, Busiel, and Maeglin 39; Elliot, Facklemann 397; Grassian, Hall 60–61; Hammett, Harris, Robert, Stemmer).

The following hints may help you evaluate Internet sites:

1. Look at the Web site's commercial component. If a company has published a site to promote its products, be suspicious. In particular, notice what information the company does *not* provide.
2. Don't be satisfied with generalities. Look for specific facts, examples, or statistics. Then, check to see which of these "facts" can be verified by other sources.
3. Try to verify the accuracy of quoted facts and statistics by contacting other sources or by checking for similar results in other studies or experiments.
4. Look at your own attitudes and beliefs to see if you're predisposed to automatically accept certain things that you read.
5. Exercise extreme caution in using anything picked up from usenet discussion groups.
6. When considering material provided in a listserv academic discussion group, look at the author's credentials: Does the author have a solid track record of publications or other contributions to the field discussed by that group?
7. In general, maintain a suspicious mindset: Demand evidence for any assertions you read.

Evaluating the Evidence

Evidence is any finding used to support or refute a particular conclusion. While evidence can serve the truth, it also can create distortion, misinformation, and deception. For example, how much money, material, or energy does recycling really save? How good for your heart is oat bran? How well are public schools educating our children? Which investments or automobiles are safest? Conclusions about such matters are based on evidence that often can be manipulated in support of one view or another. As consumers of research, we have to assess for ourselves the quality of the evidence presented.

We assess the quality of evidence by examining it critically to understand its limitations, to see if findings conflict; to discover connections, similarities, trends, or relationships; to determine the need for further enquiry; and to raise new questions.

"Is there enough evidence?"

Is the Evidence Sufficient? Evidence is sufficient when it enables us to reach an accurate judgment or conclusion. A study of the stress-reducing benefits of low-impact aerobics, for example, would require a broad survey sample: people who have practised aerobics for a long time; people of different genders, different ages, different occupations, and different lifestyles before they began aerobics, etc. Even responses from hundreds of practitioners might constitute insufficient evidence unless those responses were supported by laboratory measurements of metabolism, heart rates, and blood pressure.

Personal experience usually offers insufficient evidence from which to generalize. You cannot tell whether your experience is representative, no matter how long you might have practised aerobics. Although anecdotal evidence ("This worked great for me!") might offer a good starting point for an investigation, personal experience should be evaluated within the broader context of *all* available evidence.

"Is the evidence hard or soft?"

Can the Evidence Be Verified? *Hard evidence* consists of factual statements, expert opinion, or statistics that can be verified (shown to be true). *Soft evidence* consists of uninformed opinion or speculation, data obtained or analyzed unscientifically, and findings that have not been replicated or reviewed by experts. Reputable news organizations employ "fact-checkers" to verify information before it appears in print.

Evidence that seems scientific can turn out to be soft. For example, information obtained from polling often is reported in fancy charts, graphs, and impressive statistics—but it is based on public opinion, which is almost always changing (Crossen 104).

Base your conclusions on hard evidence. For example, suppose an article makes positive claims about low-impact aerobics but provides no data on measurements of pulse, blood pressure, or metabolic rates. Although these claims might coincide with your own experience, your evidence so far consists of only two opinions: yours and the author's—without scientific support. Any conclusion at this point would rest on soft evidence. Only after carefully assessing dependable sources can you decide which conclusions are supported by the bulk of the evidence.

Interpreting the Evidence

Interpreting means trying to reach the truth of the matter: an overall judgment about what the evidence means and what conclusion or action it suggests. Unfortunately, research does not always yield answers that are conclusive or about which we can be certain. Instead of settling for the most *convenient* answer, we should pursue the most *reasonable* answer by examining critically a full range of possible meanings.

What Level of Certainty Is Warranted? As possible outcomes of research, we can identify three distinct and very different levels of certainty:

1. The definitive truth: the *conclusive answer:*

A practical definition of "truth"

   Truth is *what is so* about something, the reality of the matter, as distinguished from what people wish were so, believe to be so, or assert to be so. From another perspective, in the words of Harvard philosopher Israel Scheffler, truth is the view "which is fated to be ultimately agreed to by all who investigate." The word *ultimately* is important. Investigation may produce a wrong answer for years, even for centuries. . . . Does the truth ever change? No. . . . One easy way to spare yourself any further confusion about truth is to reserve the word *truth* for the final answer to an issue. Get in the habit of using the words, *belief, theory,* and *present understanding* more often. (Ruggiero 21–22).

We often are mistaken in our certainty about the *truth.* For example, in the second century A.D., Ptolemy's view of the universe concluded that the earth was its centre. Though untrue, this judgment was based on the best information available at that time. Ptolemy's view survived for thirteen centuries, even after new information had discredited this belief. When Copernicus and Galileo proposed more truthful views in the fifteenth century, they were labelled heretics.

Conclusive answers are the research outcome we seek, but often we have to settle for answers that are less than certain.

2. The *probable answer:* the answer that stands the best chance of being true or accurate—given the most we can know at this particular time. Probable answers are subject to revision in the light of new information.

3. The *inconclusive answer:* the realization that the truth of the matter is far more elusive, ambiguous, or complex than we expected.

"Exactly how certain are we?"

To ensure an accurate outcome, we must decide what level of certainty the findings warrant. For example, we are *highly certain* about the perils of smoking or sunburn, *reasonably certain* about the benefits of fruits and vegetables and moderate exercise, but *far less certain* about the perils of coffee drinking, or electromagnetic waves, or the benefits of vitamin supplements.

Are the Underlying Assumptions Sound? Assumptions are notions we take for granted, things we accept without proof. The research process rests on assumptions like these: that a sample group accurately represents a larger target group, that survey respondents remember certain facts accurately, and that mice and humans share enough biological similarities for meaningful research. For a particular study to be valid, the underlying assumptions must be accurate.

Consider this example: You are an education consultant evaluating the accuracy of IQ testing as a predictor of academic performance. Reviewing the evidence, you perceive an association between low IQ scores and low achievers. You then check your statistics by examining a cross-section of reliable sources. Can you then conclude that IQ tests do predict performance accurately? This conclusion might be invalid unless you could verify the following assumptions:

1. That neither parents, teachers, nor children had seen individual test scores, which could produce biased expectations.

2. That, regardless of score, each child had completed an identical curriculum at an identical pace, instead of being "tracked" on the basis of his or her score.

Do I Have a Personal Bias? To support a particular version of the truth, our own bias might cause us to overestimate (or deny) the certainty of our findings.

Personal bias is a fact of life

> Expect yourself to be biased, and expect your bias to affect your efforts to construct arguments. Unless you are perfectly neutral about the issue, an unlikely circumstance, at the very outset . . . you will believe one side of the issue to be right, and that belief will incline you to . . . present more and better arguments for the side of the issue you prefer. (Ruggiero 134)

Because personal bias is hard to transcend, *rationalizing* often becomes a substitute for *reasoning:*

Reasoning versus rationalizing

> You are reasoning if your belief follows the evidence—that is, if you examine the evidence first and then make up your mind. You are rationalizing if the evidence follows your belief—if you first decide what you believe and then select and interpret evidence to justify it. (Ruggiero 44)

Personal bias often is unconscious until we examine our own value systems, attitudes long held but never analyzed, notions we've inherited from our own backgrounds, and so on. Recognizing our own biases is a crucial first step in managing them.

"What else could this mean?"

Are Other Interpretations Possible? Perhaps other researchers would disagree with the meaning of these findings. Some controversial issues (the need for defence spending or causes of inflation) will never be resolved. Although we can get verifiable data and can reason persuasively on some subjects, no close reasoning by any expert and no supporting statistical analysis will prove anything about a controversial subject to everyone's satisfaction. For instance, one could only *argue* (more or less effectively) that federal funds will or will not alleviate poverty or unemployment.

Settling on a final meaning can be difficult. For example (Ledermen 5): What does a reported increase in violent crime on North American college campuses mean—especially in light of national statistics that show violent crime decreasing?

- That college students are becoming more violent?
- That some drugs and guns in high schools end up on campuses?
- That off-campus criminals see students as easy targets?

Or could these findings mean something else entirely?

- That increased law enforcement has led to more campus arrests—and thus, greater recognition of the problem?
- That crimes haven't increased, but more are being reported?

Depending on our interpretation, we might conclude that the problem is worsening—or improving!

Avoiding Errors in Reasoning

Finding the truth, especially in a complex issue or problem, often is a process of elimination, of ruling out or avoiding errors in reasoning. As we interpret, we make *inferences:* We derive conclusions about what we don't know by reasoning from what we do know (Hayakawa 37). For example, we might infer that a drug that boosts immunity in laboratory mice will boost immunity in humans, or that a rise in campus crime statistics is caused by the fact that young people have become more violent. Whether a particular inference is on target or dead wrong depends largely on our answers to one or more of these questions:

- *To what extent can these findings be generalized?*
- *Is Y really caused by X?*
- *How much can the numbers be trusted, and what do they mean?*

Following are three major reasoning errors that can distort our interpretations.

"How much can we generalize?"

Faulty Generalizations. When we accept research findings uncritically and jump to conclusions about their meaning, we commit the error of *hasty generalization.* When we overestimate the extent to which the findings reveal some larger truth, we commit the error of *overstated generalization.*

A study in Greece on the role of fruits, vegetables, and olive oil in lowering breast cancer risk was widely publicized in 1995 because of the alleged benefits of olive oil for women who consume it twice or more a day. Subsequent analysis of this study revealed that data about the women's food consumption covered only one year and were based on a single questionnaire asking respondents to estimate their previous year's diet. (Estimates of this type tend to be highly inaccurate.) Also, the study did not identify the quantities of olive oil individual users consumed. In this instance, the study's generalization about olive oil was shown to be *hasty* (based on insufficient evidence).

Further analysis revealed that only 99 respondents (of the nearly 2,500 surveyed) claimed to have consumed olive oil twice or more a day ("Olive Oil" 1). In this instance, the study's generalization was shown to be *overstated* (a limited generalization made to apply to all cases). Something true in one instance need not be true in other instances.

Although this particular study was flawed, many other studies support the generalization that fruits and vegetables do help lower the risk of cancer. Generalizing is vital and perfectly legitimate—when it is warranted.

Faulty Causal Reasoning. Causal reasoning tries to explain *why* something happened or *what* will happen: often very complex questions. Faulty causal reasoning oversimplifies or distorts the cause-effect relationship through errors like these:

Ignoring other causes

Investment builds wealth. [*Ignores the role of knowledge, wisdom, timing, and luck in successful investing.*]

Ignoring other effects	Running improves health. [*Ignores the fact that many runners get injured, and that some even drop dead while running.*]
Inventing a cause	Right after buying a rabbit's foot, Felix won the 649 lottery. [*Posits an unwarranted causal relationship merely because one event follows another.*]
Confusing correlation with causation	Poverty causes disease. [*Ignores the fact that disease, while highly associated with poverty, has many causes unrelated to poverty.*]
Rationalizing	My grades were poor because my exams were unfair. [*Denies the real causes of one's failures.*]

Because of bias or impatience, we can be tempted to settle for a hasty cause or to confuse possible, probable, and definite causes.

"Did X possibly, probably, or definitely cause Y?"

Sometimes a definite cause is apparent (e.g., "The engine's overheating is caused by a faulty radiator cap"), but usually much analysis is needed to isolate a specific cause. Suppose you want to answer this question: Why does our local college not have day-care facilities? Brainstorming yields these possible causes:

- lack of need among students
- lack of interest among students, faculty, and staff
- high cost of liability insurance
- lack of space and facilities on campus
- lack of trained personnel
- prohibition by law
- lack of government funding for such a project

Say you proceed with interviews, questionnaires, and research into provincial laws, insurance rates, and availability of personnel. You begin to rule out some items, and others appear as probable causes. Specifically, you find a need among students, high campus interest, an abundance of qualified people for staffing, and no provincial laws prohibiting such a project. Three probable causes remain: lack of funding, high insurance rates, and lack of space. Further inquiry shows that lack of funding and high insurance rates *are* issues. These obstacles, however, could be eliminated through new sources of revenue: charging a fee for each child, soliciting donations, or diverting funds from other campus organizations.

Finally, after examining available campus space and speaking with school officials, you arrive at one definite cause: lack of space and facilities. One could argue that lack of space and facilities is somehow related to funding, and the college's being unable to find funds or space may be related to student need, which is not sufficiently acute or interest sufficiently high to exert real pressure. Lack of space and facilities, however, appears to be the *immediate* cause.

When you report on your research, be sure readers can draw conclusions identical to your own on the basis of the evidence. The process might be diagrammed like this:

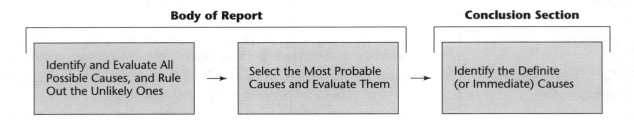

Initially you might have based your conclusions hastily on soft evidence (an opinion—buttressed by a newspaper editorial—that the campus was apathetic). Now you base your conclusions on solid, factual evidence. You have moved from a wide range of possible causes, to a narrow range of probable causes, and finally to one definite cause.

Sometimes, finding a single cause is impossible, but this reasoning process can be tailored to most problem-solving analyses. Anything but the simplest effect is likely to have more than one cause. By narrowing the field, you can focus on the real issues.

Faulty Statistical Reasoning. The purpose of statistical analysis is to determine the meaning of a collected set of numbers. In primary research, our surveys and questionnaires often lead to some kind of numerical interpretation ("What percentage of respondents prefer X?" "How often does Y happen?"). In secondary research, we rely on numbers collected by primary researchers. Numbers seem more precise, more objective, more scientific and less ambiguous than words. They are easier to summarize, measure, compare, and analyze. But numbers can be misleading. For example, radio or television phone-in surveys produce grossly distorted data: Although 90 percent of callers might express support for a particular viewpoint, callers tend to be those with the greatest anger or the strongest feelings about the issue—representing only a fraction of overall attitudes (Fineman 24). Mail-in surveys can produce similar distortion because only people with certain attitudes might choose to respond.

"How much can we trust these numbers?"

Before relying on any set of numbers, we need to know exactly where they came from, how they were collected, and how they were analyzed (Lavin 275–76). Can the numbers be trusted, and if so, what do they mean?

Faulty statistical reasoning produces conclusions that are unwarranted, inaccurate, or downright deceptive. The following are some common statistical fallacies:

- *The sanitized statistic:* Numbers are manipulated (or "cleaned up") to obscure the facts. For instance, a recently revised formula enables the government to exclude from its unemployment figures an estimated 5 million people who remain unemployed after one year—thus creating a far rosier economic picture than the facts warrant. Similar formulas allow for all sorts of sugarcoating in reports of wages, economic growth, inflation, and

"Exactly how well are we doing?"

other statistics that affect the political climate (Morgenson 54). The College Board's recentring of SAT scores has raised the average math score from 478 to 500 and the average verbal score from 424 to 500 (a boost of almost 5 and 18 percent, respectively) although actual student performance remains unchanged (Samuelson 44).

- *The meaningless statistic:* Exact numbers are used to quantify something so inexact or vaguely defined that it should only be approximated (Huff 247; Lavin 278): "Only 38.2 percent of college graduates end up working in their specialty." "Toronto has 3,247,561 rats." "Zappo detergent makes laundry 10 percent brighter." An exact number looks impressive, but certain subjects (child abuse, cheating in college, virginity, drug and alcohol abuse on the job, eating habits) cannot be quantified exactly because respondents don't always tell the truth (because of denial, embarrassment, or merely guessing). Or they respond in ways they think the researcher expects.

- *The undefined average:* The mean, median, and mode are confused in determining an average (Huff 244; Lavin 279). The *mean* is the result of adding up the value of each item in a set of numbers, then dividing by the number of items. The *median* is the result of ranking all the values from high to low, then choosing the middle value (or the 50th percentile, as in calculating SAT scores). The *mode* is the value that occurs most often in a set of numbers.

"How many rats was that?"

Each of these three measurements represents some kind of average, but unless we know which average is being presented, we cannot interpret the figures accurately. Assume that we are computing the average salary among female vice presidents at XYZ Corporation:

Vice President	Salary
A	$90,000
B	90,000
C	80,000
D	65,000
E	60,000
F	55,000
G	50,000

In the above example, the mean salary (total salaries divided by people) equals $70,000; the median salary (middle value) equals $65,000; the mode (most frequent value) equals $90,000. Each is legitimately an average, and each could be used to support or refute a particular assertion (for example, "Women vice presidents are paid too little" or "Women vice presidents are paid too much").

"Why is everybody griping?"

Research expert Michael Lavin sums up the potential for bias in reporting averages:

> Depending on the circumstances, any one of these measurements [mean, median, or mode] may describe a group of numbers better than the other two. . . . [But] people typically choose the value which best presents their case, whether or not it is the most appropriate to use. (279)

Although the mean is the most commonly computed average, this measurement can be misleading when values on either end of the scale are extremely high or low. Suppose, for instance, that vice president A received a $200,000 salary. Because this figure deviates so far from the normal range of salary figures for B through G, it distorts the average for the whole group—increasing the mean salary by more than 20 percent (Plumb and Spyridakis 636).

- *The distorted percentage figure:* Percentages are reported without explanation of the original numbers used in the calculation (Adams and Schvaneveldt 359; Lavin 280): "Seventy-five percent of respondents prefer our brand over the competing brand"—without mention that only four people were surveyed. Or "Sixty-six percent of employees we hired this year are women and minorities, compared to the national average of 40 percent"—without mention that only three people have been hired this year, by a company that employs 300 (mostly white males).

  Another fallacy in reporting percentages occurs when the *margin of error* is ignored. This is the margin within which the true figure lies, based on estimated sampling errors in a survey. For example, a claim that most people surveyed prefer brand X might be based on the fact that 51 percent of respondents expressed this preference; but if the survey carried a 2 percent margin of error, the true figure could be as low as 49 percent or as high as 53 percent. In a survey with a high margin of error, the true figure may be so uncertain that no definite conclusion can be drawn.

"Is 51 percent really a majority?"

- *The bogus ranking:* Items are compared on the basis of ill-defined criteria (Adams and Schvaneveldt 212; Lavin 284): "Last year, the Batmobile was the number-one selling car in Canada"—without mention that some competing car makers actually sold *more* cars to private individuals, and that the Batmobile figures were inflated by hefty sales to rental-car companies and corporate fleets. Unless we know how the ranked items were chosen and how they were compared (the criteria), a ranking can produce a scientific-seeming number based on a completely unscientific method.

"Which car should we buy?"

- *The fallible computer model:* Computer models process complex assumptions to produce impressive but often inaccurate statistical estimates about costs, benefits, risks, or probable outcomes.

  Assumptions are notions we take for granted, things we often accept without proof. The research process rests on assumptions like these: that a sample group accurately represents a larger target group, that survey respondents remember certain facts accurately, that mice and humans share enough biological similarities for meaningful research. For a particular study to be valid, the underlying assumptions have to be accurate.

Computer models to predict global warming levels, for instance, are based on differing assumptions about wind and weather patterns, cloud formations, ozone levels, carbon dioxide concentrations, sea levels, or airborne sediment from volcanic eruptions. Despite their seemingly scientific precision, different global warming models generate fifty-year predictions of sea-level rises that range from a few inches to several feet (Barbour 121). Other models suggest that warming effects could be offset by evaporation of ocean water and by clouds reflecting sunlight back to outer space (Monatersky 69). Still other models suggest that the 0.56°C (1°F) warming over the last 100 years may not be the result of the greenhouse effect at all, but of "random fluctuations in global temperatures" (Stone 38). The estimates produced by any model depend on the assumptions (and data) programmed in.

"Garbage in, garbage out."

Choice of assumptions might be influenced by researcher bias or the sponsor's agenda. For example, a prediction of human fatalities from a nuclear plant meltdown might rest on assumptions about availability of safe shelter, evacuation routes, time of day, season, wind direction, and structural integrity of the containment unit. But the assumptions could be manipulated to produce an overstated or understated estimate of risk (Barbour 228). For computer-modelled estimates of accident risk (oil spill, plane crash) or of the costs and benefits of a proposed project or policy (a space station, welfare reform), consumers rarely know the assumptions behind the numbers. We wonder, for example, about the assumptions underlying NASA's pre-*Challenger* risk assessment, in which a 1985 computer model reportedly showed an accident risk of less than 1 in 100,000 shuttle flights (Crossen 54).

■ *Confusion of correlation with causation: Correlation* is the measure of association between two variables (between smoking and increased lung cancer risk, or between education and income). *Causation* is the demonstrable production of a specific effect (smoking causes lung cancer). Correlations between smoking and lung cancer or education and income signal a causal relationship that has been proven by studies of all kinds. But not every correlation implies causation. For instance, a recently discovered correlation between moderate alcohol consumption and decreased heart disease risk offers insufficient proof that moderate drinking *causes* less heart disease.

"Does a beer a day keep the doctor away?"

Many highly publicized correlations are the product of "data dredging." In this process, computers randomly compare one set of variables (various eating habits) with another set (a range of diseases). From these countless comparisons, certain relationships are revealed (say, between coffee drinking and pancreatic cancer risk). As dramatic as such isolated correlations may be, they constitute no proof of causation and often lead to hasty conclusions (Ross 135).

"Is this good news or bad news?"

- *Misleading terminology:* The terms used to interpret statistics sometimes hide their real meaning. For instance, the widely publicized figure that people treated for cancer have a "50 percent survival rate" is misleading in three ways: (1) *survival* to laypersons means "staying alive," but to medical experts, staying alive for only five years after diagnosis qualifies as survival; (2) the "50 percent" survival figure covers *all* cancers, including certain skin or thyroid cancers that have extremely high cure rates, as well as other cancers (such as lung or ovarian) that rarely are curable and have extremely low survival rates; (3) more than 55 percent of all cancers are skin cancers with a nearly 100 percent survival rate, thereby greatly inflating survival statistics for other types of cancer ("Are We" 6; *Facts and Figures* 2).

  Even the most valid and reliable statistics require that we interpret the reality behind the numbers. For instance, the overall cancer rate today is higher than it was in 1910. What this may mean is that people are living longer and thus are more likely to die of cancer and that cancer today rarely is misdiagnosed—or mislabelled because of stigma ("Are We" 4). The finding that rates for certain cancers double after prolonged exposure to electromagnetic waves may really mean that cancer risk actually increases from 1 in 10,000 to 2 in 10,000.

These are only a few examples of statistics and interpretations that seem highly persuasive but that in fact cannot always be trusted. Any interpretation of statistical data carries the possibility that other, more accurate interpretations have been overlooked or deliberately excluded (Barnett 45).

How Standards of Proof Vary for Different Audiences and Cultural Settings

How much evidence is enough to "prove" a particular claim? The answer often depends on whether the enquiry occurs in the science lab, the courtroom, the boardroom—as well as on the specific cultural setting:

- The scientist demands evidence that indicates at least 95 percent certainty. A scientific finding must be evaluated and replicated by other experts. Good science looks at the entire picture. Findings are reviewed before they are reported. Enquiries and answers in science are never "final," but open-ended and on-going: What seems probable today may be shown improbable by tomorrow's research.

- The juror demands evidence that indicates only 51 percent certainty (a "preponderance of the evidence").

  Jurors are not scientists. Instead of the entire picture, jurors get only the information made available by lawyers and witnesses. A jury bases its opinion on evidence that exceeds "reasonable doubt"

(Monastersky 249; Powell 32+). Courts have to make decisions that are final.

- The corporate executive demands immediate (even if insufficient) evidence. In a global business climate of overnight developments (in world markets, political strife, military conflicts, natural disasters) important business decisions often are made on the spur-of-the-moment, often on the basis of incomplete or unverified information—or even hunches—in order to react to crises and capitalize on opportunities (Seglin 54).

- Specific cultures may have their own standards for authentic, reliable, and persuasive evidence. "For example, African cultures rely on story telling for authenticity. Arabic persuasion is dependent on universally accepted truths. And Chinese value ancient authorities over recent empiricism."

(Carolyn Young, University of Wyoming)

Reassessing the Entire Research Process

Chapters 6 and 7 show that the research process is a minefield of potential errors, in what we do and how we reason: We might ask the wrong questions; we might rely on the wrong sources; we might collect or record data incorrectly; we might analyze or document data incorrectly. We therefore need to critically examine our methods and our reasoning before reporting findings and conclusions. The following research checklist helps guide our assessment.

Checklist for the Research Process

Use this checklist to assess your research process.

METHOD

❑ Did I ask the right questions?

❑ Are the sources appropriately up to date?

❑ Is each source reputable, trustworthy, and relatively unbiased?

❑ Does the evidence clearly support all of the conclusions?

❑ Can all of the evidence be verified?

❑ Is a fair balance of viewpoints presented?

❑ Has the research achieved adequate depth?

❑ Has the entire research process been valid and reliable?

❑ Is all quoted material clearly marked throughout the text?

❑ Are direct quotations used sparingly and appropriately?

❑ Are all quotations accurate and integrated grammatically?

❑ Are all paraphrases accurate and clear?

❑ Have I documented all sources not considered common knowledge?

❑ Is the documentation consistent, complete, and correct?

REASONING

❑ Am I reasonably certain about the meaning of these findings?

❑ Does my final answer seem definitive, only probable, or inconclusive?

❑ Am I reasoning instead of rationalizing?

❑ Is this the most reasonable conclusion (or merely the most convenient)?

❑ Can I rule out other possible interpretations or conclusions?

❑ Have I accounted for all sources of bias, including my own?

❑ Are my generalizations warranted by the evidence?

❑ Am I confident that my causal reasoning is correct?

❑ Can all of the numbers and statistics and interpretations be trusted?

❑ Have I resolved (or at least acknowledged) any conflicts among my findings?

❑ Should the evidence be reconsidered?

☑ EXERCISES OR COLLABORATIVE PROJECTS

1. Assume you are an assistant communications manager for a new organization that prepares research reports for decision makers worldwide. (A sample topic: "What is the expected long-term impact of the North American Free Trade Agreement on the Canadian computer industry?") These clients expect answers based on the best available evidence and reasoning.

   Although your recently hired co-workers are technical specialists, few have experience in the kind of wide-ranging research required by your clients. Training programs in the research process are being developed by your communications division but will not be ready for several weeks.

   Meanwhile, your manager directs you to prepare a one- or two-page memo that introduces employees to major procedural and reasoning errors that affect validity and reliability in the research process. Your manager wants this memo to be comprehensive but not vague.

2. Assume the scenario from Exercise 1. In a memo to colleagues, offer guidelines for avoiding unintentional plagiarism in quoting, paraphrasing, and citing the work of others. Explain what to document and how, using MLA style for a parenthetical reference and a works cited entry. (Illustrate with examples, but not those from the book!)

3. From print or broadcast media or from personal experience, identify an example of each of the following sources of distortion or of interpretive error:
   - A study with questionable sponsorship or motives.
   - Reliance on soft evidence.
   - Overestimating the level of certainty.
   - Biased interpretation.
   - Rationalizing.
   - Faulty causal reasoning.
   - Hasty generalization.
   - Overstated generalization.
   - Sanitized statistic.
   - Meaningless statistic.
   - Undefined average.
   - Distorted percentage figure.
   - Bogus ranking.
   - Fallible computer model.
   - Misinterpreted statistic.

   Submit your examples to your instructor, along with a memo explaining each error, or be prepared to discuss your material in class.

Documenting Research Findings

D OCUMENTING research findings means acknowledging one's debt to each information source. Proper documentation satisfies professional requirements for ethics, efficiency, and authority.

Why You Should Document

Documentation is a matter of *ethics* in that the originator of borrowed material deserves full credit and recognition. Moreover, all published material is protected by copyright law. Failure to credit a source could make you liable to legal action, even if your omission was unintentional.

Documentation also is a matter of *efficiency*. It provides a network for organizing and locating the world's recorded knowledge. If you cite a particular source correctly, your reference will enable interested readers to locate that source themselves.

Finally, documentation is a matter of *authority*. In making any claim—for example, "A Honda Accord is more reliable than a Ford Taurus"—you invite challenge: "Says who?" Data on road tests, frequency of repairs, resale value, workmanship, and owner comments can help validate your claim by showing its basis in *fact*. A claim's credibility increases in relation to the expert references supporting it. For a controversial topic, you may need to cite several authorities who hold various views, as in this next example, instead of forcing a simplistic conclusion on your material:

Citing a balance of views

> Opinion is mixed as to whether a marketable quantity of oil rests beneath Georges Bank. Cape Cod geologist John Blocke feels that extensive reserves are improbable ("Geologist Dampens Hopes" 3). Oil geologist Donald Marshall is uncertain about the existence of any oil in quantity at this location ("Offshore Oil Drilling" 2). But the U.S. Interior Department reports that the Atlantic continental shelf may contain 5.5 billion barrels of oil (Kemprecos 8).

Readers of your research report expect the *complete* picture.

What You Should Document

Document any insight, assertion, fact, finding, interpretation, judgment, or other "appropriated material that readers might otherwise mistake for your own" (Gibaldi and Achtert 155)—whether the material appears in published form or not. Specifically, you must document:

Sources that require documentation

- any source from which you use exact wording
- any source from which you adapt material in your own words
- any visual illustration: chart, graph, drawing, or the like (see Chapter 12 for documenting visuals)

In some instances, you might have reason to preserve the anonymity of unpublished sources: for example, to allow people to respond candidly without fear of reprisal (as with employee criticism of the company), or to protect their privacy (as with certain material from e-mail enquiries or electronic newsgroups). You still must document the fact that you are not the originator of this material by providing a general acknowledgment in the text ("A number of employees expressed frustration with . . .") along with a general citation in your list of references or works cited ("Interviews with Polex employees, May 2008").

You don't need to document anything considered *common knowledge:* material that appears repeatedly in general sources. In medicine, for instance, it is common knowledge that foods high in fat correlate with higher incidences of cancer, so in a report on fatty diets and cancer, you probably would not need to document that well-known fact. But you would document information about how the fat/cancer connection was discovered, subsequent studies (e.g., the role of saturated versus unsaturated fats), and any information for which some other person could claim specific credit. If the borrowed material can be found in only one specific source, and not in multiple sources, document it. When in doubt, document the source.

How You Should Document

Borrowed material has to be cited twice: at the exact place that you use the material, and at the end of your document. Documentation practices vary widely, but all systems work almost identically: a brief reference in the text names the source and refers readers to the complete citation, which enables the source to be retrieved.

Many disciplines, institutions, and organizations publish their own style guides or documentation manuals. Here are a few:

Style guides from various disciplines

Geographical Research and Writing
Style Manual for Engineering Authors and Editors
IBM Style Manual
NASA Publications Manual

This chapter illustrates citations and entries for three styles widely used for documenting sources in respective disciplines:

- Modern Language Association (MLA) style, for the humanities
- American Psychological Association (APA) style, for social sciences
- Council of Biology Editors (CBE) style, for natural and applied sciences

Unless your audience has a particular preference, any of these three styles can be adapted to most research writing. Another widely used format is that of the *Chicago Manual of Style,* which covers documentation in the humanities, related fields, and natural sciences. Whichever style you select, use it consistently throughout the document.

MLA Documentation Style

Traditional MLA documentation of sources used superscript numbers (like this: [1]) in the text, followed by the full reference at the bottom of the page (footnotes) or at the end of the document (endnotes) and, finally, by a bibliography. A more current form of documentation appears in the *MLA Handbook for Writers of Research Papers*. In the new MLA style, an in-text parenthetical reference briefly identifies the source. Full documentation then appears in a "Works Cited" section at the end of the document. Footnotes or endnotes now are used only to comment on material in the text.

A parenthetical reference usually includes the author's surname and the exact page number of the borrowed material:

Parenthetical reference in the text

> A recent study indicates an elevated risk of leukemia among children exposed to certain types of electromagnetic fields (Bowman et al. 59).

Readers seeking the complete citation for Bowman can move easily to "Works Cited," listed alphabetically by author:

Full citation at document's end

> Bowman, J. D., et al. "Hypothesis: The Risk of Childhood Leukemia Is Related to Combinations of Power-Frequency and Static Magnetic Fields." Bioelectromagnetics 16.1 (1995): 48–59.

This complete citation includes page numbers for the entire article.

MLA Parenthetical References

For clear and informative parenthetical references, observe these guidelines:

- If your discussion names the author, do not repeat the name in your parenthetical reference; simply list the page number:

Citing page numbers only

> Bowman et al. explain how their recent study indicates an elevated risk of leukemia for children exposed to certain types of electromagnetic fields (59).

- If you cite two or more works in a single parenthetical reference, separate the citations with semicolons:

Three works in a single reference

> (Jones 32; Leduc 41; Gomez 293–94)

- If you cite two or more authors with the same last name, include the first initial in your parenthetical reference to each author:

Two authors with identical last names

> (R. Jones 32)
>
> (S. Jones 14–15)

- If you cite two or more works by the same author, include the first significant word from each work's title, or a shortened version:

Two works by one author

(Lamont, <u>Biophysics</u> 100–01)

(Lamont, <u>Diagnostic Tests</u> 81)

- If the work is by an institutional or corporate author or if it is unsigned (that is, author unknown), use only the first few words of the institutional name or the work's title in your parenthetical reference:

Institutional, corporate, or anonymous author

(American Medical Assn. 2)

("Distribution Systems" 18)

To avoid distracting your readers, keep each parenthetical reference as brief as possible. One method is to name the source in your discussion, and to place only the page number in parentheses.

Where to place a parenthetical reference

For a paraphrase, place the parenthetical reference *before* the closing punctuation mark. For a quotation that runs into the text, place the reference *between* the final quotation mark and the closing punctuation mark. For a quotation set off (indented) from the text, place the reference two spaces *after* the closing punctuation mark.

MLA Works Cited Entries

The Works Cited list includes each source you have paraphrased or quoted. Double space the list for academic papers in the humanities. In all other situations, single space the list. Key the first line of each entry flush with the left margin. Indent the second and subsequent lines five spaces (1.25 cm, ½"). Use a one-character space after any period, comma, or colon.

How to space and indent entries

Following are examples of complete citations as they would appear in the Works Cited section of your document. Shown italicized below each citation is its corresponding parenthetical reference as it would appear in the text. Note capitalization, abbreviations, spacing, and punctuation in sample entries.

Index to Sample MLA Works Cited Entries

MLA Works Cited Entries for Books. Any citation for a book should contain the following information (found on the book's title and copyright pages): author, title, editor or translator, edition, volume number, and facts about publication (city, publisher, date).

1. Book, Single Author—MLA

Bender, Peter Urs. <u>Secrets of Power Presentations</u>. 5th ed. Toronto: The Achievement Group, 1991.

Parenthetical reference: (Bender 29–30)

Identify the province or state of publication by Canada Post or U.S. Postal Service abbreviations. If the city of publication is well known (Toronto, Vancouver, etc.), omit the province or state abbreviation. If several cities are listed on the title page, give only the first. For other countries, except the U.S., include an abbreviation of the country name.

2. Book, Two or Three Authors—MLA

Aronson, Linda, Roger Katz, and Candide Moustafa. <u>Toxic Waste Disposal Methods</u>. New Haven: Yale UP, 1996.

Parenthetical reference: (Aronson, Katz, and Moustafa 121–23)

Shorten publishers' names, as in "Simon" for Simon & Schuster or "Yale UP" for Yale University Press. For page numbers having more than two digits, give only the final two digits for the second number.

3. Book, Four or More Authors—MLA

Beebe, Morton, et al. <u>Cascadia: A Tale of Two Cities, Seattle and Vancouver, B.C.</u> New York: Henry N. Abrams, 1996.

Parenthetical reference: (Beebe et al. 14)

"Et al." is the abbreviated form of the Latin "et alia," meaning "and others."

4. Book, Anonymous Author—MLA

<u>Structured Programming.</u> Boston: Meredith, 1995.

Parenthetical reference: (<u>Structured</u> 67)

5. Multiple Books, Same Author—MLA

Chang, John W. <u>Biophysics</u>. Boston: Little, 1997.

---. <u>Diagnostic Techniques</u>. New York: Radon, 1994.

Parenthetical references: (Chang, <u>Biophysics</u> 123–26) (Chang, <u>Diagnostic</u> 87)

When citing more than one work by the same author, do not repeat the author's name; simply key three hyphens followed by a period. List the works alphabetically by title.

6. Book, One or More Editors—MLA

Gunn, John. M.,ed. <u>Restoration and Recovery of an Industrial Region: Sudbury</u>. New York: Springer-Verlag, 1995.

Parenthetical reference: (Gunn 34)

For more than three editors, name only the first, followed by "et al."

7. Book, Indirect Source—MLA

Kline, Thomas. <u>Automated Systems</u>. Boston: Rhodes, 1992.

Stubbs, John. <u>White-Collar Productivity</u>. Miami: Harris, 1996.

Parenthetical reference: (qtd. in Stubbs 116)

When your source (as in Stubbs, above) has quoted or cited another source, include each source in its appropriate alphabetical place in your Works Cited list. Use the name of the original source (here, Kline) in your text and begin the parenthetical reference with "qtd. in"—or "cited in" for a paraphrase.

8. Anthology Selection or Book Chapter—MLA

Bowman, Joel P. "Electronic Conferencing." <u>Communication and Technology: Today and Tomorrow</u>. Ed. Al Williams. Denton, TX: Assn. for Business Communication, 1994. 123–42.

Parenthetical reference: (Bowman 129)

Page numbers in the entry cover the selection cited from the anthology.

MLA Works Cited Entries for Periodicals. Give all available information in this order: author, article title, periodical title, volume and issue, date (day, month, year), and page numbers for the entire article—not just pages cited.

9. Article, Magazine—MLA

Jenish, D'Arcy. "A Car That Just May Fly." <u>Maclean's</u> 21 June, 1999: 46–47.

Parenthetical reference: (Jenish 46)

No punctuation separates the magazine title and date. Nor is the abbreviation "p." or "pp." used to designate page numbers. If no author is given, list all other information:

"Distribution Systems for the New Decade." <u>Power Technology Magazine</u> 18 Oct. 1996: 18+.

Parenthetical reference: ("Distribution Systems" 18)

This article began on page 18 and then continued on page 21. When an article does not appear on consecutive pages, give only the number of the first page, followed immediately by a plus sign. A three-letter abbreviation denotes any month spelled with five or more letters.

10. Article, Journal with New Pagination Each Issue—MLA

Ackerman, Nancy. "Landfill Landscape." <u>Canadian Geographic</u> 119.4 (1999): 56–63.

Parenthetical reference: (Ackerman 56–63)

Because each issue for that year will have page numbers beginning with "1," readers need the number of the issue. The "119" denotes the volume number; the "4" denotes the issue number. Omit "The" or "A" or any other introductory article from a journal or magazine title.

11. Article, Journal with Continuous Pagination—MLA

Norcliffe, Glen. "John Cabot's Legacy in Newfoundland." <u>Geography: an International Journal</u> 84 (1999): 97–109.

Parenthetical reference: (Norcliffe 104)

When page numbers continue from issue to issue for the full year, readers do not need the issue number, because no other issue in that year repeats these same page numbers. (Include the issue number if you think it will help readers retrieve the article more easily.) The "84" denotes the volume number.

12. Article, Newspaper—MLA

> DeGroot, Paul. "Web Site Is Built on Address, Content." Globe and Mail
>   26 March, 1999, national ed., sec. R:5.

Parenthetical reference: (DeGroot 5)

When a daily newspaper has more than one edition, cite the specific edition after the date. Omit any introductory article in the newspaper's name (not The Globe and Mail). If no author is given, list all of the other information. If the newspaper's name does not contain the city of publication, insert it, using brackets: "Northern Miner [LaRonge, SK]."

MLA Works Cited Entries for Other Sources. Miscellaneous sources range from unsigned encyclopedia entries to conference presentations to government publications. A full citation should give this information (as available): author, title, city, publisher, date, and page numbers.

13. Encyclopedia, Dictionary, Other Alphabetic Reference— MLA

> "Communication." The Business Reference Book. 1999 ed.

Parenthetical reference: ("Communication")

Begin a signed entry with the author's name. For any work arranged alphabetically, omit page numbers in the citation and the parenthetical reference. For a well-known reference book, only an edition (if stated) and a date are needed. For other reference books, give the full publication information.

14. Report—MLA

> MacHutchon, Arthur, S. Himmer, and C.A. Bryden. Khatzeywateen Valley
>   Grizzly Bear Study: Final Report. Victoria: BC Ministry of Forests,
>   Oct. 1993.

Parenthetical reference: (MacHutchon, Himmer and Bryden 29)

If no author is given, begin with the organization that sponsored the report; e.g., Canadian Professional Sales Association (CPSA). For any report or other document with group authorship include the group's abbreviated name in your first parenthetical reference; e.g., (Canadian Professional Sales Association [CPSA] 49), and then use only that abbreviation in any subsequent reference; e.g., (CPSA 78).

15. Conference Presentation—MLA

> Smith, Abelard A. "Radon Concentrations in Molded Concrete." First British
>   Symposium in Environmental Engineering. London, 11–13 Oct. 1995.
>   Ed. Anne Hodkins. London: Harrison, 1996. 106–21.

Parenthetical reference: (Smith 109)

The previous example shows a presentation that has been included in the published proceedings of a conference. For an unpublished presentation, include the presenter's name; the title of the presentation; and the conference title, location, and date, but do not underline or italicize the conference information.

16. Interview, Personally Conducted—MLA

Turner, Dan. Operations Manager for Prairie Power. Personal Interview. Winnipeg. 4 Mar. 2008

Parenthetical reference: (Turner)

17. Interview, Published—MLA

Lescault, James. "The Future of Graphics." <u>Executive Views of Automation</u>. Ed. Karen Prell. Miami: Haber, 1997. 216–31.

Parenthetical reference: (Lescault 218)

The interviewee's name is placed in the entry's author slot.

18. Letter, Unpublished—MLA

Singh, Jopal. Letter to the author. 15 May 2008.

Parenthetical reference: (Singh)

19. Questionnaire—MLA

Sakamoto, Yoshi. Questionnaire sent to 612 Quebec business executives. 14 Feb. 2007.

Parenthetical reference: (Sakamoto)

20. Brochure or Pamphlet—MLA

<u>Portfolio Strategy</u>: Fall 2008. Toronto: RBC Dominion Securities, 2008

Parenthetical reference: (<u>Portfolio Strategy</u>)

If the work is signed, begin with its author.

21. Lecture—MLA

Jack, David. "Energy Levels and Spectrum of the Hydrogen Atom." Lecture. Concordia University, Montreal, 3 Nov. 1999.

Parenthetical reference: (Jack)

If the lecture title is not known, write Address, Lecture, or Reading but do not use quotation marks. Include the sponsor and the location if available.

22. Government Document—MLA

British Columbia. Ministry of Highways. <u>Standard Specifications for Bridge Maintenance</u>. Victoria: B.C. Ministry of Highways, 1999.

Parenthetical reference: (B.C. Ministry of Highways 49)

If the author is unknown (as shown), list the information in this order: name of the government, name of the issuing agency, document title, place, publisher, and date.

23. Document with Corporate Authorship—MLA

Canada Post Corporation. <u>The Canadian Addressing Standard</u>. Ottawa: Canada Post Corporation, 1995.

Parenthetical reference: (Canada Post 5)

24. Map or Other Visual—MLA

<u>Deaths Caused by Breast Cancer, by County</u>. Map. <u>Scientific American</u> Oct. 1995: 32D.

Parenthetical reference: (<u>Deaths Caused</u>)

If the creator of the visual is listed, list that name first. Identify the type of visual ("Map," "Graph," "Table," "Diagram") immediately following its title.

25. Unpublished Dissertation, Report, or Miscellaneous Items—MLA

Author (if known), title (in quotes), sponsoring organization or publisher, date, page numbers.

For any work that has group authorship (corporation, committee, task force), cite the name of the group or agency in place of the author's name.

MLA Works Cited Entries for Electronic Sources. In general, citation for an electronic source with a printed equivalent should begin with that publication information (see relevant sections above). But any citation should enable readers to retrieve the material electronically whether or not a printed equivalent exists.

26. On-line Database Source—MLA

Sahl. J. D. "Power Lines, Viruses, and Childhood Leukemia." <u>Cancer Causes Control</u> 6.1 (Jan. 1995): 83. <u>MEDLINE</u>. On-line. DIALOG. 7 Nov. 1995.

Parenthetical reference: (Sahl 83)

For entries with a printed equivalent, begin with complete publication information, then the database title (underlined), the "On-line" designation to indicate the medium, service provider, and date of access. The access date is important because frequent updatings of databases can produce different versions of the material.

For entries with no printed equivalent, give the title and date of the work in quotation marks, followed by the electronic source information:

Argent, Roger R. "An Analysis of International Exchange Rates for 2008." <u>Accu-Data</u>. On-line. Dow Jones News Retrieval. 10 Jan. 2009.

Parenthetical reference: (Argent 4)

If the author is not known, begin with the work's title.

27. Computer Software—MLA

<u>Virtual Collaboration</u>. Diskette. New York: Harper, 1994.

Parenthetical reference: (<u>Virtual</u>)

Begin with the author's name, if known.

28. CD-ROM—MLA

Cavanaugh, Herbert A. "EMF Study: Good News and Bad News." <u>Electrical World</u> Feb. 1995: 8. <u>ABI/INFORM</u>. CD-ROM. Proquest. Sept. 1995.

Parenthetical reference: (Cavanaugh 8)

If the material is also available in print, begin with complete publication information, followed by the name of the database (underlined), "CD-ROM" designation, vendor's name, and electronic publication date. If the material has no printed equivalent, list its author (if known) and its title (in quotation marks), followed by the electronic source information.

For CD-ROM reference works and other material that is not routinely updated, give the work title followed by the "CD-ROM" designation, place, electronic publisher, and date:

<u>Time Almanac</u>. CD-ROM. Washington: Compact, 1994.

Parenthetical reference: (<u>Time Almanac</u> 74)

Begin with the author's name, if known.

29. Internet (Bulletin Board, Discussion List)—MLA

Templeton, Brad. "10 Big Myths about Copyright Explained." 29 Nov. 1994. On-line posting. Listserv law/copyright-FAQ/myths/part 1. BITNET. 6 May 1995.

Parenthetical reference: (Templeton)

Begin with the author's name (if known), followed by the title of the work (in quotation marks), publication date, "On-line posting" designation, name of discussion group, name of network, and date of your access. If appropriate, include the on-line address at the end of the entry, after the word "Available." The parenthetical reference should not include a page number as none is given in an on-line posting.

30. E-mail—MLA

> Wallin, John Luther. "Frog Reveries." E-mail to author. 12 Oct. 2006.

Cite personal e-mail as you would printed correspondence. If the document has a subject line or title, enclose it in quotation marks. For publicly posted e-mail (for a newsgroup or discussion list) include the address and the date of access.

31. Web Source (on-line article or posting)—MLA

> Dumont, R. A. "An Online Course in Technical Writing." 10 Dec. 1995.
>   On-line posting. http://www.umassd.edu/englishdepartment
>   (6 Jan. 1996).

Parenthetical reference: (Dumont 7–9)

Begin with the author's name (if known), followed by title of the work (in quotation marks), posting date, "On-line" designation, Web address, and date of access. In place of (or in addition to) the Web address, include the name of the Web site (underlined), if available:

> Rogers, S. E. "Chemical Risk Assessment Guidelines." 12 Feb. 1996. OTA
>   Online. http://www.ota.gov (10 Mar. 1996).

"OTA" stands for Office of Technology Assessment.

32. Web Source (Home Page, Professional Site)—MLA

> Sunshine Ski Development—list of documents. Canadian Environmental
>   Assessment Agency. 14 Jan. 1999 <http://www.ceaa.gc.ca>

33. Web Source (Home Page, Personal Site)—MLA

> McCoy Gobessi, Linda. Home page. Last update not indicated.
>   Intellego Interactive Designs. 21 June 1999
>   <www.intellegodesigns.com>

MLA Sample Works Cited Page

Place your Works Cited section on a separate page at the end of the document. Arrange entries alphabetically by author surname. When the author is unknown, list the title alphabetically according to its first word (excluding introductory articles). For a title that begins with a digit ("5," "6," etc.), alphabetize the entry as if the digit were spelled out.

See the list of works cited in Figure 8.1. In the left margin, large numbers refer to the elements discussed on the page facing Figure 8.1. Bracketed labels identify different types of sources the first time a particular type is cited.

Works Cited

Broad, William J. "Cancer Fear Is Unfounded, Physicists Say." <u>New York Times</u>
14 May 1995, sec. A: 19.   *[newspaper article]*

Brodeur, Paul, "Annals of Radiation: The Cancer at Slater School."
<u>New Yorker</u> 7 Dec. 1992: 86+.   *[magazine article]*

Castleman, Michael. "Electromagnetic Fields." <u>Sierra</u> Jan./Feb. 1992: 21–22.

Cavanaugh, Herbert A. "EMF Study: Good News and Bad News." <u>Electrical
World</u> Feb. 1995: 8. <u>ABI/INFORM</u>. CD-ROM. Proquest. Sept. 1995.
                    [trade-magazine article from CD-ROM database]

Dana, Amy, and Tom Turner. "Currents of Controversy." <u>Amicus Journal</u>
Summer 1993: 29–32.   *[alternative press]*

de Jager, L., and L. deBruyn. "Long-Term Effects of a 50 HZ Electric Field on
the Life-Expectancy of Mice." <u>Review of Environmental Health</u> 10.3
(1994): 221–24. <u>MEDLINE</u>. On-line. DIALOG. 8 Mar. 1996.
                    [journal article from on-line database]

Des Marteau, Kathleen. "Study Links Sewing Machine Use to Alzheimer's
Disease." <u>Bobbin</u> Oct. 1994: 36-38. <u>ABI/INFORM</u>. CD-ROM. Proquest.
Aug. 1995.

"Electrophobia: Overcoming Fears of EMFs." <u>University of California Wellness</u>
Letter Nov. 1994: 1.   *[newsletter]*

Goodman, E. M., B. Greenebaum, and M. T. Marron. "Effects of
Electromagnetic Fields on Molecules and Cells." <u>International Review of
Cytology</u> 158 (1995): 279–338. <u>MEDLINE</u>. On-line. DIALOG. 8 Mar. 1996.

Halloran-Barney, Marianne B. Energy Service Advisor for County Electric.
E-mail to author. 3 Apr. 1996.   *[E-mail enquiry]*

Jauchem, J. "Alleged Health Effects of Electromagnetic Fields: Misconceptions in
the Scientific Literature." Journal of Microwave Power and Electromagnetic
Energy 26.4 (1991): 189–95.   *[journal article from print source]*

Kirkpatrick, David. "Can Power Lines Give You Cancer?" <u>Fortune</u> 31 Dec.
1990: 80–85.

Lee, J. M., Jr., et al. <u>Electrical and Biological Effects of Transmission Lines: A Review</u>.
U.S. Dept. of Energy. NTIS no. PC A06/MF A01. Washington: GPO, 1989.

Figure 8.1   A List of Works Cited (MLA Style)   (*Continued*)

Discussion of Figure 8.1

1. Centre the Works Cited title at the top of the page. Use 2.5 cm (1") margins. Single space *within* the entries, double space *between* the entries. Order the entries alphabetically. For numbering Works Cited pages, follow numbering of text pages.

2. Indent five spaces (1.25 cm, ½") for the second and subsequent lines of an entry.

3. Place quotation marks around article titles. Underline or italicize periodical or book titles. Capitalize the first letter of key words in all titles (also articles, prepositions, and conjunctions only if they come first or last).

4. Do not cite a magazine's volume number, even if it is given.

5. For a CD-ROM database that is updated often (such as Proquest), conclude your citation with the date of electronic publication.

6. For additional perspective beyond "establishment" viewpoints, examine "alternative" publications (such as *The Amicus Journal* and *In These Times,* in this list).

7. Conclude an on-line database citation with the date you accessed the source.

8. Use a period and one space to separate a citation's three major items (author, title, publication data). Leave one space after a comma or colon. Use no punctuation to separate magazine title and date.

9. Alphabetize hyphenated surnames according to the name that appears first.

10. Include the issue number for a journal with new pagination in each issue. For page numbers of more than two digits, give only the final digits in the second number.

11. For government reports, name the sponsoring agency and include all available information for retrieving the document. Use the first author's name and "et al." for works with four or more authors or editors.

Maugh, Thomas H. "Studies Link EMF Exposure to Higher Risks of Alzheimer's." Los Angeles Times 31 July 1994, sec A: 3.

12   Mevissen, M., M. Keitzmann, and W. Loscher. "In Vivo Exposure of Rats to a Weak Alternating Magnetic Field Increases Ornithine Decarboxylase Activity in the Mammary Gland by a Similar Extent as the Carcinogen DMBA." Cancer Letter 90.2 (1995): 207–14. MEDLINE. On-line. DIALOG. 8 Mar. 1996.

Miller, M. A., et al. "Variation in Cancer Risk Estimates for Exposure to Powerline Frequency Electromagnetic Fields: A Meta-analysis Comparing EMF Measurement Methods." Risk Analysis 15.2 (1995): 281–87. MEDLINE. On-line. DIALOG. 8 Mar. 1996.

Miltane, John. Chief Engineer for County Electric. Personal Interview. Adams, MA. 5 Apr. 1996.   *[personal interview]*

Moore, Taylor. "EMF Health Risks: The Story in Brief." EPRI Journal Mar./Apr. 1995: 7–17.

13   Moulder, John. "Power Lines and Cancer" 6 Oct. 1995. On-line posting. Newsgroup powerlines.cancer.FAQ: USENET. 10 Mar. 1996.

[World Wide Web newsgroup]

Palfreman, Jon. "Apocalypse Not." Technology Review 24 April 1996: 24–33.

Pinsky, Mark A. The EMF Book: What You Should Know about Electromagnetic Fields, Electromagnetic Radiation, and Your Health. New York: Warner, 1995.

[book—one author]

Reiter, R. J. "Melatonin Suppression by Static and Extremely Low Frequency Electromagnetic Fields: Relationship to the Reported Increased Incidence of Cancer." Review of Environmental Health 10.3 (1994):171–86. MEDLINE. On-line. DIALOG. 8 Mar. 1996.

Schneider, David. "High Tension: Researchers Debate EMF Experiments on Cells."
14   Scientific American Oct. 1995: 26+.

Taubes, Gary. "Fields of Fear." Atlantic Monthly Nov. 1994: 94–108. On-line. U of Virginia Electronic Text Center. Internet. 15 Mar. 1996. Available
15   www:http://etext. libvirginia.edu/english.html.   *[Internet source]*

United States Environmental Protection Agency. EMF in Your Environment.
16   Washington: GPO, 1992.

White, Peter. "Bad Vibes." In These Times 28 June 1993: 14–17.

Figure 8.1   A List of Works Cited (MLA Style)

Discussion of Figure 8.1 *Continued* ━━━━━━━━━

12. Use three-letter abbreviations for months with five or more letters.

13. Because an on-line conference source such as a listserv or newsgroup provides no page numbers, you can eliminate the in-text parenthetical reference by referring directly to that source in your discussion ("Dr. Jones of Harvard points out that").

14. When an article skips pages in a publication, give only the first page number followed by a plus sign.

15. When the privacy of the electronic source is not an issue (e.g., a library versus an e-mail correspondent), consider including its electronic address in your entry, after the word *Available.*

16. Shorten publishers' names (as in "Simon" for Simon & Schuster; "Knopf" for Alfred A. Knopf, Inc.; "GPO" for Government Printing Office; or "U of T Press" for University of Toronto Press).

ACW Documentation for Unconventional Electronic Sources[1]

Unconventional electronic sources include MUDs (multi-user dungeons), MOOs (MUD Object-Oriented software), IRC (Internet Relay Chat); FTPs (File Transfer Protocols), and others listed below. Conventions for documenting these sources continue to evolve. One useful system has been developed by Professor Janice R. Walker and endorsed by The Alliance for Computers and Writing (ACW).

Begin the citation with the name of the communicator(s) and indicate the type of communication (e.g., personal interview).

> Pine-Guest. Personal Interview. telnet world.sensemedia.net 1234 (12 Dec. 1995).

Gopher Site—ACW. Gopher is a software tool for locating and searching Internet databases and retrieving and downloading files.

> Quittner, Joshua. "Far Out: Welcome to Their World Built of MUD." Published in <u>Newsday</u>, 7 Nov. 1993. gopher/University of Koeln/About MUDs, MOOs and MUSEs in Education/Selected Papers/newsday (5 Dec. 1995).

Listserv and Newslist—ACW. In one of these sites, messages are posted about a single topic. Indicate the subject line of the posting in quotes.

> Seabrook, Richard H.C. "Community and Progress." cybermind@jefferson. village.virginia.edu (22 Jan. 1994).

E-mail—ACW. Indicate the author and the subject line of the posting. For personal e-mail entries, the address usually is omitted.

> Mah, Jodie. "Electronic Documentation." Personal e-mail (1 May 2006).

The ACW system observes MLA conventions wherever possible, but also provides formats for unique documentation often required when citing unconventional sources. For example, if the author is not named, your parenthetical reference might include the Internet or Web site and date:

> (MediaMOO 10 Mar. 2006)

If page numbers are not given, a reference might include author and date:

> (Patrese Apr. 2005)

The full citation for each parenthetical reference appears alphabetically on a Works Cited page at the end of the document. A typical entry contains the following information (as available or appropriate):

> Author's Last Name, First Name. "Title of Work." Title of Complete Work. [protocol (e.g., ftp, telnet, gopher) and address] [search path] (date of message or visit).

---

1. Discussion adapted and examples reproduced from the style sheet prepared by Janice R. Walker and its version published in Hairston, Maxine, and John J. Ruskiewicz. *The Scott, Foresman Handbook for Writers.* 4th ed. New York: Harper, 1996: 671–75.

Following are some examples of specific entries as they would appear in the Works Cited section of your document—along with MLA entries for conventional print and electronic sources.

FTP Site—ACW. A File Transfer Protocol site enables files to be transferred between computers via telephone lines.

> Bruckman, Amy. "Approaches to Managing Deviant Behavior in Virtual Communities." ftp.media.mit.edupub/asb/papers/deviance-chi94 (4 Dec. 1995).

WWW Site—ACW. A World Wide Web site is accessed via a web browser such as *Yahoo, Netscape, InfoSeek, WebCrawler,* or *Lynx.*

> Burka, Lauren P. "A Hypertext History of Multi-User Dimensions." Mud History. http://www.ccs.neu.edu/home/1pb/mud-history.html (5 Dec. 1995).

Telnet Site—ACW. Telnet provides users direct access to files in other computers on the Internet.

> Gomes, Lee. "Xerox's On-Line Neighborhood: A Great Place to Visit." Mercury News 3 May 1992. telnet lambda.parc.xerox.com 8888, @go#50827, press13 (5 Dec. 1995).

Synchronous Communication (MOOs, MUDs, IRC)—ACW. Synchronous communication happens in "real time": The message keyed in by the sender appears instantly on the screen of the recipient, as in a personal interview.

APA Documentation Style

One popular alternative to MLA style appears in the *Publication Manual of the American Psychological Association.* APA style is useful when writers wish to emphasize the publication dates of their references. A parenthetical reference in the text briefly identifies the source, date, and page number:

Reference cited in the text

> In a recent study, mice continuously exposed to an electromagnetic field tended to die earlier than mice in the control group (de Jager & de Brun, 1994, p. 224).

The full citation then appears in the alphabetic listing of "References," at the end of the report:

Full citation at the end of the document

> de Jager, L., & de Brun, L. (1994). Long term effects of a 50 Hz electric field on the life-expectancy of mice. Review of Environmental Health, 10 (3–4), 221–224.

APA style (or some similar author-date style) is preferred in the sciences and social sciences, where information quickly becomes outdated.

APA Parenthetical References

APA's parenthetical references differ from MLA's as follows: the citation includes the publication date; a comma separates each item in the reference; and "p." or "pp." precedes the page number (which is optional in the APA system). When a subsequent reference to a work follows closely after the initial reference, the date need not be included. Here are specific guidelines:

- If your discussion names the author, do not repeat the name in your parenthetical reference; simply give the date and page number:

Author named in the text

> Researchers de Jager and de Brun explain that experimental mice exposed to an electromagnetic field tended to die earlier than mice in the control group (1994, p. 224).

When two authors of a work are named in your text, their names are connected by "and," but in a parenthetical reference their names are connected by an ampersand, "&."

- If you cite two or more works in a single reference, list the authors in alphabetical order and separate the citations with semicolons:

Two or more works in a single reference

> (Jones, 2007; Gomez, 1999; Leduc, 2008)

- If you cite a work with three to five authors, try to name them in your text, to avoid an excessively long parenthetical reference:

A work with three to five authors

> Franks, Oblesky, Ryan, Jablar, and Perkins (1993) studied the role of electromagnetic fields in tumour formation.

In any subsequent references to this work, name only the first author, followed by "et al."

- If you cite two or more works by the same author published in the same year, assign a different letter to each work:

Two or more works by the same author in the same year

> (Lamont 2006a, p. 135)
> (Lamont 2006b, pp. 67–68)

Other examples of parenthetical references appear with their corresponding entries in the following discussion of the list of references.

APA Reference List Entries

How to space and indent entries

The APA reference list includes each source that you cited in your document. In preparing the list, which you should single space, key the first line of each entry flush with the left margin. Indent the second and subsequent lines five spaces 1.25 cm, ½". Use one character space after any period, comma, or colon.

Following are examples of complete citations as they would appear in the "References" section of your document. Shown immediately below each entry is its corresponding parenthetical reference as it would appear in the text. Note the capitalization, abbreviation, spacing, and punctuation in the sample entries.

Index to Sample Entries for APA References

Books

1. Book, single author
2. Book, two to five authors
3. Book, six or more authors
4. Book, anonymous author
5. Multiple books, same author
6. Book, one or more editors
7. Book, indirect source
8. Anthology selection or book chapter

Periodicals

9. Article, magazine
10. Article, journal with new pagination each issue
11. Article, journal with continuous pagination
12. Article, newspaper

Other Sources

13. Encyclopedia, dictionary, alphabetic reference
14. Report
15. Conference presentation

16. Interview, personally conducted
17. Interview, published
18. Personal correspondence
19. Brochure or pamphlet
20. Lecture
21. Government document
22. Miscellaneous items

Electronic Sources

23. On-line database abstract
24. On-line database article
25. Computer software or manual
26. CD-ROM abstract
27. CD-ROM reference work
28. Electronic bulletin boards, discussion lists, e-mail
29. Web source (home page—professional site)
30. Web source (home page—personal site)

APA Entries for Books. Any citation for a book should contain all applicable information in the following order: author, date, title, editor or translator, edition, volume number, and facts about publication (city and publisher).

1. Book, Single Author—APA

Bender, P.U. (1991) <u>Secrets of power presentations</u> (5th Ed.). Toronto: The Achievement Group.

Parenthetical reference: (Bender, 1991, pp. 29–30)

Use only initials for an author's first and middle name. Capitalize only the first words of a book's title and subtitle and any proper names. Identify a later edition in parentheses.

2. Book, Two to Five Authors—APA

Aronson, L., Katz, R., & Moustafa, C. (1996). <u>Toxic waste disposal methods</u>. New Haven: Yale University Press.

Parenthetical reference: (Aronson, Katz, & Moustafa, 1993)

Use an ampersand (&) before the name of the final author listed in an entry. As an alternative parenthetical reference, name the authors in your text and include date (and page numbers, if appropriate) in parentheses.

3. Book, Six or More Authors—APA

> Fogle, S. T., et al. (1995). <u>Hyperspace technology</u>. Boston: Little, Brown.

Parenthetical reference: (Fogle, et al., 1995, p. 34)

For more than five authors, name only the first followed by "et al."

4. Book, Anonymous Author—APA

> <u>Structured programming</u>. (1995). Boston: Meredith Press.

Parenthetical reference: (Structured Programming, 1995, p. 67)

In your list of references, place an anonymous work alphabetically by the first key word (not *The, A,* or *An*) in its title. In your parenthetical reference, capitalize all key words in a book, article, or journal title. But in your list of references, capitalize only journal titles in this way.

5. Multiple Books, Same Author—APA

> Chang, J. W. (1997a). <u>Biophysics</u>. Boston: Little, Brown.
> Chang, J. W. (1997b). <u>MindQuest</u>. Chicago: John Pressler.

Parenthetical references: (Chang, 1997a) (Chang, 1997b)

Two or more works by the same author not published in the same year are distinguished by their respective dates alone, without the added letter.

6. Book, One or More Editors—APA

> Gunn, J.M. (Ed.). (1995). <u>Restoration and recovery of an industrial region:</u>
> <u>Sudbury</u>. New York: Springer-Verlag.

Parenthetical reference: (Gunn, 1995, p. 34)

For more than five editors, name only the first, followed by "et al."

7. Book, Indirect Source

> Stubbs, J. (1996). <u>White-collar productivity</u>. Miami: Harris.

Parenthetical reference: (cited in Stubbs, 1996, p. 47)

When your source (as in Stubbs, above) cites another source, list your source in the References section, but name the original source in your text: "Kline's study (cited in Stubbs, 1996, p. 47) supports this conclusion."

8. Anthology Selection or Book Chapter—APA

> Bowman, J. (1994). Electronic conferencing. In A. Williams (Ed.),
> <u>Communication and technology: Today and tomorrow</u>. (pp.
> 123–142). Denton, TX: Association for Business Communication.

Parenthetical reference: (Bowman, 1994, p. 126)

The page numbers in the complete reference are for the selection cited from the anthology.

APA Entries for Periodicals. A citation for an article should give this information (as available), in order: author, publication date, article title (without quotation marks), volume or number (or both), and page numbers for the entire article—not just the page cited.

9. Article, Magazine—APA

Jenish, D. (1999, 21 June). A car that just may fly. <u>Maclean's</u>, 112, 46–47.

Parenthetical reference: (Jenish, 1999, p. 46)

If no author is given, provide all other information. Capitalize the first word in an article's title and subtitle, and any proper nouns. Capitalize all key words in a periodical title. Underline or italicize the periodical title, volume number, and commas (as above).

10. Article, Journal with New Pagination for Each Issue—APA

Ackerman, N. (1999). Landfill landscape. <u>Canadian Geographic, 119</u> (4), 56–63.

Parenthetical reference: (Ackerman, 1999, 56–58).

Because each issue for a given year has page numbers that begin at "1," readers need the issue number ("1"). The "119" denotes the volume number, which is underlined or italicized.

11. Article, Journal with Continuous Pagination—APA

Norcliffe, G. (1999). John Cabot's legacy in Newfoundland. <u>Geography: an international journal 84</u>

Parenthetical reference: (Norcliffe, 1999, p. 104)

The "84" denotes the volume number. When page numbers continue from issue to issue for the full year, readers do not need the issue number, because no other issue in that year repeats these same page numbers. (You can include the issue number if you think it will help readers retrieve the article more easily.)

12. Article, Newspaper—APA

DeGroot, P. (1999, March 26). Web site is built on address, content. <u>The Globe and Mail</u>, p. R2.

Parenthetical reference: (DeGroot, 1999, p. R2)

In addition to the year of publication, include the month and day. If the newspaper's name begins with "The," include it in your citation. Include "p." or "pp." before page numbers. For an article on non-consecutive pages, list each page, separated by a comma.

APA Entries for Other Sources. Miscellaneous sources range from unsigned encyclopedia entries to conference presentations to government documents. A full citation should give this information (as available): author, publication date, work title (and report or series number), page numbers (if applicable), city, and publisher.

13. Encyclopedia, Dictionary, Alphabetic Reference—APA

Communication. (1993). In <u>The business reference book</u>. Boston: Business Resources Press.

Parenthetical reference: ("Communication," 1993)

For a signed entry, begin with the author's name and publication date.

14. Report—APA

MacHutchon, A. Himmer, S., and Bryden, C.A. (1993). <u>Khatzeywateen Valley grizzly bear study: final report</u>. Victoria: BC Ministry of Forests, Oct. 1993.

Parenthetical reference: (MacHutchon, Himmer, and Bryden, 1993, p. 29)

If the authors are named, list them first, followed by the publication date. When citing a group author; e.g., Canadian Professional Sales Association, include the group's abbreviated name in your first parenthetical reference; e.g., (Canadian Professional Sales Association [CSPSA]), and use only that abbreviation in any subsequent reference; e.g., (CPSA). When the agency (or organization) and publisher are the same, list "Author" in the publisher's slot.

15. Conference Presentation—APA

Smith, A. A. (1996). Radon concentrations in molded concrete. In A. Hodkins (Ed.), <u>First British Symposium on Environmental Engineering</u> (pp. 106–121). London: Harrison Press.

Parenthetical reference: (Smith, 1995, p. 109)

The example shows a presentation included in the published proceedings of a conference. The name of the symposium is a proper name, and so is capitalized. For an unpublished presentation, include the presenter's name, year and month, title of the presentation (underlined or italicized), and all available information about the conference or meeting: "Symposium held at . . ." Do not underline or italicize this information.

16. Interview, Personally Conducted—APA

Parenthetical reference: (D. Turner, personal interview, March 4, 2008)

This material is considered a non-recoverable source, and so is cited in the text only, as a parenthetical reference. If you name the interviewee in your text, do not repeat the name in your parenthetical reference.

17. Interview, Published—APA

Jable, C. K. (1997). The future of graphics [Interview with James Lescault]. In K. Prell (Ed.), <u>Executive Views of Automation</u> (pp. 216–231). Miami: Haber Press.

Parenthetical reference: (Jable, 1997, pp. 218–223)

Begin with the name of the interviewer, followed by the publication date, title, designation (in brackets), and publication information.

18. Personal Correspondence—APA

Parenthetical reference: (L. Nguyen, personal correspondence, May 15, 2006)

This material is considered non-recoverable data, and so is cited in the text only, as a parenthetical reference. If you name the correspondent in your text, do not repeat the name in your citation.

19. Brochure or Pamphlet—APA

This material follows the citation format for a book entry. After the title of the work, include the designation "Brochure" in brackets.

20. Lecture—APA

Jack, D. (1999, November 3). <u>Energy levels and spectrum of the hydrogen atom</u>. Lecture presented at Concordia University.

Parenthetical reference: (Jack, 1999)

If you name the lecturer in your text, do not repeat the name in your citation.

21. Government Document—APA

British Columbia Ministry of Highways. (1999). <u>Standard specifications for bridge maintenance</u>. Victoria: Author.

Parenthetical reference: (British Columbia Ministry of Highways, 1999, p. 49)

If the author is unknown, present the information in this order: name of the issuing agency, publication date, document title, place, and publisher. When the issuing agency is both author and publisher, list "Author" in the publisher's slot.

22. Miscellaneous items (unpublished manuscripts, dissertations, etc.)—APA

Author (if known), date of publication, title of work, sponsoring organization or publisher, page numbers.

For any work that has group authorship (corporation, committee, etc.), cite the name of the group or agency in place of the author's name.

APA Entries for Electronic Sources. APA documentation standards for electronic sources continue to be refined and defined. A sampling of currently preferred formats follows. Any citation for electronic media should enable the reader to identify the original source (printed or electronic) and provide an electronic path for retrieving the material.

Begin with the publication information for the printed equivalent. Then in brackets name the electronic source ([On-line], [CD-ROM], [Computer software]), the protocol[2] (Bitnet, Dialog, FTP, Telnet), and any other items that define a clear path (service provider, database title, access code, retrieval number, or site address).

23. On-line Database Abstract—APA

Sahl, J. D. (1995). Power lines, viruses, and childhood leukemia [On-line]. Cancer Causes Control, 6 (1), 83. Abstract from: DIALOG File: MEDLINE Item: 93–04881.

Parenthetical reference: (Sahl, 1995)

Note the absence of closing punctuation in the path statement. Any punctuation added to the path could interfere with retrieval.

24. On-line Database Article—APA

Alley, R. A. (1995, January). Ergonomic influences on worker satisfaction [29 paragraphs]. Industrial Psychology [On-line serial], 5(11). Available FTP: Hostname: publisher.com Directory: pub/journals/industrial. psychology/1995.

Parenthetical reference: (Alley, 1995)

Give the length of the article [in paragraphs], after its title. Do not add any terminal punctuation to the availability statement.

25. Computer Software or Software Manual—APA

Virtual collaboration [Computer software]. (1994). New York: HarperCollins.

Parenthetical reference: (Virtual, 1994)

For citing a manual, replace the "Computer software" designation in brackets with "Software manual."

26. CD-ROM Abstract—APA

Cavanaugh, H. (1995). An EMF study: Good news and bad news [CD-ROM]. Electrical World, 209(2), 8. Abstract from: Proquest File: ABI/Inform Item: 978032.

Parenthetical reference: (Cavanaugh, 1995)

The "8" in the above entry denotes the page number of this one-page article.

27. CD-ROM Reference Work—APA

Time almanac. (1994). Washington: Compact, 1994.

Parenthetical reference: (Time almanac, 1994)

---

2. A protocol is a body of standards that ensures compatibility among the different products designed to work together on a particular network.

If the work on CD-ROM has a printed equivalent, APA currently prefers that it be cited in its printed form. As more works appear in electronic form, this convention may be revised.

28. Electronic Bulletin Boards, Discussion Lists, E-mail—APA

Parenthetical reference: Teo Hakinnen (personal communication, May 10, 2006) provided these statistics.

29. World Wide Web Home Page, Professional Site—APA

Sunshine ski development—list of documents. [On-line]. Canadian Environmental Assessment Agency. http://www.ceaa.gc.ca [1999, Jan 14].

30. World Wide Web Home Page, Personal Site—APA

McCoy Gobessi, Linda. (1999, June 21). Home page [On-line]. Intellego Interactive Designs. <www.intellegodesigns.com>

This material is considered personal communication in APA style. Instead of being included in the list of references, it is cited directly in the text. According to APA's current standards, material from discussion lists and electronic bulletin boards has limited research value because it does not undergo the kind of review and verification process used in scholarly publications.

APA Sample List of References

APA's References section is an alphabetic listing (by author) equivalent to MLA's Works Cited section. Like Works Cited, the reference list includes only those works actually cited. (A bibliography usually would include background works or works consulted as well.) One notable difference from MLA style is that the APA style calls for only "recoverable" sources to appear in the reference list. Therefore, personal interviews, e-mail messages, and other unpublished materials are cited in the text only.

The list of references in Figure 8.2 accompanies the report on technical marketing, pages 483–492. In the left margin, coloured numbers denote elements discussed on the page facing Figure 8.2. Bracketed labels on the right identify different types of sources the first time a particular type is cited.

1   **References**

2   Alderman, L. (1995, July). How you can take control of your own career.
         Money, 24(7), 38–40.   *[magazine article]*

3   Basta, N. (1988, September). Take a good look at sales engineering. Graduating
         Engineer, 32, 84–87.

4   Baxter, N. (1994). Is there another degree in your future? Washington, DC: U.S.
         Department of Labor.   *[govt. publication—author named]*

5   Campbell, M. K. (1993). Wanted: Sales reps with EE degrees. IEEE Potentials,
         31(1), 28–29.   *[journal article]*

6   College Placement Council. (1995). CPC annual (39th ed.). Bethlehem, PA:
         Author.   *[book—author as publisher]*

7   Cornelius, H., & Lewis, W. Career guide for sales and marketing (2nd ed.). New
         York: Monarch Press.   *[book with two authors]*

8   Electronic sales positions. (1996). The national job bank. Holbrook, MA: Bob
         Adams, Inc.   *[directory entry—no author named]*

         Engineering careers. (1995). The encyclopedia of careers and vocational
         guidance (9th ed.). Chicago: J. G. Ferguson.   *[encyclopedia]*

         Gradler, C., & Schrammel, K. (1994). The 1992–2005 job outlook in brief.
         Washington, DC: U.S. Department of Labor.

         Resnick, R. R. (1995, June). Business is good, NOT. Internet World, 6(6), 71–73.

         Schranke, R. W. (1985). EE and MBA: A winning combination? IEEE Potentials,
         28 (1), 13–15.

9   Solomon, S. D. (1996, January). An engineer goes to Wall Street [10 pages].
         Technology Review [On-line serial], 99(1). Available
         www:http://web.mit.edu/techreview/www/   *[on-line article]*

10   Tolland, M. (1996, April). Alternate careers in marketing. Presentation at Electro
         '96, Conference in Boston.   *[unpublished conf. presentation]*

         U.S. Department of Labor. (1994). Tomorrow's jobs. Washington, DC: Author.
                                                    [govt. publication—no author named]

         Young, J. (1995, August). Can computers really boost sales? Forbes ASAP,
         84–101.   *[magazine article—no vol. or issue number]*

Figure 8.2   A List of References (APA Style)

Discussion of Figure 8.2

1. Centre the References title at the top of the page. Use 2.5 cm (1") margins. For numbering reference pages, follow numbering of text pages. Include only recoverable data (material that readers can retrieve for themselves); cite personal interviews, unpublished lectures, electronic discussion lists, and e-mail and other personal correspondence parenthetically in the text only. See also item 10 in this list.

2. Single space *within* entries, double space *between* entries. Order the entries alphabetically by author's last name (excluding *A, An,* or *The*). List the initials only for the authors' first and middle names. Write out the names of all months. In student papers, indent the second and subsequent lines of an entry five spaces (1.25 cm, ½"). In papers submitted for publication in an APA journal, indent the *first* line instead.

3. Do not enclose article titles in quotation marks. Underline or italicize periodical titles.

4. Capitalize the first word in article or book titles and subtitles, and any proper nouns. Capitalize all key words in magazine or journal titles.

5. Use italics or a continuous underline for a journal article's title, volume number, and the comma. Give the issue number in parentheses only if each issue begins on page 1. Do not include "p." or "pp." before journal page numbers (only before page numbers from a newspaper).

6. Identify the edition of a book in parentheses. If the author is also the publisher, use the word "Author" after the place of publication. Otherwise, write out the publisher's name in full.

7. For more than one author or editor, use ampersands instead of spelling out "and."

8. Use the first key word in the title to alphabetize works whose author is not named.

9. Omit punctuation at the end of an electronic address.

10. Treat an unpublished conference presentation as a recoverable source; include it in your List of References instead of merely citing it parenthetically in your text.

CBE Numerical Documentation Style

In the numerical system of documentation preferred by the Council of Biology Editors, each work is assigned a number the first time it is cited. This same number then is used for any subsequent reference to that work. Numerical documentation often is used in the physical sciences (astronomy, chemistry, geology, physics) and the applied sciences (mathematics, medicine, engineering, computer science).

Preferred documentation styles for particular disciplines are defined in style manuals such as:

- American Chemical Society. *The ACS Style Guide for Authors and Editors* (1985)
- American Institute of Physics. *AIP Style Manual* (1990)
- American Mathematical Society. *A Manual for Authors of Mathematical Papers* (1990)
- American Medical Association. *Manual of Style* (1989)

One widely consulted guide for numerical documentation is *Scientific Style and Format: The CBE Manual for Authors, Editors, and Publishers.* 6th ed., 1994, from the Council of Biology Editors.

CBE Numbered Citations

In one version of CBE style, a citation in the text appears as a raised number immediately following the source to which it refers:

Numbered citations in the text

> A recent study[1] indicates an elevated leukemia risk among children exposed to certain types of electromagnetic fields. Related studies[2-3] tend to confirm the EMF/cancer hypothesis.

When referring to two or more sources in a single note (as in "[2-3]" above) separate the numbers with a hyphen if they are in sequence and by commas but no space if they are out of sequence: ("[2,6,9]").

The full citation for each source then appears in the numerical listing of references at the end of the document:

REFERENCES

Full citations at the end of the document

> 1. Bowman JD, et al. Hypothesis: the risk of childhood leukemia is related to combinations of power-frequency and static magnetic fields. Bioelectromagnetics 1995; 16(1): 48–59.
>
> 2. Feychting M, Ahlbom A. Electromagnetic fields and childhood cancer: meta-analysis. Cancer Causes Control 1995 May; 6(3): 275–277.

To refer again to any of these sources later in your document, use the same number.

CBE Reference List Entries

CBE's References section lists each source in the numerical order in which it was first cited. In preparing the list, which should be single spaced, begin each entry on a new line. Key the number flush with the left margin, followed by a period and a space. Align subsequent lines directly under the first word of line one.

Following are examples of complete citations as they would appear in the References section for your document.

Index to Sample CBE Entries

1 Book, single author
2. Book, multiple authors
3. Book, anonymous author
4. Book, one or more editors
5. Anthology selection or book chapter

6. Article, magazine
7. Article, journal with new pagination each issue
8. Article, journal with continuous pagination
9. Article, newspaper
10. Article, on-line source

CBE Entries for Books. Any citation for a book should contain all available information in the following order: number assigned to the entry, author or editor, work title (and edition), facts about publication (place, publisher, date), and number of pages. Note the capitalization, abbreviation, spacing, and punctuation in the following sample entries.

1. Book, Single Author—CBE

1. Kerzin-Fontana JB. Technology management: a handbook. 3rd ed. Delmar, NY: American Management Assn.; 1997. 356p.

2. Book, Multiple Authors—CBE

2. Aronson L, Katz R, Moustafa C. Toxic waste disposal methods. New Haven: Yale Univ. Pr.; 1996. 316p.

3. Book, Anonymous Author—CBE

3. [Anonymous]. Structured programming. Boston: Meredith Pr.; 1995. 267p.

4. Book, One or More Editors—CBE

4. Morris AJ, Pardin-Walker LB, editors. Handbook of new information technology. New York: Harper; 1996. 345p.

5. Anthology Selection or Book Chapter—CBE

5. Bowman JP. Electronic conferencing. In: Williams A, editor. Communication and technology: today and tomorrow. Denton, TX: Assn. for Business Communication; 1994. p. 123–42.

CBE Entries for Periodicals. Any citation for an article should contain all available information in the following order: number assigned to the entry, author, article title, periodical title, date (year, month), volume and issue number, and inclusive page numbers for the article. Note the capitalization, abbreviation, spacing, and punctuation in the sample entries.

6. Article, Magazine—CBE

6. DesMarteau K. Study links sewing machine use to Alzheimer's disease. Bobbin 1994 Oct: 36–38.

7. Article, Journal with New Pagination each Issue—CBE

7. Thackman-White JR. Computer-assisted research. American Library Jour 1997; 51(1): 3–9.

8. Article, Journal with Continuous Pagination—CBE

8. Barnstead MH. The writing crisis. Jour of Writing Theory 1994; 12: 415–433.

9. Article, Newspaper—CBE

9. DeGroot, P. Web site is built on address, content. Globe and Mail 1999 Mar 26; Sect R:5 (col 3).

10. Article, On-line Source—CBE

10. Alley RA. Ergonomic influences on worker satisfaction. Industrial Psychology [serial on-line] 1995 Jan; 5(11). Available from: ftp. pub/journals/industrial psychology/1995 via the INTERNET. Accessed 1996 Feb 10.

For more detailed guidelines on CBE style, consult the CBE manual.

✅ EXERCISES

1. Locate the style manual for your discipline. (Ask the faculty in your major or a librarian). Redesign Figure 8.1 according to the guidelines in this manual. Submit your document along with a memo outlining the main differences in the two documentation styles. If your discipline stipulates no particular style, use the *APA Manual* for this assignment.

2. Locate the latest updates for MLA and APA documentation of electronic sources at the following Web sites:

   http://www.westwords.com/guffey/apa.html
   http://www.uvm.edu/~xli/reference/apa.html
   http://www.mla.org/main_stl.htm
   *http://www.english.ttu.edu/kairos/1.2/inbox/
       mla.html*

✅ COLLABORATIVE PROJECT

Work in groups of three. Examine the documentation format each of you has used in your major report assignment, to confirm that you have correctly used the documentation system stipulated by your project supervisor.

Summarizing Information

Purpose of Summaries

Elements of a Summary

Critical Thinking in the Summary Process

A Sample Situation

Forms of Summarized Information

Closing Summary

Informative Abstract (Summary)

Descriptive Abstract (Abstract)

A SUMMARY is a short version of a longer document. An economical way to communicate, a summary saves time, space, and energy.

Purpose of Summaries

Chapter 6 shows how abstracts (a type of summary) aid our research by providing an encapsulated glimpse of an article or other long document. As we record our research findings, we summarize and paraphrase to capture the main ideas in a compressed form. In addition to this dual role as a research aid, summarized information is vital in day-to-day workplace transactions.

On the job, you have to write concisely about your work. You might report on meetings or conferences, describe your progress on a project, or propose a money-saving idea. A routine assignment for many new employees is to provide superiors (decision makers) with summaries of the latest developments in their field.

Given today's pace and volume of information, summaries are more vital than ever. Some reports and proposals can be hundreds of pages long. Those who must act on this information need to rapidly identify what is most important in a document. From a good summary, busy readers can get enough information to decide whether they should read the entire document, parts of it, or none of it.

Whether you summarize someone else's document or your own, your job is to communicate the *essential message* accurately and in the fewest words. The essential message in any well-written document is easy enough to identify, as in the following passage:

The original passage

> The lack of technical knowledge among owners of television sets leads to their suspicion about the honesty of television repair technicians. Although television owners might be fairly knowledgeable about most repairs made to their automobiles, they rarely understand the nature and extent of specialized electronic repairs. For instance, the function and importance of an automatic transmission in an automobile are generally well known; however, the average television owner knows nothing about the flyback transformer in a television set. The repair charge for a flyback transformer failure is roughly $150—a large amount to a consumer who lacks even a simple understanding of what the repairs will accomplish. In contrast, a $450 repair charge for the transmission on the family car, though distressing, is more readily understood and accepted.

Three significant ideas comprise the essential message: (1) television owners lack technical knowledge and are suspicious of repair technicians; (2) an owner usually understands even the most expensive automobile repairs; and (3) owners do not understand or accept expenses for television repairs. A possible summary might read like this:

A summarized version

> Because television owners lack technical knowledge about their sets, they are often suspicious of repair technicians. Although consumers may understand expensive automobile repairs, they rarely understand or accept repair and parts expenses for their television sets.

This summary is almost 30 percent of the original length because the original itself is short. With a longer original, a summary might be 5 percent or less. But length is less important than informative value: an effective summary gives readers just what they need and no more. For letters, memos, or other short documents that can be read quickly, the only summary needed is usually an *opening thesis* or *topic sentence* that previews the contents.

Summaries are vital to some key executives who do not have time to read in detail everything that crosses their desks. For example, some executives ask that all significant world news for the last twenty-four hours be condensed into one page and placed on their desks, first thing each morning. Others employ writers who summarize articles from relevant and reputable magazines.

Elements of a Summary

All effective summaries display the following elements.

- *The essential message*: The essential message is the significant material from the original: controlling ideas (thesis and topic sentences); major findings; important names, dates, statistics, and measurements; and conclusions or recommendations. Significant material does not include background; the author's personal comments or conjectures; introductions; long explanations, examples, or definitions; visuals; or data of questionable accuracy.

- *Non-technical style*: More people generally read the summary than any other part of a document. Write at the lowest level of technicality. Translate technical data into plain English. "The patient's serum glucose measured 240 mg%" can be translated: "The patient's blood sugar remained critically high." Of course, if you know all your readers are experts, you don't need to simplify.

- *Independent meaning*: In meaning as well as style, your summary should stand alone as a self-contained message. Readers should have to read the original only for more detail—not to make sense of the basic ideas.

- *No personal assessment*: Avoid personal comments ("This interesting report" or "The author is correct in assuming"). Add nothing to the original except for a brief clarifying definition, if needed.

- *Conciseness*: Conciseness is vital, but never at the expense of clarity and accuracy. Make the summary short enough to be economical, but long enough to be clear and comprehensive.

Critical Thinking in the Summary Process

Follow these guidelines for summarizing your own writing or another's.

1. *Read the entire original.* When summarizing another's work, get a complete picture before writing a word.
2. *Reread and underline.* Reread the original, underlining essential material. Focus on the thesis and topic sentences.
3. *Edit the underlined information.* Reread the underlined material and cross out whatever does not advance the meaning.
4. *Rewrite in your own words.* Include all essential material in the first draft, even if it's too long; you can trim later.
5. *Edit your own version.* When you have everything readers need, edit for conciseness.

   a. Cross out all needless words without harming clarity or grammar. Use complete sentences.

   > The summer internship in journalism gives the ~~journalism~~ student ~~first-hand~~ experience ~~at what goes~~ on ~~within~~ a ~~real~~ newspaper.

   b. Cross out needless prefaces such as "The writer argues" or "Also discussed is."

   c. Use numerals for numbers, except to begin a sentence.

   d. Combine related ideas in order to emphasize relationships (pages 255–257).

6. *Check your version against the original.* Verify that you have preserved the essential message and added no comments.
7. *Rewrite your edited version.* Add transitional expressions to reinforce the connection between related ideas.
8. *Document your source.* If summarizing another's work, cite the source immediately below the summary, and place directly quoted statements within quotation marks. (See Chapter 8 for documentation formats.)

Although the summary is written last by the writer, it is read *first* by the reader. Take time to do a good job.

A Sample Situation

Imagine that you work in the information office of your province's Ministry of the Environment. In a coming election, citizens will vote on a referendum proposal for constructing municipal trash incinerators. Referendum supporters argue that incinerators would help solve the growing problem of waste disposal in highly populated parts of the province. Opponents argue that incinerators cause air pollution.

To clarify the issues for voters, the Ministry is preparing a newsletter to be mailed to each registered voter. You have been assigned the task of researching the recent data and summarizing it. Here is one of the articles marked and then summarized to show the critical thinking process outlined above.

INCINERATING TRASH: A HOT ISSUE GETTING HOTTER

Combine as orienting sentence (controlling idea)

<u>Alarmed by</u> the tendency of <u>landfills</u> to <u>contaminate the environment</u>, both public officials and citizens are vocally seeking <u>alternatives</u>. The <u>most commonly discussed</u> alternative is something called a *<u>resource recovery facility</u>*. <u>Nearly 40 Canadian cities have built such in the last 15 years</u>, and <u>another 50</u> or so are in various stages of <u>planning</u>.

Include definition

These recovery facilities are a new form of an old technology. <u>Basically</u>, they're <u>incinerators</u>. But, unlike the incinerators of old, they don't just burn waste. <u>They also recover energy</u>. The energy is <u>sold</u> as steam to an industrial customer, or it is converted to electricity and sold to the local utility. (A few facilities, but not many, also recover metals or other materials before using the waste as fuel.)

Include major fact

<u>A ton of trash</u> possesses the <u>energy</u> content of <u>a barrel and a half of oil</u>. This is not a trivial amount. Canada discards <u>50 million tons</u> of <u>municipal refuse</u> a

Include major statistic

year. If all of it were <u>converted to energy</u>, we <u>could replace</u> the equivalent of <u>12 percent of our oil imports</u>.

Include major fact

At the local level, <u>selling energy</u> or materials not only replaces non-renewable resources; but it also provides a source of income that <u>partly offsets</u> the <u>cost of operating</u> the facility.

Include major fact

The <u>new facilities are</u>, on average, <u>much cleaner than the</u> municipal incinerators of <u>old</u>. Many have two-stage combustion units, in which the second-stage

Delete explanation

burns exhaust gases at high temperature, converting many potential organic pollutants to less harmful emissions such as carbon dioxide. Some, especially the larger and newer facilities, also come equipped with the latest in pollution control devices.

Delete questionable point

The environmental community is uneasy with this new technology. Environmentalists have argued for many years that the best method of handling municipal trash is to recycle it—i.e., to separate the glass, metal, paper, and other materials and use them again, either without reprocessing or as raw materials in producing new products. The thought of the potential resources in municipal solid waste simply being burned, even with energy recovery, has made many environmentalists opponents of resource recovery.

Include key finding and explanation

More recently, opponents have found a stronger reason to oppose <u>burning waste</u>: *<u>dioxin in the plants' emissions</u>*. The <u>amounts</u> present are <u>extremely small</u>, measured in trillionths of a gram per cubic metre of air. <u>But dioxin can be deadly, at least to animals, at very low levels</u>.

What is Dioxin?

Include definition

<u>Dioxin</u> is a <u>generic term for any of 75 chemical compounds</u>, the technical name for which is poly-chlorinated dibenzo-p-dioxins (PCDDs). A related group of 135

Delete technical details

chemicals, the PCDFs or furans, are often found in association with PCDDs.

Include major fact	The most infamous of these substances, 2,3,7,8-TCDD, is often <u>referred to as the "most toxic chemical known."</u> This judgment is <u>based on animal test data</u>. In laboratory tests, 2,3,7,8-TCDD is lethal to guinea pigs at a concentration of *500 parts per trillion*. A part per trillion is roughly equivalent to the thickness of a human hair compared to the distance across the Canada.
Include major point	<u>The effects on humans are less certain</u>, for many reasons: it is difficult to measure the amounts to which humans have been exposed; difficult to isolate the effects of dioxin from the effects of other toxic substances on the same population; and the latency period for many potential effects, such as cancer, may be as long as 20 to 30 years.
Delete long explanation	
Include continuation of major point	<u>Nevertheless</u>, because of the <u>extreme effects</u> of this substance <u>on animals</u>, known releases of dioxin have generated <u>considerable public alarm</u>. One of the most publicized releases occurred at Seveso, Italy, in July 1976, where a pharmaceutical plant explosion resulted in the contamination of at least 700 acres of fields and affected more than 5,000 people. Dioxin was found in the soil in concentrations of 20 to 55 parts per billion.
Delete long example	
	The immediate effects on humans were nausea, headaches, dizziness, diarrhea, and an acute skin condition called chloracne, which causes burn-like sores. The effects on animals were more severe: birds, rabbits, mice, chickens, and cats died by the hundreds, within days of the explosion. In response to the explosion, the Italian provincial authorities evacuated 730 people from the zone nearest the plant, and sealed off an area containing another 5,000 people from contact with non-residents.
Delete long example	In North America, perhaps the best known dioxin contamination incident occurred at Times Beach, Missouri, where used oil, contaminated with dioxin, was sprayed on roads as a dust suppressant. Soil samples showed dioxin at levels exceeding 100 parts per billion. While no human health effects were documented at Times Beach, a flood in December 1982 led to widespread dispersal of the contamination, as a result of which the entire town was condemned, the population evacuated, and over $30 million of the U.S.'s Superfund money used to purchase the condemned property.
Include the most striking and familiar example	<u>Dioxin was among the substances</u> of concern <u>at Love Canal</u>. And it was <u>the major contaminant</u> in the chemical defoliant, <u>Agent Orange</u>, the subject of a <u>lawsuit by 15,000 Vietnam veterans</u> and dependents and an out-of-court settlement of those complaints valued at $180 million.
Include key findings	<u>As early as 1978, trace amounts of dioxin were found in the routine emissions of a municipal incinerator. Virtually every incinerator tested since</u> that date <u>has shown traces of dioxin.</u>

The Meaning of it All

Include major fact	<u>At the request of the U.S. Congress, the Environmental Protection Agency began in 1994</u> a major research effort on dioxin, the <u>National Dioxin Study</u>. The study is intended to provide a context in which to place mounting concerns about dioxin. Research for the study was organized into seven "tiers," each tier including a <u>group of sites at which dioxin contamination may be present</u>.

Condense list

- Tier 1, <u>production sites,</u> includes the 10 sites at which 2,4,5-TCP, a pesticide known to have been contaminated by dioxin, was produced, <u>and</u> additional <u>sites</u> where <u>waste materials</u> from its production were <u>disposed.</u>
- Tier 2, <u>precursor sites,</u> includes 9 sites where 2,4,5-TCP was used as a precursor <u>to make other chemical products,</u> and related waste disposal sites. The chemical products included the herbicides 2,4,5-T and silvex, and hexachlorophene, a disinfectant that was widely used in soaps and deodorants, but was banned from non-prescription uses by the U.S. Food and Drug Administration in 1981.
- Tier 3 includes 60 to 70 <u>sites at which</u> 2,4,5-TCP and its derivatives were <u>formulated into herbicide products,</u> and associated waste disposal sites.
- Tier 4 includes a wide range of <u>combustion sources, including internal combustion engines, wood stoves, fireplaces, forest fires, oil burners and other sources</u> burning waste oil, and many others.
- Tier 5 includes 20 to 30 of the thousands of <u>sites at which dioxin-contaminated pesticides have been used,</u> for example, power line rights-of-way, forests, and rice and sugar cane fields.
- Tier 6 includes about 20 of the <u>chemical and pesticide production facilities</u> where improper quality control may have led to the <u>accidental production of dioxin.</u>
- Tier 7 includes samples from sites where the Agency least expected to find dioxin, to determine whether there are background levels of dioxin in the environment. <u>Soil samples</u> have been taken at 500 <u>randomly selected locations</u> across the country—200 in rural areas, 300 in urban areas—and fish have been <u>sampled</u> from over 400 locations.

Include key finding

While the study is not yet complete, data from a variety of sources have already produced disturbing—yet, perhaps, in an odd way, reassuring—<u>results. Dioxin in trace amounts appears to be widely present in the environment, even in remote locations where industrial activity and waste combustion are unlikely to be the source.</u>

Delete long example

Environment Canada, the Canadian EPA, also has an extensive dioxin testing program under way. One of the more startling findings of its research, conducted at a resource recovery facility on picturesque Prince Edward Island, is that the garbage delivered to the plant contained more dioxin than the plant's emissions. The source of the dioxin in this case is not known, though it could include pesticide residues or other products contaminated with dioxin during manufacturing processes.

Delete speculation

Include key conclusion

In short, <u>dioxin</u> is <u>not just</u> a problem <u>created by burning municipal waste.</u> It is <u>not clear</u> at this time <u>whether municipal waste combustion is even the major source of dioxin in the environment.</u>

Include conclusion

Ultimately, the dioxin problem is <u>like other toxic substance issues. We know less than we need to know to thoroughly evaluate the risk.</u> The more we find out, the more complex the issues tend to become. There is <u>no risk-free solution, since all</u> the potential <u>disposal methods may</u> result in some <u>release</u> of <u>toxic substances</u> to the environment. Yet those who counsel delay, to allow the collection of more data, are met with the suspicion that their real agenda is to prevent action entirely.

Delete personal comment

*Include
recommendations*

What we do know at present <u>does not seem</u> to suggest <u>that we should stop planning</u> to build <u>resource recovery facilities</u>. What it does suggest is that we <u>proceed cautiously, inform the public</u> of both what is known and what is unknown, <u>install pollution controls</u> if the plants' uncontrolled emissions are significant or if the exposed population wants added protection, and <u>hope that continued examination</u> of all the sources and effects of dioxin <u>will eventually produce a consensus</u>.

Adapted from James E. McCarthy, *Congressional Research Service Review* Apr. 1986: 19–21.

Assume that in two early drafts of your summary, you rewrote and edited; for coherence and emphasis, you inserted transitions and combined related ideas. Here is your final draft.

INCINERATING TRASH: A HOT ISSUE GETTING HOTTER (A Summary)

Because landfills often contaminate the environment, trash incinerators (resource recovery facilities) are becoming a popular alternative. Nearly 40 are operating in Canadian cities, and 50 more are planned. Besides their relatively clean burning of waste, these incinerators recover energy, which can be sold to offset operating costs. One ton of trash has roughly the energy content of 1.5 barrels of oil. Converting all Canadian refuse to energy could reduce oil imports by 12 percent.

However, incinerator emissions contain very small amounts of dioxin (a generic name for any of 75 related chemicals). Even low dioxin levels can be deadly to animals. In fact, animal tests have helped label one dioxin substance "the most toxic chemical known." Although effects on human beings are less certain, news of dioxin in the environment creates public alarm, as evidenced at Love Canal and by the successful Agent Orange lawsuit by 15,000 Vietnam veterans. Almost every municipal incinerator tested since 1978 has shown traces of dioxin.

At the U.S. Congress' request, the Environmental Protection Agency in 1994 began the National Dioxin Study. Sites included herbicide and pesticide production and waste-disposal facilities, combustion sources such as woodstoves and forest fires, areas of dioxin-contaminated pesticide use such as rice and sugarcane fields, and random soil and fish samples nationwide. Findings indicate that trace amounts of dioxin are widely present in the environment, even in areas remote from industry and waste combustion. Waste incineration is by no means the only source of environmental dioxin—and may not even be the major source.

At this stage, we know too little to evaluate the risk. No risk-free waste-disposal solution exists. But the evidence so far does not suggest that we stop planning incinerators. We should, however, move cautiously, fully informing the public, installing pollution controls as needed, and searching for a better solution.

Adapted from James E. McCarthy, *Congressional Research Service Review* Apr. 1986: 19–21.

The version above is trimmed, tightened, and edited: word count is reduced to roughly 20 percent of the original. A summary this long serves well in many situations, but other audiences might want a briefer and more compressed summary—say, 10 to 15 percent of the original:

A More Compressed Summary

Because landfills often contaminate the environment, trash incinerators (resource recovery facilities) are becoming a popular alternative across Canada. Besides their relatively clean burning of waste, these incinerators recover energy, which can be sold to offset operating costs.

However, incinerator emissions contain very small amounts of dioxin, a chemical proven so deadly to animals, even at low levels, that it has been labelled the most toxic chemical known. Although its effects on human beings are less certain, news of dioxin in the environment creates public alarm. Almost every municipal incinerator tested since 1978 has shown traces of dioxin.

Findings of a U.S. study begun in 1994 suggest that trace amounts of dioxin are widely present in the environment, even in areas remote from industry and waste combustion. The dioxin source is by no means only waste incineration.

We lack risk-free disposal solutions and know too little to evaluate risks. But nothing so far suggests that we should stop planning incinerators. We should, however, move cautiously, fully informing the public, installing pollution controls as needed, and continuing to search for better solutions.

Notice that the essential message is still intact; related ideas are again combined and fewer supporting details are included. Clearly, length is adjustable according to your audience and purpose.

Forms of Summarized Information

In preparing a report, proposal, or other document, you might summarize others' material as part of your presentation. But you will often summarize your own material as well. For instance, if your document extends to several pages, it might include three forms of summary, in different locations, with different levels of detail: *closing summary, informative abstract,* or *descriptive abstract.*[1] Figure 9.1 depicts these forms.

---

1. Adapted from Vaughan. Although we take liberties with his classification, Vaughan's insightful article helped clarify our thinking about the overlapping terminology that perennially seems to confound discussions of these distinctions.

Forms of Summarized Information

Closing Summary
- comes in Conclusion
- reviews main findings in preceding sections

Informative Abstract (called "Summary")
- condenses the full report; gives all of the important information, conclusions, and recommendations
- precedes the full report

Descriptive Abstract (called "Abstract")
- appears on title page or separate from report
- talks *about* the report's purpose, contents, and information sources

Figure 9.1   Summarized Information Assumes Various Forms

Closing Summary

A *closing summary* refers to summarized information at the beginning of a Conclusion section or at the end of a report's central Body sections. It helps readers review and remember the preceding major findings. This look back at the "big picture" helps readers appreciate the conclusions and recommendations that follow.

Informative Abstract ("Summary")

Many report readers appreciate condensed versions of reports. Some of these readers like to see a capsule version of a report before reading the complete document; others simply want to know basically what a report says without having to read the full document.

In order to meet reader needs, the *informative abstract* appears just after the title page. This summary tells the reader essentially what the full version says: It identifies the need or issue that has prompted the report; it describes the report's analytical method; it reviews the main facts and findings; and it condenses the report's conclusions and recommendations.

Actually, the term "Informative Abstract" is not used much these days. You are more likely to encounter the term "Summary." The heading, "Executive Summary," is used for material summarized for managers who may not understand all the technical jargon a report might contain. By contrast, a "Technical Summary" is written for readers at the same technical level as the author of the report. It's possible that you may need two or three levels of summary for report readers who have different levels of technical expertise.

See Chapter 20 for more discussion of the Summary section in a report.

Descriptive Abstract ("Abstract")

A *descriptive abstract* talks about a report; it doesn't give the report's main points. Such an abstract helps potential readers decide whether to read the report. Thus, a descriptive abstract conveys only the nature and extent of a document. It presents the broadest view and offers no major facts from the original. It indicates whether conclusions and recommendations are included, but doesn't list them.

Descriptive abstracts usually appear in special publications or in electronic databases, both of which name and briefly describe hundreds of reports. One such publication is the widely used *Fisheries Abstracts*. However, some reports place a one-to-three sentence abstract on the report's title page. In all these placements, the term "Abstract" will signal a brief description, not all of the report's highlights.

Revision Checklist for Summaries

Use this checklist to refine your summaries.

CONTENT

❑ Does the summary contain only the essential message?

❑ Does the summary make sense as an independent piece?

❑ Is the summary accurate when checked against the original?

❑ Is the summary free of any additions to the original?

❑ Is the summary free of needless details?

❑ Is the summary economical yet clear and comprehensive?

❑ Is the source documented?

❑ Does the descriptive abstract tell what the original is about?

ORGANIZATION

❑ Is the summary coherent?

❑ Are there enough transitions to reveal the line of thought?

STYLE

❑ Is the summary's level of technicality appropriate for its audience?

❑ Is the summary free of needless words?

❑ Are all sentences clear, concise, and fluent?

❑ Is the summary written in correct English?

✔ EXERCISES

1. Read each of these two paragraphs, and then list the significant ideas comprising each essential message. Write a summary of each paragraph.

In recent years, ski-binding manufacturers, in line with consumer demand, have redesigned their bindings several times in an effort to achieve a non-compromising synthesis between performance and safety. Such a synthesis depends on what appear to be divergent goals. Performance, in essence, is a function of the binding's ability to hold the boot firmly to the ski, thus enabling the skier to change rapidly the position of his or her skis without being hampered by a loose or wobbling connection. Safety, on the other hand, is a function of the binding's ability both to release the boot when the skier falls, and to retain the boot when subjected to the normal shocks of skiing. If achieved, this synthesis of performance and safety will greatly increase skiing pleasure while decreasing accidents.

Contrary to public belief, sewage-treatment plants do not fully purify sewage. The product that leaves the plant to be dumped into the leaching (sievelike drainage) fields is secondary sewage containing toxic contaminants such as phosphates, nitrates, chloride, and heavy metals. As the secondary sewage filters into the ground, this conglomeration is carried along. Under the leaching area develops a contaminated mound through which groundwater flows, spreading the waste products over great distances. If this leachate reaches the outer limits of a well's drawing radius, the water supply becomes polluted. And because all water flows essentially toward the sea, more pollution is added to the coastal regions by this secondary sewage.

2. Attend a campus lecture on a topic of interest and take notes on the significant points. Write a summary of the lecture's essential message.

3. Find an article about your major field or area of interest and write both an informative abstract and a descriptive abstract of the article.

4. Select a long paper that you have written for one of your courses; write an informative abstract and a descriptive abstract of the paper.

5. After reading the article in Figure 9.2, on page 216, prepare a summary, using the steps under "Critical Thinking in the Summary Process" (page 207) as a guide. Identify a specific audience and use for your material.

A possible scenario: You are assistant communications manager for a leading software development company. Part of your job involves publishing a monthly newsletter for employees. After finding this article, you decide to summarize it for the upcoming issue. (Aspirin is a popular item in this company, given the headaches, stiff necks, and other medical problems that often result from prolonged computer work.) You have 350–375 words of newsletter space to fill. Consider carefully what this audience needs and doesn't need. In this situation, what information is most important?

Bring your abstracts to class and exchange them with a colleague's for editing according to the revision checklist. Revise your edited copies before submitting them to your instructor.

✔ COLLABORATIVE PROJECT

Organize into small groups and choose a topic for discussion: an employment problem, a campus problem, plans for an event, suggestions for energy conservation, or the like. (A possible topic: Should employers have the right to require lie detector tests, drug tests, or AIDS tests for their employees?) Discuss the topic for one class period, taking notes on significant points and conclusions. Afterward, organize and edit your notes in line with the directions for writing summaries. Next, write a summary of the group discussion in no more than 200 words. Finally, as a group, compare your individual summaries for accuracy, emphasis, conciseness, and clarity.

ASPIRIN
A New Look at an Old Drug
by Ken Flieger

Canadians consume millions of aspirin tablets a year. The *Physician's Desk Reference* lists more than 50 over-the-counter drugs in which aspirin is the principal active ingredient. Yet, despite aspirin's having been in routine use for nearly a century, both scientific journals and the popular media are full of reports and speculation about new uses for this old remedy.

Almost a century after its development aspirin is the focus of extensive laboratory research and some of the largest clinical trials ever carried out in conditions ranging from cardiovascular disease and cancer to migraine headache and high blood pressure in pregnancy.

How Does It Work?

The mushrooming interest in aspirin has come about largely because of advances in understanding how it works. What is it about this drug that, at small doses, interferes with blood clotting, at somewhat higher doses reduces fever and eases minor aches and pains, and at comparatively large doses combats pain and inflammation in rheumatoid arthritis and several other related diseases?

The answer is not yet fully known, but most authorities agree that aspirin achieves some of its effects by inhibiting the production of prostaglandins. Prostaglandins are hormone-like substances that influence the elasticity of blood vessels, control uterine contractions, direct the functioning of blood platelets that help stop bleeding, and regulate numerous other activities in the body.

In the 1970s, a British pharmacologist, John Vane, Ph.D., noted that many forms of tissue injury were followed by the release of prostaglandins. In laboratory studies, he found that two groups of prostaglandins caused redness and fever, common signs of inflammation. Vane and his co-workers also showed that by blocking the synthesis of prostaglandins, aspirin prevented blood platelets from aggregating, one of the initial steps in the formation of blood clots.

This explanation of how aspirin and other non-steroidal anti-inflammatory drugs (NSAIDs) produce their intriguing array of effects prompted laboratory and clinical scientists to form and test new ideas about aspirin's possible value in treating or preventing conditions in which prostaglandins play a role. Interest quickly focused on learning whether aspirin might prevent the blood clots responsible for heart attacks.

A heart attack or myocardial infarction (MI) results from the blockage of blood flow not *through* the heart, but *to* the heart muscle. Without an adequate blood supply, the affected area of muscle dies and the heart's pumping action is either impaired or stopped altogether.

The most common sequence of events leading to an MI begins with the gradual build-up of plaque (atherosclerosis) in the coronary arteries. Circulation through these narrowed arteries is restricted, often causing the chest pain known as angina pectoris.

An acute heart attack is believed to happen when a tear in plaque inside a narrowed coronary artery causes platelets to aggregate, forming a clot that blocks the flow of blood. Approximately 100,000 Canadians suffer heart attacks each year and about 60% of them die. Those who survive a first heart attack are at greatly increased risk of having another.

Could Aspirin Help?

To learn whether aspirin could be helpful in preventing or treating cardiovascular disease, scientists have carried out numerous large randomized controlled clinical trials. In these studies, similar groups of hundreds or thousands of people are randomly assigned to receive either aspirin or a placebo, an inactive, look-alike tablet. The participants—and in double-blind trials the investigators, as well—do not know who is taking aspirin and who is swallowing a placebo.

Over the last two decades, aspirin studies have been conducted in three kinds of individuals: persons with a history of coronary artery or cerebral vascular disease; patients in the immediate, acute phases of a heart attack; and healthy persons with no indication of current or previous cardiovascular illness.

The results of studies of people with a history of coronary artery disease and those in the immediate phases of a heart attack have proven to be of tremendous importance in the prevention and treatment of cardiovascular disease. The studies showed that aspirin substantially reduces the risk of death and/or non-fatal heart attacks in patients with a previous MI or unstable angina pectoris, which often occurs before a heart attack.

On the basis of such studies, these uses for aspirin (unstable angina, acute MI, and survivors of an MI) are described in the professional labelling of aspirin products and in information provided to physicians and other

Figure 9.2   An Article to be Summarized
Adapted from *FDA Consumer* Jan./Feb. 1994: 19–21.

(Continued)

health professionals. Aspirin labelling intended for the general public does not discuss its use in arthritis or cardiovascular disease because treatment of these serious conditions—even with a common over-the-counter drug—has to be medically supervised. The consumer labelling contains a general warning about excessive or inappropriate use of aspirin, and specifically warns against using aspirin to treat children and teenagers who have chickenpox or the flu because of the risk of Reye syndrome, a rare but sometimes fatal condition.

Aspirin for Healthy People?

Once aspirin's benefits for patients with cardiovascular disease were established, scientists sought to learn whether regular aspirin use would prevent a first heart attack in healthy individuals. The findings regarding that critical question have thus far been equivocal. The major American study designed to find out if aspirin can prevent cardiovascular deaths in healthy individuals was a randomized, placebo-controlled trial involving just over 22,000 male physicians between 40 and 84 with no prior history of heart disease. Half took one 325-milligram aspirin tablet every other day, and half took a placebo.

The trial was halted early, after about four-and-a-half years, and the findings quickly made public in 1988 when investigators found that the group taking aspirin had a substantial reduction in the rate of fatal and non-fatal heart attacks compared with the placebo group. There was, however, no significant difference between the aspirin and placebo groups in number of strokes (aspirin-treated patients did slightly worse) or in overall deaths from cardiovascular disease.

A similar study in British male physicians with no previous heart disease found no significant effect nor even a favourable trend for aspirin on cardiovascular disease rates. The British study of 5,100 physicians, while considerably smaller than the American study, reported three-quarters as, many vascular "events." FDA scientists believe the results of the two studies are inconsuitable.

The U.S. Preventive Services Task Force, a panel of medical-scientific authorities in health promotion and disease prevention, is one of many groups looking at new information on the role of aspirin in cardiovascular disease. In its *Guide to Clinical Preventive Services*, issued in 1989, the task force recommended that low-dose aspirin therapy "should be considered for men aged 40 and over who are at significantly increased risk for myocardial infarction and who lack contraindications" to aspirin use. A revised *Guide*, published in the fall of 1994, included a slightly revised recommendation

concerning aspirin and cardiovascular disease but no major change in advice to physicians about aspirin's possible role in preventing heart attacks.

Better understanding of aspirin's myriad effects in the body has led to clinical trials and other studies to assess a variety of possible uses: preventing the severity of migraine headaches, improving circulation to the gums thereby arresting periodontal disease, preventing certain types of cataracts, lowering the risk of recurrence of colorectal cancer, and controlling the dangerously high blood pressure (called preeclampsia) that occurs in 5 to 15 percent of pregnancies.

None of these uses for aspirin has been shown conclusively to be safe and effective, and there is concern that people may be misusing aspirin on the basis of unproven notions about its effectiveness. In October 1993, the FDA proposed a new labelling statement for aspirin products advising consumers to consult a doctor before taking aspirin for new and long-term uses. The proposed statement would read: "IMPORTANT: See your doctor before taking this product for your heart or for other new uses of aspirin because serious side effects could occur with self-treatment."

The Other Side of the Coin

While examining new possibilities for aspirin in disease treatment and prevention, scientists do not lose sight of the fact that even at low doses aspirin is not harm-less. A small subset of the population is hypersensitive to aspirin and cannot tolerate even small amounts of the drug. Gastrointestinal distress—nausea, heartburn, pain—is a well-recognized adverse effect and is related to dosage. Persons being treated for rheumatoid arthritis who take large daily doses of aspirin are especially likely to experience gastrointestinal side effects.

Aspirin's antiplatelet activity apparently accounts for hemorrhagic strokes, caused by bleeding into the brain, in a small but significant percentage of persons who use the drug regularly. For the great majority of occasional aspirin users, internal bleeding is not a problem. But aspirin may be unsuitable for people with uncontrolled high blood pressure, liver or kidney disease, peptic ulcer, or other conditions that might increase the risk of cerebral hemorrhage or other internal bleeding.

New understanding of how aspirin works and what it can do leaves no doubt that the drug has a far broader range of uses than imagined [nearly a century ago]. The jury is still out, however, on a number of key questions about the best and safest ways to use aspirin. And until some critical verdicts are handed down, consumers are well-advised to regard aspirin with appropriate caution.

Figure 9.2   An Article to be Summarized

PART III

Structural, Style, and Format Elements

Organizing for Readers

CHAPTER

10

O NE of your biggest writing challenges is to transform your material into manageable form. First, you need to unscramble information to make sense of it for yourself; then you need to shape it for the reader's understanding.

In order to follow your thinking, readers need a message organized in a way that makes sense to *them*. But data rarely materializes or thinking rarely occurs in neat, predictable sequences. You cannot merely report ideas or data in the same random order they occur. Instead you must *shape* this material into an organized unit of meaning. In trying to organize, you will face questions like these:

Typical Questions in Organizing for Readers	
■ What major question am I answering for my reader(s)?	■ What should I emphasize?
■ What secondary questions will help answer the main question?	■ What belongs where?
	■ What do I place first? Why?
■ What relationships and answers do the gathered data suggest?	■ What comes next?
	■ How do I end?

Writers rely on the following strategies for organizing material: topical arrangement, outlining, paragraphing, and sequencing.

Topical Arrangement

Whenever you analyze something, you break it down to discover constituents, connections, similarities, trends, associations, correlations, relationships, and perspectives. You break the topic into sub-topics (that's commonly called *partition*). You also see which things share similarities and should therefore be discussed at the same level in a certain category (that's called *classification*). The following example explains how this can be achieved.

> A CD collection could be divided (partitioned) into categories, to discuss the collection in an orderly way: jazz, rock, blues, country, classical, new age, world music, etc. The rock CDs might further be sub-divided by the decade of the albums' release or by other descriptions—heavy metal, progressive rock, country rock, rock fusion, etc. The heavy metal bands could then be grouped together (classification) to identify the distinctive features of this rock genre.
>
> However, someone might use a different approach to discuss a CD collection. The collection might be grouped according to how various albums have influenced selected current, popular musicians. Why use this topical arrangement instead of the arrangement described in the previous paragraph? Your choice depends on your audience and purpose—see the above list of questions.

The following case study illustrates how authors arrange and develop topics for a report.

> In December 1998, the Canadian Council for Tobacco Control and British Columbia Ministry of Health released a report relating to cigarette additives and cigarette smoke constituents. The report had a persuasive purpose—to discourage smoking by releasing facts about cigarette ingredients and additives, as well as the detailed chemical analysis of the smoke of each brand of cigarette sold in British Columbia.
>
> The information in the report emanated from the tobacco companies themselves, in response to a July 1998 British Columbia government requirement. The writers of the report were faced with two challenges: (1) to arrange the information so that readers could easily make sense of what they read, and (2) to present a progression of facts so that readers could draw the "right" conclusions about cigarette smoke.
>
> The authors started by preparing an Introduction to the report. After the Introduction, they developed the following four main topics:
>
> 1. *background* information about British Columbia's requirements
> 2. *cigarette additives and ingredients* for each brand sold in B.C.
> 3. *analysis of cigarette smoke* for the 11 leading brands
> 4. *"light"* cigarettes' test results
>
> The authors then further developed one of the report's more contentious parts, the light cigarettes' test results, by presenting the following groups of data:
>
> ■ B.C. tests show little difference in substances in light and regular cigarettes
> ■ labels on cigarette packages mislead consumers
> ■ filter vents on cigarettes help "fool" test machines
> ■ machine tests don't simulate real smoking
> ■ using more accurate test methods gives more accurate results
> ■ a majority of smokers are fooled by the "light" label
>
> Then, the authors further developed the first sub-topic, "differences in substances in light and regular cigarettes." They did this in a series of tables that showed tar, nicotine, and carbon monoxide values for each of the 11 corporate brands sold in British Columbia. ■

Table 10.1 shows the full set of relationships among the report's topics, which essentially operate at three levels. These levels are differentiated in Table 10.1 by decreasing levels of capitalization. As you move from left to right through the four main topics, there is a logical development, all leading to the report's culminating point about smokers being "fooled" by the "light cigarette" designation. Further, within the fourth main topic, the six sub-topics are presented equally, but in an order that supports the authors' main point about the problem with so-called "light" cigarettes.

Table 10.1   Relationships Within a Report's Topical Arrangement (based on B.C. Ministry of Health report)

Background	Additives and Ingredients	Smoke Analysis	Impact of "Light" Cigarettes on Smokers
B.C. Regulations Reporting Requirements	Nature of Disclosure	The Test Methods • test conditions • methodology The Test Results • four values for each brand Impact on Health • carbon monoxide • cadmium • benzene The Chemicals • 29 toxic chemicals in cigarettes	Little Difference In Light And Regular Cigarettes • tar values • nicotine values • CO values Misleading Labels Filter Vents Lower Readings Machine vs Real Smoking Better Tests. Better Results Smokers' Beliefs

The report is available on-line at <http://www.cctc.ca/bcreports>

In organizing their documents, writers use partition and classification routinely, in a process we know as *outlining*.

Outlining

With an outline you move from a random listing of items to a deliberate map that will guide readers from point to point. Readers more easily understand and remember material organized in a sequence they find logical. Organize in the sequence in which you expect readers to approach the material.

A Document's Basic Shape

How should you organize the document to make it logical from your audience's point of view? Begin with the basics. Useful writing of any length—a book, chapter, news article, letter, or memo—typically follows this organizing pattern:

■ The *introduction* provides orientation by doing any of these things: explaining the topic's origin and significance and the document's purpose; identifying briefly your intended audience and your information sources; defining specialized terms or general terms that have special meanings in your document; accounting for limitations such as incomplete or questionable data; previewing the major topics to be discussed in the body section.

   Some introductions need to be long and involved; others, short and to the point. Reports too often waste readers' time with needless background information. If you don't know your readers well enough to give them only what they need, use subheadings so that they can choose what they want to read.

- The *body* delivers on the promise implied in your introduction ("Show me!"). Here you present your data, discuss your evidence, lay out your case, or tell readers what to do and how to do it. Body sections come in all different sizes, depending on how much readers need and expect.

    Body sections are titled to reflect their specific purpose: "Description and Function of Parts," for a mechanical description; "Required Steps," for a set of instructions; "Collected Data," for a feasibility analysis; "Operating Instructions," for a user's manual.

- The *conclusion* of a document has assorted purposes: It might evaluate the significance of the report, re-emphasize key points, take a position, predict an outcome, offer a solution, or suggest further study. If the issue is straightforward, the conclusion might be brief and definite. If the issue is complex or controversial, the conclusion might be lengthy and open ended. Whatever the conclusion's specific purpose, readers expect a clear perspective on the whole document.

    Conclusions vary with the document. You might conclude a mechanical description by reviewing the mechanism's major parts and then briefly describing one operating cycle. You might conclude a comparison or feasibility report by offering judgments about the facts you've presented and then recommending a course of action.

Most workplace documents display this basic shape

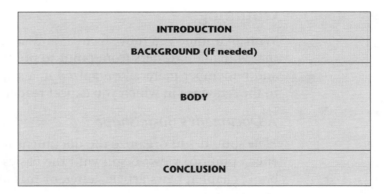

| INTRODUCTION |
| BACKGROUND (if needed) |
| BODY |
| CONCLUSION |

A suitable beginning, middle, and ending are essential, but alter your outline as you see fit. No single form of outline should be followed exactly by any writer. *The organization of any document ultimately is determined by its audience's needs and expectations.* In many cases, specific requirements about a document's organization and style are spelled out in a company's style guide. Structures for specific types of documents are provided in various sections of this text.

The computer is especially useful for rearranging outlines until they reflect the sequence in which you expect readers to approach your message.

The Formal Outline

A simple list usually suffices for organizing short documents. However, long or complex documents call for a systematic, formal outline, to mark divisions and to show how categories relate. Here, for example, is a formal outline for a report examining the health effects of electromagnetic fields:

Children Exposed to EMFs: A Risk Assessment

I. INTRODUCTION
   A. Definition of electromagnetic fields
   B. Background on the health issues
   C. Description of the local power-line configuration
   D. Purpose of this report[1]
   E. Brief description of data sources
   F. Scope of this report

II. DATA SECTION [Body]
   A. Sources of EMF exposure
      1. home and office
         a. kitchen
         b. workshop[2] [etc.]
      2. power lines
      3. natural radiation
      4. risk factors
         a. current intensity
         b. source proximity
         c. duration of exposure
   B. Studies of health effects
      1. population surveys
      2. laboratory measurements
      3. workplace links
   C. Conflicting views of studies
      1. criticism of methodology in population studies
      2. criticism of overgeneralized lab findings
   D. Power industry views
      1. uncertainty about risk
      2. confusion about risk avoidance
   E. Risk-avoidance measures
      1. nationally
      2. locally

III. CONCLUSION
   A. Summary and overall interpretation of findings
   B. Recommendations

---

1. Long reports often begin directly with a statement of purpose. For the intended audience (i.e., generalists) of this report, however, the technical topic first must be defined for the readers' clear understanding of the context.

2. Note that each level of division yields at least two items. If you cannot divide a major item into at least two subordinate items, retain only your major heading.

A formal outline easily converts to a table of contents for the finished report, as shown in Chapter 20. (Because they serve mainly to guide the *writer*, omit minor outline headings, such as a and b [under II.A.1 in our example] from the table of contents or the report itself. Excessive headings make a document seem fragmented.)

In technical documents, the alphanumeric form of notation shown above often is replaced by decimal notation:

Decimal notation in a technical document

2.0 DATA SECTION
   2.1 Sources of EMF Exposure
      2.1.1 home and office
         2.1.1.1 kitchen
         2.1.1.2 workshop [etc.]
      2.1.2 power lines
      2.1.3 natural radiation
      2.1.4 risk factors
         2.1.4.1 current intensity
         2.1.4.2 source proximity
         2.1.4.3 [etc.]

The decimal outline makes it easier to refer readers to specifically numbered sections of the document: ("See 2.1.2"). While both systems achieve the same organizing objective, decimal notation usually is preferred in business, government, and industry.

In some cases, you may want to expand the above *topic outline* into a *sentence outline,* in which each sentence serves as a topic sentence for a paragraph in the report:

A sentence outline

2.0. DATA SECTION
   2.1. Although the several million miles of power lines crisscrossing North America have been the focus of the EMF controversy, potentially harmful waves also are emitted by household wiring, appliances, electric blankets, and computers.
      2.1.1. [etc.]

Sentence outlines are used mainly in collaborative projects in which various team members prepare different sections of a long document.

The Importance of Being Organized

The neat and ordered outline shown earlier represents the *product* of outlining, not the *process*. Beneath any finished outline (or document) lies *planning*. Whether you work alone or as part of a team, planning is an essential element of the writing process. Initially, planning may take the form of general discussions and brainstorming. The ideas generated are often written on a whiteboard or displayed on a computer screen as notes or flowcharts (see "Getting Started," Chapter 3).

The second stage of planning involves *organizing* the ideas into specific topics. Ideas may be discarded because they are not within the scope of the project; other ideas may be generated as the topics are being identified. When you know the main topics you need to cover for your project, you are ready to put them into an outline. If you have used a computer during your planning and organizing, you already have a draft outline. The next step is to rearrange your outline so that it flows logically (has a sequence). Various types of sequencing are covered later in this chapter.

Two rules of effective and efficient writing are:

1. NEVER start writing until you have *thoroughly* planned the topics to be included in your document and created an organized, logical outline.
2. When you start writing, follow your outline precisely; don't start planning again!

Outlining and Reorganizing on a Computer

Most word processing programs enable you to work on your document and your outline simultaneously. An "outline view" of the document helps you to see relationships among ideas at various levels, to create new headings, to add text beneath headings, and to move headings and their subtext (Figure 10.2). You also can *collapse* the outline view to display the headings only.

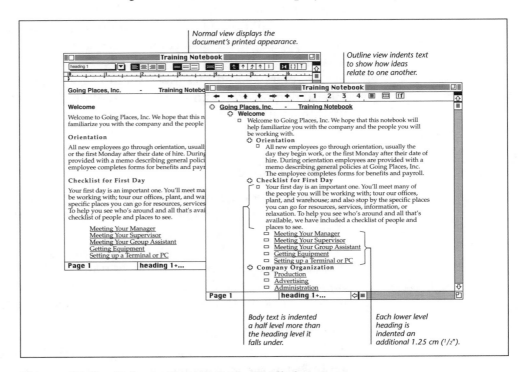

Figure 10.2   Using a Computer's Outlining Feature
Adapted from *Microsoft Word User's Guide, Macintosh version 5.0,* 1992: 502. Reprinted by permission of Microsoft Corporation.

Switch between "normal view" (to compose your text) and "outline view" (to examine the arrangement of material). You can add or delete headings or text and reorganize whole sections of your document. (*Microsoft Word* 504–05).

As a visual alternative to traditional outlining, many computer graphics programs enable you to display prose outlines as tree charts.

Organizing for Cross-cultural Audiences

Different cultures often have different expectations as to how information should be organized. A document considered well organized by one culture may confuse or offend another. For instance, a paragraph in English typically begins with a main idea directly expressed as a topic or orienting sentence followed by specific support; any digression from this main idea is considered harmful to the paragraph's *unity*. Some cultures, however, consider digression a sign of intelligence or politeness. To native readers of English, the long introductions and digressions in certain Spanish or Russian documents might seem tedious and confusing, but a Spanish or Russian reader might view the more direct organization of English as overly abrupt and simplistic (Leki 151).

Expectations can differ even among same-language cultures. British correspondence, for instance, typically expresses the bad news directly up front, instead of the indirect approach preferred in North America. A bad-news letter or memo appropriate for North American readers could be considered evasive by British readers (Scott and Green 19).

Despite all our electronic communication tools, connecting with readers—especially in a global context—requires, above all, human sensitivity and awareness of audience.

Chapters 19 and 21 show structures for long and short reports. Chapter 19 also demonstrates how three levels of outlines (planning outlines, detailed working outlines, and paragraph outlines) can be used to efficiently write a complex document.

Paragraphing

Readers look for orientation, for shapes they can recognize. Beyond its larger shape (introduction, body, conclusion), a document depends on the smaller shapes of each paragraph.

Although paragraphs can have various structures and purposes (paragraphs of introduction, conclusion, or transition), our focus here is on s*tandard support paragraphs*. While part of the document's larger design, each of these middle blocks of thought usually can stand alone in meaning and emphasis.

The Standard Paragraph

All the sentences in a standard paragraph relate to the main point, which is expressed as the *topic sentence:*

Topic sentences

> Computer literacy has become a requirement for all "educated" people.
>
> A video display terminal can endanger the operator's health.
>
> Chemical pesticides and herbicides are both ineffective and hazardous.

Each topic sentence introduces an idea, judgment, or opinion. But in order to grasp the writer's exact meaning, readers need explanation. Consider the third statement:

> Chemical pesticides and herbicides are both ineffective and hazardous.

Imagine you are a researcher for the *Epson Electric Light Company* and have been asked to determine whether the company should (1) begin spraying pesticides and herbicides under its power lines, or (2) continue with its manual (and non-polluting) ways of minimizing foliage and insect damage to lines and poles. If you simply responded with the preceding assertion, your employer would have questions:

- *Why, exactly, are these methods ineffective and hazardous?*
- *What are the problems?*
- *Can you explain?*

To answer these questions and to support your assertion, you need a fully developed paragraph:

Intro. (topic sent.)
Body (2–6)

Conclusion (7–8)

> [1]**Chemical pesticides and herbicides are both ineffective and hazardous.** [2]Because none of these chemicals has permanent effects, pest populations invariably recover and need to be resprayed. [3]Repeated applications cause pests to develop immunity to the chemicals. [4]Furthermore, most of these products attack species other than the intended pest, killing off its natural predators, thus actually increasing the pest population. [5]Above all, chemical residues survive in the environment (and living tissue) for years, often carried hundreds of miles by wind and water. [6]This toxic legacy includes such biological effects as birth deformities, reproductive failures, brain damage, and cancer. [7]Although intended to control pest populations, these chemicals ironically threaten to make the human population their ultimate victims. [8]We therefore recommend continuing our present control methods.

Most standard paragraphs in technical writing have an introduction-body-conclusion structure. They begin with a clear topic (or orienting) sentence stating a generalization. Details in the body support the generalization.

The Topic Sentence

Readers look to a paragraph's opening sentences for a framework. When they don't know exactly what the paragraph is about, readers struggle to grasp your meaning. Read this next paragraph once only, and then try answering the questions that follow.

A paragraph with its topic sentence omitted

> Besides containing several toxic metals, it percolates through the soil, leaching out naturally present metals. Pollutants such as mercury invade surface water, accumulating in fish tissues. Any organism eating the fish—or drinking the water—in turn faces the risk of heavy metal poisoning. Moreover, acidified water can release heavy concentrations of lead, copper, and aluminum from metal plumbing, making ordinary tap water hazardous.

Can you identify the paragraph's main idea? Probably not. Without the topic sentence, you have no framework for understanding this information in its larger meaning. And you don't know where to place the emphasis: on polluted fish, on metal poisoning, on tap water?

Now, insert the following opening sentence and reread the paragraph:

The missing topic sentence

> Acid rain indirectly threatens human health.

With this orientation, the exact meaning becomes obvious.

The topic sentence should appear *first* in the paragraph, unless you have a good reason to place it elsewhere. Think of your topic sentence as the one sentence you would keep if you could keep only one (U.S. Air Force Academy 11). In some instances, a paragraph's main idea may require a "topic statement" consisting of two or more sentences, as in this example:

A topic statement can have two or more sentences

> The most common strip-mining methods are open-pit mining, contour mining, and auger mining. The specific method employed will depend on the type of terrain that covers the coal.

The topic sentence or topic statement should immediately tell readers what to expect. Don't write: *Some pesticides are less hazardous and often more effective than others* when you mean: *Organic pesticides are less hazardous and often more effective than their chemical counterparts.* The first topic sentence leads everywhere and nowhere; the second helps the reader focus, tells the reader what to expect from the paragraph. Don't write: *Acid rain poses a danger,* leaving readers to decipher your meaning of *danger.* If you mean that: *Acid rain is killing our lakes and polluting our water supplies,* say so. Uninformative topic sentences keep readers guessing.

Paragraph Unity

A paragraph is unified when all its material belongs there—when every word, phrase, and sentence directly supports the topic sentence.

A unified paragraph

> **Solar power offers an efficient, economical, and safe solution to eastern Canada's energy problems.** To begin with, solar power is highly efficient. Solar collectors installed on fewer than 30 percent of roofs in the East would provide more than 70 percent of the area's heating and air-conditioning needs. Moreover, solar heat collectors are economical, operating for up to twenty years with little or no maintenance. These savings recoup the initial cost of installation in only ten years. Most important, solar power is safe. It can be transformed

into electricity through photovoltaic cells (a type of storage battery) in a noiseless process that produces no air pollution—unlike coal, oil, and wood combustion. In sharp contrast to its nuclear counterpart, solar power produces no toxic waste and poses no catastrophic danger of meltdown. Thus, massive conversion to solar power would ensure abundant energy and a safe, clean environment for future generations.

One way to damage unity in the paragraph above would be to discuss the differences between active and passive solar heating, or manufacturers of solar technology, or the advantages of solar power over wind power. Although these matters do *broadly* relate to the general issue of solar energy, none directly advances the meaning of *efficient, economical,* or *safe.*

Every topic sentence has a key word or phrase that carries the meaning. In the pesticide-herbicide paragraph (page 229), the key words are *ineffective* and *hazardous.* Anything that fails to advance their meaning throws the paragraph—and the reader—off track.

Paragraph Coherence

In a unified paragraph, everything belongs. In a coherent paragraph, everything sticks together: Topic sentence and support form a connected line of thought, like the links in a chain. To convey precise meaning, a paragraph must be unified. To be readable, a paragraph must also be coherent.

Paragraph coherence can be damaged by (1) short, choppy sentences, (2) sentences in the wrong sequence, or (3) insufficient transitions and connectors (Appendix) for linking related ideas. Here is how the solar energy paragraph might become incoherent:

An incoherent paragraph

> Solar power offers an efficient, economical, and safe solution to eastern Canada's energy problems. Unlike nuclear power, solar power produces no toxic waste and poses no danger of meltdown. Solar power is efficient. Solar collectors could be installed on fewer than 30 percent of roofs in the East. These collectors would provide more than 70 percent of the area's heating and air-conditioning needs. Solar power is safe. It can be transformed into electricity. This transformation is made possible by photovoltaic cells (a type of storage battery). Solar heat collectors are economical. The photovoltaic process produces no air pollution.

Here, in contrast, is the original, coherent paragraph with sentences numbered for later discussion and with transitions and connectors shown in boldface. Notice how this version reveals a clear line of thought:

A coherent paragraph

> [1]Solar power offers an efficient, economical, and safe solution to eastern Canada's energy problems. [2]**To begin with**, solar power is highly efficient. [3]Solar collectors installed on fewer than 30 percent of roofs in the East would provide more than 70 percent of the area's heating and air-conditioning needs. [4]**Moreover**, solar heat collectors are economical, operating for up to twenty years with little or no maintenance. [5]**These savings** recoup the initial cost of

installation within only ten years. **⁶Most important**, solar power is safe. **⁷It** can be transformed into electricity through photovoltaic cells (a type of storage battery) in a noiseless process that produces no air pollution—unlike coal, oil, and wood combustion. **⁸In sharp contrast** to its nuclear counterpart, solar power produces no toxic waste and poses no danger of catastrophic meltdown. **⁹Thus**, massive conversion to solar power would ensure abundant energy and a safe, clean environment for future generations.

We easily can trace the sequence of thoughts in this paragraph.

1. The topic sentence establishes a clear direction.
2–3. The first reason is given and then explained.
4–5. The second reason is given and explained.
6–8. The third and major reason is given and explained.
9. The conclusion sums up and reemphasizes the main point.

Within this line of thinking, each sentence follows logically from the one before it. Readers know where they are at any place in the paragraph. To reinforce the logical sequence, related ideas are combined in individual sentences, and transitions and connectors signal clear relationships. The whole paragraph sticks together.

Paragraph Length

Paragraph length depends on the writer's purpose and the reader's capacity for understanding. Actual word count is less important than how thoroughly the paragraph makes your point. Consider these guidelines:

- In writing that carries highly technical information or complex instructions, short paragraphs (perhaps in a vertically displayed list) give readers plenty of breathing space. A clump of short paragraphs, however, can make a document seem choppy and poorly organized.

- In writing that explains concepts, attitudes, or viewpoints, support paragraphs generally run from 100 to 300 words. But long paragraphs can be tiring and hard to follow, especially if important ideas get buried in the middle. On average, report paragraphs should be kept to 100 words, while paragraphs in letters and memos should average about 60 words.

- Long paragraphs can be broken into parts—using bullets, for example—to make the information more accessible to the reader.

- In letters, memos, or news articles, paragraphs of only one or two sentences focus the reader's attention. A short paragraph (even a single-sentence paragraph) can highlight an important idea in any document.

- Avoid long paragraphs at the beginning or end of a document because they can discourage the reader or obscure the emphasis.

Sequencing

Research demonstrates that readers more easily understand and remember material that is organized in a logical sequence (Felker et al. 11). Items in sequence follow some pattern that reveals a certain relationship: cause-and-effect, comparison-contrast, and so on. For instance, a progress report usually follows a *chronological* sequence (events presented in order of occurrence). An argument for a companywide exercise program likely would follow an *emphatic* sequence (benefits presented in order of importance—least to most, or vice versa).

A single paragraph usually follows one particular sequence. A longer document may use one particular sequence or a combination of sequences. Some common sequences are described below.

Spatial Sequence

A spatial sequence begins at one location and ends at another. It is most useful in describing a physical item or a mechanism. Describe the parts in the sequence in which readers would actually view them or in the order in which each part functions: left to right, inside to outside. This description of a hypodermic needle proceeds from the needle's base (hub) to its point:

"What does it look like?"

> A hypodermic needle is a slender, hollow steel instrument used to introduce medication into the body (usually through a vein or muscle). It is a single piece composed of three parts, all considered sterile: the hub, the cannula, and the point. The hub is the lower, larger part of the needle that attaches to the neck-like opening on the syringe barrel. Next is the cannula (stem), the smooth and slender central portion. Last is the point, which consists of a bevelled (slanted) opening, ending in a sharp tip. The diameter of a needle's cannula is indicated by a gauge number; commonly, a 24–25 gauge needle is used for subcutaneous injections. Needle lengths are varied to suit individual needs. Common lengths used for subcutaneous injections are 0.85 cm (⅜"), 1.25 cm (½"), 1.5 cm (⅝"), and 1.85 cm (¾"). Regardless of length and diameter, all needles have the same functional design.

Product and mechanism descriptions almost always have some type of visual to support or amplify the verbal description.

Chronological Sequence

Explanations of how to do something or how something happened generally are arranged according to a strict time sequence: first step, second step, and so on.

"How is it done?"

> Instead of breaking into a jog too quickly and risking injury, take a relaxed and deliberate approach. Before taking a step, spend at least ten minutes stretching and warming up, using any exercises you find comfortable. (After your first week, consult a jogging book for specialized exercises.) When you've completed your

warmup, set a brisk walking pace. Exaggerate the distance between steps, taking long strides and swinging your arms briskly and loosely. After roughly 100 metres at this brisk pace, you should feel ready to jog. Immediately break into a very slow trot: lean your torso forward and let one foot fall in front of the other (one foot barely leaving the ground while the other is on the pavement). Maintain the slowest pace possible, just above a walk. *Do not bolt out like a sprinter!* The biggest mistake is to start fast and injure yourself. While jogging, relax your body. Keep your shoulders straight and your head up, and enjoy the scenery—after all, it is one of the joys of jogging. Keep your arms low and slightly bent at your sides. Move your legs freely from the hips in an action that is easy, not forced. Make your feet perform a heel-to-toe action: land on the heel; rock forward; take off from the toe.

The paragraph explaining how acid rain endangers human health (page 230) is another example of chronological sequence.

Effect-to-Cause Sequence

A sequence that first identifies a problem and then traces its causes is typically found in problem-solving analyses.

"How did this happen?"

Modern whaling techniques have brought the whale population to the threshold of extinction. In the nineteenth century, invention of the steamboat increased hunters' speed and mobility. Shortly afterward, the grenade harpoon was invented so that whales could be killed quickly and easily from the ship's deck. In 1904, a whaling station opened on Georgia Island in South America. This station became the gateway to Antarctic whaling for the nations of the world. In 1924, factory ships were designed that enabled round-the-clock whale tracking and processing. These ships could reduce a thirty-metre whale to its by-products in roughly thirty minutes. After World War II, more powerful boats with remote sensing devices gave a final boost to the whaling industry. The number of kills had now increased far beyond the whales' capacity to reproduce.

Cause-to-Effect Sequence

A cause-to-effect sequence follows an action to its results. The topic sentence identifies the causes, and the remainder of the paragraph discusses its effects.

"What will happen if I do this?"

Some of the most serious accidents involving gas water heaters occur when a flammable liquid is used in the vicinity. The heavier-than-air vapours of a flammable liquid such as gasoline can flow along the floor—even the length of a basement—and be explosively ignited by the flame of the water heater's pilot light or burner. Because the victim's clothing frequently ignites, the resulting burn injuries are commonly serious and extremely painful. They may require long hospitalization, and can result in disfigurement or death. *Never, under any circumstances, use a flammable liquid near a gas heater or any other open flame.* (Consumer Product Safety Commission)

Emphatic Sequence

Reasons offered in support of a specific viewpoint or recommendation often appear in workplace writing, as in the pesticide-herbicide paragraph on page 229 or the solar energy paragraph on page 230. For emphasis, the reasons or examples usually are arranged in decreasing or increasing order of importance.

"What should I remember about this?"

> Although strip mining is safer and cheaper than conventional mining, it is highly damaging to the surrounding landscape. Among its effects are scarred mountains, ruined land, and polluted waterways. Strip operations are altering our country's land at the rate of 2,023 hectares (5,000 acres) acres per week. An estimated 27,195 kilometres (10,500 miles) of streams have been poisoned by silt drainage in Appalachia alone. If strip mining continues at its present rate, 41,400 square kilometres (16,000 square miles) of U.S. land eventually will be stripped barren.

In this paragraph, the most dramatic example is saved for the end, for greatest emphasis.

Problem-Causes-Solution Sequence

The problem-solving sequence proceeds from description of the problem, through diagnosis, to solution. After outlining the cause of the problem, this next paragraph explains how the problem has been solved:

"How was the problem solved?"

> On all waterfront buildings, the unpainted wood exteriors had been severely damaged by the high winds and sandstorms of the previous winter. After repairing the damage, we took protective steps against further storms. First, all joints, edges, and sashes were treated with water-repellent preservative to protect against water damage. Next, three coats of non-porous primer were applied to all exterior surfaces to prevent paint from blistering and peeling. Finally, two coats of wood-quality latex paint were applied over the non-porous primer. To keep coats of paint from future separation, the first coat was applied within two weeks of the priming coats, and the second within two weeks of the first. Two weeks after completion, no blistering, peeling, or separation has occurred.

Comparison-Contrast Sequence

Evaluation of two or more items on the basis of their similarities or differences often appears in job-related writing.

"How do these items compare?"

> The ski industry's quest for a binding that ensures good performance as well as safety has led to development of two basic types. Although both bindings improve performance and increase the safety margin, they have different release and retention mechanisms. The first type consists of two units (one at the toe, another at the heel) that are spring-loaded. These units apply their retention forces directly to the boot sole. Thus the friction of boot against ski allows for the kind of ankle movement needed at high speeds over rough terrain, without causing the boot to release. In contrast, the second type has one spring-loaded

> unit at either the toe or the heel. From this unit extends a boot plate that travels the length of the boot to a fixed receptacle on its opposite end. With this plate binding, the boot has no part in release or retention. Instead, retention force is applied directly to the boot plate, providing more stability for the recreational skier, but allowing for less ankle and boot movement before releasing. Overall, the double-unit binding performs better in racing, but the plate binding is safer.

For comparing and contrasting more specific data on these bindings, two lists would be most effective.

> The Salomon 555 offers the following features:
>
> 1. upward release at the heel and lateral release at the toe (thus eliminating 80 percent of leg injuries)
> 2. lateral antishock capacity of 15 millimetres, with the highest available return-to-centre force
> 3. two methods of re-entry to the binding: for hard and deep-powder conditions
> 4. five adjustments
> 5. (and so on)
>
> The Americana offers these features:
>
> 1. upward release at the toe as well as upward and lateral release at the heel
> 2. lateral antishock capacity of 30 millimetres, with moderate return-to-centre force
> 3. two methods of re-entry to the binding
> 4. two adjustments, one for boot length and another for comprehensive adjustment for all angles of release and elasticity
> 5. (and so on)

Instead of this block structure (in which one binding is discussed and then the other), the writer might have chosen a point-by-point structure (in which points common to both items, such as "Re-entry Methods" are listed together). The point-by-point comparison is favoured in feasibility and recommendation reports because it offers readers a meaningful comparison between common points.

☑ EXERCISES

1. Locate, copy, and bring to class a paragraph that has the following features:

   - an orienting topic sentence
   - adequate development
   - unity
   - coherence
   - a recognizable sequence
   - appropriate length for its purpose and audience

   Be prepared to identify and explain each of these features in a class discussion.

2. For each of the following documents, indicate the most logical sequence. (For example, a description of a proposed computer lab would follow a spatial sequence.)

   - a set of instructions for operating a power tool
   - a campaign report describing your progress in political fund raising
   - a report analyzing the weakest parts in a piece of industrial machinery
   - a report analyzing the desirability of a proposed oil refinery in your area
   - a detailed breakdown of your monthly budget to trim excess spending
   - a report investigating the reasons for student apathy on your campus
   - a report evaluating the effects of the ban on DDT in insect control
   - a report on any highly technical subject, written for a general reader
   - a report investigating the success of a no-grade policy at other colleges
   - a proposal for a no-grade policy at your college

☑ COLLABORATIVE PROJECT

Organize into small groups. Choose *one* of these topics, or one your group settles on, and then brainstorm to develop a formal outline for the body section of a report. One representative from your group can write the final draft and display it (using a data projection unit, overhead projector, or similar equipment) for class revision.

- job opportunities in your career field
- a physical description of the ideal classroom
- how to organize an effective job search
- how the quality of your higher educational experience can be improved
- arguments for and against a formal grading system
- an argument for an improvement you think your college needs most.

Editing for Readable Style

You might write for a diverse or specific audience, or for experts or non-experts. But no matter how technically appropriate your document, audience needs are not served unless your style is *readable*.

A definition of style

What is *writing style*, and how does it influence reader response to a document? Your writing style is the product of:

- the words you choose
- the way in which you put a sentence together
- the length of your sentences
- the way in which you connect sentences
- the tone you convey

Readable sentences require correct grammar, punctuation, and spelling. Granted, basic mechanical errors do distract readers; but correctness alone is no guarantee of readability. For example, this response to a job applicant is mechanically correct but inefficient:

Inefficient style

> We are in receipt of your recent correspondence indicating your interest in securing the advertised position. Your correspondence has been duly forwarded for consideration by the personnel office, which has employment candidate selection responsibility. You may expect to hear from us relative to your application as the selection process progresses. Your interest in the position is appreciated.

Notice how hard you have worked to extract information that could be expressed this simply:

More efficient

> Your application for the advertised position has been forwarded to our personnel office. As the selection process moves forward, we will be in touch. Thank you for your interest.

Inefficient style makes readers work harder than they should.

Style can be inefficient for many reasons, but it is especially inept when it:

- makes the writing impossible to interpret
- takes too long to make the point
- reads like a Dick-and-Jane story from primary school
- uses imprecise or needlessly long words
- sounds stuffy and impersonal

Regardless of its cause, inefficient style results in writing that is less informative and less persuasive. Moreover, inefficient style can be unethical—by confusing or misleading readers.

To help your audience spend less time reading, you must spend more time editing for a style that is *clear, concise, fluent, exact,* and *likeable*.

Editing for Clarity

A clear sentence requires no more than a single reading. It avoids ambiguous constructions, signals relationships among its parts, and emphasizes the main idea. The following guidelines will help you edit for clarity.

Avoid Ambiguous Phrasing. Workplace writing ideally has *one* meaning only and allows for *one* interpretation. Does one's "suspicious attitude" mean that one is "suspicious" or "suspect"?

Ambiguous phrasing	All managers are not required to submit reports. (*Are some or none required?*)
Revised	Managers are **not all required** to submit reports.

or

Managers are **not required** to submit reports.

Ambiguous phrasing	Most city workers strike on Friday.
Revised	Most city workers **are planning to strike** Friday.

or

Most city workers **typically strike** on Friday.

Avoid Ambiguous Pronoun References. Each pronoun you use (*he, she, it, their,* etc.) must refer to one clearly identified noun. If the pronoun's referent (or antecedent) is ambiguous, readers will be confused.

Ambiguous referent	Our patients enjoy the warm days while they last. (*Are the patients or the warm days on the way out?*)

Depending on whether the referent for *they* is *patients* or *warm days*, the sentence can be clarified.

Clear referent	While these warm days last, our patients enjoy them.

or

Our terminal patients enjoy the warm days.

Ambiguous referent	Jack resents his assistant because he is competitive. (*Who's the competitive one—Jack or his assistant?*)
Clear referent	Because his assistant is competitive, Jack resents him.

or

Because Jack is competitive, he resents his assistant.

Avoid Ambiguous Punctuation. A missing hyphen, comma, or other punctuation mark can obscure your meaning.

Missing hyphen	Replace the trailer's inner wheel bearings. (*The inner-wheel bearings or the inner wheel-bearings?*)
Missing comma	Does your company produce liquid hydrogen? If so, how[,] and where do you store it? (*Notice how the meaning changes with a comma after "how."*)
	Police surrounded the crowd[,] attacking the strikers. (*Without the comma, the crowd appears to be attacking the strikers.*)

Although missing hyphens and commas are prime culprits, other omissions can cause ambiguity as well. A missing colon after *kill* yields the headline "Moose Kill 200." A missing " *'s* " after *Mills* creates this gem: "Mills Remains Buried in Saskatoon." Punctuation *does* affect meaning.

Exercise 1
Revise the following sentences to eliminate ambiguities in phrasing, pronoun reference, or punctuation.

a. Call me any evening except Tuesday after 7 o'clock.

b. The benefits of this plan are hard to imagine.

c. I cannot recommend this candidate too highly.

d. Visiting colleagues can be tiring.

e. Janice dislikes working with Claire because she's impatient.

f. Despite his efforts, Joe misinterpreted Sam's message.

g. Our division needs more effective writers.

h. Tell the reactor operator to evacuate and sound a general alarm.

i. If you don't pass any section of the test, your flying days are over.

j. Dial "10" to deactivate the system and sound the alarm.

Avoid Telegraphic Writing. *Function words* show relationships between the *content words* (nouns, adjectives, verbs, and adverbs) in a sentence. Some examples of function words:

- articles (*a, an, the*)
- prepositions (*in, of, to*)
- linking verbs (*is, seems, looks*)
- relative pronouns (*who, which, that*)

Some writers mistakenly try to compress their writing by eliminating these function words.

Ambiguous	Proposal to employ retirees almost dead.
Revised	The proposal to employ retirees **is** almost dead.
Ambiguous	Uninsulated end pipe ruptured. (*What ruptured? The pipe or the end of the pipe?*)
Revised	**The** uninsulated end **of the** pipe ruptured.

or

The uninsulated pipe **on the** end ruptured.

Ambiguous	The reactor operator told management several times she expected an accident. (*Did she tell them once or several times?*)
Revised	The reactor operator told management several times **that** she expected an accident.

or

The reactor operator told management **that** several times she expected an accident.

Avoid Ambiguous Modifiers. Modifiers explain, define, or add detail to other words or ideas. If a modifier is too far from the words it modifies, the message can be ambiguous.

Misplaced modifier	Only press the red button in an emergency. (*Does only modify press or emergency?*)
Revised	Press **only** the red button in an emergency.

or

Press the red button in an emergency **only**.

Another problem with ambiguity occurs when a modifying phrase has no word to modify.

Dangling modifier	**Being so well known in the computer industry,** I would appreciate your advice.

The writer meant to say that the *reader* is well known, but with no word to join itself to, the modifying phrase dangles. Eliminate the confusion by adding a subject:

Revised	Because **you** are so well known in the computer industry, I would appreciate your advice.

Exercise 2
Revise the following sentences to repair telegraphic writing or to clarify ambiguous modifiers.

a. The manager claimed repeatedly she reported the danger.

b. I want the final Amex report written by your division.

c. Replace main booster rocket seal.

> *d.* The president refused to believe any internal report was inaccurate.
>
> *e.* Only use this phone in a red alert.
>
> *f.* After offending our best client, I am deeply annoyed with the new manager.
>
> *g.* Send memo to programmer requesting explanation.
>
> *h.* Do not enter test area while contaminated.

Unstack Modifying Nouns. One noun can modify another noun (as in "software development"). But when two or more nouns modify a noun, the string of densely packed words becomes hard to read and ambiguous.

> **Stacked**   Be sure to leave enough time for a **training session participant** evaluation. (*Evaluation of the session or of the participants?*)

With no function words (articles, prepositions, verbs, relative pronouns) to break up the string of nouns, readers cannot see the relationships among the nouns. What modifies what?

Stacked nouns also deaden your style. Bring your style *and* your reader to life by using action verbs (*complete, prepare, reduce*) and prepositional phrases.

> **Revised**   Be sure to leave enough time **for** participants **to evaluate** the training session.
>
> *or*
>
> Be sure to leave enough time **to evaluate** participants **in the** training session.

No such problem with ambiguity occurs when *adjectives* are stacked in front of a noun.

> **Clear**   He was a **nervous, angry, confused,** but **dedicated** employee.

Readers can readily see that the adjectives modify *employee*.

Arrange Word Order for Coherence. In coherent writing, everything sticks together; each sentence builds on the preceding sentence and looks ahead to the following sentence. Sentences generally work best when the beginning looks back at familiar information and the end provides the new (or unfamiliar) information:

Familiar		Unfamiliar
My dog	has	fleas.
Our supervisor	just won	the lottery.
This company	is planning	a merger.

Exercise 3

Revise the following sentences to unstack modifying nouns.

a. Develop on-line editing system documentation.

b. We need to develop a unified construction automation design.

c. Install a hazardous materials dispersion monitor system.

d. I recommend these management performance improvement incentives.

e. Sarah's job involves fault analysis systems troubleshooting handbook preparation.

Use Active Voice Often. A verb's *voice* signals whether a sentence's subject acts or is acted upon. The active voice ("I did it") is more direct, concise, and persuasive than the passive voice ("It was done by me"). In the active voice, the agent performing the action serves as the subject:

Active	*Agent*	*Action*	*Recipient*
	Joe	lost	your report.
	Subject	*Verb*	*Object*

The passive voice reverses the pattern, making the recipient of an action serve as subject.

Passive	*Recipient*	*Action*	*Agent*
	Your report	was lost	by Joe.
	Subject	*Verb*	*Prepositional phrase*

Sometimes the passive eliminates the agent altogether:

Passive	Your report was lost. (*Who lost it?*)

Some writers mistakenly rely on the passive voice because they think it sounds more objective and important. But the passive voice often makes writing wordy, indecisive, evasive, and unethical.

Concise and direct (active)	I underestimated labour costs for this project. (*7 words*)
Wordy and indirect (passive)	Labour costs for this project were underestimated by me. (*9 words*)
Evasive (passive)	Labour costs for this project were underestimated. (*7 words*)

Do not evade responsibility by hiding behind the passive voice:

Passive not responsible	A **mistake** was made in your shipment.
	It was decided not to hire you.
	A **layoff** is recommended.

Use the active voice when reporting errors or bad news. Readers appreciate clarity and sincerity.

The passive voice creates a weak and impersonal tone.

Weak and impersonal	An offer will be made by us next week.
Strong and personal	We will make an offer next week.

Use the active voice when you want action. Otherwise, your statement will have no power.

Weak passive	If my claim is not settled by May 15, the Better Business Bureau will be contacted, and their advice on legal action will be taken.
Strong active	If you do not settle my claim by May 15, I will contact the Better Business Bureau for advice on legal action.

Notice how this active version emphasizes the new and significant information by placing it at the end.

Use the active voice for giving instructions.

Faulty passive	The bid should be sealed. Care should be taken with the dynamite.
Correct active	**Seal** the bid. **Be careful** with the dynamite.

Avoid shifts from active to passive voice in the same sentence.

Faulty shift	During the meeting, project members spoke and presentations were given.
Correct	During the meeting, project members spoke and **gave** presentations.

Unless you have a deliberate reason for choosing the passive voice, use the *active* voice for making forceful connections like the one described here:

> By using the active voice, you direct the reader's attention to the subject of your sentence. For instance, if you write a job-application letter that is littered with passive verbs, you fail to achieve an important goal of that letter: to show the readers the important things you have done, and how prepared you are to do important things for them. That strategy requires active verbs, with clear emphasis on *you* and what you have done/are doing. (Pugliano 6)

Exercise 4

The following sentences are wordy, weak, or evasive because they are in the passive voice. Revise each sentence as a concise, forceful, and direct expression in the active voice, to identify the person or agent performing the action.

a. The evaluation was performed by us.

b. The report was written by our group.

c. Unless you pay me within three days, my lawyer will be contacted.

d. Hard hats should be worn at all times.

e. It was decided to reject your offer.

f. Gasoline was spilled on your Ferrari's leather seats.

g. It is believed by us that this contract is faulty.

h. Our test results will be sent to you as soon as verification is completed.

i. The decision was made that your request for promotion should be denied.

Use Passive Voice Selectively. Passive voice is appropriate in lab reports and other documents in which the agent's identity is immaterial to the message.

Use the passive voice when your audience does not need to know the agent.

Correct passive	Mr. Jones was brought to the emergency room.
	The bank failure was publicized provincewide.

Use the passive voice to focus on events or results when the agent is unknown, unapparent, or unimportant.

Correct passive	All memos in the firm are filed in a database.
	Josef's article was published last week.

Use the passive voice when you want to be indirect or inoffensive (as in requesting the customer's payment or the employee's cooperation, or to avoid blaming someone—such as your supervisor) (Ornatowski 94).

Active but offensive	**You** have not paid your bill.
	You need to overhaul our filing system.
Inoffensive passive	**This bill** has not been paid.
	Our filing system needs to be overhauled.

Use the passive voice if the person behind the action has reason for being protected.

Correct passive	The criminal was identified.
	The embezzlement scheme was exposed.

Exercise 5

The following sentences lack proper emphasis because of an improper use of the active voice. Revise each ineffective active as an appropriate passive, to emphasize the recipient rather than the actor.

a. Joe's company fired him.

b. Someone on the maintenance crew has just discovered a crack in the nuclear-core containment unit.

c. A power surge destroyed more than 2,000 lines of our new applications program.

d. You are paying inadequate attention to worker safety.

e. You are checking temperatures too infrequently.

f. The tornado destroyed the barn.

g. You did a poor job editing this report.

Avoid Overstuffed Sentences. A sentence crammed with ideas makes details hard to remember and relationships hard to identify:

> Overstuffed   Publicizing the records of a private meeting that took place three weeks ago to reveal the identity of a manager who criticized our company's promotion policy would be unethical.

Clear things up by sorting out the relationships.

> Revised   In a private meeting three weeks ago, a manager criticized our company's policy on promotion. It would be unethical to reveal the manager's identity by publicizing the records of that meeting. (*Other versions are possible here, depending on the writer's intended meaning.*)

Give your readers no more information than they can retain in one sentence.

Exercise 6

Unscramble this overstuffed sentence by making shorter, clearer sentences:

A smoke-filled room causes not only teary eyes and runny noses but also can alter people's hearing and vision, as well as creating dangerous levels of carbon monoxide, especially for people with heart and lung ailments, whose health is particularly threatened by second-hand smoke.

Editing for Conciseness

Writing can suffer from two kinds of wordiness: one kind occurs when readers receive information they don't need (think of an overly detailed weather report during local television news). The other kind of wordiness occurs when too many words are used to convey information readers *do* need (as in saying "a great deal of potential for the future" instead of "great potential").

Every word in the document should advance your meaning.

> Writing improves in direct ratio to the number of things we can keep out of it that shouldn't be there. (Zinsser 14)

Concise writing conveys the most information in the fewest words. But it includes the details necessary for clarity.

Use fewer words whenever fewer will do. But remember the difference between *clear writing* and *compressed writing* that is impossible to decipher.

Impenetrable	Give new vehicle air conditioner compression cut-off system specifications to engineering manager advising immediate action.

First drafts rarely are concise. The following strategies will help you "trim the fat."

Avoid Wordy Phrases. Each phrase here can be reduced to one word:

Wordy		Concise
at a rapid rate	=	rapidly
due to the fact that	=	because
the majority of	=	most
on a personal basis	=	personally
give instruction to	=	instruct
would be able to	=	could
readily apparent	=	obvious
a large number	=	many
prior to	=	before
aware of the fact that	=	know
conduct an inspection of	=	inspect
in close proximity	=	near

Eliminate Redundancy. A redundant expression says the same thing twice, in different words, as in *fellow colleagues*.

a **dead** corpse	**end** result
completely eliminate	cancel **out**
basic essentials	consensus **of opinion**
enter **into**	**utter** devastation
mental awareness	**the month of** August
mutual cooperation	**utmost** perfection

Avoid Needless Repetition. Unnecessary repetition clutters writing and dilutes meaning.

Repetitious	In trauma victims, breathing is restored by **artificial respiration**. Techniques of **artificial respiration** include mouth-to-mouth **respiration** and mouth-to-nose **respiration.**

Repetition in the above passage disappears when sentences are combined.

Concise	In trauma victims, breathing is restored by artificial respiration, **either mouth-to-mouth or mouth-to-nose.**

Repetition can be useful. Don't hesitate to repeat, or at least rephrase, material (even whole paragraphs in a longer document) if you feel that readers need reminders. Effective repetition helps avoid cross-references like this: "See page 23" or "Review page 10."

Exercise 7

Revise the following wordy sentences to eliminate needless phrases, needless repetition, and redundancy.

a. I have admiration for Professor Singh.
b. Due to the fact that we made the lowest bid, we won the contract.
c. On previous occasions we have worked together.
d. She is a person who works hard.
e. We have completely eliminated the bugs from this program.
f. This report is the most informative report on the project.
g. Through mutual cooperation, we can achieve our goals.
h. I am aware of the fact that Sam is trustworthy.
i. This offer is the most attractive offer I've received.

Avoid There *Sentence Openers.* Avoid *There is* and *There are* sentence openers.

Weak	**There is** a coaxial cable connecting the antenna to the receiver.
Revised	A coaxial cable connects the antenna to the receiver.

Weak	**There is** a danger of explosion in Number 2 mineshaft.
Revised	Number 2 mineshaft is in danger of exploding.

Dropping these openers places the key words at sentence end, where they are best emphasized. Of course, in some contexts, proper emphasis would call for a *there* opener.

Correct	People often have wondered about the rationale behind Boris's sudden decision. Actually, there are several good reasons for his dropping out of the program.

Avoid Some It *Sentence Openers.* Avoid beginning a sentence with *It*—unless the *It* clearly points to a specific referent in the preceding sentence: "This document is excellent. It deserves special recognition."

Weak	It was his bad attitude that got him fired.
Revised	His bad attitude got him fired.
Weak	It is necessary to complete both sides of the form.
Revised	Please complete both sides of the form.

Delete Needless Prefaces. Instead of delaying the new information in your sentence, get right to the point.

Wordy	**I am writing this letter because** I wish to apply for the position of copy editor.
Concise	Please consider me for the position of copy editor.
Wordy	**As far as artificial intelligence is concerned,** the technology is only in its infancy.
Concise	Artificial-intelligence technology is only in its infancy.

Exercise 8

Revise the following sentences to eliminate *There* and *It* openers and needless prefaces.

a. There was severe fire damage to the reactor.

b. There are several reasons why Jenna left the company.

c. It is essential that we act immediately.

d. It has been reported by Clayton that several safety violations have occurred.

e. This letter is to inform you that I am pleased to accept your job offer.

f. The purpose of this report is to update our research findings.

Avoid Weak Verbs. Use verbs that express a definite action: *open, close, move, continue, begin.* Avoid weak verbs that express no specific action: *is, was, are, has, give, make, come, take.* In some cases, such verbs are essential to your meaning: "Dr. Yang is operating at 7 a.m." "Take me to the laboratory." But in other cases, weak verbs add words without advancing meaning. All forms of the linking verb *to be* (*am, are, is, was, were, will, have been, might have been*) generally are weak. This next sentence achieves conciseness because of the strong verb *consider:*

Concise	Please **consider** my offer.
Weak and wordy	Please **take into consideration** my offer.

Don't disappear behind weak linking verbs and their baggage of needless nouns and prepositions.

| | Weak | My recommendation **is** for a larger budget. |
| | Strong | I **recommend** a larger budget. |

Strong verbs, or action verbs, suggest an assertive, positive, and confident writer. Here are some weak verbs converted to strong:

Weak		Strong
is in conflict with	=	conflicts
has the ability to	=	can
give a summary of	=	summarize
make an assumption	=	assume
come to the conclusion	=	conclude
take action	=	act
make a decision	=	decide

Exercise 9

Revise the following wordy and vague sentences to eliminate weak verbs.

a. Our disposal procedure is in conformity with federal standards.

b. Please make a decision today.

c. We need to have a discussion about the problem.

d. I have just come to the realization that I was mistaken.

e. Your conclusion is in agreement with mine.

f. This manual gives instructions to end users.

Delete Needless To Be Constructions. The preceding section showed that forms of *to be* (*is, was, are,* etc.) are weak. Sometimes the *to be* form itself mistakenly appears behind such verbs as *appears, seems,* and *finds.*

| | Wordy | Your product seems **to be** superior. |
| | | I consider this employee **to be** highly competent. |

Avoid Excessive Prepositions. Needless prepositions combined with forms of *to be* make wordy sentences.

| | Wordy | The recommendation first appeared **in** the report written **by** the supervisor **in** January **about** that month's productivity. |
| | Concise | The recommendation first appeared in the supervisor's productivity report for January. |

The following prepositional phrases can be reduced.

Excessive		Reduced
with the exception of	=	except for
in reference to	=	about (or regarding)
in order that	=	so
in the near future	=	soon
in the event that	=	if
at the present time	=	now
in the course of	=	during
in the process of	=	during (or in)

Fight Noun Addiction. Nouns manufactured from verbs (nominalizations) often accompany weak verbs and needless prepositions.

Weak and wordy	We ask for the **cooperation** of all employees.
Strong and concise	We ask that all employees **cooperate.**

Weak and wordy	Give **consideration** to the possibility of a career change.
Strong and concise	**Consider** a career change.

Besides causing wordiness, a nominalization can be vague—by hiding the agent of an action.

Wordy and vague	**A valid requirement** for immediate action exists. (*Who should take the action? We can't tell.*)
Precise	We **must act** immediately.

Here are nominalizations restored to their verb forms:

Vague		Precise
conduct an investigation of	=	investigate
provide a description of	=	describe
conduct a test of	=	test
make a discovery of	=	discover

Nominalizations drain the life from your style. In cheering for your favourite team, you wouldn't say "Blocking of that kick is a necessity!" instead of "Block that kick!"

Write as you would speak, but avoid slang or overuse of colloquialisms. Also avoid excessive economy. For example, "Employees must cooperate" would not be a desirable alternative to the first example in this section. But, for the final example, "Block that kick" would be.

Exercise 10

Revise the following sentences to eliminate needless prepositions and *to be* constructions, and to cure noun addiction.

a. Igor seems to be ready for a vacation.

b. Our survey found 46 percent of users to be disappointed.

c. In the event of system failure, your sounding of the alarm is essential.

d. These are the recommendations of the chairperson of the committee.

e. Our acceptance of the offer is a necessity.

f. Please perform an analysis and make an evaluation of our new system.

g. A need for your caution exists.

h. I consider Bjorn to be an excellent technician.

i. The appearance of this problem was just yesterday.

j. Power surges are associated, in a causative way, with malfunctions of computers.

Make Negatives Positive. A positive expression is easier to understand than a negative one.

| **Indirect and wordy** | Please do not be late in submitting your report. |
| **Direct and concise** | Please submit your report on time. |

Readers work even harder to translate sentences with multiple negative expressions:

| **Confusing and wordy** | Do **not** distribute this memo to employees who have not received a security clearance. |
| **Clear and concise** | Distribute this memo only to employees who have received a security clearance. |

Besides the directly negative words (*no, not, never*), some words are indirectly negative (*except, forget, mistake, lose, uncooperative*).

Confusing and wordy	Do **not neglect** to activate the alarm system.
	My diagnosis was **not inaccurate.**
Clear and concise	**Be sure** to activate the alarm system.
	My diagnosis was **accurate.**

The positive versions are more straightforward *and* persuasive.

Some negative expressions, of course, are perfectly correct, as in expressing disagreement.

Correct negatives	This is **not** the best plan.
	Your offer is **unacceptable.**
	This project **never** will succeed.

Select positives over negatives whenever your meaning allows:

Negatives		**Positives**
did not succeed	=	failed
does not have	=	lacks
did not prevent	=	allowed
not unless	=	only if
not until	=	only when
not absent	=	present

Clean Out Clutter Words. Clutter words stretch a message without adding meaning. Here are some of the commonest: *very, definitely, quite, extremely, rather, somewhat, really, actually, currently, situation, aspect, factor.*

| **Cluttered** | **Actually,** one **aspect** of a business **situation** that could definitely make me **quite** happy would be to have a **somewhat** adventurous partner who **really** shared my **extreme** attraction to risks. |
| **Concise** | I seek an adventurous business partner who enjoys risks. |

Delete Needless Qualifiers. Qualifiers such as *I feel, it seems, I believe, in my opinion,* and *I think* soften the tone and impact of a statement. Use qualifiers to express uncertainty or to avoid seeming arrogant or overconfident.

| **Appropriate qualifiers** | Despite Frank's poor grades last year he will, **I think,** do well in college. |
| | Your product **seems** to be what we need. |

But when you are certain, eliminate the qualifier so as not to seem tentative or evasive.

Needless qualifiers	**It seems** that I've made an error.
	We **appear to** have exceeded our budget.
	In my opinion, this candidate is outstanding.

In communicating across cultures, keep in mind that a direct, forceful style might be considered offensive (page 228).

Exercise 11

Revise the following sentences to eliminate inappropriate negatives, clutter words, and needless qualifiers.

a. Our design must avoid non-conformity with building codes.

b. Never fail to wear protective clothing.

c. Do not accept any bids unless they arrive before May 1.

 d. I am not unappreciative of your help.

 e. We are currently in the situation of completing our investigation of all aspects of the accident.

 f. I appear to have misplaced the contract.

 g. Do not accept bids that are not signed.

 h. It seems as if I have just wrecked a company car.

Editing for Fluency

Fluent sentences are easy to read because of clear connections, variety, and emphasis. Their varied length and word order eliminate choppiness and monotony. Fluent sentences enhance *clarity,* allowing readers to see the most important ideas. Fluent sentences enhance *conciseness,* often replacing several short, repetitious sentences with one longer, economical sentence. The following strategies will help you write fluent sentences.

Combine Related Ideas. A series of short, disconnected sentences is not only choppy and wordy, but also unclear.

Disconnected	Jogging can be healthful. You need the right equipment. Most necessary are well-fitting shoes. Without this equipment you take the chance of injuring your legs. Your knees are especially prone to injury. (*5 sentences*)
Clear, concise, and fluent	Jogging can be healthful if you have the right equipment. Shoes that fit well are most necessary because they prevent injury to your legs, especially your knees. (*2 sentences*)

Most sets of information can be combined in different relationships, depending on what you want to emphasize. Imagine that this set of facts describes an applicant for a junior-management position with your company.

- Roy Dupius graduated from an excellent management school.
- He has no experience.
- He is highly recommended.

Assume you are a personnel director, conveying to upper management your impression of this candidate. To convey a negative impression, you might combine the facts in this way:

Strongly negative emphasis	Although Roy Dupius graduated from an excellent management school and is highly recommended, **he has no experience.**

The *independent* idea (in boldface) receives the emphasis. To continue with our example: If you are undecided, but leaning in a negative direction, you might write:

| Strongly negative emphasis | Roy Dupuis graduated from an excellent management school and is highly recommended, **but** he has no experience. |

In the sentence above, the ideas before and after *but* are both independent. These independent ideas are joined by the coordinating word *but,* which suggests that both sides of the issue are equally important (or "coordinate"). Placing the negative idea last, however, gives it slight emphasis.

Finally, to emphasize strong support for the candidate, you could say:

| Strongly positive emphasis | Although Roy Dupuis has no experience, **he graduated from an excellent management school and is highly recommended.** |

In the above version the earlier idea is subordinated by *although,* leaving the two final ideas independent.

Caution: Combine sentences only to advance your meaning, to ease the reader's task. A sentence with too much information and too many connections can be difficult for readers to sort out.

| Overstuffed | Our night supervisor's verbal order from upper management to repair the overheated circuit was misunderstood by Leslie Kidd, who gave the wrong instructions to the emergency crew, thereby causing the fire within 30 minutes. |
| Clearer | Upper management issued a verbal order to repair the overheated circuit. When our night supervisor transmitted the order to Leslie Kidd, it was misunderstood. Kidd gave the wrong instruction to the emergency crew, and the fire began within 30 minutes. |

Vary Sentence Construction and Length. We have just seen how related ideas often need to be linked in one sentence, so that readers can grasp the connections:

| Disconnected | The nuclear core reached critical temperature. The loss-of-coolant alarm was triggered. The operator shut down the reactor. |
| Connected | As the nuclear core reached critical temperature, triggering the loss-of-coolant alarm, the operator shut down the reactor. |

But an idea that should stand alone for emphasis needs a sentence of its own:

| Correct | Core meltdown seemed inevitable. |

However, an unbroken string of long or short sentences can bore and confuse readers, as can a series with identical openings:

| Dreary | There are some drawbacks about diesel engines. **They** are difficult to start in cold weather. **They** cause vibration. **They** also give off an unpleasant odour. **They** cause sulfur dioxide pollution. |

Varied   Diesel engines have some drawbacks. Most obvious are their noisiness, cold-weather starting difficulties, vibration, odour, and sulfur dioxide emission.

Similarly, when you write in the first person, overusing *I* makes you appear self-centred. (Some organizations require use of the third person, avoiding the first person completely, for all manuals, lab reports, specifications, product descriptions, etc.)

Do not avoid personal pronouns if they make the writing more readable (by eliminating passive constructions).

Use Short Sentences for Special Emphasis. All this talk about combining ideas, might suggest that short sentences have no place in good writing. Wrong. Short sentences show connections and clarify relationships, short sentences (even one-word sentences) provide vivid emphasis. They stick in a reader's mind.

Exercise 12

Combine each set of sentences into one fluent sentence that provides the requested emphasis. For example,

Sentence set	John is a loyal employee. John is a motivated employee. John is short-tempered with his colleagues.
Combined for positive emphasis	Even though John is short-tempered with his colleagues, he is a loyal and motivated employee.
Sentence set	This word processor has many features. It includes a spelling checker. It includes a thesaurus. It includes a grammar checker.
Combined to emphasize thesaurus	Among its many features, such as spelling and grammar checkers, this word processor includes a thesaurus.

a. The job offers an attractive salary.
It demands long work hours.
Promotions are rapid.
(Combine for negative emphasis.)

b. The job offers an attractive salary.
It demands long work hours.
Promotions are rapid.
(Combine for positive emphasis.)

c. Our office software is integrated.
It has an excellent database management program.
Most impressive is its word processing capability.

It has an excellent spreadsheet program.
(Combine to emphasize the word processor.)

d. Company X gave us the lowest bid.
Company Y has an excellent reputation.
(Combine to emphasize Company Y.)

e. Superinsulated homes are energy efficient.
Superinsulated homes create a danger of indoor air pollution.
The toxic substances include radon gas and urea formaldehyde.
(Combine for a negative emphasis.)

Finding the Exact Words

Too often, language can be a vehicle for *camouflage* rather than communication. People see many reasons to hide behind language, as when they:

- speak for their company but not for themselves
- fear the consequences of giving bad news
- are afraid to disagree with company policy
- make a recommendation some readers will resent
- worry about making a bad impression
- worry about being wrong
- pretend to know more than they do
- avoid admitting a mistake or ignorance

Inflated and unfamiliar words, borrowed expressions, and needlessly technical terms camouflage meaning. Whether intentional or accidental, poor word choices have only one result: inefficient and often unethical writing that resists interpretation and frustrates the reader.

Following are strategies for finding words that are *convincing, precise,* and *informative.*

Use Simple and Familiar Words. Don't replace technically precise words with non-technical words that are vague or imprecise. Don't write *a part that makes the computer run* when you mean *central processing unit.* Use the precise term, and define it in a glossary for non-technical readers:

Correct   Central processing unit: the part of the computer that controls information transfer and carries out arithmetic and logical instructions.

Certain technical words may be indispensable in certain contexts, but the non-technical words usually can be simplified. Instead of *answering in the affirmative, say yes;* or instead of *endeavouring to promulgate* a new policy, *try to announce* it.

Unfamiliar words	Acoustically attenuate the food-consumption area.
Revised	Soundproof the cafeteria.

Don't use three syllables when one will do. Generally, trade for less:

Three Syllables		One Syllable
aggregate	=	total
demonstrate	=	show
effectuate	=	cause
endeavour	=	effort, try
eventuate	=	result
frequently	=	often
initiate	=	begin
is contingent upon	=	depends on
multiplicity of	=	many
optimum	=	best
subsequent to	=	after
utilize	=	use

Trim wherever you can. Most important, choose words you hear and use in everyday speaking—words that are universally familiar.

Don't write *I deem* when you mean *I think,* or *keep me apprised* instead of *keep me informed,* or *I concur* instead of *I agree,* or *securing employment* instead of *finding a job,* or *it is cost prohibitive* instead of *we can't afford it.*

Don't write like the author of a report from the Federal Aviation Administration, who recommended that manufacturers of the DC–10 re-evaluate *the design of the entire pylon assembly to minimize design factors which are resulting in sensitive and/or critical maintenance and inspection procedures* (25 words, 50 syllables). A plain English translation: *Redesign the pylons so they are easier to maintain and inspect* (11 words, 18 syllables).

Besides the annoyance they cause, needlessly long or unfamiliar words can be *ambiguous.*

Ambiguous	Make an improvement in the clerical situation.

Should we hire more clerical personnel or better personnel or should we train the personnel we have? Words chosen to impress readers too often confuse them instead. A plain style is more persuasive because "it leaves no one out" (Cross 6).

Of course, now and then the complex or more elaborate word best expresses your meaning. For instance, we would not substitute *end* for *terminate* in referring to something with an established time limit.

Correct	Our trade agreement terminates this month.

If a complex word can replace a handful of simpler words—and can sharpen your meaning—use the complex word.

Weak	Six rectangular grooves **around the outside edge** of the steel plate **are needed for** the pressure clamps **to fit into.**
Informative and precise	Six rectangular grooves on the steel plate **perimeter accommodate** the pressure clamps.
Weak	We need a **one-to-one exchange of ideas and opinions.**
Informative and precise	We need a **dialogue.**
Weak	Sexist language **contributes to the on-going prevalence** of gender stereotypes.
Informative and precise	Sexist language **perpetuates** gender stereotypes.

Exercise 13

Revise the following sentences for straightforward and familiar language.

a. May you find luck and success in all endeavours.

b. I suggest you reduce the number of cigarettes you consume.

c. Within the copier, a magnetic-reed switch is utilized as a mode of replacement for the conventional microswitches that were in use on previous models.

d. A good writer is cognizant of how to utilize grammar in a correct fashion.

e. I will endeavour to ascertain the best candidate.

f. In view of the fact that the microscope is defective, we expect a refund of our full purchase expenditure.

g. I wish to upgrade my present employment situation.

Avoid Useless Jargon. Every profession has its own "shorthand." Among specialists, technical terms are a precise and economical way to communicate. For example, *stat* (from the Latin "statim" or "immediately") is medical jargon for *drop everything and deal with this emergency.* For computer buffs, a *glitch* is a momentary power surge that can erase the contents of internal memory; a *bug* is an error that causes a program to run incorrectly. Such useful jargon conveys clear meaning to a knowledgeable audience.

Technical language, however, can be used appropriately or inappropriately. The latter is useless jargon, meaningless to insiders as well as outsiders. In the world of useless jargon people don't *cooperate* on a project; instead, they *interface* or *contiguously optimize their efforts.* Rather than *designing a model,* they *formulate a paradigm.* Instead of *observing limits or boundaries,* they *function within specific parameters.*

A popular form of useless jargon is adding *-wise* to nouns, as shorthand for *in reference to* or *in terms of.*

Useless jargon	**Expensewise** and **schedulewise,** this plan is unacceptable.
Revised	In terms of expense and scheduling, this plan is unacceptable.

Writers create another form of jargon when they invent verbs from nouns or adjectives by adding an *-ize* ending: Don't invent *prioritize* from *priority;* instead use *to rank priorities.*

Jargon's worst fault is that it makes the person using it seem stuffy and pretentious:

Pretentious	Unless all parties interface synchronously within given parameters, the project will be rendered inoperative.
Possible translation	Unless we coordinate our efforts, the project will fail.

Beyond reacting with frustration, readers often conclude that useless jargon is camouflage for a writer with something to hide.

Before using any jargon, think about your specific readers and ask yourself: "Can I find an easier way to say exactly what I mean?" Use jargon only if it *improves* your communication.

If your employer insists on needless jargon or elaborate phrasing, then you have little choice. What is best in matters of style is not always what some people consider appropriate. Use the style your employer or organization expects, but remember that most documents that achieve superior results are in plain English.

Use Acronyms Selectively. Acronyms are another form of specialized shorthand, or jargon. They are formed from the first letters of words in a phrase (as in *LOCA* from *loss of coolant accident*) or from a combination of first letters and parts of words (as in *bit* from *binary digit* or *pixel* from *picture element*).

Computer technology has spawned countless acronyms, including:

Acronym		Meaning
ISDN	=	Integrated Services Digital Network
Telnet	=	Telephone Network
URL	=	Uniform Resource Locator

Acronyms *can* communicate concisely—but only when the audience knows their meaning, and only when you use the term often in your document. Whenever you first use an acronym, spell out the words from which it is derived.

An acronym defined

Modem ("modulator+demodulator"): a device that converts, or "modulates," computer data in electronic form into a sound signal that can be transmitted via phone line and then reconverted, or "demodulated," into electronic form for the receiving computer.

For lay audiences, try to avoid acronyms altogether or be sure to define the terms that make up the acronym.

Avoid Triteness. Writers who rely on tired old phrases (clichés) like the following seem too lazy or too careless to find exact ways to say what they mean.

make the grade	the chips are down
in the final analysis	not by a long shot
close the deal	last but not least
hard as a rock	welcome aboard
water under the bridge	over the hill
holding the bag	bite the bullet
up the creek	work like a dog

Exercise 14

Revise the following sentences to eliminate useless jargon and triteness.

a. For the obtaining of the X-33 printer, our firm will have to accomplish the disbursement of funds to the amount of $3,000.

b. To optimize your financial return, prioritize your investment goals.

c. The use of this product engenders a 50-percent repeat consumer encounter.

d. We'll have to swallow our pride and admit our mistake.

e. We wish to welcome all new managers aboard.

f. Not by a long shot will this plan succeed.

g. Managers who make the grade are those who can take daily pressures in stride.

h. Intercom utilization will be employed to initiate substitute employee operative involvement.

Avoid Misleading Euphemisms. Euphemisms are expressions aimed at politeness or at making unpleasant subjects seem less offensive. Thus, we *powder our nose* or *use the boys' room* instead of *using the bathroom;* we *pass away* or *meet our Maker* instead of *dying.* Euphemisms make the truth seem less painful.

When euphemisms avoid offending or embarrassing our audience, they are perfectly legitimate. Instead of telling a job applicant he or she is *unqualified,* we might say, *your background doesn't meet our needs.* In addition, there are times when friendliness and interoffice harmony are more likely to be preserved with writing that is not too abrupt, bold, blunt, or emphatic (Mackenzie 2).

Euphemisms are unethical if they understate the truth when only the truth will serve. In the sugar-coated world of misleading euphemisms, bad news disappears:

- Instead of being *laid off* or *fired,* workers are *surplused* or *deselected,* or the company is *downsized.*

- Instead of *lying* to the public, the government *engages in a policy of disinformation.*

■ Instead of *wars* and *civilian casualties,* we have *conflicts* and *collateral damage.*

Language loses all meaning when *criminals* become *offenders,* when *rape* becomes *sexual assault,* and when people who are just plain *lazy* become *under-achievers.* Plain talk is always better than deception. If someone offers you a job *with limited opportunity for promotion,* expect a *dead-end job.*

Avoid Overstatement and Unsupported Generalizations. Exaggerating destroys credibility. Be cautious when using words such as *best, biggest, brightest, most,* and *worst.*

Overstated	**Most** businesses have no loyalty toward their employees.
Revised	**Some** businesses have little loyalty toward their employees.

Overstated	You will find our product to be the **best.**
Revised	You will **appreciate the high quality** of our product.

Unsupported generalizations harm your credibility. Be aware of the vast differences in meaning among these words:

few	never
some	rarely
many	sometimes
most	often
all	always

Unless you specify *few, some, many,* or *most,* readers can interpret your statement to mean *all.*

Misleading	Assembly-line employees are doing shabby work.

Unless you mean *all* qualify your generalization with *some, most*—or even better, specify *20 percent.*

Exercise 15
Revise the following sentences to eliminate euphemism, overstatement, or unsupported generalizations.

a. I finally must admit that I am an abuser of intoxicating beverages.

b. I was less than candid.

c. This employee is poorly motivated.

d. Most entry-level jobs are boring and dehumanizing.

e. Clerical jobs offer no opportunity for advancement.

f. Because of your absence of candour, we no longer can offer you employment.

Avoid Imprecise Words. Even words listed as synonyms carry different shades of meaning. Do you mean to say *I'm slender, you're slim, she's lean,* or *he's scrawny?* The wrong choice could be disastrous.

A single wrong word can offend readers, as in this statement by a job applicant:

> **Offensive**   Another attractive feature of your company is its **adequate** training program.

While "adequate"might convey honestly the writer's intended meaning, the word seems inappropriate in this context (an applicant expressing a judgment about a program). Although the program may not have been highly ranked, the writer could have used any of several alternatives (*solid, respectable, growing—* or no modifier at all).

Be especially aware of similar words with dissimilar meanings, as in these examples:

affect/effect	farther/further
all ready/already	fewer/less
almost dead/dying	healthy/healthful
among/between	imply/infer
continual/continuous	invariably/inevitably
eager/anxious	uninterested/disinterested
fearful/fearsome	worse/worst

Don't write *skiing is healthy* when you mean that skiing promotes good health. Healthful things keep us healthy.

Be on the lookout for imprecisely phrased (and therefore illogical) comparisons.

> **Imprecise**   Your bank's interest rate is higher than Central Bank. (*Can a rate be higher than a bank?*)
>
> **Precise**   Your bank's interest rate is higher than Central Bank's.

Imprecise language can create ambiguity. For instance, is *send us more personal information* a request for *more* information that is personal or for information that is *more* personal?

Precision ultimately enhances conciseness, when one exact word replaces multiple inexact words.

> **Wordy and less exact**   I have **put together** all the financial information.
> **Keep doing** this exercise for ten seconds.
>
> **Concise and more exact**   I have **assembled** all the. . . .
> **Continue** this exercise. . . .

Be Specific and Concrete. General words name broad classes of things, such as *job, computer,* or *person.* Such terms usually need to be clarified by more specific ones.

General		Specific
job	=	senior accountant for Softbyte Press
computer	=	Acer 9000
person	=	Sarah Chu, production manager

The more specific your words, the sharper your meaning.

General	structure
	dwelling
	vacation home
	log cabin
Specific	log cabin in Ontario
	a three-room log cabin on the banks of Green Lake

Notice how the picture becomes more vivid as we move to lower levels of generality.

Abstract words name qualities, concepts, or feelings (*beauty, luxury, depression*) whose exact meaning has to be nailed down by *concrete* words—words that name things we can know through our five senses.

Abstract		Concrete
a **beautiful** view	=	snowcapped mountains, a wilderness lake, pink granite ledge, ninety-foot birch trees
a **luxurious** condominium	=	imported tiles, glass walls, oriental rugs
a **depressed** worker	=	suicidal urge, insomnia, feelings of worthlessness, no hope for improvement

Informative writing *tells* and *shows*.

> **General**   One of our **workers** was **injured** by a **piece of equipment recently**.

The boldface words only *tell* without showing.

> **Specific**   **Arlene Kowalchuk** suffered a **broken thumb** while working on a **lathe yesterday**.

Choose informative words that express exactly what you mean. Don't write *thing* when you mean *lever, switch, micrometer,* or *disk*. Instead of evaluating an employee as *good, great, disappointing,* or *terrible,* use terms that are more concrete, such as *reliable, skillful, dishonest,* or *incompetent*—further clarified by examples, such as *never late for work*.

In some instances, of course, you may wish to generalize for the sake of diplomacy. Instead of writing *Bill, Mary, and Sam have been tying up the office phones with personal calls,* you might prefer to generalize: *Some employees have been*. The second version makes the point without accusing anyone in particular.

When you can, provide solid numbers and statistics that get your point across:

General	In 1972, thousands of people were killed or injured on America's highways. Many families had at least one relative who was a casualty. After the speed limit was lowered to 55 miles per hour in late 1972, the death toll began to drop.
Specific	In 1972, 56,000 people died on America's highways; 200,000 were injured; 15,000 children were orphaned. In that year, if you were a member of a family of five, chances are that someone related to you by blood or law was killed or injured in an auto accident. After the speed limit was lowered to 55 miles per hour in late 1972, the death toll dropped steadily to 41,000 in 1975.

Concrete and specific expressions not only are more informative; they are more persuasive as well.

Exercise 16

Revise the following sentences to make them more precise or informative.

a. Our outlet does more business than Montreal.

b. Anaerobic fermentation is used in this report.

c. Confusion is in control of this office.

d. Your crew damaged a piece of office equipment.

e. His performance was admirable.

f. This thing bothers me.

Use Analogies to Sharpen the Image. Ordinary *comparison* shows similarities between two things *of the same class* (two computer keyboards, two methods of cleaning dioxin-contaminated sites). *Analogy* shows some essential similarity between two things of *different classes* (report writing and computer programming, computer memory and post office boxes).

Analogies are good for emphasizing a point (*Some rain is now as acidic as vinegar*). They are especially useful in translating something abstract, complex, or unfamiliar, as long as the easier subject is broadly familiar to readers. Analogy therefore calls for particularly careful analyses of audience.

Analogies can save words and convey vivid images. *Collier's Encyclopedia* describes the tail of an eagle in flight as "spread like a fan." The following sentence from a description of a trout feeder mechanism uses an analogy to clarify the positional relationship between two working parts:

Analogy	The metal rod is inserted (and centred, **crosslike**) between the inner and outer sections of the clip.

Without the analogy *crosslike,* we would need something like this to visualize the relationship:

> **Missing analogy**
>
> The metal rod is inserted, **perpendicular to the long plane and parallel to the flat plane,** between the inner and outer sections of the clip.

This second version is doubly inefficient: more words are needed to communicate, and more work is needed to understand the meaning.

Besides naming things vividly, analogies help *explain* things. The following analogy from the *Congressional Research Report* helps us understand something unfamiliar (dangerous levels of a toxic chemical) by comparing it to something more familiar (human hair).

> **Analogy**
>
> A dioxin concentration of 500 parts per trillion is lethal to guinea pigs. One part per trillion is roughly equal to the thickness of a human hair compared to the distance across North America.

Adjusting the Tone

Your tone is your personal stamp—the personality that takes shape between the lines. The tone you create depends on (1) the distance you impose between yourself and the reader, and (2) the attitude you show toward the subject.

Assume that a friend is going to take over a job you've held. You've decided to write your friend instructions for parts of the job. Here is your first sentence:

Informal

> Now that you've arrived in the glamorous world of office work, put on your track shoes; this is no ordinary manager-trainee job.

First, we notice that the sentence imposes little distance between the writer and the reader (it uses the direct address, "you," and the humorous suggestion to "put on your track shoes"). The ironic use of "glamorous" suggests that the writer means just the opposite: that the job holds little glamour.

For a different reader (the recipient of a company training manual, for example), the writer would have chosen some other opening:

Semi-formal

> As a manager trainee at GlobalTech, you will work for many managers. In short, you will spend little of your day seated at your desk.

The tone now is serious, no longer intimate, and the writer expresses no distinct attitude toward the job. For yet another audience (those who will read an annual report for clients or investors), the writer again might alter the tone:

Formal

> Manager trainees at GlobalTech are responsible for duties that extend far beyond desk work.

Here the businesslike shift from second- to third-person address makes the tone too impersonal for any document addressed to the trainees themselves.

We already know how tone works in speaking. When you meet someone new, for example, you respond in a tone that defines your relationship:

Tone announces interpersonal distance

> Honoured to make your acquaintance. [formal tone—greatest distance]
>
> How do you do? [formal]
>
> Nice to meet you. [semi-formal—medium distance]
>
> Hello. [semi-formal]
>
> Hi. [informal—least distance]
>
> What's happening? [informal—slang]

Each of these greetings is appropriate in some situations, inappropriate in others.

To decide on an appropriate distance from which to address a particular audience, follow these guidelines:

- Use a formal or semi-formal tone in writing for superiors, professionals, or academics (depending on what you think the reader expects).
- Use a semi-formal or informal tone in writing for colleagues and subordinates (depending on how close you feel to your readers).
- Use an informal tone when you want your writing to be conversational, or when you want it to sound like a person talking.
- Above all, find out what the preferences are in your organization.

Whichever tone you select, be consistent throughout your document.

| **Inconsistent tone** | My office isn't fit for a pig [*too informal*]; it is ungraciously unattractive [*too formal*]. |
| **Revised** | The shabbiness of my office makes it an unfit place to work. |

In general, lean toward an informal tone without falling into slang.

In addition to setting the distance between writer and reader, your tone implies your *attitude* toward the subject and the reader:

Tone announces attitude

> We dine at seven.
>
> Dinner is at seven.
>
> Let's eat at seven.
>
> Let's chow down at seven.
>
> Let's strap on the feedbag at seven.
>
> Let's pig out at seven.

The words we choose tell readers a great deal about where we stand.

If readers expect an impartial report, try to keep your own biases out of it. But for situations in which your opinion *is* expected, or in which you perceive some danger or ethics violation, let readers know where you stand.

Plain English needed	Avoid prolix nebulosity.
Revised	Don't be wordy and vague.

Say *I enjoyed the fibre optics seminar* instead of: *My attitude toward the fibre optics seminar was one of high approval.* Say *Let's liven up our dull relationship* instead of: *We should inject some rejuvenation into our lifeless liaison.*

In an upcoming meeting about the reader's job evaluation, does your reader expect to *discuss* the evaluation, *talk it over, have a chat,* or *chew the fat?* If the situation calls for a serious tone, don't use language that suggests a casual attitude—or vice versa. Use the following strategies for making your tone conversational and appropriate.

Use an Occasional Contraction. Unless you have reason to be formal, use (but do not overuse) contractions. Balance an *I am* with an *I'm,* a *you are* with a *you're,* an *it is* with an *it's* (as we've done throughout this book).

Missing contraction	Do not be wordy and vague.
Revised	Don't be wordy and vague.

Generally, use contractions only with pronouns, not with nouns or proper nouns (names).

Awkward contractions	Barbara'll be here soon. Health's important
Ambiguous contractions	The dog's barking. Bill's skiing.

These ambiguous contractions could be confused with possessive constructions.

Address Readers Directly. Use the personal pronouns *you* and *your* to connect with readers.

Impersonal tone	Students at our college will find the faculty always willing to help.
Personal tone	As a student at our college, **you** will find the faculty always willing to help.

Research shows that readers relate better to something addressed directly to them.

Caution: Use *you* and *your* only to correspond *directly* with the reader, as in a letter, memo, instructions, or some form of advice, encouragement, or persuasion. By using *you* and *your* when your subject and purpose call for first or third person, you might write something wordy and awkward like this:

Wordy and awkward	**When you** are in northern Ontario, **you** can see wilderness lakes everywhere around **you.**
Appropriate	Wilderness lakes are everywhere in northern Ontario.

Exercise 17

The following sentences contain pretentious language, unclear expression of attitude, missing contractions, or indirect address. Adjust the tone.

a. Further interviews are a necessity to our ascertaining the most viable candidate.

b. This project is beginning to exhibit the characteristics of a loser.

c. We are pleased to tell you that you are a finalist.

d. Do not submit the proposal if it is not complete.

e. Employees must submit travel vouchers by May 1.

f. Persons taking this test should use the HELP option whenever they need it.

g. I am not unappreciative of your help.

h. My disapproval is far more than negligible.

Use **I** *and* **We** *When Appropriate.* Instead of disappearing behind your writing, use *I* or *We* when referring to yourself or your organization.

Distant	The writer would like a refund.
Revised	I would like a refund.

A message becomes doubly impersonal when both the writer and the reader disappear.

Impersonal	The requested report will be sent next week.
Personal	**We** will send the report **you** requested next week.

Use the Active Voice. Because the active voice is more direct and economical than the passive voice, it generally creates a less formal tone. (Review pages 244–246.)

Passive and impersonal	Travel expenses cannot be reimbursed unless receipts are submitted.
Active and personal	We cannot reimburse your travel expenses unless you submit receipts.

Exercise 18

The following sentences have too few *I* or *We* constructions or too many passive constructions. Adjust the tone.

a. Payment will be made as soon as an itemized bill is received.

b. You will be notified.

c. Your help is appreciated.

d. Our reply to your bid will be sent next week.

    e. Your request will be given our consideration.

    f. My opinion of this proposal is affirmative.

    g. This writer would like to be considered for your opening.

Emphasize the Positive. Whenever you offer advice, suggestions, or recommendations, try to emphasize benefits rather than flaws.

Critical tone	Because of your division's lagging productivity, a management review may be needed.
Encouraging tone	A management review might help boost productivity in your division.

Avoid an Overly Informal Tone. We generally do not write in the same way we would speak to friends at the local burger joint or street corner. Achieving a conversational tone does not mean lapsing into substandard usage, slang, profanity, or excessive colloquialisms. *Substandard usage* ("He ain't got none," "I seen it today," "She brang the book") fails to meet standards of educated expression. *Slang* ("hurling," "belted," "bogus," "bummed") usually has specific meaning only for members of a particular in-group. *Profanity* ("This idea sucks," "What the hell") not only displays contempt for the audience but often earns contempt for the person using it. *Colloquialisms* ("O.K.," "a lot," "snooze," "in the bag") are understood more widely than slang, but tend to appear more in speaking than in writing.

    Slang and profanity are almost always inappropriate in school or workplace writing. The occasional colloquial expression, however, helps soften the tone of any writing—as long as the situation calls for a measure of informality. Tone is considered offensive when it violates the reader's expectations: when it seems disrespectful, tasteless, distant and aloof, too chummy, casual, or otherwise inappropriate for the topic, the reader, and the situation.

    A formal, or academic, tone, is perfectly appropriate in countless writing situations: a research paper, a job application, a report for the company president. In a history essay, for example, we would not refer to Mackenzie King and Pierre Trudeau as "those dudes, Mac and Pierre."

    Whenever we begin with rough drafting or brainstorming, our tone might be overly informal and is likely to require some adjustment during subsequent drafts.

Avoid Bias. Even controversial subjects deserve unbiased treatment. Imagine you have been sent to investigate the causes of an employee-management confrontation at your company's Orillia branch. Your initial report, written for the Toronto central office, is intended simply to describe what happened. Here is how an unbiased description might read:

A factual account

At 9:00 a.m. on Tuesday, January 21, eighty women employees set up picket lines around the executive offices of our Orillia branch, bringing business to a halt. The group issued a formal protest, claiming that their working conditions were repressive, their salary scale unfair, and their promotional opportunities limited. The women demanded affirmative action, insisting that the company's hiring and promotional policies and wage scales be revised. The demonstration ended when Garvin Tate, vice president in charge of personnel, promised to appoint a committee to investigate the group's claims and to correct any inequities.

Notice the absence of implied judgments; the facts are presented objectively. A less impartial version of the event, from a protestor's point of view, might read:

A biased version

Last Tuesday, sisters struck another blow against male supremacy when eighty women employees paralyzed the company's repressive and sexist administration for more than six hours. The timely and articulate protest was aimed against degrading working conditions, unfair salary scales, and lack of promotional opportunities for women. Stunned executives watched helplessly as the group organized their picket lines, determined to continue their protest until their demands for equal rights were addressed. An embarrassed vice-president quickly agreed to study the group's demands and to revise the company's discriminatory policies. The success of this long-overdue confrontation serves as an inspiration to oppressed women employees everywhere.

Judgmental words (*male supremacy, degrading, paralyzed, articulate, stunned, discriminatory*) inject the writer's attitude, even though it isn't called for. In contrast to this bias, the following version patronizingly defends the status quo:

A biased version

Our Orillia branch was the scene of an amusing battle of the sexes last Tuesday, when a group of irate feminists, eighty strong, set up picket lines for six hours at the company's executive offices. The protest was lodged against supposed inequities in hiring, wages, working conditions, and promotion for women in our company. The radicals threatened to surround the building until their demands for "equal rights" were met. A bemused vice-president responded to this carnival demonstration with patience and dignity, assuring the militants that their claims and demands—however inaccurate and immoderate—would receive just consideration.

Again, qualifying adjectives and superlatives slant the tone.

Being unbiased, of course, doesn't mean burying your head—and your values—in the sand. Remaining neutral about something you know to be wrong or dangerous is unethical (Kremers 59). If, for instance, you conclude that the Orillia protest was clearly justified, say so.

Avoid Sexist Usage. Sexist usage refers to doctors, lawyers, and other professionals as *he* or *him*, while referring to nurses, administrative assistants, and homemakers as *she* or *her*. In this traditional stereotype, males do the jobs that really matter and that pay higher wages, whereas females serve only as support and decoration. When females do invade traditional "male" roles, we might express our surprise at their boldness by calling them *female executives, female sportscasters, female surgeons,* or *female hockey players.* Likewise, to demean males who have settled for "female" roles, we sometimes refer to *male secretaries, male nurses, male flight attendants,* or *male models.*

The following are guidelines for non-sexist usage:

Guidelines for non-sexist usage

1. Use neutral expressions:

chair or chairperson	rather than	chairman
businessperson	rather than	businessman
supervisor	rather than	foreman
police officer	rather than	policeman
letter carrier	rather than	postman
homemaker	rather than	housewife
humanity or humankind	rather than	mankind
actor	rather than	actor vs. actress

2. Rephrase to eliminate the pronoun, if you can do so without altering your original meaning.

> **Sexist**   A writer will succeed if **he** revises.
>
> **Revised**   A writer who revises succeeds.

3. Use plural forms.

> **Sexist**   A writer will succeed if **he** revises.
>
> **Revised**   Writers will succeed if **they** revise (but *not* A writer will succeed if **they** revise.)

When using a plural form, avoid creating an error in pronoun-referent agreement by having the *plural* pronoun *they* or *their* refer to a *singular* referent (as in ***Each writer** should do **their** best*). Note: The Oxford English Dictionary committee now approves this "error" but it is not yet widely accepted.

4. When possible (as in direct address) use *you: **You** will succeed if **you** revise.* But use this form only when addressing someone directly. (See page 269 for discussion.)

5. Use occasional pairings (*him* or *her, she* or *he, his* or *hers*): *A writer will succeed if **she** or **he** revises.*

    But note that overuse of such pairings can be awkward: *A writer should do **his or her** best to make sure that **he or she** connects with **his or her** readers.* Most handbooks now encourage alternating use between the two pronouns, and discourage pairings and *he/she: An effective writer always focuses on **her** audience; the writer strives to connect with all **his** readers.*

6. Drop diminutive endings such as *-ess* and *-ette* used to denote females (*poetess, drum majorette, actress,* etc.).

7. Use *Ms.* instead of *Mrs.* or *Miss,* unless you know that person prefers one of the traditional titles. Or omit titles completely: *Roger Tse* and *Morag Kelly; Tse* and *Kelly.*

8. In quoting sources that have ignored present standards for non-sexist usage, consider these options: Insert [*sic*] ("thus" or "so") following the first instance of sexist terminology in a particular passage. Use ellipsis to omit sexist phrasing. Paraphrase the material, instead of quoting it directly.

Avoid Offensive Usages of All Types. Enlightened communication respects all people in reference to their specific cultural, racial, ethnic, and national background; sexual and religious orientation; age or physical condition. References to individuals and groups should be as neutral as possible; no matter how inadvertent, any expression that seems condescending or judgmental or that violates the reader's sense of appropriateness is offensive. Detailed guidelines for reducing biased usage appear in these two works, among others:

Schwartz, Marilyn, et al. *Guidelines for Bias-Free Writing.* Bloomington: Indiana UP, 1995.

Publication Manual of the American Psychological Association, 4th ed. Washington, DC: American Psychological Association, 1994.

Below is a sampling of suggestions adapted from the previous works:

■ When referring to members of a particular culture, be as specific as possible about that culture's identity: Instead of *Latin American* or *Asian* or *Hispanic,* for instance, use *Cuban American* or *Korean* or *Nicaraguan.*

   Avoid judgmental expressions: Instead of *third-world* or *undeveloped nations* or the *Far East,* use *developing* or *newly industrialized nations* or *East Asia.* Instead of *non-whites,* refer to *people of colour.*

■ When referring to someone who has a disability, avoid terms that could be considered pitying or overly euphemistic, such as *victims, unfortunates, challenged,* or *differently abled.* Focus on the individual instead of the disability: Instead of *blind person* or *amputee,* refer to *a person who is blind* or *a person who has lost an arm.*

   In general usage, avoid expressions that demean those who have medical conditions: *retard, mental midget, insane idea, lame excuse, the blind leading the blind, able-bodied workers,* etc.

■ When referring to members of a particular age group, use *girl* or *boy* for people of age fourteen or under; *young person, young adult, young man,* or *young woman* for those of high-school age; and *woman* or *man* for those of college age. (*Teenager* or *juvenile* carries certain negative connotations.) Instead of *the elderly,* use *older persons.*

Exercise 19

The following sentences contain negative emphasis, excessive informality, biased expressions, or offensive usage. Adjust the tone.

a. If you want your workers to like you, show sensitivity to their needs.

b. By not hesitating to act, you prevented my death.

c. The union has won its struggle for a decent wage.

d. The group's spokesman demanded salary increases.

e. Each employee should submit his vacation preferences this week.

f. While the girls played football, the men waved pom-poms.

g. Aggressive management of this risky project will help you avoid failure.

h. The explosion left me blind as a bat for nearly an hour.

i. This dude would be an excellent employee if only he could learn to chill out.

Considering the Cultural Context

The style guidelines in this chapter apply specifically to standard English in North America. But practices and preferences can differ widely in different cultural contexts. Certain cultures might prefer long sentences and technical language, to convey an idea's full complexity. Other cultures value expressions of respect, politeness, praise, and gratitude more than clarity or directness (Hein 125–26; Mackin 349–50).

Some documents in other languages tend to be more formal than in English, and some rely heavily on passive voice (Weymouth 144). French readers, for example, may prefer an elaborate style that reflects sophisticated and complex modes of thinking. In contrast, our "plain English," conversational style might connote simple-mindedness, disrespect, or incompetence (Thrush 277).

In translation or in a different cultural context, certain words carry offensive or unfavourable connotations. A few notable disasters (Gesteland 20; Victor 44):

- The Chevrolet *Nova*—meaning "don't go" in Spanish
- The Finnish beer *Koff*—for an English-speaking market
- Colgate's *Cue* toothpaste—an obscenity in French
- A brand of bicycle named *Flying Pigeon*—imported for a North American market

Idioms ("strike out," "ground rules") hold no logical meaning for other cultures. Slang ("bogus," "fat city") and colloquialisms ("You bet," "Gotcha") can strike readers as too informal and crude.

Any form of offensive style (including profanity and inappropriate humour) can alienate audiences—toward your company *and* your culture (Sturges 32).

Avoiding Reliance on Automated Tools

Many of the strategies in this chapter could be executed rapidly with word-processing software. By using the *global search and replace function* in some programs, you can command the computer to search for ambiguous pronoun references. The computer will also detect overuse of passive voice, *to be* verbs, *There* and *It* sentence openers, negative constructions, clutter words, needless prefaces and qualifiers, overly technical language, jargon, sexist language, etc. With an on-line dictionary or thesaurus, you can check definitions or see a list of synonyms for a word you have used in your document.

But these editing aids can be extremely imprecise. No amount of automation is likely to eliminate the writer's burden of *choice*. None of the rules or advice offered in this chapter applies universally. Ultimately, the informed writer's sensitivity to meaning, emphasis, and tone—the human contact—determines the effectiveness of any document.

Using Objective Self-evaluation Tools

This chapter presents many tools for polishing writing. However, you may not know where to start, or even if much editing is needed. Moreover, you may have to evaluate the readability of your own writing, a difficult task at best. If so, you will find the following objective indexes useful.

1. *Percentage of SVO and SVC sentences.* Most clear writing features a high percentage (75% or better) of basic sentence patterns, **subject-verb-object** (SVO) and **subject-verb-complement** (SVC).

   > Hockey players need skating skills. (SVO)
   > Hockey players take risks on the ice. (SVO+C)
   >
   > Hockey players are resilient. (SVC)
   > Pro hockey players are reluctant to play in Canada. (SVC+C)
   >
   > In most cases, pro hockey players hire player agents. (Adverbial opening + SVO)
   > Consequently, they seldom participate in contract negotiations. (Adverbial opening + SVC)

   Quick index: Examine a passage of ten sentences or more. **Confirm that 75% or more of the sentences use an SVO or SVC sentence pattern.**

   Note: Other, more complicated, patterns include *compound sentences* (two or more independent clauses), *complex sentences* (one independent clause and one or more dependent clauses), and *compound-complex sentences* (two or more independent clauses and at least one dependent clause).

2. *Words before subject.* Readable sentences quickly get to the point, even though many sentences start with transition words.

Quick index: In a passage of ten or more sentences, calculate the average number of words before the sentences' subjects. **That average should be three words or less.**

3. *Words between subject and verb.* Occasionally, you can afford to place words between the subject and verb (John, *a large, ungainly man with a pronounced limp,* slowly walked home). But you should **restrict the average number of intervening words to three or less.**

4. *Percentage of linking verbs.* Forms of the verb *to be* (*is, are, has been, will be, would have been*) and words like *seems, appears,* and *looks* link subjects and predicates. In most cases, linking verbs contribute to wordy and weaker phrasing than with active verbs. (Compare "he is a trainer of dogs" with "he trains dogs".)

   Quick index: Count all the verbs in a passage of at least 100 words. Then calculate the percentage of **linking verbs; these less efficient verbs should comprise 30% or less of the total number of verbs** in the passage.

5. *Fog Index.* During World War II, two *New York Times* editors, Gunning and Mueller, worried that part of their newspaper's rapidly growing readership would not easily understand the paper's stories. So, the editors devised a readability index based on two main principles:

   - The longer the sentence, the harder it is to understand.

   - "Big" words (of three or more syllables) contribute to reading difficulty.

In practice, Gunning and Mueller's *Fog Index* is based on these guidelines:

   - A document's readability can be gauged by taking random samples.
   - Each sample passage needs to be about 100 words (or more), to give an accurate measurement of readability.
   - Each sample passage must comprise complete sentences.
   - Proper nouns of three or more syllables ("Saskatchewan") and words which *become* three syllables by adding "es" ("excesses") or "ed" ("exceeded") should not be counted as part of the "big" words.

A Fog Index calculation includes five steps. The following calculation is for the two paragraphs in point number 4, above.

1. No. of sentences		5
2. No. of words		92
3. Avg. sentence length		18.4
4. % of "big" words		5.4
5. Sub-total		23.8
		x 0.4
Fog Index		**9.52**

A Fog Index of 9.52 roughly translates to a Grade 10 reading level. But the bottom line index tells only part of the story. The examined passage has a low rating primarily because only 5 of the 92 words have three or more syllables.

By contrast, the paragraph that starts at the top of page 276 ("Many of the strategies . . . have used in your document.") has an index of 18.4, mainly because 22.5 percent of the words have three or more syllables. Literally interpreted, that index says the passage requires a Ph.D. candidate's reading level. But is the paragraph really that difficult to follow? Probably not—words such as *strategies, executed, rapidly,* and *word-processing* should not pose a problem for the readers of this textbook.

This text tries to maintain a Fog Index of 11 to 13. Most of your business and technical writing should have an index of 10 to 12. Remember, though, do not panic if the index is higher; the high reading *may* result from a high percentage of three-syllable words, most of which your readers know very well. If a high reading results from a high average sentence length, then you should edit to correct that problem.

Note: Many word-processing programs contain objective evaluation tools. Refer to your user's manual for more details.

☑ EXERCISES

1. Calculate Fog Index readings for various passages in this text. For each reading, consider:
   • Does that reading reflect the degree of difficulty?
   • Does the reading match the reading levels for anticipated readers of this book?

2. Use the five objective self-evaluation tools to assess the readability of a document important to you. (application letter, progress report, class term project report).

3. Find a passage that you find very difficult to read. Determine some of the causes of that difficulty by using the five objective indexes on pages 276–277 of this chapter.

☑ COLLABORATIVE PROJECT (ON-GOING)

Form a proofreading/editing group of three to four people. Evaluate and proofread each other's assignments. Use the editing advice in this chapter to improve conciseness, clarity, and naturalness. Compare the objective readability ratings for your writing to those of other writers in your group.

Designing Visuals

Avisual is any pictorial representation used to clarify a concept, emphasize a particular meaning, illustrate a point, or analyze ideas or data. Besides saving space and words, visuals help audiences process, understand, and remember information. Because they offer powerful new ways of looking at data, visuals reveal trends, problems, and possibilities that otherwise might remain buried in lists of facts and figures.

In printed or on-line documents, in oral presentations or multimedia programs, visuals are a staple of communication today. This chapter covers four main types of visuals: tables, graphs, charts, and illustrations.

Why Visuals Are Essential

Readers expect more than just raw information; they want the information processed for their understanding. Readers want to feel intelligent, to understand the message at a glance. Visuals help us answer many of the questions asked by readers as they process information:

Typical Reader Questions in Processing Information

- Which information is most important?
- Where, exactly, should I focus?
- What do these numbers mean?
- What should I be thinking or doing?
- What should I remember about this?
- What does it look like?
- How is it organized?
- How is it done?
- How does it work?

More receptive to images than to words, today's readers resist pages of mere printed text. Visuals help diminish a reader's resistance in several ways:

- *Visuals enhance comprehension by displaying abstract concepts in concrete, geometric shapes.* "How does the metric system work?" (Figure 12.1).
- *Visuals make meaningful comparisons possible.* "How do provinces compare in terms of environmental pollution?" (Figure 12.2). "How does one pound compare with one kilogram?" (Figure 12.1).
- *Visuals depict relationships.* "How does seasonal change affect the rate of construction in our city?" (see Figure 12.10). "What is the relationship between Fahrenheit and Celsius temperature?" (Figure 12.1).
- *Visuals serve as a universal language.* In the global workplace, carefully designed visuals can transcend cultural and language differences, and thus facilitate international communication (Figure 12.1).
- *Visuals provide emphasis.* To emphasize the change in death rates for heart disease and cancer since 1970, a table (Table 12.1) or bar graph (Figure 12.4) would be more vivid than a prose statement.

All You Need to Know About Metric
(For Your Everyday Life)

10

Metric is based on the Decimal system

The metric system is simple to learn. For use in your everyday life you will need to know only ten units. You will also need to get used to a few new temperatures. Of course, there are other units which most persons will not need to learn. There are even some metric units with which you are already familiar; those for time and electricity are the same as you use now.

BASIC UNITS

(comparative sizes are shown)

METRE: a little longer than a yard (about 1.1 yards)
LITRE: a little larger than a quart (about 1.06 quarts)
GRAM: a little more than the weight of a paper clip

1 METRE

1 YARD

COMMON PREFIXES
(to be used with basic units)

milli: one-thousandth (0.001)
centi: one-hundredth (0.01)
kilo: one-thousand times (1000)
For example
1000 millimetres = 1 metre
100 centimetres = 1 metre
1000 metres = 1 kilometre

1 LITRE

1 QUART

MILK MILK

25 DEGREES FAHRENHEIT

OTHER COMMONLY USED UNITS

millimetre: 0.001 metre diameter of a paper clip wire
centimetre: 0.01 metre a little more than the width of a paper clip (about 0.4 inch)
kilometre: 1000 metres somewhat farther than 1/2 mile (about 0.6 mile)
kilogram: 1000 grams a little more than 2 pounds (about 2.2 pounds)
millilitre: 0.001 litre five of them make a teaspoon

OTHER USEFUL UNITS
hectare: about 2 1/2 acres
metric ton: about one ton

25 DEGREES CELSIUS

1 POUND

BUTTER

WEATHER UNITS: **FOR TEMPERATURE** **FOR PRESSURE**
degrees celsius kilopascals are used
100 kilopascals = 29.5 inches of Hg (14.5 psi)

°C	−40	−20	0	20	37	60	80	100
°F	−40	0	32	80	98.6	160		212

water freezes body temperature water boils

1 KILOGRAM

BUTTER

Figure 12.1   Visuals that Clarify and Simplify
Source: National Institute of Standards and Technology, 1992.

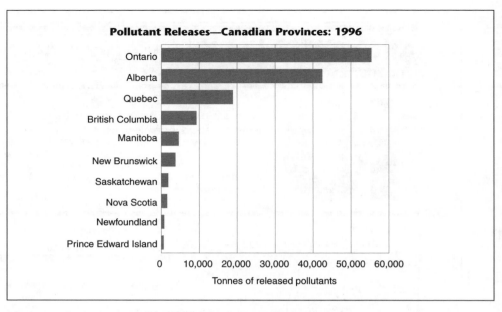

Figure 12.2   A Graph Displaying the "Big Picture"
Source: *Environment Canada's 1996 National Pollutant Release Inventory Summary Report*
available: www.ec.gc.ca/press/npn*96_b_e.htm

■ *Visuals condense and organize information, making it easier to remember and interpret.* A simple table, for instance, can summarize a long and difficult printed passage, as in the example that follows.

Assume that you are researching recent death rates for heart disease and cancer. From various sources, you collect these data:

Technical data in printed form can be hard to interpret

1. In 1970, 471.2 males and 267.4 females per 100,000 people died of heart disease; 227.6 males and 151.6 females died of cancer.
2. In 1980, 392.1 males and 213.5 females per 100,000 people died of heart disease; 240.3 males and 148.3 females died of cancer.
3. In 1990. . . .

In the written form above, numerical information is repetitious, tedious, and hard to interpret. As the amount of numerical data increases, so does our difficulty in processing this material. Arranged in Table 12.1 (page 283), these statistics become easier to compare and comprehend.

Along with your visual, analyze or interpret the important trends or the essential message you want your readers to see:

A caption explaining the numerical relationships

As Table 12.1 indicates, both male and female death rates from heart disease decreased from 1970 to 1992, but females showed a slightly larger decrease. Cancer deaths during this period increased slightly for both groups, with males showing the larger increase.

Table 12.1   Data Displayed in a Table

Death Rates for Heart Disease and Cancer, 1970–1992				
Number of Deaths (per 100,000) Population				
	Heart Disease		Cancer	
Year	Male	Female	Male	Female
1970	471.2	267.4	227.6	151.6
1980	392.1	213.5	240.3	148.3
1990	267.5	150.6	246.6	153.2
1992	255.8	141.4	244	152.8
Percent change, 1970–1992	−45.7	−47.1	+6.7	+0.8

Based on *Statistics Canada, Catalogue no. 82-221-XDE*

Besides their value as presentation devices, visuals help us analyze information. Table 12.1 is one example of how visuals enhance critical thinking by helping us to identify and interpret crucial information and to discover meaningful connections.

When to Use a Visual

Translate your writing into visuals whenever they make your point more clearly than the prose.[1] Use visuals to *clarify* and to enhance your discussion, not to *decorate* it. Use a visual display to direct the audience's focus or to help them remember something, as in the following situations (Dragga and Gong 46–48):

Use visuals in situations like these

- when you want to instruct or persuade
- when you want to draw attention to something immediately important
- when you expect the document to be consulted randomly or selectively (e.g., a manual or other reference work) instead of being read in its original sequence (e.g., a memo or letter)
- when you expect the audience to be relatively less educated, less motivated, or less familiar with the topic
- when you expect the audience to be in a distracting environment

An effective visual advances the writer's purpose and the reader's understanding.

---

1. One alternative approach to the writing process is to begin with one or more key visuals and then compose the text to introduce and interpret the visual.

What Types of Visuals to Consider

Different types of visuals serve different functions. The following overview sorts visual displays into four categories: tables, graphs, charts, and graphic illustrations. Each type of visual offers readers a new way of seeing, a different perspective.

Tables Display Organized Lists of Data. Tables display data (as numbers or words) in rows and columns for comparison. Use tables to present exact numerical values and to organize data so that readers can sort out relationships for themselves. Complex tables usually are reserved for more specialized readers.

Numerical tables present data for analysis, interpretation, and exact comparison.

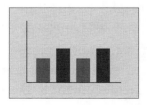

Prose tables organize verbal descriptions, explanations, or instructions for readers' access.

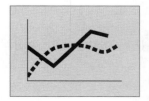

Graphs Display Numerical Relationships. Graphs translate numbers into shapes, shades, and patterns by plotting two or more data sets on a coordinate system. Use graphs to sort out or emphasize specific numerical relationships for readers. The visual representation helps readers grasp, at a glance, the approximate values, the point being made about those values, or the relationship being emphasized.

Bar graphs often show comparisons.

Line graphs often show changes over time.

Charts Display the Parts of a Whole. Charts depict relationships without the use of a coordinate system by using circles, rectangles, arrows, connecting lines, and other designs.

Pie charts show the parts or percentages of a whole.

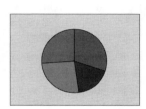

Organization charts show the links among departments, management structures, or other elements of a company.

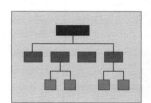

Flowcharts trace the steps (or decisions) in a procedure or stages in a process.

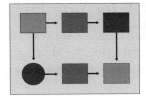

Tree charts show how the parts of an idea or a concept interrelate.

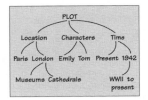

Gantt charts show when each phase of a project is to begin and end.

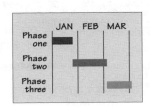

Pictorial charts (Pictograms) use icons (or isotypes) to symbolize the items being displayed or measured.

Graphic Illustrations Depict Actual or Virtual Views. Graphic illustrations are pictorial devices for helping readers visualize what something looks like, how it works, how it's done, how it happens, or where it's located. Certain diagrams present views that could not be captured by photographing or observing the object.

Representational diagrams present a realistic but simplified view, usually with essential parts labelled.

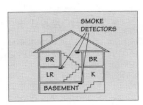
Source: Department of Energy

Exploded diagrams show the item pulled apart, to reveal its assembly.

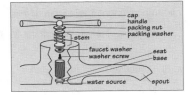

Cutaway diagrams eliminate outer layers to reveal inner parts.

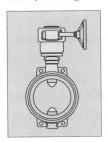

Block or schematic diagrams present the conceptual elements of a principle, process, or system to depict *function* instead of appearance.

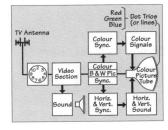

Maps enable readers to visualize a specific location or to comprehend data about a specific geographic region.

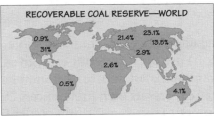
Source: Department of Energy

Photographs present an actual picture of the item, process, or procedure.

Source: SuperStock

How to Select Visuals for Your Purpose and Audience

You usually will have more than one way to display information in a visual format. To select the most effective display, consider carefully your specific purpose and the abilities and preferences of your audience.

Questions About a Visual's Purpose and Intended Audience

What is my purpose?

- What do I want the audience to do or think (know facts and figures, follow directions, make a judgment, understand how something works, perceive a relationship, identify something, see what something looks like, pay attention, other)?
- Do I want viewers to focus on one or more exact values, compare two or more values, or synthesize a range of approximate values?

Who is my audience?

- What is their technical background on this topic?
- What is their level of interest in this topic?

- Would they prefer the raw data or interpretations of the data?
- Are they accustomed to interpreting visuals?

Which type of visual might work best in this situation?

- What forms of information should this visual depict (numbers, shapes, words, pictures, symbols)?
- Which visual display would be most compatible with the type of judgment, action, or understanding I seek from this audience?
- Which visual display would this audience find most accessible?

Here are a few examples of the choices you must consider in selecting visuals:

- If you just want the audience to know facts and figures, a table might be sufficient, but if you want them to make a particular judgment about these data, a bar graph, line graph, or pie chart might be preferable.
- To depict the operating parts of a mechanism, an exploded or cutaway diagram might be preferable to a photograph.
- Expert audiences tend to prefer numerical tables, flowcharts, schematics, and complex graphs or diagrams they can interpret for themselves.
- General audiences tend to prefer basic tables, graphs, diagrams, and other visuals that direct their focus, and that interpret key points extracted from the data.

Choices to consider in selecting visuals

Although several alternatives might be possible, one particular type of visual (or a combination) usually is superior for a given purpose and audience. None of the above examples is, of course, immutable. Your particular audience or organization may express its own preferences. Or your choices may be limited by lack of equipment (software, scanners, digitizers), insufficient personnel (graphic designers, technical illustrators), or insufficient budget. In any case, your basic task is to enable the intended audience to interpret the visual correctly.

Preferred Displays for Specific Visual Purposes

PURPOSE	PREFERRED VISUAL
■ Organize numerical data	Table
■ Show comparative data	Table, bar graph, line graph
■ Show a trend	Line graph
■ Interpret or emphasize data	Bar graph, line graph, pie chart, map
■ Introduce an unfamiliar object	Photo, representational diagram
■ Display a project schedule	Gantt chart
■ Show how parts are assembled	Photo, exploded diagram
■ Show how something is organized	Organization chart, map
■ Give instructions	Prose table, photo, diagrams, flowchart
■ Explain a process	Flowchart, block diagram
■ Clarify a concept or principle	Block or schematic diagram, tree chart
■ Describe a mechanism	Photo, representational diagram, or cutaway diagram

Tables

Tables can display exact quantities, compare sets of data, and present information systematically and economically. Numerical tables such as Table 12.1 present *quantitative information* (data that can be measured). In contrast, prose tables present *qualitative information* (brief descriptions, explanations, or instructions). Table 12.2, for example, combines numerical data, probability estimates, comparisons, and instructions—all organized for the smoker's understanding of radon gas risk in the home.

Table 12.2   A Prose Table
Source: *Home Buyer's and Seller's Guide to Radon.* Washington: GPO, 1993

		Radon Risk if You Smoke		
Radon level	If 1,000 people who smoked were exposed to this level over a lifetime . . .	The risk of cancer from radon exposure compares to . . .	WHAT TO DO: Stop Smoking and . . .
20 pCi/L[a]	About 135 people could get lung cancer	← 100 times the risk of drowning	Fix your home
10 pCi/L	About 71 people could get lung cancer	← 100 times the risk of dying in a home fire	Fix your home
8 pCi/L	About 57 people could get lung cancer		Fix your home
4 pCi/L	About 29 people could get lung cancer	← 100 times the risk of dying in an airplane crash	Fix your home
2 pCi/L	About 15 people could get lung cancer	← 2 times the risk of dying in a car crash	Consider fixing between 2 and 4 pCi/L
1.3 pCi/L	About 9 people could get lung cancer	(Average indoor radon level)	(Reducing radon levels below 2 pCi/L is difficult)
0.4 pCi/L	About 3 people could get lung cancer	(Average outdoor radon level)	

Note: If you are a former smoker, your risk may be lower. [a]picocuries per litre

No table should be overly complex for its intended audience. An otherwise impressive-looking table, such as Table 12.3, is difficult for non-specialists to interpret because it presents too much information at once. We can see how an unethical writer might use a complex table to bury numbers that are questionable or embarrassing (R. Williams 12). Can you discover any hidden facts in Table 12.3? (For instance, which industry has been slowest in cleaning up its act?)

Table 12.3   A Complex Table

Toxic Release Inventory, by Industry and Source: 1990 to 1994									
In millions of pounds. Based on reports from almost 23,000 manufacturing facilities which have 10 or more full-time employees and meet established thresholds for using the list of more than 300 chemicals covered.									
INDUSTRY	1987 SIC[1] code	1990	1991	1992	1993	1994			
						Total[2]	Air[3] non-point	Air[4] point	Water
Total	(X)	2,603.7	2,684.3	2,449.6	2,157.4	1,976.9	350.0	991.0	47.0
Food and kindred prod.	20	9.9	12.0	11.9	12.0	10.3	2.5	6.3	0.1
Tobacco products	21	1.0	0.6	0.6	0.6	1.0	0.1	0.9	–
Textile mill products	22	23.4	22.2	19.1	17.6	15.9	3.2	12.5	0.1
Apparel and other textile prod.	23	1.1	1.3	1.3	1.0	1.3	0.3	1.0	–
Lumber and wood products	24	33.6	30.2	30.0	29.8	31.7	3.7	27.9	–
Furniture and fixtures	25	57.8	652.8	53.2	54.0	50.6	6.4	44.1	–
Paper and allied products	26	203.6	207.2	199.1	179.8	218.6	18.4	186.6	8.9
Printing and publishing	27	51.4	46.4	40.4	35.9	34.2	19.9	14.3	–
Chemical and allied products	28	1,007.9	960.5	991.3	874.4	700.7	87.5	220.4	33.5
Petroleum and coal products	29	62.4	56.5	61.7	50.9	43.8	28.4	13.6	0.5
Rubber and misc. plastic prod.	30	154.5	134.2	121.1	111.0	111.6	30.7	80.6	–
Leather and leather products	31	9.5	7.8	7.2	4.4	3.6	1.0	2.6	–
Stone, clay, glass products	32	20.5	16.4	14.3	14.3	12.4	2.1	8.9	–
Primary metal industries	33	438.6	386.8	341.2	304.6	293.8	21.6	68.7	1.7
Fabricated metals products	34	125.6	109.1	100.6	88.6	86.1	29.5	55.8	0.1
Industrial machinery and equip.	35	48.0	38.8	33.0	26.5	23.5	7.1	16.1	0.1
Electronic, electric equip.	36	73.4	60.2	47.1	32.9	29.0	6.1	22.7	0.1
Transportation equipment	37	157.5	137.5	125.3	123.6	119.7	29.5	89.9	0.1
Instruments and related prod.	38	38.9	34.9	29.1	22.5	15.7	4.2	11.3	0.3
Misc. manufacturing industries	39	21.6	18.4	16.9	15.2	13.7	3.9	9.8	–
Multiple codes	20–39	251.7	203.6	191.8	137.2	142.9	39.0	70.3	1.3
No codes	20–39	11.9	26.8	13.6	20.1	16.9	5.2	6.4	0.2

– Represents or rounds to zero.   (X) Not applicable.   [1]Standard Industrial Classification, see text, section 13. [2]Includes other releases not shown separately.   [3]Fugitive.   [4]Stack.
Source: U.S. Environmental Protection Agency, 1994 Toxics Release Inventory, June 1996

Readers need to understand how the table is organized, where to find what they need, and how to interpret the information they find (Hartley 90).

Tables are constructed with various tools: (a) tab markers and tab keys on a word processor, (b) row-and-column displays in a spreadsheet program, (c) the "Table" command in better word-processing programs. The "Table" command option offers a full range of table editing features: cut and paste, adjust spacing, insert text between rows, add rows or columns, adjust column width, etc.

Guidelines for using tables   *Table Guidelines:* Whichever table options you employ, use the following general guidelines:

- Use a table only when you are reasonably sure it will enlighten—rather than frustrate—readers. For non-specialized readers, use fewer tables and keep them simple.

- Try to limit the table to one page. Otherwise write "continued" at the bottom, and begin the second page with the full title, "continued," and the original column headings.

- If the table is too wide for the page, turn it 90 degrees (landscape) and place its top toward the inside of the binding. Or divide the data into two tables. (Few readers may bother rotating the page to read the table broadside.)

- In your discussion, refer to the table by number, and explain what readers should be looking for; or include a prose caption with the table. Specifically, introduce the table, show it, and then interpret it.

For more specific information about creating tables, see the Table Construction Guidelines accompanying Table 12.4.

Tables work well for displaying exact values, but for easier interpretation, readers prefer graphs or charts. Geometric shapes (bars, curves, circles) generally are easier to remember than lists of numbers (Cochran et al. 25).

Any visual other than a table usually is categorized as a *figure,* and so titled (*Figure 1 Aerial View of the Panhandle Site*). Figures covered in this chapter include graphs, charts, and illustrations.

Like all other components in the document, visuals are designed with audience and purpose in mind (Journet 3). An accountant doing an audit might need a table listing exact amounts, whereas the average public stockholder reading an annual report would prefer the "big picture" in an easily grasped bar graph or pie chart (Van Pelt 1). Similarly, an audience of scientists might find Table 12.3 perfectly appropriate, but a less specialized audience (say, environmental groups) might prefer the clarity and simplicity of Figure 12.2.

Graphs

Graphs translate numbers into pictures. Plotted as a set of points (a *series*) on a coordinate system, a graph shows the relationship between two variables.

Graphs have a horizontal and a vertical axis. The horizontal axis carries categories (the independent variables) to be compared, such as years within a period (1990, 1995, 2000). The vertical axis shows the range of values (the dependent variables) for comparing or measuring the categories, such as the number of people who died from heart failure in a specific year. A dependent variable changes according to activity in the independent variable (e.g., a decrease in quantity over a set time, as in Figure 12.3). In the equation $y = f(x)$, x is the independent variable and y is the dependent variable.

Graphs are especially useful for displaying comparisons, changes, over time, patterns, or trends. When you decide to use a graph, choose the best type for your purpose: bar graph or line graph.

TABLE 12.4   Table Construction Guidelines

HOW TO CONSTRUCT A TABLE

① ► TABLE 1 ■ Science and Engineering Graduates in 1993 and 1994: 1995 Career Status

COLUMN HEADS

STUB HEAD ② ► DEGREE AND FIELD	Graduates 1993 and 1994 (1,000)	1995—PERCENT DISTRIBUTION				Median salary ($1,000) ③
		In school[a]	Employed		Not employed	
			In S&E[b]	In other		
All science fields	④ **580.2**	⑤ **25**	**10**	**59**	**6**	**22.8**
Computer science/math	69.2	13	32	51	4	29.0
⑥ Life sciences	121.1	37	10	47	5	⑦ 21.8
Physical sciences	33.2	39	27	30	4	25.5
Social sciences	356.7	⑧ ► X	5	67	7	21.2
All engineering fields[c]	**118.4**	**15**	**62**	**20**	**4**	**33.5**
Civil	18.1	13	67	17	3	31.0
Electrical/electronics	38.6	11	64	21	4	35.0
Industrial	6.4	9	59	28	3	34.0
Mechanical	28.9	12	66	17	4	31.5

ROW HEADS

NOTE ⑨ ► [a]Full-time grad. students. [b]Science & engineering. [c]Other fields not shown. (X) Not available.

SRC ⑩ *Source: National Science Foundation/SRS, National Survey of Recent College Graduates: 1995.*
Statistical Abstract of the United States: 1997 (117th edition). Washington: GPO: 611

1. Number the table in its order of appearance and provide a title that describes exactly what is being compared or measured.

2. Label stub, row, and column heads (*Degree and Field, Median salary, Computer Science*) so readers know what they are looking at.

3. Stipulate all units of measurement using familiar symbols and abbreviations ($, hr., no.). Define specialized symbols or abbreviations ($Å$ for *angstrom, db* for *decibel*) in a footnote.

4. Compare data vertically (in columns) instead of horizontally (in rows). Columns are easier to compare than rows. Try to include row or column averages or totals, as reference points for comparing individual values.

5. Use horizontal rules to separate headings from data. In a complex table, use vertical rules to separate columns. In a simple table, use as few rules as clarity allows.

6. List the items in a logical order (alphabetical, chronological, decreasing cost). Space listed items so they are not cramped or too far apart for easy comparison. Keep prose entries as brief as clarity allows.

7. Convert fractions to decimals, and align decimals vertically. Keep decimal places for all numbers equal. Round insignificant decimals to the nearest whole number.

8. Use *x, NA,* or a dash to signify any omitted entry, and explain the omission in a footnote ("Not available," "Not applicable").

9. Use footnotes to explain entries, abbreviations, or omissions. Label footnotes with lowercase letters so readers do not confuse the notation with the numerical data.

10. Cite data sources beneath any footnotes. When adapting or reproducing a copyrighted table for a work to be published, obtain written permission from the copyright holder.

Bar Graphs

Easily understood by most readers, bar graphs show discrete comparisons, as on a year-by-year or month-by-month basis. Each bar represents a specific quantity. Use bar graphs to help readers focus on one value or compare values that change over equal time intervals (expenses calculated at the end of each month, sales figures totalled at yearly intervals). Use a bar graph only to compare values that are noticeably different. Otherwise, all the bars will appear almost identical.

Simple Bar Graphs. The simple bar graph in Figure 12.3 displays one relationship taken from the data in Table 12.1, the rate of male deaths from heart disease. To aid interpretation, you can record exact values above each bar—but only if readers need exact numbers.

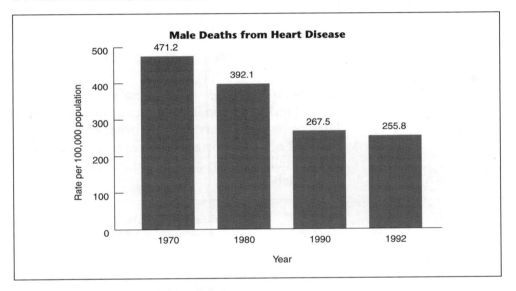

Figure 12.3   A Simple Bar Graph

Multiple-bar Graphs. A bar graph can display two or three relationships simultaneously, each relationship plotted as a separate series. Figure 12.4 displays two comparisons from Table 12.1, the rate of male deaths from both heart disease and cancer.

Whenever a graph shows more than one relationship (or series), each series of numbers is represented by a different pattern, colour, shade, or symbol, and the patterns are identified by a *legend.*

The more relationships a graph displays, the harder it is to interpret. As a rule, plot no more than three series of numbers on one graph.

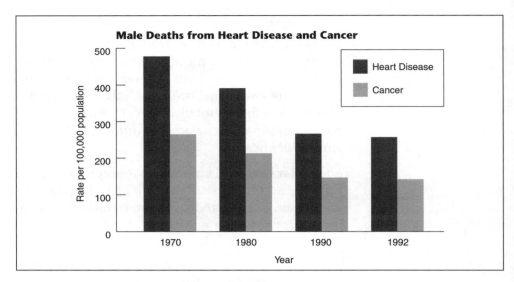

Figure 12.4   A Multiple-bar Graph

Horizontal-bar Graphs. To make a horizontal-bar graph, turn a vertical-bar graph (and scales) on its side. Horizontal-bar graphs are good for displaying a large series of bars arranged in order of increasing or decreasing value, as in Figure 12.5. The horizontal format leaves room for labelling the categories horizontally *(Service,* etc.). A vertical-bar graph would leave no room for horizontal labelling.

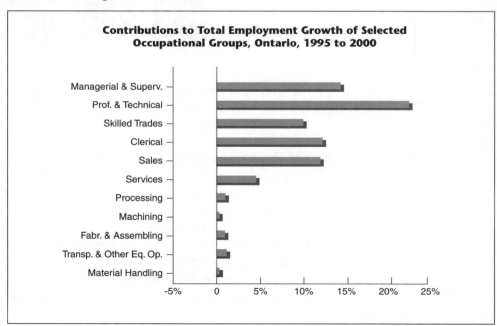

Figure 12.5   A Horizontal-bar Graph
Source: Labour Market Information and Research, Ontario Ministry of Education and Training

Stacked-bar Graphs. Instead of side-by-side clusters of bars, you can display multiple relationships by stacking bars. Stacked-bar graphs are especially useful for showing how much each item contributes to the whole. Figure 12.6 displays other comparisons from Table 12.1.

Display no more than four or five relationships in a stacked-bar graph. Excessive subdivisions and patterns create visual confusion.

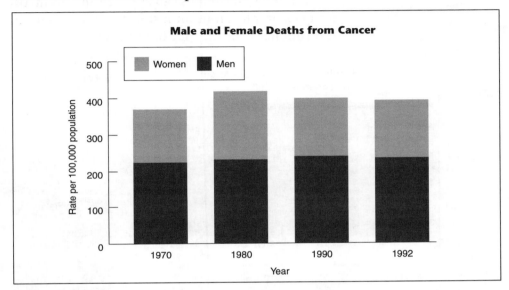

Figure 12.6   A Stacked-bar Graph

Deviation Bar Graphs. The deviation bar graph can display both positive and negative values, as in Figure 12.7. Notice how the vertical axis extends to the neg-

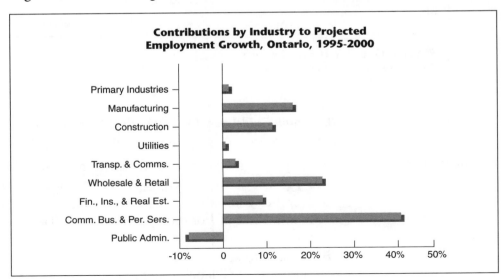

Figure 12.7   A Deviation Bar Graph
Source: Forecast using FOCUS-Ontario and PRISM-Ontario models, the Institute for Policy Analysis, University of Toronto

ative side of the zero baseline, following the same incremental division as above the baseline.

3-D Bar Graphs. Graphics software enables you to shade and rotate images and produce 3-dimensional views. The 3-D perspectives in Figure 12.8 engage our attention and add visual emphasis to the data.

Although 3-D graphs can enhance and dramatize a presentation, an overly complex graph can be almost impossible to interpret. Never sacrifice clarity and simplicity for the sake of visual effect.

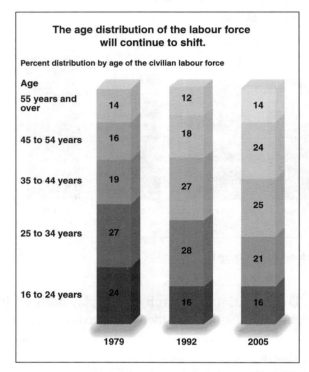

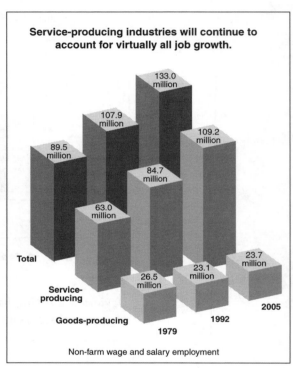

Figure 12.8   3-D Bar Graphs
Source: U.S. Bureau of Labor Statistics

Bar Graph Guidelines. Once you decide on a type of bar graph, use the following suggestions for presenting the graph to your audience.

Bar graph guidelines

- Keep the graph simple and easy to read. Avoid plotting more than three types of bars in each cluster. Avoid needless visual details.
- Number your scales in units the audience will find familiar and easy to follow. Units of 1 or multiples of 2, 5, or 10 are best (Lambert 45). Space the numbers equally.
- Label both scales to show what is being measured or compared. If space allows, keep all labels horizontal for easier reading.

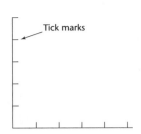 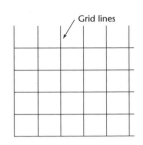

- Use *tick marks* to show the points of division on your scale. If the graph has many bars, extend the tick marks into *grid lines* to help readers relate bars to values.
- To avoid confusion, make all bars the same width (unless you are overlapping them). If you must produce your graphs by hand, use graph paper to keep bars and increments evenly spaced.
- In a multiple-bar graph, use a different pattern, colour, or shade for each bar in a cluster. Provide a legend identifying each pattern, colour, or shade.
- If you are trying for emphasis, be aware that darker bars are seen as larger, closer, and more important than lighter bars of the same size (Lambert 93).
- Cite data sources beneath the graph. When adapting or reproducing a copyrighted graph for a work to be published, you must obtain written permission from the copyright holder.
- In your discussion, refer to the graph by number ("Figure 1"), and explain what readers should be looking for; or include a prose caption along with the graph.

Many computer graphics programs automatically employ most of the design features discussed above. Anyone producing visuals, however, should know all the conventions.

Line Graphs

A line graph can accommodate many more data points than a bar graph (e.g., a twelve-month trend, measured monthly). Line graphs help readers synthesize large bodies of information in which exact quantities need not be emphasized. Whereas bar graphs display quantitative differences among items (cities, regions, yearly or monthly intervals), line graphs display data whose value changes over time, as in a trend, forecast, or other change during a specified time (profits, losses, growth). Some line graphs depict cause-and-effect relationships (e.g., how seasonal patterns affect sales or profits).

Simple Line Graphs. A simple line graph, as in Figure 12.9, uses one line to plot time intervals on the horizontal scale and values on the vertical scale. The relationship depicted here would be much harder to express in words alone.

Multiple-line Graphs. A multiple-line graph displays several relationships simultaneously, as in Figure 12.10.

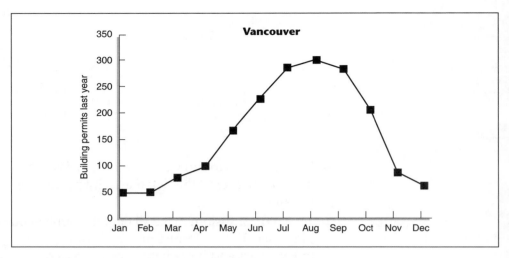

Figure 12.9   A Simple Line Graph

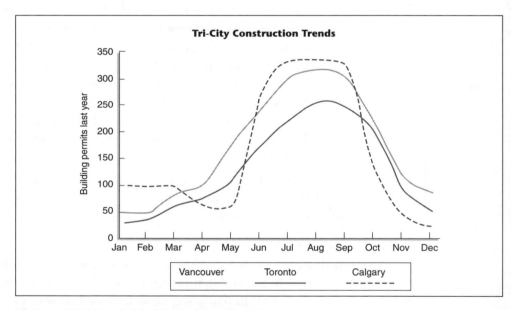

Figure 12.10   A Multiple-line Graph

For legibility, use no more than three or four curves in a single graph. Explain the relationships readers are supposed to see.

A caption explaining the visual relationships

Building permits in all three cities increased steadily as the weather warmed, but Calgary's increase was more erratic. Its permits declined for April–May, but then surpassed Vancouver's and Toronto's for June–September.

Band or Area Graphs. For emphasis and appeal, fill the area beneath each plotted line with a pattern. Figure 12.11 is a version of the Figure 12.9 line graph.

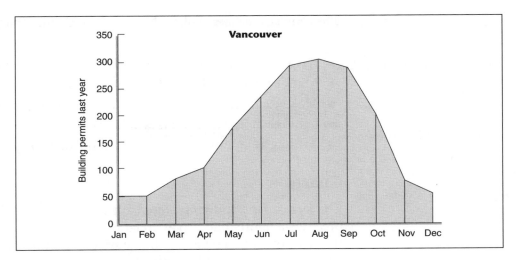

Figure 12.11   A Simple Band Graph

The multiple-bands in Figure 12.12 depict relationships among sums instead of the direct comparisons depicted in the equivalent Figure 12.10 line graph.

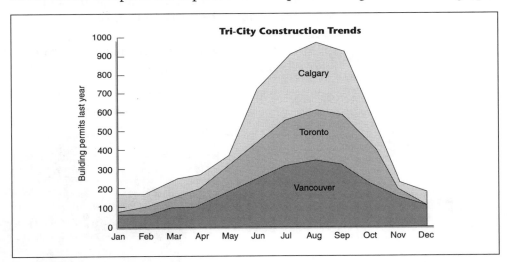

Figure 12.12   A Multiple-band Graph

Despite their visual appeal, multiple-band graphs are easy to misinterpret: In a multiple-line graph, each line depicts its own distance from the zero baseline. But in a multiple-band graph, the very top line depicts the *total*, each band below it being a part of that total (like stacked-bar graph segments). Always clarify these relationships for viewers.

Line Graph Guidelines. Follow bar graph guidelines (pages 294–295), with these additions:

Line graph guidelines

- Display no more than three or four lines on one graph.
- Mark each individual data point used in plotting each line.
- Make each line visually distinct (using colour, symbols, etc).
- Label each line so readers will know what it represents.
- Avoid grid lines that readers could mistake for plotted lines.

Charts

The terms *chart* and *graph* often appear interchangeably. But a chart is more precisely a figure that displays relationships (quantitative or cause-and-effect) that are not plotted on a coordinate system. Commonly used charts include pie charts, organizational charts, flowcharts, tree charts, and pictorial charts (pictograms).

Pie Charts

Considered easy for readers to understand, a pie chart depicts the percentages or proportions of the parts that make up a whole. In a pie chart, readers can compare the parts to each other as well as to the whole (to show how much was spent on what, how much income comes from which sources, and so on). Figure 12.13 shows a pie chart.

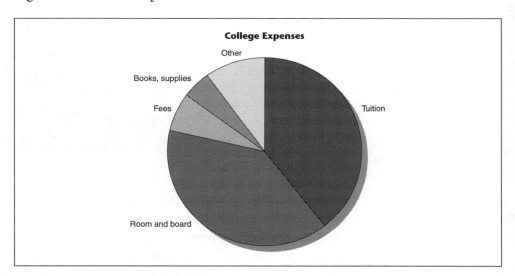

Figure 12.13   A Simple Pie Chart

Figure 12.14 shows two other versions of the pie chart in Figure 12.13. Version (a) displays dollar amounts, and version (b) the percentage relationships among these dollar amounts.

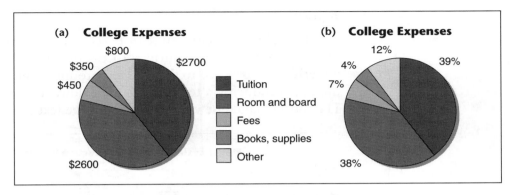

Figure 12.14   Two Other Versions of Figure 12.13

Pie Chart Guidelines. For constructing pie charts, follow these suggestions:

- Be sure the parts add up to 100 percent.
- If you must produce your charts by hand, use a compass and protractor for precise segments. Each 3.6-degree segment equals 1 percent. Include any number from two to eight segments. A pie chart containing more than eight segments is difficult to interpret, especially if the segments are small (Hartley 96).
- Combine small segments under the heading "Other."
- Locate your first radial line at 12 o'clock and then move clockwise from large to small (except for "Other," usually the final segment).
- For easy reading, keep all labels horizontal.

Organization Charts

An organization chart divides an organization into its administrative or managerial parts. Each part is ranked according to its authority and responsibility in relation to other parts and to the whole, as in Figure 12.15.

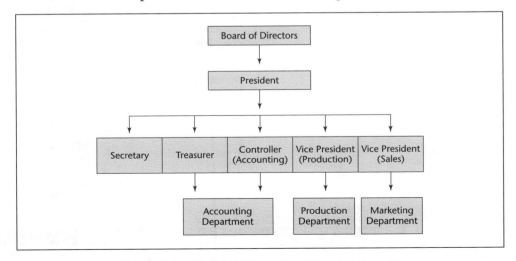

Figure 12.15   An Organization Chart for One Corporation

Flowcharts

A flowchart traces a procedure or process from beginning to end. In displaying the steps in a manufacturing process, the flowchart would begin at the raw materials and proceed to the finished product. Figure 12.16 traces the procedure for producing a textbook. (Other flowchart examples appear on pages 111 and 112, and elsewhere throughout the text.)

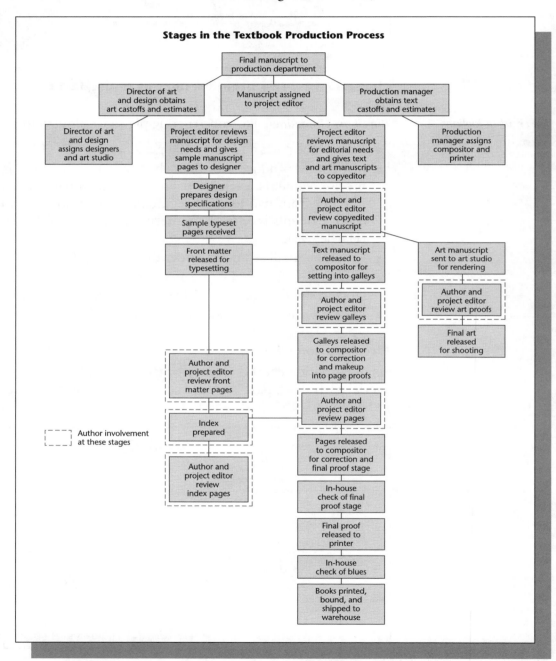

Figure 12.16   A Flowchart for Producing a Textbook
Source: *Harper & Row Author's Guide*

Tree Charts

Whereas flowcharts display the steps in a process, tree charts show how the parts of an idea or concept relate to each other. Figure 12.17 displays the parts of an outline for this chapter so that readers can better visualize relationships. The tree version seems clearer and more interesting than the prose listing.

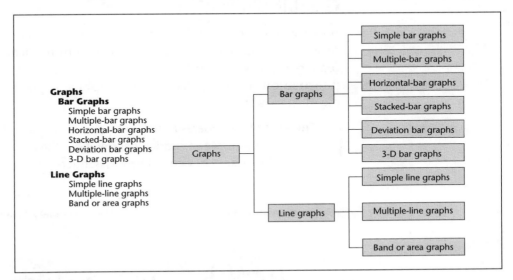

Figure 12.17   An Outline Converted to a Tree Chart

Pictograms

Pictograms depict numerical relationships with icons or symbols (cars, houses, smokestacks) of the items being measured, instead of using bars or lines. Each

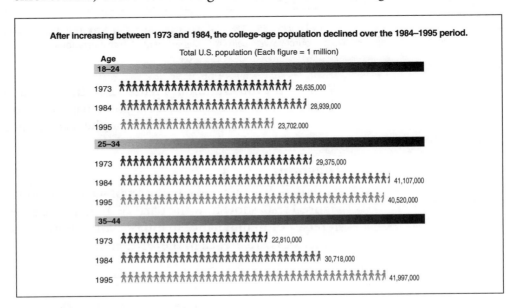

Figure 12.18   A Pictogram
Source: U.S. Bureau of the Census

symbol represents a stipulated quantity, as in Figure 12.18. Many graphics programs provide an assortment of predrawn symbols.

Use pictograms when you want to make information more interesting for non-technical audiences.

Graphic Illustrations

Illustrations consist of diagrams, maps, drawings, and photographs depicting relationships that are physical rather than numerical. Good illustrations help readers understand and remember the material (Hartley 82). Consider this information from a government pamphlet, explaining the operating principle of the seat belt:

> The safety-belt apparatus includes a tiny pendulum attached to a lever, or locking mechanism. Upon sudden deceleration, the pendulum swings forward, activating the locking device to keep passengers from pitching into the dashboard.

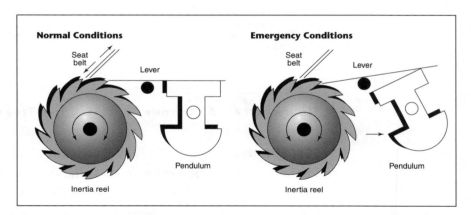

Figure 12.19   A Diagram of a Safety-belt Locking Mechanism
Source: *Safety Belts*. U.S. Department of Transportation

Without the illustration in Figure 12.19 the mechanism would be difficult to visualize. Clear and uncluttered, a good diagram eliminates unnecessary details and focuses only on material useful to the reader. The following pages illustrate some commonly used diagrams.

Diagrams

Exploded diagrams, like that of a brace for an adjustable basketball hoop in Figure 12.20, show how the parts of an item are assembled; they often appear in repair or maintenance manuals. Notice how all parts are numbered for the reader's easy reference in the written instructions.

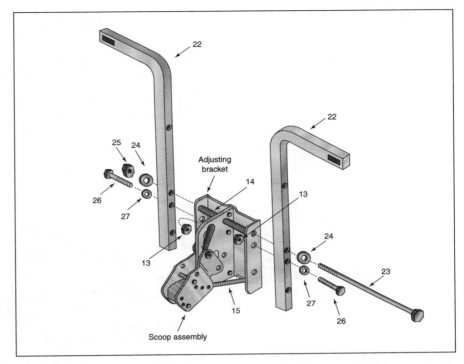

Figure 12.20   An Exploded Diagram of a Brace for a Basketball Hoop
Source: Courtesy of Spalding

Cutaway diagrams show the item with its exterior layers removed in order to reveal interior sections, as in Figure 12.21 on page 304. Unless the specific viewing perspective is immediately recognizable (as in Figure 12.21), define for readers the angle of vision: "top view," "side view," etc.

Block diagrams are simplified sketches that represent the relationship between the parts of an item, principle, system, or process. Because block diagrams are designed to illustrate *concepts* (such as current flow in a circuit), the parts are represented as symbols or shapes. The block diagram in Figure 12.22 on page 305 illustrates how any process can be controlled automatically through a feedback mechanism.

Figure 12.23 on page 305 shows the feedback concept applied as the cruise-control mechanism on a motor vehicle.

Increasingly available are electronic drawing programs, clip-art programs, image banks, and other resources for creating visuals or downloading pre-drawn images. Specialized diagrams, however, often require the services of graphic artists or technical illustrators. The client requesting or commissioning the visual provides the art professional with an *art brief* (often prepared by writers and editors) that spells out the visual's purpose and specifications for the visual.

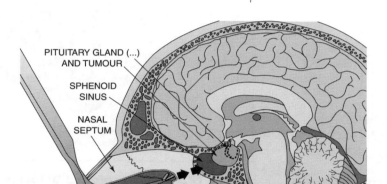

THE OPERATION

Incision

Transsphenoidal surgery is performed with the patient under general anesthesia and positioned on his back. The head is fixed in a special headrest, and the operation is monitored on a special x-ray machine (fluoroscope).

In the approach illustrated here (not used by all surgeons), a small incision is made in one side of the nasal septum **(Fig. 2)**. Part of the septum is then removed to provide access to the sphenoid sinus cavity **(Fig. 3)**.

Figure 2
Incision into nasal septum

PITUITARY GLAND (...)
AND TUMOUR

SPHENOID
SINUS

NASAL
SEPTUM

Figure 3
Removal of nasal septum to reach pituitary chamber

Figure 12.21   A Cutaway Diagram of a Surgical Procedure
Source: *Transphenoidal Approach for Pituitary Tumor.* ©1986 by The Ludann Co., Grand Rapids, MI

An art brief for Figure 12.21

For example, part of the brief addressed to the medical illustrator for Figure 12.21 might read as follows:

Purpose: to illustrate transsphenoidal adenomectomy for laypersons

- View: full cutaway, axial
- Range: descending from cranial apex to a horizontal plane immediately below the upper jaw and second cervical vertebra
- Depth: medial cross section
- Structures omitted: cranial nerves, vascular and lymphatic systems
- Structures included: gross anatomy of bone, cartilage, and soft tissue—delineated by colour, shading, and texture
- Structures highlighted: nasal septum, sphenoid sinus, and sella turcica, showing the pituitary embedded in a 1.5 cm tumour invading the sphenoid sinus via an area of erosion at the base of the sella

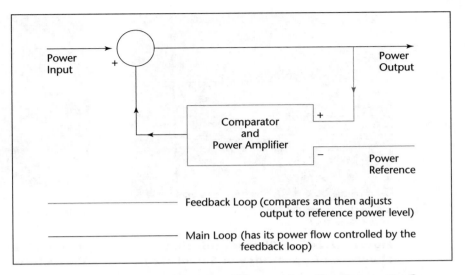

Figure 12.22   A Block Diagram Illustrating the Concept of Feedback

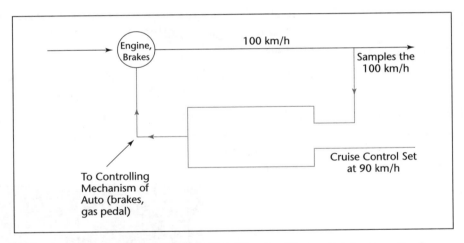

Figure 12.23   A Block Diagram Illustrating a Cruise-control Mechanism

Photographs

Photographs are especially useful for showing what something looks like (Figure 12.24) or how something is done (Figure 12.25).

No matter how visually engaging, a photograph is difficult to interpret if it includes needless details or fails to identify or emphasize the important material. One graphic design expert offers this practical advice for technical documents:

A Fixed-platform Oil Rig
Source: SuperStock

**Figure 12.24   A Photograph that
Shows the Appearance of Something**

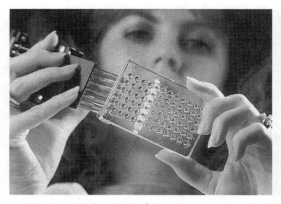

Antibody Screening Procedure
Source: SuperStock

**Figure 12.25   A Photograph that
Shows How Something Is Done**

> To use pictures as tools for communication, pick them for their capacity to carry meaning, not just for their prettiness as photographs, . . . [but] for their inherent significance to the [document]. (White, *Great Pages* 110, 122)

Specialized photographs often require the services of a professional who knows how to use angles, lighting, and special film to obtain the desired focus and emphasis.

Photograph Guidelines. Whenever you plan to include photographs in a document or a presentation, observe these guidelines:

*Guidelines for using
photographs*

- Try to simulate the approximate angle of vision readers would have in identifying or viewing the item or, for instructions, in doing the procedure (Figure 12.26).

Titration in Measuring Electron-spin Resonance
Source: SuperStock

**Figure 12.26   A Photograph that
Shows a Realistic Angle of Vision**

Replacing the Microfilter Activation Unit
Source: SuperStock

**Figure 12.27 A Photograph
that Needs to be Cropped**

Source: SuperStock

**Figure 12.28   The Cropped
Version of Figure 12.27**

- Trim (or crop) the photograph to eliminate needless details (Figures 12.27 and 12.28).
- For emphasizing selected features of a complex mechanism or procedure, consider using diagrams in place of photographs or as a supplement (Figures 12.29 and 12.30).

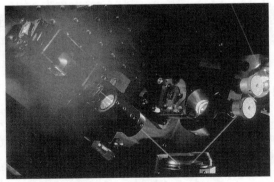

Sapphire Tunable Laser *Source: SuperStock*

**Figure 12.29   A Photograph of a
Complex Mechanism**

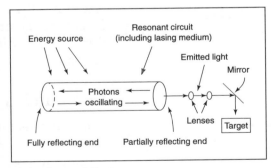

Major Parts of the Laser

Figure 12.30   A Simplified Diagram

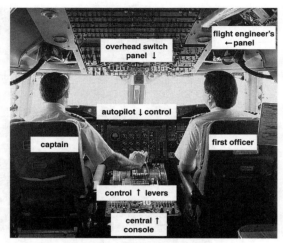

Standard Flight Deck for a Long-range Jet
Source: SuperStock

Figure 12.31   A Photograph with Essential Features Labelled

- Label all the parts readers need to identify (Figure 12.31).
- For an image unfamiliar to readers, provide a sense of scale by including a person, a ruler, or a familiar object (such as a hand) in the photo.
- If your document will be published, obtain a signed release from any person depicted in the photograph and written permission from the copyright holder. Beneath the photograph, cite the photographer and the copyright holder.
- In your discussion, refer to the photograph by figure number and explain what readers should be looking for; or include a prose caption.

Digital-imaging technology allows photographs to be scanned and stored electronically. These stored images then can be retrieved, edited, and altered. Such capacity for altering photographic content creates unlimited potential for distortion and raises questions about the ethics of digital manipulation (Callahan 64–65).

Computer Graphics

Computer technology transfers many of the tasks formerly performed by graphic designers and technical illustrators to individuals with little formal training in graphic design. In whatever career you anticipate, you probably will be expected to produce high-quality graphics for conferences, presentations, and in-house publications.

Today's computer systems create sophisticated, multicolour, graphic displays and multimedia presentations. Among the virtually countless types of computer-generated visuals are these examples:

- With an electronic stylus (a pen with an electronic signal), you can draw pictures on a graphics tablet to be displayed on the monitor, stored, or sent to other computers.
- You can create three-dimensional effects, showing an object from different angles through the use of shading, shadows, on-screen rotation, background lighting, or other techniques.
- You can recreate the visual effect of a mathematical model, as in writing equations to explain what happens when high winds strike a tall building. (As the wind deforms the structure, the equations change. Then you can take those new equations and represent them visually.)
- You can create a design, build a model, simulate the physical environment, and let the computer forecast what will happen with different variables.
- You can integrate computer-assisted design (CAD) with computer-assisted manufacturing (CAM), so that the design will direct the machinery that makes the parts themselves (CAD/CAM).
- You can create animations, to see how bodies move (as in a car crash or in athletics).
- You can practise dealing with toxic chemicals, operating sophisticated machines, or making other rapid decisions in medical or technical environments, without the cost or danger in actual situations.
- Through various types of scientific visualization, you can do "what-if" projections and explore countless ways of conceptualizing and understanding your data. Because the computer can generate and evaluate many possibilities rapidly, it enables you to test hypotheses without doing the calculations.

Selecting Design Options

Computer graphics systems allow you to experiment with scales, formats, colours, perspectives, and patterns. By testing design options on the screen, you can revise and enhance your visual repeatedly until it achieves your exact purpose.

Here is a sampling of design options:

- Update charts and graphs whenever the data change. The software will calculate the new data and plot the relationships.
- Edit your graphics on the screen, adding, deleting, or moving material as needed.
- Create your image at one scale, and later specify a different scale for the same image.
- Overlay images in one visual.
- Adjust bar width and line thickness.
- Fill a shape with a colour or pattern.
- Scan, edit, and alter pages, photos, or other images.

Most of these options are available via simple keystrokes or pull-down menus.

Using Clip Art

Clip art is a generic term for collections of ready-to-use images (of computer equipment, maps, machinery, medical equipment, etc.), all stored electronically. Various clip-art packages enable you to import into your document countless images like the one in Figure 12.32. By running the image through a drawing program, you can enlarge, enhance, or customize it, as in Figure 12.33.

Although a handy source for images, clip art often has a generic or crude look that makes a document appear unprofessional. Consider using clip art for icons only, or for in-house documents.

Figure 12.32   A Clip-art Image
Source: Desktop Art®; *Business 1*
© Dynamic Graphics, Inc.

Figure 12.33   A Customized Image
Source: Professor R. Armand Dumont

One form of clip art especially useful in technical writing is the *icon* (an image with all non-essential background removed). Icons convey a specific idea visually as in Figure 12.34. Icons appear routinely in computer documentation and in other types of instructions because the image provides readers with an immediate signal of the desired action.

Whenever you use an icon, be sure it is "intuitively recognizable" to your readers ("Using Icons" 3). Otherwise, readers are likely to misinterpret its meaning—in some cases with disastrous results.

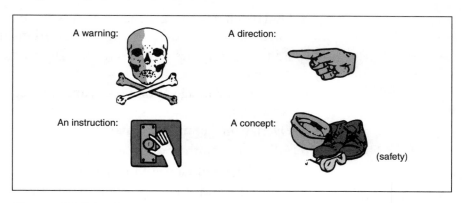

Figure 12.34   Icons
Source: Desktop Art®; *Business 1* and *Health Care 1*, © Dynamic Graphics, Inc.

Keep in mind that certain icons have offensive connotations in certain cultures. Hand gestures are especially problematic: some Arab cultures consider the left-hand unclean. A pointing index finger—on either hand—as in Figure 12.34, is a sign of rudeness in Venezuela or Sri Lanka (Bosley 5-6)

Using Colour or Shading

Colour or shading often makes a presentation more esthetically pleasing, more interesting to look at. But colour and shading serve purposes beyond visual appeal. Used effectively in a visual, they draw and direct readers' attention and help them identify the various elements.

Colour or shading can help clarify a concept or dramatize how something works. The use of bright colours against a darker, duller background enables readers to *visualize* concepts, as does the use of dark shading against white. Along with shape, type style, and position of elements on a printed page, colour or shading can guide readers through the material. Used effectively on a printed page, colour and shading help organize the reader's understanding, provide orientation, and emphasize important material. Following are just a few among many possible uses of colour and shading (White, *Colour* 39–44; Keyes 647–49).

Use Colour and Shading to Organize. Readers look for ways of organizing their understanding of a document (Figure 12.35). Colour or shading can reveal structure and break up material into discrete blocks that are easier to locate, process, and digest:

- A colour or shaded background screen can set off like elements such as checklists, instructions, or examples.
- Horizontal rules can separate blocks of text, such as sections of a report or areas of a page.
- Vertical rules can set off examples, quotations, captions, and so on.

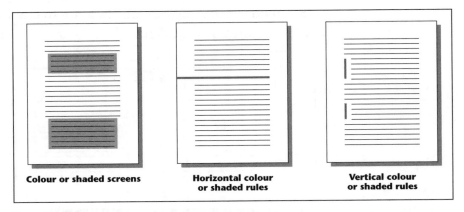

Colour or shaded screens   Horizontal colour
or shaded rules   Vertical colour
or shaded rules

Figure 12.35   Colour or Shading Used to Organize Page Elements
(A colour version of this figure can be found on Web site www.pearsoned.ca/lannon)

Use Colour or Shading to Orient. Readers look for clear bearings and signposts that help them find their place and find what they need (Figure 12.36):

- Colour or shading can help headings stand out from the text and differentiate major from minor headings.
- Coloured or shaded tabs and boxes can serve as location markers.
- Coloured or shaded sidebars (for marginal comments), callouts (for labels), and leader lines (for connecting a label to its referent) can guide the eyes.

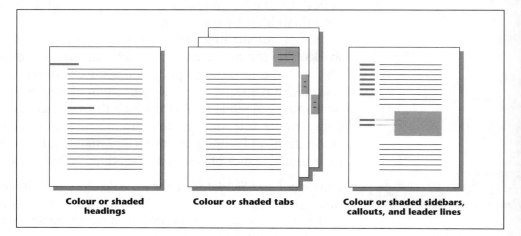

Figure 12.36   Colour or Shading Used as an Orientation Device (A colour version of this figure can be found on Web site www.pearsoned.ca/lannon)

Use Colour or Shading to Emphasize. Readers look for places to focus their attention in a document (Figure 12.37).

- Colour or shaded typefaces can highlight key words or ideas.
- Colour or shading can call attention to cross-references.
- A coloured or shaded, ruled box can frame a warning, caution, note, or hint.

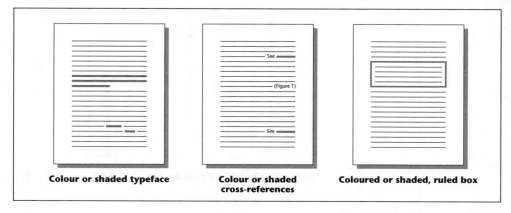

Figure 12.37   Colour or Shading Used for Emphasis (A colour version of this figure can be found on Web site www.pearsoned.ca/lannon)

Colour or Shading Guidelines. Whichever colour or shading options you use, employ the following general guidelines:

Guidelines for using colour or shading

- "Colour or shading gains impact when it is used selectively. It loses impact when it is overused." *(Aldus Guide* 39). Use colour or shading sparingly, and use no more than three or four distinct colours when using colour—including black and white (White, *Great Pages* 76).

- Apply colour or shading consistently to elements throughout your document. Inconsistent use of colour or shading can distort readers' perception of the relationships (Wickens 117).

- Make colour redundant. Be sure all elements are first differentiated in black and white: by shape, location, texture, type style, or typesize. Different readers perceive colours differently or, in some cases, not at all. A sizable percentage of readers have impaired colour vision (White, *Great Pages* 76).

- Use a darker colour or shade to make a stronger statement. The darker the colour or shade the more important the material. Readers perceive differently the sizes of variously coloured or shaded objects. Darker items can seem larger and closer than lighter objects of identical size.

- Make coloured or shaded type larger than body type. Try to avoid colour or light shading for body type, or use a high-contrast colour or shade (dark against a light background). Colour is less visible on the page than black ink on a white background. The smaller the image or the thinner the rule, the stronger or brighter the colour (White, *Editing* 229, 237).

- For contrast in a colour screen, use a very dark type against a very light background, say a 10–20 percent screen (Gribbons 70). The bigger the area of the screen, the paler the background colour (Figure 12.38).

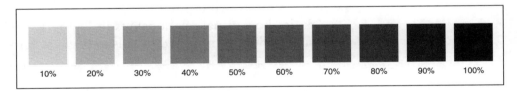

Figure 12.38   A Colour-Density Chart (A colour version of this figure can be found on Web site www.pearsoned.ca/lannon)

- A colour's connotations can vary from culture to culture. In North America, for example, red signifies danger and green traditionally signifies safety. But in Ireland, green or orange carry political connotations in certain contexts. In Muslim cultures, green is a holy colour (Cotton 169).

Using Web Sites for Graphics Support

The World Wide Web offers a growing array of visual resources. Following is a sample of useful Web sites (Martin 135–36).

- Image banks such as Graphics Web, Photo Web, and the Internet Font directory offer clip-art, photo, and font databases that can be browsed and from which material can be purchased on-line and downloaded to a personal computer.
- Some royalty-free images are available from the Digital Picture Archive.
- Samples of computer-generated and traditional art work can be browsed and purchased via Artists on Line.
- On-line versions of graphics magazines offer helpful design suggestions.
- Graphic design firms offer samples of work that often embody innovative design ideas.

Whether you seek design ideas, tools for creating your own visuals, or electronic catalogues of completed artwork, the Web is a good bet.

Be extremely cautious about downloading visuals (or any material, for that matter) from the Web and then using it. Review the copyright law (pages 152, 153). Originators of any work on the Web own the work and the copyright.

How to Avoid Visual Distortion

Although you are perfectly justified in presenting data in its best light, you are ethically responsible for avoiding misrepresentation. Any one set of data can support contradictory conclusions. Even though your numbers may be accurate, their visual display could be misleading.

Present the Real Picture

Visual relationships in a graph should portray accurately the numerical relationships they represent. Begin the vertical scale at zero. Never compress the scales to reinforce your point.

Notice how visual relationships in Figure 12.39 become distorted when the value scale is compressed or fails to begin at zero.

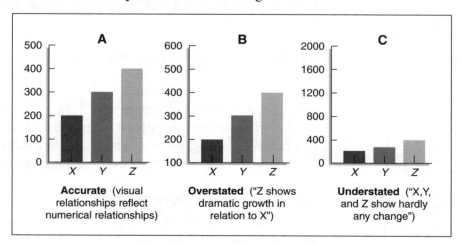

Figure 12.39   An Accurate Bar Graph and Two Distorted Versions

In version A, the bars accurately depict the numerical relationships measured from the value scale. In version B, item Z (400) is depicted as three times X (200). In version C, the scale is overly compressed, causing the shortened bars to understate the quantitative differences.

Deliberate distortions are unethical because they imply conclusions contradicted by the actual data.

Present the Complete Picture

Without bogging down in needless detail, an accurate visual includes all essential data. Figure 12.40 shows how distortion occurs when data that would provide a complete picture are selectively omitted.

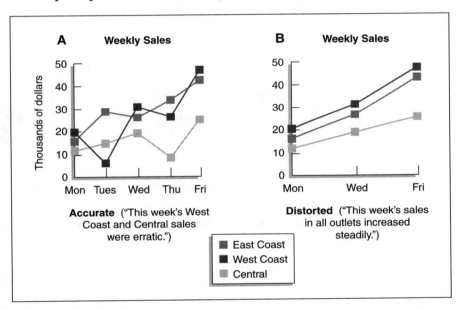

Figure 12.40   An Accurate Line Graph and a Distorted Version

Version A accurately depicts the numerical relationships measured from the value scale. In version B, too few points are plotted.

Decide carefully what to include and what to leave out of your visual display.

Never Mistake Distortion for Emphasis

When you want to emphasize a point (a sales increase, a safety record, etc.), be sure your data support the conclusion implied by your visual. For instance, don't use inordinately large visuals to emphasize good news or small ones to downplay bad news (Williams 11). When using clip art, pictograms, or drawn images to dramatize a comparison, be sure the relative size of the images or icons reflects the quantities being compared.

A visual accurately depicting a 100-percent increase in phone sales at your company might look like version A in Figure 12.41, below. Version B overstates the good news by depicting the larger image four times the size, instead of twice the size, of the smaller. Although the larger image is twice the height, it is also twice the *width,* so the total area conveys the visual impression that sales have *quadrupled.*

Visuals have their own rhetoric and persuasive force, which we can use to advantage—for positive or negative purposes, for the reader's benefit or detriment (Van Pelt 2). Avoiding visual distortion is ultimately a matter of ethics.

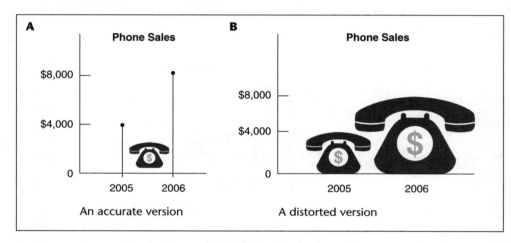

Figure 12.41   An Accurate Pictogram and a Distorted Version

How to Incorporate Visuals with the Text

An effective visual enables readers to locate and extract the information they need. To simplify the reader's task, visual and verbal elements in a document should complement each other. For example, a visual should be able to stand alone in meaning—without being isolated from the verbal text.

Visual and Verbal Element Guidelines. Following are specific guidelines for incorporating visual and verbal elements effectively.

Guidelines for fitting visuals with text

- Place the visual where it will best serve your readers. If it is central to your discussion, place the visual as close as possible to the material it clarifies. (Achieving proximity often requires that you ignore the traditional "top or bottom" design rule for placement of visuals on a page.) If the visual is peripheral to your discussion or of interest to only a few readers, place it in an appendix so that interested readers can refer to it as they wish. Tell readers when to consult the visual and where to find it.

- Never refer to a visual that readers cannot easily locate. In a long document, don't be afraid to repeat a visual if you discuss it again later.

- Never crowd a visual into a cramped space. Set your visual off by framing it with plenty of white space, and position it on the page for balance. To save space and to achieve proportion with the surrounding text, consider carefully the size of each visual and the amount of space it will occupy.

- Number the visual and give it a clear title and labels. Your title should tell readers what they are seeing. Label all of the important material.

- Match the visual to your audience. Don't make it too elementary for specialists or too complex for non-specialists. Be sure your intended audience will be able to interpret the visual correctly.

- Introduce and interpret the visual. In your introduction, tell readers what to expect:

  Informative   As shown in Table 2, operating costs have increased 7 percent annually since 1999.

  Uninformative   See Table 2.

  Visuals alone make ambiguous statements (Girill 35); pictures need to be interpreted. Instead of leaving readers to struggle with a page of raw data, explain the relationships displayed. Follow the visual with a discussion of its important features:

  Informative   This cost increase means that . . . .

  Always tell readers what to look for and what it means.

- Use prose captions to explain important points made by the visual. Captions help readers interpret a visual (as in Table 12.1). When possible, use a smaller typesize so that captions don't compete with text type (*Aldus Guide* 35).

- Never include excessive information in one visual. Any visual that contains too many lines, bars, numbers, colours, or patterns will overwhelm readers, causing them to ignore the display. In place of one complicated visual, use two or more straightforward ones.

- Be sure the visual's meaning can stand alone. Even though it repeats or augments information already in the text, the visual should contain everything readers will need to interpret it correctly.

The Visual Plan Sheet, Figure 12.42, and the Revision Checklist for Visuals on page 319 will help ensure that your visuals enhance your meaning.

VISUAL PLAN SHEET

Focusing on Your Purpose

- What is this visual's purpose (to instruct, persuade, create interest)? _____
- What forms of information (numbers, shapes, words, pictures, symbols) will this visual depict?

  _____

- What kind of relationship(s) will the visual depict (comparison, cause-effect, connected parts, sequence of steps)? _____
- What judgment, conclusion, or interpretation is being emphasized (that profits have increased, that toxic levels are rising, that X is better than Y, that time is being wasted)?

  _____

- Is a visual needed at all? _____

Focusing on Your Audience

- Is this audience accustomed to interpreting visuals?_____
- Is the audience interested in specific numbers or an overall view?_____
- Should the audience focus on one exact value, compare two or more values, or synthesize a range of approximate values (Wickens 121)? _____
- Which type of visual will be most accurate, representative, accessible, and compatible with the type of judgment, action, or understanding expected from the audience?_____

  _____

- In place of one complicated visual, would two or more straightforward ones be preferable?

  _____

Focusing on Your Presentation

- What enhancements, if any, will increase audience interest (colours, patterns, legends, labels, varied typefaces, shadowing, enlargement or reduction of some features)?_____

  _____

- Which medium—or combination of media—will be most effective for presenting this visual (slides, transparencies, handouts, large-screen monitor, data projection unit, flip chart, report text)?_____
- To achieve the greatest utility and effect, where in the presentation does this visual belong?

  _____

Figure 12.42   A Planning Sheet for Preparing Visuals

Revision Checklist for Visuals

Use this checklist to revise your visuals.

CONTENT

- ❏ Does the visual serve a legitimate purpose (clarification, not mere ornamentation) in the document?
- ❏ Is the visual titled and numbered?
- ❏ Is the level of complexity appropriate for the audience?
- ❏ Are all patterns in the visual identified by label or legend?
- ❏ Are all values or units of measurement specified (grams per ounce, millions of dollars)?
- ❏ Are the numbers accurate and exact?
- ❏ Do the visual relationships represent the numerical relationships accurately?
- ❏ Are explanatory notes added as needed?
- ❏ Are all data sources cited?
- ❏ Has written permission been obtained for reproducing or adapting a visual from a copyrighted source in any type of work to be published?
- ❏ Is the visual introduced, discussed, interpreted, integrated with the text, and referred to by number?
- ❏ Can the visual itself stand alone in meaning?

ARRANGEMENT

- ❏ Is the visual easy to locate?
- ❏ Are all design elements (title, line thickness, legends, notes, borders, white space) positioned for balance?
- ❏ Is the visual positioned on the page to achieve balance?
- ❏ Is the visual set off by adequate white space or borders?
- ❏ Does the top of a wide visual face the inside binding?
- ❏ Is the visual in the best report location?

STYLE

- ❏ Is this the best type of visual for your purpose and audience?
- ❏ Are all decimal points in each column vertically aligned?
- ❏ Is the visual uncrowded and uncluttered?
- ❏ Is the visual engaging (patterns, colours, shapes), without being too busy?
- ❏ Is the visual in good taste?
- ❏ Is the visual ethically acceptable?

☑ EXERCISES

1. The following statistics are based on data from three colleges in a large western city. They give the number of applicants to each college over six years.

    • In 1999, X College received 2,341 applications for admission, Y College received 3,116, and Z College 1,807.

    • In 2000, X College received 2,410 applications for admission, Y College received 3,224, and Z College 1,784.

    • In 2001, X College received 2,689 applications for admission, Y College received 2,976, and Z College 1,929.

    • In 2002, X College received 2,714 applications for admission, Y College received 2,840, and Z College 1,992.

    • In 2003, X College received 2,872 applications for admission, Y College received 2,615, and Z College 2,112.

    • In 2004, X College received 2,868 applications for admission, Y College received 2,421, and Z College 2,267.

    Illustrate these data in a line graph, a bar graph, and a table. Which version seems most effective for a reader who (a) wants exact figures, (b) wonders how overall enrollments are changing, or (c) wants to compare enrollments at each college in a certain year? Include a caption interpreting each of these versions.

2. Devise a flowchart for a process in your field or area of interest. Include a title and a brief discussion.

3. Devise an organization chart showing the lines of responsibility and authority in an organization where you hold a part-time or summer job.

4. Devise a pie chart to depict your yearly expenses. Title and discuss the chart.

5. Obtain enrollment figures at your college for the past five years by sex, age, race, or any other pertinent category. Construct a stacked-bar graph to illustrate one of these relationships over the five years.

6. Keep track of your pulse and respiration at thirty-minute intervals over a four-hour period of changing activities. Record your findings in a line graph, noting the times and specific activities below your horizontal coordinate. Write a prose interpretation of your graph and give it a title.

7. In textbooks or professional journal articles, locate each of these visuals: a table, a multiple-bar graph, a multiple-line graph, a diagram, and a photograph. Evaluate each according to the revision checklist, and discuss the most effective visual in class.

8. Choose the most appropriate visual for illustrating each of these relationships. Justify each choice in a short paragraph.

    a. A comparison of three top brands of fibreglass skis, according to cost, weight, durability, and edge control.

    b. A breakdown of your monthly budget.

    c. The changing cost of an average cup of coffee, as opposed to that of an average cup of tea, over the past three years.

    d. The percentage of college graduates finding desirable jobs within three months after graduation, over the last ten years.

    e. The percentage of college graduates finding desirable jobs within three months after graduation, over the last ten years—by gender.

    f. An illustration of automobile damage for an insurance claim.

    g. A breakdown of the process of radio wave transmission.

    h. A comparison of five cereals on the basis of cost and nutritive value.

9. Anywhere on campus or at work, locate at least one visual that needs revision for accuracy, clarity, appearance, or appropriateness. Look in computer manuals; lab manuals; newsletters;

financial aid or admissions or placement brochures; student, faculty, or employee handbooks; newspapers; or textbooks. Use the Visual Plan Sheet and the Revision Checklist as guides to revise and enhance the visual. Submit to your instructor a copy of the original, along with a memo explaining your improvements. Be prepared to discuss your revision in class.

☑ COLLABORATIVE PROJECT

Compile a list of twelve World Wide Web sites that offer graphics support by way of advice, image banks, design ideas, artwork catalogues, and the like. Provide the address for each site, along with a description of the resources offered and the cost. Report your findings in a format stipulated by your instructor.

Designing Pages and Documents

Pᴀɢᴇ design determines the *look* of a page, the layout of words and graphics. Well-designed pages invite readers in, guide them through the material, and help them understand and remember it.

Readers' *first* impression of a document tends to be a purely visual, esthetic judgment. Readers are attracted by documents that appear inviting and accessible.

Page Design in Workplace Writing

Page design becomes especially significant when we consider these realities about writing and reading in the workplace:

1. *Technical information generally is designed differently from material in novels, news stories, and other forms of writing.* To be accessible, a technical document requires more than just an unbroken sequence of paragraphs. To find their way through complex material, readers may need the help of charts, diagrams, lists, various typesizes and fonts, different headings, and other page-design elements.

2. *Technical documents rarely get readers' undivided attention.* Readers may be skimming the document while they jot down ideas, talk on the phone, or drink coffee. Or they may refer to sections of the document during a meeting or presentation. Amid frequent distractions, readers must be able to leave the document and return easily.

3. *People read work-related documents only because they have to.* Novels, general newspapers, and magazines are read for relaxation, but work-related documents (trade magazines, reports, newsletters) often require the reader's *labour*. The more complex the document, the harder readers have to labour. If these readers had other ways of getting the information, they might not read at all.

4. *As computers generate more and more paper, any document is forced to compete for readers' attention.* Even brilliant writing is useless unless it gets read by its intended audience. Suffering from information overload, today's readers resist any document that appears overwhelming. They want formats that will help them find the information they really need. A user-friendly document has an accessible format: At a glance, readers can see how the document is organized, where they are in the document, which items matter most, and how the items relate.

Having decided at a glance whether your document is inviting and accessible, readers will draw conclusions about the value of your information, the quality of your work, and your credibility.

Notice how the information in Figure 13.1 (page 324) resists our attention. Without design cues, we have no way of grouping this information into organized units of meaning. Now look at Figure 13.2 (page 325) which shows the same information after a design overhaul.

Sunspaces

Either as an addition to a home or as an integral part of a new home, sunspaces have gained considerable popularity.

A sunspace should face within 30 degrees of true south. In the winter, sunlight passes through the windows and warms the darkened surface of a concrete floor, brick wall, water-filled drums, or other storage mass. The concrete, brick, or water absorbs and stores some of the heat until after sunset, when the indoor temperature begins to cool. The heat *not* absorbed by the storage elements can raise the daytime air temperature inside the sunspace to as high as 37.8°C (100°F). As long as the sun shines, this heat can be circulated into the house by natural air currents or drawn in by a low-horsepower fan.

In order to be considered a passive solar heating system, any sunspace must consist of these parts: a collector, such as a double layer of glass or plastic; an absorber, usually the darkened surface of the wall, floor, or water-filled containers inside the sunspace; a storage mass, normally concrete, brick, or water, which retains heat after it has been absorbed; a distribution system, the means of getting the heat into and around the house by fans or natural air currents; and a control system, or heat-regulating device, such as movable insulation, to prevent heat loss from the sunspace at night. Other controls include roof overhangs that block the summer sun, and thermostats that activate fans.

Figure 13.1   Ineffective Page Design
Adapted from U.S. Department of Energy. *Sunspaces and Solar Greenhouses.* Washington: GPO, 1984

Sunspaces

Either as an addition to a home or as an integral part of a new home, sunspaces have gained considerable popularity.

How Sunspaces Work

A sunspace should face within 30 degrees of true south. In the winter, sunlight passes through the windows and warms the darkened surface of a concrete floor, brick wall, water-filled drums, or other storage mass. The concrete, brick, or water absorbs and stores some of the heat until after sunset, when the indoor temperature begins to cool.

The heat *not* absorbed by the storage elements can raise the daytime air temperature inside the sunspace to as high as 37.8°C (100°F). As long as the sun shines, this heat can be circulated into the house by natural air currents or drawn in by a low-horsepower fan.

The Parts of a Sunspace

In order to be considered a passive solar heating system, any sunspace must consist of these parts:

1. A *collector,* such as a double layer of glass or plastic.

2. An *absorber,* usually the darkened surface of the wall, floor, or water-filled containers inside the sunspace.

3. A *storage mass,* normally concrete, brick, or water, which retains heat after it has been absorbed.

4. A *distribution system,* the means of getting the heat into and around the house (by fans or natural air currents).

5. A *control system* (or heat-regulating device), such as movable insulation, to prevent heat loss from the sunspace at night. Other controls include roof overhangs that block the summer sun, and thermostats that activate fans.

Figure 13.2   Effective Page Design

Desktop Publishing

Planning, drafting, and writing at their workstations, writers themselves are increasingly responsible for all stages in document preparation. Because they combine word processing, typesetting, and graphics, *desktop publishing* (DTP) systems mean less reliance on inputters (word processing clerical/secretarial staff, etc.), print shops, and graphic artists.

Using page-design software, scanners, and laser printers, writers at their desks can control the entire production cycle: designing, illustrating, laying out, and printing the final document:

- Text can be keyed or scanned into the program and then edited, checked for spelling and grammar, displayed in columns or other spatial arrangements, set in a variety of sizes and fonts—or sent electronically.
- Page highlights and orienting devices can be added: headings, ruled boxes, vertical or horizontal rules, coloured background screens, marginal sidebars or labels, page-locator tabs, shadowing, shading, etc.
- Images can be drawn directly or imported into the program via scanners; charts, graphs, and diagrams can be created via graphics programs. These visuals then can be enlarged, reduced, cropped, and pasted electronically on the text pages.
- At any point in the process, entire pages can be viewed and evaluated for visual appeal, accessibility, and emphasis, then revised as needed.
- All work at all stages can be stored in the computer for later use, adaptation, or upgrading. Documents or parts of documents used repeatedly (*boiler plate*) can be retrieved as needed, modified, or inserted in some other document.

You might work alone or in collaboration with colleagues and graphic design professionals. In either case, you will need to understand the basic principles of effective page design.

As automated design continues to improve the look of workplace writing, audiences raise their expectations for inviting and accessible documents.

Page-design Guidelines

Approach your design decisions from the top down. First, consider the overall look of your pages; next, the shape of each paragraph; and finally, the size and style of individual letters and words (Kirsh 112). Figure 13.3 depicts how design considerations follow a top-down sequence, moving from large matters to small. (All design considerations are influenced by the size of the budget for a publication. For instance, adding a single colour, say, to major heads, can double the printing cost.)

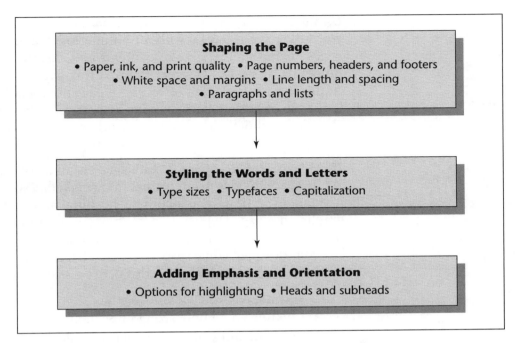

Figure 13.3   A Flowchart for Decisions in Page Design

If your organization prescribes no specific guidelines, the following design principles should satisfy most readers' expectations.

Shaping the Page

In shaping a page, we consider its look, feel, and overall layout. The following suggestions will help you shape appealing and usable pages.

Use the Right Paper and Ink. For routine documents (memos, letters, in-house reports) key or print in black ink, on 21.5 cm x 28 cm (8½" x 11") low-gloss, white paper. Use rag-bond paper (20 pound or heavier) with a high fibre content (25 percent minimum). Shiny paper produces glare and tires the eyes. Flimsy or waxy paper feels inferior.

For documents that will be published (manuals, marketing literature, etc.), the grade and quality of paper are important considerations. Paper varies in weight, grain, and finish—from low-cost newsprint, with noticeable wood fibre, to wood-free, specially coated paper with custom finishes. Choice of paper finally depends on the artwork to be included, the type of printing, and the intended esthetic effect; for example, specially coated, heavyweight, glossy—for an elegant effect in an annual report (Cotton 73).

Use High-quality Type or Print. Print hard copy on an inkjet or laser printer. If your inkjet's output is blurry, consider purchasing special inkjet paper for the best output quality.

Use Consistent Page Numbers, Headers, and Footers. For a long document, count your title page as page i, without numbering it, and number all front-matter pages, including the table of contents and abstract, with lower case Roman numerals (ii, iii, iv). Number the first text page and subsequent pages with Arabic numerals (1, 2, 3). Along with page numbers *headers* or *footers* appear in the top or bottom page margins, respectively. These provide chapter or article titles, authors' names, dates, or other publication information. (See, for example, the headers at the top of the pages in this book.)

Use Adequate White Space. White space is all of the space not filled by text. White space divides printed areas into small, digestible chunks. For instance, it separates sections in a document, headings and visuals from text, and paragraphs on a page (Figure 13.4). White space can be designed to enhance a document's appearance, clarity, and emphasis.

Well-designed white space imparts a shape to the whole document, a shape that orients readers and lends a distinctive visual form to the printed matter by:

1. keeping related elements together
2. isolating and emphasizing important elements
3. providing breathing room between blocks of information

Use white space to orient the readers

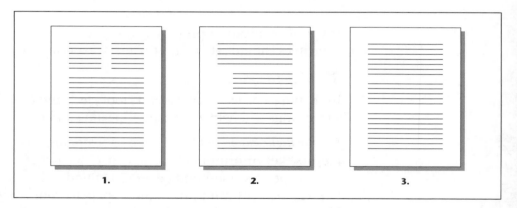

Figure 13.4   Using White Space

Pages that look uncluttered, inviting, and easy to follow convey an immediate sense of user-friendliness.

Provide Ample and Appropriate Margins. Small margins make a page look crowded and difficult. On your 21.5 cm x 28 cm (8½" x 11") page, leave margins of at least 2.5 cm (1"). For a document that will be bound, widen the left margin an extra 1.25 cm (½").

Choose between *unjustified* text (uneven or "ragged" right margins) and *justified* text (even right margins). Each arrangement creates its own "feel."

Justified lines

To make the right margin even in justified text, the spaces vary between words and letters on a line, sometimes creating channels or rivers of white space. The reader's eyes are then forced to adjust continually to these space variations within a line or paragraph. Because each line ends at an identical vertical space, the eyes must work harder to differentiate one line from another (Felker 85). Moreover, to preserve the even margin, words at line's end are often hyphenated, and frequently hyphenated line endings can be distracting.

Unjustified lines

Unjustified text, on the other hand, uses equal spacing between letters and words on a line, and an uneven right margin. For some readers, a ragged right margin makes reading easier. These differing line lengths can prompt the eye to move from one line to another (Pinelli 77). In contrast to justified text, an unjustified page seems to look less formal, less distant, and less official.

Justified text seems preferable for books, annual reports, and other formal materials. Unjustified text seems preferable for more personal forms of communication such as letters, memos, and in-house reports.

Keep Line Length Reasonable. Long lines tire the eyes. The longer the line, the harder it is for readers to return to the left margin and locate the next line (White, *Visual Design* 25).

Notice how your eye labours to follow the apparently endless message that here seems to stretch in lines that continue long after your eye was prepared to move down to the next line. After reading more than a few of these lines, you begin to feel tired and bored and annoyed, without hope of ever reaching the end.

Short lines force the eyes back and forth (Felker 79). "Too-short lines disrupt the normal horizontal rhythm of reading" (White 25).

Lines that are too
short cause your eye
to stumble from one
fragment to another
at a pace that too
soon becomes
annoying, if not
nauseating.

A reasonable line length is 70–80 characters (or 12 to 15 words) per line for an 21.5 cm x 28 cm (8½" x 11") single-column page. The number of characters will depend on print size. Longer lines call for larger type and wider spacing between them (White, *Great Pages* 70).

Line length, of course, is affected by the number of columns (vertical blocks of print) on your page. Two-column pages often appear in newsletters and brochures, but research indicates that single-column pages work best for complex, specialized information (Hartley 148).

Keep Line Spacing Consistent. For any document likely to be read completely (letters, memos, instructions), single-space within paragraphs and double-space between. Instead of indenting the first line of single-spaced paragraphs, separate them with a line of space.

Tailor Each Paragraph to Its Purpose. Readers often skim a long document to find what they want. Most paragraphs therefore begin with a topic sentence forecasting the content.

Shape each paragraph

Use a long paragraph (no more than fifteen lines) for clustering material that is closely related (such as history and background, or any body of information best understood in one block).

Use short paragraphs for making complex material more digestible, for giving step-by-step instructions, or for emphasizing vital information.

Instead of indenting a series of short paragraphs, separate them by inserting an extra line of space (as here).

Avoid "widow" and "orphan" lines: The last line of a paragraph printed at the top of a page is called a *widow*. The first line of a paragraph printed on the bottom of a page is called an *orphan*.

Make Lists for Easy Reading. Readers prefer information in list form rather than in continuous prose paragraphs (Hartley 51).

Types of items you might list: advice or examples, conclusions and recommendations, criteria for evaluation, errors to avoid, materials and equipment for a procedure, parts of a mechanism, or steps or events in a sequence. Notice how the preceding information becomes easier to grasp and remember when displayed in the list below.

Types of items you might list:

- advice or examples
- conclusions and recommendations
- criteria for evaluation
- errors to avoid
- materials and equipment for a procedure
- parts of a mechanism
- steps or events in a sequence

A list of brief items usually needs no punctuation at the end of each line. A list of full sentences or questions requires appropriate punctuation after each item.

Depending on the list's contents, set off each item with some kind of visual or verbal signal. If the items require a strict sequence (as in a series of steps, or parts of a mechanism), use Arabic numbers (1, 2, 3) or the words *First, Second, Third,* etc. If the items require no strict sequence (as in the bulleted list above), use dashes, asterisks, or bullets. For a checklist use open boxes. See Figure 13.5.

Use lists to help readers organize their understanding

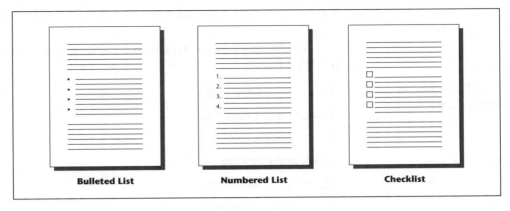

Figure 13.5   Types of Lists

Introduce your list with an explanation. Phrase all listed items in parallel grammatical form. If the items suggest no strict sequence, try to impose some logical ranking (most important to least important, alphabetical, or some such). Set off the list with extra white space above and below.

Keep in mind that a document with too many lists appears busy, disconnected, and splintered (Felker 55). And long lists could be used by unethical writers to camouflage bad or embarrassing news (Williams 12). As with all format options, use restraint and good judgment.

Styling the Words and Letters

In styling words and letters, we consider typographic choices that will make the text easy to read.

Use Standard Type Sizes. Word-processing programs offer a wide variety of type sizes:

Select the appropriate type size

9 point

10 point

12 point

14 point

18 point

24 point

The standard type size for most documents is 10 to 12 point. Use larger or smaller sizes for headings, titles, captions (brief explanation of a visual), sidebars (marginal comments), or special emphasis. Use a consistent type size for similar elements throughout the document.

Select Appropriate Fonts. A font, or typeface, is the style of individual letters and characters. Each font has its own *personality:* "The typefaces you select for . . . [heads], subheads, body copy, and captions affect the way readers experience your ideas" (*Aldus Guide* 24).

Particular fonts can influence reading speed by as much as 30 percent (Chauncey 26).

Word-processing programs offer a variety of fonts like the examples below, listed by name.

Select a font for its personality

11-point New York

11-point Courier

11-point Palatino

11-point Geneva

11-point Monaco

11-point Chicago

11-point Helvetica

11-point Times

Can you assign a personality to each of the above fonts?

For greater visual unity, try to use different sizes and versions (**bold,** *italic,* expanded, condensed) of the same font throughout your document—with the possible exception of headings, captions, sidebars, or visuals.

All fonts divide into two broad categories: *serif* and *sans serif.* Serifs are the fine lines that extend horizontally from the main strokes of a letter.

Decide between serif and sans serif type

Serif type makes body copy more readable because the horizontal lines "bind the individual letters" and thereby guide the reader's eyes from letter to letter—as in the type you are now reading (White, *Visual Design* 14).

In contrast, sans serif type is purely vertical (like this). Clean looking and "businesslike," sans serif is considered ideal for technical material (numbers, equations, etc.), marginal comments, headings, examples, tables, and captions to pictures and visuals, and any other material set off from the body copy (White 16).

European readers generally prefer sans serif type throughout their documents, and other cultures have their own preferences as well. Learn all you can about the design conventions of the culture you are addressing.

Except for special emphasis, stick to the more conservative styles and avoid ornate ones altogether.

Avoid Sentences in Full Caps. Sentences or long passages in full capitals (uppercase letters) are difficult to read because all uppercase letters and words have the same visual outline (Felker 87). The longer the passage, the harder readers work to grasp your emphasis.

MY DOG HAS MANY FLEAS.

My dog has many fleas.

FULL CAPS *are good for emphasis but hard to read*

Hard	ACCORDING TO THE NATIONAL COUNCIL ON RADIATION PROTECTION, YOUR MAXIMUM ALLOWABLE DOSE OF LOW-LEVEL RADIATION IS 500 MILLIREMS PER YEAR.
Easier	According to the National Council on Radiation Protection, your MAXIMUM allowable dose of low-level radiation is 500 millirems per year.

Lowercase letters take up less space, and the distinctive shapes make each word easier to recognize and remember (Benson 37).

Use full caps as section headings (INTRODUCTION) or to highlight a word or phrase (WARNING: NEVER TEASE THE ALLIGATOR). As with other highlighting options discussed below, use full caps sparingly in your document.

Highlighting for Emphasis

Effective highlighting helps readers distinguish the important from the less important elements. Highlighting options include fonts, type sizes, white space, and other graphic devices that:

- emphasize key points
- make headings prominent
- separate sections of a long document
- set off examples, warnings, and notes

You can highlight with <u>underlining</u>, FULL CAPS, dashes, parentheses, and asterisks.

> You can indent to set off examples, explanations, or any material that should be distinguished from other elements in your document.

Using ruled (or keyed) horizontal lines, you can separate sections in a long document:

Using ruled lines, broken lines, or ruled boxes, you can set off crucial information such as a warning or a caution:

- -

Caution: A document with too many highlights can appear confusing, disorienting, and tasteless.

- -

In adding emphasis and orientation, consider design elements that will direct readers' focus and help them navigate the text. See pages 311–312 for more on background screens, ruled lines, and ruled boxes.

Word processing software offers highlighting options that might include **boldface,** *italics,* small caps, varying type sizes and fonts, and colour. For specific highlighted items, some options are better than others:

Not all highlighting is equal

Boldface works well for emphasizing a single sentence or brief statement, and is perceived by readers as being "authoritative" (*Aldus Guide* 42).

Italics suggest a more subtle or "refined" emphasis than boldface (Aldus Guide 42). Italics can highlight words, phrases, book titles, etc. But multiple lines (like these) of italic type are difficult to read.

SMALL CAPS WORK FOR HEADINGS AND SHORT PHRASES. BUT ANY LONG STATEMENT ALL IN CAPS IS DIFFICULT TO READ.

Small type sizes (usually sans serif) work well for captions, labels for visuals, or to set off other material from the body copy.

Large type sizes and dramatic typefaces are both difficult to miss and difficult to digest. Be conservative—unless you really need to convey forcefulness.

Colour is appropriate only in some documents, and only when used sparingly. (Pages 311–313 discuss how colour or shading can influence readers' perception and interpretation of a message.)

Whichever highlights you select for a document, be consistent. Make sure that all headings at one level are highlighted identically, that all warnings and cautions are set off identically, etc. Use the "styles" feature of your word processor to ensure this consistency.

Never combine too many highlights.

Using Headings for Access and Orientation

Readers of long documents often look back or jump ahead to sections that interest them most.

Headings announce how a document is organized, point readers to what they need, and divide the document into accessible blocks or "chunks." An informative heading can help a reader decide whether a section is worth reading (Felker 17). Besides cutting down on reading and retrieval time, headings help readers remember information (Hartley 15).

Make Headings Informative. A heading should be informative but not wordy. Informative headings orient readers, showing them what to expect. Vague or general headings can be more misleading than no headings at all (Redish et al. 144). Whether your heading takes the form of a phrase, a statement, or a question, be sure it advances thought.

Uninformative heading	Document Formatting

What should we expect here: specific instructions, an illustration, a discussion of formatting policy in general? We can't tell.

Informative versions	How to Format Your Document
	Format Your Document in This Way
	How Do I Format My Document?

When you use questions as headings, phrase the questions in the same way as readers might ask them.

Make Headings Specific as Well as Comprehensive. Focus the heading on a specific topic. Do not preface a discussion of the effects of acid rain on lake trout with a broad heading such as "Acid Rain." Use instead "The Effects of Acid Rain on Lake Trout."

Also, provide enough headings to contain each discussion section. If chemical, bacterial, and nuclear wastes are three *separate* discussion items, provide a heading for each. Do not simply lump them under the sweeping heading "Hazardous Wastes." If you have prepared an outline for your document, adapt major and minor headings from it.

Make Headings Grammatically Consistent. All major topics or all minor topics in a document share equal rank; to emphasize this equality, express topics at the same level in identical—or parallel—grammatical form.

Non-parallel headings	How to Avoid Damaging Your Disks:
	1. Clean Disk-Drive Heads
	2. Keep Disks Away from Magnets
	3. Refraining from Exposing the Magnetic Surface
	4. It is Crucial that Disks Be Kept Away from Heat
	5. Disks Should Be Kept Out of Direct Sunlight
	6. Keep Disks in a Dust-free Environment

In items 3, 4, and 5, the lack of parallelism (no verbs in the imperative mood) obscures the relationship between individual steps and confuses readers. This next version emphasizes the equal rank of these items.

Parallel headings	3. Refrain from Exposing the Magnetic Surface
	4. Keep Disks Away from Heat
	5. Keep Disks Out of Direct Sunlight

Parallelism helps make a document readable and accessible.

Make Headings Visually Consistent. "Wherever heads are of equal importance, they should be given similar visual expression, because the regularity itself becomes an understandable symbol" (White, *Visual Design* 104). Use identical type size and typeface for all headings at a given rank. (Use the "styles" feature of your word processing software.)

Lay Out Headings by Rank. Like a road map, your headings should announce clearly the large and small segments in your document.

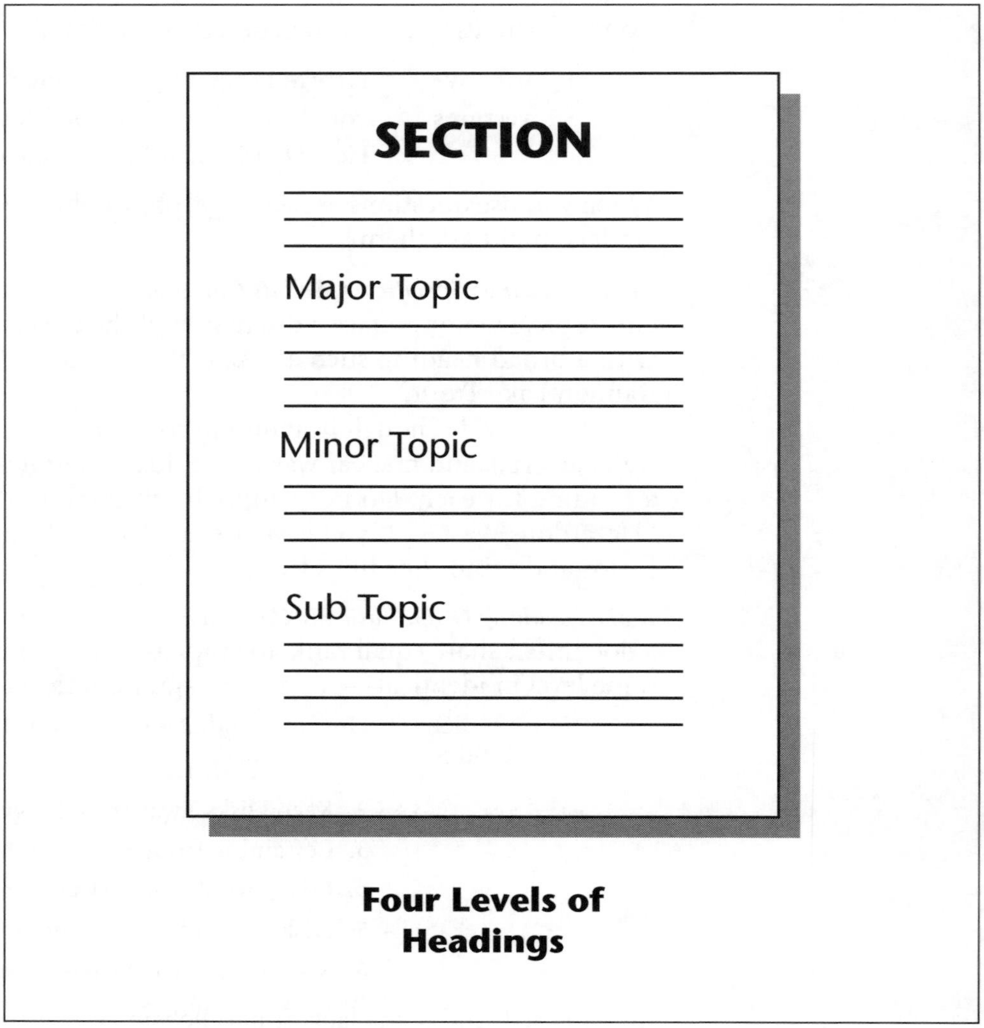

SECTION

Major Topic

Minor Topic

Sub Topic

Four Levels of Headings

Figure 13.6   Heading Levels

(Use the logical divisions from your outline as a model for heading layout.) Think of each heading at a particular rank as an "event in a sequence" (White *Visual Design* 95).

Figure 13.7 shows how headings vary in positioning and highlighting, depending on their rank.

SECTION HEADING

In formal reports, always centre section headings at the top of a new page. Use a type size roughly 4 points larger than body copy (say, 16-point section heads for 12-point body copy). Avoid *overly* large heads, and use no other highlights. Fully capitalize the heading. (Some documents use colour for section headings and capitalize just the first letter of each word.) Leave a full line space above the following text (as in this example). In most cases, use the same font for heads as for the text.

Major Topic Heading

Place major topic headings at the left margin (flush left), and begin each word with an uppercase letter. Use a type size roughly 2 points larger than body copy, with no other highlights. Start the copy immediately below the heading (as shown), or leave one space below the heading.

Minor Topic Heading

Use boldface and the same type size as the body copy, with no other highlights. Start the copy immediately below the heading (as shown), or leave one space below the heading.

Subtopic Heading. Incorporate subtopic headings into the body copy they head. Place subtopic heads flush left and set them off with a period. Use boldface and the same type size as in the body copy, with no other highlights.

1. ***Alternate subtopic heading.*** If numbering is appropriate, place the subtopics in a list, with the numbers flush left and the body copy indented. Use italics *and* boldface if you want to draw particular attention to this fourth level of heading.

- **Bulleted variation**. When the sequence of items in a list is not important, use bullets to precede the indented subtopic headings.

Figure 13.7   Recommended Format for Headings

Many variations of the above format are used successfully. One such variation is shown in Figure 13.8, page 338. Another variation is demonstrated by the engineering report in Figure 19.6, starting on page 499.

SECTION HEADING

Use a type size roughly 4 points larger than body copy (say, 16-point section heads for 12-point body copy). Use colour to draw attention to the main heading.

Major Topic Heading

Place major topic headings at the left margin (flush left), and begin each word with an uppercase letter. Use a type size roughly 2 points larger than body copy, with no other highlights. Start the text one line space below the heading.

Minor topic heading

Indent minor topic headings. Use boldface and the same type size as the body copy, with no other highlights. Start the body copy immediately below the heading (as shown).

Subtopic heading. Incorporate subtopic headings into the body copy they head. Place subtopic heads flush left and set them off with a period. Use boldface and the same type size as in the body copy, with no other highlights.

Figure 13.8   Alternate Format for Headings

The layout in Figures 13.7 and 13.8 embody the following guidelines:

- *Ordinarily, use no more than four levels of heading (section, major topic, minor topic, subtopic).* Excessive heads and subheads can make a document seem cluttered or fragmented.

- *To divide logically, be sure each higher-level heading yields at least two lower-level headings.*

- *Make sure that the headings system has a consistent, logical progression.* Each succeeding heading level in Figure 13.8 has less capitalization than the preceding level.

- *Never begin the sentence right after the heading with "this," "it," or some other pronoun referring to the heading.* Make the sentence's meaning independent of the heading.

- *Use boldface for all headings.*

- *Never leave a heading floating on the final line of a page.* Unless two lines of text can fit below the heading, carry it over to the top of the next page.

Figure 13.9   A Floating Head

Figure 13.9 illustrates a poor heading format (floating head).

When the headings show the relationships among all the parts, readers can grasp at a glance how a document is organized.

Audience Considerations in Page Design

Like any writing decisions, page design choices are by no means random. An effective writer designs a document for specific use by a specific audience.

In deciding on a format, work from a detailed audience/purpose profile (Wight 11). Know who your readers are and how they will use your information. Design a document to meet their particular needs and expectations, as in these examples:

- If readers will use your document for reference only (as in a repair manual), make sure you have plenty of headings.

- If readers will follow a sequence of steps, show that sequence in a numbered list.
- If readers will need to evaluate something, give them a checklist of criteria (as in this book at the end of most chapters).
- If readers need a warning, highlight the warning so that it cannot possibly be overlooked.
- If readers have asked for your one-page résumé, save space by using a 10-point type size.
- If readers will be facing complex information or difficult steps, widen the margins, increase all white space, and shorten the paragraphs.

How effectively you combine your options will depend mostly on how carefully you have analyzed your audience. But regardless of the audience, never make the document look "too intellectually intimidating" (White, *Visual Design* 4).

Consider also your audience's specific cultural expectations. For instance, Arabic and Persian text is written from right to left instead of left to right (Leki 149). In other cultures, readers move up and down the page, instead of across. Be aware that a particular culture might be offended by certain icons or by a typeface that seems too plain or too fancy (Weymouth 144). Ignoring a culture's design conventions can be interpreted as a sign of disrespect.

Finally, keep in mind that even the most brilliant page design cannot redeem a document whose content is worthless, organization chaotic, or style unreadable. The value of a document ultimately depends on elements that are more than skin deep.

Designing On-screen Pages

To be read on a computer screen, pages must accommodate small screen size, reduced resolution, and reader resistance to scrolling—among other restrictions. Some special design requirements of on-screen pages are:

Elements of on-screen page design

- Sentences and paragraphs are short and more concise than their hard-copy equivalents.
- Sans-serif type is preferred for on-screen readibility.
- The main point usually appears right up front on each screen.
- Each "page" often stands alone as a discrete "module," or unit of meaning. Instead of a traditional introduction-body-conclusion sequence of pages, material is displayed in screened-sized chunks, each linked as hypertext.
- Links, navigation bars, hot buttons, and help options are displayed on each page.

Special authoring software (Adobe FrameMaker® or RoboHelp®) automatically converts hard-copy documents to various on-screen formats, chunked and linked for easy navigation.

Provide margins for on-screen pages, so that your text won't bump against (or run off) the edge of the user's screen. Also, avoid using underlines for emphasis because these might be confused with hyperlinks (Munger).

Revision Checklist for Page Design

Use this checklist to revise your page design.

- ❑ Is the paper white, low-gloss, rag bond, with black ink?
- ❑ Is all type or print neat and legible?
- ❑ Does the white space adequately orient the readers?
- ❑ Are the margins ample?
- ❑ Is the line length reasonable?
- ❑ Is the right margin unjustified?
- ❑ Is the line spacing appropriate and consistent?
- ❑ Does each paragraph begin with a topic sentence?
- ❑ Does the length of each paragraph suit its subject and purpose?
- ❑ Are all paragraphs free of "widow" and "orphan" lines?
- ❑ Do parallel items in strict sequence appear in a numbered list?
- ❑ Do parallel items of any kind appear in a list whenever a list is appropriate?

- ❑ Are pages numbered consistently?
- ❑ Is the body type size 10 to 12 points?
- ❑ Do full caps highlight only words or short phrases?
- ❑ Is the highlighting consistent, tasteful, and subdued?
- ❑ Are all format patterns distinct enough so that readers will find what they need?
- ❑ Are there enough headings for readers to know where they are in the document?
- ❑ Are headings informative, comprehensive, specific, parallel, and visually consistent?
- ❑ Are headings clearly differentiated according to rank?
- ❑ Is the overall design inviting without being overwhelming?
- ❑ Does this design respect the cultural conventions of my audience?

☑ EXERCISES

1. Find an example of effective page design, in a textbook or elsewhere. Photocopy a selection (two or three pages), and attach a memo explaining to your instructor and colleagues why this design is effective. Be specific in your evaluation. Now do the same for an example of poor formatting. Bring your examples and explanations to class, and be prepared to discuss why you chose them.

2. These are headings from a set of instructions for listening. Rewrite the headings to make them parallel.
   - You Must Focus on the Message
   - Paying Attention to Non-verbal Communication
   - Your Biases Should Be Suppressed
   - Listen Critically
   - Listening for Main Ideas
   - Distractions Should Be Avoided
   - Provide Verbal and Non-verbal Feedback
   - Making Use of Silent Periods
   - Are You Allowing the Speaker Time to Make His or Her Point?
   - Keeping an Open Mind Is Important

3. Using the revision checklist on page 341, redesign an earlier assignment or a document you've prepared on the job. Submit to your instructor the revision and the original, along with a memo explaining your improvements. Be prepared to discuss your format design in class.

4. Anywhere on campus or at work, locate a document with a design that needs revision. Candidates include career counselling handbooks, financial aid handbooks, student or faculty handbooks, software or computer manuals, medical information, newsletters, or registration procedures. Redesign the document or a two-to-five page selection from it. Submit to your instructor a copy of the original, along with a memo explaining your improvements. Be prepared to discuss your revision in class.

☑ COLLABORATIVE PROJECT

Working in small groups, redesign a document you select or your instructor provides. Prepare a detailed explanation of your group's revision. Appoint a group member to present your revision to the class, using an opaque or overhead projector, a large-screen computer monitor, data projection unit, or photocopies.

PART

IV

Descriptive Writing

Definitions

T O DEFINE a term is to explain the precise meaning you intend by using that term. Clear writing depends on definitions that both reader and writer understand. Unless you are sure readers know the exact meaning you intend, always define the term upon first use.

Purpose of Definitions

Every specialty has its own technical language. Engineers, architects, or programmers talk about "torque," "tolerances," or "microprocessors"; lawyers, real estate brokers, and investment counsellors discuss "easements," "liens," "amortization," or "escrow accounts." Whenever such terms are unfamiliar to an audience, they need defining.

For colleagues, you rarely have to define specialized terms (unless the term is new), but reports often are written for the layperson—the client or some other general reader. When you write for non-specialists, clarify your meaning with definitions.

Most of the specialized terms previously mentioned are concrete and specific. Once "microprocessor" has been defined for the reader, its meaning will not differ appreciably in another context. When a term is highly technical, a writer can figure out that it should be defined for some readers. However, familiar terms like "disability," "guarantee," "tenant," "lease," or "mortgage" acquire very specialized meanings in specialized contexts. Here definition becomes crucial. What "guarantee" means in one situation is not necessarily what it means in another. Contracts are detailed (and legal) definitions of the specific terms of an agreement.

Assume you're shopping for disability insurance to protect your income in case of injury or illness. Besides comparing prices, you want each company to define "physical disability." Although Company A offers the cheapest policy, it might define physical disability as inability to work at *any* job. Therefore, if a neurological disorder prevents you from continuing work as designer of electronic devices, without disabling you for some menial job, you might not qualify as "disabled." In contrast, Company B's policy, although more expensive, might define physical disability as inability to work at your *specific* job. Both companies use the term "physical disability," but each defines it differently. Because they are legally responsible for the documents they prepare, all communicators rely on the technique of clear definition.

Growth in technology, specialization, and global communication makes definition increasingly vital. Know for whom you're writing, and why. If you are unable to pinpoint your audience, assume a general readership and define generously.

Elements of Definitions

For all definitions, use these guidelines:

Plain English

Clarify meaning by using language readers understand.

Unclear	A tumour is a neoplasm.
Better	A tumour is a growth of cells that occurs independently of surrounding tissue and serves no useful function.
Unclear	A solenoid is an inductance coil that serves as a tractive electromagnet. *(A definition appropriate for an engineering manual, but too specialized for general readers.)*
Better	A solenoid is an electrically energized coil that converts electrical energy to magnetic energy capable of performing mechanical functions.

Basic Properties

Convey the properties of an item that differentiate it from all others. A thermometer has a singular function; it measures temperature. Without this essential information, a definition would have no real meaning for uninformed readers. Any other data about thermometers (types, special uses, materials used in construction) are secondary. A book, on the other hand, cannot be defined according to functional properties because books have multiple functions. A book can be used to write in or to display pictures, to record financial transactions, to read, and so on. Also, other items (individual sheets of paper, posters, newspapers, picture frames) serve the same functions. The basic property of a book is physical: it is a bound volume of pages. Readers would have to know this *first,* to understand what a book is.

Objectivity

Unless readers understand that your purpose is to persuade, omit your opinions from a definition. "Bomb" is defined as "an explosive weapon detonated by impact, proximity to an object, a timing mechanism, or other predetermined means." If you define a bomb as "an explosive weapon devised and perfected by hawkish idiots to blow up the world," you are editorializing, *and* ignoring a bomb's basic property.

Likewise, in defining "diesel engine," simply tell what it is and how it works. You might think that diesels are too noisy and sluggish for automobiles, but omit these judgments from your definition.

Types of Definition

Definitions vary greatly in length and detail: from a few words in parentheses, to one or more complete sentences, to multiple paragraphs or pages.

Your choice of definition type depends on what information readers need, and that, in turn, depends on why they need it. "Carburetor," for instance, could be defined in one sentence, briefly telling readers what it is and how it works. But this definition would be expanded for the student mechanic who needs to know the origin of the term, how the device was developed, what it looks like, how it is used, and how its parts interact. Audience needs should guide your choice.

Parenthetical Definition

A parenthetical definition explains the term in a word or phrase, often as a synonym in parentheses following the term:

Parenthetical definitions

> The effervescent (bubbling) mixture is highly toxic.
> The leaching field (sievelike drainage area) requires crushed stone.

Another option is to express your definition as a clarifying phrase:

> The trees on the site are mostly deciduous; that is, they shed their foliage at season's end.

Use parenthetical definitions to convey the general meaning of specialized terms so that readers can follow the discussion where these terms are used. A parenthetical definition of "leaching field" might be adequate in a progress report to a client whose house you are building. But a public-health report titled "Groundwater Contamination from Leaching Fields" would call for an expanded definition.

Sentence Definition

A definition may require one or more sentences with this structure: (1) the item or term being defined, (2) the class (specific group) to which the term belongs, and (3) the features that differentiate the term from all others in its class.

Elements of sentence definitions

Term	Class	Distinguishing Features
carburetor	a mixing device	in gasoline engines that blends air and fuel into a vapour for combustion within the cylinders
transit	a surveying instrument	that measures horizontal and vertical angles
diabetes	a metabolic disease	caused by a disorder of the pituitary gland or pancreas and characterized by excessive urination, persistent thirst, and decreased ability to metabolize sugar

Term	Class	Distinguishing Features
liberalism	a political concept	based on belief in progress, the essential goodness of people, and the autonomy of the individual, and advocating protection of political and civil liberties
brief	a legal document	containing all the facts and points of law pertinent to a specific case, and filed by a lawyer before the case is argued in court
stress	an applied force	that strains or deforms a body
laser	an electronic device	that converts electrical energy to light energy, producing a bright, intensely hot, and narrow beam of light
fibre optics	a technology	that uses light energy to transmit voices, video images, and data through hair-thin glass fibres

These elements can be combined into one or more sentences.

A complete sentence definition

> Diabetes is a metabolic disease caused by a disorder of the pituitary gland or pancreas. This disease is characterized by excessive urination, persistent thirst, and decreased ability to metabolize sugar.

Sentence definition is especially useful for stipulating the precise working meaning of a term that has several possible meanings. State your working definitions at the beginning of your report:

A working definition

> Throughout this report, the term "disadvantaged student" means . . .

Classifying the Term. Be specific and precise in your classification. The narrower your class, the more specific your meaning. "Transit" is correctly classified as a "surveying instrument," not as a "thing" or an "instrument." "Stress" is classified as "an applied force"; to say that stress "takes place when . . ." or "is something that . . ." fails to reflect a specific classification. Be sure to select precise terms of classification: "Diabetes" is precisely classified as "a metabolic disease," not as "a medical term."

Differentiating the Term. Differentiate the term by separating the item it names from every other item in its class. Make these distinguishing features narrow enough to pinpoint the item's unique identity and meaning, yet broad enough to be inclusive. A definition of "brief" as "a legal document introduced in a courtroom" is too broad because the definition doesn't differentiate "brief" from all other legal documents (wills, written confessions, etc.). Conversely, differentiating "carburetor" as "a mixing device used in automobile engines" is too narrow because it ignores the carburetor's use in all other gasoline engines.

Also, avoid circular definitions (repeating, as part of the distinguishing features, the word you are defining). Thus, "stress" should not be defined as "an applied force that places stress on a body." The class and distinguishing features must express the item's basic property ("an applied force that strains or deforms a body").

Categorical v. Operational Definitions. So far, our sample definitions have placed the defined term in a category; we could use the term, *categorical definition,* for this common method of defining things in sentences. Categorical definitions are static, but a second type of sentence definition, *operational definition,* defines things in active terms. Here's an example:

Operational definition

> **Technologists** translate engineering designs into working plans and then see that these plans are carried out.

In the example, technologists are defined in terms of *what they do,* rather than in terms of *what they are.*

Operational definitions work best in proposals, progress reports, and résumés because the active verbs contribute to the sense of an active and successful person, plan, or activity. Also, operational definitions use fewer words to convey meaning. Compare the above example to its categorical equivalent:

Categorical definition

> A technologist **is someone who** translates engineering designs into working plans and then sees that these plans are carried out.

Expanded Definition

An expanded definition can include parenthetical and sentence definitions, but it provides greater detail for readers who need it. The sentence definition of "solenoid" on page 346 is good for a general reader who simply needs to know what a solenoid is. But a manual for mechanics or mechanical engineers would define solenoid in detail (as on pages 355–357); these readers need to know also how a solenoid works and how to use it.

The problem with defining an abstract and general word, such as "condominium" or "loan," is different. "Condominium" is a vaguer term than "solenoid" (solenoid A is pretty much like solenoid B) because the former refers to many types of ownership agreements.

Concrete, specific terms such as "diabetes," "transit," and "solenoid" often can be defined in a sentence, and they require expanded definition only for certain audiences. But terms such as "disability" and "condominium" require an expanded definition for almost any audience. The more general or abstract the term, the more need for an expanded definition.

An expanded definition may be a single paragraph (as for a simple tool) or may extend to scores of pages (as for a digital dosimeter—a device for measuring radiation exposure); sometimes the definition itself *is* the whole report.

Expansion Methods

How you expand a definition depends on the questions you think readers need answered, as shown in Figure 14.1. Begin with a sentence definition, and then use only those expansion strategies that serve your reader's needs.

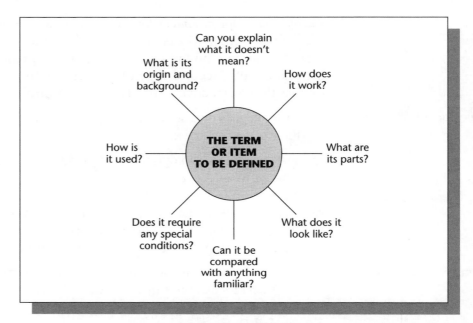

Figure 14.1   Directions in Which a Definition can be Expanded

Etymology

A word's origin (its development and changing meanings) can clarify its definition. *Biological control* of insects is derived from the Greek "bio," meaning *life* or *living organism,* and the Latin "contra," meaning *against* or *opposite.* Biological control, then, is the use of living organisms against insects. College dictionaries contain etymological information, but your best bet is *The Oxford English Dictionary* and encyclopedic dictionaries of science, technology, and business.

Some technical terms are acronyms, derived from the first letters or parts of several words. *Laser* is an acronym for *light amplification by stimulated emission of radiation.*

Sometimes a term's origin can be colourful as well as informative. *Bug* (jargon for *programming error*) is said to derive from an early computer at Harvard that malfunctioned because of a dead bug blocking the contacts of an electrical relay. Because programmers, like many of us, were reluctant to acknowledge error, the term became a euphemism for *error.* Correspondingly, *debugging* is the correcting of errors in a program.

History and Background

The meaning of specialized terms such as "radar," "bacteriophage," "silicon chips," or "x-ray" often can be clarified through a background discussion: discovery or history of the concept, development, method of production, applications, etc. Specialized encyclopedias are a good background source.

"Where did it come from?"

> The idea of lasers . . . dates back as far as 212 B.C., when Archimedes used a [magnifying] glass to set fire to Roman ships during the siege of Syracuse. (Gartaganis 22)

"How was it perfected?"

> The early researchers in fibre optic communications were hampered by two principal difficulties—the lack of a sufficiently intense source of light and the absence of a medium which could transmit this light free from interference and with a minimum signal loss. Lasers emit a narrow beam of intense light, so their invention in 1960 solved the first problem. The development of a means to convey this signal was longer in coming, but scientists succeeded in developing the first communications-grade optical fibre of almost pure silica glass in 1970. (Stanton 28)

Negation

Readers can grasp some meanings by understanding clearly what the term *does not* mean. For instance, an insurance policy may define coverage for "bodily injury to others" partly by using negation:

> "We will *not* pay: 1. For injuries to guest occupants of your auto."

In this next example, negation clarifies the definition of "lasers":

> "Lasers are not merely weapons from science fiction."

Operating Principle

Most items work according to an operating principle, whose explanation should be part of your definition:

"How does it work?"

> A clinical thermometer works on the principle of heat expansion: As the temperature of the bulb increases, the mercury inside expands, forcing a mercury thread up into the hollow stem.

> Air-to-air solar heating involves circulating cool air, from inside the home, across a collector plate (heated by sunlight) on the roof. This warmed air is then circulated back into the home.

> Basically, a laser [uses electrical energy to produce] coherent light, light in which all the waves are in phase with each other, making the light hotter and more intense. (Gartaganis 23)

> [A fibre optics] system works as follows: An electrical charge activates the laser . . . , and the resulting light . . . energy passes through the optical fibre. At the other end of the fibre, a . . . receiver . . . converts this light signal back into electrical impulses. (Stanton 28)

Even abstract concepts or processes can be explained on the basis of their operating principle:

> Economic inflation is governed by the principle of supply and demand: If an item or service is in short supply, its price increases in proportion to its demand.

Analysis of Parts

When your subject can be divided into parts, identify and explain them:

"What are its parts?"

> The standard frame of a pitched-roof wooden dwelling consists of floor joists, wall studs, roof rafters, and collar ties.

> Psychoanalysis is an analytic and therapeutic technique consisting of four parts: (1) free association, (2) dream interpretation, (3) analysis of repression and resistance, and (4) analysis of transference.

In discussing each part, of course, you would further define specialized terms such as "floor joists" and "repression."

Analysis of parts is particularly useful for helping non-technical readers understand a technical subject. This next analysis helps explain the physics of lasing by dividing the process into three discrete parts:

> 1. [Lasers require] a source of energy, [such as] electric currents or even other lasers.
> 2. A resonant circuit . . . contains the lasing medium and has one fully reflecting end and one partially reflecting end. The medium—which can be a solid, liquid, or gas—absorbs the energy and releases it as a stream of photons [electromagnetic particles that emit light]. The photons . . . vibrate between the fully and partially reflecting ends of the resonant circuit, constantly accumulating energy—that is, they are amplified. After attaining a prescribed level of energy, the photons can pass through the partially reflecting surface as a beam of coherent light and encounter the optical elements.
> 3. Optical elements—lenses, prisms, and mirrors—modify size, shape, and other characteristics of the laser beam and direct it to its target. (Gartaganis 23)

Figure 1 shows the three parts of a laser.

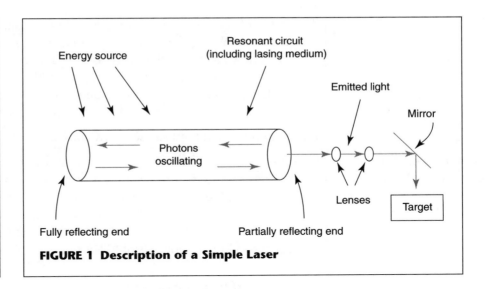

FIGURE 1 Description of a Simple Laser

Visuals

Well-labelled visuals (such as the laser description) are excellent for clarifying definitions. Always introduce your visual and explain it. If your visual is borrowed, credit the source. Unless the visual takes up one whole page or more, do not place it on a separate page. Include the visual near its discussion.

Comparison and Contrast

Comparisons and contrasts help readers understand. Analogies (a type of comparison) to something familiar can help explain the unfamiliar:

"Does it resemble anything familiar?"

> To visualize how a simplified earthquake starts, imagine an enormous block of gelatin with a vertical knife slit through the middle of its lower half. Gigantic hands are slowly pushing the right side forward and pulling the left side back along the slit, creating a strain on the upper half of the block that eventually splits it. When the split reaches the upper surface, the two halves of the block spring apart and jiggle back and forth before settling into a new alignment. Inhabitants on the upper surface would interpret the shaking as an earthquake. ("Earthquake Hazard Analysis" 8)

> The average diameter of an optical cable is around two-thousandths of an inch, making it about as fine as a hair on a baby's head (Stanton 29–30).

Here is a contrast between optical fibre and conventional copper cable:

"How does it differ from comparable things?"

> Beams of laser light coursing through optical fibres of the purest glass can transmit many times more information than the present communications systems. . . . A pair of optical fibres has the capacity to carry more than 10,000 times as many signals as conventional copper cable. A 1.25 cm (½") optical cable can carry as much information as a copper cable as thick as a person's arm. . . .

> Not only does fibre optics produce a better signal, [but] the signal travels far-ther as well. All communications signals experience a loss of power, or attenuation, as they move along a cable. This power loss necessitates placement of repeaters at 1.5- or 3.0-kilometre intervals of copper cable in order to regenerate the signal. With fibre, repeaters are necessary about every 50 or 65 kilometres, and this dis-tance is increasing with every generation of fibre. (Stanton 27–28)

Here is a combined comparison and contrast:

"How is it both similar and different?"

> Fibre optics technology results from the superior capacity of lightwaves to carry a communications signal. Sound waves, radio waves, and light waves can all carry signals; their capacity increases with their frequency. Voice frequencies car-ried by telephone operate at 1000 cycles per second, or hertz. Television sig-nals transmit at about 50 million hertz. Light waves, however, operate at frequencies in the hundreds of trillions of hertz. (Stanton 28)

Required Materials or Conditions

Some items or processes need special materials and handling, or they may have other requirements or restrictions. An expanded definition should include this important information.

"What is needed to make it work (or occur)?"

> Besides training in engineering, physics, or chemistry, careers in laser technology require a strong background in optics (study of the generation, transmission, and manipulation of light).

Abstract concepts might also be defined in terms of special conditions:

> To be held guilty of libel, a person must have defamed someone's character through written or pictorial statements.

Example

Familiar examples showing types or uses of an item can help clarify your def-inition. This example shows how laser light is used as a heat-generating device:

"How is it used or applied?"

> Lasers are increasingly used to treat health problems. Thousands of eye operations involving cataracts and detached retinas are performed every year by ophthal-mologists. . . . Dermatologists treat skin problems. . . . Gynecologists treat prob-lems of the reproductive system, and neurosurgeons even perform brain surgery—all using lasers transmitted through optical fibres. (Gartaganis 24–25)

The next example shows how laser light is used to carry information:

> The use of lasers in the calculating and memory units of computers, for example, permits storage and rapid manipulation of large amounts of data. And audiodisc players use lasers to improve the quality of the sound they reproduce. The use of optical cable to transmit data also relies on lasers. (Gartaganis 25)

And this final example shows how optical fibre can relay a video signal:

> Acting, in essence, as tiny cameras, optical fibres can be inserted into the body and relay an image to an outside screen. (Stanton 28)

Examples are a most powerful communication tool—as long as you tailor the examples to the readers' level of understanding.

Whichever expansion strategies you use, be sure to document your information sources.

Sample Situations

The following definitions employ expansion strategies appropriate to their audiences' needs. Specific strategies are labelled in the margin. Each definition, like a good essay, is unified and coherent: Each paragraph is developed around one main idea and logically connected to other paragraphs. Visuals are incorporated. Transitions emphasize the connection between ideas. Each definition is at a level of technicality that connects with the intended audience.

To illustrate the importance of audience analysis in a writer's decision about "How much is enough?" this example, like many throughout the text, is preceded by an audience/purpose profile based on the worksheet on page 34.

An Expanded Definition for Semi-technical Readers

AUDIENCE/PURPOSE PROFILE. The intended readers of this material are beginning student mechanics. Before they can repair a solenoid, they will need to know where the term comes from, what a solenoid looks like, how it works, how its parts operate, and how it is used. This definition is designed as merely an *introduction,* so it offers only a general (but comprehensive) view of the mechanism.

Because the intended readers are not engineering students, they do *not* need details about electromagnetic or mechanical theory (e.g., equations or graphs illustrating voltage magnitudes, joules, lines of force). ■

EXPANDED DEFINITION: SOLENOID

Formal sentence definition

A **solenoid** is an electrically energized coil that forms an electromagnet capable of performing mechanical functions. The term "solenoid" is derived from the word "sole," which in reference to electrical equipment means "a part of," or "contained inside, or with, other electrical equipment." The Greek word *solenoides* means "channel," or "shaped like a pipe."

Etymology

Description and analysis of parts

A simple plunger-type solenoid consists of a coil of wire attached to an electrical source, and an iron rod, or plunger, that passes in and out of the coil along the axis of the spiral. A return spring holds the rod outside the coil when the current is de-energized, as shown in Figure 1.

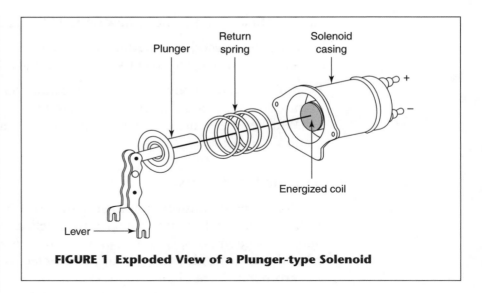

FIGURE 1 Exploded View of a Plunger-type Solenoid

Special conditions and operating principle

When the coil receives electric current, it becomes a magnet and thus draws the iron rod inside, along the length of its cylindrical centre. With a lever attached to its end, the rod can transform electrical energy into mechanical force. The amount of mechanical force produced is the product of the number of turns in the coil, the strength of the current, and the magnetic conductivity of the rod.

Example and analysis of parts
Explanation of visual

The plunger-type solenoid in Figure 1 is commonly used in the starter motor of an automobile engine. This type is 11.5 cm (4½") long and 5 cm (2") in diametre, with a steel casing attached to the casing of the starter motor. A linkage (pivoting lever) is attached at one end to the iron rod of the solenoid, and at the other end to the drive gear of the starter, as shown in Figure 2.

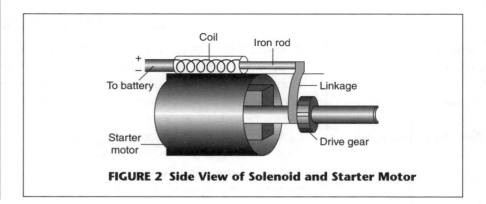

FIGURE 2 Side View of Solenoid and Starter Motor

When the ignition key is turned, current from the battery is supplied to the solenoid coil, and the iron rod is drawn inside the coil, thereby shifting the attached linkage. The linkage, in turn, engages the drive gear, activated by the starter motor, with the flywheel (the main rotating gear of the engine).

Comparison of sizes and applications

Because of the solenoid's many uses, its size varies according to the work it must do. A small solenoid will have a small wire coil, hence a weak magnetic field. The larger the coil, the stronger the magnetic field; in this case, the rod in the solenoid can do harder work. An electronic lock for a standard door would, for instance, require a much smaller solenoid than one for a bank vault.

The audience for the following definition (an entire community) is too diverse to define precisely, so the writer wisely addresses the lowest level of technicality—to ensure that all readers will understand.

An Expanded Definition for Non-technical Readers

AUDIENCE/PURPOSE PROFILE. The following definition is written for members of a community whose water supply (all obtained from wells, because the town has no reservoir) is doubly threatened: (1) by chemical seepage from a recently discovered toxic dump site, and (2) by a two-year drought that has severely depleted the water table. This definition forms part of a report that analyzes the severity of the problems and explores possible solutions.

To understand the problems, these readers first need to know what a water table is, how it is formed, what conditions affect its level and quality, and how it figures into town planning decisions. The concepts of *recharge* and *permeability* are vital to readers' understanding of the problem here, so these terms are defined parenthetically. These readers have no interest in geological or hydrological (study of water resources) theory. They simply need a broad picture. ∎

EXPANDED DEFINITION: WATER TABLE

Formal sentence definition
Example

The water table is the level below the earth's surface at which the ground is saturated with water. Figure 1 shows a typical water table that might be found in the East. Wells driven into such a formation will have a water level identical to that of the water table.

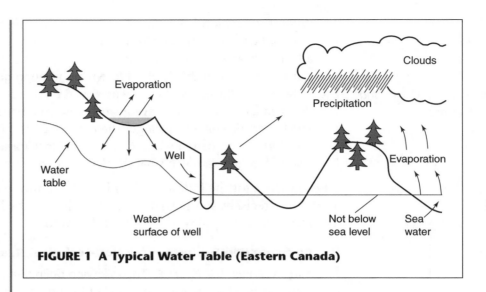

FIGURE 1 A Typical Water Table (Eastern Canada)

Operating principle

The world's fresh-water supply comes almost entirely as precipitation that originates with the evaporation of sea and lake water. This precipitation falls to earth and follows one of three courses: It may fall directly onto bodies of water, such as rivers or lakes, where it is directly used by humans; it may fall onto land, and either evaporate or run over the ground to the rivers or other bodies of water; or it may fall onto land, be contained, and seep into the earth. The latter precipitation makes up the water table.

Comparison

Similar in contour to the earth's surface above, the water table generally has a level that reflects such features as hills and valleys. Where the water table intersects the ground surface, a stream or pond results.

Operating principle

A water table's level, however, will vary, depending on the rate of recharge (replacement of water). The recharge rate is affected by rainfall or soil permeability (the ease with which water flows through the soil). A water table then is never static; rather, it is the surface of a body of water striving to maintain a balance between the forces which deplete it and those which replenish it. In areas of Nova Scotia and some western provinces where the water table is depleted, the earth caves in, leaving sinkholes.

Example

Special conditions and examples

The water table's depth below ground is vital in water resources engineering and planning. It determines an area's suitability for wastewater disposal, or a building lot's ability to handle sewage. A high water table could become contaminated by a septic system. Also, bacteria and chemicals seeping into a water table can pollute an entire town's water supply. Another consideration in water-table depth is the cost of drilling wells. These conditions obviously affect an industry's or homeowner's decision on where to locate.

Special conditions

The rising and falling of the water table give an indication of the pumping rate's effect on a water supply (drawn from wells) and of the sufficiency of the recharge rate in meeting demand. This kind of information helps water resources planners decide when new sources of water must be made available.

Placement of Definitions

Poorly placed definitions interrupt the information flow. If you have only a few parenthetical definitions, place them in parentheses after the terms. Any more than a few definitions per page will be disruptive. Rewrite them as sentence definitions and place them in a "Definitions" section of your introduction, or in a glossary.

If your sentence definitions are few, place them in a "Definitions" section of your introduction; otherwise, in a glossary. Definitions of terms in the report's title belong in your introduction.

Place expanded definitions in one of three locations:

1. If the definition is essential to the reader's understanding of the *entire* document, place it in the introduction. A report titled "The Effects of Aerosols on the Earth's Ozone Shield" would require expanded definitions of "aerosols" and "ozone shield" early.

2. When the definition clarifies a major part of your discussion, place it in that section of your report. In a report titled "How Advertising Influences Consumer Habits," "operant conditioning" might be defined early in the appropriate section. Too many expanded definitions *within* a report, however, can be disruptive.

3. If the definition serves only as a reference, place it in an appendix. For example, a report on fire safety in a public building might have an expanded definition of "carbon monoxide detectors" in an appendix.

Electronic documents pose special problems for placement of definitions. In a hypertext document, for instance, each reader explores the material differently (Chapter 25). One option for making definitions available when they are needed is the "pop-up note": The term to be defined is highlighted in the text, to indicate that its definition can be called up and displayed in a small window on the actual text screen (Horton 25).

Revision and Editing Checklist For Definitions

Use this checklist to revise your definitions.

CONTENT

- ❑ Is the type of definition (parenthetical, sentence, expanded) suited to its purpose and readers' needs?
- ❑ Does the definition convey the basic property of the item?
- ❑ Is the definition objective?
- ❑ Is the expanded definition adequately developed?
- ❑ Are all information sources documented?
- ❑ Are visuals employed adequately and appropriately?

ARRANGEMENT

- ❑ Does the sentence definition describe features that distinguish the item from other items in the same class?
- ❑ Is the expanded definition unified and coherent (like an essay)?
- ❑ Are transitions between ideas adequate?
- ❑ Does the definition appear in the appropriate location?

STYLE AND PAGE DESIGN

- ❑ Is the definition in plain English?
- ❑ Will the level of technicality connect with the audience?
- ❑ Are sentences clear, concise, and fluent?
- ❑ Is word choice precise?
- ❑ Is the definition ethically acceptable?
- ❑ Is the page design inviting and accessible?

☑ EXERCISES

1. Sentence definitions require precise classification and differentiation. Is each of these definitions adequate for a general reader? Rewrite those that seem inadequate. Consult dictionaries and encyclopedias as needed.

   a. A bicycle is a vehicle with two wheels.

   b. A transistor is a device used in transistorized electronic equipment.

   c. Surfing is when one rides a wave to shore while standing on a board specifically designed for buoyancy and balance.

   d. Bubonic plague is caused by an organism known as *pasteurella pestis.*

   e. Mace is a chemical aerosol spray used by the police.

   f. A Geiger counter measures radioactivity.

   g. A cactus is a succulent.

   h. In law, an indictment is a criminal charge against a defendant.

   i. A prune is a kind of plum.

   j. Friction is a force between two bodies.

   k. Luffing is what happens when one sails into the wind.

   l. A frame is an important part of a bicycle.

   m. Hypoglycemia is a medical term.

   n. An hourglass is a device used for measuring intervals of time.

   o. A computer is a machine that handles information with amazing speed.

   p. A Ferrari is the best car in the world.

   q. To meditate is to exercise mental faculties in thought.

2. Standard dictionaries define for the general reader, whereas specialized reference books define for the specialist. Choose an item in your field and copy the definition (1) from a standard dictionary and (2) from a technical reference book. For the technical definition, label each expansion strategy. Rewrite the specialized definition for a general reader.

3. Using reference books as necessary, write sentence definitions for these terms or for terms from your field.

biological insect control	gyroscope
generator	coronary bypass
dewpoint	oil shale
microprocessor	chemotherapy
capitalism	estuary
local area network	Boolean logic
marsh	classical conditioning
artificial intelligence	hypothermia
economic inflation	thermistor
anorexia nervosa	aquaculture
low-impact camping	nuclear fission
hemodialysis	modem

4. Select an item from the list in Exercise 3 or from an area of interest. Identify an audience and purpose. Complete an audience/purpose profile (page 85). Begin with a sentence definition of the term. Then write an expanded definition for a first-year student in that field. Next, write the same definition for a layperson (client, patient, or other interested party). Leave a margin at the left side of your page to list expansion strategies. Use at least four expansion strategies in each version, including at least one visual or an art brief (page 304) and a rough diagram. In preparing each version, consult no fewer than four outside references. Cite and document each source, using one of the documentation styles discussed in Chapter 8. Submit, with your two versions, an explanation of your changes from the first version to the second.

☑ COLLABORATIVE PROJECTS

1. Divide into small groups on the basis of academic majors or interests. Appoint one person as group manager. Decide on an item, concept, or process that would require an expanded definition for a layperson. For example:

   - From computer science: an algorithm, an applications program, artificial intelligence, binary coding, top-down procedural thinking, or systems analysis
   - From nursing: a pacemaker, coronary bypass surgery, or natural childbirth

   Complete an audience profile (page 85).

   Once your group has decided on the appropriate expansion strategies (etymology, negation, etc.), the group manager will assign each member to work on one or two specific strategies as part of the definition. As a group, edit and incorporate the collected material into an expanded definition, revising as often as needed.

   The group manager will assign one member to present the definition in class, using either opaque or overhead projection, a large-screen monitor, data projection unit, or photocopies.

2. Beyond informative definition, your group's goal in this next project is to develop a *persuasive* definition.

   Assume you work for an organization that has recently formulated a policy to eliminate sexual harassment. Your charge as the communications group is to develop printed material that will publicize this new policy. Your specific task is to develop an expanded definition of *sexual harassment* to be published in the company newsletter.

   At this stage, the company is plagued by confusion, misunderstanding, resentment, and paranoia about the harassment issue. Therefore, beyond compliance with legal requirements, your organization seeks to improve gender relations between co-workers, in the hope of boosting productivity.

   Thus, you face an informative, persuasive, and ethical challenge: to move beyond the usual matters of clarity so that your definition promotes real understanding and reconciliation. In short, you need to amplify the legal definition so that employees are able to recognize harassment and to understand clearly what does and what does not constitute harassment. But unless you also do something to change their us-against-them *attitude,* you will only create greater tension and over-reaction.

   In other words, you want your definition not merely to *inhibit* behaviour, but to *enlighten* the readers. Insensitive readers, of course, are likely to change their behaviour only if they feel coerced. But appeals to fear almost always have limited success, and people generally tend to be reasonable in the long run. You want your definition to have rational appeal, to cause readers to *internalize* the values that underlie the issue. No sermons, please.

Descriptions and Specifications

D ESCRIPTION (creating a picture with words) is part of all writing. But technical descriptions convey information about a product or mechanism to someone who will use it, buy it, operate it, assemble it, manufacture it, or to someone who has to know more about it. Any item can be visualized from countless different perspectives. Therefore, *how* you describe—your perspective—depends on your purpose and the needs of your audience.

Two kinds of description are featured in this chapter, mechanism description and specifications. We start with a mechanism description (see Figure 15.1).

Purpose of Description

Manufacturers use descriptions to sell products; banks require detailed descriptions of any business or construction venture before approving a loan; and medical personnel maintain daily or hourly descriptions of a patient's condition and treatment.

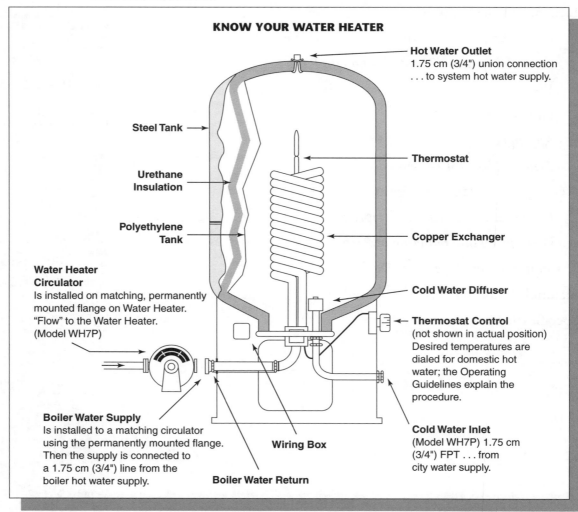

Figure 15.1   A Mechanism Description
Source: Courtesy of AMTROL Inc.

No matter what the subject of description, readers expect answers to as many of these questions as are applicable: *What is it? What does it do? What does it look like? What is it made of? How does it work? How was it put together?* The description in Figure 15.1, part of an installation and operation manual, answers applicable questions for do-it-yourself homeowners.

Objectivity in Description

Descriptions are mainly *subjective* or *objective:* based on feelings or fact. Subjective description emphasizes the writer's attitude toward the thing, whereas objective description emphasizes the thing itself.

Essays describing "An Unforgettable Person" or "A Beautiful Moment" express opinions, a personal point of view. Subjective description aims at expressing feelings, attitudes, and moods. You create an *impression* of your subject ("The weather was miserable"), more than communicating factual information about it ("All day, we had freezing rain and gale-force winds").

Objective description shows an impartial view, filtering out personal impressions and focusing on observable details.

Except for promotional writing, descriptions on the job should be impartial, if they are to be ethical. Pure objectivity is, of course, humanly impossible. Each writer filters the facts and their meaning through her or his own perspective. Nonetheless, we are expected to communicate the facts as we know them and understand them. One writer offers this useful distinction: "All communication requires us to leave something out, but we must be sure that what is left out is not essential to our [reader's] understanding of what is put in" (Coletta 65).

An ethical writer "is obligated to express her or his opinions of products, as long as these opinions are based on objective and responsible research and observation" (Mackenzie 3). Being "objective" does not mean forsaking personal evaluation in cases in which a product may be unsafe or unsound. Even positive claims made in promotional writing (for example, "reliable," "rugged," etc.) should be based on objective and verifiable evidence.

Here are guidelines for remaining impartial.

Record the Details That Enable Readers to Visualize the Item. Ask these questions: *What could any observer recognize? What would a camera record?*

Subjective	His office has an *awful* view, *terrible* furniture, and a *depressing* atmosphere.

The italicized words only *tell;* they do not *show.*

Objective	His office has broken windows looking out on a brick wall, a rug with a 15-cm hole in the centre, chairs with bottoms falling out, missing floorboards, and a ceiling with plaster missing in three or four places.

Use Precise and Informative Language. Use high-information words that enable readers to *visualize*. Name specific parts without calling them "things," "gadgets," or "doohickeys." Avoid judgmental words ("impressive," "poor"), unless your judgment is requested and can be supported by facts. Instead of "large," "long," and "near," give exact measurements, weights, dimensions, and ingredients.

Use words that specify location and spatial relationships: "above," "oblique," "behind," "tangential," "adjacent," "interlocking," "abutting," and "overlapping." Use position words: "horizontal," "vertical," "lateral," "longitudinal," "in cross-section," "parallel."

Indefinite	Precise
a late-model car	a 2005 Ford Taurus sedan
an inside view	a cross-sectional, cutaway, or exploded view
next to the foundation	adjacent to the right side
a small red thing	a red activator button with a 2.5-cm diameter and a concave surface

Do not confuse precise language, however, with overly complicated technical terms or needless jargon. Don't say "phlebotomy specimen" instead of "blood," or "thermal attenuation" instead of "insulation," or "proactive neutralization" instead of "damage control." The clearest writing uses precise but plain language. General readers prefer non-technical language, as long as the simpler words do the job. Always think about your specific readers' needs.

Elements of Description

Clear and Limiting Title

Promise exactly what you will deliver—no more and no less. "A Description of a Velo Ten-Speed Racing Bicycle" promises a complete description, down to the smallest part. If you intend to describe the braking mechanism only, be sure your title so indicates: "A Description of the Velo's Centre-Pull Caliper Braking Mechanism."

Overall Appearance and Component Parts

Let readers see the big picture before you describe each part.

> The standard stethoscope is roughly 61 cm long and weighs about 140 grams. The instrument consists of a sensitive sound-detecting and amplifying device whose flat surface is pressed against a bodily area. This amplifying device is attached to rubber and metal tubing that transmits the body sound to a listening device inserted in the ear.
>
> Seven interlocking pieces contribute to the stethoscope's Y-shaped appearance: (1) diaphragm contact piece, (2) lower tubing, (3) Y-shaped metal piece, (4) upper tubing, (5) U-shaped metal strip, (6) curved metal tubing, and (7) hollow ear plugs. These parts form a continuous unit.

Visuals

Use drawings, diagrams, or photographs generously. Our overall description of the stethoscope is greatly clarified by Figure 1.

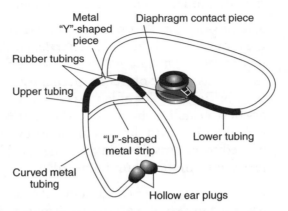

FIGURE 1   Stethoscope with Diaphragm Contact Piece (Front View)

Function of Each Part

Explain what each part does and how it relates to the whole.

> The diaphragm contact piece is caused to vibrate by body sounds. This part is the heart of the stethoscope that receives, amplifies, and transmits the sound impulse.

Appropriate Details

Give enough detail for a clear picture, but do not burden readers needlessly. Identify your readers and their reasons for reading your description.

Assume you set out to describe a specific bicycle model. The picture you create will depend on the details you select. How will your reader use this description? What is the reader's level of technical understanding? Is this a customer interested in the bike's appearance—its flashy looks and racy style? Is it a repair technician who needs to know how parts operate? Or is it a helper in your bicycle shop who needs to know how to assemble this bike? If you had designed the bike, you would give the manufacturer detailed specifications.

The description of the hot-water maker in Figure 15.1 focuses on what this model looks like and what it's made of. Its intended audience of do-it-yourselfers will know already what a hot-water maker is and what it does. That audience needs no background. A description of how it was put together appears with the installation and maintenance instructions later in the manual.

Specifications for readers who will manufacture the hot-water maker would describe each part in exact detail (e.g., the steel tank's required thickness and pressure rating as well as required percentages of iron, carbon, and other constituents in the steel alloy).

Clearest Descriptive Sequence

Any item usually has its own logic of organization, based on (1) the way it appears as a static object, (2) the way its parts operate in order, or (3) the way its parts are assembled. We describe these relationships, respectively, in a spatial, functional, or chronological sequence.

Spatial Sequence. Part of all physical descriptions, a spatial sequence answers these questions: *What is it? What does it do? What does it look like? What parts and material is it made of?* Use this sequence when you want readers to visualize the item as a static object or mechanism at rest (a house interior, a document, the CN Tower, a plot of land, a chainsaw, or a computer keyboard). Can readers best visualize this item from front to rear, left to right, top to bottom? (What logical path do the parts create?) A retractable pen would logically be viewed from outside to inside. The specifications in Figure 15.2 on page 376 proceed from the ground upward.

Functional Sequence. The functional sequence answers: *How does it work?* It is best used in describing a mechanism in action, such as a 35-millimetre camera, a nuclear warhead, a smoke detector, or a car's cruise-control system. The logic of the item is reflected by the order in which its parts function. Like the hot-water maker in Figure 15.1, a mechanism usually has only one functional sequence. The stethoscope description on page 369 follows the sequence of parts through which sound travels.

In describing a solar home-heating system, you would begin with the heat collectors on the roof, moving through the pipes, pumping system, and tanks for the heated water, to the heating vents in the floors and walls—from source to outlet. After this functional sequence of operating parts, you could describe each part in a spatial sequence.

Chronological Sequence. A chronological sequence answers: *How has it been put together?* The chronology follows the sequence in which the parts are assembled.

Use the chronological sequence for an item that is best visualized by its assembly (such as a piece of furniture, an umbrella tent, or a prehung window or door unit). Architects might find a spatial sequence best for describing a proposed beach house to clients; however, they would use a chronological sequence (of blueprints) for specifying to the builder the prescribed dimensions, materials, and construction methods at each stage.

Combined Sequences. The description of a bumper jack on pages 372–374 alternates among all three sequences: a spatial sequence (bottom to top) for describing the overall mechanism at rest, a chronological sequence for explaining the order in which the parts are assembled, and a functional sequence for describing the order in which the parts operate.

A General Model for Description

Description of a complex mechanism almost invariably calls for an outline. This model is adaptable to any description.

I. Introduction: General Description[1]
   A. Definition, Function, and Background of the Item
   B. Purpose (and Audience—where applicable)
   C. Overall Description (with general visuals, if applicable)
   D. Principle of Operation (if applicable)
   E. List of Major Parts
II. Description and Function of Parts
   A. Part One in Your Descriptive Sequence
      1. Definition
      2. Shape, dimensions, material (with specific visuals)
      3. Subparts (if applicable)
      4. Function
      5. Relation to adjoining parts
      6. Mode of attachment (if applicable)
   B. Part Two in Your Descriptive Sequence (and so on)
III. Summary and Operating Description
   A. Summary (used only in a long, complex description)
   B. Interrelation of Parts
   C. One Complete Operating Cycle

This outline is tentative, because you might modify, delete, or combine certain parts to suit your subject, purpose, and reader.

Introduction: General Description

Give readers only as much background as they need to get the picture.

A Description of the Standard Stethoscope

Introduction

Definition and function

The stethoscope is a listening device that amplifies and transmits body sounds to aid in detecting physical abnormalities.

History and background

This instrument has evolved from the original wooden, funnel-shaped instrument invented by a French physician, R. T. Lennaec, in 1819. Because of his female patients' modesty, he found it necessary to develop a device, other than his ear, for auscultation (listening to body sounds).

Purpose and audience

This report explains to the beginning paramedical or nursing student the structure, assembly, and operating principle of the stethoscope. [*Omit this section if you submit to your instructor an audience/purpose profile or if you write for a workplace audience.*]

---

1. In most descriptions, the subdivisions in the introduction can be combined and need not appear as individual headings in the document.

Finally, give a brief, overall description of the item, discuss its principle of operation, and list its major parts, as in the overall stethoscope description on page 366.

Description and Function of Parts

The body of your text describes each major part. After arranging the parts in sequence, follow the logic of each part. Provide only as much detail as your readers need.

Readers of this description will use a stethoscope daily, so they need to know how it works, how to take it apart for cleaning, and how to replace worn or broken parts. (Specifications for the manufacturer would require many more technical details—dimensions, alloys, curvatures, tolerances, etc.)

Diaphragm Contact Piece

Definition, size, shape, and material
Subparts

The diaphragm contact piece is a shallow metal bowl, about the size of a silver dollar (and twice its thickness), which is caused to vibrate by various body sounds.

Three, separate parts make up the piece: hollow steel bowl, plastic diaphragm, and metal frame, as shown in Figure 2.

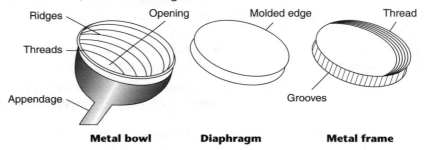

FIGURE 2   Exploded View of a Diaphragm Contact Piece

The stainless steel metal bowl has a concave inner surface, with concentric ridges that funnel sound toward an opening in the tapered base, then out through the hollow appendage. Lateral threads ring the outer circumference of the bowl to accommodate the interlocking metal frame. A fitted diaphragm covers the bowl's upper opening.

The diaphragm is a plastic disk, 2 millimetres thick, 10.2 cm in circumference, with a molded lip around the edge. It fits flush over the metal bowl and vibrates sound toward the ridges. A metal frame that screws onto the bowl holds the diaphragm in place.

The stainless steel frame fits over the disk and metal bowl. A 0.75-cm ridge between the inner and outer edge accommodates threads for screwing the frame to the bowl. The frame's outside circumference is notched with equally spaced, perpendicular grooves—like those on the edge of a dime—to provide a gripping surface.

Function and relation to adjoining parts

Mode of attachment

The diaphragm contact piece is the heart of the stethoscope that receives, amplifies, and transmits sound through the system of attached tubing. The piece attaches to the lower tubing by an appendage on its apex (narrow end), which fits inside the tubing.

Each part of the stethoscope, in turn, is described according to its own logic of organization.

Summary and Operating Description

Conclude by explaining how the parts work together to make the whole item function.

Summary and Operating Description

How parts interrelate

One complete operating cycle

The seven major parts of the stethoscope provide support for the instrument, flexibility of movement for the operator, and ease in auscultation.

In an operating cycle, the diaphragm contact piece, placed against the skin, picks up sound impulses from the body surface. These impulses cause the plastic diaphragm to vibrate. The amplified vibrations, in turn, are carried through a tube to a dividing point. From here, the amplified sound is carried through two separate but identical series of tubes to hollow ear plugs.

A Sample Situation

The following description of an automobile jack, aimed toward a general audience, follows our outline model.

A Mechanism Description for Non-technical Readers

AUDIENCE/PURPOSE PROFILE. Some readers of this description (written for an owner's manual) will have no mechanical background. Before they can follow instructions for using the jack safely, they will have to learn what it is, what it looks like, what its parts are, and how, generally, it works. They will not need precise dimensions (e.g., "The rectangular base is 20.25 cm long and 16.5 cm wide, sloping upward 3.75 cm from the front outer edge to form a secondary platform 2.5 cm high and 7.5 cm square"). The engineer who designed the jack might include such data in specifications for the manufacturer. Laypersons, however, need only the dimensions that will help them recognize specific parts and understand their function, for safe use and assembly.

Also, this audience will need only the broadest explanation of how the leverage mechanism operates. Although the physical principles (torque, fulcrum) would interest engineers, they would be of little use to readers who simply need to operate the jack safely. ∎

Description of a Standard Bumper Jack

Introduction—General Description

Definition, purpose, and function

The standard bumper jack is a portable mechanism for raising the front or rear of a car through force applied with a lever. This jack enables even a frail person to lift one corner of a 2-tonne automobile.

Overall description (spatial sequence)

The jack consists of a molded steel base supporting a free-standing, perpendicular, notched shaft (Figure 1). Attached to the shaft are a leverage mechanism, a bumper catch, and cylinder for insertion of the jack handle. Except for the main shaft and leverage mechanism, the jack is made to be dismantled and to fit neatly in the car's trunk.

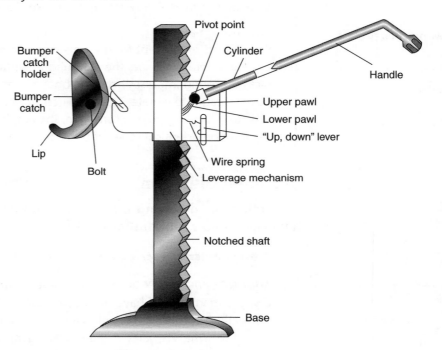

FIGURE 1 A Side View of the Standard Bumper Jack

Operating principle

The jack operates on a leverage principle, with a human hand travelling 46 cm and the car only 1 cm during a normal jacking stroke. Such a device requires many strokes to raise the car off the ground but may prove a lifesaver to a motorist on some deserted road.

List of major parts

Five main parts make up the jack: base, notched shaft, leverage mechanism, bumper catch, and handle.

(chronological sequence)
First major part

Description of Parts and Their Function

Base

The rectangular base is a molded steel plate that provides support and a point of insertion for the shaft (Figure 2). The base slopes upward to form a platform containing a 1.25-cm depression that provides a stabilizing well for the shaft. Stability is increased by a 1.25-cm cuff around the well. As the base rests on its flat surface, the bottom end of the shaft is inserted into its stabilizing well.

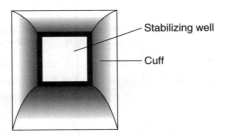

FIGURE 2   A Top View of the Jack Base

Notched Shaft

The notched shaft is a steel bar (80 cm long) that provides a vertical track for the leverage mechanism. The notches, which hold the mechanism in its position on the shaft, face the operator.

The shaft vertically supports the raised automobile, and attached to it is the leverage mechanism, which rests on individual notches.

Leverage Mechanism

The leverage mechanism provides the mechanical advantage needed for its operator to raise the car. It is made to slide up and down the notched shaft. The main body of this pressed-steel mechanism contains two units: one for transferring the leverage and one for holding the bumper catch.

The leverage unit has four major parts: the cylinder, connecting the handle and a pivot point; a lower pawl (a device that fits into the notches to allow forward and prevent backward motion), connected directly to the cylinder; an upper pawl, connected at the pivot point; and an "up-down" lever, which applies or releases pressure on the upper pawl by means of a spring (Figure 1). Moving the cylinder up and down with the handle causes the alternate release of the pawls, and thus movement up or down the shaft—depending on the setting of the "up-down" lever. The movement is transferred by the metal body of the unit to the bumper-catch holder.

The holder consists of a downsloping groove, partially blocked by a wire spring (Figure 1). The spring is mounted in such a way as to keep the bumper catch in place during operation.

Bumper Catch

The bumper catch is a steel device that attaches the leverage mechanism to the bumper. This 23-cm molded plate is bent to fit the shape of the bumper. Its outer 0.5 cm is bent up to form a lip (Figure 1), which hooks behind the bumper to hold the catch in place. The two sides of the plate are bent back 90 degrees to leave a 5.0-cm bumper-contact surface, and a bolt is riveted between them. This bolt slips into the groove in the leverage mechanism and provides the attachment between the leverage unit and the car.

Handle
The jack handle is a steel bar that serves both as lever and lug-bolt remover. This round bar is 56 cm long, 1.5 cm in diameter, and is bent 135 degrees roughly 13 cm from its outer end. Its outer end is a wrench made to fit the wheel's lug bolts. Its inner end is bevelled to form a blade-like point for prying the wheel covers and for insertion into the cylinder on the leverage mechanism.

Conclusion and Operating Description

Assembly

One quickly assembles the jack by inserting the bottom of the notched shaft into the stabilizing well in the base, the bumper catch into the groove on the leverage mechanism, and the bevelled end of the jack handle into the cylinder. The bumper catch is then attached to the bumper, with the lever set in the "up" position.

One complete operating cycle (functional sequence)

As the operator exerts an up-down pumping motion on the jack handle, the leverage mechanism gradually climbs the vertical notched shaft until the car's wheel is raised above the ground. When the lever is in the "down" position, the same pumping motion causes the leverage mechanism to descend the shaft.

Specifications

Airplanes, bridges, smoke detectors, and countless other items are produced according to certain specifications. A particularly exacting type of description, specifications (or "specs") prescribe standards for performance, safety, and quality. For almost any product, specifications spell out:

- the methods for manufacturing, building, or installing the product
- the materials and equipment to be used
- the size, shape, and weight of the product

Because these requirements define an acceptable level of quality, specifications have ethical and legal implications. Any product "below" specifications provides grounds for a lawsuit. When injury or death results (as in a bridge collapse caused by inferior reinforcement), the contractor, subcontractor, or supplier who cut corners is criminally liable.

Federal and provincial regulatory agencies routinely issue specifications to ensure safety. Health Canada specifies standards for a wide variety of materials and devices, from the operation of seat belts to the fire retardant qualities of cloth used for infant pyjamas. Meanwhile, the Canadian Standards Association designates safety and operating specifications for nearly every product sold in this country. Further, provincial and local agencies issue specifications in the form of building codes, electrical codes, and property development requirements, to name just a few.

Government departments (Defence, Interior, etc.) issue specifications for all types of military hardware and other equipment. A set of NASA specifications for spacecraft parts can be hundreds of pages long, prescribing the standards for even the smallest nuts and bolts, down to screw-thread depth and width in millimetres.

The private sector issues specifications for countless products or projects, to help ensure that customers get exactly what they want. Figure 15.2 on page 376 shows partial specifications drawn up by an architect for a building that will house a small medical clinic. This section of the specs covers only the structure's "shell." Other sections detail the requirements for plumbing, wiring, and interior finish work.

The detailed building specifications partially shown in Figure 15.2 provide the basis for the comprehensive agreement between the builder and the client. In addition, the specifications (along with properly drawn building plans) are important in convincing the municipal authority to issue a building permit. Subsequently, building inspectors will use the plans and specifications as part of their criteria when they inspect the clinic in various stages of the building process.

Specifications like those in Figure 15.2 must be clear enough for *identical* interpretation by the widest possible range of readers (Glidden 258–59):

- *the customer*, who has the big picture of what is needed and who wants the best product at the best price

- *the designer* (architect, engineer, computer scientist, etc.), who must translate the customer's wishes into the actual specifications

- *the contractor or manufacturer*, who won the job by making the lowest bid, and so must preserve profit by doing only what is prescribed

- *the supplier*, who must provide the exact materials and equipment

- *the workforce*, who will do the actual assembly, construction, or installation (managers, supervisors, subcontractors, and workers—some working on only one part of the product, such as plumbing or electrical)

- *the inspectors* (such as building, plumbing, or electrical inspectors), who evaluate how well the product conforms to the specifications

Ruger, Filstone, and Grant Architects

SPECIFICATIONS FOR THE POWNAL CLINIC BUILDING

Foundation
Footings: 8" x 16" concrete (load-bearing capacity: 3000 lbs. per sq. in.)
Frost walls: 8" x 4' @ 3000 psi
Slab: 4" @ 3000 psi, reinforced with wire mesh over vapour barrier

Exterior Walls
Frame: eastern pine #2 timber frame with exterior partitions set inside
    posts
Exterior partitions: 2" x 4" kiln-dried spruce set at 16" on centre
Sheathing: 1/4" exterior-grade plywood
Siding: #1 red cedar with a 1/2" x 6' bevel
Trim: finished-pine boards ranging from 1" x 4" to 1" x 10"
Painting: 2 coats of Clear Wood Finish on siding; trim primed and finished
    with one coat of bone-white, oil base paint

Roof System
Framing: 2" x 12" kiln-dried spruce set at 24" on centre
Sheathing: 5/8" exterior-grade plywood
Finish: 240 Celotex 20-year fibreglass shingles over #15 impregnated felt
    roofing paper
Flashing: copper

Windows
Anderson casement and fixed-over-awning models, with white exterior
    cladding, insulating glass and screens, and wood interior frames

Landscape
Driveway: gravel base, with 3" traprock surface
Walks: timber defined, with traprock surface
Cleared areas: to be rough graded and covered with wood chips
Plantings: 10 assorted lawn plants along the road side of the building

Figure 15.2   Specifications for a Building Project (Partial)

Each of these parties has to understand and agree on exactly *what* is to be done and *how* it is to be done. In the case of a lawsuit over failure to meet specifications, the readership broadens to include judges, lawyers, and jury. Figure 15.3 depicts how a clear set of specifications unifies all readers (their various viewpoints, motives, and levels of expertise) in a shared understanding.

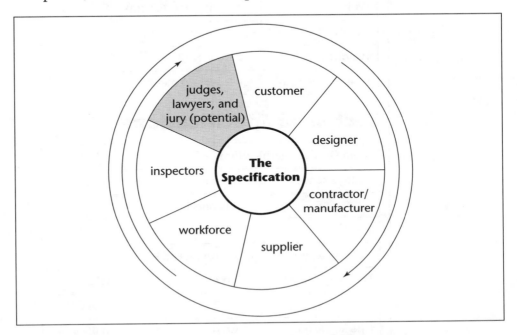

Figure 15.3   Readers and Potential Readers of Specifications

In addition to guiding a product's design and construction, specifications can facilitate the product's use and maintenance. For instance, specifications in a computer manual include the product's performance limits, or *ratings*: its power requirements, work or processing or storage capacity, environment requirements, the make-up of key parts, etc. Product support literature for appliances, power tools, and other items routinely contains ratings to help readers select a good operating environment or replace worn or defective parts (Riney 186). The ratings in Figure 15.4 are taken from the owner's manual for a power supply.

Physical Dimensions

Height	4.5 inches (11.4 cm)
Width	10.5 inches (26.7 cm)
Depth	7.5 inches (19 cm)
Weight	7 lbs 6 oz (3.4 kg)
Line cord length	4 feet (1.20 metres)

Technical Specifications

Main Output Specifications		Min	Max
Voltage Range	Channel A	12.5 V	±20.00 V
	Channel B	12.5 V	±20.00 V
	Ch A and B	12.5 V	±40 V or +20/−20 V
Current Range:	Ch A/B, A and B	0.003 A	0.500 A
Load Regulation:	Ch A	1.164%	
	Ch B	1.266%	
Line Regulation:	Ch A	0.05%	
	Ch B	*0.00%	
Ripple and Noise		2 mV	6–8 mV
Bandwidth			120 Hz
Transient Response:		<220us within 50 mV of set level for 90% load change	
Temperature Coefficient		<100 ppm/°C	
Output Protection:	Voltage	Outputs will withstand up to 40 V forward voltage	
	Current	Reverse protection by diode clamp = up to 1.0 A	

Figure 15.4   Specifications for the Spider Power Supply
Source: Courtesy of Curt Willis

Revision and Editing Checklist For Descriptions

Use this checklist to refine the content, arrangement, and style of your description.

CONTENT

❑ Does the title promise exactly what the description delivers?

❑ Are the item's overall features described, as well as each part?

❑ Is each part defined before it is discussed?

❑ Is the function of each part explained?

❑ Do visuals appear whenever they can provide clarification?

❑ Will readers be able to visualize the item?

❑ Are any details missing, needless, or confusing for this audience?

❑ Is the description ethically acceptable?

ARRANGEMENT

❑ Does the description follow the clearest possible sequence?

❑ Are relationships among the parts clearly explained?

STYLE AND PAGE DESIGN

❑ Is the description sufficiently impartial?

❑ Is the language informative and precise?

❑ Will the level of technicality connect with the audience?

❑ Is the description written in plain English?

❑ Is each sentence clear, concise, and fluent?

❑ Is the page design inviting and accessible?

☑ EXERCISES

1. Select an item from the following list or a device used in your major field. Using the general outline as a model, develop an objective description. Include (a) all necessary visuals; or (b) rough diagram for each visual; or (c) a "reference visual" (a copy of a visual published elsewhere) with instructions for adapting your visual from that one. (If you borrow visuals from other sources, provide full documentation.) Write for a specific use by a specified audience. Attach your written audience/purpose profile (based on the worksheet, page 85) to your document.

soda-acid fire extinguisher	algorithm
breathalyzer	Skinner box
sphygmomanometer	radio
transit	distilling apparatus
sabre saw	bodily organ
hazardous waste site	brand of woodstove
photovoltaic panel	catalytic converter

Remember, you are simply describing the item, its parts, and its function: *do not* provide directions for its assembly or operation.

As an optional assignment, describe a place you know well. You are trying to convey a visual image, not a mood; therefore, your description should be impartial, discussing only the observable details.

2. The bumper-jack description in this chapter is aimed toward a general reading audience. Evaluate it by using the revision checklist. In one or two paragraphs, discuss your evaluation, and suggest revisions.

3. Locate a description and specifications for a particular brand of automobile or some other consumer product. Evaluate this material for promotional and descriptive value and ethical appropriateness.

☑ COLLABORATIVE PROJECTS

1. Divide into small groups. Assume that your group works in the product-development division of a large and diversified manufacturing company.

Your division has just invented an idea for an inexpensive consumer item with a potentially vast market. (Choose one from the following list.)

- flashlight
- nail clippers
- retractable ballpoint pen
- scissors
- stapler
- any simple mechanism—as long as it has moving parts

Your group's assignment is to prepare three descriptions of this invention:

a. for company executives who will decide whether to produce and market the item
b. for the engineers, machinists, and so on, who will design and manufacture the item
c. for the customers who might purchase and use the item

Before writing for each audience, be sure to collectively complete audience/purpose profiles (page 85).

Appoint a group manager, who will assign tasks (visuals, keying, etc.) to members. When the descriptions are fully prepared, the group manager will appoint one member to present them in class. The presentation should include explanations of how the descriptions differ for the different audiences.

2. Assume your group is an architectural firm designing buildings at your college. Develop a set of specifications for duplicating the interior of the classroom in which this course is held. Focus only on materials, dimensions, and equipment (whiteboard, desk, etc.) and use visuals as appropriate. Your audience includes teachers, school administrators, and the firm that will construct the classroom. Use the same format as in Figure 15.2, or design a better one. Appoint one member to present the completed specifications in class. Compare versions from each group for accuracy and clarity.

Process Analyses, Instructions, and Procedures

A PROCESS is a series of actions or changes leading to a product or result. *Instructions* describe how to carry out a "process"; a *procedure* is a special kind of instructional set. This chapter discusses all three types of process-related description.

Although process descriptions and instructions both present chronological steps which lead to a predicted result, that's where the similarity ends. The reasons for writing and reading a process description are quite different from the motivations for writing and reading instructions. These fundamental differences lead to the differences in content, structure, voice, mood, appearance, and style summarized in Table 16.1 on pages 384–385.

Process Analysis

Readers of process descriptions want to know *how* and *why* the processes occur, so the writer's first order of business is to divide the process into its parts or principles. Usually, those parts occur in chronological order. Moreover, the first part or step of the process usually leads to the second step and often creates the conditions that allow that second step to occur. Then, the second step leads to the third step, and so on.

This chronological development of dependent steps is particularly noticeable to writers who analyze mechanical processes (operation of a piston-driven engine), geological processes (formation of icebergs), or chemical processes (chemical hydration within concrete). Even electronic processes, which occur at blinding speed, can be understood as a series of causative actions: It's possible to know the exact order, duration, and effect caused by each sub-process within an electronic circuit.

The electronic example raises another very interesting point about most processes. They depend on the "conditions" which cause them. The process of an electronic circuit's operation depends on the design of the circuit itself. In a less confining way, perhaps, the process by which a road is washed by heavy spring run-off depends on the physical conditions of water volumes, soil composition, and terrain.

As Table 16.1 illustrates, a process analysis must include enough detail to enable readers to follow the process step by step. However, that level of detail depends on the reader's needs. For example, a back-country skier who wants to avoid avalanches will be satisfied with a basic description of the forces and conditions that affect the slab-avalanche process. However, a civil engineer studying avalanches will need to know much more about snow compaction forces, changes in crystalline structures, and the forces that cause snow layers to shear apart.

Because it emphasizes the process itself, rather than the reader's role, process analysis is written in the third person. Indeed, all aspects of a process description resemble a technical essay:

- It uses standard paragraphs, most of which use chronological patterns.
- It employs serious, reflective phrasing.
- It employs precise, accurate vocabulary.
- It presents a formal appearance, usually with headings, formal illustration format, and formal documentation of sources.

In order to help the reader fully understand the process, the writer must carefully plan the structure of a process description. The writer's first step is to analyze the process itself, at the level of the reader's interests and needs. This analysis will help the writer produce a detailed outline.

For an idea of the components of such an outline, see the structure for process description summarized in Table 16.1, pages 384–385.

The following process description has used a structure like the one outlined in Table 16.1. The document's writer, Bill Kelly, belongs to an environmental group studying the problems of acid rain in its southern Ontario community. To gain community support, the environmentalists must educate citizens about the problem. Bill's group is publishing and mailing a series of brochures. The first brochure explains how acid rain is formed.

Here is Bill's audience/purpose profile for the document.

A Process Analysis for Non-technical Readers

AUDIENCE/PURPOSE PROFILE. My audience will consist of general readers. Some already will be interested in the problem; others will have no awareness (or interest). Therefore, I'll keep my explanation at the lowest level of technicality (no chemical formulas, equations). But my explanation needs to be vivid enough to appeal to less aware or less interested readers. I'll use visuals to create interest and to illustrate simply. To give an explanation thorough enough for broad understanding, I'll divide the process into three chronological steps: how acid rain develops, spreads, and destroys. ■

This is the document resulting from Bill's analysis of both his subject and his audience.

HOW ACID RAIN DEVELOPS, SPREADS, AND DESTROYS

Introduction

Definition

Acid rain is environmentally damaging rainfall that occurs after fossil fuels burn, releasing nitrogen and sulphur oxides into the atmosphere. Acid rain, simply stated, increases the acidity level of waterways because these nitrogen and sulphur oxides combine with the air's normal moisture. The resulting rainfall is far more acidic than normal rainfall. Acid rain is a silent threat because its effects, although slow, are cumulative. This analysis explains the cause, the distribution cycle, and the effects of acid rain.

Purpose

Brief description of the process

Most research shows that power plants burning oil or coal are the primary cause of acid rain. The burnt fuel is not completely expended, and some residue

Table 16.1   Process Analysis Compared to Instructions   (Continued)

PURPOSE	Helps reader understand how and why the process occurs
AUDIENCE	Aimed at interested persons who want to understand how something works or how it happens
CONTENT	*Explanations* are essential, in addition to straight *chronological description* of the process' stages. Description of process' *physical environment* is part of some descriptions. *Illustrations* are often very useful. Descriptions are *specific* and *detailed*.
STRUCTURE	*General idea* (lead-in) • names and defines process and its special features • where, when, why, how often the process occurs • where necessary, gives background theory • lists the process' main stages or actions *Individual stages* (chronological) • each stage is described in detail and related to the stages that precede and follow; the importance of particularly important *stages* is noted • each stage includes applicable measurements of time, distance, direction, density, volume, etc. *Conclusion* (lead out to practical considerations) • where applicable, comments about time needed for overall process, cost, process' applications, special problems, immediate and long-term results
VOICE/MOOD	Uses indicative mood; e.g., "the next stage takes three hours..." Stays detached, in 3rd person; e.g., "the skier's first move..." Active or passive voice; e.g., "the signal travels..." or, "the signal is next transferred to the filtering stage..."
APPEARANCE AND STYLE	Usually looks formal (headings, paragraphs, standard spacing) Reads like a "serious" discussion Uses a mixture of sentence types and lengths Uses precise, accurate vocabulary

enters the atmosphere. Although this residue contains several potentially toxic elements, sulphur oxide and, to a lesser extent, nitrogen oxide are the major problem, because they are transformed when they combine with moisture. This chemical reac-

Table 16.1 Instructions Compared to Process Analysis (*Continued*)

Helps the reader perform the process that is described	**PURPOSE**
Aimed at persons who need to complete a task or want to improve performance	**AUDIENCE**
Provides no more detail than is necessary (**Note:** Analysis and explanations <u>may</u> be necessary.) Features a very careful *chronological listing of steps* Very carefully describes *exact steps* to take Includes *frequent visual illustrations*	**CONTENT**
Introduction • concisely explains the overall actions to be performed • in some cases, provides background information and, where necessary, lists materials/equipment to be used or the conditions necessary for successful action • in some cases, cautions reader about safety factors *Chronological list of steps* (plus necessary explanations) • where appropriate, combines groups of steps together under sub-headings; e.g., "Setting the Timer," "Selecting Programs" • shows the interrelations and sequence of actions by using numbered steps and sequence transitions; e.g., "next," "then," "10 minutes later," "after the liquid cools" • gives reasons for performing certain actions in a specific way or at a specific time • uses illustrations to show the *results* of performed actions, not just the techniques for performing the actions *Brief practical conclusion* • reminds the reader of expected results/performance times	**STRUCTURE**
Uses imperative mood; e.g., "Set the timer by choosing..." Directly addresses reader; e.g., "Your first task will be to..." Uses active voice; e.g., "Choose one of three settings..."	**VOICE/MOOD**
Uses some paragraphs, but mostly uses numbered point form Looks "user friendly" Writes in phrases or short sentences Features direct, straightforward vocabulary Employs lots of open space	**APPEARANCE AND STYLE**

Preview of stages

tion forms sulphur dioxide and nitric acid, which then rain down to earth.

The major steps explained here are (1) how acid rain develops, (2) how acid rain spreads, and (3) how acid rain destroys.

The Process

How Acid Rain Develops

Once fossil fuels have been burned, their usefulness is over. Unfortunately, it is here that the acid rain problem begins.

First stage

Fossil fuels contain a number of elements that are released during combustion. Two of these, sulphur oxide and nitrogen oxide, combine with normal moisture to produce sulphuric acid and nitric acid. (Figure 1 illustrates how acid rain develops.) The released gases undergo a chemical change as they combine with atmospheric ozone and water vapour. The resulting rain or snowfall is more acid than normal precipitation.

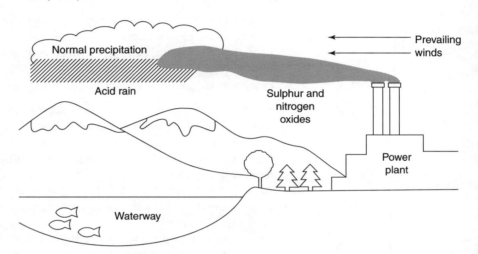

FIGURE 1 How Acid Rain Develops

Definition

Acid level is measured by pH readings. The pH scale runs from 0 through 14—a pH of 7 is considered neutral. (Distilled water has a pH of 7.) Numbers above 7 indicate increasing degrees of alkalinity. (Household ammonia has a pH of 11.) Numbers below 7 indicate increasing acidity. Movement in either direction on the pH scale, however, means multiplying by 10. Lemon juice, which has a pH value of 2, is 10 times more acidic than apples, which have a pH of 3, and is 1,000 times more acidic than carrots, which have a pH of 5.

Because of carbon dioxide (an acid substance) normally present in air, unaffected rainfall has a pH of 5.6. At this time, the pH of precipitation in the northeastern United States and Canada is between 4.5 and 4. In Massachusetts, rain and snowfall have an average pH reading of 4.1. A pH reading below 5 is considered to be abnormally acidic, and therefore a threat to aquatic populations.

How Acid Rain Spreads

Second stage

Although it might seem that areas containing power plants would be most severely affected, acid rain can in fact travel thousands of miles from its source. Stack gases escape and drift with the wind currents. The sulphur and nitrogen oxides are thus able to travel great distances before they return to earth as acid rain.

For an average of two to five days after emission, the gases follow the prevailing winds far from the point of origin. Estimates show that about 50 percent of the acid rain that affects Canada originates in the United States; at the same time, 15 to 25 percent of the U.S. acid rain problem originates in Canada.

The tendency of stack gases to drift makes acid rain a widespread menace. More than 200 lakes in the Adirondacks, hundreds of miles from any industrial centre, are unable to support life because their water has become so acidic.

How Acid Rain Destroys

Third stage

Acid rain causes damage wherever it falls. It erodes various types of building rock such as limestone, marble, and mortar, which are gradually eaten away by the constant bathing in acid. Damage to buildings, houses, monuments, statues, and cars is widespread. Some priceless monuments and carvings already have been destroyed, and even trees of some varieties are dying in large numbers.

Substage

More important, however, is acid rain damage to waterways in the affected areas. (Figure 2 illustrates how a typical waterway is infiltrated.)

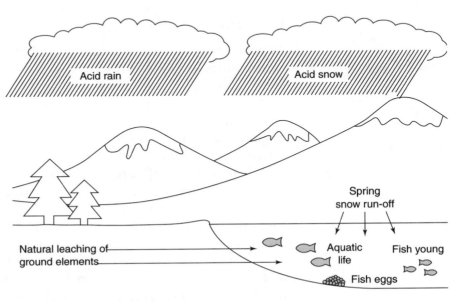

FIGURE 2 How Acid Rain Destroys

Because of its high acidity, acid rain dramatically lowers the pH in lakes and streams. Although its effect is not immediate, acid rain eventually can make a waterway so acidic it dies. In areas with natural acid-buffering elements such as limestone, the dilute acid has less effect. The northeastern United States and Canada, however, lack this natural protection, and so are continually vulnerable.

The pH level in an affected waterway drops so low that some species cease to reproduce. In fact, a pH level of 5.1 to 5.4 means that fisheries are threatened; once a waterway reaches a pH level of 4.5, no fish reproduction occurs. Because each creature is part of the overall food chain, loss of one element in the chain disrupts the whole cycle.

In the northeastern United States and Canada, the acidity problem is compounded by the run-off from acid snow. During the cold winter months, acid snow sits with little melting, so that by spring thaw, the acid released is greatly concentrated. Aluminum and other heavy metals normally present in soil are also released by acid rain and run-off. These toxic substances leach into waterways in heavy concentrations, affecting fish in all stages of development.

Summary

One complete cycle

Acid rain develops from nitrogen and sulphur oxides emitted by industrial and power plants burning fossil fuels. In the atmosphere, these oxides combine with ozone and water to form acid rain: precipitation with a lower-than-average pH. This acid precipitation returns to earth many miles from its source, severely damaging waterways that lack natural buffering agents. The northeastern United States and Canada are the most severely affected areas in North America.

Elements of Instruction

As consumers, we need instructions to learn how to operate everything from automobiles to VCRs. But we also seek instruction on topics that we know reasonably well. Because of our recreation activities, for instance, we often read instructional magazine articles on how to ski steep slopes or how to hit a particular golf shot or how to perform an aerobics sequence, even though we might already be able to perform the activity. Why? We want to perform the activity more skillfully!

Almost anyone with a responsible job writes and reads instructions. The new employee uses instructions for operating office equipment or industrial machinery; the employee going on vacation writes instructions for the replacement person. The person who buys a computer reads the manuals (or documentation) for instructions on connecting a printer or running a program.

Instructions carry profound ethical and legal implications. Each year, as many as 10 percent of workers are injured on the job (Clement 14). Countless injuries also result from misuse of consumer products such as power tools and car jacks—misuse often caused by defective instructions.

A reader injured because of inaccurate, incomplete, or misleading instructions can sue the writer. Courts have ruled that a writing defect in product support literature carries liability, as would a design or manufacturing defect in the product itself (Girill 37). Some legal experts argue that writing defects carry even greater liability than product defects because they are more easily demonstrated to a non-technical jury (Bedford and Stearns 28).

To ensure that your own instructions meet professional and legal requirements for accuracy, completeness, and clarity, observe the following guidelines.

Clear and Limiting Title

Make your title promise exactly what your instructions deliver—no more and no less. The title "Instructions for Cleaning the Drive Head of a Laptop Computer" tells readers what to expect: instructions for a specific procedure on a selected part. But the title "The Laptop Computer" gives no forecast. A reader of a document so titled might think the document contains a history of the laptop, or a description of each part, or a wide range of related information.

Informed Content

Make sure that you know exactly what you're talking about. Ignorance on your part makes you no less liable for instructions that are faulty or inaccurate:

Never count on ignorance as an excuse

> If the author of [a car repair] manual had no experience with cars, yet provided faulty instructions on the repair of the car's brakes, the home mechanic who was injured when the brakes failed may recover [damages] from the author. (Walter and Marsteller 165)

Do not write instructions unless you know the procedure in detail and unless you actually have performed it.

Visuals

In addition to showing what to do, instructional visuals attract the attention of today's graphic-oriented readers and help keep words to a minimum. Instructions also often include a persuasive dimension: to motivate interest, commitment, or action.

Types of visuals especially suited to instructions include icons, representational and schematic diagrams, flowcharts, photographs, and prose tables.

Illustrate any step that might be difficult for readers to visualize. Show the same angle of vision the reader will have when doing the activity or using the equipment—and name the angle (*side view, top view*) if you think readers will have trouble figuring it out for themselves.

The less specialized your audience, the more visuals they are likely to need. But do not illustrate any action simple enough for readers to visualize on their own, such as "Press RETURN" for any user familiar with a keyboard.

Figure 16.1 depicts an array of visuals and their specific instructional functions. Virtually each of these visuals is easily constructed and some could be further enhanced, depending on your production budget and graphics capability. Writers and editors often provide a *brief* (page 304) and a rough sketch describing the visual and its purpose for the graphic designer or art department.

how to locate something

Installing a communication card

1 If your communication card has ports for connecting equipment, remove the plastic access cover from the vertical plate.

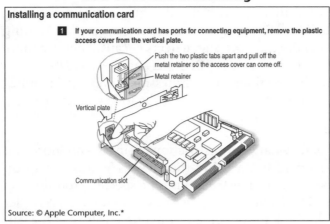

Source: © Apple Computer, Inc.*

how to operate something

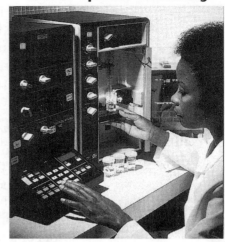

Source: SuperStock

how to handle something

Handling floppy disks

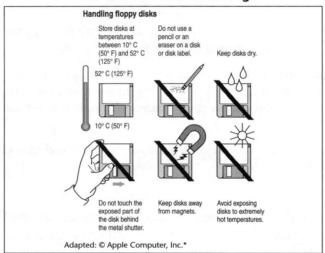

Adapted: © Apple Computer, Inc.*

how to assemble something

Extension Cord Retainer

1. Look into the end of the Switch Handle and you will see 2 slots. The WIDER end of the Retainer goes into the TOP slot (Figure 8).
2. Plug extension cord into Switch Handle and weave cord into Retainer, leaving a little slack (Figure 9).

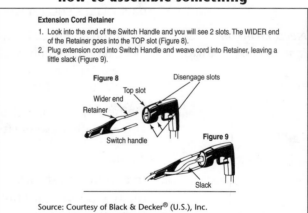

Source: Courtesy of Black & Decker® (U.S.), Inc.

how to position something

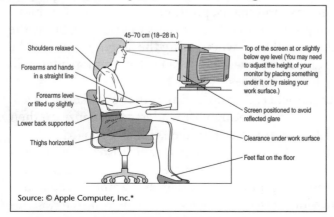

Source: © Apple Computer, Inc.*

how to avoid damage or injury

△ **Important:** The fixing assembly in the printer operates at very high temperatures. When you need to open the printer, be careful not to touch the fixing assembly. △

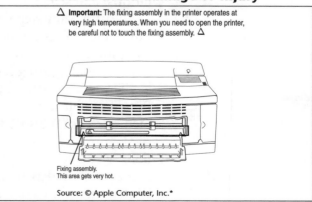

Source: © Apple Computer, Inc.*

Figure 16.1   Common Types of Instructional Visuals and Their Functions   **(Continued)**

how to diagnose and solve problems

GENERAL TROUBLESHOOTING CHART

If the amplifier is otherwise operating satisfactorily the more common causes of trouble may generally be attributed to the following:
1. Incorrect connections or loose terminal contacts. Check the speakers, record player, tape deck, antenna and line cord.
2. Improper operation. Before operating any audio component, be sure to read the instructions.

3. Improper location of audio components. The proper positioning of components, such as speakers and turntable, is vital to stereo.
4. Defective audio components.

Following are some other common causes of malfunction and what to do about them.

PROGRAM	SYMPTOM	PROBABLE CAUSE	WHAT TO DO
AM, FM or MPX reception	a. Constant or intermittent noise heard at certain times or in a certain area	* Discharge or oscillation caused by electrical appliances, such as fluorescent lamps, TV sets, D.C. motors, rectifier and oscillator * Natural phenomena, such as atmospherics, static, and thunderbolt * Insufficient antenna input due to reinforced concrete walls or long distance from the station * Wave interterence from other electrical appliances	* Attach a noise limiter to the electrical appliance that causes the noise, or attach it to the power source of the amplifier. * Install an outdoor antenna and ground the amplifier to raise the signal-to-noise ratio. * Reverse the power cord plug-receptacle connections. * If the noise occurs at a certain frequency, attach a wave trap to the ANT. input. * Place the set away from other electrical appliances

Source: Courtesy of Sansui Electronic Co. Ltd.

how to proceed systematically

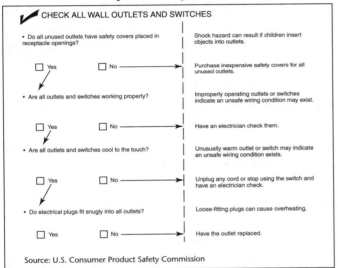

✔ CHECK ALL WALL OUTLETS AND SWITCHES

- Do all unused outlets have safety covers placed in receptacle openings?

☐ Yes   ☐ No → Shock hazard can result if children insert objects into outlets.

Purchase inexpensive safety covers for all unused outlets.

- Are all outlets and switches working properly?

☐ Yes   ☐ No → Improperly operating outlets or switches indicate an unsafe wiring condition may exist.

Have an electrician check them.

- Are all outlets and switches cool to the touch?

☐ Yes   ☐ No → Unusually warm outlet or switch may indicate an unsafe wiring condition exists.

Unplug any cord or stop using the switch and have an electrician check.

- Do electrical plugs fit snugly into all outlets?

☐ Yes   ☐ No → Loose-fitting plugs can cause overheating.

Have the outlet replaced.

Source: U.S. Consumer Product Safety Commission

how to make the right decisions

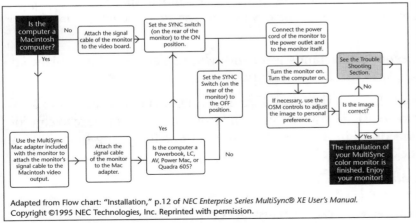

Adapted from Flow chart: "Installation," p.12 of *NEC Enterprise Series MultiSync® XE User's Manual.* Copyright ©1995 NEC Technologies, Inc. Reprinted with permission.

how to identify safe or acceptable limits

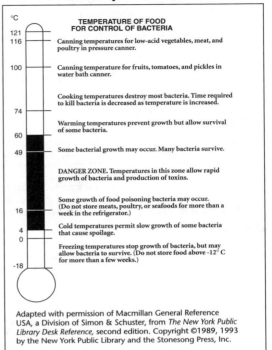

Adapted with permission of Macmillan General Reference USA, a Division of Simon & Schuster, from *The New York Public Library Desk Reference,* second edition. Copyright ©1989, 1993 by the New York Public Library and the Stonesong Press, Inc.

why action is important

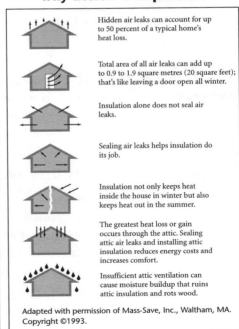

Hidden air leaks can account for up to 50 percent of a typical home's heat loss.

Total area of all air leaks can add up to 0.9 to 1.9 square metres (20 square feet); that's like leaving a door open all winter.

Insulation alone does not seal air leaks.

Sealing air leaks helps insulation do its job.

Insulation not only keeps heat inside the house in winter but also keeps heat out in the summer.

The greatest heat loss or gain occurs through the attic. Sealing attic air leaks and installing attic insulation reduces energy costs and increases comfort.

Insufficient attic ventilation can cause moisture buildup that ruins attic insulation and rots wood.

Adapted with permission of Mass-Save, Inc., Waltham, MA. Copyright ©1993.

Figure 16.1   Common Types of Instructional Visuals and Their Functions

Appropriate Level of Technicality

Unless you know your readers have the relevant background and skills, write for general readers, and do three things:

1. Give them enough background to understand why they need your instructions.
2. Give them enough detail to understand *what* to do.
3. Give them enough examples to visualize the procedure clearly.

Page 394 shows how you might adapt instructions titled "How to Initialize Your Blank Disk" for a general audience.

Background Information. Begin by explaining the purpose of the procedure.

Tell readers why they are doing this

> You might easily lose information stored on a floppy disk if:
>
> 1. the disk is damaged by direct sunlight, extreme temperature, or moisture.
> 2. the disk is erased by a faulty disk drive, a power surge, or a user error.
> 3. the stored information is scrambled by a nearby magnet (telephone, computer terminal, or the like).
> Always make a backup copy of any important material.

Also, state your assumptions about your reader's level of technical understanding.

Tell them what they should know already

> To follow these instructions, you should be able to identify these parts of a Macintosh system: computer, monitor, keyboard, mouse, disk drive, and a 3.5-inch floppy disk.

Define any specialized terms that appear in your instructions.

Tell them what each key term means

> **Working Definition**
>
> *Initialize:* Before you can store or retrieve information on a disk, you must initialize the blank disk (unless you are using preformatted disks). Initializing creates a format the computer can understand—a directory of specific memory spaces (like post office boxes) on the disk, where you can store and retrieve information as needed.

When your reader understands *what* and *why*, you are ready to explain *how* the reader can carry out the procedure.

Adequate Detail. Explain the procedure in enough detail for readers to know exactly what to do. Vague instructions result from the writer's failure to consider the readers' needs, as in these unclear instructions for giving first aid to an electrical shock victim:

Inadequate detail for general readers

> 1. Check vital signs.
> 2. Establish an airway.
> 3. Administer external cardiac massage as needed.

4. Ventilate, if cyanosed.
5. Treat for shock.

These instructions might be clear to medical experts, but not to general readers. Not only are the details inadequate, but also terms such as "vital signs" and "cyanosed" are too technical for laypersons. Such instructions posted for workers in a high-voltage area would be useless. The instructions need illustrations and explanations, as in the following instruction for item 2, establishing an airway:

MOUTH-TO-MOUTH BREATHING

Adequate detail for general readers

If there are no signs of breathing, place one hand under the victim's neck and gently lift. At the same time, push with the other hand on the victim's forehead. This will move the tongue away from the back of the throat to open the airway.

Source: Reprinted with permission of Macmillan General Reference USA, a Division of Simon & Schuster, from *The New York Public Library Desk Reference,* second edition. Copyright ©1989, 1993 by the New York Public Library and the Stonesong Press, Inc.

It's easy to overestimate what people already know, especially when the procedure is almost automatic for you. (Think about when a relative or friend was teaching you to drive a car, or perhaps you tried to teach someone else.) Always assume the reader knows less than you. A colleague will know at least a little less; a layperson will know a good deal less—maybe nothing—about this procedure.

Exactly how much information is enough? These suggestions can help you find an answer:

How to provide adequate detail

- Give everything readers need, so the instructions can stand alone.
- Give only what readers need. Don't tell them how to build a computer when they need to know only how to copy a disk.
- Instead of focusing on the *product* ("How does it work?"), focus on the *task* ("How do I use it?" or "How do I do it?") (Grice, "Focus" 32).
- Omit steps (*Seat yourself at the computer*) obvious to readers.
- Adjust the information rate ("the amount of information presented in a given page," Meyer 17) to the reader's background and the difficulty of the task. For complex or sensitive steps, slow the information rate. Don't make readers do too much too fast.
- Reinforce the prose with visuals. Don't be afraid to repeat information if it saves readers from flipping pages.
- When writing instructions for consumer products, assume "a barely literate reader" (Clement 151). Simplify.
- Recognize the persuasive dimension of the instructions. You may need to persuade readers that this procedure is necessary or beneficial, or that they can complete this procedure with relative ease and competence.

Examples. Procedures require specific examples (how to load a program, how to order a part), to help readers follow the steps correctly.

Use plenty of examples

To load your program, key this command:

> Load "Style Editor"

Then press RETURN.

Like visuals, examples *show* readers what to do. Examples in fact often appear as visuals.

In the sample procedure that follows, careful use of background, detailed explanation, and visual examples create a user-friendly level of technicality for readers just learning to use a computer.

First Step: How to Initialize Your Blank Disk

Before you can copy or store information on a blank disk, you must initialize the disk (unless you are using preformatted disks). Follow this procedure:

1. Switch the computer on.
2. Insert your application disk in the main disk drive.

Begin each instruction with an action verb

3. Insert your blank disk in the external disk drive. Unable to recognize this new disk, the computer will respond with a message asking whether you wish to initialize the disk (Figure 1).

Let the visual repeat, restate, or reinforce the prose

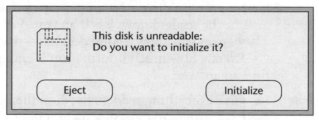

FIGURE 1 The "Initialize" Message

4. Using your mouse, place the tip of the on-screen pointer (a small arrow) inside the "Initialize" box.
5. Press and quickly release the mouse button. Within 15–20 seconds the initializing will be completed, and a message will appear, asking you to name your disk (Figure 2).

Place the visual close to the step

FIGURE 2 The "Disk-naming" Message

Second Step: How to Name Your Initialized Disk (and so on)

In the sample, notice that instructions and illustrations repeat the same information—they are redundant (Weiss 100). You may recall from Chapter 11 that writers avoid *style redundancy* (extra words that give no extra information). For instructions, however, a writer deliberately seeks *content redundancy*, giving the same information in prose and then in visuals. Granted, this prose-visual redundancy makes a longer document, but such repetition helps prevent misinterpretation. When you can't be sure how much is enough, risk over-explaining rather than under-explaining.

Logically Ordered Steps

Instructions not only divide the procedure into steps; they also guide users through the steps in *chronological order*. They organize the facts and explanations in ways that make sense to the reader.

Show how steps are connected

> You can't splice two wires to make an electrical connection until you have removed the insulation. To remove the insulation, you will need . . . .

Try to keep all information for one step close together.

Warnings, Cautions, and Notes

Here are the only items that should interrupt the steps in a set of instructions (Van Pelt 3):

- A *note* clarifies a point, emphasizes vital information, or describes options or alternatives.

  > NOTE: The computer will not initialize a disk that is scratched or imperfect. If your blank disk is rejected, try a new disk.

- A *caution* prevents possible mistakes that could result in injury or equipment damage:

  > CAUTION: A momentary electrical surge or power failure will erase the contents of internal memory. To avoid losing your work, every few minutes save on disk what you have just keyed into the computer.

- A *warning* alerts users against potential hazards to life or limb:

  > WARNING: To prevent electrical shock, always disconnect your printer from its power source before cleaning internal parts.

- A *danger* notice identifies an immediate hazard to life or limb:

  > DANGER: The red canister contains **DEADLY** radioactive material. **Do not break the safety seal** under any circumstances.

In addition to prose warnings, attract readers' attention and help them identify hazards by using symbols or icons (Bedford and Stearns 128):

Use symbols to alert readers

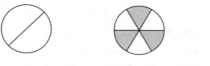

Do not enter   **Radioactivity**   **Fire danger**

Preview the warnings, cautions, and notes in your introduction, and place them, *clearly highlighted*, immediately before the respective steps.

Note: A recent study found that product users were six times more likely to comply with warnings included with the directions for using the product instead of on a separate warning label ("Notes" 2).

Use notes, warnings, and cautions only when needed; overuse will dull their effect, and readers may overlook their importance.

Appropriate Words, Sentences, and Paragraphs

Of all communications, instructions have the strictest requirements for clarity, because they lead to *immediate action.* Readers are impatient, and often will not read the entire instructions before plunging into the first step. Poorly phrased and misleading instructions can be disastrous.

Like descriptions, instructions name parts, use location and position words, and state exact measurements, weights, and dimensions. Instructions additionally require your strict attention to phrasing, sentence structure, and paragraph structure.

Transitions to Mark Time and Sequence. Transitional words provide a bridge between related ideas. Some transitions ("in addition," "next," "meanwhile," "finally," "ten minutes later," "the next day," "before") mark time and sequence. They help readers understand the step-by-step process:

Preparing the Ground for a Tent

Use transitions to mark time and sequence

Begin by clearing and smoothing the area that will be under the tent. This step will prevent damage to the tent floor and eliminate the discomfort of sleeping on uneven ground. *First,* remove all large stones, branches, or other debris within a level 3 x 4-metre (10 x 13-foot) area. Use your camping shovel to remove half-buried rocks that cannot easily be moved by hand. *Next,* fill in any large holes with soil or leaves. *Finally,* make several light surface passes with the shovel or a large, leafy branch to smooth the area.

Carefully Shaped Paragraphs and Sentences. Much of the introductory and explanatory material in instructions take the form of standard prose paragraphs, with enough sentence variety to keep readers interested. But the steps themselves have unique paragraph and sentence requirements. Unless the procedure consists of simple steps (as in the "Preparing the Ground for a Tent," example), separate each step by using a numbered list—one step for one activity. If the activity is especially complicated, use a new line (not indented) to begin each sentence in the step.

Instructions ordinarily employ short sentences. But brief is not always best, especially when readers have to fill in the information gaps. Never telegraph your message by omitting articles (a, an, the).

Unlike many types of documents, instructions call for very little sentence variety. Use sentences with similar structure ("Do this. Then do that.") to avoid confusing readers trying to follow the procedure.

If a single step covers two related actions, follow the sequence of actions that are required:

Confusing sequence	Insert the disk in the drive before switching on the computer.

The second action required is mistakenly given before the first.

Logical sequence	Before switching on the computer, insert the disk in the drive.

Make your explanations easier to follow by using a familiar-to-unfamiliar sequence:

Difficult	You must initialize a blank disk before you can store information on it.

This sentence is clearer if the familiar material comes first:

Easier	Before you can store information on a blank disk, you must initialize the disk.

Shape every sentence and every paragraph for the reader's access.

Active Voice and Imperative Mood. Use the active voice and imperative mood ("Insert the disk") to address the reader directly. Otherwise, your instructions can lose authority ("You should insert the disk"), or become ambiguous ("The disk is inserted"). In the ambiguous example, we can't tell if the disk is to be inserted or if it already has been inserted.

Indirect or confusing	The user keys in his or her access code.
	You should key in your access code.
	It is important to key in the access code.
	The access code is keyed in.
Direct and clear	Key in your access code.

The imperative makes instructions more definite and easier to understand because the action verb—the crucial word that tells what the next action will be—comes first. Instead of burying your verb in midsentence, *begin* with an action verb ("raise," "connect," "wash," "insert," "open"), to give readers an immediate signal.

Affirmative Phrasing. Research shows that readers respond more quickly and efficiently to instructions phrased affirmatively rather than negatively (Spyridakis and Wenger 205).

Weaker	Verify that your disk is not contaminated with dust.
Stronger	Examine your disk for dust contamination.

Parallel Phrasing. Like any items in a series, steps should be in identical grammatical form. Parallelism is important in all writing but in instructions especially, because repeating grammatical forms emphasizes the step-by-step organization of the instructions.

Not parallel	To log on to the VAX 950, follow these steps: 1. Switch the terminal to "on." 2. The CONTROL key and C key are pressed simultaneously. 3. Keying LOGON, and pressing the ESCAPE key. 4. Key your user number, and press the ESCAPE key.
Parallel	To log on to the VAX 950, follow these steps: 1. Switch the terminal to "on." 2. Press the CONTROL key and C key simultaneously. 3. Key LOGON, and press the ESCAPE key. 4. Key your user number, and press the ESCAPE key.

Parallelism increases readability and lends continuity to the instructions.

Effective Page Design

Instructions rarely get undivided attention. The reader, in fact, is doing two things more or less at once: interpreting the instructions and performing the task. Effective instructional design is *accessible* and *inviting*. An effective design conveys the sense that the task is within a qualified user's range of abilities.

Here are suggestions for designing instructions that help users find, recognize, and remember what they need:

How to design your instructions

- Use informative headings that tell readers what to expect, that emphasize what is most important, and that serve as an aid to navigation. A heading such as "How to Initialize Your Blank Disk" is more informative than "Disk Initializing." Also, the second version sounds less like a person speaking and more like a robot!
- Arrange all steps in a numbered list.
- Single-space within steps and double-space between, to separate steps visually. (Use the Spacing Before and After Paragraph feature of your word processing program for maximum editing flexibility.)

- Double-space to signal a new paragraph, instead of indenting.
- Use white space and highlighting to separate discussion from step.

> Set off your discussion on a separate line (like this), indented or highlighted or both. You can highlight with underlining, capitals, dashes, parentheses, and asterisks. Alternatively, you can use **bold-face**, *italics,* varying type sizes, and varying `typefaces`.

- Set off warnings, cautions, and notes in ruled boxes or use highlighting and plenty of white space.
- Keep the visual and the step close together. If room allows, place the visual right beside the step; if not, right after the step. Set off the visual with plenty of white space.
- Strive for format variety that is appealing but not overwhelming or inconsistent. Readers can be overwhelmed by a page with excessive or inconsistent graphic patterns.

The more accessible and inviting the design, the more likely your readers will follow the instructions. Don't be afraid to experiment until you find a design that works.

Measurements of Usability

When we evaluate how well a document achieves its objectives, we measure its *usability*. In measuring the usability of instructions, we ask this question: *How effectively do these instructions enable users to complete the intended task safely, efficiently, and appropriately?*

Consumers look for products that are easy to use. As a result, companies routinely measure the usability of their products—including the product's *documentation* (assembly, operating, or troubleshooting instructions, warnings, manuals). To win customer goodwill—and to avoid lawsuits—a company will go to great lengths to anticipate all of the ways a product might be used or misused.

Usability testing is a complex process in which testers have to know (1) how to design tests that are valid and reliable, and (2) how to interpret their findings accurately. Primary research methods from Chapter 6 are employed in usability testing (interviews, questionnaires, observation, experiment).

Ideally, usability tests are conducted in a situation that simulates the actual situation, with people who actually will use the document (Redish and Schell 67; Ruhs 8). But even in a classroom setting we can make reasonable assessments of a document's effectiveness on the basis of usability criteria.

Usability criteria for a specific document are defined by its intended use and by characteristics of the user and the environment that affect its use, as depicted in Figure 16.2.

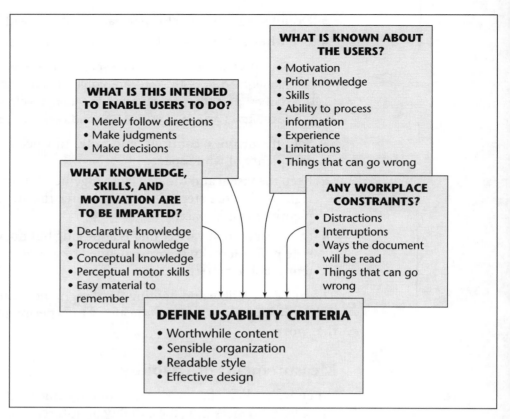

Figure 16.2   Assessing a Document's Usability

Intended Use

A first step in evaluating usability is to define what we want users to be able to do as a result of reading the document:

- Will users merely carry out a desired action ("What do I do next?"), as in copying a disk correctly? Or will they navigate a complex task that requires decisions ("What option should I choose?") or judgments ("Is this good enough?"), as in diagnosing or treating an ailment? What kinds of knowledge and skills does the task require?

- Besides procedural knowledge (how to do things), what kinds of declarative knowledge (knowing facts) or conceptual knowledge (understanding principles or theories) underlie the procedure? How much learning versus performing is required (Mirel et al. 79; Wickens 243)?

- Are we trying to impart perceptual motor skills (swinging a golf club, making a surgical incision), which are less easily forgotten—as opposed to procedural skills (using a computer program, cleaning a fuel-injection system), which are more easily forgotten (Wickens 250)?

- Will users need to remember this information for a short or long period (Wickens 232)? Will they always have the document in front of them while performing the task?
- Do we need to *persuade* the user to pay attention, be careful, or the like?

Human Factors

Those characteristics of the user and the environment that enhance or limit job performance are known as *human factors*. These include the user's attitudes, abilities, and limitations, and the constraints of the work environment (Wickens 3).

- Who are the users? What do they know already? How informed are they in general? How accustomed to such procedures? How educated? How motivated?
- Will readers be scanning the document, studying it, memorizing it, or merely referring to it periodically and randomly?
- Can we anticipate ways in which the document could be misinterpreted or misunderstood (Boiarsky 100)?
- Can we anticipate possible distractions or interruptions from the work environment?

For a closer look at human factors, review the audience/purpose profile sheet (page 85).

Usability Criteria for the Document

Only after identifying its intended use and the possible human factors can we decide on criteria for evaluating the document's effectiveness.

- Is everything easy to find, appropriate to this reader for this task, easy to understand, and complete and accurate (Haynes 239)?
- Is the document organized in a way the readers are expected to proceed? Is everything easy to read and follow (style, format, visuals)?

The revision and editing checklist (page 409) offers one approach for a detailed assessment of usability.

IN BRIEF

Usability Issues with On-Line or Multimedia Documents

In contrast to paper documents, on-line or multimedia documents create unique usability issues (Holler 25; Humphreys 754–55):

- On-line documents tend to focus more on doing than on detailed explanations. Workplace readers typically use on-line documents for reference or training rather than for study or memorizing.
- Users of on-line instructions rarely need persuading (e.g., to pay attention or follow instructions) because they are guided interactively through each step of the procedure.
- Visuals play an increasingly essential role in on-line instruction.
- On-line documents typically are organized to be read interactively and selectively rather than in linear sequence. Users move from place to place, depending on their immediate needs. Organization therefore is flexible and modular, with small bits of easily accessible information that can be combined to suit a particular user's needs and interests.
- On-line readers easily can lose their bearings. Unable to shuffle or flip through a stack of printed pages in linear order, readers need constant orientation (to retrieve some earlier bit of information or to compare something on one page with another). In the absence of page or chapter numbers, index, or table of contents, "Find," "Search," "Back," "Home," and "Help" options need to be plentiful and complete.
- Studies often suggest that reading an on-line document is slower than a paper document.

As increasing applications materialize for online and multimedia instruction, usability criteria will continue to be defined.

★   ★   ★

A Sample Set of Instructions

The instructions for *doing something* (felling a tree) in Figure 16.3 on pages 403–406 are patterned after our general outline, shown earlier. They will appear in a series of brochures for forestry students about to begin summer jobs with a Forestry Service.

Instructions for Semi-technical Readers

AUDIENCE/PURPOSE PROFILE. I'm writing these instructions for partially informed readers who know how to use chainsaws, axes, and wedges but who are approaching this dangerous procedure for the first time. Therefore, I'll include no visuals of cutting equipment (chainsaws and so on) because the audience already knows what these items look like. I can omit basic information (such as what happens when a tree binds a chainsaw) because the audience already has this knowledge. Likewise, these readers need no definition of general forestry terms such as *culling* and *thinning*, but they *do* need definitions of terms that relate specifically to tree felling (*undercut, holding wood*, and so on).

To ensure clarity, I will illustrate the final three steps with visuals. The conclusion, for these readers, will be short and to the point—a simple summary of major steps with emphasis on safety. ■

1

INSTRUCTIONS FOR FELLING A TREE

INTRODUCTION

Forestry Service personnel fell (cut down) trees to cull or thin a forested plot, to eliminate the hazard of dead trees standing near power lines, to clear an area for construction, and the like.

These instructions explain how to remove sizable trees for personnel who know how to use a chainsaw, axe, and wedge safely.

When you set out to fell a tree, expect to spend most of your time planning the operation and preparing the area around the tree. To fell the tree, you will make two chainsaw cuts, severing the stem from the stump. Depending on the direction of the cuts, the weather, and the terrain, the severed tree will fall into a predetermined clearing.

> **WARNING:** Although these instructions cover the basic procedure, felling is very dangerous. Trees, felling equipment, and terrain vary greatly. Even professionals sometimes are killed or injured because of judgment errors or misuse of tools.
>
> Your main concern is safety. Be sure to have an expert demonstrate this procedure before you try it. Also, pay attention to warnings in steps 1 and 4.

To fell sizable trees, you will need this equipment:
—a 3- to 5-horsepower chainsaw with a 51-cm (20-inch) blade
—a single-blade splitting axe
—two or more 31-cm (12-inch) steel wedges

The major steps in felling a tree are (1) choosing the lay, (2) providing an escape path, (3) making the undercut, and (4) making the backcut.

REQUIRED STEPS

1. *How to Choose the Lay*

   The "lay" is where you want the tree to fall. On level ground in an open field, which way you direct the fall makes little difference. But such ideal conditions are rare.

   Consider ground obstacles and topography, surrounding trees, and the condition of the tree to be felled. Plan your escape path and the location of your cuts depending on surrounding houses, electrical wires, and trees. Then follow these steps:

   a. Make sure the tree still is alive.

Figure 16.3   A Set of Instructions   **(Continued)**

2

b. Determine the direction and amount of lean.

> **WARNING:** If the tree is dead and leaning substantially, do not try to fell it without professional help. Many dead, leaning trees have a tendency to split along their length, causing a massive slab to fall spontaneously.

c. Find an opening into which the tree can fall in the direction of lean or as close to the direction of lean as possible.

Because most trees lean downhill, try to direct the fall downhill. If the tree leans slightly away from your desired direction, use wedges to direct the fall.

2. *How to Provide an Escape Path*

Falling trees are unpredictable. Avoid injury by planning a definite escape path. Follow these steps:

a. Locate the path in the direction opposite of the fall (Figure 1).

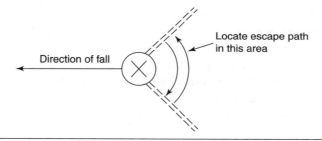

FIGURE 1 Escape-path Location

b. Clear a path 70 cm (2 feet) wide extending beyond where the top of the tree could land.

3. *How to Make the Undercut*

The undercut is a triangular slab of wood cut from the trunk on the side toward which you want the tree to fall. Follow these steps:

a. Start the chainsaw.

b. Holding the saw with blade parallel to the ground, make a first cut 70 to 92 cm (2 to 3 feet) above ground. Cut horizontally, to no more than 1/3 the tree's diameter (Figure 2).

Figure 16.3   A Set of Instructions   (*Continued*)

3

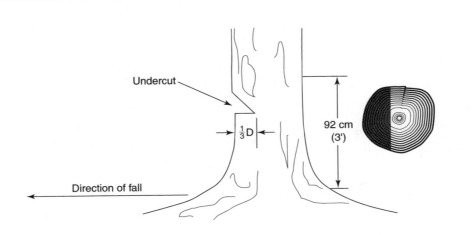

FIGURE 2 Making the Undercut

c. Make a downward-sloping cut, starting 10 to 15 cm (4 to 6 inches) above the first so that the cuts intersect at 1/3 the diameter (Figure 2).

4. *How to Make the Backcut*

After completing the undercut, you make the backcut to sever the stem from the stump. This step requires good reflexes and absolute concentration.

> **WARNING:** Observe tree movement closely during the backcut. If the tree shows any sign of falling in your direction, drop everything and move out of its way. Also, do not cut completely through to the undercut; instead, leave a narrow strip of "holding wood" as a hinge, to help prevent the butt end of the falling tree from jumping back at you.

To make your backcut, follow these steps:

a. Holding the saw with the blade parallel to the ground, start your cut about 7.5 cm (3 inches) above the undercut, on the opposite side of the trunk. Leave a narrow strip of "holding wood" (Figure 3).

Figure 16.3 A Set of Instructions (*Continued*)

4

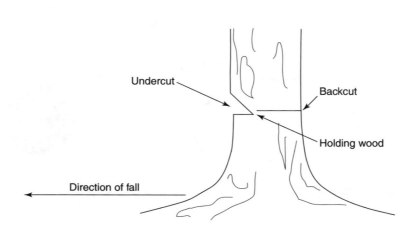

FIGURE 3 Making the Backcut

If the tree begins to bind the chainsaw, hammer a wedge into the backcut with the blunt side of the axe head. Then continue cutting.

b. As soon as the tree begins to fall, turn off the chainsaw, withdraw it, and step back immediately—the butt end of the tree could jump back toward you.

c. Move rapidly down the escape path.

CONCLUSION

Felling is a complex and dangerous procedure. Choosing the lay, providing an escape path, making the undercut, and making the backcut are the basic steps—but trees, terrain, and other circumstances vary greatly.

For the safest operation, seek professional advice and help whenever you foresee *any* complications whatsoever.

Figure 16.3   A Set of Instructions

Procedures

Procedures differ from instructions in two major respects:

1. The reader already knows how to perform the tasks outlined in the procedure and thus does not need detailed instructions.
2. The reader does not necessarily know the order in which tasks are to be performed, or how and when to coordinate with other members of a work team.

Therefore, procedures are usually aimed at groups of readers; the procedures describe how the group members will coordinate their activities, or when they will perform their particular functions. Examples include evacuation procedures (in case of a fire or toxic spill), maintenance procedures, or installation procedures.

Not all procedures are aimed at groups, however. A software installation will likely be performed by a single technician who has the skills and general knowledge to do the job but who needs to know the specific variations of the procedure required by a given software program. Other procedures such as a union grievance or a procedure for reporting an on-site accident will assume that the reader needs to know whom to contact, when to contact, and what form to use. In these circumstances, the assumption is that the reader doesn't need to be told *how* to grieve the perceived infraction or *how* to phrase the accident report.

The following excerpt from a group procedure comes from a Canadian power utility. The procedure demonstrates how workers must coordinate their skills with others. In the conductor repair procedure, that coordination is essential in preventing the instant death that could result from a botched maneuver.

CONDUCTOR REPAIR ON 72/138 Kv H-FRAME

(INSTALL PRE-FORMED ARMOUR SPLICES USING A SECOND UNIT TO SUPPORT CONDUCTORS)

1. Operate in a crew that has a minimum of four (4) certified Journeymen Power Line Technicians.

2. Conduct a tailboard session to confirm the order in which this procedure is to be performed.

3. Position the aerial device in the best position to maintain safe working clearances while allowing two line technicians to work satisfactorily on the line. Verify safe working clearances with the measuring stick, as outlined in the General Rules.

   NOTE: Position the aerial device directly under the centre phase. Back in with the turret two (2) metres from the centre of the structure. Park the boom truck, which has a wire holder on an insulated jib, on the other side of the structure in such a way that the truck can support each conductor without having to move the truck. Install unit grounding on both vehicles.

4. *Line technicians*—Carry all tools and materials along in the buckets.

5. *Line technicians*—Test the insulators. Install a temporary jumper if it's necessary.

6. *Second unit operator*—Support the outside conductor with the jib and raise the conductor slightly.

7. *Line technician in the insulated aerial bucket*—Move into position while maintaining both phase-to-phase and phase-to-ground clearance. Disconnect the clamp from the insulators with hot sticks.

8. *Second unit operator*—Move the conductor to a position where pre-formed armour rod may be installed without reducing the limits of approach.

   The line technicians may now bond on and complete the repairs.

9. *Line technicians*—Remove the bonds and back away. Move the conductor back to the insulators and use hot line tools to attach a suspension clamp to the insulators again.

10. Repeat this operation on the other outside phase.

11. *Line technicians*—Connect the centre phase and loosen the suspension clamp with hot sticks. The clamp may be slid out on the conductor to a point where the technician in the insulated aerial device can maintain clearances and bond on to the line. After replacing the suspension clamp, you may remove the bonds and move into position to use hot line tools to apply the armour rod.

Figure 16.4   Sample Technical Procedure

Revision and Editing Checklist for Instructions

Use this checklist to evaluate the usability of instructions.

CONTENT

- ❑ Does the title promise exactly what the instructions deliver?
- ❑ Is the background adequate for the intended audience?
- ❑ Do explanations enable readers to understand what to do?
- ❑ Do examples enable readers to see how to do it correctly?
- ❑ Are the definition and purpose of each step given as needed?
- ❑ Is all needless information omitted?
- ❑ Are all obvious steps omitted?
- ❑ Do notes, cautions, or warnings appear whenever needed, before the step?
- ❑ Is the information rate appropriate for the reader's abilities and the difficulty of this procedure?
- ❑ Are visuals adequate for clarifying the steps?
- ❑ Do visuals repeat prose information whenever necessary?

PAGE DESIGN

- ❑ Does each heading clearly tell readers what to expect?
- ❑ Are steps single-spaced within, and double-spaced between?
- ❑ Do white space and highlights set off discussion from steps?
- ❑ Is everything accurate?
- ❑ Are notes, cautions, or warnings set off or highlighted?
- ❑ Are visuals beside or near the step, and set off by white space?

ORGANIZATION

- ❑ Is the introduction adequate without being excessive?
- ❑ Do the instructions follow the exact sequence of steps?
- ❑ Is all the information for a particular step close together?
- ❑ For a complex step, does each sentence begin on a new line?
- ❑ Is the conclusion necessary and, if necessary, adequate?

STYLE

- ❑ Do introductory sentences have enough variety to maintain interest?
- ❑ Does the familiar material appear *first* in each sentence?
- ❑ Do steps generally have short sentences?
- ❑ Does each step begin with the action verb?
- ❑ Are all steps in the active voice and imperative mood?
- ❑ Do all steps have parallel phrasing?
- ❑ Are transitions adequate for marking time and sequence?

☑ EXERCISES

1. Improve the readability of the following instructions by editing them for a more appropriate voice and design.

   What to Do Before Jacking Up Your Car

   Whenever the misfortune of a flat tire occurs, some basic procedures should be followed before the car is jacked up. If possible, your car should be positioned on as firm and level a surface as is available. The engine has to be turned off; the parking brake should be set; and the automatic transmission shift lever must be placed in "park," or the manual transmission lever in "reverse." The wheel diagonally opposite the one to be removed should have a piece of wood placed beneath it to prevent the wheel from rolling. The spare wheel, jack, and lug wrench should be removed from the luggage compartment.

2. Select a specialized process that you understand well and that has several distinct steps. Using the process analysis on pages 383–388 as a model, explain this process to colleagues who are unfamiliar with it. Begin by completing an audience/purpose profile (page 85). Some possible topics: how the body metabolizes alcohol, how economic inflation occurs, how the federal deficit affects our future, how a lake or pond becomes a swamp, how a volcanic eruption occurs.

3. Choose a topic from the following list, your major, or an area of interest. Using the general outline in this chapter as a model, outline instructions that require at least three major steps. Address a general reader, and begin by completing an audience/purpose profile. Include (a) all necessary visuals; or (b) a brief (page 304) and a rough diagram for each visual; or (c) a "reference visual" (a copy of a visual published elsewhere) with instructions for adapting your visual from that one. (If you borrow visuals from other sources, provide full references.)

planting a tree	hitting a golf ball
hot-waxing skis	removing the rear
hanging wallpaper	wheel of a bicycle
filleting a fish	avoiding hypothermia

4. Select any one of the instructional visuals in Figure 16.1 and write a prose version of those instructions—without using visual illustrations or special page design. Bring your version to class and be prepared to discuss the conclusions you've derived from this exercise.

5. Locate an example of five or more visuals from the following list.
   A visual that shows:
   - how to locate something
   - how to operate something
   - how to handle something
   - how to assemble something
   - how to position something
   - how to avoid damage or injury
   - how to diagnose and solve a problem
   - how to identify safe or acceptable limits
   - how to proceed systematically
   - how to make the right decision
   - why an action or procedure is important

   Bring your examples to class for discussion, evaluation, and comparison.

☑ COLLABORATIVE PROJECTS

Any of the exercises may be a collaborative project.

Manuals

Manuals consist primarily of instructions, often printed and bound in book form. Their use has increased, as products become increasingly complex. Even an electric wok comes with a manual. And relatively simple printers often come with 60-page operating manuals.

Why are manuals so common and so detailed? The majority of published manuals exist to help users get the most out of purchased equipment. Also, well-written manuals endear the company to consumers, instead of alienating them. Further, companies who purchase equipment and software programs do so in order to improve productivity; that goal is undercut if employees can't properly use the equipment or software.

Equipment and software suppliers have found that clearly presented, properly documented, "user-friendly" manuals reduce the number of complaints, enquiries, and warranty claims from customers. In effect, good manuals pay for themselves. Poor manuals, on the other hand, lead to over-use of the company's customer service staff and alienate users. Besides, badly written manuals require frequent revisions, an expensive process.

Even when a product supplier provides extensive employee training along with its product, user and maintenance manuals refresh employees' memories and reduce the incidence of equipment breakdowns.

Types of Manuals

There is a manual for every purpose. Table 17.1 shows a partial list:

Table 17.1   Types of Manuals and Their Purpose   *(Continued)*

Type of Manual	Purpose
Software manuals	Help users navigate the intricacies of computer software
Operating manuals	Instruct users how to use and care for equipment and operating systems
Repair and service manuals	Provide detailed technical information for technicians (the complete service manual for your automobile is much more detailed and probably 20 times thicker than your operator's manual)
Maintenance and troubleshooting manuals	Provide users with detailed information on how to maintain equipment and troubleshoot common problems. They are vital for many businesses, including large-scale installations. For example, Doppelmayr's maintenance manual for its detachable chair lift system provides several hundred pages of specific maintenance instructions, covering every aspect of the system's hardware and operation

Table 17.1 Types of Manuals and Their Purpose

Type of Manual	Purpose
Test manuals	Describe techniques, equipment, and ideal results for lab and field tests of everything from soil samples to sludge samples to electronic equipment
Installation manuals	Outline how to install complicated equipment or software
Construction manuals	Describe construction procedures, pertinent building codes, and contract requirements
Reference manuals	Allow users to easily find specific information
Tutorial manuals	Take trainees through page after page of skill development exercises and explanations of how a system works
Documentation manuals	Include tutorials and descriptions (instructions) of how to do things and explanations of how certain things work (process analysis)
Business practice manuals	Describe procedures for business operation, advertising policies, customer service methods, collections and complaint handling, business travel procedures, and a multitude of business guidelines. (One of the first, and most famous, business practice manuals was written by Ray Kroc as he began to franchise the McDonald's restaurants across North America.)
User manuals	Provide detailed descriptions of how to use equipment. These are the most common types of manuals. If you want to program your VCR, you turn to the manual; if you want to re-configure your computer's hard drive, you refer to the appropriate manual.

Manual Writing

Writing manuals is quite complex: many are book-length, with a variety of topics to cover. Full-length manuals usually require more skills and time than one person can devote to the project. Even full-time manual writers collaborate with product designers, page designers, and graphic artists, all of whom add their specialized skills and perspective to the project.

The main challenge in writing (and designing) a manual is reducing the reader's reluctance to use the document; manuals, especially long ones, can overwhelm readers. So, manual writers must employ all the aspects of "user-friendly" instructions described in Chapter 16.

Planning

You should begin the writing process by analyzing your manual's purpose. Each type of manual requires a primary purpose that you can clarify by analyzing who will read your manual and how they will use it. That analysis will guide your choice of what to include in the manual. The readers' needs and knowledge levels will later dictate the technical level and the amount of detail included in each section.

After your preliminary analysis of audience and purpose, you need to talk with the product developers and the project manager to learn more about the product and its uses. This consultative stage may take several meetings. Among other things, you need to determine:

- the product's features and specifications
- exactly how the product works
- the product's full range of uses and applications
- how to troubleshoot problems and malfunctions
- how to install or set up the product
- how to operate, maintain, and adjust the device
- how to obtain parts and accessories
- how to claim warranty work
- which aspects of the product's use could result in damage to the product itself or the operator or to the system in which the product's installed

The manual should be organized in the order in which readers will use various sections.

It's important to revise the manual's contents *before* completing a detailed writing outline and it's essential to examine (and possibly revise) that outline before composing the first draft. Also, you should show your completed outline to members of the manual production team before starting to write the manual. The outline should have the entire headings system in place, along with the names and locations of all illustrations and a brief description of each paragraph or block of instructions.

Drafting

Writing the actual instructions and technical descriptions will be relatively easy if the outline has been thoroughly prepared. Perhaps all the paragraphs and instruction blocks will be written by one person, or perhaps various sections will be written by their respective developers. In the latter case, one person or a small group of editors will revise and edit all of the sections to ensure consistent style and to avoid duplication. In some cases, the writer will create the manual's graphics; however, most large organizations employ graphic artists to create artwork and technical illustrations.

Testing and Revising

Measurements of usability can be very helpful (see Chapters 11 and 16), but the best way to determine audience reaction is to use members of the target market to test the manual. This is especially important for the instructions sections—ask readers to follow their literal interpretations of the instructions. You'll see which instructions are unclear or incomplete, and you can revise accordingly. Then, after revising the content and editing the phrasing, retest the manual on a new batch of readers to see if the revisions have helped.

The remaining task is to ruthlessly edit all the manual's phrasing to make it as direct, clear, and concise as possible. The advice in Chapter 11 certainly applies to the descriptive writing in manuals.

Parts of Manuals

The two main parts of manuals are: (1) body sections, and (2) supplementary sections.

Body Sections

Manuals do not strictly follow a beginning/middle/closing sequence. However, an introductory section (or two) is needed to orient the reader.

Introduction. At its beginning, a manual should include:

- the manual's purpose and scope
- an overview of how to use the manual
- key definitions and principles
- introductory descriptions of equipment or procedures
- accompanying illustrations (photographs or diagrams of equipment, flow charts which show the relationships among sets of instructions)

Early on, a manual might also provide:

- specifications for equipment and equipment operation
- background information, such as an overview of the equipment or procedures that are being replaced
- a list of accessories and/or related equipment

The heading title for an introductory section could be topical; for example, the title "Introductions and Specifications" would suit a user's manual for a sophisticated piece of electronics test equipment, especially if the manual were aimed at electronics technicians. On the other hand, the opening sections for a mass-marketed CD player might use talking headings such as:

- Key Facts About Your CD Player
- How To Install the CD Player in Your Stereo System

Remaining Sections. The number of remaining sections varies with the manual's purpose and readers. Table 17.2 illustrates this:

Table 17.2   Section Variations

380-page operating and service manual for a Phillips oscilloscope:	60-page operating manual for a Sony video cassette recorder:	Onkyo Tuner/ Amplifier instruction manual:
• Operating Instructions • Theory of Operations • Maintenance Instructions • Calibration Instructions	• Preliminaries • Preparation • Operation • Other Information	• Features, Safeguards, and Precautions • Before Using This Unit • System Connections • Controls • Operations • Troubleshooting Guide • Specifications

Table 17.3   Order of Manual Sections

Order	Example/Description
Chronological development	Sets of instructions for an electronic power supply could be provided in the order in which a user would use the device: • Unpacking and Installing the Power Supply • Connecting the Power Supply to a Load • Operating and Adjusting the Supply • Maintaining and Calibrating the Supply • Troubleshooting Operational Problems • Ordering Parts and Accessories
Order of importance	This structure is often used for reference manuals and test manuals. The most important (and most-used) sections are placed first.
Spatial development	The physical structure of a system can form the basis for organizing that system's corresponding manual. For example, the maintenance manual for a ski lift could be divided into sections such as: • Cable Maintenance • Chairs and Grips • Loading Ramps • Drive Systems • Housings, etc.

Order of Sections. The order of sections within a manual may be based on chronological development, order of importance, or spatial development, as illustrated in Table 17.3.

In organizing the components of a manual, you might consider creating two or more separate, related documents. For, example, ACCPAC International uses three manuals for its Simply Accounting® software: (1) Getting Started, (2) Workbook, and (3) User Guide.

Conclusion. Manuals do not usually include a separate Conclusion section at the end of the manual. If conclusion material is included, it is placed at the end of a body section. For example, the end of a set of repair instructions might indicate the standard length of time to perform the repair and might reiterate key steps to check if the repair hasn't solved the identified problem.

Supplementary Sections

Manuals include supplementary matter to help readers use the document. Depending on the type of manual, you should include some or all of the following *front matter.*

Cover and Title Page. Essentially, a cover's purpose is to protect the manual, but the cover also carries the manual's title and, where appropriate, the company name and logo, and equipment model number. As Figures 17.1 and 17.2 on pages 418 and 419 illustrate, a manual's corresponding title page carries more information. At a minimum, the title page names the document's intended use (in the title), the manufacturer's name and logo, the date (or year) of publication, and the name and model number of the product. Very seldom do manual writers' names appear on the title page. Well-designed covers carry design principles from the cover to the title page.

Tables of Contents and Illustrations. The longer and more complex a manual is, the more its readers need a table of contents and a list of illustrations to find particular topics within the manual. See Chapter 20, for detailed advice on how to format a table of contents and list of figures and tables.

Warnings and Cautions. Manuals often require warnings and cautions, especially for electrically powered equipment. Often, these warnings will appear on the inside front cover. Sometimes warranty information appears with the warnings and cautions.

Glossary. A glossary might appear in the front matter, if a reader needs to know the meaning of certain terms before starting to use the manual. Alternatively, the introductory section could define key terms for the reader.

CUTTING EDGE TECHNOLOGIES

Operating and Service Manual

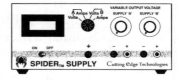

SPIDER™ SUPPLY

Model 001a

Figure 17.1 Sample Manual Cover
Source: Courtesy of Curt Willis

OPERATING AND SERVICE MANUAL

SPIDER™ SUPPLY

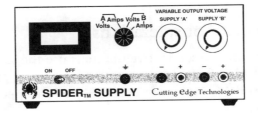

Variable Dual 20-Volt Channel
Voltage Regulated Power Supply
Model 001a
Series 0.1.0-98a

Copyright © Cutting Edge Technologies 1998
4131 Web Crescent, Kelowna, British Columbia V1W 1V8

Figure 17.2 Sample Manual Title Page

Source: Courtesy of Curt Willis

Depending upon the type of manual, you may need to include some back matter.

Back Matter. A manual's back matter might include some or all of the following:

- replacement parts and ordering
- schematics
- dealers and service depots
- service log
- component specifications tables
- construction codes

There are as many possible combinations of back matter as there are types of manuals. You can determine the best combination of back matter sections for your manual by examining a variety of manuals in your field.

Indexes. Indexes are commonly used in long or complex manuals, such as computer user manuals.

Format Considerations

In many ways, effective manuals use the same design principles that can be applied to formal reports and books. These principles are outlined in Chapters 13 and 16. However, certain special aspects of manual format should be remembered.

Section Identification

In order to constantly orient your manual's reader, use headers (or footers) that combine the page number with a diminutive section identifier. (This text uses a version of that system.) Your reader will then have three methods to easily find particular sections in the manual:

1. the table of contents
2. the index
3. the page headers/footers

Figure 17.3 shows one method of designing a section identifier. Some manuals also use sturdy card stock or plastic tabs along the right-hand edge to distinguish one section from another.

Section 6: CALIBRATION

To keep your SPIDER SUPPLY running at an optimal level, you may need to calibrate it. Calibrating the power supply is simple and will not likely need to be performed often.

Several possible circumstances could cause your power supply to drift from its specified settings: extreme temperature changes, over-drawing output current, abuse, or long-term use. The following calibration instructions will help you bring your supply back to specifications, should need be.

6.1 Non-Powered Tests

If you plan to calibrate your supply, you should do these quick no-power tests as well. They take little time and require minimal equipment.

To ensure that all connections are indeed *connected*, perform the following checks:

✓ Check every component solder joint and header connection to confirm that they are sound and properly affixed.
✓ Check the following resistances with a DMM:

6.1: Non-Powered Tests continued...

✓ Confirm the following resistances with a DMM:

Table 6-5 Variable voltage resistor (dials) checks

Point	Front Panel Voltage Dial Adjustment	Resistance measurement
Between J1 & J2	SUPPLY 'A' fully CCW	150 Ω
Between J1 & J2	SUPPLY 'A' fully CW	2.60 Ω
Between J3 & J4	SUPPLY 'B' fully CCW	150 Ω
Between J3 & J4	SUPPLY 'B' fully CW	2.60 Ω

Figure 17.3   Variations in Section Identifiers Used for the First and Second Pages of a Section

Source: Courtesy of Curt Willis

Headings System

Headings and sub-headings are particularly valuable in lengthy, complex manuals so make headings stand out by using bolding or colour. Clearly distinguish among levels of headings by using capitalization, font size, and headings placement. You might also use one kind of font for the main headings and another kind of font for the other levels of headings. Figure 17.4 shows subtle shadowing being used in an electronics student's manual for the power supply he has built.

Section 1: INTRODUCTION

We hope you're as excited as we are about the new 1999 version of the industrious SPIDER SUPPLY. The SPIDER SUPPLY Dual 20VDC Voltage Regulated Power Supply is a reliable, user-friendly DC output device.

1.1 Features

The Basics (batteries are included)

The SPIDER SUPPLY comes with many easy-to-use features for your convenience. The new liquid crystal digital display allows you to view the output with more clarity and accuracy than our past analogue meters.

Our new voltage regulated 20 volt DC supplies power for both a single- or dual-channel output, ideal for use with OP-Amp circuits. Your power supply also includes a circuit common ground as well as a true earth ground. And new cutting edge regulators in accordance with our vented case result in improved heat dissipation, and thus a more durable output.

Figure 17.4   Subtle Shading Used to Distinguish Headings (For a version where colour has been used to distinguish headings instead, see Web site www.pearsoned.ca/lannon) Source: Courtesy of Curt Willis

Flashy graphics attract attention, but the headings must also be clearly phrased to be usable. Notice how effectively the following heading (from Hewlett-Packard's *HP Desk Jet 720 Series Printer Users' Guide*) signals the content of its section:

How to Print on Different Paper Sizes

Compare that heading to much less useful headings such as:

Printing and Paper Size Variations

or

Paper Differentiation Techniques

Page Layout

Chapter 16 discusses effective page design for instructions. Follow that advice, but also remember to use a physical format that can comfortably accommodate both point-form instructions and paragraphed explanations.

Hints for Effective Page Layout. The following useful hints for effective page layout are illustrated in Figures 17.1 to 17.4:

- Use lots of open (white) space.
- Use pictures, diagrams, or graphs to show the *results* of the manual user's actions as well as how to achieve those results.
- Place lengthy explanations in boxes.
- Use fonts wisely:
  a. bold, italicize, or change font size before changing font type
  b. use strong fonts (Times New Roman, Garnet, Boston, Fritz, Palamino)

Symbols and Design Graphics

Hints, warnings, explanations, and special instructions can be highlighted by placing them in boxes and by using symbols to capture the reader's attention. Think of how you might use some of the following symbols that are found in MS Word's "Insert" pull-down menu. Many more symbols are available from various locations on the Internet.

Design Graphics Benefits: Design graphics, such as those illustrated in Figures 17.3 and 17.4, provide three main benefits:

1. They contribute to a professional appearance.
2. They help set up a balanced page layout.
3. They help create an inviting, accessible look that encourages readers to use the manual.

Design Techniques. The simplest design technique is to use italics, bolding, underlining, and quotation marks for special effects, and to use each of those techniques for one effect. For example, you could use:

- italics for emphasizing key words or phrases
- bolding for headings and definitions
- underlining for names of printed publications or for emphasizing important words, warnings, etc.
- quotation marks for quoted words or for words used in a special way

Remember to use such techniques consistently within a manual. For example, don't use italics to emphasize a phrase in one place, and bolding to emphasize a phrase in another place.

☑ EXERCISES

1. Select part of a technical manual in your field, or instructions for a general reader, and make a copy of the material. Use the revision/editing checklist (page 409) to evaluate the sample's usability. In a memo to your instructor, discuss the strong and weak points of the instructions; or be prepared to explain to the class why the sample is effective or ineffective.

2. Create an operating or user manual for a product or system you've developed in one of your classes. Alternatively, write a procedures manual for a series of related techniques and procedures which you've learned in your program of studies. (Examples could include CAD methods, test procedures, fabrication techniques, design principles, or procedures for complying with government regulations.)

☑ COLLABORATIVE PROJECT

In conjunction with other members of your class, research suitable material for a "Survival Manual for First-year College Students." Include such things as study habits, listening and note-taking techniques, how to gain access to college services, student loans and employment services, student housing, parking and bus service, methods for relieving stress, social activities, athletics and intramural activities, library services, computer access, etc.

As a group, make notes from your own experiences and plan a method of collectively researching the topic. Include in your planning a clear idea of the purpose and length of the manual. Then, after having interviewed campus resource personnel and researched secondary material, organize and write the manual at the level of a first-year student's experience. Also, look for partners who would consider a joint venture to publish and distribute such a manual.

Proposals

A PROPOSAL offers to do something or recommends that something be done. A proposal's general purpose is to improve conditions, authorize work on a project, present a product or service (for payment), or otherwise support a plan for solving a problem or doing a job.

Your proposal may be a letter to your college's Dean of Engineering to suggest an interdisciplinary program of studies linked with the Computer Science and Arts programs; it may be a memo to your firm's general manager to request funding for computer training; or it may be a 100-page document to the provincial highways ministry to bid for a contract to design a series of highway overpasses. You may write the proposal alone or as part of a team. It may take hours or months.

Types of Proposals

Proposals are as varied as the situations which generate them, but we can identify three main types:

1. *sales proposals*, which promote business
2. *research proposals*, which are used in academic institutions and in business
3. *improvement proposals* (or *planning proposals*), which suggest how to improve situations or ways of doing things, or which present solutions to problems.

Some proposals are sent internally; others are sent to external readers. Either way, the proposal writer has reasons for sending the proposal. But, internal or external, the success or failure of the proposal depends almost entirely on the writer's ability to look at the situation from the reader's point of view. Table 18-1 shows a variety of proposals whose writers have tried to use supporting arguments that appeal to their readers.

Some of the proposals in Table 18-1 have been solicited by their readers. These may have to be presented differently from proposals that have not been solicited and which will likely not be anticipated by their receivers.

A s*olicited proposal* is received by a client who is not surprised or annoyed to receive that proposal. However, the client usually states definite requirements and expects to see those requirements fully answered. Also, frequently, the client indicates the conditions and/or the format for the proposal. In these cases, the proposal writer has to pay strict attention to the reader's expectations.

The writer of an *unsolicited proposal* has a different challenge: Often, the reader initially feels reluctant to accept the proposal. Perhaps the reader doesn't see a problem or is happy with the current way of doing things. Perhaps the reader is not aware of the product you have to sell, or has other priorities. However, if you can convince the reader of the need for your proposed solution, you have a chance of persuading the reader. If you can't establish that need in the reader's mind, there's no point in proposing how to meet the need!

Table 18.1   Types of Proposals

Type	Internal	External
Sales	The design unit in a company that designs and manufactures auto parts solicits proposals for testing new magnesium-alloy brake parts. In keeping with the company's budgetary policies, the company's design unit can choose the company's own research lab's proposals or an external lab's proposal. Either way, the design unit will be billed for the testing. If the company lab wins the testing contract, it gains credits for salaries and new equipment.	An engineering firm that specializes in environmental studies proposes the assessment methods, timeline, staffing, and budget for assessing the potential environmental impact of a proposed golf course. The proposal responds to a "Request for Proposal" (RFP) issued by the provincial Ministry of the Environment. The RFP lists several pages of requirements that a successful proposal must meet.
Research	A truck manufacturing company's engine design team proposes a project to determine methods of reducing engine vibration. In arguing its case, the design team points to negative customer and dealer feedback about excessive engine vibration and noise. The design team also cites examples of how engine vibration has created warranty problems for the manufacturer.	A university physicist proposes a four-year computer modeling study of the properties of surface molecules. The physicist knows that his readers at the Natural Sciences and Engineering Research Council will understand his highly technical proposal, but for possible public consumption he attaches an executive summary that explains the potential applications of his research to the upper ozone layer.
Improvement	A research chemist in a petroleum firm's product development branch proposes a new way of blending methanol with gasoline. This new blending method would reduce production costs. In response to her supervisor's request, a fisheries biologist proposes a software package that tracks costs of extended research studies.	A software development firm, after reading newspaper reports about sailing delays and operating cost overruns for an East coast ferry fleet, proposes a software program that fully coordinates the ferries' sailing schedules, maintenance schedules, staff training, supply loading, and fueling. Before submitting the proposal, the software firm's partners learn all they can about who screens proposals at the ferry corporation.

The Proposal Process

The basic proposal process can be summarized simply: Someone offers a plan for something that needs to be done. In business and government, this process has five stages:

1. Client X recognizes a need for a service or product.
2. Client X draws up detailed requirements and advertises its need in a Request for Proposal (RFP).
3. Firms A, B, and C research Client X and its needs. (Likely they will request a more detailed version of the RFP.)
4. Firms A, B, and C propose a plan for meeting the need.
5. Client X awards the job to the firm offering the best proposal.

The complexity of each phase will, of course, depend on the situation. In practice, the process could look like the following.

John Sand, a computer network designer in Vernon, British Columbia, spots the following RFP in a local newspaper.

 Province of British Columbia
Ministry of Transportation

Request for Proposal
19991209-EIS

The Ministry of Transportation requires the computers in its Vernon engineering field office to be networked. Proposals for the design and installation of such a network are being accepted.

Proposals will be evaluated primarily on the following criteria:
- ability to integrate existing computer equipment
- understanding of the engineering office's needs
- providing the least amount of disruption to current operations
- cost and value of the proposed products and services

For details of the Vernon office's needs, contact Sandra Mazzini, 549-3099.

Submit proposals no later than December 20, 1999 to:
Mr. Richard Janvier
Engineering Information Systems Coordinator
Ministry of Transportation
784 Jasper Avenue
Kamloops, BC V2C 1L7
Phone: (250) 371-3935
Fax: (250) 371-3928

After phoning his partner, Tom Glavine, who is working on a project in Cranbrook, John phones Sandra Mazzini to learn more about the Vernon office's needs, current computer equipment, type of work performed, and methods of filing data and designs. He takes detailed notes and asks Sandra to confirm key points at the end of the 20-minute conversation.

The conversation with the local office confirms what John had suspected:

1. The Ministry of Transportation has a limited capital budget and therefore wants to reduce costs by using the current group of computers. The client does not wish to buy any new computers unless absolutely necessary.

2. The engineers at the office are currently very busy preparing for upcoming spring and summer projects, so they cannot be interrupted for long periods by equipment installation or staff network training.

John Sand again consults with his partner. They agree that the best way to meet the client's needs is to design a peer-to-peer network which uses the engineering office's existing computers. The office's networking and file management needs do not require a more sophisticated (and more expensive) system. Such a network will not make much money for Sand and Glavine Systems because they will not earn their normal mark-up on equipment, so the partners agree to try to make money on the contract by offering system support, which the client can purchase as an add-on. (System support does not require money from the capital budget. John's conversation with Sandra Mazzini revealed that her office has more leeway with its annual services budget.)

Other firms will compete for this project. The client will award it to the firm submitting the best proposal, based on the criteria listed in the RFP, and the following criteria which are generally used to assess proposals:

- understanding of the client's needs
- soundness of the firm's technical approach
- quality of the proposed project's organization and management
- ability to complete the job by the deadline
- ability to control costs
- specialized experience of the firm in this type of work
- qualifications of staff assigned to the project
- the firm's record for similar projects

Note: Sometimes an RFP will list the client's specific criteria in a point scale, as in the following excerpt from an RFP for harvesting timber on Crown land:

Criteria	Weighting
Employment	30
Proximity	10
Existing plant	10
New capital investment	10
Labour value-added	10
Change in value-added	20
Revenue	10
Total Weighting	100

All applicants must submit a proposal that contains a business case for lumber manufacturing or specialty wood products manufacturing and addresses the development objectives of the Crown.

Source: Adapted from a format used by the Ministry of Forests, Province of British Columbia

Some clients hold a pre-proposal conference for the competing firms. During this briefing, the firms are informed of the client's needs, expectations, specific start-up and completion dates, criteria for evaluation, and other details to guide proposal development. Such a conference is not necessary for a relatively small project such as networking a small engineering office.

Nor does the Vernon engineering office do what some municipal and government agencies do: restrict a given project to a list of pre-selected firms. Usually, this is done on a rotation basis—if, say, a city department has 15 firms on its contractor list, it might send invitations to bid to the first five firms on the list, and then the next five firms for the next project, and so on. Or, an agency might require firms to present their qualifications for a certain kind of project before actually soliciting proposals for it. Only those firms who clear the qualifications hurdle will be allowed to submit a proposal.

In the networking case, John Sand knows that the merits of his firm's proposed plan will be evaluated *solely* on the basis of what he puts *on paper*. Still, it helps to know who will make the final decision about the competing proposals. In the conversation with Sandra Mazzini, John had learned that Richard Janvier will make the decision at the regional office. So, being a local vendor will not be a major advantage for Sand and

Glavine Systems. Also, Mazzini hints that Janvier is a no-nonsense person who dislikes high-pressure sales. With that in mind, John takes pains to design a simple, functional system and write a proposal which is businesslike and free from unnecessary jargon.

The Sand and Glavine Systems proposal appears in this chapter, starting on page 451. ■

Proposal Guidelines

Readers will evaluate your proposal according to how clearly, informatively, and realistically you answer these questions:

- *What are you proposing?*
- *What problem will you solve?*
- *Why is your plan worthwhile?*
- *What is unique about your plan?*
- *What are your (or your firm's) credentials?*
- *How will the plan be implemented?*
- *How long will the project take to complete?*
- *How much will it cost?*
- *How will we benefit if we accept your plan?*

In addition to answering the questions above, successful proposal writers adhere to the following guidelines.

Design an Accessible and Appealing Format. Format is the *look* of a document, including such features as:

- the layout of words and graphics
- typeface, type size, and white space
- highlights and lists
- headings

A poorly designed proposal suggests to readers the writer's careless attitude toward the project.

Signal Your Intent with a Clear Title. Decision makers are busy people who have no time for guessing-games. The title should clearly signal the proposal's purpose and content.

> **Unclear**   PROPOSED OFFICE PROCEDURES FOR VISTA FREIGHT, INC.

What kinds of office procedures are being proposed? This title is too broad.

> **Revised**   A PROPOSAL FOR AUTOMATING VISTA'S FREIGHT
> BILLING SYSTEM

Don't write "Recommended Improvements" when you mean "Recommended Wastewater Treatment." A specific and comprehensive title signals the proposal's intent.

Include Supporting Material and Appropriate Supplements. Both short and long proposals may include supporting materials (maps, blueprints, specifications, calculations, and so forth). Place supporting material in an appendix to avoid interrupting the discussion.

Depending on your readers, appropriate supplements for a long proposal might include a title page, cover letter, table of contents, summary, abstract, and appendices. Readers with various responsibilities will be interested in different parts of your proposal. Some know about the problem and will read only your plan; some will look only at the summary; others will study recommendations or costs; still others will need all the details. If you're unsure as to which supplements to include in an internal proposal, ask the intended reader or study other proposals. For a solicited proposal (one written for an outside agency) follow the agency's instructions *exactly*.

Focus on the Problem and the Objective. Readers want specific suggestions for filling specific needs. Their biggest question is "What's in this for me?" Show them that you understand their problem and offer a plan for improving their products, sales, or services.

Notice in the following example how proposal writer Gerald Beaulieu focuses on Vista's inefficient office procedures, and then outlines specific solutions.

Statement of the Problem

Gives background

Vista provides two services: (1) It locates freight carriers for its clients. The carriers, in turn, pay Vista a 6 percent commission for each referral; (2) Vista handles all shipping paperwork for its clients. For this auditing service, clients pay Vista a monthly retainer.

Describes problem and its effects

Although Vista's business has increased steadily for the past three years, record-keeping, accounting, and other paperwork still are done *manually*. These inefficient procedures have caused a number of problems, including late billings, lost commissions, and poor account maintenance. Unless its office procedures are updated, Vista stands to lose clients.

Objective

Enables readers to visualize results

This proposal offers a realistic and efficient plan for Vista to streamline office procedures. We first identify the burden imposed on your staff by the current system, and then we show how to reduce inefficiency, eliminate client complaints, and improve your cash flow by automating most office procedures.

Treat Contingencies and Limitations Realistically. Do not under-estimate the project's complexity. Identify contingencies (occurrences subject to chance) readers might not anticipate, and propose realistic methods for dealing with the unexpected. Here is how the Vista proposal qualifies its promises:

Assesses contingencies realistically

As outlined below, Vista can realize tangible benefits by automating office procedures. But, as countless firms have learned, *imposing* automated procedures on a staff can create severe morale problems—particularly among senior staff who feel coerced. To diminish employee resistance, invite your staff to comment on this proposal. To help avoid hardware and software problems once the system is operational, we have included recommendations and a budget for staff training. (Firms have learned that inadequate training is counterproductive to the automation process.)

If the best available solutions have limitations, let readers know. Otherwise, you and your firm could be liable in the case of project failure. Avoid overstatement. Notice how the above solutions are qualified ("diminish" and "help avoid" instead of "eliminate") so as not to promise more than the writer can deliver. Ethical communication is essential.

Explain the Benefits of Implementing Your Plan. A persuasive proposal shows readers how they (or their organization) will benefit by adopting your plan.

The Vista proposal specifies the following benefits. (Each benefit will be described at length in the body section.)

Relates benefits directly to reader's needs

Once your automated system is operational, you will be able to:
- identify cost-effective carriers
- coordinate shipments (which will ensure substantial discounts for clients)

- print commission bills
- track shipments by weight, kilometres, fuel costs, and destination
- send clients weekly audit reports on their shipments
- bill clients on a 25-day cycle
- produce weekly or monthly reports

Additional benefits include eliminating repetitive tasks, improving cash flow, and increasing productivity.

Provide Concrete and Specific Information. Vagueness is a fatal flaw in a proposal. Before you can persuade readers, you must inform them; therefore, you need to *show* as well as *tell*. Instead of writing, "We will install state-of-the-art equipment," write,

Spells out details

To meet your automation requirements, we will install twelve Power Macintosh computers with 6-Gigabyte hard drives. The system will be networked for rapid file transfer between offices. The plan also includes interconnection with four HP printers, and one HP Desk Jet colour printer.

To avoid any misunderstanding and to reflect your ethical commitment, a proposal must elicit *one* interpretation only.

Include Effective Visuals. If they enhance your proposal, use visuals, properly introduced and discussed. Page 437 shows one visual from the Vista proposal.

Gives a framework for interpreting the visual

As the flowchart illustrates (Figure 1), your routing and billing system creates a good deal of redundant work for your staff. The routing sheet alone is handled at least six times. Such extensive handling leads to errors, misplaced sheets, and late billing.

Use a Tone That Connects with Readers. Your tone is the voice and personality that appear between the lines. Make the tone confident, encouraging, and diplomatic. Show readers you believe in your plan; urge them to act, and anticipate how they will react to your suggestions. But do not come across with a bossy or insulting tone, as in this example:

Had Vista's managers been better trained they could have streamlined office procedures by eliminating some of the more obvious paper-shuffling problems. Moreover, the clerical staff could have avoided errors had they been more vigilant.

Here is a more diplomatic version:

Avoids blaming anyone

Vista's manual office procedures have resulted in an inefficient flow of information. The problems include repetitive tasks, late billings, lost documents, and poor account maintenance.

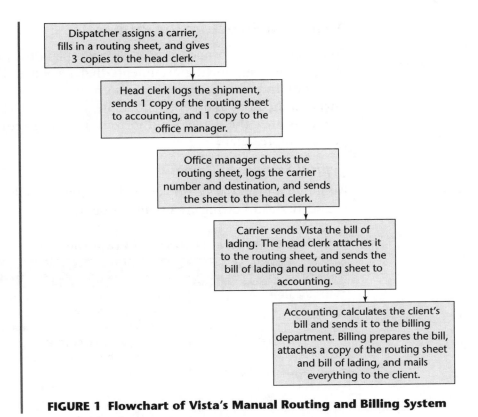

FIGURE 1 Flowchart of Vista's Manual Routing and Billing System

Analyze Audience Needs. Proposals address diverse audiences. A research proposal might be read by experts, who would then advise the granting agency whether to accept or reject it. Planning and sales proposals might be read by colleagues, superiors, and clients (often laypersons). Informed and expert readers will be most interested in the technical details. Non-technical readers will be interested in the expected results, but will need an explanation of technical details as well. Learn all you can about the needs, interests, and biases of your audience.

If the primary audience is expert or informed, keep the proposal itself technical. For uninformed secondary readers (if any), provide an informative abstract, a glossary, and appendices explaining specialized information. If the primary audience has no expertise and the secondary audience does, follow this pattern: Write the proposal itself for laypersons, and provide appendices with the technical details (formulas, specifications, calculations) that the informed readers will use to evaluate your plan.

A General Structure for Proposals

To be successful, a proposal must clearly explain the proposed actions and it must present supporting arguments that recognize the reader's needs and priorities. In practice, a proposal also needs to open with an overview of its purpose, method, and benefits. Finally, it needs to close with a request for action—either the reader's authorization or a meeting to discuss the proposal in more detail.

Typical Sections of Proposals

Although a proposal's complexity determines exactly which sections will be included, the following are usually present.

Table 18.2   Typical Sections of Proposals   (*Continued*)

Section	What to Include
Introduction	• Connect with your reader by referring to the reader's request or to a problem that has led to this proposal. • Briefly summarize the proposed plan, service, or product. Perhaps highlight your (or your team's) qualifications. • "Hook" the reader by previewing the proposal's main benefit. • Describe the scope of the project and list the topics covered in the proposal. • Match the length of the introduction to the length of the proposal. For example, use a single paragraph for a short letter proposal or one or more pages for a report-length document. Alternatively, you may put the introduction in the transmittal letter that accompanies the proposal.
Background	• Discuss the problem or need that has led to the proposal. This discussion will be more extensive in an unsolicited proposal. In a solicited proposal, show that you understand the problem completely. • Discuss the general situation that has led to the current problem (when appropriate) and discuss the significance of solving that problem. • Talk about the requirements for a solution.

Project Description	• Describe your solution to the problem:
	  – What will be done
	  – When
	  – Where
	  – By which methods
	• Include headings such as:
	  – Plan of the work
	  – Schedule
	  – Task breakdown
	  – Projected results

Table 18.2   Typical Sections of Proposals

Section	What to Include
Project Description (*Continued*)	• Incorporate the project components specified in the client's detailed guidelines, if you are responding to an RFP.

Supporting material: **Facilities/equipment** **Personnel** **Past experience**	• Provide evidence of ability to complete all aspects of the project:
	  – Show that you have access to required facilities, equipment, and other resources.
	  – Show that the project leaders have the required qualifications and experience to complete the project.
	• Provide examples of similar work performed by your team.
	• Include résumés (where appropriate).

Supporting Arguments	• Show that the proposed plan is feasible (For example, that it can indeed be completed in the projected time frame, or that a similar solution has been successfully implemented in a similar situation). • Discuss the benefits of the proposed action and, if necessary, address potential reader concerns.
Budget	• Complete this section carefully, to avoid problems due to potential increases in your costs—you're legally bound during the time period you specify. Some proposals need detailed cost breakdowns; others need only a bottom-line figure.
Authorization	• Use this closing action statement to request your reader to authorize your proposed plan, or request a meeting to present your proposal. • Include the authorization request in the closing paragraph of informal proposals (along with a reminder of the proposal's main benefits). For formal proposals, place the authorization request in the transmittal letter.

Additional Sections in Formal Proposals

In addition to the standard seven sections found in informal proposals, include the following sections in longer, formal proposals (Table 18.3).

Table 18.3   Additional Sections in Formal Proposals   (*Continued*)

Section	What to Include
Copy of RFP	• Include a copy of the RFP when you know or suspect that the receiving organization has recently issued more than one RFP.
Transmittal Document (Letter)	• Use this persuasive letter to address the person who receives the proposal or is responsible for the final decision. This is your only chance to directly address the gatekeeper or decision-maker who will decide the fate of the proposal, so word this letter very carefully. • Refer to the RFP. • Describe (briefly) the main points and benefits of the proposal. • Indicate the time limit of your bid. • Ask for the action you desire.
Summary	• Summarize the proposal's highlights in one page or less. • Use the headings "Summary" or "Abstract" for technical readers. • Use the heading "Executive Summary" for less technical summaries designed for managers and others. • Include both types of summaries if more than one type of reader may read the proposal.
Title Page	• Include, in order: – The title of the proposal – The name of the client organization – The RFP number or other identifier – The author's name (if appropriate) and that of the organization – The date of submission
Table of Contents	• Include all section headings and the pages on which they appear. • Do not list parts that appear before the table of contents page: – RFP – Transmittal letter – Summary – Title page • List the names of appendices.
List of Illustrations	• Include a list of figures and tables if the document contains a total of three or more figures and tables.

Table 18.3   Additional Sections in Formal Proposals

Section	What to Include

Supporting Documents	• Include such appendices as:
	  – Testimonials from satisfied clients
	  – Résumés
	  – Technical evidence
	  – Relevant news or magazine articles, brochures, or photos of previous projects

Sample Proposals

Now, let's see how the identified sections are implemented in three different proposals:

1. An informal improvement proposal
2. An informal research proposal
3. A formal sales proposal

An Informal Improvement Proposal

Here's a planning proposal titled "A Proposal for Solving the Noise Problem in the University Library."

Jill Sanders, a library student on a co-op work placement, addresses her proposal to the chief librarian. Because this proposal is unsolicited, it must first make the problem vivid through details that arouse concern and interest. This introduction is longer than it would be in a solicited proposal, whose readers would agree on the severity of the problem. Notice that Jill has chosen to use a three-level heading system, based on the traditional *introduction/body/conclusion* pattern. ■

INTRODUCTION

Statement of Problem

During the October 2005 Convocation at Margate University, students and faculty members complained about noise in the library. Soon afterward, areas were designated for "quiet study," but complaints about noise continue. To create a scholarly atmosphere, the library should take immediate action to decrease noise.

Objective

This proposal examines the noise problem from the viewpoint of students, faculty, and library staff. It then offers a plan to make areas of the library quiet enough for serious study and research.

Concise descriptions of problem and objective immediately alert the readers

Figure 18.1   An Informal Improvement Proposal   **(Continued)**

This section comes early because it is referred to in next section

Details enable readers to understand the problem

Shows how campus feels about problem

Shows concern is widespread and pervasive

Identifies specific causes

Sources

My data come from a university-wide questionnaire, interviews with students, faculty, and library staff, enquiry letters to other college libraries, and my own observations for three years on the library staff.

Details of the Problem

This subsection examines the severity and causes of the noise.

Severity. Since the 2005 Convocation, the library's fourth and fifth floors have been reserved for quiet study, but students hold group-study sessions at the large tables and disturb others working alone. The constant use of computer terminals on both floors adds to the noise, especially when students converse. Moreover, people often chat as they enter or leave study areas.

On the second and third floors, designed for reference, staff help patrons locate materials, causing constant shuffling of people and books, as well as loud conversation. At the computer service desk on the third floor, conferences between students and instructors create more noise.

The most frequently voiced complaint from the faculty members interviewed was about the second floor, where people using the Reference and Government Documents services converse loudly. Students complain about the lack of a quiet spot to study, especially in the evening, when even the "quiet" floors are as noisy as the dorms.

More than 80 percent of respondents (530 undergraduates, 30 faculty, 22 graduate students) to a university-wide questionnaire (Appendix A) insisted that excessive noise discourages them from using the library as often as they would prefer. Of the student respondents, 430 cited quiet study as their primary reason for wishing to use the library.

The library staff recognizes the problem but has insufficient personnel. Because all staff members have assigned tasks, they have no time to monitor noise in their sections.

Causes. Respondents complained specifically about these causes of noise (in descending order of frequency):

1. Loud study groups that often lapse into social discussions.
2. General disrespect for the library, with some students' attitudes characterized as "rude," "inconsiderate," or "immature."
3. The constant clicking of computer terminals on all five floors.
4. Vacuuming by the evening custodians.

All complaints converged on lack of enforcement by library staff.

Because the day staff works on the first three floors, quiet-study rules are not enforced on the fourth and fifth floors. Work-study students on these floors have no authority to enforce rules not enforced by the regular staff. Small, black-and-white "Quiet Please" signs posted on all floors go unnoticed, and the evening security guard provides no deterrent.

Figure 18.1   An Informal Improvement Proposal   **(Continued)**

This statement of need evolves logically and persuasively from earlier evidence

Needs

Excessive noise in the library is keeping patrons away. By addressing this problem immediately, we can help restore the library's credibility and utility as a campus resource. We must reduce noise on the lower floors and eliminate it from the quiet-study floors.

Previews the plan

Scope

The proposed plan includes a detailed assessment of methods, costs and materials, personnel requirements, feasibility, and expected results.

PROPOSED PLAN

This plan takes into account the needs and wishes of our campus community, as well as the available facilities in our library.

Methods

Tells how the plan will be implemented

Noise in the library can be reduced in three complementary phases: (1) improving publicity, (2) shutting down and modifying our facilities, and (3) enforcing the quiet rules.

Describes first phase

Improving Publicity. First, the library must publicize the noise problem. This assertive move will demonstrate the staff's interest. Publicity could include articles by staff members in the campus newspaper, leaflets distributed on campus, and a freshman library orientation acknowledging the noise problem and asking cooperation from new students. All forms of publicity should detail the steps being taken by the library to solve the problem.

Shutting Down and Modifying Facilities. After notifying campus and local newspapers, you should close the library for one week. To minimize disruption, the shutdown should occur between the end of summer school and the beginning of the fall term.

During this period, you can convert the fixed tables on the fourth and fifth floors to cubicles with temporary partitions (six cubicles per table). You could later convert the cubicles to shelves as the need increases.

Then you can take all unfixed tables from the upper floors to the first floor, and set up a space for group study. Plans already are under way for removing the computer terminals from the fourth and fifth floors.

Describes third phase

Enforcing the Quiet Rules. Enforcement is the essential, long-term element in this plan. No one of any age is likely to follow all the rules all the time—unless the rules are enforced.

First, you can make new "Quiet" posters to replace the present, innocuous notices. A visual-design student can be hired to draw up large, colourful posters that attract attention. Either the design student or the university print shop can take charge of poster production.

Next, through publicity, library patrons can be encouraged to demand

Figure 18.1   An Informal Improvement Proposal   **(Continued)**

quiet from noisy people. To support such patron demands, the library staff can begin monitoring the fourth and fifth floors, asking study groups to move to the first floor, and revoking library privileges of those who refuse. Patrons on the second and third floors can be asked to speak in whispers. Staff members should set an example by regulating their own voices.

Costs and Materials

Estimates costs and materials needed

- The major cost would be for salaries of new staff members who would help monitor. Next year's library budget, however, will include an allocation for four new staff members.
- A design student has offered to make up four different posters for $200. The university printing office can reproduce as many posters as needed at no additional cost.
- Prefabricated cubicles for 26 tables sell for $150 apiece, for a total cost of $3,900.
- Rearrangement on various floors can be handled by the library's custodians.

The Student Fee Allocations Committee and the Student Senate routinely reserve funds for improving student facilities. A request to these organizations presumably would yield at least partial funding for the plan.

Personnel

The success of this plan ultimately depends on the willingness of the library administration to implement it. You can run the program itself by committees made up of students, staff, and faculty. This is yet another area where publicity is essential to persuade people that the problem is severe and that you need their help. To recruit committee members from among students, you can offer Contract Learning credits.

The proposed committees include an Anti-noise Committee overseeing the program, a Public Relations Committee, a Poster Committee, and an Enforcement Committee.

Feasibility

Assesses probability of success

On March 15, 2006, I mailed survey letters to 25 Canadian colleges, enquiring about their methods for coping with noise in the library. Among the respondents, 16 stated that publicity and the administration's attitude toward enforcement were main elements in their success.

Improved publicity and enforcement could work for us as well. And slight modifications in our facilities, to concentrate group study on the busiest floors, would automatically lighten the burden of enforcement.

Benefits

Offers a realistic and persuasive forecast of benefits

Publicity will improve communication between the library and the campus. An assertive approach will show that the library is aware of its patrons' needs and is willing to meet those needs. Offering the program for public inspection will draw the entire community into improvement

Figure 18.1   An Informal Improvement Proposal   **(Continued)**

efforts. Publicity, begun now, will pave the way for the formation of committees.

The library shutdown will have a dual effect: It will dramatize the problem to the community, and also provide time for the physical changes. (An anti-noise program begun with carpentry noise in the quiet areas would hardly be effective.) The shutdown will be both a symbolic and a concrete measure, leading to reopening of the library with a new philosophy and a new image.

Continued strict enforcement will be the backbone of the program. It will prove that staff members care enough about the atmosphere to jeopardize their friendly image in the eyes of some users, and that the library is not afraid to enforce its rules.

CONCLUSION AND RECOMMENDATION

Re-emphasizes need and feasibility and encourages action

The noise in Margate University library has become embarrassing and annoying to the whole campus. Forceful steps are needed to restore the academic atmosphere.

Aside from the intangible question of image, close inspection of the proposed plan will show that it will work if you take the recommended steps and—most important—if daily enforcement of quiet rules becomes a part of the library's services.

Figure 18.1   An Informal Improvement Proposal

An Informal Research Proposal

An informal student research proposal is illustrated on page 447. This proposal memo describes a computer student's idea for a research project required by the English 116 class that she's taking. That project will culminate in an analytical report for a "real-world" reader.

The student, Amy Suen, chooses to examine firewall systems that might provide network security for the networked systems at 2020 Design, an electronics design and manufacturing company. Amy does some preliminary research to confirm that she can find information on firewalls. Also, through a contact at 2020 Design she learns that her report would interest Mark Reuters, 2020's computer networking specialist. Mark has been too busy designing and installing his company's new array of computers to pay much attention to the external security issue. Still, 2020 is committed to marketing its products on the Internet and therefore risks incursions into its internal communications, including its proprietary designs.

Amy knows that 2020 Design will not make decisions based on a first-year computer student's report, but Mark Reuters assures her that her report could provide a springboard for his own investigation of firewall software. For that reason, he is willing to help Amy with her preliminary research.

In preparing her proposal for her instructor, Devon Koenig, Amy starts by analyzing her reader and her purpose for writing the proposal, as follows:

Audience: Devon Koenig, project supervisor. He will use my proposal to decide whether to approve my proposed approach. If my proposal is rejected, I'll have to prepare another.

His knowledge: severely limited (so I'll have to provide background)

His questions: (in the assignment memo dated January 17)

1. What's your topic? Who's the reader for your proposed report?

2. What main question does your reader want answered? (Identify the report's specific analytical purpose.)

3. How will the proposed report achieve that purpose? (Here, an attached detailed outline would help establish that you do indeed have a plan.)

4. Do you have the time, resources, and commitment to complete the project? (You should include a time budget and a resources budget.)

5. Will you find sufficient information to answer the report's overall question? (Attach a tentative bibliography.)

Purpose: Convince Prof. Koenig that the topic has merit and that the project is feasible. (Show that I can research, that I can manage the project, that I can afford it, that I can think, that I can write well enough to handle a report of this complexity.)

Audience attitude and temperament: Has high standards and expectations. Therefore, I'll have to answer all his questions thoroughly. He said he'll be skeptical, so I'll have to support all my statements. This won't be an easy sell! I don't think he cares much about how much the project will cost me, as long as I can prove I can afford it. He's a tough marker, so I'll need to phrase the memo carefully and get it proofread.

Audience expectations: He doesn't want more than three pages, not including attachments. His comments in class emphasized our need to provide proof of all positive statements. That's the only way I'll get his support. I'll need to use a direct, businesslike tone—he doesn't like extra words or pompous language. (I'd better stay away from words like "utilize.") And I'd better stick pretty close to the proposal structure he recommended: Connect with reader/provide "hook" in the proposal pre-summary/give background/show need for report/describe planned approach/propose schedule/prove that it's feasible—sources/my qualifications/budget/request authorization. ■

Now, here's the memo that Amy Suen presents to her project supervisor.

English 116 Memorandum

Date: February 4, 2005
To: Professor Devon Koenig, English Department
From: Amy Suen, Computer Systems 1st year
Re: **Proposed Research Project for English 116**

In response to the proposal assignment which you announced in our January 25 class, this memo outlines my proposal to research firewall products. The research will lead to a recommendation of which product will best suit the needs of 2020 Design, a local electronics company. Its networking specialist, Mark Reuters, has indicated his interest in my findings.

Background

Mark Reuters has recently revamped 2020 Design's total network of computers. He is now in the process of installing new networking software, and will continue fine tuning the network and training 2020 Design personnel for the next three months. At that time he will turn his attention to the challenges of partially linking 2020's internal network to the Internet.

One of the major problems to solve will be the issue of internal network security. 2020 Designs stays competitive by developing new electronic designs, so it doesn't want outsiders tapping into its research and development work. Still, the company wants to market its products on the Internet and engage in e-commerce.

Recently, "firewall" has come to mean software products for blocking unwanted access to protected information, but its original meaning included all aspects of network security strategy—software, hardware, and personnel. Mark Reuters has asked me to focus on software products.

Developing appropriate software is very expensive, so most companies purchase rather than develop. Firewall software ranges from a few thousand dollars to about $100,000, depending on performance and user requirements. Each product has advantages and disadvantages which depend on network configurations and the method of implementing the software. Therefore, it's not easy to choose an appropriate firewall product.

Proposed Plan

My initial research into the topic indicates that the following process would be best.

1. **Determine the client's needs**. Subject to your approval of my proposal, Mark Reuters will provide me with details of the network he administers. Those details will include the special features and challenges built into that network, (which apparently is quite unique). With Mark Reuters' help, I'll be able to choose the criteria that I can use to evaluate and compare firewall software products.

2. **Research available software**. As the attached tentative bibliography shows, there seems to be plenty of information available. In addition, I have tentatively arranged interviews with Marsha Campbell, one of my computer instructors, and Guy Lariviere, the network administrator for our College. I'll proceed with those interviews if I receive your authorization to proceed.

3. **Evaluate information gathered about firewall products**. Please see the attached outline, which describes the general approach I plan to take. So far, I have identified three products (Alta Vista, CheckPoint, and CyberGuard), but I'll continue to look for others. I expect to discuss three to five products in the final report; that means that I may have to do a preliminary assessment to weed out inappropriate firewall products.

4. **Rigourously apply the assessment criteria and choose the best product for 2020 Designs**. Part of this assessment can come from the specifications and product information provided by the manufacturers on their Web sites. The full assessment will come from actually testing the software.

Figure 18.2   A Student Research Proposal   **(Continued)**

Prof. Koenig
February 4, 2005
Page 2

Feasibility of Project

I've looked at this project quite carefully and I think it's feasible because:
- Information is available and I have access to expert opinion here at the College.
- My strong interest in this subject has already prompted me to read all the sources listed in the attached bibliography and I've made notes on three of the articles.
- Professor Campbell has agreed to help me assess software on the network in computer lab 218, and she is accepting this project for credit in her Networking class.
- I can get access to firewall products through Mark Reuters, who will request demo. software from manufacturers.

Schedule

According to your January comments about task requirements, I have over-estimated the time required for the following tasks, but my semester time budget can still accommodate the following:

Activity	Time Required	Dates	Document Produced
Research re: firewalls (types and leading products) and 2020 system configuration	10-15 hrs	Feb. 2-14	Refine planning outline
Interview Campbell and Lariviere	2-2 1/2 hrs	Feb. 15 Feb. 16	Refine planning outline
Evaluate data	5-8 hrs	Feb. 22	Adjusted research plan (?)
Analyze/organize data	6-10 hrs	Feb. 27-28	Working outline (due Mar. 8)
Plan/write progress report	4 hrs	Mar. 5-6	Progress report (due Mar. 8)
Write report from outline	6-10 hrs	Mar. 14-16	Analytical report—draft
Edit report and polish format	5-8 hrs	Mar. 24-27	Analytical report—due Mar. 31

Budget

Because I won't have to buy firewall products, and because I use my home Internet connection for many purposes, my budget for this project is minimal:

Photocopy articles	$20
Bus travel for interviews	$15
Report printing and binding	$14
Total:	$49

Authorization

I hope that you agree that my proposal topic and approach is appropriate for the English 116 project, because I'm committed to doing an excellent job. For one thing, I'm also doing the project for my Networking class, and I can afford to put more effort into a project that fulfills two sets of requirements. Also, I think I may be able to get a student co-op job at 2020 Designs this May if I do well on this project. May I have your authorization to proceed? If you wish to contact me outside of class, please e-mail me at amysuen@silk.net

AS

Attachments: Tentative Bibliography
Planning Outline

Figure 18.2   A Student Research Proposal   (*Continued*)

PLANNING OUTLINE: REPORT PROJECT
English 116

Topic: Firewalls

Reader (needs/reason for reading/knowledge level):

Mark Reuters, 2020 Design interested in firewall products for his firm's network/very knowledgeable, but not about current products

Purpose: Assess firewall products suitable for 2020 Design (maybe recommend best one)

Tentative Structure/Topics:

Reason for report
Background re: current firewall technology
    List of products (CyberGuard, Alta Vista, CheckPoint, and others)
    Manufacturers
    Concepts behind the products
2020 Design's network structure
Client's general and special requirements
Product evaluations:
    Supporting operating system and services
    Performance
    Price
    Installation and training
    Does it meet client's particular requirements?
Conclusion re: which products satisfy the criteria/which best satisfies the criteria

Tentative List of Sources:

Interviews: Prof. Campbell, Guy Lariviere, and Mark Reuters

Alta Vista firewall 98. [On-line]. Digital Equipment Corp. <http://www.altavista.software.digital.com> [29 January 2005]

CSI firewall matrix. [On-line]. Computer Security Institute. <www.gosci.com> [31 January 2005]

CyberGuard firewall for Windows NT. [On-line]. CyberGuard Corp. <http://cybg.com> [29 January 2005]

Firewall-1 products and solution. [On-line]. Check Point Technologies Ltd. <www.checkpoint.com> [1 February 2005]

Firewall software for NT and Unix. (1997, June) <u>BYTE</u>, 130-134.

Rubin, A., Geer, D., and Ranum, M.J. (1997). <u>Web security source book</u>. New York: Wiley Computer Publishing.

Stein, L.S. (1998). <u>Web security, a step-by-step reference guide</u>. Reading: Addison-Wesley.

Figure 18.2   A Student Research Proposal Attachment

A Formal Sales Proposal

The formal proposal that begins on page 451 presents a commercial sales pitch. Its writer, John Sand, uses a formal report format to impress his reader with a professional-looking document. John does not include a copy of the RFP; the receiver doesn't have any other RFPs circulating at the moment. Also, the proposal does not include a Conclusion section or a Summary, because the transmittal letter contains a summary of the proposal and states the author's conclusions and request for authorization.

Other aspects of the writer's audience and purpose analysis have been discussed in "The Proposal Process" section of this chapter (page 430).

Sand and Glavine Systems

Suite 106-204 Kalamalka Lake Road, Vernon, BC   V2C 1L7 Phone (250) 558-5704 Fax: (250) 558-1554

December 19, 1999

Mr. Richard Janvier
Engineering Information Systems Coordinator
Ministry of Transportation
784 Jasper Avenue
Kamloops BC   V2C 1L7

Dear Mr. Janvier:

Response to RFP 1999120-EIS, Office Computer Network

The enclosed proposal details the methodology that Sand and Glavine Systems would use to complete the computer network system outlined in your recent request for proposal.

Sand and Glavine Systems is well qualified to supply the network design and implementation outlined in RFP 19991209-EIS, "Office Computer Network." We are an established business in the Okanagan Valley with a reputation for providing outstanding quality and customer service. We have designed and installed many computer network systems including several for engineering firms.

Based on the information supplied by Sandra Mazzini and on our extensive experience with computer networks, we recommend the use of a small peer-to-peer network. Networks like these are cost-effective, efficient, and easy to administer. We could supply this system by upgrading your existing hardware and software. By using this strategy, we will keep costs to a minimum and shorten the time line for getting a system in place and operating. Our proposal calls for upgrading your equipment, installing a network, and orientating the staff, all to be completed within one week of being awarded the contract.

We will design and supply this system, including all necessary hardware, software, cables, and taxes for under $4000. This price also includes a brief orientation for staff who will be using the system.

If you have any questions about the proposal after you have had the opportunity to review and evaluate it, please call me at 558-5704.

Sincerely,

John Sand

Figure 18.3   A Formal Sales Proposal   (*Continued*)

PROPOSAL FOR
OFFICE COMPUTER NETWORK
RFP 19991209-EIS

Prepared for
Richard Janvier
Engineering Information Systems Coordinator

Ministry of Transportation
Engineering Services
784 Jasper Avenue
Kamloops, BC
V2C 1L7

Prepared by

Sand and Glavine Systems
Suite 106-204 Kalamalka Lake Road
Vernon, BC
V1T 7M3

December 19, 1999

Figure 18.3   A Formal Sales Proposal   (*Continued*)

TABLE OF CONTENTS

Figure 18.3   A Formal Sales Proposal   (*Continued*)

Sand and Glavine Systems

INTRODUCTION

Sand and Glavine Systems is well qualified to supply the network design and implementation outlined in RFP 19991209-EIS, "Office Computer Network." We are an established business in the Okanagan Valley with a reputation for providing outstanding quality and customer service. We have extensive experience in networking computer systems, including several engineering offices. This proposal details our plan to create an efficient, low-maintenance computer network.

Statement of Need

Background

The Ministry of Transportation currently operates a field engineering office in Vernon. Working as a team, the office staff produces engineering plans ranging from preliminary drawings and estimates to detailed design packages. This team relies heavily on the use of computerized engineering and drafting tools as well as traditional office software. To handle the high volume and variety of documents produced, the office is equipped with seven personal computers (PCs), two plotters, and one laser printer. The PCs have varying configurations, processors, and attached peripherals. The objective of Sand and Glavine Systems is to maximize the use of the existing equipment into a seamless cost-effective network, making the job of the staff easier and the office more productive.

Impacts

With such a high emphasis on a team concept, many or all of the staff can be involved in a project. Having so many people involved in a single project using separate personal computers can lead to complications in file management and resource sharing.

Unless a stringent file management system is followed, duplicate copies of files will exist. The possibility of having files in more than one location can lead to serious complications. Modifications performed on any one copy will result in different versions of the same document. Updating one of the duplicate documents to contain all modifications wastes time, if the error is even detected. Worse, the probability of having the latest version of a file overwritten with an earlier version is high, leaving disastrous results.

To remedy this, work units sometimes rely on a catalogue of floppy disks containing the latest version of a file. Updating a file requires transferring it from the floppy disk to the hard disk of a PC, making the modifications, saving the file, and transferring it back to the floppy. A fail-safe system will have have a back-up floppy of the original. Using this method will ensure data integrity but staff will spend much of their time transferring files and making back-up copies. Also, it only works if strict guidelines are followed. The longer the project, the greater the chance a breakdown in file management will occur.

Figure 18.3   A Formal Sales Proposal   (*Continued*)

Sand and Glavine Systems

Sharing hardware resources, such as plotters, and printers, between individual PCs is difficult and will lead to productivity losses. Options include dedicating one computer to printing and plotting or connecting the plotters and printer to different computers and sharing time with the operators. Neither choice is efficient.

Unless a computer is used full-time, dedicating it to printing and plotting is a waste of a costly resource. Sharing a workstation is complicated because the operator must handle printing and plotting chores as well as his or her own duties. In both cases the method for getting the information to the printer or plotter involves transferring files to and from floppy disks: a time consuming task.

An alternative used by some companies is to purchase additional equipment to spread the workload. The problem, though, is not that the printer or plotter cannot handle the existing tasks, but that people cannot freely access them when needed. Adding equipment is not a cost-effective approach for pieces of hardware that see only heavy use in spurts and sit idle for great lengths of time.

Needs

The Ministry of Transportation needs to cut productivity losses. This must be achieved at a minimal cost. Staff of the engineering field office need an effective and hassle-free way of performing their duties. Methods considered for achieving this cannot introduce new problems or unreasonable demands for the staff.

Any system used will require a safe and practical method for the engineering office staff to share and store electronic documents. It must also provide a way to produce hard copies of these documents, on demand, from any computer on the system.

To successfully meet these needs, Sand and Glavine Systems proposes a local area network be established using the Ministry's existing computers.

Meeting the Need

Local Area Networks

Since the arrival of the personal computer there has been a drive to share information and computing resources. Local Area Networks (LANs) were created to fulfill that desire. A LAN is a data communications system that allows any connected device to send and/or receive information. This connectivity allows users to share information and computer resources including storage devices, software applications, data files, printers, and plotters.

LANs cover relatively short distances usually within an office, a department, or perhaps a building or campus. LANs consist of network interface cards attached to the connected computers, cables to connect the computers, and software to manage both data flow and the user interface to the network.

$- 2 -$

Figure 18.3   A Formal Sales Proposal   **(Continued)**

Sand and Glavine Systems

The main goal of a LAN is to bring connectivity and savings to a company. Once installed, a network distributes a company's informational resources to the people who need it. People can then do their jobs more quickly, efficiently, and with less trouble than individual PCs. The LAN will also provide savings through sharing of expensive computer resources—printers, plotters, software, and information.

LAN solutions

Once a decision to network has been made, the next step is to decide how to distribute the workload. There are three ways to do this—through a dedicated server, a non-dedicated server, or a peer-to-peer network.

1. A network with a **dedicated server** has a computer set aside to handle the network traffic and tasks for the LAN. The server can be optimized with large storage disks, lots of memory, and a fast processor. A network with a dedicated server provides the greatest amount of security and is the simplest to administer. Although the most powerful arrangement of the three, the dedicated server also brings the highest price in cost of equipment and administration. If the network being designed is large, having a dedicated server is the only option to consider.

2. With smaller networks a **non-dedicated server** can be considered. The server acts as both a network host and a workstation. The system software manages requests from the network as well as from the user sitting in front of the system. A priority ratio determines how the requests are handled. The setting of the priority ratio depends on whether the server will be performing more network requests or more local user requests. This set-up gets more use from the server, but if network traffic is heavy the local user will notice a degradation in performance. Also, if the applications of the local user require a great amount of processing, this processing demand will have a detrimental effect on the network.

3. The alternative to using either type of server is for each individual computer to act as **both a server and workstation**. Any computer connected to the network can share resources, such as disk space and printers, with any other computer on the network. These **peer-to-peer networks** provide a very cost-effective way to share information and limited resources. On peer-to-peer networks, users have easy access to each other's computer. Each user is also responsible for backing up the data on his/her computer. So, if security or data administration is a concern, a peer-to-peer network is not the system to choose.

Recommended solution

The needs and current practices of the Ministry of Transportation field engineering office suggest the most suitable system would be a peer-to-peer network (Figure 1).

– 3 –

Figure 18.3   A Formal Sales Proposal   **(Continued)**

Sand and Glavine Systems

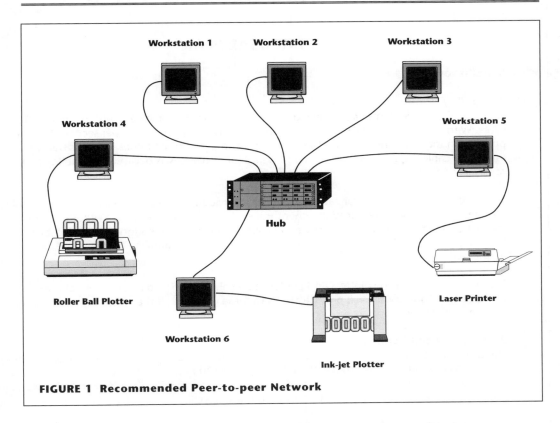

FIGURE 1 Recommended Peer-to-peer Network

The main needs include the ability to easily store and retrieve data, to occasionally share information, and to readily access the plotters or laser printer. This type of activity does not place a heavy burden on a network, so a network server is unjustified. A peer-to-peer network can smoothly handle these tasks without the costs and administration involved in using a system with a server.

As noted above, the drawbacks to a peer-to-peer network are data security and data administration. Since data security is not an issue at this time, a peer-to-peer network poses no threat. Data administration is already performed on an individual basis with each workstation having its own tape back-up system. A peer-to-peer network would retain the same data security and administration.

It should be noted that installing a network does not negate the need for good file management. The possibility of having duplicate files or newer files being overwritten with older versions still exists. This is especially true for a peer-to-peer network, where central storage does not exist.

– 4 –

Figure 18.3   A Formal Sales Proposal   **(Continued)**

Sand and Glavine Systems

PROPOSAL PLAN

Installation

1. Cabling
Sand and Glavine Systems will install high-quality, category 5 unshielded twisted pair (UTP) cable. With category 5 UTP cable, data transmission rates of 10 megabits per second (Mbs) are possible on today's standards, and the system will comply with the future 100 Mbs transmission rates. UTP cable is quickly becoming the standard for smaller LANs because of reliability and ease of installation.

The most common practice for cable installation is through a suspended ceiling, with the cable dropped to each computer location either through the wall or a drop-post. Without seeing the installation site first, we cannot specify exact cable locations, but we suggest that all cables be hidden, eliminating the potential for network interruptions and damage that exposed cables might cause.

Our proposal calls for the plotters and printer to be linked directly to one or more of the workstations. The network will provide access to these devices as if they were connected directly to each workstation.

2. Topology and hardware
The topology for the network will be a bus-star configuration using a 12-port Ethernet switching hub. Each computer will be fitted with an Ethernet 10/100 network interface card (NIC) following the 10Base-T standard. These reliable cards supply data transmission speeds of up to 10 Mbs and will accommodate future 100 Mbs transmission rates as well.

We will not install the office's 486 Wang computer on the network, thus saving the cost of one NIC. While this computer's architecture would run the software we plan to install, the performance would be sluggish. Using this computer as a printer server for the plotter will not be required once the network is operating.

3. Software
Since each computer already has a registered copy of Windows 98 installed, an upgrade to Windows NT 4.0 will provide the most cost-effective network software. While there is a nominal cost for this upgrade, it is less expensive than purchasing separate networking software.

Using this strategy will lower training costs and time. Most computer users are familiar with the Windows environment and they will have little to learn about the network portion of this software.

Figure 18.3   A Formal Sales Proposal   **(*Continued*)**

Sand and Glavine Systems

4. Testing

Once the network is installed, extensive testing will guarantee that it is operating properly. Testing the system will include the following:

1) Executing all software applications to check for memory conflicts with the network software drivers. All conflicts will be resolved.

2) Successfully transferring files from each computer to every other connected computer to ensure that all computers are "talking" to each other.

3) Printing from every computer to each plotter and the printer to ensure they are recognized by the network and configured properly.

Training

A good computer network is invisible to the operator. The network to be installed is designed for ease of use. All computers will operate as they did before, only with added functionality. Because of this simplicity, extensive training is not required.

However, an introduction to the network's capabilities is advisable. We recommend a three-hour orientation for all employees who will use the system. We will show the staff the added functionality and the benefits of using the network. The orientation can be done in a group setting at the office and is provided at no additional cost.

Schedule

Once notice of approval has been received and a contract signed, Sand and Glavine Systems is prepared to have the network operational within one week. A break down of approximate time requirements is listed below.

1) Two days to acquire the necessary hardware and the software licences.

2) One day for an on-site visit. During this visit we will interview staff to establish a design criterion for the network. Cable requirements will also be determined and finalized.

3) One day to design the system and cable layout.

4) One day for the physical installation, including cabling. To minimize disruption to personnel and ease the process, we recommend the installation be scheduled for a weekend.

5) A three-hour network orientation for the staff. It would be best to schedule this for the Monday morning following the physical installation.

Figure 18.3   A Formal Sales Proposal   (*Continued*)

Sand and Glavine Systems

Support

Our standard support packages are available to purchase on a contract basis. The monthly and yearly packages offer unlimited phone support for the length of the contract. Our knowledge base is exceptional and past experience shows the majority of problems are resolved over the phone. An outline of all available packages, including prices, is in the Costs section.

Staffing

Sand and Glavine Systems is a well-established computer network business located in Vernon. We have a solid reputation for superior technical expertise and product support. Computer network design and installation is our specialty and we have successfully completed large and small projects for many businesses located in the Okanagan Valley. Appendix A contains a list of satisfied clients.

We will assign our most qualified and senior staff to this project.

Mr. John Sand—B.Sc., CNE
Mr. Sand is co-founder of Sand and Glavine Systems. He has a degree in project management from the University of Alberta as well as network certification from Novell. Mr. Sand will manage the project and oversee installation.

Mr. Tom Glavine—B.Sc.
Mr. Glavine is co-founder of Sand and Glavine Systems. He has a degree in computer science from the University of Toronto and specializes in computer network design. Mr. Glavine will design the network system and oversee installation.

Mr. Roger Clemenceau—CNCI
Mr. Clemenceau has been with Sand and Glavine Systems since its inception. He has certification in network cable layout and installation. Mr. Clemenceau will be responsible for the cable layout and will oversee the cable installation.

Costs

Determining the total cable needed for this project requires an on-site visit. We have approximated the cable required from the floor plan that Sandra Mazzini faxed to us. We anticipate our estimate to very close. Should we need more cable, we will bill the Ministry of Transportation separately for this item. If we have over-estimated the cable requirements, we will show the credit on the invoice.

The total cost for this project is shown in the table on the following page:

Figure 18.3   A Formal Sales Proposal   (*Continued*)

Sand and Glavine Systems

Software	Windows NT 4.0 upgrade	6 × $89	$534.00
Hardware	3Com Fast Etherlink XL 10/100	6 × $99	$594.00
	3Com 12 Port Switching Hub	1 × $675	$675.00
Cable	Category 5 Unshielded Twisted Pair	300' @ $0.25/ft.	$ 75.00
Services	System design and installation labour		$2,090.00
Total			**$3,968.00**

System support can be purchased separately on a monthly or yearly contract basis. This base entitles you to unlimited phone support with on-site service charged at an additional hourly rate. Support can also be purchased on an on-site, as-needed basis. Support costs are as follows:

Monthly—$60 per month—on site service $60/hr., minimum 1/2 hour charge
Yearly—$480 per year—on-site service $50/hr., minimum 1/2 hour charge
On-site, as-needed—$75/hr., minimum 1-hour charge

Scope of services
The prices in this proposal are valid until April 15, 2000. The scope of the network services offered is only for the computer systems located within Suite 102-2380, 35th Avenue, Vernon, British Columbia.

Figure 18.3   A Formal Sales Proposal   (**Continued**)

Sand and Glavine Systems

APPENDIX A

CLIENT LIST

Blade Architectural Engineering, Penticton

CivilTech Consulting and Engineering, Vernon

Douglas Benton & Associates, Vernon

GLP Engineering, Vernon

Ministry of Forests, Kamloops

McAfee and Sons, Kelowna

Osoyoos Growers Coop, Osoyoos

Premium Foods, Winfield

Robinson Agencies, Vernon

School District 103, Kelowna

The Video Shop, Kelowna

References are available upon request.

– 9 –

Figure 18.3   A Formal Sales Proposal

An Interpersonal Perspective

Some of the examples on the preceding pages show external proposals, most of which attempt to win business contracts. Often, however, as employees we feel the need to improve workplace conditions or ways of doing things. If we try to ignore our feelings, we can end up feeling bitter and helpless. But, if we have methods of convincing others to make necessary changes, we can feel better about ourselves and the place where we work.

The following action gradient, which becomes more positive as it moves to the right, illustrates the values of suggesting improvements.

negative	neutral	positive
Emotional response	*Complaint re: specific incident*	*Rational analysis*
Childish reaction		Adult reaction
Emphasis on momentary relief	Emphasis on specific compensation	Emphasis on improving the overall situation
Employee feels powerless and bitter	Employee feels good if specific problem is handled	Employee feels empowered

Figure 18.4   The Action Gradient

Here's an example of the action gradient at work.

> Let's assume that you work as an engineering technologist for a civil engineering firm that specializes in developing city subdivisions. Because you're frequently placed in charge of projects, you essentially act as an assistant manager. Your office manager is technically competent and works hard, but she uses negative feedback as her primary motivational tool; the only time she comments on a person's work is when that person has made a mistake. Usually, she presents her criticisms in a hostile, aggressive manner. Employee morale and productivity are starting to suffer.
>
> By contrast, your co-workers prefer your positive motivational techniques. You give credit for work well done. When you have to comment on incomplete or shoddy work, you take care to focus on the work itself, not on the worker. Lately, though, the manager's attitude and behaviour have been particularly hard to stomach because everyone has been working extra hard to meet a contract deadline. ∎

Avoiding Action

If you operate at the left side of the action gradient, you don't confront the problem directly; instead, you use passive aggression by talking behind your manager's back. This approach allows you and the other employees to take care of your resentment and frustration for a moment, but you don't feel good about yourself, and meanwhile, the interpersonal climate steadily worsens.

Taking Limited Action

If you operate in the middle ground, you may comment about a specific incident and ask for an apology. However, even if you receive that apology, the basic situation hasn't changed because you haven't confronted the underlying problem.

Taking Positive Action

The advantage of operating on the right side of the gradient is that you try to improve the overall situation. This response pattern requires a rational analysis of the problem and the formulation of a workable solution. Once you believe you have a valid solution, you have a choice of presenting it as a proposal or as recommendations. In the proposal, you single-mindedly argue in favour of a definite course of action, while the recommendations report assesses two or more possible solutions and then chooses one of those solutions.

Whether you chose the proposal route or the (apparently) more objective recommendations report, you have set in motion a series of productive possibilities. For example, your proposal of an incentive plan for managers and staff may get adopted. But even if it doesn't gain approval, you will feel good about yourself for positively confronting the situation. Moreover, you could be perceived as a positive influence within the organization, which will not hurt your subsequent chances for promotion. And, in the long run, positive actions improve the working climate, which was your goal in the first place.

Graphics in Proposals

Proposals tend to feature text, not graphics. Still, as Table 18.4 suggests, visuals can help make proposals more persuasive.

Table 18.4   Graphics in Proposals[1]

The Message	The Graphic
We offer high performance at low costs	• Line, bar, and pie charts • Tables
Our plan is logical	• Flow chart
Our system or equipment does the job	• Schematic diagram • Hybrid graphic (such as drawings, photos, and tabular data pasted onto a flow diagram)
The parts are easy to assemble	• Exploded view drawing
We can meet the schedule	• Timeline with milestones • Critical path diagram
We have the resources and experience	• Data charts • Résumés with experience timelines • Photos (people, facilities, and equipment)

1. Adapted from G. Edward Quimby, "Make Text and Graphics Work Together," *Intercom*, January 1996, p.34.

Revision and Editing Checklist for Proposals

Use this checklist as a guide to revising and refining your proposals.

FORMAT

❑ Have you chosen the best format (letter, memo, report) for your purpose and audience?
❑ Does the long proposal include adequate appendices?
❑ Does the title forecast the proposal's subject and purpose?

CONTENT

❑ Is the problem clearly identified?
❑ Is the objective clearly identified?
❑ Does everything in the proposal support its objective?
❑ Does the proposal *show* as well as *tell*?
❑ Does the proposed plan, service, or product benefit the reader's personal or organizational needs?
❑ Are the proposed methods practical and realistic?
❑ Are all foreseeable limitations and contingencies identified?
❑ Is the proposal free of overstatement?
❑ Is the proposal's length appropriate to the subject?

ARRANGEMENT

❑ Does the proposal include all *relevant* sections of the recommended structure?
❑ Does the introduction provide sufficient orientation to the problem and the plan?
❑ Does the plan explain *how, where,* and *how much*?
❑ Are there clear transitions between related ideas?

STYLE

❑ Is the writing style clear, concise, and fluent?
❑ Is the level of technicality appropriate for the primary reader?
❑ Do supplements follow the appropriate style guidelines?
❑ Does the tone connect with the readers?
❑ Is the language convincing and precise?
❑ Is the proposal grammatically correct?
❑ Is the proposal ethically acceptable?

✔ EXERCISES

1. Assume the head of your high school English Department has asked you, as a recent graduate, for suggestions about revising the English curriculum to prepare students for writing. Write a proposal, based on your experience since high school. (Primary audience: the English Department head and faculty; secondary audience: school committee.) In your external, solicited proposal, identify problems, needs, and benefits and spell out a realistic plan. Review the outline on page 438 before selecting specific headings.

2. After identifying your primary and secondary audience, compose a short planning proposal for improving an unsatisfactory situation in the classroom, on the job, in your dorm, or in your apartment (e.g., poor lighting, drab atmosphere, health hazards, poor seating arrangements). Choose a problem or situation whose resolution is more a matter of common sense and lucid observation than of intensive research. Be sure to (a) identify the problem clearly, give brief background, and stimulate the readers' interest; (b) state clearly the methods proposed to solve the problem; and (c) conclude with a statement designed to gain readers' support for your proposal.

3. Write a research proposal to your instructor (or an interested third party) requesting approval for the final term project (an analytical report or formal proposal). Identify the subject, background, purpose, and benefits of your planned enquiry, as well as the intended audience, scope of enquiry, data sources, methods of enquiry, and a task timetable. Be certain that adequate primary and secondary sources are available. Convince your reader of the soundness and usefulness of the project.

4. As an alternate term project to the formal analytical report (Chapter 19), develop a long proposal for solving a problem, improving a situation, or satisfying a need in your college, community, or job. Choose a subject sufficiently complex to justify a formal proposal, a topic requiring research (mostly primary). Identify an audience (other than your instructor) who will use your proposal for a specific purpose. Compose an audience/purpose profile, using the sample on pages 430–432 as a model. Here are possible subjects for your proposal:

   - improving living conditions in your dorm or fraternity/sorority
   - creating a student-oriented advertising agency on campus
   - creating a day-care centre on campus
   - creating a new business or expanding a business
   - saving labour, materials, or money on the job
   - improving working conditions
   - improving campus facilities for the disabled
   - supplying a product or service to clients or customers
   - increasing tourism in your town
   - eliminating traffic hazards in your neighbourhood
   - reducing energy expenditures on the job
   - improving security in dorms or in the college library
   - improving in-house training or job-orientation programs
   - creating a one-credit course in job hunting or stress management for students
   - improving tutoring in the learning centre
   - making the course content in your major more relevant to student needs
   - creating a new student government organization

- finding ways for an organization to raise money
- improving faculty advising for students
- purchasing new equipment
- improving food service on campus
- easing first-year students through the transition to college

- changing the grading system at your school
- establishing more equitable computer use

☑ COLLABORATIVE PROJECT

Exercises 1, 2, or 4 may be used for a collaborative project.

Formal Analytical Reports

A FORMAL analytical report is used when an analysis requires lengthy discussion (usually ten pages or more) and/or when the topic is important enough to warrant formal presentation (title page, table of contents, formal heading system, formal documentation, etc.)

Less formal reports can use memo formats, letter formats, or a relaxed, semi-formal version of the formal report format. Chapter 21 illustrates short, informal formats.

Analytical reports answer the questions:

1. *What data, observations, ideas, and background information can we gather about the topic discussed in this report? (What do we know?)*
2. *What conclusions can we draw from this material? (What does it all mean?)*
3. *What recommendations stem from our conclusions? (What should we do about it?)*

All readers of analytical reports want the first two questions answered. Most readers want the third question answered as well.

"Real-world" analytical reports answer questions for decision makers. Often, such reports provide the main basis for a reader's practical business decision. By contrast, "academic" analytical reports usually employ a more theoretical model although, increasingly, academic researchers are being approached by business firms for answers to difficult "real-world" questions.

Four Main Types of Analysis

As an employee you may be asked to *evaluate* a new assembly technique on the production line, or to locate and purchase (*recommend*) the best equipment at the best price. You might have to *identify the cause* of a monthly drop in sales, the reasons for low employee morale, the causes of an accident, or the reasons for equipment failure. You might need to assess the *feasibility* of a proposal for a company's expansion or investment. There are many varieties of these four main types of analysis, but the procedure remains the same: (1) ask the right questions, (2) search for information, (3) evaluate and interpret your findings, and (4) draw conclusions and possibly recommend actions.

Typical Analytical Problems

Far more than an encyclopedia presentation of information, the analytical report shows how you arrived at your conclusions and recommendations. Here are some typical analytical problems.

Will X Work for a Specific Purpose? Analysis can answer practical questions. For example, imagine that your employer is concerned about the effects of stress on employees. She asks you to investigate the claim that low-impact aerobics has therapeutic benefits—with an eye toward such a program for employees.

You design your analysis to answer this question: *Do low-impact aerobics programs significantly reduce stress?* The analysis follows a *questions-answers-conclusions* sequence. Because the report could lead to action, you include recommendations based on your conclusions.

The questions posed in such a *feasibility report* are also termed *assessment criteria*. In order to answer the main question of whether low-impact aerobics reduce stress, supporting questions have to be asked (assessment criteria have to be applied):

- *What causes stress?*
- *How is stress revealed physiologically?*
- *Can the physical manifestations of stress be measured?*
- *What kinds of activities reduce stress? How strenuous do they have to be?*
- *How long do these activities have to be followed before measurable effects are detected?*
- *Do the stress-reducing activities work equally well for all subjects?*

Has X Worked As Well As Expected? *Evaluation* (*assessment*) *reports,* like feasibility studies, use a series of evaluation criteria to assess the performance or value of equipment, facilities, or programs. Unlike feasibility reports, however, assessment reports apply those criteria *after* a decision has been made.

Let's imagine, for example, that your engineering firm decided last year to network all of the firm's computers. Now, in assessing that network's performance, your report might use the following criteria to determine if the predicted gains have actually happened:

- *performance gains, if any: (the amount and quality of design work)*
- *communication within the firm: savings in meeting time*
- *compatibility with the firm's design and communication software*
- *network reliability and down time*
- *the firm's ability to accept more complex projects*

Is X or Y Better for a Specific Purpose? Analysis is essential in comparing machines, processes, business locations, computer systems, or the like. Assume that you manage a ski lodge and need to answer this question: *Which of the two most popular ski bindings is best for our rental skis?* In a comparative analysis of the Salomon 555 and the Americana bindings, you would assess the strengths and weaknesses of each binding on the basis of specific criteria (safety, cost, ease of repair, ease of adjustment, dependability, and so on) which you would rank in order of importance.

The comparative analysis follows a *questions-answers-conclusions* sequence and is designed to help the reader make a choice. Examples appear in magazines such as *Consumer Reports* and *Consumer's Digest.*

Why Does X Happen? The causal analysis is designed to answer questions like this: *Why do small businesses have a high failure rate?* This kind of analysis follows a variation of the questions-answers-conclusions structure: namely, *problem-causes-solution*. Such an analysis follows this sequence:

1. identify the problem
2. examine possible and probable causes, and isolate definite ones
3. recommend solutions

An analysis of low employee morale would investigate causal relationships.

How Can X Be Improved or Avoided? Another form of problem solving focuses on desired results and recommends methods of achieving these results. This type of analysis answers questions like these: *How can we operate our division more efficiently? How can we improve campus security?*

Usually, a *recommendations report* first identifies causes of a problem or components of a desired result. Then, the report presents possible solutions and uses a consistent set of criteria to evaluate each solution in turn. Finally, the report recommends which solution or combination of solutions to implement.

Many readers of solicited recommendations prefer to see the final recommendations first, *before* the full analysis that leads to those recommendations. Chapter 21 describes when a direct recommendations pattern would be more suitable than an indirect pattern.

What Are the Effects of X? An analysis of the consequences of an event or action would answer questions like these: *How has air quality been affected by the local power plant's change from burning oil to coal? Does electromagnetic radiation pose a significant health risk?*

Another kind of problem-solving analysis is done to predict an effect: *What are the consequences of my changing majors?* Here, the sequence is *proposed action–probable effects–conclusions and recommendations.*

Is X Practical in This Situation? The feasibility analysis assesses the practicality of an idea or plan: *Will the consumer interests of Hicksville support a computer store?* In a variation of the questions-answers-conclusions structure, a feasibility analysis presents *reasons for–reasons against*, with both sides supported by evidence. Business owners often use this type of analysis.

Combining Types of Analysis. Types of analytical problems overlap considerably. Any one study may in fact require answers to two or more of the previous questions. The sample report on pages 483–492 is both a feasibility analysis and a comparative analysis. It is designed to answer these questions: *Is technical marketing the right career for me? If so, how do I enter the field?*

Elements of Analysis

Successful analytical reports feature the following elements.

Clearly Identified Problem or Question

Know what you're looking for. If your car's engine fails to turn over when you switch on the ignition, you would wisely check battery and electrical connections before dismantling parts of the engine. Apply a similar focus to your report.

On page 470, a hypothetical employer posed this question: *Will a low-impact aerobics program significantly reduce stress among my employees?* The aerobics question obviously requires answers to three other questions: *What are the therapeutic claims for aerobics? Are they valid? Will aerobics work in this situation?* How aerobic exercise got established, how widespread it is, who practices, and other such questions are not relevant to this problem (although some questions about background might be useful in the report's introduction). Always begin by defining the main questions and thinking through any subordinate questions they may imply. Only then can you determine the data or evidence you need.

With the main questions identified, the writer of the aerobics report can formulate her statement of purpose:

Definite

> The purpose of this report is to examine and evaluate claims about the therapeutic benefits of low-impact aerobic exercise.

The writer might have mistakenly begun instead with this statement:

Vague

> This report examines low-impact aerobic exercise.

Words such as *examine* and *evaluate* (or *compare, identify, determine, measure, describe,* and so on) enable readers to understand the specific analytical activity that is the subject of the report.

Notice how the first version sharpens the focus by expressing the precise subject of the analysis: not aerobics (a huge topic), but the alleged *therapeutic benefits* of aerobics.

Define your purpose by condensing your approach to a basic question: *Does low-impact aerobic exercise have therapeutic benefits?* or *Why have our sales dropped steadily for three months?* Then restate the question as a declarative sentence in your statement of purpose.

Subordination of Personal Bias

Interpret evidence impartially. Throughout your analysis, stick to your evidence. Do not force viewpoints on your material that are not substantiated by dependable evidence.

Accurate and Adequate Data

Do not distort the original data by excluding vital points. Say you are asked to recommend the best chainsaw for a logging company. Reviewing test reports, you come across this information.

> Of all six brands tested, the Bomarc chainsaw proved easiest to operate. It also had the fewest safety features, however.

If you cite these data, present *both* findings, not simply the first—even though you may prefer the Bomarc brand. *Then* argue for the feature you think should receive priority.

As space permits, include the full text of interviews or questionnaires in appendices.

Fully Interpreted Data

Explain the significance of your data. Interpretation is the heart of the analytical report. You might interpret the chainsaw data in this way:

> Our cutting crews often work suspended by harness, high above the ground. Also, much work is in remote areas. Safety features therefore should be our first requirement in a chainsaw. Despite its ease of operation, the Bomarc saw does not meet our safety needs.

By saying "therefore" you engage in analysis—not mere information sharing. *Merely listing your findings is not enough.* Tell readers what your findings mean.

Clear and Careful Reasoning

Each stage of your analysis requires decisions about what to record, what to exclude, and where to go next. As you evaluate your data *(Is this reliable and important?)*, interpret your evidence *(What does it mean?)*, and make recommendations based on your conclusions *(What action is needed?)*, you might have to alter your original plan. Remain flexible enough to revise your thinking if contradictory new evidence appears.

Appropriate Visuals

Use visuals generously (Chapter 12). Graphs are especially useful in an analysis of trends (rising or falling sales, radiation levels). Tables, charts, photographs, and diagrams work well in comparative analyses.

Valid Conclusions and Recommendations

Along with the informative abstract, conclusions and recommendations are the sections of a long report that receive most attention from readers. The goal of analysis is to reach a valid *conclusion*—an overall judgment about what all the material means (that X is better than Y, that B failed because of C, that A is a good plan of action). Here is the conclusion of a report on the feasibility of installing an active solar heating system in a large building:

Offer a final judgment

> 1. Active solar space heating for our new research building is technically feasible because the site orientation will allow for a sloping roof facing due south, with plenty of unshaded space.

2. It is legally feasible because we are able to obtain an access easement on the adjoining property, to ensure that no buildings or trees will be permitted to shade the solar collectors once they are installed.

3. It is economically feasible because our sunny, cold climate means high fuel savings and faster payback (fifteen years maximum) with solar heating. The long-term fuel savings justify our short-term installation costs (already minimal because the solar system can be incorporated during the building's construction—without renovations).

Conclusions are valid when they are logically derived from accurate interpretation.

Having explained *what it all means*, you then recommend *what should be done*. Taking into account all possible alternatives, your recommendations urge specific action (to invest in *A* instead of *B*, to replace *C* immediately, to follow plan *A*, or the like). Here are the recommendations based on the previous interpretations:

Tell what should be done

1. I recommend we install an active solar heating system in our new research building.

2. We should arrange an immediate meeting with our architect, building contractor, and solar-heating contractor. In this way, we can make all necessary design changes before construction begins in two weeks.

3. We should instruct our legal department to obtain the appropriate permits and easements immediately.

Recommendations are valid when they propose an appropriate response to the problem or question.

Because they culminate your research and analysis, recommendations challenge your imagination, your creativity, and—above all—your critical thinking skills. Having reached a valid conclusion about *what is*, you now must decide *what ought to be done*. But what strikes one person as a brilliant idea might be seen by others as idiotic or offensive. Depending on whether recommendations are carefully thought out or off the wall, writers earn an audience's respect or its scorn. Figure 19.1 depicts the types of decisions writers encounter in formulating, evaluating, and refining their recommendations.

When you do achieve definite conclusions and recommendations, express them with assurance and authority. Unless you have reason to be unsure, avoid non-committal statements ("It would seem that" or "It looks as if"). Be direct and assertive ("The earthquake danger at the reactor site is acute," or "I recommend an immediate investment"). Let readers know where you stand.

If, however, your analysis yields nothing definite, do not force a simplistic conclusion on your material. Instead, explain your position ("The contradictory responses to our consumer survey prevent me from reaching a definite conclusion. Before we make any decision about this product, I recommend a full-scale market analysis"). The wrong recommendation is far worse than no recommendation at all.

Consider All the Details

- What exactly should be done?
- How exactly should it be done?
- When should it begin and be completed?
- Who will do it, and how willing are they?
- Any equipment, material, or resources needed?
- Any special conditions required?
- What will this cost, and where will the money come from?
- What consequences are possible?
- Whom do I have to persuade?
- How should I order my list (priority, urgency, etc.)?

Locate the Weak Spots

- Is anything unclear or difficult to follow?
- Is it unrealistic?
- Is it risky or dangerous?
- Is it too complicated or confusing?
- Is anything about it illegal or unethical?
- Will it cost too much?
- Will it take too long?
- Could anything go wrong?
- Who might object or be offended?
- What objections might be raised?

Make Improvements

- Can I rephrase anything?
- Can I change anything?
- Should I consider alternatives?
- Should I reorder my list?
- Can I overcome objections?
- Should I get advice or feedback before I submit this?

Figure 19.1 How to Think Critically About Your Recommendations
Source: Questions adapted from Ruggiero, Vincent R. *The Art of Thinking*, 3rd ed. New York: Harper, 1991: 162–65.

A General Model for Analytical Reports

Every analytical report identifies an issue to be examined or an overall question to be answered for the intended audience. That issue or question is eventually settled in the report's conclusion section. In between, the report employs a series of supporting questions (analytical criteria) to lead to the bottom-line answer. Figure 19.2 illustrates the line of reasoning one might use for a feasibility report about a proposed downtown location for a multi-purpose arena. The city council likes the idea of a downtown location, but wants to be certain that the location is practical, so it instructs the consultant to question traffic flow in the area, potential parking problems, and the ability of existing city services to handle increased demands. The city also asks the consultant to predict the impact on surrounding businesses.

Figure 19.2 shows the relationships among the introduction, the central sections, and the conclusion in one particular type of analytical report. Though other reports will use the same basic *introduction-analysis-conclusion* pattern, no general model can cover all formal analytical reports. Some reports will have one central section; others will have several. Much depends on the scope of the report and on the complexity of the analysis.

INTRODUCTION	BACKGROUND	ASSESSMENT	CONCLUSION
Question ———————————————————————————————→			**Answer**
Report's purpose: *Assess feasibility of proposed arena location* To be evaluated on basis of: ① Cost of land ② Impact on traffic ③ City services infrastructure (water, sewer, gas) ④ Parking ⑤ Impact on business	Explain process by which this site was identified Explain why other sites will be assessed later: *priority given to downtown development* Explain information sources	**Cost of Land** • City property—reserved for public • Equivalent value **Impact on Traffic** • Concerts and conventions • Hockey games **Availability of Parking** • Concerts and conventions • Hockey games **City Infrastructure** • Water • Sewer • Gas **Parking** • Requirements for various events • On-site parking • Parking within 4-block radius **Impact on Business** • Restaurants • Shopping	*Land cost makes location desirable* *Feasible in terms of traffic flow, parking, existing infrastructure* *Little positive impact on local business* Recommendation: *Retain this site as feasible option, but look at other sites also*

Figure 19.2   A Question-to-Answer Development Pattern for Analytical Reports

Parts of a Formal Report

Table 19.1 presents the sections that usually appear in formal reports, in the order they most often follow. (*The numbers in brackets refer to the suggested order for preparing the sections; following that order of preparation will help you write the report efficiently.*)　Your supervisor will tell you which sections are required for the specific report you're writing.

Table 19.1　Parts of a Formal Report

Front Matter	Body	Back Matter
Transmittal Document (13) Cover (14) Title Page (8)	Introduction (3)	Sources Cited (6)
Summary (4)	Central Section(s) (1)	Additional Sources Consulted (7)
Table of Contents (12)	Conclusion (2)	
List of Illustrations (11)	Recommendation (2)	
Glossary (9) List of Symbols (9) Acknowledgements (10)		Appendices (5)

Strictly speaking, the transmittal document (letter or memo) does not belong in the front matter (i.e., between the title page and introduction). Transmittal documents *accompany* reports. For information and advice about transmittal documents and other parts of the front matter and back matter, see Chapter 20.

Introduction

The most important function of an analytical report's introduction is to identify the report's analytical purpose and preview how that purpose will be achieved. Usually that preview includes a list of supporting questions that will be used to answer the report's major question. In other words, the introduction lists the criteria used in the report's assessment or outlines the process used to determine causes, or previews the logical path to be used in arriving at a recommended action. In some cases, you will need to justify your choice of criteria or explain your analytical method.

An introduction may also require some or all of the following elements:

1. The context, situation, or problem prompting this report (background)
2. Type of data on which the report is based and the type of source
3. Other pertinent theoretical or background information
4. Useful illustrations

An introduction also indirectly sets the tone of the report. The phrasing reflects whether the report takes an aggressive stance, or uses a more cautious or conciliatory approach. For example, a causal report's direct, no-nonsense approach is signalled as follows:

> The Forest Ministry assembled an investigation team to determine if:
>
> 1. forestry activities in the area contributed to the large destructive debris flow that killed three people, and if
> 2. additional investigation is required to assess the future risk of mass mudslides in the area.

Body Sections

Some reports need just one central section. For example, a ten-page causal analysis report might use a central section called "Contributory Causes," with a sub-section for each of the factors that may have helped cause the problem or situation.

Other reports may need several central sections. For example, a 35-page assessment of three submitted proposals for a truck-leasing contract might have <u>four</u> central sections, one for each proposal and one entitled "Comparison of Alternatives." Each of four central sections would use the same set of assessment criteria to organize the analysis within each section. The report's conclusion section would identify the best of the three proposals and recommend whether to accept that proposal in its entirety, or to negotiate a modified version.

As you read the body sections of the two sample reports in this chapter, notice how the analytical criteria (supporting or exploratory questions) are presented in the introduction and then used to form logical structures in the report's main body. Notice also that the sample reports use clear, informative headings that identify exactly where you are at any point in the discussion.

Conclusion

The conclusion of an analytical report will interest readers because it answers the questions that sparked the analysis in the first place. Some workplace reports, therefore, place the conclusion *before* the introduction and body sections.

In the conclusion you summarize, interpret, and (perhaps) recommend. Although you have interpreted evidence at each step in the analysis, your conclusion pulls the strands together in a broader interpretation. In other words, you lead out from the material, to put it in perspective. This final section must be consistent in three ways:

1. The summary must reflect accurately the body of the report, and the bottom-line conclusions must be firmly based on information, ideas,

and analysis already presented in the report. Do not introduce new material in the conclusion section.

2. Your overall interpretation must be consistent with the findings in your summary, and must present an honest and objective appraisal of the material.

3. If you include recommendations, they must be consistent with the purpose of the report, the evidence presented, and the interpretations given.

Often recommendations form the last part of the conclusion section, especially if the report's primary purpose is to assess or to identify causes, but if the report's main purpose is to advise the reader what action to take, create a separate recommendations section. Remember also that not all reports require a set of recommended actions.

A Sample Situation

The report in Figure 19.3, patterned after our model outline, combines a feasibility analysis with a comparative analysis.

> Richard Larkin, author of the following report, has a work-study job fifteen hours weekly in his school's placement office. His supervisor, Mimi Lim (placement director), likes to keep abreast of trends in various fields. Larkin, an engineering major, has become interested in technical marketing and sales. In need of a report topic for his writing course, Larkin offers to analyze the feasibility of a technical marketing and sales career, both for himself and for technical and science graduates in general. Lim accepts Larkin's offer, looking forward to having the final report in her reference file for use by students choosing careers. Larkin wants his report to be useful in three ways: to satisfy a course requirement, to help him in choosing his own career, and to help other students with their career choices.

> With his topic approved, Larkin begins gathering his primary data, using interviews, letters of enquiry, telephone enquiries, and lecture notes. He supplements these primary sources with articles in recent publications. He will document his findings in APA (author-date) style.

> As a guide for designing his final report, Larkin completes the following audience/purpose profile. ■

Audience/Purpose Profile for a Formal Report

AUDIENCE IDENTITY AND NEEDS

My primary audience consists of Mimi Lim, Placement Director, and the students who will be referring to my report as they choose careers. The secondary audience is my writing instructor. The data I've uncovered will help me make my own career choice.

Lim is highly interested in this project, and she has promised to study my document carefully and to make copies available to interested students. Because she already knows something about the technical marketing field, Lim will need very little background to understand my report. Many student readers, however, may know little or nothing about technical marketing, and so will need background, definitions, and detailed explanations. Here are the questions I can anticipate from my collective audience:

- *What, exactly, is technical marketing and sales?*
- *What are the requirements for this career?*
- *What are the pros and cons of this career?*
- *Could this be the right career for me?*
- *How do I enter the field?*
- *Is there more than one option for entering the field? If so, which option would be best for me?*

ATTITUDE AND PERSONALITY

Readers likely to be most affected by my document are students who will be making career choices. I would expect my readers' attitudes to vary widely:

1. Some readers will approach my document with great interest, especially those seeking a career that is more people oriented than technology oriented.
2. Some readers will be only casually interested in my document as they investigate a range of possible careers.
3. Some readers are likely to feel overwhelmed by the variety and importance of the career choices they face. Members of this group might be looking for easy answers to the problem of choosing a career.
4. Other readers may approach my document skeptically, perhaps unwilling to re-examine their earlier decisions about a more traditional career.

To connect with this array of readers, I will need to persuade them that my conclusions are based on dependable data and careful reasoning.

EXPECTATIONS ABOUT THE DOCUMENT

Although I initiated this document, Lim has been greatly supportive, and eager to read the final version. All my readers will expect me to spell things out. But I know that my readers are busy and impatient, so I'll want to make this report concise enough to be read in no more than fifteen or twenty minutes.

Essential information will include an expanded definition of technical marketing and sales, the skills and attitudes needed for success, the career's advantages and drawbacks, and a description of various paths for entering the career. Throughout, I'll relate my material to many technical and science majors, not just engineers.

The body of this report combines a feasibility analysis with a comparative analysis. Therefore, I'll use a reasons-for and reasons-against structure in the feasibility section. In the comparison section, I'll use a block structure followed by a table that presents a point-by-point comparison of the four entry paths. Because I want this report to lead to informed decisions, I will include concrete recommendations that are based solidly on my conclusions.

To address various readers who may not want to read the entire report, I will include an informative abstract.

My tone throughout should be conversational. Because I am writing for a mixed audience (placement director, students, and writing instructor), I will use a third-person point of view. ■

This report's front matter (title page and so on) and end matter are shown and discussed in Chapter 20, pages 521–530.

INTRODUCTION

The escalating cutbacks in aerospace, defence-related, and other industries have narrowed career opportunities for many of today's science and engineering graduates. A study by the Massachusetts Institute of Technology, for example, found that leading industries hired 80 to 90 percent fewer engineers in the mid 1990s than in the mid 1980s (Solomon, 1996, p. 24). This trend is expected to continue—if not worsen—in the foreseeable future.

Employment opportunities in all engineering specialties (except for computer engineering) are projected to grow at rates that range from average to far below average to near-static through the year 2005. In some specialties (such as petroleum engineering) employment actually will decline (Gradler & Schrammel, 1994, pp. 14-16).

Given such bleak employment prospects, recent graduates would do well to consider careers that are more promising. One especially attractive alternative is technical marketing, a career that involves identifying, reaching, and selling to customers a technical product or service.

Customer orientation is an ever-growing part of today's business and manufacturing climate. As early as the mid 1980s, North American industry ceased to be "manufacturing driven" (where customers would buy any products available). Instead, companies became "service driven" by customers demanding products that were designed to exact specifications and that could be serviced efficiently (Basta, 1988, p. 84). These customer demands account for the fact that top technical managers typically have sales and marketing experience in addition to their technical background.

Nationwide, roughly 75 percent of top managers have worked their way up through sales and marketing ranks (Campbell, 1993, p. 28). Figure 1 shows how a marketing background has become a fast track to top management.

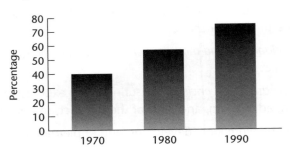

Figure 1   **Top Managers with Sales/Marketing Backgrounds**

Source: Data from Campbell (1993)

1.

Figure 19.3   An Analytical Report   **(Continued)**

In the product-oriented industries of 1970, technical marketing accounted for only 39 percent of top-management backgrounds. But that number nearly doubled by 1990 because of growth in customer orientation. Also, in 1995, employment listings for recent graduates showed more than one hundred major companies offering positions in technical marketing and sales (College Placement Council, 1995, p. 393).

Any undergraduates interested in this career need answers to these basic questions:

- Is this the right career for me?
- How do I enter the field?

To help answer these questions, this report analyzes information gathered from professionals as well as from the literature.

The following analysis includes these areas: definition of technical marketing, employment outlook, technical skills required, other skills and qualities required, career advantages and drawbacks, and a comparison of four entry options.

COLLECTED DATA

Key Factors in Technical Marketing as a Career

Anyone considering technical marketing needs to assess whether this career is practical, considering the individual's interests, abilities, and expectations.

The technical marketing process. Although the terms *marketing* and *sales* usually occur interchangeably, technical marketing involves far more than sales work. The process itself (identifying, reaching, and selling to customers) entails six major activities (Cornelius & Lewis, 1993, p. 44):

1. *Market research:* gathering information about the size and character of the market for a product or service.

2. *Product development and management:* producing the goods to fill a specific market need.

3. *Cost determination and pricing:* measuring every expense in the production, distribution, advertising, and sales of the product, to determine its price.

4. *Advertising and promotion:* developing and implementing all strategies for reaching customers.

2.

Figure 19.3   An Analytical Report

(Continued)

5. *Product distribution:* coordinating all elements of a technical product or service, from its conception through its final delivery to the customer.

6. *Sales and technical support:* creating and maintaining customer accounts, and servicing and upgrading products.

Fully engaged in all these activities, the marketing professional gains a good understanding of the industry, the product, and the customer's needs.

Employment outlook. For graduates with the right combination of technical and personal qualifications, the employment outlook for technical marketing appears excellent, as depicted in Figure 2. Compared with jobs in engineering, which will increase at roughly the same rate as overall employment, jobs in marketing management will increase at nearly a 50 percent higher rate.

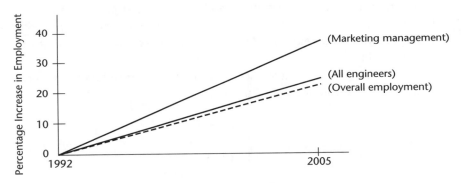

Figure 2   The Employment Outlook for Technical Marketing
Source: Data from Gradler & Schrammel (1994)

Although highly competitive, these marketing positions will call for the very kinds of technical, analytical, and problem-solving skills that engineers can offer (Solomon, 1996, p. 24)—especially in an increasingly automated environment.

Technical skills required. Computer networks, the Internet, interactive media, and multimedia will exert an increasing impact on the way products are advertised and sold. Admittedly, initial sales volume on the Net has been disappointing because of problems with navigation, security, and overall buyer hesitation (Resnick, 1995, pp. 71-72). However, despite these short-term deficiencies, on-line marketing specialist Graham Albatro is among many experts who predict unlimited long-term potential for marketing via the Internet and World Wide Web (Internet discussion list, April 4, 1996).

3.

Figure 19.3   An Analytical Report   *(Continued)*

To enhance the level of direct customer contact, marketing representatives increas-ingly work out of a "virtual" office. Using laptop computers, fax networks, and personal digital assistants, representatives in the field have real-time access to electronic catalogues of product lines, multimedia presentations, pricing for customized products, inventory data, product distribution, and customized sales contracts (Young, 1995, pp. 86-93).

With their rich background in problem-solving, computer, and technical skills, engineering graduates are ideally suited for: (a) working in an automated environment, and (b) implementing and troubleshooting these complex and often sensitive electronic systems.

Other skills and qualities required. In marketing and sales, not even the most sophisticated automation can substitute for the "human factor": the ability to connect with customers on a person-to-person level (Young, 1995, p. 95). One senior sales engineer praises the efficiency of her automated sales system, but thinks that automation "will get in the way" of direct customer contact. Other technical marketing professionals express similar views about the continued importance of human interaction (94).

Besides a strong technical background, marketing requires a generous blend of those traits summarized in Figure 3.

Figure 3 **Requirements for a Technical Marketing Career**

Motivation is essential for marketing work. Professionals must be energetic and able to function with minimal supervision. Ideal candidates are creative people who can plan and program their own tasks, who can manage their time, and

4.

Figure 19.3   An Analytical Report   (*Continued*)

who have no fear of hard work (personal interview, February 22, 1996). Leadership potential, as demonstrated by extracurricular activities, is an asset.

Motivation, however, is no guarantee of success. Marketing professionals are paid to communicate the virtues of their products or services to customers. This career therefore calls for skill in communication, both written and oral. Writing for readers outside the organization includes advertising copy, product descriptions, sales proposals, sales letters, and operating instructions for customers. In-house writing includes recommendation reports, feasibility studies, progress reports, and assorted memos (U.S. Department of Labor, 1994, p. 7).

Skilled presentation is vital to any sales effort. Technical marketing professionals need to speak with a level of confidence that will enable them to be persuasive—to represent their products and services in the best possible light (personal interview, February 8, 1996). Sales presentations require public speaking at conventions, trade shows, and similar forums.

Besides motivation and communication skills, interpersonal skills are the ultimate requirement for success in marketing (Solomon, 1996, pp. 28-29). Consumers are more likely to buy a product or service if they like the person selling it. Marketing professionals are extroverted and friendly; they enjoy meeting people. Because they understand diplomacy, they are able to motivate customers without alienating them.

Advantages of the career. A technical marketing career offers diverse experience in every phase of a company's operation, from the design to the sale of a product. Many companies encourage employees to rotate periodically between marketing and their technical specialties (Basta, 1988, p. 84). Because of its broad exposure, a marketing position can provide a direct path to upper-management jobs. In fact, sales engineers with solid experience often open their own firms as "manufacturers' agents" representing a variety of companies ("Engineering careers," 1995, p. 247).

Another benefit is the possibility of a high salary. Most marketing professionals receive a base pay plus commissions. According to John Turnbow, managing recruiter of National Electric's Technical Marketing Program, some of NE's new marketing engineers earn over $60,000 in their first year. In fact, many salaries in this field reach six figures—sometimes higher than a company's executive salaries (personal communication, April 5,1996).

This career is particularly attractive for its geographic and job mobility. Companies nationwide seek recent graduates, but especially in Ontario and Quebec and on east and west coasts ("Electronic sales," 1996, pp. 1134-37). In addition, one develops

5.

Figure 19.3   An Analytical Report   *(Continued)*

and refines the kinds of interpersonal and communication skills that are highly portable. This is especially important at a time in which more than one out of seven jobs created since 1991 has been temporary and in which job security is disappearing (Alderman, 1995, p. 37).

Drawbacks of the career. Technical marketing is not a career for everyone. Personnel might spend 50 to 75 percent of work time travelling. Success requires hard work for long hours and occasional weekends (Campbell, 1993, p. 24). Above all, the job is stressful because of constant pressure to sell and to meet quotas. Anyone considering this career should be willing and able to work and thrive in a highly competitive environment.

Comparison of Entry Options

Engineers and other technical graduates enter technical marketing through one of four options. Some graduates join small companies and begin marketing work immediately. Others join companies that offer formal training programs. Some begin by acquiring experience in their specialty. Others earn a graduate degree beforehand. Each option is described below and then evaluated on the basis of specific criteria.

Option 1: Entry level marketing without training programs. Direct positions in marketing are available with smaller companies and with firms that represent an array of manufacturers. Because this option offers no formal training, candidates must be motivated and enterprising.

Elaine Carto, president of Abco Electronics, believes small companies can offer a unique opportunity; entry-level salespersons learn about all facets of an organization, and have a good possibility for rapid advancement (personal interview, February 10, 1996). Career counsellor Phil Hawkins says, "It is all a matter of whether you want to be a big fish in a small pond or a small fish in a big pond" (personal interview, February 12, 1996).

Manufacturers' representatives constitute another entry-level position. These professionals represent products for manufacturers who have no marketing staff of their own. Manufacturers' representatives are, in effect, their own bosses, choosing from among many offers the products they wish to represent (Tolland, 1996).

Entry-level marketing offers immediate income and a chance for early promotion. A disadvantage, however, might be the gradual loss of any technical edge that one might have acquired in college.

6.

Figure 19.3   An Analytical Report   (*Continued*)

Option 2: A marketing and sales training program. Formal training programs offer the most popular route into sales and marketing. Large to mid-size companies typically offer two formats: (a) a product-specific program, in which trainees learn about a particular product or line of products, or (b) a rotational program, in which trainees learn about various products and work in various positions. Programs last from several weeks to several months, covering products, markets, competition, and customer relations.

Former trainees speak of the diversity and satisfaction offered by such training programs. Ralph Lang, of Allied Products, enjoyed the constant interaction with company personnel (phone interview, April 10, 1996). Bill Collins, sales engineer with Intrex Computers, values his broad knowledge of Intrex's product line, instead of being narrowly focused on one technical area. Sarah Watts, also with Intrex, enjoys applying her training to a variety of sales challenges (Campbell, 1993, p. 29). Like direct entry, this option offers immediate income. A possible disadvantage, however, is that trainees might find their technical expertise compromised because they have had no chance to practise in their specialty.

Option 3: Practical experience in one's specialty. Instead of directly entering marketing, some candidates first gain practical experience in their specialty. This option provides direct exposure to the workplace environment and a chance to sharpen technical ability in practical applications. Moreover, some companies will offer marketing and sales positions to their outstanding engineers as a first step toward upper-management ("Engineering careers," 1995, p.183).

Many industry experts consider the practical-experience option the wisest choice. Jane Doser, recruitment manager for Trans Electric, has this view of on-the-job experience: "Until you've done some work in your specialty, you really don't know yourself as a person or know what kind of person you're going to be" (Schranke, 1985, p. 15).

This option ensures technical expertise, but delays a candidate's entry to technical marketing.

Figure 19.3   An Analytical Report   (*Continued*)

Option 4: Graduate program. Instead of direct entry, some people choose to pursue either a Master's of Science (MS) degree in their specialty, a Master's of Business Administration (MBA) degree, or both. According to engineering professor Mary McClane, MS degrees usually are unnecessary for technical marketing unless a particular sale is highly complex (1996). The MBA carries a real advantage in terms of general business and marketing skills. In general, jobseekers with an MBA have a distinct competitive advantage (Gradler & Schrammel, 1994, p. 3). More significantly, new MBAs with a technical bachelor's degree and 1 to 2 years of experience command salaries more than 30 percent higher than MBAs who have neither work experience nor a technical bachelor's degree (Baxter, 1994, p. 7).

A motivated student might combine degrees. Dora Anson, president of Susimo Cosmic Systems, sees the MS and MBA as the ideal combination for technical marketing (lecture, January 15, 1996). To employers, the advanced degree means greater technical competence, stronger motivation, and higher performance levels.

One disadvantage of a full-time graduate program is lost salary, compounded by school expenses. These costs must be weighed against the prospect of promotion and monetary rewards later in one's career.

An overall comparison by relative advantages. Table 1 compares the four technical marketing entry options on the basis of three criteria: immediate income, rate of advancement through marketing ranks, and long-term potential.

Table 1   Relative Advantages Among Four Technical-Marketing Entry Options

Option	Relative Advantages		
	Early Immediate Income	Rapid Advancement In Marketing	Long-term Potential
Entry level, no experience	yes	yes	no
Training program	yes	yes	no
Practical experience	yes	no	yes
Graduate program	no	no	yes

As Table 1 shows, the choice of any particular entry option can have important career implications.

8.

Figure 19.3   An Analytical Report   (*Continued*)

CONCLUSION

Summary of Findings

Technical marketing and sales involves identifying, reaching, and selling the customer a technical product or service. Besides a solid technical background, anyone entering the field will need motivation, communication skills, and interpersonal skills. This career offers job diversity and excellent income potential, balanced against hard work and relentless pressure to perform.

College graduates who seek a career in technical marketing and sales have four entry options:

1. Direct entry with no formal training
2. A formal training program
3. Practical experience in a technical specialty prior to entry
4. Graduate programs

Each option has advantages and disadvantages in immediacy of income, rate of advancement, and long-term potential.

Interpretation of Findings

For graduates with a strong technical background and the right skills and motivation, technical marketing offers attractive prospects for income and advancement. Anyone contemplating this field, however, needs to enjoy customer contact and be able to thrive in a highly competitive environment.

Those who decide that technical marketing is for them can choose among four entry options:

- If immediate income is unimportant, graduate school is an attractive option.
- For hands-on experience, an entry-level job is the logical option.
- For sharpening technical skills, prior work in one's specialty is invaluable.
- For sophisticated sales training, a formal program with a large company is best.

9.

Figure 19.3   An Analytical Report (*Continued*)

Recommendations

If your interests and abilities match the requirements outlined earlier, follow these suggestions in planning for a technical marketing career.

1. To get a firsthand view, seek the opinions and advice of people in the field.

2. Before settling on an entry option, consider all its advantages and disadvantages and decide whether this particular option best coincides with your personal goals.

3. Remember that you are never committed to one entry option only. For a fuller understanding of technical marketing, you might pursue any combination of options during your professional life.

4. When making any vital career decision, consider career counsellor Warren Polgar's advice: "Listen to your brain and your heart" (lecture, November 19, 1995). Choose an option or options that offer not only professional advancement, but personal satisfaction as well.

REFERENCES

[The complete list of references is shown and discussed in Chapter 8, page 198] [Note: References normally start on a new page. In this report, the REFERENCES page would be page 11.]

10.

Figure 19.3   An Analytical Report

The Process of Writing Reports

The efficient writing process described in Chapter 3 certainly applies to writing lengthy reports. Also, the research advice in Chapters 6, 7, and 8 applies mostly to gathering, recording, and documenting information for formal reports. To avoid unnecessary effort and to save time in writing a lengthy report, follow the advice in Chapters 3 and 6.

Using Outlines

You can use three types of outlines to write top-quality reports efficiently:

1. Use a *planning outline* to guide your research and initial planning. That outline will change as you gather material, but such an outline will continually remind you of the report's purpose and the analytical criteria to achieve that purpose. Figure 19.4, on page 494, shows a planning outline for a comparative assessment report.

2. When you have chosen, evaluated, and analyzed the material for your report, write a detailed formal *working outline*, including:

   - the report's working title
   - a purpose/audience statement to remind yourself of the reason for the report
   - a thesis statement to further remind yourself that everything in the report contributes to a "bottom-line" answer
   - all headings and sub-headings, named and formatted as they will be in the finished report's body
   - a brief description of every paragraph in the finished report
   - the name and number of each illustration, placed where it will appear in the report

   This working outline will take some time to write because it forms a complete blueprint for the first draft, but a thorough, well-conceived outline will dramatically decrease the time required to compose, revise, and edit your first draft. Also, *each keystroke that goes into the working outline will appear in that first draft*; the headings and illustration labels will all be in place, and even the paragraph description phrases will likely end up in their respective paragraphs. Compare the headings and paragraph descriptions in Figure 19.5 on pages 495–497 with the corresponding report in Figure 19.6 on pages 500–514.

3. As you use the working outline to compose the first draft, you can refer to your note cards to establish the exact content of each paragraph, or you can write a brief, informal *paragraph outline* for each one. See page 497 for an example. Such "quickie" outlines don't have to be neat; they merely help you write coherent, unified paragraphs quickly. You may prefer to create a paragraph outline for each new paragraph as you come to it, or you may prefer to write outlines for several paragraphs in succession.

Now, let's see this sequence of outlines at work. First we'll look at the outline for writing the report that was referred to in the proposal in Chapter 3. In Chapter 21, we'll look at the outline for writing the progress report.

The writer is Art Basran, Kelowna Branch Manager for MMT Consulting. The primary reader is Jessica Proctor, Director of Mining Development for Jackson Mining Ltd. of Grand Forks, British Columbia. First, Art's planning outline forms the basis for his project plan and the report that will present the project's results. ■

Project: Determine best method to haul coal from the proposed Othello mine.

Jackson Mining has suggested four haul methods, based on its previous experience:
- Diesel trucks
- Diesel trains
- Electric trains
- Electric fleets

Method:
In order to help Jackson Mining select the most cost-effective method of hauling coal from the Othello mine, we'll need to calculate :

1. Annual Costs (fuel consumption, labour, maintenance): Will survey rough-cleared roadway; will calculate all grades and energy needed to haul loads on those grades; will calculate tractive resistances for each of four haul methods; will project haul times; will investigate potential for electric fleet energy recycling
2. Construction Costs: For roads and for rail roads (road bed and track); for electric installations; for maintenance building
3. Capital Costs: For each of the four haul methods—Note: Start by calculating number of units required to haul daily mine output (client does not plan to store coal on site, for environmental reasons). Then, use Merrill Lynch Guide for unit costs.
4. Communication System Costs: GPS, radio system and back-ups, on-board computers

Special Problem:
Need a method to uniformly compare all components of all four types of operations—Is there such a method? (maybe ask Courtland Petersen at KPMG)

Also:
- Should we consider expansion of haul fleet, in case production exceeds projections?
- What about interest rates?
- Who's going to be the primary reader of the report? How much civil engineering and transport engineering background does he/she have?

Information Sources:
Merrill Lynch Industrial Guide
Chartwell's *Power Consumption Calculations*
Find specs books for diesel and electric trains
Internet Web sites for Western Star Trucks, Kenworth, Volvo Industrial Trucks
Jackson Mining's Minesite report for Environment Ministry

Figure 19.4   A Planning Outline

After weeks of hard work by Art Basran's team, and after consulting an accountant (see Chapter 3, page 56), Art analyzes all the data his team has generated, and organizes it into the following working outline. Notice that the detailed calculations are placed in 38 pages of appendices to ensure that the calculations don't clutter the main body of the report.

Title: Cost Analysis of Four Alternatives for Hauling Coal from the Proposed Othello Mine

Purpose/Audience
The report will help the client, Jackson Mining Company, select the most cost-effective method of hauling coal from its proposed Othello mine. <u>Primary reader</u>: Jessica Proctor, Director of Mining Development.

Thesis Statement
If the investors know the interest rate and the amortization period for capitalizing the Othello mine, and if other factors in choosing a coal hauling method are less important than cost, the investors can select the haul method from the EUAC tables.

1.0   INTRODUCTION
    1.1   The Situation
- Jackson Mining's new find: Where, when developed, name, MMT's involvement
- Four transport alternatives to be analyzed and main criterion of analysis
- Guidelines for analysis

    1.2   Limitations
- Basic assumption

    1.3   Background
- Sales and expansion overview (transition paragraph)

    1.3.1   Diesel trucks
- Why?

    1.3.2   Diesel trains
- Haul requirements

    1.3.3   Electric trains
- Haul requirements

    1.3.4   Electric fleets
- Description of planned operation
- Sidings
- Transition: Refer to specifications in Appendix G

2.0   COST ANALYSIS
    2.1   Annual Costs
- Annual cost components

    2.1.1   Fuel consumption
- Why important, and how calculated (refer to Appendix A)
- Table 1: Tractive and Grade Resistances for Diesel Trucks
- Explain Table 1
- Refer to Appendix E—lead into next table
- Table 2: Speed, Power, and Fuel Consumption for Diesel Trucks
- Explain Table 2

Figure 19.5   A Working Outline   **(Continued)**

2.1.2   Labour
- Method of calculating (refer to Appendix B)

2.1.3   Maintenance
- Components

2.2   Capital Costs
- Three components (list)

2.2.1   Transportation units
- Calculation method

2.2.2   Construction costs
- Three main factors (list)
- Calculation method
- Maintenance buildings

2.2.3   Communication system
- Name components

2.3   Cost Comparisons
- Refer to Table 3
- Table 3: Capital and Operating Costs
- Explain Table 3 and lead into Equivalent Uniform Annual Costs

2.4   Equivalent Uniform Annual Costs
- Definition and purpose of EUAC comparison
- Refer to Figure 1: What to see there
- Why the sharp decline in EUAC
- Refer to Appendix D (transition paragraph)
- Figure 1: EUAC for Four Alternatives at 6%

3.0   POTENTIAL FOR EXPANSION
Why examine potential for expansion (lead-in)

3.1   Diesel Trucks
- Explain how an immediate increase of 23.3% could be achieved

3.2   Diesel and Electric Trains
- Show room for a 53.5% increase in production and refer to increases past this amount

3.3   Electric Fleets
- Show room for a 130% increase in production and refer to increases past this amount

4.0   CONCLUSION
- Tables in Appendix D show that the diesel and electric train options give much better results than the diesel trucks and the electric train fleets
- Which is better, diesel train option or electric train option?
- Table 4: Diesel Trains as Best Alternative
- Table 5: Electric Trains as Best Alternative
- Comment on Tables 4 and 5
- Factors beyond the scope of this report which must be decided by the investors

Figure 19.5   A Working Outline   (*Continued*)

APPENDIX A: FUEL CONSUMPTION CALCULATIONS
- Tables 6, 8, 10, and 12: Tractive and Grade Resistances
- Tables 7, 9, 11, and 13: Speed, Power, and Fuel Consumption
- Figures 2, 3, 4, and 5: Fuel Consumption by Section

APPENDIX B: ANNUAL OPERATING COSTS
- Tables 14, 15, 16, and 17: Annual Operating Costs

APPENDIX C: CAPITAL COSTS
- Tables 18, 19, 20, and 21: Capital Costs

APPENDIX D: EQUIVALENT UNIFORM ANNUAL COSTS
- Tables 22, 23, 24, 25, 26, and 27: Capital and Operating Cost Comparisons
- Figures 6, 7, 8, 9, and 10: EUAC for Alternatives at 6%, 7%, 8%, 9%, and 10%

APPENDIX E: SAMPLE CALCULATIONS RE: ENERGY REQUIREMENTS

APPENDIX F: MINESITE TOPOGRAPHICAL MAP

APPENDIX G: UNIT SPECIFICATIONS

Figure 19.5   A Working Outline

As an example of how Art Basran develops paragraph outlines to efficiently write paragraphs, consider his working outline note for section 2.1.1:

2.1.1   Fuel consumption
Why important, and how calculated (refer to Appendix A)

The third-level heading is already in place, and the basic idea of the paragraph has been identified. He develops this idea in the following paragraph outline:

2.1.1   Fuel consumption
Major factor because calculations are complicated
Appendix A—calculations based on example: Table 1

Now, with the key points in place, Art writes sentences in a *statement + explanation* paragraph sequence:

2.1.1   Fuel consumption

Fuel consumption is a major factor because of the large amounts of energy required to transport five million tons of coal annually. Calculating fuel requirements is complicated—Appendix A contains the full breakdown of fuel calculations for each of the alternative hauling methods. Such calculations are based on the total resistance faced by each particular method of hauling the coal. For an example of how total resistance is calculated, see the following table, which calculates the resistance for diesel trucks on the proposed road.

Clearly, Art writes in a deliberate, painstaking way. He writes this way to avoid duplicating effort—nearly everything he keys into his working and paragraph outlines appear in the first draft of his report. This disciplined approach suits Art's working style. *You* may prefer to write your paragraph outlines in pen or pencil, perhaps in whole sequences of paragraphs, and then key the paragraphs as you compose sentences. Find the method that best suits your working style, *but use outlines*!

A Formal Analytical Report

The following pages illustrate excerpts from the report Art Basran produced from his working outline. For the purposes of this textbook, only a few of the report's 38 appendix pages have been included.

As you review the report, notice the following aspects of the format:

- *Margins, headers, and page numbering*: Are used to distinguish first pages of a section from the other pages of that section.
- *Spacing and indentation*: Paragraphs are not indented; rather, double spacing is used between paragraphs. Note: Only main headings are followed by an open line of space.
- *Headings system*: Multiple-decimal:
  - *First order* (1.0): 14 pt., bolded, fully capitalized, at left margin, 4 cm (1.5") from top edge of page, followed by one open line of space
  - *Second order* (1.1): 14 pt., bolded, first letter of each word capitalized, indented one tab from left margin, followed by a line of type
  - *Third order* (1.3.1): 12 pt., bolded, indented two tabs from left margin, first letter of entire heading capitalized, followed by a line of type
- *Documentation system*: APA format
- *Letter of transmittal*: Accompanies report

MMT Consulting

#12-1542 Dickson Avenue, Kelowna, British Columbia V1V 2W6   Ph. (250) 868-4040   Fax (250) 868-5060

April 14, 2009

Ms. Jessica Proctor
Director of Mining Development
Jackson Mining Ltd.
174 Central Avenue
Grand Forks, British Columbia
V2P 6W9

Dear Ms. Proctor:

Re: Othello Mine Transportation Alternatives

Enclosed is a copy of the report, "Cost Analysis of Four Alternatives for Hauling Coal from the Proposed Othello Mine." As you requested, MMT Consulting has considered the annual costs and the capital costs for each of diesel trucks, diesel trains, electric trains, and electric fleets.

We found that the best method of comparing the four transportation alternatives relies on the accounting vehicle known as Equivalent Uniform Annual Costs (EUAC). Using this vehicle, we have calculated costs for all alternatives in a consistent manner. After all costs are compared, your choice will depend on the cost of borrowing and on the length of time you operate the Othello mine. For example, at a rate of 6%, diesel trains provide the best alternative for the first 12 years of operation, while at the same rate, electric trains give the best value for operations lasting beyond 12 years.

I would be pleased to discuss this report's findings with your Board of Directors. Please phone me at (250) 868-4040 during business hours, or call my cell number, (250) 868-3445 at other times.

This project has been very interesting, in all respects. If you would like to discuss how MMT Consulting could further assist with the Othello project, you will find me eager to do so.

Sincerely,

Art Basran, P.Eng.
Kelowna Branch Manager

Figure 19.6   A Formal Analytical Report—Transmittal Document   **(Continued)**

COST ANALYSIS OF FOUR ALTERNATIVES FOR HAULING COAL FROM THE PROPOSED OTHELLO MINE

For the Jackson Mining Company
Grand Forks, British Columbia

Prepared by MMT Consulting
Kelowna, British Columbia

Submitted:
April 14, 2009

Figure 19.6   A Formal Analytical Report   (*Continued*)

MMT Consulting

EXECUTIVE SUMMARY

The proposed Othello mine has an expected annual production of five million tons. The mine requires a cost-effective method of transporting the coal from the minesite to the mainline railroad.

Four suggested alternatives were analyzed, considering various interest rates and study periods:
1. Diesel trucks
2. Diesel trains
3. Electric trains
4. Electric fleets

Capital costs and annual operating costs were determined for each alternative, and combined to form an Equivalent Uniform Annual Cost. Figure 1 shows the results for the preferred interest rate of 6%.

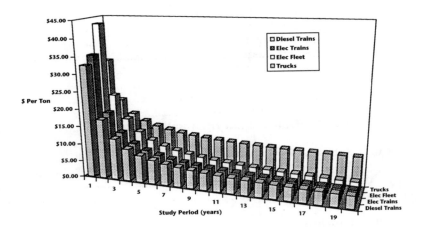

Figure 1: EUAC for Alternatives at 6%

Diesel trains and electric trains were the two preferred alternatives. The EUAC calculations revealed that the cost curves for diesel trains and electric trains cross at different points, depending on the interest rate. At an interest rate of 6%, the curves cross at 12 years. Therefore, from 1 to 12 years, diesel trains are preferred, and after 12 years, electric trains are preferred. This crossover year increases with increasing interest rates.

Therefore, if both the study period and the interest rate are known to the investors, the preferred alternative can be chosen from the calculations provided in this report. Other factors may affect the investors' choice of transportation for Othello mine coal, but these factors are outside the scope of this report.

ii.

Figure 19.6   A Formal Analytical Report   **(Continued)**

MMT Consulting

TABLE OF CONTENTS

iii.

Figure 19.6　A Formal Analytical Report

(Continued)

LIST OF ILLUSTRATIONS

Figures

Tables

iv.

Figure 19.6   A Formal Analytical Report   **(Continued)**

1.0 INTRODUCTION

1.1 The Situation

The Jackson Mining Company has discovered a high-grade coal deposit in the mountains about 55 miles due north of Grand Forks, British Columbia. The company expects the market for this grade of coal to increase dramatically in the near future, and thus anticipates developing the deposit if development and transportation costs are acceptable. Jackson Mining has tentatively named its proposed minesite as the Othello mine. MMT Consulting has been authorized to determine the most cost-effective method(s) of transporting the coal from that minesite to the mainline railroad, a distance of approximately 50 miles (Jackson Mining, 1999, p.16).

Four transport alternatives will be considered in the following analysis:

1. Diesel trucks
2. Diesel trains
3. Electric trains
4. Electric fleets.

The criterion used to evaluate each option is the Equivalent Uniform Annual Cost (the EUAC). EUAC is a cost measure that considers startup (capital) costs as well as annual operating and maintenance costs. The EUAC discussed in this report is in dollars per ton, or how much it costs to haul one ton of coal from the minesite to the railhead.

The alternatives will be studied over study periods ranging from one to twenty years, and at interest rates varying from 6% to 10%. A short evaluation of each alternative's capacity to handle an increase in production is also provided.

1.2 Limitations

All calculations and recommendations are based on the assumption that fuel and electricity costs will remain constant or comparable throughout the study period.

1.3 Background

The Othello mine under study has anticipated coal sales of five million tons annually (Jackson Mining, 1999, p. 6). Each of the following transportation alternatives would have to handle this volume. Also, the ability to expand in the future would be an asset.

1.3.1 Diesel trucks

The CAT 777B truck was chosen for this study because of its load capacity of 95 tons and its output of 920 horsepower. These trucks would be running 24 hours a day.

1.3.2 Diesel trains

Each train would be running with six diesel engines and 98 coal cars. It takes 11.2 hours to complete a round trip, and the time it takes to produce the amount of coal the train hauls is 17.2 hours. Thus, the train would haul a complete load and then idle for about 6 hours until the next load was ready.

1.

Figure 19.6   A Formal Analytical Report   (*Continued*)

1.3.3 Electric trains

Each train would run four electric engines and 98 coal cars. The haul times are the same as quoted for the diesel train.

1.3.4 Electric fleets

Each fleet would consist of three of the above electric trains. The first train would be loaded and sent off. While it was enroute, the second train would be loading, and this load-and-go process would be repeated for the third train. The departures would be timed so that the second train leaves just as the first train crests the highest point of the pass through which the rail line runs. This would also be repeated for the third train. In this way, the electricity generated by the first and second trains on their downgrades could be conserved and used to assist in powering the second and third trains on their upgrades.

Four sidings would need to be constructed in order to allow the outgoing and returning trains to pass each other. However, these sidings are proposed for options 2 and 3 as well.

Complete specifications for all four alternatives can be found in Appendix G.

2.0 COST ANALYSIS

Data has been collected for the capital costs and for the annual operating costs for all alternatives. Much of this data is available in Merrill Lynch's *Industrial Guides* (Jacobs, 1994, pp.140-175 and Ringness, 1998, pp. 242-63).

2.1 Annual Costs

The annual costs involve three main components:

1. fuel
2. labour, and
3. maintenance.

2.1.1 Fuel consumption

Fuel consumption is a major factor because of the large amounts of energy required to transport five million tons of coal annually. Calculating fuel requirements is complicated—Appendix A contains the full breakdown of fuel calculations for the alternative hauling methods. Such calculations are based on the total resistance faced by a particular method of hauling the coal. For an example of how total resistance is calculated, see Table 1, which calculates the resistance for diesel trucks on the proposed road.

2.

Figure 19.6   A Formal Analytical Report

(Continued)

MMT Consulting

Table 1: Tractive and Grade Resistances for Diesel Trucks

Section	Grade (%)	Truck Wt (ton)	Load Wt	Total Wt	Rt (lb)	Rg	Tr
G	2.0	66.3	95.0	161.3	16,125.0	6,450.0	22,575.0
F	1.8	66.3	95.0	161.3	16,125.0	5,805.0	21,930.0
E	2.0	66.3	95.0	161.3	16,125.0	6,450.0	22,575.0
D	2.1	66.3	95.0	161.3	16,125.0	6,772.5	22,897.5

The first column in Table 1 lists the sections into which the road has been divided for analytical purposes. These sections of road have varying grades. Grade resistance (Rg) and tractive resistance (Tr) are found for each section. (Sample calculations for these are given in Appendix E.) The calculated total resistance (Tr) is then used in the next table (Table 2).

Table 2: Speed, Power, and Fuel Consumption for Diesel Trucks

Section	Grade (%)	Tr (lb)	Power (hp)	Speed (mph)	Dist (mi)	Time (hr)	BTU (x1000)	Fuel Burned	Total Fuel
G	2.0	22,575.0	920.0	12.55	8.4	0.67	1,572.5	11.34	42.62
F	1.8	21,930.0	920.0	12.92	7.2	0.56	1,309.3	9.44	35.49
E	2.0	22,575.0	920.0	12.55	5.4	0.43	1,010.9	7.29	27.40
D	2.1	22,897.5	920.0	12.38	4.8	0.39	911.4	6.57	24.70

As in Table 2, the speed for each section is calculated, given the maximum power output of the alternative, to a maximum of 30 mph. The distance and time are then calculated and used to find total BTU per section of road. Finally, the total fuel consumed per section is determined; this depends on the fuel efficiency of that transportation alternative. All the calculated values for the various sections of road are added together to find the fuel consumed per trip. Then, given the cost of fuel, a total cost per trip is found.

2.1.2 Labour
The next component of annual cost is labour. The method used to calculate labour differs from the trucks to the trains. Since the trucks are assumed to run 24 hours a day, the total hours per year is multiplied by the number of drivers and further by their hourly wage rate. In the other approach, the time per trip for the trains is calculated. That figure is multiplied by the number of engine staff and train persons needed, and further by their hourly rate. The results of these calculations can be found in Appendix B.

2.1.3 Maintenance
This third component of annual operating costs can be further divided into unit maintenance and road maintenance. Road or rail maintenance is given as a cost per mile, and then multiplied by the total distance covered. The results of these calculations appear in Appendix B.

3.

Figure 19.6   A Formal Analytical Report   **(Continued)**

2.2 Capital Costs

Capital costs for each of the four alternatives consist of:

1. cost of the transportation units
2. cost of construction, and
3. cost of communication systems.

2.2.1 Transportation units

The number of required units was found by taking the annual output of the mine and calculating the number of units that would haul the coal with the maximum efficiency. It was found that 30 diesel trucks and trains of 98 cars were needed. Seven extra trucks would be purchased, to allow for expansion and also to allow trucks to be taken off the road for maintenance.

2.2.2 Construction costs

Construction costs can be determined by examining three main factors:

1. road and rail construction
2. the maintenance building, and
3. electrical installations (where applicable).

Road and rail construction were found by multiplying the cost per mile by the total distance covered. For the rail alternatives, the costs of switches, loops, and sidings must be added. Overall, then, the railroad construction costs outweigh road construction costs by more than $45 million. In the case of the maintenance building costs, the truck maintenance facility would be $1.6 million more than the building required for the train options.

The two electric train options involve an additional expense—They require an electric installation, at a cost of $15.7 million. This figure was calculated by multiplying the cost per mile by the total distance and adding the cost of tapping into existing power sources. The full calculations are given in Appendix C.

2.2.3 Communication system

This is the third main component of the capital costs for this project. Such a system is necessary to control the movements of any of the four alternative transportation methods, so the same figure has been used for all four alternatives. A Global Positioning System, on-board computers, and two-way radios make up the complete system.

2.3 Cost Comparisons

The costs for the four alternatives are provided in Table 3 below.

Table 3: Capital and Operating Costs

Option	Capital Costs	Annual Operating Costs
Diesel Trucks	$115,539,000	$38,027,700
Diesel Trains	$149,083,000	$4,574,400
Electric Trains	$161,783,000	$3,061,000
Electric Fleets	$201,463,000	$2,766,600

4.

Figure 19.6   A Formal Analytical Report   **(Continued)**

MMT Consulting

Table 3 makes it clear that there is a direct correlation between the two cost parameters: The more expensive the system is to purchase and install, the less it will cost to operate. However, the investors must also consider the cost of borrowing the required capital funds. This expense, which can be considerable, is factored into a comprehensive comparative tool called the Equivalent Uniform Annual Costs; this measure is discussed next.

2.4 Equivalent Uniform Annual Costs

Once the capital and annual costs are found, they can be combined with varying interest rates and study periods to calculate tables of Equivalent Uniform Annual Costs (EUAC). The purpose of converting all costs into an EUAC is to provide a common means of comparing all the alternatives. The capital costs are spread over the length of the study period, and added to the annual costs. Thus, a comparison of EUACs will yield a qualitative assessment of the alternatives to go with the quantitative assessment suggested by Table 3 (Winters, October 7, 1999).

Figure 1 below gives a graphic representation of EUAC for the four alternatives, with study periods ranging from one to twenty years, at an interest rate of 6%. The format of the graph makes it easy to compare the four alternatives at this interest rate. For example, at an interest rate of 6% diesel trains provide the most cost-effective method of transporting coal from the mine for study periods from two to twelve years.

The sharp decline in EUAC after the early study periods reflects the fact that the capital costs are being spread over longer and longer study periods. For shorter study periods, the capital costs play a larger role in determining EUAC, while for longer periods the annual operating cost is the more significant determinant. A full summary of EUAC for interest rates of 6%, 7%, 8%, 9%, and 10% appears in Appendix D.

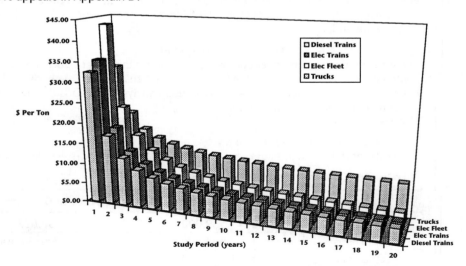

Figure 1: EUAC for Four Alternatives at 6%

5.

Figure 19.6   A Formal Analytical Report   (*Continued*)

MMT Consulting

3.0 POTENTIAL FOR EXPANSION

Market conditions or additional discoveries of coal seams may result in mine expansion. If this proves to be the case, it would require an increase in the transportation of coal. Thus, it is prudent to examine each transport alternative's potential for expansion.

3.1 Diesel Trucks

In order to protect against breakdowns, 37 diesel trucks would be purchased, although only 30 are needed to effectively haul the coal from the minesite at a time. This leaves seven trucks for immediate expansion. In other words, an immediate increase of 23.3% could be achieved. Also, it is very easy for a trucking system to grow with the mine, because one or two additional units can readily be purchased as needed.

3.2 Diesel and Electric Trains

It takes both the diesel and electric trains 11.2 hours to complete a round trip, while it takes the mine 17.2 hours to produce enough coal for a full load. Therefore, six hours are spent idle waiting for the next load. This leaves room for a 53.5% increase in production. Increases past this amount would result in either adding more cars and engines to the trains, or switching to fleets of trains. Both of these are expensive capital options.

3.3 Electric Fleets

It takes the electric fleets 22.4 hours to complete a round trip, while it takes the mine 51.6 hours to produce enough coal for a full load. Therefore, 29.2 hours are spent idle waiting for the next load. This idle time leaves room for a 130% increase in production. Increases past this amount would result in either adding more cars and engines to the trains, or adding more fleets. Again, this expansion involves expensive capital options.

Figure 19.6   A Formal Analytical Report   **(Continued)**

4.0   CONCLUSION

The tables in Appendix D (pages 30-41) contain the Equivalent Uniform Annual Cost values for the four options at varying interest rates. Using the EUAC method clearly shows that the diesel and electric train options give much better results than the diesel trucks and the electric train fleets.

However, it is not easy to choose between the diesel train and electric train options, as the following tables show. The diesel train option is the better alternative for the first 12 or so years, after which the electric train option becomes slightly better.

Table 4: Diesel Trains as Best Alternative

% Interest Rate	Study Period (yrs)
6	1 to 12
7	1 to 13
8	1 to 14.5
9	1 to 16
10	1 to 19

Table 5: Electric Trains as Best Alternative

% Interest Rate	Study Period (yrs)
6	1 to 12
7	over 13
8	over 14.5
9	over 16
10	over 17

Although Tables 4 and 5 show that the diesel train option has a slight overall edge in EUAC, the figures throughout the study periods are quite close. For more details of just how close these figures are, see the following appendices.

In any event, the choice between diesel and electric trains may depend on additional factors, not just transportation cost analysis. One prime consideration will be how long the investors plan to operate the mine. This in turn will depend on factors such as the continuing quality of the coal deposits, the market demand, and the market price of coal. Other criteria might include the availability of diesel fuel or electricity, expected fuel or wage increases, or environmental concerns.

These additional factors are beyond the scope of this report and must be decided by the investors.

7.

Figure 19.6   A Formal Analytical Report   (*Continued*)

MMT Consulting

REFERENCES CITED

Jackson Mining. (1999). *Othello minesite proposal.* Presented to the British Columbia Ministry of the Environment and the Ministry of Small Business, Tourism, and Culture.

Jacobs, G. (1994). *Merrill Lynch industrial calculation guide.* New York: Wiseman Press.

Ringness, A. (1998). 1998 *update: Merrill Lynch industrial calculation guide.* New York: Wiseman Press.

Winters, Brendan. Letter to MTM Consulting. October 7, 1999.

8.

Figure 19.6   A Formal Analytical Report   (*Continued*)

ADDITIONAL SOURCES CONSULTED

Chartwell, Y. K. (January, 1994). Power consumption calculations: A planners' guide. *Transportation Today*, pp. 123-182.

Connors, C. S. (May 24, 1994). *Mining feasibility of the proposed Othello mine.* Confidential report for Jackson Mining, prepared by Connors Bowles, Mining Engineer Consultants, Calgary.

Siemens Electrical Corporation. (1995). *Siemens electric engines: Specifications and fleet rates.* Seattle: Siemens International Sales Department.

9.

Figure 19.6   A Formal Analytical Report   (*Continued*)

MMT Consulting

APPENDIX A: FUEL CONSUMPTION CALCULATIONS

> Note: For purposes of this text, only page 12 has been included.

Figure 19.6   A Formal Analytical Report[1]   (*Continued*)

1. The remainder of the 38 pages of appendices has been omitted, to save space.

MMT Consulting

Table 6: Tractive and Grade Resistances for Diesel Trucks

	Section	Grade (%)	Truck Wt (ton)	Load Wt	Total Wt	Rt (lb)	Rg	Tr
Trip from mine	G	2.0	66.3	95.0	161.3	16,125.0	6,450.0	22,575.0
	F	1.8	66.3	95.0	161.3	16,125.0	5,805.0	21,930.0
	E	2.0	66.3	95.0	161.3	16,125.0	6,450.0	22,575.0
	D	2.1	66.3	95.0	161.3	16,125.0	6,772.5	22,897.0
	C	-1.7	66.3	95.0	161.3	16,125.0	-5,482.0	10,642.0
	B	-2.2	66.3	95.0	161.3	16,125.0	-7,095.0	9,030.0
	A	-2.0	66.3	95.0	161.3	16,125.0	-6,450.0	9,675.0
Trip to mine	A	2.0	66.3	0.0	66.3	6,625.0	2,650.0	9,275.0
	B	2.2	66.3	0.0	66.3	6,625.0	2,915.0	9,540.0
	C	1.7	66.3	0.0	66.3	6,625.0	2,252.5	8,877.5
	D	2.1	66.3	0.0	66.3	6,625.0	2,782.5	9,407.5
	E	2.0	66.3	0.0	66.3	6,625.0	2,650.0	9,275.0
	F	-1.8	66.3	0.0	66.3	6,625.0	-2,385.0	4,240.0
	G	-2.0	66.3	0.0	66.3	6,625.0	-2,650.0	3,975.0

12.

Figure 19.6   A Formal Analytical Report

Revision and Editing Checklist for Analytical Reports

Use this checklist to refine the content, arrangement, and style of your report.

CONTENT

- ❏ Does the report grow from a clear statement of purpose?
- ❏ Is the report's length adequate and appropriate for the subject?
- ❏ Are all limitations of the analysis clearly acknowledged?
- ❏ Are visuals used whenever possible to aid communication?
- ❏ Are all data accurate?
- ❏ Are all data unbiased?
- ❏ Are all data complete?
- ❏ Are all data fully interpreted?
- ❏ Is the documentation adequate, correct, and consistent?
- ❏ Are the conclusions logically derived from accurate interpretation?
- ❏ Do the recommendations constitute an appropriate response to the question or problem?

ARRANGEMENT

- ❏ Is there a distinct introduction, body, and conclusion?
- ❏ Are headings appropriate and adequate?
- ❏ Are there enough transitions between related ideas?
- ❏ Is the report accompanied by all needed front matter?
- ❏ Is the report accompanied by all needed end matter?

STYLE AND PAGE DESIGN

- ❏ Is the level of technicality appropriate for the stated audience?
- ❏ Is the writing style throughout clear, concise, and fluent?
- ❏ Is the language convincing and precise?
- ❏ Is the report written in grammatical English?
- ❏ Is the page design inviting and accessible?

☑ EXERCISE

Prepare an analytical report, using some sequence of these guidelines:

a. Choose a subject for analysis from the list your instructor provides, from your major, or from a subject of interest.

b. Identify the problem or question so that you will know exactly what you are looking for.

c. Restate the main question as a declarative sentence in your statement of purpose.

d. Identify an audience—other than your instructor—who will use your information for a specific purpose.

e. Hold a private brainstorming session to generate major topics and subtopics.

f. Use the topics to make an outline based on the model outline in this chapter. Divide as far as necessary to identify all points of discussion.

g. Make a tentative list of all sources (primary and secondary) that you will investigate. Verify that adequate sources are available.

h. Write your instructor a proposal memo, describing the problem or question and your plan for analysis. Attach a tentative bibliography.

i. Use your planning outline as a guide to research and observation. Evaluate sources and evidence, and interpret all evidence fully. Modify your outline as needed.

j. Read Chapter 21 and then submit a progress report to your instructor describing work completed, problems encountered, and work remaining. Attach a detailed working outline.

k. Compose an audience/purpose profile. (Use the sample on pages 480–482 as models, along with the profile worksheet on page 85).

l. Write the report for your stated audience. Work from a clear statement of purpose, and be sure that your reasoning is shown clearly. Verify that your evidence, conclusions, and recommendations are consistent. Be especially careful that your recommendations observe the critical-thinking guidelines in Figure 19.1.

m. After writing your first draft, make any needed changes in the outline and revise your report according to the revision checklist. Include all necessary supplements.

n. Exchange reports with a colleague for further suggestions for revision.

o. Prepare an oral report of your findings for the class as a whole.

☑ COLLABORATIVE PROJECTS

1. Divide into small groups. Choose a subject for group analysis—preferably, a campus issue—and partition the topic by group brainstorming. Next, select major topics from your list and classify as many items as possible under each major topic. Finally, draw up a working outline that could be used for an analytical report on this subject.

2. Prepare a questionnaire based on your work above, and administer it to members of your campus community. List the findings of your questionnaire and your conclusions in clear and logical form. (Review pages 137–142, on questionnaires and surveys.)

Adding Document Supplements

Purpose of Supplements

Cover

Transmittal Document

Title Page

Summary

Table of Contents

List of Figures and Tables

Documentation

Glossary

Appendices

SUPPLEMENTS are reference items generally added to a long report or proposal to make the document more accessible. A document's supplements accommodate readers with various interests: The title page, letter of transmittal, table of contents, and abstract give summary information about the content of the document. The glossary, appendices, and list of works cited can either provide supporting data or help readers follow technical sections. According to their needs, readers can refer to one or more of these supplements or skip them altogether. All supplements, of course, are written only after the document itself has been completed.

Some companies and organizations require that a full range of supplements routinely accompany any long document: others do not. For situations in which your audience has not stipulated its requirements, select only those supplements that enhance the informative value of your particular document. Avoid using supplements merely as decoration.

Purpose of Supplements

Documents must be accessible to varied readers for many purposes. Supplements address these workplace realities:

- *Confronted by a long document, many readers will try to avoid reading the whole thing.* Instead they look for the least information they need to complete the task, make the decision, or take some other action.

- *Different readers often use the same document for different purposes.* Some look for an overview; others want details; others want only conclusions and recommendations, or the "bottom line." Technical personnel might focus on the body of a highly specialized report and on the appendices for supporting data (maps, formulas, calculations). Executives and managers might read only the transmittal letter and the executive summary. If the latter audience reads any parts of the report proper, they are likely to focus on conclusions and recommendations.

A document with carefully planned supplements accommodates the needs of diverse audiences.

Report supplements can be classified into two groups:

1. *supplements that precede your report* (front matter): transmittal document, cover, title page, summary, table of contents, and list of illustrations.
2. *supplements that follow your report* (back matter): glossary, appendices, footnotes, endnote pages.

Cover

Use a sturdy, plain cover with page fasteners. With the cover on, the open pages should lie flat. Use covers only for long documents.

Centre the report title and your name four to five inches below the upper edge of your page (many workplace reports include a company name and logo instead of the report author's name).

THE FEASIBILITY OF A TECHNICAL MARKETING CAREER
by
Richard B. Larkin

Transmittal Document

For college reports, the transmittal document (memo or letter) sometimes follows the title page and is bound as part of the report. For workplace reports, the transmittal document usually is not bound in the report, but is presented separately. Include a transmittal document with any formal report or proposal addressed to a specific reader. Your letter or memo adds a note of courtesy and gives you a place for personal remarks. For instance, your letter or memo might:

What to include in a transmittal document

- acknowledge those who helped with the report
- refer to sections of special interest: unexpected findings, key visuals, major conclusions, special recommendations, and the like
- discuss the limitations of your study, or any problems gathering data
- discuss the need and approaches for follow-up investigations
- describe any personal (or off-the-record) observations
- suggest some special uses for the information
- urge the reader to immediate action

The transmittal document can be tailored to a particular reader, as is Richard Larkin's in Figure 20.1 on page 520. If a report is being sent to a number of people who are variously qualified and bear various relationships to the writer, individual transmittal documents may vary, within the following basic structure:

Introduction. Open with reference to the reader's original request. Briefly review the reasons for your report or include a brief descriptive abstract. Maintain a confident and positive tone throughout. Indicate pride and satisfaction in your work. Avoid implied apologies, such as "I hope this report meets your expectations."

Body. In the body, include items from your prior list of possibilities (acknowledgments, special problems). Although your informative abstract will summarize major findings, conclusions, and recommendations, your letter or memo gives a brief and personal overview of the *entire project*.

Conclusion. State your willingness to answer questions or discuss findings. End positively with something like "I believe that the data in this report are accurate, that they have been analyzed rigourously and impartially, and that the recommendations are sound."

7409 Trinity Court
Niagra Falls, ON   L2H 3A6
April 29, 2008

Ms. Mimi Lim
Placement Director
Seneca College
1750 Finch Avenue East
North York, ON   M2J 2X5

Dear Ms. Lim:

Here is my analysis to determine the feasibility of a career in technical marketing. In preparing my report, I've learned a great deal about the requirements and modes of access to this career, and I believe my information will help other students as well.

Although committed to their specialities, some technical and science graduates seem interested in careers in which they can apply their technical knowledge to customer and business problems. Technical marketing may be an attractive choice of career for those who know their field, who can relate to different personalities, and who are good communicators.

Technical marketing is competitive and demanding, but highly rewarding. In fact, it is an excellent route to upper-management and executive positions. Specifically, marketing work enables one to develop a sound technical knowledge of a company's products, to understand how these products fit into the marketplace, and to perfect sales techniques and interpersonal skills. This is precisely the kind of background that paves the way to top-level jobs.

I've enjoyed my work on this project, and would be happy to answer any questions.

Sincerely,

Richard B. Larkin

Richard B. Larkin

Figure 20.1   A Letter of Transmittal for a Formal Report

Feasibility of a Career
in Technical Marketing

for
Mimi Lim
Placement Director
Seneca College
North York, Ontario

by
Richard B. Larkin,
English 266 Student

May 1, 2008

Figure 20.2   A Title Page for a Formal Report

Title Page

How to prepare a title page

The title page (see page 521) lists the report title, author's name, name of person(s) or organization to whom the report is addressed, and date of submission.

Title. Your title announces the report's purpose and subject. The previous title (given as an example for the cover) is clear, accurate, comprehensive, and specific. But even slight changes can distort this title's signal.

An unclear   A TECHNICAL MARKETING CAREER
title

The version above is unclear about the report's purpose. Is the report *describing* the career, *proposing* the career, *giving instructions* for career preparation, or *telling one person's career story*? Insert descriptive words ("analysis," "instructions," "proposal," "feasibility," "description," "progress") that accurately state your purpose.

To be sure that your title forecasts what the report delivers, write its final version *after* completing the report.

Placement of Title Page Items. Do not number your title page but count it as page i of your preliminary pages. Centre the title horizontally, 8–10 cm (3″–4″) below the upper edge. Place other items in the spacing and order shown in Figure 20.2 on page 521, the title page to a report. Or devise your own system, as long as your page is balanced.

Summary

Chapter 9 defines varieties of summary writing, including the summary (or executive summary) which *accompanies* a formal report or proposal (as shown in Figure 20.3). Many readers who don't have the time or willingness to read your entire report will consider the summary to be the most useful part of the material you present.

Chapter 9 also recommends a step-by-step process that will help you find and condense the elements of a good summary:

- the issue or need which led to the report
- the report's key facts, statistics, findings, and in some cases, illustrations—this is the material your reader *must* know
- the report's conclusions and recommendations

When you write and edit the summary, make clear connections between the report's data and interpretations. If you find yourself unable to do this in the summary, you'll probably need to revise the original report.

Follow these guidelines for the report summary:

1. Make the summary about 1/10 the length of the original, but remember that summaries rarely are shorter than 3/4 page or longer than five pages.
2. Where appropriate, use a table to summarize key facts and findings.

SUMMARY

The feasibility of technical marketing as a career is based on a college graduate's interests, abilities, and expectations, as well as on possible entry options.

Technical marketing is a feasible career for anyone who is motivated, who can communicate well, and who knows how to get along. Although this career offers job diversity and excellent potential for income, it entails almost constant travel, competition, and stress.

College graduates enter technical marketing through one of four options: entry-level positions that offer hands-on experience, formal training programs in large companies, prior experience in one's specialty, or graduate programs. The relative advantages and disadvantages of each option can be measured in resulting immediacy of income, rapidity of advancement, and long-term potential.

Anyone considering a technical marketing career should follow these recommendations:

- Speak with people who work in the field.
- Weigh carefully the implications of each entry option.
- Consider combining two or more options.
- Choose options for personal as well as professional benefits.

Figure 20.3   A Summary

3. Add no new information. Simply give the report's highlights.
4. Use the same order of topics in the summary as in the original.
5. Adjust the vocabulary to suit the intended reader. An executive summary, for example, includes little technical jargon. When you send report copies to readers with varying levels of expertise, write a different summary for each type of reader.
6. Include a graph or other figure in the summary *only* if the illustration is absolutely necessary in understanding the report.

TABLE OF CONTENTS

Figure 20.4   A Table of Contents for a Formal Report

Table of Contents

Your table of contents serves as a road map for readers and a checklist for you. If you are using a high-end word processing program, you can generate a table of contents automatically provided that you have assigned styles or codes to all of the headings in your report. If your word processing program does not have this feature, compose the table of contents by assigning page numbers to headings from your outline. Keep in mind, however, that not all levels of outline headings appear in your table of contents or your report. Excessive headings can fragment the discussion.

Follow these guidelines:

How to prepare a table of contents

- List front matter (summary, list of illustrations), numbering the pages with small Roman numerals. (The title page, though not listed, is counted as page i.) List back matter such as glossary, appendices, and endnotes. Number these pages with Arabic numerals, continuing the page sequence of your main report.
- Include in the table of contents only headings or subheadings that are in the report; the report may, however, contain subheadings not listed in the table of contents.
- Phrase headings in the table of contents exactly as in the report.
- List various levels of headings with varying typefaces and indentions.
- Use *leader lines* (. . . . .) to connect the heading text to the page number. Align rows of dots vertically, each above the other.

Figure 20.4 on page 524 shows the table of contents for Richard Larkin's feasibility analysis.

List of Figures and Tables

Following the table of contents is a list of figures and tables, if needed. When a report has three or more visuals, place this table on a separate page. List the figures first, then the tables. Figure 20.5 on page 526 shows the list of figures and tables for Larkin's report. Also see the extensive list of illustrations in Figure 19.6 on page 503.

Documentation

As Chapter 8 demonstrates, reference pages are organized according to the format required by your workplace or academic discipline. MLA and APA formats require references to be listed in alphabetical order on a Works Cited page or References page. The CBE format lists sources in the same numerical order as they are cited in the report.

Whichever documentation format you use, consider including a separate list of sources you consulted, but did not cite. For these, use a heading like Additional Sources Consulted. Thus, you will:

FIGURES AND TABLES

Figure 20.5   A List of Figures and Tables for a Formal Report

- show your reader that you have indeed covered all the bases
- acknowledge that certain sources influenced your thinking, even if you didn't have reason to cite them specifically, and
- serve the reader who wishes to explore the topic further

Glossary

A glossary alphabetically lists specialized terms and their definitions, following or preceding your report. Specialized reports often contain glossaries, especially when written for both technical and non-technical readers. A glossary makes key definitions available to non-technical readers without interrupting the flow of the report for technical readers. If fewer than five terms need defining, place them in the report introduction as working definitions, or use footnote definitions. If you use a separate glossary, inform readers of its location: "(see the glossary at the end of this report)." Note, though, that some readers prefer the glossary in the front matter, just before the introduction.

How to prepare a glossary

Follow these guidelines for a glossary:

- Define all terms unfamiliar to a general reader (an intelligent layperson).
- Define all terms that have a special meaning in your report (e.g., "In this report, a small business is defined as").
- Define all terms by giving their class and distinguishing features, unless some terms need expanded definitions.
- List your glossary and its first page number in your table of contents.
- List all terms in alphabetical order. Boldface each term. You may use a colon to separate the term from its single-spaced definition. This is not necessary if you use a tablar format.
- Define only terms that need explanation. In doubtful cases, over-defining is safer than underdefining.

Figure 20.6 shows part of a non-tabular glossary for a comparative analysis of two techniques of natural childbirth, written by a nurse practitioner for expectant mothers and student nurses. Figure 20.7 illustrates a partial tabular glossary.

Appendices

An appendix follows the text of your report. It expands items discussed in the report without cluttering the report text. Typical items in an appendix include:

What an appendix might include

- complex formulas
- details of an experiment
- interview questions and responses
- long quotations (one or more pages)
- maps or photographs
- material more essential to secondary readers than to primary readers

GLOSSARY

Analgesic: a medication given to relieve pain during the first stage of labour.

Cervix: the neck-shaped anatomical structure that forms the mouth of the uterus.

Dilation: cervical expansion occurring during the first stage of labour.

Episiotomy: an incision of the outer vaginal tissue, made by the obstetrician just before the delivery, to enlarge the vaginal opening.

First stage of labour: the stage in which the cervix dilates and the baby remains in the uterus.

Induction: the stimulating of labour by puncturing the membranes around the baby or by giving an oxytoxic drug (uterine contractant), or both.

Figure 20.6   A Non-tabular Glossary (Partial)

GLOSSARY

| **Analgesic:** | A medication given to relieve pain during the first stage of labour. |
| **Cervix:** | The neck-shaped anatomical structure that forms the mouth of the uterus. |

Figure 20.7   A Tabular Glossary (Partial)

- related correspondence (letters of enquiry, and so on)
- sample questionnaires and tabulated responses
- sample tests and tabulated results
- some visuals occupying more than one full page
- statistical or other measurements
- texts of laws and regulations

The appendix is a catch-all for items that are important but difficult to integrate within your text. Figure 20.8 on page 530 shows an appendix to a budget proposal. Also see appendix pages in the sample report in Figure 19.6 on page 513.

Do not stuff appendices with needless information. Do not use them unethically for burying bad or embarrassing news that belongs in the report proper. Follow these guidelines:

How to prepare an appendix

- Include only material that is relevant.
- Use a separate appendix for each major item.
- Title each appendix clearly: "Appendix A: Projected Costs."
- Limit an appendix to a few pages, unless more length is essential.
- Mention your appendix early in your introduction, and refer readers to it at appropriate points in the report: "(see Appendix A)."

Use an appendix for any material that is essential but might harm the unity and coherence of your report. Remember that readers should be able to understand your report without having to turn to the appendix. Distill the essential facts from your appendix and place them in your report text.

APPENDIX A

Table 1 Allocations and Performance of Five College Newspapers

	Red Deer College	Durham College	Kelsey College	Holland College	Yukon College
Enrollment	1,600	1,400	3,000	3,000	5,000
Fee paid (per year)	$65.00	$85.00	$35.00	$50.00	$65.00
Total fee budget	$88,000	$119,000	$105,000	$150,000	$334,429.28
Newspaper budget	$10,000	$6,000	$25,300	$37,000	$21,500
Yearly cost per student	$6.25	$4.29	$8.43	$12.33	$25,337.14[a] $4.06 $5.20[a]
Format of paper	Weekly	Every third week	Weekly	Weekly	Weekly
Average no. of pages	8	12	18	12	20
Average total pages	224	120	504	336	560 672[a]
Yearly cost per page	$44.50	$50.00	$50.50	$110.11	$38.25 $38.69[a]

[a]These figures are next year's costs for the Yukon *Torch*.

Source: Figures were quoted by newspaper business managers in April 2008.

Figure 20.8   An Appendix

☑ EXERCISES

1. These titles are intended for investigative, research, or analytical reports. Revise each inadequate title to make it clear and accurate.

   a. The Effectiveness of the Prison Furlough Program in Our Province

   b. Drug Testing on the Job

   c. The Effects of Nuclear Power Plants

   d. Woodburning Stoves

   e. Interviewing

   f. An Analysis of Vegetables (for a report assessing the physiological effects of a vegetarian diet)

   g. Wood as a Fuel Source

   h. Oral Contraceptives

   i. Lie Detectors and Employees

2. Prepare a title page, transmittal document (for a definite reader who can use your information in a definite way), table of contents, and informative abstract for a report you have written earlier.

3. Find a short but effective appendix in one of your textbooks: In a journal article in your field, or in a report from your workplace. In a memo to your instructor and colleagues, explain how the appendix is used, how it relates to the main text, and why it is effective. Attach a copy of the appendix to your memo. Be prepared to discuss your evaluation in class.

☑ COLLABORATIVE PROJECT

Collect samples of various document supplements. As a group, critique the format and content of the supplements.

Short Reports

Short reports form the bulk of the writing done by technologists, technicians, research scientists, and engineers. Such reports provide information and analysis that readers use to stay informed and to make practical decisions.

Some reports emphasize <u>information</u>:

- progress reports
- trip reports
- field observations
- project completion reports
- periodic activity reports
- meeting minutes

Other reports focus on <u>analysis</u>:

- feasibility reports
- causal analysis
- assessment reports
- yardstick (comparison) reports
- justification reports
- recommendations reports

Formats

When a document is quite short (1 to 3 pages), or when its subject matter suits a direct, informal address to the reader, use a *correspondence format* such as a letter, memo, or e-mail. For details of letter, memo, and e-mail formats, see Chapter 22.

When a document is somewhat longer (4 to 10 pages), and when its subject matter is serious enough to warrant a more formal approach, use a *semi-formal report format*. However, use a *formal report format*, as illustrated in Chapter 19, when you want to influence policy within your organization: The more formal the document, the better chance of its being heeded. So, consider "dressing up" even 6- to 10-page reports in formal report clothing if you really want to impress the reader. Table 21.1 summarizes the differences between semi-formal and formal report formats.

Table 21.1   Semi-formal and Formal Report Formats   (*Continued*)

Item	Semi-formal	Formal
Length	4-10 pages	6 pages +
Required Sections		
Transmittal document	optional	yes
Cover	no	optional
Title page	optional—title could be placed on first page of report body	yes
Summary	no	yes
Table of contents	optional	yes
List of illustrations	optional	yes
Glossary	incorporate into text	optional
Introduction	yes	yes
Background	optional	optional
Central analysis	one or more sections	one or more sections

Table 21.1   Semi-formal and Formal Report Formats

Item	Semi-formal	Formal
Conclusion	yes	yes
Recommendations	optional	optional
Sources cited	optional	yes (if sources were cited)
Sources consulted	optional	optional
Format and Appearance		
Headings system	more relaxed; seldom more than two levels of headings; main headings placed where they come on the page	formal; usually three or four levels; each main heading placed at the top of a page
Page numbering	all page numbers placed at same location on page	different for first page of a section than for subsequent pages in that section
Margins	all pages use same margins layout	top and bottom margins for first page of a section are larger than for subsequent pages
Indentation	paragraphs not indented (double-space between paragraphs); bulleted and numbered lists may be indented	paragraphs not indented; double-space between paragraphs bulleted and numbered lists may be indented
Headers	seldom used	optional, but headers used in most professional reports

A Structure for all Purposes

Readers of business reports are generally busy people. They want reports to be as brief as possible. They usually want a report's main point in the first or second paragraph and they want clear, logical idea patterns. The *action structure* illustrated in Figure 21.1, on page 535, satisfies those readers' desires.

Action Opening

Using the action structure, you immediately "connect" with your reader by:

- referring to an issue that concerns the reader (and you); or
- referring to comments made in a recent meeting; or
- responding to the reader's previous communication (memo, e-mail, letter, telephone call) on the subject

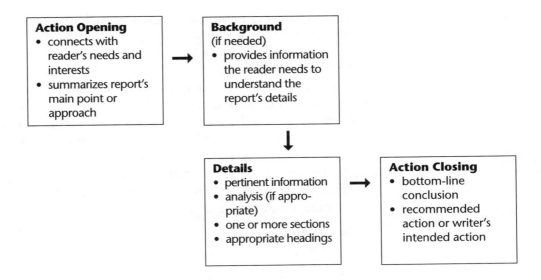

Figure 21.1   An Action Structure for Informal and Semi-formal Reports

By making such a connection, you gain the reader's attention. Then, in the same paragraph you summarize the report's main point *or* you preview the approach taken in the report.

Background

Next, you provide any background needed by your reader to understand the report's detailed information and analysis. You may have to:

- review the circumstances leading to the issue discussed in the report
- define terms
- provide technical background
- review a problem or a proposed solution

Not all reports require background information. Your audience/purpose analysis will help you determine whether your reader needs to be briefed. You may be able to go straight from the opening paragraph to the Details section of the report.

   Most readers appreciate subject headings for both the Background and the Details sections, even for a one-page report. Clearly, the number of headings you use depends on the depth and complexity of the report's topic. See this chapter's sample reports for examples of headings usage. As you read the reports, distinguish between standard topical headings ("Project Costs") and talking headings, that speak directly to the reader ("How Much We've Spent").

Details

Essentially, a report's Details section answers most, if not all, of the questions posed by any good reporter: *What? Where? When? Who? How? How much?*

Why? The order in which you answer such questions depends on the subject matter and your reader's priorities.

Action Closing

Finally, the report provides bottom-line conclusions. Most reports also discuss what should be done next. Some reports recommend action to be taken by the reader or the reader's organization; others state what action the writer intends or proposes. Still other reports simply list possible actions without indicating who might take responsibility.

The action structure can be adapted to develop any type of correspondence or short report. The remainder of this chapter demonstrates the action structure's valuable adaptability to various reports:

- Progress reports
- Project completion reports
- Periodic activity reports
- Incident reports
- Inspection reports
- Field trip reports
- Meeting minutes
- Feasibility reports
- Causal analyses
- Assessment reports
- Recommendations reports
- Lab reports
- Form reports

Let's take a look at each of these reports.

Progress Reports

Large organizations depend on progress (or status) reports to keep track of activities, problems, and progress on various projects. Daily progress reports are vital in a business that assigns crews to many projects. Managers use progress reports to evaluate a project and its supervisor, and to decide how to allocate funds. Managers also need to know about delays that could dramatically affect outcomes and project costs.

Also, managers need information to coordinate the efforts of the work groups. For example, a hydro manager responsible for restoring power transmission lines after a severe ice storm will have to coordinate clean-up crews, construction crews, and line crews. A large project such as a major power line restoration would require several written *periodic progress reports.*

When work is performed for an external client, the reports explain to the client how time and money have been spent and how difficulties have been overcome. The reports can therefore be used to assure the clients that the work will be completed on schedule and on budget. Many contracts stipulate when progress will be reported. Failure to report on time may invoke contractual penalties.

To meet managers' and clients' needs, progress reports must answer these questions:

1. *How much has been accomplished since the last report?*
2. *Is the project on schedule?*
3. *If not, what went wrong?*
   a) *How was the problem corrected?*
   b) *How long will it take to get back on schedule?*
4. *What else needs to be done?*
5. *What is the next step?*
6. *Have you encountered any unexpected developments?*
7. *When do you anticipate completion?* Or, (on a long project): *When do you anticipate completion of the next phase?*

The following general structures adapt the action structure to periodic progress reporting. Exactly how you structure the report depends on the nature of the project and on the aspect you want to stress. You could organize the report by:

- the different tasks or sub-contracts involved
- the amount of work completed versus the amount remaining
- phases or time frames identified by the contact or the project manager

---

VARIATION 1: Organized by Task

- Intro: connect with reader/refer to project
- Project description or summary

ROAD BASE PREPARATION
  Progress to date
  - in previous reporting period(s)
  - work done in period just closing
  Work to be completed
  - work planned for next work period
  - work planned for periods thereafter

PAVING
  Progress to date
  - in previous reporting period(s)
  - work done in period just closing
  Work to be completed
  - work planned for next work period
  - work planned for periods thereafter

COST ANALYSIS
- costs to date
- costs in period just closing

CONCLUSION
- overall appraisal of work to date
- cost appraisal
- conclusions and recommendations re: work

Figure 21.2   A Progress Report Organized by Project Task

VARIATION 2: Organized by Work Completed

- Intro: connect with reader/refer to project
- Project description or summary

WORK COMPLETED
    Road base preparation
- in previous reporting period(s)
- work done in period just closing

    Paving
- work planned for next work period
- work planned for periods thereafter

WORK REMAINING
    Road base preparation
- work planned for next work period
- work planned for periods thereafter

    Paving
- work planned for next work period
- work planned for periods thereafter

COST ANALYSIS
- costs to date
- costs in period just closing

CONCLUSION
- overall appraisal of work to date
- cost appraisal
- conclusions and recommendations re: work

Figure 21.3   A Progress Report Organized by Degree of Project Completed

VARIATION 3: Organized by Time Frame

- Intro: connect with reader/refer to project
- Project description/set up chronologically

PHASE 1 (specific dates go here)
    Road base preparation
- work completed
- work to be done or changed

    Paving
- work completed
- work to be done or changed

PHASE 2 (specific dates go here)
    Road base preparation
- work completed
- work to be done or changed

    Paving
- work completed
- work to be done or changed

COST ANALYSIS
- costs to date
- costs in period just closing

CONCLUSION
- overall appraisal of work to date
- cost appraisal
- conclusions and recommendations re: work

Figure 21.4   A Progress Report Organized by Project Time Frame

Figures 21.2–21.4, on pages 537 and 538, illustrate outlines for the three possible structures. These outlines relate to the third in a series of reports for a six-month highway reconstruction project. Which structure would you use?

Any of the three variations could incorporate a special category for "Problems and Setbacks," where appropriate. This category would describe methods for overcoming any problems and setbacks. Alternatively, the report might discuss problems and setbacks under other headings, if the difficulties do not require special treatment. Also, notice that the three sample structures each show only two main sections for reporting progress, but three or more sections may be required.

Two Sample Progress Reports

Figure 21.5, on pages 541–546, illustrates a periodic progress report with its information organized in a manner that distinguishes between "work completed" and "work in progress."

Art Basran is the writer of the report shown in Figure 21.5. As you may recall, he manages the Kelowna, British Columbia, office of MMT Consulting. Art's report is the fourth in a series of oral and written progress reports for his regional manager, Brenda Backstrom, regarding a project that is very important to MMT Consulting. (Chapter 19 features the formal analytical report that Art later presents to the client, Jackson Mining.)

For this progress report, Art has chosen a semi-formal report format instead of a memo. He has selected this format because of the six-page length and because he is trying to persuade his supervisor to support a new method of analyzing combined engineering and accounting data. ■

The second sample progress report, illustrated in Figure 21.6, on pages 546–547, is written by an engineering technology student, Tim Anders.

Tim is reporting progress on a research project to his project supervisor. Tim has had some setbacks in the project, so he takes care of those setbacks before discussing his recent progress. He modifies the "Work Completed/Work to be Completed" structure to suit his particular situation. ■

PROGRESS REGARDING MMT's COST ANALYSIS OF FOUR ALTERNATIVES FOR HAULING COAL FROM JACKSON MINING'S PROPOSED OTHELLO MINE

For Brenda Backstrom, Regional Manager
MMT Consulting, Calgary Regional Office

Prepared by Art Basran
Kelowna Branch Office Manager
MMT Consulting

Submitted:
March 5, 2009

Figure 21.5   Semi-form Progress Report Organized by Degree of Completion

(*Continued*)

INTRODUCTION

The Jackson Mining Company has discovered a high-grade coal deposit in the mountains about 55 miles due north of Grand Forks, British Columbia. The company expects the market for this grade of coal to increase dramatically in the near future, and thus anticipates developing the deposit if development and transportation costs are acceptable. Jackson Mining has tentatively named its proposed minesite as the Othello mine. MMT Consulting has been authorized to determine the most cost-effective method(s) of transporting the coal from that minesite to the mainline railroad, a distance of approximately 50 miles.

Four transport alternatives are being considered:

1. Diesel trucks
2. Diesel trains
3. Electric trains
4. Electric fleets.

The criterion used to evaluate each alternative is the Equivalent Uniform Annual Cost (EUAC). The EUAC discussed in this report is in dollars per ton for the haul to the railhead. The four alternatives will be studied over periods ranging from one to twenty years, and at interest rates varying from 6% to 10%.

The EUAC formula provides clear comparisons of the transportation alternatives. Using this method, and capitalizing on hard work by our staff and good surveying weather, the project seems certain to be completed under budget and ahead of schedule. Details are provided in the following sections.

BACKGROUND

The Othello mine under study has anticipated coal sales of five million tons annually. Each of the following transportation alternatives would have to handle this volume. Also, the ability to expand in the future would be an asset.

1. **Diesel trucks**
   The CAT 777B truck was chosen for this study because of its load capacity of 95 tons and its output of 920 horsepower. These trucks would be running 24 hours a day.
2. **Diesel trains**
   Each train would be running with six diesel engines and 98 coal cars. It would take 11.2 hours to complete a round trip, and 17.2 hours to produce the amount of coal the train would haul. Thus, the train would haul a complete load and then idle for about six hours until the next load was ready.
3. **Electric trains**
   Each train would run four electric engines and 98 coal cars, with the same haul times as for the diesel train.
4. **Electric fleets**
   Each fleet would consist of three of the above electric trains. The first train would be loaded and then depart. While enroute, the second train would be loaded, and this load-and-go process would be repeated for the third train. The departures would be timed so that the second train would leave just as the first train crested the highest point of the rail line pass. In this way, the electricity generated by the downgrade trains would be conserved and used to assist in powering the upgrade trains.

1.

Figure 21.5   Semi-formal Progress Report Organized by Degree of Completion

(*Continued*)

MMT's INVOLVEMENT

After the initial negotiations between the respective head offices of Jackson Mining and MMT, our Kelowna office prepared a detailed proposal which Jackson Mining approved on January 6. Since then, two engineers and three technologists from our Kelowna office have researched this project with advice from Brendan Winters, a Penticton chartered accountant who has special expertise in mining projects.

Work Completed

Since January 6, our team has completed the following tasks:

- completed a preliminary survey of the proposed rail line and haul road; the elevations and other data collected from this survey are being used to help calculate tractive and grade resistances for the diesel trucks and for the two types of trains
- researched construction costs for both a rail line and a haul road, and for associated construction costs (such as maintenance buildings)
- researched maintenance costs for both a rail line and a haul road
- researched labour costs for operating the trucks and the trains
- researched the costs of purchasing trucks, diesel trains, and electric trains
- designed and researched the full costs of a complete communications system which is required to control the proposed mine's transportation system.

Work in Progress

We now have all the data required to complete our calculations and analyses. This work will progress in three stages:

1. Using the data collected from our surveys, we will calculate tractive and grade resistances for the diesel trucks and for the two types of trains. A sample of those calculations is provided below in Table 1. Next, to supplement the information regarding resistances, we will calculate the speed, power, and fuel consumption of each transportation type. A sample of those calculations appears in Table 2 on page 541.

Table 1:   Tractive and Grade Resistances for Diesel Trucks

Section	Grade (%)	Truck Wt (ton)	Load Wt	Total Wt (lb)	Rt	Rg	Tr
G	2.0	66.3	95.0	161.3	16,125.0	6,450.0	22,575.0
F	1.8	66.3	95.0	161.3	16,125.0	5,805.0	21,930.0
E	2.0	66.3	95.0	161.3	16,125.0	6,450.0	22,575.0
D	2.1	66.3	95.0	161.3	16,125.0	6,772.5	22,897.5

The first column in Table 1 lists the sections into which the road has been divided for analytical purposes. These sections of road have varying grades. Grade resistance (Rg) and tractive resistance (Rt) are found for each section.

2.

Figure 21.5   Semi-formal Progress Report Organized by Degree of Completion

(Continued)

Table 2:   Speed, Power, and Fuel Consumption for Diesel Trucks

Section	Grade (%)	Tr (lb)	Power (hp)	Speed (mph)	Dist (mi)	Time (hr)	BTU (x1000)	Fuel (gal)	Total Fuel
G	2.0	22,575.0	920.0	12.55	8.4	0.67	1,572.5	11.34	42.62
F	1.8	21,930.0	920.0	12.92	7.2	0.56	1,309.3	9.44	35.49
E	2.0	22,575.0	920.0	12.55	5.4	0.43	1,010.9	7.29	27.40
D	2.1	22,897.5	920.0	12.38	4.8	0.39	911.4	6.57	24.70

The final calculations for resistances and fuel consumption will be added to labour and maintenance costs to determine annual operating costs for each of the alternatives under study. Thus, we will be able to complete the Cost Comparison table, a draft of which is shown in Table 3 below.

Draft Table 3:   Cost Comparisons

Option	Capital Costs	Annual Operating Costs
Diesel Trucks	$115,539,000	$
Diesel Trains	$149,083,000	$
Electric Trains	$161,783,000	$
Electric Fleets	$201,463,000	$

2. Once the capital and annual costs are found, they can be combined with varying interest rates and study periods to calculate tables of Equivalent Uniform Annual Costs (EUAC). The purpose of converting all costs into an EUAC is to provide a common means of comparing all the alternatives. The capital costs are spread over the length of the study period, and added to the annual costs. Thus, a comparison of EUACs will yield a qualitative assessment of the alternatives to go with the quantitative assessment suggested by Draft Table 3.

To provide an idea of how these EUAC tables (and corresponding graphs) will look in the final analysis, we have estimated figures for the four transportation alternatives and placed them in Draft Table 4 and Draft Figure 1 (Appendix).

The final phase of our work for this project will be to produce a comprehensive report of our findings. This report has been outlined, and some of the preliminary material has been drafted. We expect the final version of this report to total about 40 pages, with the bulk of those pages presenting our detailed calculations. We're using the format that we learned from Mykon Communications last March and which proved successful in our final report to the City of Kelowna regarding the proposed multi-purpose arena.

3.

Figure 21.5   Semi-formal Progress Report Organized by Degree of Completion
(Continued)

CONCLUSION

Appraisal of Work To Date

We're satisfied with both the quantity and the quality of the data gathered for the required analysis. Part of this is due to the hard work performed by our Kelowna project team, part is due to our recent connection to the Internet, and part of the credit should go to Brendan Winters whose experience in gathering and analyzing financial data has been invaluable.

Also, we had some good fortune with the weather during the survey work. Unseasonably warm weather and light snowfalls allowed the surveys to finish one week ahead of our anticipated February 2 completion date, and under budget by 15%. (We would have been even more under budget, but we had to rent a helicopter three days more than anticipated because of very difficult terrain in the Kelso Pass area.)

Overall, it seems that we will be about $14,000 under budget for the project, partly because of the savings in the surveys and partly because Brendan Winters' research expertise has cut our estimated research time. Full figures will be provided in our final progress report.

Anticipated Completion Date

We expect to have all calculations completed by March 7. After that, it should take two of our staff (one engineer and one technologist) two working days to produce a final draft of the report for examination at Regional Office. Allowing for examination time and for final editing at the Kelowna office, we should be able to have the finished copy of our report produced by March 14, which is 14 days ahead of the date we had scheduled for delivering our analysis to Jackson Mining.

Recommendations

We have forged a positive working relationship with Jessica Proctor, Director of Mining Development at Jackson Mining. Jessica has indicated that her company would like us to bid on the construction engineering contract for the anticipated road/rail line construction project, which may begin as early as this July. In connection with this possible contract, we recommend two courses of action:

1. Have the Jackson Mining report produced professionally by a graphics firm. We have money to spend because we're under budget for this project. Also, a graphics firm such as Apex Graphics (which does annual reports and similar documents for major businesses in the Okanagan) could produce a high-quality colour report in one day if we provide a disk prepared in Microsoft Office, the software we use. My main reason for suggesting this extra expenditure of under $1,000 is that Jackson Mining's Directors place a high value on professional work. I think it would help project a positive image which will benefit any future proposals we make to this company.
2. Do some preliminary investigation of the parameters and requirements of road construction and rail line construction for Othello Mine's proposed transportation routes. If Jackson Mining presents a Request for Proposal on this construction project in the near future, MMT Consulting will be prepared.

4.

Figure 21.5   Semi-formal Progress Report Organized by Degree of Completion
(Continued)

APPENDIX

Draft Table 4: EUAC for Alternatives at 6% (Based on preliminary estimates)

Study Period	Diesel Trains	Electric Trains	Electric Fleets	Trucks
1	$32.52	$34.91	$43.26	$32.10
2	17.18	18.26	22.53	20.21
3	12.07	12.72	15.63	16.25
4	9.52	9.95	12.18	14.27
5	7.99	8.29	10.12	13.09
6	6.98	7.19	8.75	12.30
7	6.26	6.41	7.77	11.74
8	5.72	5.82	7.04	11.33
9	5.30	5.37	6.48	11.00
10	4.97	5.01	6.03	10.75
11	4.70	4.71	5.66	10.54
12	4.47	4.47	5.36	10.36
13	4.28	4.27	5.10	10.22
14	4.12	4.09	4.89	10.09
15	3.98	3.94	4.70	9.98
16	3.87	3.81	4.54	9.89
17	3.76	3.70	4.40	9.81
18	3.67	3.60	4.27	9.74
19	3.59	3.51	4.16	9.68
20	3.51	3.43	4.07	9.62

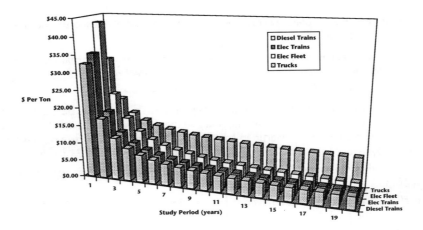

Draft Figure 1: EUAC for Four Alternatives at 6% (Based on preliminary estimates)

5.

Figure 21.5   Semi-formal Progress Report Organized by Degree of Completion

Okanagan University College   *Memo*

To: Don Klepp, English 124 Instructor   **Date:** 19 February 19, 2005

From: Tim Anders, Civil Engineering Technology 1

Re: **Progress of My Research Project**

As I mentioned in our conversation yesterday, my research project is progressing despite the delay caused by choosing a dead-end topic. This memo presents the details of my progress and outlines the work remaining.

Background
You'll recall that I started to research the process used to choose the site for the city's new multi-purpose arena. I found information about the site itself (city maps and infrastructure services), but the site selection process seems to have been cut and dried. The arena is being built on city-owned land; no other site came close to matching the current site's cost or other advantages, as I learned from Jim McElroy's report submitted for last year's English 124 class.

So, following your suggestion, I'm exploring the feasibility of using the Internet to learn the equivalent of the English 124 class.

Progress: Planning and Research
I started on February 10 by identifying TerraTech Engineering as the reader for my report, for two reasons:

1. According to a friend who works in TerraTech's Cranbrook office, TerraTech needs to upgrade the report writing skills of employees in several of its locations because the firm has been restructured and almost everybody in the firm is now responsible for producing reports for clients. TerraTech is not sure how to improve its employees' writing skills in a cost-effective manner. Perhaps the Internet could form the basis for guided self-improvement.
2. I hope to get a co-op position with TerraTech this summer and fall. Maybe my report will show my interest in the firm.

As instructed, I wrote a planning outline, which is attached. I've used this outline to guide my research in two main areas:

1. Locating and examining Web sites for several topic areas—grammar and English language basics; letters, memos, and e-mail; job reports (progress reports, project completion reports, test reports, etc.); analytical reports; proposals; graphics and illustrations; and technical talks.

2. Locating and reading articles in education journals. The attached bibliography lists two articles that I'm finding very useful. The material I've gleaned from those articles, along with an interview I did with Billie Martin in the Distance Education Department, has led to the section called "Relevant Learning Theory," that appears in the attached working outline.

The bulk of that outline sets up a report that will describe and assess the various Web sites on the basis of the:

1. usefulness of the site's material compared to *Technical Communication* and your lectures
2. clarity of the explanations in each site
3. site's ease of use.

See my working outline for more details.

Figure 21.6   A Student Research Progress Report   (*Continued*)

Professor Klepp | February 19, 2005 | Page 2

Analysis and Organization of Gathered Data

As the working outline shows, I have completed my analysis of all the Web site data, except for the job reports. This week, my friend at TerraTech is sending me a list of all the short job reports written by TerraTech employees. I'll see if the reports on this list are discussed on any Web sites.

My assessments are leading to definite conclusions about the feasibility of using Internet sites to teach oneself to be a better business communicator. Also, I'm pleased with the report's structure. The order of assessed sites follows the order of topics in English 124. This order presents a logical progression for a self-directed study program.

Work To Be Completed

When I receive your feedback on my working outline, I'll compose the report, probably on the March 6-7 weekend. Then I'll edit the report on the following weekend and exchange it with Jan Bath's and Phil Strain's reports—we have formed a proofreading group. I look forward to your March 12 lecture on editing and finishing techniques.

The attached Work Schedule shows the hours required and deadline dates for all remaining tasks.

Conclusion

I'm now confident that this project will be completed before the submission deadline of March 22. In case I have any last-minute questions, may I book 10 minutes of your office time on Friday, March 19?

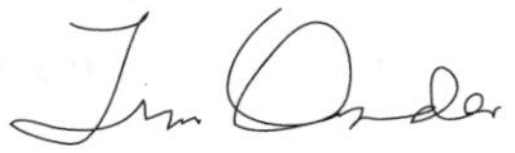

Tim Anders

Attachments: Bibliography
Working Outline
Work Schedule

Figure 21.6 A Student Research Progress Report

Occasional progress reports are written for short-term projects that do not have scheduled reporting dates. Either the writer responds to a supervisor's request (or a client's request), or the writer reports progress in order to elicit reader support.

Project Completion Reports

A project completion report is presented as the concluding progress report for a lengthy project, or the only report arising from a short project. Either way, the action structure can form the report's backbone. (Note, though, that in Table 21.2 the Details section is expanded into Project Highlights and Exceptions.)

Table 21.2   Project Completion Report Structure

Section	Contents
Action Opening	The reader connection depends on the type of reader: client? writer's supervisor? (What are the reader's main concerns?) State that the project is complete; briefly describe the outcome.
Background	Review the job's features: purpose, schedule, budget, location, people involved.
Project Highlights	Describe the project's main accomplishments (work completed, targets met, results obtained). Discuss problems encountered, the impact of these problems on the project, and how the problems were handled.
Exceptions	Describe the deviations from the contract or project plan (if any)—the work not completed or done differently than planned. Give the reason for each deviation and explain the effect of each on the final project result.
Action Closing	Analyze the reader's main concerns. What types of follow-ups are needed?

Periodic Activity Reports

The periodic activity report is similar to a progress report in that it summarizes activities over a specified period. But unlike a progress report, that describes activity on a given *project*, a periodic reports summarizes the general activities during a given *period*. Manufacturers requiring periodic reports often have prepared forms, because most of the tasks are quantifiable; i.e., units produced, etc. Still, not all jobs lend themselves to prepared-form reports, and you will probably have to develop your own format. If so, the action structure can be readily adapted to your purpose.

Incident Reports

An incident report resembles news accounts of events. Most of the description is provided as past tense narrative. Note, however, that some incident reports also use present tense to refer to the current situation and future tense to discuss what needs to be done.

Inspection Reports

Building inspectors, park wardens, gas inspectors, quality control technicians, and others sometimes use forms to report the results of their inspections. However, often a form is not available or does not suit a particular inspection. In these cases, the following adaptation of the action structure works very well.

Table 21.3   Inspection Report Structure

Section	Reader Questions to Answer
Action Opening	• Why should I read this report? • What is the main result of the inspection?
Background	• Why was this inspection conducted? • What was inspected? • Who did the inspection? • When and where did the inspection occur?
Details	What did the inspection reveal? 1. Conditions found: What did the inspectors observe re: the quality of work performed or items provided at the site? In what condition were equipment, facilities, or materials? 2. Deficiencies: What conditions, if any, need to be corrected? Does any work need to be done or re-done?
Action Closing	• Overall, what is the state of the site (facilities, equipment, etc.)? • Does the writer suggest specific actions?

The inspection report on page 550 deals with a troubling incident: a family, against its will, had been evacuated from its home because of dangerous carbon monoxide levels in the home. The writer, who is relatively new in her position, phrases her observations and opinions very cautiously. In particular, notice that she records details very clearly and that she uses passive voice wherever possible to emphasize the *results* of the inspection, *not her part in the inspection and subsequent actions.*

Prairie POWER Corporation

INSPECTION MEMORANDUM

DATE: January 7, 2005

TO: Randall Johnson, Gas & Electrical Inspections Coordinator

FROM: Miranda Ocala, Gas Inspector

RE: **Clogged Masonry Chimney – 322 Montcalm Crescent, Saskatoon, SK**

On the evening of January 3, an elderly member of the Smith family resident at 322 Montcalm Crescent was rushed to the U of S Hospital Emergency Department. An alert resident suspected CO poisoning and alerted SaskEnergy. Later that day, Melvin Trask of SaskEnergy advised the occupants of the two-storey, single family residence to vacate because:
* the chimney was blocked with ice
* CO concentrations of .02% were present apparently due to spillage of gas combustion products.

On January 4, Keith McLeod and I inspected the gas equipment and found:
* the masonry chimney was blocked with ice. (We noted a white, lime-like substance on the exterior portion of the chimney that is exposed in the garage.)
* the furnace and the water heater were spilling.
* the home had evidence of excessive moisture – the windows were frozen shut. A serviceperson from Prairie Heating was present; she opened a small passageway at the top of the chimney's interior. Soon after a draft was established, (i.e., in 30 minutes), the ice began to melt.
* the gas equipment was in good condition. That equipment consists of:
    1.   a 137,000 BTUH standard Lennox furnace with a 6" vent draft hood
    2.   a 36,000 John Wood water heater with draft hood (3" vent).

Both operated satisfactorily as soon as the chimney passage was reasonably clear.
* The 1", two-outlet supply pipe was in good condition
* The masonry chimney, constructed of bricks and concrete and lined with tile throughout, seemed in good condition, although our initial inspection was unable to confirm the chimney's interior condition because of the ice build-up.

On January 6, after the ice had thawed, our subsequent inspection revealed damaged tile liner around the vent connector's entry point. This defect, coupled with the exposure of all four sides of the chimney and the recent cold weather, seems to have led to the icing condition. There is evidence that severe icing has occurred before: There is a white substance on the chimney exterior in the garage.

Because the tile liner measures 6 1/4" by 6 1/4", and a flexible liner measures 6 3/8" OD, I have approved the use of a traditional (shop made) sectional 6" aluminum liner. This is the most economical method of any acceptable corrections.

Still, the owner, Rod Smith, is annoyed that corrections are necessary to a house built just 14 years ago. He is also very angry that an owner's defect has been issued precluding occupancy until satisfactory corrections have been made. He has threatened to sue for the costs of housing his family in a hotel until the residence is cleared for occupancy. I suggest that our customer service people speak with Mr. Smith to explain all the ramifications of allowing a family to occupy a home with potential for CO-induced deaths.

Miranda Ocala

Miranda Ocala

Figure 21.7   A Sample Inspection Report

Field Trip Reports

Usually, a field assignment is complete only after you have reported on what you observed and what you did. The field trip may have involved a four-hour hike along an abandoned forestry road, or required two weeks of testing pollution levels in salmon spawning rivers. Regardless of the trip's duration and complexity, you need to perform two main tasks, in advance of the inevitable report:

1. Make careful, detailed observations and record them in a notebook or on an audio cassette recorder.
2. Organize those notes to answer your reader's questions in the order your reader would prefer.

Table 21.4 illustrates a structure that could be used for most field trip reports.

Table 21.4   Field Trip Report Structure

Section	Reader Questions to Answer
Action Opening	• Why are you reporting this? (optional) • In brief, what have you been doing? What did you accomplish?
Background	• Who went where? When? Why? • On whose authority? (optional) • How did the writer travel? (optional) • What was the project? (optional)
Details of Work Accomplished	• What did you do? What routine work? Which work specifications were followed? • What work did you perform beyond the routine requirements? • What did you observe? • What meetings, if any, did you have? With whom? What were the results?
Problems Encountered	• What were the specific problems, if any? Did you identify the causes of these problems? • What specific actions did you take to solve the problems? • Were you successful? If not, why not?
Action Closing	• What remains to be done? What resources are necessary? Who should perform the work? Have you assigned the work? • Are you requesting support or authorization from me, your reader?

Meeting Minutes

Many team or project meetings require someone to record the proceedings. Minutes are the records of such meetings. Copies of minutes are distributed to all members and interested parties, to track the proceedings and to remind members of their designated responsibilities. The appointed secretary records the minutes. When you record minutes, answer these questions:

- *What group held the meeting? When, where, and why?*
- *Who chaired the meeting? Who else was present?*
- *Were the minutes of the last meeting approved (or disapproved)?*
- *Who said what? Was anything resolved?*
- *Who made which motions and what was the vote? What discussion preceded the vote?*
- *Who was given responsibility for which actions?*

See Figure 21.8 on page 554 for a sample set of minutes.

The reports discussed so far in this chapter focus on factual information. Now the focus shifts to short analytical reports, all of which logically arrive at a conclusion. Readers of analytical reports want more than the facts; they want to know what the facts mean.

The four major varieties of formal analytical reports (feasibility reports, causal analyses, assessment reports, and recommendations reports) have all been discussed in Chapter 19. Therefore, this chapter discusses only how to modify them for letter, memo, and semi-formal report versions. Like short informational reports, short analytical reports can profitably use the four-part action structure.

As you examine the structures suggested for short analytical reports, notice a key difference between formal and informal analytical reports. A formal report places its main point, its "bottom line," at the end of the report and satisfies a reader's immediate "need to know" by placing a Summary in the front matter. An informal report, on the other hand, places the report's main finding in the first or second paragraph, to satisfy the reader's curiosity. While this "front-loading" technique suits most informal reports, it doesn't suit every situation, as you'll see in the discussion of indirect recommendations reports, later in this chapter.

Feasibility Reports

Your reader for a feasibility analysis will likely want your answer at the beginning, so the structure in Table 21.5 should work well. See Figure 21.9 on page 555 for a sample report.

Causal Analyses

Your reader's immediate interest in what caused a problem, a failure, or an incident should direct you to state the report's main point in the lead para-

Table 21.5   Short Feasibility Report Structure

Section	Content	Comments
Action Opening	Refer to reader's request or the situation requiring analysis. State whether the examined project or equipment is feasible.	The reader connection might be placed in a transmittal document if a semi-formal format is used. A letter or memo does not need a heading for the opening paragraph.
Background	Describe the situation leading to this feasibility study. Explain exactly what kind of feasibility is studied and list the assessment criteria.	The amount of background depends on the reader's familiarity with the subject. The criteria may have to be justified.
Details of Assessment	Apply each assessment criterion, step by step, to the data. Choose suitable criteria—a proposed equipment purchase, for example, could look at cost, warranty, equipment reliability, performance, and compatibility with current equipment.	The title of this section will depend on the kind of feasibility being discussed, and on the reader's priorities.
Action Closing	Summarize the results of applying all criteria and and state the bottom-line conclusion. If appropriate, recommend approval.	A summary table could be effective. Brochures, test data, financial projections, or other detailed supporting data could be attached.

graph, as in Table 21.6 on page 556. Incidentally, not all causal analyses deal with problems, breakdowns, or failures. You might be asked to identify the causes of an unexpected rise in factory productivity, a steady increase in fish breeding stock, or an improvement in the employee turnover rate.

The causal analysis illustrated in Figure 21.10 on page 558 was commissioned by a homeowner who suspected that a gaping hole under her driveway resulted from her neighbour's faulty driveway design. TerraTech, the consulting firm engaged by the homeowner, presents its findings in detached, carefully measured language. The report writer uses the classic causal analysis technique of identifying and eliminating possible causes until the most likely, primary cause has been found and proved.

A letter format is used for this report because of its length and relatively straightforward content.

MEETING OF THE CAMPUS RECYCLING COMMITTEE
Room 125, Student Services Building, March 28, 2006

Chair: T. Maguire, Jordan College Student
Association President

Present: R.W. Siggia, V.P., Administration   T. Singh, 3rd year Arts
J. Klym, Campus Services   J. Cormier-Bauer, 2nd year Engineering
M. O'Connor, Print Services   H. Calvin, 4th year Business
P. Masinkowski, 4th year Phys. Ed.

Guest: John Maravich, Canadian Waste Disposal, Ltd.

1. Approval of Agenda
T. Maguire asked to add a presentation by John Maravich and suggested that discussion of bottle recycling as a student association fundraiser be tabled to the next meeting, in order to accommodate the address. T. Maguire called for approval of the amended agenda.   **Passed Unanimously.**

2. Other Business
John Maravich proposed a business arrangement wherein Canadian Waste Disposal would have exclusive rights to recycle paper products at Jordan College in return for an annual $5,000 scholarship to a Jordan College Business student, and a commitment to hire Jordan College students on a part-time basis. The projected total volume of business was discussed, along with other details provided in Canadian's written proposal (see attached). The committee agreed to hold a special meeting in two weeks to discuss the proposal.

Action by: T. Singh and J. Cormier-Bauer will press class presidents to poll students re: their on-campus paper usage.

M. O'Connor and R.W. Siggia will review administrative and academic paper usage.

J. Klym will determine recycling potential for calendars, phone books, and all other campus service publications.

3. Approval of Previous Meeting
After revision of the numbers relating to recycling of library culls, the previous meeting minutes were accepted.
MOVED: R.W. Siggia   SECONDED: J. Klym   **Passed Unanimously.**

4. Recycling Ink Products
H. Calvin and J. Klym presented a report on the types and volume of ink used by on-campus photocopiers and computer printers. Their main findings were that in the last fiscal year:
1. $212,700 was spent on ink cartridges for laser printers, inkjet printers, and photocopiers
2. of that amount, $192,654 was used to purchase new cartridges and the remainder was spent on recycled cartridges. On average, recycled cartridges cost 62% as much as new ones.
3. the latest editions of Consumer Journal and Computer Equipment Monthly report 93% reliability with recycled cartridges.

MOVED: J. Klym   SECONDED: H. Calvin

That Jordan College adopt a one-year trial period of using recycled cartridges. Discussion centred on the issue of whether this committee has a legitimate right to take this action. R.W. Siggia contended it is Administration's prerogative, but agreed to approach President Monroe with the committee's decision. **Passed Unanimously.**

Call for adjournment at 5.05 p.m.   **Carried.**

Figure 21.8   A Sample Set of Meeting Minutes

Ministry of Transportation   **Internal Memo**

DATE: January 10, 2000

TO: Richard Janvier, Engineering Information Systems Coordinator

FROM: Sheri Prasso, Science and Technical Officer

RE: **Sand and Glavine Proposal For Office Networking
             (RFP 19990209-EIS)**

As you requested, this report assesses the proposal submitted by Sand and Glavine Systems for an office network for our Vernon Engineering Services office. The proposal has merit, but requires changes before the Ministry of Transportation can accept it.

The RFP placed its focus on making better use of the computer information systems by creating a local area network (LAN). Therefore, I used the following criteria to assess the Sand and Glavine computer network proposal:

1. Technical considerations
2. Cost
3. Training and support
4. Efficiency gains.

Information for the assessment was collected from current books on the subject, staff at the Vernon Engineering office, and local businesses.

Technical Considerations and Cost

The proposed network will meet Engineering Information Systems' requirements, with minor changes. (In particular, the Wang 486 needs to be retained as part of the network (see the attached technical analysis for more detail). These changes put the cost of the network slightly over budget. However, anticipated reductions in cable requirements and installation time should lower the cost. The overall cost of the modified network will be close to the proposal's quoted price of $4,000.

Training and Support

Technically, the Sand and Glavine Systems proposed network is simple. Because of this simplicity, and the competence of the staff at the Vernon Engineering Office, the proposed training will be sufficient. Unlike training, support was not included in the proposal's quoted price. It was offered at additional cost through monthly service contracts. The Ministry of Transportation has qualified computer support personnel on staff. Purchasing support from Sand and Glavine Systems would duplicate service and add to the direct cost of this network.

Efficiency Gains

Sand and Glavine's proposed computer network will meet Engineering Service's Information Systems' objective of increasing the efficiency of its Vernon office. The network will save time and allow staff to focus their efforts on engineering rather than on file management. Also, Sand and Glavine will install the system on a weekend, saving two days of down time.

Recommendation

If Sand and Glavine Systems re-submits the proposal with the requested changes, it should be adopted.

S Prasso

Sheri Prasso

Attachments: Technical analysis (cable, topology, hardware, and software)
             Cost analysis

Figure 21.9   A Sample Feasibility Report

Table 21.6   Informal or Semi-formal Causal Analysis Structure

Section	Content	Comments
Action Opening	Refer to the reader's request or to the writer's role in analyzing the identified situation. State whether the cause(s) can be identified and, if so, name the main cause.	The reader connection might be placed in a transmittal letter or memo if a semi-formal format is used. A letter or memo report does not need a heading for the opening paragraph or two.
Background	Describe the situation (or environment) in which the event occurred or in which the problem developed. Provide background about similar problems or situations.	This section should not exceed two paragraphs. If more detail is necessary, it can be placed as attachments.
Details of Analysis	Describe the step-by-step analytical process and give the results of that process.	Causal analysis usually names possible causes identified from previous experience and based on the relation between an event and prior conditions. See Chapter 7 re: correlation and causation.
Action Closing	Summarize the report's main findings. State the bottom line. If appropriate, recommend remedial or preventative action.	A summary table could be effective. Attached brochures, performance tests, financial projections, or other detailed supporting data could be appropriate.

Assessment Reports

Assessment reports essentially use the same approach as feasibility reports, except that assessments (also known as *evaluation reports or investigation reports*) are conducted *after* a project has been conducted, or *after* changes have been made.

One special type of assessment report is the *yardstick* or *benchmark report*, which assesses and compares two or more alternative solutions or equipment proposals. In this type of analysis, appropriate criteria act as yardsticks by which the competing alternatives can be compared. Thus, the analysis is handled consistently and fairly. See Table 21.7 for the structure of these types of reports.

Table 21.7 Yardstick Assessment Report Structure

Section	Content	Comments
Action Opening	Define the situation requiring assessment—the problem or challenge. Report the main conclusion.	Only one or two paragraphs are necessary for a letter or memo. Use the heading, "Introduction," for a semi-formal report.
Background	Briefly explain possible alternative solutions. Name the assessment criteria and explain how these were developed and selected.	The section could be called "Background" or "Assessment Method." Extensive technical data should be attached to the end of the report, not placed in the Background section.
Details of Assessment	Evaluate each alternative, according to the assessment criteria. The assessment could be organized by criteria (such as cost, durability, product support). Or the alternatives could be examined, one by one: All the criteria would be applied to the first alternative before moving on to the next alternative.	Use a title like "Data and Assessment." Organize by criteria to allow the alternatives to be ranked by each criterion in turn (e.g., the least to the most expensive). Focus on each alternative in turn.
Action Closing	Conclude which alternative, or combination of alternatives, best meets the assessment criteria.	An implementation plan could be included, but it shouldn't be the focus of an assessment report.

Recommendations Reports

Many recommendations reports respond to reader requests for a solution to a problem; others originate with the writer, who has recognized a problem and developed a solution. This latter type is often called a *justification report.*

Both kinds of recommendations reports could use either a direct pattern or an indirect pattern, depending on the reader's needs and attitudes.

The *direct pattern* suits situations where you can anticipate reader support. Perhaps the reader has accepted similar recommendations in the past. Perhaps your recommended choice is so obvious and clear-cut that there is no other course of action. (See Figure 21.11, on page 562, for such a situation.) Perhaps your recommended action matches company policy and practice. Perhaps the recommendation reflects the reader's own preferred approach or administrative bias.

TerraTech ENGINEERING

1714 Kalamalka Lake Road, Vernon, British Columbia V1G 2N6   Ph. (250) 545-0919
Fax (250) 545-2020   terra@junction.net

June 21, 2006

Ms. L. P. Garcia
306 Melville Court
Vernon, BC   V1B 2W9

Dear Ms. Garcia:

Re: Causes of the Undercut Driveway at 306 Melville Court

At your request, we have examined the extent of the undercutting of your 17-month old driveway and have identified the primary cause of that problem to be water directed from a neighbouring driveway.

Background

In similar situations that we have analyzed, we've determined that open space can develop under a concrete pad if the base soil has not been properly packed, or if flowing water has eroded soil away, or if water has pooled under the pad and thus caused the soil to settle.

Much depends on the soil's composition. In the case of your driveway, the base soil primarily consists of glacial till, a combination of sand, gravel, larger rocks, and small amounts of organic material. Typically, when glacial till gets saturated with water, it turns into a slurry that either flows downhill or collapses into itself, as all loose spaces among the particles are filled.

Investigation and Results

We conducted the investigation in four stages:

1. We determined the nature and extent of damage by examining the concrete deck and by probing the empty space beneath it. Our visual inspection of the concrete revealed no cracks or sagging of the deck; the driveway has stood up very well. We then interviewed your builder, Mark Lambton, who showed us his construction notes. The notes say that the concrete sub-contractor used twice the normal amount of reinforcing bar within the concrete slab.

   The driveway has not pulled away from the rebar fitted into the garage footings, despite 9" of open space under the concrete along the intersection of driveway and footings. The drawing on page 2 shows the extent of open space under the driveway, and other features of the existing situation. (Numbers show the depth of settling or erosion at various points.) The undercutting is quite extensive, as the drawing shows.

2. We ruled out inadequate packing as a cause of the settling. Mark Lambton's notes reveal that the driveway base was packed uniformly, that it was watered between packings, and that it was packed five times over a four-day period. This exceeds normal practice.

Figure 21.10   A Causal Analysis   **(Continued)**

Ms. L.P. Garcia
June 21, 2006
Page 2

3. We ruled out erosion as a major causative factor. There may have been some minor initial erosion along the north edge of the driveway but erosion could not have caused the irregular pattern of open space beneath the slab. That irregular pattern suggests that pooled water has led to irregular soil settling.

4. We determined the source of the amounts of water required to cause the degree of observed settling. We do not believe that the water has come from your driveway, say in last fall's heavy rains. Your driveway has been designed to channel water down toward a collection drain located two metres from the centre of the garage door. To test our belief, we ran water onto your driveway from two hoses simultaneously. All the water was easily channeled down to the drain.

Then, we investigated water flow from the north-neighbouring driveway that slopes away from the garage, toward the street. That driveway is higher than yours at every point of its length, and the entire driveway slopes down towards the rock-covered depression between the two drives. Moreover, a one-metre wide diagonal depression in the neighbouring driveway channels water toward the catchment area immediately adjacent to the spot where your driveway begins to be undercut (see the diagram).

With your neighbour's permission, we ran water onto his driveway for 45 minutes. All of the released water ran down to the catchment area A, from which the water seeped under your driveway and formed pools of settling water. When we re-inspected in three hours, all that water had soaked in.

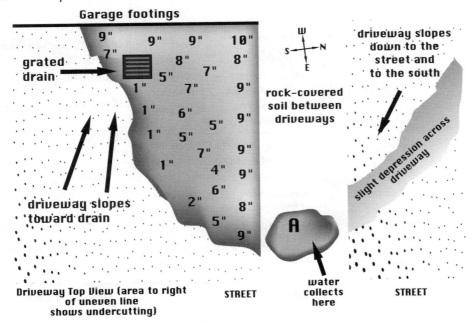

Conclusion
We're confident that the driveway undercutting has resulted from water-induced settling and that the majority of the water has come from your north neighbour's driveway.

Figure 21.10   A Causal Analysis

(Continued)

Ms. L.P. Garcia
June 21, 2006
Page 3

Corrective action will require shoring up the space under the driveway with an impermeable base and diverting water away from possible entry points along the north edge of your driveway. We can recommend Majestic Mudjacking for the former task—this company will pump a rapidly hardening slurry of cement, sand, water, clay, and loam under the exposed slab. If you wish, we'll undertake the water diversion.

We believe that you have grounds for requiring your neighbour to pay the costs of all repair work; local bylaws require each homeowner to control the passage of water off their property, so that the water doesn't flow onto a neighbour's property. Please let us know if we can be of further service. Our invoice is enclosed.

Sincerely,
TerraTech Engineering

Dimitri J. Jones, C.E.T.

Figure 21.10   A Causal Analysis

Table 21.8   Indirect Recommendations Report Structure

Section	Content	Comments
Action Opening	Refer to the need or problem in a way that your reader will recognize and accept. Use active verbs to recommend action.	Use a heading like "Recommendation" or "Problem and Solution."
Background	Name the alternative solutions you considered and explain the criteria used to assess the alternatives. Briefly explain why you discarded alternatives other than the one you selected.	In some cases, it may not be wise to quickly dismiss potential solutions; your approach may seem arbitrary. In such cases, fully apply the assessment criteria to all alternatives.
Details of Assessment	Discuss the benefits, comparative advantages, and drawbacks of your recommended solution. Detail the required resources and costs of your recommended solution.	Use a title like "Features of the Solution," or "Advantages and Requirements," or "How Our Firm Will Benefit."
Action Closing	Summarize the main reasons for choosing the recommended solution and provide a plan for implementing it. Request authorization for your actions or specify the actions you're asking of the reader.	You could attach detailed supporting information such as performance tests, brochures, quotes, and financial projections.

Table 21.8 shows the direct pattern for the kind of recommendations that would be received favourably.

The direct recommendations report in Figure 21.11, on page 562, responds to the following identified need.

> At a coal-fueled electrical power plant, steel outflow pipes carry ash from the coal furnaces to storage lagoons (known as "ash pits" or "lagoons"). Some of these pipes (known as "ash lines") have been eroded and are in danger of failing. The writer knows, as does the reader, that the plant must replace the lines when they are in danger of failing; no other alternative action is available. Still, the recommended action needs to be justified. Also, the report needs to include some background information for the reader, who has recently transferred from a hydroelectric plant. ■

An *indirect approach* works better in situations where your reader may be unreceptive to your recommendations, or where the recommendations deal with a sensitive issue such as workplace harassment or strained employer-employee relations. Table 21.9 suggests the sequence for an indirect recommendations report.

Table 21.9   Indirect Recommendations Report Structure

Section	Content	Comments
Action Opening	Refer to the situation in such a way that your reader realizes there's a problem or a need to be addressed. Briefly describe the approach used in this report.	A semi-formal report could have an "Introduction"; a letter or memo would not need a heading for this section. In a letter or memo, "connect" with the reader in the first sentence.
Background	Show the extent of the need or problem by presenting quotes, examples, or supporting statistics. List alternative solutions and explain the criteria used to assess the alternatives.	Either semi-formal or informal reports could use a heading such as "Background" or "Problem and Solutions."
Details of Assessment	Evaluate the alternatives with the identified criteria, starting with the least applicable solution. Present the best alternative last; apply the criteria vigorously.	Use titles like "Assessment of Alternative Solutions" or "Possible Solutions."
Action Closing	Summarize your recommendation. Show how it can be implemented. Ask for authorization or specify the actions you're asking your reader to take.	You might attach detailed supporting information such as performance tests, brochures, quotes, and financial projections.

Direct POWER Corporation   MEMORANDUM

DATE: April 17, 2005
TO: Martin Scherre, Head Engineer, Correl Park Power Station
FROM: Judy Shohat, Plant Engineer, Correl Park Power Station *JS*

RE: Ash Line Replacement

As I mentioned in our plant meeting two weeks ago, some of the ash lines will need replacing. Shimon Barak and I have since examined Production Units 1 through 6 and found potential line failures for the lines leading from Unit 5 and Unit 6.

Recommendation
Correl Park should purchase 915 m of 300 mm (319 mm OD, 9.5 mm WT) commercial-grade black steel pipe for replacement ash line, at an estimated cost of $60,000.

Background
Approximately 2/3 of all ash line failures are detected and repaired with only some welding time required. However, if an ash line fails in the early evening and is not detected until morning, the line downstream of the failure will plug due to reduced flow velocity. When this has happened, we have had to contract a high-pressure washing truck to clean the line at a cost of from $5,000 to $10,000. In order to maximize line life, we rotate the lines 1/3 turn every three or four years, to distribute the wear around the inner circumference of the pipe.

Findings
Correl Park Unit 6 has three ash lines. 6A and 6B each have one rotation to go, so they will be fine for at least three more years. However, 6C ash line received its third and final turn in May, 2004. Last week this line was examined and rotated in whatever direction exposed the thickest remaining wall to the area of highest wear. A random sampling of thickness readings along this pipe showed an average thickness of 4.47 mm, that is down from the original thickness of 9.5 mm. Experience has shown that an average thickness of equal to or less than 1/2 the original significantly increases the failure frequency. About 765 metres needs replacing.

Currently, No. 5 ash pit is being cleaned out, with the ash being used for road construction. Once the cleaning is complete, it will be necessary to install about 150 metres of ash line to make this pit functional again. (We could then restore Unit 5 to service.) We considered installing the required line with used pipe that we have in stock, but that used pipe is no better than the 6C line that needs to be replaced.

Authorization
I request authorization for the recommended replacement so that bidding for the pipe supply contract can proceed. A Purchase Recommendation and a Technical Specification for the required pipe are attached.

Att.

Figure 21.11   A Direct Recommendations Report

To illustrate the indirect pattern at work, consider the challenge faced by Kim Briere and her colleagues in an Engineering Technology Diploma Program.

> Like many of her colleagues, Kim's writing skills are not adequate for the Applied English 140 course offered in the first semester of her five-semester program. After lengthy consultations with her colleagues, with a college academic counsellor, and with the chairperson of the Engineering Technology Program, Kim sends the recommendation illustrated in Figure 21.12 (see page 564) to Jake Stroud, the Applied English 140 instructor.
>
> As a result of her audience/purpose analysis, Kim realizes that her needs and those of her colleagues are different from those of Professor Stroud. She's also aware that he is opposed to teaching what he calls "remedial English." He has said that the English 140 class "applies university-level writing skills to real-world situations; there's no time to develop basic skills that university students should bring with them."
>
> Kim suspects that Professor Stroud will philosophically oppose her recommendations and that he'll resist her recommended action because it means more work for him. Therefore, she places her recommendations at the end of the report, after leading her reader through an analysis that shows that the majority of the Applied English 140 students really have only one viable option. ■

Lab Reports

The academic lab reports you write during your studies are different from the reports you'll write in industry. First, the names are different; at college, you submit *lab reports*; at work, you'll produce *laboratory reports* or *test reports*. The purpose also differs: Your college lab reports help you learn material or prove a theory, while "real-world" laboratory tests have practical applications such as the following:

- Water samples are tested to determine if a water treatment plant is working properly.
- Car seat child-restraint systems are tested to see if they are safe and effective.
- Soil core samples are tested to determine if a PCB-contaminated site has been decontaminated.

Various formats and requirements exist for academic and industrial settings. You will have to adapt to the specific requirements at your workplace. However, all laboratory and test reports use the general pattern shown on page 566.

MEMORANDUM

TO: Professor Stroud, English Department   **DATE:**   October 16, 2006

FROM: Kim Briere, Applied English 140

RE: **Improving Performance in English 140**

As you have stated in class, we have a severe problem in English 140: The overwhelming majority of the 38 students have failed at least two of the first three assignments so far. Students like me, who are committed to success, are very concerned. So, we've consulted a College Counsellor and the Engineering Dean and we've identified the solution that is presented in this memo.

Thirty-one of us have met three times to discuss the issue. We need to solve the problem of low grades and we need to pass this class to move on to English 150 next semester. Many of us have also discussed the issue with our Department Chair, who warns us that we need a solid grounding in English to do well in our engineering program.

We see a problem for you, too. It must be difficult to have to correct so many things in our memos, letters, and reports. Also, we ask so many questions about grammar and sentence basics in class that you don't have time to present your full lecture.

The cause of the problem seems to be our "inadequate grasp of the English language" (your comment in the October 12 class). We agree with your assessment. In our meeting yesterday, 29 of us found that we lost an average 21 marks for mechanical errors and poor paragraphing on the last assignment!

So, what can we do? We must satisfy three criteria. We need to:

1. improve our English grades to succeed in our program of study
2. build our writing skills for future careers
3. find a practical, immediate solution.

Following the advice of an Academic Counsellor, who showed us the Harvard Case Study model, we've applied the above criteria to four options:

1. Work harder and spend more time on our assignments
2. Lobby the college to reinstate the drop-in Writing Centre, that disappeared after last year's budget cuts
3. Drop the English 140 course now
4. Arrange for special tutorial sessions

The table on page 2 summarizes our thoughts about the four options.

Figure 21.12   An Indirect Recommendations Report   **(Continued)**

Options	Improve Grades	Build for Future?	Practical and Immediate?
Work harder and longer	Not likely—we still need basic skills	No—we're held back by lack of basic skills	No—we carry seven classes each and spend too much time on English now!
Lobby for writing centre	Yes—individual examples and instruction could help us develop basics	Yes—could build the base we need	No—the College is still in a deficit situation and the bureaucracy moves too slowly
Drop the course	Perhaps, if we take the course later, we'll succeed	We don't know how to build writer skills on our own	No—we need a solution this semester
Arrange for tutor(s)	Yes—we can develop the skills, individually and collectively	Yes—we need to build skills to get to the next level	This is the only practical possibility of the four options, **if** we can get the needed assistance

As you can see, we have only one viable option. In order to make that option work, two things have to happen:

1. We need times and a place to meet. Dean Cartwright has arranged a classroom for 4-7 p.m. on Mondays, Wednesdays, and Fridays. She has also found $1,000 to pay a tutor or tutors.

2. We need your help to direct a tutor (or tutors); you have the best idea of our needs. Also, can you help us find one or two tutors? Perhaps you know capable retired professors or graduate students.

Please support our recommendation action. We'd like to start no later than next Monday, so may we have your response in Thursday's class?

Kim Briere

Kim Briere

Figure 21.12 An Indirect Recommendations Report

Table 21.10 Lab Report Structure

Section	Content	Comments
Introduction	Name and define the subject; review the subject's significance. Or, indicate how this test fits into a project or routine procedure.	Could also include the scope of the research. Might discuss the rationale for the research or the objective of the research. Sometimes this is expressed as a question to be answered, sometimes as a hypothesis to be proved or disproved.
Equipment and Procedure	Where appropriate, describe the design of the investigation. List materials instruments, and equipment. Describe, step by step, how the test, experiment, or study was done. Describe methods for observing, recording, and interpreting results.	Might also be called "Materials and Methods." Use passive voice, third person narrative, in the past tense. Use passive voice, third person narrative, in the past tense.
Results	List recorded observations Provide detailed relevant calculations.	Relate these results to the methods used to achieve them.
Conclusion	Analyze the percentage of error and the possible causes of error. Answer: • Do the results answer the questions? • Was the research objective met? • Do you have doubts about the results? Why?	Often called "Discussion." Might also answer: • Was the hypothesis proved? • Are these results consistent with other research? • Are there implications for further research?

Form Reports

Many reporting situations can be handled with pre-printed forms (or electronic templates). Daily and weekly progress reports, for example, often use forms to keep clients and supervisors informed about a project. In many jobs, the best time to learn how to use job-specific forms is during the orientation period, the first two to three weeks on the job. Ask questions about the purpose of each form and the expected standard of completion. Also ask to see completed sample forms. (Some supervisors will prefer to show you how to use a given form only when that form is needed, and not before.)

Employers have passed on the following hints for successfully completing form reports:

Hints for completing form reports

- Read headings or questions on the form carefully. If necessary, ask directions, or look for models (precedents). Do not assume you've guessed correctly.
- Before writing or keying the form, read the entire form and make some quick notes of what to include.
- Choose <u>exact</u> words and phrases, not approximate descriptive language.
- Use jargon only if necessary; perhaps a non-technical person will read your report.
- Analyze the reader and the purpose for the report, and provide <u>all</u> necessary detail.
- Write or print neatly. On multiple-copy forms, press firmly!
- Check for errors in facts and figures, spelling, or logic.
- Know deadlines and stick to them! Remember that form reports are not designed for the writer's convenience; they're used to help you provide information quickly, while the information is still useful to the reader.

Writing a Short Report Efficiently

Most short reports are written in the middle of busy days, with other tasks waiting to be completed. Thus, it's important to use an efficient writing process, such as the following, which assumes a report of two to three pages.

Efficient writing process

1. Analyze the report's purpose and audience. (*2 to 3 minutes*)
2. Quickly list the report's content; then evaluate and revise that content. (up to *5 minutes*)
3. Construct a rough outline, perhaps with headings in place. (up to *5 minutes*)
4. Then, **and only then**, compose the first draft. (*40 to 60 minutes*)
5. Revise the content where necessary. (*5 minutes*)
6. Edit phrasing to ensure it's clear and readable, and that the tone suits the proposal and the reader's likely reaction. (*10 minutes*)
7. Proofread for errors and correct them. (*5 minutes*)

Revision and Editing Checklist for Short Reports

Use this checklist as a guide to revising and refining your short reports.

❑ Have you chosen the best report format for your purpose and audience?

❑ Does the letter or memo use proper format?

❑ Does the subject line forecast the letter or memo's contents?

❑ Does the semi-formal report format contain the appropriate elements?

❑ Are readers given enough information for an informed decision?

❑ Are the conclusions and recommendations clear?

❑ Did you make the right choice between the direct and indirect patterns of presenting the report's bottom line?

❑ Are paragraphs single-spaced within and double-spaced between?

❑ Do headings, charts, or tables appear whenever needed?

❑ If more than one reader is receiving copies, does the letter or memo include a distribution notation to identify other readers?

❑ Does the semi-formal report's title page name other readers?

❑ Is the writing style clear, concise, exact, fluent, appropriate, and direct?

❑ Does the document's appearance create a favourable impression?

❑ Have you included useful details such as supplementary attachments, enclosures, or appendices?

✔ EXERCISES

1. Identify a dangerous or inconvenient area or situation on campus or in your community (endless cafeteria lines, a poorly lit intersection, slippery stairs, a poorly adjusted traffic light). Observe the problem for several hours during a peak-use period. Write a justification report to a *specifically identified* decision maker, describing the problem, listing your observations, making recommendations, and encouraging reader support or action.

2. Assume you have received a $10,000 scholarship, $2,500 yearly. The only stipulation for receiving installments is that you send the scholarship committee a yearly progress report on your education, including courses, grades, school activities, and cumulative average. Write the report.

3. In a memo to your instructor, outline your progress on your term project. Describe your accomplishments, plans for further work, and any problems or setbacks. Conclude your memo with a specific completion date.

4. Keep accurate minutes for one class session (preferably one with debate or discussion). Submit the minutes in memo form to your instructor.

5. Conduct a brief survey (e.g., of comparative interest rates from various banks on a car loan, comparative tax and property evaluation rates in three local towns, or comparative prices among local retailers for an item). Arrange your data and report your findings to your instructor in a memo.

6. Recommendations Report (choose one)

   a. You are a consulting engineer to an island community of 200 families suffering a severe shortage of fresh water. Some islanders have raised the possibility of producing drinking water from salt water (desalination). Write a report for the Island Trust, summarizing the process and describing instances in which desalination has been used successfully or unsuccessfully. Would desalination be economically feasible for a community of this size? Recommend a course of action.

b. You are a health officer in a town less than one mile from a massive radar installation. Citizens are disturbed about the effects of microwave radiation. Do they need to worry? Should any precautions be taken? Find the facts and write your report.

c. You are an investment broker for a major firm. A longtime client calls to ask your opinion. She is thinking of investing in a company that is fast becoming a leader in fibre optics communication links. "Should I invest in this technology?" your client wants to know. Find out, and give her your recommendations in a short report.

d. The "coffee generation" wants to know about the properties of caffeine and the chemicals used on coffee beans. What are the effects of these substances on the body? Write your report, making specific recommendations about precautions that coffee drinkers can take.

e. As a consulting dietitian to the school cafeteria in Blandville, you've been asked by the school board to report on the most dangerous chemical additives in foods. Parents want to be sure that foods containing these additives are eliminated from school menus, insofar as possible. Write your report, making general recommendations about modifying school menus.

f. Dream up a scenario of your own in which information and recommendations would make a real difference. (Perhaps the question could be one you've always wanted answered.)

☑ COLLABORATIVE PROJECT

Organize into groups of four or five and choose a topic upon which all group members can take the same position. Here are some possibilities:

- Should your college abolish core requirements?
- Should every student in your school pass a writing proficiency exam before graduating?
- Should courses outside one's major be graded pass/fail at the student's request?
- Should your school drop or institute student evaluation of teachers?
- Should all students be required to be computer literate before graduating?
- Should campus police carry guns?
- Should dorm security be improved?
- Should students with meal tickets be charged according to the type and amount of food they eat, instead of paying a flat fee?

As a group, decide your position on the issue. Brainstorm collectively to justify your recommendation to a stipulated primary audience in addition to your colleagues and instructor. Complete an audience/purpose profile (page 85), and compose a justification report. Appoint one member to present the report in class.

Workplace Correspondence

Areport may be completed by a team of writers for multiple readers, but letters, memos, and e-mail (electronic mail) are usually written by a single writer for one or more definite readers. Because workplace correspondence is more direct and personal than reports and often has a persuasive purpose, proper tone is essential. You want your reader to be on your side. Because successful business depends on a two-way transaction in which both participants meet their needs, you must use a "you" attitude. You must look at the situation from the reader's viewpoint.

This chapter looks at four correspondence media: letters, memos, e-mail, and faxes. The chapter presents current formats, introduces considerations common to all four media, and discusses issues that concern each different medium.

Letters appeared on the scene first, followed in the mid-20th century by memos. Then, as that century drew to a close, new technologies brought facsimile transmission (faxes) and e-mail messaging. As we begin a new century, we can be sure of three things:

1. Rapid technological change will bring new varieties of electronic correspondence, **but**
2. We will want relatively permanent records of that correspondence, **and**
3. The basic principles of successful correspondence will work in any correspondence medium, paper-based or electronic.

Letter Format

North American business correspondence blends ordered, elaborate formatting with streamlined, direct phrasing. (By contrast, European letters often *look* less formal, but are phrased more formally and elaborately than Canadian and American letters.)

As the 21st century begins, two traditional formats are out of fashion and a third may soon lose favour. The *block* and *semi-block formats* shown in Figures 22.1 and 22.2 on page 573, were both popular in the 1960s and early 1970s in Canada, but neither format is widely used now.

In the 1970s and early 80s, IBM and others championed the *full-block format* because its left-justified set-up saved keying time. The full-block format (Figure 22.3 on page 573) led the way through the 80s and 90s, but as the 90s drew to a close, it started to give way to an even more streamlined layout which had been introduced as the "simplified letter" by the U.S. National Office Management Association in the early 1960s. Figure 22.4 on page 573, shows a contemporary version of the *simplified format*.

Today's version of the simplified format responds to a growing discomfort with the formal greeting ("Dear ...") and complimentary close ("Yours..."), which seem characteristic of an earlier era. Notice that a subject line replaces the salutation and that the complimentary close is eliminated. In other respects, a simplified letter copies a full-block letter, although the simplified format's overall appearance resembles contemporary memos.

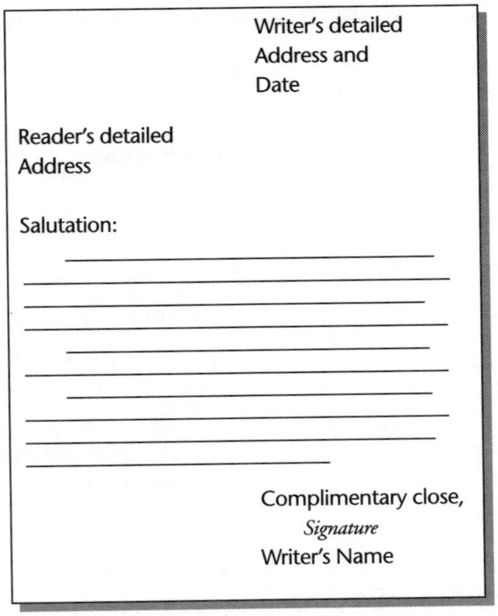

Figure 22.1 shows a Semi-block Format with the Writer's detailed Address and Date at top right, Reader's detailed Address, Salutation, body text, and Complimentary close, Signature, Writer's Name at bottom right.

Figure 22.1　A Semi-block Format

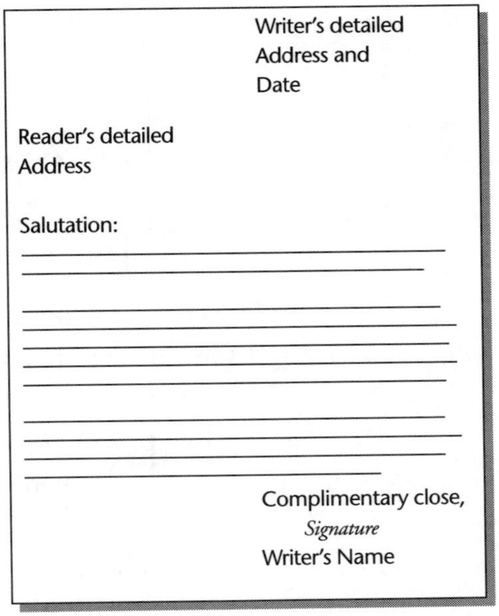

Figure 22.2 shows a Block Format with the Writer's detailed Address and Date at top right, Reader's detailed Address, Salutation, body text, and Complimentary close, Signature, Writer's Name at bottom right.

Figure 22.2　A Block Format

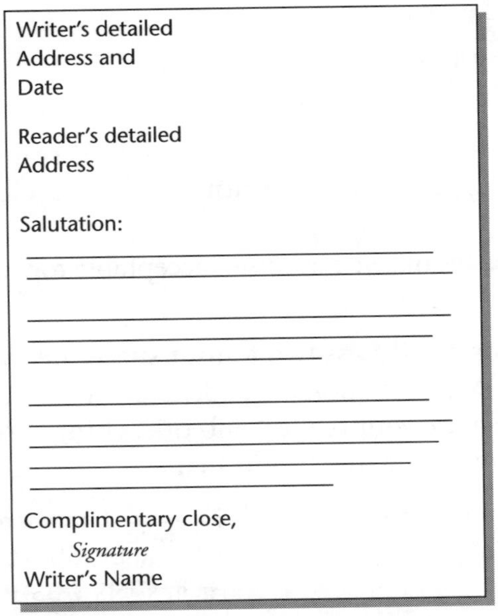

Figure 22.3 shows a Full-block Format with the Writer's detailed Address and Date at top left, Reader's detailed Address, Salutation, body text, and Complimentary close, Signature, Writer's Name at bottom left.

Figure 22.3　A Full-block Format

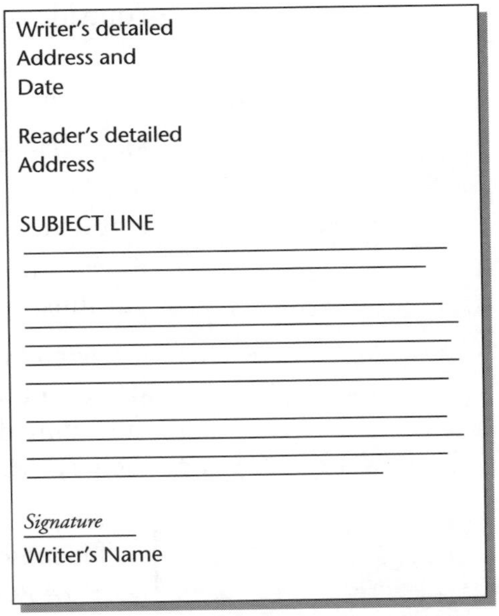

Figure 22.4 shows a Simplified Format with the Writer's detailed Address and Date at top left, Reader's detailed Address, SUBJECT LINE, body text, and Signature, Writer's Name at bottom left.

Figure 22.4　A Simplified Format

Basic Elements of Letters

Business letters have traditionally included five elements (in order from top to bottom): heading and date, inside address, salutation, letter text, and closing.

Heading and Date. Your personal business letters start with your detailed address (but not your name) at the top of the page, followed by the date of the letter.

If you're sending a letter on company stationery, place the date a line or two below the letterhead.

127 Marchbank Avenue
Barrie ON   K9M 7H3

June 23, 2005

ROCKWOOD INDUSTRIES CO. LTD.
1222 Terminal Road Rockwood ON   N0B 2K3 (413) 554-7863

June 23, 2005

Canadian usage includes four correct ways of writing addresses:

1. 127 Marchbank Avenue
   Barrie ON   K9M 7H3

2. 127 Marchbank Avenue
   Barrie ON   K9M 7H3

3. 127 Marchbank Avenue
   Barrie, Ontario
   K9M 7H3

4. 127 Marchbank Avenue
   Barrie, Ont.
   K9M 7H3

The first of the acceptable forms has been instituted by Canada Post Corporation to help its computerized optical scanners operate. Notice that Canada Post's address standard eliminates internal punctuation. Actually, Canada Post's "optimum requirements" for the address on the envelope (the "outside address") look like this:

127 MARCHBANK AVENUE
BARRIE ON   K9M 7H3

Note: The majority of businesses, with the exception of some government offices, use the second acceptable form of writing addresses. Check with your employer.

For the purposes of this book, we have used acceptable forms 1, 2, and 3 in our illustrations.

Inside Address. Place the inside address two to four spaces below the date and abutting the left margin. Wherever possible, address your letter to a specifically named reader, and include your reader's job title. Using a form of address such as "Mr." or "Ms." before the name is optional.

Mr. Saul Kaufman, General Manager   *or,*   Bluenose Engineering Co.
Bluenose Engineering Co.   1774 Robie Street
1774 Robie Street   Halifax NS   B3H 3G7
Halifax NS   B3H 3G7

Attention: Mr. Saul Kaufman
                    General Manager

Note: Depending on the length of your letter, adjust the vertical placement of the heading and inside address to achieve a page that appears balanced.

Salutation. The salutation usually appears two line spaces below the inside address. A standard salutation begins with *Dear* and ends with a colon (*Dear*

Mr. Kaufman:). If you don't know the person's name, an attention line (*Attention: General Manager*) is preferable to using the position title (*Dear General Manager:*).

No satisfactory guidelines exist for addressing several people within an organization. *Gentlemen* or *Dear Sirs* shows implied bias. *Ladies and Gentlemen* sounds too much like the beginning of a speech. *Dear Sir or Madam* is too old-fashioned. *To Whom It May Concern* is vague and impersonal. Your best bet is to use an attention line (*Attention: Personnel Department*) and eliminate the salutation (use a simplified format).

Letter Text. The text of your letter begins two spaces below the salutation or subject line. Workplace letters typically include: (1) a brief *introduction* paragraph (two or three sentences) that identifies your purpose and connects with the reader's interest; (2) one or more paragraphs that present the *details* of your message; and (3) a *closing* paragraph that sums up and encourages action. Some letters will need to provide *background* information immediately after the introduction.

Keep your paragraphs short, usually fewer than eight lines. If a paragraph goes beyond eight lines, or if the paragraph contains detailed supporting facts or examples, consider using bulleted or numbered lists to make the paragraph readable. On average, letter paragraphs should not exceed 60 words per paragraph.

Closing. The closing, placed one line space below the last line of text, includes three components in traditional formats: complimentary close, signature, and writer's name and position.

> Yours truly,
>
> *Maris McGovern* (signature)
>
> Maris McGovern
> Sales Manager

Yours truly and *Sincerely* are the most commonly used complimentary closes. Others, in order of decreasing formality, include:

> Respectfully,
> Cordially,
> Best Wishes,
> Warmest Regards,
> Regards,
> Best,

Align the three-part closing with the letter's heading.

If you are representing a company or group that bears legal responsibility for the correspondence, key the company's name in full caps two spaces below your complimentary closing; place your keyed name and title four spaces below the company name and sign in the triple space between.

Yours truly,

ROCKWOOD INDUSTRIES

[signature]

Mary Baxter
Research Coordinator

Specialized Parts of Letters

Some letters require one or more of the following specialized parts. *Examples appear in sample letters in this chapter and in Chapter 23.*

Attention Line. Use an attention line when you direct a letter to a specific department or position within an organization, but you don't know the reader's name. (Or, use it in the simplified letter format.)

Rockwood Industries Inc.
335 – 11th Avenue S.W.
Calgary AB   T2R 1L9

Attention: Director of Research and Development
or,
ATTENTION: Director of Research and Development

Subject Line. Because it announces the topic of your letter, the subject line is a good device for attracting a busy person's attention.

Subject: Improvements in Client Service
or,
SUBJECT: Improvements in Client Service

Place the subject line below the salutation with one line space before and after it.

Dear Mr. Patrese:

SUBJECT: Improvements in Client Service

If you are using a simplified style letter, place the subject line below the inside address with two line spaces before and after it.

Initials. If someone keys your letter, your initials (in caps) and his/hers (in lower case letters) should appear below the writer's keyed name, flush with the left margin. This practice is disappearing because the overwhelming majority of writers key their own letters these days.

J. Mansonneau
Manager

JM/to

Enclosure Notation. When other documents accompany your letter, add an enclosure notation one line below the initials (or writer's name and position) flush with the left margin. State the number of enclosures.

> Enclosure
> Enclosures 2
> Encl. 3

Distribution Notation. If you distribute copies of your letter to other readers, insert the notation *Copy*, or *c*, or *pc*, or *Distribution*, one line below the previous line (such as an enclosure line).

> Copy: B. Grammel
>
> c: M. Henderson
>
> Distribution: Hamilton Better Business Bureau
> Hamilton Chamber of Commerce
> Ontario Ombudsman

Most copies are distributed on an FYI (For Your Information) basis, but writers sometimes use the distribution notation to maintain a paper trail or to signal that the letter is being shared with others (e.g., superiors or legal authorities).

Note: The notation *bc* means blind copy. It appears on copies *other than* the original and indicates that the recipient of the letter is not aware that a copy is being sent to others.

Design Factors

Design starts with a choice of formats. Currently, the format most favoured by Canadian business writers is the full-block layout, but the simplified format is gaining in popularity. Both these forms look businesslike and eliminate the need to tab and centre.

Additional design factors enable workplace letters to appear inviting, accessible, and professional:

Quality Stationery. Use high-quality 20-pound or 24-pound, 21.5 cm x 28 cm (8½" x 11") white paper with a minimum fibre content of 25 percent. Hundreds of varieties of coloured, specially textured papers are available, but you should exercise caution in using anything other than white stationery.

Uniform Margins and Spacing. When using stationery without a letterhead, frame your letter with 2.5 cm to 3.75 cm (1"–1½") margins, depending on the amount of space required by the letter's text. Strive for a balanced look. Use single spacing within paragraphs and double spacing between paragraphs.

Page Continuation Format. If your letter continues beyond a first page, begin each additional page with a notation identifying the addressee, date, and page number.

| Saul Kaufman   June 25, 2005   Page 2

If there's sufficient space, you can stack the notation at the left margin.

| Saul Kaufman
| June 25, 2005
| Page 2

Begin the text two spaces below the page continuation notation. Never use an additional page solely for the closing section. Instead, re-format the letter so that the closing appears on the first page or so that at least two lines of text appear above the closing on the subsequent page.

Envelope Preparation. Your 24 cm x 10.5 cm (9½″ x 4⅛″) envelope (also called a #10 envelope) should be of the same quality as your stationery. Place your reader's name and address at a fairly central point on the envelope (13-15 line spaces from the top of the envelope and 1.25 cm (½″) left of the horizontal centre of the envelope. Place your own name and address in the upper left corner. Single-space these elements. Most likely, your word processor will have an envelope printing function which will automatically place these elements in the correct location on the envelope. (See your printer's operating manual for instructions.)

Memo Usage and Format

Memoranda (usually called "memos") are used within organizations for a wide variety of messages. Originally, memos were intended for relatively brief messages, but now they're also used for longer messages, including informative and analytical reports of up to four pages, as Chapter 21 demonstrates. Memos are also used for proposals and other persuasive messages.

The major form of communication in most organizations, memos leave a paper trail of directives, enquiries, instructions, requests, recommendations, and daily reports needed to run an organization.

Organizations rely heavily on memos to trace decisions and responsibilities, track progress, and recheck data. Therefore, any memo you write can have far-reaching ethical and legal implications. Be sure your memo includes the date and your initials or signature. Also, make sure your information is specific, unambiguous, and accurate. Finally, remember that your memos must provide the information and analysis that the reader needs, but *no more* than the reader needs.

Format

Basically, there are two varieties of memos: intra-office (within an office) and inter-office (between offices of the same firm.) Both use the same type of format, with minor variations.

Memohead. Intra-office memos usually feature the designation, Memorandum (or Memo) at the top of the page, sometimes in conjunction with the company's name and logo, sometimes by itself. (See Figure 21.6, page 546 and Figure 21.7, page 550.) Inter-office memos usually name the company at the top of the page, followed by the term, "Inter-office Memo." (See Figure 3.4, page 56.)

Heading Guides. Four heading guides are mandatory: date line, receiver's name and title, sender's name and title, and subject line.

> **DATE:**   June 25, 2006
>
> **TO:**   John Tarnowski, Purchasing Coordinator
>
> **FROM:**   May Krienke, Explorations Chief
>
> **RE:**   **Cost Estimates for the Churchill River Project**

Provide the titles held by you and your reader, even if you are both well aware of each other's position. Why? First, it's a formal courtesy used within most organizations. Second, the title designations provide a record which may prove useful in the future.

Additional heading information might include file locators (FILE, or OUR FILE, or YOUR FILE), the sender's phone number or e-mail address, or a distribution line. Distribution lines more often appear at the end of a memo, but if you prefer to include your distribution list in the heading, incorporate that list in the TO section or place a DISTRIBUTION line between the TO and FROM sections. If you want to direct copies of a memorandum to certain personnel, include a COPIES or COPY TO line either after the TO or FROM section.

Margins and Spacing. Use block format for memos: Do not indent paragraphs. Instead, single space within paragraphs and double space between paragraphs. Leave 2.5 cm (1″) left and right margins. Do not right justify paragraphs; leave a ragged right edge. Do not worry about balancing memos on the page; start the heading guides one or two open spaces below the memohead and continue until the memo is complete.

Normally, memo writers leave an open space between each pair of heading guides. Also, it's common practice to tab the information following the heading guides so that the information is aligned. (See the above example of heading guides usage.)

Signature versus Initials. Many memo writers simply sign their initials beside their name in the FROM section (see Figure 21.11 on page 562). Others choose the more formal (and, they say, the more businesslike) practice of signing their name or placing their initials, at the end of the memo.

> J. Mansonneau
>
> J. Mansonneau

This practice has the added advantage of identifying the writer on each page of a two-page memo.

Attachments. An effective way of including detailed useful or corroborative data is to attach it to the memo. If such material were included in the body of the data, it might interfere with the smooth development and easy reading of that memo, so it's better placed where the readers can read it if they want to do so. For example, an internal proposal concerning a proposed expansion of the firm's advertising program might attach a demographic analysis of the firm's target market and some sample newspaper ads.

Graphic Highlighting. Memo readers are usually busy people who want easily understood documents. One way to provide readability is to use bulleted or numbered lists of information and ideas. Headings also make documents easier to read. Tables or columns of information can present material concisely and clearly. So, remember to use combinations of these techniques, even for relatively short memos.

Facsimile Transmission

A fax (short for facsimile) machine electronically scans a page, converts the scanned image to digital code, and sends the code through a telephone cable to another fax machine, which decodes the digital message so that it can print an exact copy (facsimile) of the scanned page. Fax transmissions can also be generated by your word processor and sent via fax modem. For example, Microsoft Word allows you to send a Word document via fax; simply go the **File** menu, choose *Send To…* and then, *Fax Recipient,* and follow the instructions. Other computer systems have similar capabilities.

Faxed messages offer the advantage of speedy delivery for both internal memos and external letters. The technology also provides a confirmation that the receiving fax machine has indeed received the message. However, faxes also have some disadvantages. They don't transmit colour, and often the lines and even letters in faxed messages are broken or blurred. In addition certain kinds of fax paper break down and thus do not provide a permanent record unless photocopied by the recipient. So, if time is of the essence, send a fax message, but if you want your reader to have a crisp, professional-looking copy on file, send that copy as a follow-up.

Note: Recipients with fax modems in their computers can print faxes on their laser printer and thus avoid the "paper breakdown" problem.

Format

Documents transmitted by fax usually are accompanied by a cover sheet or transmittal sheet. The actual format for such sheets varies widely, but they should include:

1. The name and fax number of the receiver
2. The name and fax number of the sender
3. The number of pages sent, including the cover sheet
4. The name and phone number of the person to contact if the fax isn't satisfactorily sent

Figure 22.5 shows a sample cover sheet.

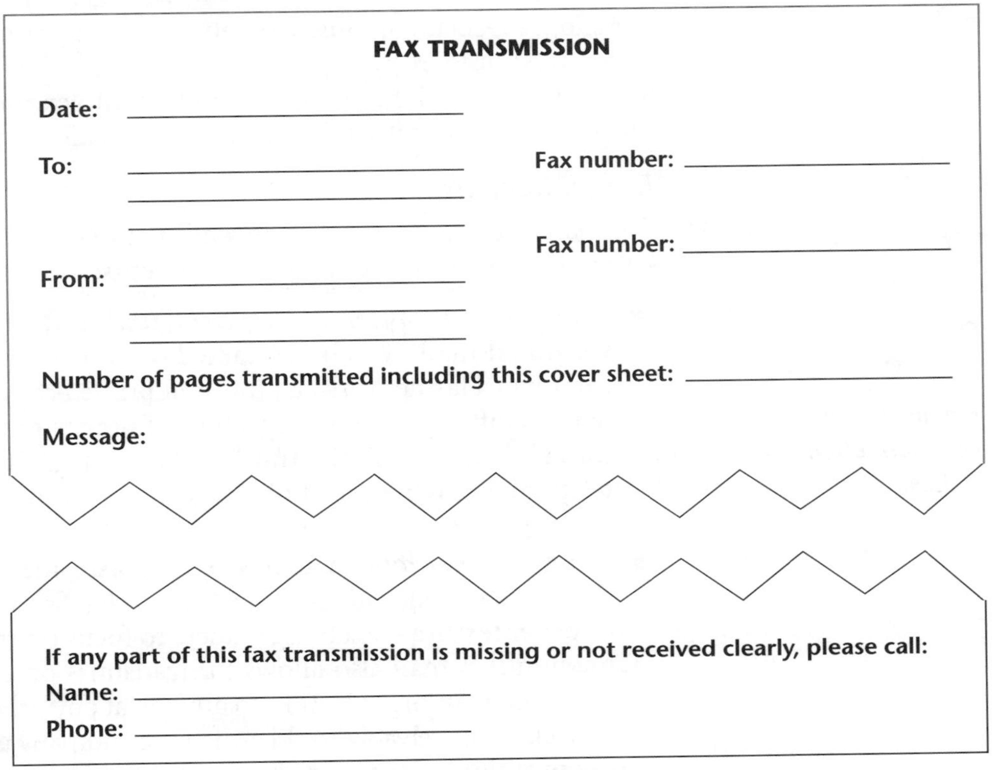

FAX TRANSMISSION

Date: _____

To: _____   Fax number: _____
       _____
       _____
                                         Fax number: _____

From: _____
       _____
       _____

Number of pages transmitted including this cover sheet: _____

Message:

If any part of this fax transmission is missing or not received clearly, please call:

Name: _____

Phone: _____

Figure 22.5   A Fax Transmission Cover Sheet

Electronic Mail

Perhaps the most widely used application on the Internet is electronic mail, known simply as e-mail. The Electronic Messaging Association estimated that Internet users sent more than two trillion messages in 1997. Who knows what that figure might be this year?

E-mail connects users to discussion forums on Listserv and Usenet and carries routine, day-to-day communication as well. E-mail transmits an electronic document via networked computer terminals to recipients in the same building or across the globe. Specific codes direct the message to any electronic mailbox designated by the sender, or to all the mailboxes on a mailing list. Alerted by an audio signal or on-screen message, the recipient opens the on-screen mailbox, reads the message, and then either responds, files the message, prints it out, forwards it, or deletes it. E-mail messages can be exchanged instantly or at the convenience of the communicating parties.

In effect, e-mail is a new hybrid of written correspondence and one-on-one conversation. Most e-mail messages are relatively casual in tone and format, reflecting the democratic, "free" nature of the medium. However, as uses for e-mail increase and as software becomes more sophisticated, e-mail messages are starting to look more formal and writers are taking more care with their phrasing, especially in business settings. Until recently, e-mail has been best suited to simple messages. Now, however, new software with enriched formatting and the ability to attach more complex documents means that you can send fully formatted documents via e-mail.

E-mail Benefits

Compared to phone, fax, or conventional mail (or even face-to-face conversation, in some cases), e-mail offers benefits:

E-mail facilitates communication and collaboration

- *E-mail is fast, convenient, efficient, and relative unintrusive.* Unlike conventional mail, which can take days to travel, e-mail travels instantly. Although a fax network can transmit printed copy rapidly, e-mail eliminates paper shuffling, dialing, and a host of other steps. Moreover, e-mail makes for efficiency by eliminating "telephone tag." It is less intrusive than the telephone, leaving the choice of when to read and respond to a message entirely up to the recipient.

- *E-mail is democratic.* With few exceptions, e-mail messages appear as plain print on a screen, with no special typestyles, fancy letterheads, paper design, or paper texture—enabling readers to focus on the message instead of the medium.[1] E-mail also allows for transmission of messages by anyone at any level in an organization to anyone at any other level. For instance, the mail clerk conceivably could e-mail the company president directly, whereas a conventional memo or phone call would be routed through the chain of management or screened by administrative assistants (Goodman 33–35). In addition, people who are ordinarily shy in face-to-face encounters may be more willing to express their views in an e-mail conversation.

- *E-mail can foster creative thinking.* E-mail dialogues involve give-and-take, much like a conversation. Writers feel encouraged to express their thoughts spontaneously, thinking as they write, without worrying about page design, paragraph structure, perfect phrasing, or the like. The focus is on conveying your meaning to the recipients who in turn will respond with thoughts of their own. This relatively free exchange of views can lead to all sorts of new insights or ideas (Bruhn 43).

- *E-mail is excellent for collaborative work and research.* Collaborative team keep in touch via e-mail, and researchers contact people who have the answers they need. Especially useful for collaborative work is the e-mail function that enables documents or electronic files of any length to be attached and sent for downloading by the receiver.

---

1. Multimedia allows charts, graphs, 3-D images, sound, voice, animation, or video to be added to certain e-mail messages, but many of these features would be considered inappropriate—if not frivolous—in routine correspondence.

E-mail Privacy Issues

Although e-mail connects increasing millions of users, no specific laws protect any computer conversation from eavesdropping or snooping.[2] Gossip, personal messages, or complaints about the boss or a colleague—all might be read by unintended receivers. Employers often claim legal right to monitor *any* of their company's information, and some of these claims can be legitimate:

Monitoring of e-mail by an employer is legal

> In some instances it may be proper for an employer to monitor e-mail, if it [the employer] has evidence of safety violations, illegal activity, racial discrimination, or sexual improprieties, for instance. Companies may also need access to business information, whether it is kept in an employee's drawer, file cabinet, or computer e-mail. (Bjerklie, "E-Mail" 15)

E-mail privacy can be compromised in other ways as well. Some notable examples:

E-mail offers no privacy

- Everyone on a group mailing list—intended reader or not—automatically receives a copy of the message.
- Even when deleted from the system, messages often live on for years, saved in a back-up file.
- Anyone who gains access to your network and your private password can read your document, alter it, use parts of it out of context, pretend to be its author, forward it to whomever, plagiarize your ideas, or even author a document or conduct illegal activity in your name. (One partial safeguard is encryption software, which scrambles the message, enabling only those who possess the special code to unscramble it.)

E-mail Quality Issues

Free exchange via computer screen adds to the *quantity* of information exchanged, but not always to its *quality*:

A useful definition of "information"

> Claude Shannon, father of communication theory...once said, "Information is news that makes a difference. If it doesn't make a difference, it isn't information." A radio traffic report about a car crash up ahead is information if you can still change your route. But if you are already stuck in traffic, the message is . . . useless. (Rothschild 25)

Following are specific ways in which information quality can be compromised by e-mail communication:

E-mail does not always promote quality in communication

- The ease of sending and exchanging messages can generate overload and junk mail—a party announcement sent to 300 employees on a group mailing list, or the indiscriminate mailing of a political statement to dozens of newsgroups (*spamming*).
- Some electronic messages may be poorly edited and long-winded.

---

2. Whereas the phone company and other private carriers are governed by federal laws protecting privacy, no such legal protection has been developed for communication on the Internet (Peyser and Rhodes 82).

- Off-the-cuff messages or responses might offend certain recipients. E-mail users often seem less restrained about making rude remarks (*flaming*) than they would be in a face-to-face encounter.
- Recipients might misinterpret the tone. *Emoticons* or *Smileys*, punctuation cues that signify pleasure :-), displeasure :-(, sarcasm ;-), anger >:-< and other emotional states, offer some assistance but are not always an adequate or appropriate substitute for the subtle cues in spoken conversation. Also, common e-mail abbreviations (FYI, BTW, HAND—which mean "for your information," "by the way," and "have a nice day") might strike some readers as too informal.

IN BRIEF

Spamming

Spam is defined as "unsolicited e-mail, sent en masse and often promoting an electronic sex site, pyramid-type scheme, or niche product." (D1) By clicking onto e-mail lists, spammers can send thousands, even millions of e-mails simultaneously. Spam can be very annoying; worse, the large potential volume of simultaneous e-mails can crash internet service provider (ISP) systems.

Legislation may eventually make it possible to convict illegal purveyors of spam, but other measures are needed to protect against receiving such messages. Simon Tuck offers the following advice for individual Internet users[3]:

- *Lie low.* Industry officials say the best way to avoid spam is to stay off the spammers' lists by keeping your e-mail address to friends and business contacts. Spammers use automated programs to reap addresses from chat rooms and electronic bulletin boards.
- *Filters.* Use filters that recognize and eliminate spam before it reaches your e-mail account. You can filter out messages with certain words such as "sex" or "rich" or go even further and set up an account that accepts mail only from a predetermined set of addresses.

- *Code names.* Use a different on-line identity from your e-mail address. That way you can protect your privacy from stalkers and fool the spammers' programs that dig for addresses.
- *No directories.* Don't list yourself in the member directory of your ISP, which can be used like a telephone book by spammers.
- *Gripe.* Complain about spam and spammers to your ISP and make sure it does something about your complaint.
- *Avoid bombs.* Industry officials say "mail bombings"—sending a huge number of e-mails to crash a computer system—only provokes spammers into taking worse actions.
- *Don't respond.* Some spams ask you to send a return e-mail to get yourself off their list. Some mass e-mailers are making a genuine offer—but others use the response to confirm that they've found a live address.

3. Source: Simon Tuck "Canning Spam" page D1 and page D5, *Globe and Mail*, Thursday, October 15, 1998

★   ★   ★

E-mail Guidelines

Recipients who consider an e-mail message poorly written, irrelevant, offensive, or inappropriate will only end up resenting the sender. These guidelines offer suggestions for effective e-mail use.[4]

Guidelines for effective e-mail use

- Use e-mail to reach a lot of people quickly with a relatively brief, informal message.
- Don't use e-mail to send confidential information: employee evaluations, criticism of people, proprietary information, or anything that warrants privacy.
- Don't use e-mail to send formal correspondence to clients or customers, unless they request or approve this method beforehand.
- Don't use the company e-mail network for personal correspondence or for anything that is not work related.
- Check your distribution list before each mailing, to be sure the message reaches all intended primary and secondary readers but no unintended ones.
- Assume your e-mail correspondence is permanent and could be read by anyone anytime. Ask yourself whether you've written anything you couldn't say to another person face-to-face. Avoid spamming and flaming.
- Before you forward an incoming message to other recipients, be sure to obtain permission from the sender.
- Limit your message to a single topic, and keep the whole thing focused and concise. (Yours may be just one of many messages confronting the recipient.) Don't ramble.
- Use a clear subject line to identify your topic ("Subject: Request for Beta Test Data for Project #16"). This helps recipients decide whether to read the message immediately and makes it easier to file and retrieve for later reference.
- Refer clearly to the message to which you are responding ("Here are the Project 16 Beta test data you requested on Oct. 10").
- Try to keep the sentences and paragraphs short, for easy reading.
- Don't write in FULL CAPS—unless you want to SCREAM at the recipient!
- Close with a signature section that names your company or department, telephone and fax number, and any other information the recipient might consider relevant.

---

4. Adapted from Bruhn 43; Goodman 33–35, 167; Kawasaki 286; Nantz and Drexel 45–51; Peyser and Rhodes 82.

Interpersonal Elements of Workplace Correspondence

In addition to presenting the reader with an accessible and inviting design, effective correspondence enhances the relationship between writer and reader. Interpersonal elements forge a *human* connection. Observe the following guidelines.

Focus on Your Reader's Interests: The "You" Perspective. In speaking face to face, you unconsciously modify your statements and expression as you read the listener's signals: a smile, a frown, a raised eyebrow, a nod. In a telephone conversation, a voice provides cues that signal approval, dismay, anger, or confusion. Writing a letter, memo, fax, or e-mail, however, carries a major disadvantage; you can easily forget that a flesh-and-blood person will be reacting to what you are saying—or seem to be saying.

Workplace correspondence displaying a "you" perspective subordinates the writer's interests to those of the reader. In addition to focusing on what is important to the reader, the "you" perspective conveys respect for the reader's feelings and attitudes.

To achieve a "you" perspective, put yourself in the place of the person who will read your correspondence; ask yourself how the reader will react to what you have written. Even a single word, carelessly chosen, can offend. In writing to correct a billing error, for example, you might feel tempted to say this:

A needlessly offensive tone

> Our record keeping is very efficient and so this obviously is your error.

Such an accusatory tone might be appropriate after numerous failed attempts to achieve satisfaction on your part, but in your initial correspondence it will alienate the reader. The following is a more considerate version:

A tone that conveys the "you" perspective

> If my paperwork is wrong, please let me know and I will send you a corrected version immediately.

Instead of indicting the reader, this second version conveys respect for the reader's viewpoint.

Use Plain English. Workplace correspondence too often suffers from *letterese*, those tired, stuffy, and overblown phrases some writers think they need, to make their communications seem important. Here is a typically overwritten closing sentence:

Letterese

> Humbly thanking you in anticipation of your kind cooperation, I remain Faithfully yours,

Although no-one *speaks* this way, some writers lean on such heavy prose instead of simply writing this:

Clear phrasing

> I will appreciate your cooperation.

Here are a few of the many old standards that are popular because they are easy to use but that make correspondence unimaginative and boring:

Letterese	*Plain-English*
As per your request	As you requested
Contingent upon receipt of	As soon as we receive
I am desirous of	I want, I would like
Please be advised that I	I
This writer	I
In the immediate future	Soon
In accordance with your request	As you requested
Due to the fact that	Because
I wish to express my gratitude.	Thank you.

Be natural. Write as you would speak in a classroom or office.

Anticipate Your Reader's Reaction. Like any effective writing, good correspondence does not just happen. It is the product of a deliberate process. As you plan, write, and revise, answer these questions:

1. *What do I want the reader to do, think, or feel after reading this correspondence?* (offer me a job, give me advice or information, answer my enquiry, follow my instructions, grant me a favour, enjoy good news, accept bad news)
2. *What facts will my reader need?* (measurements, dates, costs, model numbers, enclosures, other details)
3. *To whom am I writing?* (Do you know the reader's name? When possible, write to a person, not a title.)
4. *What is my relationship to my reader?* (Is the reader a potential employer, an employee, a person doing a favour, a person whose products are disappointing, an acquaintance, an associate, a stranger?)

Answer those four questions *before* drafting correspondence. After you have a draft, answer the following three questions, which pertain to the *effect* of your correspondence. Will readers be inclined to respond favourably?

5. *How will my reader react to what I've written?* (with anger, hostility, pleasure, confusion, fear, guilt, resistance, satisfaction)
6. *What impression of me will my reader get from this correspondence?* (intelligent, courteous, friendly, articulate, pretentious, illiterate, confident)
7. *Am I ready to sign my correspondence with confidence?* (Think about it.)

Send correspondence only when you have answered each question to your satisfaction.

Decide on a Direct or Indirect Plan. The reaction you anticipate from your reader should determine the organizational plan of your correspondence: either *direct* or *indirect*.

- Will the reader feel pleased or neutral about the message?
- Will the message cause resistance, resentment, or disappointment?

Each reaction calls for a different organizational plan. The direct plan puts the main point right in the first paragraph, followed by the explanation. Use the direct plan when you expect the reader to react with approval or when you want the reader to know immediately the point of your letter (e.g., in good-news, enquiry, or application letters—or other routine correspondence).

If you expect the reader to resist or to need persuading, consider an indirect plan. Give the explanation *before* the main point (as in refusing a request, admitting a mistake, or requesting a pay raise). An indirect plan might make readers more tolerant of bad news or more receptive to your argument.

Whenever you consider using an indirect plan, think carefully about its ethical implications. Never try to deceive the reader—and never create an impression that you have something to hide.

Structures for Workplace Correspondence

Trial and error, along with perceptive analysis of readers and purposes for letters, memos, etc., will allow you to find the best ways to organize your workplace correspondence. The best structure for each message will depend on the circumstances. You can start by using the audience/purpose analysis form to choose the content of the message. Then you can adapt the action structure described in Chapter 21 for virtually any letter, memo, or e-mail you write. Let's review that structure:

1. *Action opening:* Connect with reader's interest and, (where appropriate), summarize the full message in one or two sentences.
2. *Background:* Provide any information the reader needs to understand the main message that follows. Many letters and memos don't need this section; in others, you'll be able to fit a one-sentence background overview into the introductory paragraph.
3. *Details:* Present the main message. (Answer the reader's questions; describe your idea; present your information and analysis; argue your case; explain your point of view.)
4. *Action Closing:* Request the desired action from your reader and/or describe the action you intend to take. Provide information that the reader needs to perform the requested action.

Now let's see some examples of how that structure can work for common workplace messages. The scope of this book does not allow coverage of every kind of letter or memo you might eventually write in your working life, but a careful study of the following examples will help you learn how to adapt the action structure to many other kinds of messages.

Notice that some messages require a *direct approach*: the letter or memo's main point or bottom line is provided in the opening paragraph because you've realized that's what the reader wants and you've concluded that your own purpose will not be jeopardized by doing so. Other messages require an *indirect plan* where the opening paragraph previews the document's structure and the main point comes at the end of the document.

The enquiry described in Table 22.1 (and later illustrated by Figure 22.6) employs a direct pattern; the reader will want to immediately know the message's main purpose. Then, seeing the potential for business, the reader will be motivated to read carefully.

Table 22.1   Sample Enquiry (letter or e-mail) Structure

Section	Situation: Enquiry about updates for PURE anti-virus software Reader: PURE Inc. Client Services Department
Action Opening	State purpose for writing/general nature of enquiry (paragraph 1)
Background	Say how long you've had the PURE software installed; say whether you purchased a CD-ROM version or downloaded it from the Internet (paragraph 2)
Details	Ask detailed questions about the updates: • range of virus types detected • methods of receiving updates/frequency of updates • company's main strategy for discovering viruses • costs of updates/types of payment accepted by PURE (paragraph 3 uses numbered or bulleted list)
Action Closing	Provide e-mail address and phone number; ask PURE rep. to respond; give deadline for response, if that's an issue (paragraph 4)

Figure 22.6 illustrates the phrasing that might be used for the message that Table 22.1 outlines.

From: **Bart Nickel [bartn@peg.net]**
Sent: **February 11, 2004 10.56 am**
To: **custserv@pure.com**
Subject: Updates

The PURE anti-virus software is installed on my PC. Lately, when the machine boots up, I have been prompted to update the software. I've checked your Web site, but I still have some questions about ordering updates.

The software was installed three months ago from a CD-ROM which I purchased at Future Computers in Winnipeg. I understood from the salesperson that the software would not need updating for a year or more.

Before requesting an update, I'd like to know:
• why I might need an update so soon after the software purchase
• whether your send out software update information to all your customers, regardless of when they purchased the software
• which new viruses the updated version might detect and eliminate
• how your company discovers viruses that the software removes
• how you provide updates to your customers, and how frequently
• whether you charge for the update, and if so, how much

Please contact me at my e-mail address, or phone me at (906) 449-6390.

Bart Nickel

Figure 22.6   A Sample E-mail Enquiry

The situation outlined in the following table *also* uses a direct pattern: stating the requested action and its contribution to the *reader's* goals will get the reader's attention and help hold that attention throughout the memo.

Table 22.2   Sample Request Memo Structure

Section	Situation: Request for funds to design a company Web site Reader: General Manager Writer: Sales Representative
Action Opening	The main action that needs to be taken and the primary reason for that action, connect with reader's interests relative to this action (paragraph 1)
Background	Circumstances leading to this situation or events affecting the situation (paragraph 2)
Details	Detailed description of what is being requested or needs to be done: • staffing required • equipment and software required and whether the company currently has these requirements in inventory • time lines and schedule • costs (one or more paragraphs)
Action Closing	Request the specific desired action or reader's approval for the writer's proposed action (final paragraph)

Figure 22.7, on page 591 illustrates the phrasing that might be used for the message outlined above.

Next, the following claim letter (also know as an adjustment letter or a complaint letter) also uses a direct pattern. The writer immediately gets to the point.

Table 22.3   Claim Letter (or e-mail) Structure

Section	Situation: Claim for damages Reader: Manager, Shipping Department, Genesis Computer Systems Co. (an Edmonton wholesaler) Writer: Home-based computer consultant, Fort MacMurray Alberta
Action Opening	State the problem or the action requested (in this case, claim for a system damaged in shipment because of poor packing) (paragraph 1)
Background	Name the original order no., the packing slip no., the invoice no., and the method and date of shipment (paragraph 2)
Details	Details of the claim: • Describe the nature and extent of the equipment damage and estimate the damage. • Refer to how the damaged equipment is being returned to the supplier. (paragraph 3)

(Continued on page 592)

MEMO   *Magnum Mine Machinery*

DATE: June 23, 2005

TO: Kordell Dobson, General Sales Manager

FROM: Marc Bessier, Sales Representative *MB*

RE: **Company Web Site**

In Monday's monthly sales meeting, you mentioned the possibility of using e-commerce as a way of building our market base. Recent development in my sales territory reinforce the need to establish a company Web site as a first step toward e-commerce.

Background

My territory primarily consists of mining operations in northern Ontario and northern Manitoba. Because many of the mines are quite remote, they use the Internet to keep in touch with the world and to shop for equipment and supplies. I've been using the mail, phone calls, and fax messages to send product information and answer their enquiries, but I'm on the road 7 days out of 10, so it's difficult for me to respond promptly.

Several purchasing officers have told me that they'd prefer to go to the Internet for product information, prices, and availability. And they'd like to order on the Net, too.

Action Required

Our chief competitor, Allan-Price, has set up a home page. There's not much on it right now, and it's not very well organized, but Allan-Price has a presence on the Web, as Marco Corrazini of Canway's Musquean Mine pointedly told me on the phone yesterday. I think we have to keep up with Allan-Price.

What will establishing a Web site require? I called a friend at Merced Industrial Machines to learn how his company set up its top-quality site. He told me that some of the Merced head office people had computer experience, so they tried to do the work themselves. In the end, though, they had to call in a consultant, who charged about $5,000 to design and build the site. In addition, Merced purchased about $1500 worth of software. And it continues to pay a part-time Webmaster $400 per month to update and troubleshoot the site.

I contacted that same consultant, June Paschke, yesterday. She has three years' experience as a Web page designer. She said that building a site for us would take about the same amount of time (10 working days) and cost about the same as the Merced contract. Of course, she would have to meet with us before presenting a detailed proposal of her work plan and fees.

Authorization

May I arrange a meeting next Monday for June Paschke to discuss our needs and her solutions with you, me, and our other three regional sales representatives? We'll all be in town for the AGM. Also, may I meet with you to discuss my possible involvement in the project? I have a special interest in a Web site project because of its potential for building business. I'll be in Cochrane and Kapuskasing for the next two days, but I'll check frequently for messages on my pager, 689-4352.

Figure 22.7 A Sample Request

Table 22.3   Claim Letter (or e-mail) Structure   (Continued)

Section	Situation: Claim for damages
Details	• Describe the loss of business (the customer went to another dealer). • Refer to enclosed documents.
Action Closing	Close politely, but firmly—say what you expect to be done, and confirm that you desire continued business relations with the reader (paragraph 4)

As the preceding samples show, the direct, four-part action structure can be adapted for a variety of situations. Some of those situations, such as a refusal of a request, will require an indirect pattern. Here's a suggested structure for refusing a request.

Table 22.4   Refusal Message Structure

Section	Situation: Respond to request for funds to design a company Web site Reader: Sales Representative Writer: General Manager
Action Opening	Express appreciation for the sales rep's initiative; acknowledge that there has recently been discussion of creating a company Web site (paragraph 1)
Background	Without actually saying "no" just yet, explain the circumstances which preclude creating a Web site at this time (perhaps the firm is in the process of contracting a Web consultant or joining forces with another firm, or perhaps the company is analyzing its entire marketing strategy) (paragraph 2)
Details	Soften the bad news by: • placing it in the middle of the paragraph • using the passive voice (not, "we cannot grant your request at this time," but, "Funds are therefore not available for this project at this time.") • focusing on the reasons for the refusal, not on the refusal itself (part of paragraph 2, or perhaps a new paragraph)
Action Closing	Thank the reader for his/her commitment and ideas; encourage him/her to pursue an interest in Web site design; assure the reader that he/she will be consulted when the project is next discussed (final paragraph)

When Kordel Dobson writes to refuse Marc Bessier's request, here's the phrasing Kordell uses.

MEMO   *Magnum Mine Machinery*

DATE: June 23, 2005

TO: Marc Bessier, Sales Representative

FROM: Kordell Dobson, General Sales Manager

RE: **Your Ideas for a Company Web Site**

Thank you for your initiative in promoting the creation of our own Web site. Over the past few months there have indeed been some recent discussions about establishing a presence on the Web.

I'm going to be in Montreal until next week, so I'm faxing this memo to your hotel in Timmins. Next week my preparations for the AGM and my participation in the AGM's follow-up meetings will occupy my time.

We are in negotiations to merge with a Western Canadian firm, in order to give both firms a national presence. (I'm sure you've heard the rumours.) If indeed that merger happens, we will combine our strategies and resources with that firm on many fronts. In the meantime, all new projects are on hold, including the creation of new marketing vehicles and e-commerce. We haven't discussed the possibility of establishing a Web site with our potential merger partner; too many other issues need to be resolved first.

I appreciate your commitment to the firm's goals. Please continue your interest in Web page design, so that you can contribute to future discussion and actions in this exciting method of communicating with our present and future customers. Perhaps we can grab a few minutes to discuss your ideas, after the CEO's address on Monday.

Kordell

Kordell Dobson

Figure 22.8   A Sample Refusal of a Request

Length of Workplace Correspondence

All letters and memos should be as short as you can make them. Restrict them to one page, if you can. Although one-page messages are not always possible—see several samples in Chapter 21, for example—you can restrict some messages to one page by placing the main message in a cover letter and the remaining details in enclosures. For instance, a complex order for supplies might be organized in order sheets enclosed with a cover letter which:

- authorizes the purchase, designates the delivery method, and names the source of your information about the supplies
- quickly summarizes the nature of the order and refers to the enclosed order "forms" (which provide details of items, quantities, order numbers, prices, taxes, shipping, and overall costs)
- closes by saying how you will pay and when you expect delivery

A Final Word

When you write workplace correspondence, write efficiently. Very few one-page messages should take more than 45 minutes to plan, compose, and polish. You will, however, take longer if you have to re-write major sections of letters or memos. That kind of re-writing can be avoided by clear thinking in the early stages of the process.

So, remember:

- Consider your audience's needs, interests, and priorities and the purpose of the document.
- Use your audience/purpose analysis to choose the content and arrange that content.
- Work from an outline that identifies the content and/or purpose of each paragraph.
- Revise the content and structure before writing sentences and paragraphs.

You'll be amazed at how efficiently you'll write.

☑ EXERCISES

1. Design a letterhead and a memohead for a business that you would like to start.

2. Collect samples of workplace writing—letters, memos, and e-mail messages. In those samples, look for instances of letterese, clichés, and wordy and unclear phrasing. Improve the phrasing where necessary.

3. Check the tone of memos and letters which you examine. Do you see phrasing that might antagonize the reader? Do you see phrasing that places the writer's needs and interests ahead of the reader's? If so, re-phrase.

4. Examine workplace letters and memos to see if they use a variation of the four-part action structure. (See pages 588 to 592 and Chapter 21.) If the action structure has not been used for a given message would the message be more effective if it were re-structured?

5. Monitor your next composition of a one-page letter, memo, or e-mail. Record how long you take to complete each stage of the writing process. (See Chapter 3.)

☑ COLLABORATIVE PROJECT

In conjunction with other members of your class, survey correspondence practices of businesses in your part of Canada.

Ask about:

- which page format (block, full-block, simplified) the business prefers its employees to use and whether those employees are encouraged to use attention lines and/or subject lines
- which addressing format is favoured by the business
- whether the business allows its employees to use abbreviations in external messages

Also, ask for a sample letter and a sample internal memo.

Members of your group could conduct the survey in person. If so, send a copy of the survey questions with an accompanying letter first, and then telephone for an appointment. Emphasize that information in the sample letters and memos will be held confidential. Also offer to make a copy of the survey's statistical results available to each participating business.

Alternatively, the entire survey could be conducted by mail.

Note: All letters sent during the survey should be approved by an editing team appointed by the class.

Job-search Communications

Self-assessment Inventory

Completing a Self-inventory

Your Transferable Skills

Personal Job Assessment

Your Career Orientation

Choosing Positions to Pursue

Job Market Research

Identify Information Needs

Identify Information Sources

Enquiries

Networking

Producing Job-search Materials

Uses for Résumés

Preparing Your Résumé

Organizing Your Résumé

Image Projection

Electronic Résumés

Contacting Employers

Campaign Strategies

Contact Methods

Employment Interviews

Interview Preparation

Questions

Answers

Follow-ups to Interviews

Responding to Job Offers

Technology has added new tools for job seekers, but today's job searches require the same basic approach and communication skills which have been used for some time. This chapter discusses seven steps in a successful job search:

1. Assessing what you have to offer
2. Identifying which kinds of jobs to pursue
3. Researching the job market
4. Producing résumés and other job-search documents
5. Devising a campaign strategy of contacting employers
6. Performing well in interviews
7. Responding to job offers

Being informed about careers and specific positions in your field, preparing to meet professional requirements, and then following a systematic job-search strategy will increase your future *job satisfaction.*

Self-assessment Inventory

Assessing what you have to offer employers is not easy to do, especially if you have not received detailed, accurate job performance appraisals from previous employers. Self-assessment is even more difficult for those of you who have had little job experience to use as a basis for evaluating your skills and aptitudes. Assessing your package of employable characteristics requires objectivity and an organized approach. Fortunately, tools such as the self-inventory shown in Figure 23.1 help provide that structured objectivity.

Apparent to Audience	Subtle or Not Obvious
1. Strengths	2. Strengths
3. Limitations	4. Limitations

Figure 23.1   A Self-inventory

Completing a Self-inventory

The self-inventory chart's four sections (quadrants) can be completed in any sequence. The chart can be very useful if you fill each quadrant with lists of your transferable skills (see next section), work habits, attitudes, and/or knowledge which make up the full package you bring to an employer. You can use this chart to choose content for your résumés, or to help write an application letter, or to prepare for a job interview.

Quadrant 1. Quadrant 1, "apparent strengths," features those qualities that an employer would discover by reading your résumé, interviewing your references, or by asking you certain questions in an interview. For example, you may have had several years work experience in which you developed skills required by the position you're applying for. Or, your college major may have developed skills required by the position. By highlighting such strengths in your résumé and cover letters, you can create the image you want to project. Reviewing quadrant 1 will also help you prepare your strategy for job interviews.

Quadrant 2. The "subtle strengths" in quadrant 2 will be more difficult to project to employers. These strengths may include such qualities as your loyalty, capacity for long hours and hard work, or desire to succeed in your career. Such qualities are difficult to build into traditional (reverse chronological) résumés, but you could use some of the following techniques to highlight your subtle strengths:

- Start your résumé with a profile section that summarizes the main positive features you bring to a particular position.
- Use a functional résumé or hybrid résumé that includes sections of relevant skills and attitudes.
- Attach reference letters that mention your less obvious strengths.
- Refer to your "quiet strengths" in your application letter.

Quadrant 3. Quadrant 3 includes those characteristics that you and the employer will readily identify as potential limitations on your ability to do the job. The most common limitation for applicants trying to enter a given field would be lack of experience in that area. You can be certain that these limitations will be considered when the employer chooses which applicants to interview, and that the interviewer will either ask about these limitations or will wait to see what you have to say about them.

So, what can you do? Trying to avoid discussing your obvious limitations does not work. You need to directly address the issue by showing that you have indeed developed the skills and understanding needed for the job, through college work placements, realistic class projects, volunteer work, and/or leisure activities. (If you have not in fact developed the requirements for the position, you should not apply!)

Quadrant 4. Quadrant 4 houses those limitations that the employer will not discover unless you blurt them out. You may have an aversion to writing the daily reports required by your job, for example. Or you may be a "night person" who has difficulty getting to work on time in the morning. Or you may not like the customer service component of a position that otherwise appeals very much to you. Or perhaps your perfectionist tendencies bring you into conflict with others.

There are two main issues here, an ethical issue and a practical one. Ethically, you should not present yourself for a position where you are not prepared to work wholeheartedly. You should also not apply for a position if you have attitudes that you are not prepared to change and that you know will hamper your performance in the job. On the other hand, if you are aware of a potential limitation and you are in the process of overcoming the problem, there may be no need to reveal the problem when the interviewer asks you to comment about your limitations.

Your Transferable Skills

Another very useful tool in determining your employable characteristics is a list of the transferable skills which you have previously developed. As Figure 23.2 demonstrates, such a list includes proof ("validating experience") as well as the skills themselves.

Skill	Above Average	Average	Below Average	Validating Experience
Programming in Java	✔			• Programming project in CoSci 356—mark: 92% • Co-op work experience at Fundy Industries—good evaluation
Supervising/coaching /leading	✔			• Coached Jr. lacrosse 3 yrs • Bell captain at Lakeshore Lodge for two summers
Report writing		✔		• Completed 5 major reports at college—avg grade: 70% • Collaborated on documentation report at Fundy Industries—involved in all phases of 95-page report
Keying	✔			• Timed at 64 words per minute
Problem solving	✔			• Won software troubleshooting competition 2 yrs at college

Figure 23.2   A Segment of a Transferable Skills Inventory

Many of the transferable skills valued by employers are communication skills: writing, speaking, listening, reading, and interpersonal. Such skills are featured in the "Critical Skills Required of the Canadian Workforce" identified by the Corporate Council on Education, a program sponsored by the Conference Board of Canada. (See the "In Brief" box on page 601 for more details.)

Personal Job Assessment

The long-term goal for your job search should be job satisfaction, so after you have thoroughly examined what makes you employable, you should choose what kinds of positions to pursue. Before drawing up a list of positions for which to apply, you will benefit from thinking about your life goals and reasons for working. After all, most of us spend a large portion of our lives at work.

Your Career Orientation

What motivates you to work? What benefits and satisfactions most attract you to certain types of positions? Knowing the answer to these questions may help you choose your career path and help you in your job-search activities.

Here is a set of categories that reflect what workers hope to "get" from their jobs:

1. *Getting ahead.* This worker looks for advancement within an organization, and starts looking elsewhere if the organization doesn't have such opportunities.
2. *Getting rich.* This worker is primarily interested in a position's financial benefits. Even though he/she may find the work stimulating, this person will take less interesting positions if the pay is better.
3. *Getting secure.* Some workers will sacrifice organizational status and high salaries for long-term security.
4. *Getting control.* This employee wants to control his/her work day, to reduce stress and to be more productive. Sometimes this person equates "control" with controlling others.
5. *Getting high on work.* This person loves the work he/she does, and would likely do it for no pay if a pay cheque wasn't necessary.
6. *Getting balanced.* Many employees stay in jobs that no longer challenge them because they see their work as just one part of their lives; their families and their leisure activities or community activities are as important or more important than their work.

IN BRIEF

Employability Skills Profile: The Critical Skills Required of the Canadian Workplace

Academic Skills	Personal Management Skills	Teamwork Skills
Those skills that provide the basic foundation to get, keep, and progress on a job and to achieve the best results	The combination of skills, attitudes, and behaviours required to get, keep, and progress on a job and to achieve the best results	Those skills needed to work with others on a job and to achieve the best results
Canadian employers need a person who can:	Canadian employers need a person who can demonstrate:	Canadian employers need a person who can:

Communicate

- Understand and speak the languages in which business is conducted
- Listen to understand and learn
- Read, comprehend, and use written materials, including graphs, charts, and displays
- Write effectively in the language in which business is conducted

Think

- Think critically and act logically to evaluate situations, solve problems, and make decisions
- Understand and solve problems involving mathematics, and use the results
- Use technology, instruments, tools, and information systems effectively
- Access and apply specialized knowledge from various fields (e.g., skilled trades, technology, physical sciences, arts, and social sciences

Learn

- Continue to learn for life

Positive Attitudes and Behaviours

- Self-esteem and confidence
- Honesty, integrity, and personal ethics
- A positive attitude toward learning, growth, and personal health
- Initiative, energy, and persistence to get the job done

Responsibility

- The ability to set goals and priorities in work and personal life
- The ability to plan and manage time, money, and other resources to achieve goals
- Accountability for actions taken

Adaptability

- A positive attitude toward change
- Recognition of and respect for people's diversity and individual differences
- The ability to identify and suggest new ideas to get the job done creatively

Work with Others

- Understand and contribute to the organization's goals
- Understand and work within the culture of the group
- Plan and make decisions with others and support the outcomes
- Respect the thoughts and opinions of others in the group
- Exercise "give and take" to achieve group results
- Seek a team approach as appropriate
- Lead when appropriate, mobilizing the group for high performance

★ ★ ★

Source: This document was developed by the Corporate Council on Education, a program of the National Business and Education Center, The Conference Board of Canada.

IN BRIEF

Today's New Worker

Barbara Moses, a career development specialist, has put a new spin on what she calls "today's new worker." She describes six profiles of "new workers":

1. **Independent thinkers:** Want to own or build their own work; impatient with corporate norms; little allegiance to the company; detest endless meetings.
2. **Lifestylers:** Determined to balance outside interests and responsibilities with career. Motto: "I work to live, not live to work."
3. **Personal developers:** Evaluate their work in terms of whether they're being challenged; will take career risks if they thus develop new skills; identify with their work, not with their employer.
4. **Careerists:** Ambitious; aspire to management roles; motivated by prestige and status.
5. **Authenticity seekers:** Motto: "I gotta be me." Won't sacrifice their own personality in order to play a corporate role; can be creative, but difficult to manage if employer demands conformity to corporate norms.
6. **Collegiality seekers:** Associate strongly with their team or work group and derive much of their identity from belonging to it; what's important is working with people they enjoy; not happy working by themselves.

Source: Barbara Moses, "The challenge: How to satisfy the new worker's agenda," *Globe and Mail*, p.B15, Nov. 10, 1998.

Choosing Positions to Pursue

Choosing what types of work to do involves a simple four-step process:

- *Step 1.* List the positions you would like to have, the jobs you would like to do. Don't worry about your qualifications for these positions just yet.
- *Step 2.* List the positions that you could currently handle, based on your self-inventory of employable characteristics and transferable skills. If you're close to completing an educational or training program, you could also list those positions you'll soon be able to handle successfully.
- *Step 3.* Check which positions are on both lists and organize them on the basis of two criteria: (1) which positions appeal to you the most, and (2) which positions best suit your qualifications. It's important to be realistic at this point, but it's also important to try to identify what you consider ideal employment. You might also list positions for which you'll be qualified after you gain more work experience.
- *Step 4.* Confirm that you have included the full range of positions open to people with your interests and qualifications. For example, a person with a degree in technical writing might consider working as a web page designer and webmaster, or a B.Sc. graduate with a major in botany might

look at developing new varieties of plants for a commercial greenhouse, or a civil engineering technologist might explore the opportunities for a consultant contracting for small towns in a rural region.

So, now you have a list of what types of positions to pursue. The next task in your job search is to learn what's available.

Job Market Research

Again, you need an organized approach:

- identify information needs
- identify information sources
- use a variety of research tools to ensure that you find all available positions, including those in the "hidden job market"

Identify Information Needs

Unfortunately, wanting to hold a particular position does not guarantee that such a position is currently available. You'll need to research the job market to learn several key things:

- which of your desired positions are available now, and which might be available in the near future
- which companies are expanding and thus requiring additional workers
- which companies have internship programs or will accept "volunteer employees"
- what qualifications are required for specific positions
- when and how companies recruit for seasonal employees and/or permanent employees
- which firms contract some or all of their work and how you can monitor these firms' on-going contract requests
- which business trends and expansion of government or commercial operations can be anticipated for the foreseeable future

Your first research step, then, should be to decide the scope of your information search. In your current job search, do you need to know only which companies are hiring, or will soon be hiring, people like you? Or, are you interested in the full range of information listed in the previous paragraph? Your information requirements will determine which of the following job market information sources you use.

Identify Information Sources

Literally hundreds of information banks can help you find employers and jobs. Some of these will list available positions; others will help you direct your spoken or written enquiries.

The following information sources should provide valuable leads:

Useful information sources

1. **Campus Placement Office.** Most universities and colleges have placement offices. Those institutions that offer co-op work programs provide information about co-op employers; also, evaluation reports written by former co-op students are on file.
2. **Canada Employment Centres** and **Job Futures** publications.
3. **Career Planning Annual** published by the University and College Placement Association provides information on employer-members who recruit at the college and university level.
4. **College Placement Annual** published by the College Placement Council contains a list of companies in both Canada and the U.S. who are seeking college and university graduates.
5. **Canadian Trade Index** provides information about Canadian manufacturers.
6. **Dun & Bradstreet Canadian Key Business Directory** has information about businesses in Canada.
7. **Standard & Poor's Register of Corporations, Directors, and Executives** contains an alphabetical listing of more than 35,000 corporations in Canada and the U.S. showing products and services, officers, and telephone numbers.
8. **Financial Post's 100 Best Companies** groups companies according to their service or product and includes information on work environment and benefits.
9. **Canadian Miner's Handbook** includes information about the Canadian mining industry.
10. **Lumberman's Green Book** provides information on the forest industry.
11. **Newspaper feature articles** focus on companies and executives, expansion plans, new products, and key appointments.
12. **Trade or professional journals and associations** list opportunities, trade shows, seminars, and meetings that provide opportunities for networking.
13. **Job postings in government publications.**
14. **The Internet** provides information (labour markets, companies, job postings, job-search skills) and offers services (for a fee) to individuals wishing to post a résumé. The following sites will be of interest:

    www.monster.com

    www.careermag.com

    canada.careermosaic.com

    www.theglobeandmail.com/careerconnect (ads, job-search tips, on-line résumé submissions)

    www.careerhunters.com

www.careerbridge.com

ngr.schoolnet.ca/ (National Graduate Register database by Industry Canada, plus many hotlinks)

jb-ge.hrdc-drhc.gc.ca

www.activemploi.com

In addition to information gleaned from Web sites such as the ones listed above, you can learn a great deal about some companies by visiting their home pages. Besides telling about their operations, many companies list job openings on their Web pages.

Enquiries

Statistics Canada's 1997 survey of job hunting techniques revealed that 69% of Canadian job seekers contacted employers directly in the early stages of a job search. Many of those contacts were enquiries about potential openings.

Why Enquire? You should enquire about potential employment if you don't know if a company will have a position for someone like you **and** if you're not sure whether the company's available position would suit your interests and qualifications. Also, a well-crafted enquiry will tell you which additional skills you will have to develop.

The following advice applies particularly to letter enquiries but much of the advice could also be applied to telephone and in-person enquiries.

Your main challenge in sending unsolicited enquiries is getting the reader to respond. To meet that challenge, you must do two main things:

1. You must show your reader that you have something to offer the company. The best way to do this is to quickly review your qualifications and refer your reader to an enclosed résumé for more details. Remember, though, that you're not applying for a named position in this letter, so do not write a sales pitch. Save that for any application letter that you later send to this same reader.

2. You must make it easy for the reader to respond. Even the kindest, best-intentioned reader will place your enquiry at the bottom of a priority list if a response to your letter requires a lot of time and effort.

Tips. Here are some tips for reducing your reader's effort, and thus increasing the chances of getting a response to your enquiry:

- Use a structure that the reader can easily follow. (See chapter 22, page 588, for details.)
- Place your questions in a numbered or bulleted word list.
- Make sure those questions follow a logical order (the first logical question for most job enquiries will be whether the employer has, or anticipates having, openings in your field).

- Make each question absolutely clear. (Show your letter to others before sending it.)
- Ask a reasonable number of questions; five seems to be the limit.
- Do not ask questions that you could easily answer by reading the company's annual report, visiting its Web site, or phoning the company's personnel office.
- Use appropriate tone and phrasing: positive, assertive, polite, concise, business-like, fresh (no clichés), and energetic (active verbs).
- Make it easy for the reader to respond: Where feasible, offer to phone or visit your reader to get the information.
- Display the "you" attitude by focusing on the nature of the work involved, rather than on how you might benefit.

The enquiry illustrated in Figure 23.3 on page 607 was sent by a Civil Engineering Technology student who was responding to an invitation he had received while on co-op job placement.

Chris Hendsbee's accompanying résumé is shown in Figure 23.9, on pages 618 and 619.

Networking

Surprisingly, in 1997 only 22 percent of Canadian job seekers contacted friends, relatives, and/or former colleagues, students, or teachers as part of a job search. That statistic is slightly higher for better-educated job seekers: In 1997, about 25 percent of university graduates asked friends and relatives to pass on information about job opportunities.

The other three-quarters of job seekers missed a very powerful two-way communication tool. Let's examine the power of networking.

Jenny Roy, age 25, recently graduated from the Environmental Sciences program at the University of Waterloo. After graduation, she landed a four-month contract with Cambrian Consultants, a private firm investigating the link between water quality and fish stocks in Georgian Bay. But that contract ran its course and Jenny had had no luck finding other employment through newspaper ads, Internet sites, environmental journals, or her enquiries to a variety of private and government operations.

In desperation, she turned to several people who had been influential in her life:

- her mother, Adrienne Lavois, who worked as an administrative secretary in the Department of Indian Affairs in Ottawa
- her uncle, Pierre Riley, a retired geologist in Montreal
- her mentor, Dr. Howard Cash, who taught freshwater biology at the University of Waterloo
- a former classmate, Sandy Travers, who worked as a lab assistant at the University of Guelph
- her high school volleyball coach, Nancy St. Jean, who ran a fishing lodge on Lake Temagami

453B Gordon Drive
Kelowna BC V1W 2T1
January 27, 1999

Mr. Miro Betts
International Survey Systems
1199 – 11th S.W.
Calgary AB T2R 1K7

Dear Mr. Betts:

In late October, at Greenwood Consultants in Nelson, your demonstration of real-time kinematics further kindled an interest I've developed in GPS surveying techniques. Your invitation to contact ISS this winter has led to this enquiry.

As you may remember, I'm studying Civil Engineering Technology at Okanagan University College. Also, my interest in GPS has prompted me to read widely on the subject. That's partly why I was so enthusiastic about the accuracy of the equipment you demonstrated in Nelson. Now, I'm eager to get a chance to work with a company such as yours.

Consequently, I'm wondering:

1. whether ISS will have an opening for someone like me, this May to September
2. what the work would entail and what equipment might be used
3. what qualifications ISS would require, and
4. whether I should upgrade my qualifications to be ready to work for ISS this summer. (Please see the attached résumé for my current qualifications.)

Would it be possible for me to meet with you or another representative to discuss what I might contribute to ISS? I am willing to travel wherever you set up a meeting in Alberta or B.C. You can contact me at my e-mail address, chris@silk.net, or you can leave a phone message at (250) 876-3422, and I'll return your call as soon as I return from class.

Sincerely,

Chris Hendsbee

Chris Hendsbee

Enclosure: Résumé

Figure 23.3 A Sample Job Enquiry

Initially, these five people agreed to watch for possible positions for Jenny. They offered to distribute résumés for her and to talk to their friends, relatives, business acquaintances, and colleagues. At that point, Jenny had five people "searching" for job leads. Figure 23.4 shows how she might have diagrammed her network:

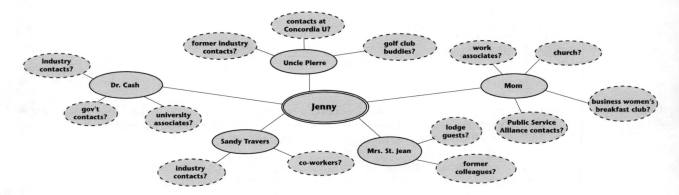

Figure 23.4   A Basic Network

Jenny originally thought only in terms of her five front-line searchers. She didn't anticipate how far the network could develop. Indeed, she didn't know that dozens of strangers would be contributing to her job search. Let's see how just one of the contact lines developed (Figure 23.5):

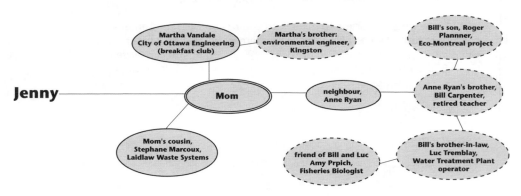

Figure 23.5   An Expanded Network

In addition to Jenny's mother, eight other people became aware of a bright, eager, young person looking for work. For various reasons, all of them were on alert for suitable employment opportunities and were prepared to pass their information along. The amazing thing is that only two of them, Jenny's mother's neighbour and Jenny's mother's cousin, have ever met Jenny! ■

If you think that the basic assumption behind the networking concept is naïve, and if you say that there's no motivation for people to actively seek employment for someone whom they've never met, remember two things:

1. The person farther down the network (Bill Carpenter's brother-in-law, for example) is not really doing a favour for Jenny; he's doing it for his friend (or brother-in-law, in this case).

2. Each person in the network only has to pass on information, which is not a time-consuming or onerous task. Most often, this type of information is passed along during casual, friendly conversation.

Jenny's situation, though fictional, is common enough. She can get a tip about an opportunity from any one of the many "researchers" in her network. Thus, she has a strong chance of tapping into the huge hidden job market—the vast majority of available positions are not formally advertised.

To further confirm the power of networking, let's look at a rather dramatic real-life example. The central figure's name has been changed, but the details of his story are accurate.

In 1990, Jim Landon lost his sawmill job when Simpson Timber closed its operation in Hudson Bay, Saskatchewan. Jim had worked at the mill since leaving high school in 1970. In a job-search program sponsored by his employer, Jim learned how to use networking for his job search. It appealed to Jim: He'd used the concept successfully in raising funds for minor hockey in his community.

Jim tied the networking idea to a rather novel approach: He produced snapshot résumés on 8 cm x 9 cm (3" x 3½") filing cards, as shown in Figure 23.6.

Basic contact information	**Jim Landon** Box 309 Hudson Bay SK S0D 3T4 Phone: (306) 334-7429
Names positions, but doesn't restrict his chances	<u>Preferred Position</u> Production line worker, loader, or yard worker in sawmill or plywood mill
Quick summary of relevant experience. Shows potential for adapting to a variety of positions	<u>Experience</u> 20 years at Simpson Timber, Hudson Bay (Mill to close this summer.) Have performed all sawmill production jobs. Expert in sorting and grading lumber. Skilled with wide variety of power tools and equipment.
Suggests high level of motivation	<u>Personal Characteristics</u> Hard working and conscientious. Loyal. Eager to earn living for family of four. Will relocate. Willing to work any hours.

Figure 23.6   Snapshot Résumé

Jim worked part-time pumping gas and diesel fuel at the Co-op station on the Yellowhead Highway which runs through Hudson Bay. He gave copies of his mini-résumé to truckers on their way from Quebec and Ontario to British Columbia. He asked the truckers to leave the résumés at truck stops in Alberta and British Columbia.

A month after his campaign began, Jim received a call from a mill near Sparwood, British Columbia. The mill manager's brother had found a copy of Jim's card résumé on a bulletin board in Fernie, 29 kilometres down the road from Sparwood. After going to Sparwood for an interview, Jim accepted a job offer. ■

Producing Job-search Materials

Jim Landon's card is just one kind of sales material produced by job searchers. The most common sales tool is called a *résumé*. It provides an objective, organized record of key facts about the applicant and summarizes the applicant's skills.

Uses for Résumés

Résumés accompany letters of introduction, application letters, and enquiries. You can send them by fax or e-mail; you can send them as follow-ups to self-introduction telephone calls; and you can leave them at each employer in a campaign of visiting business offices and other places of employment. You can also use a résumé to accompany a business proposal.

Preparing Your Résumé

You may need two or more résumés, depending on the range of positions you decide to pursue. Indeed, it's a good idea to modify your basic résumé to match each position for which you apply. Different positions emphasize certain requirements more than others, so you might place your education first in one résumé and your work experience first in another. A third résumé might expand the amount of detail regarding your volunteer experiences, if you've developed relevant skills through that experience.

Basic Considerations. Employers generally spend 15 to 45 seconds initially scanning a résumé. They look for an obvious and persuasive answer to the question, "What can you do for us?"

Employers are impressed by a résumé that:

1. looks good (conservative, tasteful, uncluttered, on quality paper)
2. reads easily (headings, typeface, spacing, and punctuation that provide clear orientation)
3. provides information the employer needs to decide whether to interview the applicant

Employers generally discard résumés that are mechanically flawed, cluttered, sketchy, or difficult to follow. Don't leave readers guessing or annoyed; make the résumé perfect.

Most résumés organize the information within these categories:

- name and contact information
- job and career objectives
- educational background
- work experience
- personal data
- interests, leisure pursuits, volunteer activities, awards, and skills
- references

Select and organize material to emphasize what you can offer. Don't just list *everything*; be selective. (We're talking about *communicating*, not just delivering information.) Don't abbreviate, because some readers might not know the referent and because other readers may infer that you're lazy and take shortcuts. Use punctuation to clarify and emphasize, not to be "artsy."

Begin your résumé well before you plan to use the document as part of your job search. You'll need time to do a first-class job. Your final version can be duplicated for various similar targets, but each new type of job requires a new résumé that is tailored to fit the advertised demands of the job. Most job seekers find it useful to create two or three different résumés that have different emphases and different lengths, so that these can be quickly modified to suit positions which suddenly appear.

> *Caution:* Never invent or misrepresent credentials. Your résumé should make you look as good as the facts allow. Distorting the facts is unethical and counter-productive. Companies routinely investigate claims made in résumés and people who have lied are fired.

Name and Address. As a heading, include your full name, mailing address, phone number, and e-mail address. Make your name stand out by using a larger font and by bolding it. If you anticipate an address change after a certain date, include both your current and future addresses and the date of the change. Make it easy for an employer to contact you!

Job and Career Objectives. Your job market research should give you a good idea of the specific jobs for which you *realistically* qualify. Resist the impulse to be all things to all people. Be prepared to have different statements of objectives to meet the requirements of different job descriptions.

The key to a successful résumé is the image of you it projects. That image should *accurately* reflect your package of qualities and qualifications, but it should also match the position's requirements. For example, the following Career Objective appeared in a résumé submitted to a municipal engineering department by a civil engineering technologist with 11 years' work experience and several courses in business administration.

Career Objective
Project planning and administration for a municipal engineering office, with responsibility for cost-effective solutions to urban traffic and transportation problems.

To save space, you can omit your statement of career objectives and include it in the accompanying letter.

Educational Background. If your education is more substantial than your work experience, place it first for emphasis. Begin with your most recent school and work backward, listing degrees, diplomas, and schools attended beyond high school (unless the high school's prestige, its program, or your achievements warrant its inclusion). List the courses that have directly prepared you for the job you seek. Where applicable, name co-op work placements or special projects that have helped you develop relevant skills and knowledge.

Work Experience. If you have solid experience that relates to the job you seek, list it before your education. Begin by listing your most recent experience and then work backward, listing each significant job you've had. Describe your exact duties in each job, indicating promotions. Where applicable, describe skills developed in certain positions.

The standard heading, "Work Experience," might not adequately describe your situation. If that's the case, here are some alternative ways of highlighting your valuable experience:

- Provide two categories, "Related Experience" and "Other Work Experience." In the first category, include related volunteer experience, as long as it is substantial enough to merit inclusion. In the second category, list those positions not related to the position for which you're currently applying. Include details of non-related work experience to show that you've had significant experience and to highlight such qualities as loyalty, leadership ability, or ability to learn new skills quickly.
- Feature a special category called "Volunteer Experience." A person's experience in a service club or other organization will develop skills needed for a particular position, sometimes at a very high level.
- Create a separate category called either "Practicum Experience" or "Co-op Experience" if you've had significant work experience through a college work placement.

Personal Data. An employer cannot legally discriminate on the basis of gender, age, religion, race, national origin, disability, or marital status. Therefore, you aren't required to provide this information. But if you believe that any of this information could advance your prospects, by all means include it.

Personal Interests, Activities, Awards, and Skills. List leisure activities, sports, and other pastimes. Employers use this information to learn whether you will easily fit into an existing work team. Also list memberships and offices held in teams and organizations. Employers value team skills and leadership potential. If your volunteer experience is not directly related to the position for which you're applying, include that volunteer work in this personal activity section; employers know that people with well-rounded lifestyles are likely to take an active interest in their jobs. But be selective—list only those items that reflect qualities employers seek.

References. List three to five people *who have agreed to provide* strong, positive assessments of your qualifications and personal qualities. Some of their support will come in the form of requested letters or e-mail responses. Other references will be asked to complete reference forms. Or, you could request reference letters from previous employers, teachers, or others who have closely observed your work habits and skills. Still other reference requests will come in the form of telephone calls from employers who are doing reference checks.

Some employers use references to narrow the list of applicants to a shortlist. Others will contact references after interviews have been conducted. Usually, the motivation for these follow-up calls is to confirm interviewers' perceptions or to investigate aspects which troubled the interviewers during the interview.

Often, then, your references' comments can make or break your application. So, choose those references carefully:

- Select references who can speak with authority about your ability and character.
- Choose among previous employers, professors, and respected community figures who know you well enough to *comment concretely* on your behalf. (Opinions without detailed, concrete observations will not usually convince alert employers.)
- Do not choose members of your family or friends not in your field.
- When asking someone to be a reference, don't simply ask, "Could you please act as one of my references?" This question leaves the person little chance to refuse, but this person might not know you well or might be unimpressed by your work and therefore might provide a watery reference that does you more harm than good. Instead, ask: "Do you know me and my work well enough to provide a strong reference?" This second approach gives your respondent the option of declining gracefully or it elicits a firm commitment to a positive recommendation.

Your listing of references should include each person's name, position title or occupation, full address, phone number, e-mail address, or other method of contacting the person. You might also indicate the nature of the person's reference (work, academic, character, supervisory) if that's not obvious from your listing of the person's occupation.

Note: There is some controversy about whether to include references in a résumé. Some job-search counsellors suggest a line saying "References available upon request." These advisors argue that the employer will then call you to get those references and you'll have an opportunity to make a positive impression. The problem is that if other qualified applicants *have* listed references in *their* résumés, the employer will save time and effort by interviewing them instead of you.

Counsellors at colleges that have job placement offices will sometimes advise graduates to list the address of the placement office where employers can get your list of references. The problem with that arrangement is that you lose control of which references are provided for certain applications.

Organizing Your Résumé

Organize your résumé in the order that conveys the strongest impression of your qualifications, skills, and experience. Depending on your background, you can arrange your material in reverse chronological order, functional order, or a combination of both.

Reverse Chronological Organization. In a reverse chronological résumé you list your most recent experience first, moving backward through your earlier experiences. Use this arrangement to show a pattern of job experiences or progress along a specific career path. Reverse chronology suits applicants who have a well-established record of relevant experience and education. Many employers like this traditional organization because they're used to it and they find it easy to read. Marcel Dionne's résumé in Figure 23.7 on page 616 shows an example of the traditional reverse chronological order.

Functional Organization. In a functional résumé, you emphasize skills, abilities, and achievements that relate specifically to the job for which you are applying. Use this arrangement if you have limited job experience, gaps in your employment record, or are changing careers. See Carol Hampton's résumé in Figure 23.8 on page 617 for an example.

Combined Organization. Most employers prefer chronologically ordered résumés because they are easier to scan. However, electronic scanning of résumés calls for a more functional pattern. One alternative is a modified-functional résumé which preserves the logical progression that employers prefer but which also highlights your abilities and job skills (as in Christopher Hendsbee's résumé shown in Figure 23.9 on pages 618 and 619).

Image Projection

When you plan, write, edit, and periodically adjust your résumés, evaluate them according to how well they project your desired image. If, for example, you want to be seen as energetic, active, and enthusiastic, be sure to include information about your volunteer activities and outdoor leisure pursuits. Further project the desired image by choosing active verbs such as "led," "organized," "built," maintained," and "completed."

Also, have your résumé project an image consistent with the position's requirements. For example, if you're applying for a position where you'd spend half your time in the field collecting samples and the other half assessing those samples and reporting the results, use language and provide facts which reveal your writing skills and the meticulous side of your nature, as well as your physical fitness.

Electronic Résumés

Today's electronic résumés usually are on-line versions of hard copy résumés (with differences explained below). Increasingly, these will appear as hypertext documents with links to the applicant's placement dossier, publications, and other support material. Multimedia résumés will incorporate sound, visuals, and animation.

Electronic Scanning of Résumés. Although present job hunting largely continues to depend on hard copy résumés, these often are scanned electronically. Electronic storage of on-line or hard copy résumés offers employers an efficient way to screen countless applicants, to compile a database of applicants for later openings, and to evaluate all applicants fairly.

How Scanning Works. The computer captures and searches the printed image for key words (nouns instead of traditional "action verbs"). Those résumés containing the most key words ("hits") make the final cut (Pender).

How to Prepare a Scannable Résumé. Using nouns as key words, list all your skills, credentials, and job titles. (Help-wanted ads are a useful source for key words.)

- List specialized skills: *Marketing, C++ programming, database management, user documentation, Internet collaboration, software development, graphic design, hydraulics, fluid mechanics, editing, surveying, soils testing, water-quality monitoring, job-site management.*
- List general skills: *Teamwork coordination, conflict management, oral communication, report and proposal writing, troubleshooting, bilingual in French and English.*
- List credentials: *Student member, Institute of Electrical and Electronic Engineers, certified PADI Open Water diver, B.S. Electrical Engineering, top 5 percent of class.*
- List job titles: *Manager, director, supervisor, intern, coordinator, project leader, technician, trainer.*

If you lack skills or experience, emphasize your personal qualifications: *analytical skills, energy, efficiency, flexibility, imagination, motivation.*

In preparing a scannable résumé, use a plain typeface, 10 to 14 point type, and white paper. Use boldface or FULL CAPS for emphasis. Avoid fancy fonts, italics, underlining, bullets, slashes, dashes, parentheses, or ruled lines (Pender). Left justify all information within the résumé: many searchable résumé systems do not understand indenting or columns. Avoid a two-column format, which often is jumbled by scanners that read across the page. Figure 23.10 on page 621 illustrates a computer-scannable résumé.

Marcel Dionne

144 Avenue Champlain
Quebec PQ   G7E 1R6
Cell Ph. 451-3565   E-mail: mdionne@avoir.ca

EDUCATION   **Software Engineering** (Bachelor degree)
1995-1999   *University of Waterloo*
Learned to apply a full range of sofware engineering principles through scenarios based on concurrent object-oriented software system designs.
<u>Projects</u>: 2nd year—helped Prof. Warsaw develop tracking software for Kitchener Trucking's "smart tire" program
3rd year—developed software reliability model and automatic detection of software failures for Kitchener Board of Education
4th year—re-designed maintenance scheduling software for the University of Waterloo's boiler heating system

EXPERIENCE   **Software Consultant** (contract position)
Nov. 1999   *City of Quebec*
to present   Work with City engineers to re-design Quebec City's transit management software. Co-responsible for designs and responsible for implementing the program, including training 12 city employees to work with the software. The project will be complete June 10, 2000.

Summer Relief Worker
Summers   *Canada Courier*, Montreal and Hamilton
1995-1998,   Worked in all aspects of the parcel delivery business: truck driver, dispatch worker, delivery
and May to   tracking troubleshooter, order desk clerk, packing department clerk. A highlight of this
Oct., 1999   experience was the opportunity to troubleshoot problems with Canada Courier's parcel tracking software. Re-wrote the software to make it more reliable.

PROFILE   Interests include distance running, computers, and computer-generated music
Single. 24 years old. Capable of working long, productive hours

REFERENCES   *Professor John Marks*   *Bill Spender*
Computer Engineering Dep't.   Operations Manager
University of Waterloo   Canada Courier
Ph. (519) 888-4532, ex.5430   1780 Boulevard St. Laurent
E-mail: marks@coulomb.uwaterloo.ca   Montreal PQ   G9T 2W2
Ph. (514) 986-2987

Professor Viktor Warsaw   *Lise Tremblay*
Computer Engineering Dep't.   Engineering Contract Manager
University of Waterloo   City of Quebec
Ph. (519) 888-4532, ex.5444   Place Centrale
E-mail: warsaw@coulomb.uwaterloo.ca   Quebec PQ   G7E 4R4
Ph. (418) 655-2517

Figure 23.7   A Reverse Chronological Format Résumé (compressed to fit on one page)

Carol Hampton

196-4068 Minster Avenue
Toronto ON   M6W 2R5
Phone: (416) 445-5333
E-mail: comphamp@collect.ca

OBJECTIVE
To apply computer installation, configuration, and troubleshooting skills to a networked environment

SKILLS AND ABILITIES

Analytical
- Have shown an aptitude for determining client network requirements
- Proficient at solving math-based problems (top marks in Mathematics in first two semesters of College program)
- Proficient at discovering programming errors

Design
- Won city-wide competition for high school Web page design, May 2000
- Proficient in desktop publishing operations—currently design advertising for George Brown College's student newspaper

Research
- Researched comparative study of firewall software packages for Professional Communications II class
- For a 30-minute class oral presentation, researched the San Francisco Project's development of Java applications
- Industry experience with Farnham Industries, Mississauga—found ready- made solutions for problems with a networked configuration. Saved the firm $6000, the cost of a custom-designed solution. (Summer experience, 2001)

Interpersonal
- Worked closely with the staff at Farnham Industries to implement network solutions. Gained the trust and cooperation of staff who were at first reluctant to try new methods, especially those introduced by a "student."
- Engaged in peer counselling in high school and at George Brown College

EDUCATION
Currently completing the last semester of the two-year **Computer System Technician** diploma program at *George Brown College*, Toronto. Qualified to function as a user support specialist, network administrator, or business network trainer.

REFERENCES

Terry MacArthur
Systems Analyst Consultant
Toronto
(416) 442-3454
tersystem@toronto.ca

Jens Husted
Computer Networking Instructor
Information Technology Department
George Brown College
(416) 415-2010
husted@gbc/scitech.ca

Marjorie Prystai-Alvarez
Personnel Coordinator
Farnham Industries
Mississauga
(905) 657-7439
staff@farnham.on.ca

Figure 23.8   A Functional Format Résumé

Christopher Hendsbee

453B Gordon Drive
Kelowna BC   V1W 2T1
Phone: (250) 876-3422
E-mail: chris@silk.net

Objective   GPS surveying position, with a chance to use and further develop current skills

Education   **Civil Engineering Technology**
Okanagan University College, Kelowna BC   1997-present
The program stresses practical applications of civil engineering theory.

Experience   **Surveyor**
Deep Woods Consultants, Nelson BC   May-Nov, 1998
Surveyed forestry roads, property lines, bridge sites, and topographics.
Became familiar with many types of total stations and data collectors.
Led and supervised a surveying crew. Responsible for all the notes.

Equipment Operator
Lucky Logging, Keremeos BC   July-Aug, 1997
Operated a 966 Cat loader and stacked processed logs. Operated the excavator with a Styer processing head, and worked on the grapple skidder.
Built landings and fire guards.
Greased and repaired equipment.

Release Driver
Sterile Insect Release Program, Osoyoos BC   Aug-Sept, 1996
Followed a marked route on an ATV. Every morning the manager would drop the sterile moths and I would release them over my route. Recorded field notes and addressed questions and problems raised by farmers.

Labourer
Worked as a ranch hand, fencing company assistant, and assistant orchardist.

Special Skills   Proficient with Windows 98 and NT 4.0. Also proficient with software programs: WordPerfect 2000; Microsoft Works (spreadsheets, word processing, databases, charts/graphs, communications); Microsoft Office 2000 (Word, Excel, Access, PowerPoint); Harvard Graphics presentation package; Microsoft Publisher; AutoCAD version 14, AutoCAD Light; and MiniCAD
Proficient with compasses
Very familiar with GPS
Proficient at operating heavy equipment
Proficient at operating chainsaws and a large variety of hand and power tools

. . . 2

Figure 23.9   A Combination Format Résumé: Chronological and Functional   **(Continued)**

Interests and Activities	Archery (bronze medal in the BC Summer Games), hunting, hiking, swimming, weight lifting, trap shooting
Accreditations Licences, and Memberships	S100 Wild Fire Suppression Certificate Hunters licence Avalanche course Drivers licence Level one first aid Firearms acquisition certificate Student member, Applied Science Technologists and Technicians
References	**Dave Muster** Owner, Lucky Logging, Nelson BC RR#1 Newhouse Road Keremeos BC V0X 1D0 Ph. (250) 499-5609 **Jean McElroy** Survey Manager Deep Woods Consultants Nelson BC V1L 5T9 Ph. (250) 825-4565 **Bill Waterburn** SIR Supervisor RR#1 Barcello Road Cawston BC V8X 5Y2 Ph. (250) 499-2366 **Bob Bradley** Department Chair Civil Engineering Technology Okanagan University College 1000 K.L.O. Road Kelowna BC V1Y 4X8 Ph. (250) 762-5445 (ext. 4590)

Figure 23.9   A Combination Format Résumé: Chronological and Functional

Remember, an electronic résumé does not have to be as attractive as your "normal" résumé. Personnel departments who use computer databases are looking for content, not appearance.

When you send e-résumés, remember:

- Always ask before faxing a scannable résumé format. Many personnel departments are not automated and would prefer to see your formatted résumé.

- Be cautious about sending résumés via e-mail. The receiving software may not be able to "read" the document you send. Do not send your résumé as part of the e-mail itself; attach the résumé in a common format such as Word or WordPerfect. (But be sure that your receiver's software is compatible with the document you're attaching.)

Contacting Employers

It's important to have a plan for contacting employers. Much time and money can be wasted on pursuing the wrong positions or pursuing them at the wrong time. You need to plan whom you contact, how you contact them, in what order, and when. You also need to follow up initial contacts. Pick suitable times to contact employers by phone or in person; for example, do not phone a government manager late on a Friday afternoon. Don't drop off a résumé at a restaurant during its lunch or dinner rush. Try to pick a time when you know that the recipient will have time to speak with you. If possible, call a receptionist to learn the best time to call or appear.

Campaign Strategies

The job-search campaign you wage will vary with your circumstances. If you search for a new job while employed, your search will be more selective and discreet than if you are unemployed or at college.

Searching for a satisfying job involves a carefully planned campaign of contacting employers. The following excerpt from a campaign log (Figure 23.11) illustrates the required planning and detailed record keeping. Such a

Employer	Contact	Response	Interview	Follow-up	Status	Comments
Trendmark Electronics, Kanata	Enquiry letter/ Mar. 17 (see file)	Mar. 28; phone call Jim Lund, R&D encouraged me to apply	Not yet	Mar. 29—sent thank-you letter; asked to tour Ottawa plant	Hopeful— J.D. said my qualifications "looked fine"	Phone by April 10 if no further news
Ames Research, Hull	Applied—letter Mar. 21 for Electronics Researcher	None so far	Not yet	Not yet	Highly desirable but doubtful; many experienced people will apply	Will send positive follow-up letter if no response by April 4— prepare letter!

Figure 23.11   An Excerpt from a Campaign Log

Carol Hampton
196-4068 Minster Avenue
Toronto ON   M6W 2R5
Phone: (416) 445-5333
E-mail: comphamp@collect.ca

OBJECTIVE
To apply computer installation, configuration, and troubleshooting skills in collaboration with others.

QUALIFICATIONS
Programming in Java, HTML, Logo, Pascal, C++. Network design and troubleshooting.
Determining client network requirements. Advanced computer mathematics. Web page design. Newspaper advertising design. Internet research. Usability testing. Desktop publishing of installation and maintenance manual. Writing, designing, and testing hardware upgrade manuals. Research on comparative study of firewall software packages.

EXPERIENCE
FARNHAM INDUSTRIES, 7800 CONCEPT COURT, MISSISSAUGA. Solutions for problems with a networked configuration. Network solution implementation. Liaison with staff. Positive relations. Development of trust and cooperation.

EDUCATION
GEORGE BROWN COLLEGE, TORONTO. **Computer System Technician** diploma.
Qualified as a user support specialist, network administrator, or business network trainer.

REFERENCES
Terry MacArthur
Systems Analyst Consultant
Toronto
(416) 442-3454
tersystem@toronto.ca

Marjorie Prystai-Alvarez
Personnel Coordinator
Farnham Industries
Mississauga
(905) 657-7439
staff@farnham.on.ca

Jens Husted
Computer Networking Instructor
Information Technology Department
George Brown College
(416) 415-2010
husted@gbc/scitech.ca

Figure 23.10   A Computer-scannable Résumé

log becomes especially important if your campaign involves many contacts over a prolonged period.

Many employment advisors recommend tiered campaigns. For example, Tom Smith, a 25-year old graduate of the Industrial Electronics program at Saskatoon's Kelsey Institute, used the following strategy to win a position that would give him job satisfaction after his May graduation.

Tier 1:

Because of his military supervisory service, Tom wanted to start his electronics career as a quality control supervisor or production shift supervisor. He found four firms that had such positions, three in Saskatoon and one in Calgary. Using the library and the Internet, he set out to learn all he could about the four companies, their business prospects, and their range of positions. He used his contact network, which included friends (and friends of friends) who worked at three of the companies, to try to learn about possible openings.

He devised a detailed campaign of introduction letters, follow-ups, and requests for informational interviews, to exhaust every possibility of being employed by one of the four companies. He placed a time limit of six weeks on Tier 1 activities before moving on to Tier 2.

Tier 2:

Tom's secondary interest was in electronics research, so he identified several firms in Halifax, Moncton, Ottawa, Saskatoon, Calgary, Montreal, and Vancouver engaged in such research. He did some preliminary research on these firms, but delayed further action until Tier 1 activities were completed.

Tier 3:

In case the first three months of job searching at Tom's Tier 1 and Tier 2 levels proved fruitless, Tom was prepared to go to his back-up plan, Tier 3. Here, Tom would look for a position as a glider flight instructor (developed in the military and as a personal interest), or as an electronics research assistant.

Result:

Tom did not have to go to Tier 2 or Tier 3 of his plan. In week 2 of his campaign, one of the Saskatoon firms advertised a quality control position; also, early in week 3 Tom learned that the other three firms were sufficiently interested in Tom's qualifications to invite him for an exploratory meeting. The Calgary firm brought him back for a second meeting, and then for a formal interview for a production shift manager position.

He was also formally interviewed for the quality control position in Saskatoon. One week later, he was offered both positions for which he had been formally interviewed. He accepted the production manager job in Calgary, though the pay was lower, because that company would give Tom more opportunities to pursue a management career.

Perhaps *your* next campaign will not need to be so elaborate as Tom's. But his approach had one major advantage—he gave himself every chance to land the kind of position that would give him *maximum job satisfaction* at that stage of his career.

Contact Methods

An enquiry letter (or in-person enquiry) offers a good method of getting noticed by an employer. Indeed, it's not uncommon for the authors of well-written enquiries to be invited for exploratory interviews; sometimes, an employer will offer positions to an impressive interviewee, even if the employer hadn't intended on hiring just yet.

Still, the enquiry is primarily a research tool, not a method of selling your qualifications. (See the advice about enquiries earlier in this chapter.) So, if you already know that you would like to work for a particular employer, but it doesn't seem that this employer currently has openings, you may want to introduce yourself.

A letter of introduction is really quite straightforward. You introduce your qualifications and your interest in the company. You name the position(s) which would appeal to you and refer the reader to the pertinent experience in your enclosed résumé. The action closing should indicate when you're available and how the reader can easily contact you. Perhaps you'll also request a meeting to discuss future employment opportunities.

An introduction letter does not apply for a specific available position, so you can't present a full sales pitch which shows your suitability for a given position. But you can say enough about yourself and your career goals to engage the reader's interest. The introduction letter should be short, though; you have to know when to stop and let your résumé speak for you.

An application letter is more formal and persuasive in tone. You will write an application when you know that a position is available and when you're certain that you have what it takes to fulfill the position's requirements. Each application must be tailored to the specific position for which you're applying, so you have to think clearly about the letter's content and phrasing.

First, you need to remember that *unsolicited applications* require a different approach from *solicited applications*.

Unsolicited Applications. If your contact network has informed you of an opening, and if that position has not been formally advertised, your main challenge is to deal with a reader who is not anticipating your application. It's possible that the reader doesn't even *want* applications; the reader may be using his/her own contacts to find candidates. If that's the case, you must get and hold the reader's interest by immediately appealing to the reader's needs and preferences.

Finding the right appeal is not easy. For starters, you'll have to research the position, to learn what type of work is done, which qualifications are essential, and if possible, what characteristics the employer would like the new employee to have. If the employer has not yet drawn up a set of position requirements or employee characteristics, that employer may be receptive to a wider range of candidates than if the position had been advertised. The following is an unsolicited application scenario.

Unsolicited Application

Royale Ltee., a Montreal-based courier company, is expanding from metropolitan Montreal to all of southern Quebec and southern Ontario. It has recently been purchased by a trucking consortium, Bouchard Transport, which has injected cash into the operation.

The writer of the following letter, Marcel Dionne, is a 24-year old graduate of the University of Waterloo. His cousin, Michelle Legaree, who works as an accountant for Bouchard Transport, gives Marcel the background details and says that she's heard that Royale Ltee. will need someone to help develop the logistics of expanding the courier operation. Also, Marcel worked four summers for Canada Courier when he was at university, so he has a good idea of what Michelle means. His recent degree in software engineering has led to an 8-month contract to help redesign Quebec City's transit management software, but that contract will finish in three weeks. Acting quickly, he learns what he can about Royale Ltee. Among other things, he learns that Jean-Guy Ryan is the General Manager, at age 29, and that Ryan and the other Royale Ltee. managers have been successful running an informal, democratic style of operation that encourages employees to suggest ways of improving service and controlling operating costs. ■

Figure 23.12 on page 625 shows how Marcel appeals to Ryan in his (Marcel's) unsolicited application.

Solicited Applications. Solicited applications illustrated in Figure 23.12 require a similar structure to the unsolicited letter. However, the *opening paragraph* will be more straightforward—you simply apply for the position by name, you refer to the advertisement, and you preview your sales pitch.

The application letter's *sales pitch* depends on your accurate analysis of the advertised position's requirements. The employer has carefully chosen those requirements and will expect your application to show how you can fulfill them. Therefore, if your reading of the position description leaves you with questions, write or phone the employer to get answers. Your main challenge is to prove that you have what the employer needs, so you *must* understand those needs.

When you construct your sales argument, look at your application from the employer's point of view. As in all business letters, answer the reader's question: *What's in it for me?* Two hints for answering that question are:

1. Sell your qualifications and personal qualities as a *package.* The whole is greater than the sum of its parts, but only if you show how one set of skills complements and strengthens another set. For example, a former McDonald's manager who has earned a Computer Science degree will be better able to apply that computer knowledge because of previous business experience.

2. Highlight that package with a phrase or fact that identifies you and you only. Marketers refer to this technique as "positioning your product."

Pension Champlain
144 Avenue Champlain
Quebec PQ   G7E 1R6
May 18, 2000

M. Jean-Guy Ryan, General Manager
Royale Ltee.
2408 Boulevard Laurentian
Montreal PQ   G6H 5T5

Dear Monsieur Ryan:

Michelle Legaree, an accountant with Royale's parent company, Bouchard Transport, has told me about your expansion plans. Please consider my offer to help your courier firm develop software and logistics to allow a rapid, smooth transition from an urban courier to a regional operation.

My background in software engineering, my experience with Canada Courier, and my current work for the City of Quebec place me in a unique position to contribute to your firm. The enclosed résumé provides details of my software engineering degree; you'll notice that most of my class projects focused on developing solutions for logistical problems. That focus resulted from my experience at Canada Courier in Montreal and Hamilton; as a summer relief worker, I became familiar with all aspects of the delivery business. In my last stint with Canada Courier, I was asked to troubleshoot problems with its parcel tracking software. That experience has helped me manage several very difficult logistical issues in Quebec City's transit management software.

A growing company needs energetic, innovative people who wish to grow with the organization. The enclosed reference letters show that I match that description. Two of the references listed in my résumé, Professor Marks and Canada Courier's Bill Spender, will be able to comment on my problem-solving abilities and work ethic.

I'll be available for employment in three weeks, when my project contract in Quebec City finishes. However, my supervisor has given his approval for me to go to Montreal to discuss my application for a position with your firm, at any time you set. I really hope you do invite me for an interview because I believe that my skills and interests match Royale's upcoming needs. You can contact me at my e-mail address (on the résumé) or at my cell phone, 451-3565.

Sincerely,

Marcel Dionne

Marcel Dionne

Enclosure: Résumé

Figure 23.12   An Unsolicited Application

You "position" yourself in a special place in the reader's mind. That positioning idea should reflect the strongest connection between your package and the employer's set of requirements.

Three letters in this chapter illustrate successful positioning:

1. The enquiry letter on page 607 positions the writer's enthusiasm for GPS surveying.
2. The unsolicited application in Figure 23.12 on page 625 presents three faces of the writer's special collection of relevant skills. (The opening sentence in paragraph 2 even uses the term, "unique position".)
3. The solicited application in Figure 23.13 on page 628 positions the applicant's unusual and special combination of electronics training, leadership skills, and communications skills.

In phrasing your sales pitch, project a *you* attitude by:

- discussing the position's requirements *before* matching your qualifications to those requirements
- using objective, third-person phrasing wherever possible ("the enclosed résumé lists that related experience") or "you" phrasing ("you can reach me at…", rather than "I can be reached at…")

Application letters require a *positive, business-like closing*. Say when you're available for work or for an interview, and indicate the easiest way for the reader to reach you. Request an interview, or express your desire for an interview, because gaining an interview invitation is the reason you wrote this letter! Finally, you might close by stating your desire for the position or by reiterating your key argument for considering your application.

Figure 23.13 on page 628 shows Tom Smith's response to an opening for a quality control supervisor. This is the advertisement to which Tom replied:

Quality Control Supervisor

The company: Altitude Electronics specializes in electronic instrumentation and controls for the aerospace industry – satellites, launch rockets, and high-altitude weather balloons. Its award-winning products result from superior design and meticulous attention to detail in the various stages of the manufacturing process.

The position: You will be one of two quality control supervisors. You will test products, report deficiencies, supervise production-worker methods, and work in conjunction with the Production Manager to train production line assemblers.

The successful candidate will have: A two-year Electronics diploma from an accredited Canadian college, or equivalent. Demonstrated leadership skills and above-average communications skills (interpersonal, oral, written, listening). Familiarity and some skill in fabrication, component assembly, soldering, and product finishing. Demonstrated skills in electronics troubleshooting and CAD/CAM.

Apply to   Dirk Benefeld, General Manager, Altitude Electronics
            2310 Hanselman Avenue
            Saskatoon SK   S7L 6A4

Tom's first response was to think, "it's as if they wrote this ad for me!" Then he analyzed the advertisement as follows:

- The position requires a combination of technical skills and communication skills. That's exactly what I have to offer, so I should be able to make a good case.
- The ad expresses pride in the company's accomplishments ("award-winning," "superior design"), so I should emphasize my own drive to succeed.
- Mr. Benefeld is on the Industrial Electronics industry advisory board, so I shouldn't have to sell the program to him, just remind him of how practical and comprehensive it is.
- Probably my competitive advantage is my background of leadership positions and communications experience, so that should be stressed in the résumé as well as in the letter. And I'll choose my references and reference letters to emphasize the leadership communications.
- The ad mentions "meticulous attention to detail," so I'd better show that side of my character.

Employment Interviews

When your application is successful, you will be invited to an interview, sometimes to a series of interviews. (Weyerhaueser Canada, for example, often subjects applicants to two days of interviews and tests.) Sometimes, just one person will interview you. More often, you can expect to be quizzed by a panel. At a minimum, expect to be interviewed by your potential immediate supervisor and by someone from the company's personnel division. Smaller firms might be represented by the firm's manager, a project supervisor, and a member of the work team that has the open position.

Interview Preparation

Careful preparation is the key to a productive interview. Prepare by learning about the company in trade journals and industrial indexes. (Learn about the company's products or services, history, prospects, branch locations.) Request company literature, including its annual report if the company's publicly traded. Speak with people who know about the company.

If you're applying to a government or municipal agency, try to learn what will affect the growth or downsizing of that agency, and try to learn if there's room for personal growth or career advancement within the agency. Also, learn about the agency's range of services. If you can't find information of this sort before the interview, ask questions during the interview.

Prepare also by thinking about your reasons for wanting the job and what you have to offer the employer. Your self-inventory and list of transferable skills will help you prepare. Also, look at your résumé from the interviewer's point of view—Think of the questions you would ask if you were the inter-

108-3118D 33rd Street West
Saskatoon SK   S7L 6K3
May 7, 2005

Mr. Dirk Benefeld, General Manager
Altitude Electronics
2310 Hanselman Avenue
Saskatoon SK   S7L 6A4

Dear Mr. Benefeld:

Re: Quality Control Supervisor

Please consider my application for the quality control supervisor position which you advertised on page D18 of yesterday's Star-Phoenix. This position requires exactly what I have to offer.

As the enclosed résumé details, I'm about to graduate from Kelsey's Industrial Electronics program, which provides a comprehensive and practical overview of current electronics applications. The course also teaches us how to think and how to keep abreast of the rapidly changing electronics field. My marks have consistently been in the top three of the class in each of the six trimesters of the program. This reflects my work ethic and my attention to detail. It also reflects the solid theoretical grounding I received from two years of engineering studies at the University of Saskatchewan.

Instructor Al Schlatter, who's listed as a reference in my résumé, has agreed to tell you about my fabrication, assembly, troubleshooting, and CAD skills.

From my enquiries, I've learned that your quality control position requires strong leadership communications skills. The attached reference letters comment on my performance as President of the Kelsey Students' Association this year. As President, I've been able to hone skills which I've developed as a cadet leader and glider pilot instructor for the Department of National Defence.

I'd appreciate the opportunity to discuss the quality control supervisor position with you. If you agree that my qualifications match the position's requirements, you can contact me, Monday through Saturday, 7.30 a.m. to 11.00 p.m., by calling the Students' Association office, 652-0980. I can be available for an interview at any time you arrange. I'll be available for work after May 29, the final day of exams.

Yours sincerely,

Tom Smith

Tom Smith

Enclosures: Résumé
               Industrial Electronics Course Overview and Grades
               Reference letters (3)

Figure 23.13   A Solicited Application

viewer. If you have difficulty thinking of such questions, have friends go through your résumé to look for issues that will elicit questions.

As you prepare, you will find the following "game plan" helpful.

Interview Preparation

1. Strengths to emphasize, in order of priority

2. Subtle strengths I need to bring out

3. Apparent limitations I should be ready to counteract

4. Subtle limitations I need not introduce

5. My overall strategy for making my case (for projecting my image)

6. Things I want to learn about the job and the company

Questions

It's possible to anticipate many of the questions you'll be asked at an interview. You can prepare for obvious questions like:

- Why do you want to work here?
- What do you know about our company?
- What do you see as your biggest weakness? biggest strength?
- What type of supervisor do you prefer?
- Do you prefer to work under close supervision in a structured environment, or more independently within broadly stated guidelines?
- What are your short-term and long-time career goals?

You can anticipate three categories of questions: information questions, high-risk questions, and opportunity questions.

Categories of interview questions

Information Questions. These easy questions come early in the interview and enable you to provide factual background information about your education and experience. The interviewer will assess how you present yourself, what you know about the firm, and how you "fit" the culture of the organization. (*Why did you apply for this job? Tell me about your program at the college.*)

High-risk Questions. These questions can destroy your chances for a job if handled poorly. These questions probe what the interviewer believes to be your potential weaknesses related to the job requirements. If you can successfully deflect these questions in the middle of the interview, then you will have an opportunity to sell yourself in the next stage. (*Why did you leave your previous job? What difficulties have you faced in previous jobs? What are your limitations?*)

Opportunity Questions. These questions usually are asked at the end of the interview and provide the opportunity for you to convince the interviewer that you can make a contribution to the organization. Your answers should be bold (not arrogant) and confident. (*What are your strengths? How can you contribute to our product or service? How do you see yourself fitting into our organization?*)

Also, you will have a chance to ask your own questions. Have a list of written questions with you, in an unobtrusive notebook. Refer to this notebook when you're asked if you have questions. Focus on the work you would be doing and the conditions of employment—ratio of office work and field work, travel involved, level of responsibility, opportunities for further training and skill development. If your questions have already been answered in the interview's give-and-take, mention them anyway; show that your primary interest is in the work.

If at all possible, do not ask questions about salary and benefits. After you receive an offer of employment, you can discuss employment benefits. Or, if you must know, call the company's personnel office. Usually however, these issues will not pose a problem because a company representative will review salary and benefits in a closing stage of the interview.

Answers

Answer questions directly and fully. Some closed-ended questions such as: *Are you familiar with Microsoft Office Pro?* probably only merit a short response of one to three sentences. However, the majority of interview questions are open-ended, as in: *What are your main strengths?* Such questions need to be answered fully enough to satisfy the interviewer's interest, though not so fully that you totally exhaust that interest. If you don't provide enough detail to support your responses, the interviewer will doubt your assertions. So, give examples of your strengths, skills, and achievements; back up your statements with reasons and specific details; recount incidents which establish that you've used certain techniques or completed certain tasks in the past.

Interviews can place you under pressure, so two kinds of preparation are essential:

1. Anticipate questions and rehearse ways to answer them.
2. Practise using impromptu speaking techniques. Chapter 24 describes impromptu organizing methods that will allow you to control nervousness and to perform under pressure.

Here are some other hints for successful job interviews:

Job interview hints

- If possible, research the range of candidates who might apply for the same position as you. Know your competition, and how you compare to them.

- Dress appropriately for the interview—as if this were your most important day at work.
- Arrive early for the interview. Occasionally, the interview team will give a task to perform or a case study before you're called into the interview room.
- Remember that you'll be the "guest" and the lead interviewer will be the "host," so don't be too socially aggressive—wait for the host to initiate a handshake; wait to be asked to take a chair; allow the interviewers to guide the conversation.
- Maintain eye contact much of the time, but don't stare.
- Maintain a relaxed but alert posture. Don't slouch. Don't fidget. Show your interest by leaning forward. Smile when appropriate. Be yourself, your best self.
- Answer questions truthfully; skilled interviewers will ask the same controversial question or probe the same issue in different ways to see if your answers are consistent.
- When you don't know the answer to a question, say so. In some cases, you could explain how you would determine the answer to the question.
- Don't blurt things you don't need to mention. (See Quadrant 4 of the self-inventory.)
- Don't be afraid to allow silence. An interviewer may stop talking, to observe your reaction and to induce you into revealing your inner thoughts.
- Remember to smile, and show other non-verbal responsiveness to your interviewers. You'll improve your chances of getting the job—no-one likes to work with a grouch!
- When the interviewer says the interview is ending, or hints that it's drawing to a close (closes the question folder or puts away his/her pen), don't wear out your welcome. Restate your interest, ask when you might expect further word, thank the interviewer, and leave.
- In general, treat the interview as potentially one of the most important conversations in your life!

Follow-ups to Interviews

Within a few days after the interview, refresh the employer's memory with a letter restating your interests. Here's an example:

> Thank you for the opportunity to discuss your technologist position on Wednesday.
>
> Learning about your planned plant expansion has strengthened my desire to work for Kraftsteel Industries. Also, our conversation has confirmed my belief that I could contribute to your company's continuing growth, through my CAD skills and design capabilities.
>
> If you require further information, please call my pager number, 767-9901.

Responding to Job Offers

Hopefully, your strategy will result in an offer for a position in your first tier of choices. If so, you'll likely have no difficulty accepting with enthusiasm. If you receive an offer by phone, ask when you'll receive a written offer. Respond to that letter with a formal *letter of acceptance*. Your response may serve as part of your contract, so spell out the terms you are accepting. Here's an acceptance letter, written by the same person as the above follow-up letter.

> I am delighted to accept your offer of the mechanical engineering technologist position at your Hampstead plant, with a starting salary of $32,400. I understand that there will be a six-month probationary period and that I will be eligible for raises after one year.
>
> As you requested, I will phone Pat Larsen in your Human Resources office for instructions on reporting date, physical exam, and employee orientation.
>
> I look forward to a satisfying career with Kraftsteel Industries.

You may have to refuse offers, perhaps because you learned things during the job interview which gave you reason to believe that the position was not for you, or perhaps because you have accepted another position which better meets your current job objectives. So, even if you refuse by telephone, write a prompt, cordial letter of refusal, explaining your reasons and allowing for future possibilities. The writer of the above acceptance letter phrased a refusal this way:

> Although I was impressed with your new hydroforming technology and the efficiency of your auto parts plant, I am unable to accept your offer of a position as an assistant shift foreman at your plant.
>
> I have accepted a position with Kraftsteel Industries because Kraftsteel has offered me the chance to join its design team. CAD design, as I mentioned in our recent interview, is one of my main interests.
>
> In the future, if opportunities arise with your hydroforming design group, I would appreciate the chance to be considered for a position with that group.
>
> Thank you for your interest in me and for your courtesy.

IN BRIEF

Evaluating a Job Offer

Fortunately, most organizations will not expect you to accept or reject an offer on the spot. You probably will be given at least a week to make up your mind. Although there is no way to remove all risks from this career decision, you will increase your chances of making the right choice by thoroughly evaluating each offer—weighing all the advantages against all the disadvantages of taking the job.

The Organization

Background information on the organization—be it a company, government agency, or non-profit concern—can help you decide whether it is a good place for you to work.

Is the organization's business or activity in keeping with your own interests and beliefs? It will be easier to apply yourself to the work if you are enthusiastic about what the organization does.

How will the size of the organization affect you? Large firms generally offer a greater variety of training programs and career paths, more managerial levels for advancement, and better employee benefits than small firms. Large employers also have more advanced technologies in their laboratories, offices, and factories. However, jobs in large firms tend to be highly specialized—workers are assigned relatively narrow responsibilities. On the other hand, jobs in small firms may offer broader authority and responsibility, a closer working relationship with top management, and a chance to clearly see your contribution to the success of the organization.

Should you work for a fledgling organization or one that is well established? New businesses have a high failure rate, but for many people, the excitement of helping create a company and the potential for sharing in its success more than offset the risk of job loss. It may be almost as exciting and rewarding, however, to work for a young firm which already has a foothold on success.

Does it make any difference to you whether the company is private or public? A private company may be controlled by an individual or a family, which can mean that key jobs are reserved for relatives and friends. A public company is controlled by a board of directors responsible to the stockholders. Key jobs are open to anyone with talent.

Is the organization in an industry with favourable long-term prospects? The most successful firms tend to be in industries that are growing rapidly.

Where is the job located? If it is in another city, you need to consider the cost of living, the availability of housing and transportation, and the quality of educational and recreational facilities in the new location. Even if the place of work is in your area, consider the time and expense of commuting and whether it can be done by public transportation.

Where are the firm's headquarters and branches located? Although a move may not be required now, future opportunities could depend on your willingness to move to these places.

It frequently is easy to get background information on an organization simply by accessing its Web site or telephoning its public relations office. A public company's annual report to the stockholders tells about its corporate philosophy, history, products or services, goals, and financial status. Most government agencies can furnish reports that

(Continued)

IN BRIEF

describe their programs and missions. Press releases, company newsletters or magazines, and recruitment brochures also can be useful. Ask the organization for any other items that might interest a prospective employee.

Background information on the organization also may be available at your public or school library. If you cannot get an annual report, check the library for reference directories that provide basic facts about the company, such as earnings, products and services, and number of employees.

Stories about an organization in magazines and newspapers can tell a great deal about its successes, failures, and plans for the future. You can identify articles on a company by looking under its name in periodical or computerized indexes—such as the *Business Periodicals Index*. It probably will not be useful to look back more than two or three years.

The library also may have government publications that present projections of growth for the industry in which the organization is classified. Long-term projections of employment and output for industries, covering the entire economy, are developed by the Department of Labour and Statistics Canada. Trade magazines also have frequent articles on the trends for specific industries.

Career centres at colleges and universities often have information on employers that is not available in libraries. Ask the career centre librarian how to find out about a particular organization. The career centre may have an entire file of information on the company.

The Nature of the Work

Even if everything else about the job is good, you will be unhappy if you dislike the day-to-day work. Determining in advance whether you will like the work may be difficult. However, the more you find out about it before accepting or rejecting the job offer, the more likely you are to make the right choice. Ask yourself questions like the following.

Does the work match your interests and make good use of your skills? The duties and responsibilities of the job should be explained in enough detail to answer this question.

How important is the job in this company? An explanation of where you fit in the organization and how you are supposed to contribute to its overall objectives should give an idea of the job's importance.

Are you comfortable with the supervisor?

Do employees seem friendly and cooperative?

Does the work require travel?

Does the job call for irregular hours?

How long do most people who enter this job stay with the company? High turnover can mean dissatisfaction with the nature of the work or something else about the job.

The Opportunities

A good job offers you opportunities to grow and move up. It gives you chances to learn new skills, increase your earnings, and rise to positions of greater authority, responsibility, and prestige.

The company should have a training plan for you. You know what your abilities are now. What valuable new skills does the company plan to teach you?

The employer should give you some idea of promotion possibilities within the organization. What is the next step on the career ladder? If you have to wait for a job to become vacant before you can be promoted, how long does this usually take? Employers differ on their policies regarding promotion from within the organization. When opportunities for advancement do arise, will you compete with applicants from outside the company? Can you apply for jobs for which you qualify elsewhere within the organization or is mobility within the firm limited?

(Continued)

IN BRIEF

The Salary and Benefits

Wait for the employer to introduce these subjects. Most companies will not talk about pay until they have decided to hire you. In order to know if their offer is reasonable, you need a rough estimate of what the job should pay. You may have to go to several sources for this information. Talk to friends who recently were hired in similar jobs. Ask your teachers and the staff in the college placement office about starting pay for graduates with your qualifications. Scan the help-wanted ads in newspapers and on the Internet. Check the Internet, the library, or your school's career centre for salary surveys. If you are considering the salary and benefits for a job in another geographic area, make allowances for differences in the cost of living, which may be significantly higher in a large metropolitan area than in a smaller city, town, or rural area. Use the research to come up with a base salary range for yourself, the top being the best you can hope to get and the bottom being the least you will take. An employer cannot be specific about the amount of pay if it includes commissions and bonuses. The way the plan works, however, should be explained. The employer also should be able to tell you what most people in the job earn.

Also take into account that the starting salary is just that, the start. Your salary should be reviewed regularly—many organizations do it every 12 months. If the employer is pleased with your performance, how much can you expect to earn after 1, 2, or 3 or more years?

Don't think of your salary as the only compensation you will receive—consider benefits. Benefits can add a lot to your base pay. Health insurance and pension plans are among the most important benefits. Other common benefits include life insurance, paid vacations and holidays, and sick leave. Benefits vary widely among smaller and larger firms, among full-time and part-time workers, and between the public and private sectors. Find out exactly what the benefit package includes and how much of the costs you must bear.

Asking yourself these kinds of questions won't guarantee that you make the best career decision—only hindsight could do that—but you probably will make a better choice than if you act on impulse.

Source: Adapted excerpts from U.S. Department of Labor. *Tomorrow's Jobs*. Washington, D.C.: GPO, 1995.

Revision and Editing Checklist for Job-search Correspondence

Use this checklist to refine the content, arrangement, and style of your letters and résumés.

CONTENT

❑ Is the letter addressed to a specifically named person?

❑ Does the letter contain all of the standard parts?

❑ Does the letter have all needed specialized parts?

❑ Have you given the reader all necessary information?

❑ Have you identified the name and position of your reader?

ARRANGEMENT

❑ Does the introduction immediately engage the reader and lead naturally to the body?

❑ Are transitions between letter parts clear and logical?

❑ Does the conclusion encourage the reader to act?

❑ Is the format correct?

❑ Is the design acceptable?

STYLE

❑ Is the letter in conversational language (free of letterese)?

❑ Does the letter reflect a "you" perspective throughout?

❑ Does the tone reflect your relationship with your reader?

❑ Is the reader likely to react favourably to this letter?

❑ Is the style throughout clear, concise, and fluent?

❑ Is the letter grammatical? (Appendix)

❑ Does the letter's appearance enhance your image?

RÉSUMÉS

❑ Have you adapted the content, structure, and format of your résumé to suit the specific position you're pursuing?

❑ Have you made sure that your résumé is absolutely free of errors in content, spelling, and grammar?

❑ Have you used section headings that accurately identify your package of employable characteristics?

❑ Have you made it easy for your reader to find key pieces of information?

❑ Does your résumé's appearance enhance your image?

☑ EXERCISES

1. Complete a self-inventory and a list of transferable skills. Use these self-assessment tools to:
   - identify the employable characteristics that form the core package you'll "sell" for any position you may pursue
   - identify which skills, qualifications, and personal qualities you will emphasize for particular positions
   - prepare for questions job interviewers will ask you

2. Develop a job-search strategy for your next job search.
   - List the types of positions you should pursue.
   - Determine which positions are currently available and which may become available soon.
   - Decide which position(s) to pursue in the first tier of your campaign and the methods you'll use to contact employers.

3. Design and write two or more résumés that you can adapt for the range of positions you expect will interest you.

4. Analyze an advertisement that describes a position that interests you. Which qualifications does the employer's advertisement stress? How? Do you have the qualifications and personal attributes required by the position? If you have relevant skills that have not been developed (and demonstrated) through directly relevant work experience, how will you show that you can indeed perform the tasks required in the position?

5. Write a letter applying for an advertised position. Show how your combined qualifications, skills, and personal qualities match the employer's stated needs.

6. Write a letter applying for a non-advertised position. Show that you understand the position's requirements and that you can meet them. Place your primary appeal in the opening paragraph and elaborate in subsequent paragraphs.

7. Prepare a strategy sheet for a real or imagined job interview. As you do so, plan answers for questions likely to be asked.

☑ COLLABORATIVE PROJECT

In conjunction with other members of your class, prepare an inventory of positions that may be available to graduates of your program of study. Alternatively, prepare an inventory of summer part-time jobs.

Among other information, provide:
- descriptions of the positions, their related duties, and required qualifications
- expected dates of availability and whether the positions will be advertised externally
- background information about the companies offering the positions
- salary ranges and benefit packages
- names of contact persons, their telephone or fax numbers, and mailing or e-mail addresses

Oral Presentations

Think about the kinds of situations where your speaking skills will lead to success at work. Include informal situations (your firm's general manager stops you in the hallway to ask how a project is progressing) as well as formal situations (you make a half-hour sales presentation to an important client).

Think about opportunities you'll have to:

- persuade people to consider, perhaps even accept, your ideas
- provide listeners with the information they need
- foster the image you want and need to project (knowledgeable? skillful? dynamic? competent? supportive?)
- help listeners solve problems, find answers, or resolve issues
- maintain or improve working relationships with your colleagues
- show your clients that you value their business
- explain how things work
- instruct others how to perform tasks
- maintain or build your status within the organization

Now, take your reflections a step further. Think about your reactions to a speaker you've recently heard in a classroom or meeting room. What judgments did you make about that speaker's competence based on the way the speaker spoke? To what degree did the speaker's presentation style affect your willingness to believe the speaker's information and agree with the speaker's ideas? Did you "buy" what the speaker had to say?

As a result of these sets of reflections, are you more aware of how effective presentation skills could advance or hinder your career?

Speaking Situations for Technical People

Many engineers, technologists, technicians, scientists, and other "technical workers" prefer to design, test, build, or improve things, rather than to talk or write about the details of their work. But often these same people can succeed only by communicating their information, instructions, explanations, and analyses. Also, they must communicate effectively to get the facilities, staff, or equipment they need.

Here is a random selection of situations where a technical person's speaking skills could be very important:

- answering key questions in a job interview
- presenting an informal proposal at a department meeting
- introducing a sewer line plan to residents who don't want the line extended into their rural subdivision
- announcing a layoff to the employees affected
- selling a formal proposal to a client

- presenting a technical paper or describing a successful project at a convention

Your degree of success in such situations depends upon your speaking skills and the preparation you put into each presentation.

Factors in Success

Ask almost anyone about the number one factor in speaking successfully and that person will reply, "confidence." Or, possibly, the response might reflect a negative view—"you have to overcome fear and anxiety to speak well." Certainly, many people fear public speaking—Peter Urs Bender, Canada's guru of business presentations, points to a survey which found that people fear public speaking more than death.[1] It seems that cartoonist Scott Adams has heard of the same survey:

Source: *Globe and Mail*, p. B27, March 3, 1999. DILBERT reprinted by permission of United Feature Syndicate, Inc.

Fear, anxiety, nervousness—these feelings are understandable. After all, others judge us by the way we speak and our work effectiveness frequently depends on our ability to explain and persuade. However, there's no point in dwelling on non-productive feelings. Instead, we need to focus on the factors that make us successful.

You already know the secret to effective speaking—confidence! However, if you currently don't have much confidence, you might find that statement rather hollow. If that's the case, the following hints will probably interest you.

1. *Have something to say.* Usually, you'll be asked to speak if your experience or role means that you ought to have information and insights which the audience will be glad to hear. But even if you're not an expert on a sub-

---

1. Peter Urs Bender, *The Secrets of Power Presentations*. 5th edition. Toronto: The Achievement Group, 1991.

ject, you can research that subject so that you have plenty to offer. The net result is that your confidence level should rise because you know that you have a worthwhile message.

2. *Know your purpose.* Being clear about the purpose of your presentation really helps you focus on the key ideas and information to stress. When you have that focus, when you know exactly what you're trying to accomplish, and when you know how to achieve your purpose, you'll feel a surge of confidence.

   Here are some common purposes for talks: inform, explain, persuade, entertain, teach, involve emotions, inspire. Usually, you will try to combine two or more purposes.

3. *Know your audience.* Knowing your listeners' needs and interests should help to further boost your confidence because you can shape your talk to meet your audience's expectations and priorities. Some presenters also prefer to speak to people whom they know because they feel supported by a familiar group of faces. However, the main advantage of a known audience is that you can anticipate audience reactions and you can plan accordingly.

4. *Know the speaking environment and situation.* You can reduce pre-talk jitters and the chance of being flustered during a presentation if you know what to expect. Will the audience have heard other speakers before you get up? Will you be introduced as the highlight speaker? If you're making a sales presentation or oral proposal, how many people will be at the meeting and who will be the prime decision makers? Also, will your competitors have already presented their sales pitches or will they present later?

   You'll also find it useful to *scout the room in advance.* Learn the location of the AC outlets, the lectern, the viewing screen, and the light switches. Plan your placement of VCRs, data projection units, or overhead projectors. Check whether sight lines are obscured by pillars or by your AV placement. Determine where you can move around. Check that the seating arrangements suit your planned presentation. Above all, get a "feel" for the room. You'll feel more confident.

5. *Know how to perform.* This last factor is the most difficult to manage because it takes practice to develop one's performing style. However, here's a good starting point: **BE YOURSELF!** Whatever style you develop, it should grow out of your normal conversational patterns. Depending on your personality and the style required for the situation, you will eventually be able to move to one or more of the following levels.

   a. *Conversational level.* At its best, the conversational style is intimate, relaxed, and natural, but not particularly forceful. It may include bursts of liveliness, but generally stays rather low-key, with just enough volume and projection to allow the audience to hear.

b. *Heightened conversational level.* Speaking at an augmented conversational level may be the best level for beginning speakers. At this level, the speaker pumps up the volume. He/she increases the energy level and emphasizes key words more forcefully. The speaker is somewhat animated and involved with the audience.

c. *Performance level.* Now, the speaker is more dramatic. He/she uses vocal emphasis, pacing, pauses, varying volume, and varying vocal tones to really engage listener interest and to signal the speaker's full meaning. Both speaker and listener are aware that this is a performance, but the speaker retains his/her natural spontaneity.

d. *Oratorical level.* This is suitable for large audiences only. In every way possible, the speaker uses dramatic techniques and theatrical gestures to enflame audience interest and to amplify the speaker's message. This is definitely not a normal way of speaking, but the oratorical style works for political rallies, big religious meetings, and calls to war.

So, where do you fit on that scale? Perhaps you can operate on any one of the levels, depending on the situation. In order to assess your speaking strengths and limitations, complete Exercise 5 on page 661.

Four Presentation Styles

Really there are only four main ways to deliver oral presentations:

1. You can read a prepared script.
2. You can memorize the whole talk.
3. You can speak impromptu, with little or no prior preparation.
4. You can speak extemporaneously, with a rehearsed set of note cards.

Only highly trained professionals are proficient at *reading* presentations. Untrained readers lose eye contact with their audience, so the audience feels excluded. Also, most people do not read well—their delivery sounds artificial and the audience quickly becomes bored. Further, a scripted presentation allows little chance for revision in mid-delivery.

For several reasons, then, you should not read a speech, not even a complex technical presentation. Your audience for such a presentation would prefer a handout along with your comments about how to read and interpret that document. Still, your job might require you to read a prepared statement. If so, use a double-spaced, large-type script with extra space between paragraphs. Rehearse until you are able to glance up from the script periodically without losing your place.

Like scripted deliveries, most *memorized* speeches don't sound natural. They sound, well, "memorized." Also, you cannot change the content or tone of the speech, even if audience reactions make it obvious that you need to take a different approach. And, of course, the pressure of giving a speech easily plays havoc with your memory. You only have to forget one phrase, and then whole sections of the memorized talk could temporarily disappear from your memory.

The *impromptu* style brings what the previous two styles lack—spontaneity and real contact with the audience. However, "speaking off the cuff" has its own dangers, most notably the lack of a clear line of development. Impromptu speakers can ramble, and thus make very little sense to their listeners. Also, the impromptu approach can put so much pressure on you that you can't retrieve from memory what you know and believe. Further, you run the risk of phrasing things rather awkwardly and ineffectively.

The *extemporaneous* style makes the most sense for nearly all presentations because it provides the benefits of careful preparation (research, structured outline, strong introduction and conclusion, planned transitions, and rehearsed AV aids) as well as the direct contact and spontaneity that this method allows.

Delivering Extemporaneous Talks

Briefly, here's how the extemporaneous technique works. The speaker:

1. chooses appropriate material and organizes that material in an outline
2. carefully prepares an introduction and conclusion
3. transfers the whole talk to a series of brief notes on note cards
4. rehearses with the notes and with the planned audio visual materials
5. refers to notes while delivering the talk

The rehearsals are critical to success. In the rehearsals, the speaker can:

- find the most effective ways of expressing points
- develop clear bridges between various parts of the talk
- learn the best way to integrate AV aids and supporting examples or stories
- determine how long the planned talk takes to deliver and modify the content accordingly
- modify the note cards where necessary

It's important to rehearse thoroughly, but not to the point where you memorize the talk. At that point, you can get trapped into saying things one way only, and thus lose your ability to respond to audience feedback. One of the major advantages of the properly rehearsed talk is that you know what you are about to say, and have the freedom to use the best way to phrase ideas to reach a given audience at a given moment. You talk directly to the audience with occasional glances at your note cards.

In the end, speaking directly to the audience is the best way of overcoming stage fright. If you concentrate on getting your message to your audience, and if you heed your audience's reactions, you soon forget about yourself and your natural stage fright. You focus on communicating!

Impromptu Speaking

Although impromptu speaking is not recommended for any situation where you have adequate time to prepare, certain situations occur where impromptu skills can help you achieve your goals. Job interviews come immediately to mind, for example. Also, you'll frequently be asked questions after your presentations or you'll be asked for your opinion during meetings.

There's Nothing to Fear but Fear Itself

Quite simply, many people don't perform well as impromptu speakers because of panic. Suddenly, the pressure is on and your brain freezes. Later, perhaps just a few seconds later, you know exactly what you should have said, but it's too late. You have spouted some gibberish, and feel like a fool.

Here's What To Do

Flustered speakers need something that will allay the panic long enough to get their brain moving again. At the same time, they need a device to comb through their brain to retrieve what they know about the subject. And finally, that magic "something" must be used to make sense of what the speakers have found in their brain.

Sound impossible? Actually, the solution is really quite simple and effective—the speaker needs an *instant organizing device* such as a *statement-elaboration pattern*. If you're asked in a job interview why you chose to study at a certain university, you might pause for a second and say:

> "I chose this university mainly because the graduates from my program are qualified for a wide range of positions and most of those graduates get employed in their field."

The above statement buys you a little time to think, but more importantly you have an idea and you have an organizing method! The statement-elaboration pattern allows you to expand upon each of the main parts of the statement:

- when and how you chose your university and which other colleges you investigated
- the "wide range of positions"
- some of the "employed graduates" you know (or statistics which you may happen to know)

Knowing that you have a "method" allows the panic to subside long enough for you to retrieve and organize what you really do have to say. You're not stuck! Now, this method requires practice before you can get really proficient with it, but you'll be amazed at how well you can teach yourself to use this pattern and the following impromptu organizing patterns.

Use Additional Impromptu Patterns

1. *Chronological.* Time patterns are built into our language and thinking. For example, we readily understand the *past/present/future* pattern. Or, we can organize our thoughts according to a series of dates that lead up to the present.

> This technique could work for a 28-year old female who has completed an engineering program. In a job interview she is asked why she chose engineering. She might reply that starting when she was 10 years old, she used to help her father repair equipment at the family-run amusement arcade. Then, when she was 14 she won a science contest with a design for a gravity pump for the family home's fish pond. When she was 19...

   And, so it goes. Chronological patterns are easy to use because we organize our brains with certain milestones and accompanying memories.

2. *Narrative.* Similarly, we can use story patterns to retrieve key bits of information from our brains and then use the same story (or "narrative") to organize our thoughts on a subject. For example:

> If the female engineering grad in the job interview mentioned above were asked to explain whether she could effectively supervise a work crew on a forest road deactivation project, she could tell a story about a parallel experience she had during a work placement last year. At various points she could interrupt her narrative to point out the skills she demonstrated during that earlier experience.

3. *Topical arrangement.* In a job interview for an technologist position, a 37-year old graduate of an engineering technology program might be asked about his strengths relative to the position being discussed. He might say:

> "I can answer that by discussing three main areas: my previous factory experience, my talent for computer drafting and design, and the valuable experience I gained during my four-month work placement at your firm last year." Then, he would discuss each topic in turn.

4. *Cause-effect.* This two-part structure is described by its name. It can start with causative factors and work toward the results of those factors, or it can start with a description of a situation and work back to the causes of that situation. For example:

> The head of a highway maintenance team was recently asked why a certain highway had so many potholes during the previous winter. He began by briefly describing the physical features of some of the more common types of potholes and then recounted the special factors which result in those types of potholes, factors which were particularly prevalent that winter.

Now, before we get lost in a consideration of potholes, let's remember the main benefit of that highway maintenance spokesperson's use of the cause-effect pattern—long after listeners forgot the details of his explanation, they remembered that he seemed sensible and trustworthy!

Preparing Your Presentation

Plan the presentation systematically, to stay in control and build confidence. For our limited purposes here, we will assume your presentation is extemporaneous.

Research Your Topic

Do your homework. Be prepared to support each assertion, opinion, conclusion, and recommendation with evidence and reason. Check your facts for accuracy. Your listeners expect to hear a knowledgeable speaker; don't disappoint them.

Begin gathering material well ahead of time. Use summarizing techniques from Chapter 8 to identify and organize major points. If your presentation is a spoken version of a written report, most of your research has been done, but you may need to introduce material not found in the written version in order to appeal to listeners rather than readers.

Aim for Simplicity and Conciseness

Keep your presentation short and simple. Boil the material down to a few main points. Listeners' normal attention span is about twenty minutes. After that, they begin tuning out. Time yourself in practice sessions and trim as needed. If the material requires a lengthy presentation, plan a short break, with refreshments if possible, about half way.

Anticipate Audience Questions

Consider those parts of your presentation that listeners might question or challenge. You might need to clarify or justify information that is new, controversial, disappointing, or surprising.

Outline Your Presentation

Review Chapter 10 for organizing and outlining strategies. When you're preparing a talk, especially a lengthy, complex presentation, you can use the same kinds of organizing techniques as in a written document. However, the patterns in a written report might not suit an oral presentation. For example, see the report outline on pages 493 and 494, Chapter 19. That outline suits a written technical report, but not an oral version of the report. If Art Basran, the report's author, is asked to present his report orally to Jackson Mining's Board of Directors, he might revise his working outline as follows:

INTRODUCTION
- Express appreciation for opportunity to address Board.
- Review Jackson Mining's requirements and the four transport alternatives and analysis method.
- Show **O'head** of 4 alternatives.
- Show **O'head** of guidelines for analysis.
- Discuss **handout**: background info re: 4 haul alternatives.

CONCLUSION
- The diesel and electric train options give much better results than diesel trucks and electric train fleets.
- Which is better, diesel train option or electric train option?
- Show **O'heads** of Table 4: Diesel Trains as Best Alternative and Table 5: Electric Trains as Best Alternative.
- Figures are actually closer than Tables 4 and 5 might indicate at first.
- *MMT Consulting cannot recommend which specific option to choose because of the factors beyond the scope of this report which you must decide.*
- **My purpose here today:**
  Help you understand the analysis behind our findings so you can make the best decision for your operation.

COST ANALYSIS

Annual Costs
- *Fuel consumption*: Why important, and how calculated (Refer to Appendix A of report). Show **O'head** of Table 1: Tractive and Grade Resistances for Diesel Trucks
- *Labour*: Method of calculating. Refer to Appendix B.
- *Maintenance*: Quick reminder only

Capital Costs
- *Transportation units*: Quick overview of calculation method
- *Construction costs:* Show 3 main factors—**O'head**
  Show calculation method—**O'head**
  Comment re: maintenance buildings

Communication System
- Name components (brief).

Cost Comparisons
- Show **O'head** of Table 3.
- Explain Table 3 and lead into Equivalent Uniform Annual Costs.

Equivalent Uniform Annual Costs
- Why we chose EUAC comparisons
- Show **O'head** of Figure 1: Show how to read it.
  Refer to Appendix D (report **handouts**).
  Explain the sharp decline in EUAC.

Stop for questions at this point

POTENTIAL FOR EXPANSION
- Refer to conversation with Jessica Proctor re: flexibility (potential for expansion).
- Use **O'heads** to show how:
  - an immediate increase of 23.3% could be achieved for diesel trucks
  - diesel and electric trains could handle up to a 53.5% increase in production
  - electric fleets have room for 130% increase in production

LEAD-OUT
- Wish Board success with this venture.
- Indicate MMT's willingness to oversee road construction.
- Invite further questions.

Carefully Prepare Your Introduction and Conclusion

Speech *introductions* are very important; first, you must gain audience attention, establish your credibility, and lead in to the content of your talk. In the process, establish the mood of your presentation. Three groups of related techniques for immediately engaging your listeners are listed in Table 24.1.

Table 24.1   Effective Methods for Engaging Listeners

Establish the Topic:	Grab Audience Attention:	Connect with Your Audience
• Refer directly to subject.	• Refer to recent events.	• Establish common ground.
• Provide a pre-summary.	• State a startling fact or idea.	• Promise a reward.
• Delimit the topic.	• Give illustration or story.	• Present your credentials.
• Provide background info.	• Ask a rhetorical question.	• Justify the topic.
• Define terms.		

The *conclusion* to your talk provides your last chance to confirm your main point. Sometimes you may also want to finish on an emotional high or persuade your listeners to act in a certain way. And, no matter what the purpose of your talk has been, your closing phrasing should signal a strong sense of conclusion; you should never have to tell your audience: "that's the end of my talk."

Here are some techniques for closing strongly:

- Summarize your main points.
- Request a specific action from your audience.

- Challenge the audience to reach certain goals.
- Declare *your* intended action.
- Quote a memorable phrase or piece of poetry.
- Finish with a powerful example or story.
- Repeat a key phrase from the introduction.
- Show how you've fulfilled a promise made in the introduction.

Some combination of two or more of the above techniques will suit any presentation.

Build Bridges for Your Listeners

Most audience members don't listen attentively all the time; they tune in and out. When they *do* tune back in, you need to help them understand what direction the talk has taken while they were "away." Not all audience members wander, but even the best listeners find it difficult to follow speakers who do not provide bridges from one section of a talk to the next.

The following bridging techniques can help the best and worst of listeners stay on your idea track:

1. *Build bridges at the beginning.* Preview the presentation's structure so that your listeners know where you're headed and can anticipate the relationships among the topics you'll be discussing. If your presentation is lengthy and complex, an agenda in poster form or a handout would help the audience.

2. *Use the organization structure that best suits the topic.* A presentation about overcoming speaker nervousness could use a problem-solution pattern. A presentation about the development process for a residential subdivision could employ a chronological pattern, perhaps with key deadline dates assigned to each stage of the process.

3. *Build word bridges during the presentation.* Transitional phrases can take several forms:
   - Confirm the direction of the presentation. (*Now let's consider some other methods of reducing waste.*)
   - Change the direction of the presentation. (*We've identified the problem; now it's time to find a solution.*)
   - Lead into an example or a detailed list of evidence. (*If you want assurance that this program actually works, here's a case for you to consider…*)
   - Develop an idea further. (*In addition to their contribution to the local ecology, these marsh lands help local tourism …*)

4. *Use repetition to confirm key ideas and to re-orient wayward listeners.* You could repeat a key phrase (such as Martin Luther King's "I have a dream"). Or, you could repeat an idea without making the repetition obvious

(*Nothing to fear but fear itself*; *You're your own worst critic*; *Believe in your abilities as much as we do*). You could summarize the points you've just made in the preceding section—these *stage summaries* help those who've not listened as attentively as they might have.

Plan Your Visuals

Visuals increase listeners' interest, focus, understanding, and memory. Select visuals that will clarify and enhance your talk—without making you fade into the background.

Decide Where Visuals Will Work Best. Use visuals to emphasize a point and enhance your presentation whenever *showing* would be more effective than merely *telling*.

Decide Which Visuals Will Work Best. Will you need numerical or prose tables, graphs, charts, graphic illustrations, computer graphics? How fancy should these visuals be? Should they impress or merely inform? Use the visual planning sheet in Chapter 12 to guide your decisions.

Create a Storyboard. A storyboard is a double-column format in which your discussion is outlined in the left column, aligned with the specific supporting visuals in the right column.

Pollution Threats to Local Groundwater

1.0   Introduce the Problem

    1.1   Do you know what you are drinking when you turn on the tap and fill the glass?

    1.2   The quality of our water is good, but not guaranteed to last forever.

    1.3   St John's rapid population growth poses a serious threat to our freshwater supply.   (Transparency: *a line graph showing 20-year population growth*)

    1.4   Measurable pollution in some town water supplies already has occurred.   (Transparency: *two side-by-side tables showing 20-year increases in nitrate and chloride concentrations in three city wells*)

    1.5   What are the major causes and consequences of this problem and what can we do about it?   (Poster: *a multi-coloured list that previews my five subtopics*)

2.0   Describe the Aquifer

    2.1   The groundwater is collected and held in an aquifer.

        2.1.1.   This porous rock formation forms a broad, continuous arch beneath the entire city.   (Transparency: *a cutaway view of the aquifer's geology*)

Figure 24.1   A Partial Storyboard

Decide How Many Visuals Are Appropriate. Use an array of lean, simple visuals that present material in digestible amounts instead of one or two overstuffed visuals that people end up staring at endlessly.

Decide Which Visuals Are Achievable. Fit each visual to the situation. The visuals you select will depend on the room, the equipment, and the production resources available.

Fit each visual to the situation

How large is the room and how is it arranged? Some visuals work well in small rooms, but not large ones, and vice versa. How well can the room be darkened? Which lights can be left on? Can the lighting be adjusted selectively? What size should visuals be, to be seen clearly by the whole room? (A smaller, intimate room usually is better than a room that is too big and cavernous.)

What hardware is available (slide projector, opaque projector, overhead projector, film projector, videotape player, data projection unit, projection screen)? How far in advance does this equipment have to be requested? What graphics programs are available? Which is best for your purpose and listeners?

What resources are available for producing the visuals? Can drawings, charts, graphs, or maps be created as needed? Can transparencies (for overhead projection) be made or slides collected? Can handouts be keyed and reproduced? Can multimedia displays be created?

Select Your Media. Fit the medium to the situation. Which medium or combination is best for the topic, setting, and listeners? How fancy do listeners expect this to be? Which media are appropriate for this occasion? Examples appear on pages 652–653.

Fit the medium to the situation

- For a weekly meeting with colleagues in your department, scribbling on a blank transparency, chalkboard, or dry-erase markerboard might suffice.
- For interacting with listeners, you might use a whiteboard or chalkboard to record audience responses to your questions.
- For immediate orientation, you might begin with a poster or flip chart sheet listing key visuals/ideas/themes to which you will refer repeatedly.
- For helping listeners take notes, absorb technical data, or remember complex material, you might distribute a presentation outline as a preview or provide handouts.
- For displaying and discussing written samples listeners bring in, you might use an opaque projector.
- For a presentation to investors, clients, or upper management, you might require polished and professionally prepared visuals, including computer graphics, multimedia, and state-of-the-art technology.

Figure 24.2 presents the various common media in approximate order of availability and ease of preparation.

Whiteboard/Chalkboard

Uses
- simple, on the spot visuals
- recording audience responses
- very informal settings
- small, well-lighted rooms

Tips
- copy long material in advance
- write legibly
- make it visible to everyone
- use washable markers on whiteboard
- speak to the listeners—not to the board

Poster

Uses
- overviews, previews, emphasis
- recurring themes
- formal or informal settings
- small, well-lighted rooms

Tips
- use 51 cm x 76.5 cm (20" x 30") posterboard or larger
- use intense, washable colours
- keep each poster simple and uncrowded
- arrange/display posters in advance
- make each visible to the whole room
- point to what you are discussing

Flip Chart

Uses
- a sequence of visuals
- back-and-forth movement
- formal or informal settings
- small, well-lighted rooms

Tips
- use an easel pad and easel
- use intense, washable colours
- work from a storyboard
- check your sequence beforehand
- point to what you are discussing

Handouts

Uses
- present complex material
- help listeners follow along
- help listeners take notes
- help listeners remember

Tips
- staple or bind the packet
- number the pages
- try saving for the end
- if you must distribute up-front, ask listeners to await instructions before reading the material

Figure 24.2   Selecting Media for Visual Presentations   (*Continued*)

Opaque Projection

Uses
- direct display of paper documents
- samples listeners bring in
- pages from books, reports
- informal settings
- very small and dark rooms
- when spontaneity is more important than image quality

Tips
- allow projector to warm up
- don't shut off projector until you're done
- never stare at the bright bulb
- use a light source for viewing your notes
- use a laser or telescoping pointer
- place listeners close enough to see clearly

Slide Projection

Uses
- professional-quality visuals
- formal setting
- small or large, dark rooms

Tips
- work from a storyboard
- check the slide sequence beforehand
- use a light source for viewing your notes
- use a laser or telescoping pointer

Overhead Projection

Uses
- on-the-spot or prepared visuals
- overlaid visuals[1]
- formal or informal settings
- small- or medium-sized rooms
- rooms needing to remain lit

Tips
- use cardboard mounting frames for your acetate transparencies
- write discussion notes on each frame
- check your sequence beforehand
- turn off projector when not using it
- face the audience—not the screen
- point directly on the transparency

Computer Projection

Uses
- sophisticated charts, graphs, maps
- multimedia presentations
- formal settings
- small, dark rooms

Tips
- take lots of time to prepare/practise
- work from a storyboard
- check the whole system beforehand
- have a default plan in case something goes wrong

1. The overlay technique begins with one transparency showing a basic image, over which additional transparencies (with coordinated images, colours, labels, etc.) are added to produce an increasingly complex image.

Figure 24.2   Selecting Media for Visual Presentations

Prepare Your Visuals

As you prepare visuals, focus on economy, clarity, and simplicity.

Be Selective. Use a visual only when it truly serves a purpose. Use restraint in choosing what to highlight with visuals. Try not to begin or end the presentation with a visual. At those times, listeners' attention should be focused on the presenter instead of the visual.

Make Visuals Easy to Read and Understand. Think of each visual as an image that flashes before your listeners. They will not have the luxury of studying the visual at leisure. Listeners need to know at a glance what they are looking at and what it means. The following are guidelines for achieving readability.

Guidelines for Readable Visuals

- Make visuals large enough to be read anywhere in the room.
- Don't cram too many words, ideas, designs, or typestyles onto a visual.
- Keep wording and images simple.
- Boil your message down to the fewest words.
- Break things into small sections.
- Summarize with key words, phrases, or short sentences.
- Use 18–24 point type size and sans serif typeface (White, Great Pages 80).

In addition to being able to *read* the visual, listeners need to *understand* it. Following are guidelines for achieving clarity.

Guidelines for Understandable Visuals

- Display only one point per visual—unless previewing or reviewing (White 79).
- Give each visual a title that announces the topic.
- Use colour, sparingly, to highlight key words, facts, or the bottom line.
- Use the brightest colour for what is most important (White, Great Pages 78–79).
- Label each part of a diagram or illustration.
- Proofread each visual carefully.

When your material is extremely detailed or complex, distribute handouts to each listener.

Look for Alternatives to Word-filled Visuals. Instead of presenting mere overhead versions of printed pages, explore the full *visual* possibilities of your media. For example, anyone who tries to write a verbal equivalent of the visual message in Figure 24.3 soon will appreciate the power of images in relation to words alone. Whenever possible, use drawings, graphs, charts, photographs, and other visual representation discussed in Chapter 12.

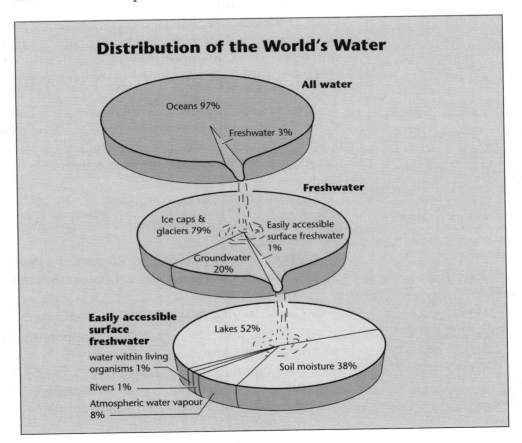

Figure 24.3   Images More Powerful Than Words
Source: "Distribution of the World's Water," as appeared in *WWF Atlas of the Environment* by Geoffrey Lean and Don Hinrichsen. Copyright ©1994 Banson Marketing Ltd. Reprinted with permission.

Use all Available Technology. Using desktop publishing systems and presentation software such as Powerpoint™ or Inspiration™ you can create professional-quality visuals and display technical concepts. Using hypertext and multimedia systems, you can create dynamic presentations that appeal to the listener's multiple senses. Using an automatic, remote-controlled transparency feeder and a laser pointer (pencil-sized), you can deliver a smooth and elegant presentation. These are just a few of the possibilities inherent in the technology.

Check the Room and Setting Beforehand. Make sure that you have enough space, electrical outlets, and tables for your equipment. If you will be addressing a large audience by microphone and plan to point to features on your visuals, be sure the microphone is movable. Pay careful attention to lighting, especially for white-boards, chalkboards, flipcharts, and posters. Don't forget a pointer if you need one.

Prepare Note Cards

Note cards build your confidence—you know that you won't be stuck for some-thing to say. Think of note cards as insurance against going blank in front of your audience. More importantly, note cards help keep you from wandering. When you work from a structured set of notes, there's less chance of going off on tangents.

However, you do need to discipline yourself. Notes will help only if you reg-ularly check them to make sure that you're still on course and that you haven't omitted key points. And you do need to rehearse with the cards so that you're sure that you can read them and that you're comfortable with them. Rehearsal builds confidence.

Here are some tips for creating usable note cards:

Note card creation tips

1. Use card stock or heavy paper (32 lb. or heavier), so the notes don't shake or droop.
2. Choose a size that suits you. Probably the smallest effective size is 7.5 cm x 12.5 cm (3″ x 5″). Remember that the larger the card, the more you can place on it.
3. Use no more than ten cards. Four to six cards will suffice for most talks.
4. Write on one side of each card. Number the cards sequentially in the upper right corner.
5. Use point form to remind yourself of the things you want to say. Write large, legible points. Do not print your speech out in full; you'll be tempted to read the material, and if you succumb to the temptation, you'll lose your audience.
6. Write sentences for the few critically important statements that you want to get exactly right (no more than three to five per talk).
7. Include:

   - headings or names of sections of the talk
   - your main points, in point form
   - key statistics, facts, or quotes that you may not remember
   - reminders to yourself—Breathe! Don't pace! Pause here. Slow down! Look at them!
   - AV usage cues—O'head: Table 1; draw on whiteboard; dim lights
   - time limits for certain parts of the presentation

Figure 24.4 illustrates note cards that Art Basran might use for his presentation to the Jackson Mining Board:

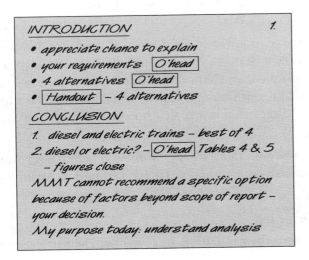

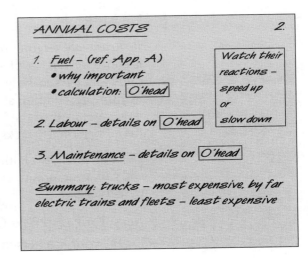

Figure 24.4   Sample Note Cards

Rehearse Your Talk

See the advice on page 643 to refresh your memory of how and what to rehearse. Pay particular attention to the introduction and conclusion, both of which must be presented smoothly and confidently. If possible, videotape one of your rehearsed deliveries to determine what might be improved. Then, use the evaluation sheet on page 664 to guide your improvements.

> **Note:** most speakers find that their rehearsal time is about 80% of actual performance time, unless nervousness causes them to forget material or to speak too quickly.

Delivering Your Presentation

You have planned and prepared carefully. Now consider the following simple steps to make your actual presentation enjoyable instead of terrifying.

Cultivate the Human Landscape

A successful presentation involves relationship building between presenter and audience.

Get to Know Your Audience Try to meet some audience members before your presentation. We all feel more comfortable with people we know. Don't be afraid to smile.

Display Enthusiasm and Confidence. Nobody likes a speaker who seems half dead. Clean up verbal tics ("er," "ah," "uuh"). Overcome your shyness; research indicates that shy people are seen as less credible, trustworthy, likable, attractive, and knowledgeable.

Be Reasonable. Don't make your point at someone else's expense. If your topic is controversial (layoffs, policy changes, downsizing), decide how to speak candidly and persuasively with the least chance of offending anyone. For example, in your presentation about groundwater pollution, you don't want to attack the developers, since the building trade is a major producer of jobs, in St. John. Avoid personal attacks.

Don't Preach. Speak like a person talking—not someone giving a sermon. Use *we, you, your, our,* to establish commonality with the audience. Avoid jokes or wisecracks.

Keep Your Listeners Oriented

Enable your listeners to focus their attention and organize their understanding. Give them a map, some guidance, and highlights.

Introduce Your Topic Clearly. Open with a preview of your discussion:

A presentation preview

> Today, I want to discuss A, B, and C.

Use visuals to highlight your main points and reveal your organization. For example, you might outline main points on a poster, flipchart, whiteboard, chalkboard, or transparency, or hand out a presentation outline.

Focus on Listeners' Concerns. Say something to establish immediate common ground. Show how your presentation has meaning for the audience, personally.

An appeal to listener's concerns

> Do you know what you will be drinking when you turn on the tap?

Listeners who have a definite stake in the issues will be far more attentive and receptive.

Provide Explicit Transitions. Alert your listeners whenever you are preparing to switch gears:

Explicit transitions

> For my next point. . . .
> Turning now to my second point. . . .
> The third point I want to emphasize. . . .

Repeat key points or terms to keep them fresh in listeners' minds.

Give Concrete Examples. Mobilize the informative and persuasive force of good examples.

A concrete example

> Overdraw from town wells in St. John has resulted in measurable salt infusion at a yearly rate of 0.1 mg per litre.

Use examples that focus on listener concerns.

Review and Interpret. Last things are best remembered. Help listeners remember the main points:

A review of main points

| To summarize the dangers to our groundwater. . . .

Manage Your Presentation Style

Think about how you are moving, how you are speaking, where you are looking. These all are elements of your personal style.

Use Natural Movements and Reasonable Postures. Move and gesture as you normally would in conversation, and maintain reasonable postures. Avoid foot shuffling, pencil tapping, swaying, slumping, or fidgeting.

Adjust Volume, Pronunciation, and Rate. With a microphone, don't speak too loudly. Without one, don't speak too softly. Be sure you can be heard clearly without shattering eardrums.

Nervousness causes speakers to gallop along and mispronounce things. Slow down and pronounce clearly. Usually, a rate that seems a bit slow to you will be just right for listeners.

Maintain Eye Contact. Look directly into listeners' eyes. With a small audience, eye contact is one of your best connectors. As you speak, establish eye contact with as many listeners as possible. With a large group, maintain eye contact with those in the first rows. Establish eye contact immediately—before you even begin to speak—by looking around.

Manage Your Speaking Situation

Do everything you can to keep things running smoothly.

Be Responsive to Listener Feedback. Assess listener feedback continually and make adjustments as needed. If you are labouring through a long list of facts or figures and people begin to doze or fidget, you might summarize. Likewise, if frowns, raised eyebrows, or questioning looks indicate confusion, skepticism, or indignation, you can backtrack with a specific example or explanation. By tuning in to your audience's reactions, you can avoid leaving them confused, hostile, or simply bored.

Stick to Your Plan. Say what you came to say, then summarize and close—politely and on time. Don't punctuate your speech with digressions that pop into your head. Unless a specific anecdote was part of your original plan to clarify a point or increase interest, avoid excursions. We often tend to be more interested in what we have to say than our listeners are!

Leave Listeners with Something to Remember. Before ending, take a moment to summarize the major points and re-emphasize anything of special importance. Are listeners supposed to remember something, have a different attitude, take a specific action? Let them know! As you conclude, thank your listeners.

Allow Time for Questions and Answers. At the very beginning, tell your listeners that a question-and-answer period will follow. Observe the following guidelines for managing listener questions diplomatically and efficiently.

Guidelines for Managing Listener Questions

- Announce a specific time limit, to avoid prolonged debates.
- Listen carefully to each question.
- If you can't understand a question, ask that it be rephrased.
- Repeat every question, to ensure that everyone hears it.
- Be brief in your answers.

- If you need extra time, arrange for it after the presentation.
- If anyone attempts lengthy debate, offer to continue *after* the presentation.
- If you can't answer a question, say so and move on.
- End the session with, "We have time for one more question," or some such signal.

IN BRIEF

Oral Presentations for Cross-cultural Audiences

Imagine you've been assigned to represent your company at an international conference or before international clients (e.g., of passenger aircraft or computers). As you plan and prepare your presentation, remain sensitive to various cultural expectations.

For example, some cultures might be offended by a presentation that gets right to the point without first observing formalities of politeness, well wishes, and the like.

Certain communication styles are welcomed in some cultures, but considered offensive in others. In southern Europe and the Middle East, people expect direct and prolonged eye contact as a way of showing honesty and respect. In Southeast Asia, this may be taken as a sign of aggression or disrespect (Gesteland 24). A sampling of the questions to consider:

- Should I smile a lot or look serious? (Hulbert 42)
- Should I rely on expressive gestures and facial expressions?
- How loudly or softly, rapidly or slowly should I speak?

- Should I come out from behind the podium and approach the audience or keep my distance?
- Should I get right to the point or take plenty of time to lead into and discuss the matter thoroughly?
- Should I focus on only the key facts or on all the details and various interpretations?
- Should I be assertive in offering interpretations and conclusions, or should I allow listeners to reach conclusions on their own?
- Which types of visuals and which media might work or not work?
- Should I invite questions from this audience, or would this be offensive?

To account for language differences, prepare a handout of your entire script for distribution after the presentation, along with a copy of your visuals. This way, your audience will be able to study your material at leisure.

★　★　★

☑ EXERCISES

1. In a memo to your instructor, identify and discuss the kinds of oral reporting duties you expect to encounter in your career.

2. Design an oral presentation for your class. (Base it on a written report.) Make a sentence outline, and a storyboard that includes at least three visuals. Practise with a tape recorder or a friend. Use the peer evaluation sheet (page 664) to evaluate your delivery.

3. Observe a lecture or speech, and evaluate it according to the peer evaluation sheet. Write a memo to your instructor (without naming the speaker), identifying strong and weak areas and suggesting improvements.

4. In an oral presentation to the class, present your findings, conclusions, and recommendations from the analytical report assignment in Chapter 19.

5. Prepare a speaker self-assessment. You'll find the self-assessment form on pages 662 and 663 very useful if the assessment is done objectively and thoroughly. In order to improve objectivity, either enlist the aid of one or more committed, objective observers, or videotape a presentation and analyze it with the help of the self-assessment form. Alternatively, you can view and analyze the tape together with some supportive critics.

You may find the definitions, comments, and advice on page 663 helpful.

☑ COLLABORATIVE PROJECT

Exercise 3 may be done as a collaborative project.

SPEAKER SELF-ASSESSMENT

Item	Description	Audience Reactions?	Improvements?
Appearance Physical presence Style of dress/grooming			
Voice Timbre Volume/projection Resonance			
Vocal Delivery Clear sounds Tonal range/skill Tonal variety Inflections Emphasis Pacing: rate & variety Vocal fillers			
Other **Non-verbals** Eye contact Facial expressions Body movements Hand/arm gestures Nervous habits			
Language Use Slang Clear phrasing Appropriate vocabulary level			
Performance Level Conversational Heightened Performance Oratorical			

Appearance

Physical presence . . . . Sheer size gives an advantage, but smaller people can compensate by being physically active.

Dress/grooming . . . . Your appearance is particularly important in a talk's opening moments.

Voice

Timbre . . . . The nature of your vocal cords: bass? reedy? shrill? birdlike? throaty? etc.

Volume/projection . . . . "Volume" ranges from a whisper to a shout, but a whisper can be projected nearly as far as a shout.

Resonance . . . . To achieve more resonance, vibrate your vocal cords more vigorously.

Vocal Delivery

Clear sounds? . . . . To avoid slurring sounds, take care to say **each sound** distinctly.

Tonal range/skill . . . . Can you convey a full range of emotions by changing vocal tones?

Tonal variety . . . . It's essential to vary your tones and avoid the dreaded monotone.

Inflections . . . . Downward inflections at the end of statements sound confident and authoritative, but upward inflections make you sound unsure .

Emphasis . . . . Emphasizing key words is a distinguishing feature of "public" speaking.

Delivery rate . . . . Speaking quickly is O.K. **if** you emphasize key words and speak clearly.

Pacing: variety . . . . Effective speakers vary their pace and use pauses to emphasize points.

Vocal fillers . . . . "Like," "uh," "um," "O.K.," and "eh" are the most common fillers used by Canadians; these fillers can distract listeners.

Other Non-verbals

Eye contact . . . . If you want to keep audience interest, you **must** look at your listeners.

Facial expressions . . . . Lively facial expressions show interest in your listeners.

Body movements . . . . These can vary with the situation, but they should be controlled in business presentations.

Hand/arm gestures . . . . These should be used naturally, not in a contrived or wooden manner.

Nervous habits . . . . Our bodies reveal our real feelings, so we can't eliminate nervous signs completely; however, we should stifle those which distract audiences.

Language Use

Slang? . . . . Slang is inappropriate in all formal business settings.

Clear phrasing? . . . . Public talks require well-conceived, clear descriptions and explanations.

Level of vocabulary . . . . Carefully match your level of vocabulary to your audience, without talking down to them, or overusing jargon.

Peer Evaluation Sheet for Oral Presentations

Presentation Evaluation for (name/topic) _____

Comments

Content

☐ Began with a clear purpose.   _____

☐ Showed command of the material.   _____

☐ Supported assertions with evidence.   _____

☐ Used adequate and appropriate visuals.   _____

☐ Used material suited to this audience's
   needs, knowledge, concerns, and interests.   _____

☐ Acknowledged opposing views.   _____

☐ Gave the right amount of information.   _____

Organization

☐ Presented a clear line of reasoning.   _____

☐ Used transitions effectively.   _____

☐ Avoided needless digressions.   _____

☐ Summarized before concluding.   _____

☐ Was clear about what the listeners
   should think or do.   _____

Style

☐ Seemed confident, relaxed, and likable.   _____

☐ Seemed in control of the speaking situation.   _____

☐ Showed appropriate enthusiasm.   _____

☐ Pronounced, enunciated, and spoke well.   _____

☐ Used appropriate gestures, tone,
   volume, and delivery rate.   _____

☐ Had good posture and eye contact.   _____

☐ Answered questions concisely and convincingly.   _____

Overall professionalism: Superior _____ **Acceptable** _____ **Needs work** _____

Evaluator's signature: _____

Web Sites and On-line Documentation

Except for manuals and reference books, paper documents (letters, memos, reports, proposals) usually are structured to be read in linear sequence: front-to-back. Information builds on the information that precedes it. E-mail documents, often printed out at their destination, usually display this linear structure.

But some types of electronic documents enable users to design their own information sequence as they search for specific chunks of information or merely browse through parts of a topic in no particular order, as one might read a newspaper or encyclopedia (Grice and Ridgway 35-43). Because readers design their own information sequence, these documents are written in small, discrete modules, that can stand alone in meaning.

This chapter introduces types of electronic documents essential to workplace communication.

On-line Documentation

People who use computers in their jobs need instructions and training for operating the systems and understanding their equipment's many features. On-line documentation is designed to support specific tasks and provide answers to specific questions.

Although computers come with printed manuals, the computer itself is becoming the preferred training medium. In computer-based training, documentation on the screen itself explains how the system works and how to use it. Examples of on-line help include:

Types of on-line documentation

- error messages and troubleshooting advice
- reference guides to additional information or instructions
- tutorial lessons that include interactive exercises with immediate feedback
- help and review options to accommodate different learning styles

Instead of leafing through a printed manual, users find what they need by keying a simple command, clicking a mouse, using a help menu, or following an electronic prompt.

The documentation itself might appear (a) in dialogue boxes that ask the user to input a response or click on an option, or (b) pop-up or balloon help that appears when the user clicks on an icon or points to an item on the screen for more information. (For examples, explore the on-line help resources on your own computer.)

Hypertext

One extension of on-line documentation increasingly used in tutorial and training software is *hypertext*, information in electronic form designed for non-linear reading. Unlike printed text, designed to be read front-to-back, a hypertext document offers various informational paths through the material, the particular path (or paths) determined by what and how much a reader wants to know. *Hypermedia*, expands the applications of hypertext by adding graphics, sound, video, and animation.

In addition to on-line documentation, hypertext is used as a research and reference tool for navigating complex cross-references and retrieving information electronically. In a hypertext system, a topic can be explored from any angle, at any level of detail. Assume, for instance, that you are using a hypertext database to research the AIDS epidemic. The database contains chunks of related topics organized in a network (or web) of files linked electronically (Horton 22), as illustrated in Figure 25.1.

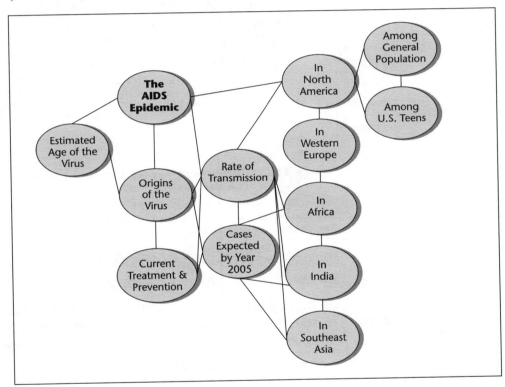

Figure 25.1   Topics (or files) in a Hypertext Network are Linked Electronically

Hypertext accommodates enquiry in various directions

After accessing the initial file ("The AIDS Epidemic"), you navigate the network in any direction, choosing which file to open and where to go next. The files themselves might be printed words, graphics, sound, video, or animation. Freed from the fixed-page sequence of a printed document, you customize the direction of your search.

Because hypertext offers multiple layers of information, from general to specific (Figure 25.2), you also customize the depth of your search.

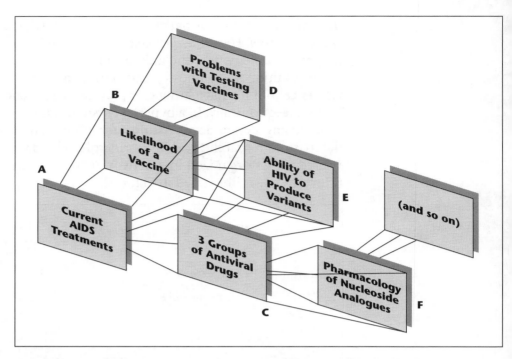

Figure 25.2   Hypertext Topics can be Layered to serve Different Audiences

Source: Visual adapted from Horton, William. "Is Hypertext the Best Way to Document Your Product?" *Technical Communications* 39.1 (1991):25. Used with permission from the Society for Technical Communication, Arlington, VA.

Communication specialist William Horton explains the instructional power achieved through hypertext layering:

Hypertext accommodates enquiry at various depths

> Paper…lacks depth. All information must be on the same level or layer. With hypertext, however, the screen can have deeper reserves of information. These deeper layers do not clutter the screen, but are available if needed. ("Is Hypertext" 25)

Persons navigating a hypertext document invent their own "text" and so can discover combinations, relationships, and chains of knowledge impossible to express in the sequential pages of a printed document (Bernstein 42).

Following is an application of hypertext instruction in the auto industry:

A hypertext application

> A mechanic can zoom from a picture of a car engine to a video of a specific malfunctioning part, and then move directly to the text that tells how to fix it. (Morse 7)

For all their potential as research and instructional tools, hypertext documents carry limitations:

Limitations of hypertext documents

> • Confronting countless possible paths through the material, readers can get lost in "hyperspace." (*Where do I go next? How do I get out? How do I organize?*) Ease of navigation depends on how effectively individual chunks (or "nodes") of information are segmented and linked.

- Readers may resist a document that leaves them responsible for organizing their own learning. They generally rely on the writer to help organize their thinking (Horton, "Is Hypertext" 26).
- Instead of always enhancing learning, hypertext documents can in fact interfere with understanding and impede performance (Barfield, Haselkoam and Weatbrook 22, 27). Users in one study took longer to read a hypertext document than the equivalent paper document (Rubens 36).
- Some hypertexts can be too highly structured, thus leaving users with *fewer* navigational choices than they would have with a printed document (Selber).

These problems can be addressed by communicators making the right decisions (Horton "Is Hypertext" 27; Nickels-Shirk 191):

Decisions in creating hypertext documents

- How much information should be included on one screen?
- What level of detail should be presented?
- How can each chunk be written so it can be read in any order and still make sense?
- How can the material best be linked for easiest navigation of various possible paths?
- Which combination of media should be employed (printed words, speech, sound effects, animation, music)?

Creating hypertext documents usually is not a one-person job; it often requires writers, graphic artists, computer specialists, animators, and the like. This is one example of how communication technology makes collaboration both possible and necessary.

The most rapidly expanding application of hypertext occurs via the Internet, on the World Wide Web. (Chapter 6 covers Internet research.)

The Web

Like a CD-ROM or electronic database, the Web offers a collection of electronic documents and multimedia. But hypertext enables the Web to link information in non-linear patterns, providing countless routes to be explored—worldwide—according to the user's special needs (Hunt 377). Some unique characteristics of the Web (December 371-72) are:

How the Web differs from other media

- *The Web is interactive.* Users construct their own hypertextual path through the material and can respond/add to the message.
- *The Web allows reciprocal use.* Besides obtaining information, users can also provide it.
- *The Web is porous.* A work can be entered at various points because a Web site usually offers multiple files which are linked.
- *The Web is ever changing.* A Web page or site is continually "a work in progress"—not only in its content but also in the technology itself (software, hardware, modems, servers). Unlike paper, software, or CD-ROM, the Web has no "final state."

These features enable Web users to discover and create their own connections among an endless array of ideas.

Note: Keep in mind that Web pages, like all on-line screens, take at least 25 percent longer to read than paper documents. One possible solution: high-resolution screens that are as readable as paper copy. These should be widely available and affordable within a decade (Neilsen "Be Succinct" 1).

IN BRIEF

How Web Sites Enhance Workplace Transactions

The Web is a tool for advertising, learning about new products or companies, updating product information, or ordering products (Teague 236, 238). Each organization advertises its services and products via its own *home page*, a type of electronic billboard that introduces the organization and provides links to additional pages users can explore as they wish.

Specific Benefits

- **Visibility.** A site attracts business by establishing a presence in markets worldwide.
- **Access.** A site is accessible 24 hours a day (Dulude 47).
- **Customer relations.** Through enhanced customer service and support and rapid response, a site increases customer satisfaction and enhances a company's caring persona (Hoger, Cappel, and Myerscough 41).
- **Efficiency.** Two way, real-time communication enables sudden problems, errors, or areas of danger to be broadcast rapidly. The audience can control the viewing of messages and respond immediately. On-screen instructions (for example, for assembling a modem) can be enhanced with high-resolution, 3-D graphics, parts can be colour-coded for assembly, and material can be updated instantly (Dulude 49-60).

- **Economy.** The cost of an Internet/Web bank transaction drops from over a $1 to roughly 1 cent; the cost of processing an airline ticket drops from $8 to $1 (IBM 13). A site enables mass publishing. Radically reduced printing, mailing, and distribution costs facilitate mass publishing. Also, an advertiser can embed deeper and deeper levels of product details, without consuming extra page space. Ultimately, as the cost of business transactions drops, so does the number of required employees.
- **Data Gathering.** Tracking software provides customer data by recording who uses the Web site, how often they use it, and exactly where they go. Employees access reference materials from journal and trade-magazines, and addresses of researchers, and remain current about legal issues, and government regulations (Ritzenthaler and Ostroff 17-18).
- **Information Sharing.** Intranets and extranets increase the flow of ideas up and down, and down and up, from outside to inside the company and vice versa. Knowledge audits identify who knows what and this information is then listed in the company intranet directory ("yellow pages").
- **Collaboration.** Company sites help reduce the length/need for face-to-face meetings. And people who do meet are better prepared because they have shared information beforehand.

Elements of a Usable Web Site

Although more diverse than typical users of paper documents, Web users share common expectations. The following are basic usability indicators for a Web site.

Accessibility

Users expect a site that is easy to enter, exit, and navigate. Instead of reading word-for-word, they tend to skim, looking for key material without having to scroll through pages of text. They look for chances to interact and they want to download material at a reasonable speed.

Worthwhile Content

Users expect the site to contain all the explanations they need (help screens, links, etc.). They want material that is accurate and constantly up to date. They expect clear error messages that spell out appropriate corrective action. They look for links to other, high-quality sites as indicators of credibility. They look for an e-mail address and other contact information being prominently displayed.

Sensible Arrangement

Users always want to know where they are, and where they are going. They expect a recognizable design and layout, with links easily navigated forward or backward, back links to the home page, and no dead ends. They look for navigation bars and hot buttons explicitly labelled ("Company Information," "Ordering," "Job Openings," and so on).

Instead of a traditional introduction, discussion, and conclusion, users expect the punch line right up front. Because they hate to scroll, users often get only what is on the first screen.

Good Writing and Page Design

Users expect a writing style that is easy to read and error-free. They look for concise pages that are quick to scan, with short sentences and paragraphs, headings, and bulleted lists. Instead of having to wade through overstatement and exaggeration to "get at the fact," readers expect restrained, impartial language (Neilsen "Be Succinct" 2). Table 25.1 on page 673 illustrates the impact of good writing on usability.

Good Graphics and Special Effects

Some users look for images or multimedia special effects—as long as these are not excessive or gratuitous. Since other users often disable their browser's visual capability (to save memory and downloading time) they look for a prose equivalent of each visual (*visual/prose redundancy*). They expect to recognize each icon and screen element—hot buttons, links, help options, etc.

Scripting a Web Document with HTML

HTML (hypertext markup language) is a computer scripting language that can be understood by all Web browsers and that specifies the positioning of each element on a Web page: text, art, headings, lists, hot-buttons, etc. For any type of computer or operating system, HTML provides a common "interface" enabling all users on a network to create, access, exchange, or edit information (Culshaw 34).

An HTML document is coded by use of *tags*: the command, enclosed in angle brackets, appears on both ends of the content to be acted upon. The tagged command plus the related text are known as an *HTML element*.

A typical HTML element   ▌   <TITLE>English 266 Technical Writing</TITLE>

Figure 25.3 shows basic HTML commands. Figure 25.4 shows one Web page created by Professor R.A. Dumont; Figure 25.5 shows that page's partial HTML script (obtained from "View Source" on the desktop menu).

> **Note:** To visit a Web site offering HTML advice, instruction, and useful links, go to <http://utoronto/websites/HTMLdocs/NewHTML/into.html>. Also, keep in mind that <u>Wysiwyg</u> ("what you see is what you get") editing programs, such as Adobe PageMill™, Microsoft FrontPage™, or Symantec Visual Page™ largely eliminate the need for HTML coding by hand. These authoring tools provide step-by-step instructions and templates for creating Web pages, positioning graphics and other page elements, adding clip art, etc.

Site Version	Sample Paragraph	Usability Improvement (relative to control condition)
Promotional writing (control condition) using the "marketese" found on many commercial Web sites	Nebraska is filled with internationally recognized attractions that draw large crowds of people every year, without fail. In 1996, some of the most popular places were Fort Robinson State Park (355,000 visitors), Scotts Bluff National Monument (132,166), Arbor Lodge State Historical Park & Museum 100,000), Carhenge (86,598), Stuhr Museum of the Prairie Pioneer (60,002), and Buffalo Bill Ranch State Historical Park (28,446).	0% (by definition)
Concise text with about half the word count as the control condition	In 1996, six of the best-attended attractions in Nebraska were Fort Robinson State Park, Scotts Bluff National Monument, Arbor Lodge State Historical Park & Museum, Carhenge, Stuhr Museum of the Prairie Pioneer, and Buffalo Bill Ranch State Historical Park.	58%
Scannable layout using the same text as the control condition in a layout that facilitated scanning	Nebraska is filled with internationally recognized attractions that draw large crowds of people every year, without fail. In 1996, some of the most popular places were: • Fort Robinson State Park (355,000 visitors) • Scotts Bluff National Monument (132,166) • Arbor Lodge State Historical Park & Museum (100,000) • Carhenge (86,598) • Stuhr Museum of the Prairie Pioneer (60,002) • Buffalo Bill Ranch State Historical Park (28,446)	47%
Objective language using neutral rather than subjective, boastful, or exaggerated language (otherwise the same as the control condition)	Nebraska has several attractions. In 1996, some of the most-visited places were Fort Robinson State Park (355,000 visitors), Scotts Bluff National Monument (132,166), Arbor Lodge State Historical Park & Museum (100,000), Carhenge (86,598), Stuhr Museum of the Prairie Pioneer (60,002), and Buffalo Bill Ranch State Historical Park (28,446).	27%
Combined version using all three improvements in writing style together: concise, scannable, and objective	In 1996, six of the most-visited places in Nebraska were: • Fort Robinson State Park • Scotts Bluff National Monument • Arbor Lodge State Historical Park & Museum • Carhenge • Stuhr Museum of the Prairie Pioneer • Buffalo Bill Ranch State Historical Park	124%

Table 25.1   The Impact of Good Writing on Usability

Source: Neilsen, Jakob, "Reading on the Web." Oct. 1997. Alertbox. 8 Aug. 1997 <http://www.useit.ccm/alertbox/9710a.html>

IN BRIEF

How Site Needs and Expectations Differ Across Cultures

Despite its United States origin, the Internet rapidly has become international and cross-cultural. And yet, countries vary greatly in their level of "Internet maturity," with much of the world several years behind North America (Neilsen "Global" 2). A useful international site therefore reflects careful regard for cost, clarity, and cultural sensitivity.

Cost

High telephone rates in many countries hike Internet costs. In Japan, for example—whose Internet use ranks second to that in North America—monthly cost for a one-hour daily on-line is more than double the North American cost for unlimited access (Neilsen "Global"). A usable site therefore omits graphics that are slow to load.

Clarity

To facilitate access and avoid misunderstandings, international communication via the Internet incorporates measures like these:

- Sites often provide home-page versions in various languages (or links to a translation package).
- Time zones, currencies, and other units of measurement differ (10 a.m. in Vancouver equals 6 p.m. in London, 7 p.m. in Stockholm, or 3 a.m. in Tokyo). In arranging real-time interactions (e.g., an on-line conference) the host specifies the recipient's time as well as the home time (Neilsen "International" 1).
- Because the value of a "dollar" in countries such as Australia, U.S., Singapore, or Zimbabwe differs from the value of the Canadian dollar, businesses specify "$12.50 Canadian," and so on. Also, offering payment options in the culture's own currency helps avoid currency-exchange ambiguities (Hodges 18-19).
- A date listed as "6/10/08" might be confusing in other cultures. Preferable would be "10 June, 2008" or "June 10, 2008."
- Temperature measurements are specified as "Fahrenheit" or "Celsius."

Cultural Sensitivity

A site truly "international" in ambiance—and not merely "North American"—enables anyone, anywhere to feel at home (Neilsen "Global" 2). For example, it avoids sarcasm or irreverence (which some cultures consider highly offensive), and exclusive references or colloquialisms such as "bear markets," "the wild west," and "Stanley Cup."

Java enhances HTML documents

HTML produces only static pages, with limited possibilities for data display. However, a programming language called *Java* can be embedded in an HTML script to provide "dynamic" content (graphics, motion, and sound). Java-enhanced Web pages allow more sophisticated, interactive applications such as simulations and computer-based training.

HTML Commands

- To denote a Web page (so browsers can identify this page as an HTML file):
  <HTML> entire HTML file </HTML> (slash [/] denotes an ending tag)

- To mark main elements in the text:
  <TITLE>....</TITLE>
  <BODY>....</BODY>
  <BLOCKQUOTE>....</BLOCKQUOTE> (sets off quoted material)

- To signify a break in the text*:

    (line break; begins next line at left margin)
  <P>   (paragraph)
  <HR>   (displays horizontal ruled line, across text width of page)
  * No closing tag is needed for a mere insertion into the page, in which no specific content is modified. These are called *empty tags*.

- To specify headings:
  <H1>....</H1>   (for highest-level head)
  <H2>....</H2>   (and so on, down to as far as sixth-level heads)

- To align elements elsewhere than at left margin (centre, right, justify):
  <H2 ALIGN=right>....</H2> (aligns head on right margin)
  <P ALIGN=center>....</P>   (centres the paragraph)

- To display a list:
  <UI>   (unnumbered list, with bullets displayed before each item)
  <LI>   (1st item in list)
  <LI>   (2nd item, and so on)
  </UL>   (end of list)

  <OL>   (numbered list, with a number displayed before each item)
  <LI>   (1st item in list)
  <LI>   (2nd item in list)
  </OL>   (end of list)

- To specify typestyles:
  <Q>....</Q>   (Show enclosed content in quotation marks)
  <B>....</B>   (Boldface)
  <I>....</I>   (Italics)
  <U>....</U>   (Show underlined text)
  <BIG>....</BIG>   (Larger than current font)
  <SMALL>....</SMALL>   (Smaller than current font)

- To insert a figure in the text:
  <FIGURE>filename or URL where figure is stored</FIGURE>

- To create links (HREF stands for Hypertext Reference):
  <A HREF="some URL">Go to some URL</A>   (to other Web sites)
  <A HREF="#price list">price list</A>   (to another part of document)

- To receive e-mail from site users:
  <A HREF>="mail to your e-mail address">Your e-mail address</A>

Figure 25.3   A Sample of HTML Commands

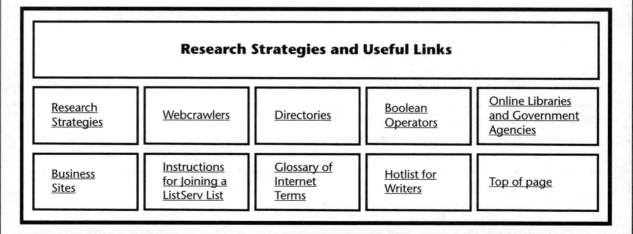

UMass Dartmouth

Course Guidelines and Syllabus for Enl. 600

<u>Syllabus - Part II</u>:   **Assignments 3 through 5**

<u>Syllabus - Part III</u>:   **Assignments 6 and 7**

Textbook: Technical Communication, 8th ed., John M. Lannon, 2000, published by Longman.

Getting the necessary background for working in cyberspace

This course focuses on honing your skills in technical writing; however, since it is a cybered course, you will need to learn the basics of the Internet within the first week so that you can exchange documents with your peer editors and with me. You also will have to tag the documents (using Hypertext Markup Language, HTML), link them to your welcome page, and use FTP (file transfer protocol) to put them in your folder.

Read these <u>procedures for submitting assignments</u>, and you will understand why you need the background. If you're new to much of this jargon and the procedures, start reviewing the material covered at our <u>Cybered Help Desk</u>. The many links will lead you to information on the basics of tagging, downloadable software, explanations of procedures, and guidelines for performing the procedures. You also can get technical help at the help desk and from Robert Epstein, my able assistant and all-around technical guru. Robert has an excellent background in both PCs and Macs, and so can help you with cross-platform or HTML problems. As one of the top graduate students in our professional writing program for the past two years, he also can answer any questions you might have about our program and courses. You can reach him at **<u>REpstein@umassd.edu</u>**

Research Strategies and Useful Links				
<u>Research Strategies</u>	<u>Webcrawlers</u>	<u>Directories</u>	<u>Boolean Operators</u>	<u>Online Libraries and Government Agencies</u>
<u>Business Sites</u>	<u>Instructions for Joining a ListServ List</u>	<u>Glossary of Internet Terms</u>	<u>Hotlist for Writers</u>	<u>Top of page</u>

Figure 25.4   A Web Page

<P>A NAME=top></A><IMG SRC="umdlogo.gif" X-CLARIS-USEIMAGEWIDTH
X-CLARIS-USEIMAGEHEIGHT ALIGN=bottom></P>

<P><IMG SRC="thinbluestripe.GIF" WIDTH=512 HEIGHT=6 ALIGN=bottom></P>

<H2><FONT COLOR="#0000AF">Course Guidelines and Syllabus for Enl. 600</FONT></H2>

<P><A HREF="syllabus2.html">Syllabus - Part II:</A>
<FONT COLOR="#0000FF"><B>Assignments 3 through 5</B></FONT></P>

<P>A HREF="syllabus3.html">Syllabus - Part III</A>:
<FONT COLOR="#0000FF"><B>Assignments 6 and 7</B></FONT></P>

<P><IMG SRC="thinbluestripe.GIF" WIDTH=512 HEIGHT=6 ALIGN=bottom></P>

<P><FONT COLOR=#0000CC"><B>Textbook</B>:</FONT> Technical Communication, 8th ed., John M.
Lannon, 2000, published by Longman.</P>

<P> </P>

<P><FONT COLOR=#0000AF"><STRONG>Getting the necessary background for working in
cyberspace</STRONG></FONT></P>

<BLOCKQUOTE>This course focuses on honing your skills in technical writing; however, since it is a cybered
course, you will need to learn the basics of the Internet within the first week so that you can exchange
documents with your peer editors and with me. You also will have to tag the documents (using Hypertext
Markup Language, HTML), link them to your welcome page, and use FTP (file transfer protocol) to put them
in your folder.

<P>Read these <A HREF="submissions.html">procedures for submitting assignments</A>, and you will
understand why you need the background. If you're new to much of this jargon and the procedures, start
reviewing the material covered at our <A HREF="http://www3.umassd.edu/Public/CyberEdhelp/
welcome.html"> Cybered Help Desk</A>. The many links will lead you to information on the basics of
tagging, downloadable software, explanations of procedures, and guidelines for performing the
procedures.</P>

Figure 25.5   The Partial HTML Script for Figure 25.4

Symantec Visual Page™ largely eliminate the need for HTML coding by hand. These authoring tools provide step-by-step instructions and templates for creating Web pages, positioning graphics and other page elements, adding clip art, etc.

Java enhances HTML documents

HTML produces only static pages, with limited possibilities for data display. However, a programming language called *Java* can be embedded in an HTML script to provide "dynamic" content (graphics, motion, and sound). Java-enhanced Web pages allow more sophisticated, interactive applications, such as simulations and computer-based training.

Guidelines for Creating a Web Site

Note: Organizational Web sites generally are developed by a Web team: content developers, graphic designers, programmers, and managers. Whether or not you are an actual team member, expect to play a collaborative role in your organization's site development and maintenance.

Planning Your Site

1. *Identify the site's intended audience.* Are they potential customers seeking information; people purchasing a product or service; or customers seeking product support, updates, or troubleshooting advice (Wilkinson 33)? Will different audiences be seeking different material?

2. *Identify the site's purpose.* Is the purpose to publish information, sell a product, promote an idea, solicit customer feedback, advertise talents, or create goodwill? Should the site convey the image of a "cool" cutting-edge company (or individual), displaying skill with the latest Web technologies (animation, interaction, fancy design)? For specific ideas, look for and examine other sites that display the features you seek.

3. *Identify what the site will contain.* Will it display only print documents or graphics, audio, and video as well? Will links be provided and, if so, how many and to where? Will user feedback be solicited and, in what form: survey questions, e-mail comments, or the like?

4. *Identify the level of user interaction.* Will this be a document-only site, offering no interaction beyond downloading and printing? Will it offer dynamic marketing (Dulude 69): on-line questions and answers, technical support, downloadable software, on-line catalogues? Will users be able to download documents, software, or documentation? Will an e-mail button be included?

Laying Out Your Pages

1. *Design your pages to guide the user.* Highlight important material with headings, lists, typestyles, colour, and white space. Remember that too much white space causes excessive scrolling. Use sans-serif fonts. Use

storyboards (page 650) to sketch the basic elements of each page. Limit page size to 30 k, to speed downloading.

2. *Use graphics that download quickly.* Avoid excessive complexity and colour, especially in screen background. Keep maximum image size below 30 k. Create an individual file for each graphic and use thumbnail sketches on the home page, with links to the larger images, each in its own file.

3. *Include text-only versions of all visual information.* Roughly 20 percent of users turn off the graphics function on their browsers (Gannon 22-23).

4. *Provide orientation.* Structure the content to reflect its relative importance and how often it's used. Place the material most important to your readers right up front and create links to more detailed information. Date each page to announce the exact time of each update—or include a "What's New" head, so readers can stay abreast of changes.

5. *Provide navigational aids.* Keep links logical and always link back to the home page. Don't overwhelm the user with excessive choices. Label each link explicitly (for example, "Product Updates" instead of merely "Click here").

6. *Define and shape the content.* Use hypertext to chunk information into subtopics, each in a digestible node and link it—but remember that hypertext takes longer to download and print (Neilsen "Be Succinct 1–2). Structure each hypertext node as an "inverse pyramid," in which you begin with the conclusion (Neilsen "How Users Read" 1). The inverted pyramid works like a newspaper article, in which the major news/conclusion appears first (e.g., "The jury deliberated only 2 hours before returning a guilty verdict") followed by the details. (Neilsen "Inverted Pyramids"). Last but not least, use restraint: Give users the opportunity to receive less information (Outing 2). Think hard about what users need and give them only that.

7. *Sharpen the style.* Make the on-line text at least 50 percent shorter than its hard copy equivalent. Try to summarize (Chapter 9). Use short sentences and paragraphs. Avoid "marketese" or promotional language that exaggerates ("breakthrough," "revolutionary," "cutting edge").

8. *Check your site.* Double check the accuracy of all numbers, dates, data, etc., and check for broken links and correct spelling, grammar, and so on.

9. *Attend to legal considerations.* Have your legal department approve all material before you post it (Wilkinson 33). Obtain written permission before linking to other Web pages or borrowing any graphic element from another site. Display a privacy notice that explains how each transaction is being recorded, collected, and used. To protect your own intellectual property, display a copyright notice on every page of the site (Evans 48, 50).

10. *Test your site for usability.* Test for usability with unfamiliar users (beta testing) and keep track of their problems and questions. What do users like or dislike? Can they navigate effectively to get to what they need? Are the icons recognizable? Is the site free of needless complexity or inter-activity? Test your document with various browsers to be sure it can be downloaded.

11. *Maintain your site.* Review the site regularly, update often, and redesign as needed. If the site accommodates e-mail queries, respond within one business day (Dulude 117).

IN BRIEF

Privacy Issues on the Web

Information sharing between computers is what makes the Internet and World Wide Web possible. For instance, when a user visits a site, the host computer needs to know what browser is being used. Also, for improved client service, a host site can track the links visitors follow, the files they open or download, and the pages they visit most often (Reichard 106).

Too often, however, more information gets "shared" than the user intended. For instance, the host computer can record the user's domain name, place of origin, and usage patterns (James-Catalano 32).

Some servers and sites display privacy notices explaining how usage patterns or transactions are being recorded, collected, and used. But this offers only limited protection. Any Internet transaction is routed through various browsers and servers and can be intercepted anywhere along the way.

In the workplace, monitoring increasingly compromises employee privacy. As early as 1993—with monitoring technology in its infancy—an estimated 20 million American workers were subject to computer monitoring (Karaim 72). Some types of workplace monitoring, of course, have legitimate purposes.

Legitimate Purposes for Monitoring a Workplace Web Site

- **Troubleshooting.** Monitoring software (AlertPage™, Net.Medic™) can scan a company site for broken lines, and identify server glitches, software bugs, modem problems, or faulty hardware connections (Reichard 106).

- **Productivity.** Companies track intranet use for the number of queries per employee, types of questions asked, by whom, and the length of time required for employees to find what they need. These data help decide whether the search mechanism (user interface) can be improved or whether on-line documents can be organized or written more clearly (Cronin 103).

- **Security.** Software can track employees' visits to other Web sites, as well as files opened for recreational or personal use, e-mail sent and received, and even provide snapshots of an employee's computer screen (Karaim 72). They can deny access to unauthorized Web sites and also inform the employer about the employee's attempt. Such monitoring can be a justifiable precaution against employee theft, drug abuse, security violations (such as publishing trade secrets on the Internet)—or wasted time. For example, businesses lose millions of worker hours yearly to computer game-playing by employees (Hutheesing 369). Beyond its legitimate uses, monitoring also carries potential for the abuse of personal privacy.

IN BRIEF

Privacy Abuses in Workplace Monitoring

- Employers have more freedom to violate employee privacy than the police (Karaim 72). Andre Bacard, author of *The Computer Privacy Handbook*, points out that supervisors can "tap an employee's phones, monitor her e-mail, watch her on closed-circuit TV, and search her computer files, without giving her notice" (qtd. in Karaim 72).

- Some companies notify their employees that their electronic transactions are subject to monitoring, but many do not.
- Even face-to-face transactions are subject to monitoring: An electronic "Active Badge" tracks employees as they move about their work site, recording how much time they spend in the bathroom or at the water cooler and who they talk to during the work day. (Karaim 72).

Checklist for Web Site Usability

Use this checklist to assess Web site usability.

ACCESSIBILITY
- ❑ Is the site easy to enter, navigate, and exit?
- ❑ Is required scrolling kept to a minimum?
- ❑ Is downloading speed reasonable?
- ❑ If interaction is offered, is it useful—not superfluous?
- ❑ Does the site avoid overwhelming the user with excessive choices?

CONTENT
- ❑ Are all needed explanations, error messages, and help screens provided?
- ❑ Is the time of each update clearly indicated?
- ❑ Is everything accurate and up-to-date?
- ❑ Are links connected to high-quality sites?
- ❑ Does everything belong (nothing excessive or superfluous or needlessly complex)?
- ❑ Is an e-mail button or other contact method prominently displayed?
- ❑ Does the content accommodate international users?

ARRANGEMENT
- ❑ Is the key part of the message on the first page?
- ❑ Are navigation bars, hot buttons, and help options clearly displayed and explicitly labelled?
- ❑ Are links easily navigated—backwards and forward—with back links to the home page?

WRITING AND PAGE DESIGN
- ❑ Is the text easy to scan, with short sentences and paragraphs, and do headings, lists, typestyles, and colour highlight important material?
- ❑ Is the overall word count roughly one-half of the hard copy equivalent?
- ❑ Is the tone reasonable and restrained—free of overstatement and "marketese"?

GRAPHICS AND SPECIAL EFFECTS
- ❑ Is each graphic easy to download?
- ❑ Is each graphic backed up by a text-only version?
- ❑ Is each graphic or special effect necessary?

LEGAL CONSIDERATIONS
- ❑ Does the site display a privacy notice that explains how the transaction is being recorded, collected, and used?
- ❑ Does each page of the site display a copyright notice?
- ❑ Has written permission been obtained for each link to other sites and for each graphic element borrowed from another site?
- ❑ Has all posted material received prior legal approval?

☑ EXERCISES

1. Consult page 671 and evaluate a Web site for usability. You might select a site at your school or place of employment. You might begin by deciding on specific information you seek (such as "internship opportunities," "special programs," "campus crime statistics," or "average SAT scores of admitted students") and use this as a basis for assessing the site's accessibility, content, arrangement, etc.

   Complete your evaluation and report any problems or suggested improvements in a memo to a designated decision maker. (Your instructor might ask different class groups to evaluate the same site, and to compare their findings in class.)

2. Download and print pages from a Web site. Edit these pages to improve layout and writing style. Submit copies to your instructor.

3. Examine Web sites from three or four competing companies (e.g., computer makers IBM™, Apple™, Gateway™, Dell™, and Compaq™—or auto makers, etc). Which site do you think is the most effective, the least effective, and why? Report your findings in a memo to your colleagues.

☑ COLLABORATIVE PROJECTS

Any of the exercises may be used as collaborative projects.

Review of Grammar, Usage, and Mechanics

Common Sentence Errors
    Sentence Fragment
    Comma Splice
    Run-on Sentence
    Faulty Coordination
    Faulty Subordination
    Faulty Agreement—Subject and Verb
    Faulty Agreement—Pronoun and Referent
    Faulty or Vague Pronoun Reference
    Faulty Pronoun Case
    Faulty Modification
    Faulty Parallelism
    Sentence Shifts
Effective Punctuation
    End Punctuation
    Semicolon
    Colon
    Comma
    Apostrophe
    Quotation Marks
    Ellipses
    Italics
    Parentheses
    Brackets
    Dashes
    Hyphen
Transitions and Other Connectors
Effective Mechanics
    Abbreviations
    Capitalization
    Numbers

No MATTER how vital and informative a message may be, its credibility is damaged by basic errors. Any of these errors—an illogical, fragmented, or run-on sentence; faulty punctuation; or a poorly chosen word—stands out and mars otherwise good writing. Not only do such errors annoy the reader, but they also speak badly for the writer's attention to detail. Your career will make the same demands for good writing that your English classes do. The difference is that evaluation (grades) in professional situations usually shows in promotions, reputation, and salary.

The Correction Symbol Table, on the last page of this book, lists correction symbols.

Common Sentence Errors

Any piece of writing is only as good as each of its sentences. Here are common sentence errors, with suggestions for easy repairs.

Sentence Fragment

frag

A sentence expresses a logically complete idea. Any complete idea must have a subject and a verb and must not depend on another complete idea to make sense. Your sentence *might* contain several complete ideas, but it *must* contain at least one!

> Although Mary was nervous, she grabbed the line, and she saved the sailboat.
>   *(incomplete idea)*   *(complete idea)*   *(complete idea)*

If the idea is not complete—if your reader is left wondering what you mean—you probably have omitted some essential element (the subject, the verb, or another complete idea). Such a piece of a sentence is a *fragment*.

> Grabbed the line. *(a fragment because it lacks a subject)*
> Although Mary was nervous. *(a fragment because, although it has a subject and a verb, it needs to be joined with a complete idea)*

The only exception to the sentence rule applies when we give a command (Run!), in which the subject (you) is understood. Logically complete, this statement is properly called a sentence. So is this one:

> Sam is an electronics technician.

Readers cannot miss your meaning: Somewhere is a person; the person's name is Sam; the person is an electronics technician. Suppose instead we write:

> Sam an electronics technician.

This statement is not logically complete, therefore not a sentence. The reader is left asking, "What about Sam the electronics technician?" The verb—the word that makes things happen—is missing. By adding a verb we can easily change this fragment to a complete sentence.

> Simple verb   Sam **is** an electronics technician.
>
> Verb and adverb   Sam, an electronics technician, **works hard**.
>
> Dependent clause, verb, and subjective complement   **Although he is well paid,** Sam, an electronics technician, **is not happy**.

Do not, however, mistake the following statement—which seems to have a verb—for a complete sentence:

| Sam being an electronics technician.

Such "ing" forms do not function as verbs unless accompanied by such other verbs as **is**, **was**, and **will be**. Again, readers are confused unless you complete your idea with an independent clause.

| **Sam**, being an electronics technician, checked all **circuitry**.

Likewise, remember that the "to + verb" form does not function as a verb.

| To become an electronics technician.

The meaning is unclear unless you complete the thought.

| To become an electronics technician, **Sam had to pass an exam**.

Sometimes we inadvertently create fragments by adding certain words (**because**, **since**, **if**, **although**, **while**, **unless**, **until**, **when**, **where**, and others) to an already complete sentence, transforming our independent clause (complete sentence) into a dependent clause.

| **Although** Sam is an electronics technician.

Such words subordinate the words that follow them so that an additional idea is needed to make the first statement complete. That is, they make the statement dependent on an additional idea, which must itself have a subject and a verb and be a complete sentence. (See "Faulty Subordination.") Now we have to round off the statement with a complete idea (independent clause).

| Although Sam is an electronics technician, **he hopes to be an engineer**.

Note: Be careful not to use a semicolon or a period, instead of a comma, to separate elements in the preceding sentence. Because the dependent clause depends on the independent clause for its meaning, you need only a *pause* (symbolized by a comma), not a *break* (symbolized by a semicolon), between these ideas. In fact, many fragments are created when too strong a mark of punctuation (period or semicolon) severs the connection between a dependent and an independent clause. (See the later discussion of punctuation.)

Here are some fragments from technical documents. Each is repaired in more than one way. Can you think of other ways of making these statements complete?

Fragment	She spent her first week on the job as a researcher. **Compiling information from digests and journals**.
Correct	She spent her first week on the job as a researcher, compiling information from digests and journals.
	She spent her first week on the job as a researcher. She compiled information from digests and journals.
Fragment	**Because the employee was careless**. The new computer was damaged.
Correct	Because the employee was careless, the new computer was damaged.
	The employee's carelessness resulted in damage to the new computer.

cs

Comma Splice

In a comma splice, two complete ideas (independent clauses), which should be *separated* by a period or a semicolon, are incorrectly *joined* by a comma:

Comma splice   Sarah did a great job, she was promoted.

You can choose among several possibilities for correcting this error:

1. Substitute a period followed by a capital letter:
    Sarah did a great job. She was promoted.
2. Substitute a semicolon to signal the relationship:
    Sarah did a great job; she was promoted.
3. Use a semicolon with a connecting adverb (a transitional word):
    Sarah did a great job; **consequently**, she was promoted.
4. Use a subordinating word to make the less important sentence incomplete, thereby dependent on the other:
    Because Sarah did a great job, she was promoted.
5. Add a connecting word after the comma:
    Sarah did a great job, **and** she was promoted.

Your choice of construction will depend, of course, on the exact meaning or tone you want to convey. The following comma splice can be repaired in the ways described above.

Comma splice   This is a new technique, therefore, some people mistrust it.
     Correct   This is a new technique. Some people mistrust it.
                    This is a new technique; therefore, some people mistrust it.
                    Because this is a new technique, some people mistrust it.
                    This is a new technique, **so** some people mistrust it.

ro

Run-on Sentence

The run-on sentence, a cousin to the comma splice, crams too many ideas without needed breaks or pauses.

Run-on   The hourglass is more accurate than the water clock because water in a water clock must always be at the same temperature to flow at the same speed since water evaporates and must be replenished at regular intervals, thus being less effective than the hourglass for measuring time.

Like a runaway train, this statement is out of control. Here is a corrected version:

Revised   The hourglass is more accurate than the water clock because water in a water clock must always be at the same temperature to flow at the same speed. Also, water evaporates and must be replenished at regular intervals. These temperatures and volume problems make the water clock less effective than the hourglass for measuring time.

coord

Faulty Coordination

Give equal emphasis to ideas of equal importance by joining them, within simple or compound sentences, with coordinating conjunctions: **and**, **but**, **or**, **nor**, **for**, **so**, and **yet**.

This course is difficult **but** worthwhile.

My horse is old **and** grey.

We must decide to support **or** reject the manager's proposal.

But do not confound your meaning by coordinating excessively.

Excessive coordination	The climax in jogging comes after a few miles **and** I can no longer feel stride after stride **and** it seems as if I am floating **and** jogging becomes almost a reflex **and** my arms **and** legs continue to move **and** my mind no longer has to control their actions.
Revised	The climax in jogging comes after a few miles when I can no longer feel stride after stride. By then I am jogging almost by reflex, nearly floating, my arms and legs still moving, my mind no longer having to control their actions.

Notice how the meaning becomes clear when the less important ideas (**nearly floating, arms and legs still moving, my mind no longer having**) are shown as dependent on, rather than equal to, the most important idea (**jogging almost by reflex**)—the idea that contains the lesser ones.

Avoid coordinating ideas that cannot be sensibly connected:

Faulty	Josh had a drinking problem **and** he dropped out of school.
Revised	Josh's drinking problem depressed him so much that he couldn't study, so he quit school.

Faulty	I was late for work **and** wrecked my car.
Revised	Late for work, I backed out of the driveway too quickly, hit a truck, and wrecked my car.

Instead of *try and,* use *try to.*

Faulty	I will try and help you.
Revised	I will try to help you.

sub

Faulty Subordination

Proper subordination shows that a less important idea is dependent on a more important idea. By using subordination you can combine simple sentences into complex sentences and emphasize the most important idea. Consider these complete ideas:

Joe studies hard. He has severe math anxiety.

Because these ideas are expressed as simple sentences, they appear to be coordinate (equal in importance). But if you wanted to indicate your opinion of Joe's chances of succeeding in math, you would need a third sentence: **His disability probably will prevent him from succeeding**, or **His willpower will help him succeed**. To communicate the intended meaning concisely, combine ideas and subordinate the one that deserves less emphasis:

Despite his severe math anxiety *(subordinate idea)*, Joe studies hard *(independent idea)*.

This first version suggests that Joe will succeed. Below, subordination is used to suggest the opposite meaning:

Despite his diligent studying *(subordinate idea)*, Joe has severe math anxiety *(independent idea)*.

A dependent (or subordinate) clause in a sentence is signalled by a subordinating conjunction: **because, so, if, unless, after, until, since, while, as,** and **although,** among others. Be sure to place the idea you want emphasized in the independent clause; do not write

> Although Moira is receiving excellent medical treatment, she is seriously ill.

if you mean to suggest that Moira has a good chance of recovering.

Do not coordinate when you should subordinate:

> **Weak**   Television viewers can relate to an athlete they idolize and they feel obliged to buy the product endorsed by their hero.

Of the two ideas in the sentence above, one is the cause, the other the effect. Emphasize this relationship through subordination:

> **Revised**   Because television viewers can relate to an athlete they idolize, they feel obliged to buy the product endorsed by their hero.

When combining several ideas within a sentence, decide which is most important, and subordinate the other ideas to it—do not merely coordinate:

> **Faulty**   This employee is often late for work, and he writes illogical reports, and he is a poor manager, and he should be fired.
>
> **Revised**   Because this employee is often late for work, writes illogical reports, and has poor management skills, **he should be fired.** (*The last clause is independent.*)

Do not overstuff sentences by subordinating excessively:

> **Overstuffed**   This job, which I took when I graduated from college, while I waited for a better one to come along, which is boring, where I've gained no useful experience, makes me anxious to quit.
>
> **Revised**   Upon college graduation, I took this job while waiting for a better one to come along. Because I find it boring and have gained no useful experience, I am eager to quit.

Faulty Agreement—Subject and Verb

agr sv

The subject should agree in number with the verb. We are not likely to use faulty agreement in short sentences, where subject and verb are not far apart. Thus, we are not likely to say "Jack eat too much" instead of "Jack eats too much," but in more complicated sentences—those in which the subject is separated from its verb by other words—we sometimes lose track of the subject-verb relationship.

> **Faulty**   The lion's **share** of diesels **are** sold in Europe.

Although **diesels** is closest to the verb, the subject is **share,** a singular subject that must agree with a singular verb.

> **Correct**   The lion's **share** of diesels **is** sold in Europe.

Agreement errors are easy to correct when subject and verb are identified.

> **Faulty**   A **system** of lines **extend** horizontally to form a grid.
> **Correct**   A **system** of lines **extends** horizontally to form a grid.

A second problem with subject-verb agreement occurs when we use indefinite pronouns such as **each, everyone, anybody,** and **somebody.** They function as subjects and usually take a singular verb.

| Faulty | **Each** of the crew members **were** injured. |
| Correct | **Each** of the crew members **was** injured. |

| Faulty | **Everyone** in the group **have** practised long hours. |
| Correct | **Everyone** in the group **has** practised long hours. |

Agreement problems can be caused by collective nouns such as **herd, family, union, group, army, team, committee,** and **board.** They can call for a singular or plural verb—depending on your intended meaning. When denoting the group as a whole, use a singular verb.

| Correct | The **committee meets** weekly to discuss new business. |
| | The editorial **board** of this magazine **has** high standards. |

To denote individual members of the group, however, use a plural verb.

| Correct | Not all members of the editorial **board are** published authors. |

Yet another problem occurs when two subjects are joined by **either ... or** or **neither ... nor.** Here, the verb is singular if both subjects are singular, and plural if both subjects are plural. If one subject is plural and one is singular, the verb agrees with the subject closest to the verb.

Correct	Neither **Al** nor **Bill works** regularly.
	Either apples or **oranges are** good vitamin sources.
	Either Felix or his **friends are** crazy.
	Neither the boys nor their **father likes** the home team.

If, on the other hand, two subjects (singular, plural, or mixed) are joined by **both ... and,** the verb will be plural. Whereas **or** suggests "one or the other," **and** announces a combination of the two subjects, thereby requiring a plural verb.

| Correct | **Both** Hal and Will **are** resigning. |
| | The **book and** the **briefcase appear** expensive. |

A single *and* between singular subjects makes for a plural subject.

Faulty Agreement—Pronoun and Referent

agr p

A pronoun can make sense only if it refers to a specific noun (its referent or antecedent), with which it must agree in gender and number.

| Correct | **Tao** lost **his** blueprints. |
| | The **workers** complained that **they** were treated unfairly. |

Some instances, however, are not so obvious. When an indefinite pronoun such as **each, everyone, anybody, someone,** and **none** serves as the pronoun referent, the pronoun itself is singular.

| Correct | **Anyone** can get **his or her** degree from that college. |
| | **Each** candidate described **her** plans in detail. |

Faulty or Vague Pronoun Reference

ref

Whenever a pronoun is used, it must refer to one clearly identified referent; otherwise, your message will be confusing.

Ambiguous	**Sally** told **Sarah** that **she** was obsessed with her job.
Correct	Sally told Sarah, "I'm obsessed with my job."
	Sally told Sarah, "I'm obsessed with your job."
	Sally told Sarah, "You're obsessed with [your, my] job."
	Sally told Sarah, "She's obsessed with [her, my, your] job."

Avoid using **this**, **that**, or **it**—especially to begin a sentence—unless the pronoun refers to a specific antecedent (referent).

Vague	He drove away from his menial **job**, boring **lifestyle**, and damp **apartment**, happy to be leaving **it** behind.
Correct	He drove away, happy to be leaving behind his menial job, boring lifestyle, and damp apartment.
Vague	The problem with our **defective machinery** is compounded by the **operator's incompetence. That** annoys me!
Correct	I am annoyed by the problem with our defective machinery as well as by the new operator's incompetence.

ca

Faulty Pronoun Case

A pronoun's case (nominative, objective, or possessive) is determined by its role in a sentence: as subject, object, or indicator of possession.

If the pronoun serves as the subject of a sentence (**I**, **we**, **you**, **she**, **he**, **it**, **they**, **who**), its case is *nominative*.

She completed her graduate program in record time.

Who broke the chair?

When a pronoun follows a version of **to be** (a linking verb), it explains (complements) the subject, and so its case is nominative.

It was **she.**

The chemist who perfected our new distillation process is **he.**

If the pronoun serves as the object of a verb or a preposition (**me**, **us**, **you**, **her**, **him**, **it**, **them**, **whom**), its case is *objective*.

Object of the verb	The employees gave **her** a parting gift.
Object of the preposition	Several colleagues left with **him.**
	To **whom** do you wish to complain?

If a pronoun indicates possession (**my**, **mine**, **ours**, **your**, **yours**, **his**, **her**, **hers**, **its**, **their**, **theirs**, **whose**), its case is *possessive*.

The brown briefcase is **mine.**

Her offer was accepted.

Whose opinion do you value most?

Here are some frequent errors in pronoun case:

Faulty	**Whom** is responsible to **who**? *(The subject should be nominative and the object should be objective.)*

Correct	**Who** is responsible to **whom**?
Faulty	The debate was between Marsha and **I**. (*As object of the preposition, the pronoun should be objective.*)
Correct	The debate was between Marsha and **me**.
Faulty	**Us** board members are accountable for our decisions. (*The pronoun accompanies the subject, "board members," and thus should be nominative.*)
Correct	**We** board members are accountable for our decisions.
Faulty	A group of **we** managers will fly to the convention. (*The pronoun accompanies the object of the preposition, "managers," and thus should be objective.*)
Correct	A group of **us** managers will fly to the convention.

Hint: By deleting the accompanying noun from the two latter examples, we can easily identify the correct pronoun case ("We . . . are accountable"; "A group of us . . . will fly").

mod

Faulty Modification

A sentence's word order (syntax) helps determine its effectiveness and meaning. Words or groups of words are modified by adjectives, adverbs, phrases, or clauses. Modifiers explain, define, or add detail to other words or ideas. Prepositional phrases, for example, usually define or limit adjacent words:

the foundation **with the cracked wall**

the repair job **on the old Ford**

the journey **to the moon**

As do phrases with "-ing" verb forms:

the student **painting the portrait**

Opening the door, we entered quietly.

Phrases with "to + verb" form limit:

To succeed, one must work hard.

Some clauses limit:

the person **who came to dinner**

Problems with word order occur when a modifying phrase begins a sentence, and has no word to modify.

Dangling modifier	**Dialing the telephone**, the cat ran out the open door.

The cat obviously did not dial the telephone, but because the modifier **Dialing the telephone** has no word to modify, the word order suggests that the noun beginning the main clause (*cat*) names the one who dialed the phone. Without any word to join itself to, the modifier *dangles*. By inserting a subject, we can repair this absurd message.

Correct	As Moe dialed the telephone, the cat ran out the open door.

A dangling modifier also can obscure your meaning.

Dangling modifier	**After completing the student financial aid application form,** the Financial Aid Office will forward it to the appropriate agency.

Who completes the form—the student or the financial aid office?

Here are some other dangling modifiers that make the message confusing, inaccurate, or downright absurd:

Dangling modifier	**While walking**, a cold chill ran through my body.
Correct	While **I** walked, a cold chill ran through my body.
Dangling modifier	Impurities have entered our bodies **by eating chemically processed foods**.
Correct	Impurities have entered our bodies by **our** eating chemically processed foods.
Dangling modifier	**By planting different varieties of crops,** the pests were unable to adapt.
Correct	By planting different varieties of crops, **farmers** prevented the pests from adapting.

The order of adjectives and adverbs in a sentence is as important as the order of modifying phrases and clauses. Notice how changing word order affects the meaning of these sentences:

I **often** remind myself of the need to balance my checkbook.

I remind myself of the need to balance my checkbook **often**.

Be sure that modifiers and the words they modify follow an order that reflects your meaning.

Misplaced modifier	Cal keyed another memo on our computer **that was useless**. (*Was the computer or the memo useless?*)
Correct	Cal keyed another useless memo on our computer.
	or
	Cal keyed another memo on our useless computer.
Misplaced modifier	He read a report on the use of non-chemical pesticides **in our conference room**. (*Are the pesticides to be used in the conference room?*)
Correct	In our conference room, he read a report on the use of non-chemical pesticides.
Misplaced modifier	She volunteered **immediately** to deliver the radioactive shipment. (*Volunteering immediately, or delivering immediately?*)
Correct	She immediately volunteered to deliver . . .
	or
	She volunteered to deliver immediately . . .

Faulty Parallelism

par

To reflect relationships among items of equal importance, express them in identical grammatical form:

Correct	. . . We here highly resolve . . . that government **of the people, by the people, for the people** shall not perish from the earth.

The statement above describes the government with three modifiers of equal importance. Because the first modifier is a prepositional phrase, the others must be also. Otherwise, the message would be garbled, like this:

| Faulty | We here highly resolve . . . that government **of the people, which the people created and maintain, serving the people** shall not perish from the earth. |

If you begin the series with a noun, use nouns throughout the series; likewise for adjectives, adverbs, and specific types of clauses and phrases.

| Faulty | The new apprentice is **enthusiastic, skilled,** and **you can depend on her.** |
| Correct | The new apprentice is **enthusiastic, skilled,** and **dependable.** *(all subjective complements)* |

| Faulty | In his new job, he felt **lonely** and **without a friend.** |
| Correct | In his new job, he felt **lonely** and **friendless.** *(both adjectives)* |

| Faulty | She plans **to study** all this month and **on scoring well** in her licensing examination. |
| Correct | She plans **to study** all this month and **to score well** in her licensing examination. *(both infinitive phrases)* |

| Faulty | She **sleeps** well and **jogs** daily, **as well as eating** high-protein foods. |
| Correct | She **sleeps** well, **jogs** daily, and **eats** high-protein foods. *(all verbs)* |

To improve coherence in long sentences, repeat words that introduce parallel expressions:

| Faulty | Before buying this property, you should decide whether you will settle down and raise a family, travel for a few years, or pursue a graduate degree. |
| Correct | Before buying this property, you should decide whether **to settle** down and raise a family, **to travel** for a few years, or **to pursue** a graduate degree. |

Sentence Shifts

shift

Shifts in point of view damage coherence. If you begin a sentence or paragraph with one subject or person, do not shift to another.

| Shift in person | When **you** finish the job, **one** will have a sense of pride. |
| Correct | When **you** finish the job, **you** will have a sense of pride. |

| Shift in number | **One** should sift the flour before **they** make the pie. |
| Correct | **One** should sift the flour before **one** makes the pie. (Or better: Sift the flour before making the pie.) |

Do not begin a sentence in the active voice and then shift to passive.

| Shift in voice | **He delivered** the plans for the apartment complex, and the building site **was also inspected by him.** |
| Correct | **He delivered** the plans for the apartment complex and also **inspected** the building site. |

Do not shift tenses without good reason.

| Shift in tense | She **delivered** the blueprints, **inspected** the foundation, **wrote** her report, and **takes** the afternoon off. |
| Correct | She **delivered** the blueprints, **inspected** the foundation, **wrote** her report, and **took** the afternoon off. |

Do not shift from one mood to another (as from imperative to indicative mood in a set of instructions).

| Shift in mood | **Unscrew** the valve and then steel wool **should be used** to clean the fitting. |
| Correct | **Unscrew** the valve and then **use** steel wool to clean the fitting. |

Do not shift from indirect to direct discourse within a sentence.

Shift in discourse	Jim wonders **if he will get the job** and **will he like it?**
Correct	Jim wonders **if he will get the job** and **if he will like it.**
	Will Jim get the job, and will he like it?

Effective Punctuation

Punctuation marks are like road signs and traffic signals. They govern reading speed and provide clues for navigation through a network of ideas; they mark intersections, detours, and road repairs; they draw attention to points of interest along the route; and they mark geographic boundaries. In short, punctuation marks give us a simple way of making ourselves understood.

End Punctuation

The three marks of end punctuation—period, question mark, and exclamation point—work like a red traffic light by signaling a complete stop.

Period. A period ends a sentence. Periods end some abbreviations.

| Ms. | Assn. | Dr. |
| M.D. | Inc. | B.A. |

Periods serve as decimal points for figures.

$15.95
2.14%

Question Mark. A question mark follows a direct question.

Where is the balance sheet?

Do not use a question mark to end an indirect question.

| Faulty | He asked if all students had failed the test? |
| Correct | He asked if all students had failed the test. |
| *or* |
| | He asked, "Did all students fail the test?" |

Exclamation Point. Because exclamation points symbolize strong feeling, don't overuse them. Otherwise you might seem hysterical or insincere.

| Correct | Oh, no! |
| | Pay up! |

Use an exclamation point only when expression of strong feeling is appropriate.

Semicolon

A semicolon usually works like a blinking red traffic light at an intersection by signaling a brief but definite stop.

Semicolon Separating Independent Clauses. Semicolons separate independent clauses (logically complete ideas), whose contents are closely related and are not connected by a coordinating conjunction.

> The project was finally completed; we had done a good week's work.

The semicolon can replace the conjunction-comma combination that joins two independent ideas.

> The project was finally completed, and we were elated.
> The project was finally completed; we were elated.

The second version emphasizes the sense of elation.

Semicolons Used with Adverbs as Conjunctions and Other Transitional Expressions. Semicolons accompany conjunctive adverbs, and other expressions that connect related independent ideas (**besides, otherwise, still, however, furthermore, consequently, therefore, in contrast, in fact,** or the like).

> The job is filled; however, we will keep your résumé on file.
> Your background is impressive; in fact, it is the best among our applicants.

Semicolons Separating Items in a Series. When items in a series contain internal commas, semicolons provide clear separation between items.

> We are opening branch offices in the following cities: Halifax, Nova Scotia; Moncton, New Brunswick; Montreal, Quebec; and Windsor, Ontario.
> Members of the survey crew were Laura Joe, a geologist; Hector Lightweight, a draftsperson; and Mary Shelley, a graduate student.

Colon

Like a flare in the road, a colon signals you to stop and then proceed, paying attention to the situation ahead, the details of which will be revealed as you move along. Usually, a colon follows an introductory statement that requires a follow-up explanation.

> We need the following equipment immediately: a voltmeter, a portable generator, and three pairs of insulated gloves.
> She is an ideal colleague: honest, reliable, and competent.
> Two candidates clearly are superior: Don and Marsha.

With the exception of **Dear Sir:** and other salutations in formal correspondence, colons follow independent (logically and grammatically complete) statements. Because colons, like end punctuation and semicolons, signal a full stop, they never are used to fragment a complete statement.

> **Faulty** My plans include: finishing college, travelling for two years, and settling down in Edmonton.

No punctuation should follow "include."

Colons can introduce quotations.

> The supervisor's message was clear enough: "You're fired."

A colon normally replaces a semicolon in separating two related, complete statements when the second statement explains or amplifies the first.

> His reason for accepting the lowest-paying job offer was simple: He had always wanted to live in the Northwest.

The statement following the colon explains the "reason" mentioned in the statement preceding the colon.

Comma

,/

The comma is the most frequently used—and abused—punctuation mark. Unlike the period, semicolon, and colon, which signal a full stop, the comma signals a *brief pause*. The comma works like a blinking yellow traffic light, for which you slow down without stopping. Never use a comma to signal a *break* between independent ideas; it is not strong enough.

Comma as a Pause Between Complete Ideas. In a compound sentence where a coordinating conjunction (**and**, **or**, **nor**, **for**, **but**) connects equal (independent) statements, a comma usually precedes the conjunction.

> This is a high-paying job, but the stress is high.
> This vacant shop is just large enough for our juice bar, and the location is excellent for walk-in customer traffic.

Without the conjunction, these statements would suffer from a comma splice, unless the comma were replaced by a semicolon or period.

Comma as a Pause Between an Incomplete and a Complete Idea. A comma usually appears between a complete and an incomplete statement in a complex sentence to show that the incomplete statement depends for its meaning on the complete statement. (The incomplete statement cannot stand alone, separated by a break such as a semicolon, colon, or period.)

> **Because he is a plump person**, Mel diets often.
> **When he eats too much**, Mel gains weight.

Above, the first idea is made incomplete by a subordinating conjunction (**since, when, because, although, where, while, if, until**), which here connects a dependent with an independent statement. The first (incomplete) idea depends on the second (complete) for wholeness. When the order is reversed (complete idea followed by incomplete), the comma usually is omitted.

> Mel diets often **because he is a plump person**.
> Mel gains weight **when he eats too much**.

Because commas take the place of speech signals, reading a sentence aloud should tell you whether or not to pause (and use a comma).

Commas Separating Items (Words, Phrases, or Clauses) in a Series. Use a comma to separate items in a series.

> **Ann**, **Ned**, **Shelley**, and **Philip** are joining us on the hydroelectric project.
> The office was **beige, blue**, and **burgundy**.

> She works hard **at home, on the job,** and even **during her vacation.**
> The employee claimed **that the hours were long, that the pay was low, that the work was boring,** and **that the supervisor was paranoid.**

Use no commas when *or* or *and* appears between all items in a series.

> She is willing to work in Winnipeg or Regina or even in Toronto.

Add a comma when *or* or *and* is used only before the final item in the series.

> Our luncheon special for Thursday will be rolls, steak, beans, and ice cream.

Without the comma, the sentence might cause readers to conclude that beans and ice cream is an exotic new dessert.

Comma Setting off Introductory Phrases. Infinitive, prepositional, or verbal phrases introducing a sentence usually are set off by commas.

Infinitive phrase	**To be or not to be,** that is the question.
Prepositional phrase	**In Rome,** do as the Romans do.
Participial phrase	**Moving quickly,** the army surrounded the enemy.

When an interjection introduces a sentence, it is set off by a comma.

> **Oh,** is that the final verdict?

When a noun in direct address introduces a sentence, it is set off by a comma.

> **Mary,** you've done a great job.

Commas Setting off Non-restrictive Elements. A restrictive phrase or clause limits or defines the subject in such a way that deleting the modifier would change the meaning of the sentence.

> All candidates **who have work experience** will receive preference.

The clause, **who have work experience,** defines **candidates** and is essential to the meaning of the sentence. Without this clause, the meaning would be entirely different.

> All candidates will receive preference.

This next sentence also contains a restriction:

> All candidates **with work experience** will receive preference.

The phrase, **with work experience,** defines **candidates** and thus specifies the meaning of the sentence. Because this phrase *restricts* the subject by limiting the category, **candidates,** it is essential to the sentence's meaning and so is not separated from the sentence by commas.

A non-restrictive phrase or clause does not limit or define the subject; a non-restrictive element could be deleted without changing the basic meaning of the sentence.

> Our draftsperson, **who has little experience,** is highly competent.
> This house, **riddled with carpenter ants,** is falling apart.

In each of those sentences, the modifying phrase or clause does not restrict the subject; each could be deleted:

> Our new draftsperson is highly competent.
> This house is falling apart.

A non-restrictive clause or phrase is set off from the sentence by commas.

Commas Setting off Parenthetical Elements. Items that interrupt sentence flow are called parenthetical and are enclosed by commas. Expressions such as **of course**, **as a result**, **as I recall**, and **however** are parenthetical and may denote emphasis, afterthought, clarification, or transition.

Emphasis	This deluxe model, **of course,** is more expensive.
Afterthought	Your report format, **by the way,** was impeccable.
Clarification	The loss of my job was, **in a way,** a blessing.
Transition	Our warranty, **however,** does not cover tire damage.

Direct address is parenthetical.

> Listen, **my children,** and you shall hear . . .

A parenthetical expression at the beginning or the end of a sentence is set off by a comma.

> **Naturally,** we will expect a full guarantee.
> **My friends,** I think we have a problem.
> You've done a good job, **Jim.**
> **Yes,** you may use my name in your advertisement.

Commas Setting off Quoted Material. Quoted items included within a sentence are often set off by commas.

> The customer said, **"I'll take it,"** as soon as he laid eyes on our new model.

Commas Setting off Appositives. An appositive, a word or words explaining a noun and placed immediately after it, is set off by commas.

> Lindsay O'Shea, **our new president,** is overhauling all personnel policies.
> Alpha waves, **the most prominent of the brain waves,** are typically recorded in a waking subject whose eyes are closed.
> Please make all cheques payable to Sam Sawbuck, **company treasurer.**

Commas Used in Common Practice. Commas set off the day of the month from the year, in a date.

> May 10, 2006

They set off numbers in three-digit intervals.

> 11,215
> 6,463,657

They set off street, city, and state in an address.

> The bill was sent to Jaspal Singh, 184 Sea Street, Victoria, BC V9W 4D6.

When the address is written vertically, however, the omitted commas are those which would otherwise occur at the end of each address line.

Jaspal Singh
184 Sea Street
Victoria, BC V9W 4D6

Commas set off an address or date in a sentence.

Room 3C, Margate Complex, is the site of our newest office.
December 15, 2007 is my retirement date.

They set off degrees and titles from proper names.

Roger P. Cayer, M.D.
Gordon Browne, Jr.
Sandra Mello, Ph.D.

Commas Used Erroneously. Avoid needless or inappropriate commas. You are probably safer using too few commas than too many. Reading sentences aloud is one way to identify inappropriate pauses.

Faulty	As I opened the door, he told me, that I was late. *(separates the indirect from the direct object)*
	The universal symptom of the suicide impulse, is depression. *(separates the subject from its verb)*
	This has been a long, difficult, project. *(separates the final adjective from its noun)*
	Poon, Henri, and Parvis, are joining us on the design phase of this project. *(separates the final subject from its verb)*
	An employee, who expects rapid promotion, must quickly prove her or his worth. *(separates a modifier that should be restrictive)*
	I spoke in a conference call with Jaswinder, and Gemma. *(separates two words linked by a coordinating conjunction)*
	The room was, eighteen feet long. *(separates the linking verb from the subjective complement)*
	We painted the room, red. *(separates the object from its complement)*

ap/

Apostrophe

Apostrophes serve three purposes: to indicate the possessive, a contraction, and the plural of numbers, letters, and figures.

Apostrophe Indicating the Possessive. At the end of a singular word, or of a plural word that does not end in *s,* add an apostrophe plus *s* to indicate the possessive.

The people's candidate won.
The chain saw was Lyle's.
The men's locker room burned.
I borrowed Doris's book.
Have you heard Olga Charles's speech?

Do not use an apostrophe to indicate the possessive form of either singular or plural pronouns:

> The book was hers.
> Ours is the best sales record.
> The fault was theirs.

At the end of a plural word that ends in *s,* add an apostrophe only.

> the cows' water supply
> the Jacksons' wine cellar

At the end of a compound noun, add an apostrophe plus *s.*

> my father-in-law's false teeth

At the end of the last word in nouns of joint possession, add an apostrophe plus *s* if both own one item.

> Elke and Tran's lakefront cottage

Add an apostrophe plus *s* to both nouns if each owns specific items.

> Elke's and Tran's passports

Apostrophe Indicating a Contraction. An apostrophe shows that you have omitted one or more letters in a phrase that is usually a combination of a pronoun and a verb.

> I'm (I am)   they're (they are)
> he's (he is)   we're (we are)
> you're (you are)   who's (who is)

Don't confuse *they're* with *their* or *there.*

> **Faulty**   there books
>   Their now leaving.
>   living their
> **Correct** their books
>   They're now leaving.
>   living there

Remember the distinction in this way:

> Their boss knows they're there.

Don't confuse **it's** and **its. It's** means "it is." **Its** is the possessive.

> It's watching its reflection in the pond.

Don't confuse **who's** and **whose. Who's** means "who is," whereas **whose** indicates the possessive.

> Who's interrupting whose work?

Other contractions are formed from the verb and the negative.

> isn't (is not)   can't (cannot)
> don't (do not)   haven't (have not)
> won't (will not)   wasn't (was not)

Apostrophe Indicating the Plural of Numbers, Letters, and Figures. Use an apostrophe only when its absence would create ambiguity.

> The 6's look like smudged G's, the 9's are illegible, and the %'s are unclear.

Quotation Marks

Quotation marks set off exact words borrowed from another speaker or writer. At the end of a quotation the period or comma is placed within quotation marks.

> "Hurry up," he whispered.
> She told me, "I'm depressed."

The colon or semicolon is always placed outside quotation marks:

> Our contract clearly defines "middle-management personnel"; however, it does not state salary range.
> You know what to expect when Honest Al offers you a "bargain": a piece of junk.

Sometimes a question mark is used within a quotation that is part of a larger sentence. (Do not follow a question mark with a comma.)

> "Can we stop the flooding?" inquired the supervisor.

When the question mark or exclamation point is part of the quotation, it belongs within quotation marks, replacing the comma or period.

> "Help!" he screamed.
> She asked Dal, "Can't we agree about anything?"

When the question mark or exclamation point denotes the attitude of the person quoting instead of the person quoted, it belongs outside the quotation mark.

> Why did he wink and tell me, "It's a big secret"?
> He actually accused me of being an "elitist"!

When quoting a passage of fifty words or longer, indent the entire passage five spaces and single-space between its lines to set it off from the text. Do not enclose the indented passage in quotation marks.

Use quotation marks around titles of articles, book chapters, poems, and unpublished reports.

> The enclosed article, "The Job Market for College Graduates," should provide some helpful insights.

The title of a published work—book, journal, newspaper, brochure, or pamphlet—should be underlined or italicized.

Finally, use quotation marks (with restraint) to indicate your ironic use of a word.

> He is some "friend"!

Ellipses

Three dots in a row (...) indicate that you have omitted some material from a quotation. If the omitted words come at the end of the original sentence, a fourth dot indicates the period. Use several dots centred in a line to indicate that a paragraph or more has been left out. Ellipses help you save time and zero in on the important material within a quotation.

"Three dots . . . indicate that you have omitted some material . . . . A fourth dot indicates the period. . . . Several dots centred in a line · · · indicate a paragraph or more. . . . Ellipses help you . . . zero in. . . .

Italics

ital

In longhand writing, indicate italics by *underlining*. On a word processor, use italic print for titles of books, periodicals, films, newspapers, and plays; for the names of ships; for foreign words or scientific names; for emphasizing a word (use sparingly); for indicating the special use of a word.

The Gage Canadian Dictionary is a handy reference tool.

The *Lusitania* sank rapidly.

She reads the *Globe and Mail* often.

My only advice is *caveat emptor.*

Bacillus anthracis is a highly virulent organism.

Do *not* inhale these spores, under any circumstances!

Our contract defines a *full-time employee* as one who works a minimum of thirty-five hours weekly.

Parentheses

( ) /

Use commas normally to set off parenthetical elements, dashes to give some emphasis to the material that is set off, and parentheses to enclose material that defines or explains the statement that precedes it.

This organism requires an anaerobic (oxygenless) environment.

The cost of manufacturing our Beta II fuel cells has increased by 10 percent in one year. (See Appendix A for full cost breakdown.)

This new three-colour model (made by Ilco Corporation) is selling well.

Notice that material within parentheses, like all other parenthetical material discussed earlier, can be deleted without harming the logical and grammatical structure of the sentence.

Also, use parentheses to enclose numbers or letters that segment items of information in a series.

The three basic steps in this procedure are (1) . . . , (2) . . . , and (3) . . . .

Brackets

[ ] /

Use brackets within a quotation to add material that was not in the original quotation but is needed for clarification. Sometimes a bracketed word will provide an antecedent (or referent) for a pronoun.

"She [Melanchuk] was the outstanding candidate for the job."

Brackets can enclose information from some other location within the context of the quotation.

"It was in early spring [April 2, to be exact] that the tornado hit."

Use brackets to correct a quotation.

"His report was [full] of mistakes."

Use *sic* ("thus" or "so") when quoting a mistake in spelling, usage, or logic.

> Her assistant's comment was clear: "She don't [sic] want any of these."

Dashes

~~/

Dashes can be effective indicators of meaning—as long as they are not overused. Make dashes by selecting en-dash (–) or em-dash (—) from the special characters feature of your word processor. Alternatively, make an en-dash using a space, a hyphen, and another space; and make an em-dash or by placing two hyphens side by side. Parentheses de-emphasize enclosed material; dashes emphasize it.

Used selectively, dashes can provide emphasis, but they are not a substitute for all other punctuation. When in doubt, do not use a dash!

Dashes can denote an afterthought.

> Have a good vacation—but don't get sunstroke.

They can enclose an interruption in the middle of a sentence.

> This building's designer—I think it was Wright—was, above all, an artist.
> Our new team—Wong, Tse, and Lau—already is compiling outstanding statistics.

Although they can often be used interchangeably with commas, dashes dramatize a parenthetical statement more than commas do.

> Julie, a true friend, spent hours helping me rehearse for my interview.
> Julie—a true friend—spent hours helping me rehearse for my interview.

Notice the added emphasis in the second version.

Hyphen

– /

Use a hyphen to join compound modifiers (two or more words preceding the noun as an adjective), but not compound nouns.

> the rough-hewn wood
> the well-written report
> the all-too-human error
> a three-part report

Do not hyphenate these same words if they *follow* the noun

> The wood was rough hewn.
> The report is well written.
> The error was all too human.

Hyphenate an adverb-participle compound preceding a noun.

> the high-flying glider

Do not hyphenate compound modifiers if the adverb ends in **-ly**.

> the finely tuned engine

Hyphenate most words that begin with the prefix **self-**. (Check your dictionary.)

> self-reliance
> self-discipline
> self-actualizing

Hyphenate to avoid ambiguity.

> re-creation *(a new creation)*
> recreation *(leisure activity)*

Hyphenate words that begin with **ex-** only if **ex-** means "past."

> ex-employee
> expectant

Hyphenate all fractions, along with ratios that are used as adjectives and that precede the noun.

> a two-thirds majority
> In a four-to-one ratio they defeated the proposal.

Do not hyphenate ratios if they do not immediately precede the noun.

> The proposal was voted down four to one.

Hyphenate compound numbers from twenty-one through ninety-nine.

> Thirty-eight windows were broken.

Hyphenate a series of compound adjectives preceding a noun.

> The subjects for the motivation experiment were fourteen-, fifteen-, and sixteen-year-old students.

Use a hyphen to divide a word at the right-hand margin. Consult your dictionary for the correct syllable breakdown:

> com-puter
> comput-er

Actually, it is best to avoid altogether this practice of dividing words at the ends of lines.

Transitions and Other Connectors

trans

Transitions help make your meaning clear, signaling readers that you are in a specific time or place, that you are giving an example, showing a contrast, shifting gears, or concluding your discussion. Here are some common transitions and the relations they indicate:

Addition	I am majoring in naval architecture; **furthermore,** I spent three years crewing on a racing yawl.

> moreover   and
> in addition   again
> also   as well as

Place	Here is the switch that turns on the stage lights. **To the right** is the switch that dims them.

> beyond   to the left
> over   nearby
> under   adjacent to
> opposite to   next to
> beneath   where

Time	The crew will mow the ball field this morning; **immediately afterward**, we will clean the dugouts.

first	the next day
next	in the meantime
second	in turn
then	subsequently
meanwhile	while
at length	since
later	before
now	after

Comparison	Our reservoir is drying up because of the drought; **similarly**, water supplies in neighbouring towns are low.

likewise
in the same way
in comparison

Contrast	Felix worked hard; **however**, he received poor grades.

however	but
nevertheless	on the other hand
yet	to the contrary
still	notwithstanding
in contrast	conversely

Results	Jack fooled around; **consequently**, he was fired.

thus	thereupon
hence	as a result
therefore	so
accordingly	as a consequence

Example	Competition for part-time jobs is fierce; **for example**, eighty students applied for the sales associate's job at Sears.

for instance	namely
to illustrate	specifically

Explanation	She had a terrible semester; **that is**, she flunked four courses.

in other words	in fact
simply stated	put another way

Summary or conclusion	Our credit is destroyed, our bank account is overdrawn, and our debts are piling up; **in short**, we are bankrupt.

in closing	to sum up
to conclude	all in all
to summarize	on the whole
in brief	in retrospect
in summary	in conclusion

Pronouns serve as connectors, because a pronoun refers back to a noun in a preceding clause or sentence.

> As the **crew** neared the end of the project, **they** were all willing to work overtime to get the job done.
>
> **Low employee morale** is damaging our productivity. **This** problem needs immediate attention.

Repetition of key words or phrases is another good connecting device—as long as it is not overdone. Here is another example of effective repetition:

> Overuse and drought have depleted our water supply critically. Because of our **depleted supply**, we need to enforce strict **water**-conservation measures.

Here, the repetition also emphasizes a critical problem.

Because this next paragraph lacks transitions, sentences seem choppy and awkward:

> Choppy   Technical writing is a difficult but important skill to master. It requires long hours of work and concentration. This time and effort are well spent. Writing is indispensable for success. Good writers derive pride and satisfaction from their effort. A highly disciplined writing course should be part of every student's curriculum.

Here is the same paragraph rewritten to improve coherence:

> Revised   Technical writing is a difficult but important skill to master. It requires long hours of work and concentration. This time and effort, **however**, are well spent **because** writing is an indispensable tool for success. **Moreover**, good writers derive pride and satisfaction from their effort. A highly disciplined writing course, **therefore**, should be part of every student's curriculum.

Besides increasing coherence *within* a paragraph, transitions and connectors emphasize relationships **between** paragraphs by linking related groups of ideas. Here are two transitional sentences that could serve as conclusions for some paragraphs or as topic sentences for paragraphs that would follow; or they could stand alone for emphasis as single-sentence paragraphs:

> Because the A-12 filter has decreased overall engine wear by 15 percent, it should be included as a standard item in all our new models.
>
> With the camera activated and the watertight cover sealed, the diving bell is ready to be submerged.

Topic headings, like those in this book, are another connecting device. A topic heading is both a link and a separation between related yet distinct groups of ideas.

Sometimes a whole paragraph can serve as a connector between major sections of your report. Assume that you have just completed a section in a report on the advantages of a new oil filter and are now moving to a section on selling the idea to the buying public. Here is a paragraph you might write to link the two sections:

> Because the A-12 filter has decreased overall engine wear by 15 percent, it should be included as a standard item in all our new models. However, tooling and installation adjustments will add roughly $100 to the list price of each model. Therefore, we have to explain to customers the filter's long-range advantages. Let's look at ways of explaining these advantages.

Notice that this transitional paragraph *contains* transitional expressions as well.

Effective Mechanics

Correctness in abbreviation, capitalization, use of numbers, and spelling is an important sign of your attention to detail.

Abbreviations

ab

Whenever you abbreviate, consider your audience; never use an abbreviation that might confuse your reader. Abbreviations are often inappropriate in formal writing. When in doubt, write the word out.

Abbreviate some words and titles when they precede or immediately follow a proper name.

Correct	Ms. Seligman	Mr. Trautwein
	Dr. Jekyll	Raymond Dumont, Jr.
	St. Simeon	Loretta Della Savo, Ph.D.

Do not however, write abbreviations such as these:

| **Faulty** | Tess is a Dr. |
| | Pray hard and you might become a St. |

In general, do not abbreviate military, religious, and political titles.

Correct	Reverend Ormsby
	Captain Hook
	Prime Minister Jean Chrétien

Abbreviate time designations only when they are used with actual times.

Correct	A.D. 576
	400 B.C.
	5:15 a.m.

Do not abbreviate these designations when they are used alone.

| **Faulty** | Plato lived sometime in the B.C. period. |
| | She arrived in the a.m. |

In formal writing, do not abbreviate days of the week, months, words such as **street** and **road**, or names of disciplines such as **English**. Avoid abbreviating provinces, such as **Que.** for **Quebec**; countries, such as **U.S.** for **United States**; and book parts such as **Chap.** for **Chapter**, **pp.** for **pages**, and **fig.** for **figure**.

Use **no.** for **number** only when the actual number is given.

| **Correct** | Check switch No. 3. |

Abbreviate a unit of measurement only when it appears often in your report and is written out in full on first use. Use only abbreviations you are sure readers will understand. Abbreviate items in a visual aid only if you need to save space.

Here are common abbreviations for units of measurement:

AC	alternating current	kn	knot
amp; A	ampere	kw	kilowatt
Å	angstrom	kwh	kilowatt hour
az	azimuth	l; L	litre
bbl	barrel	lat	latitude
BTU	British Thermal Unit	lb	pound
C	Celsius, coulomb	lin	linear
cal	calorie	long	longitude
cc	cubic centimetre	log	logarithm
cd	candela	m	metre
circ	circumference	m^2	square metre
cm	centimetre	m^3	cubic metre
cm^2	square centimetre	M	nautical mile
cm^3	cubic centimetre	max	maximum
CPS	cycles per second	mg	milligram
cu ft	cubic foot	mi	mile
cu m; m^3	cubic metre	min	minute
dB	decibel	ml; mL	millilitre
DC	direct current	mm	millimetre
dm	decimetre	mo	month
doz	dozen	mol	mole
DP	dewpoint	mph	miles per hour
eV	electronvolt	N	newton
F	Fahrenheit; farad	oct	octane
fbm	foot board measure	oz	ounce
fl oz	fluid ounce	Pa	pascal
FM	frequency modulation	psf	pounds per square foot
freq	frequency	psi	pounds per square inch
ft; '	foot	qt	quart
ft lb	foot pound	r	roentgen
gal	gallon	rpm	revolutions per minute
GPM	gallons per minute	s	second
gr; g	gram	sp gr	specific gravity
ha	hectare	sq	square
hp	horsepower	t	ton; tonne
hr; h	hour	temp	temperature
Hz	hertz	tol	tolerance
in; "	inch	ts	tensile strength
IU	international unit	V	volt
J	joule	VA	volt ampere
K	kelvin	W	watt
ke	kinetic energy	wk	week
kg	kilogram	WL	wavelength
km	kilometre	yd	yard
km^2	square kilometre	yr	year

Here are some common abbreviations for reference in manuscripts:

anon.	anonymous	fig.	figure
app.	appendix	i.e.	that is
b.	born	illus.	illustrated
©	copyright	jour.	journal
c., ca.	about (c. 1999)	l., ll.	line(s)
cf.	compare	ms., mss.	manuscript(s)
ch.	chapter	no.	number
col.	column	p., pp.	page(s)
d.	died	pt., pts.	part(s)
ed.	editor	rev.	revised or review
e.g.	for example	sec.	section
esp.	especially	sic	thus, so (to cite an error in the quotation)
et al.	and others		
etc.	and so on	trans.	translation
ex.	example	vol.	volume
f. or ff.	the following page or pages		

For abbreviations of other words, consult your dictionary. Most dictionaries list abbreviations at the front or back or alphabetically with the word entry.

Capitalization

cap

Capitalize these items: proper nouns, titles of people, books and chapters, languages, days of the week, the months, holidays, names of organizations or groups, races and nationalities, historical events, important documents, and names of structures or vehicles. In titles of books, films, and so on, capitalize first and following words, except articles or short prepositions.

A Tale of Two Cities	the Chevrolet Corvette
Protestant	Russian
Wednesday	Labour Day
the *Queen Elizabeth II*	DuPont Chemical Company
the CN Tower	Senator John Pasteur
April	France
Charlottetown	the War of 1812
the Charter of Rights	the Motor Vehicle Act

Do not capitalize the seasons, names of college classes (**senior**, **junior**), or general groups (**the younger generation**, or **the leisure class**).

Capitalize adjectives that are derived from proper nouns.

Chaucerian English
Roman numerals

Capitalize titles preceding a proper noun but not those following:

Provincial Premier, Penny Nguyen
Penny Nguyen, provincial premier

Capitalize words such as **street**, **road**, **corporation**, **college** only when they accompany a proper noun.

> George Brown College
> High Street
> the Rand Corporation

Capitalize **north**, **south**, **east**, and **west** when they denote specific locations, not when they are simple directions.

> the South
> the Northwest
> Turn east at the next set of lights.

Begin all sentences with capitals.

Numbers

If numbers can be expressed in one or two words, you can write them out or you can use the numerals.

> fourteen   14
> eighty-one   81
> ninety-nine   99

For larger numbers, use numerals.

> 4,364 or 4 364   2,800,357 or 2 800 357
> 543   200 million
> 3¼

Use numerals to express decimals, precise technical figures, or any other exact measurements. Numerals are more easily read and better remembered than numbers that are spelled out.

> 50 kilowatts   15 pounds of pressure
> 14.3 milligrams   4,000 rpm or 4 000 rpm

Express these in numerals: dates, census figures, addresses, page numbers, exact units of measurement, percentages, ages, times with a.m. or p.m. designations, and monetary and mileage figures.

> page 14   1:15 p.m.
> 18.4 kilos   9 metres
> 115 kilometres   12 litres
> the 9-year-old tractors $15
> 15.1 percent or 15% (financial documents and statistics)

Do not begin a sentence with a numeral.

> Six hundred students applied for the 102 available jobs.

Do not use numerals to express approximate figures, time not designated as a.m. or p.m., or streets named by numbers less than 100.

[#]

> about seven hundred fifty
> four fifteen
> 108 East Fifth Street

If one number immediately precedes another, spell out the first and use a numeral for the second:

> Please deliver twelve 5-metre rafters.

In contracts and other documents in which precision is vital, a number can be stated both in numerals and in words:

> The tenant agrees to pay a rental fee of three hundred seventy-five dollars ($375.00) monthly.

Works Cited

Adams, Gerald R., and Jay D. Schvaneveldt. <u>Understanding Research Methods</u>. New York: Longman, 1985.

<u>The Aldus Guide to Basic Design</u>. Aldus Corporation, 1988.

American Psychological Association. <u>Publication Manual of the American Psychological Association</u>. 4th ed. Washington: Author, 1994.

"Are We in the Middle of a Cancer Epidemic?" <u>University of California at Berkeley Wellness Letter</u> 10.9 (1994): 4–5.

Bailey, Edward P. <u>Writing Clearly: A Contemporary Approach</u>. Columbus, OH: Merrill, 1984.

Barbour, Ian. <u>Ethics in an Age of Technology</u>. New York: Harper, 1993.

Barfield, Woodrow, Mark Haselkorn, and Catherine Weatbrook. "Information Retrieval with a Printed User's Manual and with Online Hypercard Help." <u>Technical Communication</u> 37.1 (1990): 22–27.

Barker, Larry J. et al. <u>Groups in Process</u>. 3rd ed. Englewood Cliffs, NJ: Prentice Hall, 1987.

Barnett, Arnold. "How Numbers Can Trick You." <u>Technology Review</u> Oct. 1994: 38–45.

Barnum, Carol, and Robert Fisher, "Engineering Technologists as Writers: Results of a Survey." <u>Technical Communication</u> 31.2 (1984): 9–11.

Baumann, K. E., et al. "Three Mass Media Campaigns to Prevent Adolescent Cigarette Smoking." <u>Preventive Medicine</u> 17 (1988): 510–30.

Beamer, Linda. "Learning Intercultural Communication Competence." <u>Journal of Business Communication</u> 29.3 (1992): 285–303.

Bedford, Marilyn S., and F. Cole Stearns. "The Technical Writer's Responsibility for Safety." <u>IEEE Transactions on Professional Communication</u> 30.3 (1987): 127–32.

Begley, Sharon. "Is Science Censored?" <u>Newsweek</u> 14 Sept. 1992.

Benson, Phillipa J. "Visual Design Considerations in Technical Publications." <u>Technical Communication</u> 32.4 (1985): 35–39.

Bernstein, Mark. "Deeply Intertwingled Hypertext: The Navigation Problem Reconsidered." <u>Technical Communication</u> 38.1 (1991): 41–47.

Bjerklie, David. "E-Mail: The Boss Is Watching." <u>Technology Review</u> 14 Apr. 1993: 14–15.

Bogert, Judith, and David Butt. "Opportunities Lost, Challenges Met: Understanding and Applying Group Dynamics in Writing Projects." <u>Bulletin of the Association for Business Communication</u> 53.2 (1990): 51–53.

Boiarsky, Carolyn. "Using Usability Testing to Teach Reader Response." <u>Technical Communication</u> 39.1 (1992): 100–02.

Brody, Herb. "Great Expectations: Why Technology Predictions Sometimes Go Awry." <u>Technology Review</u> July 1991: 38–44.

Brownell, Judi, and Michael Fitzgerald. "Teaching Ethics in Business Communication: The Effective/Ethical Balancing Scale." <u>Bulletin of the Association for Business Communication</u> 55.3 (1992): 15–18.

Bruhn, Mark J. "E-Mail's Conversational Value." <u>Business Communication Quarterly</u> 58.3 (1995): 43–44.

Bryan, John. "Down the Slippery Slope: Ethics and the Technical Writer as Marketer." <u>Technical Communication Quarterly</u> 1.1 (1992): 73–88.

Burghardt, M. David. <u>Introduction to the Engineering Profession</u>. New York: Harper, 1991.

Burnett, Rebecca E. "Substantive Conflict in a Cooperative Context: A Way to Improve the Collaborative Planning of Workplace Documents." <u>Technical Communication</u> 38.4 (1991): 532–39.

Callahan, Sean. "Eye Tech." <u>Forbes ASAP</u> 7 June 1993.

Caswell-Coward, Nancy. "Cross-Cultural Communication: Is It Greek to You?" <u>Technical Communication</u> 39.2 (1992): 264–66.

Chauncey, Caroline. "The Art of Typography in the Information Age." <u>Technology Review</u> Feb./Mar. (1986): 26+.

Christians, Clifford G., et al. <u>Media Ethics: Cases and Moral Reasoning</u>. 2nd ed. White Plains, NY: Longman, 1978.

Clark, Gregory. "Ethics in Technical Communication: A Rhetorical Perspective." <u>IEEE Transactions on Technical Communication</u> 30.3 (1987): 190–95.

Clement, David E. "Human Factors, Instructions, and Warnings, and Product Liability." <u>IEEE Transactions on Professional Communication</u> 30.3 (1987): 149–56.

Cochran, Jeffrey K., et al. "Guidelines for Evaluating Graphical Designs." <u>Technical Communication</u> 36.1 (1989): 25–32.

Coletta, W. John. "The Ideologically Biased Use of Language in Scientific and Technical Writing." <u>Technical Communication Quarterly</u> 1.1 (1992): 59–70.

Communication Concepts, Inc. "Electronic Media Poses New Copyright Issues." <u>Writing Concepts</u> ©. Reprinted in <u>INTERCOM</u> [Newsletter of the Society for Technical Communication] Nov. 1995: 13+.

Consumer Product Safety Commission. <u>Fact Sheet No. 65</u>. Washington: GPO, 1989.

Cotton, Robert, ed. <u>The New Guide to Graphic Design</u>. Secaucus, NJ: Chartwell, 1990.

Council of Biology Editors. <u>Scientific Style and Format: The CBE Manual for Authors, Editors, and Publishers</u>. 6th ed. Chicago: Cambridge UP, 1994.

Cronin, Mary J. "Knowing How Employees Use the Intranet Is Good Business." <u>Fortune</u> 21 July 1997: 103.

Cross, Mary. "Aristotle and Business Writing: Why We Need to Teach Persuasion." <u>Bulletin of the Association for Business Communication</u> 54.1 (1991): 3–6.

Crossen, Cynthia. <u>Tainted Truth: The Manipulation of Fact in America</u>. New York: Simon, 1994.

Dana-Farber Cancer Institute. <u>Facts and Figures about Cancer</u>. Boston: Author, 1995.

Davenport, Thomas H. <u>Information Ecology</u>. New York: Oxford, 1997.

Debs, Mary Beth, "Collaborative Writing in Industry." <u>Technical Writing: Theory and Practice</u>. Ed. Bertie E. Fearing and W. Keats Sparrow. New York: Modern Language Assn., 1989: 33–42.

———. "Recent Research on Collaborative Writing in Industry." <u>Technical Communication</u> 38.4 (1991): 476–85.

Dombrowski, Paul M. "Challenger and the Social Contingency of Meaning: Two Lessons for the Technical Communication Classroom." <u>Technical Communication Quarterly</u> 1.3 (1992): 73–86.

Dragga, Sam, and Gwendolyn Gong. <u>Editing: The Design of Rhetoric</u>. Amityville, NY: Baywood, 1989.

Dulude, Jennifer. "The Web Marketing Handbook." Thesis. University of Massachusetts Dartmouth, 1997.

Dumont, R. A. "Writing, Research, and Computing." <u>Critical Thinking: An SMU Dialogue</u>, 1988.

Dumont, R. A., and J.M. Lannon, <u>Business Communications</u>. 3rd ed. Glenview, IL: Scott, 1990.

Dyson, Esther. "Intellectual Value." <u>Wired</u> July 1995: 134+.

Dyson, Esther, and Nicholas Negroponte. "How Smart Agents Will Change Selling." <u>Forbes ASAP</u> 28 Aug. 1995: 95.

"Earthquake Hazard Analysis for Nuclear Power Plants." <u>Energy and Technology Review</u> June 1984: 8.

Elbow, Peter. <u>Writing without Teachers</u>. New York: Oxford, 1973.

"Electronic Mentors." <u>The Futurist</u> May 1992: 56.

Evans, James. "Legal Briefs." <u>Internet World</u> Feb. 1998: 22.

———. "Whose Web Site Is It Anyway?" <u>Internet World</u> Sept. 1997: 46+.

<u>Facts and Figures about Cancer</u>. Boston: Dana-Farber Cancer Institute, 1990.

Felker, Daniel B., et al. <u>Guidelines for Document Designers</u>. Washington: American Institutes for Research, 1981.

Figgins, Ross. "The Future of Business Communication Technology: Where Are We Headed, Captain?" <u>Communication and Technology: Today and Tomorrow</u>. Ed. Al Williams. Denton, TX: Assn. for Business Communication, 1994. 123–42.

Fineman, Howard, "The Power of Talk." Newsweek 8 Feb. 1993: 24–28.

Finkelstein, Leo, Jr. "The Social Implications of Computer Technology for the Technical Writer." Technical Communication 38.4 (1991): 466–73.

Florman, Samuel, quoting Donald D. Rikard. "Toward Liberal Learning for Engineers." Technology Review Mar. 1986: 18–25.

Franke, Earnest A. "The Value of the Retrievable Technical Memorandum System to the Engineering Company." IEEE Transactions on Professional Communication 32.1 (Mar. 1989): 12–16.

Garfield, Eugene, "What Scientific Journals Can Tell Us about Scientific Journals." IEEE Transactions on Professional Communication 16.4 (1973): 200–02.

Gartiganis, Arthur. "Lasers." Occupational Outlook Quarterly Winter 1984: 22–26.

Gesteland, Richard R. "Cross-Cultural Compromises." Sky May 1993: 20+.

Gibaldi, Joseph. MLA Handbook for Writers of Research Papers. 4th ed. New York: Modern Language Assn., 1995.

Gibaldi, Joseph, and Walter S. Achtert. MLA Handbook for Writers of Research Papers. 3rd ed. New York: Modern Language Assn., 1988.

Gilbert, Nick, "1-8000-ETHIC." Financial World 16 Aug. 1994: 20+.

Gilsdorf, Jeanette W. "Executives' and Academics' Perception of the Need for Instruction in Written Persuasion." Journal of Business Communication 23.4 (1986): 55–68.

———. "Write Me Your Best Case for . . ." Bulletin of the Association for Business Communication 54.1 (1991): 7–12.

Girill, T. R. "Technical Communication and Art. Technical Communication 31.2 (1984): 35.

———. "Technical Communication and Ethics." Technical Communication 34.3 (1987): 178–79.

———. "Technical Communication and Law." Technical Communication 32.3 (1985): 37.

Glidden, H. K. Reports, Technical Writing, and Specifications. New York: McGraw, 1964.

Golen, Steven, et al. "How to Teach Ethics in a Basic Business Communications Class." Journal of Business Communication 22.1 (1985): 75–84.

Goodall, H. Lloyd, Jr., and Christopher L. Waagen. The Persuasive Presentation. New York: Harper, 1986.

Goodman, Danny. Living at Light Speed. New York: Random, 1994.

Goubil-Gambrell, Patricia. "Designing Effective Internet Assignments in Introductory Technical Communication Courses." IEEE Transactions on Professional Communication 39.4 (1996): 224–31.

Gouran, Dennis S., et al. "A Critical Analysis of Factors Related to Decisional Processes Involved in the Challenger Disaster." Central States Speech Journal 37.3 (1986): 119–35.

Gribbons, William M. "Organization by Design: Some Implications for Structuring Information." Journal of Technical Writing and Communication 22.1 (1992): 57–74.

Grice, Roger A. "Document Development in Industry." Technical Writing: Theory and Practice. Ed. Bertie E. Fearing and W. Keats Sparrow. New York: Modern Language Assn., 1989. 27–32.

———. "Focus on Usability: Shazam!" Technical Communication 42.1 (1995): 131–33.

Grice, Roger A., and Lenore S. Ridgway. "Presenting Technical Information in Hypermedia Format: Benefits and Pitfalls." Technical Communication Quarterly 4.1 (1995): 35–46.

Grossman, Wendy M. "Downloading as a Crime." Scientific American Mar. 1998: 37.

Gruman, Galen. "The Paper Chase." MACWORLD Apr. 1995: 126–31.

Guffey, Mary Ellen et. al. Business Communication. 2nd Canadian ed. Toronto: Nelson, 1999.

Hafner, Kate, "Have Your Agent Call My Agent." Newsweek 27 Feb. 1995: 76–77.

Halpern, Jean W. "An Electronic Odyssey." Writing in Nonacademic Settings. Ed. Dixie Goswami and Lee Odell. New York: Guilford, 1985. 157–201.

Hamblen, Matt. "Volvo Taps AT&T for Global Net." Computerworld 1 Dec. 1997: 51+.

Harcourt, Jules. "Teaching the Legal Aspects of Business Communication." Bulletin of the Association for Business Communication 53.3 (1990): 63–64.

Hartley, James. Designing Instructional Text. 2nd ed. London: Kogan Page, 1985.

Haskin, David. "The Extranet Team Play." Internet World Aug. 1997: 57-60.

Hauser, Gerald. Introduction to Rhetorical Theory. New York: Harper, 1986.

Haynes, Kathleen J. M., and Linda K. Robertson. "An Application of Usability Criteria in the Classroom." Technical Writing Teacher 18.3 (1991): 236–42.

Hays, Robert. "Political Realities in Reader/Situation Analysis." Technical Communication 31.1 (1984): 16–20.

Hein, Robert G. "Culture and Communication." Technical Communication 38.1 (1991): 125–26.

Hill-Duin, Ann. "Terms and Tools: A Theory and Research-Based Approach to Collaborative Writing." Bulletin of the Association for Business Communication 53.2 (1990): 45–50.

Hoger, Elizabeth, James J. Cappel, and Mark A. Myerscough. "Navigating the Web with a Typology of Corporate Uses." Business Communication Quarterly 61.2 (1998): 39–47.

Holler, Paul F. "The Challenge of Writing for Multimedia." INTERCOM [Newsletter of the Society for Technical Communication] July/Aug. 1995: 25.

Hopkins-Tanne, Janice. "Writing Science for Magazines." A Field Guide for Science Writers. Eds. Deborah Blum and Mary Knudson. New York: Oxford, 1997. 17–26.

Horton, William. "Is Hypertext the Best Way to Document Your Product?" Technical Communication 38.1 (1991): 20–30.

———. "Mix Media, Not Metaphors." <u>Technical Communication</u> 41.4 (1994): 781–83.

Howard, Tharon. "Property Issue in E-Mail Research." <u>Bulletin of the Association for Business Communication</u> 56.2 (1993): 40–41.

Huff, Darrell. <u>How to Lie with Statistics</u>. New York: Norton, 1954.

Hulbert, Jack E. "Developing Collaborative Insights and Skills." <u>Bulletin of the Association for Business Communication</u> 57.2 (1994): 53–56.

———. "Overcoming Intercultural Communication Barriers." <u>Bulletin of the Association for Business Communication</u> 57.2 (1994): 41–44.

Humphreys, Donald S. "Making Your Hypertext Interface Usable." <u>Technical Communication</u> 40.4 (1993): 754–61.

Hutheesing, Nikhil. "Who Needs the Middleman?" <u>Forbes</u> 28 Aug. 1995.

Hyakawa, S. I. <u>Language in Thought and Action</u>. 3rd ed. New York: Harcourt, 1972.

James-Catalano, "The Virtual Library." <u>Internet World</u> June 1995: 26+.

Jameson, Daphne A. "Using a Simulation to Teach Intercultural Communication in Business Communication Courses." <u>Bulletin of the Association for Business Communication</u> 56.1 (1993): 3–11.

Janis, Irving L. <u>Victims of Groupthink: A Psychological Study of Foreign Policy Decisions and Fiascos</u>. Boston: Houghton, 1972.

Johannesen, Richard L. <u>Ethics in Human Communication</u>. 2nd ed. Prospect Heights, IL: Waveland, 1983.

Journet, Debra. Unpublished review of <u>Technical Writing</u>. 3rd ed.

Karaim, Reed. "The Invasion of Privacy." <u>Civilization</u> Oct./Nov. 1996: 70–77.

Kawasaki, Guy. "The Rules of E-Mail." <u>MACWORLD</u> Oct. 1995: 286.

Kelley-Reardon, Kathleen. <u>They Don't Get It Do They?: Communication in the Workplace—Closing the Gap between Women and Men</u>. Boston: Little, 1995.

Kelman, Herbert C. "Compliance, Identification, and Internalization: Three Processes of Attitude Change." <u>Journal of Conflict Resolution</u> 2 (1958): 51–60.

Keyes, Elizabeth. "Typography, Color, and Information Structure." <u>Technical Communication</u> 40.4 (1993): 638–54.

Kiely, Thomas. "The Idea Makers." <u>Technology Review</u> Jan. 1993: 31–40.

Kipnis, David, and Stuart Schmidt. "The Language of Persuasion." <u>Psychology Today</u> Apr. 1985: 40–46. Rpt. in Raymond S. Ross, <u>Understanding Persuasion</u>. 3rd ed. Englewood Cliffs: Prentice, 1990.

Kirsh, Lawrence. "Take It from the Top." <u>MACWORLD</u> Apr. 1986: 112–15.

Kleimann, Susan D. "The Complexity of Workplace Review." <u>Technical Communication</u> 38.4 (1991): 520–26.

Kohl, John R., et al. "The Impact of Language and Culture on Technical Communication in Japan." <u>Technical Communication</u> 40.1 (1993): 62–72.

Kotulak, Ronald. "Reporting on Biology of Behavior." <u>A Field Guide for Science Writers</u>. Eds. Deborah Blum and Mary Knudson. New York: Oxford, 1997. 142–51.

Kraft, Stephanie. "Whistleblower Bill's Holiday Adventures." <u>The Valley Advocate</u> [Northhampton, MA] 6 Jan. 1994: 5–6.

Kremers, Marshall. "Teaching Ethical Thinking in a Technical Writing Course." <u>IEEE Transactions on Professional Communication</u> 32.2 (1989): 58–61.

Lambert, Steve. <u>Presentation Graphics on the Apple® Macintosh</u>. Bellevue, WA: Microsoft Corporation, 1984.

Lang, Thomas A., and Michelle Secic. <u>How to Report Statistics in Medicine</u>. Philadelphia: American College of Physicians, 1997.

LaPlante, Alice. "Brainstorming." <u>Forbes ASAP</u> 25 Oct. 1993: 45–61.

———. "Imaging Your Sea of Data." <u>Forbes ASAP</u> 29 Aug. 1994: 37–41.

Larson, Charles U. <u>Persuasion: Perception and Responsibility</u>. 7th ed. Belmont, CA: Wadsworth: 1995.

Lavin, Michael R. <u>Business Information: How to Find It, How to Use It</u>. 2nd ed. Phoenix, AZ: Oryx, 1992.

Lederman, Douglas. "Colleges Report Rise in Violent Crime," <u>Chronicle of Higher Education</u> 3 Feb. 1995, sec. A: 31–42.

Leki, Ilona. "The Technical Editor and the Non-native Speaker of English." <u>Technical Communication</u> 37.2 (1990): 148–52.

Levi, Stephen. "Optimism about the Net." <u>MACWORLD</u> July 1994: 179–80.

Lewis, Philip L., and N. L. Reinsch. "The Ethics of Business Communication." <u>Proceedings of the American Business Communication Conference. Champaign, IL., 1981</u>. In <u>Technical Communication and Ethics</u>. Ed. John R. Brockman and Fern Rook. Washington: Society for Technical Communication, 1989: 29–44.

Littlejohn, Stephen W. <u>Theories of Human Communication</u>. 2nd ed. Belmont, CA: Wadsworth, 1983.

Littlejohn, Stephen W., and David M. Jabusch. <u>Persuasive Transactions</u>. Glenview, IL: Scott, 1987.

McDonald, Kim A. "Some Physicists Criticize Research Purporting to Show Links between Low-Level Electromagnetic Fields and Cancer." <u>Chronicle of Higher Education</u> 3 May 1991, sec. A: 5+.

Machlis, Sharon. "Surfing into a New Career as Webmaster." <u>Computerworld</u> 1 Dec. 1997: 45+.

MacKenzie, Nancy. Unpublished review of <u>Technical Writing</u>. 5th ed.

Mackin, John. "Surmounting the Barrier between Japanese and English Technical Documents." <u>Technical Communication</u> 36.4 (1989): 346–51.

McWilliams, Gary, and Marcia Stepanik. "Taming the Info. Monster." <u>Business Week</u> 22 June 1998: 170+.

Maeglin, Thomas. Unpublished review of <u>Technical Writing</u>, 7th ed.

Martin, James A. "A Road Map to Graphics Web Sites." MACWORLD Oct. 1995: 135–36.

Martin, Jeanette S., and Lillian H. Chaney. "Determination of Content for a Collegiate Course in Intercultural Business Communication by Three Delphi Panels." Journal of Business Communication 29.3 (1992): 267–83.

Max, Robert R. "Wording It Correctly." Training and Development Journal Mar. 1985: 5–6.

McGuire, Gene. "Shared Minds: A Model of Collaboration." Technical Communication 39.3 (1992): 467–68.

Meyer, Benjamin D. "The ABCs of New-Look Publications." Technical Communication 33.1 (1986): 13–20.

Meyerson, Moe. "Grand Illusions." Inc. Tech 2 (1997): 35–36.

Microsoft Word User's Guide: Word Processing Program for the Macintosh, Version 5.0. Redmond, WA: Microsoft Corporation, 1992.

Mirel, Barbara, Susan Feinberg, and Leif Allmendinger. "Designing Manuals for Active Learning Styles." Technical Communication 38.1 (1991): 75–87.

Mokhiber, Russell. "Crime in the Suites." Greenpeace May 1989: 14–16.

Monatersky, R. "Do Clouds Provide a Greenhouse Thermostat?" Science News 142 (1992): 69.

Morgan, Meg. "Patterns of Composing: Connections between Classroom and Workplace Collaborations." Technical Communication 38.4 (1991): 540–42.

Morgenson, Gretchen. "Would Uncle Sam Lie to You?" Worth Nov. 1994: 53+.

Morse, June. "Hypertext—What Can We Expect?" STC Intercom [Newsletter of the Society for Technical Communication] Feb. 1992: 6–7.

Moses, Barbara. "The Challenge: How to Satisfy the New Worker's Agenda." Globe and Mail 10 Nov. 1998, B15.

Nantz, Karen S., and Cynthia L. Drexel. "Incorporating Electronic Mail with the Business Communication Course." Business Communication Quarterly 58.3 (1995) 45–51.

Neilsen, Jakob. "Be Succinct! (Writing for the Web)." 15 Mar. 1997. Alertbox. 8 Aug. 1998 <http://www.useit.com/alertbox/9719a.html>.

———. "How Users Read on the Web." Oct. 1997. Alertbox. 8 Aug. 1998 <http://www.useit.com/alertbox/9710a.html>.

———. "Inverted Pyramids in Cyberspace." June 1996. Alertbox. 8 Aug. 1998 <http://www.useit.com/alertbox/9710a.html>.

Nelson, Sandra J., and Douglas C. Smith. "Maximizing Cohesion and Minimizing Conflict in Collaborative Writing Groups. Bulletin of the Association for Business Communication 53.2 (1990): 59–62.

Nickels-Shirk, Henrietta. "'Hyper' Rhetoric: Reflections on Teaching Hypertext." Technical Writing Teacher 18.3 (1991): 189–200.

"Notes." Technology Review July 1993: 72.

Nydell, Margaret K. <u>Understanding Arabs: A Guide for Westerners</u>. New York: Logan, 1987.

"On Line." <u>Chronicle of Higher Education</u> 21 Sept. 1992, sec. A: 1.

"Olive Oil and Breast Cancer: How Strong a Connection?" <u>University of California at Berkeley Wellness Letter</u> 11.7 (1995): 1–2.

Ornatowski, Cezar M. "Between Efficiency and Politics: Rhetoric and Ethics in Technical Writing." <u>Technical Communication Quarterly</u> 1.1 (1992): 91–103.

Pace, Roger C. "Technical Communication, Group Differentiation, and the Decision to Launch the Space Shuttle Challenger." <u>Journal of Technical Writing and Communication</u> 18.3 (1988): 207–20.

Pender, Kathleen. "Dear Computer, I Need a Job." <u>Worth</u> Mar. 1995: 120–21.

Perelman, Lewis, J. "How Hypermation Leaps the Learning Curve." <u>Forbes ASAP</u> 25 Oct. 1993: 78+.

Perloff, Richard M. <u>The Dynamics of Persuasion</u>. Hillsdale, NJ: Erlbaum, 1993.

Peterson, Ivars. "Web Searches Fall Short." <u>Science News</u> 153.18 (1998): 286.

Peyser, Marc, and Steve Rhodes. "When E-Mail Is Oops-Mail." <u>Newsweek</u> 16 Oct. 1995: 82.

Pinelli, Thomas E., et al. "A Survey of Typography, Graphic Design, and Physical Media in Technical Reports." <u>Technical Communication</u> 33.2 (1986): 75–80.

Plumb, Carolyn, and Jan H. Spyridakis. "Survey Research in Technical Communication: Designing and Administering Questionnaires." <u>Technical Communication</u> 39.4 (1992): 625–38.

Porter, James E. "Truth in Technical Advertising: A Case Study." <u>IEEE Transactions on Professional Communication</u> 30.3 (1987): 182–89.

Presidential Commission. <u>Report to the President on the Space Shuttle Challenger Accident</u>. Vol I. Washington: GPO, 1986.

Pugliano, Fiore. Unpublished review of <u>Technical Writing</u>. 5th ed.

Quimby, G. Edward. "Make Text and Graphics Work Together." <u>Intercom</u> Jan. 1996: 34.

Redish, Janice C., and David A. Schell. "Writing and Testing Instructions for Usability." <u>Technical Writing: Theory and Practice</u>. Ed. Bertie E. Fearing and W. Keats Sparrow. New York: Modern Language Assn., 1987: 61–71.

Redish, Janice C., et al. "Making Information Accessible to Readers." <u>Writing in Nonacademic Settings</u>. Ed. Lee Odell and Dixie Goswami. New York: Guilford, 1985.

Richards, Thomas O., and Ralph A. Richards, "Technical Writing." Paper presented at the University of Michigan, 11 July 1941. Published by the Society for Technical Communication.

Riney, Larry A. <u>Technical Writing for Industry</u>. Englewood Cliffs: Prentice, 1989.

Ritzenthaler, Gary, and David H. Ostroff. "The Web and Corporate Communication: Potentials and Pitfalls." <u>IEEE Transactions on Professional Communication</u> 39.1 (1996): 16–20.

Rokeach, Milton. The Nature of Human Values. New York: Free, 1973.

Ross, Philip E. "Lies, Damned Lies, and Medical Statistics." Forbes 14 Aug. 1995: 130–35.

Ross, Raymond S. Understanding Persuasion. 3rd ed. Englewood Cliffs: Prentice, 1990.

Rothschild, Michael. "When You're Gagging on E-Mail." Forbes ASAP 6 June 1994: 25–26.

Rottenberg, Annette, T. Elements of Argument. 3rd ed. New York: St. Martin's, 1991.

Rowland, D. Japanese Business Etiquette: A Practical Guide to Success with the Japanese. New York: Warner, 1985.

Rowland Robert C. "The Relationship between the Public and the Technical Spheres of Argument: A Case Study of the Challenger Seven Disaster." Central States Speech Journal 37.3 (1986): 136–46.

Rubens, Philip M. "Reading and Employing Technical Information in Hypertext." Technical Communication 38.1 (1991): 36-40.

———. "Reinventing the Wheel?: Ethics for Technical Communicators." Journal of Technical Writing and Communication 11.4 (1981): 329–39.

Ruggiero, Vincent R. The Art of Thinking. 3rd ed. New York: Harper, 1991.

Ruhs, Michael A. "Usability Testing: A Definition Analyzed." Boston Broadside [Newsletter of the Society for Technical Communication] May/June 1992: 8+.

Samuelson, Robert. "Merchants of Mediocrity." Newsweek 1 Aug. 1994: 44.

Schenk, Margaret T., and James K. Webster. Engineering Information Resources. New York: Decker, 1984.

Schwartz, Marilyn, et al. Guidelines for Bias-Free Writing. Bloomington, IN: Indiana UP, 1995.

Scott, James C., and Diana J. Green. "British Perspectives on Organizing Bad-News Letters: Organizational Patterns Used by Major U.K. Companies." Bulletin of the Association for Business Communication 55.1 (1992): 17–19.

Selber, Stuart. Unpublished review of Technical Writing, 7th ed. 1998.

Selzer, Jack. "Composing Processes for Technical Discourse." Technical Writing: Theory and Practice. Ed. Bertie E. Fearing and W. Keats Sparrow. New York: Modern Language Assn., 1989: 43–50.

Sherblom, John C., Claire F. Sullivan, and Elizabeth C. Sherblom, "The What, the Whom, and the Hows of Survey Research." Bulletin of the Association for Business Communication 56:12 (1993): 58–64.

Sherif, Muzapher, et al. Attitude and Attitude Change: The Social Judgment-Involvement Approach. Philadelphia: Saunders, 1965.

Snyder, Joel. "Finding It on Your Own." Internet World June 1995: 89–90.

Spruell, Geraldine. "Teaching People Who Already Learned How to Write, to Write." Training and Development Journal Oct. 1986: 32–35.

Spyridakis, Jan H. "Conducting Research in Technical Communication: The Application of True Experimental Design." Technical Communication 39.4 (1992): 607–24.

Spyridakis, Jan H., and Michael J. Wenger. "Writing for Human Performance: Relating Reading Research to Document Design." <u>Technical Communication</u> 39.2 (1992): 202–15.

Stanton, Mike. "Fiber Optics." <u>Occupational Outlook Quarterly</u> Winter 1984: 27–30.

Staudennmaier, S. J. "Engineering with a Human Face." <u>Technology Review</u> July 1991: 66–67.

Stedman, Craig. "Extranet Brokers Access to Funds Data." <u>Computerworld</u> 20 Oct. 1997: 49+.

Steinberg, Stephen. "Travels on the Net." <u>Technology Review</u> July 1994: 20–31.

Stevenson, Richard W. "Workers Who Turn in Bosses Use Law to Seek Big Rewards." <u>New York Times</u> 10 July 1989, sec A: 1.

Stone, Brad, and T. Trent Gegax. "Your Favorite Sites." <u>Newsweek</u> 20 Nov. 1995: 16.

Stone, Peter H. "Forecast Cloudy: The Limits of Global Warming Models." <u>Technology Review</u> Feb./Mar. 1992: 32–40.

Stonecipher, Harry. <u>Editorial and Persuasive Writing</u>. New York: Hastings, 1979.

Sturges, David L. "Internationalizing the Business Communication Curriculum." <u>Bulletin of the Association for Business Communication</u> 55.1 (1992): 30–39.

Teague, John H. "Marketing on the World Wide Web." <u>Technical Communication</u> 42.2 (1995): 236–42.

Templeton, Brad. "10 Big Myths about Copyright Explained." 29 Nov. 1994. Online posting. Listserve law/copyright/FAQ/myths/part 1 BITNET. 6 May 1995.

Thrush, Emily A. "Bridging the Gap: Technical Communication in an Intercultural and Multicultural Society." <u>Technical Communication Quarterly</u> 2.3 (1993): 271–83.

Tuck, Simon. "Canning Spam." <u>Globe and Mail</u> 15 Oct. 1998, D1 and D5.

Unger, Stephen H. <u>Controlling Technology: Ethics and Responsible Engineer</u>. New York: Holt, 1982.

U.S. Air Force Academy. <u>Executive Writing Course</u>. Washington: GPO, 1981.

U.S. Department of Commerce. <u>Statistical Abstract of the United States</u>. Washington: GPO, 1994.

U.S. Department of Labor. <u>Tips for Finding the Right Job</u>. Washington: GPO, 1993.

———. <u>Tomorrow's Jobs</u>. Washington: GPO 1995.

U.S. General Services Administration. <u>Your Rights to Federal Records</u>. Washington: GPO, 1995.

"Using Icons As Communication." <u>Simply Stated</u> [Newsletter of the Document Design Center, American Institutes for Research] 75 (Sept./Oct. 1987): 1+.

van der Meij, Hans, and John M. Carroll. "Principles and Heuristics for Designing Minimalist Instruction." <u>Technical Communication</u> 42.2 (1995): 243–61.

Van Pelt, William. Unpublished review of <u>Technical Writing</u>. 3rd ed.

Varner, Iris I., and Carson H. Varner. "Legal Issues in Business Communications." <u>Journal of the American Association for Business Communication</u> 46.3 (1983): 31–40.

Vaughan, David K. "Abstracts and Summaries: Some Clarifying Distinctions." <u>Technical Writing Teacher</u> 18.2 (1991): 132–41.

Velotta, Christopher. "How to Design and Implement a Questionnaire." <u>Technical Communication</u> 38.3 (1991): 387–92.

Victor, David A. <u>International Business Communication</u>. New York: Harper, 1992.

Walker, Janice R. "MLA-Style Citations of Electronic Sources." April 1995. The Alliance for Computers and Writing. http://prarie-island.ttu.edu/acw.html (10 Jan. 1996).

Wallace, Bob. "Restaurant Franchiser Puts Intranet on Menu." <u>Computerworld</u> 10 Nov. 1997: 12.

Walter, Charles, and Thomas F. Marsteller. "Liability for the Dissemination of Defective Information." <u>IEEE Transactions on Professional Communication</u> 30.3 (1987): 164–67.

Watkins, Beverly T. "Many Campuses Start Building Tomorrow's Electronic Library." <u>Chronicle of Higher Education</u> 2 Sept. 1992, sec. A: 1+.

Weinstein, Edith K. Unpublished review of <u>Technical Writing</u>. 5th ed.

Weiss, Edmond H. <u>How to Write a Usable User Manual</u>. Philadelphia: ISI, 1985.

Welz, Gary. "Job Seeking on the Net." <u>Internet World</u> May 1995: 52.

Weymouth, L. C. "Establishing Quality Standards and Trade Regulations for Technical Writing in World Trade." <u>Technical Communication</u> 37.2 (1990): 143–47.

White, Jan. <u>Color for the Electronic Age</u>. New York: Watson-Guptill, 1990.

———. <u>Editing by Design</u>. 2nd ed. New York: Bowker, 1982.

———. <u>Great Pages</u>. El Segundo, CA: Serif, 1990.

———. <u>Visual Design for the Electronic Age</u>. New York: Watson-Guptill, 1988.

Wicclair, Mark, R., and David K. Farkas. "Ethical Reasoning in Technical Communication: A Practical Framework." <u>Technical Communication</u> 31.2 (1984): 15–19.

Wickens, Christopher D. <u>Engineering Psychology and Human Performance</u>. 2nd ed. New York: Harper, 1992.

Wight, Eleanor, "How Creativity Turns Facts into Usable Information." <u>Technical Communication</u> 32.1 (1985): 9–12.

Wilkinson, Theresa A. "Defining Content for a Web Site." <u>INTERCOM</u> June 1998: 33-34.

Williams, Joseph. <u>Style</u>. 4th ed. New York: Harper, 1994.

Williams, Robert I. "Playing with Format, Style, and Reader Assumptions." <u>Technical Communication</u> 30.3 (1983): 11–13.

Winsor, D. A. "Communication Failures Contributing to the Challenger Accident: An Example for Technical Communicators." <u>IEEE Transactions on Professional Communication</u> 31.3 (1988): 101–07.

Wojahn, Patricia G. "Computer-Mediated Communication: The Great Equalizer between Men and Women?" <u>Technical Communication</u> 41.4 (1994): 747–51.

Wriston, Walter. <u>The Twilight of Sovereignty</u>. New York: Scribner's, 1992.

Yoos, George. "A Revision of the Concept of Ethical Appeal." <u>Philosophy and Rhetoric</u> 12.4 (1979): 41–58.

Zinsser, William. <u>On Writing Well</u>. New York: Harper, 1980.

Index

Correction Symbols

Symbol	Meaning	Symbol	Meaning
ab	abbreviation	– – /	dashes
agr p	faulty pronoun/referent agreement	. . . /	ellipses
agr sv	faulty subject/verb agreement	! /	exclamation point
amb	ambiguity	– /	hyphen
appr	inappropriate diction	*ital*	italics
bias	biased tone	( ) /	parentheses
ca	faulty pronoun case	. /	period
cap	capitalization	? /	question mark
chop	choppy sentences	" / "	quotation marks
cl	clutter word	; /	semicolon
coh	paragraph coherence	*qual*	needless qualifier
cont	contraction	*red*	redundancy
coord	faulty coordination	*rep*	needless repetition
cs	comma splice	*ref*	faulty or vague pronoun reference
dgl	dangling modifier	*ro*	run-on sentence
euph	euphemism	*seq*	sequence of development in a paragraph
exact	inexact word	*sexist*	sexist usage
frag	sentence fragment	*shift*	sentence shift
gen	generalization	*st mod*	stacked modifiers
jarg	needless jargon	*str*	paragraph structure
len	paragraph length	*sub*	faulty subordination
lev	level of technicality	*th op*	"th" sentence openers
mng	meaning unclear	*trans*	transition
mod	misplaced modifier	*trite*	triteness
noun ad	noun addiction	*un*	paragraph unity
om	omitted word	*v*	voice
over	overstatement	*var*	sentence variety
par	faulty parallelism	*w*	wordiness
pct	punctuation	*wo*	word order
ap/	apostrophe	*ww*	wrong word
[ ] /	brackets	#	numbers
: /	colon	¶	begin new paragraph
, /	comma	*ts*	topic sentence